ENCYCLOPEDIA OF
Hinduism

ENCYCLOPEDIA OF WORLD RELIGIONS

ENCYCLOPEDIA OF
Hinduism

Constance A. Jones and James D. Ryan

J. Gordon Melton, Series Editor

An imprint of Infobase Publishing

Encyclopedia of Hinduism

Facts On File, Inc.
An imprint of Infobase Publishing
132 West 31st Street
New York NY 10001

ISBN-10: 0-8160-5458-4
ISBN-13: 978-0-8160-5458-9

Library of Congress Cataloging-in-Publication Data

Jones, Constance A., 1961–
  Encyclopedia of Hinduism / Constance A. Jones and James D. Ryan.
   p. cm. — (Encyclopedia of world religions)
  Includes index.
  ISBN 978-0-8160-5458-9
  1. Hinduism—Encyclopedias. I. Ryan, James D. II. Title. III. Series.
  BL1105.J56 2006
  294.503—dc22   2006044419

Text design by Erika K. Arroyo
Cover design by Cathy Rincon

Printed in the United States of America

VB Hermitage 10 9 8 7 6 5 4 3 2 1

This book is printed on acid-free paper.

CONTENTS

ABOUT THE EDITOR

Series editor J. Gordon Melton is the director of the Institute for the Study of American Religion in Santa Barbara, California. He holds an M.Div. from the Garrett Theological Seminary and a Ph.D. from Northwestern University. Melton is the author of *American Religions: An Illustrated History, The Encyclopedia of American Religions, Religious Leaders of America,* and several comprehensive works on Islamic culture, African-American religion, cults, and alternative religions. He has written or edited more than three dozen books and anthologies as well as numerous papers and articles for scholarly journals. He is the series editor for Religious Information Systems, which supplies data and information in religious studies and related fields. Melton is a member of the American Academy of Religion, the Society for the Scientific Study of Religion, the American Society of Church History, the Communal Studies Association, and the Society for the Study of Metaphysical Religion.

LIST OF ILLUSTRATIONS

PREFACE

The Encyclopedia of World Religions series has been designed to provide comprehensive coverage of six major global religious traditions—Buddhism, Hinduism, Islam, Judaism, Roman Catholicism, and Protestant Christianity. The volumes have been constructed in an A-to-Z format to provide a handy guide to the major terms, concepts, people, events, and organizations that have, in each case, transformed the religion from its usually modest beginnings to the global force that it has become.

Each of these religions began as the faith of a relatively small group of closely related ethnic peoples. Each has, in the modern world, become a global community, and, with one notable exception, each has transcended its beginning to become an international multiethnic community. Judaism, of course, largely defines itself by its common heritage and ancestry and has an alternative but equally fascinating story. Surviving long after most similar cultures from the ancient past have turned to dust, Judaism has, within the last century, regathered its scattered people into a homeland while simultaneously watching a new diaspora carry Jews into most of the contemporary world's countries.

Each of the major traditions has also, in the modern world, become amazingly diverse. Buddhism, for example, spread from its original home in India across southern Asia and then through Tibet and China to Korea and Japan. Each time it crossed a language barrier, something was lost, but something seemed equally to be gained, and an array of forms of Buddhism emerged. In Japan alone, Buddhism exists in hundreds of different sect groupings. Protestantism, the newest of the six traditions, began with at least four different and competing forms of the religious life and has since splintered into thousands of denominations.

At the beginning of the 19th century, the six religious traditions selected for coverage in this series were largely confined to a relatively small part of the world. Since that time, the world has changed dramatically, with each of the traditions moving from its geographical center to become a global tradition. While the traditional religions of many countries retain the allegiance of a majority of the population, they do so in the presence of the other traditions as growing minorities. Other countries—China being a prominent example—have no religious majority, only a number of minorities that must periodically interface with one another.

The religiously pluralistic world created by the global diffusion of the world's religions has made knowledge of religions, especially religions practiced by one's neighbors, a vital resource in the continuing task of building a good society, a world in which all may live freely and pursue visions of the highest values the cosmos provides.

In creating these encyclopedias, the attempt has been made to be comprehensive if not exhaustive. As space allows, in approximately 800 entries, each author has attempted to define and explain the basic terms used in talking about the religion, make note of definitive events, introduce the most prominent figures, and highlight the major organizations. The coverage is designed to result in both a handy reference tool for the religious scholar/specialist and an understandable work that can be used fruitfully by anyone—a student, an informed lay person, or a reader simply wanting to look up a particular person or idea.

Each volume includes several features. They begin with an essay that introduces the particular tradition and provides a quick overview of its historical development, the major events and trends that have pushed it toward its present state, and the mega-problems that have shaped it in the contemporary world.

A chronology lists the major events that have punctuated the religion's history from its origin to the present. The chronologies differ somewhat in emphasis, given that they treat two very ancient faiths that both originated in prehistoric time, several more recent faiths that emerged during the last few millennia, and the most recent, Protestantism, that has yet to celebrate its 500-year anniversary.

The main body of each encyclopedia is constituted of the approximately 800 entries, arranged alphabetically. These entries include some 200 biographical entries covering religious figures of note in the tradition, with a distinct bias to the 19th and 20th centuries and some emphasis on leaders from different parts of the world. Special attention has been given to highlighting female contributions to the tradition, a factor often overlooked, as religion in all traditions has until recently been largely a male-dominated affair.

Geographical entries cover the development of the movement in those countries and parts

of the world where the tradition has come to dominate or form an important minority voice, where it has developed a particularly distinct style (often signaled by doctrinal differences), or where it has a unique cultural or social presence. While religious statistics are amazingly difficult to assemble and evaluate, some attempt has been made to estimate the effect of the tradition on the selected countries.

In some cases, particular events have had a determining effect on the development of the different religious traditions. Entries on events such as the St. Bartholomew's Day Massacre (for Protestantism) or the conversion of King Asoka (for Buddhism) place the spotlight on the factors precipitating the event and the consequences flowing from it.

The various traditions have taken form as communities of believers have organized structures to promote their particular way of belief and practice within the tradition. Each tradition has a different way of organizing and recognizing the distinct groups within it. Buddhism, for example, has organized around national subtraditions. The encyclopedias give coverage to the major groupings within each tradition.

Each tradition has developed a way of encountering and introducing individuals to spiritual reality as well as a vocabulary for it. It has also developed a set of concepts and a language to discuss the spiritual world and humanity's place within it. In each volume, the largest number of entries explore the concepts, the beliefs that flow from them, and the practices that they have engendered. The authors have attempted to explain these key religious concepts in a nontechnical language and to communicate their meaning and logic to a person otherwise unfamiliar with the religion as a whole.

Finally, each volume is thoroughly cross-indexed using small caps to guide the reader to related entries. A bibliography and comprehensive index round out each volume.

—J. Gordon Melton

ACKNOWLEDGMENTS

We are particularly indebted to colleagues who have generously shared the products of their research and have edited our work: Dev Ashish, Bettina Baeumer, Mariana Caplan, Laura Cornell, George Chryssides, Mark Dyczkowski, Gilles Farcet, Jennifer Saunders, and Stuart Sovatsky. We are especially grateful to Gail Harley and Robert Schimpelfenig, who wrote many entries on contemporary leaders and movements.

The assiduous research of our assistants, Maria Albergato, Laura Amazzone, Kate Hendon, Erin Johansen, Simmy Makhijani, Pei-hsuan Wu, and Reuben Rutledge, added greatly to the inclusiveness of this volume.

Insight into specific movements, and photographs, have been provided by Arumugaswami Sannyasi, knowledgeable sources Jennifer Burns, Carol Lee Flinders, Nancy Friedberg, Nick and Sultana Harvey, Krishnapriya Hutner, Sean and Pervin Mahoney, Sundari Michaelian, Ravin Nadarajah, Hema Patankar, Penelope Phipps, Krishnakant, Paramacharya Palaniswami, Hamsa Stainton, Madhu Tandan, Peter Walsh, Indrani Weber, and Mary Young. Support on many levels came from Dr. Ralph Ortiz and Dr. Ching Chun Ou.

We are extremely grateful to J. Gordon Melton, general editor of the series, who offered expertise and encouragement at every step of the way.

—Constance A. Jones and James D. Ryan

NOTE ON
TERMS AND SPELLING

Because the spelling of Hindu terms today relies upon transliteration from several different languages from different language groups, perfect consistency in English spellings is not possible. Moreover, alternate spellings of Hindu terms and names are in common use throughout the English-speaking world.

We have chosen in most cases to cite the academically accepted and/or current spellings, even though these spellings may not be the same as common usage and/or historical usage. For example, the name of one wife of Shiva, the goddess Minakshi, is popularly rendered Meenakski, while scholars predominantly favor the former spelling. Also, a number of variations appear over time in the names of cities, so that Banaras is now commonly spelled Benares. Similarly, the honorific Sri is also spelled Shri, Shrii, and Shree. When proper names such as these appear in published volumes in bibliographical citations in this volume, the spelling follows the Library of Congress listing exclusively. Consequently, there often appear differences between spellings of names in text entries and spellings in the further reading associated with those entries.

Another point of possible confusion is current alternate spellings of Hindu terms such as *sannyasi* and *sannyasin* (meaning renunciant), which are synonymous. A closely related term, *sannyas*, is the vow that *sannyasis* or *sannyasins* take to enter into their lives of austerity.

In the last 20 years, the names of several important cities in India have been changed to their historical pre-British names. In this work, names of cities are generally left in the form found in the scholarly literature of the period. In most instances present-day changes are indicated in the text, such as Madras (Chennai), Bombay (Mumbai), Benares (Varanasi), and Calcutta (Kolkata).

Due to the dissemination of Hindu ideas in the West, many terms have become part of the English language and are not italicized to indicate that they are foreign words. For example, atman, bhakti, karma, maya, mudra, nirvana, and various types of yoga (such as hatha, jnana, ashtanga, and siddha yoga) are treated as English words.

INTRODUCTION
HINDUISM

The Origins of Hinduism

Until the 19th century, Hinduism was considered the indigenous religion of the subcontinent of India and was practiced largely in India itself and in the places where Indians migrated in large numbers. In the 21st century, while still centered in India, Hinduism is practiced in most of the world's countries and can thus rightly be considered a world religion. Its creation, unlike that of some world religions founded by known historical leaders, reaches into prehistory; we do not know the individuals who first practiced the religion (or set of religions that have merged to constitute present-day Hinduism) nor know exactly when its earliest forms emerged.

Hindu is a term from the ancient Persians. The Sindhu River in what is now Pakistan was called the "Hindu" by the Persians (the first textual mention occurred perhaps in the last centuries before the Common Era [C.E.]). The people who lived in proximity to the Sindhu therefore came to be called Hindus.

In academic terms the Hindu tradition, or Hinduism, is usually referred to as Brahmanism in its earlier phase, before circa 300 B.C.E., and referred to as Hinduism after that. In common usage, the term *Hinduism* is used for the entire span of the tradition.

For at least two reasons the Hindu tradition contains the greatest diversity of any world tradition. First, Hinduism spans the longest stretch of time of the major world religions, with even the more conservative views setting it as well over 3,000 years old. Throughout this expanse of time, the Hindu tradition has been extremely conservative about abandoning elements that have been historically superseded. Instead, these elements have often been preserved and given new importance, resulting in historical layers of considerable diversity within the tradition. Second, Hinduism has organically absorbed hundreds of separate cultural traditions, expressed in as many as 300 languages. As a result, Hindu tradition is metaphorically like the Grand Canyon gorge, where the great river of time has sliced through the landscape, leaving visible successive historical layers.

Some practices of Hinduism must have originated in Neolithic times (c. 4000 B.C.E.). The worship of certain plants and animals as sacred, for instance, could very likely have very great antiquity. The worship of goddesses, too, a part of Hinduism today, may be a feature that originated in the Neolithic.

The first attested elements that can be argued to be "Hindu" are found in the Indus Valley civilization complex, which lay geographically in present-day Pakistan. This civilization complex, which is contemporaneous with Sumeria and matches it in complexity and sophistication, is dated 3600–1900 B.C.E. Many seals found at Indus Valley sites were apparently used to mark commercial goods and had engraved upon them pictures that some have related to later Hinduism. One is the "proto-Shiva" seal, which shows a person, seated in a cross-legged position, with a headdress with horns on it and what appears to be an erect phallus. The headdress is said to relate to the later god Shiva's title of "Lord of the Animals," and the erect phallus is said to be related to the common icon of Shiva, the lingam, which is phallic in shape. Some see his seated posture as being the yogic lotus position. Shiva is known for his yogic practices.

Other Indus Valley seals seem to depict what came to be known as the "Seven Mothers," still worshipped in contemporary Hinduism. Additionally, B. B. Lal, the most prominent Indian archaeologist of the Indus Valley culture, argues that other artifacts and fire sites of the Indus Valley complex appear to be designed for rituals associated with the Vedic ritual tradition, which is usually dated many centuries later.

The Sacred Texts of Hinduism: The Vedas

Considerable debate exists with regard to the relationship of the Indus Valley civilization and the later Vedic tradition that focused on fire worship. The scholarly consensus for many years held that the Aryans, people who migrated from the west through Iran, arrived in India no earlier than 1200 B.C.E., much too recently to have participated in the Indus Valley world. These people were, the view holds, associated with the transmission of the Vedas, India's most sacred and revered texts. This consensus has been challenged, primarily from the Indian side, and continues to undergo scrutiny. The alternative view rejects the notion that the people who gave India the Vedas were originally foreign to India and sees a continuity between India's earliest civilization and the people of the Vedas.

The Rig Veda (c. 1500 B.C.E.), which everyone agrees is the most ancient extant Indian text, is the foundational text of Hinduism. It consists of about a thousand hymns. The great majority of the hymns are from five to 20 verses in length. The Rig Veda contains hymns of praise to a pantheon of divinities as well as a few cosmogonic hymns that tell of the creation of the universe. These stories are extremely important for the development of later Hinduism.

By far the greatest number of the thousand plus hymns of the Rig Veda are devoted to Indra, king of the gods, a deity connected with rain and storms who holds a thunderbolt, and Agni, the god of fire. The rest of the hymns are devoted to an array of gods, most prominently Mitra, Varuna, Savitri, Soma, and the Ashvins. Less frequently mentioned are the gods who became most important in the later Hindu pantheon, Vishnu and Rudra (one of whose epithets was *shiva,* the benign). A number of goddesses are mentioned, most frequently Ushas, goddess of the dawn, and Aditi, said to be the mother of the gods. The goddess of speech, Vach (Vak), however, may be most important, since speech is one of the most powerful sacred realities in Hindu tradition, although there are not many references to her.

The religion of the Rig Veda has for a long time been referred to as henotheistic, meaning that the religion was polytheistic, but it recognized each divinity in turn as, in certain ways, supreme. Certainly, later Hinduism continued and enriched this henotheistic concept, and, through time, Hinduism has been able to accept even Christ and Allah as being supreme "in turn." The Rig Veda, though, was the central text in a very powerful ritual tradition. Rituals public and private, with sacred fire always a central feature, were performed to speak to and beseech the divinities. Sacrifices of animals were a regular feature of the larger public rites of the Vedic tradition.

Two other Vedas, the Yajur and Sama Vedas, were based on the Rig Veda. That is, most of their text is from the Rig Veda, but the words of the prior text are reorganized for the purposes of the rituals. Yajur Veda, the Veda of sacrificial formulas, which has two branches called the Black and the White Yajur Vedas, contains the chants that accompany most of the important ancient rites. The Sama Veda, the Veda of sung chants, is very much focused on the praise of the god Soma, the personification of a drink taken at most rituals that probably had psychedelic properties. Priests of the three Vedas needed to be present for any larger, public ritual. Later a fourth Veda, the Atharva Veda, became part of the tradition. This text consists primarily of spells and charms used to ward off diseases or to influence events. This text is considered the origin of Indian medicine, the system of Ayurveda. There are also a number of cosmogonic hymns in the Atharva Veda, which show the development of the notion of divine unity in the tradition. A priest of the Atharva Veda was later included in all public rituals and the tradition evolved to include four Vedas rather than three.

Two important points must be understood about the Vedic tradition. First, none of the Vedas is considered composed by humans. All are considered to be "received" or "heard" by the *rishis,* divinely inspired sages, whose names are noted at the end of each hymn. Second, none of the text of the Vedas was written down until the 15th century C.E. The Vedic tradition was passed down from mouth to ear for millennia and is, thus, the oral tradition par excellence. The power of the word in the Vedic tradition is considered an oral and aural power, not a written one. The chant is seen as a power to provide material benefit and spiritual apotheosis. The great emphasis, therefore, was on correct pronunciation and on memorization. Any priest of the tradition was expected to have an entire Veda memorized, including its nonmantric portions (explained later).

Any of the four Vedas is properly divided into two parts, the mantra, or verse portion, and the Brahmana, or explicatory portion. Both of these parts of the text are considered revelation, or *shruti.* The Brahmanas reflect on both the mantra text and the ritual associated with it, giving very detailed, varied, and arcane explication of them. The Brahmanas abound in equations between ritual aspects, the ritual performers, and cosmic, terrestrial, and divine realities. Early Western scholars tended to discount these texts, as being nothing but priestly mumbo-jumbo. But most recent work recognizes the central importance of the Brahmanas to the development of Indian thought and philosophy.

The name *Brahmana* derives from a central word in the tradition, *brahman. Brahman* is generically the term for "prayer" but technically refers to the power or magic of the Vedic mantras. (It also was used to designate the one who prays, hence the term *Brahmin.) Brahman* is from the root *brih,* "to expand or grow," and refers to the expansion of the power of the prayer itself as the ritual proceeds; this power is understood as something to be "stirred up" by the prayer. In later philosophy, the term *brahman* refers to the transcendent, all-encompassing reality.

The culmination of Brahmana thought is often considered to be the Shatapatha Brahmana of the White Yajur Veda. It makes explicit the religious nature of the *agnichayana* fire ceremony, the largest public ritual of the tradition. Shatapatha Brahmana makes clear that this public ritual is, in fact, a reenactment of the primordial ritual described in Rig Veda X. 90, the most important cosmogonic hymn of the Vedas. This myth describes the ritual immolation of a cosmic "Man," whose parts are apportioned to encompass all of the visible universe and everything beyond it that is not visible. That is, the cosmic "Man" is ritually sacrificed to create the universe. Shatapatha Brahmana delineates how, at the largest public ritual in the tradition, the universe is essentially re-created yearly. The Brahmana understands that, at its most perfect, the Vedic ritual ground is identical to all of the universe, visible and invisible.

Within the Brahmanas two subdivisions are important in the development of later tradition. One of the subdivisions is called the Aranyaka. From its name one can understand that this portion of the text pertained to activity in the forest (*aranya*). These specially designated portions of the Brahmanas contain evidence that some Vedic *yajna,* or ritual, was now performed internally, as an esoteric practice. This appears to be a special practice done by adepts, who would essentially perform the ritual mentally, as though it were being done in their own body and being. This practice was not unprecedented, since the priests of the Atharva Veda did not chant as other priests, but rather were required at public rituals to perform mentally the rituals that other priests performed externally. But the Aranyaka notion was distinctive in that the ritual was performed *only* internally. From this interpretation originated the notion that the ritualist himself was the *yajna,* or ritual.

Last, the Brahmanas included (commonly within the Aranyaka portion) the Upanishads, the last of the Vedic subdivisions or literary modes (no one really knows when these subdivisions were designated). As do the Brahmanas, many of these texts contained significant material that reflected on the nature of the Vedic sacrifice. Thus the division between Brahmana proper, Aranyaka, and Upanishad is not always clear. The most important feature of the Upanishad was the emergence of a clear understanding of the unity of the individual self or atman and the all-encompassing *brahman,* understood as the totality of universal reality, both manifest and unmanifest.

The genesis of the Upanishadic understanding, that the self and cosmic reality were one, is clear. First, the Shatapatha Brahmana stated that the most perfect ritual was, in fact, to be equated to the universe itself, visible and invisible. Second, the Aranyakas made clear that the individual initiated practitioner was the ritual itself. So, if the ritual equals all reality and the individual adept equals the ritual, then the notion that the individual equals all reality is easily arrived at. The

Upanishads were arrived at, then, not by philosophical speculation, but by ritual practice. Later Upanishads of the orthodox variety (that is, early texts associated with a Vedic collection) omitted most reference to the ritual aspect and merely stated the concepts as they had been derived. Most importantly, the concepts of rebirth (reincarnation) and the notion that actions in this life would have consequence in a new birth (karma) were first elaborated in the Upanishads.

This evidence shows that the concept of karma, or ethically conditioned rebirth, had its roots in earlier Vedic thought. But the full expression of the concept was not found until the later texts, the Upanishads, which are called the Vedanta, or the end or culmination of the Vedas. Therefore, the notion of reaching unity with the ultimate reality was seen as not merely a spiritual apotheosis, but also a way out of the trap of rebirth (or redeath).

Epic Hinduism and Classical Hinduism

In the sixth century B.C.E., a large-scale revolt against Vedic practice occurred in India. The Buddha, a great reformer, decried the supremacy of Brahmins in Vedic practice and in Indian society and called for a path that was open to all without discrimination. He criticized the animal sacrifices made by the Brahmins and their corruption in monetary pursuits. He was joined in this era by the Jain leader Mahavira. Both of these leaders began movements on the eastern plain of the Ganges valley, near the area of Benares (Varanasi), which represented a shift in the center of the culture from the area of the Punjab, in what is now present-day Pakistan, to eastern India.

Buddhism achieved supremacy in early India through the influence of the empire of the great king Ashoka in the third century B.C.E., but, although it enjoyed periods of state glory over the centuries, it never succeeded in supplanting traditions that looked to the Vedas. Thus, the culture and tradition represented by the great epics Ramayana and Mahabharata showed the emergence of the forms of religion called, in current academic terms, *Hinduism*. These specifically show a contrast to the forms found in earlier Vedic "Brahminism."

In the Sanskrit epics, still widely known in myriad versions in India today, the gods Shiva and Vishnu begin to emerge as the focal points for cultic worship. Shiva appears to be a god of the Himalayas who was identified by the Brahmins with the god Rudra of the Vedas. In all likelihood the cultic Shiva was fashioned from an amalgam of traditional sources over many centuries. This pattern of taking local traditions and creating direct connection of them with the Vedas was an ongoing feature in the evolution of the Brahminical tradition.

Similarly, Vishnu and his numerous avatars emerged from a mélange of cultural sources. Vishnu in the Vedas was not at all a significant divinity. But the cult of Vishnu was organized around a sense of continuity with this Vedic divinity and the larger monistic philosophy that developed in the Vedic tradition. The epic Ramayana is understood to be a story of the descent of Vishnu to Earth in order to defeat the demons. Likewise, Krishna, as warrior, another important avatar of Vishnu, was central to the Mahabharata epic. In both epics, stories of Shiva are also found scattered throughout.

A similar phenomenon occurs in the career of the great Goddess, Shakti, in Hindu tradition. *Shakti* forms the third large cultic center in Hinduism, whose worshippers, called *shaktas,* believe in the supremacy of the goddess. The development of *shakti* worship began to take shape at the beginning of the Common Era, some centuries later than the developments in the other cultic contexts.

The Bhagavad Gita (c. 100 B.C.E.), which is found in the Mahabharata (MBh), identifies the god Krishna with the *brahman* of the Upanishads. The likelihood is that Krishna was a divinity of certain western Indian groups, who had reached such popularity that he could not be ignored. It

may have been that Krishna was originally a tribal chieftain. In the Mahabharata itself he is spoken of consistently as God only in the Bhagavad Gita, which is clearly a later addition to the MBh. This identification of a local god with the highest divinity (and further with Vishnu) shows a pattern that leads to the incredible diversity of Hinduism. All across India in the next thousand years numerous local gods and goddesses are taken up into the larger Hindu tradition.

Examples from as far away as South India, the last area of India to accept the Aryan ethos, demonstrate the process of absorption of local divinities into the larger Hindu pantheon. Lord Venkateshvara of Tirupati, in Andhra Pradesh, a hill divinity who may have been worshipped in the same spot for several thousand years, was first identified with Shiva and then later identified as the god Vishnu himself. Tirupati thereupon became part of the Vaishnavite tradition and a pilgrimage site of great importance. Similarly, the goddess Minakshi in the temple city of Madurai, most probably a goddess of her home region in Tamil Nadu for many, many centuries, was associated with Shiva by being identified as his wife. In fact, she appears late enough not to be identified with Parvati, his usual spouse, but as a separate wife. Likewise, the Tamil god Murugan became identified as the youngest son of Shiva and Parvati.

Over the era from perhaps 600 B.C.E. until as late as the 14th century various local divinities were slowly but systematically absorbed into the Vedic or Brahmanical tradition. The Sanskrit texts, the *puranas,* composed from the fourth to the 12th centuries C.E., tell tales of the complicated and varied lives of Vishnu, Shiva, and the Goddess, but many local tales in local languages and Sanskrit tell the more hidden tales of how these local godly kings and queens became part of the larger tradition. The earliest additions to the pantheon of Hinduism were clearly those gods and goddesses who formed the basis of the Vishnu and Shiva cults. Parvati was likely a mountain goddess who may have ruled the mountains on her own at one time but became absorbed in the Shaivite tradition. Likewise, Lakshmi, the wife of Vishnu, has characteristics of a local nature divinity who became identified with Sri of the Vedas.

Vedic ritual tradition saw a revival in the kingdoms of the Guptas during the fourth through sixth centuries C.E. This period is often described as a golden age of Indian tradition, when Sanskrit literature flourished with such poets as Kalidasa, and the kings patronized Brahmins and reestablished Vedic rites that had long languished. Except for this passing phase, however, Vedic ritual tradition lost its supremacy very early. By the turn of the Common Era worship of the major cults had expanded greatly and by the sixth century C.E. temples to these divinities began to be created in stone.

Temple Hinduism represented a real shift in worship from that of the Vedas. Vedic worship had no permanent cultic sites, and no icons or images, nor was it locally bound. Following the traditions of the non-Aryan substratum in India, temple Hinduism focused its worship around icons placed in permanent temples. Most of these temples were built at places that had been sites of worship for hundreds of years. Part of the shift, however, very much connected the new temple sites with the Aryan tradition: the priests in the major temples now were all Brahmins and they all used Sanskrit in the rituals to the gods, where other languages had been used exclusively.

Caste

In the transition from Vedic religion to Hinduism proper, one important feature is the development of the stratified social system that in India became known as the caste system. Texts dating from the late centuries before the Common Era, such as the *Laws of Manu*, began to make clear that the four classes found in the Vedas were now seen as stratified social entities. Rules and social laws began to be passed down, not universally, but in terms of each class or "birth" (*jati*) division. Brahmins, here, were placed at the apex of the pyramid,

because of their priestly positions. (However, they were also not allowed to accumulate large amounts of wealth and could not hold positions of direct political power.) Next were the warriors, or Kshatriyas, who held kingly and administrative power. The large body of the people, the Vish, or Vaishya, were farmers or merchants. The lowest class were the Shudras, born, it was thought, to be servants.

As time went on and the tradition expanded its reach into all parts of India, indigenous tribes and other groups entering the society of Aryans were absorbed at an even lower rung of the social ladder. Eventually the concept of the untouchable (contemporary Dalit) was created to refer to people whom the upper castes would not even allow to be near or to touch them. Hinduism developed into a society where people became ranked rigidly by occupation. The sacerdotal position, or priestly work, was considered purest. Work that involved dealing with the dead, carrion, cleaning of sewers, sweeping, and other such tasks, was considered "unclean" and was performed only by hereditary untouchables.

Islam

In the 11th and 12th centuries, Islam entered an India that was flourishing. As the devotional movements that embodied the new tendency of the culture to worship the iconic divinity developed, saints emerged to sing poetry at the many shrines. Cultic Hinduism displayed a vast array of poet singers and wanderers who embodied the devotion for which ordinary Hindus strove. The ascetic wanderer had emerged even before Buddha, who was one of them. And through time the developing tradition looked to the wandering sadhu, or saint, to exemplify the purest devotion to the divine. The often eccentric holy man remains a distinctive feature of Hinduism today.

Islam entered India with a vengeance and stayed to rule. As Islamic presence expanded over North India, the Mughal empire was established in the 15th century C.E. For several centuries

Islam presided over India. Its reach encompassed nearly the entire country, although the far reaches of the south were spared its iconoclasm and its heaviest hand.

The Islamic era (c. 1100 to 1750 C.E.) produced religious interaction that may be unique in the world. Many of the Muslims who entered India were Turks, who often had an appreciation for the Sufi traditions. Sufis were often patronized by the Islamic courts. As the Sufi wandering holymen, many of whom were as otherworldly and eccentric as their Indian counterparts, began to meet with the local wanderers and saints, new religious ideas began to develop. The long tradition of Hindu saints who were lower caste, anticaste, or anti-Brahminical were supplemented by Sufi wanderers who held similar views. What emerged were powerful spiritual traditions that condemned *all* orthodoxy and were socially revolutionary in that they decried caste as spiritually bankrupt and laughed at the Brahmins as scoundrels and worse. The Sant tradition of North India that emerged in this era was well represented by such people as Kabir, who spoke most radically about the stupidity of untouchability and the foolishness of the orthodox.

The Sant and Sufi sentiments that developed in this era merged in the tradition of Guru Nanak (15th century) and the Sikhs, who eschew all ritual, icons, and ritual leaders. For the Sikhs there is no guru except the Granth Sahib, their holy book, which has many verses from the poet-saints of this era.

Other movements, such as the Bauls, remained less institutionalized than the Sikh tradition. They too combined elements from devotional Hinduism, Sufi love poetry and music, and anti-Brahminical sentiments into cultic groups that exist today outside the orthodox umbrella of Hinduism.

British Era

By the beginning of the 18th century, the British had arrived in India and had become powerful in Bengal. They succeeded in developing political power through the use of intermediaries carefully chosen from corrupt Muslim potentates and Hindu kings in the chaotic aftermath of Mughal rule.

It is no accident that Hindu modernism begins in Bengal, as it represented the longest contact point between the Western ruler, Britain, and its new subjects. English education became the norm for well-educated Bengalis by the early 18th century. When other parts of the country were just becoming accustomed to the heavy hand of the British, the Bengalis had already become more than familiar with their views and ways. What emerged were both a reform movement in Hinduism and the roots of the Indian nationalist movement.

Groups emerged in the late 18th century who, influenced in part by Christian ideas, sought to reform Hinduism. Groups such as the Brahmo Samaj of Ram Mohan Roy sought to end child marriage, to allow widows to remarry, to eliminate the custom of widows' burning themselves on the funeral pyres of their husband, to eliminate caste, and to end worship of icons. Many of these people worked from a notion that India had been dominated by the British because the Indian culture had become spiritually corrupt. They felt that if they had had a stronger social sense and greater solidarity, the British could not have so easily gained preeminence. This view was held by nearly every major fighter for Indian independence, including Mahatma Gandhi and Sri Aurobindo.

The caste system received significant criticism for more than two millennia by various groups who argued from the point of view of a different spiritual vision. The Buddha and Mahavira are the first we know of, starting in 600 B.C.E., but the Virashaivas of Karnataka, a South Indian state, eliminated caste from their reform tradition in the 11th century C.E., and many groups of mendicant wanderers such as the Siddhas routinely criticized caste and Brahminical cultural dominance, from the Buddha's time forward. The medieval poet-saints of North India who followed the views of Kabir were only maintaining a long countertradition. So when the "reformists" of Bengal began to attack the social evils of Hinduism their actions must not be seen as merely a mimicking of Christians and the British. It should be noted, as well, that the antiiconic view of the Brahmo Samaj of Calcutta (Kolkata) were also not new. The Virashaivas were essentially antiiconic (except for the Shiva lingam, which they kept in their personal homes), and the traditional Vedanta of the Upanishads looked to *brahman* alone without characteristics (or icons) as the ultimate divinity. The Brahmo Samaj takes its name, in fact, from this *brahman*, spelled as *Brahmo* in *Bengali*.

In the rich matrix of Hindu reform in Bengal in the 19th century emerged the great saint Ramakrishna and his student Swami Vivekananda. They maintained the reformist notions that caste must be uprooted, but Ramakrishna himself was not opposed to worship of icons. What Ramakrishna does, though, is round out the syncretic movements of the Sants, who melded Islamic and Hindu notions while decrying orthodoxy. Ramakrishna directly experienced Islam and Christianity and saw them as alternate paths to the one goal of the Divine. Ramakrishna then takes Hinduism full circle from its Vedic roots, where God could be seen as having any face and still be God. But now the social evils that had accrued in Hinduism over the centuries were seen by many to be superfluous to any religious need.

Post-Independence India (after 1947)

The Indian Constitution was written by an untouchable (now referred to as a Dalit), B. R. Ambedkar. Dr. Ambedkar's selection as the person to head the Constitutional Commission was a sign that the reform values that the Indian independence fighters held were going to be instituted in law in independent India. In the Indian Constitution, "scheduled castes and tribes," those "out-casted" by traditional Hindu society, were given a specified percentage of guaranteed seats in the Indian Parliament

until such time as the Constitution could be amended. (This guarantee was also instituted in nearly every state of the new Indian Union.) Additionally, separate electorates were established for Muslims to ensure that they would have adequate representation in the new Indian state. Along with these reforms, inheritance and marriage laws established legal practices to aid women and to counter long-held traditions detrimental to women. Dowry, for instance, a burden for every woman's family, was outlawed. (This law, regrettably, has never been rigorously enforced.) Most importantly, the new state of India was declared a secular state with its own unique definition: it was a state that respected all religions and made accommodations for them, but a state that privileged no single religion. This respect for religion went to the extent of institution, by request of Muslim leaders, of certain laws regarding marriage and property that only applied in the Muslim community. (Muslims, for instance, were allowed to maintain the practice of polygamy, in which men may have as many as four wives.)

Independent India began in the chaos of partition. Many Muslims, Hindus, and Sikhs were killed in the days after independence, when the state of Pakistan was created. Millions crossed the borders on India's east and west to enter the state that they felt would most protect their interests. Blame has been assigned in many places for the tragic fact of partition. Muslim leaders, Hindu leaders, and the British certainly all bore some share of the blame. Conflict ensued over the state of Kashmir, where a Hindu king ceded his majority Muslim state to India at the last minute. This began a long history of wars and disagreement between Pakistan and India that continues in the present day. (Pakistan itself was split in two in 1972, when the state of Bangladesh was created from East Pakistan.)

For a long time these disagreements did not greatly affect the relationship between Indian Muslims and the Hindu majority. In the 1980s a new political movement emerged in India, based on the assertion of Hindu majority privilege. It is often referred to as Hindu fundamentalism, but this phraseology glosses over the complexities and competing values it represents. Nation-states need to justify their existence ideologically. Pakistan shaped its identity from the beginning around Islam, and Hindus and other religions found themselves marginalized there from the beginning. India, however, had preserved the values of a secular state. Muslims regularly held the office of president of India and cabinet posts and were kept visibly in government offices and in positions in the army.

It can be argued that the movement for privileging Hinduism in India and for a call to "Hinduize" India was directly related to the need for a national ideology. Formation of national identity for new nations is extremely complex, and flows of power are difficult to track, but the emergence of Hindu fundamentalism seems clearly related to this need for the creation of national identity. Hindu assertion was not new in India. Certain groups, such as the Rashritriya Swayam Sevak Sangh (The National Self-Help Organization), who admired the fascists in Italy and Germany and taught regimented military tactics for their followers (along with hatred of Muslims), had their roots in Hindu nationalist groups of the 19th century. Suffice it to say that hatred of Muslims, conversion of non-Hindu minorities (including Christians), and reassertion of caste privilege were all part of this larger movement. In the 1990s the Bharatiya Janata Party (BJP) gained power with this platform, and some of its officials presided over a bloody anti-Muslim massacre in the Indian state of Gujarat. In 2004 they were ousted from power in favor of the Congress Party, the same party that had led India to independence and created the secular state of India. In the interim, great damage was done to relationships between Hindus and Muslims in India. Many Muslims began to retreat into their own fundamentalisms, now global in scope. Others simply left India, if they could. This relationship is in deep crisis at this time and will need skillful diplomacy and cultivation to be repaired, if it ever is.

Dissemination

Through European scholarship and interest, Hindu texts and practices became known in Western Europe and North America as early as the 18th century. In the 19th century, German philosophy, French scholarship, and the American transcendentalist movement served to disseminate Hindu ideas among Western readers, without contributions from Indian emigrants. A diaspora, which involved the resettlement of significant numbers of emigrants from India, began as early as the 17th century and reached significant size in the 18th through 20th centuries. The pattern of the diaspora was first characterized by the arrival of indentured laborers in Indonesia, Africa, and the Caribbean region to work the fields of large landowners. From the 20th century, Hindus from India migrated to the West for education. From the first days of the diaspora, groups of Hindus have cohered to transfer their faith and practices from native India to their new homes, temples, and communities. Thus, the dissemination of Hinduism around the world has followed two main routes: the route of scholarship and study, as the religion has been studied by non-Indians and introduced to non-Indian populations, and the route of immigration, as devoted Hindus have created Hindu homes and institutions in their places of resettlement.

The acceptance of Hindu ideals and practices in the West has depended upon a succession of Hindu practitioners who visited the West. Beginning with P. C. Moozumdar and Swami Vivekananda at the World Parliament of Religions in Chicago in 1893 and continuing through the residence of Paramahansa Yogananda in the United States from the 1920s, the West has received ever-larger numbers of Hindu teachers, especially since new immigration laws that allowed South Asian migration to the West.

Philosophical and theological ideas from Hinduism have been incorporated into Western thought on a large scale, primarily through the publications and activities of the Theosophical

Society and the teachings of many Hindu adepts in the West. Today, every major form of Hindu practice and belief has its Western form, which, although modified from traditional Hinduism, nevertheless contains the character of Hinduism.

An Encyclopedic Approach

In some 800 entries, *Encyclopedia of Hinduism* explores the vast world of Hinduism that emerges from prehistory and lives today in astonishing variety. This volume focuses on the most significant groups within Hinduism, the religious and cultural movements that enriched its history, significant teachers and their contributions, and the diaspora of Hindu thought and practice around the world. Two major religious traditions that sprang from a Hindu milieu, Jainism and Sikhism, have many entries; Buddhism, also a tradition that evolved from within Hinduism, is the subject of another encyclopedia in this series.

Inevitably, one volume cannot fully describe a history of at least 3,000 years and a staggering diversity in the present. The authors had to choose one topic over another and one person over another. Yet, the *Encyclopedia of Hinduism* represents major events, specific groups, central concepts, and major teachers who have given Hinduism its unique place as a world religion. Importantly, the many women leaders and teachers who have been valued in the evolution of Hinduism retain a focus in these entries. This volume, though selective, gives the interested reader a reliable window into the vast and enduring tradition of Hinduism, and some of its sister traditions in the land of India.

—Constance A. Jones and James D. Ryan

CHRONOLOGY

3600 B.C.E. to 1700 B.C.E.

⬩ Indus Valley civilization, including sites at Mohenjodaro and Harappa, prospers. Archaeological finds include a seal that some scholars identify as a proto-Shiva.

2050

⬩ Indo-Iranian people settle in Iran (Persia) and Afghanistan.

1900

⬩ Drying up of Sarasvati River due to climate changes. End of Indus-Sarasvati culture; center of civilization in ancient India relocates from the Sarasvati River to the Ganges River.

1500

⬩ Compilation of Rig Veda Samhita (the earliest extant text in Hinduism).

1350

⬩ At Boghaz Koy, Turkey, stone inscription of the treaty with Mitanni lists as divine witnesses the Vedic deities Mitra, Varuna, Indra, and the Nasatyas (Ashvins).

1000

⬩ End of compilation of the three original Vedas: Rig, Yajur, and Sama.

950

⬩ Decline of Sanskrit as a spoken language occurs over the next 300 years.

800 to 400

⬩ Orthodox Upanishads are compiled.

750

⬩ Prakrits (vernacular or "natural" languages) develop among India's various cultures, as evidenced from later Buddhist and Jain works.

c. 600

⬩ Death of Zoroaster, founder of Zoroastrianism, original religion of the Persians. His Zend Avesta, holy book of that faith, has much in common with the Rig Veda, sharing many verses.

599

⬩ Birth of Mahavira Vardhamana (c. 599–527), 24th Tirthankara, Jain master who stresses vegetarianism, asceticism, and nonviolence.

563

♦ Birth of Siddhartha Gautama (563–483), the Buddha.

c. 500 to 200

♦ Over these 300 years numerous secondary Hindu scriptures (*smriti*) are composed: Shrauta Sutras, Grihya Sutras, Dharma Sutras, Mahabharata, Ramayana, *puranas*, and others.

c. 450

♦ Panini composes his Sanskrit grammar, the *Ashtadhyayi*.

c. 400

♦ *Dharmashastra* of Manu develops. Its verses codify cosmogony, four *ashramas*, government, domestic affairs, caste, and morality.
♦ The Ajivikas, an ascetic, atheistic sect of naked sadhus reaches the height of its popularity. Adversaries of the Buddha and the Jain Mahavira, they have a philosophy that is deterministic, holding that everything is inevitable.

305

♦ Chandragupta Maurya, founder of first pan-Indian empire. At its height under the Buddhist emperor Ashoka (r. 273 b.c.e.–232 b.c.e.), the Mauryan Empire includes all India except the far south.

c. 302

♦ Kautilya (Chanakya), minister to Chandragupta Maurya, writes *Arthashastra*, a compendium of laws, procedures, and advice for ruling a kingdom.

300 B.C.E. to 100 C.E.

♦ Tamil Sangam age begins. Sage Agastya writes *Agattiyam*, first known Tamil grammar. Tolkappiyar writes *Tolkappiyam*, a summary of earlier works on grammar, poetics, and rhetoric, indi-cating prior high development of Tamil. Gives rules for absorbing Sanskrit words. At this time Tamil literature refers to worship of Vishnu, Indra, Murugan, and Supreme Shiva.
♦ Pancharatra Vaishnavite sect is prominent. All later Vaishnavite sects are based on the Pancharatra beliefs (formalized by Sandilya about 100 c.e.).

297 B.C.E.

♦ According to Jain history, Emperor Chandragupta Maurya abdicates; becomes Jain monk.

273

♦ Ashoka, the greatest Mauryan emperor, grandson of Chandragupta, seizes power and rules until 232. He converts to Buddhism. India's national emblem features the lion capital from his pillar.

c. 200 B.C.E. to 200 C.E.

♦ Patanjali writes the Yoga Sutra.

c. 200 B.C.E. to 100 C.E.

♦ Jaimini writes the Mimamsa Sutra.

c. 75 C.E.

♦ A Hindu prince from Gujarat invades Java.

c. 80

♦ Jains divide, on points of rules for monks, into the Shvetambara, "White-Clad," and the Digambara, "Sky-Clad."

c. 100

♦ Birth of Kapila, founder of the Samkhya philosophy, one of six classical systems of Hindu philosophy.
♦ Birth of Sandilya, first systematic promulgator of the ancient Pancharatra doctrines. His Bhakti Sutras, devotional aphorisms on Vishnu, inspire a Vaishnavite renaissance. By 900 c.e.

the sect has left a permanent mark on many Hindu schools. The Samhita of Sandilya and his followers embody the chief doctrines of present-day Vaishnavites.

c. 200

- Hindu kingdoms are established in Cambodia and Malaysia.

c. 250

- Pallava dynasty (c. 250–885) is established in Tamil Nadu. They erect the Kamakshi temple complex at the capital of Kanchipuram and the great seventh-century stone monuments at Mahabalipuram.

320

- Imperial Gupta dynasty (320–540) emerges. During this "Classical Age" norms of literature, art, architecture, and philosophy are established. This North Indian empire promotes both Vaishnavism and Saivism and, at its height, rules or receives tribute from nearly all India. Buddhism also thrives under tolerant Gupta rule.

c. 380

- Birth of Kalidasa (380–460), the great Sanskrit poet and dramatist, author of *Shakuntala* and *Meghaduta*

c. 400

- Vatsyayana writes *Kama Sutra,* the famous text on erotics.
- Death of Karaikkalammaiyar, a woman, first of the 63 Shaivite saints of Tamil Nadu.

c. 500

- Sectarian folk traditions are revised, elaborated, and recorded in the *puranas,* Hinduism's encyclopedic compendium of culture and mythology.

c. 570

- Birth of Shaivite saint Appar (c. 570–670).
- Birth of Shaivite saint Sambanthar (c. 570–670).

c. 600–900

- Twelve Vaishnava Alvar saints of Tamil Nadu flourish, writing 4,000 songs and poems praising Vishnu and narrating the stories of his avatars.

c. 700

- Over the next hundred years the small Indonesian island of Bali receives Hinduism from neighboring Java.
- Stone-carving and sculptural works completed at Mahabalipuram.

c. 710

- Death of Bhavabhuti, Sanskrit dramatist, second only to Kalidasa.

712

- Muslims conquer Sind region (Pakistan).

c. 750

- Rashtrakuta dynasty carves Kailasanatha Temple out of a rock hill at Ellora.

788

- Shankara (788–820) is born in Malabar. The famous monk-philosopher establishes 10 traditional monastic orders.

c. 800

- Birth of Vasugupta, modern founder of Kashmiri Shaivism, a monistic, meditative school.
- Birth of Andal, girl saint of Tamil Nadu. Writes devotional poetry to Lord Krishna, disappears at age 16.

c. 825

- Birth of Tamil Shaivite saint Sundarar.

c. 850

♦ Birth of Manikkavacakar, Tamil Shaivite saint.

c. 880

♦ Birth of Nammalvar (c. 880–930), greatest of Alvar saints. His poems shape beliefs of southern Vaishnavites to the present day.

c. 900

♦ Birth of Matsyendranatha, exponent of the Nath sect emphasizing kundalini yoga practices.

950

♦ Birth of Kashmiri Shaivite guru Abhinavagupta (950–1015).

960

♦ Chola king Vira, after having a vision of Shiva Nataraja, commences enlargement of the Shiva temple at Chidambaram, completed in 1250 C.E.

1001

♦ Turkish Muslims invade Afghanistan and the Punjab, the first major Muslim conquest in India.

c. 1010

♦ Tirumurai, Tamil devotional hymns of Shaivite saints, is collected as an anthology by Nambiandar Nambi.

1025

♦ Chola ruler Rajendra I sends victorious naval expeditions to Burma, Malaysia, and Indonesia.

1077

♦ Birth of Ramanuja (1077–1157) of Kanchipuram, Tamil philosopher-saint of Sri Vaishnavite sect.

1106

♦ Birth of Basavanna (1106–1167), founder and guru of the Virashaiva sect.

c. 1130

♦ Birth of Nimbarka (c.1130–1200), Vaishnavite teacher of Vedanta. Birth of Sekkilar, author of Periya Puranam, epic hagiography of the 63 Tamil Shaivite saints.

c. 1150

♦ Khmer ruler completes Angkor Wat temple (in present-day Cambodia), the largest Hindu temple in Asia.

1197

♦ Birth of Ananda Tirtha Madhva (1197–1276), venerable Vaishnavite dualist philosopher.

c.1200

♦ Birth of Gorakhnath, famous Nath yogi.
♦ All of North India is now under Muslim domination.

1230 to 1260

♦ Temple to the Sun (Surya) is constructed at Konarak, Orissa.

c. 1300

♦ Birth of Lalleshvari (c. 1300–1372) of Kashmir, Shaivite renunciant and mystic poet. She contributes significantly to the Kashmiri language.

1336

♦ Vijayanagara empire (1336–1646) of South India is founded.

1398/9

♦ Tamerlane (Timur) invades India with 90,000 cavalry and sacks Delhi (1398) and Haridvar, a Ganges pilgrimage town (1399).

c. 1400

◆ Birth of Kabir, Vaishnavite reformer who has both Muslim and Hindu followers. His Hindi songs remain immensely popular to the present day.

1450

◆ Birth of Mirabai (1450–1547), Vaishnavite Rajput princess-saint devoted to Lord Krishna.

1469

◆ Birth of Guru Nanak (1469–1539), founder of Sikhism, a faith that rejects caste and renunciation.

1473

◆ Birth of Vallabhacharya (1473–1531), a saint who teaches *pushtimarga,* "path of grace."

1486

◆ Birth of Chaitanya (1486–1533), Bengali founder of popular Vaishnavite sect that proclaims Krishna as Supreme God and emphasizes group chanting and dancing.

c. 1500

◆ Shaivite Hindu princes resettle on Bali and construct a separate kingdom.

1526

◆ Muslim conqueror Babur (1483–1530) occupies Delhi and founds the Indian Mughal Empire (1526–1761).

1532

◆ Birth of monk-poet Tulsidas (1532–1623), author of Ramcharitmanasa (1574–77) (based on Ramayana), which advances worship of Rama.

1556

◆ Akbar (1542–1605), grandson of Babur, becomes third Mughal emperor, promoting religious tolerance.

1595

◆ Construction begins on Hall of a Thousand Pillars at famous Shaivite temple in Chidambaram and is completed in 1685.

1600

◆ Royal charter forms the East India Company, setting in motion a process that ultimately results in the subjugation of India under British rule.
◆ Birth of Surdas (c. 1600), sightless Hindi bard of Agra, whose hymns to Krishna are collected in the *Sursagar.*

1603

◆ Guru Arjun compiles Adi Granth, Sikh scripture.

1605

◆ Akbar's son Jehangir succeeds his father as fourth Mughal emperor.
◆ Sikh Golden Temple at Amritsar, Punjab, is finished; later covered with gold leaf.

1608

◆ Birth of Tukaram (1608–1649), saint famed for his poems to Krishna. Considered greatest Marathi spiritual composer.

1647

◆ Shah Jehan completes Taj Mahal in Agra on the Yamuna River.

1658

◆ Zealous Muslim Aurangzeb (1618–1707) becomes Mughal emperor.

1675

♦ Aurangzeb executes Sikh Guru Tegh Bahadur, beginning the Sikh-Muslim tensions that continue to this day.

1708

♦ Gobind Singh, 10th and last Sikh guru, is assassinated.

1718

♦ Birth of Ramprasad Sen (1718–1780), Bengali poet-saint and worshipper of goddess Kali.

1751

♦ Robert Clive is victorious in the British fight for control of South India.

1764

♦ British defeat the weak Mughal emperor and gain full control of Bengal, richest province of India.

1781

♦ Birth of Sahajanand Swami (1781–1830), Gujarati founder of the Swaminarayan sect (with 1.5 million followers today).

1784

♦ Judge and linguist Sir William Jones founds Calcutta's (Kolkata's) Royal Asiatic Society, first such scholastic institution.

1786

♦ Sir William Jones uses the Rig Veda term *Aryan* (noble) to name the parent language of Sanskrit, Greek, Latin, and Germanic tongues.

1792

♦ Britain's Lord Cornwallis, governor-general of India, defeats Tipu Sultan of Mysore, the most powerful ruler in South India, which constituted the main bulwark of resistance to British expansion in India.

1803

♦ Second Anglo-Maratha war results in British capture of Delhi and control of large parts of India.
♦ Birth of Ralph Waldo Emerson (1803–1882), American poet who helps popularize Bhagavad Gita and Upanishads in the United States.

1818

♦ Birth of Swami Shiv Dayal Singh (1818–1878), founder of the esoteric reformist Radhasoami Vaishnavite sect in Agra.

1820

♦ First Indian immigrants arrive in the United States.

1824

♦ Birth of Swami Dayananda Sarasvati (1824–1883), founder of Arya Samaj (1875), Hindu reformist movement stressing a return to the values and practices of the Vedas.

1828

♦ Rammohan Roy (1772–1833) founds Brahmo Samaj in Calcutta (Kolkata). Influenced by Islam and Christianity, he denounces polytheism and idol worship.

1831

♦ Birth of Russian mystic Madame Helena P. Blavatsky (1831–1891), cofounder of Theosophical Society in 1875. Introduces amalgam of psychism, Buddhism, and Hinduism to the West.

1835

♦ Mauritius receives 19,000 indentured laborers from India. Last ship carrying workers arrives in 1922.

1836

◆ Birth of Sri Paramahansa Ramakrishna (1836–1886), God-intoxicated Bengali saint, devotee of goddess Kali, and guru of Swami Vivekananda.

1837

◆ Britain formalizes importation of Indian indentured laborers throughout the Commonwealth.

1838

◆ Birth of Keshab Chunder Sen (1838–1884), Hindu reformer.

1840s

◆ Hindus from India enter the Caribbean region as indentured laborers.

1841

◆ First U.S. chair of Sanskrit and Indology established at Yale University.

1850

◆ First English translation of the Rig Veda, by H. H. Wilson.

1851

◆ Sir M. Monier-Williams (1819–1899) publishes *English-Sanskrit Dictionary*.

1853

◆ Birth of Sri Sarada Devi (1853–1920), wife of Sri Ramakrishna, lineage holder in the Ramakrishna tradition and inspiration for the Sarada Math convent for women.
◆ Max Müller (1823–1900), German Sanskrit scholar in England, advocates the term *Aryan* to describe speakers of Indo-European languages.

1857

◆ First major Indian revolt against British rule, the "Sepoy Mutiny."

1860

◆ First indentured servants from Madras (Chennai) and Calcutta (Kolkata) arrive in Durban, South Africa to work on sugar plantations.

1861

◆ Birth of Bengali poet Rabindranath Tagore (1861–1941), awarded the Nobel Prize in literature in 1913.

1863

◆ Birth of Swami Vivekananda (1863–1902), dynamic missionary to West and catalyst of Hindu revival in India.

1869

◆ Birth of Mohandas Karamchand Gandhi (1869–1948), Indian nationalist and Hindu political activist, who develops the strategy of nonviolent disobedience that leads to the independence of India (1947) from Great Britain.

1872

◆ Birth of Sri Aurobindo Ghose (1872–1950), Bengali Indian nationalist and yoga philosopher.

1873

◆ Birth of Swami Rama Tirtha (1873–1906), who lectures throughout Japan and America spreading "practical Vedanta."

1875

◆ Madame Blavatsky, with others, founds Theosophical Society in New York, later headquartered at Adyar, Madras (Chennai).

1876

◆ British queen Victoria (1819–1901) is proclaimed empress of India (r. 1876–1901).
◆ Birth of Dada Lekhraj (1876–1969), Hindu founder of Brahma Kumaris, an international

social reform movement led by women that stresses meditation and world peace.

1876 to 1890

◆ Max Müller (1823–1900), pioneer of comparative religion as a scholarly discipline, publishes 50-volume *Sacred Books of the East,* English translations of Indian and other Asian scriptures.

1879

◆ First emigrant ship to Fiji adds 498 Indian indentured laborers to the nearly 340,000 already working in other colonies of the British Empire.
◆ Birth of Sri Ramana Maharshi (1879–1950), Hindu *advaita* renunciant saint of Tiruvannamalai, South India.

1884

◆ Birth of Swami Ramdas (1884–1963), known as Papa, Indian saint and devotee of Lord Rama.

1885

◆ Indian National Congress founded.

1886

◆ René Guénon (1886–1951), first European philosopher of note to become a Vedantin, is born.

1887

◆ Birth of Swami Shivananda (1887–1963), renowned universalist teacher, author of 200 books, founder of Divine Life Society in Rishikesh, and guru to many teachers who brought Hinduism to the West.

1888

◆ Birth of Sarvepalli Radhakrishnan (1888–1975), philosopher, eminent writer, and free India's first vice president and second president.

1893

◆ World Parliament of Religions in Chicago recognizes Eastern religious traditions through presentations by representatives of Hinduism, Buddhism, Jainism, and Sikhism. Swami Vivekananda receives acclaim as spokesperson for Hinduism.

1894

◆ Birth of Meher Baba (1894–1969) of Poona, silent sage whose mystical teachings stress love, self-inquiry, and God consciousness.

1896

◆ Birth of Anandamayi Ma (1896–1982), God-intoxicated yogini and mystic saint of Bengal.
◆ Birth of Bhaktivedanta Swami Prabhupada (1896–1977). In 1966 he founds International Society of Krishna Consciousness (ISKCON) in the United States.

1897

◆ Swami Vivekananda founds Ramakrishna Math and Mission near Calcutta (Kolkata).

1908

◆ Birth of Swami Muktananda (1908–1982), a guru of the Kashmiri Shaivite school who founds Siddha Yoga Dham to promulgate Indian mysticism, kundalini yoga, and philosophy throughout the world.

1912

◆ Anti-Indian racial riots on the U.S. West Coast expel large Hindu immigrant population.

1916

◆ Birth of Swami Chinmayananda (1916–1993), Vedantist scholar, lecturer, teacher, and founder of Chinmaya Mission.

1917

+ Last Hindu Indian indentured laborers are taken to British colonies of Fiji and Trinidad.
+ U.S. government severely restricts Indian citizens from immigration. Restriction stands until 1965.

1918

+ Sai Baba of Shirdi (1856–1918), saint to Hindus and Muslims, dies at approximately age 62.

1920

+ Mohandas K. Gandhi (1869–1948) uses *satyagraha,* "truth power," first articulated in South Africa, as a strategy of noncooperation and nonviolence against India's British rulers.
+ Paramahansa Yogananda (1893–1952), famous author of *Autobiography of a Yogi,* teacher of *kriya yoga* and Hindu guru with many Western disciples, enters the United States, where he founds the Self-Realization Fellowship (1935).

1922

+ Tagore's school at Shantiniketan (founded 1901) is made into Visva Bharati University and becomes a national university in 1951.

1923

+ U.S. law excludes Indian nationals from naturalization.

1924

+ Sir John Marshall (1876–1958) discovers relics of Indus Valley pre-Hindu civilization. Begins systematic large-scale excavations.

1925

+ K. V. Hedgewar (1890–1949) founds Rashtriya Swayam Sevak Sangh (RSS), a militant Hindu nationalist movement.

1926

+ Birth of Satya Sai Baba, charismatic Hindu guru, educationalist, and worker of miracles.

1927

+ Shivaya Subramuniyaswami (1927–2001), founder of Saiva Siddhanta Church and *Hinduism Today* magazine, is born in Oakland, California.
+ Maharashtra bars tradition of dedicating girls to temples as Devadasis, ritual dancers. Karnataka, Andhra Pradesh, and Orissa soon follow suit. Twenty years later, Tamil Nadu bans devotional dancing and singing by women in its temples and in all Hindu ceremonies.

1928

+ Hindu leader and future prime minister of India Jawaharlal Nehru (1889–1964) drafts plan for a free India; becomes president of Congress Party in 1929.

1931

+ Birth of Sri Chinmoy, yogi, artist, master of self-transcendence, and United Nations peace ambassador, in Bengal.
+ Some 2.5 million Indian Hindus reside overseas; largest communities are in Sri Lanka, Malaya, Mauritius, and South Africa.

1934

+ Paul Brunton's popular *A Search in Secret India* introduces Hindu teachers such as Ramana Maharshi to the West.

1938

+ Bharatiya Vidya Bhavan is founded in Bombay (Mumbai) by K. M. Munshi to conserve, develop, and honor Indian culture.

1947

+ India gains independence from Britain on August 15.

1948

- Establishment of Sarva Seva Sangh, Gandhian movement for new social order (*sarvodaya*).
- Mohandas Gandhi is assassinated on January 30 in retaliation for his embracing of Muslim demands in India.
- The last British troops leave India on February 28.

1949

- India's new constitution, authored chiefly by B. R. Ambedkar, declares there shall be no "discrimination" against any citizen on the grounds of caste, *jati,* and abolishes the practice of "untouchability."

1950

- India is declared a secular republic. Prime Minister Jawaharlal Nehru (r. 1947–64) is determined to abolish caste and industrialize the nation.

1964

- India's Vishva Hindu Parishad (VHP), a Hindu religious nationalist movement, is founded to counter secularism.
- Rock group the Beatles practice Transcendental Meditation (T.M.), making Maharshi Mahesh Yogi famous.

1965

- U.S. immigration law is rewritten to cancel racial qualifications and restore rights of naturalization to Asians. The first Hindu teacher to benefit from the lifting of immigration quotas is Bhaktivedanta Swami Prabhupada, famous Vaishnavite guru and founder of International Society of Krishna Consciousness. Annual immigration from India shifts from 100 (1925) to 170,000 (1985) per year.

1966

- Jawaharlal Nehru's daughter, Indira Gandhi, becomes prime minister of India, world's largest democracy.

1973

- Neem Karoli Baba (1900–1973), Hindu mystic and *siddha,* dies.

1975

- Netherlands gives independence to Dutch Guyana, which becomes Suriname; one-third of Hindus (descendants of Indian plantation workers) immigrate to Netherlands for better social and economic conditions.

1979

- Shivaya Subramuniyaswami founds *Hinduism Today,* international journal to promote Hindu solidarity.

1980

- Hindu nationalist party, Bharatiya Janata Party (BJP), is founded.

1984

- Indian soldiers under orders from Prime Minister Indira Gandhi storm Sikh Golden Temple in Amritsar and crush rebellion. Gandhi is assassinated later in the year by her Sikh bodyguards. Her son Rajiv takes office.

1986

- Swami Satchidananda (1914–2002) dedicates Light of Truth Universal Shrine (LOTUS) at Yogaville, Virginia, in the United States.
- Jiddu Krishnamurti (1895–1986), Indian philosopher, lecturer, and author, known for his teaching of radical self-awareness, dies.

1992

- Hindu radicals demolish Babri Masjid, built in 1548 on Rama's birthplace in Ayodhya by Muslim conqueror Babur after he destroyed a Hindu temple marking the site.

1993

- Chicago hosts centenary Parliament of World Religions, in September.

1994

- Harvard University study identifies more than 800 Hindu temples open for worship in the United States.

1998 to 2004

- Bharatiya Janata Party (BJP) serves as India's ruling party.

2001

- History's largest human gathering, 70 million people, worship at Kumbha Mela 2001, Allahabad, at the confluence of the Ganges and Yamuna Rivers.
- Swami Amar Jyoti, 73, founder of four Jyoti ashrams in the United States and India, dies.

2006

- Hinduism continues to grow in most countries of the old diaspora: Fiji, Guyana, Trinidad, Mauritius, Malaysia, and Suriname. Europe and the United States continue to be destinations for the current participants in the diaspora. Descendants maintain their faith and identity.

ENTRIES A TO Z

A

abhaya mudra

The *abhaya mudra* (*see* MUDRAS) is an important gesture in Indian iconography. In it, the right hand is raised and opened, straight up and facing forward (divinities with more than two hands raise one of their right hands). *Abhaya* literally means "no fear," and the gesture indicates blessing, protection, and reassurance. The gesture is ancient and widespread and is found in the iconography of Buddhists, Jains, and Hindus.

The Buddha(s) and the TIRTHANKARAS are frequently seen using this hand gesture. The Lord SHIVA in his NATARAJA, or divine dancer, pose has his upper right hand in the *abhaya mudra*. In fact, this *mudra* may be used when any divinity is represented in Indian dance/dramas.

Further reading: Fredrick W. Bunce, *A Dictionary of Buddhist and Hindu Iconography, Illustrated: Objects, Devices, Concepts, Rites, and Related Terms* (New Delhi: D. K. Printworld, 1997); Eva Rudy Jansen, *The Hindu Book of Imagery: The Gods and Their Symbols* (Havelte, Holland: Binkey Kok, 1995); Margaret Stutley, *An Illustrated Dictionary of Hindu Iconography* (Boston: Routledge & Kegan Paul, 1985).

Abhedananda, Swami (1866–1939) *pioneer Hindu leader in the United States*

The Indian monk Swami Abhedananda founded the New York City Vedanta Society at the end of the 19th century, pioneering the spread of Hindu thought in America.

Abhedananda was born Kaliprasad Chandra in Calcutta (Kolkata). As a teenager, he was interested in yoga, philosophy, and the religious life and, though quite intelligent, did not attend college. Rather, at the age of 18 he had his first meeting with Sri RAMAKRISHNA, who immediately recruited the youthful Kaliprasad to his inner circle. Kaliprasad moved into the Ramakrishna residence at Dakshineswar, where he lived until Ramakrishna died two years later.

Shortly after Ramakrishna's passing, Kaliprasad joined the other men who had gathered around the master in taking the vows of the renounced life (see SANNYASI), at which time he took the name Abhedananda. He spent the next several years in concentrated study of the Hindu holy books and in meditation. For a brief period he left his brother monks to wander around India.

In 1893, one of his fellow monks, Swami VIVE-KANANDA, traveled to America to address the WORLD

PARLIAMENT OF RELIGIONS. Abhedananda organized the celebration in Calcutta of the swami's American success, and three years later Vivekananda called him to assist his work in the West. Abhedananda remained in London for a year speaking and building a following for the Vedanta Society.

In 1897, Abhedananda began a 25-year stay in New York City. He succeeded in organizing a Vedanta Society (Vivekananda had failed to do so), and built it into a relatively strong organization. He moved in the intellectual circles of his day and was invited to speak at a number of colleges and universities. He also made some 17 lecture tours in Europe. All his teachings and lecturing consistently reflected the ADVAITA VEDANTA perspective of Ramakrishna; together with his learned colleagues he argued for the unity of Truth and the confluence of science and religion.

In 1921, Abhedananda returned to India, where he was received as a celebrity. He went on to establish two Ramakrishna centers, in Darjeeling (1923) and Calcutta (1929). Among his last duties was presiding at the 1937 Parliament of Religions in Calcutta, organized to celebrate the Ramakrishna Centennial. Abhedananda died two years later in 1939.

See also VEDANTA SOCIETIES/RAMAKRISHNA MATH AND MISSION; UNITED STATES.

Further reading: Swami Abhedananda, *Doctrine of Karma: A Study in the Philosophy and Practice of Work* (Calcutta: Ramakrishna Vedanta Math, 1965); ———, *The Religion of the Twentieth Century* (Calcutta: Ramakrishna Vedanta Math, 1984); ———, *Spiritual Teachings of Swami Abhedananda.* Translated by P. Sheshadri Aiyer (Calcutta: Ramakrishna Vedanta Math 1962); ———, *Swami Vivekananda and His Work* (Calcutta: Ramakrishna Vedanta Math, 1968); Ashutosh Ghosh, *Swami Abhedananda, the Patriot Saint* (Calcutta: Ramakrishna Vedanta Math, 1967).

Abhidhyan Yoga Institute (est. 1991)

The Abhidhyan Yoga Institute, also called Modern Seers, headquartered at Swarthmore, Pennsylvania, is a training center for All Embracing (*Abhidhyan*) Yoga, a somewhat rare form of TANTRA that has survived within several lesser-known Hindu and Buddhist sects. All Embracing Yoga incorporates the four major yoga paths: JNANA YOGA, the path of study; BHAKTI YOGA, the path of devotion to the Divine; KARMA YOGA, the path of action; and RAJA YOGA, the path that unites mind, heart, and body in pursuit of the Divine.

The revival of All Embracing Yoga, and its spread from India to the United States and several other countries is attributed to Sri Acharya Abhidhyanananda Avadhuta (Anatole Ruslanov) (b. May 5, 1965), a Russian computer scientist who apprenticed in BENARES (Varanasi) India, with Sri ANANDAMURTI (1921–90), founder of the ANANDA MARGA YOGA SOCIETY. As a monastic student of the guru, Anatole became a vital transmitter and spiritual master of this largely overlooked form of tantric practice.

A year after the death of Sri Anandamurti (1990), Anatole established the Abhidhyanananda Yoga Institute with its headquarters in the United States. He added his own teaching methods to those of his teacher, synthesized what he had learned during his monastic life in India, and refined his tantric abilities. In 1998, Anatole revealed to his students that he had had a transformational experience that had lifted his religious and practical focus to a higher level, thus requiring a revision of the discipline required of practitioners.

Students of All Embracing Yoga engage in regular meditation, follow strict moral codes, and practice postures (ASANAS) and breathing techniques (PRANAYAMA). Abhidhyanananda recommends solitary spiritual work for a year prior to entering this specific yoga path.

The institute publishes a periodical, *The Tantrik Path*, at its headquarters in Nevada City, California. No publications in book form are used at the institute. Rather, all teachings are found online on the Internet.

Abhinavagupta (c. middle of 10th century to middle of 11th century) *Kashmiri Shaivite philosopher*

Abhinavagupta, who lived his entire life in the northern Indian region of Kashmir, is one of the giants of Indian philosophical and intellectual history. His work represents the pinnacle of the tantric (*see* TANTRISM) school of KASHMIRI SHAIVISM, which sees the world as both real and divine. He is also recognized as one of India's foremost theorists in the field of aesthetics, or the appreciation of art.

Abhinavagupta interwove the diverse threads of the earlier schools of Kashmiri Shaivism into a coherent and cogent philosophy and practice. He wrote numerous books and commentaries, all in Sanskrit. Most well known is the magnum opus, the massive *Tantraloka;* it deals with the philosophy, religion, and yogic practice of the Kashmir Shaiva tradition.

Abhinavagupta's exceptional work on the theory of art derives its interest from his belief in the divinity of the senses and sense experience. His most well known book in this area is his commentary on the *Dhvanyaloka,* an important text on aesthetics, which has become a source book for much of later Indian aesthetic theory. Abhinavagupta's influence is most evident in the traditions of Swami MUKTANANDA and his disciple Swami CHIDVILASANANDA, two of the most prominent modern teachers in the Kashmiri Shaivite tradition.

See also SHAIVISM.

Further reading: Raniero Gnoli, *The Aesthetic Experience According to Abhinavagupta* (Varanasi: Chowkhamba Sanskrit Series Office, 1968); Paul Eduardo Muller-Ortega, *The Triadic Heart of Siva: Kaula Tantricism of Abhinavagupa in the Non-Dual Shaivism of Kashmir* (Albany: State University of New York Press, 1989); K. C. Pandey, *Abhinavagupta: An Historical and Philosophical Study* (Varanasi: Chowkhamba Sanskrit Series Office, 1963); R. Raghavan, *Abhinavagupta and His Works* (Varanasi: Chokambha Orientalia, 1981); Y. S. Walimbe, *Abhinavagupta and Indian Aesthetics* (Delhi: Ajanta, 1980).

Abhishiktananda, Swami (1910–1973) *pioneer in Hindu-Christian monasticism*

Born Henri Le Saux, Abhishiktananda was a pioneer in the field of spiritual and theological dialogue between Christianity and Hinduism.

He was born on August 30, 1910, at Saint Briac in Brittany, France. At an early age he felt a call to the vocation of a Roman Catholic priest, and in 1929 he entered the Benedictine Monastery of Saint Anne de Kergonan in Plouharnel. During his 19 years there he worked as librarian and master of ceremonies. He served in the French army during World War II and experienced a miraculous escape after being captured by German troops in 1940.

Seeking a more radical path for living a spiritual life, Le Saux was attracted to India as early as 1934. In Tamil Nadu state he met Father Jules Monchanin, a Roman Catholic priest serving in a Tamil village in southern India, who was formulating a path for living a contemplative life that combined Indian asceticism (see SANNYASI) and Christian practice. Le Saux joined Fr. Monchanin in 1948 at Kulitalai; the two began a small ashram near the CAUVERY RIVER at the village of Tannirpalli in Tiruchirappalli District, South India. In 1950, they settled in Shantivanam (Forest of Peace) and named their new foundation Saccidananda Ashram after the Hindu trinity.

In 1950 Le Saux adopted the dress of a Hindu ascetic and changed his name to Swami Abhishiktananda (the Bliss of the Anointed One). He began studying Tamil and Sanskrit and immersed himself in Indian traditions and practices. A meeting in 1949 with RAMANA MAHARSHI (1879–1950) at Ramana's ashram in Tiruvannamalai had a strong influence on his developing spirituality, and between 1950 and 1955 he spent many months in deep meditation in the caves near Ramana's ashram at the holy mountain Arunachala. After Ramana's death in 1950, he became a disciple of Gnanananda Giri of Tirukoylur.

When the ailing Fr. Monchanin returned to France and died in 1957, Abhishiktananda felt a growing attraction to the north of India and the Himalayas. He undertook several pilgrimages and often visited the holy city of BENARES, (Varanasi), where he found others, such as Dr. Raimon Panikkar, engaged in Hindu-Christian dialogue. In 1968, he left Shantivanam under the leadership of Father Bede Griffiths (1968–93) and went to live in a hermitage in Uttarkashi in the Himalayas. In 1980, Shantivanam, under the leadership of Father Bede, was received in the Camaldolese Congregation of the Benedictine Confederation.

In 1969 Abhishiktananda participated in the All-India Seminar on the Church in India Today in Bangalore, the aim of which was to adapt the principles of Vatican II to the Indian context. There he was recognized as a pioneer in the field of Hindu-Christian dialogue, whose life and work inspired several religious communities, such as Jyotiniketan Ashram formed in 1969 at Bareilly.

Abhishiktananda's books and teaching are largely addressed to Christians, with the aim of helping them discover the spirit and principles of ADVAITA (non-dual) Hinduism. While always remaining a Christian, he discerned elements of Christianity in the spiritual wisdom of India that helped him toward resolving for himself the tensions between the two religions and finding an inner integration. His goal was to move beyond the limits of institutional religions and churches to encourage spiritual renewal, which he considered essential for human survival in the modern world.

On July 14, 1973, Abhishiktananda suffered a heart attack on the road in Rishikesh, where he was on retreat with another French religious. He died December 7, 1973, at Indore, Madhya Pradesh.

See also CHRISTIAN-HINDU RELATIONS.

Further reading: Abhishiktananda, *Saccidananda: A Christian Approach to Advaitic Experience* (Delhi: I.S.P.C.K., 1974); ———, *The Further Shore* (Delhi: I.S.P.C.K., 1975); ———, *The Secret of Arunchala* (Delhi: I.S.P.C.K., 1979); ———, *Guru and Disciple: An Encounter with Sri Gnanananda* (Delhi: I.S.P.C.K., 1990); ———, *Swami Abhishiktananda: Ascent to the Depth of the Heart: The Spiritual Diary (1948–1973)*. Edited and selected by Raimon Panikkar, translated by David Fleming and James Stuart (Delhi: I.S.P.C.K., 1998); H. Ralston, *Christian Ashrams: A New Religious Movement in Contemporary India* (Lewiston, N.Y.: Edwin Mellen Press, 1987); James Stuart, *Swami Abhishiktananda: His Life Told through His Letters*, rev. ed. (Delhi: I.S.P.C.K., 1995).

Abu, Mount

Mount Abu is a small peak (some 4,000 feet high) in the southwest of the Indian state of Rajasthan that figures in Hindu legend. It is especially holy to Jains (see JAINISM), who built beautifully adorned temples there. It was once a British hill station for retreat from the summer heat.

According to one legend, the sage Vasishtha's cow Nandini was once trapped in a deep gorge and could not free herself. The sage appealed to Lord SHIVA for assistance. The Lord sent SARASVATI, the divine stream, to help flood the gorge so that the cow could float up. Vasishtha then decided to ensure that such mishaps would not occur in future. He asked the youngest son of HIMALAYA, the king of mountains, to fill the chasm permanently. This he did with the assistance of Arbud, the mighty snake. This spot came to be known as Mount Arbud, and the name was later changed to its present form—Mount Abu.

It is said that this mountain was visited and blessed in the sixth century B.C.E. by MAHAVIRA, the 24th and last Jain TIRTHANKARA of this half of the cosmic era. It is known for its marble Jain temples, two of which are famous. The first, built in the 11th century, is devoted to RISHABHA, the first Tirthankara of the line leading to Mahavira, The other, from the 13th century, is dedicated to Neminatha, the 22nd Tirthankara in the line. The temples are not large but are known for their stunning and intricately carved statuary and ornamentation.

Further reading: Lothar Clermont, *Jainism and the Temples of Mount Abu* (New Delhi: Prakash Books, 1998); Sehdev Kumar, *A Thousand Petalled Lotus: Jain Temples of Rajasthan: Architecture and Iconography* (New Delhi: Abhinav, 2001); Jodh Singh Mehta, *Abu to Udaipur (Celestial Simla to City of Sunrise)* (Delhi: Motilal Banarsidass, 1970); Muniraj Jayanta Vijayi, *Holy Abu: A Tourist's Guide to Mount Abu and Its Jaina Shrines* (Bhavnagar: Shri Yashovijaya Jaina Granthmala, 1954).

Acharanga Sutra (c. 300 B.C.E.–400 C.E.)

The Acharanga Sutra is the first of the 12 texts accepted as canonical by SHVETAMBARA Jains. The DIGAMBARA Jains believe that the original version of this sutra was lost and reject the text held sacred by the Shvetambaras. The sutra outlines, with some details, the rigorous limitations that Jain monks must observe and answers difficulties that might occur in their struggle to prevent injury to any creatures, including microscopic ones.

To cite some examples, the Acharanga Sutra prohibits monks from digging in the earth (to prevent injury to any earth being); bathing, swimming, wading, or walking in the rain (to prevent injury to any water being); kindling or extinguishing any flame (to prevent injury to beings that live in fire); waving the arms or making any other sudden movement (to prevent injury to air beings); and walking in any greenery or stepping on any plant (to prevent injury to beings living in plants). The sutra also demands the strictest vegetarianism.

Further reading: Hermann Jacobi, trans., *Jain Sutras*, Part 1, Sacred Books of the East, XVL (Delhi: Motilal Banarsidass, 1964); P. S. Jaini, *The Jain Path of Purification* (Berkeley: University of California Press, 1979); Bimala Churn Law, *Some Jain Canonical Sutras* (Bombay: Bombay Branch Royal Asiatic Society, 1949).

acharya

An *acharya* is any spiritual guide or teacher. In ancient times the term referred specifically to the one who initiated a student and taught him the complete VEDA or sacred literature. In later times it became a general honorific indicating great learning and/or spiritual accomplishment. The term was, for example, appended to the names of all the great VEDANTA teachers: SHANKARA, RAMANUJA, MADHVA, and NIMBARKA, become Shankaracharya, Ramanujacharya, Madhvacharya, and Nimbarkacharya.

This practice is followed in the JAIN tradition as well; for example, GUNABHADRA will be called Gunabhadracharya. Furthermore, Jains honor *acharyas* in the *panchanamaskara* MANTRA, the central mantra of the Jain faith, immediately after the ARHATS and SIDDHAS; this indicates their exalted status.

Further reading: Brian K. Smith, "Ritual, Knowledge and Being: Initiation and Veda Study in Ancient India," *Numen* 33, no. 1 (1986): 65–89.

achintya bhedabheda   *See* CHAITANYA, SRI KRISHNA.

adhvaryu

The *adhvaryu* is the priest of the YAJUR VEDA at the traditional Vedic public ritual. He oversees all the ritual activity, carrying out most of the actions himself. He prepares and uses the implements, pours clarified butter, kills the ritual animal, and recites the appropriate verses (of either the Black or the White Yajur Veda) as the ritual actions are performed. The priests of the RIG, SAMA, and ATHARVA VEDAS are usually much less active on the ritual ground.

Further reading: Julius Eggeling, trans., *The Satapatha-Brahmana*, Part I, *According to the Text of the Madhyandina School* (Delhi: Motilal Banarsidass, 1982); Jan Gonda, *The Ritual Sutras* (Wiesbaden: Otto Harrassowitz, 1977); Arthur B. Keith, trans., *The Veda of the Black Yajus School* (Delhi: Motilal Banarsidass, 1967); J. Frits Staal, *The Science of Ritual* (Poona: Bhandarkar Oriental Research Institute, 1982).

adhyasa

Adhyasa, or "superimposition" of an unreal thing upon a real one, is an important concept in the ADVAITA (non-dual) philosophy of SHANKARA, the renowned teacher of VEDANTA.

A pedestrian example would be a person looking at a rope in a dark place and briefly seeing a snake. This sort of superimposition involves two physical objects, but the central superimposition or *adhyasa* in Shankara's system is the ignorant superimposition of the empirical world upon the attribute-free BRAHMAN or ultimate reality. Humans imagine that the empirical world is real, but, just as the rope is not the snake, so is the empirical world not the *brahman.* Shankara holds that the phenomenal world is false (*mithya*) and illusory (MAYA). Ignorance (AVIDYA), leads us to see the world as real, but when knowledge (VIDYA or JNANA) dawns, we see the truth: that the only existence is *brahman,* the actionless, attribute-free ground of being that can be described as SAT-CHIT-ANANDA, being-consciousness-bliss.

Further reading: S. N. Dasgupta, *History of Indian Philosophy,* Vol. 1 (Delhi: Motilal Banarsidass, 1975); ———, *History of Indian Philosophy,* Vol. 2 (Delhi: Motilal Banarsidass, 1975); Daya Krishna, *New Perspectives in Indian Philosophy* (Jaipur: Rawat, 2001); Karl Potter, ed., *Encyclopedia of Indian Philosophies,* vol. 3 (Delhi: Motilal Banarsidass, 1981).

adhyatma   See VEDANTA.

Adi Da Samraj (1939–   ) *teacher of "Crazy Wisdom"*

Adi Da Samraj, a U.S.-born guru, teaches his idiosyncratic philosophy and discipline to a small but devoted international following, mostly in English-speaking countries.

According to Adi Da Samraj's autobiography, he experienced a state of perfect awareness of ultimate reality from the day of his birth as Franklin Jones on November 3, 1939, on Long Island, New York. At age two he relinquished that state in order to experience human limitations completely. From 1957 he studied philosophy at Columbia University in New York. Beginning in his college years Jones engaged in a spiritual quest that led him to Swami RUDRANANDA in New York City and eventually to Swami MUKTANANDA, the famous practitioner of Shaivism and *siddha* yoga. From childhood, Jones reported many experiences of KUNDALINI (awakening divine energy), mystical revelation, astral travel, and superconscious identification with higher beings, but he found that these powers were not valuable because they were not expressions of his real nature. In 1970 at the Vedanta temple in Hollywood, he experienced a reawakening and realization of his ultimate nature; he knew his oneness with SHAKTI, divine energy. He left Muktananda and became a devotee of Shakti.

In 1972, Jones began to teach his "radical" understanding of a spiritual path that includes devotion to a guru and self-observation. He opened a small ashram in Los Angeles and began to attract devotees. During a trip to India he adopted the first of what would become many new names for himself, Bubba Free John. At first he worked with students in a traditional way, but in the late 1970s he adopted the "Crazy Wisdom" approach to spirituality. In 1979, he changed his name to Da Free John. In 1986, his name became Da Love-Ananda. In the late 1980s he became Da Avabhasa (the Bright), in 1990 Da Kalki, and finally, in 1995, Adi Da Samraj. The completion of his work of revelation, he says, is signified in this last change of name and his title of AVATAR.

In 1983, he acquired an island in Fiji for his community, then called the Johannine Daist Communion. Today Adi Da's spiritual movement is named Adidam, or the Way of the Heart. A central teaching of this path is that all seeking requires constant activity, a factor that, in itself, prevents conscious realization and perfect happiness. Because the means used on any path are always changing, no method of seeking is ever permanently successful. Adi Da asserts that he has attained the Most Perfect Happiness and can transmit this divine Self-realization to others. Thus, a devotional relationship with Adi Da is the source of divine Self-realization. The Way of the Heart employs meditation, study, worship, communal living, and dietary and sexual disciplines as means for "radical" understanding and communion with Adi Da.

The educational organization of Adidam is the Laughing Man Institute, which propagates the teaching of Adi Da around the world. Adidam also has a publishing vehicle, the Dawn Horse Press, which publishes *The Adidam Revelation Magazine* and books about and by Adi Da.

At the turn of the 21st century Adidam reported over 1,000 members worldwide, the majority of whom live in the United States. Centers have been opened in New Zealand, Australia, Great Britain, and Fiji. Ashrams currently are located in Fiji, Hawaii, and northern California.

See also BONDER, SANIEL.

Further reading: Saniel Bonder, *The Divine Emergence of the World-Teacher Heart-Master Da Love-Ananda* (Clearlake, Calif.: Dawn Horse Press, 1990); Adi Da Samraj, *Avatar Adi Da Samraj and the First 25 Years of His Divine Revelation Work* (Middletown, Calif.: Dawn Horse Press, 1997); ———, *The Knee of Listening* (Clearlake, Calif.: Dawn Horse Press, 1973); ———, *See My Brightness Face to Face: A Celebration of the Rachira Buddha* (Middletown, Calif.: Dawn Horse Press, 1997).

Adidam   *See* ADI DA SAMRAJ.

Adi Granth   *See* SIKHISM.

Adinatha   *See* RISHABHA.

Adipurana

The Adipurana is an important SANSKRIT text of the DIGAMBARA Jains (*see* JAINISM). It records the lives of the 63 great men of Jain history and myth (which are also recorded later in the larger compendium of HEMACHANDRA, *The History of the 63 Famous Men*). It was begun in Karnataka state by JINASENA around the ninth century C.E. and completed by one of his students, GUNABHADRA, whose addition bears the separate name of Uttarapuranam.

The Adipurana was the first major Jain text that openly integrated elements of Hinduism into the Jain philosophical framework. Jinasena provides for Jain BRAHMINS (who are not, however, allowed the haughtiness and privilege of Hindu Brahmins), the caste system (which in the Jain view is a political institution, not a birthright), various Hindu life transition rituals, and elements of Hindu temple ritual, which are given different philosophical interpretations. For example, Jinasena provided the first Jain fire rituals, which are clearly Vedic, Brahmanical rituals revalorized for the Jain context. Jinasena also establishes a set of "traditional" Jain MANTRAS to mirror the Hindu tradition.

See also JAINISM.

Further reading: P. S. Jaini, *The Jaina Path of Purification* (Delhi: Motilal Banarsidass, 1979); ———, "Jaina Puranas: A Puranic Counter Tradition." In *Purana Perennis: Reciprocity and Transformation in Hindu and Jaina Texts.* Edited by Wendy Doniger (Albany: State University of New York Press, 1993); George Ralph Strohl, "The Image of the Hero in Jainism: Rsabha, Bharata and Bahubali in the Adipurana of Jinasena" (Diss., University of Chicago, 1984); Moriz Winternitz, *History of Indian Literature* (Delhi: Motilal Banarsidass, 1967).

Adishesha   (also Shesha or Ananta)

Adishesha, the divine thousand-headed serpent, is the couch for Lord VISHNU as he sleeps between eras on the vast ocean of milk. When the MILK OCEAN was churned by the demons and gods to produce the nectar of immortality,

Adishesha was the churning rope, according to some versions of the story. It is also said that, when time begins again in a new era, the world sits on the head of Adishesha; whenever he stirs, earthquakes result. At the end of each cosmic era he vomits out the fire of destruction, which incinerates the universe.

In the story of PRAHLADA and HIRANYAKASHIPU, Prahlada prays to Adishesha when forced by his father to eat poison and is saved. Other stories associate Adishesha with cosmic poison in different ways.

Many different personages in Indian tradition have been said to be incarnations of Adishesha, most notably BALARAMA, the brother of Lord KRISHNA. Adishesa is usually described as the son of a *rishi*, a seer. However, as is common in Indian mythology many contradictory stories exist, and some say that he was born of SHIVA. He has even been identified with the eternal, all-encompassing *BRAHMAN* itself.

Further reading: Cornelia Dimmitt and J. A. B. van Buitenen, *Classical Hindu Mythology: A Reader in the Sanskrit Puranas* (Philadelphia: Temple University Press, 1978); E. Washburn Hopkins, *Epic Mythology* (Delhi: Motilal Banarsidass, 1986).

Aditi

Aditi (she who has no limit) is one of the few goddesses mentioned by name in the RIG VEDA, the earliest extant Indian text. There she is said to be the mother of the ADITYAS, a group of seven (sometimes eight or 12) important divinities, including VARUNA and MITRA. However, the list of her children varies in other texts; SURYA, the Sun God; AGNI, the god of fire; or even INDRA, the king of the gods, is referred to as *aditya,* that is, "having Aditi as mother." Aditi is said to have sprung from the RISHI DAKSHA (although in Rig Veda, Daksha is also simultaneously her son). There is no iconography of Aditi (*see* ICONS).

Further reading: Joel Peter Brereton, *The Rgvedic Adityas* (New Haven, Conn.: American Oriental Society, 1981); Cornelia Dimmitt and J. A. B. van Buitenen, *Classical Hindu Mythology: A Reader in the Sanskrit Puranas* (Philadelphia: Temple University Press, 1978); E. Washburn Hopkins, *Epic Mythology* (Delhi: Motilal Banarsidass, 1986); M. P. Pandit, *Aditi and Other Deities in the Veda* (Pondicherry: Dipti, 1970); W. J. Wilkins, *Hindu Mythology, Vedic and Puranic* (Calcutta: Rupa, 1973).

Adityas

Aditya means "whose mother is ADITI," the Vedic goddess. The father of the Adityas is usually said to be the RISHI Kashyapa, a famous Vedic *rishi*. The Adityas are sometimes referred to as seven, sometimes eight, and sometimes 12 in number. The Vedic list is seven or eight. The list of seven includes VARUNA, MITRA, ARYAMAN, BHAGA, DAKSHA, ANSHA, and SURYA or SAVITRI. The list of eight sometimes includes Martanda, who is said to have been excluded by his mother.

When 12 Adityas are listed, in later times, they represent the 12 months of the year; they are Dhatri, MITRA, ARYAMAN, RUDRA, SURYA, Bhaga, VIVASVAT, PUSHAN, SAVITRI, TVASHTRI, and VISHNU. In some lists AGNI, the god of fire, or even INDRA, the king of the gods, is referred to as an "Aditya."

Further reading: Joel P. Brerton, *The Rg Vedic Adityas* (New Haven, Conn.: American Oriental Society, 1981); Pravesh Saxena, *Aditya from Rgveda to the Upanisads* (Delhi: Parimal, 1992); W. J. Wilkins, *Hindu Mythology, Vedic and Puranic* (Calcutta: Rupa, 1973).

adrishta

Adrishta literally means the "unseen," a category in MIMAMSA and VAISHESHIKA traditions.

In Mimamsa the term refers to any invisible result of a ritual act that accrues to a person; it bears fruit upon that person's death. *Adrishta* has lent itself to extensive commentary in the Mimamsa literature. It is intangible and ineffable, but also the instrument through which Vedic rites come to fruition.

In Vaisheshika, the term is sometimes synonymous with *adharma*, the equally invisible negative karmic accrual. In a larger sense in Vaisheshika, *adrishta* is the unknown quality of things and of the soul; it brings about the cosmic order and arranges for souls according to their merits and demerits.

Further reading: Arthur B. Keith, *The Karma-Mimamsa* (London: Oxford University Press, 1921); S. N. Klostermaier and K. Klaus, *A Survey of Hinduism* (Albany: State University of New York Press, 1989); Karl H. Potter, *Indian Metaphysics and Epistemology: The Tradition of Nyaya-Vaisesika Up to Gangesa* (Delhi: Motilal Banarsidass, 1977).

advaita

Advaita (non-dual, from the root *dvi*, or two) is a term used to describe the unitary philosophies and religious movements in India. Rather than a definition of these schools of thought as unitary or monist, the negative description is generally used. *Advaita* is usually translated as "non-dual." Duality would imply that there is more than one reality; non-duality implies that there is nowhere a second to the one reality.

A number of philosophies in Indian tradition are conventionally called *advaita*. Their characteristics vary considerably. Best known is "absolute *advaita*," formulated by the Vedanta founder SHANKARA, in which the individual self, and all apparently separate selves, are understood to be nothing but the ultimate Self, that is, non-dual with it; there are no distinctions between selves. A further aspect of Shankara's *advaita* system is that the world is false or MAYA, illusion. Only the one BRAHMAN is true.

The views of RAMANUJA and VALLABHA are also technically referred to as *advaita* or non-dualistic,

as both their systems maintain that individual selves are nothing but the ultimate Self. However, they both also include qualifying language to show that they do not hold Shankara's absolute view. In their understanding, the highest Self or *brahman* is God and therefore has certain inherent characteristics that distinguish it from any other self. No individual self can possess the power and supremacy of the divinity; in fact, both Ramanuja and Vallabha see the individual selves as being distinct from each other. Similarly, Ramanuja and Vallabha qualify their *advaita* belief that the world or universe is in fact nothing but the divinity: from another perspective the world is different from the divinity.

Many other Vedantins similarly could be called *advaita* with these sorts of reservations. They sometimes use terms like Dvaitadvaita (nondualist and dualist) or BHEDABHEDA (both different and non-different). Philosophically they are quite similar to Ramanuja and Vallabha.

Finally, most TANTRIC philosophical systems are also termed *advaita* or non-dual. In these cases, the individual self is understood as being precisely *brahman*, God or Goddess, with no reservations. The power inherent in the divinity is understood to belong to any individual, at the highest level of realization. The world too is understood to be non-dual with the divinity.

Further reading: M. M. Agarwal, *The Philosophy of Nimbarka* (Varanasi: Chaukhamba Surbharati Prakashan, 1983); Surendranath Dasgupta, *A History of Indian Philosophy,* 5 vols. (New Delhi: Motilal Banarsidass, 1975); Julius J. Lipner, *The Face of Truth: A Study of Mean and Metaphysics in the Vedantic Theology of Ramanuja* (Houndmills: Macmillan, 1986); Unmesha Mishra, *Nimbarka School of Vedanta* (Allahabad: Tirabhukti, 1966); G. V. Tagare, *Brahma-vada Doctrine of Sri Vallabhacarya* (New Delhi: D. K. Printworld, 1998); Swami Tapasyananda, *Bhakti Schools of Vedanta (Lives and Philosophies of Ramanuja, Nimbarka, Madhva, Vallabha and Chaitanya)* (Madras: Sri Ramakrishna Math, 1990); P. B. Vidyarthi, *Divine Personality and Human Life in*

Ramanuja (New Delhi: Oriental, 1978); Ramnarayan Vyas, *The Bhagavata Bhakti Cult and the Three Acaryas, Sankara, Ramanuja and Vallabha* (Delhi: Nag, 1977).

advaita Fellowship   *See* NISARGADATTA MAHARAJ.

Africa, Hinduism in

Hinduism is practiced throughout the African continent but is primarily focused in South Africa, Kenya, Tanzania, and Ghana. According to 2000 census data, nearly 1 million Hindus live in South Africa, the largest concentration of followers on the continent.

India has had a long history of interaction with East Africa, first recorded as trade during the time of the Roman Empire, which exported products and slaves from East Africa and imported Indian cloth and spices. An Indian presence in Africa has been discovered at archaeological sites in Zimbabwe and the Swahili coast. Remains of small Indo-African colonies have also been identified on Madagascar and Zanzibar. Zanzibar appears to have been the center of South Asian mercantilism, which predated the entry of the Europeans. Even today words from Indian languages can be found in the Swahili language.

The trade initiated by the Roman Empire ebbed for centuries, but the onset of European colonization of Africa and India, and particularly the British Empire, renewed communication between East Africa and India, as Kenya, Uganda, and South Africa became part of the British Empire and began to be settled by South Asian colonists. Europeans presided over a flourishing of trade across the Indian Ocean that included the German colony of Tanzania (German East Africa), although they also suppressed the slave trade. The Indian community in Zanzibar grew to include Hindus, Muslims, Roman Catholics from Goa, Buddhists from Sri Lanka, Sikhs, and Parsees (Zoroastrians from India).

Construction by the British of the Kenya-Uganda railway generated another emigration of South Asian workers to East Africa. First Muslims, and later Hindus, arrived as construction laborers. After completion of the railway, many remained to create Indian bazaars and shops along the new line. The British practice of separating different ethnic groups into homogeneous colonies kept Indian immigrants in segregated communities. Racist attitudes and policies among the European colonists prompted various South Asian groups to organize politically. Schools were founded in order to educate South Asians. After World War II, nationalist movements among the indigenous African population channeled resentment of the financial success of the Asians and threatened the South Asian communities. Even under duress, South Asians continued to immigrate to East Africa and to assist in the development of Hindu communities there.

The majority of the Hindu population in East Africa is from the Gujarat (70 percent) and Punjab regions; all but the lowest castes are represented. As a result of constant communication with India, Hindus in East Africa practice the religion of the subcontinent, although members of the different castes interact more freely in East Africa than in India. Various temples allow the Hindu population to worship their respective deities.

In 1972 Idi Amin expelled all Hindus from Uganda. Twenty years later Uganda allowed the Hindu population to return. Today there are two Hindu temples in Uganda, and 65 percent of the South Asian population in Uganda is Hindu.

The Hindu population continues to be separate from other ethnic and religious groups in Africa, as the indigenous and European populations of Africa tend to be primarily Christian or Muslim. Modern movements, such as the VEDANTA SOCIETIES and RAMAKRISHNA MATH AND MISSION and the SATYA SAI BABA movement can be found, although traditional Hinduism and Hindu movements remain of interest to the immigrants and their descendants.

In contrast to free Hindu immigration in Uganda, Hindus first appeared in South Africa, Zimbabwe, and MAURITIUS as indentured servants for the British Empire. It was the same indentured servant scheme that took other Indian populations to Guyana and Trinidad and Tobago. Hindus arrived at the South African port of Natal in 1860 to work on plantations. The laborer population increased over the following decades with the construction of continental railroads. Uttar Pradesh, Gujarat, and Tamil Nadu are among the Indian states from which the first Hindus emigrated. During the early decades, Hindus preserved a broad array of rituals and customs even through they shared temple space across various sects. The temples became eclectic places of worship and helped to solidify a cultural identity for Hindus living far away from their Indian homes.

Most laborers remained in Africa after their contracts of servitude ended and established permanent settlements. An Indian merchant class soon formed around the developing communities. Revenues accumulated for the construction and maintenance of the first temples, built on plantations or at the outskirts of towns. Large temples built as early as the 1880s still stand in Durban at the Umgeni Road Temple Complex. The Umbilo Shree Ambalavanaar Alayam Temple of Durban, built in 1875, is recorded as the first proper Hindu temple built on the continent. After it was destroyed in 1905 by the flooding of the Umbilo River, the temple was revitalized in 1946 and was dedicated as a national monument in 1980. The Umbilo Temple continues to operate as a favored place of Hindu worship, celebrating the annual fire walking ceremony each spring.

In 1913 laws were passed in South Africa to curb immigration. Nevertheless, before strict apartheid appeared, South Asians were relatively free to travel and to own land. In response to the policies of apartheid, MOHANDAS KARAMCHAND GANDHI, during his 21-year residency in South Africa, first developed his method of social action and nonviolent protest. In 1947 the South African government passed the Group Areas Act, which enforced strict segregation of all people of color. Previously, South Asians and indigenous Africans had worked together and shared traditions through free intercommunication. The Group Areas Act precluded the possibilities of free communication and forced South Asians and Africans to leave desirable locations and settle in segregated townships in more undesirable areas. Hindu congregations were scattered across the country, isolated from each other and cut off from India. Temples and community centers were created in these highly segregated communities. Between 1968 and 1973 the government of South Africa established a policy of conversion to Christianity for the Hindu population, which left Hindu communities cut off from their traditions and unable to socialize youth into the Hindu heritage.

The ARYA SAMAJ movement fought the South African policies of apartheid. The movement, begun in India in 1875, entered South Africa in 1906 and Kenya and Tanzania later on. As a social service and educational organization, the Arya Samaj served poor Hindus, but it also affirmed the Vedic tradition and established schools. The movement effectively dissuaded Hindus from converting to Christianity, despite the presence of influential Christian missions. In Tanzania the Hindu Mandal, established in 1910, offered welfare programs, youth activities, and medical services.

Other Hindus from diverse backgrounds joined to retain their tradition in the face of significant challenges to its existence. With the end of apartheid in the early 1990s, Hindus were again able to travel and have contact with India.

A number of active Hindu missions countered the growing influence of Christian missionaries. One exemplary mission was begun by Swami Shankarananda. The swami arrived in South Africa in 1907 and helped organize

Hindu practice, spread Hindu teaching, and revive festivals. Schools were established under his direction, focused on the study of traditional Hindu scripture. In 1912 Shankarananda organized the first South African Hindu Conference, which established the South African Maha Sabha, which maintained ties among 44 institutes. Shankarananda's work opened the way for other missionaries, including Swami Adhyananda and Pandit Rishi Ram, to establish their own work in the country. The work of these early missionaries inspired movements in the later decades of the 20th century.

Hindus entered Mauritius in the early 19th century as indentured workers for French sugar plantations. After Great Britain suppressed the slave trade, the colonial French farmers needed a new source of cheap labor. In time the population of Indians in Mauritius grew considerably. Today Hindus make up 68 percent of the total population. Most Hindus live in the rural areas and still work on plantations. Arya Samaj is also active in Mauritius.

Recently neo-Hindu movements have grown in popularity on the continent. In both Kenya and South Africa the INTERNATIONAL SOCIETY FOR KRISHNA CONSCIOUSNESS became influential in the latter part of the 20th century. The RAMAKRISHNA MATH AND MISSION, and the Divine Life Society of Swami SHIVANANDA Saraswai have also become popular. In Ghana, where Indian merchants arrived during the 20th century, a missionary known as the Black Monk of Africa founded a monastery in Accra in 1977. With a small but devoted following, the monastery provides services to Hindu communities. The ANANDA MARGA YOGA SOCIETY has also established a popular following in Ghana. Only five Hindu families live in Senegal at present.

The observance of Hindu festivals continues in Africa largely unchanged from Indian sources. Each year in October DIVALI, or the festival of lights, is celebrated across Africa. In South Africa, the popular festival lasts into November and includes both Hindu and non-Hindu participants. In Kenya, Divali is recognized as a national holiday. Communities in Tanzania and Ghana also celebrate Divali. Other festivals observed across Africa include the popular summer celebration HOLI, the festival of colors. Several local festivals are also observed according to regional customs.

Although Hindus have maintained a cultural identity and are generally respected throughout Africa, some Hindus have become increasingly alarmed over the tactics of Christian missionaries. Some of the growing numbers of American and European Christian missionaries have instigated divisions among African communities. For example, some Christian evangelicals have disseminated portrayals of Hindus as followers of demonic gods and goddesses, fueling religious tensions. In South Africa in recent years, several Hindu organizations have petitioned Christian evangelicals to condemn attempts to convert Hindus and have protested against the use of propaganda that depicts Hindus as devil worshippers. The tactics have ignited a new call for Hindu unity and for peaceful efforts to counter Christian evangelicalism.

See also CARIBBEAN REGION; DIASPORA.

Further reading: Crispin Bates, ed., *Community, Empire, and Migration: South Asians in Diaspora* (New York: Palgrave, 2001); David Chidester et al., *Islam, Hinduism, and Judaism in South Africa: An Annotated Bibliography* (Westport, Conn.: Greenwood Press, 1997); George Delf, *Asians in East Africa* (London: Oxford University Press, 1963); Alleyn Diesel and Patrick Maxwell, *Hinduism in Natal: A Brief Guide* (Pietermaritzburg: University of Natal Press, 1993); Dhram P. Ghai, ed., *Portrait of a Minority: Asians in East Africa* (London: Oxford University Press, 1965); J. S. Mangay, *A History of the Asians in East Africa* (Oxford: Clarendon Press, 1969); Martin Prozesky and John W. De Gruchy, *Living Faiths in South Africa* (New York: St. Martin's Press, 1995); Steven Vertovec, *The Hindu Diaspora: Comparative Patterns* (London: Routledge, 2000).

agama

In the tantric tradition (*see* TANTRISM) *agama* most commonly means "authoritative scripture." Different systems of tantric tradition may designate different texts as *agamas*. In South India, for instance, there is a tradition called Agamanta SHAIVISM that relies upon 28 *agamas*. In this tradition, the VEDAS are referred to as NIGAMA.

Agamas tend to be fairly late texts (compared to the Vedas); the earliest *agama* could hardly have been written before the sixth century C.E. Though many of the *agamas* of the diverse tantric traditions are philosophical, others focus on Shaivite temple ritual, including the layout of temples, the installation of icons, and the ritual forms to be used. In this sense, they are foundational texts for temple Hinduism.

In a more limited sense, an *agama* is a tantric text that takes the form of a teaching by SHIVA to PARVATI or another goddess. (In this context, a *Nigama* is a text taught by the goddess to Shiva.) Finally, *agama* is a linguistic term used in PANINI, The great Sanskrit grammarian, for an augment added to a base to form a complete word.

Further reading: J. A. B. van Buitenen, trans., *Yamana's Agamapramanyam or Treatise on the Validity of Pancaratra* (Madras: Ramanuja Research Society, 1971); Bruno Dagens, *Architecture in the Ajitagama and the Rauravagama: A Study of Two South Indian Texts* (New Delhi: Sitaram Institute of Scientific Research, 1984); Mark Dyczkowski, *The Canon of the Saivagama and the Kubjika Tantras of the Western Kaula Tradition* (Albany: State University of New York Press, 1988); Kamalakar Mishra, *Kashmir Saivism: The Central Philosophy of Tantrism* (Portland, Ore.: Rudra Press, 1993); S. K. Ramachandra Rao, *Agama-Kosa: Agama Encyclopedia* (Bangalore: Kapatharu Research Academy, 1994).

Agastya (also Agasti)

Agastya was one of the Vedic RISHIs (inspired poets); his name is given as the author of several hymns in the first of the 10 chapters of the RIG VEDA. He is said to be the son of both MITRA and VARUNA, both of whose seed was emitted upon sight of the celestial APSARAS URVASHI. Agastya then was born in a water jar. (A similar story exists about the conception of DRONA in a bucket.)

In the MAHABHARATA and later literature Agastya became an important *rishi*. In the Mahabharata itself there are a number of stories about him. One tale frequently mentioned in Indian literature relates how Agastya helped the gods destroy demons who had hidden in the ocean by drinking up the entire ocean. In another tale Agastya restores the world to order: the VINDHYA mountain grew jealous of mount MERU, the central mountain of our universe around which the Sun and Moon always go, so he began to raise his head in order to block the path of the celestial orbs. Agastya, GURU of the Vindhya mountain, went to Vindhya and forced him to lower his head in obeisance, and to keep his head lowered while Agastya headed in the southern direction. Agastya, however, never returned.

This notion of the Vindhya's bowing to Agastya is associated with the migration of the ARYANS and particularly the BRAHMINS to South India. Agastya is venerated in the south of India, where he is said to have been the first to organize the Tamil grammar. Tolkappiyar, the author of the oldest known Tamil grammar, is considered one of Agastya's 12 students. Agastya was also said to have been a member of the first two Tamil Sangams or literary academies, which were inundated by the sea. (The literature of the third and last Sangam is understood to be still extant, but, of course, the Sangams are not historically verifiable.)

In Tamil Nadu Agastya is mythologically associated with SHIVA, who it is said to have sent Agastya to the south. In the tantric tradition of the SRI VIDYA, Agastya is said to be the husband of LOPAMUDRA, the female founder of one of the *sri vidya* lineages.

In the Ramayana Agastya was visited at his ASHRAM by RAMA and became an adviser to him. In the end Agastya became a star—Canopus, which shines in the southern sky in India.

Further reading: G. S. Ghurye, *Indian Acculturation: Agastya and Skanda* (Bombay: Popular Prakashan, 1977); E. Washburn Hopkins, *Epic Mythology* (Delhi: Motilal Banarsidass, 1986); K. N. Sivaraja Pillai, *Agastya in the Tamil Land* (New Delhi: Asian Educational Services, 1985).

Agehananda Bharati, Swami (1923–1991)
Western Hindu monastic

Swami Agehananda Bharati was an Austrian-born Hindu monk and an important scholar of Indian culture and languages.

Leopold Fischer was born in Vienna, Austria, on April 20, 1923, to a retired cavalry captain, Hans Fischer, and his wife, Margarete. In a youth of considerable privilege, Leopold and his brother Hans were closer emotionally to their governess, Frau Blumel, than to their parents, who, according to Leopold, were not interested in understanding and communicating with their sons. At age 13 Leopold joined the Indian Club, as he was already keen on India and all things Indian, and began to study HINDI and classical SANSKRIT; the next year he decided to become a professional Indologist. On his 16th birthday, after Hitler took over Austria, Fischer took an oath to fight for India's freedom and became a member of Hitler's "Free India" Legion, an organization based on anti-British politics and Aryan racist thought. Also on his birthday, he took vows to become a Hindu by honoring the five things of the cow (milk, buttermilk, butter, urine, and dung) while renouncing the sixth thing of the cow, namely, its flesh. He was given the Hindu name Ramachandra by a traveling Hindu preacher, Bhai Sachidanand. During the war, he served with the Indian Legion of the German army in the European theater, expanding his language skills to include several contemporary Indian languages.

In January 1949, Fischer landed in Bombay (Mumbai), having written to many Indian contacts he had made in Europe. He lived in RAMAKRISHNA ashrams, first in Calcutta (Kolkata), then in Almora. After two years, he decided that the Ramakrishna Math was not his ordained path; nor was its founder, Swami VIVEKANANDA (1863–1902), his ordained teacher, and he became a novice in a Hindu monastery. He was initiated into the Dasanami SANNYASI order of Hinduism by Swami Vishvananda Bharati on the banks of the Ganges at BENARES (Varanasi), where he became Agehananda Bharati (bliss through homelessness). In this initiation into monasticism (DIKSHA), he became the first Westerner to embrace monastic Hinduism fully. He then began a 1,500-mile trek of India on foot as a mendicant monk with a begging bowl.

Agehananda Bharati continued his scholarly activities in such diverse subjects as cultural anthropology, South Asian studies, linguistics, and comparative philosophy. He taught at Delhi University, Banaras Hindu University, and Nalanda Institute in India; at a Buddhist academy in Bangkok, Thailand; and at the University of Tokyo.

In 1956, Bharati immigrated to the United States as a research associate for Washington University. In 1957 he joined the anthropology faculty at Syracuse University and became the Ford-Maxwell Professor of South Asian studies. He became a U.S. citizen in 1968. His publications include 500 articles, essays, and books that report on Hindu monasticism and worldview and have been widely read by scholars and general readers alike.

His interpretation of Hinduism through anthropological and personal lenses have been influential among Western Hindus as well as scholars.

Agehananda Bharati died of cancer at a friend's house in Pittsford, New York, on May 14, 1991, at the age of 68.

Further reading: Swami Agehananda Bharati, *The Tantric Tradition* (London: Rider, 1965); ———, *The Light at the Center: Context and Pretext of Modern Mysticism* (Santa Barbara, Calif.: Ross-Erikson, 1976); ———, *The Ochre Robe: An Autobiography,* 2d ed. (Santa Barbara, Calif.: Ross-Erikson, 1980).

Aghora   *See* AGHORI SADHUS.

Aghori sadhus

Paradoxically named, the Aghori ("non-terrible") SADHUS are among the most strange and frightening of all the mendicants of India. Their practice is similarly called *aghora*—"non-terrible." They inhabit cremation grounds, where they perform their esoteric rituals. They eat the flesh of human corpses and smear their bodies with ashes from human cremations. They carry begging bowls made from human skulls (they do not beg but will not refuse anything) and eat their food from them. They are popularly known as evil sorcerers who command fearsome magic powers.

The practices of the Aghoris are calculated to outrage; they are known copraphages (eaters of human excrement), and folklore reports their kidnapping and sacrificing children for their outrageously transgressive rites. They trace their sect to the great guru of the NATHS, GORAKHNATH; they embody the extreme left-handed tantra (see TANTRISM), which finds the divinity everywhere, and they believe that complete release is to be found in discovering the essence of the divinity in that which is most horrific. They are often devotees of the fierce aspect of the GODDESS, but also, of SHIVA. Their origins are probably to be found in the ancient SHAIVA cult of the Kapalikas. These sadhus are given a wide berth by most contemporary Indians and are looked down upon as evil.

Further reading: R. G. Bhandarkar, *Vaisnavism, Saivism and Minor Religious Systems* (Banares: Indological Book House, 1965); N. N. Bhattacharya, *The History of the Tantric Religion* (Delhi: Manohar, 1982.); Shashibhusan Das Gupta, *Obscure Religious Cults* (Calcutta: Firma KLM, 1995); *Sadhus: India's Holy Men,* 3, *Aghori, Living with the Dead* (videorecording)/a Bedi Films/Denis Whyte Films Production for BBC TV, Canal Plus, Premiere (Princeton, N.J.: Films for the Humanities and Sciences, 1995); Robert Svoboda, *Aghora: At the Left Hand of God* (Albuquerque: Brotherhood of Life, 1986).

Agni

Agni, the god of fire, is one of the most central divinities in the early Vedic tradition. There are more hymns to Agni in the RIG VEDA, the earliest SANSKRIT text, than to any other divinity. Agni is sometimes said to be the son of earth and sky. He is also sometimes said to be the offspring of BRAHMA. He is sometimes called the son of ADITI and the RISHI Kashyapa. Finally, he is also sometimes called the son of the *rishi* Angiras.

Agni's most important role is in the Vedic ritual, where he is the messenger between humanity and the gods. He is called upon always to take the gods to the ritual place so that they can hear the pleas and praises of the chanters. In Vedic poetry he is called a domestic priest, a poet, and a sage, as though to identify him directly with the RISHIS. There is a sense of his presence in every home as the hearth fire, and there are a closeness and intimacy expressed in the Vedic poetry with him that are lacking with many of the other Vedic divinities. He is seen to extend protection to humans in many ways and to grant wealth and length of life.

Iconographically, in later times Agni is seen as red or black in color, riding a ram. He is guardian of the southeastern direction among the eight guardians of the directions. Fire is considered one of the five elements (*PANCHA BHUTAS*).

Further reading: Cornelia Dimmitt and J. A. B. van Buitenen, *Classical Hindu Mythology: A Reader in the Sanskrit Puranas* (Philadelphia: Temple University Press, 1978); Alfred Hillebrandt, *Vedic Mythology* (Delhi: Motilal Banarsidass, 1990); E. Washburn Hopkins, *Epic*

Mythology (Delhi: Motilal Banarsidass, 1986); Sachidananda Mahapatra, *Concept of Jatavedas in Vedic Literature* (Delhi: Eastern Book Linkers, 2003); W. J. Wilkins, *Hindu Mythology, Vedic and Puranic,* 2d ed. (Calcutta: Rupa, 1973).

agnichayana

The *agnichayana,* or "ritual of building the fire altar," was one of the grandest rituals in the Vedic sacrificial tradition; it played an extremely important role in the development of Hinduism. It is most completely described in the sixth book of the SHATAPATHA BRAHMANA, which is attached to the YAJUR VEDA. The ritual involves building a temporary shelter of posts and roof thatching to serve as the site for the ritual and all of its adjuncts, which last for more than two weeks. Once the shelter has been created, a huge falcon is built from consecrated bricks. This bird is homologized or understood to be PRAJAPATI or the PURUSHA, the Universal Being. Seventeen specialized priests are required for this most elaborate of Vedic rituals. A sacrifice of 14 goats formed a central part of the early ritual.

The *agnichayana* is understood as a renewal or re-creation of the universe through ritual. A late verse in the RIG VEDA recounts how the Primordial Man offered himself in sacrifice to create all of the universe; the *agnichayana* reenacts this process. SOMA, the special drug taken by the Vedic BRAHMINS, was used during this ritual.

The *agnichayana* ritual, and the theory that developed around it, helped define Indian notions of ADVAITA or non-duality—the equation of the individual self with the Universal Self or Reality. The Shatapatha Brahamana, where this ritual is described, says that it must be understood as the universe itself. As the later Vedic texts, the Aranyakas, show, this Vedic ritual can be done esoterically within the body and being of one person. If the *agnichayana* is the Universal Reality and a person's being is the ritual, then one can conclude that a person's being is the Universal Reality, or all that is. This insight leads to the philosophical identification of the individual self and the Ultimate Reality, later found explicitly in the Upanishads.

Further reading: Julius Eggeling, trans., *The Satapatha-Brahmana,* Part 1, *According to the Text of the Madhyandina School* (Delhi: Motilal Banarsidass, 1982); J. Frits Staal, *AGNI: The Vedic Ritual of the Fire Altar,* 2 vols. (Berkeley: University of California Press, 1983); Robert Gardner and Frits Staal, *Altar of Fire* (videorecording) (Cambridge, Mass.: Film Study Center at Harvard University, 1983).

Agni Yoga Society (est. 1920)

The Agni Yoga Society was founded in New York in 1920 by the Russian artist Nicholas Roerich (October 9, 1874–December 13, 1947) and his wife, Helena (February 12, 1879–October 5, 1955), and was incorporated in New York City as a nonprofit educational organization. The society's philosophy emphasizes the evolution of planetary consciousness as a necessary and attainable goal for humankind.

Agni Yoga, sometimes referred to as the teaching of "Living Ethics," does not rely on a physical or meditative discipline. It is rather a way of life offering a practice and commitment to directing thought and prioritizing actions for the common good. It is reportedly practiced by thousands in Russia and by several thousand others around the world. Although the teaching reveres Hinduism, Agni Yoga is not considered exclusively Hindu in nature; rather, it involves a synthesis of religious teachings of all ages from around the world.

Agni Yoga evolved from Nicholas Roerich's encounters in London with Mahatma Morya and Mahatma Koot Hoomi (ascended masters in the tradition of THEOSOPHY). In March 1920, Nicholas produced the first of the group's writings; they were followed by several books by Helena. At the request of the Mahatmas the Roerichs moved to New York to share the teachings and to open cultural centers in America. Several institutes and museums were established, including the Agni Yoga Society.

The society has published a set of books called the Agni Yoga Series, which encapsulates their philosophy, a teaching that integrates Eastern beliefs with Western spiritual and scientific thought. Although the society does not offer courses, it provides information on Agni Yoga and welcomes correspondence.

Further reading: Agni Yoga Series (New York: Agni Yoga Society, 1977); Ruth Drayer, *Nicholas and Helena Roerich: The Spiritual Journeys of Two Great Artists and Peacemakers* (Wheaton, Ill.: Theosophical Pub. House, 2005); *Helena Roerich, Letters of Helena Roerich* (New York: Agni Yoga Society, 1954–67); Nicholas Roerich, *Altai-Himalaya: A Travel Diary* (New York: Frederick A. Stokes, 1929).

Ahalya

The wife of the RISHI Gautama, Ahalya was seduced by INDRA while her husband was taking his morning bath. Indra took the form of her husband, and though Ahalya knew that Indra was not her husband, she consented to his advances. When the *rishi* was returning to the hut Indra took the form of a cat and escaped. The *rishi*, however, knew through his supranormal powers what had occurred. He cursed his wife, turning her to stone, and put a curse on Indra as well.

In some versions of the Ahalya story Indra is cursed with the testicles of a ram; in other versions he is cursed with 1,000 vaginas. In the later tale, Indra beseeched the gods to relieve the curse and the vaginas were transformed into 1,000 eyes. This colorful story explains how Indra acquired the epithet "thousand-eyed one."

In the RAMAYANA, RAMA comes upon the stone form of a woman, who, with the touch of his foot, becomes alive again. She is Ahalya. This well-known myth has generated many books and novels in contemporary Indian languages.

Further reading: Wendy Doniger, *Splitting the Difference: Gender and Myth in Ancient Greece and India* (Chicago: University of Chicago Press, 1999); Stephanie W. Jamison, *Sacrificed Wife/Sacrificer's Wife: Women, Ritual, and Hospitality in Ancient India* (New York: Oxford University Press, 1996); C. Rajagopalachari, *Ramayana* (Bombay: Bharatiya Vidya Bhavan, 1962).

aham brahmasmi   *See* MAHAVAKYAS.

ahamkara

Ahamkara means "ego" (literally, I-doing, or conceiving of everything in terms of I.) In nearly every tradition of Hinduism *ahamkara* is considered the great spiritual enemy. In YOGA one transcends the ego through the calming of the mind and eventually learns to ignore the pernicious pull of *ahamkara*. In non-dual Vedantic practice, ego is seen as false self, which must be rejected in favor of the transcendent Self that is Ultimate Reality.

In the practice of BHAKTI, or devotional YOGA, through chants and MANTRAS one connects to the inner godhead and uproots the ego with service to the Divine. Only in the tantric (*see* TANTRISM) traditions is Ahamkara seen as a positive word, but there, also, it is understood that one's ego must be transformed into divine "I-ness," where the mundane ego is totally supplanted in identification with God. In Jain and SIKH traditions *ahamkara* is seen also as a supreme negative; ego must be controlled and finally eliminated.

Further reading: Usharbudh Arya, *Philosophy of Hatha Yoga* (Glenview, Ill.: Himalayan Institute of Yoga Science and Philosophy of the U.S.A., 1977); Gasper M. Koelman, *Patanjala Yoga: From Related Ego to Absolute Self* (Poona: Papal Athenaeum, 1970); Swami Muktananda, *So'ham Japa: A Meditation Technique for Everyone* (Ganeshpuri: Shree Gurudev Ashram, 1972); Frank R. Podgorski, *Ego-Revealer, Concealer: A Key to Yoga* (Lanham, Md.: University Press of America, 1984).

ahimsa

Ahimsa means "non-killing." This is a concept that seems to emerge in late Vedic times (c. 800 B.C.E.) and is primarily associated with the Jain (see JAINISM) and Buddhist traditions at that time. It gradually is taken into the Brahminical tradition and becomes central to it up to the present day. The notion of *ahimsa* is applied toward animal life primarily but in Jain tradition is recognized in the case of plants also.

Ahimsa understands that all animals (and for the Jains certain plants) have souls and that the killing of any animal (or certain plants) whether for eating or not accumulates karmic (see KARMA) demerit to the one who does it. The Jains were the most radical in this regard, and their monks were enjoined to sweep their path clear with whisks to prevent stepping on insects and sometimes wore (and wear) masks over their mouths to prevent the breathing in and killing of small invisible beings and insects. Jains would never eat meat and would not countenance the eating of meat or the killing of any animal for any reason in their tradition.

Because Jains believe that there were small invisible beings everywhere, monks were required to walk and move extremely circumspectly and slowly. Agriculture was traditionally forbidden to all Jains because it involved violence to beings, invisible and visible, who live in the ground. Buddhists in India adhered to a strict notion of *ahimsa*, but Buddhist monks would accept meat if given it, while Jain monks would never do so. The notion of *ahimsa* is the primary motive for Indian vegetarianism and orthodox BRAHMINS too avoid all meat, animal products, and eggs (which are seen to be living embryos).

Because of *ahimsa* there are certain orthodox Hindu ascetics who will not wear leather shoes or sandals, but will wear only wooden shoes. Mohandas Karamchand GANDHI expanded the notion of *ahimsa* to the interpersonal realm and developed it into a philosophy of personal action. Gandhi took the word to mean "nonviolence" in all its aspects, and, while he was very strictly vegetarian as part of his vow of *ahimsa,* he believed that it should become a general principle of human conduct, in all relations between people. Particularly he trained people in the notion of "nonviolent" response to all violence and provocation as a moral as well as a political matter. His political use of *ahimsa* was adopted by many great political leaders of the 20th century, including Martin Luther King Jr.

Further reading: Christopher Key Chapple, *Nonviolence to Animals, Earth and Self in Asian Traditions* (Albany: State University of New York Press, 1993); Erik H. Erikson, *Gandhi's Truth on the Origins of Militant Nonviolence* (New York: Norton, 1969); Vilas Sangave, *The Jain Path of Ahimsa* (Solapur: Bhagawan Mahavir Research Centre, 1991); Tara Sethia, ed. *Ahimsa, Anekanta and Jainism* (Delhi: Motilal Banarsidass, 2004); Unto Tahtinen, *Ahimsa: Non-Violence in Indian Tradition* (London: Rider, 1976); Koshelya Walli, *The Conception of Ahimsa in India Thought, According to Sanskrit Sources* (Varanasi: Bharata Manisha, 1974).

Airavata (Airavana)

Airavata is the huge, four-tusked white elephant who is the vehicle of the king of the gods, INDRA. When the elephants of the eight directions are listed, Airavata is the elephant of the western direction. Airavata appears in the MAHABHARATA as the mount of Indra, but is particularly referenced in the RAMAYANA in the battle with the *raksasas*. In this battle, he is attacked by the *raksasas* and loses his tusks, whereupon he turns and gouges RAVANA, the demon king. In the myth of the churning of the MILK OCEAN, Airavata emerges along with many other auspicious beings and things. For this reason, it is understood, he is named "the one from the waters."

Further reading: Cornelia Dimmitt and J. A. B. van Buitenen, *Classical Hindu Mythology: A Reader in the Sanskrit Puranas* (Philadelphia: Temple University

Press, 1978); E. Washburn Hopkins, *Epic Mythology* (Delhi: Motilal Banarsidass, 1986); T. G. Gopinatha Rao, *Elements of Hindu Iconography*, 4 vols. (Delhi: Motilal Banarsidass, 1997); Margaret Stutley, *An Illustrated Dictionary of Hindu Iconography* (Boston: Routledge & Kegan Paul, 1985).

Aishtanemi   *See* NEMINATHA.

Aitareya Upanishad

Aitareya is a matronymic or patronymic deriving from the SANSKRIT root *itara*. It means "son of *itara*" (either masculine or feminine), who would be his mother or father. This is an ancient RIG VEDIC sage who also goes by the name of Mahidasa. Credited to him are the Aitareya Brahmana, the Aitareya Aranyaka, and the Aitareya Upanishad, all texts attached to the RIG VEDA. The Aitareya Upanishad is found in the Aitareya Aranyaka, constituting chapters 4 to 6 of that work.

The Aitareya Upanishad begins with cosmological verses showing how the ultimate being, the ATMAN or Self, created the worlds, the elements, and human beings. Important here is the connection between each of the elements of the divine PURUSHA, which is the template Person, and the elements of nature aspects of the cosmos and the human being. From the original Person fire, air, Sun, the quarters of space, the Moon, death, and water emerge. All of these elements again go into making up the human being. Once this takes place the Self enters into the human being that has emerged as the result of his creation. This then makes clear that the self of a human being is the Ultimate Self, which is the source of everything.

Further reading: S. N. Dasgupta, *A History of Indian Philosophy,* Vol. 1 (Delhi: Motilal Banarsidass, 1975); Arthur B. Keith, *The Aitareya Aranyaka* (Oxford: Clarendon Press, 1909); Swami Nikhilananda, trans., *The Upanishads,* Vol. 3 (New York: Ramakrishna-Vivekananda Center, 1975); S. Radhakrishnan, *The Princi-*

pal Upanishads (Atlantic Highlands, N.J.: Humanities Press, 1994).

Aiyanar

Aiyanar is a demigod represented as a warrior mounted on a horse who is the night guardian in Tamil Nadu. He is sometimes accompanied in iconography or painted representation by other martial figures and dogs. He patrols the boundaries of fields, chasing away evil forces. Figurines of horses and elephants are found in his shrines. Horses in Tamil Nadu will be devoted to Aiyanar. He is regarded as a local son of SHIVA.

Further reading: R. Srinivasan, *Aiyanar's Domain: Political and Social Conditions and Attitudes in Tamil Folk Literature* (Bombay: Research Book Centre, 1993); Henry Whitehead, *The Village Gods of South India* (Delhi: SumitPublications, 1976).

Ajanta

At Ajanta in the Aurangabad District of Maharashtra are some of the most famous ancient caves of India. Here are preserved some of India's most beautiful ancient painting and sculpturing. The caves date from the second century B.C.E. to seventh century C.E. There are 29 caves at Ajanta, which are carved into solid stone halfway up a large hill that curves gently away, to the left of the visitor. In the middle of the steep incline is a walkway, which appears made on a natural cliff.

All of the caves at Ajanta were done by the Buddhists. Some were clearly used as monastic dwellings, and others were *chaityas* or shrine rooms. Some of the caves have beautiful frescoes depicting scenes from the Buddhist Jatakas (tales of the life of the BUDDHA). The frescoes of Ajanta show a development of nearly 1,000 years of fresco art. Other caves have impressive figures of the Buddha in high relief.

Further reading: Benoy K. Behl, *The Ajanta Caves: Ancient Paintings of Buddhist India* (New York: Thames

& Hudson, 2004); *Guide to the Ajanta Paintings* (New Delhi: Munshiram Manoharlal Publishers, 1999–2003); Swati Mitra, ed., *From Ajanta to Ellora: Travel Guide* (New Delhi: Eicher Goodearth Ltd., 2005); Lachu Moorjani, *Ajanta: Regional Feasts of India* (Layton, Utah: Gibbs Smith, Publisher, 2005); Walter Spink, *Ajanta to Ellora* (Bombay: Marg Publications, 1967).

Ajapa Yoga Foundation (est. 1974)

The Ajapa Yoga Foundation was established in 1974 by followers of Guru Janardan Paramahansa (1888–1980). It promotes *ajapa,* a breathing and meditation technique not widely known but practiced for centuries by RISHIS (spiritual adepts) in India. Practitioners believe that it is the pure and original YOGA and not a derivative of any prior teaching.

The primary teaching of the foundation is that humans see themselves as living in a world of suffering and desire because they have lost their true sense of self. Through the practice of *ajapa* yoga, they can realize their true identity. Today, five ashrams are maintained in India, Bangladesh, and California.

The modern teaching traces back to the 1860s, when Swami Purnananda Paramahansa (1834–1928) learned the ancient technique from Matang Rishi at Siddhashrama, a remote Tibetan monastery. After five years of training, Purnananda returned to Bengal and established ashrams with the purpose of reintroducing *ajapa.*

Upon Purananda's death, leadership passed to Swami Bhumananda Paramahansa (1873–1958), who was in turn succeeded by his disciple, Guru Janardan. In the 1960s Janardan organized the World Conference on Scientific Yoga in New Delhi, where he made the acquaintance of many Westerners. He then toured Europe and North America and established ashrams and centers in Hamburg, Montreal, New York, and California. In 1966, Janardan found a baby on the bank of the Ganges River in India, named him Guru Prasad (b. 1966), and raised him to be his successor as a living master of *ajapa* yoga. Guru Prasad assumed

leadership of the ashrams and foundation at age 14 and continues to teach practitioners and to maintain the ashrams and centers.

Further reading: Mitchell Radow, *Search for Peace* (New York: Ajapa Yoga Foundation, 1983); Swami Shraddhanand, trans., *Tattwa Katha: A Tale of Truth, Parts I and II* (New York: Ajapa Yoga Foundation, 1976–79).

Ajivikas

The Ajivikas were an ancient cult known mostly through references in contemporaneous Buddhist and Jain literature. The founder of the cult was Maskariputra (d. 484 B.C.E.), who had learned from earlier teachers in the tradition. The last element of Ajivika tradition died in India around the 15th century.

As did the followers of SAMKHYA, the Ajivikas did not believe in a god or gods. They believed only in KARMA and the round of births and rebirth, and were strictly deterministic. Each of us, they thought, must live through these cycles for a fabulously long period of time—8,400,000 great eons; no amount of good or bad deeds would make any difference. The Ajivikas were criticized in some texts for licentiousness, but the evidence indicates that, compelled as they believed by fate, they were devoted ascetics.

Further reading: B. M. Barua, *The Ajivikas* (Calcutta: University of Calcutta, 1920); A. L. Basham, *History and Doctrine of the Ajivikas* (London: Luzac, 1951); ———, *The Wonder That Was India: A Survey of the History and Culture of the Indian Sub-Continent before the Coming of the Muslims* (Calcutta: Rupa, 2001); R. G. Bhandarkar, *Vaisnavism, Saivism and Minor Religious Systems* (New York: Garland, 1980); Shashibhusan Das Gupta, *Obscure Religious Cults* (Calcutta: Firma KLM, 1995).

ajna chakra

The *ajna* (command) chakra is the sixth chakra (energy center) from the base of the spine in the

KUNDALINI YOGA systems. It is located between the eyebrows. The realization of *ajna* chakra yields undifferentiated cosmic awareness transcending all emotion. Some take the "element" associated with this chakra to be Prakriti, the source of the natural world, and her three GUNAS, or strands. Others associate this chakra with the elements of consciousness—BUDDHI (higher mind), AHAMKARA (ego), and MANAS (mind). In either case, the *ajna* chakra's presiding deity is ARDHANARISHVARA, the form of SHIVA when he is half-goddess and half-god. This form symbolizes the end of differentiation and the integration of the transcendent and the worldly. The SHAKTI, or energy, of the chakra is *hakini*. This chakra has two petals of luminescent, translucent whiteness.

Further reading: Harish Johari, *Chakras: Energy Centers of Transformation* (Rochester, Vt.: Destiny Books, 2000); Swami Nityabodhananda Saraswati, *Ajna Cakra* (Monghyr: Bihar School of Yoga, 1973); Lilian Silburn, *Kundalini: The Energy of the Depths: A Comprehensive Study Based on the Scriptures of Nondualistic Kasmir Saivism.* Translated from the French by Jacques Gontier (Albany: State University of New York Press, 1988); Sir John Woodroffe, trans., *The Serpent Power* (Madras: Ganesh, 1978).

Akal Takht

"The Seat of the Eternal," Akal Takht is the center of SIKH religious authority. It is located in the Golden Temple compound in the Punjabi city of AMRITSAR.

The Sikh community meets twice a year in front of the Akal Takht. Decisions must be unanimous; once made they are then considered "decisions of the Guru" and must be observed by all members of the Sikh community.

This tradition goes back to the 10th SIKH GURU GOBIND SINGH, who decreed before his death in 1708 that there would be no more personal, human gurus and that the Sikhs should consider their sacred book—the Granth Sahib (Adigranth)—as their guru. Any disputes concerning interpretations of tradition must be decided by the entire community gathered together.

Further reading: W. H. McLeod, *The Evolution of the Sikh Community: Five Essays* (Delhi: Oxford University Press, 1975); ———, "Kabir, Nanak and the Early Sikh Panth," in David N. Lorenzen, ed., *Religious Change and Cultural Domination* (Mexico City, Mexico: El Colegio de Mexico, 1981).

akasha   *See* ELEMENTS, FIVE.

Akka Mahadevi   *Virashaiva saint*

Akka Mahadevi, a talented mystical poet who died while still a young woman, is regarded as one of the early saints of the VIRASHAIVA sect founded by BASAVANNA.

Akka Mahadevi was born in the 12th century in Karnataka. As a young and beautiful maiden, she was seen by the then king Kaushika, who fell hopelessly in love with her. Despite the attempts of his ministers to distract him from marrying a commoner, he persisted in asking them to arrange for her to be his wife. Because the king was not a SHAIVITE and she was a devotee of SHIVA Akka Mahadevi persisted in refusing to marry the king. Finally the king threatened her parents with death if she did not marry him. Mahadevi could no longer refuse, but she exacted a high price: she was to be allowed to worship Shiva as she liked, spend time with Shiva devotees as she liked, and be with the king only as she liked. These conditions would be permanent; the king would have the right to overrule them only three times.

Mahadevi sadly proceeded through the marriage rites. Once married, by day she would focus on the Shiva LINGAM in prayer and spend time with Shaivite teachers and devotees; at night she would suffer the attentions of the king. Before she would go to meet him she would remove all her jewelry and makeup in order to appear bedraggled and disheveled.

Time passed; eventually the king in his impatience to be with his beautiful wife used up his three exceptions by interfering with her devotions. Mahadevi then abandoned the king and set out to be near the form of Shiva on a mountain outpost some distance away. There she worshipped continuously, abandoning all care for her body or for the world. She had already begun to go naked in the palace, uninterested in worldly things; her trip to the mountain was also without clothes. Mahadevi is depicted in all iconography as naked, her privacy protected by her long full hair. Her parents begged her to return to the king, but she refused. The king tried to lure her back by converting to Shaivism, but this too failed.

Though the stories vary, it seems certain that Mahadevi met Allamaprabhu of the Virashaivas and joined the sect. She is said to have died after her visit to the mountain, but there must have been a long enough interlude for her to produce her beautiful mystical poetry, in which she finally found Shiva in a formless reality beyond even the notion of God.

Further reading: Swami Ghanananda and Sir John Stewart Wallace, eds., *Women Saints East and West* (Hollywood, Calif.: Vedanta Press, 1979); K. Ishwaran, *Speaking of Basava: Lingayat Religion and Culture in South Asia* (Boulder, Colo.: Westview, 1992); A. K. Ramanujan, trans. and introduction, *Speaking of Siva* (New York: Penguin Books, 1973).

akshamala

An *akshamala* is a necklace of seeds or beads used for keeping track of a prayer litany, in other words, an Indian rosary. SHAIVITE *akshamalas* are typically made of the *rudraksha* (*Eleocarpus ganitrus*) seed—spherical, brownish red, with a texture similar to that of a peach pit. VAISHNAVA *akshamalas* are typically made of seeds of tulasi, the Indian basil plant, sacred to Vaishnavites. *Akshamalas* can also be made of coral, crystal, or other gems; some TANTRICS use small skulls carved

of ivory. Many *akshamalas* have 50 beads to correspond with the number of letters of the alphabet. Others have 108 or other numbers of beads.

Further reading: Kim Kaur Khalsa, *Mala Meditation for Physical, Mental, and Spiritual Prosperity: Yogic Use of Malas (Prayer Beads) to Maintain a State of Union with the Infinite Based on the Teachings of Yogi Bhajan* (Los Angeles: Sacred Gems, 1994).

Akshapada (Gautama)   *See* NYAYA.

Allahabad (Prayag)

Prayag is the traditional name for the city of Allahabad in Uttar Pradesh. *Prayaga* in SANSKRIT means "confluence," and it is the place where the holy YAMUNA and the most sacred GANGES meet. It is also understood that an ancient sacred river mentioned in the VEDAS, the Sarasvati, invisibly joins these two. Thus, this city is considered most holy because these three rivers join there.

Prayag is one of the seven holy pilgrimage cities of India. It is said that BRAHMA did the first *ashva medha* or HORSE SACRIFICE there. Every 12 years during the month of Magha (January–February), the great KUMBHA MELA festival is held in Prayag, attracting millions of pilgrims and devotees.

Further reading: S. K. Dubey, *Kumbh City Prayag* (New Delhi: Centre for Cultural Resources and Training, 2001); Anne Feldhaus, *Connected Places: Region, Pilgrimage and Geographical Imagination in India* (New York: Palgrave Macmillan, 2003); Baidyanath Saraswati, *Traditions of Tirthas in India: the Anthropology of Hindu Pilgrimage* (Varanasi: N. K. Bose Memorial Foundation, 1983).

Alvars

The Alvars, "those who are immersed in God," are the 12 poet-saints of South Indian VAISHNAVISM.

They lived between the seventh and 10th centuries. Their devotional songs, written in the Tamil language, were collected in the Nalayira Divya Prabandham (The sacred collection of the four thousand songs) by Nathamuni, the first of the great Vaishnavite teachers of Tamil Nadu.

The songs of the Alvars are used today in Tamil Vaishnava temples and in ritual contexts alongside the sacred SANSKRIT recitations. They praise Lord VISHNU in an intimate, highly passionate style, frequently referring to his incarnations as RAMA, KRISHNA, and other deities. The acts and adventures of all these incarnations are lovingly recalled and praised. The poems frequently refer to the well-known shrines of the Tamil country, which were visited by the Alvars in their pilgrimages and travels.

The Tamil Alvars are Periyalvar, ANDAL, Kulasekalvar, Tirumalisai, Tondaradipodi Alvar, Tirupanalvar, Maturakavi, Tirumankai, NAMMALVAR, Poykai, Putam, and Pey. The latter three are the earliest, dating from 650 to 700 C.E. Two Alvars stand out for their brilliance: Periyalvar (c. ninth century), who composed beautiful verses in praise of Lord Krishna as a child, and Nammalvar (c. 880–930 C.E.), who is the most prolific poet in the Nalayira Divya Prabandham. Nammalvar's main work, the 1,102-stanza Tiruvaymoli (The divine words from the mouth) was intended to encapsulate the Vedas. The only female Alvar was Andal; her poems expressing her love for Ranganatha, the form of Vishnu found at the most sacred Tamil Vaishnavite shrine at Srirangam, are used in Vaishnava wedding ceremonies in Tamil Nadu.

Further reading: S.M.S. Chari, *Philosophy and Theistic Mysticism of the Alvars* (Delhi: Motilal Banarsidass, 1997); Vidya Dehejia, *Antal and Her Path of Love: Poems of a Woman Saint from South India* (Albany: State University of New York Press, 1990); Alkondavilli Govindacharya, *The Holy Lives of the Azhvars or the Dravida Saints* (Bombay: Ananthacharya Indological Research Institute, 1982); David N. Lorenzen, ed., *Religious Movements in South Asia, 600–1800* (Delhi: Oxford University Press, 2004); V. K. S. N. Raghavan, *A Brief Study of the Tirpallandu of Sri Periyalvar, the Tirupalliyeluchi of Sri Sondaradippodiyarlvar, and the Kanninunsiruttambu of Sri Madhurakaviyalvar* (Madras: Sri Visishtadvaita Pracharini Sabha, 1983); A. K. Ramanujan, trans., *Hymns for the Drowning: Poems for Visnu by Nammalvar* (Princeton, N.J.: Princeton University Press, 1981); Kamil Zvelibil, *Tamil Literature*. Vol. 10, fascicle 1, *A History of Indian Literature*. Edited by Jan Gonda (Weisbaden: Otto Harrassowitz, 1974).

amangala

Amangala means "inauspicious" (See MANGALA). It is one of four crucial terms in Indian culture; the others are *mangala* (auspicious), SHUBHA (purity), and *ashubha* (impurity).

Further reading: John B. Carman and A. Marglin, eds., *Purity and Auspiciousness in Indian Society* (Leiden: E. J. Brill, 1985); B. Holland, compiler, *Popular Hinduism and Hindu Mythology: An Annotated Bibliography* (Westport, Conn.: Greenwood Press, 1963).

Amarnath

Amarnath is a famous shrine to SHIVA in Kashmir, located some 80 miles from Shrinagar, in a mountain cave roughly 7,500 feet high. A Shiva LINGAM shape of ice covered with snow is visible at the far end of the cave. This is considered a "natural" or "self-generated" Shiva lingam, created by nature.

It is said that Shiva revealed the secret of immortality to PARVATI at this cave. Beneath the tiger skin on which Shiva sat, pigeon eggs later hatched. Those who do pilgrimage to this place often see the immortal pigeons incubated by the Lord Shiva himself. Some say that the first to make the pilgrimage to this shrine was Bhrigu *Rishi*.

In modern times it is said that a Muslim shepherd, Buta Malik, was given a sack of coal by a holy man at this site. When the shepherd returned home, he discovered that the coal had turned to gold; at the same time a Shiva lingam made of ice had appeared in the famous cave. The principal pilgrimage to this shrine is during the full moon of Shravana (July–August). The full pilgrimage, a widely observed custom since 1850, takes a total of 40 days from the lowlands upward and back.

Further reading: F. M. Hassnain, Yoshiaki Miura, and Vijay Pandita, *Sri Amarnatha Cave, the Abode of Shiva* (New Delhi: Nirmal, 1987); Karan Singh, *The Glory of Amarnath* (Bombay: Shanti Svarup Nishat, 1954).

Ambuvachi

Ambuvachi is a rite observed in most of North and central India, but most elaborately in Bengal. During four days in the Hindu month of Ashadha (June–July), just before the rainy season is to begin, the earth goddess is said to menstruate in order to prepare herself for fertility. During this period all plowing, sowing, and other farmwork are suspended. Widows may be required to observe special taboos during Ambuvachi, as they are not involved in procreation.

Further reading: Abbe J. A. Dubois, *Hindu Manners, Customs and Ceremonies*. Translated from the French by Henry K. Beauchamp (Oxford: Clarendon Press, 1959); Swami Harshananda, *Hindu Festivals and Sacred Days* (Bangalore: Ramakrishna Math, 1994).

American Meditation Society

The American Meditation Society was founded in 1976 by Purushottam Narshinhran Valodia (March 3, 1932–May 17, 1988), also known as Gururaj Ananda Yogi. Its teaching is focused on MEDITATION.

Drawn as a child to spiritual concerns, the guru ran away from his home in Gujarat at age five to visit temples. He wandered from village to village for six months, until found by his parents. As he wandered, he discovered that the temple gods were lifeless and did not speak to him. Con-tinuing his search into adulthood, he eventually discovered that what he sought lay within himself. After SELF-REALIZATION, he set about to become a spiritual teacher in the West.

He moved from his native Gujarat to South Africa and became a successful businessman. In 1975, he retired from business to become a full-time spiritual teacher, founding the International Foundation for Spiritual Unfoldment in 1975. By 1976, the organization had spread to nine countries in the British Commonwealth, Europe, and America, where the American Meditation Society was founded that year in California.

Gururaj Ananda Yogi taught that his path is not a religion, but the basis that underlies all religions. His teaching is to awaken each individual to the same reality that he discovered, primarily through the practice of meditation. The society offers courses in meditation and the intonation of sound during meditation. During his lifetime, students would send pictures of themselves to Gururaj, who would meditate upon the pictures and hear each person's unique sound in the universe, which became the student's personal mantra for meditation.

Further reading: Ted Partridge, *Jewels of Silence* (Farmborough, England: St. Michael's Abbey Press, 1981); Savita Taylor, *The Path to Unfoldment* (London: VSM, 1979).

American Yoga Association (est. 1968)

The American Yoga Association, the first nonprofit organization in the United States dedicated to yoga education, was founded by Alice Christensen (no date of birth) in 1968. Located in Sarasota, Florida, it serves as a resource center for both students and teachers, focusing on VEDANTA philosophy, HATHA YOGA, and MEDITATION techniques.

In 1953 Christensen began to have visionary experiences of a white light followed by transcendental communications from Swami SHIVANANDA SARASWATI (1887–1963) of Rishikesh. Subsequent dreams encouraged her to pursue the path of yoga. Sivananda became Christensen's guru and they maintained their correspondence by mail until his death. She then began to study with SWAMI RAMA (1900–72) and to travel in India.

Christensen began to teach yoga in 1965. As a student of Swami Rama she represented his teachings in the West. In 1968 she founded the Light Society (known later as the American Yoga Association) in Cleveland Heights, Ohio. By 1972 11 yoga centers were established in India, Australia, and the United States. During this time the first book published by the association was released, *The American Yoga Association Beginner's Manual*. After Swami Rama's death in 1972, Christensen continued to study yoga as a student of Sri LAKSH-MANJOO (1907–92), a teacher of KASHMIRI SHAIVISM. Christensen would remain his student, frequently traveling to Kashmir, until his death in 1992.

The American Yoga Association provides educational services to program developers in health-related fields as well as writers seeking information on yoga. During the late 1960s Christensen inaugurated a program called Easy Does It Yoga, which the association continues to offer to seniors and those with physical limitations. The program has gained wide respect for its effectiveness in helping older adults regain independence. Following the Kashmiri Shaivism system, the association emphasizes a self-directed approach to yoga that encourages its participants to engage in inner awareness for the purpose of releasing potential for self-knowledge. The association offers books and videotapes by Christensen.

Further reading: Alice Christensen, *The American Yoga Association Beginner's Manual* (New York: Simon & Schuster, 2002); ———, *The American Yoga Association's Easy Does It Yoga* (New York: Fireside Books, 1999).

amrita

Amrita is the term used in the VEDAS for *SOMA*, comparable to the ambrosia of the Greeks. It is considered a nectar of immortality of sorts and is taken during certain rites to achieve transcendent insight. Perhaps because the Moon is sometimes called Soma, *amrita* in the Vedic context is said to be found on the Moon; it feeds the Fathers in the dark half of the Moon's phases and the gods in the bright half.

The story goes that the gods and antigods (*asuras*) once joined together to churn the MILK OCEAN to make *amrita*. A huge mountain was used as a churning stick and the divine snake ADISHESHA (or Vasuki) was used as the rope around the stick. Many things emerged from the Milk Ocean at that time including the special divine wish-giving cow who appears in later mythology. Finally, the *amrita* emerged held in a cup by the divine physician Dhanvantari. The gods then plotted with VISHNU so that the antigods (*asuras*) would not be able to drink the nectar. Vishnu took on his form of the dazzling maiden, MOHINI, and as he distracted the *asuras*, the gods drank all the *amrita* themselves.

One story says that when the gods drank the *amrita* it spilled at four sites: HARDVAR, Nasik, Ujjain, and ALLAHABAD (Prayag). In esoteric HATHA YOGA it is thought that *amrita* can be accumulated in the skull above the posterior of the nasal passage. This *amrita* is understood to be transformed semen that can create bodily immortality. By severing the frenulum, or skin attachment under the bottom of the tongue, a yogi can force his tongue backward into what is called the Khechara MUDRA, in order to drink the *amrita*.

Further reading: Cornelia Dimmitt and J. A. B. van Buitenen, *Classical Hindu Mythology: A Reader in the Sanskrit Puranas* (Philadelphia: Temple University Press, 1978); Alfred Hillebrandt, *Vedic Mythology* (Delhi: Motilal Banarsidass, 1990); E. Washburn Hopkins, *Epic Mythology* (Delhi: Motilal Banarsidass, 1986); W. J. Wilkins, *Hindu Mythology, Vedic and Puranic* (Calcutta: Rupa, 1973).

Amrita Foundation (est. 1970s)

The Amrita Foundation was founded in Dallas, Texas, during the 1970s by former associates of the

SELF-REALIZATION FELLOWSHIP (SRF), who felt the need for independent development and wanted to publish their own version of the teachings of Paramahansa YOGANANDA (1893–1952). Since the 1920s, SRF had taken prime responsibility for publishing and circulating Yogananda's writings, but after his death some followers thought that the SRF's editing distorted the texts.

As SRF owned the copyrights to most of Yogananda's writings, the Amrita Foundation set about reprinting materials that had passed into the public domain, including the original editions of Yogananda's writings. Among the reprints were the initial writings and essential teachings of the infrastructure of Yogananda's work—the lessons on KRIYA YOGA distributed to students.

The home study course is a hallmark feature of the foundation's services, making the *kriya* lessons available to everyone. Issues are sent out each month to subscribers. The focal points of these lessons include the principles of MEDITATION and concentration, as well as physical practices designed to facilitate the spiritual development that *kriya yoga* can help achieve. Advice on diet and nutrition is also promoted; an important aspect of *kriya yoga* is promotion of a healthy body in order to awaken KUNDALINI energy as the vehicle to spiritual bliss (ANANDA).

The foundation has reprinted a substantial number of the first editions of Yogananda's early writings, including *The Second Coming of Christ*, *Songs of the Soul*, and *Whispers from Eternity*. The foundation remains based in Dallas, Texas.

Further reading: Paramahansa Yogananda, *Second Coming of Christ* (Dallas: Amrita Foundation, 1984); ———, *Songs of the Soul* (Dallas: Amrita Foundation, 1980).

Amritanandamayi Ma (1953–) *teacher who embodies the Divine Mother*

Ammachi (beloved Mother), as Amritanandamayi Ma is affectionately known, is a world-renowned Hindu guru recognized as an incarnation of the Holy Mother of Hinduism.

Sudhamani (her birth name) was born on September 27, 1953, to a poor fisherman in the small village of Parayakadavu in the state of Kerala, showing signs of divinity from the start. The birth itself, which was foreseen by a wandering religious mendicant, was said to be painless for her mother, and the infant did not cry, beaming a happy smile instead. At six months she began speaking prayers and singing songs in praise of Krishna. Her fervor increased, and by age six she was found daily immersed in JAPA (MANTRA recitation), devotional singing, and quiet MEDITATION. This practice estranged her from family and friends who did not understand. She took refuge in a deep spirituality.

In the mid-1970s she had a series of profound visions and meditative experiences, which firmly established her intimate relationship with the Divine Mother and set her on her present mission to

Amritanandamayi Ma (b. 1953), a famous devotional teacher from South India known for physically embracing all who go to her *(Ma Amritananda Center, San Ramon, California)*

"Give solace to suffering humanity." Her mission has matured into a dynamic global congregation. She runs an orphanage near her ASHRAM, housing about 400 poor villagers. She has built hospitals in Bombay and Ernakulam and industrial and computer training centers to help poor students learn vocational skills. She advocates the establishment of schools at every ashram to impart religious education.

The house where Ammachi was born has become an ashram and the headquarters of Mata Amritananda Mayi Trust. The ashram, Amritapuri, offers food and accommodations for travelers, funds social services for indigents, and sponsors humanitarian activities around the world. Hundreds of devotees work there on social service projects all day and attend daily sessions with Ammachi. At each of her daily appearances, Ammachi sits on a simple chair on stage with 30 male students, *brahmacharis,* seated on mats on her right and 30 female students, *brahmacharinis,* seated on her left, all dressed in white. Each DARSHAN, which can last for six to eight hours, includes the singing of BHAJANS while each of the attendees walks forward for a blessing and an embrace from Ammachi, who remains on stage until all have experienced her embrace.

Ammachi tours the globe with a constant schedule of appearances held at major cities in many countries. She does not deliver teachings or speeches. Instead, she blesses all those who go forward. Often thousands of admirers stand in line for hours to be hugged by Ammachi. She says that her life itself is her message and teaching. "An unbroken stream of love flows from me towards all beings in the universe," she has said. "That is my inborn nature."

At gatherings she disappears behind a screen, where she puts on the clothes of KRISHNA or DEVI, the goddess. She returns to serve as a channel for God, blessing the audience. She says, "The ATMAN, or Self, that is in me is also within you. If you can realize that Indivisible Principle ever shining in you, you will become That."

Ammachi has initiated 11 senior disciples into the order of *sannyas* (renunciants), two of whom are women. She has followed Hindu tradition by having Swami Dhruvananda of the RAMAKRISHNA MATH AND MISSION give the rites of *sannyas* to Swami Amritaswarupananda, her first disciple to renounce worldly life. Since then, Amritaswarupananda has performed the rites with Ammachi in attendance.

In 1993 Ammachi was named one of three presidents of Hinduism by the Parliament of the World's Religions in Chicago. That same year *Hinduism Today* bestowed a "Hindu of the Year" award upon her. In 1995 she spoke at the interreligion meeting of the United Nations. A movie, *Darshan,* released in 2006, portrays her life and the services organized by the headquarters of her trust.

Further reading: Amritanandamayi, *Awaken Children: Dialogues with Sri Sri Mata Amritanandamayi.* Adaptation and translation by Swami Amritaswarupananda 3d ed. (Kerala: Mata Amritanandamayi Mission Trust, 1992); ———, *Eternal Wisdom.* Compiled by Swami Jnanamritananda Puri. English translation from the original Malayalam by M. N. Namboodiri (San Ramon, Calif.: Mata Amritanandamayi Center, 1999); Swami Amritaswarupananda, *Ammachi: A Biography of Mata Amritanandamayi* (San Ramon, Calif.: Mata Amritanandamayi Center, 1991).

Amritsar

Amritsar is the sacred city of the SIKHS, located in Punjab state. The land was given to the fourth Sikh guru Ramdas by the Muslim Mughal emperor Akbar, and Ramdas shortly thereafter, in 1577, founded a city there. The city was built around a sacred spring, called Amrita Saras, "the flow [*saras*] of the nectar of immortality [AMRITA]."

The famous AKAL TAKHT or "eternal seat," of central importance in Sikhism, is located in Amritsar within the GOLDEN TEMPLE. The Adigranth, or Granth Sahib, the sacred book of the Sikhs, is enshrined in the temple; it is the sole true

Sikh devotees outside the Golden Temple in Amritsar, the international center for Sikh spirituality. *(www.shutterstock.com/Paul Prescott)*

guide for the Sikh faith, which no longer recognizes any human gurus.

Further reading: J. S. Grewal, *From Guru Nanak to Maharaja Ranjit Singh* (Amritsar: Guru Nanak University, 1982); W. H. McLeod, *The Evolution of the Sikh Community: Five Essays* (Delhi: Oxford University Press, 1975).

anahata chakra

The *anahata* CHAKRA, or the "chakra of the unsounded sound," is the fourth chakra (energy center) from the base of the spine in KUNDALINI YOGA systems. It is located on the spine at the heart. The *anahata* chakra is associated with righteousness, sanctity, and an emerging clarity of consciousness. Dedication, devotion, and calmness are also linked to the *anahata* chakra. Its deity is a form of SHIVA, Isana Shiva. Its SHAKTI is Kakini. It has 12 deep red petals.

Further reading: Harish Johari, *Chakras: Energy Centers of Transformation* (Rochester, Vt.: Destiny Books, 2000); Lilian Silburn, *Kundalini: The Energy of the Depths: A Comprehensive Study Based on the Scriptures of Nondualistic Kasmir Saivism.* Translated from the French by Jacques Gontier (Albany: State University of New York Press, 1988); Sir John Woodroffe, trans., *The Serpent Power* (Madras: Ganesh, 1978).

ananda

Ananda literally means "bliss." In Hinduism, *ananda* is the bliss beyond comprehension that is experienced when one is in communion with or has realized in totality the Godhead.

Ananda is seen as an aspect of the Divine and is often mentioned together with *sat* (divine being) and *cit* (divine consciousness). The term *SAT-CHIT-ANANDA* (divine being, consciousness, bliss) often appears in Vedantic contexts (*see* VEDANTA) and has become a proper name for SWAMIS or holy men.

Many teachers also have *"ananda"* appended to their names, such as Nikhilananda, "He who has realized total divine bliss," or Satyananda, "He who has realized the divine bliss of the One Truth," or Muktananda, "He who has realized the divine bliss in liberation from birth and rebirth."

Further reading: John Dudley Ball, *Ananda—Where Yoga Lives* (Bowling Green, Ohio: Bowling Green University Popular Press, 1982); J. A. B. van Buitenen, "Ananda, or All Desires Fulfilled," in *Studies in Indian Literature and Philosophy: Collected Articles of J. A. B. van Buitenen.* Edited by L. Rocher (Delhi: Motilal Banarsidass, 1988); Nalini Devdas, *Ananda: The Concept* *of Bliss in the Upanisads* (Madras: Christian Literature Society for the Christian Institute for the Study of Religion and Society, 1974).

Ananda Ashram, Monroe, New York
(est. 1964)

Ananda Ashram was founded in 1964 in Monroe, New York, as the headquarters of the Yoga Society of New York, Inc., which was founded by Ramamurti S. Mishra, M.D. (1923–93), also known as Swami Brahmananda Saraswati, a teacher of Raja YOGA. The ashram serves as a spiritual retreat and educational center that integrates principles of yoga and VEDANTA with a commitment to an East-West "cultural exchange." The center offers instruction in MEDITATION, Vedanta philosophy, HATHA YOGA, Sanskrit, dance, and music, as well as regular workshops and retreats. Guest teachers and artists from diverse traditions offer courses.

By the 1950s Mishra had gained renown in the East and West for his expertise in Eastern and Western medicine, including the system of AYURVEDA. In 1966 he quit the practice of Western medicine and left the United States. He later returned as a doctor of acupuncture and led a number of his ashrams into holistic health, including Ayurveda. In 1984 he took the vow of *sannyas* (renunciation) from Swami Gangeshvarananda and was given the name Brahmananda Saraswati.

Sri Brahmananda Saraswati also established the Brahmananda Ashram (the Yoga Society of San Francisco, Inc.), in 1972, as well as several meditation centers in the United States and around the world. He was a prolific writer who published texts on yoga, a commentary on the writing of the great ADVAITA philosopher Shankaracharya, and translations of Sanskrit texts, in addition to many essays and stories. Much of his teaching is recorded in audio and video formats. Brahmananda died in 1993.

Ananda Ashram is open year round and offers teachings to people of all faiths. Programs offered are nonsectarian and place an emphasis on self-awareness and meditation. The Baba Bhagavandas Publication Trust was established by Brahmananda in 1993 to publish important works in philosophy, medicine, and yoga.

Further reading: Ramamurti S. Mishra, *Fundamentals of Yoga* (Monroe, N.Y.: Baba Bhagavandas Publication Trust, 1996); ———, *Self Analysis and Self Knowledge* (Monroe, N.Y.: Baba Bhagavandas Publication Trust, 1997); ———, *The Textbook of Yoga Psychology* (Monroe, N.Y.: Baba Bhagavandas Publication Trust, 1997).

Ananda Ashrama and Vedanta Centre
(est. 1923)

Ananda Ashrama of La Crescenta, California, was founded in 1923 by Swami PARAMANANDA (1884–1940) to facilitate a better understanding between Eastern and Western spiritualities and to disseminate VEDANTA philosophy. The 120-acre retreat features Viswamandir, a temple established in 1928 and dedicated to the world's great religions. The ashram upholds a model of tolerance and nonsectarianism. By upholding the teachings of Sri RAMAKRISHNA and Swami Paramananda, the ashram assists individuals in discovering principles for spiritual practice. It teaches the basic tenets of the Vedanta tradition: God is one, human nature is divine, all paths lead to the same goal, and the purpose of life is the realization of God in one's soul.

In line with Paramananda's belief in equality of the sexes, he ordained women to teach Vedanta, entrusting them to undertake major responsibilities in his work in India and the United States. In both countries, he founded schools and orphanages to assist women and children in need. In fact, he designated a woman, Sri Mata Gayatri Devi (1906–95), to succeed him as director of the ashram. As a result, the parent order in India, the RAMAKRISHNA MATH AND MISSION, excommunicated his centers. Nevertheless, for 55 years Gayatri Devi continued teaching Vedanta in the tradition of Sri Ramakrishna and Swami Paramananda. At her death in 1995, Dr. Susan Schrager (1942–), known as the Reverend Mother Sudha Puri, accepted the spiritual leadership of the ashram.

Residents of Ananda Ashrama are primarily women monastics. MEDITATION classes, weekly worship services, a lending library, and retreats are offered to the public. Membership is offered to anyone who attends regular services. Through its company, Vedanta Centre Publishers, the ashram publishes and sells books, compact disks, and cassette tapes by and about Swami Paramananda.

In addition to two ashrams in Calcutta, India, and Ananda Ashrama, Swami Paramananda founded the Vedanta Centre in Cohasset, Massachusetts, in 1929.

Further reading: Sister Devamata, *Swami Paramananda and His Work,* 2 vols. (Crescenta, Calif.: Ananda Ashrama, 1926 and 1941); Sara Ann Levinsky, *A Bridge of Dreams: The Story of Paramananda, a Modern Mystic, and His Ideal of All-Conquering Love* (West Stockbridge, Mass.: Lindisfarne Press, 1984); ———, *Christ and Oriental Ideals* (Cohasset, Mass.: Vedanta Centre, 1912); ———, *Creative Power of Silence* (La Crescenta, Calif.: Vedanta Centre; 1923); ———, *Emerson and Vedanta* (Boston: Vedanta Centre, 1918); Swami Paramananda, *The Path of Devotion* (New York: Vedanta Society, 1907).

Ananda Marga Yoga Society (est. 1955)

The Ananda Marga Yoga Society describes itself as "an international socio-spiritual movement involved in the twin pursuit of SELF-REALIZATION and service to all of creation." Ananda Marga, through its educational and charitable affiliates in over 160 countries, claims more than a million followers worldwide.

The movement was founded in 1955 in the state of Bihar, India, by Prabhat Ranjan Sarkar (1921–90), better known as Marga Guru Sri SRI ANANDAMURTI, which means "He who attracts others as the embodiment of bliss." He received enlightenment quite early in his life—he is reported to have been an accomplished yogi by

the age of four—and he attracted his first devotees when he was only six. After marrying and getting a job with the railway system, he founded Ananda Marga. From then until his death he authored more than 250 books as Sri Sri Anandamurti.

After founding Ananda Marga, Sarkar began to train missionaries to carry his teachings beyond India; today the society has a complex international organization. Three levels of membership are offered: (1) *acharyas*—teachers and devotees who devote their lives to the movement and may be employed in many locales around the world; (2) local full-time workers; and (3) *margis*—members who are initiated but hold jobs outside the movement. The number of active members is not known, but estimates run as high as several hundred thousand.

The teaching of the movement involves three dimensions: the practice of tantra yoga, MEDITATION, and engagement in social service with the goal of bringing about a more just and humane world. Part of the movement's discipline is Sarkar's Sixteen Points, a system of spiritual practices that helps initiates balance the physical, mental, and spiritual aspects of life. Rituals include KIRTAN (singing) and recitation of the mantra *Baba Nam Kevalam* (the universal Father is everywhere).

Ananda Marga stresses public service, including care of the sick and elderly. Service to others is a means of transformation from the needs of oneself to the needs of others, which is also the path to enlightenment. Because of the movement's dedication to human service, many organizations have been formed within its ambit. The Ananda Marga Universal Relief Team (AMURT), founded in 1965, and the Ananda Marga Universal Relief Team Ladies (AMURTEL), founded in 1977, address disaster relief around the world. Renaissance Universal, founded in 1958, encourages intellectuals to design and create programs for improving the human condition. The Education, Relief, and Welfare Section (ERWS) is another organization created to propagate Ananda Marga's agenda of social service.

Sarkar tried to conceptualize and mobilize new ways of education. He advocated a form of education that encourages simultaneous development of the physical, mental, and spiritual aspects of humanity. His philosophy extends his emphasis on human development to include animals and plants. He established a global plant exchange program and animal sanctuaries around the world.

Sarkar proposed a political program in 1959, called Progressive Utilization Theory (PROUT), which calls for economic democracy and human rights. He also advocated a global bill of rights, constitution, and system of justice.

In India, Sarkar's political activism generated much controversy regarding the movement during the 1960s and 1970s. He ran unsuccessfully for political office in 1967 and 1968, representing the Proutist Bloc. Many in India saw the Proutists as a terrorist organization, and both PROUT and Ananda Marga were banned in India during the period of national emergency declared by Indira Gandhi. Sarkar was accused, convicted, and sentenced to life imprisonment for conspiring to murder former members. In 1978 he won a new trial and was acquitted of the charges.

Since the acquittal of its leader, Ananda Marga has recovered slowly in India but has spread widely outside India, including Germany, the United Kingdom, Australia, and the United States. Led by Acharya Vimala-ananda, the movement entered the United States in 1969 and gained many followers.

Ananda Marga has adherents and social betterment activities in more than 160 countries and claims more than a million followers worldwide. It supports a variety of schools, clinics, and children's homes. It is attempting to put its larger economic program into effect through the formation of cooperative communities, the largest of them Ananda Nagar (the City of Bliss) in West Bengal, and promoting rural development. International headquarters of the movement is in West Bengal.

The society produces several periodicals, including a monthly newsletter and a magazine.

Sadvipra, begun in 1973. A branch of Ananda Marga, Renaissance Universal, is dedicated to working toward a renaissance of social institutions based on neohumanistic values. This renaissance will involve a redesign of the major institutions of society and will foster individual growth and self-realization. Twice a year Renaissance Universal organizes a worldwide forum on contemporary issues. Its quarterly journal, *New Renaissance,* features articles on neohumanism, art, and science in service of self-realization, and social justice.

Further reading: Shrii Shrii Anandamurti, *Ananda Marga in a Nutshell,* 4 vols. (Calcutta: Ananda Marga, 1988); Acarya Vijayananda Avadhuta, *The Life and Teachings of Shrii Shrii Anandamurti* (Calcutta: Aananda Marga, 1994); *Shrii P. R. Sakar and His Mission* (Calcutta: Ananda Marga, 1993); *Way of Tantra: Ananda Marga Yoga Philosophy* (Calcutta: Ananda Marga, 1989).

Anandamayi Ma (1896–1982) *mystic and avatar of Shakti*

Born Nirmala Sundari Bhattacharya in Vadyakuta, East Bengal (now Bangladesh), on April 30, 1896, Anandamayi Ma was a mystic considered by her disciples as an AVATAR of SHAKTI, the manifest energy of the divine, and as God in the form of the goddess KALI.

Her father, Bipin Behari Bhattacharya, was head of a poor Brahmin family and was often in religious ecstasy as he sang songs from the Vaishnavite tradition. Her mother, Moksada Sundari Devi, also experienced states of religious emotion and reported visits by avatars and deities who appeared surrounded by light. Moksada eventually took vows of renunciation.

As a child, Nirmala also behaved as an ecstatic. She fell into trances, saw visions of religious figures, and gazed into space with eyes not focused on physical objects. Her education was limited and her writing skills minimal.

Married at age 13 to Ramani Mohan Chakravarti, she spent a few years living in her brother-in-law's house, often in a trance. At age 18, when her brother-in-law died, she went to live with her husband; there she met a young man who was impressed by her quiet way of being. He called her Ma (*mother* in Bengali) and said that one day the entire world would address her with that name.

Her marriage remained celibate because Nirmala's body would grow stiff and faint when her husband approached the topic of sexuality. She would regain normal consciousness only after he repeated MANTRAS. He eventually accepted her as his GURU and took initiation from her.

Throughout her life, Nirmala exhibited bodily states of trance, physical stiffness, and fainting. She could hold difficult yogic positions (ASANAS)

Anandamayi Ma (1896–1982), a renowned 20th-century mystic of Bengal and North India *(Courtesy Anandamayi Ma Ashram, Haridwar)*

for long periods and form complex hand positions (MUDRAS) and gestures. After examination by exorcists and physicians, she was diagnosed as having a kind of god intoxication, a divine madness. Her status as a holy woman was based entirely on her spontaneous ecstatic states, as she did not receive formal religious training or initiation from a guru. Instead, she heard voices that told her which spiritual practices to perform and which images to visualize. She would variously shed profuse tears, laugh for hours, talk at great speed, roll in the dust, dance for long periods, and fast for days.

At age 26 Nirmala began a stage of spiritual discipline (SADHANA) without a guru. She performed her own initiation (DIKSHA), spontaneously visualizing the ritual and initiatory sacred words, after which she entered three years of complete silence. In 1925, Sri Jyotish Chandra Roy named her Anandamayi Ma.

Although her parents worshipped KRISHNA, Anandamayi is not properly placed in a specific Hindu sect; rather, her influence was felt in many religious traditions of India. She traveled widely, staying at abandoned temples and other inhospitable sites, with little care for her physical body. She taught detachment from the world, religious devotion, and service to others. She was known for her SIDDHIS, or yogic powers, particularly telepathy, healing, and a variety of psychic states. Her chaotic states of consciousness, she believed, derived from spontaneous eruptions of the divine will that arise out of the state of nothingness or the void (*mahasunya*). She explained that her emotional states were the play of the Lord acting through her body, and that she as an individual person did not exist. She died on August 27, 1982. The Sri Sri Anandamayi Sangha of Varanasi coordinates many ASHRAMS built for her by her disciples throughout India.

Further reading: Gopinath Kaviraj, ed., *Mother as Seen by Her Devotees* (Varanasi: Shri Shri Anandamayee Sangha, 1967); ———, *Shri Shri Ma Anandamayi* (Calcutta: Basyant Prakasani, 1982); Lisa Lassell Hallstrom,

Mother of Bliss (Oxford: Oxford University Press, 1999); Richard Lannoy, *Anandamayi: Her Life and Wisdom* (Rockport, Mass.: Element, 1996); Alexander Lipski, *Life and Teachings of Shri Anandamayi Ma* (Delhi: Motilal Banarsidass, 1977).

Ananda movement (est. 1968)

Ananda is a worldwide movement based on the teachings of Paramahansa YOGANANDA (1893–1952) and founded by Swami Kriyananda (b. 1926). The Ananda World Brotherhood includes the Ananda Church of Self-Realization, several Ananda communities around the world, educational institutions, and several publishing ventures.

When he was 22 years of age, Kriyananda became a disciple of Yogananda, and he lived with him until his death, receiving the vow of SANNYAS (renunciation) from him in 1948. Until 1961 Kriyananda served in a variety of capacities—as minister, director, lecturer, and vice president—at the SELF-REALIZATION FELLOWSHIP (SRF) at Mount Washington, California, the primary organization founded by Yogananda. As a monk in Yogananda's order, he initiated students into KRIYA YOGA, traveled, and taught.

Along the way, Kriyananda received what he perceived as a summons from God, calling him to serve in another way. His intentions were perceived as divisive by officials of SRF and he was asked to resign from the organization in 1962. He left SRF to expand upon the meaning of Yogananda's teachings of *kriya yoga*. He initially offered himself as teacher and leader to lay people and students who wished to know his viewpoints. In 1968, observing Yogananda's vision of a world brotherhood community, he constructed a retreat center and house in Nevada City, California, on 750 acres of woodland and natural forest in the Sierra foothills. At present Ananda Village has almost 300 members, making it one of the largest religious communities in the United States. The village and adjoining areas support about 600 people drawn from some 25 nationalities. All residents of the village are also members of the local congregation of the Ananda Church of Self-Realization.

Kriyananda saw himself as responding to Yogananda's plea to "cover the Earth with world-brotherhood colonies, demonstrating that simplicity of living plus high thinking lead to the greatest happiness." Kriyananda took this mission seriously and laid out the rationale for Ananda in his booklet *Cooperative Communities: How to Start Them and Why* (1968).

Members of Ananda Village work in a number of capacities. Some own their own businesses; others work for Ananda. Residents operate the Ananda Education-For-Life, a school for children through the junior high school level. Youth then attend Nevada City High School to complete their education. A governing village council is elected every year. The Expanding Light, a guest facility, offers retreats, a variety of special events, workshops, and seminars. Residents engage in *kriya yoga* as taught by Yogananda. They also sponsor a worldwide outreach program for those interested in becoming practitioners. The village includes a farm, a natural food store, and a vegetarian restaurant.

Founded in 1990, Ananda Church of Self-Realization, similar in many ways to SRF, has 2,000 members who worship in the congregational way, quite different from temple worship, where individuals go alone to commune with God. The goal of the Ananda Church is to provide fellowship and teaching to inspire others to find spiritual nourishment in serving humanity. The purpose is to engage in the practice introduced to the West by Yogananda. The church has over 150 trained and ordained ministers who serve at home or in missions abroad. There are five branches: in Sacramento and Palo Alto, California; Seattle, Washington; Portland, Oregon; and Assisi, Italy. Ananda's Crystal Clarity Publishers issues books on yoga, including Kriyananda's own writings, and the periodical *Clarity Newsletter*. East-West Bookstore in Palo Alto is a thriving business begun by members of the Ananda Community.

In the 1990s, Ananda went through a significant court struggle with SRF concerning copyrights and trademarks related to Yogananda's writings and images and the name of the Ananda Church of Self-Realization. The church prevailed in most of the issues and is now free to use pictures of Yogananda and reproduce his early writings. On the other hand, the movement suffered from a lawsuit brought by a former member claiming sexual abuse at the hands of an Ananda minister. A court judgment in 2001 against the minister and the church sent the Nevada City community into bankruptcy, from which it is only slowly recovering.

Further reading: John Ball, *Ananda: Where Yoga Lives* (Bowling Green, Ohio: Bowling Green University Popular Press, 1982); Swami Kriyananda [Donald Walters], *Cooperative Communities: How to Start Them and Why* (Nevada City, Calif.: Ananda, 1968); ———, *Crises in Modern Thought* (Nevada City Calif.: Ananda, 1972); ———, *The Path* (Nevada City, Calif.: Ananda, 1977); Ted A. Nordquist, *Ananda Cooperative Village* (Uppsala: Borgstroms Tryckeri, Ab, 1978); J. Donald Walters, *Awaken to Superconsciousness* (Nevada City, Calif.: Crystal Clarity, 2000); Paramahansa Yogananda, *Autobiography of a Yogi* (Los Angeles: Self-Realization Fellowship, 1971).

Anandamurti, Sri (1921–1990) *founder*
Ananda Marga Yoga Society

Sri Sri Anandamurti, the founder of the Ananda MARGA YOGA SOCIETY, was born Prabhat Ranjan Sarkar. His father died while Prabhat was still a youth, putting an end to his formal education. As his father had, he took a job with the railroad. However, he gradually developed a discipline of YOGA and MEDITATION, and in 1955 he announced to his acquaintances that he had achieved enlightenment. He resigned from his job and founded the ANANDA MARGA (Path of Bliss) YOGA SOCIETY. It was at this time that he assumed his religious name, Anandamurti. In 1962, he initiated the first monks and four years later the first nuns.

The new organization taught a form of tantric yoga but also became socially active. As it expanded, it founded and supported several hundred elementary schools and homes for children. The social activism was underlain by Anandamurti's developing theories about the reorganization of society. He had begun to feel that both capitalism and communism, the two main economic and political options being debated in India, were lacking the elements necessary to build the good society. In 1958 he formally introduced his new plan, which he termed Progressive Universal Theory (PROUT), and founded Renaissance Universal as an organization to propagate his perspective.

PROUT was introduced in the context of widespread criticism of government corruption. As Ananda Marga grew, it became involved in a number of violent clashes and was charged with illegal political activities and terrorism. In 1967, five members of the group were murdered. The new government of Prime Minister Indira Gandhi (r. 1966–77) restricted the organization by issuing a ban on government employees joining it. In 1971, Anandamurti was arrested on what some say were fabricated charges that he had ordered the murder of some former adherents. In 1975, under severe political pressure Gandhi declared emergency rule. Ananda Marga was one of a number of organizations that were banned. The organization was suppressed, its assets seized, and a number of its leaders arrested. Gandhi was voted out of office in 1977 and Anandamurti and his followers were released when emergency rule ended.

After the drama of the Gandhi era, Ananda Marga was reorganized in India and resumed its program of propagating the spiritual and social teachings of its founder. Controversy has surrounded Anandamurti and his movement since its inception. In this period Anandamurti developed his concept of Neo-Humanism, in reaction to the neglect of the spiritual dimension of human life that he saw in communism and capitalism. He suggested that human beings were an expression of the Supreme Consciousness. If this concept were accepted, he believed, humanity would enter a state of love toward all sentient beings. He died in 1990.

Further reading: Didi Anandamitra, *The Philosophy of Shrii Shrii Anandamurti: A Commentary on Ananda Sutram* (Calcutta: Ananda Marga, n.d.); Shrii Shrii Anandamurti, *Baba's Grace: Discourses of Shrii Shrii Anandamurti* (Los Altos Hills, Calif.: Ananda Marga, 1973); Ácárya Vijayánanda Avahuta, *The Life and Teachings of Shrii Shrii Ánandamúrti* (Calcutta: Ananda Marga, 1994); ———, *Shrii P. R. Sakar and His Mission* (Calcutta: Ananda Marga, 1993); ———, *The Spiritual Philosophy of Shrii Shrii Anandamurti* (Denver, Colo.: Ananda Marga, 1981).

Ananda Yogi, Gururaj   *See* AMERICAN MEDITATION SOCIETY.

Ananta   *See* ADISHESHA.

Anasuya Foundation (est. 1975)

The Anasuya Foundation (also known as the Tripura Yoga Foundation) was created in 1975. It was a response to a revelation of Lord Dattatreya that Swami Punitachariji received while meditating on Mount Girnar in Gujarat state. Lord Dattatreya appeared as the Vedic trinity—the union of BRAHMA, VISHNU, and SHIVA. His classic form of three heads and six arms appeared as the supreme being who is omnipresent, omnipotent, and omniscient.

Lord Dattatreya represents the divine spark contained in true wisdom. He is a transmitter of the secrets that when known empower others to understand the universal energies and know the meaning of life. In the vision, Swami Punitachariji (also known as *Bapu*, a fond name for a grandfather figure) saw Lord Dattatreya seated on a large rock. Legendary saints and holy people were worshipping him with flowers. Bapu recognized Lord Dattatreya from traditional statuary and paintings and knew that the Lord's all-knowingness and spiritual prowess could transform ordinary existence into divine life.

Lord Dattatreya gave Bapu a mantric chant: "*Hari Om Tatsat Jai Guru Datta,* a mantra recited for the effects of its sound, rather than its meaning." From his own training in the Hindu tradition, Bapu believed that the world and everything in it were created through sound. He believed that repeated mantras of power make the invisible creative planes of existence reverberate to enrich and enhance the physical plane of the Earth. Bapu believed that repetition of the mantra of Lord Dattatreya sends forth the Lord's spiritual essence to those who seek his divine wisdom. Through the union of sound, between the visible and invisible worlds, one's spiritual teacher need not be on the physical plane sharing an earthly life. Chanting in this way allows spiritual interaction between GURU and *chela* (student) without time constraints. Bapu believed that Lord Dattatreya had specifically given him this insight to promote the elevated consciousness of humankind and to enhance the spirituality of the people on the planet.

The religious beliefs of Bapu were exported to North America in the late 1970s, when Shantibaba, an early devotee of Bapu, who wished to share with students in other countries the mystical teachings about sacred sound, immigrated to the United States. Not long afterward, teaching centers were also founded in the United Kingdom and Germany. Today there are centers located in California, New York, Colorado, and New Jersey. International headquarters are at Girnar Sadhana Ashram in Gujarat state, India. The American headquarters is the Tripura Yoga Foundation in Snowmass, Colorado.

Further reading: Datta Mission. Available online. URL: http://www.jaiguru.com. Accessed August 15, 2005; "Mantras and Meditation," *Hinduism Today,* August 1986.

Available online. URL: http://www.hinduism-today.com/archives/1986/08/1986-08-06.shtml. Accessed August 15, 2005; Emily Matulay and Shantibaba, *Spontaneous Meditation* (Basalt, Colo.: Anasuya, 1983).

ancestor worship

Worship of the ancestors (*pitris*) is a tradition in India dating to Vedic times (c. 1500 B.C.E.) Traditionally, a man is expected to offer libations of oil and water to his deceased father, grandfather, and great-grandfather. The anniversary of the deaths of one's mother and father must also be celebrated with formalities, including the offering of balls of rice to the ancestors. (Ancestors are presumed to be in heaven but must be fed by their progeny.) Funeral rituals always include a worship of ancestors with offerings of rice balls. Among five sacrificial rites that are enjoined daily for BRAHMINS, worshippers must "sacrifice to the ancestors" by ritually pouring out a glass of water to them.

There is an inherent paradox in this practice. The very ancient Vedic rites assume that the departed have gone to a heavenly realm. However, such notions have long been superseded by the orthodox Hindu understanding that most departed souls will be reincarnated in a new form in this realm.

Further reading: Abbe J. A. Dubois, *Hindu Manners, Customs and Ceremonies.* Translated by Henry K. Beauchamp. 3rd ed. (Oxford: Clarendon Press, 1959); Klaus K. Klostermaier, *A Survey of Hinduism* (Albany: State University of New York Press, 1994); Dakshina Ranjan Shastri, *Origin and Development of Rituals of Ancestor Worship in India* (Calcutta: Bookland, 1963).

Andal (c. ninth century C.E.)

Andal was the only woman among the ALVARS, the 12 Tamil Vaishnavite saints.

There are no reliable historical data on Andal, only two hagiographies. Tradition says she was born in Srivilliputtur in the southern state of Tamil Nadu. Her father, Vishnucitta, who was also a saint under the name Periyalvar, is said to have found her as an infant girl while he was hoeing his sacred basil (basil or TULSI is sacred to VISHNU). The infant was recognized as an incarnation of Bhudevi, the goddess of the Earth, who is consort and wife of VISHNU and a form of sri.

Andal's father raised her as though she were Sri herself. As a young girl, when her father was absent, she would dress up as a bride and put on the garland her father had set aside to be offered to the Lord Vishnu. Any handling of PUJA flowers ordinarily makes them unfit for offering, and when her father discovered her doing this, he was very upset. He put the flowers aside and did his puja without the garland. That night Vishnu appeared to Periyalvar in a dream, saying that Andal's wearing of the garland had increased its desirability to him.

After this time Andal became even more focused on worship of Vishnu. She refused ordinary marriage, wishing only to be a bride of Vishnu. She composed Tiruppavai and Nacciyar Tirmoli, two poetic works in devotion to Vishnu. Not knowing which form of Vishnu his daughter was obsessed with, Periyalvar sang songs to each of the 108 manifestations of the Lord in various places. Andal responded to the song to the Lord of SRIRANGAM, the most prominent South Indian Vaishnavite (see VAISHNAVISM) shrine. Once again, in a dream, Vishnu appeared to Periyalvar and said that he would accept Andal as his bride. It is said that Vishnu himself arranged for Andal to be taken from Srivilliputtur to Srirangam with a fabulous marriage party. When she arrived at the shrine she approached the reclining image of Vishnu there and disappeared into his image, never to be seen again.

Both of Andal's short poems, which are included in the Tamil Vaishnavite sacred text Nalayira Divya Prabandhan, use Tamil motifs to praise Vishnu. Her Nacciyar Tirumoli focuses particularly on Vishnu's forms as Krishna and Venkatanatha (see TIRUPATI). The sixth hymn of *Nacciyar Tirumoli,* which reenacts all the marriage rites, is recited at all Vaishnavite weddings in South India.

Further reading: S. M. S. Chari, *Philosophy and Theistic Mysticism of the Alvars* (Delhi: Motilal Banarsidass, 1997); Norman Cutler, *Consider Our Vows: An English Translation of Tiruppavai and Tiruvempavai* (Madurai: Muthu Patippakam, 1979); Vidya Dehejia, *Antal and Her Path of Love: Poems of a Woman Saint from South India* (Albany: State University of New York Press, 1990); Alkondavilli Govindacharya, *The Holy Lives of the Azhvars or the Dravida Saints* (Bombay: Ananthacharya Indological Research Institute, 1982).

Andhaka

Andhaka (Blind One) is the blind demon born to SHIVA and PARVATI in the following way: Parvati was joking with Shiva and covered up his three eyes with her hands. As she did this, the entire cosmos fell into darkness. Parvati's hands began to sweat as they covered Shiva's potent third eye. From the sweat of her hands, heated up by the third eye of Shiva, arose Andhaka, an angry black blind demon.

Andhaka is thus considered the son of Parvati, but when the childless demon king HIRANYAKSHA, after performing strict austerities, requested a son as a boon from Shiva, he gave him Andhaka. After a short time, Hiranyaksha died and Andhaka became the king of the demons. After horrific austerities, in which he offered every ounce of his own flesh to a sacrificial fire, Andhaka was given a boon. His request was very strange: If he were ever to desire the most desirable woman of all, he asked to be destroyed. The "most desirable woman of all," however, could only have been his own mother, Parvati. Eventually, he did in fact manifest this desire, and he was impaled by Shiva on his trident. Existing half-dead there, Andhaka became purified and a complete devotee of Shiva and Parvati and ceased being a demon.

Further reading: Cornelia Dimmitt and J. A. B. van Buitenen, *Classical Hindu Mythology: A Reader in the Sanskrit Puranas* (Philadelphia: Temple University Press, 1978); E. Washburn Hopkins, *Epic Mythology* (Delhi: Motilal Banarsidass, 1986); Stella Kramrisch, *The Presence of Siva* (Princeton, N.J.: Princeton University Press, 1981).

Anekantavada

One of the underlying philosophical ideas in JAINISM is Anekantavada, "the assertation that everything is many-sided." This historical Jain concept, which for centuries remained largely at the level of theory rather than practice, has received more focused attention from many modern Jains, especially those in the diaspora. One must take a position of Anekantavada when one realizes that no ordinary human can have a full view of anything—as only the Omniscient SIDDHA or TIRTHANKARA can. It logically follows that all views are partial and subject to many-sided analysis.

Further reading: Paul Dundas, *The Jains* (London: Routledge, 1992); P. S. Jaini, *The Jaina Path of Purification* (Berkeley: University of California Press, 1979); Bimal K. Matilal, *The Central Philosophy of Jainism (anekantavada)* (Ahmedabad: L. D. Institute of Indology, 1981); Satkar Mookerji, *The Jaina Philosophy of Non-Absolutism, a Critical Study of Anekantavada* (Calcutta: Bharati Mahvidyalaya, 1944).

Anga (c. 400 B.C.E. to 500 C.E.)

The Angas are the 12 main texts that are seen as fundamental by all Jains (see JAINISM). SHVETAMBARA Jains believe that 11 of these are still extant; DIGAMBARAS believe that none of the original texts any longer exist and that the existing versions are not authoritative. The Angas cover ecclesiastical law, doctrine, determination of false views, and narratives for the laity. The texts were all originally written in Jain Prakrit; however, Jains most commonly refer to them by their SANSKRIT names.

See also ACHARANGA SUTRA.

Further reading: Padmanabh S. Jaini, *The Jaina Path of Purification* (Delhi: Motilal Banarsidass, 1990); Hermann Jacobi, trans., *Jaina Sutras,* Sacred Books of the East Series, vols. 22 and 45 (Delhi: Motilal Banarsidass, 1964); K. C. Lalwanti, *Sudharma Svami's Bhagavati Sutra: Prakrit Text with English Translation and Notes Based on the Commentary of Abhayadeva Suri* (Calcutta: Jain Bhagwan, 1980); Jogendra Chandra Sikdar, *Studies in the Bhagawatisutra* (Muzaffarpur: Research Institute of Prakrit, Jainology and Ahimsa, 1964).

Anirvan, Sri (1896–1978) *Baul and Samkhya author and guru*

Sri Anirvan was an important scholar and writer of commentaries on traditional Hindu sacred texts, a practicing BAUL, and a spiritual seeker who espoused the SAMKHYA philosophy of Hinduism.

The future guru was born Narendra Chandra Dhar on July 8, 1896, in Mymensingh, East Bengal (now Bangladesh). His parents, Raj Chandra Dhar and Sushila Devi, were cultured, pious middle-class Hindus of the Kayastha caste. Poor but deeply committed to spiritual values, they provided Narendra with an environment of love and harmony. He learned PANINI'S SANSKRIT grammar at an early age and daily recited chapters from the BHAGAVAD GITA. At the age of seven, he had a vision of an exquisitely beautiful young girl, whose image became for him a symbol of a mystery to be addressed. This image was a benign influence that deeply influenced his SADHANA (spiritual path) and became a presiding deity of his life. Later he recognized in this vision the Divine Mother, born of perfect wisdom, the Uma Haimavati of the *Kenopanishad.*

At age nine, in a state of SAMADHI (blissful consciousness), he experienced the boundless Void and saw the sky (AKASHA) with its myriad stars enter into him. The *akasha* became his symbol of freedom and detachment; his meditation on it became part of his teaching. At age 16, upon completion of his secondary education, he left Mymensingh to live in Assam with his family's guru, Swami

Nigamananda, who was building a new ashram near Jorhat. Narendra worked on the building site until he was awarded a state scholarship to study Sanskrit and Indian philosophy. He specialized in study of the VEDAS and stood first in the University of Calcutta (Kolkata) Sanskrit examinations at both the bachelor's and the master's levels.

At age 22, having completed his studies, Narendra returned to the ashram, where his guru initiated him into *sannyas* (renunciation) and gave him the name Nirvanananda. In 1920, at age 34, he left the ashram after serving as teacher and administrator. He changed his name to Anirvan to signify that he was no longer bound by the vows of *sannyas.* He spent the next 12 years traveling widely in the Himalayas in quiet retreat and MEDITATION.

In 1944 he began living in a house near Almora, Uttar Pradesh, where he began to translate Sri AUROBINDO'S *The Life Divine* from English to Bengali and began to write his own commentaries on the Vedas. Here he met a Swiss woman, Lizelle Reymond, who became his pupil and biographer. Her work became his line of transmission to the West, and they remained in intimate contact for the rest of his life.

Living in Almora, Shillong, and finally Calcutta, Anirvan continued to write and to give lectures on the UPANISHADS to small groups of disciples. Bedridden after a fall in 1971, he remained in the care of two disciples in Calcutta. He continued to be a quiet seeker with a spiritual journey based on the teachings of PATANJALI and the SAMKHYA philosophy of Hinduism. He identified himself as a BAUL, although he did not belong to a formal organization of Bauls. He especially liked the freedom of spiritual expression taught by the Bauls and some of his writing is collected as "Letters from a Baul."

His statement of his mission was clear: "My ambition is not very great. It is to live a life rich in impressions, luminous to the end; to leave behind a few books embodying my life-long search for Truth, and a few souls who have caught fire. My aim? Simply to inspire people and give them the most complete freedom to live their own life. No glamour, no fame, no institution—nothing. To live simply and die luminously." Anirvan wrote some 20 books, most of them commentaries on the scriptures and philosophical systems of India. All but two English volumes were published in Bengali. Anirvan died on Fern Road in Calcutta on May 31, 1978.

Further reading: Shri Anirvan and Lizelle Reymond, *To Live Within: Teachings of a Baul* (North Yorkshire, England: Coombe Springs Press, 1984); Sri Anirvan, *Inner Yoga (Antaryoga)*. Translated from the Bengali by Simanta Narayan Chatterjee (New Delhi: Voice of India, 1988); ———, *Buddhiyoga of the Bhagavad Gita and Other Essays* (Madras: Samata Books, 1991).

Annapurna

Literally "She who is abundant [*purna*] with food [*anna*]," the goddess Annapurna is considered a form of DURGA or sometimes of PARVATI, both being wives of SHIVA. In her iconography she is light colored and stands on a lotus or sits on a throne. She has only two hands; in one she holds a bowl of rice and in the other a spoon that is used to stir rice while cooking it. Sometimes Shiva, as a mendicant, is receiving alms from her. For many Hindus she is a protecting deity; those who worship her are said never to want for food.

The most elaborate festival to Annapurna takes place in BENARES (Varanasi) in the fall, when she is celebrated as the sustainer of life. She is also celebrated there in the springtime during the *annakuta* or "food-pile" festival, in which a pile of food fills her temple in worship to her. In the spring, she is worshipped in association with the new sprouts of rice in the fields; at that time her temple is decorated with rice sprouts.

In the Linga Purana there is a story about Annapurna that purports to tell how Shiva took the form of ARDHANARISHVARA, or "half-man, half-woman." Once when Shiva was unable to do his

usual begging to support his family as a result of marijuana intoxication, there was nothing in the house to eat. Shiva thereupon went out to beg, while Durga, his wife, in anger, started out for her father's house. On the way she and her children ran into the famous sage NARADA. Narada told her that in her aspect as Annapurna she should make it impossible for Shiva to get food by begging. She did this and went home, still in her aspect as Annapurna. When Shiva returned home she offered him food. He was so pleased that he merged his being with her, creating Ardhanarishvara.

The name of this goddess is given to one of the highest peaks in the HIMALAYAS.

Further reading: John Stratton Hawley and Donna Wulff, eds., *The Divine Consort Radha and the Goddesses of India* (Berkeley, Calif.: Berkeley Religious Studies Series, 1982); David Kinsley, *Hindu Goddesses: Visions of the Divine Feminine in the Hindu Religious Tradition* (Berkeley: University of California, 1986); W. J. Wilkins, *Hindu Mythology, Vedic and Puranic* (Calcutta: Rupa, 1973).

Anoopam Mission (est. 1965)

The Anoopam Mission was founded in 1965 as an independent branch of the SWAMINARAYAN MOVEMENT. It is dedicated to the worldwide spread of the theistic devotional Hinduism (BHAKTI YOGA) and strict moral code of Sri Sahajanand Swami, better known to his followers as Swaminarayan (1781–1830).

Swaminarayan believed that God was not the impersonal deity portrayed in the writings and oral tradition of VEDANTA. Saints and RISHIS (wise souls) were teachers who had traveled to Earth to help a suffering humanity find the way to God; the swami considered himself to be an incarnation of an earlier guru, Lord Swami Narayan, who was believed by his followers to be God.

In the mid-20th century, His Supreme Holiness Brahmaswarup Param Pujya Yogiji Maharaj (d.

1971) sent what he called the Anoopam Mission to the United States. Its success was due to the dedication of a young man named Jashbhai, born on March 23, 1940 in Sokhada, Gujarat, who had as a young college student crossed paths with Yogiji Maharaj. Yogiji was so impressed with the young man that he called him *Saheb,* a term of great respect. Saheb organized meetings and recruited his peers onto the path of bhakti, especially as expressed through the lineage of Yogiji Maharaj. He encouraged the young men to live a life based on spirituality, service to others, and positive assistance in their community.

Those attracted to his teachings developed a new way to live as SADHUS. They did not renounce the world but accepted it. They did not take vows of chastity, obedience, and poverty; instead they had families and participated in life on an everyday level but focused on a mission of service to others. Their aim was to integrate the life of holy people with that of lay people.

Saheb was expelled from the larger movement in 1965, after a dispute with conservatives who did not want women to become sadhus. He and his followers established the Brahmajyoti (light of God), in Mogri, Gujarat, which became the new movement's international headquarters. Groups developed in the surrounding countryside and areas adjacent to the mother organization, with similar institutions set up for community service. Followers began to migrate to the United States in the 1960s, and Saheb traveled to visit them in 1973.

The Anoopam Mission in the United States encourages members to live frugally in a community atmosphere. The excess income they make in their careers is saved to enhance and carry forth the obligations of the mission. Over 100 American members (called *sadhaks*) engage as a group to work with devotees toward spiritual goals.

Sadhaks are distinguished by attire that reveals their commitment. Blue shirts and cream colored slacks are worn by the men. Cream is the symbol of the Earth; blue is symbolic of the sky and the greatest of spiritual attainments, which is to unite with God into the bliss of Oneness. These colors reflect the transformation of each person's mission from Earth-bound to spiritual-bound.

Members also wear a saffron and white badge showing an eight-spoked wheel. The hub of the wheel represents Saheb, while the spokes are the internal purification rituals required in the movement. The spokes also represent eight brothers who were blessed by Yogiji Maharaj as the leaders of the mission.

Saheb has continued to extend the mission to 25 countries throughout the world. After beginning in India, the United Kingdom, the United States, and Australia, the mission now has centers in several countries in Europe, Africa, and the Far East. The mission now sponsors educational institutions, health-care organizations, social welfare programs, and relief programs for assistance in floods, earthquakes, and water conservation. The international headquarters remains in Mogri, Gujarat, India.

Further reading: *Saheb—Profile of a Guru and His Mission* (Uxbridge, England: Anoopam Mission, 1989).

anumana

In Indian philosophies *anumana* or inference is almost universally recognized as one of the valid means for gaining knowledge. Buddhism and VAISHESHIKA accepted only two valid means—*anumana* and direct perception (PRATYAKSHA). The SAMKHYA school recognized direct perception, inference, and verbal testimony (*shabda*). NYAYA added a fourth: analogy (*upamana*). In JAINISM, *anumana* is admitted as valid under the wider category of "non perceptual" knowledge, which includes other elements such as memory. Only the CHARVAKAs or materialist philosophers denied the validity of *anumana*, thinking truth could be gained only by direct perception.

Further reading: S. N. Dasgupta, *A History of Indian Philosophy,* 5 vols. (Delhi: Motilal Banarsidass, 1975); Karl

Potter, *Presuppositions of India's Philosophies* (Englewood Cliffs, N.J.: Prentice Hall, 1963).

ap (also *jala*)   *See* ELEMENTS, FIVE.

Apabhramsha

Sanskrit linguists use the term Apabramsha, "that which is badly fallen," to refer to the languages spoken in North India between approximately 600 and 1200 C.E. These languages developed from certain of the earlier Prakrits (themselves evolutes of SANSKRIT), and evolved to become the various modern languages of North India. There are important extant Apabramsha texts, particularly among the Jains. Examples of Jain text are the Paumacariu of Svayambhu and the Mahapurana of Pushpadanta. Some later Buddhist sages also composed in this language; some of their texts are still extant.

Further reading: H. C. Bhayani, *Apabhramsa Language and Literature: A Short Introduction* (Delhi: B. L. Institute of Indology, 1989); ———, *Indological Studies: Literary and Performing Arts, Prakrit and Apabhramsa Studies* (Ahmedabad: Parshva, 1998); Moriz Winternitz, *History of Indian Literature* (Delhi: Motilal Banarsidass, 1967).

apana   *See* PRANA.

Appar (Tirunavakkarasu) (c. 570–670 C.E.)
Tamil Shaivite poet and saint
APPAR was one of the three most prominent Tamil Shaivite saints (*see* SHAIVISM, NAYANARS), whose hymns appear in the central liturgical and literary text of the the Tamil Shaivites, the TEVARAM.

Appar was born under the name Marunaikkiyar to a Vellala (agricultural class) family in Tiruvamur. His family were Shaivite but he converted to JAINISM as a youth, taking on the name Dharmasena. Afflicted by a painful abdominal disease, the young Jain monk turned to his sister, a Shaivite, for help. At her request he put his faith in Shiva, and was miraculously cured. He immediately converted back to the faith of his birth. He began to sing passionate hymns to Lord Shiva, which angered his former Jain associates. It was said that he was persecuted and even tortured by the angry Jains but by the grace of Shiva was unharmed.

Appar is said to have led the Pallava king, who had also converted to Jainism, back to Shiva. He was recognized as a saint and spent his time traveling from one shrine to the next singing hymns at each sacred location. Iconographically, Appar is often showing holding a hoe, for he was known for clearing the temple grounds of weeds and grass in service to Lord Shiva. His beautiful lyrics and speech earned him the name Tirunavakkarasu, "He who is the king of eloquence." It is said that he was first called Appar (my father) by his younger contemporary SAMBANTHAR, who addressed him thus.

Further reading: *Appar: A Sketch of His Life and Teachings* (Madras: G. A. Natesa, n.d.); Ratna Ma Navaratnam, *The Vision of Periyapuranam* (Bombay: Bharatiya Vidya Bhavan, 1987); Indira Viswanathan Peterson, *Poems to Siva: The Hymns of the Tamil Saints* (Princeton, N.J.: Princeton University Press, 1989); J. M. Nallaswami Pillai, trans., *Periyapuranam (the Lives of the Saiva Saints)* (Madras: Rajan, 1955); T. N. Ramachandran, trans., *St. Sekkizhar's Periya Puranam* (Thanjavur: Tamil University, 1990); Dorai Rangaswamy, *The Religion and Philosophy of Tevaram* (Madras: University of Madras, 1958–59); G. G. Vanmikanathan, *Appar* (New Delhi: Sahitya Akademi, 1983); ———, *Periyapuranam, a Tamil Classic on the Great Saiva Saints of South India by Sekkizhar* (Madras: Shri Ramakrishna Math, 1985); R. Vijayalakshmy, *An Introduction to Religion and Philosophy—Tevaram and Tivviyappirapantam* (Chennai: International Institute of Tamil Studies, 2001).

apsaras

The *apsaras* are celestial nymphs. These beautiful young women appear first in the Vedic literature and play a role in the *puranas*. Late tradition says that *apsaras* either were born from BRAHMA's fancy or are the daughters of the RISHI DAKSHA or of Kashyapa. The Vedic *apsaras* born from the daughters of Daksha are Menaka, Sahajanya, Parnini, Punjakasthala, Gritasthala, Ghritachi, Vishvachi, Urvashi, Anulocha, Pramlocha, and Manovati. Other well known *apsaras* of later times are Tilottama, Rambha, and Mishrakeshi.

The most famous *apsaras* is perhaps Urvashi, whom King Pururavas fell in love with and begged to stay with him. She agreed upon several conditions, one of which was that she never see him undressed. As fate would have it, one night she saw him without his clothes and was forced to return to her celestial home. Pururavas was heartbroken and searched everywhere for her. One day he was able to reach her abode and persuaded her to promise that she would meet him yearly and have his son. After he had gone to see her several times she told him how he might obtain her as his bride permanently. Through a ritual sacrifice he was able to become a celestial (GANDHARVA singer) and gain her as his bride forever.

Tilottama is also well known, as the *apsaras* who tempted Lord BRAHMA when he was doing austerities. She appeared before him in turn on all sides and caused him to form heads in all directions. Eventually he was humiliated, because he had been doing austerities to gain the throne of INDRA. *Apsarases* are often depicted in temple architecture.

Further reading: Projesh Banerjee, *Apsaras in India Dance* (New Delhi: Cosmo, 1982); E. Washburn Hopkins, *Epic Mythology* (Delhi: Motilal Banarsidass, 1986); Kanwar Lal, *Apsaras of Khajuraho* (Delhi: Asia Press, 1966); W. J. Wilkins, *Hindu Mythology* (Calcutta: Rupa, 1973); J. C. Wright, "Pururavas and Urvasi," *Bulletin of the School of Oriental and African Studies* 30 (1967): 526–547.

Aranyaka

The Aranyakas or "forest books," originally part of the BRAHMANA sections within the VEDAS, contain esoteric interpretations of the Vedic rituals. They show the ritual actors performing aspects of the ritual internally and esoterically while meditating in the forest. In the development of Indian tradition, the Aranyakas are in one sense transitional between the typical Brahmana philosophy, which explains the Vedic acts in practical terms, and the UPANISHADS, which delve into the higher philosophical vision of the Vedas.

Only four Aranyakas have been preserved: the *Brhad Aranyaka* in the SHATAPATHA BRAHMANA of the White YAJUR VEDA, the Taittariya Aranyaka of the Taittariya Brahmana of the Black Yajur Veda, the Aitareya Aranyaka in the Aitareya Brahmana of the RIG VEDA, and the Kaushitiki Aranyaka in the Kaushitiki Brahmana, also in the Rig Veda.

Further reading: Julius Eggeling, trans., *The Satapatha Brahmana, According to the Text of the Madhyamdina School* (Delhi: Motilal Banarsidass, 1972); Jan Gonda, *Vedic Literature: Samhitas and Brahmanas,* Jan Gonda, ed., in *A History of Indian Literature,* Vol. 1, fascicle 1 (Wiesbaden: Otto Harrassowitz, 1975); Arthur B. Keith, *Aitareya Aranyaka* (Oxford: Clarendon Press, 1969).

arati   *See* PUJA.

Ardhamagadhi

Ardhamagadhi is one of the Prakrit languages that immediately descended from ancient SANSKRIT. The canonical works of the Jains (*see* JAINISM) were written in this language; the Jains only later began to write in Sanskrit. Stray records of Ardhamagadhi survive in the dialogue sections of Sanskrit high literature, and some Ardhamagadhi poetry is still extant.

Further reading: Siegfried Lienhard, *A History of Classical Poetry: Sanskrit, Pali, Prakrit.* Vol. 3, Fascicle 1, *History of Indian Literature,* edited by Jan Gonda (Wiesbaden: Otto Harrassowitz, 1984); Moriz Winternitz, *History of Indian Literature* (Delhi: Motilal Banarsidass, 1967).

Ardhanarishvara

Ardhanarishvara, "The Lord Who is Half Woman," is a form of SHIVA whose left half is the GODDESS PARVATI or SHAKTI, with breast and sari drape. The iconic image is a popular one at temples and shrines to Shiva everywhere in India. Images were present very early in the development of stone architecture and are found at various rock cut temples such as at MAHABALIPURAM.

It is said that BRAHMA, the creator god, tried many times to create beings who would procreate properly. Usually the beings he created, god or human, would take up asceticism and not reproduce. Finally, he asked Lord Shiva to separate out his female goddess aspect, so that procreation could take place. Shiva did so; this feminine aspect stood before Brahma and at his request gave him the feminine energy that allowed him to become the creator of the human line.

Through this story all human beings are seen to be descended from Brahma via his feminine, procreative energy. The Ardhanarishvara depiction of Shiva as half goddess is a reminder of this story.

A different explanation for the Ardhanarishvara is found in another story, in which the sage Bhringi respectfully circumambulated Shiva every day but ignored Parvati, unlike all the other *rishis*, who customarily circumambulated them both. To induce him to honor Parvati, Shiva and Parvati joined together as one, but the stubborn sage became a bee and bored between them so as only to go around Shiva (explaining the name *bhringa*, which means bee). Still other explanations exist (*see* ANNAPURNA).

Further reading: Ellen Goldberg, *A Lord Who Is Half Woman: Ardhanarisvara in Indian and Feminist Perspective* (Albany: State University of New York Press, 2002); Stella Kramrisch, *The Presence of Shiva* (Princeton, N.J.: Princeton University Press, 1981); Neela Yadav, *Ardhanarisvara in Art and Literature* (New Delhi: D. K. Printworld, 2001).

arhat

In the Jain tradition (see JAINISM), an *arhat* (one worthy of worship) is an omniscient being who teaches in the world. As Jains do not believe in living liberated beings (*jivanmukta*), the *arhat* while living is not released from the cycle of birth and rebirth, but will be upon his/her death. A person becomes an *arhat* when he or she has destroyed nearly all KARMAS except those that hold him or her in bodily existence. Technically, one becomes an *arhat* at the 12th *gunasthana* (progression level) out of the 14 that take one to posthumous NIRVANA. All the TIRTHANKARAS in the Jain pantheon are referred to in their texts as *arhat*s.

The term *arhat* is also used in the Buddhist context, where it refers to someone who has attained nirvana—who has attained enlightenment and will be released from the cycle of birth and rebirth upon death. In the Buddhist tradition also one can be referred to as an *arhat* before one is dead.

Further reading: M. A. Dhaky, ed., *Arhat Parsva and Dharanendra Nexus* (Delhi: Motilal Banarsidass, 1997); P. S. Jaini, *Jaina Path of Purification* (Berkeley: University of California Press, 1979); K. C. Lalwani, *Kalpa Sutra* (Delhi: Motilal Banarsidass, 1979); Kristi Wiley, *Historical Dictionary of Jainism* (Lanham, Md.: Scarecrow Press, 2004).

Arjuna

Arjuna was one of the five PANDAVAS in the MAHABHARATA epic, all of them sons of Kunti by different gods. Arjuna's father was the king of the gods, Indra, hence his prominent role in the epic.

It is Arjuna who won the Pandavas' wife Draupadi at her "self-choice" ceremony, where the contestants competed in various challenges of strength and skill. The rule was that each of the five brothers would stay at night with Draupadi alone. No other brother was to enter their chamber on penalty of exile. Arjuna broke this agreement and was sent away from the other brothers for 12 years.

During his exile Arjuna had relationships with many women. He married Krishna's sister Subhadra, to whom was born their son Abhimanyu, who played an important role in the Mahabharata war. Arjuna at this time also met up with Parashurama, the BRAHMIN warrior and incarnation of VISHNU; he taught Arjuna the use of magical weapons. For helping the god AGNI and KRISHNA burn down the Khandava forest, Arjuna received his bow Gandiva, his most cherished weapon.

Returning home Arjuna was forced into solitary exile again for 13 years when his brother Yudhisthira lost everything to the Kauravas in a dice game. In his wanderings he met a hunter—Shiva in disguise—from whom he received the devastating Pashupata weapon. In the last year of his exile he served Virata, king of the Matsya people, disguised as a eunuch. There he taught music and dance to the women. He also helped Virata fight his enemies.

In the final battle of Kurukshetra, the conclusive battle of the Mahabharata, Krishna served as Arjuna's charioteer. The BHAGAVAD GITA details Arjuna's momentary failure of will as the battle is about to begin and Krishna's teachings to him. After the victory, when the customary *ashva medha* (HORSE SACRIFICE) was done, Arjuna followed the sacrificial horse on its wide wanderings, fighting many kings and claiming many countries for the Pandavas. During these wanderings he encountered his own son Babhruvahana, whom he fought and killed. The son was revived, however, by a Naga princess (*see* NAGAS) who had once been his lover.

After the war, in which most of Krishna's Yadava tribe were killed, Arjuna himself performed the funeral rites for Krishna, who had accidentally been killed by a hunter, and for Krishna's father, Vasudeva. Arjuna took the remnants of the Yadava tribe and their women back to Hastinapura, the Pandava capital.

In his old age Arjuna went to live in the Himalayas with his brothers and Draupadi, leaving the kingdom to his grandson, Parikshit (Abhimanyu's son).

Further reading: J. A. B. van Buitenen, trans., *The Mahabharata.* Vol. 1, *The Book of the Beginnings,* Vol. 2., *The Book of the Assembly Hall,* vol. 3., *The Book of Virata and the Book of Effort* (Chicago: University of Chicago Press, 1973–78); Ruth C. Katz, *Arjuna in the Mahabharata: Where Krishna Is, There Is Victory* (Columbia: University of South Carolina Press, 1989); P. C. Roy, trans., *The Mahabharata of Krishna-Dwaipayana Vyasa,* 12 vols. (Calcutta: Oriental, 1952–62).

Arsha Vidya Gurukulam (est. 1986)

The Arsha (from the RISHIS) Vidya (knowledge) Gurukulam (spiritual learning center and residence) at Saylorsburg, Pennsylvania, was founded in 1986 by SWAMI DAYANANDA SARASWATI (1930–) in the tradition of the ancient gurukulams of India. The institute is dedicated to the traditional study of *advaita* VEDANTA, SANSKRIT, HATHA YOGA, AYURVEDA, Vedic chanting, MEDITATION, astrology, and other classical Indian disciplines. It offers courses in the UPANISHADS, BHAGAVAD GITA, VEDANTA SUTRA, and other classical Vedic texts in English. The more than 15 teachers have all studied with Dayananda Saraswati. The center offers short- and long-term study programs and on-site accommodations. The 54-acre campus includes a temple dedicated to Lord Dakshinamurti, considered the first teacher of Vedic knowledge.

The Gurukulam also sponsors the All India Movement (AIM) for Seva, established in New Delhi in 2000, as its service outreach. It hopes to unite Indian society through service and caring, in a way that promotes self-sufficiency and dignity among those served. It seeks to transform Indian society by bridging the gap between privileged and less-privileged people through a policy of Indians' caring for fellow Indians. AIM has 22 branches in different states of India and publishes many books on various topics in Vedanta, including a Bhagavad Gita Home Study course and a Vedic Heritage Teaching Program for children. The Arsha Vidya bookstore in Pennsylvania has over 3,000 publications on Vedanta, Hinduism, Sanskrit, yoga, astrology, Ayurveda, philosophy, and Indian history.

Further reading: Swami Dayananda Saraswati, *Arsha Vidya: The Vision of the Rishis* (Rishikesh: Sri Gangadhareswar Trust, Swami Dayananda Ashram, 1999); ——, *Collection, Talks and Essays of Swami Dayananda Saraswati* (Rishikesh: Sri Gangadhareswar Trust, Swami Dayananda Ashram, 2000).

artha   See ENDS OF LIFE, FOUR.

Arthashastra (c. 300 C.E.)

The *Arthashastra*, the *"Authoritative Treatise on Worldly Affairs,"* is generally attributed to Kautilya (Chanakya) (c. 300 B.C.E.), the minister of the famous Chandragupta Maurya kingdom, although it was apparently expanded at a later time, as the received text includes references to later phenomena.

The *Arthashastra* resembles in many ways *The Prince,* written in the 16th century by the Italian Nicolò Machiavelli. It is a complete and elaborate treatise on statecraft and law, clearly designed for use by a king. It includes sections dealing with clans and tribes who do not belong to the state proper, the conduct of ministers, government officials, city government, taxation, law, punishments, spies, types of conquest, the army, slavery, divorce, women's property, indigent women, prostitutes, gambling, alcoholic drinks, and interest rates, among other topics.

The book is part of the tradition of authoritative treatises (*shastras; artha* means "worldly affairs") that relate to the four ENDS OF LIFE. It parallels the *DHARMASHASTRA* and the *Kamashastra*

(among which is the *KAMA SUTRA*). The fourth end of life—MOKSHA—is not generally associated with *shastras*; its subject, liberation from birth and rebirth, relies on gurus instead.

Further reading: Roger Boesche, *The First Great Political Realist: Kautilya and His Arthashastra* (Lanham, Md.: Lexington Books, 2002); Subhash C. Kashyap, *Concept of Good Governance and Kautilya's Arthashastra* (New Delhi: Indian Council of Social Science Research, 2003); L. N. Rangarajan, trans., *The Arthashastra by Kautilya* (New Delhi: Penguin Books India, 1992); Sujata Reddy, *Laws of Kautilya Arthasastra* (New Delhi: Kanishka, 2004); Manabendu Banerjee Sastri, ed., *Occasional Essays on Arthasastra* (Calcutta: Sanskrit Pustak Bhandar, 2000); Bijay Dhari Singh, *Bibliography of Kautilya Arthasastra* (Varanasi: Kishor Vidya Niketan, 2004).

Art of Living Foundation (est. 1982)

The Art of Living Foundation promotes the spiritual endeavors of Sri Sri Ravi SHANKAR (b. 1956) (not to be confused with the prominent musician of the same name). It focuses on the use of ancient Hindu methods for reaching serenity.

Shankar is a native of Bangalore, India. As a child he demonstrated great intellectual skills. He could read and discuss BHAGAVAD GITA by the age of four. In childhood he read Indian literature and was able to grasp complex text material and philosophy.

As an adult, Shankar traveled the world from his home in India, teaching the methods revealed in classical texts for developing a serene life, which he called the Art of Living. Shankar's teachings emphasize ancient science, especially Sudharsha Kriya, a meditative breathing technique that balances natural rhythms in mental, emotional, and physical life. Sudharsha Kriya gained celebrity in 1998 and 1999 when scientific studies confirmed its benefits. The meditative practice is used for stress reduction, conflict resolution, and personal development.

The Art of Living Foundation was officially established in Bangalore, India, in 1982 as a non-profit educational and humanitarian organization. It now has more than 4,000 chapters around the world. Although the foundation claims no religious affiliation, it upholds basic spiritual tenets through its offering of compassionate service around the world, including charitable and educational programs in 142 countries. It is a consulting nongovernmental organization (NGO) registered with the Economic and Social Council (ECOSOC) of the United Nations. Services include the 5-H program, a holistic endeavor that focuses on homes, health, hygiene, harmony in diversity, and human values. All programs follow the general philosophy of the foundation, emphasizing the practical and intellectual development of human values and the potential of individuals to strengthen society. The Art of Living Foundation has provided many workshops over the years at United Nations summits and conferences.

According to the foundation an estimated 2 million people around the world have benefited from Sudharsha Kriya through Art of Living courses. The foundation has also established the Research and Health Promotion Center, which provides scholarships for research into the health benefits of Sudharsha Kriya. The foundation publishes an online journal, *Prana.* A sister organization, the International Association for Human Values, coordinates volunteer efforts for aid and relief.

In 1995, the president of India recognized Shankar's spiritual accomplishments by giving him the title of Yogi Shiromani (Supreme Flowering of Enlightenment) during a major World Conference of Yoga.

The center in Bangalore, India, administers the various programs to spread the spiritual precepts of the movement, heighten knowledge of Vedic texts, and engage in community service. In England, the United States, and Canada, the work is pursued under the name *Art of Living;* in Europe it is called the *Association for Inner Growth.* In January 2005 the Art of Living Foundation donated over $34 million for tsunami relief. The foundation has also established orphanages for children and homes for women in the affected areas of India and Sri Lanka. Many of the services offered by the foundation are provided almost entirely by volunteers.

Further reading: François Gautier, *The Guru of Joy: Shri Shri Ravi Shankar and the Art of Living* (New Delhi: Books Today/The India Today Group, 2002); Ravi Shankar, *Bang on the Door: A Collection of Talks* (Santa Barbara, Calif.: Art of Living Foundation, 1990); ———, *Celebrating Silence* (Santa Barbara, Calif.: Art of Living Foundation, 2001); Ravi Shankar and Judith S. Clark, *Waves of Beauty* (Santa Barbara, Calif.: Art of Living Foundation, 1998).

Arunachala   *See* RAMANA MAHARSHI.

Arundhati

Arundhati was the wife of the Rishi Vasishtha and one of the nine daughters of Prajapati by his wife Devahuti. Along with her husband, she is one of the mythical seven *rishis,* for whom the seven stars of the Great Bear or Pleiades are named. Vasishtha is the middle of the three stars that form the tail. Arundhati is the small faint star (Alcor) beside it. Arundhati is considered the paragon of wifely faithfulness. In the Hindu marriage rites, after the main ceremony and after the marriage meal, the priest takes the couple outside and points out the star Arundhati to the bride.

Further reading: Abbé J. A. Dubois, *Hindu Manners, Customs and Ceremonies.* Translated from the French by Henry K. Beauchamp (Oxford: Clarendon Press, 1959); Alfred Hillebrandt, *Vedic Mythology,* 2 vols. (Delhi: Motilal Banarsidass, 1990); E. Washburn Hopkins, *Epic Mythology* (Delhi: Motilal Banarsidass, 1986).

Arya   *See* ARYAN.

Aryaman

Aryaman (friend or companion) is a Vedic divinity listed among the ADITYAS. When invoked he is usually paired with some other divinity. He is chief of the "Fathers" or Manes, those who have passed from this world and exist in heaven. There are no MANTRAS in the Rig Veda that focus solely on Aryaman.

Further reading: Paul Thieme, *Mitra and Aryaman* (New Haven, Conn.: American Oriental Society, 1957).

Aryan (Arya)

In the VEDAS, the earliest Indian texts, the SANSKRIT word *Arya* had the sense of noble or worthy person. It was used by the tribes or peoples who recited the Vedas to distinguish themselves from other peoples. Sometimes, in early Sanskrit the term was used to refer to the "respectable" upper three classes of the Indian tradition, to distinguish them from the disreputable classes such as the SHUDRAS and those below them, the untouchables. Most Brahmins still refer to themselves as Aryas, as do all Buddhists and Jains (see JAINISM).

The earliest text of the Vedic tradition, the RIG VEDA, which is set in ancient India, has been dated to around 1500 B.C.E. This rough estimate refers to the time the text was compiled as an anthology. Parts of the text may thus date back some centuries earlier, an indication that the Aryas were in India as early as c. 2000 B.C.E.

Vedic references to the Aryas are thus synchronous with the theoretical migration of Indo-European-speaking peoples into India from the northwest. Much scholarship and speculation have been focused on this issue since at least the 18th century, when it was discovered that Sanskrit was an Indo-European language related to Latin and Greek, while the languages of southern India seemed unrelated. The term *Arya* also appears in ancient Persian texts (it is reflected in the name of the country Iran), and in Hittite inscriptions from the Middle East around 1500 B.C.E. The name *Ireland* may also reflect the word, which would be evidence for a simultaneous Aryan migration to Europe. Recent attempts have been made in India to refute the notion that the Aryans arrived from outside the country. It is prudent to say that the issue is not yet settled.

Within India itself there are various different understandings of the nature of the Aryans. The linguistic term *Dravidian,* referring to the tongues spoken in South India, was sometimes used in the 20th century to designate a people or race different and distinct from the Aryans of the north. The term *Aryan* was taken up in Europe in the 20th century by the Nazis to designate a person of a "superrace."

Further reading: Edwin F. Bryant, *The Quest for the Origins of Vedic Culture: The Indo-Aryan Migration Debate* (Oxford: Oxford University Press, 2001); Madhav Deshpande and Peter Edwin Hook, eds., *Aryan and Non-Aryan in India* (Ann Arbor: Center for South and Southeast Asian Studies, University of Michigan, 1979); George Erdosy, ed., *The Indo-Aryans of Ancient South Asia: Language, Material Culture and Ethnicity* (Berlin: Walter De Guyter, 1995); J. P. Malory, *In Search of the Indo-European Language, Archaeology and Myth* (London: Thames & Hudson, 1991); Colin Renfrew, *Archaeology and Language: The Puzzle of Indo-European Origins* (New York: Cambridge University Press, 1990).

Arya Samaj (est. 1875)

The Arya Samaj, formerly known as Arya Pratinidhi Sabha, is a reformist Hindu sect founded in 1875 in Mumbai by Mul Shankara (1824–83). It aims to synthesize ancient orthodox ritual practice with modern anticaste and universalistic principles.

Shankara was born a Brahmin and was educated into orthodox Brahminism in Gujarat state. In 1948 he renounced ordinary life and took vows of a SANNYASI in the Saraswati Dandi Order of Yogis. As Dayananda Saraswati, his name given at initiation, he wandered all of India for 12 years, finally taking residence in Mathura to study the VEDAS under the scholar Varajananda. Dayananda understood the Vedas to teach gender equality and rejection of caste, a message that clearly opposed the orthodoxy of the day. The movement grew among liberal, educated Indians and became strong in the state of Punjab, where it remains important.

The Arya Samaj seeks to restore the centrality of the Vedas to Hinduism and to reject much of Hinduism's SANATANA DHARMA (eternal way), including worship of images and PUJA (traditional rituals). The society teaches 10 basic principles: (1) The source of all that is true is God. (2) God is a single, eternal, fully conscious being. (3) All true knowledge is contained in the Vedas. (4) All people should be prepared to accept truth. (5) All acts should be performed with righteousness and duty. (6) The movement should promote physical, spiritual, and social progress for all humans. (7) All relations among humans should be guided by love and justice. (8) Knowledge and realization should be provided for all people. (9) The movement should work for the uplift of all, not only personal development. (10) All members should be devoted to the social good.

The Arya Samaj sponsors the Purohit Academy to train students in philosophy and in the repetition of Sanskrit MANTRAS. After training, practitioners are certified by the academy to perform traditional rituals and marriages.

With its message of social reform and the universalization of spiritual truth, the Arya Samaj has proselytized since its inception and has become an important element of the Indian DIASPORA around the world, including North America, South America, Europe, Africa, Australia, and Oceania. Prominent countries in the Indian diaspora all have multiple worship centers, although membership numbers are difficult to estimate.

Further reading: Shiv Kumar Gupta, *Arya Samaj and the Raj, 1875–1920* (New Delhi: Gitanjali, 1991); Lala Lajpat Rai, *The Arya Samaj: An Account of Its Origin, Doctrines, and Activities* (New Delhi: Reliance, 1991); S. S. Yoginder, "The Fitna of Irtidad: Muslim Missionary Response to the Shuddhi of Arya Samaj in Early Twentieth Century India," *Journal of Muslim Minority Affairs* 17, no. 1 (1997): 65–83.

asana

Asana is the term for a stance or posture in HATHA YOGA. It is from the root *as* (to sit). Some say that there were originally 8,400,000 asanas to represent the 8,400,000 births that each individual must pass through before he or she becomes liberated. There are said to be only a few hundred in practice today; 84 is the number most often presented to students.

An asana is a means to focus the mind so that it becomes steady, calm, and quiet. It is not intended as any sort of physical exercise per se, despite being commonly understood that way in the West. The various asanas are intended to open up different subtle energy channels in the body and the psychic centers (CHAKRAS) that run along the spine. It is understood that the total command of the body at both gross and subtle levels is a path to the total command of the mind. Total command of the mind can lead to the steady, calm, and quiet poise of being, where the highest reality of self and universe can be directly perceived. Breath control, or *pranayama,* is always a part of asana practice.

Further reading: Nicolai Bachman, *The Language of Yoga: Complete A–Y Guide to Asana Names, Sanskrit Terms and Chants* (Boulder, Colo.: Sounds True, 2005); B. K. S. Iyengar, *Light on Yoga,* rev. ed. (New York: Schocken Books, 1979); Ajit Mookerjee, *Tantra Asana: A Way to Self-Realization* (Basel: Ravi Kumar, 1971); Swami Satyananda Saraswati, *Asana Pranayama Mudra Bandha* (Bihar: Bihar School of Yoga, 1999); Jayadeva Yogendra, *Cyclopedia Yoga with Special Information on Asana* (Bombay: Yoga Institute, 1988).

Ashish, Sri Madhava (1920–1997) *Vaishnavite guru*

Sri Madhava Ashish was the successor to Sri Krishna PREM as head of the Uttar Brindavan Ashram at Mirtola village, near Almora in the foothills of the Himalayas in Uttaranchal state.

Alexander Phipps was born on February 23, 1920, to Protestant parents, Lt. Col. Henry Ramsey Phipps and Lorna Campbell Phipps. His father was an artillery officer and his great-grandfather, a Scottish laird. Alexander attended Sherborne Public School and the College of Aeronautical Engineering at Chelsea, London. He was described as an avid reader but "not successful at school." In general, he was shy and reserved. Before completing a degree, he went to India to help in the World War II war effort as an aircraft engineer by repairing crashed planes at Dum Dum Airport, Kolkata.

While in India he met Sri Ramana MAHARSHI in Tiruvannamalai. Fired by his meeting with the South Indian saint, he decided not to return to England after the war ended. He joined the Uttar Brindavan Ashram (founded in 1929) at Mirtola village in the Kumaon region of the Himalayas as a BRAHMACHARYA under his guru, Sri Krishna Prem. In 1947, Krishna Prem gave him the vows of *sannyas* (renunciation) under the Gaudiya Sampradaya (*see* GAUDIYA MATH) and named him Madhava Ashish. The Gaudiya Sampradaya of VAISHNAVISM is associated with Sri Radha Raman Temple at BRINDABAN, the birthplace of Lord KRISHNA; it follows strict vegetarianism and devotion to the deity Krishna.

After taking up discipleship, Ashish followed a strict Vaishnavite regimen in food, dress, conduct, and sacramental worship. However, in 1957 he and his guru, Sri Krishna Prem, decided to simplify the rigid framework of full Vaishnavite orthodox discipline, so that it would speak directly to the seekers who increasingly visited Mirtola for spiritual guidance. They advocated a system of self-inquiry, which encouraged disciples to search for the mystery at the root of their own being and to find their essential nature apart from the psychophysical ego personality. The attempt was to merge individual consciousness with the uniting source of all life, a higher center of awareness accessible to all.

Madhava Ashish oversaw a discipline that included MEDITATION; service in the temple; assiduous self-inquiry through introspection, dream analysis, self-remembering, and development of a witnessing awareness in all activities in order to harmonize the inner and outer life. In addition to practices of the Vaishnavite tradition, his teaching drew on the wisdom of others, including NISARGADATTA Maharaj and the Greek-Armenian teacher G. I. Gurdjieff.

In addition to guiding disciples at Uttar Brindavan Ashram, Madhava Ashish served as a member of the Committee for Hill Development (of the Himalaya region) for India's premier planning body. He was awarded the Padma Shree by the government of India in 1993 for his contribution to scientific farming. He was also actively involved with environmental work, including sustainable farming, water harvesting, animal husbandry, environmental education, and efforts against deforestation.

After his death on April 13, 1997, leadership of Uttar Brindavan Ashram was taken up by his disciple Dev Ashish. The ashram does not have a Web site; its address is P.O. Mirtola, Via Panwanaula, District Almora, Uttaranchal-263 623.

Further reading: Madhava Ashish, *Man, Son of Man* (London: Rider, 1970); ———, *Man, Son of Man in the Stanzas of Dzyan* (Wheaton, Ill.: Theosophical Publishing House, 1970); ———, *Relating to Reality* (New Delhi: Banyan Books, 1998); ———, *Relating to Reality: Relating the Metaphysical Roots of Value to Their Applications in Every Field of Human Activity* (New Delhi: Banyan Books, 1998); Seymour B. Ginsburg, *In Search of the Unitive Vision* (Boca Raton, Fla.: New Paradigm, 2001); Krishna Prem and Madhava Ashish, *Man, the Measure of All Things, in the Stanzas of Dzyan* (London: Rider, 1969); Madhu Tandan, *Faith and Fire: A Way Within* (New Delhi: HarperCollins, 1997).

ashram

The Sanskrit *ashrama* was a place for ascetics to perform austerities (practices of renouncing bodily and psychological comfort), usually at a distance from and in isolation from the larger world (*shram,* means to exert oneself strongly). In later times the word came to designate a place organized for spiritual practice, a refuge where devotees could pursue their paths. Most often the ashram would be under the tutelage and guidance of a particular guru or lineage of teachers. Isolation is no longer the determining factor of an ashram, though many are still deliberately sited away from the hustle and bustle of everyday life.

Further reading: Anne Cushman and Jerry Jones, *From Here to Nirvana: The Yoga Journal Guide to Spiritual India* (New York: Riverhead Books, 1998); R. P. Saxena, and Vinay Laksmi, eds., *A Directory of Ashrams in India and Abroad* (Mathura, India: Ashram Publications, 1975) Susan Vickerman, "An Examination of the Indian Ashram and Its Potential for Women's Spiritual Fulfillment" (Ph.D. Diss., Graduate Theological Union, 1990).

ashramas

The *ashramas* were the four traditional stages of life that BRAHMIN males were expected to follow, according to the authoritative Hindu texts. People of other twice-born castes, such as Brahmins, warriors, or merchants, could optionally take on the *ashramas*. SHUDRAS and Dalits (Untouchables) were not included in this system.

The four traditional *ashramas* are BRAHMACHARYA (studentship), *grihastha* (householder stage), VANAPRASTHA (entering the forest), and SANNYASI (mendicancy). Usually, one was permitted to leave household life after one had seen one's grandchildren. During the *vanaprastha* stage of life, which ordained austerities in the forest or wildlands, one could optionally be accompanied by one's wife, as long as chastity was maintained.

Further reading: Irina Glushkova and Anne Feldhaus, *House and Home in Maharashtra* (New Delhi: Oxford University Press, 1998); Patrick Olivelle, *The Asrama System: The History and Hermeneutics of a Religious Institution* (New York: Oxford University Press, 1993); ———, *Manu's Code: A Critical Edition and Translation of the Manava-Dharmasastra* (New York: Oxford University Press, 2005); ———, trans., *Sannyasa Upanishads: Hindu Scriptures on Asceticism and Renunciation* (New York: Oxford University Press, 1992).

Ashtanga Yoga

Ashtanga (eight-limbed) Yoga is the system devised by PATANJALI, author of the YOGA SUTRA. As the name implies, eight practices are involved, divided into two groups. The five outer practices are YAMA, *niyama,* ASANA, PRANAYAMA, and *pratyahara;* the three inward-oriented practices are *dharana, dhyana,* and SAMADHI.

Ashtanga Yoga involved a sitting yoga, sometimes called *raja yoga,* focused on the breath. As one watched the breath, one developed ways of concentrating and eventually controlling the mind. The ultimate goal, as in all yogas, was liberation from birth and rebirth, but in the practice of Patanjali, the specific effort was to free the self (PURUSHA) from its false attachment to the phenomenal world, or PRAKRITI.

ASANAS, or postures, play a central role in the systems of Ashtanga Yoga that are disseminated today, but in the Yoga Sutras themselves, "sitting," or "asana" is simply one of the eight "limbs." Many of the postures known today may have been later additions to the practice or may have developed through separate practices that later merged with the Patanjali school. There are strong resemblances between the practices found in Patanjali and those of the Buddhist Pali canon, although the practice postures were never an important component in Buddhism.

Further reading: S. N. Dasgupta, *The History of Indian Philosophy,* Vol. 1, *The Kapila and the Patanjaal Sam-*

khya (Yoga) (Delhi: Motilal Banarsidass, 1975); Mircea Eliade, *Yoga, Immortality and Freedom.* Translated from the French by Willard R. Trask, Bollingen Series 56 (Princeton, N.J.: Princeton University Press, 1973); Georg Feuerstein, *The Yoga Sutra of Patanjali* (Rochester, Vt.: Inner Traditions International, 1989); K. S. Iyengar, *Light on Yog: Yoga Pradipika* (Boston: Unwin Paperbacks, 1979); Sri K. Pattabhi Jois, *Yoga Mala* (New York: North Point Press, 2002); Ian Whicher, *The Integrity of the Yoga Darsana: A Reconsideration of Classical Yoga* (Albany: State University of New York Press, 1998).

ashva medha   *See* HORSE SACRIFICE.

Ashvins

The Ashvins (horsemen) are twin gods of the sky in the VEDAS, depicted as young and beautiful males. They seem to have been associated with the predawn light. The Ashvins do not play a great role in later epic and Puranic mythology (*see* PURANAS), though they are ubiquitous as minor characters. In the Vedas they are called the children of the Sun (SURYA) or of the sky. But they also are said to emerge from the tears of AGNI or from VISHNU. They are said to have a wife in common, the daughter of another Sun divinity (SAVITRI); they won her in a race contest.

Most commonly the Ashvins are known as the physicians of the gods; they are everywhere connected with healing. In the Vedas they make an iron leg for Vishpala, restore Kanva's eyesight, and restore the youth of Cyavana (after trying to seduce his wife). Through the latter feat they are said to have earned the Vedic SOMA libation, which is offered to them.

Further reading: Alfred Hillebrandt, *Vedic Mythology* (Delhi: Motilal Banarsidass, 1990); E. Washburn Hopkins, *Epic Mythology* (Delhi: Motilal Banarsidass, 1986); G. C. Jhala, *Asvina in the Rgveda and Other Indological Essays* (New Delhi: Mushiram Manoharlal, 1978); K.

P. Jog, *Asvin: The Twin Gods in Indian Mythology, Literature and Art* (Delhi: Pratibha Prakashan, 2005); W. J. Wilkins, *Hindu Mythology, Vedic and Puranic,* 2d ed. (Calcutta: Rupa, 1973).

asura   *See* DEMONIC BEINGS.

Atharva   *See* VEDAS.

atman

The atman is the self or soul. The word is derived either from the root *at* (to move) or the root *an* (to breathe). It is used both for the individual self or soul and for the transcendent "Self" or "All-soul," which is all reality. Often the individual self is referred to as the *jivatman,* "the life self," and the transcendent Self is referred to as the *paramatman,* or "Ultimate Self."

The Upanishads and Vedanta philosophy focus on realizing the unity between the individual self and the ultimate Self, by means of various practices. When one realizes (not just intellectually knows) the unity of individual self and Ultimate Self, one breaks the bonds of KARMA and escapes from further rebirth.

Some sort of meditation or contemplation is always necessary to realize the unity of Ultimate Self and individual self. Some Indian paths emphasize "knowledge," or transcendental realization; some paths emphasize devotion; some look to combine devotion and action, or knowledge, action, and devotion, to reach this final goal. Though ADVAITA (non-dual) Vedanta emphasizes a total identity between the individual atman and the large atman, other Indian traditions understand that there are an infinite number of totally distinct individual selves or atmans that never merge into each other at the highest level. VAISHNAVISM generally holds this view, as does SHAIVA SIDDHANTA.

Further readings: J. A. B. van Buitenen, "The Large Atman," *History of Religions* 4 (1964): 103–114, reprinted in L. Rocher, ed., *Studies in Indian Literature and Philosophy: Collected Articles of J. A. B. van Buitenen* (Delhi: Motilal Banarsidass, 1988); Jan Feys, *A=B: An Inquiry into the Upanishads' Basic Insight* (Calcutta: Firma KLM, 1976); Swami Muktananda, *Reflections of the Self* (South Fallsburg, N.Y.: SYDA Foundation, 1980); H. G. Narahari, *Atman in Pre-Upanisadic Vedic Literature* (Madras: Adyar Library, 1944); A. S. Ramanathan, *Vedic Concept of Atman* (Jaipur: Rajasthan Patrika, 1997); Baldev Raj Sharma, *The Concept of Atman in the Principal Upanishads, in the Perspective of the Samhitas, the Brahmanas, the Aranyakas and the Indian Philosophical Systems* (New Delhi: Dinesh, 1972).

aum   *See* OM.

Aurobindo, Sri (Aurobindo Ghose) (1872–1950) *philosopher sage of modern India and creator of Integral Yoga*

Aurobindo Ghose, later named Sri Aurobindo, was one of the great sages of modern India. After an influential political career in the cause of Indian independence, he turned to the spiritual and developed the very influential Integral Yoga path, which combined practices from many different historic Indian yogas.

Ghose was born on August 15, 1872, in the Indian state of Bengal to a surgeon, Dr. Krishnadhan Ghose, and his wife, Swarnalata Devi. His father aimed to turn his fourth child into an Anglicized gentleman, giving him the name Aurobindo Ackroyd (he later dropped his middle name) and sending him at the age of seven to a convent school in Darjeeling. Shortly thereafter he was packed off to Manchester, England, where he was educated at home for five years and isolated from "Indian" influences. In 1889 he entered Cambridge, where he distinguished himself in Latin, Greek, and French. In 1893 he returned to India and joined Baroda Col-

Sri Aurobindo (1872–1950), founder of Integral Yoga *(Courtesy Aurobindo Archives, Pondicherry)*

lege, where he taught English and French and eventually became vice principal. In 1901 he married 14-year-old Mrinalini Bose, not long after beginning his political activity in support of Indian independence. Because of his absences from home and spiritual pursuits, this marriage, though affectionate, produced no children. Mrinalini died at the age of 32, just before her planned move to the Pondicherry ASHRAM Aurobindo had established.

In 1903 in Kashmir an important spiritual event took place in Aurobindo's life. Through the aid of a teacher, Bhaskar Lele, he realized the non-dual nature of the "characterless" divine

(*Nirguna Brahman*). Moving to Bengal in 1906 he plunged into revolutionary political activity, helping to found the journal *Bande Mataram* (Hail to the Mother India!) and writing many articles for it. As a result of these articles he was arrested on August 16, 1907, on a charge of sedition; he was arrested again in 1908 and spent a year in Alipore jail awaiting trial.

Aurobindo Ghose is known in India more for this political activity on behalf of India's independence (years before Gandhi returned from South Africa) than for his great spiritual work. It is only among Bengalis that is he well known and honored as a sage. The year in Alipore Jail was a turning point for Aurobindo Ghose. There he read the BHAGAVAD GITA, practiced yoga, and experienced a vision of Krishna that was powerful and transformative. Not long after he was released from jail he headed south to the French protectorate of Pondicherry, in part to avoid rearrest by the Indian police. In 1914 a Frenchman by the name of Paul Richard persuaded Aurobindo to write philosophy for a monthly journal called *Arya*. Aurobindo had begun to develop a reputation as a yogi and Richard was interested in his philosophy. All of Sri Aurobindo's major works except the epic poem *Savitri* were first published serially in this magazine. As fate would have it, Richard's wife, Mirra Alfassa, was to find in Aurobindo the fulfillment of her spiritual calling. In 1920 she left her husband and joined Sri Aurobindo in his spiritual quest; she would soon be dubbed the Mother.

In 1920 Ghose began to accept the name Sri Aurobindo, and he began delving more deeply into the unique yoga that he had initiated. His new ashram flourished after the arrival of Mirra Richard. On November 24, 1926, Sri Aurobindo announced that he had reached the "Overmind" in his meditations and retired from active ashram life. He left the external activities of the ashram to the care of Mother, who attended to all its affairs and developments until her death in 1973. In 1928 Sri Aurobindo released his book, *The Mother*, which declared to the doubters that the consciousness of the Mother and his consciousness were one and the same. In 1939–40 the ashram released the book *Life Divine,* one of Sri Aurobindo's masterpieces. On December 5, 1950, Sri Aurobindo left his body.

Sri Aurobindo and the Mother's yoga had unique characteristics. Sri Aurobindo argued that each of the yogas that had been developed in India had its own important and positive elements, but that practicing any one of them solely would lead to unbalanced spiritual development. In his book *Synthesis of Yoga* he outlined how the yogas of the Bhagavad Gita particularly could be harmonized into a synthesis that would serve the whole human being: the physical, emotional, mental, psychic (soul), and spiritual levels, he argued, all needed tending. The term for the yoga that would involve all these levels of the human being was in Sanskrit *Purna Yoga,* or "Complete Yoga." This term was translated by Sri Aurobindo as *Integral Yoga,* which he adopted as the name of his path.

Sri Aurobindo argued vehemently that the world was real, rejecting the Indian philosophical view that it was illusory. Equally importantly, he believed the world was evolving toward a state of perfection. He drew from science his belief that life emerged from matter and consciousness from life. He argued therefore that superconsciousness or the "Supramental" stage must develop from ordinary consciousness.

Sri Aurobindo's yoga aimed at accelerating the advance of this evolution toward "Supermanhood." His and the Mother's efforts were entirely focused on engendering what they called the "Supramental" manifestation, which would transform not only all human beings, but all life and even all matter. Their effort was effectively to unlock the divine within matter itself; thus, they referred to their philosophy as Divine Materialism. This was the vision that was developed in Sri Aurobindo's massive book *The Life Divine.*

Sri Aurobindo acknowledged at his death in 1950 that he had not yet achieved the "descent of the Supramental" and indicated that this would occur through the efforts of the Mother. In 1956 Mother indeed announced that the descent had occurred. In 1968 she inaugurated AUROVILLE, a new utopian city in southern India dedicated to the realization of her goals. It was intended as an international city, belonging to "nobody in particular." Along with the ashram in Pondicherry, this city flourishes to this day and is still developing according to the Mother's and Sri Aurobindo's principles and philosophy.

Significantly, Sri Aurobindo and Mother never desired to create a new cult or religion. Their goal was nothing less than the transformation of the conditions of existence for all of humanity. As a result, no successor was appointed to follow Mother. A loose-knit but devoted group of admirers have continued to practice the yoga in creative and ever changing ways. Perhaps the best known admirer of Sri Aurobindo in America was Dr. Haridas CHAUDHURI, who in 1968 founded the California Institute of Integral Studies in San Francisco, a graduate school dedicated to the development of "mind, body and spirit."

Ashrams devoted to Sri Aurobindo have been established at several sites in the United States. The first such ashram was the Cultural Integration Fellowship in San Francisco, founded by Chaudhuri in 1951. Another important ashram is Matagiri, founded by Sam Spanier and Eric Hughes in 1968 in the Catskill mountains of New York State. The name *Matagiri* means "Mother's mountain" in Sanskrit. A third developing ashram in America dedicated to the teachings of Sri Aurobindo and the Mother is the Lodi, California, ashram founded in the 1990s, with its well-known Auromere book outlet (books@auromere.com), the main American source for books written by and about Sri Aurobindo and the Mother.

Further reading: Peter Hees, *Sri Aurobindo: A Brief Biography* (Oxford: Oxford University Press, 1989);

Robert McDermott, ed., *The Essential Aurobindo* (New York: Lindisfarne Press, 1987); Satprem, *Sri Aurobindo or the Adventure of Consciousness.* Translated from the French by Tehmi (Pondicherry: Sri Aurobindo Ashram, 1970).

Auroville

Planned as an international experimental township, Auroville was inspired by the evolutionary vision of SRI AUROBINDO and founded by Mirra Alfassa, known as the MOTHER. The name *Auroville* has the two meanings: "city of dawn," from the French *aurore* (dawn), and "city of Aurobindo," for the theorist who inspired its foundation.

Auroville was inaugurated on February 28, 1968, in a ceremony attended by representatives from 124 nations and all the states of India. In a gesture symbolic of human unity, a boy and a girl from each nation and state poured a handful of soil from their homeland into a lotus-shaped marble urn near the center of the city-to-be. Auroville has been endorsed by three resolutions of the UNESCO general assembly and recognized as an international trust by a unique parliamentary act of the Indian government. Auroville welcomes people from all parts of the world to live together and explore cultural, educational, scientific, spiritual, and other pursuits in accordance with the Auroville Charter.

The idea for Auroville began in the Mother's thinking as early as 1952, when she called for an international center of education. She wrote: "A synthetic organization of all nations, each one occupying its own place in accordance with its own genius and the role it has to play in the whole, can alone effect a comprehensive and progressive unification which may have some chance of enduring." She continued, "The first aim then will be to help individuals to become conscious of the fundamental genius of the nation to which they belong and at the same time to put them in contact with the modes of living of other nations so that they may know and respect equally the true spirit of all the countries on the earth."

Naturally, the Mother's internationalist ideal, embedded in the statement, was firmly joined with her understanding that communal and individual progress must proceed simultaneously. She imagined in this international center that the individuals would all be in search of their highest spiritual development, while they worked toward collective "unification." When in 1956 the Mother finally experienced the "Supramental manifestation on earth," which Sri Aurobindo and she had anticipated, she understood that this was the beginning of a new order on Earth. Her notion of Auroville then was of a place where this new order could take concrete form in an international community with a charter and vision like none before.

In 1972 the Mother wrote in regard to her "dream" of Auroville:

There should be somewhere upon earth a place that no nation could claim as its sole property, a place where all human beings of good will, sincere in their aspiration, could live freely as citizens of the world, obeying one single authority, that of the supreme Truth, a place of peace, concord, harmony, where all fighting instincts of man could be used exclusively to conquer the sources of sufferings and miseries, to surmount his weakness and ignorance, to triumph over his limitations and incapacities; a place where the needs of the spirit and the care for progress would get precedence over the satisfaction of desires and passions, the seeking for material pleasures and enjoyment.

There are four principles in the Auroville Charter. In summary, they ask that each resident see himself or herself as a servant of the "Divine Consciousness," that Auroville will be a place of unending education, that Auroville will be a

place where the past and the future meet, and that Auroville will be a site to realize "Human Unity."

The ideals for an Aurovillian emphasize the INTEGRAL YOGA, the creative development of each person as a unique point of the Divine, and the synthesis of the yogas of knowledge, love, and work. Auroville's organization and administration are perhaps the most free and unbounded of any similar township on Earth (it is a flourishing community of about 3,000). It is a measure of the success of this experiment in self-governance (fully supported by the Indian government) that Auroville has several citations from the United Nations for its land use and ecological work. The world's largest solar kitchen provides meals. In support of the Mother's belief that the age of religions is past and is to be supplanted by a spiritual age beyond religion, the Auroville Charter states pointedly, "No religions." Except for the stunning hemispheric Matri Mandir (Mother's temple), no sign of any religious symbol or building can be seen in Auroville.

Further reading: Alan and Tim, *The Auroville Handbook* (Auroville: Abundance, 2003); *Auroville, the First Six Years: 1968–1974* (Auroville: Auropublication, 1974); Robert N. Minor, *The Religious, the Spiritual, and the Secular: Auroville and Secular India* (Albany: State University of New York Press, 1999); Satprem, trans. *The Mother's Agenda.* 10 vols. (Paris: Institut de recherches évolutives, 1979–91).

Australia

Mass immigration of Hindus from India to Australia occurred later than in most other regions of the British Commonwealth, largely because of the 1901 Immigration Restriction Act, a policy enacted by white Australians to limit the numbers of nonwhite citizens.

Prior to the enforcement of immigration policies, small numbers of Indians had entered Australia as merchants, indentured laborers, and domestic servants. The first immigrants from India arrived in New South Wales in 1830 on a trade ship from the Bay of Bengal to work as laborers on cotton and sugar plantations. Others followed sporadically until 1857, when a gold rush on the continent attracted a steady flow of Asian workers. Most Indian laborers were males, who arrived without their families and returned to India once their labor contracts were fulfilled. Some, however, remained in Australia and made a place for themselves and their families. Some became prosperous, such as Sri Pammull, an Indian merchant, who in the 1850s entered the opal trade in Melbourne and established a successful family business that has continued for four generations.

Approximately 1,000 Hindus resided in Australia at the time immigration restrictions were enacted. Most observed their religion privately at shrines within their homes, as formal places of worship had not yet been established. Although immigration restrictions limited the number of immigrants from India, the laws did not prevent adoption of Hinduism by white settlers. Between 1890 and 1920 an enthusiasm for Eastern mysticism spread in Australia. Spiritual dissenters, intellectuals, and artists from the middle class promoted the establishment of centers of THEOSOPHY. In the 1890s Charles Leadbeater founded the Theosophical Lodge in Sydney, which eventually became one of the largest Theosophical centers in the world. Theosophical lodges served as resource centers for YOGA, sites for lectures on Eastern wisdom, and sponsors of bookstores that disseminated works on Buddhist and Hindu thought. Theosophical lodges served as cultural centers for white Australians who sought introduction to and assimilation of Eastern spirituality.

After the immigration restrictions were lifted in the 1960s and 1970s, the population of Hindus, primarily from India, Sri Lanka, and Fiji, grew dramatically. The new arrivals established strong communities and maintained traditional Hinduism. In 1977, Australia's first Hindu temple, Sri Mandir, was established by Dr. Padmanabhan Shridhar Prabhu, Dr. Anand, and Prem Shankar. Sri Mandir has served as a center for Hindu festivals and has propagated Hindu culture and philosophy among Indians and non-Indians.

Today, many Hindu organizations and yoga schools are part of the culture of Australia, including the VEDANTA SOCIETY, SIDDHA YOGA FOUNDATION, DIVINE LIFE SOCIETY, and the INTERNATIONAL SOCIETY FOR KRISHNA CONSCIOUSNESS. Australian-born adherents have also participated in the propagation of Hindu teachings. John Mumford, known as Swami Anandakapila, has become instrumental in popularizing TANTRIC YOGA through the INTERNATIONAL YOGA FELLOWSHIP.

The current growth in Australia's Hindu population and the continuing interest in Hinduism among those of European origin have created a sort of renaissance of Hindu thought and practice. In the 1990s Hinduism became one of the country's fastest growing religions. According to current census reports approximately 95,000 people in Australia identify themselves as Hindu.

Further reading: Purusottama Bilimoria, *Hinduism in Australia: Mandala for the Gods* (Melbourne: Spectrum, 1989); ———, *Hindus and Sikhs in Australia* (Canberra: A. G. P. S., 1996); Marie M. De Lepervanche, *Indians in a White Australia* (Boston: G. Allen & Unwin, 1984).

avadhuta

An *avadhuta* is a type of SADHU or wandering mendicant. The term refers to different populations in different parts of India. In Bengal the BAULS are referred to as *avadhutas*. In the NATH sect founded by GORAKHNATH, the *avadhuta* is someone who has reached the highest state of spiritual development. In Maharashtra and in Gujarat the *Avadhuta* is the single Guru-God DATTATREYA.

Further reading: G. S. Ghurye with L. N. Chapekar, *Indian Sadhus* (Bombay: Popular Prakashan, 1964); Dolf Hartuiker, *Sadhus: India's Mystic Holy Men* (London: Thames & Hudson, 1993).

Avalon, Arthur   *See* WOODROFFE, SIR JOHN.

avatar

Avatar is a modern Hindi word from the SANSKRIT word *avatara*, which means "one who has descended to the earthly realm." The word in both its Sanskrit and its Hindi forms is used in VAISHNAVISM to refer to the incarnations of Vishnu, which usually number 10. Technically, Shiva never becomes an avatar. In recent times, the word avatar has come to be used for any enlightened teacher. It is, in effect, an honorific bestowed upon the teacher by his or her disciples or the larger community. One such example is Avatar ADI DA SAMRAJ.

Further reading: Antonio T. de Nicolas, *Avatar, the Humanization of Philosophy through the Bhagavad Gita* (New York: N. Hays, 1976).

avidya

Avidya, or "ignorance," is a centrally important term in Hinduism. The term also has an important place in Buddhism. *Avidya* is the fundamental ignorance that causes us to misperceive the phenomenal world. Ignorance causes us to imagine that what we see is the only reality, when this is not the case. There is an underlying reality that transcends the mundane sphere and also underlies it, but which cannot be seen by ordinary vision.

In the VEDANTA of SHANKARA this misunderstanding or *avidya* is often equated with MAYA, or illusion. According to Shankara *avidya* is the perception of an actual reality when there is none there, only a false or illusory reality. The only thing real is the BRAHMAN, which underlies all names and forms.

In Hindu tantrism the understanding of *avidya* is different. In that tradition, *avidya* is what makes us see the world as other than the divinity. The word is used in theistic, nontantric contexts in the sense of misperception of the nature of things.

Further reading: Aditi De, *The Development of the Concept of Maya and Avidya with Special Reference to the Concept of Vivarta: An Interpretation of Sankara Philosophy* (Patna: De, 1982); John Grimes, *The Seven Great Untenables* (Delhi: Motilal Banarsidass, 1990); Chandranarayan Mishra, *The Problem of Nescience in Indian Philosophy* (Darbhanga: Kashinath Mishra, 1977); Swami Muktananda, *From the Finite to the Infinite*, 2d ed. (South Fallsburg, N.Y.: SYDA Foundation, 1994); Bashistha Narain Tripath, *Indian View of Spiritual Bondage* (Varanasi: Aradhana Prakashan, 1987).

Ayodhya

Ayodhya is located in North India on the Gogra River (formerly the Sharayu), just east of Faizabad in the Indian state of Uttar Pradesh. It is the city where Lord RAMA, the AVATAR of VISHNU, was born and where he ruled. Rama's story is told in the ancient Indian epic the RAMAYANA.

Since the time of the Ramayana story, Ayodhya has been recognized as an important urban center and both Hindu and Jain (see JAINISM) mythological literature mentions this city and its king often. In modern times, Ayodhya has become a place of controversy because of a medieval mosque that is said to have been built upon the birth place of Lord Rama. (Because of controversy over the site the mosque had been decommissioned for many years.) Encouraged by politics, this mosque was destroyed in 1993 by fervent Hindus, commencing a time of sharpened conflict between Hindus and Muslims in India.

Further reading: Hans T. Bakker, *Ayodhya* (Groningen, Netherlands: Egbert Forsten, 1986); Ramchandra Gandhi, *Sita's Kitchen* (New Delhi: Wiley Eastern, 1994); Philip Lutgendorf, "Imagining Ayodhya: Utopia and Its Shadows in Ancient India." *International Journal of Hindu Studies* 1, no. 1 (1997), pp. 19–54.

Ayurveda

Ayurveda (from *ayus,* "life," and *veda,* "knowledge") is the ancient tradition of medicine in India. It is said to originate in the ATHARVA VEDA. The text *Ayurveda,* which is no longer extant, was said to have been written by Dhanvantari, the physician of the gods.

Ayurveda stresses the close observation and diagnosis of the patient by the doctor. Medicines are not prescribed so universally as in Western allopathic medicine; when they are prescribed they are tailored to the bodily tendencies of the patient.

Much of Ayurvedic medicine is based on the understanding of three humorlike systems in the body called wind, bile, and phlegm. Imbalances in these humors are seen to be the cause of various ailments of body and mind. Diet, herbs, water, minerals, and other treatments are used for cures. Some, but not all, of Ayurvedic treatment is homeopathic. The ancient tradition of Ayurveda was first put into textual form (the *Charaka Samhita*) by Charaka or Agnivesha, who claimed that he drew on the Ayurveda of Dhanvantari.

Further reading: Ram Karan Sharma and Bhagwan Dash, trans. and critical exposition, *Agnivesa's Carakasamhita.* Chowkhamba Sanskrit Studies, Vol. 94 (Varanasi: Chowkhamba Sanskrit Series Office, 2002); Vasant Dattatray Lad, *Secrets of the Pulse: The Ancient Art of Ayurvedic Pulse Diagnosis* (Albuquerque, N. Mex.: Ayurvedic Press, 1996); K. G. Zysk, *Religious Medicine: The History and Evolution of Indian Medicine* (New Brunswick, N.J.: Transaction, 1993).

Ayyappan

Lord Ayyappan of Sabrimali in Kerala is a divinity with a synthetic character. He is said on the one hand to be the son of SHIVA and MOHINI, VISHNU's female form. He is also said to be an incarnation of the Buddha. Furthermore he is honored in Kerala by Muslims. According to the myth, the god transformed himself into a baby who was found by the king Pandalam, who was childless. Ayyappan was then adopted as his heir. After a short time, Pandalam's queen produced her own son, and she tried afterward to get rid of Ayyappan. She pretended she was ill and said only tiger's milk could cure her.

Ayyappan went off to the forest and returned riding a tigress. In his search for tiger's milk, Ayyappan had been sent to heaven by Lord Shiva to kill a demoness, Mahishi. Ayyappan had succeeded in ejecting her from heaven and making her fall to Earth. The demoness asked him to take her as his wife, but, he, being celibate, decided not to accept her. However, Mahishi is given a prominent place at the Ayyappan shrine.

In recent years a winter pilgrimage has been instituted to the Ayyappan shrine; it takes place between December 15 and January 15, depending on the lunar calendar. This men-only event involves an arduous climb up the hills of the Western Ghats and has become popular throughout India. Participants dress in black, take a vow of celibacy for the duration of the celebration, prepare for the pilgrimage by singing praises to Ayyappan, and then head off on the long trek. All castes and creeds are allowed to enter the Ayyappan, shrine, but women in their fertile years are not permitted as Ayyappan is said to be "lord of celibacy." Ayyappan is sometimes also referred to as Shasta, or "ruler of the realm."

Further reading: E. Valentine Daniel, *Fluid Signs: Being a Person the Tamil Way* (Berkeley: University of California Press, 1984); *Lord Ayyappan, the Dharma*

Sasta (Bombay: Bharatiya Vidya Bhavan, 1966); N. T. Nair, *The Worship of Lord Ayyappan* (Singapore: Printworld Services, 1995); Radhika Sekar, *The Sabarimalai Pilgrimage and Ayyappan Cults* (Delhi: Motilal Banarsidass, 1992); P. T. Thomas, *Sabarimalai and Its Shasta* (Madras: Christian Literature Society, 1973); K. R. Vaidyanathan, *Pilgrimage to Sabari* (Bombay: Bharatiya Vidya Bhavan, 1978)

B

Baba

Baba is a word from the Hindi language that means "father" and is used commonly as an honorific for sages, gurus, and saints. A person called Baba may or may not have taken the vows of renunciation that are signified by the title SWAMI.

Babaji (birth possibly 203 C.E.) *the eternal yogi*

Babaji (Revered Father) is a legendary immortal YOGI who is said to have instructed many of the great historic yogis, in the service of his goal of human spiritual evolution. He is particularly associated with the modern yoga movement of the SELF-REALIZATION FELLOWSHIP.

Historical information regarding Babaji is difficult to obtain. Paramahansa YOGANANDA, founder of the fellowship and the first author to create wide recognition of Babaji, dedicates one chapter of his book *Autobiography of a Yogi* to Babaji, whose other names are Mahamuni Babaji Maharaj (Supreme Ecstatic Master), Maha Yogi (Great Yogi), and Trambak Baba or Shiva Baba (both incarnations of SHIVA). According to Yogananda, Babaji chooses to live in obscurity in the Himalayas, beyond a holy place called BADRINATH, and has intentionally kept secret any information about his birthplace and date of birth, which is believed to have occurred so long ago as to be beyond consideration.

Babaji is said to work in the background to guide the evolution of human consciousness; at certain times he appears and initiates certain people to advance their spiritual evolution and to promote new paths for humanity. He is not normally accessible, appearing only when he desires, often at *melas* (festivals). Babaji is not "religious"; rather, his goal is to help everyone achieve SELF-REALIZATION by means of several forms of the science of YOGA.

Babaji is said to have given yoga initiation to the historical teachers SHANKARA (seventh century C.E.) of the Swami Order and KABIR, (15th century C.E.), the famous medieval Hindi saint-poet. Around 800–900 C.E., he appeared as GORAKHNATH and initiated disciples into HATHA and KUNDALINI yoga disciplines. According to Yogananda, around 1860 Babaji taught *KRIYA YOGA* (the main teaching of the Self-Realization Fellowship), to LAHIRI MAHASAYA (1828–95), the GURU responsible for reviving the discipline. Yogananda claimed that Babaji also appeared to him early in the 20th century and gave him his mission to teach in the West.

Stories attest to Babaji's ability to become invisible at will. Because of this and his implicit instruction to his disciples to keep silent about him, little is known about his life. He can speak in any language but generally uses Hindi. His body is forever young, immortal, and not in need of food. Yogananda is said to have demonstrated this ability by the incorruptibility of his own body after his death in 1952, perhaps a capacity that develops after intense practice of *kriya yoga.*

Since Yogananda's death, many more stories relating to Babaji have emerged. He has been identified with an unnamed person who lived in the foothills of the Himalayas in the Kumaon region from around 1890 to 1922. His followers, acting on his statements, expected him to return after his departure in 1922 and established a number of ASHRAMS for him throughout India. Another teacher, Mahendra Baba (d. 1969), throughout the 1950s and 1960s predicted Babaji's return. Blessed from childhood with appearances from Babaji, Mahendra Baba (d. 1969), a sainted figure himself, devoted his life to facilitating the reappearance of Babaji. Mahendra restored the old ASHRAMS, wrote books about Babaji, and asked everyone to receive Babaji. However, Mahendra died before Babaji returned.

In June 1970, a young man identified as Haidakhan (also spelled Hariakhan) Baba appeared and moved among the Babaji ashrams for 14 years. From 1970 until his death on February 14, 1984, he traveled around India teaching and healing as more ashrams were opened for him. Tens of thousands of Hindus traveled to see him. Haidakhan Baba/Babaji stayed in the countryside, where he could teach the traditional sacred principles. He taught by example how to attain spiritual awakening silently. Babaji told his devotees that he appeared in many incarnations to restore the SANATANA DHARMA, the eternal truth of creation that has manifested and operates in harmony with Divine Will. He urged his students to live in truth and simplicity, regardless of religious affiliation.

According to Babaji, true devotion will replace material obsessions and will cultivate the presence of divine wisdom. He urged people at all times to chant the name of God, using the mantra *Om Namah Shiva,* literally "I take refuge in God." Babaji's followers sing a song to him each morning and evening in a service called an *arati.* They practice a fire ceremony called the *yagya* or *hawan.* Babaji advocated above all things a dedication to serve humanity through karma yoga, selfless action.

Leonard Orr and Sondra Ray, founders of the "rebirthing" movement, were among his American disciples, and BABA HARI DASS of Santa Cruz, California, published a book about stories collected about Haidakhan Baba, *Hariakhan Baba Known, Unknown.*

The Haidakhan Samaj was established in 1980 near Nainital, Uttar Pradesh state, India, as a central headquarters for the teachings of Haidakhan Baba/Babaji. The American headquarters of the Haidakhan Samaj is located in Crestone, Colorado. American devotees publish *American Haidakhan Samaj Newsletter.* The movement counts more than 8,000 members worldwide.

Another Indian teacher, S. A. A. Ramaiah, independently of the Haidakhan Baba movement and Self-Realization Fellowship, claimed that in 1942 he and a journalist, V. T. Neelakantan, became students of Babaji in spirit and received directly from him the texts of three books, *The Voice of Babaji and Mysticism Unlocked, Babaji's Masterkey to All Ills,* and *Babaji's Death of Death.* Ramaiah reports that Babaji revealed his actual beginning in human form in 203 C.E. in Tamil Nadu, India, as the son of a priest of Shiva.

Ramaiah reports that Babaji traveled during the third century to the southern tip of Sri Lanka, where he studied with a guru and had a vision of Lord Muruga, son of Shiva. After studies in Tamil Nadu, he eventually went to the Himalayas to practice *kriya yoga.* Through his practice he was transformed into a SIDDHA (a perfected person with supernatural abilities) and his body became free of the effects of aging, disease, and death. Since that time, he has continued to exist, maintain a youthful appearance, and become the guide and inspiration of many of India's great spiritual teachers.

In 1951 Ramaiah founded the INTERNATIONAL BABAJI KRIYA YOGA SANGAM, which now has locations in 50 countries and teaches all of the *kriya yoga* material that Yogananda deemed inappropriate for introduction to the West in the early 20th century. Since Ramaiah's death, the Babaji Kriya Yoga Sangam has been led by Marshall Govindan, who was initiated by Ramaiah in 1971.

Another guru, Swami Satyaswarananda of San Diego, California, claims to have had contact with Babaji. At Babaji's instruction, he has republished the writings of Lahiri Mahasaya in a series called Sanskrit Classics.

Further reading: Shedha Goodman, *Babaji, Meeting with Truth at Hariakhan Vishvwa Mahadham* (Farmingdale, N.Y.: Coleman, 1986); Marshall Govindan, *Babaji and the 18 Siddha Kriya Yoga Traditions.* 2d ed. (Freiberg, Germany: Hans Nietsch Verlag, 1999); Baba Hari Dass, *Hariakhan Baba Known, Unknown* (Davis, Calif.: Shri Rama Foundation, 1975); Leonard Orr and Makham Singh, *Babaji* (San Francisco: Author, 1979); Swami Satyeswarananda, *Babaji.* Vol. 1, *The Divine Himalayan Yogi,* 3d ed. (San Diego, Calif.: Sanskrit Classics, 1993); Paramahansa Yogananda, *Autobiography of a Yogi* (Los Angeles: Self-Realization Fellowship, 1971).

Badami

Badami is an archaeological site in the Bijapur District of the Indian state of Karnataka, capital of the famed Chalukya empire from around the sixth to the 11th century. Four sixth-century temples carved into solid rock there show a combination of northern and southern architectural styles. Generally they resemble the temples at ELLORA.

To the left of the visitor climbing to the top of the rocks is cave one, dedicated to SHIVA. It shows a 14-armed Shiva on one side of the entrance and a protection deity on the other side. Cave two is dedicated to VISHNU. Its stone carvings tell the full story of Vishnu's incarnation as VAMANA, the divine dwarf, to save the world from the ravages of the demon king BALI. Vishnu's boar incarnation (VARAHA) is also depicted in the cave.

Cave three is the largest and most elaborate. It contains large carved pillars and an extensive interior. It too has several images of Vishnu—standing, lying on the divine serpent ADISHESHA, as the boar incarnation Varaha, as the man-lion NARASIMHA, and as the divine dwarf Vamana. Each depiction is approximately 10 feet high and elaborately carved.

The fourth cave temple is smaller and is Jain (*see* JAINISM) in orientation. It depicts the 24 Jain TIRTHANKARAS, or divine teachers, on a wall and on pillars in relief. The central image is of PARSHVANATH. Gommateshvara, the son of the first Tirthankara, RISHABHA; he is depicted in his standing, yogic pose, overgrown by carved stone vines.

Some distance below the caves near the tank are two smaller shrines to Shiva and a small temple to the South Indian goddess Yellamma. These later shrines are from the 11th century. There are small caves scattered at the site down below, some of which were used or dug by Buddhists between the sixth and eighth centuries.

Further reading: Rakhal Das Banerji, *Bas Reliefs of Badami* (Calcutta: Government of India Central Publication Branch, 1928); Michael W. Meister, ed., *Essays in Early Indian Architecture by Ananda K. Coomarswamy* (New Delhi: Oxford University Press, 1992); S. Rajasekhara, *Karnataka Architecture* (Dharwad: Sujata, 1985); K. V. Ramesh, *Chalukyas of Vatapi* (Delhi: Agam Kala Prakashan, 1984); Henri Stierlin and Anne Stierlin, *Hindu India: From Khajuraho to the Temple City of Madurai* (New York: Taschen, 1998).

Badarayana (Vyasa) *Vedantic Philosopher*
See VEDANTA SUTRA.

Badrinath

Badrinath is an important Hindu pilgrimage site located in a glacial area some 10,000 feet high in the central Himalayas, in the Chamoli District of the Indian state of Uttar Pradesh. It is sometimes said to be one of the four shrines that a Hindu must visit in his or her lifetime to reach salvation. It is also known as Badarikashrama and has been an important pilgrimage site from ancient times, mentioned in the MAHABHARATA epic. Badrinath lies on the Alaknanda River, understood to be one of the channels that the GANGA or Ganges took when descending from heaven.

The town has a comparatively modern temple built on a peak, dedicated to a form of VISHNU called Badarinatha. The name—of the site and of the god—is taken from the berry patch, *badari vana,* that once existed there. The great ninth-century sage SHANKARA established one of his four famous centers at Badrinath.

Further reading: Anne Felhaus, *Connected Places: Region, Pilgrimage, and Geographical Imagination in India* (New York: Palgrave Macmillan, 2003); Dinesh Kumar, *The Sacred Complex of Badrinath: A Study of Himalayan Pilgrimage* (Varanasi: Kishor Vidya Niketan, 1991); Kanaiyalal M. Munshi, *To Badarinath* (Bombay: Bharatiya Vidya Bhavan, 1953).

Bahubali

In Jain mythology Bahubali was the younger son of RISHABHA, the first TIRTHANKARA (holy teacher) in this half of the cosmic cycle, renowned for his remarkable asceticism. In a contest for control of their kingdom Bahubali defeated his older brother, BHARATA, who then became a monk. Not long afterward, Bahubali himself decided to take vows of renunciation. His initial motive was just to compete with his brother, whose asceticism he envied. When his own austerities yielded no fruit, he eventually concentrated on fierce renunciation. On one occasion he was said to have stood on one leg so long that vines and other plants grew up

around him and he became covered with ants. He reached his goal of *kevalajnana,* highest knowledge, and has since been famed for it.

Bahubali is one of the 63 great beings in the DIGAMBARA Jain pantheon. He is enshrined in colossal statues, particularly in the state of Karnataka. One huge statue, the 10th-century Shravana Belagola statue in Karnataka, rises nearly 60 feet from its base atop a small mountain peak. On special occasions this statue is given a huge ritual bathing in milk along with massive offerings. Another Bahubali, built in the 15th century in Udipi District, Karnataka, is 40 feet high.

Further reading: Phyllis Granoff, ed. *The Clever Adultress and Other Stories: Treasury of Jain Literature* (Oakville, Canada: Mosaic Press, 1990); Jyotindra Jain and Eberhard Fischer, *Jaina Iconography* (Leiden: E. J. Brill, 1978); Helen M. Johnson, trans., *Trisastisalakapurusacarita* (Baroda: Oriental Institute, 1931–62); Vilas Adinath Sangave, *The Sacred Sravana Belagola* (New Delhi: Bharatiya Jnanapith, 1981).

Bailey, Alice Ann (1880–1949) *Theosophical teacher*

Alice Ann Bailey was a prominent teacher and leader in the Western Theosophical movement. She founded Lucis Trust, the Arcane School, and World Goodwill.

Bailey was born on June 16, 1880, in Manchester, England. She had a rather confined childhood. A devout member of the Church of England, as a young adult she went to India on its behalf to work with the British army. There she met her first husband, John Evans. The couple moved to the United States, where he served as an Episcopal minister, and had three children. The marriage eventually ended in divorce.

About the time of her divorce during World War I, she was introduced to the THEOSOPHICAL SOCIETY. At the society headquarters in Los Angeles she saw a picture of a man in a turban, whom she recognized as the same person who had appeared to her in England when she was only 15 years old. She later learned that the figure was Koot Houmi, one of the ascended masters who had communicated with the society founder Helena P. BLAVATSKY. Bailey went on to become an active member of the society, where she met her future husband, Foster Bailey.

While working with the society she was contacted by another of the masters, Djwhal Khul, usually referred to as D.K., or simply the Tibetan. Bailey began to channel writings from the Tibetan, later compiled into 19 books. In an appendix to her unfinished autobiography she explained her method of receiving teachings and writing texts in cooperation with the Tibetan. In the same book she stated the founding principles of the school she would later establish.

Bailey's first book, *Initiation: Human and Solar,* was initially well received. However, Annie Besant, the international president of the society, frowned upon writings independently received from the masters, and both Alice and Foster were soon relieved of their positions in the society.

The Baileys were married in 1921. Soon afterward they founded Lucis Trust and the Arcane School, to publish and disseminate the writings and teachings of the Tibetan and to facilitate the work of interested students. These teachings continued the synthesis of Western and Hindu thought first articulated by Blavatsky that had become the hallmark of Theosophy. The teachings emphasized the divine plan for humankind, the role of karma and reincarnation, and the existence of a spiritual brotherhood or hierarchy, overseeing the evolution and welfare of humanity. Of note is Bailey's prolific writing on the science of the Seven Rays, first introduced by Blavatsky.

Bailey's work also emphasized the practical aspects of spiritual discipleship, applied on a human level, in particular the importance of group consciousness and world service. To this end, she also founded World Goodwill, a nongovernmental organization dedicated to the promotion of good human relations on a global scale. The Lucis Trust has consultative status at the United Nations, and World Goodwill is affiliated with the United Nations Department of Public Information. Bailey also introduced a world prayer for peace, enlightenment, and spiritual assistance called the Great Invocation, as well as a set of creative meditations designed to be observed cyclically, primarily at the time of each full Moon, in order to create human alignment with the divine Plan.

In addition to the 19 titles written in cooperation with D. K., Bailey authored five books by herself. All 24 books carry Bailey's name. Bailey continued to head the Arcane School until her death on December 15, 1949, when Foster took over to lead the organization for several additional years. The Arcane School and the Lucis Trust, together with the service activities World Goodwill and Triangles, continue to function today. In addition, a number of other groups attempt to perpetuate the Bailey teachings.

Further reading: Alice A. Bailey, *The Externalisation of the Hierarchy* (New York/London: Lucis, 1957); ———, *Initiation, Human and Solar* (New York/London: Lucis, 1922); ———, *The Reappearance of the Christ* (New York/London: Lucis, 1948); ———, *The Unfinished Autobiography* (New York: Lucis, 1951); John R. Sinclair, *The Alice Bailey Inheritance* (Wellingborough, England: Turnstone Press, 1985); *Thirty Years Work: The Books of Alice A. Bailey and the Tibetan Master Djwhal Khul* (New York/London: Lucis, 1957).

Balarama

Balarama is the elder brother of KRISHNA. He is depicted as having a light color in contrast to Krishna's dark skin; one legend says that Balarama was created from a light hair of VISHNU, and Krishna from a black hair. Sometimes Balarama is seen as an AVATAR of Vishnu alongside his brother Krishna; sometimes the two are considered to share an avatar as two "parts" of the whole. He is also sometimes seen as an incarnation of ADISHESHA, the divine serpent on whom Vishnu rested.

Balarama's mother, DEVAKI, was the wife of VASUDEVA, minister to the evil king Kamsa. When Kamsa learned that a son of Devaki's would eventually kill him, he had the couple guarded and had six of Devaki's children killed in succession. Miraculously, however, the seventh child, Balarama, was transferred as an embryo into the womb of Rohini, a second wife of Vasudeva. When Krishna, the eighth child, was born, the guards miraculously fell asleep, and Vasudeva was able to deliver his new child to a woman from a cowherd family, YASHODA.

There are few stories about Balarama independent of those that associate him with Krishna. He is said to have gone to the ocean to meditate when he was very old, when Adishesha emerged from his mouth and returned to the ocean whence he had emerged.

Iconographically, BALARAMA is known as "Rama with the Plow" and carries a plow and axe in either hand.

Further reading: Cornelia Dimmitt and J. A. B. van Buitenen, *Classical Hindu Mythology: A Reader in the Sanskrit Puranas* (Philadelphia: Temple University Press, 1978); E. Washburn Hopkins, *Epic Mythology* (Delhi: Motilal Banarsidass, 1986); N. P. Joshi, *Iconography of Balarama* (New Delhi: Abhinav, 1979).

Bali, Hinduism in

Bali, an island in the Indian Ocean immediately east of Java, is today a part of the country of INDONESIA. Unlike the rest of predominantly Muslim Indonesia, however, Bali is overwhelming Hindu. Its unique history reaches back to the spread of Hinduism to Java in the fourth century C.E., the rise of Hindu rulers on Java by the seventh century, and the spread of Hinduism to Bali in the 11th century. The Hindu Majapahit kingdom, which emerged in eastern Java in the 13th century. at its peak ruled all of Java, Bali, and Madura. However, its upward trajectory was stymied by the arrival and spread of Islam into the Indone-sian islands. In the 15th century, Islam pushed the Majapahits out of Java and the once-powerful kingdom retreated to Bali, where it survived while Java was divided among rival Muslim sultans.

Hindu rule of Bali lasted until the mid-19th century, when the Dutch conquered the island. They held it only until the establishment of the Republic of Indonesia after World War II. Much of the Hindu leadership remained in place under Dutch rule. After the Dutch relinquished administration of the island the Hindu culture remained protected by the Indonesian government. A government-sponsored organization, the Parishad Hindu Dharma Indonesia (PHDI), or Hindu Council of Religious Affairs, is the highest religious body on Bali and has been given the power to make decisions on all spiritual matters.

Since the 16th century, Hinduism in Bali has developed somewhat in isolation from its roots in India, at the same time absorbing a variety of elements from the pre-Hindu indigenous religion of the island. These two factors shaped a distinctive form of Hindu life and practice in the islands, whose Hinduism is a blend of SHAIVISM, Buddhism, and ancient ancestor worship. The deity SHIVA is primarily associated with the ancestors of kings; consistently with the indigenous religion of Bali, Hindus there do not distinguish between the ancestors of rulers and the gods. The Balinese do not hold to the vegetarian dietary practices of India; instead, they eat such foods as beef, pork, and dog.

Balinese Hindus believe in Sanghyang Widhi, the omnipotent Supreme Being, who manifests in three main forms as BRAHMA the Creator, VISHNU the Preserver, and SHIVA the Destroyer. However, this deity is not directly worshipped through cult or prayer, and none of the Balinese temples is dedicated to him. Among the deities to whom worship is directed, Shiva is the most prominent. He is usually worshipped in association with one or more local deities whose gender is indicated by their name—*Dewa* (male) or *Dewi* (female). The deities are acknowledged through daily offerings and participation in village and temple events. Bali has become known in the wider Hindu world for its frequent and dramatic ceremonies, rather than for any intellectual or spiritual leadership.

Unlike in India, the gods of Balinese Hinduism are not seen as dwelling in their images; they live atop the great volcano Gunung Agung, which is identified with Mt. Meru, considered the axis of the world in many stories of traditional Hinduism. During worship and festivals the gods are called down from the mountain to enter their statues and the masks worn by celebrants. When the worship or festival ends, the gods return to their abode.

The Balinese generally bury their dead; cremation is performed only for the more significant members of society. When a cremation is performed, corpses of commoners who have died since the last cremation are dug up and burned along with the newly deceased. These cremations are elaborate events; a grandly built tower is burned as part of the rite. The cremation is considered to purify the souls of the deceased.

Although the images of the gods are not considered sacred, the temple sites are. Bali has more than 20,000 temples. Each village usually has three main temples: the Village Temple, the Temple of Death (in memory of dead royalty), and the Shrine of the Beginning.

At the Village Temple villagers congregate for worship and meetings, which center on shared sacred communal meals. The Temple of Death is associated with the nether world and is dedicated to the ancestors of rulers. In Bali, the dead are perceived as dangerous until they are purified by cremation; the temple keeps these negative forces in check.

The most important temple is the Shrine of the Beginning, dedicated to the Original Ancestor (the equivalent of Shiva) and His Consort. Other temples are dedicated to specific functions: water temples are responsible for irrigation and adequate water supply, sea temples hold back the forces of the underworld, and harvest temples secure abundance of food. Temples are built with inner courts containing shrines to the deities and platforms for offerings, and outer courtyards for more mundane purposes, such as the preparation of food. The inner courts also contain one or more towers that represent Mt. MERU. Outside most temples are sacred groves, usually banyan trees, where demonic forces are propitiated. Each household also contains a shrine known as the "shrine of origin," dedicated to ancestors and to the Sun god SURYA. Shiva, in the form of Bhattara Guru, the Divine Teacher, is included.

According to the Balinese, the Hindu gods migrated to Bali. Indigenous deities such as Ranga and Barong also have an extensive mythology, which has been grafted onto the tales of the imported gods. Many Balinese live in a lively world inhabited by spirits of all varieties and ghostly entities, many of whom inhabit various animals, all existing alongside the deities of the Hindu pantheon. They also fear witches (malevolent sorcerers) who live among them more or less openly. Evil spirits are still looked upon as causes of illness and misfortune. Daily offerings are designed, in part, to appease angry spirit entities.

Balinese Hinduism distinguishes between two types of priests: the *pedandas* and local *pemangkus*, or temple priests. The *pedandas* are always male BRAHMINS; they perform duties and rituals primarily for the higher castes. The *pemangkus* are in charge of specific temples and daily rituals and serve as priests for commoners. *Pemangkus* are primarily men but can be women and can be either of caste or without caste. Unlike *pedandas*, *pemangku* priests are allowed to be possessed by the gods.

Uma, sometimes called PARVATI, is the principal goddess of Bali; she is the Goddess of the Mountain Gunung Agung, where she dwells as the consort of Shiva, the Great Ancestor. She has many manifestations. As Uma, she nourishes and causes seeds to germinate. As DURGA, she is the

Goddess of Death and the Mistress of Demons. As Devi Ganga and Devi Danu, she is the goddess of both the lake Bator (the site of her chief temple) and the second largest volcano, Gunung Bator. As Sri, she is worshipped at the temples in the rice paddies. As Ibu Petri, she is the Goddess of the Earth. Her most wrathful form is that of Ranga, goddess of the cemeteries.

Among the important temples on Bali is Gunug Kawi, one of the island's oldest, dating to the 11th century. Carved out of local rock, it is located in the Gianyar Regency. The most sacred site on the island is the shrine Pura Besakih, located on the slope of Mt. Agung.

Today, over 90 percent of Bali's three million inhabitants are Hindu, making the island the largest community of Hindus outside India.

Further reading: Jane Belo, *Bali: Temple Festival* (New York: American Ethnological Society, 1953); ———, *Traditional Balinese Culture* (New York: Columbia University Press, 1970); ———, *Trance in Bali* (New York: Columbia University Press, 1960); James A. Boon, *The Anthropological Romance of Bali, 1597–1972: Dynamic Perspectives in Marriage and Caste Politics and Religion* (Cambridge: Cambridge University Press, 1977); R. Friederich, *The Civilization and Culture of Bali* (Kolkatta: Sushil Gupta, 1959); Clifford Geertz, *Person, Time, and Conduct in Bali.* South East Asia Studies (New Haven, Conn.: Yale University Press, 1966); Hildred Geertz and Clifford Geertz, *Kinship in Bali* (Chicago: University of Chicago Press, 1975); Christiaan Hooykaas, *Agama Tirtha, Five Studies in Hindu-Balinese Religion* (Amsterdam: Noord-Hollandsche Uitgaverij, 1964); ———, *Cosmogony and Creation in Balinese Tradition* (The Hague: Martinus Nijhoff, 1974); Leo Howe, *Hinduism and Hierarchy in Bali* (Santa Fe, N. Mex.: School of American Research Press, 2001); J. L. Swellengrebel, *Bali: Further Studies in Life, Thought, and Ritual* (The Hague: W. van Hoeve, 1969); ———, *Bali: Life, Thought, and Ritual* (The Hague: W. van Hoeve, 1960); Walter F. Vella, *The Indianized States of Southeast Asia* (Honolulu: East-West Center Press, 1968).

Bali, the *asura*

Bali is the *asura* (antigod) who plays the role of villain in the story of Vamana, the dwarf avatar (incarnation) of Vishnu.

The story takes many different forms. In the most common version the demon Bali succeeds, through religious austerities, in gaining supreme power over the Three Worlds, Earth, heaven, and the underworld. When he begins to monopolize the offerings that previously went to the gods, they go to Vishnu to ask for assistance. He takes on the form of Vamana and approaches the arrogant demon with a plan to trick him. The foolish demon king offers the dwarf a boon of territory—as much as he can cover in three paces. Thereupon the dwarf takes one step to possess the Earth, another to possess the sky, and another to possess heaven itself. In some versions Vamana takes two paces to step over the whole universe and a third step that ends up on Bali's head. Thus did Vamana return the worlds to the gods.

Further reading: Cornelia Dimmitt and J. A. B. van Buitenen, *Classical Hindu Mythology: A Reader in the Sanskrit Puranas* (Philadelphia: Temple University Press, 1978); Clifford Hospital, *The Righteous Demon: A Study of Bali* (Vancouver: University of British Columbia Press, 1984).

Barry Long Foundation   *See* Long, Barry.

Basavanna (1106–1167 c.e.) *saint who helped found Virashaivism*

Basavanna was a saint devoted to Shiva and was the chief founder of the reformist Virashaiva or lingayat community. He was a social reformer who opposed temple ritual and the caste system in favor of an internal religious orientation.

Born in the village of Mangavalli in the state of Karnataka to parents who apparently died when he was young, he was raised by his grandparents, and later by foster parents. He became learned in

Sanskrit and appears to have had a Brahmanical initiation. Basavanna studied the VEDAS and was a devotee of Shiva from an early age, but he was also a political activist and social reformer. He believed that the caste divisions and ritualism of traditional Indian society should be abolished.

Basavanna became a powerful minister to a king, while establishing a new religious movement in which caste, class, and sex were disregarded and only devotion to the Lord was important. He rejected traditional ritualism; in place of temples and icons to Lord Shiva, every Virashaiva was required to wear the LINGAM, or sign of Shiva, around the neck. Basavanna's *vacanas* or poems were pure expressions of BHAKTI, or devotion, declaring that one's own body was the true temple of Shiva, not some stone shrine. Virashaivas decry all external religion in favor of the religion of the heart.

Further reading: K. Ishwaran, *Speaking of Basava: Lingayat Religion and Culture in South Asia* (Boulder, Colo.: Westview Press, 1992); L. M. Menezes and S. M. Angadi, trans., *Vacanas of Basavanna* (Sirigere: Annana Balaga, 1967); A. K. Ramanujan, *Speaking of Shiva* (London: Penguin Books, 1973).

Baul sect

A loosely organized sect originating in Bengal around the seventh century C.E., the Bauls sought escape from orthodox Hindu thought and ritual practice, which they deemed lifeless, seeking ecstasy through music and dancing. They are known for their unconventional manner, as indicated by their name: the Bengali word *baul* (Hindi: *baur*) is derived from the SANSKRIT *vatula*, meaning "mad," or *vyakula*, meaning "perplexed." Bauls are referred to as "madmen drunk with God." Songs are their unwritten scriptures, yet they do not record either the words or the music.

The original Baul devotees drew inspiration from several religions that flourished at the time

in Bengal. They adopted practices from TANTRISM, the non-dual or ADVAITA conception of the Absolute from VEDANTA, YOGA disciplines, elements of Sufi dance and music, and the emphasis on the love in the human heart found in VAISHNAVISM. To these, the Bauls added a tenet that each individual must remain free and individual, and each must become a divinized subtle being.

Central to the spiritual path of Bauls is their reverence for gurus. Each guru writes his own songs from his personal experience, so that most songs remain original and individual. Some songs have become common to the community and are repeated at yearly festivals, or *melas*, which are held in Bengal, near Shanti Niketan, the university founded by Rabindranath TAGORE (1861–1941). It was Tagore who took the Baul sect out of obscurity by collecting the words of many of their songs and many of their simple melodies. He felt that these creations by the Bauls expressed the highest truth in simple language.

Most Bauls are illiterate members of the poorer classes. Others are learned Brahmins who have been rejected by their caste, Muslims disaffected with orthodoxy, and Sufis who fear persecution from Islamic law. Baul groups are scattered throughout India but remain centered in Bengal.

Recently Baul musicians and dancers have begun to tour Europe and the United States to perform their songs.

Further reading: Charles Capwell, *The Music of the Bauls of Bengal* (Kent, Ohio: Kent State University Press, 1986); Surath Chandra Chakravarti, *Bauls: The Spiritual Vikings* (Calcutta: Firma KLM, 1980); Lizelle Reymond, *To Live Within: The Story of Five Years with a Himalayan Guru* (London: George Allen & Unwin. 1971).

Benares (Varanasi, Kashi)

Benares on the GANGES is the most visited pilgrimage destination in all of India. It is one of the seven primary pilgrimage cities in India, one of the 12 *jyotir* LINGAM (lingam of light) sites, and a SHAKTI PITHA site sacred to the Divine Mother. It is considered the most desirable place where a Hindu can die and be cremated, as it is understood that liberation from birth and rebirth is conferred upon a person by the holiness of the city. Myth says that the Ganges flows through the topknot of Shiva down to Earth; for many it is understood that those who bathe in it derive special blessings from Shiva.

At Benares any act of devotion whatsoever, be it the smallest offering, act of penance or charity, or chant, yields unlimited results. Benares has been known at different times as Varanasi or Kashi (the place of the supreme light). It has been a great center of Shiva worship in particular and has known more than 3,000 years of continuous habitation. Only a few buildings are left from before the 16th century, as Muslim armies from the 12th century destroyed nearly every temple there.

The city's primary Shiva shrine, the Vishwanath Temple, dates only from 1776, when it was rebuilt across the road from its original ancient location. The *jnana vapi,* or Well of Wisdom, is adjacent to the site of the original temple and is the ritual center of Benares. The well is said to have been dug by Shiva himself, and its waters carry the liquid form of JNANA, the light of insight.

Benares contains so many hundreds of shrines and temples that it is said a pilgrim would need all the years of his or her life to visit them all. Some of these temples are named after the great pilgrimage centers, in other parts of India: RAMESHVARAM, DVARAKA, Puri, and KANCHIPURAM. In this way, visiting Benares is tantamount to visiting all the major shrines and temples of India. Most pilgrims make only short visits of days or weeks to Benares, but there are also many thousands who see it as the last port of call of their earthly existence. There are nearly 100 cremation spots in the six-mile expanse of the Ganges at Benares.

A well-worn 50-mile pilgrimage path encircles the holy city; pilgrims generally take five days to complete the walk, visiting 108 shrines along the way. A second important Benares pilgrimage route takes two days to complete and has 72 shrines.

Bustling, dusty Benares was once an area of sylvan wilderness. Sages and saints such as BUDDHA, MAHAVIRA, and TULSIDAS all at one time or another prayed and meditated here. For centuries Benares may have been the most often-visited sacred place on the planet. In any case, for Hindus there is no holier city on Earth.

Further reading: Winand Callewaert and Rober Schilder, *Banaras: Vision of a Living Ancient Tradition* (New Delhi: Hemkunt Publishers, 2000); Diana Eck, *Banaras: City of Light* (New York: Columbia University Press, 1999).

Bernard, Pierre Arnold (1875–1955) *Western tantric teacher*

Born Peter Coons in Leon, Iowa, Pierre Bernard created the Tantrik Order in America, in New York City, in 1909, perhaps the first Hindu group in the United States founded by a Westerner.

As a young man, Bernard moved from Iowa to California, where he held odd jobs. At age 30 he met Mortimer Hargis, with whom he formed the Bacchante Academy in San Francisco to teach hypnotism and "soul charming," a term that referred to sexual practices. The earthquake of 1906 leveled the academy and Bernard moved east.

In 1909 Bernard founded the Tantrik Order in America and gave himself the name Oom the Omnipotent. He taught YOGA and tantric Hinduism, a branch of the religion that focuses on sexual energies and consciousness. In 1910 he was arrested on charges filed by two women in his group that he was conducting sexual orgies and was keeping women against their will. He was allowed to continue operating his institute but was kept under the eye of the local police. He became legal guardian of his half sister, Ora Ray Baker, later to become the wife of Hazrat Inayat Khan, founder of the Sufi Order.

Using the name Dr. Pierre Arnold Bernard, he created the New York Sanskrit College and opened a physiological institute. Around 1918, he married Blanche DeVries, a woman of some means in New York society and a cousin of Mary Baker Eddy, founder of the Church of Jesus Christ, Scientist. His wife provided an entrée for him into society circles, and some wealthy socialites, Ann Vanderbilt among them, became disciples.

In 1924, Bernard founded a center and an Oriental-Occult Library on his estate in Nyack, New York. His 70-acre property included a mansion that served as his headquarters and an adjacent Inner Circle Theatre, which contained a library of thousands of books on Eastern religion and the occult. Here he hosted gurus and other visiting teachers of religious and occult subjects. He became a prominent citizen, offering his estate to refugees from Nazi Germany. His nephew, Theos Bernard, lived at the Nyack estate and later attended Columbia University, where in 1944 he wrote a thesis on HATHA YOGA that has become a classic text.

A colorful and intriguing character, Bernard interpreted tantric practices in a manner uniquely his own. His claims of having attained a teaching degree in Hinduism in India are unsubstantiated. His frequent name changes and questionable credentials made him the object of ridicule in journalistic reports of the day, but he did gain an expertise in Hindu thought and practice that made him an important figure in the growth of interest in Hinduism in the United States, in part through his connections with spiritual leaders and occultists of his day.

Bernard died quietly after a brief illness on September 27, 1955, in Nyack, New York.

Further reading: Pierre Bernard, "In Re Fifth Veda." *International Journal of the Tantrik Order* American Edition (New York: Tantrik Press, 1990); Charles Boswell, "The Great Fume and Fuss Over the Omnipotent Oom," *True* (January 1965): 31–33, 86–91; Leslie Shepard, *Encyclopedia of Occultism and Parapsychology*, 2d ed., 3 vols. (Detroit: Gale Research, 1984–85).

Besant, Annie Wood (1847–1933) *English socialist and president of the Theosophical Society*

Annie Besant was an English socialist reformer who converted to THEOSOPHY after reading the works of H. P. BLAVATSKY. She became an influential figure in the growth of Theosophy as a worldwide movement and helped spread appreciation of Hinduism in the West.

Annie Wood was born in London to a middle-class Irish couple on October 1, 1847. She was raised after her father's death by her mother in a very religious environment. She followed convention by marrying a minister and schoolmaster, Frank Besant, in 1867. They had two children, but she left the marriage in 1893 and took the children with her in order to realize the ideals of her emerging progressivism. The couple was legally separated five years later.

Besant had begun to write while still with her husband; once separated she started to air her skeptical views in essays. She joined the National Secular Society and lectured on feminist issues. She joined forces with Charles Bradlaugh, the atheist freethinker, to found the Free-thought Publishing Company. In 1877, with Bradlaugh, she was arrested for selling birth control pamphlets in London's slums. They were convicted, but the verdict was overturned and the trial helped to liberalize public attitudes. In 1888 she coordinated a strike of unskilled young women laborers at a match factory, which shed light on cruel and unsafe labor practices. She soon established a reputation as an orator, skeptic, and advocate for women's rights.

During the 1880s, Besant became a friend of George Bernard Shaw, who considered her Britain's and perhaps Europe's greatest orator; developing an interest in socialism she joined the Fabian Society.

In 1888, she read Blavatsky's *Secret Doctrine,* an event that changed her life. She later said that she found in the revelations of Theosophy answers to questions that she had not found in socialism, free thought, or Christianity. She resigned from the National Secular Society, renounced socialism, and became an ardent spokesperson for Theosophy.

After Blavatsky's death in 1891, Besant became the powerful head of the Esoteric section of the Theosophical Society. After a tour of the United States, where she addressed the World Parliament of Religions in Chicago, she moved to India, which became her home and headquarters until her death. She succeeded H. S. Olcott as president of the Theosophical Society in 1907 and retained the office until her death in 1933; she presided over a time of rapid expansion of the society, after a period of stagnation.

In 1909 Besant organized the Order of the Star in the East, in order to prepare for Theosophy's predicted appearance of a world teacher, who would help all of humanity evolve to higher consciousness. When a young South Indian BRAHMIN boy was found near the Theosophy compound at Adyar, outside Madras (Chennai), she became convinced that he, J. KRISHNAMURTI, would be the instrument for the coming world teacher. After receiving considerable grooming for the role of Lord Maitreya, Krishnamurti abdicated the title and suspended the Order of the Star in the East. He continued to call Besant "mother," but he refused to accept the role of "world teacher" that she felt he embodied.

Although she had abandoned her socialist affiliations, Besant carried her social reform values wherever she went. In India, the Theosophical Society founded many schools in India, including some of the first in the country for women. Politically, she fought for Indian independence from British rule, and she was elected president of the Indian National Congress in 1917.

To Blavatsky's emphasis on Buddhism, Besant added an emphasis on Hinduism to the Theosophical corpus. She wrote with C. W. Leadbeater, a Theosophist who was also an Anglican priest and later bishop of the Liberal Catholic Church, about the gifts of Hinduism and the East to esoteric wisdom in the West. Besant died on September 21, 1933, at the Theosophy compound.

Further reading: O. Bennett, *Annie Besant* (London: Hamish Hamilton, In Her Own Time Series, 1988); A. W. Besant, *The Ancient Wisdom* (London: Theosophical Publishing House, 1910); ———, *Autobiography* (Adyar, India: Theosophical Publishing House, 1939); ———, *The Bhagavad Gita or the Lord's Song.* Translated by Annie Besant (Madras: Theosophical Publishing House, 1953); ———, *Esoteric Christianity* (New York: J. Lane, 1902); ———, *Theosophical Lectures* (Chicago: Theosophical Society, 1907); A. H. Nethercot, *The First Five Lives of Annie Besant* (London: RupertHart-Davis, 1960); Catherine L. Wessinger, *Annie Besant and Progressive Messianism (1847–1933)* (Lewiston, N.Y.: Edwin Mellen Press, 1988).

Bhadrabahu (c. 300 B.C.E.) *early Jain leader*

Bhadrabahu is revered by both DIGAMBARA and SHVETAMBARA Jains (*see* JAINISM). Both sects regard him as the last of the persons who knew all the early sacred texts of the Jain tradition.

Bhadrabahu was born in Pundravardhan in what is now Bangladesh, during the reign of Chandragupta Maurya, the great Indian king. According to the Digambara tradition he led a large group of his adherents from North India to Karnataka and thus introduced Jain tradition to South India. That tradition further recounts that on his return to Pataliputra (Patna) in the north, he found that there had been an official recension of the Jain scriptures; he and his monk followers refused to accept this "new" Jain canon. He also found that the northern monks had taken up unacceptable practices, especially the wearing of clothing, which is forbidden to Digambara (sky-clad) monks. Bhadrabahu and his adherents declared themselves to be the only true Jains.

Another Bhadrabahu (c. sixth century) was the author of the Shvetambara work KALPA SUTRA.

Further reading: Paul Dundas, The Jains (New York: Routledge, 1992); P. S. Jaini, Jaina Path of Purification (Delhi: Motilal Banarsidass, 1973).

Bhagavad Gita

Bhagavad Gita means "Song about God." It is a segment, dating from around 200 B.C.E., of the MAHABHARATA, the classic Sanskrit epic traditionally ascribed to VYASA. It has 18 chapters totaling approximately 700 verses. In the framework of a legendary battle, the poem presents a philosophy of life and states principles guiding the practices of YOGA.

The framework story begins when the hero, ARJUNA, asks his charioteer, KRISHNA, to pull the chariot up between the two battling armies. On one side are his own PANDAVAS who have the rightful claim to the kingship. On the other side are their cousins, the KAURAVAS, who now are usurpers. Seeing that he is about to go into battle with his own guru DRONA; his grandfather, BHISHMA; and many of his cousins, Arjuna's will fails and he sits down, not wanting to fight.

Krishna scolds Arjuna and insists that he go to battle; he then begins a lecture on the nature of reality. Krishna, it eventually becomes clear, is God himself, though he has taken a role here as charioteer. He outlines several yogas that will help Arjuna fight the battle of existence.

The first of the yogas is that of knowledge (JNANA), which involves insight into the Truth of Ultimate Reality, BRAHMAN. This practice involves meditative focus on the Ultimate as beyond all forms and categories. Next is the yoga of devotion (BHAKTI), which involves focus on God—Krishna himself, in this case—in a steady, yogic poise of consciousness involving surrender to the Divinity, the being that oversees the universe. The third yoga is that of action (KARMA). Krishna explains how one can act in the world yogically without

regard to the fruits of one's actions. Underlying all the three yogas is the fourth yoga, rajayoga, or the yoga of MEDITATION (dhyana), which must be practiced in order to do any of the others.

The Gita generally favors action in the world and opposes leaving the world to become a renunciant. In the Gita, renunciation is redefined as giving up the fruits of actions, not leaving the world to try to be actionless. The Gita also emphasizes devotion to the iconic divinity with form and characteristics, although it does not deny that some might pursue the path of realizing the transcendent brahman that is beyond characteristics and action.

The Gita often cites the importance of developing what is called "steady mind," which will prevent perturbation of mind and wrong conduct whatever course we choose to take. It must be emphasized that though the Gita unfolds against a backdrop of war, it is not to be considered a prowar tract. All its commentators from earliest times interpret the text metaphorically; it refers to anyone's battle against karma and for liberation from the cycle of birth and rebirth.

The Bhagavad Gita was the favorite text of Mohandas Karamchand GANDHI, the foremost proponent of nonviolence. Today the Gita is memorized and chanted as an aid to the realization of the essence of the yogas detailed therein. Ideally, the entire text is committed to memory and chanted daily.

Further reading: Sri Aurobindo, Essays on the Gita (Pondicherry: Sri Aurobindo Ashram, 1993); Swami Chinmayananda, trans., The Holy Geeta (Bombay: Central Chinmaya Mission Trust, 1968); S. N. Dasgupta, The History of Indian Philosophy, Vol. 2 (Delhi: Motilal Banarsidas, 1975); Suryakumari Dwarakadas and C. S. Sundaram, Bhagavadgita Bibliography (Chennai: Kuppuswami Sastri Research Institute, 2000); Eknath Easwaran, trans., The Bhagavad Gita for Daily Living (Petaluma, Calif.: Nilgiri Press, 1984); S. Radhakrishnan, trans., The Bhagavadgita (London: Aquarian, 1995); Robert N. Minor, Bhagavad-Gita: An Exegetical Commentary (New Delhi: Heritage, 1982); ———, Modern Indian Interpreters of the *Bhagavadgita* (Albany: State University of New York Press, 1986).

Bhagavan

Bhagavan in Sanskrit means "one who is glorious, illustrious, revered, divine, or holy." It is the most common word for "God" in Hinduism. In its sense of "holy" or "divine" it is also used as an honorific for gurus and divine personages, for example, Bhagavan Sri RAJNEESH.

Further reading: Thomas Hopkins, *Hindu Religious Tradition* (Encino, Calif.: Dickenson, 1971); Klaus Klostermeier, *Survey of Hinduism* (Albany: State University of New York Press, 1994).

Bhagavata Purana

The Bhagavata Purana is one of the 18 principal PURANAS of Indian tradition; it may well be the most popular of them all. *Bhagavata* means "that which pertains to god" (in this case, VISHNU, and more particularly his incarnation as KRISHNA); a purana is a work describing the actions and history of a divinity. The Bhagavata Purana then is the story about those who are devoted to God. The work is sometimes attributed to VYASA, author of the Mahabharata.

The Bhagavata Purana was probably composed in South India, as it makes reference to the devotional ALVARAS Vaishnavite saints of the Tamil country. There are 18,000 verses in this work, 332 chapters and 12 sections or books. The 10th section, the most popular, recounts the tales of Krishna's life in BRINDAVAN—his killing of demons, his childhood escapades, and his dalliances with the GOPIS or cowherd girls.

The work exalts BHAKTI or devotion to God as the highest of paths. Neither by knowledge alone (JNANA) nor by action can one reach the supreme, which requires only steadfast devotion. The poem agrees with those VEDANTA philosophers who see the supreme divinity as the embodiment of innumerable auspicious characteristics and see the world as real and a manifestation of the godhead. As do these philosophers, it equates the BRAHMAN (Ultimate Reality) and the ATMAN (Ultimate Self) of the UPANISHADS with Vishnu or Krishna.

According to the Bhagavata Purana, each individual soul is eternally distinct and real, even when basking in the full effulgence of God after liberation from birth and rebirth. Liberation gives the soul its place in heaven, Goloka, where Lord Krishna resides. Commentaries on the Bhagavata Purana are numerous; the Vedanta (teachers) MADHVA and VALLABHA both wrote full commentaries.

Further reading: Subhash Anand, *The Way of Love: The Bhagavat Doctrine of Bhakti* (New Delhi: Munshiram Manoharlal, 1996); Anant Pai, *Stories from the Bhagawat* (Mumbai: India Book House, 2000); James D. Redington, trans., *Vallabhacarya on the Love Games of Krishna* (Delhi: Motilal Banarsidass, 1983); T. S. Rukmani, *A Critical Study of the Bhagavata Purana with Special Reference to Bhakti.* Chowkhamba Sanskrit Series, vol. 77 (Varanasi: Chowkhamba Sanskrit Series Office, 1970); J. M. Sanyal, trans., *The Srimad-Bhagavatam of Krishna-Dwaipayana Vyasa,* 2d ed. 5 vols. (Calcutta: Oriental, 1964–65); Graham M. Schweig and Graham M., trans., *Dance of Divine Love: The Rasa Lila of Krishna from the Bhagavata Purana, India's Classic Sacred Love Story* (Princeton, N.J.: Princeton University Press, 2005).

Bhairava

Bhairava (frightful or terrible) is a fearsome manifestation of SHIVA, whose icon has long fangs. He is sometimes also called Kalabhairava or Kalaraja, Lord of Time (as KALI is seen to be the Mistress of Time), and is seen to control time and the world.

Bhairava's frightful nature emerged when Lord BRAHMA spoke to him arrogantly, and he severed Brahma's fifth upward-looking head with his fingernail. Because he had thus killed a BRAHMIN, the skull could not be removed from his hand, where it remained, until he was released from the curse that befalls one who kills a Brahmin.

Bhairava of the very dark complexion was forced to travel the Earth begging alms with the skull as begging bowl. It was he who wandered through the three worlds to arrive at the Deodar Forest where sages (RISHIS) dwelt with their wives. The sages did not recognize Shiva in this naked, fierce beggar, but he was irresistibly attractive to their wives. In a final act of defiance against the confounded *rishis*, Bhairava brandished his erect penis before the wives to their delight and passion (as he was the ruler of the universe). The *rishis* put a curse on him to lose his penis, which flew around the worlds like a missile, destroying everything in its path. Finally, they had to call upon the Great Goddess to offer her YONI or vagina to hold it in place and pacify it. This is the origin of the Shiva LINGAM, which is always depicted as a phallus held in an encircling *yoni*.

Further reading: Don Handelman and David Shulman, *Shiva in the Forest of Pines: An Essay on Sorcery and Self-Knowledge* (New Delhi: Oxford University Press, 2004); Stella Kramrisch, *The Presence of Shiva* (Princeton, N.J.: Princeton University Press, 1981); Wendy Doniger O'Flaherty, *Shiva the Erotic Ascetic* (Oxford: Oxford University Press, 1981).

Bhajan, Yogi (1929–2004) *Sikh guru*

Harbhajan Singh Puri was instrumental in establishing the Sikh religion in North America. The future guru was born on August 26, 1929, in what is now Pakistan to a family headed by a medical doctor. He spent a privileged youth in private schools (he attended a Catholic convent school) and summer retreats. At the age of eight he began training in yoga with an enlightened teacher, Sant Hazara Singh, who proclaimed Harbhajan a master of KUNDALINI yoga at the age of 16.

During the unrest of partition in 1947, the young Harbhajan led thousands of villagers from their residence near Lahore, Pakistan, to resettle in New Delhi. He went on to study comparative religion and Vedic philosophy and received a master's degree with honors in economics from Punjab University and a Ph.D. in communications psychology. He married Inderjit Kaur in 1952 and they had two sons. He entered Indian government service, employed in the internal revenue supervision and customs service.

In 1968 Harbhajan immigrated to the United States, via Canada, with a vision of introducing YOGA to the West. He announced that he had traveled to the West "to create teachers, not to gain students." A devoted SIKH, he helped legally incorporate the Sikh Dharma (order) in the United States in 1971. That year Sant Charan Singh, president of the governing body of Sikh Temples in India, named Harbhajan Siri Singh Sahib, Chief Religious and Administrative Authority for the Western Hemisphere. The Akal Takhat, the Sikh seat of religious authority in Amritsar, assigned him responsibility to create a Sikh ministry in the West. He redirected young people who were experimenting with drugs and altered states of consciousness to seek higher consciousness, pointing to their deep desire to realize holistic and liberating states of mind.

In 1969, Yogi Bhajan created the HEALTHY, HAPPY, HOLY ORGANIZATION (3HO) to integrate kundalini yoga, MEDITATION, compassionate philosophy, and healthy living. It was one of the most popular of the new religions in the United States in the 1970s and 1980s. He died on October 6, 2004.

Further reading: Yogi Bhajan, *Guide to Aquarian Pregnancy: Birth and Child Care through Yoga* (San Diego, Calif.: 3HO Foundation, 1977); Yogiji Harbhajan Singh Khalsa, *The Inner Workout Manual: Kundalini Yoga* (San Bernardino, Calif.: Borgo Press, 1990); Yogiji Harbhajan Singh Khalsa, *Kundalini Yoga for Youth and Joy* (San Bernardino, Calif.: Borgo Press, 1990); Yogiji Harbhajan Singh Khalsa and Harijot Kaur Khalsa, *Owners Manual for the Human Body: Kundalini Yoga* (Eugene, Oreg.: KIT Catalog 1993).

bhajans

Bhajans are Hindu devotional songs, sung to a chosen deity. They are often sung in gatherings, sometimes led by a teacher or guru. The songs praise the divinity, listing his or her aspects and virtues and recounting favored elements of his or her mythology. The songs are used to establish a closeness or communion between the singers and the god.

Bhajan and KIRTAN singing are forms of BHAKTI (devotion). They are aimed at focusing the consciousness on higher reality, in order to develop the steadiness of mind that is needed to deal with the troubles and difficulties of this life. They also are seen to purify the consciousness so that one can take a step toward ending one's cycle of birth and rebirth. Thus their purest goal is MOKSHA, liberation or release from that cycle.

Further reading: Pandit Jasraj, *Hussaini Kanra: Bhajan* (Sound recording) (San Anselmo, Calif.: Moment Records, 1993); Donald S. Lopez, *Religions of India in Practice* (Princeton, N.J.: Princeton University Press, 1995); Bhakti Vilas Tirtha Goswami Maharaj, ed., *Vaishnavism and Nam-Bhajan/ Thakur Bhaktivinode and Bhakti Siddhanta Saraswati Thakur* (Madras: Shri Gaudiya Math, 1968); *Shanti Anantam Bhajan Songbook* (Agoura, Calif.: Vedantic Center, 1983); M. S. Subbalakshmi, *Bhajan-Shri* (Sound recording) (Calcutta: EMI: His Master's Voice, 1985).

bhakti

Bhakti (SANSKRIT *bhaj*, to adore, honor, worship) is a central spiritual path in Hinduism, involving devotion to and service of the chosen deity.

Vedic tradition, the chief religious practice of Hinduism from around 1500 B.C.E. to roughly

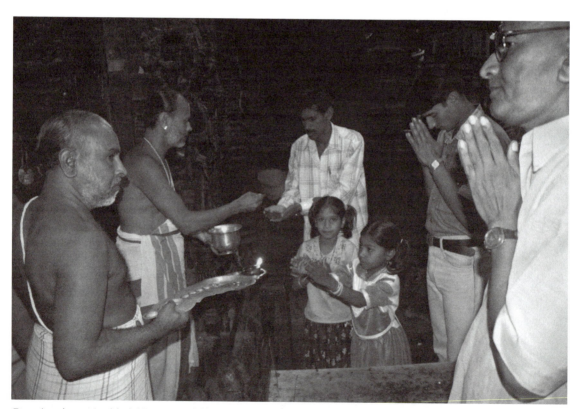

Devotional practice bhakti is a central feature of Hinduism. Here a Brahmin priest and devotees are at worship in Belur, Bengal. *(Gustap Irani)*

the start of the Common Era, relied on a ritual process of chanting and making offerings to various divinities. Compared with the later practice of bhakti, these divinities were not addressed with intimacy and a sense of connection; furthermore, they were never iconographically represented and were not generally visualized in human form; the humanity of the divinity became a very important element in later bhakti.

The devotional practices of bhakti are very old, probably originating with the non-ARYAN (thus non-Vedic) population. As the Aryans gradually spread beyond their original settlement in Northwest India and established cultural dominance over the indigenous peoples of India, they rather freely incorporated values and traditions from the local substratum. This influence began to show an obvious impact in the development of the bhakti path within Hinduism.

The Sanskrit text the BHAGAVAD GITA, written around 200 B.C.E., was the first true bhakti text in the Indian tradition, in that case focusing on the worship of KRISHNA. It depicts a very close, personal relationship with God, one with a human form and personality. However, bhakti is still seen as a restrained, austere practice that takes the form of a YOGA.

As bhakti began to emerge with full force in the extreme south of India beginning in the third century, the devotion to the gods VISHNU and SHIVA and to the Goddess became a passionate, emotional experience. Devotees such as the poet-saints who periodically emerged until the 17th or 18th century threw themselves into bhakti with complete abandon. The quintessential devotee took pride in being considered a mad person and would be often completely lost in ecstatic song and trance. One important reason why the bhakti movement eventually swept all India and transformed the face of Hinduism was that the songs of the saints were all in the local dialects and languages, not in the Sanskrit language of the priestly elite. These works were lovingly remembered and compiled by their followers.

Bhakti often involved PILGRIMAGE to and worship at sacred places where ICONS of the chosen deity could be found. The temple tradition of India developed on the basis of devotion to deities who took iconic shape in stone in temples the length and breadth of the country. Devotees yearned to see the deity and to have audience with him or her. This audience is referred to as DARSHAN, or "viewing," and is the most special and intimate aspect of the temple visit.

Further reading: Stephen P. Huyler, *Meeting God: Elements of Hindu Devotion* (New Haven, Conn.: Yale University Press, 1999); Klaus K. Klostermaier, *A Survey of Hinduism* (Albany: State University of New York Press, 1989); Donald S. Lopez, *Religions of India in Practice* (Princeton, N.J.: Princeton University Press, 1995); Donald N. Lorenzen, ed., *Bhakti Religion in North India: Community, Identity and Political Action* (Albany: State University of New York Press, 1995); A. C. Bhaktivedanta Swami Prabhupada, *The Nectar of Devotion: The Complete Science of Bhakti* (Los Angeles: Bhaktivedanta Book Trust, 1982); Karine Schomer and W. H. McLeod, ed., *Sants: Studies in a Devotional Tradition of India* (Delhi: Motilal Banarsidass, 1987); Karel Werner, *Love Divine: Studies in Bhakti and Devotional Mysticism* (Richmond, England: Curzon Press, 1993).

Bhaktivedanta, Swami A. C. Prabhupada

(1896–1977) *Vaishnavite guru and founder of the International Society for Krishna Consciousness*
Bhaktivedanta Swami played a major role in interpreting Vedanta for modern Western readers and in spreading the worship of Krishna outside India. For several decades his followers' chanting of the Hare Krishna mantra and their public distribution of literature became the face of Hinduism in the West.

Abhay Charan De was born in Calcutta on September 1, 1896, the son of a pious cloth merchant who would visit the Radha-Govinda Temple every day. When Abhay was four, his father gave him a small image of KRISHNA and taught him to worship the deity. Abjay entered Scottish Churches College in 1916. While still a student he entered into an arranged marriage with Padharani Satta in 1919; his wife never shared his devotional aspirations. He completed his college work but refused his degree, in response to Mohandas Karamchand GANDHI's call to boycott British goods.

While working as manager of a pharmaceutical company. De met Sri Srimad Bhaktisiddhanta Saraswati Goswami, head of the GAUDIYA MATH, an India-wide CHAITANYA-VAISHNAVITE religious movement, who became his spiritual master. In 1932 Sri Saraswati initiated De into the Gaudiya Math and gave him the name Abhay Charanaravinda, meaning "one who fearlessly takes shelter at the feet of the Lord." The GURU told him to prepare to spread the teachings of Krishna worship in the West, but De put aside the suggestion. After his guru's death two decades later, he wrote his first books: an *Introduction to the Geetopanishad* and the *Bhagavad Gita As It Is*. For these publications, a society called the Vaishnavites honored him with the title *Bhaktivedanta,* meaning "devotion to the knowledge of God." He left his wife and family in 1959 to study under another teacher, Acharya Goswami, at the Radha Damodara temple in BRINDAVAN (Krishna's birthplace), where he lived austerely in a small room.

In 1965 Bhaktivedanta visited the United States to proclaim the message of Krishna. In 1966 he founded the INTERNATIONAL SOCIETY FOR KRISHNA CONSCIOUSNESS (known as ISKCON), to propound the ancient tradition of Vaishnavism, as taught in the first half of the 16th century by the ecstatic Chaitanya, among modern seekers. The followers of ISKCON have made BHAKTI YOGA famous in the West through their ubiquitous chanting of the Hare Krishna mantra. The organization has published new translations of many ancient Vaishnavite scriptures, particularly the BHAGAVAD GITA and the BHAGAVATA PURANA.

The movement became one of the most prominent of the alternative religions to emerge during the 1970s in America, from which it has spread to every continent. Before his death, Srila Prabhupada (an honorific) saw the building of many temples, children's schools, rural communities, and major cultural centers around the world. Since his death, the movement has diminished in size and has fragmented.

On July 9, 1977, Bhaktivedanta Swami appointed 11 of his senior assistants to act as officiating priests (*ritviks*) to initiate all future ISKCON members on his behalf. After his death at Brindavan on November 14 that year, the appointees claimed they were in fact chosen as successor gurus, causing confusion and controversy within the movement. ISKCON members believe that Bhaktivedanta Swami still exerts his spiritual influence on anyone who follows his teachings, and that he remains a highly empowered devotee of their God, Krishna. Effigies of Bhaktivedanta Swami are installed in all ISKCON temples.

Today, in additon to ISKCON, a reform movement, the INTERNATIONAL SOCIETY FOR KRISHNA CONSCIOUSNESS REVIVAL MOVEMENT (IRM), carries on the teaching of Bhaktivedanta Swami.

Further reading: A. C. Swami Prabhupada Bhaktivedanta, *Bhagavad-Gita As It Is* (New York: ISKCon, 1972); ———, *KRSNA, The Supreme Personality of Godhead,* 3 vols. (New York: Bhaktivedanta Book Trust, 1970); ———, *The Science of Self-Realization* (New York: Bhaktivedanta Book Trust, 1977); Steven J. Gelberg, ed., *Hare Krishna, Hare Krishna* (New York: Grove Press, 1983); Satsvarupa dasa Goswami, *Srila Prabhupada-lilamrta: A Biography of His Divine Grace A. C. Bhaktivedanta Swami Prabhupada,* 3 vols. (Los Angeles: Bhaktivedanta Book Trust, 1980–83); J. Stillson Judah, *Hare Krishna and the Counterculture* (New York: John Wiley & Sons, 1974).

Bharat (Bharata)

Bharat (*Bharata* or *Bhaarata* in Sanskrit) is the Hindi name for India and the official name that the country adopted at independence. Legend traces the name to Bharata, the eponymous chief who headed the tribe from which all the people of India are said to descend and who gave his name to the MAHABHARATA. *Bharata* thus means "the homeland of those descended from Bharata."

See also RAMAYANA.

Further reading: R. C. Majumdar et al., *The History and Culture of the Indian People,* 11 vols. (London: G. Allen & Unwin, 1951–69); F. E. Pargiter, *The Purana Text of the Dynasties of the Kali Age* (Oxford: Oxford University Press, 1913).

Bharata   *See* RAMAYANA.

Bharata Natyam

Bharata Natyam is one of the oldest dance forms of India. It has been sustained in the temples and courts of southern India since ancient times. Its 108 poses are found carved on the walls of the huge gateway of the CHIDAMBARAM temple in Tamil Nadu. In the 19th century Bharata Natyam was codified and documented as a performing art by four brothers known as the Tanjore Quartet, whose musical compositions form most of the Bharata Natyam repertoire even today.

The dance was handed down from generation to generation under the DEVADASI system, in which women were dedicated to temples to serve the deity as dancers and musicians. These highly talented artists and their male gurus kept the art alive until the early 20th century, although the *devadasis* were by now no longer considered respectable. At that time, a renewal of interest in India's cultural heritage prompted the educated elite to rediscover it. The revival of Bharata Natyam by pioneers such as E. Krishna Iyer and Rukmini Devi Arundale drew the dance out of the temples and onto the stage. It did not cease, however, to be a dance devoted to the divinities.

Contemporary Bharata Natyam is based on solo dances with musical accompaniment, including singers and percussion. The dance unfolds from a base stance with the body in a lowered position with knees akimbo. From this stance the legs are moved outward rhythmically, beating tempo in play with the percussion. Most performances include a "pure dance" aspect, but hand and facial gestures (MUDRAS) are also important; they communicate, in a coded pantomime, the story being told. The stories are almost always about the gods SHIVA and VISHNU (in his various incarnations) and their wives and families. The narrative plays on familiar stories that almost always express a devotional sentiment; it is a form of choreographed worship.

Today Bharata Natyam is one of the most popular and widely performed Indian dance styles; it is practiced by male and female dancers all over India. Degree courses covering the practice and theory of Bharata Natyam are at last available at major universities of India. Important Bharata Natyam dancers of the 20th century revival include Balasaraswati, sometimes thought of as the last *devadasi;* Rukmini Devi Arundale, and Yamini Krishnamurti.

Further reading: Malati Iyengar et al., *Dance and Devotion: A Handbook on Bharatanatyam Dance and Traditional Trayers for Students Pursuing Indian Classical Dance* (Sherman Oaks, Calif.: Rangoli Foundation for Art & Culture, 2004), R. Kalarani, *Bharatanatyam in Tamilnadu, after* A.D. *1200* (Madurai: J. J., 2004); Sandhya Purecha, *Theory and Practice of Angikabhinaya in Bharatanatyam* (Mumbai: Bharatiya Vidya Bhavan, 2003).

Bharati, Baba Premanand (d. 1914)
pioneer Hindu leader in the United States
Baba Premanand Bharati was among the small group of Hindu leaders who entered the United States in the decades after the World's Parliament of Religions in 1893. He founded the Krishna Samaj in New York City soon after the start of the new century.

Born Surendranath Mukerji in India, Bharati led a life prior to his arrival in the United States in 1902 that is little known. He was a devotee of Krishna and followed a form of Vaishnavite BHAKTI YOGA similar to that popularized in the 1970s by the INTERNATIONAL SOCIETY FOR KRISHNA CONSCIOUSNESS. He advocated the repetition of the Hare Krishna mantra as a means of gaining release from the wheel of reincarnation and gaining enlightenment.

Bharati first worked in New York City, where he organized the Krishna Samaj. He lectured along the East Coast for several years and then moved to Los Angeles, where he built a temple and developed a youthful and loyal following. After only a few years, in 1909, he returned to India, where he died in 1914, still a relatively young man.

In the years after his death, Bharati was condemned by American nativists such as Elizabeth Reed, who were mobilizing public support for the Asian Exclusion Act, which passed in 1917. At about that time the Krishna Samaj was shut down. However, Bharati's followers later formed several other organizations with similar missions, including the Order of Loving Service, active only in the 1930s, and the AUM Temple of Universal Truth, which continued to operate into the 1980s, reprinting Bharati's writings in their periodicals and circulating his picture a half-century after his death.

Further reading: Baba Premanand Bharati, *American Lectures* (Calcutta: Indo-American Press, n.d.); ———, *Shree Krishna* (New York: Krishna Samaj, n.d.); Elizabeth A. Reed, *Hinduism in Europe and America* (New York: G. P. Putnam's Sons, 1914).

Bharatiya Janata Party (BJP)

The Bharatiya Janata Party (BJP), Peoples Party of India, is one of the largest political parties in India, serving as the governing party on the state and federal levels at various times in recent years.

The BJP is the political wing of the old RASHTRIYA SVAYAM SEVAK SANGH (RSS), the National Organization for Self-help. It was formed as a separate party in 1980 after internal differences within the Janata Party resulted in the collapse of its government in 1979. BJP held the prime ministership of India from 1998 to 2004 under the leadership of Atal Bihari Bajpayee. In 2004 it was defeated in parliamentary elections by a coalition led by the Congress Party.

The Bharata Janata Party considers itself to be a party of HINDU NATIONALISM; its ideology is called Hindutva, defined not in terms of the Hindu religion but as Indianness. The party points to the original meaning of the word Hindu, coined by Arab conquerors to refer to all the people living in India. However, critics have labeled the BJP a Hindu fundamentalist or even a Hindu fascist party.

The BJP rose to prominence during the turmoil surrounding the Babri Masjid Mosque in the Uttar Pradesh city of AYODHYA. This mosque was built in 1528 C.E. on a site claimed to be the birthplace of RAMA, an AVATAR of Visnu. During the 1940s RSS members erected an image of Rama in the mosque, and the government later sealed off the mosque. During the 1980s the RSS began staging violent protests against its very existence. Lal Krishnan Advani, the leader of the BJP and a leader in the VISHVA HINDU PARISHAD (World Hindu Council), was indicted on several occasions for leading the protests. This mosque was destroyed in 1992 by RSS activists, prompting nationwide riots that killed 3,000 people.

In 2006 BJP was voted out of office to a great extent because of the Gujarat violence of 2003, when 3,000 Muslims were killed, for which the BJP chief minister, Narendra Modi, was held responsible.

Further reading: Gwilym Beckerlegge and Anthony Copley, eds. *Saffron and Seva (Hinduism in Public and Private)* (New York: Oxford University Press, 2003); Chetan Bhat, *Hindu Nationalism: Origins, Ideologies, and Modern Myths* (Oxford: Oxford University Press, 2001); Blom Thomas Hanson. *The Saffron Way: Democracy and Nationalism in Modern India.* (Princeton, N.J.: Princeton University Press, 1999); Martin E. Mary and R. Scott Appleby, eds., *Religion, Ethnicity, and Self Identity: Nations in Turmoil* (Hanover, N.H.: University Press of New England, 1997); Peter van der Veer, *Religious Nationalism, Hindus and Muslims in India* (Berkeley: University of California Press, 1994).

Bhartrihari (c. fourth or fifth century)
grammarian and philosopher

Bhartrihari was a philosopher of language whose work was seminal in the development of the Indian theories of language and of MANTRA. There are several extant accounts of his life, but none seem to have a historical basis. He was primarily known as a grammarian, but his works had great philosophical impact as well.

Bhartrihari developed a philosophy that came to be known as "word ADVAITA," or non-dualism, based on the notion that the word (*shabda*) is the transcendent reality. His idea of "Shabda BRAHMAN," or Ultimate Reality, as the basis of all language, broke the barrier between grammar and philosophy. He is best known for his work *Vakyapadiya* (Treatise on words and sentences), which formulates the *sphota* theory of linguistic utterance, much debated in successive times. Bhartrihari maintained that the study of Sanskrit grammar alone could cause one to attain liberation from birth and rebirth.

Further reading: Sebastian Alackpally, *Being and Meaning: Reality and Language in Bhartrihari and Heidegger* (Delhi: Motilal Banarsidass, 2002); Harold Coward, *Bhartrihari* (Boston: Twayne, 1976); Gayatri Rath, *Linguistic Philosophy in Vakyapadiya* (Delhi: Bharatiya Vidya Prakashan, 2000).

Bhaskara (c. ninth century C.E.) *Vedantic philosopher*

Bhaskara was one of the most important philosophers of VEDANTA. He accepts the notions of non-duality—the unity of reality—as argued by the earlier SHANKARA, but does not accept their notion that the phenomenal universe, the everyday world, is illusory. He instead argues that the universe is a real evolute of the Supreme Reality BRAHMAN, regarded not as a person but as an entity. Only one of his books is extant, a commentary on the Vedantic text the VEDANTA SUTRA.

Further reading: S. N. Dasgupta, *A History of Indian Philosophy*. Vol. 3 (Delhi: Motilal Banarsidass, 1975); A. B. Khanna, *Bhaskaracarya: A Study with Special Reference to His Brahmasutrabhasya* (Delhi: Amar Granth, 1998).

Bhavabhuti (early eighth century C.E.) *Sanskrit playwright*

One of the greatest authors in Indian literature, Bhavabhuti is most famous for his three surviving Sanskrit dramas: *Mahaviracharita* (Adventures of that great hero Rama), *Uttararamacharita* (The later adventures of Rama), and *Malatimadhava* (The story of Malati and Madhava). *Mahaviracharita* tells with considerable originality the full story of RAMA from his birth to the defeat of his enemy RAVANA. The *Uttararamacharita* is a story of the children of Lord Rama as they grew up in the forest, a story not told in the original RAMAYANAS. *Malatimadhava* is basically a romance.

Further reading: Jan Gonda, ed., *A History of Indian Literature*. Vol. 1 (Wiesbaden: Otto Harrassowitz, 1976); Chittenjoor Kunhan Raja, *Survey of Sanskrit Literature* (Bombay: Bharatiya Vidya Bhavan, 1962).

Bhave, Vinoba (1885–1982) *leader in the Indian independence movement*

Vinoba Bhave, a prominent nonviolent leader of the Indian independence movement, was a prolific popular writer and a tireless organizer for land redistribution and social reform. He continued to agitate on behalf of Gandhian social values in the decades after independence.

Vinayak Narahari Bhave was born on September 11, 1885, to a Brahmin family in the village of Gagode in Maharashtra. Vinoba (an affectionate nickname) studied the works of Maharashtra's saints and philosophers as a boy. He had a passion for mathematics, but as had Sri RAMAKRISHNA before him, he seemed uninterested in the ordinary course of education. He spent two years in college dissatisfied and adrift. Early in 1916, on his way to Bombay (Mumbai) to appear for the intermediate examination, he threw his school and college certificate into a fire and decided to change course for BENARES (Varanasi), the Hindu holy city, to study Sanskrit.

At Benares, Vinoba encountered the views of Mohandas Karamchand GANDHI. Enthusiastic about Gandhi's ideas of uplifting the poor and purity of purpose he joined Gandhi's ASHRAM at Sabarmati near Ahmedabad in Gujarat state. At Gandhi's request he took charge of the ashram at Wardha in Maharashtra in 1921. In 1923 he began to publish the monthly *Maharashtra Dharma* in the regional Marathi language, to which he contributed articles on Indian philosophy, including popular studies on the *Abhangas* of the poet-saint TUKARAM. Later on, the monthly became a weekly and continued to be published for three years.

On December 23, 1932, Vinoba moved to Nalwadi (a village about two miles from Wardha), where he tried to implement his idea of supporting himself by spinning. When he grew ill in 1938, he moved to what he called Paramdham Ashram in Paunar, which remained his headquarters. Vinoba was heavily involved in the freedom movement throughout this period. In 1923, he was jailed for several months at Nagda and Akola for taking a prominent part in agitation at Nagpur. In 1925, he was sent by Gandhi to Vykon in Kerala to supervise the entry of the Harijans (Dalits, or untouchables) to the temple. In 1932, he was jailed for six months for raising his voice against British rule. In 1940, he was selected by Gandhi as the first person to do "Truth Force"

(*satyagraha*), Gandhi's nonviolent method of social action, on his own.

Vinoba was jailed three times during 1940–41 for successively longer terms. He became known nationally when Gandhi selected him for individual action, introducing him in a statement on October 5, 1940. Vinoba took part in the Quit India movement of 1942, for which he was jailed for three years at Vellore and Seoni.

Jail for Vinoba had become a place for reading and writing. He saw the proofs of his book *Gitai* (a Marathi translation of the BHAGAVAD GITA) in the Dhulia jail, where he lectured on the Gita to his jailed colleagues; the talks were collected by Sane Guruji and later published as a book. In Nagpur jail he wrote *Swarajya Shastra* (the treatise of self rule) and completed a collection of the *bhajans* (religious songs) of the saints Gyaneshwar (*see* JNANESHVARA), Eknath and Namdev. His popular books eventually treated many diverse topics in religion, philosophy, education, and the common good.

In March 1948, Gandhi's followers and workers met at Sevagram, to discuss the idea of Sarvodaya Samaj (Society for the uplift of all). Vinoba got busy with activities to soothe the wounds of partition of the nation. In the beginning of 1950, Vinoba started several idealistic reform movements.

In 1951 Vinoba launched the activity for which he became most famous, the Bhudan (Gift of the Land) movement. For the next 13 years he walked from place to place around the country asking large landowners and villages to offer land to the poor, to help bridge the great divide between the landed and landless. His efforts yielded surprising success by the time he returned to Paunar on April 10, 1964.

Over the following several years he continued in his travels, now campaigning against the various divisions within Indian society: caste, language, and class. In 1970, he announced his decision to stay in one place. He observed a year of silence from December 25, 1974, to December 25, 1975.

In 1976, he undertook a fast to stop the slaughter of cows. His spiritual pursuits intensified as he withdrew from his practical work. He passed away on November 15, 1982, at his ashram.

Vinoba's contribution to the history of the nonviolent movement remains significant. All his life he campaigned for "people's government," according to the Gandhian principle of extreme decentralization. He believed, as Gandhi did, that government and the economy should be built from the village up, not from the capital city down. Though his idealistic campaigns may have fallen short of their goals, all who encountered Vinaba saw a generous, committed, spiritually directed person. He inspired a whole generation. As a sign of respect for him and his spiritual accomplishment, Vinoba Bhave was referred to most commonly as ACHARYA, "the learned one."

Further reading: S. R. Bakshi and Sangh Mittra, *Saints of India* (New Delhi: Criterion, 2002); Verinder Grover, *Political Thinkers of Modern India* (New Delhi: Deep & Deep Publications, 1990–93); Michael W. Sonnleitner, *Vinoba Bhave on Self-Rule and Representative Democracy* (New Delhi: Promilla, 1988); Marjorie Sykes, trans., *Moved by Love: The Memoirs of Vinoba Bhave* (Hyderabad: Sat Sahitya Sahayogi Sangh, 1994).

bhavyatva   See JAINISM.

bhedabheda

Bhedabheda is a term used in some Vedantic philosophies to describe the relation between the individual self and the divinity. *Bheda* means "difference," *abheda* means "nondifference"; together the term refers to things that are different and not different at the same time. This school views the individual self as nondifferent (*abheda*) from the divinity, while recognizing that in certain respects the divinity is different from the individual self (for example, regarding its supremacy over the universe).

This point of view was expounded by BHASKARA and by the CHAITANYA school, whose approach is referred to as *achintya bhedabheda*. NIMBARKA's school refers to itself formally as Dvaitadvaita, "duality and non-duality," a different expression of the same concept, although it too is sometimes called *bhedabheda*.

Further reading: Madan Mohan Agrawal, *Essence of Vaisnavism: Philosophy of Bhedabheda* (Delhi: Ajanta, 1992); Dasgupta, Surendranath. *A History of Indian Philosophy*, 5 vols. (Delhi: Motilal Banarsidass, 1975); Swami Tapasyananda, *Bhakti Schools of Vedanta (Lives and Philosophies of Ramanuja, Nimbarka, Madhva, Vallabha and Chaitanya.)* (Madras: Sri Ramakrishna Math, 1990).

Bhima

Bhima (literally fearsome or terrible) is the second of the five PANDAVA brothers, whose story is told in the great epic MAHABHARATA.

The five Pandavas were all born of the same mother, KUNTI, with different gods as their fathers. That Bhima's father was the wind god VAYU explains his violence, temerity, and quickness to anger. He is also known for overweening pride and gluttony. Bhima was prodigiously strong and a formidable, undefeatable wrestler.

From childhood, Bhima faced an angry rival in his cousin DURYODHANA, who persistently plotted to usurp the kingdom that rightfully belonged to the sons of PANDU. One time Duryodhana poisoned Bhima and threw him into the GANGES. This action backfired: the poison was neutralized by the snake-people or NAGAS who lived in the river, who also gave Bhima a magic potion to make him superstrong. When Duhshana, one of the Kaurava sons, tried to disrobe DRAUPADI, the wife of the Pandavas, Bhima angrily vowed that he would one day kill Duryodhana and drink the blood of Duhshasana, a vow he eventually fulfilled. Bhima married the demoness Hidimba and fathered a son with her named Ghatokacha, who became a fierce fighter in the war with the KAURAVAS. In the final battle Bhima struck Duryodhana below the waist; he was forever labeled an unfair fighter on this account.

Further reading: J. A. B. van Buitenen, *The Mahabharata,* Vol. 1, *The Book of the Beginnings,* Vol. 2., *The Book of the Assembly Hall,* Vol. 3., *The Book of Virata and the Book of Effort* (Chicago: University of Chicago Press, 1973–78); P. C. Roy, trans., *The Mahabharata of Krishna-Dwaipayana Vyasa,* 12 vols. (Calcutta: Bhavata Karyalya Press, 1888–96).

Bhishma

Bhishma, "the terrible," is one of the most important characters in the great epic MAHABHARATA. He was the son of the river goddess Ganga (*see* GANGES) and the first son of the king Shantanu. In his old age, Shantanu wished to take another wife, Satyavati, but the woman insisted that any son of hers become king. As a devoted son Bhishma thereupon took a vow that he would never take the throne; as a wise man, he also vowed never to take a wife or father children.

Bhishma's efforts to obtain wives for Satyavati's son Vichitravirya proved his undoing. When he seized a woman named Amba as a potential bride, she begged to be returned to her country to marry another man, and Bhishma released her. However, her chosen love rejected her, and she returned to Bhishma. This time he refused to marry her to Vichitravirya. Enraged, Amba vowed to kill Bhishma one day, although he had earned the boon that he could not be killed without his consent. Amba angrily haunted the Earth, returning in male form as Shikhandi to fight Bhishma in the great war. Because of her presence Bhishma was killed in that battle, as he resigned himself to death.

Bhishma's half brother Vichitravirya failed to produce an heir; after his death his widows Ambika and Ambalika needed someone to father their children. Bhishma learned of another half brother, VYASA, the "author" (or compiler) of the Mahabharata. Vyasa was a renunciant, but he consented to couple with the two women. They bore PANDU and DHRITARASHTRA, the progenitors of the two sets of cousins whose war over the land of the Kurus is the subject of the great epic. Thus, Bhishma is related through his father to both sides in the conflict. He is called, therefore, great-uncle to them, though he is not their direct progenitor.

Since Dhritarashtra was blind and Pandu died when his children were very young, Bhishma became a father figure to both the PANDAVAS and the KAURAVAS. In the great battle Bhishma became the general for the Kaurava side, the side of the usurpers. He was mortally wounded when ARJUNA stepped out from behind Shikandhi (Amba reincarnated) to shoot him. He lingered for 58 days before dying, giving discourses to YUDHISHTHIRA that make up the majority of the Shantiparvan section of the Mahabharata. A chapter of the Mahabharata called Bhishmaparvan recounts his role in the story.

Further reading: Swami Veda Bharati, *Introducing Mahabharata Bhishma, Together with an English Translation of the Bhishma-Stava-Raja* (Rishikesh: Swami Rama Sadhaka Grama, 2002); J. A. B. van Buitenen, trans., *The Mahabharata,* Vol. 1, *The Book of the Beginnings,* Vol. 2, *The Book of the Assembly Hall,* Vol. 3, *The Book of Virata and the Book of Effort* (Chicago: University of Chicago Press, 1973–78); P. C. Roy, trans., *The Mahabharata of Krishna-Dwaipayana Vyasa,* 12 vols. (Calcutta: Bharata Karyalaya Press, 1888–96).

Bhubaneshwar

Bhuvaneshwar (Lord of the Worlds) is an ancient city named for SHIVA that now serves as the capital of the southern Indian state of Orissa. It is famous for its many temples, mostly dedicated to the god Shiva, all built in the Kalinga style of the region. Most characteristic of this type of architecture are the soaring, tapering towers that are decorated so as not to interrupt their straight lines. Most temples in Bhubaneshwar were built between

750 and 1250 C.E.; the most famous is Lingaraja, a temple to Shiva, or Tribhuvaneshvara (Ruler of the Three Worlds), built around 1100. Its tower is over 100 feet high.

Further reading: Department of Tourism, Government of Orissa, *Tourist Map of Bhubaneshwar* (Bhubaneshwar: The Circle, 1986); P. R. Ramachandra Rao, Bhuvanesvara Kalinga Architecture (Hyderabad: Akshara, 1980).

bija mantra

The concept of a *bija* (seed) MANTRA, originally derived from TANTRA, is widely employed in every sect of Hinduism. A *bija* is a short mantra, usually of one syllable, which is understood to be the visible or audible form of a deity. A *bija mantra* ends with the letter *m*. Examples are *Aim* for SARASVATI, *Shrim* for LAKSHMI, *Krim* for KALI, and *Gam* for GANESHA. It the tantric tradition such mantras are given to initiates only. In KUNDALINI YOGA there are *bija mantras* for each of the CHAKRAS; they are recited in order to raise the *kundalini,* the divine serpent energy coiled at the base of the spine.

Further reading: Harish Johari, *Tools for Tantra* (Rochester, Vt.: Destiny Books, 1986); Niramala Singha Kalasi, *Bija Mantra Darshana* (Vancouver, B.C.: Kalsi Technologies, 1996); Shree Rajneesh, *Seeds of Revolution: 120 Immortal Letters.* Translated by T. V. Parameshvar (Bombay: Life Awakening Movement, 1972).

bindu

The *bindu* (drop or dot) is an esoteric concept denoting the spaceless, timeless point that is the source of all manifestation. It also can denote the silent point that is the source of all sacred sound. Most YANTRAS, or ritual designs that denote particular divinities, have a dot or *bindu* at their center. Sometimes the ritual or devotional dot on the forehead (*see* FACIAL MARKINGS) is considered to represent the *bindu*. In that form the *bindu* may be seen as the infinitely dense point of consciousness out of which the universe developed. The Sanskrit writing system uses a dot where the *bindu* can be taken to represent the individual soul.

Further reading: *From Bindu to Ojas* (San Cristobal, New Mexico: Lama Foundation, 1970); Swami Pratyagatmanananda Saraswati and Sir John Woodroffe, *Sadhana for Self-Realization: Mantras, Yantras and Tantras* (Madras: Ganesh, 1963); Sir John Woodroffe, *Introduction to Tantra Shastra,* 2d ed. (Madras: Ganesh, 1952).

Birla Mandir

One of the first temples built in modern India by industrialists to celebrate their faith is the Birla Mandir, built in 1938 by G. D. Birla. Appropriate to the status of his family as one of the most wealthy in India the temple is dedicated to LAKSHMI, goddess of prosperity, and Lord VISHNU, her husband. It is called the Lakshmi Narayan Temple. The temple was opened by Mohandas Karamchand GANDHI with the specific proviso that there would be no caste restriction in regard to entry. At that time (and even to some extent today) Dalit (untouchables) were barred from entering temples.

A special characteristic of the temple is that it is explicitly (in a plaque at the front of the temple) open to people of any faith or social class; the inner carvings and statuary also pay tribute to the Buddhists, Jains (*see* JAINISM), and Sikhs (*see* SIKHISM), as well as to the many Hindu gods.

The external surface of the temple is made to resemble Delhi's prolific Mughal architecture (c. 1500–1800 C.E.); it is made of red sandstone decorated with marble. As is any temple it is decorated with many carvings showing scenes from Indian myths. The ICONS of the temple were made by specialists from BENARES (Varanasi). There were 101 experts employed in its construction, led by a learned specialist, Vishvanath Shasti. The temple was built in Orissan style, which features high, curved turrets that show a ribbed motif at the top of the temple tower.

Birla Mandir, a temple devoted to Vishnu, is an example of a modern Hindu temple in Delhi, India. *(Constance A. Jones)*

The highest tower of the temple is 160 feet. It is eastward facing with a long stairway upward that leads to the platform in which the inner sanctum is situated. The inner sanctum contains Goddess Lakshmi and Lord Narayana. Other shrines display Lord SHIVA, GANESHA, and HANUMAN. In a northern section is a shrine to KRISHNA.

Behind the temple there is a spacious area that children love containing a stone version of the chariot that Krishna and Arjuna rode in the MAHABHARATA. Several small rock temples are also found there. Included is a statue of G. D. Birla himself, facing the back of his great temple. The temple is visited by thousands of people every day.

Further reading: M. L. Gupta, *Performance Appraisal: The Birlas* (Jaipur: University Book House, 2003);

Medha M. Kudasiya, *The Life and Times of G. D. Birla* (New Delhi: Oxford University Press, 2003).

Blavatsky, Helena Petrovna Hahn (1831–1891) *cofounder of the Theosophical Society*

Better known by her initials, H.P.B., Helena Blavatsky was one of the most influential 19th-century writers in the fields of Theosophy and the occult. As cofounder of the Theosophical Society and frequent visitor to India, she also provoked wide popular interest in the religious traditions of India.

Born in Ekaterinoslav, Russia (now Dnepropetrovsk, Ukraine), on July 30, 1831, Blavatsky grew up in an affluent Russian family in which the occult and supernatural were not unknown.

As a teenager, she did automatic writing. Her mother died when Blavatsky was 12 years old and she went to live with her grandfather. At 16 she married General N. V. Blavatsky; however, claiming that marriage did not accommodate her "free spirit," she left her husband and took residence in Constantinople.

The trip to Turkey was the start of almost two decades of extensive travel, taking her to Egypt, England, India, and (it was claimed) Tibet. She traveled around the world twice in the decade 1851–61, continuing her investigations in the occult, mediumship, and spiritualism. She founded a spiritualist society in 1871 in Cairo, but the organization failed almost immediately as a result of some members' assumptions that H.P.B. had produced occult phenomena fraudulently.

H.P.B. arrived in New York in 1873 and quickly became familiar with American spiritualism. She met the Eddy brothers, mediums who conducted materialization seances. While visiting Vermont to demonstrate her own abilities at materialization along with the Eddy brothers, she met Henry Steel Olcott. In 1875, she and Olcott were joined by the lawyer William Q. Judge to found the Theosophical Society in New York City. She began to research and write her first book, *Isis Unveiled*, published in 1877.

To H.P.B., Theosophy superseded spiritualism. Whereas spiritualism claimed contact with spirits of the ordinary dead, she contacted the masters or *mahatmas*, teachers of occult wisdom who resided in elevated planes. She appeared to receive messages on paper from the *mahatmas*, which arrived, as if from the sky or from within a specially constructed cabinet, at the Theosophical headquarters. The source of the "letters from the *mahatmas*" continues to be debated—were they created by H.P.B. or delivered from the psychic realm?

H.P.B. and Olcott moved to India in 1878. The following year they began publishing *The Theosophist* magazine. A donation of land at Adyar near Madras (Chennai) in 1882 allowed them to establish a center, which still conducts education programs and retreats for members of the Theosophical Society.

After securing the land for the Theosophical Society, H.P.B. returned to London, where in 1884 she demonstrated her powers before the Society for Psychical Research. The viewers were impressed. However, her assistant in India, Emma Cutting Coulomb, destroyed this favorable impression by charging that H.P.B.'s abilities were fraudulent. In 1885, the society commissioned Richard Hodgson to investigate the charges. His report concluded that she was indeed an accomplished fraud.

While attempting to live down the scandal, H.P.B. took up residence in Germany after 1885 and returned to London in 1887. Her major work, *The Secret Doctrine*, was written there and published in 1889. It remains one of the most influential occult works to appear in the West. Blavatsky died in England on May 8, 1891. Her most famous disciple, Annie BESANT, who became a convert to THEOSOPHY after reading H.P.B.'s work, succeeded her as head of the Theosophical Society.

Further reading: Blavatsky, H. P., *Collected Writings*, 2 vols. (Wheaton, Ill.: Theosophical Press, 1950–1991); ———, *Isis Unveiled* (New York: J. W. Bouton, 1877); ———, *The Key to Theosophy* (London: Theosophical Publishing Society, 1889); ———, *The Secret Doctrine: The Synthesis of Science, Religion and Philosophy* (London: Theosophical Publishing Company, 1888); Robert S. Ellwood, *Alternative Altars: Unconventional and Eastern Spirituality in America* (Chicago: University of Chicago Press, 1979); Iverson L. Harris, *Mme. Blavatsky Defended* (San Diego, Calif.: Point Loma, 1971); Marion Meade, *Madame Blavatsky: The Woman behind the Myth* (New York: Putnam, 1980); Howard Murphet, *When Daylight Comes: A Biography of Helena Petrovna Blavatsky* (Wheaton, Ill.: Theosophical Publishing House, 1975); Charles J. Ryan, *H. P. Blavatsky and the Theosophical Movement* (Pasadena, Calif.: Theosophical University Press, 1975); Gertrude Marvin Williams, *Priestess of the Occult: Madame Blavatsky* (New York: Alfred Knopf, 1946).

Blue Mountain Center for Meditation

See EASWARAN, EKNATH.

Bonder, Saniel (1950–) *contemporary American teacher*

Saniel Bonder, formerly a leader with ADI DA SAMRAJ, left that community in 1992 and has since emerged as an independent spiritual teacher.

Bonder was born in 1950 in New York to a Jewish family who moved to North Carolina in 1957. He was awakened to spiritual matters in the later 1960s while a student at Harvard University. His turn toward Hinduism was influenced by YOGANANDA's *Autobiography of a Yogi* and by an encounter in India with Ramana MAHARSHI. In 1973 he learned of Da Free John (who is now known as Adi Da Samraj), and he joined the small community around him. He became a student of the ADVAITA VEDANTA philosophy that underlies that community.

By the beginning of the 1990s, Bonder decided that the experiment in spirituality led by Adi Da had failed, and in 1992 he withdrew from the community. He began an intense period of self-exploration with the assistance of a psychological therapist and a shaman. His experiences, including an encounter with the Goddess, led him to experience what he termed "Onlyness of Being," what traditional Hindu teachers term SELF-REALIZATION. From that point he began to conduct workshops and to lead daily MEDITATION sessions. A small initial following has grown into a new community organized around his teaching. He discovered that the new relationships were becoming what he called alchemical catalysts for transformation.

Bonder has characterized his approach to spirituality as "waking down." He contrasts his approach to the common idea that escape from mundane existence is necessary in order to become spiritual. He suggests that the ideal is to "fall" into both one's pure conscious nature and one's embodied personhood at the same time. With this "fall" we realize that we already are infinite transcendental Being incarnating as human being. Bonder has described his approach as "aspirant centered." He tries to assist seekers in realizing their divinity as a beginning point for a life of transformation. He defines *self-realization* as awareness and confidence in one's basic integration of both infinite and finite natures.

Among those who found their way to Bonder, a number of students, including his wife, have emerged as teachers and adepts. They now assist in leading the community that operates under the name Waking Down in Mutuality. Activities are carried out across the United States. Headquarters are at the Ma-Tam Temple of Being in Portland, Oregon. Bonder has written several books and regularly teaches at Ken Wilber's Integral Spiritual Center.

Further reading: Saniel Bonder, *The Divine Emergence of the World-Teacher* (Clearlake, Calif.: The Dawn Horse Press, 1990); ———, *Waking Down: Beyond Hypermasculine Dharmas—a Breakthrough Way of Self-Realization in the Sanctuary of Mutuality* (Portland, Ore.: Mt. Tam Awakenings, 1998); John W. Parker, *Dialogues with Emerging Spiritual Teachers* (Fort Collins, Colo.: Sagewood Press, 2000).

Brahma

Brahma is a divinity who makes his appearance in the post-Vedic Indian epics (c. 700 B.C.E.–100 C.E.). He has an important role in the stories of the great gods in the epics and PURANAS. He is often listed in a trinity alongside Vishnu and Shiva, where Brahma is the creator god, Vishnu is the sustainer of the world, and Shiva is the destroyer of the world. Brahma is generally considered the creator of the universe, but there are many different accounts of this act within Indian mythology; in fact, some stories credit other divinities or entities with the creation.

Unlike the other two members of the trinity (and to a lesser extent the Great Goddess),

Brahma has never had a wide following of exclusive devotees. There are only two temples in all of India devoted solely to Brahma; one is at PUSHKARA Lake near Ajmer in Rajasthan and the other is near Idar, on the border between Rajasthan and Gujarat. Brahma is born in the lotus that emerges from Vishnu's navel as he lies on the primordial MILK OCEAN. In this image he is the creator god, but still quite subsidiary to VISHNU. Iconographically Brahma's vehicle is the swan (Indian goose). Brahma's wife is SARASVATI, the goddess of the arts and learning. He is depicted carrying a vessel that pours water, prayer beads, and sometimes the VEDAS.

Brahma is always depicted as having four heads. The story is told that he was once in the midst of extended austerities in order to gain the throne of Indra, king of the gods, when the latter sent a celestial dancing girl, Tilottama, to disturb him. Not wanting to move from his meditative position, when Tilottama appeared to his right, he produced a face on his right; when she appeared behind him, he produced a face behind his head; when she appeared at his left, he produced a face on the left, and when she appeared above him he produced a face above. When SHIVA saw this five-headed Brahma he scolded him for his lust and pinched off his head looking upward, leaving Brahma humiliated and with only four heads. He did not attain the role of king of the gods.

There are a great many stories about Brahma in Indian mythology. Most commonly he is known as a boon giver who was required to grant magical powers as a reward for ascetics, whether animal, human, god, or demon. Often these beings, ascetics, gods, and the like would become problems for the gods when they became too powerful.

Further reading: Greg Bailey, *The Mythology of Brahma* (Delhi: Oxford University Press, 1983); Cornelia Dimmitt and J. A. B. van Buitenen, *Classical Hindu Mythology: A Reader in the Sanskrit Puranas* (Philadelphia: Temple University Press, 1978); E. Washburn Hopkins, *Epic Mythology* (Delhi: Motilal Banarsidass, 1986);

Rajani Mishra, *Brahma-Worship: Tradition and Iconography* (Delhi: Kanishka, 1989).

brahmacharya

Brahmacharya literally means "conducting oneself in accord with BRAHMAN." *Brahmacharya* itself has two important meanings. It refers to the ancient practice of celibacy for men, considered an indispensable aid for the most avid yogis and seekers who wish to break the bonds of SAMSARA, or worldly existence. Restraint of the senses has always been an important aspect of Indian YOGAS; complete restraint on sexuality is one of the most difficult and spiritually powerful restraints.

Brahmacharya was also used to refer to the student stage of a man's life, in the Brahmanical tradition of life stages or ASHRAMAS. One was expected to remain celibate during the 12 years of Vedic learning with one's guru, from the age of 12 to the age of 24, when one was to take up the household life. These stages of life may never have been precisely practiced by most BRAHMINS, but the ideal was widely known and respected.

Further readings: Klaus K. Klostermaier, *A Survey of Hinduism* (Albany: State University of New York Press, 1989); Patrick Olivelle, *The Asrama System: The History and Hermeneutics of a Religious Institution* (New York: Oxford University Press, 1993); ———, *Manu's Code: A Critical Edition and Translation of the Manava-Dharmasastra* (New York: Oxford University Press, 2005).

Brahma Kumaris World Spiritual Organizations (BKWSO) (est. 1937)

A worldwide family of individuals from all walks of life, the Bahma Kumaris World Spiritual Organizations offer education in human, moral, and spiritual values.

The founder, Prajapita Brahma, or Dada Lekhraj (1876–1969), was born into a humble home, the son of a village schoolmaster. He was brought up within the disciplines of the Hindu tradition but was not particularly devout at an early age. He entered the jewelry business and earned a considerable fortune as a diamond trader. At age 60, he decided to invest more time in quiet reflection and solitude. In 1936, while in a meditative state, he felt a warm flow of energy surround him and experienced a series of profound visions that revealed truths about the nature of the soul and God, the Supreme Soul. He decided to dedicate his life to understanding the significance and application of the knowledge he received and to convey this understanding to others in service of world transformation. In October 1937 he formed a managing commit-

The Universal Peace Hall, the main building of the Brahma Kumaris World Spiritual Organization on Mount Abu, Rajasthan, India *(Constance A. Jones)*

tee of eight young women, and in February 1938 he gave all of his property and assets to a trust administered by them.

Although the BKWSO is not a women's organization per se, it has been largely administered by women from its inception. The organization states that it is the need for the traditionally more feminine qualities of patience, tolerance, sacrifice, and love that keeps women in leadership positions.

The organization came into being under the name Om Mandali. At first it consisted of a handful of men, women, and children living in Hyderabad. After one year the organization moved to Karachi, Pakistan, where for 14 years, until after the partition of India and Pakistan, a group of 300 individuals lived as a self-sufficient community, spending their time in intense spiritual study and meditation.

In 1950, the community moved to Mount Abu in the state of Rajasthan, India. In 1952, Brahma Baba, as Dada Lekhraj had become known, felt that outreach was necessary to share the knowledge and experiences of the community. A few sisters left Mount ABU and moved to Bombay (Mumbai) and Delhi to serve by establishing study centers where the knowledge of Raja Yoga would be taught. The Madhuban community at Mount Abu remains the nucleus of the Brahma Kumaris centers worldwide and is a pilgrimage place for study and retreat.

In 1969, Dadi Prakashmani, one of the original eight trustees, was appointed chief administrative head of the Brahma Kumaris. Under her leadership the organization has experienced tremendous growth, expanding beyond India for the first time. It now includes 3,200 centers with over 450,000 students in 70 countries. Since 1974, Dadi Janaki has served as coordinator for all Brahma Kumaris activities outside India.

Today the BKWSO offers a varied curriculum with classes and workshops on Raja Yoga, stress-free living, MEDITATION training, community organization, and development of communication skills. As part of its 60th anniversary, the Brahma Kumaris inaugurated the Academy for a Better World as a place where men, women, and children can reach their unique human potential and cultivate common human values. The Brahma Kumaris World Spiritual University is a nongovernmental organization in general consultative status with the United Nations Economic and Social Council (ECOSOC) and the United Nations Children's Fund (UNICEF).

Further reading: Liz Hodgkinson, *Peace and Purity: the Story of the Brahma Kumaris: A Spiritual Revolution* (Deerfield Beach, Fla.: Health Communications, Inc., 1999); John Walliss, *The Brahma Kumaris as a "Reflexive Tradition": Responding to Late Modernity* (Burlington, Vt.: Ashgate, 2002).

brahman (brahma)

Brahman is one of the most important terms in the Vedic tradition, with a rich variety of meanings. It derives from the root *brih,* which means to "swell" or "grow," and evidently first referred to the swelling or growing power of the sacrifice and its MANTRAS that expand out and create efficacy.

The most common early meaning of *brahman* was simply "prayer." It is from this term that the word BRAHMIN, "one who prays," or "priest," is derived. Certain Vedic text collections are called BRAHMANAS; they are said to contain the secret of prayer.

Eventually, the term *brahman* was developed in the Upanishads to mean "the All" or "Ultimate Reality." An understanding developed that the individual self, or ATMAN, was identical to the *brahman.* These understandings developed in later VEDANTA into both theistic views, in which the *brahman* was tantamount to a god or goddess, and nontheistic views, in which the *brahman* was seen as an uncharacterized reality that constituted or underlay everything.

Often *brahman* is spelled as *brahma,* in part depending on grammatical context. Both forms are commonly used in transliterating Sanskrit. In the latter spelling the word must be carefully distinguished from BRAHMA, the creator god, whose name is pronounced with a long final *a.*

Further reading: Jan Gonda, *Notes on Brahman* (Utrecht: J. L. Beyers, 1950); Stephen H. Phillips, *Aurobindo's Philosophy of Brahman* (Leiden: E. J. Brill, 1986.) G. Sundara Ramaiah, *Brahman: A Comparative Study of the Philosophies of Sankara and Ramanuja* (Waltair: Andhra University 1974).

Brahmana

Brahmanas are texts that delineate the workings of the BRAHMAN in its oldest sense of the power, efficacy, or energy of Vedic ritual. They are considered SHRUTI or revelation and are part of the VEDAS. They accompany the MANTRA text of the four Vedas and are memorized along with them; the Brahmana of the Black YAJUR VEDA is interspersed with the mantras; the other three are stand alone texts. All the Brahmanas are written in prose.

The Brahmanas are designed to guide and explain the ritual sacrifice (YAJNA). Much Vedic mythology is found in the Brahmanas, explaining how particular rituals relate to the actions of particular divinities. For example, the SHATAPATHA BRAHMANA explains that goat hair is to be mixed with other ingredients for a ritual fire (AGNI), because the gods once collected Agni from among cattle. Brahmanas abound in much obscure, esoteric material that is not easy for the outsider to grasp, but that assure the efficacy and intelligibility of the Vedic ritual for practitioners.

Further reading: S. N. Dasgupta, *History of Indian Philosophy.* Vol. 1 (Delhi: Motilal Banarsidass, 1975; Jan Gonda, *Vedic Literature (Samhitas and Brahmanas).* Vol. 1, *A History of Indian Literature* (Wiesbaden: Otto Harrassowitz, 1975).

Brahmananda Saraswati, Swami   *See*
ANANDA ASHRAM, MONROE, NEW YORK; MISHRA, RAMAMURTI.

Brahma Sutra   *See* VEDANTA SUTRA.

Brahmin (Brahman)

A Brahmin is a member of the hereditary priestly class of India. The term is derived from the Vedic word BRAHMAN, which means (among other things) "prayer." In Sanskrit the same Vedic word designates prayer and the one who prays, the overseer of the Vedic ritual and its MANTRAS. In the ancient VARNA or class system the Brahmin was said to emerge from the mouth of the divine being, the warrior from his arms, the ordinary people from his thighs, and the servants from his feet.

Originally, Brahminical status was ensured by Vedic authority. Brahmins were responsible for the transmission of the VEDAS over the centuries via oral tradition within Brahminical families. This assured Brahminical authority over all ritual, since it was only through knowledge of the Vedas that the rituals could be performed. All public rituals had to be supervised by Brahmins and all private rituals could be learned only from Brahmins.

As the Brahminical tradition was challenged over the centuries to include more and more indigenous forms of religion, and the culture began to move away from exclusive reliance on Vedic ritual, Brahmins began to emphasize "purity" as a new justification for their superior status. This entailed special norms of conduct including very strict vegetarianism. However, they always maintained their dominant role in the transmission of knowledge and, thereby, in realms of social authority. Such knowledge extended far beyond the Vedas themselves. If there is a stereotypical or ideal role for a Brahmin in the modern world it is teaching. Transmission of knowledge is the traditional role of the Brahmin and remains so

A Brahmin priest wearing sacred thread at a village temple near Benares (Varanasi), India *(Constance A. Jones)*

today. Brahmins continue to perform the rituals at all the great temples in India, but the role of ritualist is now viewed as less important for Brahmins than the role of teacher or preceptor.

Further reading: Louis Dumont *Homo Hierarchicus: The Caste System and Its Implications* (Chicago: University of Chicago Press, 1980); Vasumath K. Duvvury, *Play, Symbolism and Ritual: A Study of Brahmin Women's Rites of Passage* (New York: Peter Lang, 1991); Brian K. Smith, *The Ancient Indian Varna System and the Origins of Caste* (Oxford: Oxford University Press, 1994); Glenn E. Yocum, "Brahman, King, Sannyasi and the Goddess in a Cage: Reflections on the 'Conceptual Order of Hinduism' at a Tamil Saiva Temple," *Contributions to Indian Sociology* 20 (1986): 15–39.

Brahmo Samaj (est. 1828)

The Brahmo Samaj (The Society of Worshippers of One God) was founded in Calcutta (Kolkata)

India, in 1828 by Raja Rammohun ROY (1772–1833), a Bengali Brahmin. Roy was a central figure in the "Indian Renaissance" and the "Bengali Renaissance," which introduced an emphasis on rationality, women's rights, and the uplift of lower castes.

The society aimed to reform Hinduism by banishing caste, idolatry, and other features it considered debased in favor of reinstituting what it considered were the traditional elements of truth, spirituality, and the unity of religion. Influenced by Christian missionaries and Western ideas that entered India during British colonialism, the society was firmly theistic, appealing to the worship of one God, omniscient and omnipotent. Distinctly Hindu, the society believes that all truth is from God and that the prophets of all religions are to be respected. Raja Rammohun Roy, Devendranath Tagore (1817–1905), and Keshub Chunder Sen (1838–84) were influential in creating the creed and practice of the society.

After Roy's death the society declined, but it was revived by Devendranath Tagore, father of the famous Indian poet Rabindranath TAGORE. Tagore was opposed to Christian missions, but he did not accept the infallibility of the Hindu scriptures. Under Tagore, the society became an active Hindu missionary organization, attracting educated Hindus in a number of cosmopolitan centers in Bengal and other states. Under Sen, the society became more universal in outlook by drawing on world scriptures. While Sen was leader a number of schisms emerged; as a result, the Brahmo Samaj movement began to include several different organizations.

Today the movement continues to uphold the Brahmo teachings of faith in a personal God, congregational worship, and condemnation of idol worship and widow burning. The society operates the Brahmo Balika Shikshalaya, a school for girls in Calcutta (Kolkata), which has stressed the emancipation of women since its founding in 1890. The school began a Montessori Section in 1930, the first Montessori school in India. The society sponsors the Raja Rammohun Roy Memorial Museum in Calcutta. Although very small today, the society provided a rational critique of traditional ritualistic observances that became part of the secularized democratic culture in Indian society. The society retains its affiliation with Unitarianism in Western countries.

See also UNITED KINGDOM; UNITED STATES.

Further reading: Piyus Kanti Das, *Raja Rammohun Roy and Brahmoism* (Calcutta: Author, 1970); David Kopf, *The Brahmo Samaj and the Shaping of the Modern Indian Mind* (Princeton, N.J.: Princeton University Press, 1979); Spencer Lavan, *Unitarians and India: A Study in Encounter and Response* (Chicago, Ill.: Exploration Press, 1991); Sivanath Sastri, *History of the Brahmo Samaj*, 2d ed. (Calcutta: Sadharan Brahmo Samaj, 1993); Keshub Chunder Sen, *The New Samhita: The Brahmo Samaj* (Bombay: Navabidhan Chittabinodini Trust, 1980).

Brihadaranyaka Upanishad (c. 700 B.C.E.)

The Brihadaranyaka Upanishad is a classical UPANISHAD connected to the White YAJUR VEDA. It is probably the oldest of the classical Upanishads and retains much material on ancient Vedic ritual, which the later classical Upanishads ignore.

The work opens with a meditation on the *ashva medha,* or HORSE SACRIFICE, seeing the horse itself as universal reality in all its particulars. This is a feature that is well established in the earlier BRAHMANA literature, which focused on the deeper meaning of ritual.

The Upanishad contains a cosmogony of the Ultimate Self or ATMAN as it differentiates into worldly reality. It also preserves several ancient dialogues about the nature of the universe, the atman, and the BRAHMAN. Particularly, it contains the disquisitions or answers of the famous sage YAJNAVALKYA to these questions.

In the course of this Upanishad, the doctrine of the two forms of *brahman,* the formed and the formless, is outlined (Bri. 2.3. 1–6). This doctrine is repeated in later Upanishads and is a central issue in the thought of later VEDANTA. Brihadaranyaka also presents for the first time the image of the divine reality as a spider and the worldly reality its spun web or threads (Bri. 2.1.20).

In the course of one of Yajnavalka's dialogues, the Brihadaranyaka Upanishad also outlines, perhaps for the first time, the three levels of consciousness: waking (*jagarita*), dreaming sleep (*svapna*), and deep sleep (*sushupti*). (The fourth level appears to be a later development: *turiya*, the transcendent state of consciousness.) The work also outlines (Bri. 4.4. 3–6) the first extended discourse on REINCARNATION and KARMA, as well as the karmic paths of the Sun and Moon: liberation is the path via the Sun and reincarnation is the path via the Moon (Bri. 6.2. 16). Finally, it introduces the negative description of the *brahman* as being "Not thus, not thus" (NETI NETI) (Bri. 4.5.15.).

Further reading: S. N. Dasgupta, *A History of Indian Philosophy,* Vol. 1 (Delhi: Motilal Banarsidass, 1975); Swami Nikhilandanda, trans., *The Upanishads,* Vol. 1 (New York: Ramakrishna-Vivekananda Center, 1975); S. Radhakrishnan, *The Principal Upanishads* (Atlantic Highlands, N.J.: Humanities Press, 1974).

Brihadishvara Temple

The Brihadishvara (Great Lord) Temple was built around 1009 C.E. by the emperor Rajaraja Chola in the Chola capital of Tanjore (Tanjavur) and is dedicated to Lord SHIVA. It is the tallest of all extant premodern Indian temples and covers the largest area. The round stone crown on top of its soaring tower is estimated to weigh 20 tons; it could have been moved to its current position, 120 feet in the air, only by a construction ramp approaching from a distance. The temple is also known for its 250 carved LINGAMs. The luxuriant and elegant artistry of this temple has been praised over the centuries. It is considered among the finest pieces of premodern Indian architecture still standing.

Further reading: R. Nagaswamy, "Iconography and Significance of the Brhadisvara Temple, Tanjavur." In *Discourses on Siva: Proceedings of a Symposium on the Nature of Religious Imagery,* edited by Michael Meister, 156–169 (Philadelphia: University of Pennsylvania Press, 1984); Pierre Richard, *Tanjavur Brhadisvara: An Architectural Study* (New Delhi: Indira Gandhi National Centre for Arts, 1995).

Brihaspati (Brahmanaspati)

Brihaspati (Lord of Prayer) is the divine priest in the VEDAS who sanctifies human rites. Later he became priest of the gods, while Shukracharya became priest for the ASURAS. He is also known as Brahmanaspati, to whom several individual hymns are addressed in the RIG VEDA.

In some myths Brihaspati is a RISHI, the son of the Rishi ANGIRAS. His wife is carried off by the Moon (SOMA), but is restored to him after a war. She later bore a son, Budha (Mercury), who was claimed by both her husband and the Moon. Still later Brihaspati became identified with the planet Jupiter, which is considered to be auspicious. Iconographically, Brihaspati holds a sacrificial pitcher and a rosary whose beads are from the *rudraksha* plant.

Further reading: Saraswati Bali, *Brhaspati in the Vedas and the Puranas* (Delhi: Nag, 1978); Ralph T. Griffith, trans., *Hinduism: The Rig Veda* (New York: Book-of-the-Month Club, 1992).

Brihatkatha (c. 200 C.E.)

The *Brihatkatha* (Great Story) is a collection of adventure tales ascribed to GUNADHYA and written around 200 C.E. It is said to have been originally composed in a dialect of the forest people, but if so, the original was not preserved. Several Sanskrit versions exist, the most famous the 11th-century KATHASARITSAGARA (The ocean of the streams of story) by Somadeva. Many of the stories of the *Brihatkatha* complex have found their way into the Jain tradition and reappear in such languages as Kannada and Tamil.

The stories tell of merchants and kings, romance and adventure, quite unlike the traditional Sanskrit PURANAS. The central hero is Naravahanadatta, the son of Udayana. Common in these stories is the appearance of semidevine wizardlike beings called Vidyadharas, who perform magic.

Further reading: J. A. B van Buitenen, *Tales of Ancient India* (Chicago: University of Chicago Press, 1969); Jagdishchandra Jain, *The Vasudevahindi: An Authentic Jain Version of the Brhatkatha* (Ahmedabad: L. D. Institute of Indology, 1977); Sarla Khosla, *Brihatkatha and Its Contributions* (Delhi: Agam Kala Prakashan, 2003).

Brindavan

For KRISHNA worshippers, the Brindavan region in Uttar Pradesh has for centuries been one of the main pilgrimage sites, a center for various cultic developments, and the focus of much Vaishnavite devotion. No prayer or song to Krishna will fail to mention it.

Although born in Mathura, Krishna spent his childhood and young life in the beautiful environs of Brindavan. There he encountered demons of various sorts and defeated them while just a child. There he became the butter thief who stole from all the families in his neighborhood. And it was there that he dallied with the cowherd maidens, the GOPIS, choosing for his favorite RADHA. In Brindavan a pilgrim can visit, walking barefoot, all the places of Krishna's young life, and sense firsthand his divine presence.

CHAITANYA's followers moved from Bengal to Brindavan to develop their philosophy and path. The region also hosts a center for followers of VALLABHA.

Further reading: Cornelia Dimmitt and J. A. B. van Buitenen, *Classical Hindu Mythology: A Reader in the Sanskrit Puranas* (Philadelphia: Temple University Press, 1978); David L. Haberman, *Journey through the Twelve Forests: An Encounter with Krishna* (New York:

Oxford University Press, 1994); John Stratton Hawley and Shrivatsa Goswami, *At Play with Krishna: Pilgrimage Dramas from Brindavan* (Princeton, N.J.: Princeton University Press, 1981).

Brunton, Paul (1898–1981) *British philosopher and spiritual teacher*

Paul Brunton was a spiritual writer and philosopher. His self-appointed task was to interpret what he learned in the East to Western audiences. He became a major figure in the spread of Eastern teachings in the West.

Brunton was born Raphael Hurst on November 27, 1898, in London. (When he first became prominent as Brunton, he never explained why or when he had changed his name.) His mother died when he was young; his father remarried, and when he too died Brunton took care of his widow. At age 16 he had a mystical experience, and by 1923 he was a member of a small bohemian group who were interested in spiritual matters. Recognizing that he had occult and clairvoyant powers, he joined the Spiritualist Society of Great Britain. He married Karen Augusta Tottrup and a son was born in 1923. Barely three years later, Brunton and his wife divorced and she married another member of their circle who became a leader in the Anthroposophical Society, another esoteric organization with roots in THEOSOPHY.

In 1930, Brunton traveled to India, where he met yogis and sages. His popular account, *A Search in Secret India,* introduced significant Indian teachers of the time, particularly MEHER BABA and RAMANA MAHARSHI, to a Western audience. His writings indicate that he practiced Ramana's technique of meditating on the question "Who am I?" and gained some degree of peace of mind and inner illumination from this discipline.

From 1934 to 1945, Brunton traveled even more extensively throughout the East and wrote six books about his experiences and his growing commitment to create a complete spiritual teaching for the modern world. Most of his writings

were in the form of organized notes and aphorisms on a host of subjects, comprising more than
7,000 pages withheld for posthumous publication. In his own words, these notes constituted an
evolving new East-West philosophy that emerged
to meet modern conditions. Brunton became a
spiritual teacher and had followers who studied
his ideas as well as his prophecies about world
affairs.

During the last 20 years of his life, Brunton
lived in Vevey, Switzerland, where he received
students and inquirers. He died there of a massive
cerebral hemorrhage on July 28, 1981.

In 1986, the Paul Brunton Philosophic Foundation (PBPF) was founded in Hector, New York,
as a resource for those seeking spiritual understanding. The foundation, under the leadership
of Brunton's son, Kenneth Thurston Hurst, completed publication of the 16-volume compendium
of his notebooks; instituted a program for donat-
ing books to libraries, prisons, and world leaders;
and initiated a circulating library of published and
unpublished writings by Brunton.

Further reading: Paul Brunton, *A Hermit in the Hima-
layas* (London: Rider, 1936); ———, *A Message from
Arunachala* (London: Rider, 1936); ———, *The Note-
books of Paul Brunton,* 16 vols. (New York: Larson,
1984–89); ———, *The Quest of the Overself* (London:
Rider, 1937); ———, *A Search in Secret India* (London:
Rider & Company, 1934); ———, *The Secret Path*
(London: Rider, 1935); J. Godwin, ed., *Paul Brunton:
Essential Readings* (Wellingborough, England: Crucible,
1990); K. T. Hurst, *Paul Brunton: A Personal View* (New
York: Larson, 1989); J. M. Masson, *My Father's Guru:
A Journey through Spirituality and Disillusion* (Reading,
Mass.: Addison-Wesley, 1993).

Buddha (c. 600 B.C.E.) *founder of Buddhism*

The Buddha (the Awakened One) is revered
among contemporary Hindus, who usually consider Buddhism to be another form of Hinduism.
The flag of India even shows the Dharma Chakra

or "wheel of the law," which is a Buddhist symbol.
The places where the Buddha was born (Lumbini
in NEPAL), preached his first sermon (Sarnath near
BENARES [Varanasi]), where he died (Vaishali), and
where he reached enlightenment (Bodhgaya) are
still visited as holy places by Hindus. Additionally, many old sites in India that preserve Buddhist
sculpture and painting, such as Barhut, AJANTA,
and ELLORA, are preserved by India and are very
popular tourist places.

The story of the Buddha's life is well known
to Hindus. The prince Gautama was shielded as
a child and young man from witnessing any sorrow: disease, old age, and death. The one time
he managed to elude the protection of his family
and went out to see the world, he was shocked
by what he saw. With the permission of his wife,
he left her and their son and ventured off as a
renunciant. He tried many different paths including severe asceticism, which withered his body
and nearly killed him. Eventually, he decided that
neither severe asceticism nor a worldly life of
indulgence was the true path, and he formulated
his famous "Middle-Way."

Finally, under the sacred Bodhi tree in Bodhgaya, Gautama reached his enlightenment; he
spent the rest of his life as an awakened teacher
wishing to lead the ignorant out of the bonds
of karma into a release from birth and rebirth.
Though recent and contemporary India looks
upon the Buddha as an AVATAR and a holy being, in
past eras Indian tradition witnessed great conflict
between Buddhism and the Brahminical tradition. Hindu saints of South India, both Shaivite
and Vaishnavite, reviled the Buddhist monks and
accused them of following a false path. The great
BHAGAVATA PURANA, which depicts the 10 incarnations of VISHNU, shows Buddha as the ninth, but
in this account he has gone to Earth to preach a
creed designed to mislead the ASURAS, or antigods,
and not to save humanity.

Further reading: Edward Conze, *Buddhist Thought in
India* (Ann Arbor: University of Michigan Press, 1982);

Richard H. Robinson, *The Buddhist Religion* (Belmont, Calif.: Wadsworth, 1986).

buddhi

Buddhi is a technical term in the SAMKHYA YOGA system that refers to discriminative intellect. Ultimately, one seeks to calm the mind so that the discriminative intellect or *buddhi* will be able to discern the clear division between the self or soul and the whirling world of phenomena. This discernment is a crucial step in the liberation of the self from the cycle of birth and rebirth. The *buddhi* is considered to have the greatest predominance of *sattva* (purity) of anything in existence. Ultimately, however, liberation can occur only when *buddhi,* too, is transcended (in consciousness), as it too is part of the world of phenomena and, in its own way, a hindrance to the highest spiritual realization.

Further reading: S. N. Dasgupta, *A History of Indian Philosophy.* Vol. 1 (Delhi: Motilal Banarsidass, 1975); Gerald Larson and Ram Shankar Bhattacharya, *Sankhya: A Dualist Tradition in Indian Philosophy, Encyclopedia of Indian Philosophies.* Vol. 4 (Princeton, N.J.: Princeton University Press, 1987); ———, *Classical Sankhya: An Interpretation of Its History and Meaning* (Santa Barbara, Calif.: Ross/Erikson, 1979); S. K. Saksena, *Essays on Indian Philosophy* (Honolulu: University of Hawaii Press, 1970).

C

Caribbean region

Hindus first entered the Americas from India as settlers in the Caribbean region in the 1840s, in what are now known as Guyana, Suriname, and Trinidad/Tobago. Most were poor lower-caste workers from the states of Eastern Uttar Pradesh and Western Bihar who were hired as indentured laborers to work on the British and Dutch sugar plantations. After their contracts of indenture ended, most of these workers remained. The British and the Dutch treated their workers differently. The Dutch tended to keep a hands-off policy toward their Hindu workers, with the result that Hindus in Suriname tended to maintain Hindi as their primary language. The British attempted to convert Hindus to Christianity and to change their culture. The result is that Hindus in Trinidad, Tobago, and Guyana speak primarily English rather than Hindi. In Trinidad a form of language known as Plantation Hindi developed, as expressed in oral histories. Missionaries from the Arya Samaj countered the Christian missionaries in the 1940s. In Suriname a small number of immigrants from Java in Indonesia, also introduced as indentured servants, converted to Hinduism. Today, approximately 27 percent of the population of Suriname, 34 percent of Guyana, and 24 percent of Trinidad and Tobago are Hindus. Smaller populations of Hindus live on the islands of Jamaica, Grenada, St. Lucia, Martinique, and Guadalupe. All are descendants of indentured servants and have faced evangelization by Christian missionaries.

Hinduism in the Caribbean is primarily Vaishnavite and centers around devotion to the monkey warrior Hanuman. Other deities such as Shiva, Durga, Kali, and Ganesha are also recognized. The primary sacred texts recognized by the laity are not the Vedas or the Upanishads, but the Ramayana and the Bhagavad Gita. Most homes have a small shrine or prayer house that serves as a site for offerings, devotion, chanting of bhajans, and meditation. Because of the schedule of plantation work, the Hindu communities have adopted Sundays as the weekly time for puja. Once a year the communities gather for the Ramayana Yajna and Divali. Arranged marriages have become the norm among some communities and serve to join Hindus around traditional culture. Apart from recognition of Brahmin families and endogamy norms, caste observance has largely disappeared from the region.

See also Africa; Diaspora.

Further reading: Crispin Bates, ed., *Community, Empire, and Migration: South Asians in Diaspora* (New York: Palgrave, 2001); Anil Mahabir, "Diaspora of Hindus in South America," *Hinduism Today* (January/February, 2001), p. 18. Steven Vertovec, *The Hindu Diaspora: Comparative Patterns* (London: Routledge, 2000).

caste

The Indian term *jati* (birth) is usually translated as "caste," which is a Portuguese word. It refers to the community into which one is born. In VEDIC tradition the concept of VARNA stratified society into four groups: BRAHMIN (priests), KSHATRIYA (warriors), VAISHYA (common people, including merchants), and SHUDRA (servant classes). The simple stratification of the Vedic tradition became the template for a much wider formal social stratification within Indian society.

In addition to the four classes of the earlier scheme, a fifth class of people known as untouchables (now referred to as Dalits) emerged, possibly when certain non-Aryan tribes began to be integrated into the larger ARYAN cultural framework. "UNTOUCHABILITY" involved cultural concepts of POLLUTION; "purer" classes and castes avoided eating food with certain other classes or taking food that had been touched by certain other classes. At its most extreme, this required that the lowest castes not touch or have physical contact with upper castes at all. The lowest strata often performed work that put them in contact with dead animals, leather, and excrement, all of which were considered polluting.

The loose array of four classes (somewhat confused in the south of India, where the British incorrectly classified many agriculturists as Shudras) sprouted additional castes that amounted to guilds that protected certain occupations from encroachment by other groups. An intricate array of occupationally defined castes and subcastes emerged. Marriage between castes is very restricted; even low-status castes jealously guard against intermarriage with groups that are lower in the hierarchy.

Brahmins are considered the purest in the hierarchy, by virtue of their cultivation of the ancient tradition of the Vedas and their strict vegetarianism. They may give food to any group, but they will only accept food from or eat food with other Brahmins. Certain Brahmins who are considered purer than others will not associate with or marry those other Brahmins.

Caste ranking has never been and is not now eternally fixed; however, it usually takes more than a generation for a given caste to move up or down the hierarchy. The primary means of advancement is to restrict meat-eating. Vegetarianism is a highly valued sign of purity, and avoiding all meat has aided more than one caste in gaining higher status, if the practice is sustained and universal. Second in importance is avoidance of marriage and association with groups that are low on the caste scale. Third, members must find different forms of employment that do not involve polluting substances. Slipping in any of these areas might cause a caste to lose status.

The Indian Constitution, which was written by the untouchable B. R. Ambedkar, outlaws caste. The national and state governments have instituted strict affirmative action in the makeup of parliaments (untouchables and disadvantaged tribals are assured a percentage of seats) and in government hiring. Many great strides have been made in modern India to abolish the evil of caste, but it is an ancient and deeply rooted system that may take generations to abolish, just as it took two centuries to dismantle discriminatory racial laws in the United States.

Further reading: Christopher J. Fuller, ed., *Caste Today* (New York: Oxford University Press, 1996); Richard Lannoy, *The Speaking Tree: A Study of Indian Culture and Society* (London and New York: Oxford University Press, 1971); McKim Marriot, *India through Hindu Categories* (New Delhi: Sage, 1990); Brian K. Smith, *Classifying the Universe: The Ancient Indian Varna System and the Origins of Caste* (New York: Oxford University Press, 1994).

Cauvery River

The Cauvery or Kaveri River begins at Talakaveri in Kodagu in the Indian state of Karnataka and flows about 600 miles, mostly through Tamil Nadu to the Bay of Bengal. It is known as the GANGES of South India. Along its course are numerous holy sites, the most important of which is SRIRANGAM, an island famous in VAISHNAVA tradition where there is a shrine to Vishnu under the name Ranganatha. The river is used as a symbol of Tamil literature and culture (*see* VAISHNAVISM).

There are various legends about the river's origin. One story says that there was once a sage Kavera who performed austerities in the mountains near the source of the current river to propitiate BRAHMA. Brahma gave him the daughter Lopamudra, who manifested herself as the river Cauvery. Later, the sage AGASTYA married Lopamudra and placed the great river in a water pot. As chance would have it, one day a crow tipped over the pot and the Cauvery flowed out.

Further reading: G. Michell with Clare Arni, eds., *Eternal Kaveri: Historical Sites along South India's Greatest River* (Mumbai: Marg, 1999).

Chaitanya, Sri Krishna (1486–1533)
Vaishnavite saint

Sri Chaitanya was born in Mayapur in what is now West Bengal to a learned teacher of the tradition. The written accounts of this great saint portray him as a miraculous child who had adventures and misadventures while still an infant that resemble those found in the stories of KRISHNA, of whom Sri Chaitanya was considered an incarnation.

As were many of the other great teachers of Indian tradition, Sri Chaitanya was a master of SANSKRIT. When he was only 16 he already knew as much as professors at Sanskrit schools. That same year his wife died of snake bite; he was then married to a daughter of a wealthy and respected teacher, a sign that his social standing was already on the rise. On a trip to Gaya to perform rituals for his ancestors he visited a Vishnu shrine and there fell into a trance. He was caught before he fell by a noted ascetic, Ishvara Puri, a practitioner of devotional VAISHNAVISM. When Chaitanya came to his senses he asked Puri to help him understand RADHA's love for Krishna.

The stories of Radha's love affair with Lord Krishna were the backdrop for the intense Vaishnavite devotion that Chaitanya was to experience. Radha's passionate, uncontrollable love for her lover Lord Krishna was the model for this devotional path. Receiving the Krishna MANTRA from Puri, Chaitanya went into a prolonged and agonizing state of mystical longing; at times he was ecstatic at realizing the presence of Lord Krishna everywhere; at times he felt deep sorrow from losing this sense of passionate contact.

At this point Sri Chaitanya ceased being a pandit or teacher, overwhelmed as he was with intense moods of frenzy and mystic passion—the passion of God-love. It was not long before he was recognized as an incarnation of Krishna. He began to attract followers with whom he would spend his days singing praises of the Lord, dancing and falling into trances. It is said that his passionate religiosity was so strong that he converted a Muslim ruler of Bengal who had previously been known to persecute Hindus as infidels.

At times Sri Chaitanya felt himself to be the embodiment of Krishna; at other times he embodied the essence of Radha. He was an exemplar of the most emotional type of devotion, wherein the devotee loses sense of himself or herself in the thrall of the mystic vision. This devotional attitude is precisely the one that SRI BHAKTIVEDANTA PRABHUPADA, the founder of the Hare Krishna movement in America, took to the shores of the West to develop and spread. Sri Prabhupada is in the direct lineage of Sri Chaitanya.

Further reading: S. N. Dasgupta, *A History of Indian Philosophy.* Vol. 4 (Delhi: Motilal Banarsidass, 1975); Edward C. Dimock Jr., *Caitanya Caritamrta of Krsnadasa Kaviraja: A Translation and Commentary* (Cambridge,

Mass.: Department of Sanskrit and Indian Studies, Harvard University, 1999); K. P. Sinha, *Sri Caitanya's Vaisnavism and Its Sources* (Kolkata: Punthi Pustak, 2001); Swami Tapasyananda, *Bhakti Schools of Vedanta* (Madras: Ramakrishna Math, n.d.).

chakra

Chakra, literally, "wheel" or "discus," is a term used in KUNDALINI yoga to designate energy centers along the spine. These centers do not reside in the gross body, at the physical level, but in what is termed the "subtle body." Though they have a physical position, they have no definite physical adjuncts or precise nervous system connections as in the case of the Chinese system of meridians in acupuncture. They are instead believed to be connected to a network of channels in the subtle body called NADIS.

The chakras are usually visualized as being lotus flowers with differing numbers of petals. Each of the chakras is a center of consciousness of sorts, playing a role in the makeup of the full human being (including his or her transcendent aspect).

There are six basic chakras found in almost every kundalini system with a seventh "highest chakra" that technically is beyond the chakras, but is often called "chakras" nonetheless. The names of these chakras vary in different systems. The most common system lists the following chakras, moving from the base of the spine to a place above the head: MULADHARA, SVADHISHTHANA, MANIPURA, ANAHATA, VISHUDDHA, AJNA. In this system the seventh level is usually called SAHASRARA, the transcendent level, which is not in most systems actually a chakra, but for convenience is sometimes designated as such.

Some accounts include an additional chakra, the *LALATA* or *soma* chakra, between *ajna* and *sahasrara*. In kundalini yoga one raises the kundalini, which is seen to be a coiled serpent, through breath control and/or MEDITATIONS so that it pierces in succession each of the chakras, giving the adapt

control or mastery over them. This movement results in complete personal transformation and, ultimately, access to the transcendent state.

Further reading: Haris Johari, *Chakras: Energy Centers of Transformation* (Rochester, Vt.: Destiny Books, 2000); John G. Woodroffe, *The Serpent Power,* 7th ed. (Madras: Ganesh, 1964).

Chamunda

Chamunda is a fearsome goddess who accepts human sacrifices and blood offerings. She is now usually assimilated to KALI, and *Chamunda* is an epithet for Kali. The first known historical mention of Chamunda is in the Sanskrit poet BHAVABHUTI's drama *Malatimadhava* (eighth century C.E.), in which the heroine Malati is captured by a female devotee of Chamunda to be sacrificed to that goddess. Chamunda's temple is depicted as near a cremation ground. That story has the goddess dancing so wildly that the world shakes; she has a gaping mouth and a garland of skulls and is covered with snakes; flames shoot from her eyes that could destroy the world, and she is encircled by goblins.

Another, South Indian description of Chamunda has her holding a skull-head mace, a snake, and a wine cup. She has a third eye, a jackal chews on a corpse below her, and her eyes show she has been drinking liquor. Another image of Chamunda, at Jaipur in Orissa, depicts her as emaciated; she holds a chopper and a pronged weapon, a skull begging bowl, and a severed head in her hands.

Chamunda is sometimes listed among the *matrikas* or "Mother Goddesses." The *Markandeya* PURANA has Chamunda emerge from the forehead of Amba or DURGA to kill two fierce demons, Chanda and Munda, and her name is explained by combining the names of these two demons.

Further reading: David R. Kinsley, *Hindu Goddesses* (Berkeley: University of California Press, 1988); ———,

The Sword and the Flute: Kali and Krsna, Dark Visions of the Terrible and Sublime in Hindu Mythology (Berkeley: University of California Press, 2000); June McDaniel, *Offering Flowers, Feeding Skulls: Popular Goddess Worship in West Bengal* (New York: Oxford University Press, 2004).

Chanakya   *See* ARTHASHASTRA.

Chandi

Chandi (the fierce) is a name for the goddess DURGA, when she is killing the demon MAHISHASURA. This name is used primarily in the 700-verse poem chanted in her honor. This poem, called either *Chandi Stotra* (Praise of Chandi) or *Durga Saptashati* (Seven hundred verses to Durga), forms an episode of 13 chapters in the Markandeya Purana, also known as the Devi Mahatmya (Glory of the Goddess). It describes Durga's victory over Mahishasura, a demon with the head of a water buffalo, and his demon hordes. It is read daily at Durga temples and is always recited at the annual celebration of Durga PUJA in the fall of each year.

Further reading: Thomas B. Coburn, *Devi-Mahatmya: The Crystalization of the Goddess Tradition* (Delhi: Motilal Banarsidass, 1984); Swami Jagadisvarananda, *The Devi Mahatmyam, or, Sri Durga-Saptashati: 700 Mantras on Shri Durga* (Madras: Sri Ramakrishna Math, 1969); Satya Nand Sarawati, trans., *Candi* (Martinez, Calif.: Devi Mandir, 1989).

Chandogya Upanishad

The classical Chandogya Upanishad is part of the Chandogya Brahmana, which is attached to the SAMA VEDA. It is one of the oldest UPANISHADS. It retains much of the character of the BRAHMANA from which it comes, in that it is largely devoted to delineating the deeper meaning and significance of the elements of the Vedic sacrifice or YAJNA (*see* VEDAS).

Much of the Chandogya Upanishad is devoted to the true meaning of the *Udigitha*, the loud chant of the Sama Vedic priest at the sacrificial ritual. The *Udgitha* is said to be tantamount to OM (Ch. 1.1.1–10) and is identified with the breath (Ch. 1.2.1–14). The esoteric meaning of each of the syllables in the word *Udgitha* is explicated (Ch. 1.3.1–12). The *Udgitha* is also identified with the Sun, with space as the ultimate, and with divinities.

The Chandoga Upanishad goes on to coordinate the sounds of the fuller Sama Vedic chant with cosmic and human entities. Through this process, the elements of the Sama Vedic chant are shown to encompass a wide range of human, worldly, and cosmic entities; it is much more important than a simple musical recitation.

Chapter three raises the familiar Upanishadic theme of the identity of ATMAN (the individual self) and the BRAHMAN (the Ultimate Reality). The fifth chapter gives the famous teaching of Uddalaka Aruni to his son, Shvetaketu; in defining the Ultimate Reality of the *brahman* he tells his son, "You are THAT" (TAT TVAM ASI). This is one of the most well known MAHAVAKYAS or "Great Sayings" quoted in the VEDANTA.

Chapters seven and eight relate the nature of the atman or individual self and show that it resides within the human heart. They tell the famous tale in which INDRA, king of the gods, at last learns the nature of the *brahman*/atman identity.

Further reading: S. N. Dasgupta, *A History of Indian Philosophy*, Vol. 1 (Delhi: Motilal Banarsidass, 1975); Swami Nikhilandanda, trans., *The Upanishads*. Vol. 1 (New York: Ramakrishna-Vivekananda Center, 1975); S. Radhakrishnan, *The Principal Upanishads* (Atlantic Highlands, N.J.: Humanities Press, 1974).

Chandra

A rich Indian mythology addresses the Earth's Moon. In the VEDAS it was called Chandra (or *candramas*). The name SOMA, who in the Vedas was a god with special characteristics, later was used for the Moon as well.

Chandra, too, is a god, one of the nine planets, and the leader of the stars. Whereas in the West the Moon's appearance is likened to the face of a man, in Indian mythology, the Moon has the form of a rabbit. The Moon is understood to be swallowed by a headless snake at the time of eclipses and regurgitated again later. The nectar of immortality (AMRITA) is found on the Moon in plenty. The crescent Moon is found in the topknot of SHIVA.

Further reading: John Dowson, *Classical Dictionary of Hindu Mythology, Religion, Geography, History, and Literature* (Portland, Oreg.: Trubner, 2003); E. Washburn Hopkins, *Epic Mythology* (Delhi: Motilal Banarsidass, 1986).

Charaka *See* AYURVEDA.

Charles, Master (1945–) *founder of Synchronicity Foundation*

Master Charles is a popular American meditation teacher, who combines the teachings of Swami MUKTANANDA (1908–82) with the insights provided by contemporary psychology and parapsychology.

Master Charles Cannon was born on March 14, 1945, in Syracuse, New York, to Italian American parents and raised as a Roman Catholic. At one point he seriously considered joining a Catholic religious order, but in his later teen years he backed away from the church. He practiced Zen Buddhism for a period and explored parapsychology. Then in 1970, some friends who had recently returned from India showed him a photograph of Swami Muktananda. Seeing the picture had an immediate and intense effect upon him. In the midst of the altered consciousness into which he had moved, he had a vision of God as Mother (a relic of his earlier devotion to the Virgin Mary), and she instructed him to go to Muktananda.

He obtained a copy of the first of Muktananda's books, *Guru,* which had just been published in the West, and soon afterward left for India.

Cannon settled in at Muktananda's ashram in Maharashtra (about 75 miles from Mumbai). He remained in India with his guru for 12 years and for a period he served as Muktananda's private secretary. Halfway through his stay, he took vows of renunciation (SANNYAS). Shortly before his death, Muktananda instructed him to return to the United States. His experience with Muktananda culminated in his reaching a state of pure consciousness, which Master Charles described in mystical language.

Back in America, he withdrew from the Siddha Yoga Dham, the organization that perpetuated Muktananda's work, and settled in rural Virginia. He also dropped the garb of an Indian monk, began wearing Western clothing, and began to call himself Brother Charles. A small community gradually gathered around him. In 1983, he founded Synchronicity Foundation to facilitate his work and built a sanctuary to hold various meetings and classes. As his leadership manifested he assumed the name Master Charles.

Unique to Master Charles's teaching activity has been his mastery of contemporary data, generated by transpersonal psychology and parapsychology, concerning MEDITATION and altered states of consciousness. He integrated this information into the meditation he learned from Muktananda to create what he termed the Synchronicity High-Tech Meditation Experience.

Master Charles continues to teach and develop his scientific form of meditation from the headquarters of the Synchronicity Foundation in Nellyford, Virginia. He publishes compact discs of meditative music that use binaural-beat technology to induce meditative states.

Further reading: Master Charles, *The Bliss of Freedom: A Contemporary Mystic's Enlightening Journey* (Malibu Calif.: Acacia, 1997); ———, *Synchronicity Experience* (Nellyford, Va.: Synchronicity Foundation, 2002).

Charvaka

Charvaka or Lokayata philosophy is an ancient materialist tradition that is known to us only through the texts of its myriad opponents. It dates from approximately 400 B.C.E. The Charvaka motto can be approximately translated as "Eat, drink, and be merry." In addition to being pure materialists, the Charvakas were strict empiricists who believed that the only valid source of knowledge is direct perception; they believed only what could be seen by the eyes directly. They rejected even inference as a method of investigation.

Though none of their texts were preserved, the Charvaka viewpoint was condemned in many philosophical contexts over two millennia. The RAMAYANA and MAHABHARATA both contained arguments against it. Nearly every subsequent Indian philosophical system, including that of the Buddhists and Jains, formulated arguments to answer them. Modern Marxists in India have sought to make this ancient system better known.

Further reading: Debiprasad Chattopadhyaya and Mrinal K. Gangopadhyaya, eds., *Carvaka/Lokayata: An Anthology of Source Materials and Some Recent Studies* (New Delhi: Indian Council of Philosophical Research, 1990); S. N. Dasgupta, *A History of Indian Philosophy*, 5 vols. (Delhi: Motilal Banarsidass, 1975); Anil Kumar Sarkar, *Dynamic Facets of Indian Thought* (New Delhi: Manohar, 1988).

Chaudhuri, Haridas (1913–1975) *follower of the philosophy of Sri Aurobindo in the United States*

A professor of philosophy in India and later in California, Haridas Chaudhuri helped spark the growing American interest in Asian religion, philosophy, and culture by founding the influential Cultural Integration Fellowship and the California Institute of Asian Studies, both of which have survived to the present day.

Chaudhuri was born in May 1913 in Shyamagram in eastern Bengal (now Bangladesh). He was orphaned at an early age. In 1929, he won the Ramtanu Gold Medal in Bengali literature upon graduating from high school. He received his M.A. and B.A. with honors in philosophy and religion from Vidyasagar College in Calcutta (Kolkata). Dr. Chaudhuri married his wife, Bina, in 1946. In 1949 he received his Ph.D. from the University of Calcutta for a dissertation on Sri Aurobindo's philosophy, "Integral Idealism." Dr. Chaudhuri then became a professor and chair of the department of philosophy at Krishnagar College in Krishnagar.

In March 1951, Dr. Chaudhuri immigrated to the United States upon the direct recommendation of Sri AUROBINDO, who had received a request from Dr. Frederick Spiegelberg of Stanford University to nominate someone for a position in the American Academy of Asian Studies in San Francisco, which was just opening. He was followed in the same year by his wife, Bina, and their two young children. Dr. Chaudhuri taught at this college for about 15 years along with several prominent scholars, including Alan Watts, who was later to become quite well known.

Haridas Chaudhuri (1913–1975), scholar and founder of the Cultural Integration Fellowship and California Institute of Integral Studies *(Cultural Integration Fellowship)*

Three months after he arrived in the United States Dr. Chaudhuri founded the Cultural Integration Fellowship in San Francisco, with the aim of furthering universal religion, cultural harmony, and creative self-development. This was the first major ASHRAM in the country dedicated to the values of Sri Aurobindo and the Mother. The Cultural Integration Fellowship in 2001 celebrated its 50th birthday and still flourishes under the guidance of Bina Chaudhuri.

In 1968 Dr. Chaudhuri founded the California Institute of Asian Studies in San Francisco (which in 1981 became the California Institute of Integral Studies). This graduate school is devoted to the promotion of cultural understanding between East and West, offering masters' and doctoral degrees in philosophy, psychology, Asian studies, and interdisciplinary studies. Dr. Chaudhuri started an accreditation process for the school that reached its fruition in 1981, six years after his untimely death of a heart attack there in June 1975.

Dr. Chaudhuri wrote numerous books in English. Among them are *Modern Man's Religion* (1966), *Philosophy of Integralism* (1954), *The Rhythm of the Truth* (1958), *Shri Aurobindo: Prophet of the Life Divine* (1959), and *Integral Yoga: The Concept of Harmonious and Creative Living* (1965). He wrote two lesser known books in Bengali: *Ma* (1944) and *Sri Auboinder Sadhana* (1949).

Dr. Haridas Chaudhuri had a strong impact on philosophical and religious studies and affairs in the San Francisco Bay area and beyond. He was host to Swami MUKTANANDA at the Cultural Integration Fellowship on one of the Swami's first trips to the United States. He also played host there to the American spiritual figures Alan Watts, Ram Dass, and Sant Keshavadas. He hosted and provided venues for such famous musicians as Ravi Shankar and Ali Akbar Khan in their early years of touring of the United States.

Among his students and those he strongly influenced can be counted Michael Murphy, cofounder of Esalen Institute, and Michael Toms, founder of New Dimensions radio, both in California. Dr. Chaudhuri also kept up an active correspondence with his Asian friend U Thant, secretary-general of the United Nations in the 1960s.

Further reading: Haridas Chaudhuri, *Integral Yoga: The Concept of Harmonious and Creative Living* (Wheaton, Ill. The Theosophical Publishing House, 1965); ———, *Modern Man's Religion* (Santa Barbara, Calif.: J. F. Rowny Press, 1966).

Chetanananda, Swami (1949–) *teacher of Kashmir Shaivism and Trika Yoga*

Swami Chetanananda is an American teacher in the tradition of Swami RUDRANANDA. At his two institutes, he propounds a SHAIVISM that generally downplays asceticism and withdrawal from life and draws on Tibetan and Kashmiri practice.

J. Michael Shoemaker was born in Kentucky the son of a pharmacist and a nurse, both devout Catholics, and he was raised in the Catholic faith. He attended school in Connersville, Indiana, where he was a football player and swimmer. He attended but dropped out of Indiana University.

Shoemaker studied with Swami Rudrananda and lived in his ashram in Big Indian, New York, until 1973, the year of Rudrananda's death. In 1971 he founded the Nityananda Institute upon instructions from Rudrananda in Bloomington, Indiana, to foster Shaivite teachings. After Rudrananda's death, he traveled to India and was initiated into SANNYAS (renunciation) by Swami MUKTANANDA in Ganeshpuri, India, in 1978 and given the name Chetanananda (the bliss of pure awareness). He was also initiated into the ancient Tibetan Buddhist ritual practices of Phowa and Chod, and others from the Longchen Nyingthing and Padampa Sangye Shi-je tradition.

After Rudrananda's sudden death, Chetanananda read the *Shiva Sutras,* a text in the Trika school of Kashmir Shaivism; he discerned a close connection with the teachings of Rudrananda.

From 1980 to 1986, he studied Kashmiri Shaivism with Swami Laksmanjoo in Srinagar. In 1983, he embraced the ancient KASHMIRI SHAIVITE practice of Trika Yoga, the philosophical framework for the practice of Kundalini YOGA. According to Rudrananda, Trika Yoga denies that renunciation is the superior path to spiritual development, but instead embraces all ethnic lifestyles as avenues to realization. Trika Yoga emphasizes a commitment to positive participation in life as a means for developing spiritual discernment.

Swami Chetanananda, as an advocate of Trika Yoga, teaches MEDITATION and the philosophy and tantric practices of Kashmiri Shaivism. He oversees a translation program for both SANSKRIT and Tibetan spiritual texts and has expertise in Indian, Tibetan, and Indonesian art, history, and archaeology. He has studied ASANA (postures in HATHA YOGA) practice, cranial osteopathy, homeopathy, and acupuncture. He is the author of several books on spiritual practice, published by Rudra Press. Although he received initiation into SANNYAS (renunciation), he does not give *sannyas* initiation to others.

Chetanananda serves as abbot of Nityananda Institute and Rudrananda Ashram, both of which are now located in Portland, Oregon. He is spiritual teacher, mentor, and guide to students. The institute emphasizes the role of the teacher in promoting spiritual growth and the importance of being engaged with a specified lineage within which the teacher was trained. The Nityananda Institute, under the imprint of Rudra Press, publishes books on Kashmir Shaivism, Trika Yoga, and hatha yoga. The institute also includes the Abhinavagupta Institute, which offers scholarly translations of Kashmiri Shaivite texts.

Further reading: Swami Chetanananda, *The Breath of God* (Portland, Ore.: Rudra Press, 1988); ———, *Dynamic Stillness*. Part 1, *The Practice of Trika Yoga* (Portland, Oreg.: Rudra Press, 1990); ———, *Songs from the Center of the Well* (Portland, Ore.: Rudra Press, 1983).

Chidambaram

Chidambaram in the South Arcot District of the Indian state of Tamil Nadu has been an important pilgrimage center for those devoted to SHIVA since about the ninth century, when the site was known as Tillai. Tradition says that a Kashmiri king who was afflicted with an incurable disease bathed in the temple tank 1,500 years ago and was cured. He is said to have enlarged the temple in appreciation. Chidambaram is known for its phallic-shaped LINGAMS of light (*jyotirlingas*), which are set in bases of the vulvic goddess; they are a primary iconic symbol of Shiva.

Chidambaram is best known as the center of the cult of Shiva as the divine dancer or NATARAJA. It is said that one of the Chola kings (ninth to 13th centuries), Vira Chola, saw a vision of Shiva performing his cosmic dance near the shrine. He then built the Golden Shrine with Shiva Nataraja in it. In another section of the temple are the 108 dance postures found in Bharata's *NATYA SHASTRA*, sculpted in high relief in honor of Shiva the cosmic dancer. Shiva himself is said to have once danced in the hall there.

The Goddess KALI was the first inhabitant of Chidambaram, but Kali and Shiva entered into a dance contest, whose loser was to leave town. Shiva then defeated the Goddess by doing a dance pose with his leg straight up in the air. Kali, out of modesty, it is said, could not duplicate the feat and left. Her shrine is found in a temple on the borders of the town. Later South Indian kings expanded the Chidambaram temple, which now is a sprawling complex with shrines to many other deities besides Shiva. The great Tamil Shaivite saints APPAR and SUNDARAR sang of the shrine, and SEKKILAR, the great compiler of the compendium of the works of the Tamil Shaivite saints, the PERIYA PURANAM, used to recite there; notables and even kings traveled to hear him.

Further reading: B. Natarajan, *The City of Cosmic Dance: Cidambaram* (New Delhi: Orient Longmans, 1974); Paul Younger, *The Home of the Dancing Sivan:*

The Traditions of the Hindu Temple in Citamparam (New York: Oxford University Press, 1995).

Chidvilasananda, Swami (Gurumayi)

(1955–) *Shaivite teacher and head of Siddha Yoga Dham*

Swami Chidvilasananda is a prominent international teacher, writer, and SIDDHA YOGA master. She was chosen by Swami MUKTANANDA to be successor to his lineage.

Chidvilasananda was born on June 24, 1955, in a village in Karnataka state, India. Following the Indian custom, the family GURU, Swami Muktananda, gave her her name—Malti. She met the swami for the first time at age five when she visited his ASHRAM with her parents. That same year Muktananda had a senior disciple take the young child several times to the nearby village of Ganeshpuri for the blessing of his own guru, Bhagawan NITYANANDA, who at that point had only a few months left to live.

From then on Malti was educated under the guidance of her guru. She lived with her family in Bombay (Mumbai) and spent weekends and school holidays in Muktananda's ashram, chanting scriptural texts, following the disciplines of yoga, and attending to her guru. Even at a young age, Malti possessed a longing to know God, which fueled an intense focus on spiritual practice. When she was 13, Swami Muktananda gave Malti SHAKTIPAT DIKSHA, the spiritual initiation that awakens KUNDALINI energy.

Beginning in 1969, Malti traveled extensively with Swami Muktananda in India and the West. In 1975, in Oakland, California, Muktananda asked her to become his translator. She was 19 at the time. Her role was to provide English translation during Muktananda's public lectures, which were sometimes delivered to audiences that numbered in the thousands, and at his private meetings with students, dignitaries, and public officials from East and West. Through her translation, Malti learned to communicate the essence of Swami

Gurumayi Chidvilasananda (b. 1955), a Shaivite teacher and the head of Siddha Yoga Dham *(SYDA Foundation)*

Muktananda's teachings. She was also called on by her guru to perform a variety of other duties, including performing administrative duties with the newly formed Siddha Yoga Dham Association (SYDA) Foundation, a global nonprofit organization; teaching courses; giving her own lectures on KASHMIRI SHAIVISM, VEDANTA, and other philosophies fundamental to Siddha Yoga practice; assisting with the translation of his books; and handling his correspondence with devotees around the globe.

In April 1982, when Malti took vows of *sannyas,* Muktananda gave her the name Swami Chidvilasananda, "the bliss of the play of consciousness." Then he initiated and installed her as a Siddha Yoga guru, the direct descendant in his lineage. In the months that followed, in a final act of tutelage, he sent Swami Chidvilasananda to teach, on her own, in India and America. Her personal skill as a teacher and her capacity to fulfill the spiritual demands of the guru's lineage were thus consolidated and guaranteed. In October 1982, Swami Muktananda died (in traditional Hindu terms, the guru "took mahasamadhi").

Since then, as head of this lineage of meditation masters, Gurumayi Chidvilasananda has taught Siddha Yoga meditation to students on six continents. Gurumayi's books, filled with her teachings and poetry, have been translated into 12 languages. She has taken a special interest in making the Siddha Yoga path available to children and young people. Gurumayi's teachings are disseminated by the SYDA Foundation.

The philanthropic aspect of Gurumayi's work is expressed through the PRASAD Project. Established by Gurumayi in 1992, this charitable organization offers aid in seven countries, administering medical, dental, and nutrition assistance as well as community development projects. In 1997, Gurumayi founded the Muktabodha Indological Institute, an educational foundation that preserves endangered elements of India's scriptural heritage and the oral tradition of the VEDAS.

As a teacher, Gurumayi directs her students to assume responsibility for making the effort needed to succeed in their spiritual path. She emphasizes the importance of spiritual practice and the necessity of integrating the fruits of practice into the fabric of one's worldly life. She imparts the Siddha Yoga teachings in a way that makes them accessible and directly applicable to the challenges and opportunities of modern life. Gurumayi teaches Siddha Yoga students to live in the awareness of the Self so that they can transform their world as well as themselves. And she continues to awaken spiritual energy in her students, through the vehicle of the Siddha Yoga Shaktipat Intensive, a course of study that teaches students a practice and discipline and that introduces them to the transmission of energy from Gurumayi to each of them, the profound spiritual awakening of kundalini SHAKTI (spiritual energy).

Further reading: Douglas Renfrew Brooks et al., *Meditation Revolution: A History and Theology of the Siddha Yoga Lineage* (South Fallsburg, N.Y.: Agama Press, 1997); Gurumayi Chidvilasananda, *Courage and Contentment* (South Fallsburg, N.Y.: SYDA Foundation, 1999); ———, *Kindle My Heart: Wisdom and Inspiration from a Living Master GuruMayi Chidvilasananda,* 2 vols. (New York: Prentice Hall, 1989–1991); Swami Shantanananda, *The Splendor of Recognition: An Exploration of the Pratyabhijna-Hrdayam, a Text on the Ancient Science of the Soul* (South Fallsburg, N.Y.: SYDA Foundation, n.d.).

Ching Hai Wu Shang   *See* SANT MAT.

Chinmaya Mission   *See* CHINMAYANANDA, SWAMI.

Chinmayananda, Swami (1916–1993)
founder of Chinmaya Mission

Swami Chinmayananda was an influential teacher of Hindu scriptures. He gave public lectures, set up ashrams, and preached to adults and children around the world. His Chinmaya Mission has worked to further Vedic education among adults and children and runs a large network of charitable institutions.

Balakrishna Menon was born on May 8, 1916, the son of Parakutti and Kuttan Menon in Ernakulam, Kerala, in South India. His aristocratic family followed strict Kerala Hindu traditions. Saints and sages often visited the family home and paid attention to the young boy. A bright student, he read widely and was good at sports. An extrovert, he got along well with others and exhibited a charming personality. He studied science in Cochin and later graduated in science at

Madras University; he received a master's degree in literature from Lucknow University.

At Lucknow University he became active in campus life. In 1942 he joined the Indian independence movement, writing and distributing leaflets, organizing strikes, and giving speeches. He became quite visible in the movement and the British issued a warrant for his arrest. He went into hiding but soon after returning was caught and put in prison, where he spent several months under difficult conditions. While in prison he studied the works of major writers of contemporary Hindu thought and practice and was inspired to follow a path of inquiry.

After working as a freelance journalist, he decided to devote himself to the quest for SELF-REALIZATION. He studied VEDANTA with Swami SIVANANDA at the Divine Life Society in Rishikesh for a number of years and in 1949 was initiated into SANNYAS (renunciation) by Swami Sivananda. His name, Swami Chinmayananda Saraswati, means the "one who revels in the bliss of pure consciousness." At Sivananda's suggestion, he studied with Swami Tapovan Maharaj high in the Himalayas at Uttarkashi. He accepted Swami Tapovan as his guru and studied with him for seven years. In 1948 he made a trek to several traditional Hindu pilgrimage centers in the Himalayas, recording his account in *My Trek through Uttarkhand*.

In 1951, Chinmayananda started his mission of teaching and preaching to public audiences, a pattern that he followed until his death. He gave discourses and held meditation camps in India and abroad. In 1963 he set up his headquarters, Sandeepany Sadhanalaya, in Bombay (Mumbai). From there he established centers, ashrams, and schools in many parts of India. He organized children's clubs to teach the principles of Hindu religion and culture. The Chinmaya Mission, which has grown considerably over the years, sponsors 62 schools for elementary education, nursing, and management in India that teach normal school curriculum as well as the Vedic heritage. The mission also sponsors free clinics, hospitals, vocational schools, orphanages, and retirement homes.

Chinmayananda was foremost a SANSKRIT pundit (scholar and teacher) and commentator on Hindu scriptures. He expounded each scripture verse by verse and then interpreted deeper levels of meaning against a backdrop of both Hindu and Western philosophy. He insisted that serious seekers find GURUS, teaching that a guru's guidance is necessary. He also taught that over time work with an external guru changes into guidance by a more pure and enlightened intellect within the student himself.

An erudite and acclaimed teacher of ADVAITA VEDANTA, Chinmayananda always stressed the importance of BHAKTI or devotion, which he defined as a consistent effort to raise the ego from its entrenchment in false values to an appreciation of selfhood. His centers contain temples and altars to several Hindu deities.

Chinmayananda was elected president of the Hindu Religion Section of the Centennial Conference of the Parliament of World Religions in Chicago in 1993, where he was to receive recognition as a world-renowned teacher of Vedanta and selfless servant of humanity. Unfortunately, he died on August 3, 1993, before the conference took place.

Further reading: Swami Chinmayananda, *The Holy Geeta: Commentary by Swami Chinmayananda* (Bombay: Central Chinmaya Mission Trust, 1976); ———, *A Manual for Self-Unfoldment* (Bombay: Central Chinmaya Mission Trust, 1985); ———, *Meditation and Life* (Madras: Chinmaya Publications Trust, 1967); ———, *Self-Unfoldment* (Piercy, Calif.: Chinmaya, 1992); Nancy Patchen, *The Journey of a Master: Swami Chinmayananda* (Berkeley, Calif.: Asian Humanities Press, 1989).

Chinmoy, Sri (1931–) *teacher of integral yoga and peace activist*

Sri Chinmoy has established centers and a following for his spiritual teachings, in the tradition of Sri Aurobindo, in many countries around the world. His teaching makes use of his own music and art, and of sports, as well as MEDITATION.

Chinmoy Kumar Ghose was born, the youngest of seven siblings, on August 27, 1931, to a Kshatriya family in Shakpura, a small village in the Chittagong District of East Bengal (now Bangladesh). His father, Shashi Kumar, was a supervisor for the railroad and later a banker. Both his father and his mother, Yogamaya Vishwas, died before Chinmoy was 12 years old. In 1944, the 12-year old child took residence at the Sri Aurobindo Ashram in Pondicherry, South India, where his eldest brother, a *sannyasi* (renunciant), and some elder members of the family were already living. Here he practiced meditation, wrote poetry and essays, and created songs as part of his spiritual practice. He also excelled in sports.

Sri Chinmoy (b. 1931), a popular yogi and peace activist, who has a worldwide following *(Courtesy Sri Chinmoy Centre)*

The young Chinmoy studied in Pondicherry for 20 years and often took the blessing of both Sri Aurobindo and the MOTHER. After achieving accomplishment in advanced states of meditation, he moved to New York City in 1964 at the age of 32 to share the spirituality of India with seekers in the West. He continues to travel widely, offering concerts, lectures, and public meditations. He does not charge a fee for his spiritual guidance or performances.

His teaching focuses on the heart's aspiration as the creative spiritual force that lies behind all great advances in religion, culture, and science. Self-transcendence and living in the heart advance fulfillment and attunement to the highest reality. His message is consistent with the basic themes of Hinduism: that God is inside each person and that God at every moment is transcending his own reality.

Sri Chinmoy has centers in various parts of the world where his students practice spiritual disciplines according to his inspiration and guidance. Each Sri Chinmoy Centre is dedicated to harmonizing the inner life of aspiration and the outer life of dedication.

Chinmoy has been creative in several fields—writing and performing songs and music, creating visual art, and engaging in sports. He sponsors many events in support of peace and international cooperation, including the Sri Chinmoy Oneness-Home Peace Run, a relay that covers more than 77 countries. His extensive Web site offers information about all of these activities.

Further reading: Sri Chinmoy, *The Garland of Nation-Souls: Complete Talks at the United Nations* (Deerfield, Fla.: Health Communications, 1995); ———, *Mother India's Lighthouse: India's Spiritual Leaders* (Blauvelt, N.Y.: R. Steiner, 1973); ———, *The Oneness of the Eastern Heart and the Western Mind,* Parts 1–3 (Jamaica, N.Y.: Agni Press, 2003–4).

chit   See SAT-CHIT-ANANDA.

Chitrabhanu, Gurudev Sri (1922–) *Jain monk and teacher of* ahimsa

Gurudev Sri Chitrabhanu is a very popular Jain preacher and advocate of nonviolence as a way of life. He was the first Jain master to leave India to preach and lecture in the West. Gurudev Sri Chitrabhanu was born on July 26, 1922, in Rajasthan, India. After an experience of spiritual awakening at the age of 20, he became sensitive to questions of the purpose and meaning of life. His search for answers led him to the JAIN religion. For 28 years he lived the life of a monk, the first five years in silence. Through his practice, Chitrabhanu came to the realization that the purpose of life is to be liberated from attachment and desire. Leaving the monastery with this wisdom, he promoted a message of enlightenment and became known to millions across India.

Chitrabhanu became an advocate of AHIMSA (nonviolence) during the same period that Mohandas Karamchand GANDHI pursued his nonviolent struggle for Indian independence. After the upsurge of violence afflicting the Western world during the 1960s, Chitrabhanu made a conscious decision to spread *ahimsa* around the world. In 1970, he was invited to the Second Spiritual Summit Conference in Geneva. He became the first Jain master ever to travel to the West, excusing himself from the doctrine that Jains should travel only by foot. The following year he attended the Third Spiritual Summit Conference at Harvard Divinity School and lectured at a number of universities in the eastern United States. In 1974, he founded the Jain Meditation International Center in the Ansonia section of New York City.

The center follows the fundamental principles of *ahimsa*, promoting the mission to create unity within the diversity of humankind. Chitrabhanu teaches that everyone must become his or her own master, believing that the approach to peace begins with oneself in everyday living. The mission of one's life is to realize this inner mastery and peace. The JAIN MEDITATION INTERNATIONAL CENTER includes 67 centers across North America as well as in England, Africa, Japan, and India.

Chitrabhanu has written over 25 books on self-realization, liberation, and peace. He continues to give talks at various centers around the world. Chitrabhanu and his wife, Pramoda, are the main advisers for the Jain Meditation International Center.

Further reading: Gurudev Shree Chitrabhanu and Leonard M. Marks, *Realize What You Are: The Dynamics of Jain Meditation* (New York: Dodd, Mead, 1978); Gurudev Shree Chitrabhanu and Lyssa Miller, *The Psychology of Enlightenment: Meditations on the Seven Energy Centers* (New York: Dodd, Mead, 1979); Gurudev Shree Chitrabhanu and Clare Rosenfield, *The Philosophy of Soul and Matter* (New York: Jain Meditation International Center, 1979); Gurudev Shree Chitrabhanu and Clare Rosenfield, *Twelve Facets of Reality: The Jain Path to Freedom* (New York: Dodd, Mead, 1980); Clare Rosenfield, *Gurudev Shree Chitrabhanu: A Man with a Vision* (Bombay: Divine Knowledge Society, n.d.).

chitta See YOGA SUTRA.

Chittirai festival

The Chittirai festival that takes place in Tamil Nadu state, in MADURAI and Alakar Kovil Temple and points in between, is one of the largest South Indian festivals. It takes place in the Sanskrit lunar month of Chaitra (Tamil, Chittirai), corresponding to April or May. It brings together the Shaivite and the Vaishnavite (*see* SHAIVISM; VAISHNAVISM) communities of the region in a single, two-part celebration. Apparently, this larger festival is in fact a combination of two festivals that once took place a few weeks apart. The joining of the two into one festival was the work of the Telegu king of Madurai Tirumala Nayak (1623–59).

The Madurai part of the celebration tells the tale of MINAKSHI, the goddess of Madurai, and her marriage to Sundreshvara (Shiva). It is focused on the monumental MEENAKSHI temple, with its four 100-foot towers, at the center of the city. Here, the festival lasts 12 full days, but it is the 10th day, when the huge temple car carrying Minakshi and her husband, Shiva, is pulled by devotees on the streets that encircle the temple, that is most dramatic. This temple car is elaborate and grand with wheels about 10 feet high and a canopy over the divinities that reaches to 40 feet. Devotees vie to pull on the heavy one-foot-thick ropes to convey the cart on a circumambulation of the temple. This temple parade is carried out each year after Minakshi and Sundereshvara (Shiva) are married.

The kings of Madurai were traditionally associated with the god Shiva. The festival's marriage of the god Shiva to Minakshi not only joins an indigenous, non-Aryan goddess to an ARYAN and Brahmanical divinity, but symbolizes a link in sovereignty between Shiva/king and the local population.

The second part of the festival starts in the mountains 70 miles west of Madurai. There the god Alakar, a form of Vishnu, proceeds toward Madurai and the Vaikai River as part of his annual outing. As it happens, VISHNU is the brother of Minakshi and is going to give the bride away to Shiva. Unfortunately, when he reaches the Vaikai River, in sight of the great temple of his sister, he discovers that he has arrived late at the wedding and must return. The Kallar community, relatively low-caste devotees of Vishnu, play a prominent role in this part of the festival, which lasts nine days.

Further reading: D. Dennis Hudson, *The Two Chitra Festivals of Madurai in Religious Festivals in South India and Sri Lanka*. Edited by Guy R. Welbon and Glenn E. Yocum (Delhi: Manohar, 1982); William P. Harman, *The Sacred Marriage of a Hindu Goddess* (Bloomington: Indiana University Press, 1989).

Christian-Hindu relations

Christianity has existed in India for almost two millennia. The Malakara Orthodox Church, head-

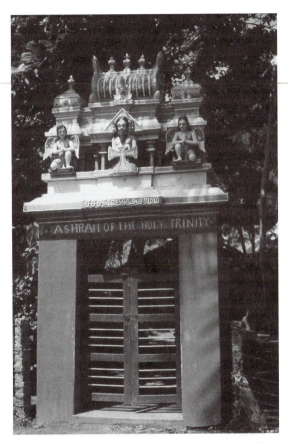

Shantivanam, a Christian ashram, in Tiruchchirapalli, Tamil Nadu, India *(Constance A. Jones)*

quartered in Kerala, has provided a Christian presence within the larger world of Hindu life. This Orthodox community has generally lived a peaceful existence over the centuries, but one largely cut off from the mainstream of the Christian world. The Roman Catholic nation of Portugal claimed portions of India in 1498, and, once a Catholic bishop was placed at the Portuguese colony of Goa, an aggressive mission program was initiated by the Jesuits. For a short time, the Orthodox realigned with the Catholics but soon saw their interests diverge and returned to an independent status.

A new era began in 1706 with the arrival of the first Protestant missionaries, Lutherans who began their missionary efforts from a base in Tranquebar. They were joined by a few other efforts to evangelize the country, but mission work did not begin in earnest until the early 19th century, when it won the backing of British colonial authorities. The number of conversions was modest, with occasional episodes of what were termed mass movements, when an entire community or caste would suddenly convert to Christianity. Often, these mass movements would originate among people at the lowest levels of the caste system, especially untouchables (Dalits), who had little to lose by abandoning Hinduism. (*See* UNTOUCHABILITY.)

During the missionary era from the 18th century onward, Protestants adopted various plans for developing a successful thrust into Indian society, including the building of modern colleges and hospitals, intellectual appeals to elites, and enticing of Dalits and various fringe groups away from lives devoid of privilege. The end result was the development of the third largest religious community in India (after Hindus and Muslims), although today the 60 million Christians represent barely 6 percent of the population.

Throughout the 20th century before Indian independence, Christianity enjoyed a favored relationship with the colonial government and often used that special status to engage in aggressive campaigns of proselytizing. Such aggressive actions created a level of hostility among Indian Hindu leaders, who developed an extended list of grievances against the church, not the least the missionaries' use of their favorable status and relative wealth to woo converts to their religion instead of teaching the merits of their faith. Moreover, Hinduism was not a missionary faith, and it saw itself at a disadvantage in the face of aggressive proselytizing. Finally, Hindu leaders complained of the ways that the Christian churches, often in league with colonial authorities, were disrupting a traditional and sacred social order.

As native Indians, such as Vedanayagam Samuel Azariah (1874–1945), the first native Anglican bishop, gained positions of authority in Indian Christianity, they began to address some of these issues. In particular, these native Indians criticized Western missionaries for failing to distinguish between the faith they expounded and the Western culture from which they emerged. Because of ignorance or thoughtlessness, they complained, missionaries frequently tried to impose Western culture, provoking more opposition than they would have if they had focused exclusively on the religious message of Christianity, which was not necessarily offensive to Indians. At the same time, a new generation of more thoughtful Western Christian missionaries, who were also students of comparative religion, arrived in India; they were willing to appropriate features of Hindu piety and spirituality, and to shape a Christianity that incorporated as many elements of Indian thought and practice as possible.

By the middle of the 19th century, Christians attempted to initiate dialogue with Hindu believers, especially groups of liberal believers that evolved from the Hindu Renaissance. Among the first results of these early conversations was a decision by the Unitarian Church that the BRAHMO SAMAJ, founded in 1823 by Raja Rammohun ROY (1772–1833), was actually preaching the same basic doctrines as traditional Hinduism, uncorrupted (by *sati* [suttee], polygamy, and the worship of idols). The Unitarians, then, withdrew from the field of proselytization and used their missionary allocations to support the Brahmo Samaj in various ways that continue to the present, including the opening of American Unitarian seminaries to train leaders of the Brahmo Samaj.

Meanwhile, various Hindu leaders began to develop a range of views on the nature of Jesus Christ. Roy saw him as a moral and religious reformer, Sri RAMAKRISHNA (1836–86) saw him as an enlightened soul leading others to enlightenment. Swami VIVEKANANDA (1863–1902) developed Ramakrishna's advaitic (non-dualist) perspective by including the life of Christ in his teaching. Roman Catholic thinkers such as Brahmabandhav Upadhyaya (1861–1907) and currently Raimundo Panikkar (b. 1918) attempted to integrate Hindu concepts into an Indian Christian theology. In 1899, in spite of British attempts to suppress his efforts, Upadhyaya established a Catholic ashram, called Kasthalic Matha. These efforts at syncretism have contributed to the development of a Christian theology that includes Hindu religious categories. Such attempts have always had to answer charges from both Western Christians and Hindus that the process of articulating an Indian Christianity distorts both faiths.

On a more practical level, two Frenchmen, Jules Monchanin (1895–1957) and Henri Le Saux (1910–73), the latter better known as ABHISHIKTANANDA, tried to combine elements of Western and Eastern monastic practice. In 1950 they founded Saccidananda Ashram in Tamil Nadu, South India. The pair adapted Benedictine monasticism to the Indian ascetic tradition, which resulted in what has been termed Christian SANNYAS (renunciation). Both Protestants and Catholics have found points of connection with Hindu and Christian practice and spirituality, ranging from the monastic experiments of Dom Bede Griffiths (1906–93) to the philosophical and scientific contributions of Ravi Ravindra to the ashram movement founded by the Methodist E. Stanley Jones (1884–1973).

In the post–World War II environment, the value of world faith communities to one another has been an increasing theme in religious writings. The World Council of Churches has emphasized interreligious dialogue, although it has taken second place to building intra-Christian relations. In like measure, in 1964, in the midst of Vatican II, the Roman Catholic Church established the Pontifical Council for Inter-Religious Dialogue. One of its major departments is designed to build new levels of understanding and respect of Hinduism. The council supported Pope John Paul II's (1920–2005) periodical meetings with Hindu and other religious leaders voicing his concern for interreligious dialogue in which the followers of the various religions can discover shared elements of spirituality, while acknowledging their differences. As the 20th century came to a close, Pope John Paul II offered an apology for the attitudes of mistrust and hostility assumed by Catholics toward followers of other religions, as part of a broad papal acknowledgment of the failings of Christians in pursuit of their missions.

Most recently, religious leaders in India have led in initiating interreligious dialogue with the founding of such organizations as the World Fellowship of Religions (1973) and the World Union (1958). In the DIASPORA, Hindus have been very active in many national interreligious councils and have been especially prominent in the Council for a Parliament of the World's Religions based in Chicago, Illinois, which holds international conferences in different parts of the world every five years. Among North American organizations that attempt to encourage and focus on dialogue between Hindus and Christians is the Society for Hindu-Christian Studies, which is currently administered by scholars at Notre Dame, Indiana, and Thiruvanmiyur, Madras (Chennai), India. They also publish the *Journal of Hindu-Christian Studies*.

As the new century begins, India has been hit with a wave of anti-Christian activity fueled by anger over the proselytizing activity of the increasing number of missionaries. Occasionally, this has erupted in violence. These violent incidents have only increased attempts by Hindu and Christian leaders to pursue understanding through dialogue.

Further reading: B. Animananda, *The Blade: The Life and Work of Brahmabandhab Upadhyay* (Calcutta: Roy & Son, 1945); Harold Coward, *Hindu-Christian Dialogue* (Maryknoll, N.Y.: Orbis Books, 1989); Stephen A. Graham, *Ordinary Man, Extraordinary Mission: The Life and Work of E. Stanley Jones* (Nashville, Tenn.: Abingdon Press, 2005); Bede Griffiths, *The Golden String* (New York: Kennedy, 1953); ———, *The Other*

Half of My Soul: Bede Griffiths and the Hindu-Christian Dialogue. Compiled by Beatrice Bruteau (Wheaton, Ill.: Theosophical Publishing House, 1996);———, *Vedanta and Christian Faith* (Los Angeles: Dawn Horse Press, 1973); Raimundo Panikkar, *The Vedic Experience* (Berkeley: University of California Press, 1977); Ravi Ravindra, *Whispers from the Other Shore: A Spiritual Search—East and West* (Wheaton, Ill.: Theosophical Publishing House, 1884); ———, *The Yoga of the Christ* (Longmead, England: Element, 1990); Philip St. Romain, *Kundalini Energy and Christian Spirituality* (New York: Crossroads, 1991); James Stuart, *Swami Abhishiktananda: His Life Told through His Letters* (Delhi: ISPCK, 1989).

Cohen, Andrew (1955–) *teacher of spirituality and evolutionary enlightenment*

Cohen is an American spiritual teacher in the tradition of H. W. L. Poonja. His influential publications and lectures focus on the evolution of consciousness.

Born in New York City on October 23, 1955, Cohen experienced a deep spiritual awakening at age 16, without the help of any spiritual path. Beginning in his early 20s, he studied and practiced martial arts, KRIYA YOGA, and Buddhism. He met his guru, H. W. L. Poonja, in Lucknow, India, in 1986 and experienced a life-changing awakening in his presence.

Cohen's teaching centers around trying to guide aspirants to a place in which the ego is tamed, and each individual is more passionate about the evolution of world consciousness than about his or her individual liberation. According to Cohen, the energy of enlightenment wants to express itself as a force of evolution. Each individual can and should serve as a portal for that energy to express itself.

In 1986 Cohen began giving teachings in London. He then moved his headquarters to Marin County, California, and now resides in Lenox, Massachusetts. He travels the world giving public talks and holding retreats. His students have formed the International Fellowship for the Realization of Impersonal Enlightenment; it has centers in Europe, Asia, and the United States and runs a retreat center in the Berkshire mountains in western Massachusetts where Cohen lives.

Cohen's magazine *What Is Enlightenment?*, founded in 1992, features interviews with spiritual and cultural leaders of the age and addresses questions of ecology, spirituality, and psychology. Since 2000, the magazine has sponsored a speaker series with presentations by evolutionary thinkers from around the world. Known as *EnlightenNEXT* since September 2005, it has become a major publication in the spiritual community in the United States.

Further reading: Andrew Cohen, *Autobiography of an Awakening* (Corte Madera, Calif.: Moksha Foundation, 1992); ———, *Embracing Heaven and Earth: The Liberation Teachings of Andrew Cohen* (Lenox, Mass.: Moksha Press, 2000); ———, *Freedom Has No History* (Lenox, Mass.: Moksha Press, 1997); ———, *Living Enlightenment: A Call for Evolution beyond Ego* (Lenox, Mass.: Moksha Press, 2002); ———, *An Unconditional Relationship to Life* (Larkspur, Calif.: Moksha Press, 1995); Moksha Foundation, *What Is Enlightenment?* (Corte Madera, Calif.: Moksha Foundation, 1992).

creation myths   *See* MYTHS OF CREATION.

cremation   *See* FUNERAL RITES.

D

Da Avabhasa   *See* ADI DA SAMRAJ.

Daksha

Daksha is a RISHI, best known as the father-in-law of SHIVA. He is the son of the god BRAHMA and father of Shiva's first wife, SATI.

Daksha is best known for the events surrounding a Vedic sacrifice that he sponsored without inviting Shiva. When Sati found out that this special sacrifice was going to take place, she confronted her father. He replied with verbal abuse, which resulted in her death, because of a curse that had been placed on him. When Shiva heard, he (or his creation Virabhadra) cut off Daksha's head and destroyed the sacrificial grounds. Daksha was later restored to life, with the head of a ram.

In the epic and PURANIC literature, Daksha the *rishi* frequently appears in different cycles of creation. He is said to have had 50 daughters, 13 of whom were married to the *rishi* Kashyapa. His daughter Svaha was married to AGNI, god of fire; Sati was married to Shiva; and the 27 remaining daughters were married to the god of the Moon, CHANDRA, and are identified with the lunar asterisms, stars that are seen to be astrologically related to the Moon.

As a Vedic divinity Daksha is listed as one of the ADITYAS—SONS OF ADITI—although he is sometimes said to be Aditi's father. Thus, in some Vedic literature he is considered to be the grandfather of the gods and the *asuras* (antigods or demons), who are all brothers in Vedic literature. (*See* DEMONIC BEINGS; VEDAS.)

Further reading: Cornelia Dimmitt and J. A. B. van Buitenen, *Classical Hindu Mythology: A Reader in the Sanskrit Puranas* (Philadelphia: Temple University Press, 1978); Stella Kramrisch, *The Presence of Siva* (Princeton, N.J. Princeton University Press, 1981).

Dakshineshwar   *See* RAMAKRISHNA, SRI.

dana

Since ancient times *dana* (giving, charity, or liberality) has been an important aspect of good conduct (DHARMA). The DHARMASHASTRA of MANU states that in this era of decline (KALI YUGA), *dana* is the most important virtue, compared to past ages, when TAPAS (spiritual power, knowledge, or the Vedic sacrifice) was paramount. The text prescribes *dana* as an important duty for all the three upper (twice-born) classes. In Vedic times a *dana* or gift was given to BRAHMINS for remission of sins.

Further reading: Kala Acharya, *Puranic Concept of Dana* (Delhi: Nag, 1993); Vijay Nath, *Dana, Gift System in Ancient India, c. 600 B.C.–c. A.D. 300: A Socio-Economic Perspective* (New Delhi: Munshiram Manoharlal, 1987); Wendy Doniger O'Flaherty and J. Duncan M. Derrett, *The Concept of Duty in South Asia* (New Delhi: Vikas Publishing House, 1978).

Danielou, Alain (1907–1994) *scholar of Hindu music and literature*

Alain Danielou was an accomplished musician and artist who developed an intense interest in Hindu music and literature. He won a respected status in the West for classical Indian music; he also wrote many popular books that expound Hinduism and Indian culture.

Danielou was born on October 4, 1907, at Neuilly-sur-Seine near Paris, France. As the son of an aristocratic family, he spent much of his time in the country being educated by tutors. He occupied his time in the library, learning piano and painting. Danielou's mother was a devoted Catholic, who founded a religious order; his father was an anticlerical politician. Danielou's artistic abilities took him to the United States, where he attended school in Annapolis, sold paintings at exhibits, and played piano at movie theaters. When he returned to France he continued to study music under Charles Panzera and Max d'Olonne.

In 1932 Danielou began to travel extensively throughout North Africa, the Middle East, and Asia with the Swiss photographer Raymond Burnier. While in India he became fascinated with its traditional culture. He became acquainted with the poet Rabindranath TAGORE, who employed him as director of the school of music in Shantiniketan, Tagore's university. Danielou later moved to BENARES (Varanasi) and met the Indian music master Shivendranath Basu. He remained in India for the next 30 years. During that time he learned both Hindi and

SANSKRIT. He was introduced to Swami Karpatri and translated some of his works. Swami Karpatri later initiated Danielou into Shaivite Hinduism (see SHAIVISM) and gave him the name Shiva Sharan. He continued a dialogue over the years with René Guénon, scholar of Sufism and ADVAITA VEDANTA, on the philosophy of Hinduism. In 1954, he left Benares to become director of the Adyar Library of Sanskrit Manuscripts in Madras (Chennai).

Danielou became sympathetic to the Indian independence movement. After India won its independence from Britain, he returned to Europe in 1963 and devoted himself to the mission of presenting a true understanding of Hinduism to the West. He founded the Intercultural Institute of Comparative Music Studies in Berlin and Venice, which he led for decades. Through this institute he organized concerts featuring Asian musicians and began recording traditional Indian music through an arrangement with UNESCO. Danielou is credited with raising the status of Indian classical music in the West to that of a recognized art form.

Danielou is best known for his scholarship on Hindu culture. He authored over 30 books on topics ranging from music to religion. In 1971, he published a *Brief History of India*, which has since been translated and republished in 12 different countries. His works on religion have significantly shaped the conversation on the relationship between ancient Western culture and Hinduism. In *Gods of Love and Ecstasy: The Traditions of Shiva and Dionysus*, Danielou illustrates the similarities in rites and beliefs between ancient Greek religion and Shaivism. He claims further that the loss of such rites has left humanity in the West alienated from nature and the divine.

Danielou's books continue to be a source of great influence to those exploring Hindu culture. His works, written in French, have been translated into eight different languages, including English, Italian, and Spanish. He has also written piano arrangements to songs by Rabindranath Tagore.

In his later years, Danielou continued interpreting the music and philosophy of India to the

West. In 1981 he received the UNESCO/CIM prize for music and in 1987 the Kathmandu medal. In 1992 he was appointed member of the Indian National Academy of Music, Dance and Theater. He died on January 27, 1994.

Further reading: Alain Danielou, *A Brief History of India* (Rochester, Vt.: Inner Traditions, 2003); ———, *A Catalogue of Recorded Classical and Traditional Indian Music* (Paris: UNESCO, 1952); ———, *Gods of Love and Ecstasy: The Traditions of Shiva and Dionysus* (Rochester, Vt.: Inner Traditions, 1992); ———, *The Myths and Gods of India* (Rochester, Vt.: Inner Traditions, 1985); ———, *The way to the Labyrinth: Memories of East and West* (New York: New Directions, 1987); ———, *While the Gods Play: Shaiva Oracles and Predictions on the Cycles of History and the Destiny of Mankind* (Rochester, Vt.: Inner Traditions, 1987).

darshan

Darshan is from the Sanskrit root *drish,* "to see." It refers to a most important element of Hinduism—the eye-to-eye contact between an iconic divinity (*see* ICONS) or a divine personage (e.g., AMRITANANDAMAYI MA, SATYA SAI BABA) and the devotee or worshipper. *Darshan* can by itself confer grace upon a seeker and result in spiritual benefit. So, Hindus eagerly visit temples as well as divine persons for *darshan.* If during a festival an icon is paraded through the streets, everyone vies to catch sight of it, to receive its glance and grace. No icon in the form of a person is considered an active divinity until the ritual opening of its eyes.

Further reading: Diana Eck, *Darsan: Seeing the Divine Image in India,* 3d ed. (New York: Columbia University Press, 1998).

Dasha Mahavidya

The Mahavidyas (*maha* great, *vidya* knowledge) are 10 (*dasha*) goddesses who are grouped together in various literary, iconographic, and mythical contexts in India. It is a tantric grouping, though some of the goddesses are from a nontantric, normative context.

In TANTRISM, a *VIDYA* is equivalent to a MANTRA, but used for goddesses (the term *mantra* is restricted to devotion to male divinities). It is understood in the tantric context that the mantra or *vidya* and the divinity are identical. Therefore this group of 10 goddesses can be logically referred to as the 10 *vidyas.* Each of these goddesses can in fact grant the ultimate "knowledge" or *vidya* that can lead to liberation from birth and rebirth.

The 10 goddesses constituting the Mahavidyas are KALI, Tara, Tripura-sundari (Sri Lalita), Bhuvaneshvari, Chinnamasta, Bhairavi, Dhumavati, Bagalamukhi, Matangi, and Kamala (LAKSHMI). Kali is the fierce black goddess, the ruler over time (*kala*), who helped DURGA defeat the demons in order to restore order to the world.

Tara, known as "She who takes one across the ocean of birth and rebirth," is more prominent in Buddhism. Iconographically, she very much resembles Kali, as she is depicted seated or standing upon the supine SHIVA. She is associated with the cremation ground and images of skulls. Tara reveals, however, a nurturing aspect that is usually not found with Kali. At Tarapith in Birbhum, Bengal, she is depicted nursing Shiva from her breast.

Tripurasundari is none other than Sri Lalita, the 16-year-old goddess who is the transcendent One. She is usually shown with a benign aspect, although she is in fact the incarnation of all goddesses, whether benign or fierce.

Bhuvaneshvari, who is often seen as the embodiment of the physical world, is vermilion in color, has three eyes, and wears a jeweled crown. She has a smiling face and a crescent Moon on her brow. She can be depicted with two, six, or 20 hands holding various objects including the lotus and a bow. She is usually depicted sitting in the cross-legged, "lotus position" yogic posture and is generally shown without clothing. A goddess described in the text Prapancasara called

Prapanceshvari appears to be identical to Bhuvaneshvari; this text is the fullest source for details on Bhuvaneshvari. In most aspects she resembles SARASVATI. In tantrism, her worship resembles in many details the worship of Sri Lalita.

Chinnamasta has the most startling representation of all these goddesses. She stands, self-decapitated, with her head in one hand and the large cutting instrument in the other. On two sides attendants drink her blood. She stands on the recumbent, copulating couple of Kama, god of love, and RATI, his mate. As does Kali she wears a necklace of human skulls, and, as does SHIVA she has a cobra encircling her upper body. Her body is naked, except for ornaments. One myth has Chinnamasta as a form of PARVATI, the consort of Shiva. Another sees her as Parvati in the form of CHANDI. In both myths the goddess is begged for food by her attendants and cuts off her head to offer them her blood. There are specific texts that outline the worship of this goddess with mantras and YANTRAS.

Bhairavi (the fierce goddess) is described as wearing red silk and a garland of severed heads (again as does Kali). Her breasts are said to be smeared with blood. She has three eyes with a crescent Moon on her forehead. She smiles, wearing a jeweled crown. She is shown with four or 10 hands. She holds a sword and a begging bowl in two of them. She is sometimes shown in sexual intercourse sitting astride Shiva. The literature often regards Bhairavi as Mahadevi, or Supreme Divinity. She is seen as supreme above even the male divinities BRAHMA, Shiva, and VISHNU. Unusual epithets call her "Fond of semen and menstrual blood" and "She who dwells in the YONI [the vagina]." Such epithets show her transgressive, tantric character.

Dhumavati, the widow goddess, is a rare and unusual personage. She is seen as black in color, ugly, old, and angry. She has hanging breasts, a long nose, and dirty clothes. She rides a conveyance that has a banner with a crow on it. She has only two arms. In one hand is a winnowing basket

and the other shows the "boon-granting" (VARADA MUDRA) gesture. (But sometimes she will hold a begging bowl made of a human skull and a spear.) Dhumavati is only rarely found independently of the Mahavidyas.

Dhumavati's origin myths show her being born from the smoke of the funeral pyre of the prototypical self-immolated goddess, SATI. Another myth shows her as a form of Sati, forced to become a widow through a curse of Shiva. Her separate temples are few. At her temples liquor, meat, and a marijuana drink are offered in addition to the usual offerings. Though her mythological history seems to depict this goddess as dangerous, she is approachable in temples and offers boons and protections, as any other local goddess.

Bagalamukhi is depicted on a lion throne. She has a yellow complexion and wears a yellow dress and yellow ornaments. She is surrounded and covered with things of yellow. One myth shows this goddess as a form of Sri Lalita. In a more popular myth she stops a demon named Madan who is killing people merely by speaking. She grasps his tongue and he becomes her devotee and therefore is not killed; there are iconographic and pictorial depictions of this event. In another myth Bagalamukhi is created by a curse of Shiva upon Parvati.

Bagalamukhi is associated with magic and occult power. She is often approached for magical powers such as the ability to immobilize or attract people. Sometimes, as with all of these tantric deities, she is associated with sexuality and sexual intercourse. As have several of the Mahavidyas, she has aspects that belong to Kali and she is sometimes said to sit upon a corpse, often while holding on to the tongue of the demon described in her myth.

Matangi is an unusual goddess who prefers offerings that are "polluted" in the Hindu sense, food that has been partially eaten or left over, things that have menstrual blood on them or have touched the dead. She is depicted as a 16-year-old girl, with blue or greenish skin and three eyes, wearing red clothing and accoutrements, seated on a corpse. She has two or four hands. In one tale she emerges from leftover food that Shiva, Parvati, Vishnu, and Lakshmi have just eaten.

Another myth calls Matangi a sister of Shiva, cursed by Parvati to be reborn in an untouchable (Dalit) family, forced to survive on leftovers and other polluted things. Matangi is also sometimes associated with the giving of magical powers.

The final of the 10 Mahavidyas is Kamala. She is identified with Lakshmi and carries Lakshmi's typical characteristics and iconography, except that she is never shown in conjunction with her husband, Vishnu.

Further reading: David Kinsley, *Tantric Visions of the Divine Feminine: The Ten Mahavidyas* (Berkeley: University of California Press, 1997); Sarbeswar Satpathy, *Dasa Mahavidya and Tantra Sastra* (Calcutta: Punthi Pustak, 1992.)

Datta Yoga Center (est. 1986)

The Datta Yoga Center in West Sunbury, Pennsylvania, is a center of KRIYA YOGA practice and teaching. It was founded in 1986 by Sri Ganapati Sachchidananda Swami (b. May 26, 1942) as the American branch of Avadhoota Datta Peetham in Mysore, India (*see* AVADHUTA). The swami also founded the Datta Temple and Hall of Trinity in Baton Rouge, Louisiana, in 1997.

As a child, Sachchidananda was fond of the religious life and became a devoted yoga practitioner. As a young adult he became known as a healer in his home village of Mekedati, Karnataka, in southern India.

To his devotees, Sachchidananda is considered an *avadhuta*, or liberated one, following in the tradition of Lord DATTATREYA. His teachings emphasize *kriya yoga*, which focuses on breath as a means of turning attention toward one's inner self and the realization of God. The Datta Yoga Center is a nonmembership organization. Centers serve

as temples for worship services and dissemination of the *avadhuta's* message of love, peace, freedom, and service and provide a place where devotees can develop spiritual values.

Music, in the form of *bhajans* (songs) and instrumentals, many of which have been composed by Sachchidananda, are a significant part of worship services. He says, "Music is my religion, music is my language, music is my soul and music is my expression." Sachchidananda has organized Music for Healing and Meditation concerts throughout the United States and Europe. He is also an advocate of ayurvedic medicine (see AYURVEDA) and the sponsor of a hospital for the underprivileged in India.

The Datta Yoga Center publishes books by Sachchidananda, a monthly newsletter called *Bhakti Mala,* and CDs of Sachchidananda's performances of his musical compositions.

Further reading: Swami Ganapati Sachchidananda, *Dattatreya the Absolute* (Mysore: Sri Ganapathi Sachchidananda Ashram, 1984); ———, *Sri Guru Gita* (Machilipatnam: Sri Ganapati Sachchidananda Publications Trust, 1988).

Davis, Roy Eugene (1931–   ) *founder of Christian Spiritual Alliance*

Roy Eugene Davis is an American teacher of KRIYA YOGA. He is associated with the Christian New Thought movement and teaches metaphysical Christianity along with Indian thought and practice through lectures and a large publishing program.

Born on March 9, 1931, in Leavittsburg, Ohio, Roy Eugene Davis was raised on a farm. He attended the Church of the United Brethren as a child and early on became interested in yoga through reading. In 1948, at age 18, while still in school, he read the influential book *Autobiography of a Yogi* by Paramahansa YOGANANDA and inwardly accepted Yogananda as his GURU. He began to take the mail-order yoga lessons offered by Yogananda's SELF-REALIZATION FELLOWSHIP (SRF). After graduation from high school in 1949, Davis went to the fellowship's headquarters in Los Angeles and became a student of Yogananda. He relates that KUNDALINI was gradually awakened in him after meeting Yogananda. He was ordained by his guru in 1951 and appointed leader of the SRF center in Phoenix, Arizona. He initiated students into Yogananda's practice of *kriya yoga*.

In 1953, after a stint in the U.S. Army Medical Corps at Fort Riley, Kansas, Davis became an independent spiritual teacher and withdrew from SRF. He founded New Life Worldwide in St. Petersburg, Florida. In the early 1960s Davis worked with Edwin O'Neal and the Christian Spiritual Alliance (CSA) in Lakemont, Georgia. He was associated with several New Thought churches, including Unity School of Christianity and Divine Science; joined the New Thought Alliance (INTA); and developed relationships with other teachers in the Hindu tradition, including SWAMI RAMA, SWAMI MUKTANANDA, and SATYA SAI BABA. When O'Neal left CSA, Davis became both chairman of the board and head of the publishing house, which was renamed the Center for Spiritual Awareness.

Davis's teaching combines metaphysical Christianity and *kriya yoga,* and he continues to give *kriya yoga* initiation. He has published over a dozen books, primarily with CSA publishers, on spiritual development, MEDITATION, *kriya yoga,* and AYURVEDA. He is the publisher of *Truth Journal* and writes monthly lessons for CSA members. He maintains a heavy schedule of lecturing to New Thought churches around the world.

Further reading: Roy Eugene Davis, *The Book of Life* (Lakemont, Ga.: CSA Press, 2000); ———, *An Easy Guide to Ayurveda: The Natural Way to Wholeness* (Lakemont, Ga.: CSA Press, 1999); ———, *God Has Given Us Every Good Thing* (Lakemont, Ga.: CSA Press, 1986); ———, *Miracle Man of Japan* (Lakemont, Ga.: CSA Press, 1970); ———, *This Is Reality* (Lakemont, Ga.: CSA Press, 1962).

Daya Mata, Sri   *See* SELF-REALIZATION FELLOWSHIP.

Dayananda Saraswati, Swami (1930–)
teacher and scholar of advaita *Vedanta*

Swami Dayananda Saraswati has contributed greatly to the spread of knowledge of VEDANTA, by training hundreds of teachers and through his own study and teaching.

Natarajan Iyer was born on August 15, 1930, the second son of Valambal and Gopala Iyer in the small village of Manjakkudi in Thanjavar District in Tamil Nadu, India. He was raised in a traditional Brahmin family who primarily made their living selling coconuts. Described by family members as quiet, reflective, dispassionate, yet daring, Natarajan helped to manage his family's small plot of land after his father died when the boy was only eight. An excellent student, Natarajan excelled in all subjects related to logic, including physics and mathematics. He was known to be a voracious reader, harboring a large collection of books in his small home, where he regularly read until early morning.

Forced to grow up rapidly, and unable to afford college, Natarajan moved to Madras (now Chennai) to find a job that would allow him to continue his studies. He learned stenography and typewriting and began a career as a journalist with a job at a weekly, *Dharmika Hind.* When the paper seemed to be failing, he joined the air force as a combatant and was posted to the Ground Training Station in Bangalore; after military service, he returned to journalism, with an interim period as campaign manager for an independent candidate for state assembly, when he fine-tuned his public speaking skills.

In 1952 he was still waiting for his promised position with the prestigious newspaper *Indian Express,* when he accidentally met Swami CHINMAYANANDA during a 41-day public teaching. At the end of the teachings Natrajan volunteered to organize the feeding of the poor, which traditionally followed a period of study and sacrifice. Swami Chinmayananda, attracted to Natrajan's earnestness and organization skills, informed him that he would return the following year for further teachings. The 22-year-old Natrajan was certain that he was meant to pursue these teachings and thus became an active member of the newly formed Chinmaya Mission, an organization inspired by the vision of Swami Chinmayananda. His previous experience in journalism and editing put him very close to Swami Chinmayananda.

In 1957 Natarajan gave up his work to follow Swami Chinmayananda. In 1962 he was the second student to be initiated into SANNYAS (renunciation) by Swami Chinmayananda and was given the name Swami Dayananda Saraswati. He would later continue his development as a teacher under the tutelage of several teachers, including Swami Pranavananda of Gudiwada.

Known today as an authoritative teacher of traditional ADVAITA VEDANTA and an accomplished scholar of Hinduism, Swami Dayananda has conducted six three-year residential courses in both India and the United Sates, producing well over 300 Vedanta teachers around the world.

He has established three institutions: two in India, the ARSHA VIDYA GURUKULUM in Coimbatore, which offers three-year residential courses, and the Swami Dayananda Ashram in Rishikesh, a retreat center and place for continued studies, and the Arsha Vidya Gurukulam in Saylorsburg, Pennsylvania, which serves as a retreat center and venue for residential courses.

Swami Dayananda is known for his scholarship, his depth of understanding, and his appreciation for Western culture, attributes that give him a wide appeal. He travels the world teaching in a variety of venues, including American universities and international conventions. He has presented papers at UNESCO and the United Nations, where he participated in the Millennium Peace Summit. In November 2001, in Delhi, he convened the First World Congress for the Preservation of Religious Diversity, inaugurated by the Dalai Lama and former Indian prime minister Vajpayee. Swami Dayananda also actively participated in forming the Women's Global Peace Initiative, which convened at the United Nations in Geneva in October 2002.

In addition to teaching, Swami Dayananda emphasizes a commitment to peace and social justice. He instituted the All India Movement (AIM) for Seva, a public service organization that provides medical, educational, nutritional, and social support to villagers in remote rural Indian communities.

Further reading: Padma Narasimhan, *Swami Dayananda Saraswati* (Madras: TT. Maps & Publications, 1990).

death ceremony   *See* FUNERAL RITES.

demonic beings

Much of Vedic mythology, epic mythology, and early Puranic mythology (*see* PURANAS) depicts an ongoing war between the gods (*devas*) and demonic beings, called usually *asuras*, but sometimes *rakshasas* (both terms now simply mean a "demonic being"). Indian tradition, it must be noted, does not see the demons in completely polarized terms, as, for instance, in Christianity, in which Satan is an absolutely evil counterpart to God. The *asuras* are known to be the sons of the same father as the gods, and both *asuras* and *rakshasas* finally go to heaven after their battle with the different gods, its being understood that they have played a role in the glorification of God by being his (or sometimes her) opponents.

In the VEDAS a special role is played by the demon (*asura*) Vritra, a serpent being who is the enemy of god INDRA, king of the gods. Indra strikes Vritra with a thunderbolt to force him to release the terrestrial waters. Sometimes Vritra in his mountain lair holds back the summer waters of the "seven streams" of the INDUS River, so important to the ARYANS; Indra must force him to release them.

A later example of a demon or *asura,* found in the epics and *puranas,* is BALI, who through severe austerities usurped the throne of Indra himself to perpetrate evil in all the worlds. VISHNU finally must take incarnation as the VAMANA AVATAR, the divine dwarf, to depose him.

Beginning with the epics, the demonic group is enhanced by the addition of the *rakshasas,* demons who are cannibilistic and blood-thirsty. In the MAHABHARATA the PANDAVA brothers encounter various such demons in their travels. BHIMA in fact had a son named Hidimba by a female demon. The most famous *rakshasa* must certainly be Ravana, ruler of Lanka. He was depicted as having 10 heads and 20 arms. It was he who abducted RAMA's wife, SITA, in the RAMAYANA; Rama destroyed him in the end, as was the divine plan. *Rashasas* are seen in later *puranas* (c. sixth through 16th centuries), as they are in the epics, often attacking sages in the wilderness and disrupting Vedic rites.

Further reading: William Buck, *Ramayana* (Berkeley: University of California Press, 1976); Robert Goldman, trans., *Ramayana of Valmiki: An Epic of Ancient India,* Vol. 1 *Balakanda* (Princeton, N.J.: Princeton University Press, 1984); Wash Edward Hale, *Asura in Early Vedic Religion* (Delhi: Motilal Banarsidass, 1990); Alfred Hillebrandt, *Vedic Mythology,* 2 vols. (Delhi: Motilal Banarsidass, 1990); M. V. Kibe, *Cultural Descendents of Ravana.* Poona Oriental Series No. 5 (Poona: Oriental Book Agency, 1941); Ajoy Kumar Lahiri, *Vedic Vrtra* (Delhi: Motilal Banarsidass, 1984); Wendy Doniger O'Flaherty, *The Origins of Evil in Hindu Mythology* (Berkeley: University of California Press, 1976); W. J. Wilkins, *Hindu Mythology, Vedic and Puranic,* 2nd ed. (Calcutta: Rupa, 1973).

Desai, Guru Amrit (1932–) *yogi and founder of Kripalu Yoga Fellowship*

Amrit Desai has been a prominent teacher of yoga in the United States for several decades. His career has survived expulsion from his own ashram on charges of sexual misconduct.

Amrit Desai was born on October 16, 1932, in Halol, Gujurat state, India. Little is reported about his family or childhood. In 1948 at age 16, he met Swami KRIPALVANANDA, student of Swami Kaivarohan, reputed to be the 28th incarnation of SHIVA. Desai studied with Kripalvananda and taught Sahaj Yoga with the SWAMI. In 1960, he traveled to the United States to study art and design at the Philadelphia College of Art, as he worked in factories to support himself. He created a successful career in the arts and his wife and son joined him in America.

In 1966 Desai founded the Yoga Society of Pennsylvania, which drew a large following. In 1970, Kripalvananda called Desai back to India to initiate him into SHAKTIPAT DIKSHA (energetic transference from master to student to awaken spiritual energy). After his initiation, Desai experienced what he called a spiritual implosion, in which he instantaneously flowed from one ASANA (yogic posture) to the next and felt powerful KUNDALINI energy.

In 1972 Desai moved his fellowship to the suburbs of Philadelphia and changed its name to the Kripalu Yoga Fellowship. In addition to teaching KRIPALU YOGA, Desai and his fellowship became pioneers of holistic health. In 1983, the ashram and fellowship moved to a 350-acre former Jesuit retreat in Lenox, Massachusetts. The practice of yoga and the ASHRAM lifestyle were strictly observed, including separation of genders, silent meals, required SADHANA (practice) and *satsang* (attendance at teaching sessions), and BHAJANS (singing of devotional songs). In 1988, Kripalu gained the legal status as a spiritual/volunteer organization and became a leading spiritual retreat center in the United States.

Throughout his teaching in the United States, Desai was a charismatic and impressive GURU. Yet, in 1994, his integrity was compromised by sexual misconduct with members of the ashram and ashram guests and he was forced to leave the spiritual center he founded. Many members of the community were saddened by the disclosure of Desai's behavior, but the Kripalu Yoga and Health Center has remained a prominent, respected spiritual and health center, reoriented around Desai's teacher, Swami Kripalananda.

Desai has returned to teaching and travels throughout the United States, offering workshops and teacher training. His new organization, Amrit Yoga Institute, teaches the Amrit Method of Yoga Nidra to provide tools for banishing unconscious fears and habits. The institute also publishes *Sacred Pathways Magazine,* a bimonthly journal of yoga and higher consciousness. The Amrit Yoga Institute is headquartered in Salt Springs, Florida.

Further reading: Richard Faulds, *Kripalu Yoga: A Guide to Practice on and off the Mat* (New York: Bantam Books, 2006); Richard Faulds, *Gurudev: The Life of Yogi Amrit Desai* (Lenox, Mass.: Kripalu Yoga Fellowship, 1982); Kaviraj (Stephen Cope), *Yoga and the Quest for the True Self* (Lenox, Mass.: Kripalu Yoga Fellowship, 2004).

Desai, Yogi Shanti (mid-20th

century) *teacher of yoga and founder of Shanti Yoga Institute*

Born in Gujarat state, India, Yogi Shanti Desai studied yoga and Hindu scriptures from an early age. As a youth he met and was initiated by Swami Kripalu, the inspiration of the Kripalu Yoga Institute. After receiving a B.S. in India, Desai immigrated in 1961 to the United States, where he received an M.S. in chemistry from Drexel University. He worked as a research chemist while teaching yoga until 1972, when he turned to teaching yoga full-time.

He opened the SHANTI YOGA INSTITUTE AND YOGA RETREAT in Ocean City, New Jersey, in 1974 to provide instruction in yoga as a way of life. From 1977 to 1985 he directed the Glassboro (New Jersey) Ashram for spiritual communal living, and after 1981 he directed Prasad, a yogic health food store and restaurant. He personally

directs the Ocean City facility with his wife, Nayana. The institute offers yoga classes, seminars, and workshops.

Further reading: Yogi Shanti Desai, *Dynamic Balanced Living* (Ocean City, N.J.: Shanti Yoga Institute, 1985); ———, *Meditation Practice Manual* (Ocean City, N.J.: Shanti Yoga Institute, 1981).

Desjardins, Arnaud (1925–) *founder of Hauteville Ashram*

Arnaud Desjardins is a French teacher of ADVAITA VEDANTA. After a successful career making documentaries about Indian and other Eastern religious leaders and traditions, Desjardins eventually founded the first ASHRAM in France. He is the most popular and influential spiritual teacher in the francophone world.

Arnaud Guerin-Desjardins (he later dropped Guerin) was born on June 18, 1925, into a devout French Protestant family. His father, Jacques Guerin-Desjardins, was a hero in both world wars, and a prominent figure in Protestant circles. Close to Baden-Powell, the founder of the scouting movement, to whom Arnaud was introduced as a young boy, Guerin-Desjardins wrote books, gave lectures, and gave his two sons and one daughter a strict religious education. He earned a middle-class living as an executive for Peugeot, while his wife, Antoinette, also a devout Protestant, cared for the children at home.

As a young boy, Arnaud, although afraid of his father, was very interested in religious subjects, but was also tormented by questions rather uncommon for most children of his age, such as What about Catholics? Could they really be so wrong? If he had been born a Catholic, would not he be convinced that the truth lay in the Catholic Church? At the end of his teens, having seen plays given at the Comédie Française in Paris as part of his cultural education, Arnaud developed a passion for theater and acting, learning whole plays by heart. His parents very reluctantly consented for him to attend the Cours Simon, at the time the most reputed drama school in France. He eventually studied law and political science, but his heart was with the Cours Simon, which opened a whole new world for him. There, he met young men and women, many of whom were to become famous actors, who lived in a different, more relaxed and open world than the one in which he had grown up. His ambition was to join the Comédie Française as an actor, yet, when he passed the first part of the exams at the national drama school, the Conservatoire, his parents put tremendous emotional pressure on him to renounce the theater. The young man finally gave in but became depressed.

The future seemed grim when he joined a bank but became bright when he fell in love with a young Protestant woman, to whom he was soon engaged. That beautiful dream came to an abrupt end when Arnaud, age 24, was struck with tuberculosis. His prospective father-in-law broke the engagement and Arnaud was sent to a sanatorium, never to see his fiancée again. Feeling abandoned and betrayed, he read voraciously and discovered the teachings of G. I. Gurdjieff and P. D. Ouspensky and learned about Hindu gurus through Jean Herbert's *Spiritualité Hindoue,* in which the author recounted his meetings with ANANDAMAYI MA, Sri AUROBINDO, RAMANA MAHARSHI, and Swami RAMDAS.

After his recovery from tuberculosis, Desjardins returned to Paris, where he joined a Gurdjieff group in the early 1950s and started working as an assistant for the embryonic French television system. In the Gurdjieff group, he met Denise, an impressive young woman a few years his senior who was an artist of growing reputation. They were married in 1957.

In 1959, having become a television director and filmmaker, Arnaud went through a difficult time in his professional life. His projects were refused one after the other, and he then decided to travel to India by car, to see for himself whether those masters he had read about lived up to Jean Herbert's description; he planned to film them with a 16-millimeter camera.

In 1959 he traveled to India, where he met and filmed Swami SHIVANANDA SARASWATI of Rishikesh, Swami Ramdas, and Anandamayi Ma. Back in France, his finished documentary was shown on national television and very well received by the public as well as critics. He then specialized in documentaries on living spiritual traditions, filming with his 16-millimeter camera, assisted only by his wife. They traveled for extensive periods, taking their two children with them. In 1965, Desjardins produced several documentaries on the Tibetans, became close to the Dalaï Lama, and went on to produce films on Zen Buddhism in Japan and Sufi brotherhoods in Afghanistan. Those films, available today on DVD and videotapes, are considered unique documents. The expeditions enabled Desjardins to spend a lot of time in close contact with some of the greatest teachers of the East and to pursue his spiritual quest while developing a growing reputation in France as a filmmaker and lecturer.

In 1965, feeling that despite his devotion to Anandamayi Ma, he could not really consider himself as her student, he went, with her blessing, to meet a swami he had only heard about, who lived a reclusive life, away from spiritual curiosity seekers, in the heart of Bengal. Sri Swami Prajnapad, while immersed in Hindu tradition, was a very unorthodox teacher. He advocated a path rooted in non-duality (*advaïta*) that takes modern psychology into account. Swami Prajnapad was an ardent admirer of Freud, whose works he had studied as early as the 1920s, and had developed an approach through which students could open to their unconscious through private interviews, which he offered every day to one or two students. In that remote ashram, where the teacher was very accessible, spoke fluent English, and had an understanding of Western culture, Desjardins felt he had found his spiritual path. He then embarked on a very intense process with Swami Prajnapad, visiting him every year for one to three months and applying his teaching in daily life.

In 1971, after going through a crisis in his personal life, Desjardins went to Swami Prajnapad and experienced a deep shift of inner perspective. Now aspiring to a quieter life, he planned to end his professional career as an administrator in French Television, but Swami Prajnapad saw a different future for his student. The guru plainly told him that his true calling lay in passing on the teaching, even if only to a few people. Since a group of people who had seen his films and read his books wanted to embark on the path with him as their guide, Desjardins started planning the opening of what was to be the first French ashram, examining it in detail with Swami Prajnapad. Having bought Le Bost, a large but modest house hidden in the heart of Auvergne, Arnaud retired from television and, in 1974, started welcoming a few students, whom he trained in the spirit of what he himself had experienced with Swami Prajnapad. A few weeks after Le Bost opened, Swami Prajnapad passed away in India.

The ashram was not open to visitors or advertised. Nevertheless, word of mouth spread and Desjardins was soon faced with an ever more demanding schedule. Nine years after he had opened Le Bost, after having experienced serious signs of utter exhaustion, he decided to rest for a few months and then open a new, more open ashram in the south of France. That was Font d'Isière, which also lasted nine years. Despite the lack of publicity, Arnaud's reputation as teacher kept growing. In 1987, he and Denise parted ways as husband and wife, although their friendship and collaboration in the work continue to this day. In 1995, at the age of 70, Desjardins embarked on a daring adventure—the foundation of a large ashram under his leadership where others could teach as well, and where many people could study and practice at different levels.

Surrounding himself with a few senior students and staff, Desjardins founded Hauteville, in the Ardèche, a place dedicated to traditional SADHANA (spiritual discipline), interreligious dialogue, and sanctuary for spiritual aspirants. Desjardins has become the best-known and most respected Hindu teacher in the French-speaking world. Seekers from all over the world travel to Hauteville for retreats where they meet not only Desjardins himself, who still is available, but also his senior students. In 1996, Desjardins married Veronique Loiseleur, one of his long-term collaborators.

Today the words of Desjardins are published by Hauteville's publishing house, La Table Ronde, in Paris. Desjardins travels widely, especially to Quebec, where he has a thriving ashram. Only two of his numerous books have been published in English. He regularly participates in interreligious dialogue at Karma Ling in the Savoie region of France with Lama Denis Teundroup, a Frenchman given the title of lama in the Tibetan tradition.

Further reading: Arnaud Desjardins, *The Message of the Tibetans.* Translated from the French by R. H. Ward and Vega Stewart (London: Stuart and Watkins, 1969); ———, *Toward the Fullness of Life: The Fullness of Love* (Putney, Vt.: Threshold Books, 1990); ———, *Yoga et Spiritualité, l'hindouism et nous* (Paris: La Palatine, 1969); Gilles Farcet, *Arnaud Desjardins, ou, L'adventure de la Sagesse* (Paris: Table Ronde, 1987); ———, *The Anti-Wisdom Manual: A Practical Guide to Spiritual Bankruptcy* (Prescott, Ariz.: Hohm Press, 2005).

deva

Deva, from the Sanskrit root meaning "to shine," is the word for *god* in Indian mythology. There are numerous gods in the VEDAS and PURANAS, so the word has a polytheistic connotation. When one calls out to a singular God one uses the term BHAGAVAN. The gods of the Vedas are numerous; the most important are INDRA, god of storms, and AGNI, god of fire. Later VISHNU, SHIVA, and the GODDESS or *DEVI* (feminine form of *deva*) became the preeminent divinities.

devadasi

Devadasi literally means, "a servant of god." This term was applied to women who lived in temples as the wives of the male divinity there. Traditionally the women were married in a solemn ceremony to the divinity. The women were seen to be the essential power and energy (SHAKTI) of the divinity incarnate; men would offer great gifts to the temple in order to have relationships and even sexual intercourse with the *devadasis*. The *devadasis* were rigorously trained in the arts and were very well educated. Several of the Indian dances that are well known today were preserved and developed by *devadasis* in the temples of India. Most notable are BHARATA NATYAM and *Odissi*.

When the British arrived they regarded these sacred women as nothing but prostitutes and banned the institution of the *devadasi* in the late 19th century. The practice continued secretly, however, for some time afterward.

Further reading: Saskia C. Kersenboom-Story, *Nityasumangali* (Delhi: Motilal Banarsidass, 1987); Frederique Marglin, *Wives of the God-King* (New York: Oxford University Press, 1985).

Deva Foundation (est. 1980s)

Dr. Deva Maharaj (b. 1948) established the Deva Foundation in Sweden and Beverly Hills, California, during the 1980s. Its mission is to provide a space where Asian and Western ideas and philosophy about holiness can meet. The foundation serves to educate individuals and groups in the areas of transformation, enlightenment, and individual growth. It offers a variety of services and treatments designed to facilitate personal growth and healing. These methods include acupressure, massage, nutrition, self-hypnosis, and SHAKTIPAT, a technique that serves as the catalyst to awaken the KUNDALINI energy believed to rest in a latent state at the base of the spine. Often pictured as a coiled serpent, this vibrant energy is believed to stimulate the opening of the CHAKRAS (energy centers) located along the spine, serving to promote spiritual enlightenment.

Dr. Deva established the foundation to serve others, using the credentials he had earned in India as a homeopathic and ayurvedic medical practitioner (*see* AYURVEDA). Members of the foundation may also take classes at the Tantra House, an auxiliary facility that functions as an esoteric school. Students at Tantra House are taught that the wedding of spirituality with sexuality hastens enlightenment and that mastery of the mysterious should be accompanied by holistic health practices. Through the years Dr. Deva has become a frequent guest on radio and television, where he demonstrates telepathy and clairvoyance. He travels often to teach and heal. In India, he frequents the Yoga Center in New Delhi, an educational center promoting his mission abroad.

The membership of the Deva Foundation includes two groups in the United States and a sole mission in Canada. The organization reports some 1,000 members through North America and at the several international centers.

Further reading: J. Gordon Melton, *Encyclopedia of American Religion* (Detroit: Gale Group, 2001).

Devaki

Devaki is the mother of KRISHNA, whose birth was assured by a miracle. Devaki's husband, VASUDEVA, was minister to the evil king Kamsa of Mathura. The king was determined to kill Devaki's children to forestall a prediction that one of her sons would assassinate him. He had the couple put under guard and had the couple's first six children killed. The seventh child, BALARAMA, was miraculously transferred while an embryo into the womb of Vasudeva's second wife, Rohini. By divine intervention, when the eighth child, Krishna, was born, all of the king's guards who kept watch over the couple fell asleep, and Vasudeva was able to deliver Krishna to his foster mother, YASHODA, with whom he was raised.

Further reading: Kenneth E. Bryant, *Poems to the Child-God: Structures and Strategies in the Poetry of Surdas* (Berkeley: University of California Press, 1978); Cornelia Dimmitt and J. A. B. van Buitenen, *Classical Hindu Mythology: A Reader in the Sanskrit Puranas* (Philadelphia: Temple University Press, 1978); E. Washburn Hopkins, *Epic Mythology* (Delhi: Motilal Banarsidass, 1986).

Devanagari

Devanagari ("of the city of the gods") is the script that is used for Hindi, Sanskrit, and Marathi. It developed out of the earlier Brahmi script toward the end of the last millennium B.C.E. It has been used regularly for Sanskrit ever since. When Hindi was recognized and developed as a separate written language in the 19th century, Devanagari was the script chosen for it.

As with most other scripts that derive from Brahmi, Devanagari uses a system of abbreviated vowel markings to show vowels after consonants, when the vowels are not the first letter of the word. Full vowel forms are made beginning a word. There are 48 to 51 letters in the Devanagari alphabet depending on whether certain unusual vowels are included and whether one includes conjunct consonants at the end. Typically the Devanagari alphabet begins with *a* and ends with *h*.

Further reading: K. C. Aryan, *Rekha, a Book on Art and Anatomy of Indian Languages and Symbols* (Delhi: Rekha Prakashan, 1952); India, Central Hindi Directorate, *Devanagari through the Ages* (New Delhi: Central Hindi Directorate, 1967); P. Visalakshy, *Nandinagari Script* (Thiruvanathapuram: Dravidian Linguistics Association, 2003).

Devayani and Yayati

Devayani and Yayati are the romantic protagonists in an old and popular myth, which also considers them to be ancestors of KRISHNA. Devayani, daughter of the famous *rishi* Ushanas Kavya, was swimming in a pond with Sharmishtha, the daughter of the king of the *asuras* (antigods or demons) and a student of Ushanas Kavya. In those days such interchange took place between gods and *asuras*. When Lord Shiva happened by they rushed to get their clothes. Sharmishtha took Devayani's clothes by mistake. Devayani upbraided Sharmishtha severely, and the latter in anger threw her friend into a well and took her clothes.

King Yayati, who was hunting, happened by and rescued Devayani. When he touched her hand, she announced that she would never touch another man's hand. Kavya gave his daughter to the king; following Devayani's wish he also handed over Sharmishtha as her slave, admonishing the king never to have carnal relations with the daughter of the *asuras*.

Devayani soon bore the king glorious sons, one of them Yadu, an ancestor of Krishna himself. Sharmishtha became jealous and managed to seduce the king to break his promise to Kavya.

When Devayani heard this she went home to her father. The king followed, chastised, and sought her return. When he reached her home, her father, Kavya, cursed the king with immediate old age as an antidote to his uncontrolled lust. The king begged a way out of the curse and was allowed to transfer the curse to someone else. He convinced his youngest son to take the curse of old age, and the son became a ruler while for a thousand years Yayati enjoyed the pleasures of love with Devayani. Finally, tiring of the life of the senses, the king took back his old age from the son and renounced the world.

Further reading: C. R. Devadhar, ed. and trans., *Yayaticarita: A Drama in Seven Acts* (Poona: Bhandarkar Oriental Research Institute, 1965); Cornelia Dimmitt and J. A. B. van Buitenen, *Classical Hindu Mythology: A Reader in the Sanskrit Puranas* (Philadelphia: Temple University Press, 1978); E. Washburn Hopkins, *Epic Mythology* (Delhi: Motilal Banarsidass, 1986).

devi   See GODDESS.

Devi, Indra (1899–2002) *Western hatha yoga teacher*

Indra Devi was a highly popular Russian-born yoga teacher. In her long, active life she established a series of learning centers in several countries on three continents, popularizing yoga among celebrities and ordinary people around the world.

Eugenie Peterson was born on May 12, 1899, in Riga, Russia, the daughter of a Russian noblewoman and a Swedish bank director. In 1920 Eugenie and her mother escaped the turmoil of the Russian Revolution and settled in Berlin, Germany. She joined a theatrical company as an actor and dancer and toured throughout Europe.

In 1927, she toured India as a member of the performing troupe and remained there for 12 years. She married Jan Trakaty, a Czechoslovakian diplomat in Bombay (Mumbai), and became a movie star in Indian films, taking the stage name Indra Devi. She met many leaders and teachers in India, including Jiddu KRISHNAMURTI, RABINDRANATH TAGORE, Jawaharlal Nehru, and the maharaja and maharani of Mysore. The maharaja requested that she be allowed to study with him. He accepted his first non-Indian female student. At the palace at Mysore, Eugenie met Tirumalai Krishnamacharya, a yoga master, whose students included B. K. S. IYENGAR.

Devi, also known as Mataji (revered mother), discovered her passion in life. She stayed in India, studying and practicing yoga until 1939. Healed of a serious heart condition through her practice, she became an avid student. She followed her teacher's methods of HATHA YOGA, which advocated a unique practice for each individual body. She studied PRANAYAMA (breath work) and *dhyana* (MEDITATION). She continued her studies in the Himalayas after the death of her first husband. She adopted the name Indra Devi for her persona as yoga teacher.

In the late 1940s, Devi traveled to Southern California. She founded a yoga studio in Holly-

wood and taught many people, including celebrities. In 1953, she married Dr. Sigrid Knauer, a physician and humanitarian. They bought a ranch in Tecate, Baja Mexico, which served as a home, school, and retreat center for 24 years. She traveled throughout the world teaching yoga and lecturing.

In 1966, Devi met SATYA SAI BABA, who profoundly affected her subsequent practice and instruction. She developed Sai Yoga, a system of moving through ASANAS (yogic postures) with spiritual consciousness.

In 1985, she moved to Argentina and established the Indra Devi Foundation. She traveled all around the world and included many famous people as her students, including Gloria Swanson, Greta Garbo, Jennifer Jones, Olivia de Haviland, and Madame Chiang Kai-shek. She popularized yoga and meditation in Hollywood in the 1940s and 1950s and, through a series of books and innovative classes, helped to promote yoga in China, the Soviet Union, and Latin America. She remained active well into her 90s, teaching two classes daily. She died on April 25, 2002, at the age of 102.

Further reading: Indra Devi, *Forever Young, Forever Healthy* (Englewood Cliffs, N.J.: Prentice Hall, 1962); ———, *Renew Your Life through Yoga* (New York: Paperback Library, 1969); ———, *Yoga for Americans: A Complete 6 Weeks' Course for Home Practice* (Englewood Cliffs, N.J.: Prentice Hall, 1959); ———, *Yoga for You* (Salt Lake City: Gibbs Smith, 2002).

Devi Mandir   See MAA, SHREE.

dharana   See YOGA SUTRA.

dharma

Dharma is a complex and multifaceted term in Hindu tradition. It can be translated as "religious law," "right conduct," "duty," and "social order." Its root, *dhri*, means "to hold up."

The social concept of dharma emerges from the VEDIC notion of *RITA* or "cosmic order." In this worldview, dharma (the social order) is maintained by dharma (right conduct and the fulfillment of duty and religious law). Social activity was traditionally very much circumscribed by tradition; following dharma meant doing what was required.

Starting as early as the fourth century B.C.E., a voluminous literature in Sanskrit was created called *DHARMASHASTRA* (authoritative texts on dharma). These included the *Dharmasutras* (aphoristic texts). Dharma later became personified as a god in mythology and literature. His son was YUDHISHTHIRA, one of the five PANDAVAS in the MAHABHARATA story.

In the Jain tradition, dharma refers to the complex of duties required of a Jain. Jains recognize 10 forms of dharma that monks are to follow (*see* JAINISM). The word dharma can be used in association with any religion or faith, such as the Zoroastrian dharma.

Further reading: Wendy Doniger and Brian K. Smith, trans., *The Laws of Manu* (New York: Penguin Books, 1991); P. V. Kane, *History of the Dharma Shastra*, 5 vols. (Poona: Bhandarkar Oriental Research Institute, 1968); Wendy Doniger O'Flaherty, J. Duncan, and M. Derrett, *The Concept of Duty in South Asia* (New Delhi: Vikas Publishing House, 1978).

Dharmashastra

The Indian literary genre of Dharmashastra (authoritative scripture prescribing the rules of right conduct) began around the fourth century B.C.E. It included the subgenre of Dharmasutras, or aphoristic works about DHARMA. Traditionally, the *LAWS OF MANU* (*Manusmriti* or *Manavadharmashastra*) is considered the first and most authoritative text, written by the legendary MANU.

Dharmashastra literature prescribes the laws, norms, rules, and regulations of life for both the individual and the community. It covers social norms, ethics, and moral tenets but also includes direction on the proper performance of rituals and ceremonies. It is usually quite specific concerning diet, domestic law, the proper conduct of kings, and, most important, the proper conduct of each caste. Major Dharmashastras were written by Apastamba, Gautama, Baudhayana, and Vasishtha, among others.

Further reading: Wendy Doniger with Brian K. Smith, *The Laws of Manu* (London: Penguin Books, 1991); P. V. Kane, *History of the Dharmasastra (Ancient and Medieval Religious and Civil Law in India)*, 5 vols. (Poona: Bhandarkar Oriental Research Institute, 1968); Patrick Olivelle, *The Dharmasutras* (Oxford: Oxford University Press. 1999).

Dhumavati   *See* DASHA MAHAVIDYA.

dhyna   *See* MEDITATION.

Diaspora

Although there is some disagreement about the term *Hindu Diaspora,* most members of the worldwide Hindu community use it to describe the millions of Hindus of South Asian origin who live outside India. While the majority of the world's Hindus reside in India, those living abroad have established Hindu practices and communities in places such as AUSTRALIA, Canada, the CARIBBEAN REGION, the UNITED KINGDOM, Fiji, MAURITIUS, and the UNITED STATES of America. The practices of overseas Hinduism have had a significant influence within India, because of frequent travel and contact between family members and institutions located in India and abroad.

While exact numbers of overseas Hindus are difficult to determine, partly because of census restrictions (for example, the United States census does not record religious affiliation), scholars have estimated the number of Hindus living in particular countries. For example, the sociologist Prema Kurien suggests that Hindus accounted for approximately 65 percent of more than 800,000 people of Indian origin reported in the 1990 United States census. Using the same calculation on the 2000 U.S. census figure of almost 1.7 million people of Indian origin, one arrives at a figure of approximately 1.1 million Hindus in the United States. Mauritius, a small country with a long history of Indian migration, is home to more than half a million Hindus, 48 percent of its total population.

Indians have been migrating since premodern times, both inside and outside India. The large-scale migration of the modern period, according to the historian Roger Daniels, may be the result of the British abolition of the slave trade and then of slavery itself during the first half of the 19th century. Without slaves, the British began to rely on indentured servants and contract laborers to work their plantations from Fiji to the Caribbean. The Indian subcontinent provided much of this cheap labor, and the British transported these workers throughout their empire. Some of these laborers eventually returned to India, but most of them remained in these distant colonies. Bhikhu Parekh, a political theorist, estimates that approximately three-quarters of the indentured laborers during the period from 1834 to 1924 were Hindu. Many Hindus were among the farmers and skilled laborers from Punjab and merchants from Gujarat who migrated as individuals to destinations such as East Africa and Canada.

Because purity and pollution are significant concerns for many classes of Hindus, orthodox Hindus, especially in the early period, were skeptical of travel abroad. At the least, international travel meant living among people who would be considered polluting. Further, many felt it would be difficult for Hindu sojourners to resist engaging in polluting activities such as MEAT-EATING or drinking alcohol. Members of the upper castes did begin to travel abroad, often for higher education,

but significant numbers did not settle abroad until the last half of the 20th century.

The patterns of global dispersal among Hindus have shifted since World War II as members of the middle and upper rungs of Hindu society began settling abroad in increasing numbers. Great Britain faced a labor shortage after the war and immigrants from India filled labor needs in the 1950s and 1960s. At first, these migrants were mostly single men, but women joined them and helped establish families there in the 1970s and 1980s. Although migration directly from South Asia slowed in Britain during the 1970s and 1980s, many East Africans of South Asian origin decided to migrate to Britain when political pressures forced them to leave Africa. Having lived abroad for multiple generations, those Hindus among them had already established Hinduism in the Diaspora and took strong orthodox traditions to Britain.

This newer wave of South Asian migrants began to arrive in the United States in the late 1960s. After decades of racist immigration laws that discriminated against Asians, among others, Lyndon Johnson signed the Immigration Act of 1965, drastically altering U.S. immigration policy. This act replaced an immigration quota based on national origins with preferences for relatives of residents of the United States and members of certain professions. The new law also increased the limits on immigrants from countries outside the Western Hemisphere. Many of the earliest post-1965 Indian immigrants were well-educated, English-speaking professionals, who tended to be from upper castes. On the basis of the family preferences in the new law, many of their relatives began to join them in the 1980s and 1990s.

These different historic immigration patterns affected religious communities in different ways. Parekh notes, for example, that the Hindus in French colonies such as Mauritius faced assimilation policies and many adopted Christianity, albeit in a hybridized form. Hindus in East Africa, by contrast, often remained connected to India and lived in more independent, homogeneous settlements, retaining strong Hindu traditions. There are, however, some common patterns of Hinduism in the sites where Hindu immigrants more recently settled, such as the United Kingdom and the United States.

In these countries the home often remains a central site of Hindu practice. Families frequently set aside space in the home for a PUJA (worship) room, in which they install images of the deities. Worship there may range from daily practice to rituals associated with important Hindu festivals and life events. Because religious specialists are harder to find outside India, many Hindus living abroad learn how to perform practices for which they would have hired a priest if they had been living in India.

Members of the community often believe that their children need to see people outside the family engaged in Hindu practice. This is one of several reasons why many overseas Hindus regularly participate in one or more religious activities outside the home. Some participate in informal groups of families from similar backgrounds who meet to perform the same ritual on a regular basis. Many overseas Hindus also participate in temple activities, which may encompass the traditions of a wider variety of Hindu practices. Transnational religious movements such as the SWAMINARAYAN group have highly developed organizations that tend to the needs of members living both in India and abroad. Other, smaller organizations send gurus abroad to tend to the needs of Hindu householders and their communities. Hindus living abroad often return to India for short periods, most often for visits to family members, but sometimes for religious pilgrimages.

It is important to note that the Hindu Diaspora properly speaking includes people who are not of South Asian descent but who have accepted Hindu practices as integral to their lives. This includes, for example, the many members of the INTERNATIONAL SOCIETY FOR KRISHNA CONSCIOUSNESS, popularly known as the Hare Krishnas, who are not of South Asian descent.

See also AFRICA; BALI; EUROPE; INDONESIA; MALAYSIA; SCANDINAVIA; SOUTH EAST ASIA.

Further reading: Roger Ballard, ed., *Desh Pardesh: The South Asian Presence in Britain* (London: Hurst, 1994); Crispin Bates, ed., *Community, Empire, and Migration: South Asians in Diaspora* (Basingstoke: Palgrave, 2001); H. Coward, J. R. Hinnells, and R. B. Williams, eds., *The South Asian Religious Diaspora in Britain, Canada, and the United States* (Albany: State University of New York Press, 2000); Roger Daniels, *History of Indian Immigration to the United States: An Interpretive Essay* (New York: Asia Society, 1989); John Kelly, "Fiji's Fifth Veda: Exile, Sanatan Dharm, and Countercolonial Initiatives in Diaspora." In P. Richman, ed., *Questioning Ramayanas: A South Asian Tradition* (Berkeley: University of California Press, 2001); Madhulika S. Khandelwal, *Becoming American, Being Indian: An Immigrant Community in New York City* (Ithaca, N.Y.: Cornell University Press, 2002); Prema Kurien, "Becoming American by Becoming Hindu: Indian Americans Take Their Place at the Multicultural Table." In R. A. Warner and J. G., Wittners, eds., *Gatherings in Diaspora: Religious Communities and the New Immigration* (Philadelphia: Temple University Press, 1998); ———, "Gendered Ethnicity: Creating a Hindu Indian Identity in the United States." *American Behavioral Scientist* 42, no. 4 (1999): 648–670; Bhikhu Parekh, "Some Reflections on the Hindu Diaspora." *New Community* 20, no. 4 (July 1994): 603–620; Ronald Takaki, *Strangers from a Different Shore: A History of Asian Americans* (New York: Penguin Books, 1989); Raymond Brady Williams, *Religions of Immigrants from India and Pakistan: New Threads in the American Tapestry* (Cambridge: Cambridge University Press, 1988); Raymond Brady Williams, ed. *A Sacred Thread: Modern Transmission of Hindu Tradition in India and Abroad* (Chambersburg, Pa.: Anima, 1992).

Digambara

Digambara is one of the two main divisions of the Jain tradition (see JAINISM). It literally means "those wearing the sky as a garment," a reference to the complete nudity of the monks of this branch. The Digambara Jains, who are relatively few in number, are concentrated in the south of India, while the SHVETAMBARAS (those wearing white garments) are concentrated in the west and north.

The Digambaras hold that during a famine in the north around 300 B.C.E., the teacher BHADRAB-AHU led a group of Jain monks southward to Karnataka. Years later, when he and his community returned north, they were shocked to find that the community of monks had deviated from the true tradition and had begun to wear white garments. The Digambara Jains believe that all of the original texts of the Jains, the PURVAS and the ANGAS, were completely lost; any text claimed by the Shvetambaras is at best a corruption of the original knowledge. (The Shvetambaras also accept that the Purvas have been lost.) Both groups agree that Bhadrabahu was the last to know all the original texts.

The oldest Digambara sacred text is Shat-khandagama, "Scripture of six parts," written in Prakrit. It is said to have been composed by the monk Dharasena (c. second century C.E., who summoned two monks, Pushpadanta and Bhutabali, to a cave to record scriptural knowledge that he feared was dwindling away; the pair later put together the Kasayapahuda, "Treatise on passion." These two texts constitute the earliest and most sacred Digambara scripture. Another very important text for Digambaras is the Tattvarthasutra, "*Aphorisms* on the meaning of the constituent aspects of the universe" by the monk Umasvati. This text, coincidentally, is the only Digambara text that is also accepted by the Shvetambaras.

It appears that the differences between the two branches of Jain tradition are due to their separate development, rather than to any direct disputation. The most important difference concerns the nudity of Digambara monks. Digambaras understand that if a monk is to be truly possessionless and therefore truly detached, he (there are no female monks) must not possess even a garment. Following this rigorous logic Digambara monks were never allowed to carry even begging bowls and were forced to beg only with their hands. Doctrinally, this concept has consequences for the potential of women to become liberated from the cycle of rebirth. Since women cannot take the final step into nudity, Digambaras judge that females cannot reach liberation until born in a male body.

Shvetambaras think that women can reach liberation in the female body. In fact Mallinatha, one of the TIRTHANKARAS, enlightened teachers, is understood by the Shvetambaras to be female, and by the Digambaras to be male. This is the only disagreement in the lists of Tirthankaras maintained by the two sects.

Until this day, there is little interchange between these two divisions of Jains, even though they share most of their doctrines. They have actively contended against each other for control of several important shrines in India, and in certain localities they are not on good terms. Generally, however, where both are present they tolerate each other, although they do not mix in festivals or in other spiritual contexts.

Further reading: Paul Dundas, *The Jains* (London: Routledge, 1992); P. S. Jaini, *The Jaina Path of Purification* (Delhi: Motilal Banarsidass, 1990); U. K. Jain, *Jaina Sects and Schools* (Delhi: Concept, 1975).

diksha

A *diksha* is an initiation, of which there are many sorts in the Hindu context. For instance, many sects and traditions require the transmission of a MANTRA to members, in some cases by one's father, in other cases by the GURU. Most mendicant orders require a formal ordination that involves a ritual that is also called a *diksha*. A SANNYASI, one who renounces the world, is required to undergo a *diksha* that includes rituals usually done at a person's cremation after death. The Hindu ceremony at which the SACRED THREAD is invested on young boys is also formally called a *diksha*.

A person may quite easily undergo several *dikshas* during his or her lifetime. TANTRIC practitioners, for instance, will almost always have an initiation after leaving their original traditions and a second one when entering a tantric circle.

Further reading: Sanjukta Gupta, Dirk Jan Hoens, and Teun Goudriaan, *Hindu Tantrism* (Leiden: Brill, 1979); Brian K. Smith, "Ritual, Knowledge and Being: Initiation and Veda Study in Ancient India," *Numen* 33, no. 1 (1986): 65–89.

Dinshah, H. Jay (1933–2000) *leader in vegetarian movement in United States*

H. Jay Dinshah was an American proponent of the vegan diet. He buttressed his arguments with Hindu concepts of nonviolence and respect for animals.

H. Jay Dinshah was born in Malaga, New Jersey, on November 2, 1933, and raised as a lactovegetarian by his parents, Irene Grace Hoger Dinshah and Dinshah P. Ghadiali, an Indian who immigrated from Bombay (Mumbai) to the United States in 1911. Ghadiali was a scientist and health educator and an early advocate of the vegetarian lifestyle. He educated his son on the value of a vegetarian diet from the time he was a small child. The boy was home-schooled by both parents.

When Dinshah was 23, out of curiosity, he visited a slaughterhouse on Front Street in Philadelphia. His wife, Freya Smith Dinshah, later recalled that the experience changed his life forever. In 1956 Dinshah read the influential book *Why Kill for Food?* by Geoffrey L. Rudd, published by the Vegetarian Society in England. Dinshah became an advocate of vegetarianism and sold copies of the book via classified ads. After reading literature from the Vegan Society in England, Dinshah stopped consuming dairy products and refused to wear leather. In 1957, he became a vegan, restricting himself to fruits, vegetables, salads, legumes, and nuts.

Dinshah founded the American Vegan Society in 1960 and served as its president for 40 years.

His efforts contributed to the steady growth of veganism throughout North America. Individuals seeking knowledge on veganism were welcome to stay at his home as long as a month to learn the ethics of veganism and ways to maintain a healthy diet. In the mid-1970s, the society purchased an office building in Malaga, New Jersey, and expanded its services.

Dinshah rooted the American Vegan Society in the doctrine of AHIMSA, a Sanskrit concept meaning no killing, no injury, and no harm, which was central to the work of both Mohandas Karamchand GANDHI and JAINISM. Dinshah did not view veganism as a mere dietary choice, but rather as an ethical responsibility to all living creatures. He taught the principles of *ahimsa* through an anagram: (1) abstinence from animal products; (2) harmlessness with reverence for life; (3) integrity of thought and deed; (4) mastery over oneself; (5) service to humanity, nature, and creation; (6) advancement of understanding and truth.

Dinshah was an accomplished orator and writer. He gave lectures and talks around the world on veganism and the mistreatment of animals. In 1975 he helped organize the World Vegetarian Congress at the University of Maine. He authored and self-published several books and was also chief editor of the American Vegan Society's periodical *Ahimsa*, which is now called *American Vegan*. He died on June 8, 2000.

Further reading: Freya Dinshah, The *Vegan Kitchen* (Malaga, N.J.: American Vegan Society, 1987); Jay H. Dinshah, *Out of the Jungle* (Malaga, N.J.: American Vegan Society, 1968); ———, *Song of India* (Surrey, England: Vegan Society, 1973); ———, *Steps in Vegetarianism* (Malaga, N.J.: American Vegan Society, 1993); William Harris and Freya Dinshah, *Veganism: Getting Started* (Malaga, N.J.: American Vegan Society, 1998).

Divali (Dipavali)

Divali may be the most popular Indian festival. Unlike some other festivals, such as RAM LILA, it is celebrated in all parts of India. It starts on the 14th day of the lunar month of Ashvayuja and extends to the second day of the lunar month of Kartikka. It usually falls around the end of October and the beginning of November.

The origin of the festival of Divali cannot be traced, but it is known to be at least 1,000 years old. As a "festival of lights" it resembles many other festivals in the world with quite ancient roots. On the first day of the festival one makes an offering to the god of death, YAMA, after praying for expiation of sins. One lights a lamp to "the underworld" where Yama lives. After feasting, rows of lamps are lighted in the evening on ledges and external places of houses. Temples and public places are also illuminated the same way. On the second day LAKSHMI, the goddess of wealth, is worshipped; in Bengal KALI is worshipped instead. Lights are also lit on this day, when late at night a huge racket is created with drums and such to drive away Alakshmi, Lakshmi's (or Kali's) inauspicious counterpart. In fact, by tradition every day of Divali is filled with the sounds of firecrackers.

The third day is devoted to the unusual worship of a demon, BALI, the demon king who was vanquished by VISHNU. One is to stay awake the whole night. On the day of Bali it is common for people to gamble, since many believe that this was the day that PARVATI defeated her husband, SHIVA, in a game of dice. On this third day cows and bulls are also worshipped, as is a pile of food that represents the hill Govardhana, which KRISHNA lifted to protect his people from storm. People also pass under a rope of grass tied to a pole and tree in order to assure safe journeys. The final day is a brother and sister day, when brothers are invited to the homes of their sisters for feasting.

Further reading: Jagadisa Ayyar, *South India Festivities* (Madras: Higginbothams, 1921); M. P. Bezbaruah, with Krishna Gopal and Phal S. Girota, eds., *Fairs and Festivals of India,* 5 vols. (Delhi: Gyan Publishing House, 2003); H. V. Shekar, *Festivals of India: Significance of the Celebrations* (Louisville, Ky.: Insight Books, 2000).

Draupadi

Draupadi is the joint wife of the five PANDAVA brothers in the Indian epic MAHABHARATA. Her name derives from her father, King Drupada, of the Panchalas.

Draupadi and her brother, Dhristhadymna, were born from the sacrificial fire in the altar of the house of Drupada. She was a partial incarnation of the goddess SRI, who is associated with kingship and kingly success. As she was supremely attractive and desirable her father decided to hold a "self-choice" festival, where, after a competition of her kingly, princely, and other suitors, she would be able to choose her husband. In the competition, whoever among the suitors could hit a revolving, fish-shaped object suspended from a tall pole would receive Draupadi in marriage.

KRISHNA and BALARAMA, the two AVATARS of VISHNU, participated in the contest, but it was the Pandava ARJUNA who successfully hit the target and was garlanded by Draupadi. The five Pandavas, accustomed to sharing travails and rewards, argued on the way home as to who should receive this lovely woman as his wife. When they arrived at home and announced that they had obtained a prize, their mother, distracted with another task, absentmindedly told them that they should share it as brothers. Because holding to one's word was more important than anything in those times, the mother, KUNTI, could not release them from her command; nor could they refuse a mother's direct requirement. Therefore, Draupadi became the wife for all five. Henceforth, she stayed two days with each husband in turn.

Draupadi figures prominently in the famous "dice scene" in the MAHABHARATA. YUDHISHTHIRA, trying to win his kingdom back from his evil cousins the KAURAVAS, wagers everything he owns—and loses. Finally he offers his wife, Draupadi, as a wager. He loses her as well. Draupadi, in menstruation, was rudely taken from her quarters into public view by the Kauravas. Draupadi argues that since Yudhishthira has already lost himself in the dice game and has become a slave, he can no longer be considered in possession of her and his wager was invalid. Angered at this "arrogance," DURYODHANA, eldest of Kauravas, commands Duhshana, one of the Kauravas, to disrobe Draupadi in order to humiliate her. As Duhshasana grasps her sari, Draupadi prays to Krishna for protection. Krishna answers her prayers and her sari becomes an endless garment that cannot be removed.

The disrobing of Draupadi is one of the most popular and reenacted parts of the Mahabharata. For this act Draupadi swears that she will not adorn her hair again until the blood of Duryodhana and Duhshasana flows in defeat on the battlefield. Draupadi accompanies her husbands through their exiles and experiences everything along with them. In the great war all five of her sons die, but she does eventually see the day when she can adorn her hair once again.

In regional mythology Draupadi is often considered the Great Goddess. This tradition is particularly well developed in the Tamil country, where she takes on not only the role of the goddess Sri, but also exhibits the characteristics of KALI and is celebrated in many shrines, rituals, and dramas. The dramas are often accompanied by possession rituals and walking on burning coals.

Further reading: J. A. B. van Buitenen, trans. *The Mahabharata*, Vol. 1, *The Book of the Beginnings*. Vol. 2, *The Book of the Assembly Hall*. Vol. 3, *The Book of Virata and the Book of Effort* (Chicago: University of Chicago Press, 1973–78); Alf Hiltebeitl, *The Cult of Draupadi*. Vol. 1, *Mythologies: From Gingee to Kuruksetra* (Chicago and London: University of Chicago Press, 1988); ———, *The Cult of Draupadi*. Vol. 2, *On Hindu Ritual and the Goddess* (Chicago and London: University of Chicago Press, 1991).

Dravidian

The adjective *Dravidian* defines a family of Indian languages that differs from the other families, mainly the Indo-Aryan, Munda, and Tibeto-Bur-

man. In the 19th and 20th centuries people speaking these languages in South India began to see themselves as possessing a separate culture, and a movement to create a separate Dravidian state, which was particularly strong between the 1930s and the 1970s, emerged.

The term itself is from the Sanskrit terms *dramila, dramida,* and *dravida,* referring in different contexts to peoples of the south of India, the South Indian region, and Tamil, one of the major Dravidian languages. The term is also sometimes used to refer to the people who speak the Dravidian languages; this usage is somewhat misleading in that it implies a racial designation such as ARYAN, while in fact there are many ethnicities represented by speakers of Dravidian languages. In the ongoing debate regarding the cultural nature of the ancient Indus Valley civilization, some believe its script reflects a Dravidian language and connect the Indus Valley peoples to contemporary Dravidian speakers. Others believe the language of the script is Indo-Aryan.

There are 26 Dravidian languages, spoken by some 250 million people. All but two of them are spoken in India; Brahui is spoken on the Afghan-Pakistani border in Baluchistan, and Kurux is spoken in Nepal. They are also spoken by old diasporic communities in Sri Lanka and Malaysia, and in newer DIASPORA countries around the world.

The largest Dravidian languages are Tamil and Telegu, each with about 70 million speakers, and Kannada and Malayalam, each spoken by about 40 million people. Other far South Indian dialects include Tulu and Toda, a tribal language. Other tribal Dravidian languages of southern and central India include Gondi, Kulumi, and Kurukh.

Great literatures have developed in all of the four major Dravidian languages. Tamil literature, however, has the most impressive corpus of extant ancient literature, dating from the second century B.C.E., as well as a large corpus of literature dating from the sixth century to the 12th century, when

Telegu and Kannada begin their literary records. Malayalam literature developed later. Scholars of Dravidian linguistics important for reference include M. B. Emeneau and T. Burrow. There are many scholars of Dravidian literatures; George Hart (Tamil), Velcheru Narayana Rao (Telegu), and A. K. Ramanujan (Tamil and Kannada) are important translators and scholars in this area.

Further reading: Robert L. Hardgrave, *The Dravidian Movement* (Bombay: Popular Prakashan, 1965); Stanford B. Steever, *The Dravidian Languages* (London: Routledge, 2004).

Drona

Drona (Bucket) is a Brahmin who played an important role in the Mahabharata epic. His unusual name derives from the fact that he was conceived in a bucket from the semen of his father, the RISHI Bharadvaja, who had been excited when the nymph Ghritaci accidentally showed herself to him naked. Drona was a descendant of Angiras, an ancient *rishi*, and the grandson of BRIHASPATI, a god. Drona's GURU was Agnivesha, son of the famous *rishi* AGASTYA.

Drona taught martial techniques and military science to both the PANDAVAS and the KAURAVAS, but he joined the latter in the great war between the two groups. After their great uncle, BHISHMA's, death, he became their commander. This was considered unusual, as he was a Brahmin and not a warrior by birth. In the battle Drona killed Drupada, the father of the Pandavas' wife, DRAUPADI. In turn he was killed by Drishtadyumna, Drupada's son and brother to Draupadi.

Further reading: J. A. B. van Buitenen, trans. and ed., *The Mahabharata*, 3 vols. (Chicago: University of Chicago Press, 1973–78); E. Washburn Hopkins and E. Washburn. *Epic Mythology* (Delhi: Motilal Banarsidass, 1986); D. A. Sadarjoshi, *Acharya Drona: A Human Drama from the Mahabharat* (Calcutta: Alpha-Beta, 1963).

Duce, Ivy O. (1895–1981) *founder of Sufism Reoriented*

Ivy O. Duce was an American proponent and leader of Sufism. She spread the universalist teachings of MEHER BABA.

Ivy Duce was born Ivy Judd and raised in the Episcopal Church. She served in the American Red Cross during World War I and after the war married and became a mother. During the 1930s she became interested in astrology. Around 1940, she became fascinated with the chart of Rabia Martin (aka Ada Ginsberg, 1871–1947) and decided to meet her. It turned out that Martin was the successor in America of the Indian Sufi teacher Hazrat Inayat Khan (1882–1927), who had offered an Islamic mysticism largely devoid of the peculiarities of Islamic thought. Duce became a follower of Martin's Sufi movement and eventually succeeded her as the leader in 1947.

In 1948, Duce met the Indian teacher MEHER BABA, of whom she had already developed a positive opinion from conversations with Martin. Over the next several years she adopted his perspectives, and he worked out a plan to redirect the Sufi movement she headed. Thus in 1952, Duce founded Sufism Reoriented, which was seen as the creation of Meher Baba. From this point on Duce viewed Sufism not as a form of Islam but as what she termed Universal Truth. She considered anyone who had reached God realization a Sufi. Meher Baba named her spiritual director or *murshida* of the organization, identified her as a seventh-plane master, and promised that her successors would be of an equally high status. He also promised that Sufism Reoriented would be a pure channel for God for the next 700 years (until his next incarnation as an AVATAR).

Duce was the only person in the West whom Meher Baba ever appointed as a spiritual teacher. Though head of a relatively small organization, she was widely recognized by the loosely organized movement that grew up around Meher Baba. Duce served for almost three decades.

Shortly before her death in 1981, she appointed James Mackie (b. 1932) as her successor.

Further reading: Ivy Duce, *How a Master Works* (Walnut Creek, Calif.: Sufism Reoriented, 1975); ———, *What Am I Doing Here?* (San Francisco: Sufism Reoriented, 1966); Ivy Duce and James Mackie, *Gurus and Psychotherapists: Spiritual versus Psychological Learning* (Lafayette, Calif.: Searchlight Seminars, 1981).

Durga

Durga (One who is hard to approach) is one of the major Indian goddesses, named perhaps for her ferocious nature. Her role is to intervene on behalf of the gods to defeat demons who threaten the cosmos.

The Devimahatmya, the most famous text to extol Durga's deeds, shows her intervening on three major occasions on behalf of the gods: against the demons Madhu and Kaitabha, against the demons Shumbha and Nishumbha, and, most famously, against Mahishasura, the buffalo demon.

In the first case, Durga fought on behalf of Lord BRAHMA and VISHNU. The story goes that Madhu and Kaitabha were born from Vishnu's ear wax. They threatened to kill Lord Brahma. As Vishnu was sleeping at the time, Brahma calls on Durga to come forth out of Vishnu as the goddess of sleep, so that Vishnu can awaken and kill the demons. She does so and Vishnu kills them.

In the case of Shumbha and Nishumbha, the two demons performed austerities that compelled SHIVA to give them riches and strength that would surpass that of the gods. Thereupon, they began a war against the divinities. Finally, the gods had to perform religious austerities to Durga to obtain her blessing. Hearing of Durga's charms (though usually ferocious in aspect, she could change her form at will), Shumbha sent his deputies one after another to win her favor. After she easily destroyed the deputies Chanda and Munda she was forced to confront their com-

mander, Raktabija, who had the power sprout up from his own blood whenever wounded. The angry Durga then sprouted KALI from her forehead; Kali went forward and systematically drank up the blood from Raktabija's wounds until he was defeated. Finally Shumbha himself, along with Nishumbha, stepped forward, and they too were defeated.

The DURGA PUJA fall festival celebrates particularly Durga's defeat of the buffalo-headed demon Mahishasura. The story of this ASURA (antigod) begins when he becomes lord of heaven after defeating all the other gods—he had won

The goddess Durga slaying Mahesha, the buffalo demon *(calendar print)*

the boon that he could not be defeated by any male god or demon. When the defeated gods approached Shiva, Vishnu, and Brahma for help, the three divinities became so angry that the light of their anger combined, taking the powers of all the gods with it to create the most formidable power (*Mahashakti*)—the goddess Durga.

Durga will be able to defeat the demon because she is female. Armed by the gods she begins a horrific battle with the buffalo-headed demon and eventually defeats him by driving her spear through him—a scene often depicted in her iconography. She is always represented in superior position over the demon, sometimes putting her foot on his neck.

Durga is the goddess of the universe, overseeing every realm. Durga's primary characteristics are that she dwells in inaccessible places and relishes meat, blood, and intoxicating drink. Durga is probably a form of the goddess from the tribal, non-Aryan realm of India, who came to be respected and adopted as the great goddess in the Brahminical tradition. Perhaps her early character is revealed in her association with the growth of plants and fertility.

The Durga Puja is held from the first through the ninth days of the first half of the month of Ashvin (September and October), as part of the NAVARATRI ceremonies in most parts of India. A bundle of nine plants is worshipped as representative of the goddess. The festival celebrates her battle against Mahishasura and her role as killer of that buffalo-headed demon. She is also cast as a married daughter, returning during the festival time from her home far away. She is particularly feted as the wife of Shiva and may be seen by some as an aspect of PARVATI. In the texts, as opposed to popular and local mythologies, her role as wife is not important.

Durga is said to have been asleep for several months when she is awakened to be worshipped at Durga Puja. The ritual of the festival includes recitation of parts of the Devimahatmya, an important goddess text.

Further reading: Robert T. Browne, *The Golden Book of Mother Durga* (New York: Hermetic Society for World Service, 2001); Sudeshana Banerjee, *Durga Puja: Yesterday, Today and Tomorrow* (New Delhi: Rupa, 2004); David Kinsley, *Hindu Goddesses* (Berkeley: University of California Press, 1988).

Durga Puja   *See* NAVARATRI.

Durvasas

Durvasas is a sage in Indian mythology known for his irascibility and for his curses. In the story of the churning of the MILK OCEAN, told in the PURANAS, Durvasas offers a beautiful garland to AIRAVATA, INDRA's white elephant. The elephant picks up the garland with its trunk and throws it on the ground. Indra tries to placate the furious sage but he will not relent, saying that he is known for his implacability and lack of forgiveness. He curses the gods to have ill fortune. It is a result of this ill fortune that they must eventually stir the Milk Ocean to obtain good results.

Another story, from the last chapter of the RAMAYANA, pits Durvasas against Lakshmana. The latter is guarding the entranceway to his palace while his brother, RAMA, talks with the god of death, YAMA. Yama has demanded that the meeting remain uninterrupted and has made Rama swear that he would kill anyone who interrupts them. Unfortunately, the perpetually angry Durvasas arrives at the entranceway and insists that he receive hospitality. Lakshmana asks for his patience but he has none. Durvasa threatens to curse all the kingdom, including Rama and Bharata, if he is not received. Lakshmana therefore tells Rama of Durvasa's arrival, knowing that Rama will be obliged to kill him. In the end Rama merely exiles Lakshmana, claiming that banishment and death are the same to noble men.

Numerous tales are told in the mythology about the angry Durvasas, but one story in the

Mahabharata credits him with giving Kunti a boon for treating him as a proper guest—she will have children by five gods. These five gods are the true fathers of the five PANDAVAS.

Further reading: Cornelia Dimmitt and J. A. B. van Buitenen, *Classical Hindu Mythology: A Reader in the Sanskrit Puranas* (Philadelphia: Temple University Press, 1978); E. Washburn Hopkins, *Epic Mythology* (Delhi: Motilal Banarsidass, 1986).

Duryodhana

Duryodhana was the eldest of the 100 KAURAVAS, the evil sons of Dhritarashtra in the MAHAB-HARATA story. He was the chief conspirator among the Kauravas against their cousins the PANDA-VAS, whose kingdom they tried to seize. He was a fierce fighter, as his Sanskrit name implies: *duryodhana* means "tough in battle." He had a particular rivalry with BHIMA, physically the strongest of the Pandavas.

When Duryodhana's cousin YUDHISHTHIRA was designated as heir to the throne, he persuaded his father to banish the Pandavas to a city where he had them placed in a house made of wax, where he planned to burn them to death. They escaped and went into hiding for some time. Later he challenged the Pandavas to a dice game in which he had the game fixed. After Yudhishthira lost everything in this game the Pandavas' wife, DRAU-PADI, was publicly humiliated. The dice game was replayed and the Pandavas lost again and went into exile for 13 years.

After they returned from exile, Duryodhana refused to split the kingdom with them and the great Mahabharata war began. Duryodhana was slain by his lifetime rival Bhima, and the Kauravas were defeated.

Further reading: Manorama Bhavanagara, *Duryod-hana* (Delhi: Anila Prakashan, 2000); J. A. B. van Buitenen, trans., *The Mahabharata*, 3 vols. (Chicago: University of Chicago Press, 1973–78); William Buck,

trans., *The Mahabharata* (Berkeley: University of California Press, 1973).

dvaita

Dvaita (from *dvi,* two) is usually translated as "dualist." In theological terms it refers to the notion that God is completely separate and different from the human soul.

Abrahamic traditions in their normative form—Judaism, Christianity, and Islam—would be seen as *dvaita* or dualistic because they believe that the human soul is a separate entity and reality from God. Normative Hinduism tends toward forms of ADVAITA, non-dualism, the opposite of *dvaita*. But there are some Indian systems that are truly *dvaita* in nature. One form of VEDANTA, championed by MADHVA, a 12th-century sage, is authentically *dvaita*. Also, the South Indian tradition of Shaiva Siddhanta can be classified as *dvaita*.

Further reading: S. N. Dasgupta, *History of Indian Philosophy,* 5 vols. (Delhi: Motilal Banarsidass, 1975); Ananta Sharan Tiwari, *Vedic Myth, Ritual, and Philoso-phy: A Study of Dvaita Interpretation of the Veda by Mad-hva* (Delhi: Pratibha Prakashan, 2001).

Dvapara Yuga

In the Indian tradition the YUGAS, or ages, refer to throws in an ancient dice game. Dvapara is named after the throw "two" (*dvi*), which is the third best throw or the second worst throw. Dvapara Yuga is 864,000 years in duration. In Dvapara the deterio-ration in human and worldly life continues. Passion, strife, greed, and war develop, and truth is no longer adhered to in the same way. In Dvapara Yuga, the once-unified VEDA was divided into four parts by VYASA. Because differences of opinion had arisen, the different Vedas (RIG, SAMA, YAJUR, ATHARVA) developed distinctions. Death arose among humankind, as well as disgust with exis-tence, calamity, suffering, and disease. In dvapara a notion of "wisdom" became necessary as a result of the perception of the faults that now existed.

Whereas in the Treta Yuga SATTVA, the pure aspect of nature (PRAKRITI) tended to prevail, in Dvapara Yuga, *rajas* (impure) and *tamas* (contaminated) aspects of nature emerged. Ritual sacrifice became a predominant feature of Dvapara; it had not been important before. VISHNU is said to preside over Dvapara, because of the need for order.

Further reading: Cornelia Dimmitt and J. A. B. van Buitenen, *Classical Hindu Mythology: A Reader in the Sanskrit Puranas* (Philadelphia: Temple University Press, 1978); W. J. Wilkins, *Hindu Mythology, Vedic and Puranic,* 2nd ed. (Calcutta: Rupa, 1973).

Dvaraka

Dvaraka is one of the seven sacred cities of India; for Vaishnavites (*see* VAISHNAVISM) it is also one of the four places renowned for the special presence of god (the other three are BADRINATH, RAMESH-VARAM, and Puri). KRISHNA is said to have fled here to escape from the evil Mathura king Kamsa, who had tried so often to kill him, and the city is considered the capital of Krishna's kingdom.

Dvaraka is on the sea in Saurashtra, a region of Gujarat. Krishna's birthday, the HOLI festival, and DIVALI are three special festival days at Dvaraka. There is a huge temple complex devoted to Krishna. The city is also the site of one of the four monastic centers established by the great sage SHANKARA in the eighth century.

Further reading: E. Washburn Hopkins, *Epic Mythology* (Delhi: Motilal Banarsidass, 1986): S. R. Rao, *The Lost City of Dvaraka* (New Delhi: Aditya Prakashan, 1999).

E

Easwaran, Eknath (1910–1999) *founder of Blue Mountain Center of Meditation*

An Indian-born proponent of MEDITATION, Eknath Easwaran was the first to teach the practice in an American academic setting. For four decades he taught nonsectarian techniques of meditation through courses, lectures, and more than two dozen books.

Eknath Easwaran was born on December 17, 1910, into an ancient matrilineal family in Kerala, India. He grew up under the guidance of his grandmother, whom he was later to honor as his spiritual teacher. From her he learned the traditional wisdom of India's ancient scriptures. When he was a boy, she sent him to the temple priest to learn SANSKRIT from one of the purest traditions in India.

Easwaran fell in love with English literature in high school. At 16 he left home to attend a Catholic college. Here he excelled in debate and read columns by Mohandas Karamchand GANDHI (1869–1948) in *Young India*. Easwaran spent his 20s as a journalist in Secunderabad, Andhra Pradesh, where he soon became recognized as a public speaker. During this time he visited the ASHRAM of Mahatma Gandhi, where Gandhi's teaching impressed him greatly, particularly Gan-

Eknath Easwaran (1910–1999), scholar and founder of the Blue Mountain Center of Meditation, Petaluma, California *(Blue Mountain Center of Meditation)*

dhi's insistence on transforming oneself before trying to transform others.

Easwaran earned graduate degrees in law and English from Nagpur University. In 1946 he began teaching at Amravati in Maharashtra. With articles appearing in the *Times of India* and the *Illustrated Weekly of India,* his reputation spread. He was soon promoted to full professor at Nagpur University and won acclaim as a writer and lecturer.

In February 1948, when his grandmother died, Easwaran recalled, "All my success had turned to ashes." Meditating on passages from Bhagavad Gita gave him peace. He developed a regular meditation practice and created a method to share his experience. He developed an Eight Point Program of meditation for solving physical and emotional problems, releasing deeper resources, and pursuing life's highest goal, SELF-REALIZATION.

Easwaran immigrated to America in 1959 through the Fulbright exchange program. Attending the University of California at Berkeley, he lectured on India's spiritual heritage and soon attracted a dedicated group of people who studied his teachings. Among them was his future wife, Christine, who helped him establish the Blue Mountain Center of Meditation, now in Petaluma, California.

In January 1968, at Berkeley, he inaugurated a course on meditation, believed to be the first of its kind offered at any major university in the United States. In 1970 the Blue Mountain Center of Meditation moved to Marin County and Easwaran transferred his teachings there. Nilgiri Press, a small publisher operating out of Oakland, began printing many publications including the *Bhagavad Gita for Daily Living* (1975), *Laurel's Kitchen* (1976), and his best-selling *Meditation* (1978), which sold over 200,000 copies. Easwaran's writings include 26 books about meditation and the classics of world mysticism, which have been translated into 26 languages, with over 1 million copies in print.

Until the end of his life, despite chronic ailments, Easwaran continued to hold regular retreats and deliver talks, drawing students from around the world. He taught nonviolence, concern for endangered species, and meditation. He died on October 26, 1999.

The Blue Mountain Center of Meditation preserves Easwaran's teachings through the leadership of Christine Easwaran. A nonprofit and nonsectarian organization, the center has a mission to share Easwaran's teachings through a quarterly journal, *The Blue Mountain,* Nigiri Press books, and video and audio products.

Further reading: Eknath Easwaran, *The Bhagavad Gita for Daily Living* (Petaluma, Calif.: Nilgiri Press, 1979); ———, *Dialogue with Death: The Spiritual Psychology of the Katha Upanishad* (Petaluma, Calif.: Nilgiri Press, 1981); ———, *Gandhi, the Man* (Petaluma, Calif.: Nilgiri Press, 1978); ———, *The Mantram Handbook: Formulas for Transformation* (Berkeley, Calif.: Nilgiri Press, 1977); ———, *Meditation: Commonsense Directions for an Uncommon Life* (Petaluma, Calif.: Nilgiri Press, 1978).

Eckankar (est. 1965)

Eckankar or ECK, the "Religion of the Light and Sound of God," was founded in 1965 by former journalist Paul Twitchell (c. 1909–70). During the 1950s Twitchell became a student of numerous esoteric and spiritual movements. He studied L. Ron Hubbard's Scientology for a time before finding a place in Swami Premananda's Self Realization Church of Absolute Monism. Later, Twitchell was initiated into Ruhani Satsang (fellowship of true seekers) in the RADHASOAMI movement, and received formal training from its founder, Sant Mat Master Kirpal Singh. Eventually he departed from Radhasoami after a disagreement and established his own teaching. He moved to San Francisco and began lecturing, writing, and practicing a form of *surat shabda* yoga, which involves contact with inner light and sound.

In 1956 Twitchell revealed that he had experienced "God-realization" after being trained by the Order of the Vairagi Masters, spiritual teachers. According to Twitchell, these beings have secretly imparted the teachings of ECK to individuals throughout history. Twitchell believed that he was entrusted by these masters to disseminate ECK teachings to the modern world. In 1965 he proclaimed himself as the Living ECK Master and the 971st Mahanta. He founded Eckankar later that year and established its headquarters in Las Vegas, Nevada.

Twitchell spent the next few years working with his wife, Gail, to build a following for the movement. He also wrote several books on the teachings of Eckankar. In 1969 Twitchell published *Eckankar: The Key to Secret Worlds*. During the same period Brad Steiger wrote a biography on Twitchell entitled *In My Soul I Am Free*. Both books increased the popularity and notoriety of the movement.

Eckankar is an eclectic religious movement. The Light and Sound of God has been described as the science of soul travel, in which the soul departs from the body in an ascent to invisible worlds. ECK beliefs and practices resemble the teachings of Radhasoami as well as the Western occult teachings of Rosicrucians. The other fundamental teachings of ECK appear to be similar to the teachings of KIRPAL SINGH (1894–1974), teacher in the SANT MAT tradition.

It was revealed after his death that Twitchell may have plagiarized teachings from Julian P. Johnson, a disciple of the Radhasomai Satsang. Eckankar maintains in response that ECK teachings have permeated various teachings throughout history, and that Twitchell has made them more accessible for the modern world. Twitchell also used different terminology than Sant Mat. Eckankar teaches that God is the source of all being flowing, from the transcendent downward to the material world. The Light and Sound of God (ECK) is the energy current from which life flows and can be understood as the Holy Spirit in Christian terms. The numerous practices offered by ECK masters aim to guide individuals to the realization of God and their place as coworkers with God. A primary means of attaining realization is through the chanting of *HU*, an ECK name for God.

After Twitchell's death in 1971, Gail Twitchell announced Darwin Gross as successor and the 972nd Living ECK Master. The choice of Gross was controversial. He was a recent inductee of the movement and his eventual marriage to Gail Twitchell fueled suspicion. Despite the loss of several devotees (known as *chelas*), ECK continued to grow. Headquarters were moved to Menlo Park, California.

Gross relinquished his position as the Living ECK Master in 1981 and named Harold Klemp as the 973rd Mahanta. Gross's status of ECK master was revoked in 1984, and he is no longer affiliated with Eckankar. Lengthy litigation over the use of the name *Eckankar* ensued between Gross and the organization, and Eckankar eventually prevailed.

Harold Klemp was born in 1942 in Wisconsin and raised on a small family farm. He had a religious upbringing at a Milwaukee boarding school and later attended college, where he studied religion. After enlisting in the U.S. Air Force he was assigned to a military installation in Japan. It was here that he first encountered Eckankar. Under Klemp's direction, Eckankar headquarters were moved to its present location in Minneapolis, Minnesota. In 1990, he established the Temple of ECK, the spiritual center of the movement. Klemp has authored over 40 books and routinely attends Eckankar conferences and seminars. Since his induction as Living ECK Master, Klemp has redirected the emphasis of ECK teachings toward divine love and service to others in daily life.

Eckankar maintains 164 centers in the United States and over 360 worldwide. The organization includes a publishing company called Illuminated Way Press, located in Crystal, Minnesota. Publications include books by Twitchell, Klemp, and other ECKists. An annual *ECKANKAR Journal* is also published. Eckankar has the status of a nonprofit religious organization and church with members in 130 countries. Its mission as an educational organization is to promote the knowledge of soul and God realization. The organization offers courses in dream interpretation, soul travel, and life service.

Further reading: Darwin Gross, *Your Right to Know* (Menlo Park, Calif.: Illuminated Way Press, 1979); Harold Klemp, *The Art of Spiritual Dreaming* (Minneapolis, Minn.: Eckankar, 1999); ———, *Autobiography of a Modern Prophet* (Minneapolis, Minn.: Eckankar, 2000); Paul Twitchell, *Dialogues with the Master* (Las Vegas, Nev.: Illuminated Way Press, 1970); ———, *ECKANKAR: The Key to Secret Worlds* (San Diego, Calif.: Illuminated Way Press, 1969).

ecology and Hinduism

The beliefs and practices of Hinduism have been a resource in ecological and environmental movements both within and outside India. Hindu religious stories, imagery, and symbolism are used to support the view that the universe is divine in all of its aspects and nature is sacred in its essence. Aspects of nature including mountains, seas, rivers, trees, flowers, animals, and even the elements of soil, water, and air have often been personified in Hindu myth as divine beings to be worshipped and cared for. Various forms of vegetarianism have been practiced widely among different Hindu groups for centuries. The deep respect for all forms of life in the beliefs and practices of Hinduism provides a natural alignment of Hindus with any concerted effort against environmental degradation.

In India, the traditional home of Hinduism, over 950 nongovernmental organizations work for environmental causes that address ecological problems from rural deforestation to urban pollution. As record rates of industrialization and urbanization press upon the limited resources of India, groups have mobilized to find ecologically sound practices in residential settlements, farming, mining, fishing, and water management. Threats to India's land, rivers, and seas, and air and the displacement of millions of people through construction of dams and mines are heightened by population expansion and the consumerism of a burgeoning middle class.

Traditionally India relied upon ecologically sound management practices in its rural areas and included a religiously based cultural order that respected the sacredness of all life. Mohandas Karamchand GANDHI's activities in the movement for Indian independence gave political legitimacy to the religious and ecological sensibilities of India, particularly Hinduism, Buddhism, and Jainism. His dedication to the values of nonviolence (AHIMSA), holding to truth (SATYAGRAHA), personal asceticism, minimal consumption, self-reliance, simplicity, sustainability, and community-based economics was based on his interpretation of Hindu values. However, since the days of Gandhi, the political leadership of the country has stressed secularization and growth so that India has continued to industrialize, urbanize, and modernize at a rapid rate. Loss of arable land, deforestation, water pollution, unplanned urbanization, dam construction, and pesticide pollution are critical problems being addressed by various ecological movements that draw on the Hindu devotion to life and the sacred.

Two locally based movements in India demonstrate the application of Hindu precepts to economic and environmental challenges: the Bishnois and the Chipko movement. The Bishnois are a small Rajasthani community who view environmental conservation as a religious duty. Their leader, Guru Maharaj Jambaji (b. 1451 C.E.), witnessed a severe drought and the cutting of trees as food for animals, which resulted in the desolation of both animals and plants. He constructed a program that prohibited the cutting of any tree and the killing of any animal. The ethic of the guru endured over centuries and the area became lush with vegetation. In the 18th century, the king of Jodhpur sent loggers to cut down the Bishnois' trees for construction of a new palace. The villagers protested, and, when their protests were not heeded, they protected the trees by surrounding the trees with their bodies. Upon hearing of the villagers' dedication, the king granted them state protection and their protection of trees and animals persists today. The Bishnois' tactic of encircling trees to protect them inspired the Chipko movement of the 20th century.

In March 1973 in Gopeshwar, Uttar Pradesh, a sports equipment factory marked trees near the village for harvesting. The villagers encircles the trees, as had the Bishnois before them, and provided a human shield against deforestation. The strategy was repeated in several villages in the Himalayas, creating the Chipko movement, which exists today as a grassroots ecodevelopment movement.

Both the Bishnoi and the Chipko movements demonstrate how environmental conservation is aligned with Hindu religion and culture. Hindu scriptures contain implicit environmental ethics that encourage respect for and stewardship of a sacred universe. The central concepts of DHARMA (right conduct) and KARMA (action in the world) have been used to support initiatives for environmental protection. Ecological writers call for a partnership between Hindu religious leaders and ecological activists to join the insight and devotion of traditional Hindu thought in collaboration with scientific strategies of sustainable development.

A series of 10 conferences on the world's religions and ecology was held at the Harvard Divinity School Center for the Study of World Religions from 1996 to 1998. Subsequently, the Forum on Religion and Ecology and its Web site were announced by the founders, Mary Evelyn Tucker and John Grim, during a report to the United Nations and subsequent press conference in 1998. In both the initial conferences and the continuing activities of the forum, scholars and practitioners promote a dialogue on the global environmental crisis and efforts to create public policy in alignment with the teachings of the world's religions. The relationship of Hinduism and ecology has become one focus of the Forum on Religion and Ecology.

Scholars and religious leaders have made presentations about Asian religious traditions and ecology at the Parliament of World Religions. The Green Yoga Association, founded by Laura Cornell in Oakland, California, in 2004, seeks to promote an ecological ethic in its practice of traditional yogic techniques and to interpret yogic texts, such as PATANJALI'S YOGA SUTRAS, in terms of environmental ethics.

Further reading: David Landis Barnhall and Roger S. Gottlieb, eds., *Deep Ecology and World Religions: New Essays on Sacred Ground* (Albany: State University of New York Press, 2001); J. Baird Callicott and Roger T. Ames, eds., *Nature in Asian Traditions of Thought: Essays in Environmental Philosophy* (Albany: State University of New York Press, 1989); Christopher Key Chapple, *Nonviolence to Animals, Earth, and Self in Asian Traditions* (Albany: State University of New York Press, 1993); Christopher Key Chapple and Mary Evelyn Tucker, eds., *Hinduism and Ecology: The Intersection of Earth, Sky, and Water* (Cambridge, Mass.: Harvard University Press, 2000); David L. Gosling, *Religion and Ecology in India and Southeast Asia* (London: Routledge, 2001); Lance E. Nelson, ed., *Purifying the Earthly Body of God: Religion and Ecology in Hindu India* (Albany: State University of New York Press, 1998); Helaine Selin, ed., *Nature across Cultures: Views of Nature and the Environment in Non-Western Cultures* (Lancaster, England: Kluwer Academic Publishers, 2003); Mary Evelyn Tucker, *Worldly Wonder: Religions Enter Their Ecological Phase* (La Salle, Ill.: Open Court, 2003).

ekadashi

Ekadashi (11th) denotes the 11th day of both the waxing and the waning lunar cycles. It is observed as a fast day by many Hindus and is an obligatory day of fasting for Vaishnavites, worshippers of VISHNU, as it is associated with his worship. When one observes *ekadashi* as a result of a vow, one must stay awake that night and worship Vishnu (as is done with SHIVA during MAHASHIVARATRI), as well as fast. The *ekadashi* in the bright half of the month of Margashirsha (November–December) is known as "heaven *ekadashi*," in reference to the heavenly abode of Vishnu. It is a very important temple day, as those who go through the temple doors on this day are believed to go to heaven.

Further reading: Abbe J. A. Dubois, *Hindu Manners, Customs and Ceremonies.* Translated from the French by Henry K. Beauchamp (Oxford: Clarendon Press, 1959); Swami Harshananda, *Hindu Festivals and Sacred Days* (Bangalore: Ramakrishna Math, 1994).

Elan Vital   *See* RAWAT, PREM.

elements, five

In Hindu science, the five gross elements that make up the universe are ether/space (*akasha*), wind/air (*vayu*), fire (*tejas* or *agni*), water (*ap* or *jala*), and earth (PRITHIVI). They are enumerated among the 24 categories of all reality of SAMKHYA, a philosophical system originating in c. 500 B.C.E., and YOGA. These elements are in fact accepted as the basic elements of all material reality by the Hindu tradition in general. Though they seem simple elemental categories, one must see them as abstractions that contain in elemental terms much more than they signify as individual words. Via the *TANMATRAS,* or subtle elements, the five basic elements relate directly to the five senses in order: hearing (ether), touch (wind), sight (fire), taste (water), smell (earth).

Further reading: Benimadhab Barua, *A History of Pre-Buddhistic Indian Philosophy* (Delhi: Motilal Banarsidass, 1970); Frits Staal, *Concepts of Science in Europe and Asia* (Leiden: International Institute for Asian Studies, 1993).

Elephanta

The famous SHIVA cave temple at Elephanta, a small island in the harbor of Bombay (Mumbai), is hollowed out from solid rock. It was created

A Brahmin householder performing water ablutions at dawn on the banks of the Ganges River in Benares (Varanasi) *(Constance A. Jones)*

A Hindu sculpture at Ellora Caves, c. 900, C.E., in Aurangabad, Maharastra *(Constance A. Jones)*

around the sixth century C.E. It is not known which dynasty built the temple.

The temple is famous for a colossal sculpture of Shiva with three heads, one each of Shiva, VISHNU, and BRAHMA. This sculpture thus presents Shiva as supreme among divinities and embodies the Hindu Trimurti, or trinity. It has been said that this sculpture with its serene aspect is the most beautiful piece of religious architecture in all of India. The statue is flanked by two other figures of Shiva as ARDHANAR-ISHVARA and Shiva as the "bearer of the GANGES."

The inner sanctum of the temple holds a typical LINGAM. Also depicted are Shiva as cosmic dancer and a depiction of the killing of the demon ANDHAKA.

Further reading: Stella Kramrisch, "The Great Cave Temple of Siva in Elephanta: Levels of Meaning and Their Form," in *Discourses on Siva: Proceedings of a Symposium on the Nature of Religious Imagery* (Philadelphia: University of Pennsylvania, 1984), pp. 156–169. Wendy Doniger O'Flaherty, George Berkson, and Carmel Berkson, *Elephanta, the Cave Temple of Shiva* (Princeton, N.J.: Princeton University Press, 1983).

Ellora

Ellora in the state of Maharashtra is a rich archaeological site containing caves, cave art, and monolithic rock architecture dating from the fifth to the eighth century C.E. Most of the work is Hindu, but some is associated with Jains (*see* JAINISM) and Buddhists. There are a total of 34 caves at Ellora. Some, cut out of solid rock, were used as dwelling places for Buddhist or Jain monks.

The most elaborate monument at Ellora is the Kailasanatha Temple (to Shiva who resides on Mount KAILASH), built by the Rastrakuta emperor Krishna I (c. 756–773 C.E.). This entire temple, cut from solid rock, includes a shrine room, hall, gateway, votive pillars, lesser shrines and cloisters. There are many carved divine figures and narratives on the walls. The ground plan is said to be about the same size as the Parthenon in Athens, Greece.

The facades for the caves inhabited by the Jain monks, as well as the Jain temples cut into the rock, exhibit sculptures featuring the full panoply of Jain religious imagery. There are images of the TIRTHANKARAS (great personages), gods and goddesses (subordinate to the Tirthankaras in importance in the Jain context), and scenes from traditional Jain stories.

Further reading: Doris Clark Chatham, "Myth, Cult, and Cetana at the Kailasa Temple, Ellora," in Michael Meister, ed., *Discourses on Siva: Proceedings of a Symposium on the Nature of Religious Imagery* (Philadelphia: University of Philadelphia Press, 1984), pp. 156–169; Jose Pereira, *Monolithic Jinas: The Iconography of the Jain Temples of Ellora* (Delhi: Motilal Banarsidass, 1977).

ends of life, four

The four ends of life or *purusharthas* (goals of man) represent a traditional scheme that has been maintained in its current form for over 2,000 years. The four are *artha* (prosperity, worldly well-being), *kama* (pleasure, erotic satisfaction), DHARMA (right conduct, adherence to social law), and *moksha* (liberation from the rounds of birth and rebirth). They offer a balanced approach to the world. Though Indian tradition is known to focus upon transcendence and the search beyond the world, VEDIC tradition always emphasized family, prosperity, pleasure, and well-being as worthy goals, as long as they are not pursued or cultivated in the extreme.

Further reading: Samiran Chandra Cakrabarti, *The Value System as Reflected in the Vedas: The Concept of Purusarthas* (Ujjain: Maharshi Sandipani Rashtriya Ved Vidya Pratishthan, 2000); Klaus Klostermaier, *A Survey of Hinduism*, 2d ed. (Albany: State University of New York Press, 1994); Rajendra Prasad et al., *Studies on the Purusarthas* (Bhubaneswar: Utkal University, 1994); Ludwik Sternbach, *Bibliography on Dharma and Artha in Ancient and Medieval India* (Wiesbaden: Otto Harrassowitz, 1973).

Europe

Excluding Great Britain and the Netherlands, Europe has had little immigration from India and today has a small Hindu population. Great Britain and the Netherlands had colonies into which South Asian laborers migrated. Many Hindus from Guyana (*see* CARIBBEAN REGION) and Kenya (*see* AFRICA) left the struggling economies and racial persecution of those countries to enter Great Britain. Over 65,000 South Asians were exiled from Uganda under the directive of Idi Amin in the 1970s and nearly all fled to Britain.

In Britain today, Hinduism flourishes in a variety of practices, and many temples exist (*see* UNITED KINGDOM). Because these Hindus remain close to their native land through Commonwealth ties, they have imported influential political and religious movements from India. Most neo-Hindu movements as well as the Vishwa Hindu Parishad are active in Great Britain.

The Netherlands also has a sizable South Asian community, populated largely by Hindus who fled economic and political hardship in Suriname. As in Great Britain, they remain in contact with Hindu movements in India and reflect the traditional practices as well as the conflicts represented in contemporary Indian Hinduism.

Eastern Europe remains the main residence for the Gypsies or Romany, who were originally Hindus from the Punjab and Afghanistan. The language and customs of the Gypsy ethnicity retain vestiges of a Hindu past, even though the Gypsy population is not considered a Hindu movement.

In the last century, native Europeans have supported an entire array of contemporary Hindu movements, particularly the INTERNATIONAL SOCIETY FOR KRISHNA CONSCIOUSNESS, the SATYA SAI BABA movement, various forms of hatha yoga, and individual teachers of Hindu practices.

See also DIASPORA; SCANDINAVIA.

Further reading: Martin Baumann, *Migration, Religion, Integration: Buddhist, Vietnamese, and Hindu Tamils in Germany* (Marburg: Diagonal-Verlag, 2000); Knut A. Jacobsen and P. Pratap Kumar, eds., *South Asians in the Diaspora: Histories and Religious Traditions* (Leiden: Brill, 2004).

F

facial markings

Various facial markings are used in India to denote sectarian affiliations or to serve other ceremonial purposes.

The most common Vaishnavite (*see* VAISHNAVISM) forehead marking is a large U-shaped mark with a vertical dot or line placed precisely in its center, not touching the bottom of the U. Variations include a more square U, and different placement of the center vertical line (which is sometimes made of a series of dots). Some Vaishnavite markings show only two parallel, vertical lines with or without a center dot, or three parallel vertical lines, sometimes with a dot placed on the middle line, or just above or below it.

Shaivite (*see* SHAIVISM) facial markings are most commonly three, equidistant, parallel lines on the forehead in varying patterns.

A dot or line of red saffron or ash might be placed on the forehead by anyone after a *PUJA* to mark an enhanced devotional state, or by a GURU or teacher at all times as a sign of devotion. In either case, the dot represents the opening of the third eye, which indicates heightened consciousness.

Women in India often wear a dot on the forehead, sometimes as a conventional decoration, but sometimes as protection from the evil eye. It might also be interpreted as a recognition of the existence of the third eye of consciousness.

Some women in North India put a mark of red saffron on the part of the hair to signify that they are married.

Further reading: Eva Rudy Jansen, *The Book of Hindu Imagery: The Gods and Their Symbols* (Havelte, Holland: Binkey Kok Publications, 1993).

fasting   *See* VOWS.

Foundation of Revelation (est. 1970)

In 1968, a young American woman, Charlotte Wallace (no b. date), attended the Spiritual Summit Conference in Calcutta (Kolkata), India, and there met an unnamed Indian beggar. Enamored by his knowledge of life, Wallace and some of her friends followed the holy man home to his native village of Gorkhara to stay with his family and learn his teachings. The holy man was born in 1913 into a Brahmin family. As a youth he spent many years studying modern knowledge but deemed this study limited and illusory. On January 14, 1966, the fire of knowledge (AGNI) vanquished all of his previous learning, and in September 1966 cosmos and consciousness became concentrated in him as the destroyer, SHIVA. Foundation devotees believe that the holy man's experience ushered in the era of Shiva Kalpa, the period of Lord Shiva's omnipotent imagination.

In 1969, the holy man took up residence in San Francisco. One year later, the foundation was established there and centers began to be created around the world. The purpose of the foundation is to break through religious, national, and racial boundaries to create a harmonious relationship of nations. The foundation reveres Shiva as the creator of all things, the destroyer of ignorance, and the force that moves each person to strive for perfection.

The foundation, still headquartered in San Francisco, has over 5,000 members in the United States. In 1997 it claimed 25,000 members worldwide. It has 21 centers in 10 countries, including India, England, France, the Netherlands, and Australia. Audio CDs of Sunday meetings and other events are sold through the foundation archives.

funeral rites

Indian *anyeshti* (funeral rites or final sacraments) are formally outlined in the *Dharmashastra* law books and other texts, including a special section of *Garuda Purana*. Actual practice, however, frequently diverges from the textual tradition.

There are rituals to be performed before death, those that relate to the disposition of the body, those that take place after death to prevent the soul from taking on the form of a ghost, and those done later when the person is honored as an ancestor. A person will almost always be cremated at death, unless he or she is an infant or a mendicant, in which case the body is most often buried. Part of the postdeath ritual involves placing the body on a bier, in either a sitting or a lying position, to be carried to the cremation ground by relatives or taken in a bullock cart or other conveyance.

At least part of this trip will be accompanied by ritual singing. The body is then lain on the funeral wood, always facing southward, as the south is the direction of death. The eldest son is the lay officiant at the cremation. After circumambulating the body, he pours oblations of water on it, cracks the skull to release the soul, and lights the funeral pyre. The funeral party will most often wait until the body is almost completely consumed.

Once the cremation is complete the funeral party returns home to do expiations, using mantras and other rituals, in order to ward off "death pollution" or the effects of being in proximity to a corpse. BRAHMINS in particular observe a period of 10 days when no one in the family is allowed to leave the house after a death. After a day or two the eldest son will return to the burning grounds to retrieve the ashes and bones. The ashes are usually put into an urn and either buried or poured into a sacred river such as the Ganges or Cauvery, thus guaranteeing liberation or heaven for the deceased. Often an 11-day ritual is performed to provide a spiritual body for the deceased, in order to prevent the deceased from becoming a ghost and wandering homeless for eternity. Later, the *shraddha* or ancestor rites are performed yearly to sustain the person in the other world.

Brahminical mendicants or SADHUS are buried in a special rite. The body is placed in a deep hole in yogic, sitting position. It is then covered in salt from bottom to chin, and the whole is covered with earth. Saints in India are usually buried in tombs. Often the tomb's covering protrudes above ground so that the constituted SAMADHI or grave site becomes a place of holy pilgrimage.

Further reading: Gian Giuseppe Filippi, *Mrtyu: Concept of Death in Indian Traditions: Transformation of the Body and Funeral Rites.* Translated by Antonio Rigopoulos. Reconstructing Indian History and Culture, 11. New Delhi, D. K. Printworld, 1996; R Beena Ghimire Poudyal and Binod Ghimire, *Hindu Death Rites: Antyeshti Samskar* (Kathmandu: Barsha Ghimire, 1998; New Delhi: D. K. Printworld, 1996); Ramashray Roy, *Samaskaras in Indian Tradition and Culture* (Delhi: Shipra, 2003).

G

ganadhara   *See* JAINISM.

gandharvas

The *gandharvas* are celestial singers and musicians. They are mentioned in the VEDAS and also play a minor role in the epics (RAMAYANA; MAHABHARATA) and PURANAS. They are minor but ubiquitous characters in Indian mythology.

KUBERA, the god of wealth, is considered the lord of the *gandharvas*. Etymologists have traced the word *gandharva* to *gandha,* or "scent." Perhaps this is why the *gandharvas* are sometimes said to have emerged from the creator god's nose. Other sources say their father is the *rishi* Kashyapa and their mothers are the daughters of another *rishi,* DAKSHA. *Gandharvas* are all said to have sweet voices, and they are seen as radiant, graceful, and beautiful. They are known to sing on various mountains including MERU, the central mountain of the earthly portion of the cosmos, but they are also heard in the sky and woods. They usually live in a sky world. The *kinnaras,* another class of beings who are sometimes considered the best of musicians, are also classified as *gandharvas*. The *gandharvas* are known to Buddhist and Jain traditions (see JAINISM) as well as to Hinduism.

Further reading: Cornelia Dimmitt and J. A. B. van Buitenen, *Classical Hindu Mythology: A Reader in the Sanskrit Puranas* (Philadelphia: Temple University Press, 1978); E. Washburn Hopkins, *Epic Mythology* (Delhi: Motilal Banarsidass, 1986).

Gandhi, Mohandas Karamchand (Mahatma) (1869–1948) *leader of the Indian independence struggle*

Mahatma Gandhi was the greatest political leader in 20th-century India. He led the Indian independence movement to success and fought for religious and social reforms as well as restoration of preindustrial cultural traditions. His philosophy of nonviolent political action has been considered an inspiration for various opposition movements around the world.

Mohandas Karamchand Gandhi was born on October 2, 1869, in the village of Porbandar in Gujarat, into a Hindu merchant family. As a young man of 13, he was married, as was the custom, to Kasturba Makharji, who was then 12 years of age. Their first son, however, was not born until 1888. He and Kasturba had three more sons.

Gandhi was considered a somewhat mediocre student; he barely won admission into the

University of Bombay in 1887. Since his father had a high position in government, and wanted the same for his son, Mohandas was persuaded to study law in England.

In 1889 at the age of 19 Mohandas entered University College at the University of London. Before he left he promised his mother to observe the strict precepts of his family's VAISHNAVISM, which forbade consumption of meat and alcohol. Once in England he made a study of vegetarianism to justify his vow intellectually and joined the Vegetarian Society, where he met various Theosophists interested in Buddhist and Hindu

scriptures. It was through them that he first read the BHAGAVAD GITA, which later became his moral guidebook. Ironically, his first study of it was in English translation. He also became interested in other religions at this time, particularly Christianity.

After admission to the British bar, Mohandas returned to India to set up a law practice in Bombay (Mumbai). He was not able to establish a practice, and after brief stints in various jobs, he took a one-year contract to work for an Indian firm in South Africa. Until this point he was not apparently interested in politics, but the treatment

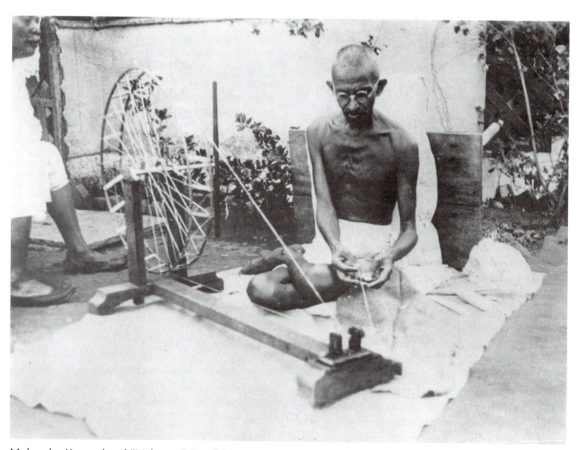

Mohandas Karamchand "Mahatma" Gandhi (1869–1948), leader in the Indian independence movement, is known for his nonviolent tactics and dedication to truth. *(Snark/Art Resource, NY)*

he received from whites in South Africa, including several famous incidents, began to change his thinking.

Gandhi was forced off a train to Pretoria after he refused to leave a first-class berth to accommodate a white passenger. Another time he was forced to travel on the footboard of a stagecoach to accommodate a white passenger. He decided to remain in South Africa, just at this time the Natal legislature was taking up a bill to deny the vote to Indians.

Gandhi was asked by the Indian community to lead the opposition to this bill. He failed to stop the measure, but he did draw attention to the grievances of Indians in South Africa. In 1894 he formed the Natal Indian Congress to fight for the rights of Indians. This organization became a great force in South African politics. In 1896 Gandhi went back to India to take his wife and children to Africa with him. In 1897 in South Africa he was attacked and nearly lynched by a white mob, but by then he had abandoned his legalistic views in favor of a stricter ethical approach, and he refused to press charges against the men who attacked him.

At the beginning of the South African War (the Boer War), Gandhi thought that Indians must support the war effort in order to legitimize their claims to full citizenship. He helped organize a volunteer ambulance corps of 300 free Indians and 800 indentured laborers. At the end of the war, however, conditions for Indians did not improve. In 1906 the Transvaal government passed a new act compelling the colony's Indian population to register. In Johannesburg that year Gandhi held a mass protest. For the first time he articulated his philosophy of *satyagraha* or "Truth Force," asking his fellow Indians to defy the new law nonviolently. In seven years of difficult struggle, Gandhi was imprisoned several times, and many other Indians were jailed, shot, or beaten for refusing to register. Finally, however, the government was forced to negotiate a compromise with Gandhi because of the negative publicity the campaign had generated.

During his years in South Africa, from 1893 until 1914, Gandhi continued to study the Bhagavad Gita. He was also influenced by Leo Tolstoy, who himself pursued an interest in Indian philosophy. Gandhi corresponded with Tolstoy for two years. Gandhi was also influenced greatly by Henry David Thoreau's essay on civil disobedience. In 1914, at the outbreak of World War I, Gandhi returned to India to begin a new phase in his life and imbue new vigor in the Indian independence struggle.

Gandhi initially supported the British war effort in World War I and the recruitment of Indians into the British army. However, when the Rowlatt Act of 1919, which allowed the government to imprison Indians without trial was passed, Gandhi launched a new call for *satyagraha*, nonviolent disobedience, his first such effort on Indian soil. The government response to this disobedience was violent, resulting in the Amritsar Massacre of Indians by the British army. The deaths shocked Gandhi and forced him to halt the agitation, but he had succeeded in organizing Indians to stand up against the British rulers.

In 1920, Gandhi was elected president of the All-India Home Rule League; the following year he became head of the Indian National Congress. Under his leadership congress became more militant, adopting the goal of self-rule in its new constitution. Gandhi helped transform congress from an elite organization to one with mass membership and mass appeal. He began to develop a policy of boycotting all foreign-made goods, especially British goods, as a way both to pressure the government and to build Indian economic self-reliance.

An enduring symbol of this policy was Gandhi's promotion of home-spun cloth in place of foreign-made fabric. The spinning wheel, which Gandhi began to use to spin thread for cloth for all his own clothing, became the symbol of the Indian independence movement. The boycott that Gandhi had begun was expanded to British educational facilities, and even to a refusal to pay taxes. Once again the agitations in 1918 ended with violent reprisals by the British, and Gandhi called off the agitation before he was jailed by the British for six years for sedition. He served two years of this sentence and was released for health reasons in 1924.

Gandhi did not play a central role in the independence movement in the early 1920s. However, he stepped forward again in 1928. The British government had appointed a constitutional reform commission with not a single Indian on it. Gandhi presented a resolution at the Calcutta Congress in 1928 asking the British government for dominion status in one year. With no response by the British in the year 1929, Gandhi launched a new nonviolent resistance campaign, this time against the tax on salt.

Gandhi's famous campaign against the salt tax included his 250-mile Dandi March from Ahmedabad to the seaside village of Dandi, where he symbolically made his own salt. This campaign gained huge attention and participation from the Indian populace; 60,000 people were imprisoned during the salt tax protest. The government in response signed the Gandhi-Irwin pact of 1931, agreeing to free all political prisoners in return for suspension of the agitation. Additionally, Gandhi was invited to the Round Table Conference in London, as the only representative of the Indian National Congress. The conference failed to yield gains for the movement; it was followed by further repression by the new head of government in India.

In 1932 Gandhi began a campaign to improve the lot of India's untouchables (now called Dalits; see UNTOUCHABILITY), whom he renamed *harijans,* "children of God." In 1933 he fasted for 21 days to protest the Indian government's treatment of Indians, the first in a series of important political fasts. In 1934 three attempts were made by the British on Gandhi's life.

In 1934 Gandhi, discouraged at the lack of commitment of those in the Indian National Congress to his program of nonviolence as a way of life for the new India, resigned as party leader and left the congress. Jawaharlal Nehru became the new leader. Gandhi disagreed with Nehru but at the same time saw him as preferable to other potential leaders of the movement. At this point Gandhi threw himself totally into efforts to educate rural India, fight against untouchability, and promote the manufacture of homespun clothing and other village-level cottage industries. For five years he lived very humbly in Sevagram, a village in central India. Gandhi was jailed by the British from 1942 to 1944 for this agitation.

Gandhi believed in cooperation between the Hindu and Muslim communities in India and maintained many friendships across religious lines. He was adamantly opposed to any partition. Eventually, however, the Indian National Congress acceded to a partition agreement that in 1947 created two states out of British India: India and Pakistan.

Gandhi personally was able to quell terrible riots between Muslims and Hindus on the eastern border between India and the new Pakistan, but when he returned to New Delhi to try to calm the communities there on January 30, 1948, he was assassinated by Nathuram Godse, a Hindu radical who opposed Gandhi's embrace of Muslims. The long journey of the champion of nonviolence was ended with a gunshot. Gandhi's last words were said to be a call to his chosen deity, "Ram." In the process of partition, millions had to flee their homes, and perhaps a million or more people were slaughtered in communal riots.

Gandhi, critical of all organized religion, also saw the value in every tradition. He once said that he was a Hindu, a Christian, a Muslim, and a Jew. More than religious, though, Gandhi was deeply spiritual and saw the search for truth and nonviolence in every aspect of life as the secrets to God. Gandhi was given the name *Mahatma,* or, "great soul," by India. He is considered the father of the modern Indian nation. More than that he was a giant on the world stage.

India was one of the few countries freed from colonial domination that relied primarily on the path of nonviolence; this was due to the enormous power and prestige of the humble, homespun cloth–clad Mahatma Gandhi. He inspired a generation of people to pursue political ends through nonviolence alone and had a tremendous impact on other great political leaders of the postwar world, notable among them Martin Luther King Jr. of the American civil rights movement.

Further reading: K. S. Bharathi. *The Social Philosophy of Mahatma Gandhi* (New Delhi: Concept, 1991); Nimal Kumar Bose, *Selections from Gandhi* (Ahmedabad: Navjivan Publishing House, 1948); Peter H. Burgess, ed., *The Sayings of Mahatma Gandhi* (Singapore: Graham Brash, 1984); M. K. Gandhi, *The Story of My Experiments with Truth* (Ahmedabad: Navajivan Press, 1927–29); Ved Mehta, *Mahatma Gandhi and His Apostles* (New York: Penguin Books, 1977); B. R. Nanda, *Mahatma Gandhi: A Biography, Complete and Unabridged* (Delhi: Oxford University Press, 1996).

Ganesha

Ganesha, lord of beginnings and remover of obstacles, is probably the most worshipped divinity of the Hindu pantheon. With the head of an elephant and a human body that shows a protruding belly—the sign of Ganesha's fondness for sweets—the god is a central figure in the cult of SHIVA, as the elder son of Shiva and PARVATI. He is also worshipped as a deity on his own, as is shown in Ganesha PURANA. Nearly every Indian PUJA or worship service commences with verses to and adoration of Ganesha. The figure of the sitting Ganesha and his incongruous vehicle, the rat, is found near the entranceway or one of the entranceways of many, many Hindu temples.

As is usual in Hindu mythology and lore, there are many and various stories about the events of Ganesha's life. The most common story of his origin is that he was made by Parvati, who rubbed off material from her skin and formed it into a shape of a person. She set this "child" Ganesha to guard her shower or inner chamber. Shiva, unaware of

Lord Ganesha, the elephant-headed god, is the son of Lord Shiva and known as remover of obstacles. *(Saiva Siddhanta Church, Kapaa, Kauai, Hawaii)*

this, found Ganesha at his post and thinking that he was a lover or intruder he cut off the child's head. Scolded by an angry Parvati, Shiva hastily rushed off to find a new head for the child and returned with the head of an elephant.

In one popular story Parvati declares a race around the universe between the ponderous Ganesha and his younger brother, Skanda or KARTTIKEYA. The younger boy takes off on his swift peacock vehicle swift as lightning, leaving the slow Ganesha with his pitiful rat vehicle far behind. Thinking a moment, Ganesha realizes that his mother and father themselves constitute the entire universe. He simply walks around his mother and father and wins the race. Ganesha is also said to have written down the MAHABHARATA epic as quickly as its reciter VYASA was able to tell it. For this Ganesha broke off one of his tusks to use as a stylus. In South India Ganesha is known as a bachelor, but in other parts of India he is seen as married.

Iconographically Ganesha appears in many poses and forms, but he is most often sitting, accompanied by the rat, with one tusk broken. Most often he is shown with two arms, but he is also depicted with several pairs. In his hands are sweets, his tusk, an axe, a noose, or an elephant goad.

After his popularity had been well established in the Brahminical tradition, Ganesha appeared in Jain tradition as well (*see* JAINISM), in which he was seen as a remover of obstacles. Outside India Ganesha is found in Buddhist contexts as a TANTRIC deity, with sometimes unbenign characteristics. He is found in Southeast Asian art, in Tibet, in China, and even in Japan.

The cult of Ganesha is probably quite old, originating in the worship of the elephant, but its actual origin is difficult to determine. The cult is visible in extant sources dating from the fourth century C.E. He is not mentioned at all in earlier texts such as the Mahabharata or the RAMAYANA, in which Shiva and VISHNU and their emerging cults are developing.

Further reading: Robert L. Brown, ed., *Ganesh: Studies of an Asian God* (Albany: State University of New York Press, 1991; Paul Courtright, *Ganesha: Lord of Obstacles, Lord of Beginnings* (New York: Oxford University Press, 1985); Satguru Sivaya Subramuniyaswami, *Loving Ganesha, Hinduism's Endearing Elephant-Faced God* (Kapaa, Hawaii: Himalayan Academy, 1996).

Gangaji (1942–) *teacher of* advaita *Vedanta*

The American-born Gangaji is a popular international teacher of VEDANTA in the tradition of Sri Harilal POONJA.

Antoinette Robertson Palmer was born on June 11, 1942, in Mississippi and graduated the University of Mississippi. She married Eli Jackson Bear, himself a spiritual teacher, and began a quest for spiritual fulfillment. She moved in 1972 to San Francisco, where she participated in several forms of Buddhist practice. She practiced Japanese Zen Buddhism and South Asian *vipassana* (insight) MEDITATION and helped manage a Tibetan Buddhist meditation center. She also took the *bodhisattva* pledge, in which a person vows to help humanity until all people reach enlightenment. Later she studied acupuncture and became a licensed acupuncturist.

Still on a quest to find a deeper level of being, Palmer went with her husband to meet the teacher of enlightenment POONJAJI in Haridwar on the GANGES River in northern India. There she found realization of the Self in the presence of her teacher, a fulfillment that he confirmed. He gave her the spiritual name *Ganga*, for the Hindu goddess of the Ganges River. Poonjaji asked her to introduce his teachings to the West.

As a popular teacher of ADVAITA (non-dualist) Vedanta, Gangaji does not base her teachings on any specific scriptures, but on her own experience of the Self. She holds regular *satsangs* (teachings) at her center in northern California and appears weekly on public access television. She travels widely and gives retreats in many places around the world. Her foundation's Prison Program provides books, audiotapes, and videotapes and organizes visits to prisons by volunteers.

Further reading: Gangaji, *Freedom and Resolve: The Living Edge of Surrender* (Ashland, Ore.: Gangaji Foundation, 1999); ———, *Just Like You: An Autobiography* (Mendocino, Calif.: D.O., 2003); ——— *You Are That! Satsang with Gangaji* (Boulder, Colo.: Satsang Press, 1995).

Ganges (Ganga)

The Ganges or Ganga is India's most sacred river. It is 1,557 miles long and sweeps a valley or basin 200 to 400 miles wide. Its scientific source is in

Morning bathing on the steps to the Ganges River in Benares (Varanasi) *(Constance A. Jones)*

glaciers on the southern slopes of the HIMALAYAS, some 10,300 feet above sea level, but its traditional source is the glacial site Gangotri. Its major flow begins where the Alaknand and Bhagirathi rivers meet at a site called Devprayag. It is joined by the YAMUNA River at ALLAHABAD (known traditionally as Prayag) in Uttar Pradesh and then flows eastward through Bihar, traversing the holy city of BENARES (Varanasi), the city of Patna, and Calcutta (Kolkata) before entering the Bay of Bengal.

Although the Ganges has long been the most sacred of Indian rivers, it is mentioned unambiguously only twice in the RIG VEDA, the oldest extant

Indian text. Its prominent mention and sacred status are fully established only in the PURANAS, Indian texts of mythology. There the river is said to have descended from heaven, taken down to Earth by the prayers of the sage Bhagiratha to sanctify the ashes of the sons of his progenitor Sagara. The latter had dug out a huge hole looking for a lost horse, but the Ganges filled this vast expanse to form the ocean. Descending from Lord VISHNU's toe, the river might have inundated all the Earth, had not SHIVA agreed to let it first flow through his topknot. Shiva has since that time been depicted with the Ganges flowing through his hair.

Ganga is considered a goddess, the eldest daughter of HIMAVAT (the Himalayas). Ganga's husband is Shantanu; their son BHISHMA plays an important role in the MAHABHARATA epic, as great uncle of both the warring factions. Ganga's water is always pure and purifying, and pilgrims take flasks and casks home for rituals and blessings. It is every Hindu's wish to have his or her ashes thrown into the Ganges after cremation. It is widely believed that such an act confers heaven or liberation on the dead person. Because of the sacredness of the Ganges and its importance to Hinduism India has made great efforts to try to clean up this very heavily polluted waterway. Activist movements have for decades agitated for cleaning up this valuable resource.

Further reading: Jagmohan Mahajan, *The Ganga Trail: Foreign Accounts and Sketches of the River Scene* (New Delhi: Clarion Books, 1984); Sudhakar Pandey, *Ganga and Yamuna in Indian Art and Literature* (Chandigarh: Indra Prakashan, 1984); Raghubir Singh, *The Ganges* (London: Thames Hudson, 1992).

Garuda

Garuda is both the mount of VISHNU and the king of birds. He is depicted with the body of a man and the face of an eagle. He is considered the son of the RISHI Kashyapa and his wife, Vinata.

Garuda is known to be an enemy of snakes, a natural characteristic of a bird of prey such as the eagle. In his case the enmity is attributed to a rivalry between his mother and her sister Kadru, mother of the serpents. Kadru had taken Vinata captive but agreed to set her free if she would give her the nectar of immortality (AMRITA). Garuda was successful in going to heaven and defeating the two snakes who guarded it there. It was this deed that gained him the reward of being Vishnu's mount.

The story did not end at this, however. INDRA, ruler of heaven, wanted his nectar returned. Finally, he allowed Garuda to feed on snakes, the traditional food of eagles, in exchange for returning the nectar of immortality. Sometimes Garuda is iconographically represented holding a pot of ambrosia (*amrita*).

Further reading: Shanti Lal Nagar, *Garuda, the Celestial Bird* (New Delhi: Book India, 1992); Margaret Stutley, *An Illustrated Dictionary of Hindu Iconography* (Boston: Routledge & Kegan Paul, 1985); W. J. Wilkins, *Hindu Mythology, Vedic and Puranic* (Calcutta: Rupa, 1973).

Gaudapada (c. 750–800 C.E.) *Vedantic philosopher*

Gaudapada is best known as the guru of Govinda, guru of the famous philosopher SHANKARA. He is the earliest writer in the movement to revive the UPANISHADIC tradition of non-dual (ADVAITA) philosophy. His is author of a commentary on the MANDUKYA Upanishad, called the Mandukya-karika, which consists of four segments or books. This work was commented on in turn by Shankara. Notable in the text of Mandukyakarika is the use of Buddhistic terminology. This has been shown to reflect not Buddhist influence on the VEDANTIC tradition, but rather an attempt to proselytize the Buddhists.

Further reading: T. M. P. Mahadevan, *Gaudapada: A Study in Early Advaita* (Madras: University of Madras, 1952).

Gaudiya Math (est. 1930s)

The Gaudiya Math (monastery) is an organization founded in the 1930s to promote Chaitanya VAISHNAVISM in India, and later around the world.

The modern revival of the BHAKTI (devotional) yoga tradition of Sri Chaitanya Mahaprabhu (1486–1534) is generally attributed to the efforts of Srila Bhaktivinode Thakur (born Kedarnath Dutta, 1838–1914). A lifelong follower of the devotion to Lord KRISHNA, he concentrated his last decades on creating various programs to spread the devotion, especially the Nama Hatta program designed to promote the chanting of the holy name. Among his accomplishments, along with his colleague Srila Jagannath das Babaji, was the rediscovery of the birthplace of Sri Chaitanya.

Bhaktivinode Thakur's work was carried forward by his son, Srila Bhaktisiddhanta Sarasvati Thakur (1874–1937). Bhaktisiddhanta, together with Kuñja Babu and other devotees, founded the Gaudiya Math in the 1930s. He emphasized the personal nature of the godhead, in distinction to the view that had become dominant in eastern India, that the divine was basically impersonal. He also worked to build the preaching centers established by his father into full ashrams. Most importantly, he tried to put into effect the desire of his father to send Vaishnavite disciples to the West.

The first center of bhakti yoga in England opened in 1933 as the Gaudiya Mission Society of London; on July 20, representatives of the Gaudiya Math had an official meeting with the king. A second European preaching center was opened in Berlin. Meanwhile, additional centers were being established across India, with a concentration in Bengal and along the route of the GANGES River to BRINDAVAN. A conscious effort was made to establish centers in the places known to have been visited by Chaitanya. An active publishing program was developed. Besides its own accomplishments, the rise of the Gaudiya Math was seen as a stimulus to other organizations that continued Chaitanya's teachings.

The math has become best known through the Western Mission started by one of his former members, A. C. Bhaktivedanta Swami Prabhupada (1896–1977), a disciple of Bhaktisiddhanta. The later told Prabhupada in 1936 to prepare himself for a mission in the West. In 1965, already of advanced years, he moved to the United States and began the INTERNATIONAL SOCIETY FOR KRISHNA CONSCIOUSNESS (ISKCON). Though independent of the math, ISKCON would become the most effective instrument in carrying out the goals of the math's founder. In the last decades of the 20th century, in spite of numerous ups and downs, it was still teaching devotion to Krishna in many countries of the world.

ISKCON's success spawned more than 20 new organizations that follow Krishna devotion. In the 1990s, most of these organizations joined with the surviving Gaudiya Math in India to create the World Vaisnava Association, as part of an attempt to coordinate and unify the global mission.

Further reading: Shukavak N. Dasa, *Hindu Encounter with Modernity: Kedarnath Datta Bhaktivinoda Vaishnava Theologian* (Los Angeles: Sri, 1999); Swami B. A. Paramadvaiti, "Our Family the Gaudiya Math: A Study of the Expansion of Gaudiya Vaisnavism and the Many Branches Developing around the Gaudiya Math." *Vrindavan Institute for Vaisnava Culture and Studies.* Available online. URL: http://www.vrindavan. org/English/Books/GMconded.html. Accessed August 15, 2005; Steven Rosen, *Contemporary Scholars Discuss the Gaudiya Tradition* (Brooklyn, N.Y.: Folk Books, 1992); Sri Srila Bhaktivinode Thakura, *The Bhagavat: Its Philosophy, Its Ethics and Its Theology* (Navadwip: Shri Goudiya Samiti, 1986); ———, *Jaiva Dharma* (Mad: Sri Gaudiya Math, 1975).

Gaudiya Vaishnavite Society

The Gaudiya Vaishnavite Society developed in the 1980s. It arose in part as a result of differences among followers of the late Swami A.C.

Prabhupada BHAKTIVEDANTA, the founder of the INTERNATIONAL SOCIETY FOR KRISHNA CONSCIOUSNESS (ISKCON). Within ISKCON, one group of conservative thinkers wanted to venerate all teachers in the organization as GURUS. A reform faction led by B. V. Tripurari opposed other ISKCON gurus' accepting veneration in the same manner as had been shown Prabhupada. Eventually Tripurari led many of the reform group away from the original organization and this group formed the Gaudiya Vaishnavite Society.

Tripurari Swami first met Prabhupada, a saintly holy man, when he visited the United States in September 1965. He became a student of the master and after a short time became a *sannyasi*, one who renounces the world to live a holy life. Amid the turmoil that follow Prabhupada's death in 1977, Tripurari remained loyal to his lineage, pointing reformists to honor Bhakti Rakshak Sridhara Maharaj (1895–1988), Prabhupada's godbrother (meaning that they had received their initiations from the same guru).

While Prabhupada had concentrated on the development of a mission in the United States. Sridhara Maharaj had developed an international following related to the work he had started through the Sri Chaitanya Saraswati Math in West Bengal, India. As knowledge of his work spread, he had built up communities abroad that supported his mission.

Several challenges emerged when the Gaudiya Vaishnavite Society became active in missionary efforts. In 1986, the city of San Francisco forbade society members to pass out their literature on the streets. The Gaudiya Society took the case to court and won. In 1988, the organization began to print its periodical *The Clarion Call*, similar in design and perspective to ISKCON's main magazine, *Back to Godhead*. This periodical was able to cross religious boundaries and reach far beyond the followers of the society. It especially addressed a variety of issues important to the New Age community, such as human and animal rights, reincarnation, holistic health ideas, vegetarianism, and spirituality.

The Gaudiya Vaishnavite Society remains in harmony with the religious beliefs and principles initially articulated by ISKCON. The major issue originally confronting ISKCON was resolved as its members spiritually realigned to Sridhara Maharaj as their leader. There was never any problem with remaining loyal to the spiritual ideal promoted by ISKCON. Society members, however, now trace their lineage from Sridhara Maharaj and not Prabhupada.

The Gaudiya Vaishnavite Society teaches a form of BHAKTI (devotional) *yoga* that encourages members to engage in temple worship, in contrast with other forms of Hinduism that focus on worshipping at a home altar. Precepts include belief in a theistic (personal) deity. The society's views thus differ from the traditional perspective of ADVAITA (non-dualist) VEDANTA, which supports a monist perspective in which the ultimate divine is conceived in impersonal terms. The Gaudiya Vaishnavite Society (and related groups such as ISKCON) build their relationship with God through personal devotion. A major element in that devotional activity concerns the frequent repetition of the following MANTRA that calls upon the name of God: Hare Krishna, *Hare Krishna, / Krishna, Krishna, Hare, Hare, / Hare Rama, Hare Rama, / Rama, Rama, Hare, Hare.*

The mantra is chanted several hours daily by devotees as a means of elevating their consciousness, quickening enlightenment, and hastening progress to SAMADHI, an elevated state of consciousness.

Further reading: Srila Bhakti Raksaka Sridhara Deva Goswami, *The Golden Volcano of Divine Love* (San Jose, Calif.: Guardian of Devotion Press, 1984); ———, *The Hidden Treasure of the Absolute* (West Bengal: Sri Chaitanya Saraswati Math, 1985); Srila Bhaktivinode Thakur, *Sri Chaitanya Mahapradhu: His Life and Precepts* (Brooklyn, N.Y.: Gaudiya Press, 1987); Swami B. V. Tripurari, *Ancient Wisdom for Modern Ignorance* (Eugene, Ore.: Clarion Call, 1994); ———, *Rasa, Love Relationships in Transcendence* (Eugene, Ore.: Gaudiya Vaishnava Society, 1993).

Gautama   *See* Nyaya-Vaisheshika.

Gayatri Mantra

Gayatri is a Vedic mantra to the Sun; it is chanted each morning by twice-born Indian men—those who have been invested with the sacred thread, whether Brahmins, Kshatriyas, or Vaishyas. In later times Gayatri was sometimes considered the wife of Brahma.

The mantra is from Rig Veda (3.62.10) to the god of the Sun Savitri. Some think it the most important Vedic mantra. It translates: "OM, Earth, Sky, Heavens! May the most excellent effulgence of the Sun-god (Savitri) inspire higher consciousness." Orthodox Indians chant the mantra three times during the day, in the morning, at noon, and at night. Gayatri is technically a Vedic meter with 24 syllables—considered the most elegant of meters.

Currently, a movement and ashram are organized around the healing benefit of repeating the mantra. It operates as Gayatri Pariwar in Haridvar, India.

Further reading: Sadguru Sant Keshavadas, *Gayatri: The Highest Meditation,* 2d rev. ed. (Delhi: Motilal Banarsidass, 1990); I. K. Taimini, *Gayatri: The Daily Religious Practice of the Hindus,* 2d ed. (Wheaton, Ill.: Theosophical Publishing, 1974); Bhagavati Sri Sri Vijayeswari Devi, *Sri Gayatri: The Inner Secrets Revealed,* 2 vols. (New York: Sri Matrudevi Visvashanti Ashram Trust, 2002).

Gayatri Pariwar, Haridwar   *See* Gayatri Mantra.

Ghose, Aurobindo   *See* Aurobindo, Sri.

Gitagovinda

Gitagovinda (Krishna in songs) is a Sanskrit poem written by the 12th-century poet Jayadeva. Made up of 12 chapters containing 24 songs, the Gitagovinda traces the passionate love affair of the young, handsome cowherd Krishna and his married lover Radha, a young woman who also herds cows (gopi). Both sacred and profane, the work details the love play of the fickle god with Radha, Radha's pain in separation from him, his eventual pain in separation from her, and their passionate reunion.

In theological terms, Radha is the devotee who seeks God, tastes the sweet pleasure of mystic union, and then is abandoned only to have the love renewed in further mystical experience. In later Vaishnavite theology Radha was seen as an extension of the fullness of the divine, who was (mysteriously) both identical and separate from him. Radha, then, becomes the energy of Krishna that allows him to experience and impart joy. This explains why in Gitagovinda god himself is seen to yearn for the devotee (Radha) in parting. Krishna needs the devotee nearly as much as the devotee needs Krishna.

Gitagovinda is a masterpiece of Sanskrit literature that was very influential among the Vaishnavites of Bengal. It was considered to be Chaitanya's favorite work, and stories tell of his relish for the songs of this book. It also influenced the Vaishnavite Sahajiyas, a tantra-influenced sect that saw sexuality as an expression of Krishna's liaisons with Radha. The Sahajiyas esoteric practice joined a man with a woman not his wife as part of the realization of the mysterious union of Radha and Krishna.

Further reading: Barbara Stoler Miller, ed. and trans., *Love Song of the Dark Lord: Jayadeva's Gitagovinda* (New York: Columbia University Press, 1977); Lee Siegel, *Sacred and Profane Dimensions of Love in Indian Traditions as Exemplified in the Gitagovinda of Jayadeva* (Delhi: Oxford University Press, 1978).

goddess

The worship of the goddess in India probably began in Neolithic times. There are several figurines from the INDUS VALLEY CIVILIZATION (c. 3600–1900 B.C.E.) that appear to be goddess figurines and indicate a focus on the divine feminine.

In the RIG VEDA (c. 1500 B.C.E.), the oldest of India's extant texts, the primary divinities AGNI and INDRA are male, as are the great majority of divinities mentioned. Some important goddesses, however, are also cited. Perhaps most important is VACH, goddess of speech. Since speech in its form as MANTRA is the locus or primary source of ritual power in the VEDIC context, the goddess of speech is all-encompassing. In fact, in Rig Veda (X.125) a verse to this goddess of speech shows her to be an all-encompassing reality, surpassing all the male gods. Other important goddesses in the VEDAS are USHAS, RATRI, and ADITI. Ushas is the goddess of the early dawn light, possibly before sunrise. Ratri is her sister, who is the goddess of the night. Aditi is understood to be the mother of the male gods. Another goddess, SARASVATI, is hailed in the Rig Veda as an important river. She gains later fame, beginning with late Vedas when the same name is used for the goddess of learning. Finally, Shaci, the wife of Indra, is frequently mentioned and sometimes taken to be all-powerful.

Hinduism developed by mythically interlinking the male gods VISHNU and SHIVA, among others, to various local divinities throughout India. Vishnu is found in the Vedas, where *shiva* (the auspicious) was an epithet of the god RUDRA. As theistic Hinduism developed, these gods emerged as a sort of cultural meeting place for various local mythic traditions. They are, in essence, amalgams of characteristics derived from different, and perhaps sundry, cultural sources. As the ARYANS moved east and south, many local divinities were identified with these greater divinities. Some of them, such as GANESHA, the elephant-headed god, for instance, became members of a larger family; Ganesha became the son of Shiva.

In this context, local goddesses were understood to be wives of Shiva and Vishnu. It is possible that SATI, Shiva's first wife, derived from just such a local non-Aryan cultural complex. PARVATI, his second wife and the daughter of the Himalaya mountain, may well have been a distinct divinity in ancient times. Later, as DURGA and KALI became recognized as wives of Shiva, many of the local goddesses lost some or all of their original character and began to be understood as Durga or Kali under other names. Parvati was probably the model, here, as many local goddesses under other names are identified with her, too—for example MINAKSHI of Madurai.

As was the case with Shiva, certain goddesses became identified with Vishnu's wife, Lakshmi; they may be seen as Rukmini or Radha the wife and lover, respectively, of Vishnu in his form as KRISHNA. Some are identified with SITA, the wife of RAMA, another AVATAR of Vishnu.

Vishnu and Shiva are the main divinities for VAISHNAVISM and SHAIVISM, respectively (the goddess-oriented sect of SHAKTAS is discussed later). They are both loosely related to the divinity BRAHMA, who has a clear post-Vedic development. Very few male divinities around India become associated with him, but there are many goddesses who are identified with his wife SARASVATI, goddess of wisdom and learning.

The development of the two main Hindu cults to Vishnu and Shiva began with the great India epics (c. 700 B.C.E. to 100 C.E.). In the early centuries of the Common Era, additional texts recounting their deeds, incarnations, and adventures began to emerge, called PURANAS. At about this time the cult of Mahadevi, or the Great Goddess, began to develop as well; texts such as the Markandeya Purana (c. 300–600 C.E.) actually praised the goddess as the supreme being above Shiva and Vishnu. This represented the beginning of the cult of the Shaktas, who focus their worship on the goddess as SHAKTI (supreme divine energy). Undoubtedly, Vedic divinities such as Vac helped form the model for this development, but the cultural roots of the Great Goddess must be seen to be in the pre-Aryan substratum of Indian culture, in which goddesses were probably worshipped from Neolithic times.

Kali or Durga became the main object of worship for goddess-oriented Hindus, but it must be understood that there are many, many goddesses throughout India of independent origin who are identified with these "greater" divinities. In the Shakta context TANTRIC forms of worship are more likely to be found, though the Shaivites have also always had a well-developed set of tantric cults drawing on the same prehistorical sources in Indian culture. There are also rare cults of Vaishnavite tantra. Sometimes these tantric cults took up the worship of the DASHA MAHAVIDYA, a pantheon of goddesses joined for specialized worship. These included well-known goddesses such as Kali and Lakshmi, who are worshipped alongside specialized cult goddesses such as SRI LALITA or other more unusual divinities such as Dasha Mahavidya, who is worshipped with polluted things such as cloth that has been stained by menstruation (see PURITY/POLLUTION).

In Shaktism ferocious, frightening forms of the divine feminine are common; they often are worshipped with the understanding that since the goddess is all of reality, we must learn to love her in the most frightening, dark forms to understand her totality. In tantrism this realization about the divinity takes the form of engaging in activities in a ritual context that are usually forbidden, such as eating beef or having sex with someone to whom one is not married. This is done in order to comprehend the divinity beyond all social or mental conception. This sort of tantric practice involves only a very small minority of goddess worshippers.

Further reading: N. N. Bhattacharya, *The History of the Tantric Religion* (Delhi: Manohar, 1982); Cornelia Dimmitt and J. A. B. van Buitenen, *Classical Hindu Mythology: A Reader in the Sanskrit Puranas* (Philadelphia: Temple University Press, 1978); John Stratton Hawley and Donna Wulff, eds., *The Divine Consort Radha and the Goddesses of India* (Berkeley: Graduate Theological Union, 1982); David Kinsley, *Hindu Goddesses: Visions of the Divine Feminine in the Hindu Religious Tradition* (Berkeley: University of California Press, 1986);

——, *Tantric Visions of the Divine Feminine* (Berkeley: University of California Press, 1997).

Golden Temple   *See* AMRITSAR.

gopi

A female cowherd. The *gopis* figure in the story of Lord KRISHNA as divine lover. When Krishna went to the woods alone at night to play on his seductive flute, the cowherds, all married women, secretly left their houses to rendezvous with him. They would dance the Rasa Lila (loosely, the divine play of the essence of divinity); with Krishna standing in the middle, each *gopi* thought he was dancing with her alone. Some versions of the story say that Krishna multiplied himself so that he could dance intimately with each of the cowgirls simultaneously.

The *gopi* becomes the symbol, in the theology of Krishna worship, of the devotee who is willing even to flout convention to go to her or his passionate "assignation" with the divine. In later versions, Radha appears as the favored *gopi* of Krishna. She, then, becomes the symbol of the passionate devotee. The love of Krishna and Radha is frequently depicted in literature, painting, and dance and is a central theme in Hindu devotion.

Further reading: Edward C. Dimock, *The Place of the Hidden Moon: Erotic Mysticism in the Vaisnava Sajiya Cult of Bengal* (Chicago: University of Chicago Press, 1966); Friedhelm Hardy, *Viraha-Bhakti: The Early History of Krsna Worship in South India* (Delhi: Oxford University Press, 1983); Milton Singer, ed., *Krishna: Myths, Rites, and Attitudes* (Chicago: University of Chicago Press, 1966).

Gorakhnath (c. 12th century) *Nath yogi and philosopher*

Gorakhnath (Sanskrit, *gorakshanatha*) (c. 12th century) is the most important figure in the NATH YOGI sect. In the North Indian Nath tradition,

Gorakhnath is variously considered the third to fifth in a series of 12 authoritative gurus.

Originally centered in western India, the practice spread throughout northern India, with both Buddhist and Hindu offshoots. Several early teachers in the lineage, including Gorakhanath, are included in Tibetan Buddhist TANTRIC lineages. Known to both is Mastyendranath, who is seen in North Indian Nath Yoga to be the guru of Gorakhnath.

There is a vast literature attributed to Gorakhanath, including several important SANSKRIT texts and numerous poems in Hindi, Bengali, and Rajasthani. A rich mythology emphasizes his magical, divine powers: he was known for being able to raise the dead at will.

The Nath Yoga practices in the tradition of Gorakhnath are tantric in orientation, but they did not involve any of the sexual practices of tantrism, as the Naths generally took a misogynistic view of women. They adopted antisocial behavior as a norm; as in earlier Shaivite sects, it was part of their esoteric practice to smear themselves with ashes from the cremation ground and even human feces, to eat disgusting things, and to act in outrageous, antisocial ways (*see* SHAIVISM).

Gorakhnath and his followers to this day are known for their propensities toward magic and their use of oxides of mercury and other secret substances and potions meant to create bodily immortality. Their practice generally conforms to that of the SIDDHAS, tantric yoga specialists, of India over many centuries.

In terms of yoga practice, those in the Gorakhnath tradition perfect forms of HATHA YOGA; they concentrate on an invisible web of bodily channels called NADIS, through which one can channel breaths to gain both occult powers and liberation from birth and rebirth. Philosophically the views of the followers of Gorakhnath varied from region to region, but generally they had a non-dual (ADVAITA) tantric character, which saw the divine as not merely a transcendent reality, but an immanent, worldly reality as well.

Further reading: Akshaya Kumar Banerjea, *Philosophy of Gorakhnath with Goraksha Vacana Samgraha* (Delhi: Motilal Benarsidass, 1988); George W. Briggs, *Gorakhnath and the Kanphata Yogis* (New Delhi: Motilal Banarsidass, 1982); David Gordon White, *The Alchemical Body* (Chicago: University of Chicago Press, 1996).

gotra

A *gotra* is an exogamous kinship division within a *jati,* or subcaste. Members of the same *gotra* within a subcaste are not allowed to marry among themselves; of course, they must marry within their *jati. Gotra* literally means "the place of the cows"; the concept may thus date back to very ancient times, when kin shared the same cow herds. BRAHMINS particularly will often trace their particular *gotra* back to one of the seven RISHIS of Vedic times.

Further reading: Morris G. Carstairs, *The Twice-Born* (Bloomington: Indiana: University Press, 1967); Purosottama Pandita, *The Early Bramanical System of Gotra and Pravara, a Translation of the Gotra-Pravara-Manjari* (Cambridge: Cambridge University Press, 1953).

Govardhana   See KRISHNA.

Grace Essence Fellowship (est. 1970s)

Grace Essence Fellowship of Taos, New Mexico, owes its development to Larry C. Short, an American with training in psychological counseling, bodywork, martial arts, MEDITATION, and YOGA. He has synthesized a path between yoga and Tibetan ideas, which he calls the Way of Radiance, a modern esoteric work school.

The fellowship was established in the late 1970s after Short discovered Swami RUDRANANDA (1928–73), the founder of the Nityananda Institute. Rudrananda was one of the first Hindu teachers to introduce KUNDALINI training to the United States. Short studied kundalini yoga with him until his death in 1973, then decided to study with his Holiness Dilgo Khyentse, a Tibetan master. He also synthesized aspects of Zen and Taoism. Rudrananda had predicted that an integration of these paths would be a universal system of spiritual work.

The synthesis, called the Way of Radiance, teaches that life is a gift and that struggling is not necessary to achieve a full and harmonious life. The goals of these teachings are to live in each moment, to dedicate one's self to growth and freedom beyond rules and regulations that squelch growth, and to transcend the struggles with ourselves, the culture, and the environment. Short has woven together strands of mindfulness practice with TANTRA to produce a novel path.

Students of the Way of Radiance have the opportunity to grow and choose their way of relating. Some become teachers, seminarians, or practitioners. Study groups for the Way are found in the United States, Venezuela, and Canada. Their headquarters are in Newton, Massachusetts.

Further reading: Martin Lowenthal, "Grace Essence Fellowship: Supporting Growth and Freedom," *Tantra* 9 (1994): 64–65; Martin Lowenthal, Lars Short, and Eli Goodwin, *Opening the Heart of Compassion: Transform Suffering through Buddhist Psychology and Practice* (Boston: Charles E. Tuttle, 1993).

Granth Sahib   *See* SIKHISM.

grihastha   *See* ASHRAMAS.

Grihya Sutra   *See* VEDAS.

Gross, Darwin   *See* ECKANKAR.

guna

In the SAMKHYA YOGA tradition, which originated around the fifth century B.C.E., the *gunas* were the strands or fabric of nature or PRAKRITI; they eternally evolved into new universes, which would be destroyed only to reemerge. *Prakriti* itself was seen to be eternal.

There are three *gunas: sattva, rajas,* and *tamas*. *Sattva* is that aspect of nature that is lucid, white, and placid. *Rajas* is that part of nature that is muddied, reddish, and agitated. *Tamas* is that part of nature that is impure, dark, and inert. Everything in worldly reality is made of the three *gunas* in lesser or greater proportions. *Sattva* predominates in discriminative intellect (BUDDHI), while *tamas* predominates in earth.

Samkhya yogic practice seeks to realize the self that is beyond and untouched by the three *gunas* of worldly existence. Samkhya became the philosophical basis for later yoga practice that focused on breath control and postures.

Further reading: S. N. Dasgupta, *The History of Indian Philosophy.* Vol. 1 (Delhi: Motilal Banarsidas, 1975); Gerald Larson and Ram Shankar Bhattacharya, eds., *Samkhya: A Dualist Tradition in Indian Philosophy* (Princeton, N.J.: Princeton University Press, 1987); Ian Whicher, *Patañjali's Metaphysical Schematic: Purusa and Prakrti in the Yogasutra* (Adyar: Adyar Library and Research Centre, 2001).

Gunadhya

Gunadhya is the author of a lost work, the BRIHATKATHA, a vast collection of tales dating from the early centuries of the Common Era. The stories generally had a secular character and imparted nuggets of wisdom.

Nothing is definitively known about Gunadhya's life, but legends do exist. One well-known legend tells the fabulous story of how the book came to be written. Gunadhya was made a minister of the great king Satavahana. One warm day, the king and his wives began to bathe in the lake. When the king splashed water on his wives, one of them asked him to stop in the SANSKRIT language. In response to her request, the king ordered sweets. His wife laughed, saying, "I never knew I had such an ignorant husband! How can we eat sweets when we are so wet? You don't understand Sanskrit well enough to know that I said, 'Stop splashing me!' 'Stop splashing' in Sanskrit sounds like 'bring sweets' if you don't understand the simple grammatical rule that two words often run together!"

The king thereupon returned to his palace and shut himself in his rooms. For the rest of the day he sat silently staring into space, refusing all food. When his two wisest ministers, Sarvavarma and Gunadhya, arrived to help, the king broke his silence, asking, "How long, my ministers, will it take me to learn Sanskrit if I work hard? What good is it to be a king, to have all this wealth, all these wives, these lands, if I am ignorant?" First Sage Gunadhya answered: "Most people need 12 years to learn Sanskrit grammar, but I will teach you in six years!" Sarvavarma jealously retorted, "The king does not have time to spend six years in such hardship. I will teach you in six months!" Gunadhya made this vow: "Sarvavarma, if you accomplish such an impossible feat, I shall renounce Sanskrit, Prakrit, and all the vernacular languages." Sarvavarma replied angrily, "And if I don't accomplish this, I shall carry your shoes on my head for 12 years!"

The king was happy, feeling he would soon be rid of his ignorance. Sarvavarma knew that what he had promised was impossible. He prayed to SARASVATI, goddess of learning. As a result of her intervention Sarvavarma was able to teach the king Sanskrit very quickly. The king bowed down to Sarvavarma, calling him "great teacher." Gunadhya, having lost the bet, left the kingdom with two of his disciples.

Gunadhya traveled in silence since he had vowed to give up all known languages. During his wanderings, he entered a wild forest, where he met a group of Paishachas, demons who spoke their seemingly incomprehensible demon language, used only in remote parts of India. The sage was able to learn this unusual language and

begin speaking again, since the language was not one of the three types he had sworn to give up.

Gunadhya was now able to understand the words of a wild-looking old forest dweller. This man greeted Gunadhya joyfully as if he had been awaiting this moment for many years, and in fact he had. He was a celestial who had been cursed to become a man, but he knew the curse would be lifted if he told a certain story to Gunadhya, who had been the cursed man's companion in a previous life. The curse would end if Gunadhya could make the story famous.

When Gunadhya realized the man's true identity, he appealed to him: "Tell the story told by SHIVA so that our curses will all end!" As the man recounted the divine tale, which comprised seven stories in the Paishachi language, the area where he sat seemed covered with a canopy of celestial beings hovering as they listened in the air above his head. Finishing his story the forest man returned to the celestial realm.

For the next seven years, Gunadhya recorded the story he had heard in 700,000 couplets, using the demon language. Since he had no ink and no paper, the great poet wrote the story's verses on tree bark in his own blood. When he finished he sent it to the king Satavahana, so that it would spread through the world. But when the king, who now knew Sanskrit, saw this disgusting book written in blood in a low language, he ordered it thrown away.

Gunadhya grew sad and depressed. He went with his students to the top of a hill and made a sacred fire. He had saved the last seventh of the tale, consisting of 100,000 verses, because his students loved it. As he was reading this tale aloud and beginning to burn its pages, every animal in the surrounding area listened and wept.

In the meantime, the king had fallen ill and needed meat, but because all the animals were listening to Gunadhya and not eating, they were too lean to kill. When the king heard this, he asked the hunters to lead him to the man telling the tale. He recognized Gunadhya, who appeared to be a forest dweller with long matted hair, sitting in the midst of the circle of weeping animals. Gunadhya then told the king the curse and the circumstances that caused the great story to descend to Earth. The king then knew that Gunadhya was a celestial. He begged him for the full story, but, unfortunately, only one-seventh remained. The king took the great story, called the *Brihatkatha*, and went to his palace. He had the work translated into Sanskrit, and that is how the story indeed became famous throughout the world.

Further reading: Sarla Khosla, *Brhatkatha and Its Contributions* (Delhi: Agam Kala Prakashan, 2003); S. N. Prasad, *Studies in Gunadhya* (Varanasi: Chaukhambha Orientalia, 1977); Arshia Sattar, trans., *Tales from the Kathasaritsagara* (New Delhi: Penguin Books, 1994).

Guptas (320–550 C.E.)

The Guptas were a powerful dynasty who ruled most of North India early in the Common Era. They patronized Jains (see JAINISM) and Buddhists (*see* BUDDHA) as well as Hindus. The famous Buddhist monastic university of Nalanda (a site now in western Pakistan) was founded by the Gupta kings and associates. Other Buddhist sites such as Bodh Gaya and Sanchi also benefited from Gupta attention and largesse.

The Gupta rulers were known for their adherence to traditional VEDIC norms in ritual and conduct. While patrons of the heterodox Buddhists and Jains, they were devotionally attached to VISHNU and remained Hindus by faith. Chandra Gupta I (320–34 C.E.) began the dynasty by consolidating power in the eastern Gangetic heartland. His successor, Sumudra Gupta (355–76 C.E.), made Pataliputra (now Patna) the center of a great empire reaching from Assam in the east to the Punjab in the west. He took tribute from other kings in the west, notably those of Rajasthan, and conquered much of the eastern Indian coastline down to KANCHIPURAM. Though he withdrew his armies, he remained overlord of southeastern India.

Chandra Gupta II (c. 376–415 C.E.) defeated the western Shaka armies and extended the rule of the empire up to the Indus River, controlling everything to the east. Chandra Gupta II ushered in a new era of cultural magnificence, becoming patron to the great poet KALIDASA and other poets and scholars. He may have had the title *Vikramaditya* cited by Kalidasa. During his reign the Chinese traveler Fa-shien, a Buddhist, traveled to India to record the wonders of the land. Chandra Gupta's son, Kumara Gupta I (c. 415–54), was killed in battles defending western India as fierce invaders, the Central Asians known as Hunas, challenged Gupta rule there. Kumara Gupta was known for his worship of SHIVA. Skanda Gupta (c. 455–67) took power upon Kumara's death. He fended off the invaders, but Gupta power had begun to weaken. The rest of Gupta rule was spent in fending off attacks from the west. The empire succumbed completely when it lost control of Bengal in 550 C.E.

Further reading: Ashvini Agrawal, *Rise and Fall of the Imperial Guptas* (Delhi: Motilal Banarsidass, 1989); A. L. Basham, *The Wonder That Was India*, 3d rev. ed. (Calcutta: Rupa, 1997); Kathryn Hinds, *India's Gupta Dynasty* (New York: Benchmark Books, 1996).

guru

The SANSKRIT word *guru* ("weighty" or "heavy" or "father") is said to derive from *gu* (the darkness of ignorance) and *ru* (driving away)—thus, "the one who drives away the darkness of ignorance." The notion of the *guru* began in VEDIC times; a student would live with a master for 12 years to acquire the Vedic learning. He treated the guru as his father and served his household as well. Today, a guru is a person's spiritual father, who is entitled to special deference, as are his wife and daughter.

The guru is a spiritual guide. Almost all traditions understand that spiritual progress and liberation from birth and rebirth cannot occur without the aid of a guru. In many contemporary

Indian traditions he is seen to be God himself and is treated as such; thus, his disciples may often refer to their devotion to the "feet of the guru" or their fealty to the "sandals [*paduka*]" of the guru. (Touching of the feet in India is a sign of deep respect.) So important is the guru that every year a holiday, Gurupurnima, is celebrated. It takes place on the full Moon in the lunar month of Ashadha (June–July). It was dedicated originally to the sage VYASA, who compiled the VEDAS and the MAHABHARATA, but it is observed by worship or honoring of one's teachers and *gurus*.

The SIKH tradition, which was founded by Guru Nanak in the 16th century, honors a line of 10 gurus whose teachings form the core of the tradition. The teachings were eventually gathered together along with the teachings of certain Indian saints into the Sikh sacred scripture, the Granth Sahib or Guru Granth. Since then the book has became the true "guru" for the Sikhs, and none other has been recognized.

Further reading: M. G. Gupta, *The Guru in Indian Mysticism* (Agra: M. G., 1994); Swami Muktananda, *The Perfect Relationship: The Guru and the Disciple,* 2d ed. (South Fallsburg, N.Y.: SYDA Foundation, 1999).

Gurupurnima   *See* GURU.

Guyana

Guyana was the first country in the Western Hemisphere to receive Hindu immigrants from India. On May 5, 1838, the British ship *Whitby* docked at Guyana's Berbice Colony with 249 immigrants on board, 164 of whom were East Indians bound for the sugar plantations of Davidson, Barclay and Company in Highbury and Waterloo. As many immigrants to the Caribbean were, these East Indians were contracted as indentured laborers to fill the labor shortage that resulted from Britain's abolition of slavery in 1833. As newly freed Africans demanded higher wages and entered different labor markets, colonial officials turned to India as a source of cheap labor.

Guyana attracted many from western Bihar, eastern Uttar Pradesh, and other regions in northern India that had been affected by famine and poverty. Between 1838 and 1917, 238,960 Indian men, women, and children immigrated to Guyana. Most were farmers, but a small number of educated Brahmins also arrived, despite British policies aimed at preventing their passage. British officials believed that Brahmins would incite dissent among workers. As many as 75,000 indentured servants returned to India at the completion of their contracts. The rest remained and settled in permanent colonies.

Hindus endured unfair treatment on the plantations and were pressured to convert to Christianity. Work in the fields had no regard for the needs of Hindu prayer, ritual, or religious ceremonies. Hindus were sequestered, placed on separate plantations, and allowed to leave designated areas only with a validated pass. Long days in the field left little time for other activities; workers quickly adapted to certain patterns of Christian worship and adopted Sunday as a day for Hindu prayer and ritual.

During the 1850s Christian missionaries frequently visited the settlements of Indians in attempts to convert Hindus to Christianity. In order to counter conversions Brahmin priests began providing spiritual rites to all Hindus regardless of caste. The rate of conversion to Christianity slowed, but a breakdown of the traditional Indian caste system followed.

Official policy of the British colony barred Hindus from employment in the civil service unless they first became Christian; many Hindus converted for this reason but privately continued to practice Hinduism. Discrimination against Hindus gradually subsided in the 1930s as the social status of Indian immigrants improved.

Hindus who immigrated to Guyana took many of the traditional forms of their religion. Although these traditions were altered to suit the conditions and circumstances of living in a multicultural society, the fundamental differences among sects found in India were reestablished in Guyana. The most popular traditions in Guyana remain VAISHNAVISM and SHAIVISM. The largest Hindu organization in the country, Guyana Sanathan Dharma Maha Sabha, sustains most of the temples. Other organizations such as the Guyana Pandits Society maintain the tradition of Hindu orthodoxy in Guyana. In the Vaishnaivite tradition, the Ramayana is the main text of Hindus in Guyana; it supports devotion to the deity HANUMAN and an annual observance of Ramayan YAJNA. Among Shaivite practitioners, daily observances include bathing a SHIVA LINGAM. Small shrines and prayer houses appear in front of homes throughout the country. Temples are the sites of chanting, MEDITATION, ritual, and worship.

As in Trinidad, DIVALI, the festival of lights, is a national holiday in Guyana. Families and communities prepare special foods and decorate their homes and neighborhoods. Another Hindu celebration, HOLI, is also a national holiday. The holiday commemorates the lore about a traditional king who was killed by his son. It represents the triumph of good over evil and features the throwing of red dye on family and friends, representing the blood of the king.

Smaller groups following the Hindu faith have emerged over recent decades, including the INTERNATIONAL SOCIETY FOR KRISHNA CONSCIOUSNESS, the SATYA SAI BABA movement, and the ARYA SAMAJ. Most notable is the Guyana Sevashram Sangha, which was established in the mid-20th century by Swami Purnananda (no dates). Purnananda went to Guyana to foster Hinduism by teaching the Hare Krishna mantra and publishing *Aum Hindutvam,* a book to help guide Hindus in Guyana. The Guyana Sevashram Sangha serves as the only institution in the Caribbean that trains young *brahmacharis* (spiritual students; *see* BRAHMACHARYA) and is the first to produce its own swami, Swami Vidyarand.

Approximately 280,000 Hindus make Guyana their home. It is the second largest religion in the country, after Christianity.

Further reading: D. A. Bisnauth, *The Settlement of Indians in Guyana, 1890–1930* (London: Peepul Tree, 2000); Hugh Desmond Hoyte, *Hinduism, Religious Diversity and Social Cohesion: The Guyana Experience* (Georgetown, British Guiana: Dynamic Graphics, 1987); Clem Seecharan, *India and the Shaping of the Indo-Guyanese Imagination, 1890s–1920s* (Leeds: Peepal Tree, 1993); Steven Vertovec, *The Hindu Diaspora: Comparative Patterns* (New York: Routledge, 2000).

H

Haidakhan Samaj (est. 1980)   *See* BABAJI.

Hanuman

The monkey god Hanuman is one of the most universally worshipped divinities of the Hindu pantheon. He is the son of Anjana, an APSARAS (nymph) who was herself born as a monkey, and VAYU, the god of the wind. In the RAMAYANA story, Hanuman is a friend to Lord RAMA, the incarnation of VISHNU. He is equally worshipped by Vaishnavites (worshippers of VISHNU) and Shaivites (worshippers of SHIVA).

It is said that Hanuman as a child saw the Sun, thought it was a fruit, and leaped up 300 leagues to catch it. BRAHMA once gave him the boon that he would not be slain in battle.

In the Ramayana, Hanuman flies over to the island of LANKA to see whether Rama's wife, SITA, is there. He finds her, but she dissuades him from taking her back lest he besmirch Rama's reputation. In a scene famous in Indian mythology, he is captured on Lanka by the demons (*rakshasas*). They march him through the streets to his execution, humiliating him by tying an oil-soaked cloth to his tail and lighting it. Furious, he jumps from building to building and sets the capital city on fire.

Hanuman fought bravely in the battle against the demons; he is remembered for going off to find herbs to revive LAKSHMANA, Rama's slain brother. Not knowing which herbs to collect he took a whole mountain of them; from them medicine was found that restored Lakshmana to life. Hanuman follows Rama back to AYODHYA to serve him; the god gives him the boon of everlasting youth and longevity. Hanuman is seen as the foremost of the devotees of Rama.

Hanuman is also found in one passage of the MAHABHARATA, where he meets BHIMA, another son of his father, Vayu. Bhima, known for his power, fights with Hanuman and is defeated. Only afterward do they realize they are half brothers.

Hanuman is known for his superhuman powers, his celibacy (though in some parts of India he is seen as married), his ability to expand and contract himself, and his learning, including grammar and the Vedic sciences. He is often regarded as a village protector and is the special divinity of wrestlers and acrobats.

Iconographically Hanuman is usually depicted with only two hands, carrying a club, but other images give him eight hands that hold several weapons and a shield, for fighting in the war against the demons. In one hand he holds the

Hanuman, monkey god, servant of Lord Rama
(*Courtesy Vedanta Society, San Francisco*)

Sanjivini mountain, the mountain of herbs that saved Laksmana's life.

Further reading: K. C. Aryan and Subhashini Aryan, *Hanuman in Art and Mythology* (Delhi: Rekha Prakashan, 1975); Devdutt Pattnaik, *Hanuman: An Introduction* (Mumbai: Vakils, Feffer & Simons, 2001).

Hanuman Foundation (est. 1974)

The Hanuman Foundation is one of the creations of the American spiritual teacher Baba RAM DASS, born Richard Alpert, April 6, 1931, in Boston, Massachusetts.

After working with psychedelics with Timothy Leary at Harvard University and being dismissed with Leary, from their teaching positions there, Alpert went to India in 1967 and met his GURU, NEEM KAROLI BABA. Neem Karoli gave him the spiritual name Ram Dass (servant of God) and introduced him to Hindu spirituality. In his time with Neem Karoli, he learned about HANUMAN, the deity depicted as a monkey who is a symbol of selfless service in the Hindu tradition. Ram Dass became an affectionate devotee of Hanuman.

The Hanuman Foundation was incorporated in 1974, after Ram Dass's pilgrimage to India in order to supply information from the teachings of Neem Karoli Baba, who, although deceased, still teaches. Ram Dass founded the Neem Karoli Baba Hanuman Temple, located in Taos, New Mexico, in a remodeled adobe building. The central focus of the temple is a 1,500-pound marble carving of Hanuman imported from India. This temple primarily serves some 300 Indian families spread between Albuquerque and Denver. Major services featuring chanting and singing are held every Tuesday (as that is considered Hanuman's day). Neem Karoli Baba's *mahasamadhi* (death/liberation day) is celebrated in September.

The foundation has become over time a central archive and headquarters of a number of projects. The Orphalese Foundation controls a tape library and the ZBS Foundation (also known as Amazing Grace) has released several recordings on spiritual topics with the assistance of Steven Levine. The foundation also works closely with the Seva Foundation, founded by Larry Brilliant (b. 1946), a devotee of Baba, on social service projects, especially the eradication of blindness.

Further reading: *Inside Out* (Nederland, Colo.: Prison Ashram Project/Hanuman Foundation, 1976); Timothy Leary, Ralph Metzner, and Richard Alpert, *The Psychedelic Experience* (New Hyde Park, N.Y.: University

Books, 1964); Baba Ram Dass, *Be Here Now* (New York: Crown, 1973); ———, *Grist for the Mill* (Santa Cruz, Calif.: Unity Press, 1977); ———, *Still Here: Embracing Aging, Changing and Dying* (New York: Riverhead Books, 2000); Baba Ram Dass with Paul Gorman, *How Can I Help?: Stories and Reflections on Service* (New York: Alfred A. Knopf, 1985).

Harappa   See INDUS VALLEY CIVILIZATION.

Hargobind   See SIKHISM.

Hari Dass, Baba (1923–) *teacher of Ashtanga Yoga*

For over 50 years, Baba Hari Dass has been teaching ASHTANGA YOGA and instituting organizations for social service in the United States, Canada, and India, while maintaining vows of monastic silence.

Born in 1923 near Almora, India, in the foothills of the Himalayas, Baba Hari Dass left home at age eight to join a sect of renunciants in the jungles of the lower Himalayas. In 1942, he took initiation as a monk in the VAIRAGI Vaishnavite order. After years of MEDITATION, he decided in 1952 to become a MUNI SADHU, a monk who practices continual silence. The observance of silence is aimed at gradually quieting the mind and eliminating unwanted thoughts. He writes on a small chalkboard to communicate his teachings. Despite this vow, he has been able to implement his plans for the extension of his version of religion and spirituality, while developing ASHRAMS and teaching YOGA.

In addition to teaching classical Ashtanga Yoga (the Yoga of the Eight Limbs, originally codified by PATANJALI), Baba Hari Dass is an author, builder, philosopher, sculptor, and proponent of AYURVEDA (the ancient Indian system of health and healing.) In 1971, he traveled to North America, and he has continued to work in India, Canada, and the United States. He and his teachings have inspired the Mount Madonna Center near Santa Cruz, California; the Dharmasara Satsang Society/Salt Spring Center near Vancouver; the Ashtanga Yoga Fellowship in Toronto; and the Sri Ram Ashram in Haridwar, India, all organizations dedicated to yoga education, retreats, service projects, and publishing. The California-based Hanuman Fellowship was formed in 1974.

In 1987, he founded (and continues to fund) a unique orphanage near HARIDVAR, Uttar Pradesh, that provides a family life for its residents,

Baba Hari Dass, silent monk, teacher of Ashtanga Yoga, author, and founder of several retreat centers and social-service organizations (*© Hanuman Fellowship*)

emulating the life of a home with parents and siblings. The orphanage now houses more than 35 children. His Hanuman Fellowship sponsors weekly gatherings, or *satsangs*, and periodic retreats at their centers. Sri Rama Foundation/ Publishing, established in 1971, publishes the writings of Hari Dass.

Hari Dass presides at weekly sessions on the YOGA SUTRA, the BHAGAVAD GITA, Ashtanga Yoga, and related subjects. He also writes commentaries on the principal yoga scriptures and teaches classes on yoga. Each Sunday he leads community gatherings that include singing, meditation, and yoga.

Further reading: Baba Hari Dass, *Ashtanga Yoga Primer* (Santa Cruz, Calif.: Sri Rama: Hanuman Fellowship, 1981); ———, *Between Pleasure and Pain: The Way of Conscious Living* (Sumas, Wash.: Dharma Sara, 1976); ———, *Fire without Fuel: The Aphorisms of Baba Hari Dass* (Santa Cruz, Calif.: Sri Rama, 1986); ———, *Hariakhan Baba: Known, Unknown* (Davis, Calif.: Sri Rama Foundation, 1975); ———, *Silence Speaks: From the Chalkboard of Baba Hari Dass* (Santa Cruz, Calif.: Sri Rama Foundation, 1977); ———, *Sweeper to Saint: Stories of Holy India* (Santa Cruz, Calif.: Sri Rama, 1980).

Haridvar (Haridwar; Hardvar; Hardwar)

Haridvar (*dvar*, doorway, to Hari, a name for VISHNU) is one of the seven sacred cities of Hindu India. SHIVA followers call the city Hardvar (Har, a name for Shiva).

Haridvar is located in the northern state of Uttaranchal, in the Himalayan foothills. The city has been called Mayapur, Gangadwar, and Kapila at different times in its history. It has been mentioned in scripture and other writings from the time of the BUDDHA (600 B.C.E.).

The city is considered the starting point for a PILGRIMAGE path that includes BADRINATH, KEDARNATH, Gangotri, and Yamanotri. It is the place where Bhagiratha is said to have taken the GANGES down to Earth in order to bless the ashes of his ancestors; pilgrims annually honor the descent of the Ganges. They also perform the special *shraddha* FUNERAL RITES for deceased loved ones. Pilgrims visit a stone footprint of Vishnu and bathe nearby. The three major gods, BRAHMA, Shiva, and Vishnu, have been said to visit the city.

Numerous temples to both Shiva and Vishnu grace the city. There are also temples to the goddess, including the Mayadevi temple, considered one of the SHAKTI PITHAS where the heart (or navel) of the goddess is said to have fallen. Notable also is the temple to DAKSHA, father-in-law of Shiva; Daksha performed his famous sacrifice here without inviting Shiva, thus provoking a quarrel and eventually the death of his daughter SATI. Haridvar/Hardvar is one of the sites for the KUMBHA MELA and the larger Maha Kumbhamela festivals.

Further reading: Reeta and Rupinder Khullar, *Gateway to the Gods, Haridwar-Rishikesh: Yamunotri-Gangotri-Kedarnath-Badrinath* (Dehradun: Uttaranchal Tourism, 2004); Survey of India, *Haridwar Guide Map* (New Delhi: Author, 1978).

Harihara

Harihara is an iconic deity who combines the forms of VISHNU (Hari) and SHIVA (Hara). He is revered by a syncretic cult based mostly in South India. There is a Harihara image in BADAMI in Karnataka that is dated to the sixth century.

The South Indian kings of the VIJAYANAGARA (1336–1565) patronized Harihara's temples. Some of their kings even took his name. A number of Harihara temples still exist in the Indian state of Karnataka today.

Harihara also appears in the iconography of Nepal. Though a minority cult, the Harihara phenomenon demonstrates the elasticity and syncretic character of Hinduism.

Harihara, iconic deity that unites Vishnu and Shiva
(calendar print)

Further reading: Michael W. Meister with M. A. Dhaky, eds., *Encyclopedia of Indian Temple Architecture* (Philadelphia: University of Pennsylvania Press, 1983).

Hariharananda Giri, Swami   *See* KRIYA YOGA CENTERS.

Har Rai   *See* SIKHISM.

hatha yoga

Hatha yoga is an amalgam of yogic practices that may have emerged separately and were later com-bined. Its origins are obscure, but it is likely that the system began to develop in the early centuries of the Common Era.

Hatha yoga includes basic practices that can be found in ASHTANGA YOGA, which relies on the YOGA SUTRA of PATANJALI. It includes different arrays of postures (ASANAS), joined to various TANTRA practices. The term *hatha* originally meant "violent," and it is possible that this style of YOGA originated in certain types of severe yoga that were later softened for protection of the body.

Some types of hatha yoga include or even focus on KUNDALINI practice. Here the focus of breath control is on the "serpent" or "Goddess Energy" at the base of the spine, which must be awakened and forced upward to pierce the psychic centers or chakras that run parallel to the spine. The NADIS, or subtle bodily channels, are used to guide breath into the central spinal channel to help the raising of the kundalini through the centers. Finally, the kundalini meets SHIVA at a point above the head called SAHASRARA CHAKRA. This meeting provokes absolute enlightenment.

Traditionally, hatha yoga has encompassed a wide range of practices including those of such sects as the NATH YOGIS, who sought bodily immortality through the ingestion (and transformation) of poisons such as oxides of mercury and practiced a physical alchemy. Today, in the West, hatha yoga is typically confined to postures and a simple focus on the breath; more advanced practitioners may begin to focus on the kundalini and the channeling of the breath in the *nadis*.

Further reading: Elsy Becherer, trans., and Hans-Ulrich Rieker, commentary, *The Yoga of Light: Hatha Yoga Pradipika, India's Classical Handbook* (New York: Herder & Herder, 1971); B. K. S. Iyengar, *The Concise Light on Yoga: Yoga Dipika* (New York: Schocken Books, 1982).

Healthy, Happy, Holy Organization
(est. 1969)

Yogi BHAJAN (1929–2004) inaugurated the Healthy, Happy, Holy Organization (3HO) in the United

States and India in 1969, with the declaration "Happiness is your birthright." The mission of 3HO is to assist the interested public in developing a happy, healthy, and holy lifestyle to meet the challenges of the modern world. Based on ancient yogic techniques taught by Yogi Bhajan, 3HO offers KUNDALINI YOGA, MEDITATION, information on a healthy diet, tantric practices, and a compassionate philosophy.

3HO is an affiliate of the larger religion of the Sikh Dharma. There are over 300 3HO centers in 39 countries including the United States, Canada, Mexico, Russia, Australia, South Africa, and countries in Europe. 3HO centers offer holistic health treatments including books, tapes, videos, and health supplements. 3HO publishes a quarterly journal called the *Aquarian Times,* featuring tips and tools for health and happiness. The organization's headquarters are located in Espanola, New Mexico.

Yogi Bhajan established the 3HO after traveling to the United States and seeing a need for yoga in the West. He reached out to the youth of the 1960s, recognizing that their experimentation with drugs expressed a need for liberation and wholeness. Yogi Bhajan introduced many young people to kundalini yoga as a natural and healthy alternative. As word of his teachings spread, the organization grew and centers were established throughout the United States. Since then the 3HO has become a popular and dynamic community dedicated to personal growth and sharing of the ancient techniques upon which the organization is founded. The organization has fulfilled one of Yogi Bhajan's stated intentions, "I did not come to collect students, but to train teachers."

The practice of kundalini as taught by Yogi Bhajan is based on *kriyas* (ritual action). It is an integrative and authentic system that combines physical exercise, breath control, and meditation. These yoga techniques constitute a spiritual technology that expands awareness, opens the potential of mind, and draws forth one's inner being. The benefits of kundalini, as cited by 3HO, include the strengthening of the nervous system, the reduction of stress, self-awareness, concentration, and peace of mind.

Further reading: Yogi Bhajan, *Guide to Aquarian Pregnancy: Birth and Child Care through Yoga* (San Diego: 3HO Foundation, 1977); Yogiji Harbhajan Singh Khalsa, *The Inner Workout Manual: Kundalini Yoga* (San Bernardino, Calif.: Borgo Press, 1990); ———, *Kundalini Yoga for Youth and Joy* (San Bernardino, Calif.: Borgo Press, 1990); Yogiji Harbhajan Singh Khalsa and Harijot Kaur Khalsa, *Owners Manual for the Human Body: Kundalini Yoga* (Eugene, Oreg.: KIT Catalog 1993).

heaven

Heaven and hell (NARAKA) have been known to Hinduism since ancient times. VEDIC Hinduism conceived of a realm beyond the sky called *svar* or *svarga,* a realm of immortality and happiness beyond this world. One reached it through proper performance of the Vedic duties, especially the rituals (YAJNA).

In later mythology, beginning in the epics RAMAYANA and MAHABHARATA, *svarga* began to be understood as the realm of INDRA, king of the gods. His paradise contained the sacred wish-giving tree and the cow who grants all wishes. The beautiful courtesans of the gods (APSARASES) reside there, along with the divine musicians (GANDHARVAS). There all desires for pleasure are instantly satisfied.

Later Hindu traditions, starting around 400 B.C.E., considered *svarga* or heaven to be only a waystation in the transmigrating life. One could enjoy one's accumulated KARMIC merit there but would still be reborn into the physical world. In Shaivite tradition, SHIVA resides in Kailash, a paradise of sorts located at an actual mountain in the HIMALAYAS, but one was only meant to visit this site once in a lifetime. It generally was not seen as a place for souls to go after death.

Among Vaishnavites (VISHNU devotees), the ancient realm that once belonged to INDRA remains as a goal, to be reached after liberation from birth and rebirth. Vishnu and his wife, Lakshmi, preside over this paradise, where souls may live in effulgent bliss eternally, in proximity to the divinity himself.

Further readings: J. A. Dowson, *A Classical Dictionary of Hindu Mythology* (Portland, Oreg.: Trubner, 2003).

Hemachandra (c. 1200 C.E.) *Jain yogi and philosopher*

Hemachandra was one of the foremost Jain SHVET-AMBARA sages and teachers. He is known for his many writings, including the vast Jain PURANA in Sanskrit, which catalogued the lives and adventures of the 63 venerated personages in the tradition of JAINISM. Included among the 63 are all the TIRTHANKARAS, enlightened teachers, of the current half-era, plus the story of BAHUBALI, one of the sons of the first Tirthankara, and even a Jain version of the story of KRISHNA. This work was highly influential in popularizing and spreading the Jain faith.

Hemachandra's Yogashastra is one of the best sources for some of the lost practices of Jain YOGA. In the area of philosophy Hemachandra wrote Pramanamimamsa and Anyayogagavyavacchedika, which are widely studied as Jain contributions to the Indian logical school of the NYAYA. The second of the two is famous for its commentary by Mallishena, entitled Syadvadamanjari, which laid out a sophisticated Jain relativistic philosophy.

Further reading: Helen M. Johnson, trans., *The Lives of the Sixty-Three Illustrious Persons,* 6 vols. (Baroda: Oriental Institute, 1962); E. Windsch, trans., *"Hemachandra's Yogasastra," Zeitschrift der Deutschen Morgenlandishcen Gesellshaft* no. 28 (Leipzig, 1874).

Himalayan International Institute of Yoga Science and Philosophy (est. 1971)

The Himalayan International Institute of Yoga Science and Philosophy was founded in 1971 by Swami Rama (1925–96); first based in Illinois, headquarters were moved to Honesdale, Pennsylvania, in 1977. The institute promotes its founder's teachings on mind-body consciousness. Courses in holistic health, HATHA YOGA, RAJA YOGA, MEDITATION, and psychology are offered there. Raja yoga, considered the royal road of yoga, is promoted as a prime way to balance mind, body, and spirit. Swami Rama always aimed to awaken the nascent consciousness, bolster its energy, and raise spiritual intensity so that the individual blends with the Universal Self. He advocated what he termed super conscious MEDITATION, a system that included relaxation, *prana* (breathing), ASANAS (postures), and chants, or MANTRAS.

After being orphaned at an early age, Swami Rama was raised by an accomplished yogi from Bengal. He spent time as a child and young man in the cave monasteries of the HIMALAYAS. He was an adept pupil eager to learn, and in 1949 he attained the level of Shankaracharya, a title that was considered a great honor. He gave up his title in 1952 and committed himself to an arduous discipline in order to prepare himself for attaining and teaching the highest spirituality.

In 1969 Swami Rama ventured to the United States; he became a research consultant for the Menninger Foundation Research Project, which viewed his project on voluntary control of external states as worthy of research. Little was known about how to induce the body to override the involuntary, autonomous nervous system. Swami Rama began to work with the husband-and-wife team of Elmer and Alyce Green, the on-site psychologists. He demonstrated an uncanny ability to control physical feats and body functions. His extraordinary skills offered significant material for laboratory analysis of mind-body connections.

The Himalayan Institute has published over 80 books on meditation and philosophy. It also publishes the bimonthly *Yoga International*. There are 37 branches, serving an international market, with affiliated centers in the United States, Canada, India, Germany, Italy, Great Britain, Trinidad,

Curaçao, and Malaysia. In 2002, there were 1,500 members in the United States alone. Swami Rama died on November 13, 1996, without naming a successor. The institute carries on his work.

Further reading: Swami Rama, *Freedom from the Bondage of* Karma, 2d ed. (New York: Himalayan Institute Press; n.d.); ———, *Living with the Himalayan Masters* (New York: Himalayan Institute Press, 1978); ———, *Path of Fire and Light,* Vol. 1, *Advanced Practices of Yoga* (New York: Himalayan Institute Press, 1986); ———, *Sacred Journey: Living Purposefully and Dying Gracefully* (Detroit: Lotus Press, n.d.); ———, *Samadhi: The Highest State of Wisdom,* Vol. 1, *Yoga the Sacred Science* (Detroit: Lotus Press., n.d.).

Himalayan Mountains

Himalaya (the abode of the snows) is a vast mountain range spreading across six countries: India, Pakistan, Nepal, Bhutan, China, and Tibet (ruled by China). Geographically it separates the Indian subcontinent from the Tibetan plateau. Fourteen of the highest peaks in the world are found in the Himalayas. The sources of several of the rivers of India are found here. Both the Indus River of Pakistan and the GANGES of India begin in these snow-covered mountains.

The Himalaya is an important mythological site for Indian tradition. Lord SHIVA and his wife, PARVATI, are said to live on the peak KAILASA, an important pilgrimage site in Tibet just across the border from Nepal. The Himalayas are personified as HIMAVAT, the father of SATI, Shiva's first wife. The Himalayan lake Mansorovar is said to be the source of the Ganges. HANUMAN the monkey god was said to have gone to the Himalaya to get the mountain of herbs that saved LAKSHMANA's life in the RAMAYANA story.

Further reading: Cornelia Dimmit and J.A. B. van Buitenen, eds. and trans., *Classical Hindu Mythology: A Reader in the Sanskrit Puranas* (Philadelphia: Temple University Press, 1978); J. A. Dowson, *A Classical Dic-* *tionary of Hindu Mythology* (Portland, Ore.: Trubner, 2003); Swami Sundaranand, *Himalaya through the Lens of a Sadhu* (Gangotri: Tapovan Kuti Prakashan, 2001).

Himavat

Literally "possessed of snow," Himavat is the personification of the Himalayas found in Indian literature and mythology. His wife is Mena.

Many stories are told of Himavat, his wife, and their family. One story holds that the couple had three daughters, Ragini, Kutila, and KALI, and one son, Sunabha. The first daughter, Ragini, was reddish colored and dressed in red. The second daughter, Kutila, was fair and wore garlands and clothes of white. The last daughter was the dark Kali.

Six years after each girl's birth they all began to practice austerities. Successful in her austerities, Kutila was taken to heaven by certain divinities to meet BRAHMA, as there was a need for someone to bear a son to SHIVA to save the universe from torment by the demons. Brahma told the divinities that this fair girl could not bear such a son, but in her temerity she insisted to Brahma that she could. This incurred his anger and he cursed her to become the river in his land (later to be taken to earth in the form of Ganga or the GANGES).

The second, ruddy, daughter, Ragini, did austerities and was also cursed by Brahma when she too became angry at him. Because of her ruddy complexion, she was turned into the twilight.

Finally, it was time for the dark one, Kali, to go to heaven because of her austerity. At this point Mena, in anguish at the prospect of losing yet another daughter, shouted out, "u! ma!" (Sanskrit for Oh, no!). UMA is another name for PARVATI, and at this point her name was officially changed. She, of course, was successful in becoming Shiva's wife.

There are many stories of Himavat's encounters with his divine son-in-law, Shiva. Usually, they show him and his wife to be uncomfortable with the antisocial ascetic with whom their daughter had fallen in love. In one example, Himavat has a ragged beggar thrown from his house only to learn later that this was Parvati's beau Shiva, with whom she had become enthralled.

Further reading: Cornelia Dimmitt and J. A. B. van Buitenen, *Classical Hindu Mythology: A Reader in the Sanskrit Puranas* (Philadelphia: Temple University Press, 1978); E. Washburn Hopkins, *Epic Mythology* (Delhi: Motilal Banarsidass, 1986).

Hinduism Today (est. 1979)

The quarterly magazine *Hinduism Today* was founded on January 5, 1979, by Satguru Sivaya SUBRAMUNIYASWAMI (1927–2001) as part of the nonprofit educational activity of the Himalayan Academy, the publishing and research organization of the SAIVA SIDDHANTA CHURCH. The publication is produced by a small monastic community on Kauai Island in Hawaii to "inform and inspire interest in Hinduism, dispel popular myths surrounding the religion, foster solidarity among sects and lineages, maintain respect for the Vedas, promote the continuing renaissance of Hinduism and serve as an educational resource for the promotion of Sanatana Dharma." It employs over 100 reporters and dozens of photographers. It is distributed across 39 countries, reaching millions of readers.

In 1951 the Himalayan Academy began publishing a series of books on Hinduism and metaphysics. The quarterly emerged in response to a growing need in the late 1970s for a nontechnical publication accessible to a wide audience that could serve as a central resource for those maintaining the faith outside India. In addition to articles directly relating to Hindu philosophy, the Hindu DIASPORA, and international news of Hindu communities and temples, the publication includes topics ranging from AYURVEDA medicine to VEGETARIANISM and YOGA. Interviews with popular Hindu teachers, reformers, and activists appear regularly.

The publication has become a reputable source on the Hindu way of life for many outside the religious community. Governments, libraries, theologians, and scholars use it to research the beliefs, practices, and contexts of Hindu groups around the world.

Hinduism Today has changed from its first distribution in 1979 as a black and white newsletter to the current full-colored magazine and Internet journal. In 1996, the publication expanded to include a CD-ROM called *Dharma Graphics,* containing 1,500 illustrations of village arts and crafts selected from 20 years of images.

Further reading: Himalayan Academy, *Himalayan Academy, 1957–1968* (Virginia City, Nev.: Himalayan Academy, 1967).

Hindu nationalism

Hindu nationalism is a contemporary movement with religious, cultural, and political aspects, oriented toward creation of a Hindu state in India and a monolithic Hindu identity, based on Hindutva (Hinduness).

Critics charge that these nationalists define *Hindu* to emphasize Brahminical and upper-caste values, ethics, and practices. The movement also includes extremists and Hindu supremacists who have targeted the economic and political rights of cultural and religious minorities. Supporters point out crimes Muslims have committed against India and the depredations of the Christians in the form of the British and call for an uprooting of "non-Hindu" elements in India as much as possible.

Hindutva declares Christians and Muslims to be "foreign" to India because their faiths have holy lands outside the boundary of the modern Indian nation-state. Critics point out that the ideology of Hindutva supports violence against religious and cultural minorities, including sexual violence against women of minority groups and Hindu women who defy Hindutva's mandates. Further, the Hindutva agenda for nation building subordinates the lives and livelihoods of *adivasis* (indigenous tribal peoples), Dalits (economically disadvantaged, former "untouchable" castes), and the poor to higher-caste Hindus. In general, Hindutva is not sympathetic to the historical and present struggles for the human rights of spiritually and politically distinct groups, such as tribal groups, Buddhists, Jains, and Sikhs, as these groups are understood to be antinational and anti-Hindu.

Hindutva's tenets were first described by V. D. Savarkar in his text *Hindutva: Who Is a Hindu?*, published in 1922. Hindutva's agenda is carried out by various groups, including the SHIV SENA and the Sangh Parivar, a network of organizations. The Sangh's major parties are Rashtriya Swayamsevak Sangh (RSS); National Volunteer Corps, formed in 1925, which provides social service and militant training; Vishwa Hindu Parishad (VHP); World Hindu Council, formed in 1964, which frames the Sangh's cultural and religious agenda and works to spread the Hindu nationalist agenda on an international level; and the Bajrang Dal, the militant youth group. Hindu nationalist political parties took various forms through the 20th century, and the BHARATIYA JANATA PARTY (BJP), "Indian People's Party," created in 1980, is the most recent incarnation of the Sangh's political wing. While the BJP advocates a clear Hindu supremacist agenda, other political parties also empathize with and support "soft" Hindutva, which contains certain aspects of Hindutva that shun violence. The Sangh also operates through a vast network of development groups and service and education organizations, such as Ekal Vidyalayas, Sewa Bharti, Utkal Bipanna Sahayata Samiti, and Vanvasi Kalyan Ashrams.

The rise of Hindu nationalism can be traced to anticolonial movements during the late 19th century, when Hindus mobilized to fight British rule. Some of these movements protected the privileges and rights of the Hindu middle and upper classes against the struggles for equal rights of other minorities and lower-class and tribal peoples. Scholarly analysis shows that Hindutva drew upon the ethnic and cultural nationalisms of Germany and Italy in the early 20th century, to promote physical training conducted in cells called *shakhas* and ideological training that linked "Hindu pride" to the subjugation of perceived enemies, such as the Christians and Muslims. The rise of Hindu nationalism is thus framed by the inequalities and struggles in India's history.

When India and Pakistan became independent nations in August 1947, divided along religious differences, widespread violence between and within religious communities accompanied the massive displacement of people across newly drawn national borders. Large groups of Muslims moved into Pakistan (a self-proclaimed Islamic state), and non-Muslims moved into India (a self-proclaimed secular state). Official estimates put the displacement at about 12 million and deaths at several million. More than 75,000 women were abducted and raped by members of their own or other communities. The forms of violence that struck within and across religious lines during the Partition still fill the social memory of India and provide rationale for mutual resentment and anger between Hindus and Muslims.

On January 30, 1948, Nathuram Godse, a former member of the RSS, shot and killed M. K. GANDHI. At the time, Hindu nationalists expressed intense dissatisfaction with what they termed Gandhi's "appeasement" of minorities, especially Muslims. Though Godse was not an official member of the RSS at the time, the RSS was banned for approximately a year. The language of "minority appeasement" continues to be a mobilizing rhetoric for Hindu nationalism.

In 1984, with Indira Gandhi's assassination as a trigger, Sikh communities were targeted by large-scale violence, concentrated in Delhi. It is widely accepted that the violence was largely the responsibility of Hindutva, abetted by the Congress government's complicity in not prosecuting instigators. In 1992, leaders of the BJP, VHP, and RSS incited Hindu nationalist crowds to destroy the 400+-year-old Babri Mosque at Aʏᴏᴅʜʏᴀ in Uttar Pradesh. According to the Sangh's mythology and grievance, the mosque stands upon the ruins of a Hindu temple, rumored to be the birthplace of Rᴀᴍᴀ, a Hindu god. The destruction of the mosque was accompanied by systematic anti-Muslim violence throughout India, concentrated in Mumbai, for which the Srikrishna Commission has held Hindu nationalists responsible.

The BJP gained power in India at the national level at the head of a coalition of political parties called the National Democratic Alliance (NDA). The NDA controlled the national government until 2004, when the Congress-led United Progressive Alliance won elections at the national level, though the BJP continued to rule in various states, alone or within political coalitions.

In the spring of 2002, the torching of 58 Hindutva activists on a train near the town of Godhra, Gujarat, set off a systematic and government-backed massacre of Muslims throughout the state. Immediately after the train fire, some of the local-language press and state-level BJP leaders insisted that local Muslims had conspired to burn the train, though the Banerjee Commission later declared this allegation to be unfounded. Starting on February 28, violence broke out in 16 of Gujarat's 24 districts, attributed by most to Hindu nationalist groups. Muslim homes, businesses, and places of worship were destroyed by large mobs armed with swords, tridents, kerosene, and liquid gas canisters. Both girls and women were subjected to sexual atrocities: gang rape and collective rape, as well as sexual mutilation with swords and sticks, before being burned to death.

Independent fact-finding groups have placed the number of dead at no fewer than 2,000, and the number of displaced at 200,000, most of whom were Muslims. Human rights observers classified the events in Gujarat as "genocide" by the standards of the United Nations Genocide Convention of 1948. India's National Human Rights Commission charged the state government with complicity at the "highest levels." Police and high-level BJP officials, according to fact-finding reports, supported the violence through inaction or active participation, including leaking electoral rolls indicating the locations of Muslim residences and businesses. Since the violence in Gujarat, impunity has reigned, as reported by Amnesty International and Human Rights Watch. Several high-profile cases were moved out of the state by the Indian Supreme Court, because of the court's lack of confidence in the ability of Gujarat's judicial system to deliver justice for the survivors.

Since these incidents in Gujarat, groups in India and the Dɪᴀsᴘᴏʀᴀ have begun to trace international political and financial support for Hindu nationalist organizations. Two reports tracked the funding of Hindu nationalist activities: the Campaign to Stop Funding Hate released one report on the activities of the India Development and Relief Fund, a United States–based charity, and Awaaz South Asia Watch released another report on the Hindu Swayamsevak Sangh, a United Kingdom–based charity.

Sangh leaders have been quoted as promising to strengthen the Hindutva movement in Orissa, a state in eastern India, and in other parts of the country. In Orissa, as of 2005, Hindutva already has a strong network of Sangh organizations and activists, who are reportedly carrying out forced conversions of Christians and tribals to Hinduism, destroying churches, committing selective murders, imposing social and economic boycotts of minorities, and imposing a ban on cow slaughter, which threatens the livelihoods of poor Muslims and Dalits.

Further reading: Partha Chatterjee, *The Nation and Its Fragments: Colonial and Postcolonial Histories* (Princeton, N.J.: Princeton University Press, 1993); Angana P. Chatterji, "Memory—Mournings: The Biopolitics of Hindu Nationalism," in Angana P. Chatterji and Lubna Nazir Chaudhry, eds. *Contesting Nation: Gendered Violence in South Asia: Notes on the Postcolonial Present* (New Delhi: Zubaan Books, 2006); Thomas Blom

Hansen, *The Saffron Wave* (Princeton, N.J.: Princeton University Press, 1999); Zoya Hasan, ed., *Forging Identities—Gender, Communities and the State* (Delhi: Kali for Women, 1994); Romila Thapar, *Cultural Pasts* (New Delhi: Oxford University Press, 2001).

hiranyagarbha

Hiranyagarbha (*hiranya,* gold; *garbha,* seed, egg, womb, embryo) is the Golden Embryo, Golden Egg, or Golden Womb identified in the Rig Veda (X.121) as the cause of the universe. Paradoxically, it has both a masculine and a feminine aspect. It is referred to as "he," but it is also the "womb" of manifest reality.

From the beginning the term *hiranyagarbha* has had multivalent and sometimes contradictory meanings. In Rig Veda X.82 it is the cosmic egg that separates into two hemispheres, in the beginning of the world, its upper portion forming the sky and its yolk becoming the Sun. This vision is elaborated in the PURANAS, where other elements of the egg make up elements of the manifest universe: the water in the cosmic egg, for instance, becomes the ocean.

Various Hindu traditions have offered various and quite different understandings of this ancient image, even within the same tradition. Influenced by SAMKHYA concepts, some say that the PURUSHA (the transcendent divine) with the cooperation of PRAKRITI (nature) made the cosmic egg from which the world emerges. In one context BRAHMA, the creator, emerged from the egg to create the universe. In other contexts, however, Brahma is himself the *hiranyagarbha;* the word can be used as an epithet or alternate name of Brahma.

In Shaivite (*see* SHAIVISM) contexts *hiranyagarbha* is seen as a creation of SHIVA that embodies aspects of him. From *hiranyagarbha,* in turn, Brahma or the universe can emerge. In Vaishnavite (*see* VAISHNAVISM) mythology, VISHNU inspires or creates the *hiranyagarbha,* from which the universe derives. In the VEDANTA of SHANKARA

the term takes on various meanings depending on the lineage and tradition expounding upon it. In this tradition it is often associated with a state of consciousness rather than an entity per se. For example, in Shankara's own commentaries *hiranyagarbha* is considered synonymous with the manifest universe, which is the product of MAYA.

Further reading: Cornelia Dimitt and J. A. van Buitenen, eds., and trans., *Classical Hindu Mythology: A Reader in the Sanskrit Puranas* (Philadelphia: Temple University Press, 1978); O'Flaherty, Wendy Doniger, *Rig Veda* (London: Penguin Books, 1981).

Hiranyakashipu

Hiranyakashipu means "he who wears a golden robe" and is the name of an arrogant *asura,* or demon king, who ruled over and tormented all the worlds. Unfortunately, he had earned boons from the gods so that he could not be killed by man or beast, by day or night, indoors or outdoors. He had become so powerful through boons that he had usurped the sovereignty of Indra, the king of the gods. VISHNU was called to take on an incarnation to deal with this cruel, ignorant tyrant.

According to the myth Hiranyakashipu felt disgraced that his son, PRAHLADA, loved and worshipped Vishnu. He tried to force his son to reveal Vishnu's whereabouts. Knowing that VISHNU was everywhere, Prahlada pointed to a pillar. The demon king brashly kicked the pillar and out sprang the man-lion or (Narasimha) incarnation of Vishnu (see NARASIMHA AVATAR), who ripped him apart. He was able to be killed here because the pillar was in the doorway (neither indoors nor outdoors), it was twilight (neither day nor night), and in the Narasimha form, Vishnu was neither man nor beast.

Further reading: Cornelia Dimmitt and J. A. B. van Buitenen, eds. and trans., *Classical Hindu Mythology: A Reader in the Sanskrit Puranas* (Philadelphia: Temple

University Press, 1978); W. J. Wilkins, *Hindu Mythology, Vedic and Puranic* (Calcutta: Rupa, 1973).

Hiranyaksha

Hiranyaksha (lit. he with golden eyes) was a demon in the story of VISHNU'S VARAHA AVATAR (incarnation in the form of a boar). Hiranyaksha had in a previous life been doorkeeper at Vishnu's palace in heaven. Because he had refused admission to many sages, they cursed him, and he was reborn as the son of Diti, the mother of the ASURAS or antigods. His father was the RISHI Kashyapa and his brother was the demon HIRANYAKASHIPU, who was killed by Vishnu in the incarnation as man-lion or NARASIMHA AVATAR.

When the Earth was at the bottom of the sea in ancient times, Vishnu took the form of an enormous boar to lift it up to the surface of the waters with his tusk. As Vishnu rose to the surface Hiranyaksha tried to take the Earth away from him so he could rule over it; as was his brother, he was killed by Vishnu.

Further reading: J. A. Dowson, *A Classical Dictionary of Hindu Mythology,* 7th ed. (London: Trubner, 2003); W. J. Wilkins, *Hindu Mythology: Vedic and Puranic,* 2d ed. (Calcutta: Rupa, 1973).

Hittleman, Richard (d. 1991) *pioneer hatha yoga instructor*

Richard Hittleman was an American writer and teacher who popularized YOGA to a mass audience starting in the late 1950s.

Hittleman was born in New York City and raised in the city's Jewish community. He initially encountered yoga through a Hindu maintenance man who worked for his parents. He sought out additional teachers and during the 1940s developed his own system of HATHA YOGA, which he began to market as "Yoga for Health." In 1957 he opened the American Academy of Yoga in Coral Gables, Florida, but within a few years he relocated to California. In 1961 he initiated the first yoga television show. Through the show and more than a dozen books, he introduced the practice of yoga ASANAS (postures) to a huge audience. Over the next decades he would sell more than 8 million books.

In 1964, in his small volume *Yoga Philosophy and Meditation,* he noted that many who had been attracted to yoga as exercise had also requested to know more about the teachings from which the practice arose. The request led to his writing several additional books on yoga philosophy and meditation, including *Guide to Yoga Meditation* (1969) and *Yoga: The 8 Steps to Health and Peace* (1976). These volumes, never as successful as his hatha yoga texts, exemplified ways hatha yoga could be used as an introductory tool to Hindu life and thought.

In 1977, Hittleman established the Yoga Universal Church, based in Rapid City, South Dakota. He had accepted ordination and chartered his church through the Universal Life Church in Modesto, California, the famous mail-order denomination set up by Kirby Hensley. Hittleman closed the Yoga Universal in the early 1980s. He subsequently formed a new organization, Yoga Universal, in 1982, not connected with the Universal Life Church. Yoga Universal continues to offer yoga-based events through Hittleman's associates John Roddy and Mary Conley.

Hittleman remained active into the 1980s. He died in 1991. His last years were spent fighting the Internal Revenue Service about back taxes. He died before the matter was settled, and the tax bill remains in litigation with his estate.

Further reading: Richard Hittleman, *Guide to Yoga Meditation* (New York: Bantam Books, 1969); ———, *Yoga: the 8 steps to Health and Peace* (New York: Bantam Books, 1976); *Richard Hittleman's Guide for the Seeker* (New York: Bantam Books, 1978); ———, *Richard Hittleman's 30 Day Yoga Meditation Plan* (New York: Bantam Books, 1978); ———, *Yoga for Total Fitness* (New York: Bantam Books, 1982); Ami Chen Mills, "Death and Taxes," Available online. http://www.metroactive.com/papers/metro/11.22.95/yogi-9547.html. Accessed August 16, 2005.

Holi

The Holi festival takes place on full Moon day in the Indian month of Phalguna (February–March) in most North Indian areas. It is very ancient, probably celebrated (with the name *Holika*) before the Common Era began.

One early form of the celebration was a rite for married women to celebrate the happiness and well-being of their families. In some areas today, the rite acquires sexual and erotic elements that may point to an origin in spring fertility rites. Sexually explicit songs may be sung and men may brandish penis-shaped objects. One of the names for the Holi festival is *Kamamahotsava* or the celebration for the God of Love.

The most popular feature of the Holi festival is the throwing or shooting of colored water on everyone. Celebrants wear white garb so that all the varied colors are visible. In villages it was not uncommon in years past for men to imbibe large quantities of *bhang,* a potent marijuana drink.

Three stories are told to explain the festival. In the first it is said that Holi is the day that SHIVA opened his third eye and turned the god of love into ashes. In another story Holika, the sister of the demon HIRANYAKASIPU, took PRAHLADA on her lap to kill him that day, but the devotee of VISHNU survived unharmed. Finally it is said that there was an ogress Dhundhi who troubled children in an ancient kingdom, until the shouts of the mischievous boys of the town (something heard often on the festival of Holi) made her run away, since she was, through a curse, made vulnerable to the taunts of children.

Further reading: Meenal Pandya, *Here Comes Holi: The Festival of Colors* (Wellesley, Mass.: MeeRa, 2003); H. V. Shekar, *Festivals of India: Significance of the Celebrations* (Louisville, Ky.: Insight Books, 2000).

Holm Community   *See* LOZOWICK, LEE.

Holy Shankaracharya Order (est. 1974)

The Holy Shankaracharya Order was founded in 1974 by Swami Lakshmy Devyashram (d. 1981), a disciple of Swami SHIVANANDA SARASWATI (1887–1963). Swami Lakshmy had started on a spiritual path alone when she met the late Shivananda, who taught her the techniques to enter *samadhi* (the highest state of mystical consciousness). The meeting occurred in a vision, which convinced her that she should travel to the Poconos and continue under his tutelage there. In 1969, she took the vows of the renounced life and was ordained by Swami Swanandashram into the Holy Order of Sannyasa, the same spiritual order in which Shivananda had been ordained.

In the early 1970s, Swami Lakshmy established contact with the ancient SHANKARACHARYA ORDER headquarters at its monastic complex in Sringiri, India. In 1974 she was selected Mahamandaleshwari or great overlord of the Holy Shankaracharya Order in the United States. By this time a small group of Indian Americans had begun to attend services at the temple's property in rural Pennsylvania. Having purchased property in Virginia, she began building a second ashram-temple there, completed in 1977. In 1978, Jagadguru Shankacharya Abhinava Vidyateertha Maharaj traveled from his seat at the Shankaracharya Order at Sringiri to visit and satisfy himself of the accomplishments of the American Shankacharya Order. Subsequently, additional Indian families began to accept the leadership provided by Swami Lakshmy.

Responding to a request by the order in Sringiri, Swami Lakshmy established a *shakti peetam* (monastery), called Sri Rajarajeshwari Peetam. As Swami Lakshmy attracted students to her teachings the ashram grew, and new instructors and teachers were ordained. They serve the order as guides for the different activities and programs developed to serve others. In 1978 a Hindu Heritage Summer Camp program was initiated. The success of this undertaking further convinced Indian Hindus that although an American, Swami Lakshmy could lead. Her leadership has also paved the way for more women to become accepted as leaders in other spiritual camps.

In 1981, Swami Saraswati Devyashram, a disciple of Lakshmy, was ordained as her successor. She assumed authority shortly before Swami Lakhsmy died. A trailblazer herself, she, much as Swami Lakshmy had, maintained and enriched the outreach program. Swami Saraswati is responsible for a new center in Tucson, Arizona. During 1982, a winter heritage camp was established there.

In 1988, Saraswati Devyashram retired and passed her lineage to Swami Parvati Devyashram. In early 1991, she moved the Holy Order from Pennsylvania to Rush, New York (near Rochester). It continues as a small organization of primarily Indian American Hindus.

Further reading: Andrew Rawlinson, *The Book of Enlightened Masters: Western Teachers in Eastern Traditions* (La Salle, Ill.: Open Court Press, 1997).

horse sacrifice

The (horse sacrifice) *ashva medha* was one of the most important and elaborate royal rituals in ancient India. The exact requirements for its performance are detailed in the 13th chapter of the SHATAPATHA BRAHMANA. The sacrifice could be performed for various purposes, but it was usually a means to demonstrate the king's power.

The chosen horse would be left to run loose for one year. The horse would be followed by a large contingent of the king's army, which would be charged to subdue whatever land the horse entered. At the end of the year, the horse would be sacrificed at a large festival.

The BRIHADARARANYAKA UPANISHAD within the Shatapatha Brahmana begins with a meditation upon the sacrificed horse as the universal reality and dwells upon the esoteric interpretation of this sacrifice. This sacrifice was performed by many kings throughout Indian history, probably for the last time in the 18th century.

Further reading: Julius Eggeling, trans. *The Satapatha Brahmana, According to the Text of the Madhyamdina School* (Delhi: Motilal Banarsidass, 1972); Steven Fuchs, *The Vedic Horse Sacrifice in Its Cultural-Historical Relations* (New Delhi: Inter-India, 1996); J. C. Heesterman, *The Inner Conflict of Tradition: Essays in Indian Ritual Kingship and Society* (Chicago: University of Chicago Press, 1985.); Wendy Doniger O'Flaherty, *Sexual Metaphors and Animal Symbols in Indian Mythology* (Delhi: Motilal Banarsidass, 1981).

I

icons

The worship of images of divinities is probably very ancient among the original inhabitants of the Indian subcontinent. In the VEDAS of the ARYANS there is no mention of image worship, and it seems unquestionable that the image worship of later Hinduism is a Brahminization or Vedicization of a common indigenous practice.

In India, icons are made from special materials—specially selected and shaped stone, metal, or wood. Icons are installed in temples or other locations with special rituals. First, the icon is consecrated and brought to life. Usually, this involves the transfer of the power of the divinity from a container, a clay pot with water and a palm frond in it, through a string that is tied to the icon. MANTRAS are used to empower the icon or bring the divinity to life within it.

Bare stone is not by itself an icon; only when the deity has been implanted within it does the image gain potency. Once the life breath (PRANA) has been established in the iconic deity, its eyes are painted in or finally formed; this prepares the icon for DARSHAN, the meeting of its eyes with those of its worshippers. An anthropomorphic icon is treated in its context as a royal human being—awakened early in the morning, sung to, bathed, clothed, fed, fanned, and entertained. Such activity is carried out throughout the day until the deity is put to bed. Icons that do not have a basically human form, such as the SHIVA LINGAM, are usually treated the same way, as though the god where present in them.

When a temple or icon is decommissioned, another careful ritual must be performed to remove the life from the image, lest it become angry at not being treated properly.

Further reading: Jitendra Nath Banerjea, *The Development of Hindu Iconography* (New Delhi: Munshiram Manoharlal, 1985); T. G. Gopinatha Rao, *Elements of Hindu Iconography,* 4 vols. (Delhi: Motilal Banarsidass, 1997); Eva Rudy Jansen, *The Hindu Book of Imagery: The Gods and Their Symbols.* (Holland: Binkey Kok, 1995); Margaret Stutley, *An Illustrated Dictionary of Hindu Iconography* (Boston: Routledge & Kegan Paul, 1985).

ida   See NADI.

Ilankovatikal (c. second century C.E.)

Ilankovatikal (Venerable ascetic prince) was the author of the Tamil Jain classic Silappatikaram (*see* JAINISM), written around the second century C.E. and considered one of the five great ancient Tamil epics.

Tamil tradition says that the author was the younger brother of the well-known Cheral (Kerala) king Senguttavan. By his name he would seem to have been a Jain monk. There is no reliable historical account of the author's life.

In the poem, he indicates that he had renounced the world upon hearing that he and not his elder brother would succeed the great king Imayavarampan Netuncharalathan (169–78 C.E.) He left the palace and joined a Jain monastery on the outskirts of Vanci.

Further reading: Parthasarathy, trans., *The Cilappatikaram of Ilanko Atikal: An Epic of South India* (New York: Columbia University Press, 1993).

Indian calendar   *See* TIME IN HINDU TRADITION.

Indo-American Yoga-Vedanta Society
(est. 1971)
The Indo-American Yoga-Vedanta Society was founded in 1971 when His Holiness Sri Swami Satchidananda Buaji (b. 1890) settled in the United States. The swami had been visiting and teaching in North America and Europe since 1948.

Satchidananda was born with a crippling birth defect, for which there was no medical treatment at the time. His parents were told he would not survive to adulthood. However, they allowed their son to be raised by a teacher and yogi, Swami Maharaj. Maharaj treated him with herbal remedies while teaching him HATHA YOGA in incremental stages to straighten out his disfigurement. Buaji began to heal. By the time he was a young man he had been successfully cured of his disability and was also a master of YOGA. He dedicated his life for a number of years to the Divine Life Society founded by Swami SHIVANANDA SARASWATI.

When he began to travel he allowed himself to be the subject of scientific studies researching how the body functions. He revealed considerable prowess in masterful demonstrations of yoga for the public. As an elderly man he settled in the United States and founded the Indo-American Yoga-Vedanta Society, headquartered in New York. Well over 100 years old, Swami Bua continued actively teaching as of 2005.

Further reading: Bhakta Wallace, "The Mysterious Story of Swami Bua (Buaji)," *VNN Vaishnava News,* January 25, 2002. Available online. URL: http://www.vnn.org/editorials/ET0201/ET25-7120.html. Accessed August 30, 2005.

Indonesia
For approximately 1,500 years the chain of islands today known as Indonesia were a part of what was known in the subcontinent as Farther India. Indian merchants began trading Indonesian spices with the West during the days of the Roman Empire. Indian-style royal courts were established on several of the Indonesian islands, with major courts in Java and Sumatra. Hinduism developed (and declined) differently on the islands of Borneo, BALI, Java, and Sumatra.

As early as the fourth century C.E., both Borneo and Sarawak were centers of both Buddhist and Hindu worship, as evidenced by statues from this period created in the Tamil style. Unlike Java and Sumatra, Borneo never developed a significant dynasty, and most of the surviving cultures there have until recently retained their indigenous forms. Hinduism can be found only among the few Indians who live there.

During the 14th century the Majapahit dynasty of Java occupied land outside its borders and extended the scope of Hindu influence to a southern portion of Borneo. On other islands, indigenous populations remained virtually untouched. Papua-New Guinea/Irianjaya and the Philippines were untouched by the Indianization of Indonesia. True Brahminic Hinduism was to be found only among the aristocracy of Java, Sumatra, and Borneo. The common people either retained their indigenous folk religions or blended them with Hindu features. The result was a form of Hinduism quite different from that in India.

The arrival of Islam caused the Hindu states to collapse. The royal courts of Java fled to Bali, leaving Bali as the only remaining Hindu state, even though pockets of Hindu belief and practice can still be found on Java and Sumatra.

After the collapse of Hindu states, Javanese Hinduism survived without a Brahminic tradition and became an amalgam of older indigenous religions, Shaivite Hinduism (*see* SHAIVISM), and Mahayana Buddhism. The result is a type of Hinduism that is similar in some ways to the folk religion found in Bali. However, Hinduism in Java has lacked a royal court and a Brahmin caste for centuries and has become primarily a folk religion in Hindu guise. All priests are laymen and not Brahmin.

Javanese Hinduism includes ancestor worship and belief in nature spirits, both malevolent and benevolent. The latter are often associated with ancestors and tend to be the ancestor spirits of each immediate family. Shiva is associated with the god of the Bromo volcano. The various gods are not seen to dwell in the temples, but rather on the mountains; the gods are ritually called out of the mountains into the temples.

Popular culture in Indonesia often includes puppet plays enacting scenes from the RAMAYANA and the MAHABHARATA. Recently a resurgence of Hinduism has appeared throughout Indonesia, resulting in the Pasek movement, the SATYA SAI BABA movement, and the Forum Hindu Dharma Indonesia. These new movements are more consistent with forms of Hinduism found in India, including several types of yoga; the older traditions with their emphasis on ancestor worship are considered backward by many.

Further reading: George Coedes, *The Indianized States of Southeast Asia.* Edited by Walter F. Vella, (Honolulu: East-West Center Press, 1968); Clifford Geertz, *The Religion of Java* (New York: Free Press, 1960); Robert W. Hefner, *Hindu Javanese* (Princeton N.J.: Princeton University Press, 1985).

Indra

Indra is the king of the gods in the VEDIC pantheon. He is a symbol of strength and has the character of a warrior. He is associated with the thunderstorm and is said to hold a lightning bolt in his hand. Many early Vedic hymns tell of his battle with the snake demon, Vritra, in the course of which Indra splits a mountain to release the terrestrial waters that Vritra has held back. Indra also fights a demon named Vala in order to release the "cows of the dawn," perhaps indicating that he was the creator of daylight.

Indra's enemies are the Dasas and Dasyus; these have often been taken to refer to the indigenous tribes of India, but the context is not at all clear. At times the terms can best be translated as "enemy," and at times they are seen to be mythological beings. In the Vedas Indra is also known as a great drinker of Soma, an intoxicant used in the Vedic ritual. SOMA itself is seen as a god.

Indra is frequently invoked ritually in Vedic ritual. There are more hymns to him in RIG VEDA than to any other god. Sometimes he is invoked along with AGNI (the god of fire), probably linking the main divinity of the heavens, Indra, with a primary terrestrial deity, Agni, who is also the messenger of the gods.

The Vedic tradition often mentions Indra's wife, Indrani. Post-Vedic mythology gives Indra the white elephant AIRAVATA as a mount to ride. Eventually Indra loses his supremacy and begins to be challenged and even ridiculed. KRISHNA protects his village from Indra by holding a mountain up as an umbrella to keep away his rains. Indra is cursed for consorting with a sage's wife (AHALYA) and is afflicted, in one version of the story, with 1,000 vaginas, which are then changed into 1,000 eyes to justify his common Vedic epithet "thousand-eyed one."

Further reading: Jan Gonda, trans., *The Indra Hymns of the Rig Veda* (Leiden: E. J. Brill, 1990); Alfred Hillebrandt, *Vedic Mythology*. Translated from the German by Sreeramula Rajeswara Sarma, Vol. I (Delhi: Motilal Banarsidass, 1990); W. J. Wilkins, *Hindu Mythology, Vedic and Puranic*. 2d ed. (Bombay: Rupa, 1973).

Indus

The Indus River is the longest river in Pakistan. It flows south from its sources in the HIMALAYAS. Its original Sanskrit name was *Sindhu.* This river became *Indos* in Greek and eventually gave its name to the country of India. The ancient Persians pronounced the name as *Hindu,* so that the people living there came to be called Hindus. The Indus was one of the two largest rivers mentioned in the VEDAS; it was included in the ancient list of the "seven rivers" praised by the Vedic sages.

It was along the Indus River in 1924 that Sir John Marshall, director general of the British Archaeological Survey, unearthed a previously unknown culture, which was dubbed the INDUS VALLEY CIVILIZATION. Later work by Sir R. E. Mortimer Wheeler at Harappa and others at Mohenjo-Daro showed it to be an extensive and elaborate city-centered culture dating from as far back as 3600 B.C.E.

Further reading: Shane Mountjoy, *The Indus River* (Philadelphia: Chelsea House, 2005).

Indus Valley civilization

The Indus Valley civilization (c. 3600 B.C.E. to 1900 B.C.E.) was one of the largest civilization complexes in the ancient world. Excavations at the primary sites of Mohenjo-Daro and Harappa show that the civilization stretched at least from the lower to the middle reaches of the Indus River, now almost entirely in Pakistan. First excavated

by Sir Mortimer Wheeler in 1921, the remains show a highly developed city culture with granaries, bath houses, city planning, sculpture, and a form of writing.

Most important for the history of Hinduism, there are elements that foreshadow later developments in the religion. Several artifacts seem to indicate goddess-oriented worship. These godlike forms, interestingly, closely resemble those excavated in Neolithic Europe.

Among the Indus Valley artifacts are numerous seals, possibly used for commercial purposes, which depict animals, humans, and possibly gods and goddesses. One of these seals seems to show a female divinity being worshipped in a tree, resembling very much the later worship of YAKSHAS, or tree beings.

One artifact that has garnered a lot of attention is a depiction of a seated figure with an erect penis and a buffalo style headdress. This figure has been called Proto-SHIVA and linked to the later concept of Shiva as Pashupati or lord of the animals.

The relationship between the Indus Valley remains, later VEDIC culture, and the ARYANS has been the subject of much controversy. Most modern Western scholarship dates the Rig Veda, India's oldest extant text, to around 1500 B.C.E., comfortably after the fall of the Indus Valley civilization. Some, particularly in India, however, seek to find in the Indus Valley the earliest Aryan and Vedic culture.

Two facts complicate this claim of a Vedic Indus Valley civilization. First, the Rig Veda barely mentions city life. Most Vedic hymns dwell on horses and herds of cows; none of them even mentions a large building, let alone any feature that might be associated with advanced city life. More importantly, the Vedas frequently mention large horses pulling men in chariots. Archaeological research indicates that large horses are not indigenous to India, but are of Middle Eastern genetic stock. Large horse remains have been found in the northern Punjab, where the Vedic people are believed to have lived, but not a single verifiable find has been made at any Indus Valley site—only remains of the smaller native Indian horse.

Undoubtedly, certain Hindu traditions may trace back to the Indus Valley civilization. Recent research has shown that elements of Indus Valley culture survived and spread in western and central India several centuries after 1900 B.C.E., previously believed to be the end date for the civilization. Additional research will probably find more examples of continuities in Indian traditions, particularly ceramic and pottery traditions. Cities did not emerge again in India until 800 B.C.E., so there is no reason to believe that the historical cities owed their existence to this early civilization.

Further reading: Bridget and Raymond Allchin, *The Rise of Civilization in India and Pakistan* (Cambridge and New York: Cambridge University Press, 1982); B. B. Lal, *The Earliest Civilization of South Asia: Rise, Maturity, and Decline* (New Delhi: Aryan Books International, 1997); Gregory L. Possehl, *The Indus Civilization: A Contemporary Perspective* (Walnut Creek, Calif.: AltaMira Press, 2002).

Integral Yoga   *See* AUROBINDO, SRI.

Integral Yoga Institutes   *See* SATCHIDANANDA, SWAMI.

Intercosmic Center of Spiritual Awareness   *See* MISHRA, RAMAMURTI.

Intergalactic Culture Foundation (est. 1981)

The Intergalactic Cultural Foundation was founded in Los Angeles in 1981 by Sri Swami Shyam Paramahansa Mahaprabho, an Indian guru with a mission to the United States. The foundation was initially known as the Lovetrance Civili-

zation Center, but the name was changed in 1986 to reflect the institute's new focus. Four sections were created to advise students along specific paths of spiritual aspiration, defined by personal proclivities and strengths: the path of the heart, the path of intellect, the path of action, and the path of reflection.

The foundation has published prolifically. Its periodicals include *Hindu Digest, Golden India,* and *Enlightenment Connoisseurs Newsletter.* Their publications catalog includes over 100 books, as well as correspondence courses, videos, and audio cassettes. Sri Swami Shyam has made speaking and teaching tours across the United States and has created the International Galactic Chronicles lecture series. By 2002, Swami Shyam had produced 2,000 pages of his own commentary on the Srimad Bhagavatam and 1,500 pages of his viewpoints on Yoga Vasistha, Viveka Chudamani, and the UPANISHADS, and 70 audio discourses on the *Bhagavat Katha.*

The headquarters of the foundation in the United States is in San Pedro, California. International headquarters is in Rishikesh, India. A number of electronic books are free.

Further reading: Swami Prem, *Galactic Chronicles Lecture Program* (Harbor City, Calif.: Aum Namo Bhagavate Vasudevay, 1995); ———, *What Is ILCC?* (Hawthorne, Calif.: Intergalactic Lovetrance Civilization Center, 1983); *Swami Prem Paramahansa and His Message* (Hawthorne, Calif.: Intergalactic Lovetrance Civilization Center, 1983); *Who Is Swami Prem Paramahansa Mahaprobho?* (Hawthorne, Calif.: Intergalactic Lovetrance Civilization, n.d.).

International Babaji Kriya Yoga Sangam (est. 1951)

The International Babaji Kriya Yoga Sangam was founded in Imperial City, California, in 1951 by Yogi S. A. A. Ramaiah, who had inherited a South Indian KRIYA YOGA lineage directly from Kriya Babaji Nagaraj, the group's official GURU. BABAJI is a semimythical figure reputedly born in 203 C.E. in the seaport town of Porto Novo, Tamil Nadu, India. After a life of adventure and spiritual accomplishment, he emerged as a master of YOGA and KUNDALINI. He then spent years in retreat in the HIMALAYAS and emerged, having overcome the limitations of death. He would become known over the centuries as the immortal Babaji (the same personage introduced to the West by Paramahansa YOGANANDA in his *Autobiography of a Yogi*).

According to S. A. A. Ramaiah, in 1944 Babaji saw the need for an organization through which he could contact his devotees throughout the world. Thus, in 1951 the International Babaji Krija Yoga Sangam was established with Ramaiah as chief administrator.

Ramaiah became a model in the 1960s for those interested in yogic methods; he traveled to the United States and demonstrated in scientific tests that he had control of a variety of bodily functions. For example, he could vary his body temperature by 15 degrees in either direction from the norm of 98.6 degrees. Ramaiah founded a mission in America with monks and disciples from India. They opened their headquarters in Norwalk, California. Kriya centers, sometimes called *sadhana* centers, were established for the more highly developed forms of yoga that had a rigorous method. These were generally set up in rural locations so as to enhance the experience of contemplation and MEDITATION for attendees.

In Imperial City, California, Ramaiah founded a shrine to Ayyappa Swami, a holy figure from the PURANAS, ancient sacred Hindu stories. Since 1970, each December the disciples conduct an annual pilgrimage from the shrine to Mount Shasta in Northern California, a distance of some 500 miles.

In India the Sangam operates the KBYS Holistic Hospital and Colleges of Yoga Therapy and Physiotherapy, located in Athanor, Tamil Nadu. There are over 50 centers for the Sangam throughout the world.

Further reading: Yogi S. A. A. Ramaiah, *Shasta Ayyappa Swami Yoga Pilgrimage* (Imperial City, Calif.: Pan American Babaji Yoga sangam, n.d.)

International Foundation for Spiritual Unfoldment   *See* AMERICAN MEDITATION SOCIETY.

International Mahavir Jain Mission   *See* JAINISM.

International Meditation Institute (est. 1970s)

The International Meditation Institute in Kulu, Himachal Pradesh, India, was founded by Swami Shyam (b. 1924), an Indian teacher who taught meditation in Canada in the early 1970s. There he developed a following of enthusiastic devotees who returned with him to India. They bestowed upon him the unofficial title of SWAMI, although he is a householder, with a wife and five children.

When Shyam was a young man, he experienced an altered spiritual state that left him forever a changed person. That space of pure consciousness, which he named *Shyam Space,* was described as pure existence and pristine consciousness where one drops the mortal self, becomes detached from the mundane world, and identifies with the pure Self. This perspective is usually expressed of terms of ADVAITA (non-dual) Vedanta, a form of Hindu thought that forms the infrastructure of various yoga techniques for enlightenment.

Today, disciples of the institute live in independent group houses near the MEDITATION center, which they visit for meditation and teaching. Swami Shyam's teachings have been taken to other areas of the world. Centers now exist in Taiwan, the United States, Europe, New Zealand, Israel, and Japan. The North American headquarters is in Montreal.

Further reading: Anne Cushman and Jerry Jones, *From Here to Nirvana: The Yoga Journal Guide to Spiritual India* (New York: Riverhead Books, 1998).

International Society for Krishna Consciousness (ISKCON) (est. 1966)

The International Society for Krishna Consciousness (ISKCON) was founded in 1966 by the Krishna devotee and Vedic scholar Swami Prabhupada BHAKTIVEDANTA (1896–1977). He entered New York City at age 69 in 1965, when the U.S. quotas on immigration from Asia were abolished, and quickly attracted a following of young men and women by chanting the Hare Krishna mantra (*Hare Krishna / Hare Krishna / Krishna Krishna / Hare Hare, / Hare Rama / Hare Rama / Rama Rama / Hare Hare*).

The first ISKCON temple was established in a tiny New York storefront at 26 Second Avenue, and from here the movement spread quickly, first throughout North America, London, and Hamburg, and then all over the world. In just over a decade Bhaktivedanta Swami had established 108 Krishna temples and published 70 volumes of books, more than 100 million copies of which were distributed by his disciples, who in the late 1970s numbered in the thousands.

ISKCON's teachings are based exclusively on Bhaktivedanta Swami's translations and explanations of classical Hindu scripture, particularly the BHAGAVAD GITA and the BHAGAVATA PURANA. ISKCON sees itself theologically as representing the monotheistic central core of Hinduism. According to this position the absolute truth is a supremely powerful being, KRISHNA, and all individual souls are of the same spiritual nature as Krishna, but never equal to him. By chanting the Hare Krishna mantra, which was introduced 500 years ago by Sri Krishna CHAITANYA (1486–1533), believed to be an incarnation of Krishna, the individual soul can reawaken its dormant love for God and at the time of death return to the spiritual realm to serve Krishna eternally in full bliss and knowledge. All other Hindu deities are seen as either subservient demigods, such as DURGA, SHIVA, and BRAHMA, or direct expansions of Krishna, such as VISHNU and Narayana.

Members of ISKCON are strict lactovegetarians and offer their food to Krishna before eating. Such offered food is called *prasadam* or the Lord's mercy. Practitioners living in temple ashrams are expected to rise early for religious observances (known as *aratis*) in the temple, the first starting at 4:30 A.M. During these ceremonies devotees sing Sanskrit songs while dancing before elaborately decorated forms of Krishna and his consort, Radha. After chanting the Hare Krishna mantra on beads and worshipping a form (or *murti*) of Bhaktivedanta Swami, the morning program ends with a class based on a verse from the Bhagavat Purana. Ceremonies and observances are standardized in all temples throughout the world.

ISKCON grew rapidly in the 1970s and 1980s but has seen a recent decline in membership, attributed by some observers to the controversies surrounding the leadership succession after Bhaktivedanta's death and the creation of subsequent reform movements.

See International Society for Krishna Consciousness Revival Movement (IRM).

Further reading: Swami A. C. Bhaktivedanta Prabhupada, *Bhagavad-Gita As It Is* (New York: Bhaktivedanta Trust, 1972); ———, *KRSNA, The Supreme Personality of Godhead,* 3 vols. (New York: Bhaktivedanta Trust, 1970); ———, *The Science of Self-Realization* (New York: Bhaktivedanta Trust, 1977); Steven J. Gelberg, ed., *Hare Krishna, Hare Krishna* (New York: Grove Press, 1983); J. Stillson Judah, *Hare Krishna and the Counterculture* (New York: Wiley, 1974).

International Society for Krishna Consciousness Revival Movement (IRM) (est. 2000)

The ISKCON Revival Movement (IRM) was formed in 2000 as a pressure group to revive and reform ISKCON on the basis of an interpretation of the directives for succession given by Swami Prabhupada BHAKTIVEDANTA (1896–1977), the founder of ISKCON.

According to IRM, the founder revealed, in a philosophical treatise called "The Final Order" issued on July 9, 1977, a signed directive appointing 11 of his senior managers to act as *ritviks* (officiating priests) to initiate new recruits into the ISKCON movement on his behalf. According to IRM, all future disciples within ISKCON were supposed to revere Bhaktivedanta Swami as their GURU, not any successor. However, shortly after Bhaktivedanta Swami's demise on November 14, 1977, these *ritviks* ignored the directive; instead, they divided the world into 11 zones, each claiming to be the guru or spiritual successor in a different area. By early 1978 the 11 *ritviks* had begun to initiate disciples on their own behalf, acting as gurus for the movement.

Over time, a number of the gurus suffered lawsuits, suicide, and other problems. The movement was plunged into confusion and acrimony. By the mid-1980s the Governing Body Commission (GBC), which managed ISKCON, issued a new interpretation of Bhaktivedanta Swami's directive. What he had really wanted, it said, was for all disciples to become initiating gurus, not just the 11 *ritviks*. Today new gurus are added to the roster via a majority vote by the GBC at its annual meetings in Mayapur. Currently ISKCON gurus number around 80.

IRM contends that both the zonal guru system and its replacement multiple-guru system are unauthorized innovations. Citing GBC resolutions and management directives approved by Bhaktivedanta Swami, the IRM insists that ISKCON will continue to flounder as long as it fails to comply with the orders of Bhaktivedanta Swami Prabhupada.

The IRM has grown quickly in the few years of its existence, claiming members and temples on every continent, including the ISKCON temple in Bangalore, the largest ISKCON temple in the world. It publishes an international magazine, *Back to Prabhupada,* and an electronic newsletter. They have also met with considerable opposition from those supporting the current multiple-guru system in ISKCON.

The IRM's followers consist of both current and former ISKCON members, ISKCON Life Members, and members of the Hindu community at large. The IRM's ultimate goal is to rebuild an ISKCON movement operating just as Bhaktivedanta Swami intended, with him as the sole guru and authority.

Further reading: Swami A. C. Bhaktivedanta Prabhupada, *Bhagavad-Gita As It Is* (New York: Bhaktivedanta Trust, 1972); Krishnakant Desai, *The Final Order* (London: Printed privately, 1996; Bangalore: International Society for Krishna Consciousness, 2001).

International Society of Divine Love
(est. 1975)

Swami H. D. Prakashanand Saraswati (b. 1929) was born into a BRAHMIN family in AYODHYA, India. His early life was fraught with intense religious feelings, and as a youth he became a reclusive mystic so that he might find God in the silence. He took the vows of SANNYAS (renunciation) at age 20 from his guru, Jagadguru Krupalu Swami of Pratapgarh. He spent the next 20 years as a wandering mendicant in the Himalayas and in the forests of central India, ending in Braj, the reputed earthly home of Lord KRISHNA. In 1975, emerging from his solitary life, he established the International Society of Divine Love. Later on he traveled to America and founded a home for devotees and disciples. By 1981 Swami Prakashanand, who had begun to be thought of as a distinguished sage and a saint, conceived of creating a global mission movement.

Swami Prakashanand is of the lineage of the great Vaishnavite sage of West Bengal Sri Krishna CHAITANYA (1485–1553). Followers of VAISHNAVISM, as well as other schools of Hinduism, understand that a great GURU can teach disciples even after the guru is no longer in a physical body. Communication between the visible and invisible is taken for granted and is an essential factor in many types of Hindu devotion. Chaitanya is assumed to be in charge of his lineage even today.

Devotees of the society believe Krishna to be the ultimate and highest God. Krishna is written about in the Mahabharata and, especially, in the BHAGAVAD GITA. According to the Gita, Krishna has the divine ability to disguise himself and give teaching and counsel while appearing to be someone else. His teaching to ARJUNA in the Gita has become one of the sacred texts of the path of BHAKTI YOGA, which emphasizes his loving activity; dedication to Krishna is considered a devotional pathway to enlightenment. This devotional approach is expressed in Prakashanand's writings based on the Vedas, Upanishads, and Bhagavata Purana. Among the significant practices of this approach is chanting the name of God while offering oneself to Krishna as a devotee.

The society has members in India, England, Ireland, Singapore, New Zealand, and Australia. During the 1990s the Society of Divine Love constructed its main Western temple and ashram complex in Austin, Texas, which was dedicated on October 8, 1995.

Further reading: *The Deity Establishment of Shree Rasehwari Radha Rani of Barsana Dham,* October 7–8 (Austin Tex.: International Society of Divine Love, 1995); H. D. Prakashanand Saraswati, *The Path to God* (Austin Tex.: International Society of Divine Love, 1995); ———, *The Philosophy of Divine Love* (Auckland, New Zealand: International Society of Divine Love, 1982); ———, The *Shikchashtek* (Philadelphia: International Society of Divine Love, 1986).

International Yoga Federation (est. 1965)

The International Yoga Federation is a loose confederation of YOGIS and YOGA associations; it is administered by the World Yoga Council, founded in 1965 by Mahavatar Kirsha Kisore Das at Bengal, India. The council is composed of grand yoga masters for each continent: Asia, America, Africa, Europe, and Oceania. The presidency rotates across continental representatives. In 2005, the executive office was located in Buenos Aires, Argentina. After 2006, the executive work rotates to Europe.

International Yoga Fellowship (est. 1980s)

The International Yoga Fellowship has grown out of the work of Swami Satyananda Saraswati (b. 1923), a former disciple of Swami Shivananda Saraswati (1887–1963).

Satyananda took the vows of the renounced life (*sannyas*) in 1943 and subsequently spent 12 years at Shivananda's Divine Life Society based in Rishikish, India. He then spent nine years wandering India in pursuit of divinity. In 1964, the year after Shivananda's death, Satyananda founded the Bihar School of Yoga, and to honor his guru and his teachings, established the Shivananda Ashram on the shores of the GANGES. Here, Satyananda continued to pursue his guru's ideas that everyone should have access to YOGA and spirituality, despite caste, marital status, or other challenges. He also explored the possibilities of a tantric path to God (*see* TANTRISM).

As did his guru, Satyananda believed in outreach programs to share their teachings. His missionary focus took him far and wide, first throughout India, then to other destinations. During the 1970s, he founded 10 ashrams in India. However, his more significant missionary activity occurred outside India. The development of the ashrams abroad had begun after his 1968 world tour to disseminate his teachings. Leaving India he encouraged missionary activity in Ireland, England, Greece, France, Sweden, Colombia, Australia, and Indonesia. Encouraged by the response, he founded the International Yoga Fellowship.

Satyananda's work entered the United States prior to his world tour. First, Llewellyn Publications in St. Paul, Minnesota, published a major work by Swami Anandakapila (aka John Mumford), who had been a major supporter and student of Satyananda in Australia. The publication of *Sexual Occultism* became the springboard of Mumford's 1976 tour to teach tantra and promote its study. Not long afterward, a New York publisher released *Yoga, Tantra and Meditation* by Janakananda Saraswati, a teacher of Satyananda's work in Scandinavia.

Meanwhile, in 1965, students and disciples of Satyananda began to migrate to the United States, taking their teachings with them from India. The new immigrants formed small gatherings. In the 1980s, Swami Niranjannan Saraswati (b. 1960) began to organize ASHRAMS for the International Yoga Fellowship in the United States. On October 28, 1980, he formed Satyanandan Ashrams USA as an affiliate of the mother organization in India. Niranjananda stayed in America to help build the work. In the summer of 1982, the American group was visited by Swami Amritananda, a major female leader in the fellowship. Her trip was followed not long afterward by Satyananda's first tour of North America.

By the time of Satyananda's American tour, he had long since developed his idea to include a complete system of tantric yoga, which begins with awakening of the KUNDALINI energy and includes sexual intercourse as a means of blending the male and female energies. Bliss is the ultimate reward for successful disciples of the so-called left-hand path.

The International Yoga Fellowship is reported to be one of the largest organizations teaching yoga. It is not always easy to find practitioners in the West, as most members live quietly in ethnic communities, but there may be tens of thousands of people affiliated in North America. International headquarters remain at the Bihar School of Yoga in Bihar, India, where the fellowship's journal, *Yoga*, is published.

Further reading: John Mumford, (Swami Anandakapila), *Sexual Occultism* (St. Paul, Minn.: Llewellyn, 1975); Swami Janakananda Saraswati, *Yoga, Tantra and Meditation* (New York: Ballantine Books, 1975); Swami Satyananda Saraswati, *Sure Ways to Self-Realization* (Mungyar: Bihar School of Yoga, 1982); ———, *Teachings of Swami Satyananda Saraswati* (Mungyar, Bihar: Bihar School of Yoga, 1981).

Isha Upanishad

The Isha Upanishad appears in the White Yajur VEDA; it constitutes the Veda's last chapter (unlike most Upanishads, which are found within the BRAHMANAS of the Veda). *Isha* literally means "lord" or "ruler," and the Upanishad clearly has theistic overtones. It is a short Upanishad of only 18 stanzas.

The Isha opens with a stanza describing the world as "indwelt by the Lord" (*ishavasya*). Stanza 5, frequently quoted, describes the BRAHMAN or ultimate reality: "It moves. It moves not. It is far and it is near. It is within all this; it is outside all this." This attempts to show the incomprehensible infinitude of the ultimate. Also quoted often is verse 11, which states that the path of ritual and the path of knowledge of *brahman* are complementary. The cryptic verses 9, 12, 13, and 14, which speak of the relationship between higher knowledge and ignorance, have been frequently explicated by the classical commentators.

Further reading: Sri Aurobindo, *Isha Upanishad* (Pondicherry: Sri Aurobindo Ashram, 1965); S. Radhakrishnan, ed. and trans., *The Principal Upanishads* (Atlantic Highlands, N.J.: Humanities Press, 1992).

Isherwood, Christopher (1904–1986)
British novelist and Western Hindu pioneer

Christopher William Bradshaw-Isherwood, a prominent Anglo-American novelist and early gay activist, was also an outspoken apologist for the VEDANTA SOCIETY and its *ADVAITA* (non-dualist) VEDANTA perspective.

Isherwood was born into a well-to-do family in Cheshire, England. He was educated at Repton School and Corpus Christi College at Cambridge, though he did not finish his degree program. In 1925 he reestablished a friendship with his fellow writer W. H. Auden, whom he had met in prep school, and, along with Stephen Spender, would constitute the so-called Auden Gang of angry young writers who made their mark on the English literary scene in the 1930s. Isherwood's initial contributions were his novels, *All the Conspirators* (1928) and *The Memorial* (1932).

In 1939 Isherwood moved to the United States and began to write for Hollywood films. At this time he became associated with the VEDANTA SOCIETY and became a disciple of Swami Prabhavananda, who headed the Los Angeles center. An emergent pacifism, fed by his experience in Germany during the 1930s, was integral to his adopting *advaita* VEDANTA as a philosophical-religious perspective. Over the next several decades, he assisted Prabhavananda in preparing translations of Hindu texts and wrote several books on Vedanta himself. His edited volume, *Vedanta for the Western World* (1945), later issued as *Vedanta for Modern Man*, was arguably his most lasting contribution. Among his later works was an autobiographical volume describing his relationship with his teacher, Prabhavananda, *My Guru and His Disciple* (1980).

Beginning in 1953, Isherwood lived with his significant other, Don Bachardy. His 1964 autobiographical novel *A Single Man* represented his public acknowledgment of his gay life. He later became involved in various gay-rights efforts. His last novel mixed his Hindu and gay experience. *A Meeting by the River* (1967) tells the story of a bisexual movie producer who tries to stop his younger brother from taking vows as a Hindu monk.

Further reading: Christopher Isherwood, *An Approach to Vedanta* (Hollywood, Calif.: Vedanta Press, 1963); ——

——, *Essentials of Vedanta* (Hollywood, Calif.: Vedanta Press 1969); ——, *My Guru and His Disciple* (New York: Farrar, Straus, Giroux, 1980); Christopher Isherwood, ed., *Vedanta for the Western World* (Hollywood, Calif.: Marcel Rodd, 1945).

ishta devata

Ishta devata (desired divinity) is an important concept in theistic Hinduism. It is understood that each person has a divinity that best fits his or her personal inclinations and way of life. Usually, the *ishta devata* will be chosen within the sectarian context—a person who has grown

A woman worships her personal divinity *(ishta devata)* at the Ganesh shrine in Belur, Bengal. *(Gustap Irani)*

up in a Shaivite family, for example, is likely to chose a Shaivite divinity, for example Subramuniya, youngest son of SHIVA, as one's personal favorite.

It is not infrequent, however, for people to choose divinities outside their sectarian context. A Bengali Vaishnavite (devotee of VISHNU) might chose KALI, the fierce goddess, as *ishta devata.* This was precisely what Sri RAMAKRISHNA did.

Further reading: Klaus Klostermeier, *Survey of Hinduism* (Albany: State University of New York Press, 1994); Thomas Hopkins, *Hindu Religious Tradition* (Encino, Calif., Dickenson, 1971).

Ishvarakrishna   *See* SAMKHYA.

Iyengar, B. K. S. (1918–   ) *yoga teacher*
Bellur Krishnamachar Sundararaja Iyengar was born on December 14, 1918, in the small village of Bellur in the Kolar District of Karnataka state in India, during the worldwide influenza pandemic. His mother had an attack of influenza while carrying and birthing Bellur. Both of them miraculously survived, but the child was left with a weak constitution, and he often suffered from malaria, typhoid, and tuberculosis.

Bellur was the 11th of 13th children, 10 of whom survived. His schoolteacher father, Sri Krishnamachar, died of untreated appendicitis when Bellur was nine years old, leaving his family in a state of poverty. His mother, Sheshamma, was known to be simple, kind-hearted, and religious in a highly orthodox way. Bellur's poor health and lack of financial resources affected his education. He struggled to stay well enough to pass exams and to collect funds to pay for his high school education.

In 1934, at age 15, he went to live with his sister in Mysore. His brother-in-law, the famous YOGI Sri T. Krishnamachar, was in need of someone to perform yoga ASANAS (postures) at the Yogashala,

the school of yoga. Bellur was initiated into the GAYATRI MANTRA and began to learn yoga practice from his brother-in-law, which slowly helped him to overcome his maladies. He began to train students at the school and soon ended his formal education in order to devote his energy to yoga instruction. He won certificates in the elementary, intermediate, and advanced diploma courses in yoga.

In 1937, Krishnamachar sent the young Bellur to Pune, India, to teach yoga. His commitment to a disciplined practice grew, as did his conviction not to publicize or beg for work or recommendations. He was devoted to living a yogic life as long as God willed.

In 1943, Iyengar married Ramamani; they had five daughters and one son. Although the 1950s continued to be financially challenging, Iyengar began to have contact with eminent personalities, such as the spiritual leader J. KRISHNAMURTI, the freedom fighter Jayaprakash Narayan, Achyut Patwardhan (commandant of the National Defense Academy), Prime Minister Nehru, and the violinist Yehudi Menuhin. Iyengar trained Menuhin in yoga, which helped him to have better control over his violin. This special friendship, begun in 1952, continued over time and gained Iyengar great respect in the West. From the 1960s onward, Iyengar traveled abroad regularly to train students and perform demonstrations.

In 1975, Iyengar opened the Ramamani Iyengar Memorial Yoga Institute (RIMYI) in Pune, named after his wife. His eldest daughter, Geeta, and son, Prashant, are actively involved in teaching yoga there.

Iyengar has based his teachings on the traditional eight limbs of yoga as presented in the YOGA SUTRAS by PATANJALI, written over 2,500 years ago. His first book, *Light on Yoga,* explains Patanjali's philosophy while introducing Iyengar's emphasis on body, mind, and spirit integration. This work, first published in 1966, has been translated into 18 languages.

Today, Iyengar is known to be one of the most influential yoga practitioners in the world.

Further reading: B. K. S. Iyengar, *Light on Life: The Yoga Journey to Wholeness, Inner Peace, and Ultimate Freedom* (Emmaus, Pa.: Rodale, 2005); ———, *Light on Yoga* (New York: Schocken Books, 1979); ———, *Yoga: The Path to Holistic Health* (London: Dorling Kindersley, 2001); B. K. S. Iyengar and 60th Birthday Celebration Committee, *Iyengar: His Life and Work* (Porthill, Idaho: Timeless Books, 1987).

J

Jagannath Temple, Puri

The Jagannath temple at Puri, in Orissa on the Bay of Bengal, is one of the most famous in India. Lord Jaggannath (Lord of the Universe) is a form of KRISHNA. Each year in the bright half of the lunar month of Ashadha (June–July) he is honored in a huge festival. The image of Jagannath is placed in a massive temple cart, 45 feet in height with 16 wheels, each seven feet high. Behind him in conveyances nearly as high are his brother, BALARAMA, and his sister, Subhadra, images constructed by youth of the area. (The English word *juggernaut* derives from the name Jagannath, as associated with these massive conveyances.)

Further reading: Anncharlott Eschmann, Hermann Kulke, and Gaya Charan Tirupathi, *The Cult of Jagannath and the Regional Tradition of Orissa* (New Delhi: Manohar, 1978); Chris Fuller, *The Camphor Flame: Popular Hinduism and Society in India* (Princeton, N.J.: Princeton University Press, 1993).

jagrat (jagarita)   See STATES OF CONSCIOUSNESS.

Jaimini (c. 200 B.C.E.) *Indian philosopher*

Jaimini is one of the great philosophers of the MIMAMSA tradition. His Mimamsa Sutras was a complete exposition of the views of one school of Mimamsa; he argued against other schools, which are no longer extant. Mimamsa is a basis for the Vedic ritualistic worldview (*see* VEDA), and the formation of the Hindu tradition in general. No biographical information about Jaimini has survived.

Further reading: S. N. Dasgupta, *History of Indian Philosophy.* Vol. 1 (Delhi: Motilal Banarsidass, 1975).

Jain festivals

True to their more austere nature and image, the festivals of the Jains (see JAINISM) are much less exuberant celebrations than those of the Hindus. Jains in fact distance themselves from the more raucous festivals of Hinduism such as HOLI. One of their religious days is devoted entirely to silence—*Maun* Ekadashi, or the eleventh of the month. This observance is celebrated in the bright part of the lunar month Margashirsha (November–December). It should be noted that there are also Hindu festivals, such as the Magha Mela at Prayag (ALLAHABAD), which are observed with vows of silence.

Both the DIGAMBARA and the SHVETAMBARA Jain communities observe the birthday of MAHAVIRA (Mahavira Jayanti). which takes place in the bright half of the month of Chaitra (March–April). Shvetambaras celebrate "Knowledge Fifth" (Jnana Panchami) on the fifth day of the bright half of Karttika (October–November), while Digambaras celebrate "Scripture Fifth" (Shrutapanchami) on the fifth day of the bright half of the month of Jyeshtha (May–June). In both these festivals books are cleaned and repaired and manuscripts are recopied.

Most important for the Jain festival cycle is the time called Chaturmas, the four months of the rainy season, when Jain monks traditionally do not travel, so as to prevent injury to water beings and other small creatures that emerge only in the monsoon. Paryushan is an eight-day observance for Shvetambaras during these four months. It is a time of fasting and concentration on purification for the lay person. One of the central events of Paryushan is the recitation of the Kalpa Sutra by monks. The final day of the festival includes a ceremony of communal confession and asking of forgiveness of creatures for the harm that may have been inflicted over the year.

The Digambara equivalent to Paryushan is called Dashalaksanaparvan, the Festival of the 10 Religious Virtues. It is conducted in the temples. The TATTVARTHA SUTRA is recited and homilies are delivered relating to the 10 virtues outlined in that text.

Divali (Dipavali) is celebrated by Jains, but the lights of the festival are intended to commemorate the final liberation of Mahavira. As among the Hindus, however, worship of LAKSHMI is performed (by laypeople only) in order to promote prosperity.

Another festival celebrated by both major sects of Jains is Akshayatritiya (Undying Third), celebrated in the bright half of Vaishakha (April–May). It is a commemoration of a gift of "undying merit" to RISHABHA, the first TIRTHANKARA in our half-era.

Further reading: John E. Cort, *Jains in the World: Religious Values and Ideology in India* (New York: Oxford

University Press, 2001); Paul Dundas, *The Jains* (London: Routledge, 1992).

Jainism

The name *Jain* derives from *jina* (victory); Jainism is thus the religion of the "victorious one"—any human being who by his or her own effort has conquered the lower passions and thus become free of attachments to things. Most Jains believe that their faith was founded by a lineage of 24 teacher/saints, the TIRTHANKARAS. The Tirthankaras have provided human beings with a means to cross the ocean of SAMSARA (the cycle of existence) by providing a vessel, namely, the DHARMA, or teachings.

Most scholars consider the 24 Tirthankaras to be mythical or at best semimythical beings. For example, one of the 24, Nemi, is said to have lived for 1,000 years. They believe that Jain history really begins with PARSHVANATHA (c. 900 B.C.E.), the son of the ruler of BENARES (Varanasi). A successful soldier and husband, at the age of 30 Parshvanatha withdrew from his elite existence to become an ascetic. As he wandered India, he gathered followers to whom he advocated four laws of life—do not take life, do not lie, do not steal, and do not own property. He built the first Jain monastery on Mount Sammeda, where he died; it is a prominent pilgrimage site for Jains.

More important for the development of Jainism was Vardhamana (c. 599–c. 527 B.C.E.), later known as MAHAVIRA, the last of the 24 Tirthankaras. Mahavira lived most of his life without clothes, the most visible symbol of the renounced life. After some 12 years as an ascetic, he managed to overcome worldly passions and become the Victor. Jains describe his state of mind as *kevala-jnana*, or perfect perception, knowledge, power, and bliss. He lived another 30 years traveling around India and attracting people to his life. A large lay community emerged to supplement the small monastic community created three centuries before by Parshvanatha. Mahavira reorganized

Jain temple in Palitana, Gujarat, a complex of white marble (*Gustap Irani*)

the Jain movement with followers assuming one of four roles: monks (*sadhu*), nuns (*sadhvi*), laymen (*shravak*), and laywomen (*shravika*).

Mahavira articulated the primary principles by which Jains live: nonviolence (AHIMSA), or the refusal to cause harm to any living things; truthfulness (*satya*), or the speaking only of harmless truth; nonstealing (*asteya*), not to take anything not properly given; chastity (brahmacharya), or refusal to indulge in sensual pleasures; nonpossession (*aparigraha*), or detachment from people, places, and material things. Monks took these as their law of life, while laypeople simply adopted a less austere existence. Several hundred years after Mahavira, the oral tradition that had until then guided the Jain community began to be written.

According to Jain tradition, Mahavira had 11 chief followers, or *ganadharas*. All these disciples are said to have achieved omniscience after 12 years of mendicancy. The last of the 11 to reach omniscience were Indrabhuti Gautama and Sudharman, who were left to lead the fledgling Jain community. It is they who probably created the various rescensions of the extant Jain canon; they also figure prominently as the chief questioners of Mahavira in the canonical dialogues.

Around 300 B.C.E, Jainism split into two basic communities, the SHVETAMBARAS (clothed) and the DIGAMBARAS (unclothed). Each subsequently divided into a number of sectarian bodies. The movement took a great leap forward in the 12th century C.E. when the ruler of Gujarat was converted and turned his realm into a Jain state. In the next century, Muslim expansion in India stopped further Jain growth, but Gujarat remains the home to the largest Jain community worldwide.

JAIN BELIEFS

Jains picture a three-story universe with humans residing in the middle level. The earthly realm is the realm of human action. Humans should be seeking the state of MOKSHA (liberation), pictured spatially as the top of the universe; there they can remain in a state of eternal bliss and peace. However, the average person goes to the lower realm at the end of earthly existence, to be punished for his or her misdeeds.

Each being has a *jiva*, or soul: humans, animals, and even some plants. This soul accumulates KARMA as dust clings to an object. Karma is considered a physical reality and can be removed only by the most concerted right conduct, which must eventually include strict asceticism. Only then can the karmic matter be scraped off the soul so that the soul may go to the top of the universe and exist in eternal effulgence forever. The three "jewels," main tenets of Jainism, are right knowledge (*samyagjnana*), right action (*samyakcaritra*), and right view (*samyagdarshana*).

One important concept for Jains is *bhavyatva*—a special quality that most souls possess that makes it possible to reach salvation through a permanent escape from the bonds of KARMA and rebirth. *Bhavyatva* is viewed as something of an inert possibility, which may or may not be triggered by the karma of the person who possesses it. The Jains, unlike most Hindus, accept the idea that some souls will never escape the round of birth and rebirth; they may lack *bhavyatva*, or they may lack the ability to activate it.

Today, a person wishing to adhere to the Jain community must profess belief in the teachings of the *jinas* and simultaneously renounce his or her attachment to any other religion. The convert then vows (1) not intentionally to take life (*ahimsa*); (2) not to lie or exaggerate (*satya*);

(3) not to steal (*achaurya*); (4) to refrain from marital unfaithfulness and unchaste thoughts (*brahmacharya*); (5) to limit accumulation of possessions and give away extras (*aparigraha*); (6) to put bounds on oneself so as to decrease the possibility of committing transgressions (*dik*); (7) to limit the number of both consumable and nonconsumable items in one's possession (*bhoga-upbhoga*); (8) to avoid unnecessary evil (*anartha-danda*); (9) to observe periods of MEDITATION (*samayik*); (10) to observe periods of self-imposed limitations (*desavakasika*); (11) to live periodically as an ascetic/monk (*pausadha*); and (12) to support the monastic community (*atithi samvibhaga*).

The vows imply that Jains will be vegetarians (most do not even consume eggs) and will refrain from vocations that include the taking of life. The more strictly observant would not, for example, take up farming, which might lead to killing of living creatures (worms, insects, etc). Jains prefer business and various intellectual activities. The monastic life is most preferred.

Jains see themselves as following a path to SELF-REALIZATION. Steps along the path include the gaining of right perceptions (*mati*), clear scriptural knowledge (*sruta*), supernatural knowledge (*avadhi*), clear knowledge of the thought of others (*manahparyaya*), and omniscience (*kevala*). Those few who attain *kevala* are considered to be perfected ones (*siddhas*). The path generally takes many lifetimes. Ultimately, the fully realized soul moves to the top of the universe to reside forever in a karma-free condition.

The many Jain temples are sites of worship and veneration of the *jinas*, which assist on the road of SELF-REALIZATION. These may be identified with the Jain symbol, a swastika above which are three dots and a half Moon. The symbol predates the German Nazi swastika by many centuries and bears no relation to it. Inside the temples one generally finds statues of one or more of the Jain saints, who in Digambara temples are usually pictured in the nude.

DIVISIONS WITHIN THE
JAIN COMMUNITY

The major division in the Jain community arose in the fifth century B.C.E. and became formalized around 300 B.C.E., when the Jain scripture was written. The division between monks who wore clothes and those who did not eventually resulted in the separation of the Digambaras from the Svetambaras.

The Digambaras teach that nudity is integral to the teachings of Mahavira; they believe that monks should be devoid of any possessions, including clothes, and should not want to protect their bodies from the elements. They depict Mahavira in complete nudity, without any ornamentation, with downcast eyes. They also teach that Mahavira never married and was celibate throughout his earthly existence.

Digambaras also teach that the words of Mahavira, reputedly contained in the 11 ANGAS of the Jain canon, were lost forever at the end of the fourth century B.C.E. That loss, they believe, caused the Jains to write the rest of their scriptures. They refuse to accept the 11 *angas* that are considered canonical by the Svetambaras, which now form part of the 41 *sutras*. Finally, the Digambaras do not allow women to join the order of the renounced life, as women are not believed to be qualified for the austerity demanded of renouncers.

In contrast, the Svetambaras teach that some of the original Tirthankaras lived as clothed persons. They emphasize that Parshvanath, the saint immediately prior to Mahavira, wore white robes. Mahavira, they note, did not become an ascetic until his parents died and he fulfilled his necessary family duties. The Svetambara believe that the words of Mahavira were not lost and may be found in the 11 surviving Angas of the Jain canon. They also believe that women can attain sainthood, noting that at least one of the Tirthankaras, Malli, was a female.

Today the Digambaras are found mostly in the southern part of India, especially in Mysore state, while the Svetambaras are primarily to be found in Gujarat and Rajasthan. Meanwhile, the modern Indian government has made various attempts to limit public nudity by the Digambara monks.

CONTEMPORARY JAIN COMMUNITIES

Today, in India, most Jains are found in business and trade. Unlike SIKHS and BUDDHISTS, they have not attempted to distinguish themselves from Hindus, and the two communities have a working relationship.

The austere Jain lifestyle tended to slow the spread of the community beyond India. Besides, many taught that travel by monks by any means other than foot was immoral. One of the earliest appearances of a Jain outside India occurred in 1893, when Virchand Gandhi made a presentation at the WORLD PARLIAMENT OF RELIGIONS in Chicago. A few other individuals, such as Champat Rai Jain, who traveled to England in the 1930s, appeared in the West through the early 20th century, but real communities did not emerge until the 1950s, when migration to England began. By the end of the century there were some 30,000 Jains in the United Kingdom, most from Gujarat, who organized the Federation of Jain Organisations in the United Kingdom.

Migration to North America followed in the 1970s, and now centers can be found throughout the eastern half of the United States plus Texas and California. These joined with Canadian centers in the Federation of Jain Associations in North America. Several Jain teachers in the United States founded organizations that attempt to spread Jain teaching among non-Indians: the International Mahavir Jain Mission is centered in New Jersey and the JAIN MEDITATION INTERNATIONAL CENTER with several branches in the United States and Canada. Jains may also be found in Australia, Singapore, Hong Kong, and Japan.

Further reading: John E. Cort, *Jains in the World: Religious Values and Ideology in India* (Oxford: Oxford University Press, 2000); ———. *Open Boundaries: Jain*

Communities and Cultures in Indian History (Albany: State University of New York Press, 1998); Paul Dundas, The Jain (New York: Routledge, 1992): Prem Suman Jain, Essentials of Jainism (Boston: Jain Center of Greater Boston, 1984); A. K. Roy, History of the Jainas (Colombia, Mo.: South Asia Books, 1984).

Jain Meditation International Center

See JAINISM

Janakananda, Swami Rajasi   See SELF-REALIZATION FELLOWSHIP.

japa   See MANTRA.

Jayadeva (late 12th–early 13th centuries)
Sanskrit poet
As with most poets, scholars, and saints in the Indian tradition, very little is verifiably known about the life of Jayadeva, the prolific Sanskrit writer best known for the devotional work GITA-GOVINDA. All that we know is gleaned from hints in the author's poetry, hints that often are subject to several interpretations. Some say that he was born in Kenduli village on the Ajaya River in the Birbhum District of West Bengal. Others say his birthplace was Kenduli village on the Praci River in the Puri District of Orissa. Other claims are made for the same village in Bihar and Maharashtra. It is evident that the poet was a Vaishnavite. Jayadeva's patron while he composed the Gitagovinda was King Lakshmanasena of Bengal (1179–1209 C.E.).

Jayadeva, as did many poets before him, became a saint for Vaishnavites. In the 17th century Nabhadas wrote a Hindi text called Bhaktamala, which retold the lives and miracles of many poet-saints, including Jayadeva. The stories are meant to inspire worship of VISHNU, while showing that the poet-saints, as ideal devotees, were themselves worthy of worship. In fact, they refer to the poet-saints as AVATARS of Vishnu, in the looser sense of the term—they are incarnations of the god for the purpose of showing all people the way to devotion.

The following is a selection from the hagiography:

1. When Jayadeva was still a child, his parents had to surrender their house to a neighbor. One day it caught fire; as soon as the boy ran inside, the fire extinguished itself.

2. It is said that Jayadeva was left as an orphan as a child. He lived in rags and survived on water alone, but he sang the praises of God wherever he went. He was said to be so ascetic that he preferred not to write poetry, but instead to perfect his soul. It is said that he did not even carry writing implements, which he felt were luxuries. He would not even sleep under the same tree two nights in a row, lest he become too attached to earthly delights and fail to think of God.

3. In order to lure him away from asceticism and to get him to write the Gitagovinda, God arranged for Jayadeva to marry a wife, Padmavati. She taught him human love, so that he could write about the divine love of Radha and KRISHNA.

4. Once in devotion to Krishna Jayadeva made a pilgrimage to Puri. On the way he fell down, fainting from thirst. It is said that Krishna in the form of a cowherd rescued him, gave him water and milk, and fanned him. It is said that Jayadeva composed his poem, the Gitagovinda, after having a direct vision of Krishna playing his flute.

5. Once Jayadeva went to the home of a merchant to be his GURU or teacher. On the way home he was accosted by two

thieves. Jayadeva told them to take what they wanted. They did so and then cut off his hands and feet and threw him into a pit. Jayadeva went into a trance, worshipping God and thinking of the irrelevance of the body. The king happened to pass by as the mutilated Jayadeva was singing the songs of the *Gitagovinda* from the pit. When the king got him out of the pit and asked how he had come to have his hands and feet amputated, Jayadeva said that he had been born that way. The king asked to become Jayadeva's disciple then began making obeisance to every devotee, giving service and alms to every SADHU or holy man. The thieves who had robbed Jayadeva heard of the king's generosity and went to him. Jayadeva asked the king to take special care of them. The thieves, fearing a stategem, told the king that Jayadeva had lost his hands and feet in another court because of the evils he had committed there. Krishna could not bear hearing this calumny against Jayadeva and the earth opened up and swallowed the thieves before everyone's eyes.

Further reading: Lee Siegel, *Sacred and Profane Dimensions of Love in the Indian Traditions as Exemplified in the Gitagovinda of Jayadeva* (London: Oxford University Press, 1978).

Jaya Sati Bhagavati, Ma (1940–)
American guru

Joyce Green was born on May 26, 1940, the youngest of four children in a working-class Jewish family in Coney Island, Brooklyn, New York. Her father, Harry Green, ran a stand selling hot corn, and her mother was a legal secretary. The family was often impoverished and the mother died when Joyce was 13 years old. Joyce attended Lincoln High School but did not graduate. At age 15, she married Salvatore DeFiore, an Italian Catholic businessman. She became a housewife and mother of three children.

In 1972, Joyce learned a yogic breath discipline in a YOGA class and practiced the breath for seven days consistently. As a result, she was awakened to spirituality by a vision of Jesus Christ, who told her, "Teach all ways, for all ways are mine." She was visited by Swami NITY-ANANDA of Ganeshpuri, not in physical form, who became a teacher to her. In 1973 her guru NEEM KAROLI BABA appeared to her, also not in physical form, and gave her teachings. As she deepened her appreciation of the teachings of these two Hindu masters, a group of students began to grow around her and she became known as Ma, or mother.

In 1976 she founded Kashi Ashram in Sebastian, Florida, where she continues to teach in the Shaivite (*see* SHAIVISM) lineage of Swami Nityananda. The ashram is a residential community with members living on the campus and nearby. In addition to interfaith services, the ashram

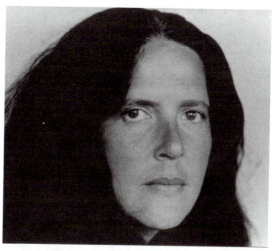

Ma Jaya Sati Bhagavati (b. 1940), American guru and founder of Kashi Ashram in Sebastian, Florida *(Kashi Church, Sebastian, Florida)*

provides a school for its own children as well as children from the larger community. First drawn to Hinduism by the inclusiveness of its tenets, Ma has incorporated many Hindu practices in an interfaith setting at Kashi Ashram. Temples devoted to GANESHA, HANUMAN, SHIVA, DURGA, KALI, LAKSHMI, SARASWATI, KRISHNA, the DASHA MAHAVIDYAS, and Ma's teachers are on the grounds of Kashi. Spiritual practices include MEDITATION, KALI YUGA, KIRTAN, and DARSHAN from Ma, and celebration of Hindu holy days. Kashi community also includes temples and shrines devoted to Judaism, SIKHISM, Christianity, and Buddhism.

In 1990, Ma founded the River Fund, Kashi's service organization, and inspired the founding of Mary's House, a home for children who have acquired immunodeficiency syndrome (AIDS). In 1994, she founded the River House, a respite for those with AIDS and other life-challenging illnesses. She and her students work with individuals who suffer from AIDS, homelessness, and abuse and those near death. She has become an advocate for those who have human immunodeficiency virus/AIDS (HIV/AIDS), for gay rights, and for the rights of women and minorities. Through the River Fund, which she founded in 1990, she and her students engage in service to communities around the world.

In 1996, Ma founded the Dattatreya Kali Saraswati Order of monks and SANNYASIS (renunciants). She has developed the teaching of Kali Yoga, a system of ASANAS (postures) drawn from ancient roots and adapted for modern times, as well as spiritual teachings in the traditions of KUNDALINI and tantric yoga (see TANTRISM). Kali Yoga emphasizes the divine feminine and selfless service to humanity.

Ma teaches internationally and regularly gives *satsang* group teaching in Florida, California, and New York. Her interest in joining people of diverse faiths led to her nomination as a trustee in the Governing Council of the Parliament of the World's Religions. She has worked with Tenzin Chogya, brother of the Dalai Lama, to establish World Tibet Day to honor the culture of Tibet and to raise awareness of the plight of the Tibetan people.

Ma has taken an active role in the interfaith movement and is a delegate to the United Religions Initiative. She serves on the advisory boards of the Institute of Religion and Public Policy and Equal Partners in Faith.

Also an artist, Ma Jaya has created works illuminating Hindu themes that have been shown in numerous galleries and museums. In 2004 Ma Jaya was honored by inclusion in the International Hall of Honor at Morehouse College, and she received the Inter-Parliamentary Paradigm of Peace Award, ratified by 26 governments around the world.

Further reading: Ma Jaya Sati Bhagavati, "Kali Who Swallows the Universe," *Parabola*, Summer 1998, pp. 18–21; ———, "There Are No Throwaway People: The Journey from Brooklyn to God." *One Heart Magazine*, November 2000, pp. 32–35; ———, "Teach All Ways for All Ways Are Mine," *Journal of the Communal Studies Association* (2002); ———, "How the AIDS Pandemic Changed My Life" in *Awakening the Spirit, Inspiring the Soul* (Sebastian, Fla.: Skylight Paths, 2004); Andrew Cohen, "Compassion in Action." *What Is Enlightenment?* Spring/Summer 2001, pp. 66–67; Lavina Melwani, "The Selfless Life of Serving Siva in All: Ma Jaya Sati Bhagavati, AIDS Angel of Kashi." *Hinduism Today*, February 1999, pp. 37–38; Regina Sara Ryan, *The Woman Awake: Feminine Wisdom for Spiritual Life* (Prescott, Ariz.: Hohm Press, 1998), 192–202; Wayne Teasdale, *The Mystic Heart* (Novato, Calif.: New World Library, 2001).

jewels of Jainism, three   *See* JAINISM.

jiva   *See* JAINISM; VEDANTA.

jivanmukta

A *jivanmukta* (living liberated one) is a person who has succeeded in escaping from the cycle of birth and rebirth but remains alive. Most Shaivite traditions, and the VEDANTA of SHANKARA, accept the possibility of *jivanmukti* (living liberation). Other Hindu traditions, such as VAISHNAVISM, do not accept the concept; they insist that full liberation occurs only at death. Neither Jains nor Sikhs believe in *jivanmukti*.

Historically, many of the earlier philosophies of India, such as SAMKHYA, had no place for the idea. A strict reading of YOGA SUTRA would not allow for it either.

Further reading: Andrew O. Fort, *Jivanmukti in Transformation: Embodied Liberation in advaita and Neo-Vedanta* (Albany: State University of New York Press, 1998).

jivatman   *See* VEDANTA.

jnana

Jnana (from the root *jna,* "to know") literally means "knowledge" but is better translated as "gnosis" or "realization." Specifically, it is the knowledge of the unity between the highest reality, or BRAHMAN, and the individual self, or JIVATMAN. The role of *jnana* is developed in the philosophy of the UPANISHADS and most clearly outlined in the ADVAITA (non-dualist) philosophy of SHANKARA.

Much thought and writing have focused on the nature of *jnana* in Indian tradition. Some see it as a cognitive function: once one understands the truth of the unity of *brahman* and the self intellectually, that is enough. Others require a realization of a mystic sort. VEDANTA has often been characterized as interested only in gaining *jnana,* but it has many paths that stress BHAKTI or devotion as the first step on the path toward the ultimate. *Jnana yoga* is one of the three major yogas mentioned in the BHAGAVAD GITA.

Further reading: S. N. Dasgupta, *History of Indian Philosophy,* vols. 1 and 2 (Delhi: Motilal Banarsidass, 1975).

Jnanasambanthar   *See* SAMBANTHAR.

jnana yoga   *See* BHAGAVAD GITA.

jnanedriya   *See* SAMKHYA.

Jnaneshvara (1275–1296) *poet-saint*

Jnaneshvara was a Vaishnavite (*see* VAISHNAVISM) poet-saint from Maharashtra, who wrote hymns of praise to VITHOBA and RUKMINI, the Maharashtran forms of KRISHNA and RADHA who are worshipped at Pandharpur. He is most famous for his commentary on the BHAGAVAD GITA written in old Marathi, a beloved and revered text in Maharashtra. It is said that Jnaneshvara died at the age of 22, at Alandi on the Krishna River. This is now an important pilgrimage site; his shrine is visited there at the time of the poet's death in November.

Further reading: P. V. Bobde, trans., *Garland of Divine Flowers: Selected Devotional Lyrics of Saint Jnanesvara* (Delhi: Motilal Banarsidass, 1987); Manu Subedar, trans., *Gita, the Mother: Commentary by Dhyaneshwar Maharaj* (New Delhi: Kalyani, 1972).

Jyoti, Swami Amar (1928–2001) *Indian guru and ashram founder*

Swami Amar Jyoti was a humanitarian activist, who founded Jyoti Ashram, Sacred Mountain Ashram, the Desert Ashram, and the Truth Consciousness movement. Born in northwest India on May 6, 1928, in a small town close to the banks of the Indus River, Swami Amar Jyoti was named Rama by his parents. As a child he was interested in science, math, writing, cycling, drama, and sports. The partition of India in 1947 interrupted his college education, causing him to transfer to a university in Bombay (Mumbai). Just a few months prior to his graduation he left school in order to obtain the remainder of his education from the world itself. At 19, without money or a destination, he took a train to Calcutta (Kolkata).

Political tensions and mass violence had broken out in India at the time, and refugees were flooding into West Bengal by the thousands. During this time Rama worked for an aviation company in Calcutta; when offered a partnership in the company, he decided to leave and instead volunteer his services to help the refugees. During this time he lived on a railway platform somewhere close to the border of India and East Bengal (now Bangladesh). He soon became the leader of the entire volunteer effort, working more than 20 hours per day. A year later, as the inflow of refugees began to subside, Rama moved back to Calcutta. Here he turned down a government position in order to work for the rehabilitation of refugees.

Rama chose to live alone on the fringes of Calcutta in an ASHRAM, where he learned classical music, sitar, religious studies, and prayer. In the contemplative atmosphere he began to have visions. His MEDITATION, YOGA, and PUJA practices increased, and soon he knew where his life's work was leading him. He lived in silence for close to a decade, focused on the goal of God realization. In those years he made many pilgrimages throughout India, but his "awakening" is attributed to the time he spent in a temple village near the source of the GANGES River.

In 1958, Rama was initiated into Vidyut Sannyas (lightninglike monasticism) in BADRINATH in the HIMALAYAS and given the name Swami Amar Jyoti (eternal light). Now he was ready to communicate to the world. He founded his first center, Jyoti Ashram, in Pune, in the state of Maharashtra close to his mother's home. In 1961 he was invited to the United States by a devotee; on this trip he gained a degree of popularity. In 1974, he set up the Sacred Mountain Ashram near Boulder,

Colorado. A few years later he established the Desert Ashram in Tucson, Arizona, under Truth Consciousness, a nonprofit organization created to disseminate Swami Amar Jyoti's teachings. He continued to travel and teach until his death on June 13, 2001.

Jyoti Ashram is a pilgrimage site. It contains a memorial temple housing the remains of the swami.

Further reading: Swami Amar Jyoti, *Immortal Light: The Blissful Life and Wisdom of Swami Amar Jyoti* (Boulder, Colo.: Truth Consciousness, 2004);———, *Spirit of Himalaya: The Story of a Truth Seeker* (Boulder, Colo.: Truth Consciousness, 2001).

Jyotipriya   *See* TYBERG, JUDITH M.

Jyotirmayananda Saraswati, Swami
(1931–   ) advaita *teacher and educator*
Swami Jyotirmayananda Saraswati founded the Yoga Research Foundation.

Born in Dumari Buzurg on February 3, 1931, in the state of Bihar, the boy who would become Swami Jyotirmayananda was a calm, reflective, and successful student. He studied at the Science College of Patna, where he first met Swami SIVANANDA of Rishikesh. He traveled to the Divine Life Society in Rishikesh, where his GURU, Sivananda, put him to work teaching others. In February 1953, he took the vow of SANNYAS (renunciation) from Sivananda and began to teach at the Yoga Vedanta Forest Academy as a professor of religion. He became the editor of the Hindi journal of the Divine Life Society, *Yoga-Vedanta*.

In 1962, after many requests, he traveled to the West, staying two years in Puerto Rico, where he founded the Sanatan Dharma Mandir. In 1969 he opened his center in Miami, Florida, where he set up a publishing center and the Yoga Research Foundation. Branches of this organization now exist throughout the world. In 1985, he founded an ashram near New Delhi that offers yoga classes, publishes the Hindi journal *Yoganjali*, and assists the needy through a medical clinic. The ashram also runs a school for children, the Bal Divya Jyoti Public School.

Jyotirmananda teaches and lectures on integral yoga and sponsors a monthly magazine, *International Yoga Guide*.

Further reading: Swami Jyotirmayananda Saraswati, *Meditate the Tantric Yoga Way* (London: Allen & Unwin, 1973); ———, *The Art of Positive Thinking* (Miami: Yoga Research Foundation, 1988).

K

Kabir (c. 15th century) *medieval Hindi saint-poet*
Kabir, a poor, illiterate man, was one of the great
saint-poets of northern India. He is revered by
Muslims, Hindus, and Sikhs, although his work
includes much social and religious criticism of
Islam and Hinduism.

The poet was born in BENARES (Varanasi) into
a weaver family who had recently converted to
Islam. As with other poet-saints such as RAM-
PRASAD and TUKARAM, the actual details of his life
are not known for certain; it is not even known
which of the poems attributed to him were
authentically his. Indian poet-saints, particularly
those who relied upon song to communicate, very
quickly became legendary figures, the possessions
of everyone. More important than the concrete
details of these people's lives or the verses that
may be authentically theirs is the collective imagination of them, which makes them part of the
cultural consciousness and makes their writings a
collective possession.

It is understood from his verses that Kabir
was illiterate, but in India this is less important
than in the bibliophilic West. Real Indian tradition, the culture that occupied the center of
Indian consciousness, was always oral and aural
first. Written texts were the abode of scholars and
pundits but less important for the transmission
of tradition.

Kabir was the disciple of the GURU Ramananda,
a famous c. 15th-century teacher. A story tells
how Kabir, a convert to Islam, tricked this orthodox Hindu into accepting him as a student. Kabir
is said to have lain upon the steps that the guru
always took in the morning to do his bathing and
ablutions in the river. Tripping in the dark over
the supine Kabir, the guru in fear uttered, "Ram!
Ram!" This is, in fact, a MANTRA in and of itself, and
so the crafty Kabir insisted he must be accepted as
a disciple since he had heard the guru's mantra.
(It should be added that Kabir's understanding of
the mantra RAMA is not an orthodox one. For him
the word did not designate the AVATAR of VISHNU
of that name, but was a divine "name" that leads
one to an undifferentiated ADVAITA (non-dual)
consciousness.)

There exists a story, probably apocryphal and
invented by Hindus, that Kabir was actually born
of a BRAHMIN woman and set afloat in a basket
on a pond to be found by a Muslim couple. Both
Hindus and Muslims still claim Kabir as their
own (while his words are included in the sacred
books of the Sikhs, the Guru GRANTH SAHIB.) It is
said that when Kabir died, Muslims and Hindus

confronted each other, each wanting to take the body for their own rituals. Before they could come to blows, however, they pulled up the shroud only to find there a heap of flowers, which they happily divided in half.

There is hardly a person who grew up in North India over the last 400 years who has not been able to recite many verses of "Kabir" by heart. His work is deeply ingrained in the culture of North India. This said, his poetry combines highly esoteric NATH YOGI symbolism, highly mystical nondual devotion that envisions a "divinity" beyond any form or description, a deep criticism of the orthodoxy of both Muslims and Hindus, and a strong social critique of the hierarchy of Hindu society. In his poetry he again and again evokes the watchword *Ram* without any sectarian content. It is a mantric word used to point toward the highest consciousness that sees beyond the veil or MAYA of this world.

Kabir's poems are found in the Guru Granth Sahib of the Sikhs (*see* SIKHISM); in the Panchvani, a compilation of sayings of five northern saints; and in the Bijak, an anthology attributed to Kabir alone. All of these were first published around the 17th century, although the Guru Granth Sahib in its formative stages may have contained these poems earlier.

Further reading: P. D. Barthwal, *The Nirgun School of Hindi Poetry* (Benares: The Indian Bookshop, 1936); Linda Hess and Shukdev Singh, trans., *The Bijak of Kabir* (San Francisco: North Point Press, 1983); David Lorenzen, *Kabir Legends and Ananda-Das's Kabir Parachai* (Albany: State University of New York Press, 1991); Karine Schomer and W. H. McCleod, eds., *The Sant Tradition of India* (Berkeley: Berkeley Religious Studies Series and Motilal Banarsidass, 1987); Charlotte Vaudeville, trans., *Kabir,* 2 vols. (Oxford: Oxford University Press, 1974).

Kailasanatha Temple   *See* ELLORA.

Kailash, Mount (Mount Kailas or Mount Kailasha)

Kailash (from *kelasa,* crystal) is the name of a mountain peak about 18,000 feet up in the HIMALAYAS. It is sacred to both Hindus and Tibetan Buddhists. In Indian mythology it is seen as the abode of the Lord SHIVA and of KUBERA, the god of wealth and of the northern direction. Mythology places it to the south of Mount MERU. Kailash is sometimes also said to be the source of the GANGES River. Throughout history it has been an important Hindu pilgrimage site.

Further reading: Bhagavan Hamsa, *The Holy Mountain, Mansarovar, and Mount Kailas: Being the Story of a Pilgrimage to Lake Marias and of Initiation on Mount Kailas* (London: Faber & Faber, 1934); Veena Sharma, *Kailash Mansarovar: A Sacred Journey* (New Delhi: Lotus Collection, Roli Books, 2004).

kaivalya

Kaivalya (from SANSKRIT *kevala,* sole or only) literally means "isolation" and refers to the liberated state of the self, when it is "isolated" completely from the pulls and distortions of PRAKRITI, or natural reality. The term originated in the ancient SAMKHYA tradition and is important in the yoga tradition of PATANJALI. Both living and dead persons may be in the state of *kaivalya.* It is a unique state where one becomes absorbed in the root-consciousness of the Self (*purusha*) alone. Bliss is not an element of traditional *kaivalya.*

Further reading: M. N. Parthasarathi, *Journey to Aloneness: Commentaries on the Kaivalya Upanishad* (Mumbai: Eeshwar, 2001); Ian Whicher, *The Integrity of the Yoga Darsana: A Reconsideration of Classical Yoga* (Albany: State University of New York Press, 1998).

Kali

The name Kali has two derivations. In the sense of "she who is black" it is from *kala* (black). In the sense of "she who is the ruler of time" it derives from *kala* (time, spelled slightly differently in SANSKRIT letters).

Kali is the most frightening of the goddesses and the most misunderstood by non-Hindus. Mythologically, she originates in the fury of the goddess DURGA and emerges physically from that goddess's forehead. She has a terrible, frightening appearance. She is originally very black (though in modern depictions she is often lighter), usually naked, emaciated, with long disheveled hair. She wears a skirt of severed arms, earrings made of the corpses of children, and a necklace of human skulls. In one hand she holds a cutting instrument, in another the severed head of a man. She has long sharp fangs, bloody lips, and a bloody lolling tongue.

In iconography Kali is often depicted as standing upon the chest of the supine corpse of SHIVA, her nominal husband. She is known to frequent the burning grounds where burned and unburned corpses abound, where she is always accompanied by female jackals. She, as does DURGA, likes liquor, meat, and blood.

There is little doubt that Kali is a fierce autochthonous non-Aryan goddess who has been absorbed into the larger Brahminized pantheon of Hinduism. Kali first appears in developed literary form in the Devibhagavatam of the 11th to 12th centuries, where she is seen to be PARVATI, wife of Shiva, who becomes completely black out of fury when battling the demons Shumbha and Nishumbha. She also appears in the 16th-century Devimahatmya, part of the Markandeya Purana; this is the source of the story that Kali emerged from the enraged Durga.

Kali is most associated with eastern India, particularly Bengal. Her devotional literature and cultic followings began to proliferate as early as the 13th and 14th centuries. Bengal is the only state to worship Kali during the all-India festival of DIVALI. The medieval Bengali poet Ram Prasad is best known for his Bengali hymns in devotion to "Mother Kali," and the

The temple to the goddess Kali, in Dakshineshwar, Bengal, where Sri Ramakrishna served as a priest *(Constance A. Jones)*

modern Bengali Saint RAMAKRISHNA, who had perhaps the greatest influence in the West of any Indian spiritual figure, was known as a devotee of Kali alone.

Devotion to Kali requires the utmost surrender and the ability to see that her chaotic and fearsome visage is only a barrier placed before the devotee, who must have the courage to seek the inner depths of her compassion and the SHAKTI or universal power she represents. When one has accomplished this step, one can learn to *become* Kali, as Sri Ramakrishna so clearly demonstrates. When one has learned to be her truth, then one's consciousness and being are completely transformed and one can live in her endless bliss for longer and longer periods.

Kali has been associated with tantric religious forms. TANTRISM in this context focuses on the cremation ground; normative elements and practices are frowned upon or forbidden. When one realizes the divinity within even the lowest realities, within the rotting corpse, within the dark of the cremation ground, then one has learned to find the limit of time and one can began to see the secrets buried in the depths of reality. Then one can begin to experience Kali as the sweet, compassionate, nurturing mother that she is.

Iconographically it is understood that Kali's nakedness symbolizes the stripping away of illusion; the severed head is a symbol of her cutting away of the ignorance that binds one to the cycle of birth and rebirth. Kali's lolling tongue is most often taken to indicate her anger, but some in India have taken it to be a gesture, like "biting the tongue" in shame.

Further reading: David Kinsley, *Hindu Goddesses: Visions of the Divine Feminine in the Hindu Religious Tradition* (Berkeley: University of California Press, 1988); ———, *The Sword and the Flute: Kali and Krsna, Dark Visions of the Terrible and the Sublime in Hindu Mythology* (Berkeley: University of California Press, 1975); Rachel Fell McDermott and Jeffrey J. Kripal, eds., *Encountering Kali: In the Margins, at the Center, In the West* (Berkeley: University of California Press, 2003).

Kalidasa (circa fourth or fifth century C.E.)
Sanskrit poet
Kalidasa is considered one of the greatest SANSKRIT dramatists and poets.

Little is known for certain about the life of the poet and dramatist Kalidasa. He appears to have lived in the time of the imperial GUPTAS, perhaps in central India, in what is now called Madhyapradesh. Three dramas are attributed to him: *Malvikagnimitra, Vikramorvashiya,* and *Shakuntala.*

Malvikagnimitra begins as a story of political alliances toward the end of the Mauryan dynasty, but the political aspect is eventually equaled or overshadowed by the love affair between the princess Malvika and the prince Agnimitra. The drama *Vikramovashiya* tells how one of the celestial nymphs, or ASPARAS, Urvashi goes to live with her lover Pururavas thanks to his prowess or *vikrama*. It has been called a drama of "luster and brilliance" with no plot or real action. In the skeleton story the celestial nymph Urvashi falls in love with an earthly king, Pururavas. She loses her celestial status but is allowed to live with him. The play is graced with nature description, beautiful poetry, and supernatural effects.

Abhijnanasakuntalam sometimes abbreviated to *Shakuntala*, is recognized as its author's masterpiece. The heroine Shakuntala is the daughter of the celestial nymph Menaka and the sage Vishvamitra. She is abandoned by her parents and is raised by the caring sage Kanva in his forest hermitage. The king Dushyanta finds the hermitage and falls in love with the beautiful, simple maiden. In Kanva's absence the lovers consummate a permitted "love marriage." The king has to leave but gives Shakuntala his signet ring and promises to send someone for her in a few days.

Shakuntala soon realizes that she is pregnant. While Shakuntala daydreams about her lover, the irascible sage DURVASAS visits; enraged at being ignored, the sage curses her that her lover will forget her. Shakuntala loses the king's signet ring, her only proof of their meeting. She visits the king in her pregnancy, but he swears he has never seen her. Finally the ring is discovered in the belly of a fish and is taken to the king, who then remembers. Eventually the king flies back to the hermitage in a celestial chariot provided by INDRA and sees a boy playing there who he recognizes must be his son. The drama ends happily.

Among Kalidasa's great poems is Raghuvamsha, a look back at the dynasty of RAMA, the hero of the RAMAYANA. The poem describes the lives of all of the ancient progenitors of his line. He also wrote *Kuma-*

rasambhava, a consummate masterpiece about SHIVA and PARVATI and their young son, Kumara. Another of his great works is *Meghaduta* (Cloud messenger), a charming poem about the God Kubera's sending a message of consolation to his lover far away by means of a cloud messenger. Nature here is beautifully described. Finally, *Ritusamhara,* a short lyric uncertainly ascribed to Kalidasa, includes a beautiful description of the four seasons and the amorous moods appropriate to each.

Further reading: Chittenoor Kuhan Raja, *Survey of Sanskrit Literature* (Bombay: Bharatiya Vidya Bhavan, 1962); Moriz Winternitz, *History of Indian Literature* (Delhi: Motilal Banarsidass, 1964–67).

Kali Yuga

All of the YUGAS or ages in the Indian tradition refer to throws in an ancient game of dice. *Kali* (spelled differently in Sanskrit from the goddess of that name) is the "four," the worst throw of the dice, comparable to "craps" in the Western dice game. Our age is understood to be the Kali Yuga, in which TAMAS, the worst aspect of nature, predominates. Trickery, envy, and even the murder of holy persons are the norm in this era, as are fatal disease, fatal hunger, fear, and instability.

Kings in the Kali Yuga are angry and debauched. People are short-lived and short in stature. Money, power, pleasure, and falsehood reign. BRAHMA, VISHNU, RUDRA, and the Sun are all worshipped in the Kali Yuga.

Further reading: Cornelia Dimmitt and J. A. B. van Buitenen, *Classical Hindu Mythology: A Reader in the Sanskrit Puranas* (Philadelphia: Temple University Press, 1978); W. J. Wilkins, *Hindu Mythology, Vedic and Puranic,* 2d ed. (Calcutta: Rupa, 1973).

Kalki Avatar

Indian tradition speaks of YUGAS or ages of history. Today we are in the KALI YUGA, or Iron Age,

a period of decline. It was preceded by the ages of gold, silver, and bronze. After the end of the KALI YUGA and a short hiatus, a new age will begin: the age of truth (KRITA YUGA), when all the wickedness, strife, and dissension of this era will be replaced by righteousness. It is understood that this age will be ushered in by Kalki, the future incarnation or AVATAR of VISHNU, riding on a magnificent white horse.

Further reading: Shakti M. Gupta, *Vishnu and His Incarnations* (Bombay: Somaiya, 1993); Pandrimalai Swamigal, *The Ten Incarnations: Dasavatara* (Bombay: Bharatiya Vidya Bhavan, 1982).

kalpa

A *kalpa* is a traditional Indian eon or unit of time, an eon. Sources differ as to its exact length, but a common measure is that a *kalpa* is made up of 1,000 MAHAYUGAS, or 4,320,000,000 years. This is considered to be a day in the life of the god BRAHMA.

Further reading: Cornelia Dimmitt and J. A. B. van Buitenen, *Classical Hindu Mythology: A Reader in the Sanskrit Puranas* (Philadelphia: Temple University Press, 1978); W. J. Wilkins, *Hindu Mythology, Vedic and Puranic,* 2d ed. (Calcutta: Rupa, 1973).

kama   See ENDS OF LIFE, FOUR.

Kamadeva (Kama)

Kamadeva or Kama is the Indian cupid, the god of love. He is found in the VEDAS as a divinity, but his character was developed in the Indian epics and PURANAS. Most famously Kamadeva is known to have been burned to ashes by the third eye of Lord SHIVA. In that tale, Shiva was in a state of MEDITATION and ascetic withdrawal. The gods desperately wanted him to marry and have progeny, because they knew that his offspring would be able to defeat the demon Taraka who was plaguing them. They sent the god of love to awaken sexual desire by shooting him with his flower arrows. Shiva became angry at Kamadeva for his presumption and he incinerated him with his third eye. Upon the mournful request of Kamadeva's wife, RATI, Shiva relented and restored the god of love to life, but without a body. This is why he is invisible. In other versions of the story, Kama is not revived, but rather reborn as Pradyumna, the son of KRISHNA.

Further reading: Catherine Benton, *God of Desire: Tales of Kamadeva in Sanskrit Story Literature* (Albany: State University of New York Press, 2005); Cornelia Dimmitt and J. A. B. van Buitenen, *Classical Hindu Mythology: A Reader in the Sanskrit Puranas* (Philadelphia: Temple University Press, 1978); E. Washburn Hopkins, *Epic Mythology* (Delhi: Motilal Banarsidass, 1986).

Kamakhya

Situated near the top of Nilachal Hill in Guwahati, overlooking the majestic Brahmaputra River, Kamakhya Temple is a famous pilgrimage site. It is the most important of the SHAKTI PITHAS, or centers of devotion for the GODDESS. According to Hindu mythology, when SHIVA carried the body of his wife, SATI, her YONI fell to Earth, where the Kamakhya Temple stands today. According to local mythology, it is here that Shiva descends to unite with the goddess's *yoni*. Thus, Nilachal Hill is the symbolic site of Shiva and the goddess's eternal sexual union and is the primordial or original seat of the goddess.

This association points to Kamakhya Temple's strong tantric tradition (*see* TANTRISM). It remains one of the holiest pilgrimage sites in India for tantra practitioners, who associate it with the powerful creative force of the mother goddess. It is a center of tantric worship and transmission of tantric traditions by devotees, adepts, and GURUS.

The image of the goddess Kamakhya (also called *Kamarupa,* the shape or form of desire) at the shrine is actually a stone, the *matri yoni* or "Mother's mound of Venus." Steep stone steps lead from the entrance of the temple to a cave deep in the earth, where Ma Kamakhya sits alongside stones of *Matangi* (SARASVATI) and Kamala (LAKSHMI).

Kamakhya herself is a form of Shodashi, or Tripura-Sundari, one of the DASHA MAHAVIDYAS, each of whom has a dedicated temple on the hill. Kamakhya is also associated through various Hindu and tantric traditions with SRI LALITA and PARVATI.

In June, during the height of monsoon season, the spring that flows inside the cave is said to turn to menstrual blood, signifying the start of one of the holiest festivals in India. In fact, the water that washes over the stone at this time of year has a reddish color due to its chemical components. During AMBUVACHI (Ameti) Festival, the temple is closed for three days, as are all the temples in the area; then it is believed to be inauspicious to start new ventures, cook food, study scripture, plant seeds, or till the earth. On the fourth day, the doors open to tens of thousands of scarlet-clad pilgrims, who carry flowers, sweets, and other offerings. The goddess's blessing is given in the form of *angadhak (ritu),* the water that is the menstrual blood of the goddess, and *angabastra,* a piece of the red sari draped over the stone during its menstruation.

The origins of the first temple on this site are shrouded in mystery. Some say it was built by the demon Narakasura, whom KRISHNA fought when he tried to marry the beautiful goddess Kamakhya (she foiled his plans by outwitting him). The original temple was destroyed in the 16th century by Mughal invaders and then rebuilt in 1665 by King Nara Narayana. This temple has a beehivelike structure, surrounded by carved panels picturing figures such as GANESHA, CHAMUNDA, temple dancers, animals, and women menstruating and giving birth. Harkening back to its origins as an ancient sacrificial site, goats are sacrificed to the goddess daily, particularly during the height of festival seasons.

Further reading: Subhendugopal Bagchi, *Eminent Indian Sakta Centres in Eastern India: An Interdisciplinary Study in the Background of the Pithas of Kalighata, Vakresvara, and Kamakhya* (Calcutta: Punthi Pustak, 1980); David Kinsley, *Tantric Visions of the Divine Feminine: The Ten Mahavidyas* (Berkeley: University of California Press, 1997).

Kama Sutra

The *Kama Sutra* (Aphorisms on love) by Vatsyayana, probably the most widely known of Indian texts, was written around the second century C.E. It consists of 1,250 verses. It is divided into seven parts, divided into 36 chapters, and further divided into 64 paragraphs.

Legend says that the author Nandi originally wrote the *Kama Sutra* in 1,000 chapters, later abbreviated to 500 chapters by the poet Shvetaketu. Babhravya, a descendent of the Panchalas (whose homeland is south of Delhi), abridged it still further to 150 chapters under seven heads or parts: Desire or Kama as a part of life; Sexual Intercourse; Acquisition of a Wife; the Wife; Wives of Other People; Courtesans and Prostitutes; the Arts of Seduction. The sixth of these parts was expounded by Dattaka at the request of the prostitutes of Pataliputra (Patna); the other parts were explained by Charayana (first part), Suvarnanabha (second part); Ghotakamukha (third part); Gonardiya (fourth part); Gonikaputra (fifth part); and Kuchumara (seventh part). Given this confusion of authors, and the length and difficulty of the original material, Vatsyayana decided to compose his own work as a sort of condensation of all the previous efforts.

A quote from the introduction to the *Kama Sutra* says that "this treatise was composed, according to the precepts of the VEDAS, for the benefit of the world, by Vatsyayana, while leading the life of a religious student at BENARES [Varanasi], and wholly engaged in the contemplation of the Deity. This work is not to be used merely as an instrument for satisfying our desires. A person acquainted with the true principles of this science, who preserves his DHARMA [virtue or religious merit], his *artha* [worldly wealth] and his *kama* [pleasure or sensual gratification], and who has regard to the customs of the people, is sure to obtain mastery over his senses. In short, an intelligent and knowing person attending to dharma and *artha* and also to *kama,* without becoming the slave of his passions, will obtain success in everything that he may do."

The *Kama Sutra's* audience is clearly male and it is oriented toward the fulfillment of male desires, particularly the sexual. Even the chapter on courtesans is intended to guide them on how males are best pleasured. Parts of the book give details on how men might increase women's sexual pleasure, but even this is framed in a male-centered way.

A brief summary of the seven parts of Vatsyayana's *Kama Sutra* is as follows: In Part I, Vatsyayana justifies the study of Kama, desire, against those who feel that it is not appropriate. They may argue, for instance, that the pursuit of prosperity, another of the sanctioned goals of life, requires giving up the pursuit of pleasure. Vatsyayana argues that pleasure is necessary for the natural maintenance of the body, although he adds that it must be sought in moderation. Part one also tells of 64 arts relating to pleasure that a young woman (and a wise man) should know; gives a detailed account of the pleasures and amusements of a citizen, such as gambling; and tells men what sort of women are appropriate for sexual intercourse.

Part II gives all the details of sexual intercourse and its elements, such as kissing, biting, and role playing. Part III discusses courtship and marriage. Part IV prescribes the conduct of a wife in her husband's absence and how she should act toward his other wives. Part V describes how a man might gain the confidence of and seduce women other than his own wife. Part VI discusses the duties and activities of courtesans and prostitutes and advises them on how to earn more money; it also discusses the different classifications of prostitutes. Part VII discusses additional methods of seduction, including aphrodisiacs.

There are two well-known commentaries on the *Kama Sutra*. *Jayamangala* or *Sutrabhasya* was written between the 10th and 13th centuries; *Sutravritti* was written somewhat later.

Further reading: Haran Chandra Chakladar, *Social Life in Ancient India: Studies in Vatsyanana's Kama Sutra* (New Delhi: Asian Educational Services, 1990); Wendy Doniger and Sudhir Kakar, trans., *Kamasutra of Vatsyayana Mallanaga: A New, Complete English Translation of the Sanskrit Text with Excerpts from the Sanskrit Jayamangala Commentary of Yashodhara Indrapada and the Hindi Jaya Commentary of Devadatta Shastri* (New York: Oxford University Press, 2002).

Kamban (c. ninth to 12th century) *classical Tamil author*

Kamban is the author of the Tamil language *Iramavataram* (The Avatar of Rama), perhaps the most ornate and aesthetically pleasing of all the many versions of the RAMAYANA written in the regional languages of India.

The details of Kamban's life, as those of many other classical Indian authors, are uncertain. Even his name, which is not his given name, can be interpreted in different ways. The traditional account has him the son of Adita, a resident of Muvalur village in Tanjore District of Tamil Nadu. He belonged to either the drummer CASTE or the caste of hereditary priests in the KALI temples. He mentions his patron, Sataiyan, in his verses. A contemporary Chola king is said to have given him the fief of a place called Kambanatu (a possible source for his name) and the title of "king of poets." Some believe that the poet was murdered by the Chola king himself out of jealousy for his fame.

The extant manuscripts of the Iramavataram, varying from 10,000 to 12,000 verses in length, probably include interpolations. From the very beginning of the poem RAMA is presented as the AVATAR of VISHNU; he is referred to by Vishnu's epithets throughout. This is quite different from the SANSKRIT version of VALMIKI, in which Rama is clearly associated with Vishnu only in the first and last chapters.

In other ways, the story as told by Kamban is very much along the lines of Valmiki; in many places it is clear that the author is familiar with the Sanskrit version. Among the noticeable variations is that Kamban omits the entire final chapter of the Sanskrit version (the Uttarakanda) of the Ramayana, which recounts a tale of Rama's children and the history of the demon king RAVANA. When Kamban's Ramayana ends Rama and SITA live happily in the ideal kingdom.

Also, although Kamban relates Sita's abduction by Ravana, in his version Ravana cannot touch Sita, who is protected by a deadly curse. Finally, in the story of AHALYA, the maiden who was turned to stone on account of her dalliance with INDRA, the curse that was put upon Indra varies between the two versions: in the Sanskrit tale he is cursed with the testicles of a goat; in the Tamil version he is cursed with 1,000 vaginas (which he begs the gods to transform into eyes—thus his epithet "the one with 1,000 eyes.")

Further reading: George L. Hart and Hank Heifetz, trans., *The Forest Book of the Ramayana of Kampan* (Berkeley: University of California Press, 1988); Kamil V. Zvelibil, *Tamil Literature*. Vol. 10, Fascile 1, *A History of Indian Literature*. Edited by Jan Gonda (Wiesbaden: Otto Harrassowitz, 1974).

Kamsa   *See* KRISHNA.

Kanada (c. 600 B.C.E.)   *See* NYAYA-VAISHESHIKA.

Kanchipuram

Kanchipuram, located about 40 miles southwest of Madras (Chennai), is one of the seven sacred cities of India. It has been an important South Indian religious and cultural center since well before the Pallava dynasty of the sixth to eighth centuries, when it served as the capital city. It also served as one of the Chola capitals in the ninth to 13th centuries and as a secondary Pandyan capital around 1000.

The city has been influenced by VAISHNAVISM, SHAIVISM, and JAINISM. Between the fourth and seventh centuries Kanchipuram was also known as one of the great centers for Buddhism, and there are still vestiges there of the Buddhist presence. SHANKARA (c. seventh century) established one of his five original Mathas or site for monks in Kanchipuram. The city has a sizable Jain population today concentrated in an area known as Jain Kanchi, where there are many Jain shrines and a few quite remarkable ancient Jain temples.

The oldest Hindu temples in Kanchipuram, dating from the seventh and eighth centuries, are the Kailasanatha temple devoted to SHIVA, and the VAIKUNTHA Perumal temple devoted to VISHNU, both built by the Pallavas. Additionally, the Kamakshi Temple, dedicated to the goddess Kamakshi, dates from the same period. Notable also are two temples in the later VIJAYANAGARA style (circa 14th through 16th centuries): one of them dedicated to Varadararaja (Vaishnavite) and also to Shiva in LINGAM form, and the other known as the Ekambaranatha temple, which has an ancient mango tree on its grounds. Kanchipuram is also famous for its beautiful saris.

Further reading: T. V. Mahalingam, *Kanchipuram in Early South Indian History* (London: Asia Publishing House, 1969).

Kanya Kumari

Kanya Kumari (Virgin maiden) is a town of approximately 200,000 people at the tip of India at the meeting place of the Arabian Sea, the Indian Ocean, and the Bay of Bengal. The local goddess Kanya Kumari is considered by some to be a form of DURGA.

The story goes that the god of Suchindram, a nearby town, was going to marry the goddess. The gods did not like this—if she married she would lose her powers to fight demonic forces. They asked the RISHI NARADA to solve the problem. When Suchindram was on the way to the ceremony, Narada made the call of a rooster. Thinking that he had departed too late for the ceremony Suchindram returned home and left the goddess in her virgin state. Because of this she was able to kill the demon Bana and protect her land.

The seashore temple of Kanya Kumari is one of the most visited PILGRIMAGE sites in India today. Offshore, a newer temple to memorialize Swami VIVEKANANDA has also been created. The town has been a pilgrimage site since very ancient times, since it is mentioned in the *aranyaka parvan* of the MAHABHARATA, which took its current form by the second century C.E. (with some sections going back to perhaps the fifth century B.C.E.).

Further reading: Francis X. Clooney, *Divine Mother, Blessed Mother: Hindu Goddess and the Virgin Mary* (New York: Oxford University Press, 2005).

Kapila (c. 100 C.E.) *philosopher*

The sage Kapila is the legendary founder of SAMKHYA tradition, and thus a key figure in the history of yoga. He is said to have passed on his knowledge to Asuri, who in turn passed it on to Panchashikha. According to the oldest commentary on the *samkhya karika*, a later text, Kapila was a "wise ascetic, . . . born of heaven, . . . and innately endowed with the four fundamental dispositions of virtue, knowledge, renunciation, and supernatural power."

The story is told that Kapila, out of pity for suffering humanity, selected a BRAHMIN householder, Asuri, as an appropriate person to whom to reveal the knowledge of Samkhya. Kapila approached him as he was performing sacrifices (as he had been doing for thousands of years). Asuri would not listen. Only after being approached two more times did he relent and become Kapila's student.

Some sources say Kapila is the son of Svambhu-va's daughter, MANU, and PRAJAPATI'S son, Kardama. Other sources say that he may be an incarnation of VISHNU who learned his wisdom directly from SHIVA; as such he would then be known as HIRANYA-GARBHA, or lord of the world. There are numerous references to Kapila in the epics and later texts, which give him various powers and statuses.

Further reading: John Davies, *Hindu Philosophy: An Exposition of the System of Kapila* (New Delhi: Cosmo, 1981).

karma

In ancient VEDIC tradition karma (action) simply referred to the Vedic rites. Indian philosophy often contrasts the *karma kanda* (action aspect) of tradition with its *jnana kanda* (knowledge aspect). Later, the term *karma* came to refer to the "law of action." According to this ethical concept, the actions or karmas of individuals in their current births shape their lives in their next births. Finally, in the context of the BHAGAVAD GITA, karma yoga refers to a YOGA of action in the world without regard to its fruits. Mohandas Karamchand GANDHI made the term *karma yoga* well known, as his political actions were all undertaken under this name. The Indian traditions of Hinduism, JAINISM, Buddhism, and SIKHISM all accept the notion of karma.

Further reading: C. F. Keyes and E. Valentine Daniel, *Karma: An Anthropological Inquiry* (Berkeley: University of California Press, 1983); Wendy Doniger O'Flaherty, ed., *Karma and Rebirth in Classical Indian Traditions* (Berkeley: University of California Press, 1980).

karmendriyas See SAMKHYA.

Karttikeya

Karttikeya is the younger son of SHIVA and PARVATI; GANESHA is the elder son. There are many versions of his life story, as is usual in Hindu tradition. In the best known version, from the PURANAS, Shiva accidentally spills his semen into fire (AGNI). The fire is distressed because of the semen's incredible power and asks the GANGES River for help. She agrees and the semen is thrown into her cool waters.

The Ganges waits 5,000 years for the seed to gestate and produce a child, but none comes forth. She goes to BRAHMA to ask for advice. He tells her to leave the seed in a vast grove of reeds for 10,000 more years. After that long period a child is indeed born in the reeds. As he cries out, the six *krittika* goddesses (the Pleiades) vie with each other to be the first to nurse him. Because of their quarreling he develops six faces around his head to look at all of them at once. As he is reared by these six goddesses, he receives the name Karttikeya, from their names.

Once the word spreads that this child is born, the god of fire suddenly renews his interest and wants to claim him. The Ganges also wants him. They go to Shiva and Parvati to settle the dispute, but this only creates complications, as the couple also want the child. They all agree to ask the child and to accept his choice. The boy, loving them all, becomes four versions of himself. The one named Karttikeya became son of Shiva, the one named Kumara becomes son of the Ganges, the one named Skanda becomes son of Parvati, and the one named Guha becomes the son of fire.

Karttikeya is depicted iconographically with a peacock vehicle, some sort of weapon in his hand, and a rooster on his banner. At times he is considered unmarried, while other stories give him a wife named Devasena; in South India he has a second wife, Valli. Karttikeya is very popular in South India, where he takes the name Murugan along with his other traditional names.

Further reading: Cornelia Dimmitt and J. A. B. van Buitenen, *Classical Hindu Mythology: A Reader in the Sanskrit Puranas* (Philadelphia: Temple University Press, 1978); E. Washburn Hopkins, *Epic Mythology* (Delhi: Motilal Banarsidass, 1986); W. J. Wilkins, *Hindu Mythology, Vedic and Puranic,* 2d ed. (Calcutta: Rupa, 1973).

Kashi Church Foundation   *See* JAYA SATI BHAGAVATI, MA.

Kashmiri Shaivism (est. ninth century)

Kashmiri SHAIVISM includes the philosophies and practices of the *ADVAITA* (non-dual) Shaivite traditions that flourished in Kashmir from approximately the ninth to the 13th centuries C.E. Kashmiri Shaivism describes ultimate reality as Paramashiva, or supreme Shiva, and teaches that nothing exists that is not one with Paramashiva. All of reality, with all of its diversity and fluctuation, is the play of this single principle. The two aspects of this single reality are inseparably united: SHIVA and SHAKTI. Shiva is the self-luminous, static consciousness, and Shakti is the dynamic, blissful power of awareness. Through their union, the universe is constantly established, sustained, and withdrawn.

Kashmiri Shaivism also teaches that Paramashiva is the true nature and Self of every human being. Through self-effort and divine grace individuals can know both their Self and the world around them as supreme Shiva. A being who lives with the constant experience of this is *jivanmukta,* liberated in this lifetime.

Within Kashmiri Shaivism, the most crucial element of this journey to liberation is the relationship between the GURU and the disciple. The disciple receives SHAKTIPAT, the descent of divine grace or power, from the guru. This essential initiation awakens the dormant spiritual energy within the individual called KUNDALINI Shakti, and ultimately leads to the realization of Paramashiva.

The earliest texts of Kashmiri Shaivism have no known human authors and are considered revealed sacred texts. According to tradition, in the ninth century C.E. Shiva revealed to Vasugupta the Shiva Sutra, a text composed of aphorisms that presents the early teachings of Kashmiri Shaivism. The Spanda Karika, whose authorship is attributed to either Vasugupta himself or his disciple Kalattabhatta, expands upon the teachings in the Shiva Sutra. In particular, the Spanda Karika describes the nature of Paramashiva as spanda, the divine pulsation or vibration. Paramashiva's nature is to expand and contract, and thereby to emanate and withdraw the universe on both a cosmic and a mundane level. A disciple can thus realize Shiva as his or her own nature by perceiving vibration as part of his or her own experience.

Somananda and his disciple Utpaladeva developed Kashmiri Shaivism further by establishing the teaching of *pratyabhijna,* the recognition of Shiva as one's own Self. They describe the experience of liberation as this recognition. Somananda first introduced this teaching in his work Soma Drishti, and Utpaladeva systematically presented it in his writings, including the Pratyabhijnakarika.

Kashmiri Shaivism reached its creative climax with the teachings of ABHINAVAGUPTA and his disciple Kshemaraja in the 10th and 11th centuries. In his magnum opus, Tantraloka, Abhinavagupta encompasses almost every aspect of Kashmiri Shaivism and gives the most sophisticated and comprehensive expression of its teachings. Kshemaraja continued his work and made Kashmiri Shaivism more accessible to wider audiences through commentaries and digests.

Kashmiri Shaivism has continued to influence and inspire people in India and throughout the world. Leading modern exponents include Swami LAKSHMANJOO (1907–91), who was raised and taught in the oral tradition of Kashmir, and Swami MUKTANANDA (1908–82), who traveled throughout the world sharing the teachings of Kashmiri Shaivism.

Further reading: J. C. Chatterji, *Kashmir Shaivism* (Albany: State University of New York Press, 1986); Mark Dyczkowski, *The Doctrine of Vibration: An Analysis of the Doctrines and Practices of Kashmir Shaivism* (Albany: State University of New York Press, 1987).

Kathakali

Kathakali (*katha,* story, *kali,* performance) is a special type of Indian dance-drama. It originated in the state of Kerala in South India more than 500 years ago. It combines drama, dance, music, and ritual. Characters with vividly painted faces and elaborate costumes reenact stories from the epics MAHABHARATA and RAMAYANA and the Puranas. The most popular stories enacted are "The Death of DURYODHANA," "The Story of Nala," "The Fight between ARJUNA and SHIVA," and "The Story of Devayani and Kacha."

As has happened for centuries new stories are added to the Kathakali repertoire from time to time when they become sufficiently popular. In recent times stories from the Bible or Shakespeare have been added to appeal to modern audiences.

The dramatic form is based, somewhat as opera is, on the notion that the audience is fully familiar with the stories being told. In the play the elaborately costumed actors (all male, even for female roles) do not speak; they pantomime the dialogue, while accompanists sing the lyrics. The language is an amalgam of Malayalam and SANSKRIT. The traditional Kathakali show begins at night and lasts till dawn; in the modern urban context in India and abroad the plays last only several hours.

The actors in Kathakali are always accompanied by drummers and singers; the lead singer controls the entire show with a special rhythm instrument. The story is conveyed purely through hand gestures (MUDRAS), facial expressions, and body movements. Complete control over facial muscles is a prerequisite for this demanding dramatic art form. It takes a minimum of eight to 10 years for a Kathakali dancer to become fully trained. The training is very demanding and includes the study of one of the traditional martial arts of Kerala to create stamina, concentration, and physical flexibility. It also, not incidentally, prepares the actors for the many dramatic fight scenes in the epics. There are 24 main mudras in Kathakali and a number of less commonly used ones.

Kathakali uses a set "color code" for the makeup of the characters. Noble characters such as ARJUNA have their faces painted green. Evil characters who have heroic roles will have green makeup with red marks on the cheeks. Very angry or very evil characters will have red makeup and a red beard. Women and mendicants have yellow painted faces. Hunters and forest dwellers have primarily black painted faces. As in most other classical Indian forms, such as BHARATA NATYAM, facial expressions for Kathakali actors accord with the nine RASAS (sentiments): love, humor, compassion, fear, disgust, anger, wonder, valor, and tranquility.

With elaborate costumes projecting larger-than-life images, loud music with a heavy percussive element, and very vigorous dance steps that require great stamina and balance, the Kathakali is the most powerful of dramatic instruments: the audience is left not merely enthralled but often completely mesmerized. This art form had its roots in shamanic costumed possessions that were taken up by Sanskritic culture and adapted to the Sanskrit language and sensibility. The primordial element, surviving from traditional pre-ARYAN Kerala culture, is quite palpable in these performances.

Further reading: David Bolland, *A Guide to Kathakali* (New Delhi: National Book Trust, 1980); Clifford R. Jones and Betty True Jones, *Kathakali: An Introduction to the Dance-Drama of Kerala* (San Francisco: American Society of Eastern Arts, 1970); Phillip Zarrilli, *The Kathakali Complex: Actor, Performance and Structure* (New Delhi: Abhinav, 1984).

Kathasaritsagara

The *Kathasaritsagara, The Ocean of the Rivers of Story,* by the Kashmiri writer Somadeva (c. 11th century), is one of the most important collections of tales deriving from the lost BRIHATKATHA of GUNADHYA. The work is the source for dozens of stories that have since been repeated over and over in various forms and versions within the Indian literary tradition, both in Sanskrit and in the vernacular languages.

The work itself consists of 22,000 verses, more than the *Iliad* and *Odyssey* combined, divided into 18 books. The first section tells stories about how the collection itself was created—for example, the story of Gunadhya and the story of king Satavahana. Among the many popular tales in the later sections are the story of Indra and King Shibi, the story of Urvashi and Pururavas (*see* APSARAS), the story of AHALYA (which appears in another form in the RAMAYANA), and the story of the BRAHMIN and the mongoose. Still other tales include the story of Udayana, the story of Kadambari, and the story of the 10 princes (*Dasakumaracarita*).

In the collection are stories of animals such as *The Mouse Merchant; The Ichneuman, the Owl, the Cat and the Mouse, the Crane and the Crocodile, the Lion and the Hare; The Parrot Who Was Taught Virtue by the King of the Parrots;* and *The Ass in the Panther's Skin.* Many of these stories closely resemble Aesop's fables in their structure and moral objectives. However, a large proportion of the hundreds of stories in this work are dedicated to the lives and adventures of kings, some of whom may have been historical, such as Satavahana and Vikramaditya.

Further reading: Aparna Chattopadhyay, *Studies in the Kathasaritsagara* (Varanasi: A. Chattopadhyay, 1993); N. M. Penzer, ed., *The Ocean of Story: Being C. H. Tawney's Translation of Somadeva's Katha Sarit Sagara (or Ocean of Streams of Story),* 10 vols. (Delhi: Motilal Banarsidass, 1968–84); J. S. Speyer, *Studies about the Kathasaritsagara* (Wiesbaden: M. Sandig, 1968); C. H. Tawney, trans., *Stories of Vikramaditya* (Bombay: Bharatiya Vidya Bhavan, 1963–64); ———, *Vetala-panchavimsati: Twenty-five stories of a Vampire from Somadeva* (Bombay: Jaico, 1956).

Katha Upanishad

The Katha Upanishad is part of the Black YAJUR VEDA. It is based on an ancient story of a young man, NACHIKETAS, who is mistakenly sent to hell by his father after he questions his father's generosity. When the boy reaches the realm of the god of death (YAMA), he finds no one at home. Since he, as a guest, is kept waiting, Yama offers the young, but very wise, boy three boons.

The story of the three boons of the god of death forms the narrative core of this Upanishad. The first boon the boy asks for is that he be returned to the upper world to live with his father. The second boon he asks for is the secret of preserving good works. His final request is to learn the secret of overcoming continuous rebirth. Death gladly assents to the first two requests, giving the boy the Nachiketas fire, named for him, to fulfill the second wish. When asked for the secret of ending rebirth, however, Death tries to dissuade the boy with offers of wealth and other boons. When Nachiketas persists he is given the secret of Ultimate Reality or the BRAHMAN.

Further reading: Swami Nikhilananda, trans., *The Upanishads* (New York: Ramakrishna-Vivekananda Center, 1975); S. Radhakrishnan, *The Principal Upanishads* (Atlantic Highlands, N.J.: Humanities Press, 1994).

kaula

Kaula is a tantric practice (*see* TANTRISM) that seeks unity with the *kula,* an esoteric term best understood to signify SHIVA (but often the menstrual blood of the goddess), sometimes focusing on Shiva as the ultimate and sometimes on SHAKTI. It includes a variety of different acts and has no definitive boundaries. It is known to make use of practices such as the PANCHA MAKARA or Five M's, which involve practicing sexual rituals, eating beef, and drinking alcohol. It focuses on raising the KUNDALINI serpent at the base of the spine up through the CHAKRAS toward the place above the head where it meets its lover Shiva to create ADVAITA (non-dual) consciousness and bliss.

Further reading: J. C. Chatterji, *Kashmir Shaivism* (Albany: State University of New York Press, 1986); Mark Dyczkowski, *The Doctrine of Vibration: An Analysis of the Doctrines and Practices of Kashmir Shaivism* (Albany: State University of New York Press, 1987).

Kauravas

The 100 Kauravas (descendants of KURU) are the chief villains in the great Indian epic the MAHABHARATA. They also descend from the ancient king Bharata. These sons of the blind king Dhritarashtra, led by Duryodhana, the eldest, conspire to steal the throne of the land from its rightful heirs, their cousins the PANDAVAS. Kaurava is only a convenient designation, as the Pandavas are also descendents of King Kuru via Pandu, Dhritarashtra's brother.

The story tells that Dhritarashtra's wife, Gandhari, receives a boon that she will bear 100 sons. She is pregnant for two years, when she hears that Kunti, wife of Pandu, has given birth. She then aborts herself, yielding a hard ball of flesh. The ball is sprinkled with water and severed into 101 parts, which are incubated and put into separate pots. From these come forth the 100 sons of Gandhari and Dhritarasthra, plus one daughter named Duhshala. (Dhritarashtra also incidentally has one bastard son, Yuyutsu.)

After his older brother Pandu dies, Dhritarashtra becomes regent and his sons (always called "the 100" although in actuality 101), led by Duryodhana, begin plotting to destroy their cousins, the five Pandavas. The story of the epic revolves around the struggle for the kingdom between these sets of brothers, culminating in the "Mahabharata" war, in which the Pandavas are triumphant, but with frightening losses.

Further reading: Peter Brook, director, *The Mahabharata* (videorecording), produced by Michael Propper (Chatsworth, Calif.: Image Entertainment, 2002); William Buck, trans., *The Mahabharata* (Berkeley: University of California Press, 1973); J. A. B. van Buitenen, trans., *The Mahabharata*, 3 vols. (Chicago: University of Chicago Press); P. C. Roy, trans., *The Mahabharata*, 12 vols. (Bombay: Bharata Karyalaya, 1888–1896).

Kautilya (Chanakya) (c. 300 B.C.E.) *See* ARTHASHASTRA.

Kaveri River *See* CAUVERY RIVER.

Kedarnath

Kedarnath is a famous Shaivite (*see* SHAIVISM) PILGRIMAGE site in the Indian state of Uttar Pradesh; one of India's *svamyambhu*, or "Self-generated" LINGAMS is located there. As in Amarnath the focus is upon an ice lingam. Pilgrimage can take place only during the middle of the summer, because of the inaccessibility of the mountainous location.

Kedarnath has been a pilgrimage site at least since the 12th century; it is listed in the eighth chapter of the text *Krityakalpataru* of Bhatta Lakshmidhara, a chief minister to King Govindachandra of the Gahadvala dynasty of Kanauj. It is usually said that there are four abodes of sanctity in all of India: BADRINATH, Puri (*see* JAGANNATH TEMPLE, PURI), RAMESHVARAM, and DWARAKA. In North India alone Kedarnath is considered one of the additional three abodes of sanctity; the other two are Yamnotri and Gangotri.

Further reading: Anne Feldhaus, *Connected Places: Region, Pilgrimage, and Geographical Imagination in India* (New York: Palgrave Macmillan, 2003); Subhadra Sen Gupta, *Badrinath and Kedarnath, the Dhaams in the Himalayas* (New Delhi: Rupa, 2002).

Kena Upanishad

The Kena Upanishad or "By Whom [*Kena*] Upanishad," takes its name from its first words, which ask the question, Who impels mind, breath and speech? Its subsidiary name, the Talavakara Upanishad, is from the *Talavakara* BRAHMANA of the SAMA VEDA, in which this Upanishad is sometimes found. The answer to the initial question is found in the second stanza: "That which is the hearing of the ear, the thought of the mind, the voice of speech and also the breathing of breath, and the sight of the eye" is the thing by which everything comes about.

This short Upanishad, with about 34 stanzas, tells a story (vss. 14–28) about the gods' first encounter with the BRAHMAN. They approached the unknown being to see whether they could overpower it, but all were defeated. INDRA himself could not overcome it, but on his way back the goddess Uma told him that the being was brahman. He passed on this information to the rest of the gods, and was recognized as the greatest of the gods because of this knowledge. Uma somehow does not get the credit.

Further reading: Sri Aurobindo, *Kena Upanishad* (Pondicherry: Sri Aurobindo Ashram, 1952); S. Radhakrishnan, *The Principal Upanishads* (Atlantic Highlands, N.J.: Humanities Press, 1994).

Keshavadas, Sant (1934–1997) advaita
Vedanta teacher

A prolific writer, composer, and international teacher, Sant Keshavadas founded the Temple of Cosmic Religion to advance his belief in the mystical unity of all religions.

Sant Keshavadas was born on July 22, 1934, on the Hindu holy day of Ekadashi, in Bhadragiri, a small village near Mysore in southern India. He was named Radha-Krishna by his parents, Venkataramana Pai and Rukmini Bai, At his birth, a priest cast his horoscope and predicted that the child would spread the devotion of God around

the world. At age 11, he received a mystical vision of Lord VISHNU, which inspired him to sing the word of God wherever he went in order to spread *sanatana* DHARMA "the eternal way"—a synonym for Hinduism—across the world.

In 1956, Radha-Krishna earned a B.A. from Mahatma Gandhi Memorial College, and two years later he received an L.L.B. at the Udipi Law College. After graduation he married Srimathi Rama Mataji, who joined him in his mission and helped him establish an ashram in Bangalore,

Sant Keshavadas (1934–1997), prominent teacher of Vedanta philosophy and yoga, known for his entrancing music and storytelling *(Courtesy Temple of Cosmic Religion, Oakland)*

Karnataka, in the 1960s. Between 1959 and 1966, Keshavadas made 47 pilgrimage tours of India, singing and speaking about his teaching.

In 1966, at the KUMBHA MELA festival in Allahabad, Keshavadas met the immortal BABAJI, who encouraged Keshavadas to go to the West to establish a following for the cosmic religion. Keshavadas and his wife (called Guru Mata) took this advice and traveled that year to Germany, England, and New York City to spread the message of *sanatana dharma*. Their message was received enthusiastically in the West and Keshavadas continued to make frequent trips across the world over the next 30 years. He established several ashrams in India, including his headquarters at the Vishwa Shanti Ashram in Bangalore, an ashram in Trinidad, and one in Oakland, California.

Keshavadas taught that mysticism or direct experience of God is the future of religion. On the basis of this belief he established the Temple of Cosmic Religion. He believed that humanity is preparing itself for cosmic consciousness, but that the ego prevents each person from reaching transformation to a higher consciousness. His main teaching focused on overcoming doctrinal differences by emphasizing unity among all religions. He offered many different approaches to unity but taught that the path to enlightenment requires repetition of God's holy name. His teachings include BHAKTI, deity worship, JNANA YOGA and VEDANTA as understood through Swami VIVEKANANDA.

Keshavadas was an accomplished composer who wrote and recorded over 6,000 songs. He often used music, storytelling, philosophy, and humor in his teachings. He spoke eight languages and lectured widely to audiences in the East and West. He also authored over 50 books including *The Bhagavad Gita and the Bible,* a work that explores the teachings of love and wisdom in Hinduism and Christianity. During the 1980s he organized construction of the Bhagavad-Gita Mandir (temple) near his Bangalore ashram. All 700 stanzas of the Bhagavad Gita are carved in black marble there, in English, Sanskrit, Hindi, and Kannada.

On December 4, 1997, at the age of 63, Keshavadas passed away while on a lecture circuit in Visakhapatnam. His work of unity and peace is continued by Guru Mata, who assumed responsibility for her husband's mission.

Further reading: Satguru Sant Keshavadas, *Essence of Bhagavad-Gita and Bible* (Oakland, Calif.: Temple of Cosmic Religion, 1982); ———, *Life and Teachings of Sadguru Sant Keshavadas* (Southfield, Mich.: Temple of Cosmic Religion, 1977); ———, *Mystic Christ* (Bangalore: Dasashrama Research, 1972); ———, *Self Realization* (Southfield, Mich.: Temple of Cosmic Religion, 1976); Mukundadas (Michael Allan Makowsky), *Minstrel of Love: A Biography of Satguru Sant Keshavadas* (Nevada City, Calif.: Hansa, 1980).

kevalin   *See* JAINISM.

Khajuraho

Khajuraho is a small village near Jhansi in the state of Madhya Pradesh. Some 22 temples are located around the village; they are considered the finest of the medieval period and are known for their erotic art.

The temples were constructed between 950 and 1050 C.E. under the Chandel empire. They show murals and a profusion of sculptures that depict explicit scenes from the KAMA SUTRA. Some have explained their frank depiction of myriad sexual positions as being tantric in origin, as TANTRISM is known to stress sexual ritual.

One legend gives a more personal explanation of the erotic artwork. The mother of the king who built the temple had been seduced by the Moon god and became a social outcast. When the boy grew up to become king, he had a dream visitation from his mother; she asked him to show all the passions of love in order that people would learn the goodness of sexuality and not condemn it. The temples of Khajuraho above all celebrate the feminine form. Women in every pose and posture, sexual and otherwise, are depicted with great care and art.

Though the temples are variously dedicated as Vaishnavite, Shaivite, GODDESS, and Jain (*see* JAINISM), they all appear quite similar; on the exterior one sees only women and men in sexual postures, and the sectarian identities are not apparent. Carvings and pictures in these temples show a dizzying profusion; every wall and ceiling is covered with painting and sculpture.

Further reading: Devagana Desai, *Khajuraho* (New Delhi: Oxford University Press, 2000); Krishna Deva, *Temples of Khajuraho* (New Delhi : Archaeological Survey of India, 1990).

khalsa   *See* SIKHISM.

Kirpal Light Satsang   *See* RADHASOAMI MOVEMENT.

kirtans

Kirtans are songs to the glories of a god. They are usually sung in groups of people, accompanied by an accordionlike instrument called the harmonium. Percussive instruments are sometimes used as well. *Kirtan* singing may be the most common form of collective devotional worship in India. Both men and women participate. Singing alternatively slows down and speeds up until the singers are in a trance, ideally experiencing the presence of, or even union, with the divinity. Both *kirtans* and *BHAJANS* are songs of worship sung in devotion.

Further reading: Gobind Singh Mansukhani, *Indian Classical Music and Sikh Kirtan* (San Bernardino, Calif.: Borgo Press, 1985); Hansadutta Swami, *Kirtan: Ancient Medicine for Modern Man* (Hopland, Calif.: Hansa Books, 1984).

Klein, Jean (c. 1916–1998)   *Western teacher of yoga and* advaita *Vedanta*

Jean Klein was an important 20th-century teacher of non-dual VEDANTA, who focused on the direct experience of the Self rather than the gradual, progressive method of enlightenment.

Klein was born around 1916 into a family that loved music, painting, and art. He describes the family as "harmonious." His childhood was spent in Brno (Czechoslovakia), Prague, and Vienna. He studied music and medicine in Vienna and Berlin, where he explored the relationships among thought, feeling, and muscle function.

He became a physician, and undertook the study of Eastern philosophies, particularly the works of Mohandas Karamchand GANDHI, Lao Tse, Chuang Tsu, Tagore, Coomaraswamy, J. KRISHNAMURTI, and Sri Aurobindo. After reading Gandhi, he became a vegetarian. He also read Dostoevsky, Nietzsche, and the Western Sufi René Guénon. Guénon's writing on cosmology and tradition proved a turning point in Klein's life. What struck him was the distinction Guénon made between traditional and tradition—the principle transmitted from teacher to disciple through initiation: "This awoke in me the feeling that it was actually humanly possible to become fully integrated and awake in the whole."

He left Germany in 1933 and spent World War II in France secretly helping thousands escape from Germany. After the war, he left Europe for India seeking an environment that would welcome self-inquiry. There he met a Pandit, a professor of SANSKRIT in Bangalore, Atmananda Krishna Menon, who became his teacher and who initiated him into the wisdom of ADVAITA (non-dual) VEDANTA. He also deepened his long study of YOGA by spending several months with Krishnamacharya, the famous hatha yoga teacher of South India. Although Klein could do ASANAS (postures) quite well, he was not attracted to yoga of the physical body. He wanted to understand how the body can become more subtle, more energized, more expanded; he began to see that the real body is energy and light, not the bone-muscle structure that we assume to be the body. As Klein taught asanas and yoga, he always gave the energy body priority, stressing that all postures could be done independently of the physical body. After he had lived intensely with this understanding, one day the teaching became a lively reality, a bright and integrated truth.

Klein's teaching sprang from his insight into the nature of being and existence. He is regarded as a prominent teacher of *advaita* in the 20th century and an embodiment of the non-dual awareness he taught. His teaching is "direct," cutting through all experiences, states, and paths of purification that depend upon progressive or sequential methods. He encourages students to experience existence directly. According to Klein, the progressive way may produce many delightful experiences, but all these are support for the ego, which is thus kept alive in a more and more subtle way. Klein's direct approach says that our real nature cannot be known or experienced as an object. When this is clearly understood there is a letting go, a giving up of trying to achieve, to become, to find, or to understand. This letting go is the beginning of real maturity and openness to our true nature.

For 40 years, Dr. Klein responded to invitations from all over the world to share his knowledge. He lived in Europe and the United States and died in February 1998 in Santa Barbara, California. He is the author of several books in English and other languages.

Klein created the nonprofit Jean Klein Foundation in 1989 to help in the process of disseminating his teaching. Based in Santa Barbara, the foundation holds meetings that are open to the public and continues to publish newsletters. It has published Klein's journal *Listening* and plans to publish several books and dialogues of Klein's.

Further reading: Jean Klein, *Be Who You Are* (Longmead, England: Element, 1989); ———, *The Ease of Being* (Durham, N.C.: Acorn Press, 1984); ———,

Transmission of the Flame (Santa Barbara, Calif.: Third Millenium, 1990).

Klemp, Harold   *See* ECKANKAR.

Konarak

Konarak in the state of Orissa is the site of the largest temple to the sun god in India. It was built around the 13th century C.E. The main building represents the sun god's chariot, which in mythology was pulled across the sky each day by fiery-maned horses. The chariot has 24 massive wheels. Pulling the chariot are seven carved horses. The

Temple to the sun god, with the god's chariot, in Konarak, Orissa *(Constance A. Jones)*

temple was decorated with erotic sculpture resembling that at KHAJURAHO. Its tower appears to have fallen but is said to have been 200 feet high.

Further reading: A. Boner, S. R. Sarma, and R. P. Das, *New Light on the Sun Temple of Konarka: Four Unpublished Manuscripts Relating to the Construction History and Ritual of the Temple* (Varanasi: Chowkhambha Sanskrit Series Office, 1972).

Kripalu Center for Yoga and Health
See DESAI, AMRIT.

Kripalu Yoga
Kripalu Yoga is a form of HATHA YOGA originally developed by Amrit DESAI (b. 1932) in the United States. The Indian-born Desai had been teaching yoga in the United States through the 1960s. However, in 1970, a significant development occurred in his work. Immediately after a visit to his teacher, Swami KRIPALVANANDA (1913–81), and while engaged in his regular practice, he experienced a spontaneous flow of yoga postures. He attributed this occurrence to the intelligence of the life force, which performed the postures without willful direction. He studied his experience and discovered the means of leading others into the same experience. As he began to teach this technique to others, he named it in honor of his guru, Sri Kripalvananda.

Kripalu Yoga begins with the eight aspects of Ashtanga Yoga derived from Patanjali's YOGA SUTRA. The postures (ASANAS) are learned in a three-step progress. One first learns the asanas consciously and practices them until some mastery of the positions is gained. In the second stage, as the practitioner holds each position, she or he withdraws attention from the outward world (in this case, the posture) and focuses attention inward on the accompanying body sensations. At this stage, one generally encounters a variety of psychological barriers and works to release all blockages on physical, mental, and spiritual levels. In the third stage, one learns to participate in "meditation in motion," allowing the wisdom of the body to move itself into the postures apart from any conscious willing. Though simply described in three stages, each stage requires a significant amount of both physical and psychological work.

Desai began teaching his new variation on yoga in 1972 through the Kripalu Yoga Fellowship, in Somneytown, Pennsylvania, which he founded. The fellowship trained and commissioned many teachers of Kripalu Yoga. In 1994, after the discovery that Desai had had sexual relations with several of his students, the board of the Kripalu Center for Yoga and Health in Lenox, Massachusetts, the showcase center of the fellowship, asked him to leave. Subsequently, the fellowship became organized as an educational institute without a focus on one teacher.

The Kripalu Center hosts a variety of programs, including yoga retreats, healing arts training, leadership instruction, and yoga teacher certification.

Further reading: Stephen Cope, *Yoga and the Quest for the True Self* (New York: Bantam, 2000); Amrit Desai, *Kripalu Yoga: Meditation in Motion* (Lenox, Mass.: Kripalu Yoga Fellowship, 1981); Richard Faulds, *Kripalu Yoga: A Guide to Practice on and off the Mat* (New York: Bantam, 2005); Deva Parnell, "Kripalu Yoga: Theory and Practice." Available online. URL: http://www.discoveryyoga.com/KYTheory.htm. Accessed August 17, 2005.

Kripalvananda, Swami Sri (1913–1981)
Popular Gujarati yogi and inspiration for kriya yoga
His Holiness Swami Sri Kripalvananda, whose teachings inspired the popular form of HATHA YOGA known as KRIPALU YOGA, was born in 1913 in Gujarat, India. His childhood was marked by several attempts to commit suicide, but after his last attempt, he met his GURU, known affectionately as Dadaji, in a visionary experience. He later learned

that Dadaji was Lakulish, the 28th incarnation of Lord SHIVA.

The vision transformed his life and, after eight months, he took initiation into *sannyas*, renunciation, from Dadaji and was guided by Dadaji for the rest of his life. Dadaji then disappeared until 1952, when Kripalvanandji saw him as a young man. In his later appearances he encouraged Kripalvananda to develop and continue intense 10-hour-a-day practice of KUNDALINI meditation that he continued for the rest of his life.

At Kayavarohan, Gujarat, Kripalvananda was inspired to build a temple to Lord Lakulish and to reestablish the town of Kayavarohan as a center of spiritual culture and learning.

As his own practice matured, Kripalvananda became the guru of two brothers, SHANTI and AMRIT DESAI (b. 1932), both of whom would later go to America and begin organizations teaching the type of kundalini and hatha yoga that inspired Kripalvananda. In 1977, Amrit Desai invited Kripalvananda to go to America, where he would stay for more than three years. In those years he was a significant influence on the emerging community of KRIYA YOGA in the United States. He returned to India shortly before his death at the end of 1981.

Further reading: Yogi Amrit Desai and Shri Kripalvananda, *The Passion of Christ: A Discourse* (Lenox, Mass.: Kripalu, 1983); Shri Kripalvanandiji, *Krpalupanisad* (St. Helena, Calif.: Sanatana Publication Society, 1979); ———, *Pilgrimage of Love,* Books 1–3 (Lenox, Mass.: Kripalu, 1992); ———, *The Stages of Kundalini Yoga* (Lenox, Mass.: Kripalu, 1976); Swami Rajarshi Muni, *Infinite Grace: The Story of My Spiritual Lineage* (Vadodara: Life Mission Publications, 2002).

Krishna

The god Krishna is understood to be an incarnation of VISHNU. None of the other incarnations of Vishnu has attracted as passionate and widespread a devotion in India as Krishna. There is some evidence that Krishna was originally a historical fig-

ure. Krishna is technically the black god, since the Sanskrit word *krishna* means "black." However, he is generally depicted with blue skin.

Krishna appears in the MAHABHARATA epic as a friend to the PANDAVA brothers. In that epic Krishna is rarely referred to with divine epithet, or as a divinity. It is only in the BHAGAVAD GITA, the famous text that recounts the teaching of Krishna to ARJUNA just before the battle, that the divinity of Krishna is clearly detailed. Some have suggested that the worship of Krishna in this context may constitute a form of euhemerism, or the deification of a famous warrior.

A second role of Krishna is as the divine lover, dancing at midnight with the cowherd maidens (GOPIS), who are drawn to his beauty, his beautiful music, and the magic of his divine presence. According to tradition he eventually favors Radha among the gopis; the passionate love of Radha for her furtive, often unavailable lover becomes the paradigm for Krishna devotionalism. Finally, Krishna appears as a child and youth, mischievous, naughty, and beloved of every mother who lays eyes upon him.

The god was born in Mathura, where his father, VASUDEVA, was minister to the evil king Kamsa. Kamsa discovered that Vasudeva's wife, DEVAKI, was to give birth to a son who would eventually kill him. Therefore, he kept Vasudeva and Devaki under guard and killed their first six children. The seventh child, BALARAMA, was miraculously transferred to the womb of Vasudeva's other wife, Rohini. When the eighth child, Krishna, was born, a profound slumber fell upon Vasudeva's guards and the father was able secretly to take the child across the YAMUNA River to BRINDAVAN and consign him to the cowherd Nanda and his wife, YASHODA, who became Krishna's foster mother.

As a child, Krishna was extremely mischievous, stealing milk and butter (one of his epithets is "butter thief"), overturning wagons, and felling trees with strength far beyond that of an ordinary child. Once Yashoda tied him to a huge mortar used for grinding things. Krishna, even though

Lord Krishna, an incarnation of Vishnu, with consort Radha *(Institute for the Study of American Religion, Santa Barbara, California)*

a baby, dragged it out of the house and used it to fell two trees.

Once when Yashoda caught him eating mud, she forced him to open his mouth; within, she saw the entire universe. Krishna's magic made her forget this incident, lest she not be able to treat him as an ordinary child.

In two stories of his childhood he outwits evil forces. Putana, a witch, was sent by the evil king Kamsa to kill the infant by suckling him with poisonous milk. Krishna was completely unharmed, but he sucked so ferociously at her breast that the demon's innards were sucked out and she died. In a later incident the snake demon Kaliya poisoned the drinking water in the Yamuna River, threatening the lives of the cowherds and the cows. Krishna found the pool where Kaliya was hiding and danced a furious dance upon him until he was killed.

In another tale the young Krishna asked people to worship the mountain Govardhana, rather than the great king of the gods Indra. Indra, learning this, sent terrible rain storms to wash away the cowherds who had defied him. Krishna with his divine strength lifted up the mountain, Govardhana, to use as an umbrella to protect the people and thus defeated Indra himself.

As a young man, Krishna began to attract the interest of the cowherd women as he played his magical flute day and night. He would flirt with them and play tricks on them. Once when the cowherd girls were bathing he took all their clothes and put them up into a big tree. When the women left the water and begged him for their garments, he bent the tree down and let them retrieve their clothes.

Particularly at night Krishna would work his divine magic. The women would yearn to see him and could not find him. They would begin to think of all his magical deeds and praise him. When they finally found him, they began to dance with him; he became many Krishnas, pairing with each woman as though she were the only one. This is referred to as the Rasalila dance and is the metaphor for the way that god is intimate with each soul while it is only one. Finally, in the stories of later times (c. 10th century) one cowherd woman alone, named RADHA, becomes Krishna's favorite. Her passionate love for him, her yearning when he does not appear at their assigned spot, and their loveplay are all celebrated in the passionate liturgy of Krishna worship, where the devotee sees himself or herself as Radha seeking passionate union with god.

After the death of Kamsa, Krishna becomes an ally of the Pandavas. He assists them in every way fair and foul and helps them triumph; the BHAGAVAD GITA makes clear that this was divine aid.

We are left here with the mystery of Krishna, a divinity who is mischievous and naughty as a child, naughty as a young man—playing games with the hearts of many women—and who in war does not hesitate to use stratagems that the SHASTRAS the authoritative texts, might find inappropriate for a warrior. Krishna effects his *LILA*, his divine game, in ways that humans cannot grasp, except through complete devotion. Krishna must eventually die, as must all the other AVATARS of

Vishnu. While in the forest doing YOGA then, he is accidentally pierced in the foot with a spear by a hunter who mistook his foot for a deer's foot. He blesses the man who threw the spear that will take him to heaven.

Many devotional Vaishnavite movements in India focus on worship of Krishna only. Most famous of these are the followers of Saint CHAITANYA of Bengal, whose Goswamis, or followers of Chaitanya's tradition, moved to Brindavan to be closer to the place where Krishna lived. The followers of Chaitanya include Sri Swami Prabhupada BHAKTIVEDANTA, who traveled to the United States to found the Hare Krishna movement. As do many Krishnaites, they worship in ecstatic devotion, while chanting MANTRAS to their god.

Further reading: W. G. Archer, *The Loves of Krishna in Indian Painting and Poetry* (London: Allen & Unwin, 1957); Cornelia Dimmitt and J. A. B. van Buitenen, eds. and trans., *Classical Hindu Mythology: A Reader in the Sanskrit Puranas* (Philadelphia: Temple University Press, 1978); David Haberman, *Journey through the Twelve Forests: An Encounter with Krishna* (New York: Oxford University Press, 1994); John S. Hawley, *Krsna the Butter Thief* (Princeton, N.J.: Princeton University Press, 1983); Alf Hiltebeitel, "Krsna and the Mahabharata," *Annals of the Bhandarkar Oriental Research Institute* 60 (1979): 65–107.

Krishna, Gopi (1903–1984) *master of Kundalini Yoga*

Gopi Krishna was an influential teacher whose impact depended on conveying his own transformative KUNDALINI YOGA experiences. He was known for his clear exposition of the awakening of kundalini. However, he never had his own spiritual teacher, was not initiated into any spiritual lineage, and did not himself train disciples.

Gopi Krishna was born in Kashmir in 1903 as an only son. In his childhood, his father renounced the world to lead a religious life and left his wife to care for three children. Since he was the only son, he bore responsibility for his family's welfare. He did not attend university because he did not pass a major examination. In reaction to his father's decision to leave the world, he vowed to live as a householder. And in shame over his failure at examination, he took on a practice of MEDITATION in order to refine his concentration.

While employed by the Indian government, he practiced meditation for 17 years and developed the ability to sit for hours in concentration without discomfort. In 1937, while meditating and imagining a lotus at the crown of the head, he felt a roar like a waterfall and felt a stream of liquid light entering the brain through the spinal cord. This was his first experience of the serpent power of kundalini, a power said to reside as a latent force at the base of the spine that can be awakened so that it travels through and opens the seven CHAKRAS (energy centers along the spine). His report of this episode, for which he was totally unprepared, described a vast circle of consciousness in which the body was but a point, bathed in light and in a state of happiness impossible to describe.

Shortly after the initial experience, he experienced a continuous "luminous glow" around his head. He began to have a variety of psychological and physiological problems and even thought he was becoming mad. Although he read accounts of this phenomenon, he found no one who could help him through this difficult period. The mental and emotional destabilization lasted for several years. Aware that a fundamental change had taken place in him, he believed that his entire nervous system would be slowly reorganized and transformed. He viewed this energy, once activated, as an intelligent force over which one has little control.

His autobiography records this experience and its aftermath in one of the most detailed accounts of the unleashing of a psychospiritual power and spiritual transformation. He describes the difficulties and dangers of the spiritual path and the pressure that it can exert on the physical body.

However unbalanced his experience, he maintained in all of his subsequent writings that the awakening of kundalini is the means of spiritual evolution for humanity.

Gopi Krishna was not a GURU in the classical sense of one who has disciples. He did not found a movement or a sect but remained a seeker who later became a teacher. He documented his experiences in a number of books that attempted to teach the reality of the kundalini experience and to help others who encounter this extraordinary phenomenon. He died on July 31, 1984.

Further reading: Gopi Krishna, *The Awakening of Kundalini* (New York: E. P. Dutton, 1975); ———, *Higher Consciousness: The Evolutionary Thrust of Kundalini* (New York: Julian Press, 1974); ———, *Kundalini: Evolutionary Energy in Man* (London: Robinson & Watkins, 1971); ———, *The Secret of Yoga* (New York: Harper & Row, 1972).

Krishnabai, Mother (1903–1989) *teacher who embodied the love of service*

The child who later became known as Mother Krishnabai was born in 1903, although little else is known of her childhood. The first years of her life were turbulent. When she was 10 her father died. At age 13 she married K. Laxman Rao, who passed away seven years later, in 1926, leaving her a young widow.

In 1928 she encountered Swami RAMDAS, who provided uplift from her sorrows. Krishnabai became a devoted disciple and attained self-realization by strictly following the swami's teaching. As the foremost disciple and successor of Swami Ramdas, she embodied the love of service and provided for the spiritual and material needs of the poor. Under Swami Ramdas's guidance she helped to establish Anandashram in Kerala, South India. She worked with her beloved teacher there, becoming a mother to all who went to the ashram. In 1963, upon the death of Swami Ramdas, she assumed leadership of Anandashram. In spite of poor health she propagated Swami Ramdas's teachings and served the poor until her death on February 12, 1989.

Further reading: Mother Krishnabai, *Guru's Grace* (Kahnangad: Anandashram, 1963); Swami Ramdas, *Krishna Bai* (Ramnagar: Anandashram, 1940); Swami Satchidananda, *Viswamata Krishnabai* (Kahnangad: Anandashram, n.d.); Sriram, *With the Divine Mother* (Kahnangad: Anandashram, n.d.).

Krishnalila   *See* RASA LILA.

Krishnamurti, Jiddu (1895–1986) *spiritual teacher of radical self-observation*

Chosen while still a child as the new messiah, or World Teacher, by the THEOSOPHICAL SOCI-ETY, the Indian J. Krishnamurti acquired world fame as he traveled and lectured on the society's universalist teachings. After a personal spiritual transformation, he rejected the society and its occultism and went on to teach his philosophy of free inquiry toward the goal of understanding the self.

Born on May 12, 1895, in Madanapalle, near Madras (Chennai) in colonial India, Krishnamurti (the image of Krishna) grew up in an orthodox BRAHMIN family steeped in tradition, ritual, and a sacred view of the world. After the death of his mother when he was only 10 years old, he moved with his father and siblings to the compound of the Theosophical Society, a rapidly growing spiritual movement, in Adyar, near Madras.

The Theosophical Society, founded in 1875 in New York City, began as an organization dedicated to a synthesis of science, religion, and philosophy with the credo "There is no religion higher than truth." Theosophical teaching includes the exploration of clairvoyant powers for discovering the hidden mysteries of nature and the esoteric powers of humanity. The Theosophists drew freely from their understanding of Eastern thought, particularly Buddhist and Hindu cosmologies, to form a worldview that included a complex cosmology, an esoteric psychology, and an evolutionary scheme that encompassed eons. Drawing upon many religious traditions and prophecies, the Theosophical Society at the time of Krishnamurti's youth was actively looking for a messiah, a world teacher, who would destroy evil and restore righteousness.

In his early teen years, Krishnamurti was chosen by the Theosophists as the young world teacher and appointed head of the Order of the Star in the East, an organization devoted to realizing his teaching mission. For a number of years he traveled and addressed audiences, maturing in

Jiddu Krishnamurti (1895–1986), philosopher and teacher of radical self-observation *(Krishnamurti Foundation America)*

his understanding of the order, the Theosophical Society, and his role in each.

Over many months in 1922–23, Krishnamurti experienced a profound transformation. Begun as MEDITATION, Krishnamurti's "process" contained moments of great beauty and clarity offset by periods of physical pain, even agony. He would fall unconscious, converse with nonphysical entities, and speak from several personas. Krishnamurti's account is consistent with other reports of mystical non-dualist transformations. His personality dissolved into communion with all that lay beyond him. In his words, "I was in everything, or rather everything was in me, inanimate and animate, the mountain, the work and all breathing things."

After "the process" was complete, he experienced a growing dissatisfaction with the authority structure of the Theosophical Society and its emphasis on occultism. At the death of his brother, which the occultists of the Theosophical Society did not foresee, his dissatisfaction became overwhelming. He declared himself in revolt against Theosophy and against all forms of spiritual authority, advising every person, "Be a light unto yourselves." He disbanded the Order of the Star in the East in 1929, declaring, "Truth is a pathless land."

From then until his death in 1986, Krishnamurti traveled around the world teaching his insights. He became a champion of freedom and inquiry and a relentless advocate of the discovery of truth without the aid of any organization, religion, or belief system. His teaching emphasized the necessity of developing awareness of one's conditioning and one's bondage to thought, fear, and time. His goal was to make people "unconditionally free" and, to this end, he invited those who listened to him to observe their inner selves, including their motives and the functions of thought. With each audience, Krishnamurti inquired into the basic nature of humanity and found that real self-transformation involves an instantaneous awareness of the psyche and its workings. Accompanied by simplicity and humility, this awareness can open a person to the reality of oneself.

The Krishnamurti Foundation of America was founded in 1969 to preserve and disseminate his teachings. Activities include the Oak Grove School, the Krishnamurti Archives, the Krishnamurti Study Center, the Krishnamurti Library, and Krishnamurti Publications of America. The Krishnamurti Foundation of England, begun in 1968, oversees the Brockwood Park School. The Krishnamurti Foundation of India sponsors the Rishi Valley School, the Krishnamurti Study Centre in Varanasi, Vasanta College of Rajghat, and other centers.

During his lifetime Krishnamurti created schools for children and young adults in India, the United States, England, and Switzerland. These alternative schools continue today in their mission to provide a new definition and practice of education, free of the conditioning and authority structures prevalent in modern educational institutions.

In his later years, Krishnamurti joined the physicist David Bohm in an exploration of the human condition through a series of dialogues. Both men recognized the limitations of traditional didactic teaching and sought a way in which truth and insight might be discovered within individuals and small groups. The dialogue process, practiced today in all Krishnamurti Foundations in the United States, India, and England, encourages individual inquiry without didactic formalism and authority structures. Krishnamurti and Bohm predicted that the actual structure of the human brain could change as a result of increased awareness and open inquiry.

Krishnamurti died on February 18, 1986, in Ojai, California, among his students.

Further reading: S. Holroyd, *The Quest of the Quiet Mind: The Philosophy of Krishnamurti* (Wellingborough, England: Aquarian Press, 1980); Pupul Jayakar, *J. Krishnamurti: A Biography* (New York: Penguin, 1986);

Constance Jones, "Krishnamurti Foundations," in J. Gordon Melton and Martin Baumann, eds., *Religions of the World* (Santa Barbara, Calif.: ABC-Clio, 2002); J. Krishnamurti, *Commentaries on Living, from the Notebooks of J. Krishnamurti.* Edited by D. Rajagopal, 3 vols. (Wheaton, Ill.: Theosophical Publishing House, 1960); ———, *Education and the Significance of Life* (San Francisco: Harper, 1953); ———, *The First and Last Freedom* (San Francisco: Harper, 1954); ———, *Freedom from the Known* (San Francisco: Harper, 1969); ———, *Talks and Dialogues of J. Krishnamurti* (New York: Avon, 1968); J. Krishnamurti and David Bohm, *The Ending of Time* (San Francisco: Harper, 1985); Mary Lutyens, *Krishnamurti,* 3 vols. (New York: Farrar, Straus Giroux, 1988).

Krishnamurti, U. G. (1918–) *unorthodox teacher of philosophy of "no self"*

U. G. Krishnamurti is an original teacher in the Hindu tradition, who believes that conscious thought is the enemy of true knowledge.

Born into a BRAHMIN family on July 9, 1918, in Andhra Pradesh, India, U. G. Krishnamurti was exposed by his family to many forms of Hinduism as well as the philosophy of the THEOSOPHICAL SOCIETY. His childhood home was visited by monks, SWAMIS, pundits, GURUS, and religious scholars, who engaged in constant conversations on philosophy, religion, occultism, and metaphysics. He studied classical yoga with Swami SIVANANDA of Rishikesh and visited Sri RAMANA MAHARSHI in Tiruvannamalai.

At the University of Madras (Chennai), U. G. Krishnamurti studied philosophy and psychology. He married in his 20s and had four children. He became a public speaker and delivered orations for the Theosophical Society, becoming acquainted with J. KRISHNAMURTI (no relation), the person chosen in 1914 by Theosophists as the "world teacher."

U. G. Krishnamurti's teaching centers around a radical notion that so-called SELF-REALIZATION is actually the discovery that there is no self to discover. There is a "natural state" for humans that simply happens, without thought and without effort. Thought is an enemy because thought cannot touch anything living and cannot capture, contain, or express the quality of life. Further, religious and spiritual teachings that reduce the quality of life to thought and systems of thought are polluting to the spirit of humanity. Anything based on knowledge through thought is an illusion. Any moment of experience cannot be captured or given expression. Once the moment is captured, it is made a part of the past. In this way, U. G. Krishnamurti challenges the way that society is organized, in its political ideologies, legal structures, and religious institutions. What is necessary for survival of the human organism are an intelligence of the body and awareness of the moment of existence.

U. G. Krishnamurti continues to teach in Switzerland, India, and the United States.

Further reading: Mahesh Bhatt, *U. G. Krishnamurti—a Life* (New Delhi: Penguin India, 2001); U. G. Krishnamurti, *Mind Is a Myth—Disquieting Conversations with the Man Called U. G.* Edited by Terry Newland (Volant: Dinesh, 1988); ———, *The Mystique of Enlightenment: The Unrational Ideas of a Man Called U. G.* Edited by Rodney Arms, 3d ed. (Bangalore: Sahasramana Prakashana, 2001); ———, *Thought Is Your Enemy: Mind-Shattering Conversations with the Man Called U. G.* Edited by Anthony Paul Frank Noronha and J. S. R. L. Narayana Moorty (Bangalore: Sowmya, 1991).

Krishnananda, Swami (1922–2001) *philosopher of* advaita *Vedanta*

Swami Krishnananda was a great scholar of Sanskrit scripture, who shared his learning in many books and lectures. He served the Divine Life Society in Rishikesh as secretary for 40 years.

Subbaraya, later named Swami Krishnananda, was born on April 25, 1922, the eldest of six siblings in an orthodox Madhva BRAHMIN family. Raised through the example of his father's holiness and piety, Subbaraya learned to maintain his family's religious tradition with earnestness. He became versed in SANSKRIT as a young boy and was a passionate learner of scripture. Subbaraya attended school in Puttur, where he excelled in all subjects, rising to the top of his class. Aside from his usual studies, he spent time reading and memorizing Sanskrit scriptural texts. At age 16 he memorized the entire BHAGAVAD GITA by heart, reciting it each day.

Subbaraya's self-study of major Hindu scriptures led him to an acceptance of ADVAITA (nondual) philosophy. His growing interest pushed him toward a renunciation of the material world, even as he was pressured by his father and uncle to seek employment and earn money. Subbaraya accepted a government post at the Hospet Government Training School in Bellary District in 1943 but soon fell ill and returned home. Succumbing to his desire for the religious life, he traveled to Rishikesh in 1944 to join the Sivananda ashram. In 1946 Swami SIVANANDA initiated Subbaraya into SANNYAS (renunciation), giving him the name Swami Krishnananda.

Swami Krishnananda was employed at the ashram as a letter writer and editor of books. Sivananda later gave him the job of handwriting and typing manuscripts. In 1948, at Sivananda's request, Krishnananda began to write books on philosophy and religion. He accepted the task with great zeal and wrote his first book, *The Realization of the Absolute,* in a mere two weeks. He spent the remainder of his life writing commentaries on Hindu scriptures and delivering lectures on Eastern and Western philosophy and religion.

In 1957, Krishnananda became secretary of the ashram and focused his attention on managing finances. In 1961, he was nominated by Sivananda to the position of general secretary of the Divine Life Society. Krishnananda retained this position for the next 30 years until his death on November 23, 2001.

Swami Krishnananda is recognized for his knowledge of scriptures, his balance of KARMA

Swami Krishnananda (1922–2001), scholar, teacher, and secretary of Divine Life Society, Rishikesh *(Courtesy Divine Life Society, Rishikesh)*

(action) and JNANA (learning) YOGA, and his ability to communicate complicated concepts to students. He was a regular lecturer, teaching three-month-long courses at the Yoga-Vedanta Forest Academy of the Divine Life Society. His literary skill was used in varying degrees throughout Sivananda's organizations. He was made president of the Sivananda Literature Research Institute because of his understanding of all 300 of his guru's works. He was later made president of the Sivananda Literature Dissemination Committee, which worked on translating Sivananda's books into the major Indian languages.

Swami Krishnananda wrote over 40 books of his own, including works of poetry. His topics included yoga, MEDITATION, traditional scriptures, mysticism, and philosophy. Many of these books convey an essential message of peace, wisdom, and SELF-REALIZATION, which the Divine Life Society continues to spread.

Further reading: Swami Krishnananda, *An Introduction to the Philosophy of Yoga* (Shivanandanagar: Divine Life Society, 1982); ———, *Meditation, Its Theory and Practice* (Shivanandanagar: Divine Life Society, 1974); ———, *The Philosophy of the Bhagavad-Gita*

(Shivanandanagar: Divine Life Society, 1980); ———, *The Realization of the Absolute* (Rishikesh: Divine Life Society, 1972).

Krishna Prem, Sri (1898–1965) *Western-born Vaishnavite guru*

British-born Sri Krishna Prem was a prominent GURU in the orthodox Vaishnavite tradition.

Ronald Nixon was born in Cheltenham, England, on May 10, 1898; served as a pilot in World War I while still a teenager; and later graduated in philosophy from King's College, Cambridge. While at Cambridge, he studied Theosophy, Buddhism, and Pali and took a Buddhist initiation.

In 1921, after graduation from Cambridge, he went to India to take a position as lecturer in English at Lucknow University and to continue his spiritual search. The vice-chancellor of Lucknow University, Dr. G. N. Chakravarti, was a Theosophist, who had known Madame BLAVATSKY and was a friend of Annie BESANT, then president of the THEOSOPHICAL SOCIETY. During a party at the home of Dr. Chakravarti and his wife, Monica, Nixon observed Monica in a meditative and devotional state in front of an image of Lord KRISHNA. In 1924, she became his guru and gave him initiation into VAISHNAVISM (the worship of incarnations of VISHNU).

In 1928, Monica took the vow of SANNYAS (called *vairagya* in the GAUDIYA Vaishnavite tradition) and assumed the name *Yashoda Ma*. Soon after, Nixon took *vairagi* vows from her and was given the name Krishna Prem. They looked for a place to start a community and found a rural area near Almora; they founded the Uttar Brindaban Ashram and dedicated a temple to Radha and Krishna there in 1931. The ASHRAM began and has continued to be aligned with strict orthodox Vaishnavism, including total vegetarianism, thrice-daily PUJAS, and a sacramental attitude toward all of life.

Yashoda Ma died in 1944, leaving Krishna Prem as her successor. He initiated two people before her death: her daughter, Moti, and an Englishman he had known at Cambridge. The ashram grew and eventually included other Indian disciples, some of whom built their own cottages near the temple.

Krishna Prem traveled little, but in 1948 he visited Sri RAMANA MAHARSHI and Sri AUROBINDO and the MOTHER. At his death on November 14, 1965, leadership of the ashram passed to Sri Madhava ASHISH, another Englishman, who collaborated with Krishna Prem on publications and edited some of his work posthumously.

Further reading: Krishna Prem, *Initiation into Yoga: An Introduction to the Spiritual Life* (Bombay: B. I., 1976); ———, *The Yoga of the Bhagavat Gita* (Longmead, England: Element Books, 1988); Krishna Prem and Madhava Ashish, *Man, the Measure of All Things, in the Stanzas of Dyzan* (London: Rider, 1969); Dilip Kumar Roy, *Yogi Sri Krishnaprem* (Bombay: Bharatiya Vidya Bhavan, 1968).

Krita Yuga

All of the YUGAS, or ages, in the Indian tradition, refer to throws in an ancient game of dice. *Krita* ("the one that made it!") is the best throw—a 4.

The Krita Yuga, which like all ages has appeared an infinite number of times and will return an infinite number of times, is also called Satya Yuga, or the age of truth. It is 1,728,000 years long. In Krita Yuga the highest virtue is said to be MEDITATION. In this age, BRAHMA is god. Eternal DHARMA is said to have all its four feet in this age, while in the others it progressively has three, two, and one. In the Krita age there is no distinction between the best and worst of creatures. Their life, happiness, and attractiveness are all equal. They are also free of sorrow, completely good, and enjoy solitude, rather than crowds. They are devoted to MEDITATION, active in spiritual restraints and austerities, and act always without self-interest. They are always joyful and have no permanent homes, but live in the mountains or by the oceans.

Further reading: Cornelia Dimmitt and J. A. B. van Buitenen, *Classical Hindu Mythology: A Reader in the Sanskrit Puranas* (Philadelphia: Temple University Press, 1978); W. J. Wilkins, *Hindu Mythology, Vedic and Puranic,* 2d ed. (Calcutta: Rupa, 1973).

Kriyananda, Goswami   *See* TEMPLE OF KRIYA YOGA.

Kriyananda, Swami (1926–)
kriya yoga *guru*

Swami Kriyananda is the founder of the ANANDA MOVEMENT of religious and communal organizations, designed to spread the teachings of KRIYA YOGA and the principles of cooperative living.

James Donald Walters was born in Toleajen, Romania, to American parents. As a youth he was sent to boarding schools in Switzerland and England and later attended Haverford College, a Quaker school in Pennsylvania, and Brown University. He left school before completing his degree and settled in South Carolina.

In South Carolina, he had his first serious contact with Hinduism, when he read the Bhagavad Gita followed by *Autobiography of a Yogi* by Paramahansa YOGANANDA. At about the same time he became a vegetarian. In 1948, he moved across the continent to meet Yogananda and offer himself as a disciple. He quickly moved into a leadership position with Yogananda's relatively small organization, the SELF-REALIZATION FELLOWSHIP (SRF), and within a year was lecturing on its behalf. His leadership role increased after Yogananda's death, and in 1955 he was named the main minister at the center in Hollywood. It was at this time he took the vows of the renounced life and became known as Kriyananda.

In 1960 he was selected as a member of SRF's board of trustees and named its vice president. However, by this time he had become focused on exploring the communal aspects of Yogananda's thought, and in 1962 he resigned all posts with SRF and decided to put his time into realizing the development of several small economically independent communities. He wrote several books underscoring the rationale for such communities, including *Cooperative Communities: How to Start Them and Why* (1968). His lectures from this time would later be compiled and published as *Crises in Modern Thought* (1972).

In 1967 he purchased land in the foothills of the Sierra as a site for the first Ananda Cooperative Community. The next decade would be spent in building the community, making it a center for teaching the *kriya yoga* he had learned with Yogananda, and writing.

In 1983, Kriyananda abandoned his vows of SANNYAS (which included celibacy) and became a lay believer/teacher. He began using his birth name again and married in 1985. Members of the community accepted this change with relative ease. In 1990, he led in the establishment of a new religious community, the Ananda Church of Self-Realization, part of the ANANDA MOVEMENT.

The progress of Ananda has been punctuated by several traumatic events. First, in 1976, a forest fire swept through the Ananda Village in the Sierras, destroying almost all its structures and threatening the survival of the community. However, it was rebuilt. After the incorporation of the church, Ananda began a lengthy litigation with SRF over usage of the term SELF-REALIZATION. SRF also sought to deny Ananda the use of a number of Yogananda's books and images. Ananda won most of the issues being litigated, although the community faced a huge bill for more than a decade of legal work. When a former member successfully sued Ananda claiming sexual harassment, Ananda was thrown into bankruptcy, from which it is slowly recovering.

Most recently, Walters has resumed his vows of *sannyas* and is once again known as Swami Kriyananda. In November 2003, he and several leaders in Ananda moved to Delhi, India, and opened an Ananda branch in India. He has continued to turn out numerous books as well as music (his role as a composer is one of the less known aspects of his career). The Ananda movement has also established a center in Assisi, Italy.

Further reading: Swami Kriyananda, *The Essence of the Bhagavad Gita* (Nevada City, Calif.: Crystal Clarity, 2006); J. Donald Walters, *The Art and Science of Raja Yoga* (Nevada City, Calif.: Crystal Clarity, 2002); ——— , *Cooperative Communities: How to Start Them and Why* (Nevada City, Calif.: Ananda, 1968); ——— , *Crises in Modern Thought* (Nevada City, Calif.: Ananda, 1972); ——— , *The Path: Autobiography of a Western Yogi* (Nevada City, Calif.: Ananda, 1977); Ted A. Nordquist, *Ananda Cooperative Village: A Study in the Beliefs, Values, and Attitudes of a New Age Religious Community*. Religion-historiska Institutionen Monograph Series (Uppsala, Sweden: Uppsala University, 1978).

kriya yoga

The "yoga of ritual action," *kriya yoga* is contrasted with *jnana* (learning) YOGA and equated with KARMA (action) yoga in the Trishikhi-Brahmana Upanishad. The practice of *kriya yoga* involves concentrating the mind upon a particular object that transmutes energy and experience. *Kriya yoga* is said to obliterate the subliminal activators (SAMSKARAS) through asceticism (TAPAS), study (*svadhyaya*), and devotion to God.

Kriya yoga is based on specific breathing patterns. Through PRANAYAMA (disciplined breathing) the devotee's focus leaves ordinary reality as it begins to climb in order to merge with the divine. It is important that the practitioner leave thoughts of mundane reality behind because such thoughts interfere with the ability to focus concentration on the other-worldly. This ability to turn inward to receive spiritual energy is believed to lead the disciple to God realization. As each CHAKRA (invisible energy wheel) is opened through MEDITATION, the KUNDALINI energy is released to travel from the base of the spine, where it is coiled in latency, through the glands of the body to release the energy of

transformation. The culmination of the process occurs when the crown chakra is energized and opened to receive energy from the divine. The process of *kriya yoga* transmutes the life force or energy that connects the physical body and the subtle anatomy described in the Hindu scriptures.

In the last century, BABAJI, LAHIRI Mayasaya, Sri YUKESWAR, and Paramahansa YOGANANDA have been responsible for a renewed interest in *kriya yoga*.

Further reading: Georg Feuerstein, *Encyclopedic Dictionary of Yoga* (New York: Paragon House, 1990).

Kriya Yoga Centers

The Kriya Yoga Centers are a set of related ashrams founded by Swami Hariharananda Giri (1907–2002), a god-brother to Swami Paramahansa YOGANANDA. Both swamis learned KRIYA YOGA under the tutelage of Sri YUKTESWAR (1855–1936), who made his home in Puri, Orissa, and who built an ASHRAM (religious community) there in 1906. Yukteswar passed his lineage to Yogananda, who left India and took the concepts of *kriya yoga* to the United States. In India, the lineage passed first to Sreemat Swami Satyananda and then in 1970 to Swami Hariharananda Giri. Hariharananda was chosen from among the members and disciples who had remained close to the ashram through the years.

Born Rabindranath Bhattacharya in Habibpur, West Bengal, on May 27, 1907, Hariharananda took initiation in the path of JNANA yoga from Sri Bijaykrishna Chattopadhyaya. In 1932, he met Sri Yukteswar, who initiated him into *kriya yoga* and gave him charge of the ashram in Puri. In 1935, Swami Yogananda gave him a second initiation into *kriya yoga*. In 1938 he renounced the world and spent 12 years in seclusion in Puri. In 1949, he had a vision of the eternal yogi BABAJI, who prophesied that he would spread the message of *kriya yoga* to the world. In 1951, Yogananda empowered him to give initiation to others. In 1959, he took formal monastic vows from the Shankaracharya of Puri and was given the name Hariharananda Giri.

After assuming leadership, Hariharananda promoted the work of the ashram throughout India, creating affiliations with other ashrams. Believing that the *kriya* path should be shared with other peoples around the world, he proceeded to make formal visits to promote knowledge of *kriya yoga* as the clearest path to enlightenment around the world.

By 1974, Hariharananda had made the decision to go west, initially with plans to develop ashrams in Switzerland. He continued to found ashrams and centers throughout Europe. His decision to start an organization in New York City introduced the work to the United States, much as Yogananda's mission had evolved into the SELF-REALIZATION FELLOWSHIP.

The United States headquarters of the Kriya Yoga Centers is located in Homestead, Florida. The international headquarters is in Orissa, India. The center publishes a periodical, *Soul Culture: A Journal of Kriya Yoga.*

Further reading: Swami Hariharananda Giri, *Isa Upanishad* (Homestead, Fla.: Kriya Yoga Ashrams, 1985); ———, *The Laughing Swami: Teachings of Swami Hariharananda* (Washington, D.C.: Yes International, 2005); ———, *Secrets and Significance of Idol Worship among the Hindus* (Puri: Karar Ashram, 1984).

Kriya Yoga Tantra Society

The Kriya Yoga Tantra Society is one of the many tantric movements (see TANTRISM) that entered the West from their spiritual homeland in India in the later decades of the 20th century. The society was founded by Andre O. Rathel, more commonly known by his spiritual name, Sunyata Saraswati.

The American tantric groups have developed through several independent sources. Sunyata was a student of the esoteric sciences, tantra, and the martial arts. During his travels he went to India, where he studied with Satyananda Saraswati, the most significant tantric teacher of the 20th century and the founder of the Bihar School of Yoga (now the International Yoga Fellowship) in Bengal. After completing his course of tantra and MEDITATION he returned to the United States and founded Beyond/Beyond in Los Angeles, California, which eventually evolved into the Kriya Yoga Tantra Society.

Sunyata availed himself of a number of teachers and teachings in order to be more fully informed about a variety of esoteric topics. He made an independent evaluation of different tantric teachers and studied with several Taoist masters in Hong Kong. From his studies he selected tantra as the most powerful of all paths to liberation and enlightenment. His central and primary path is the system called KRIYA YOGA, originally popularized by Paramahansa YOGANANDA (1893–1952), which was thought to be the original tantra of the legendary BABAJI, who is believed to live, after many centuries, in the HIMALAYAS.

Although Yogananda occasionally taught from the perspective of tantra, he did not stress left-hand tantra, the system that Sunyata adopted. According to the teachings of Sunyata, tantra promotes intense sexual energy through touch and yogic practices. The intense energy that is developed unleashes the KUNDALINI energy, a latent energy believed to be resting at the base of the spine. Once released, this power travels the spine, opening each CHAKRA (seven invisible wheels of energy along the spine) to the top of the head, when a person reaches *moksha* (spiritual liberation) or enlightenment.

Sunyata travels widely offering seminars in his method of tantric enlightenment. Retreats are offered by the society in relatively secluded areas in order to preserve the sacredness of the teachings and the privacy of the attendees. Headquarters are in San Francisco, California. The society publishes the periodical *Jyoti.*

Further reading: Andre O. Rathel and Annette B. White, *Tantra Yoga: The Sexual Path of Inner Joy and Cosmic Fulfillment* (Hollywood, Calif.: Beyond Beyond, 1981); Sunyata Saraswati, *Activating the Five Cosmic Energies* (San Francisco: Kriya Jyoti Tantra Society, 1987); Sunyata Saraswati and Bodhi Avinsha, *The Jewel in the Lotus: The Art of Tantric Union* (San Francisco: Kriya Jyoti Tantric Society, 1987).

K's, Five   *See* SIKHISM.

Kshatriya

The Kshatriyas are the warrior/kingly class in the ancient fourfold class system of India. They are second in the hierarchy beneath the BRAHMINS. Their duty was to protect and rule. They were always allied with Brahmins in their role as kings and overlords, but they vied for control of the top of the social hierarchy. In the sixth century B.C.E. the heterodox movements of Buddhism and JAINISM, which opposed Brahminical orthodoxy, were founded by men of Kshatriya lineage, respectively, Siddhartha Gautama (later, BUDDHA) and Vardhamana (later, MAHAVIRA).

As do Brahmins, Kshatriyas receive the SACRED THREAD, making them "twice-born." Up to the GUPTA era (c. 600 C.E.) they learned SANSKRIT and to some degree the scriptures. The UPANISHADS give examples of Kshatriya kings who teach Brahmins the highest wisdom.

Kshatriyas play a significant role in Indian literature, along with the Brahmins. Both the RAMAYANA and MAHABHARATA are essentially Kshatriya epics dealing with issues of kingly succession. They also, of course, highlight the two Kshatriya heroes RAMA and KRISHNA, both recognized as avatars of Lord VISHNU.

Further reading: Shanta Anand, *Ksatriyas in Ancient India: A Socio-Economic and Religious Study* (Delhi: Atma Ram, 1985); Bimla C. Law, *Ancient Mid-Indian Ksatriya Tribes* (Varanasi: Bharatiy Publishing House, 1975); C. T. Metcalfe, *The Rajpoot Tribes* (New Delhi: Cosmo, 1982).

Kubera

Kubera is the early god of wealth in India. However, he did not develop a large cult following and perhaps was overshadowed by the goddess LAKSHMI, whose attributes and realm of power were similar.

There are different stories about Kubera's birth and upbringing. Generally he is said to have ruled over Lanka (Sri Lanka) until the demon Ravana gained the power to steal some of his magical belongings and exile him. Both Kubera and Ravana are seen as descendents of the mind-born son of BRAHMA, Pulastya. Kubera apparently took up residence in the north; he is seen as the guardian of the northern direction, while INDRA guards the east, YAMA the south, and VARUNA the west. In all these stories he is always heralded as the lord of gold and riches.

Further reading: Cornelia Dimmitt and J. A. B. van Buitenen, *Classical Hindu Mythology: A Reader in the Sanskrit Puranas* (Philadelphia: Temple University Press, 1978); E. Washburn Hopkins, *Epic Mythology* (Delhi: Motilal Banarsidass, 1986); W. J. Wilkins, *Hindu Mythology, Vedic and Puranic* (Calcutta: Rupa, 1973).

Kumar, Guru Sushil (1926–1994) *Jain teacher*

Guru Sushil Kumar was a teacher of Jain tradition and of interreligious understanding. He broke with Jain convention by traveling abroad in pursuit of his mission, and he founded the International Jain Mission (*see* JAINISM).

Sushil Kumar was born on June 15, 1926, into a Hindu Brahmin family in the small village of Sikhopur in Hariyana, India. The village was later renamed Sushalgarh in his honor. When he was a very young boy, a deceased Jain YOGI and enlightened master, Sri Roop Chandji Maharaj, appeared to him in a vision and told the young Sushil to become a monk. At age seven, he left his family and village to live with a Jain monk, Sri Chotelal Maharaj, who became his guru. In 1941, at age 15, Sushil took initiation (DIKSHA) and became a monk in the STHANAKVASI sect of Jainism.

Sushil pursued an academic career in classical Indian and yogic philosophies, while experiencing directly the topics he was studying. His abilities to teach and share his experiences attracted disciples, who recognized him as a source of wisdom, truth, and understanding. He actively promoted peace and harmony throughout India and worked to establish a sense of universal brotherhood among the country's conflicting religious traditions.

In 1975 he began a controversial international tour, which broke with the Jain tradition's requirement that monks travel only by foot. He broke the ancient restraint against traveling by plane in order to share the Lord MAHAVIRA's message of nonviolence, peace, and oneness of all living beings.

His teaching of the Arhum Yoga system involves mastery of the inner self through watchfulness and direct perception. Arhum yoga includes the eight limbs of PATANJALI's yoga system, sound vibration, healing, awakening of the KUNDALINI, energy, holistic health, and the teachings of Jainism. The main text he used was the Matrika Yidya of the Namokar Mantra, a foremost mantra in the Jain tradition.

Sushil presided over a number of world religion conferences and was director and president of many organizations devoted to intercultural and interreligious cooperation, world peace, universal brotherhood, animal and environmental protection, and nonviolence. He was a founding member of the VISHWA HINDU PARISHAD.

Sushil motivated the Sikh leader Tara Singh to participate in dialogue with the Indian government to solve the animosities that were threatening the state of Punjab.

He also founded many spiritual organizations, including the World Fellowship of Religions in 1950, Vishwa Ahimsa Sangh in 1957, International Jain Mission in 1978, Arhat Sangh in 1979, and the World Jain Congress in 1981, and World Center of Nonviolence. He died on April 22, 1994.

Sushil's main ashram is Siddhachalam, in Blairstown, New Jersey, established in 1983, the first Jain pilgrimage site (tirtha) established outside India. Siddhachalam is a residential community for monks, nuns, and laymen and laywomen, as well as a retreat center. It serves as headquarters for the International Jain Mission, the World Fellowship of Religions, and the World Jain Congress. The ashram is also a wildlife sanctuary.

kumbhaka   See PRANAYAMA.

Kumbhakarna

Kumbhakarna (He with karna, ears [as big as], kumbha, pots) is a rakshasa, a demon, the brother of Ravana (see DEMONIC BEINGS). He plays a part in the RAMAYANA story and he is burned yearly in effigy during the Ramlila celebration, when the victory of Lord RAMA over the evil demons is remembered.

The story goes that Kumbhakarna was a very powerful demon, and naturally strong. Other demons, rakshasas, acquired their powers as the result of austerities and boons, but he alone had the natural power to kill any god, man, or being. Once Kumbakarna was besting INDRA, the king of the gods himself, in battle. Indra, along with other gods, RISHIS, and various beings went to BRAHMA to ask for aid. Brahma cursed Kumbhakarna at that moment, to sleep forever. Ravana, his brother, pleaded with Brahma to soften his curse and Brahma then cursed him to sleep for six months at a time, after which he would voraciously eat for one day, and then would go back to sleep again. This curse was meant to hold him in control so that he would not conquer all the worlds.

In the RAMAYANA, when the rakshasas have begun their war with RAMA, Lakshmana, and the monkeys, there is a rather humorous scene that takes place when Ravana tries forcibly to wake Kumbhakarna to fight. They beat him and scrape him in every way; they have elephants drag him; they beat a thousand drums; and so on, but Kumbhakarna continues to snore. Finally, hit with trees and doused by thousands of pitchers of water, Kumbharakarna awakes. This done, he is asked to fight and agrees, but first he must be fed vast wagon loads of food, which he takes whole into his voracious mouth. His endless hunger sated, he goes into battle. After wreaking havoc, he eventually is slain by Lord Rama himself.

Further reading: S. P. Bahadur, trans., *The Complete Works of Gosvami Tulsidas* (Varanasi: Prachya Prakashan, 1978–2005); Robert Goldman, ed., *The Ramayana of Valmiki*, 6 vols. (Princeton, N.J.: Princeton University Press, 1984–2005); C. Rajagopalachari, *Ramayana* (Bombay: Bharatiya Vidya Bhavan, 1972).

Kumbha Mela

The Kumbha Mela (pot festival) is held once every three years, moving in rotation among four riverside sites in India: Prayag (ALLAHABAD), HARIDVAR, Ujjaini, and Nasik. The first two of these locations are in Uttar Pradesh, Ujjaini is in Madhya Pradesh, and Nasik is in Maharashtra.

The Kumbha Mela may have originated in great antiquity when various seeds were taken to river banks, dipped into the water, and then sown for a bountiful harvest. One myth of the festival's origin begins with a pot of the nectar of immortality; it was carried away by Jayanta, the son of INDRA, with the gods and demons in hot pursuit. As he carried the pot for 12 divine days (12 human years) a little was dropped in each of the four festival locations. Hence the name Pot Festival.

The Kumbha Mela festival at Allahabad (Prayag), held every 12th year and called the Maha (great) Kumbha Mela, is the largest festival in India and perhaps in the world. According to astrologers, the Maha Kumbha Mela takes place when the planet Jupiter enters Aquarius and the Sun enters Aries. Millions of people assemble together at this sacred site for ceremonial processions, devotional singing, religious discourses, and other special activities for the religious. Monks and holy men and women from every Hindu sect converge together at this site to participate in this sacred and festive gathering.

Further reading: Jack Hebner and David Osborn, *Kumbha Mela: The World's Largest Act of Faith* (La Jolla, Calif.: Ganesh, 1990); D. K. Roy, *Kumbha: India's Ageless Festival* (Bombay: Bharatiya Vidya Bhavan, 1955).

kundalini

The kundalini is envisioned in Tantric Yogic practice as a serpent at the base of the spine with her head turned downward. She is the embodiment of the GODDESS. When the practioner has learned to control the breath in its channels (NADIS) in the proper way, the serpent is made to turn her head upward and begin the ascent up the spine, piercing as she goes the energy centers or CHAKRAS in their various locations along the spine. This piercing activates energies of the body to create occult powers and spiritual awakening. When the kundalini goes beyond the body to a place 12 fingers above the head called SAHASRARA, or the place of the thousand lotuses, it joins in erotic embrace Lord SHIVA, engendering complete enlightenment and liberation in this world.

Further reading: Harish Johari, *Chakras: Energy Centers of Transformation* (Rochester, Vt.: Destiny Books, 2000); Sir John Woodroffe, trans. and ed., *The Serpent Power,* 4th ed. (Madras: Ganesh, 1950).

Kundalini Research Foundation (est. 1971)

A number of gurus have introduced KUNDALINI methods to the United States for dissemination. One such yogi is Gopi KRISHNA (1903–84), who led a life of MEDITATION in search of liberation (*moksha*) and enlightenment (*samadhi*). He experimented with several types of yoga for 17 years before achieving enlightenment. After his experience with the awakening of KUNDALINI energy, he became a prolific writer, speaker, and teacher of spiritual kundalini yoga.

Kundalini energy is believed to be a wellspring of spiritual energy that is coiled at the base of the spine. Seven invisible wheels of energy (CHAKRAS) along the spine are the sites of powers that must be accessed to allow enlightenment to occur. Teachers of yoga, such as Gopi Krishna, frequently speak of opening these chakras with special breathing techniques so that the life force (*prana*) can be utilized to transform consciousness into a state of enlightenment (*samadhi*).

Gopi Krishna, with a wealth of knowledge about yoga, wrote 17 books about various aspects of the awakening of kundalini. In 1970, an American, Gene Kietter, realized the significance of what Gopi Krishna had learned and founded the Kundalini Research Foundation in New York in 1971 in order to promote his work. The foundation, now headquartered in Darien, Connecticut, seeks to promote the scientific investigation of enlightenment, inspiration, genius, and the evolution of consciousness.

Further reading: Darrell Irving, *Serpent of Fire: A Modern View of Kundalini* (York Beach, Maine: Samuel Weiser, 1994); Gopi Krishna, *Awakening of Kundalini* (New York: E. P. Dutton, 1975); ———, *The Biological Basis of Religion and Genius* (New York: Harper & Row, 1971); ———, *The Goal of Consciousness Research* (Darien, Conn.: Friends of Gopi Krishna, 1998); ———, *The Wonder of the Brain* (Norton Heights, Conn.: Kundalini Research Foundation, 1987).

Kurma Avatar

The Kurma Avatar or tortoise AVATAR (incarnation) of VISHNU plays a small role in the myth of the churning of the MILK OCEAN, which is widely repeated in Sanskrit epics, the PURANAS, and story. There, the story goes that the fate of the gods took a bad turn when the king of the gods, INDRA, was cursed by the sage DURVASAS for slighting him. The gods asked Vishnu his advice on how to restore their good fortunes. Vishnu suggested that they churn the Milk Ocean, from which they might obtain the nectar of immortality. They were advised to do this in concert with their enemies the ASURAS or antigods (demons), since the task was monumentally difficult. When they stirred the Milk Ocean, they used the divine serpent Vasuki as the churning stick. Vishnu offered himself as a huge tortoise (*kurma*) upon which to rest the churning stick.

Further reading: Cornelia Dimmitt and J. A. B. van Buitenen, *Classical Hindu Mythology: A Reader in the Sanskrit Puranas* (Philadelphia: Temple University Press, 1978); Shakti M. Gupta, *Vishnu and His Incarnations* (Bombay: Somaiya, 1993); E. Washburn Hopkins, *Epic Mythology* (Delhi: Motilal Banarsidass, 1986); Pandrimalai Swamigal, *The Ten Incarnations: Dasavatara* (Bombay: Bharatiya Vidya Bhavan, 1982); W. J. Wilkins *Hindu Mythology, Vedic and Puranic* (Calcutta: Rupa, 1973).

Kurukshetra

Kurukshetra (province of the Kurus) is a tract of land south of present-day Delhi and is the site of the great war depicted in the MAHABHARATA epic. The Kurus were a great clan, including both the PANDAVAS and the KAURAVAS, the main contenders in that war. Both groups were descended from an ancient progenitor named Kuru.

The place-name also appears in the first line of the BHAGAVAD GITA, where it takes on a metaphorical significance. The battle, as the Gita understands, actually takes place in the consciousness of every human being, who must ascertain right action (dharma) in relation to God. In the simplest terms this battle is between right and wrong, or, yogically, between higher and lower states of being. Kurukshetra has been an important pilgrimage site from ancient times (perhaps since the time of the Mahabharata). It is mentioned as such in different PURANAS.

Further reading: J. A. B. van Buitenen, trans., *The Mahabharata,* Vol. 1, *The Book of the Beginnings,* Vol. 2, *The Book of the Assembly Hall,* vol. 3, *The Book of Virata and the Book of Effort* (Chicago: University of Chicago Press, 1973–78); Cornelia Dimmitt and J. A. B. van Buitenen, *Classical Hindu Mythology: A Reader in the Sanskrit Puranas* (Philadelphia: Temple University Press, 1978); E. Washburn Hopkins, *Epic Mythology* (Delhi: Motilal Banarsidass, 1986); P. C. Roy, *The Mahabharata of Krishna-Dwaipayana Vyasa,* 12 vols. (Calcutta: Bharata Karyalaya, 1888–96); W. J. Wilkins, *Hindu Mythology, Vedic and Puranic* (Calcutta: Rupa, 1973).

Kurus   *See* MAHABHARATA.

L

Lahiri Mahasaya (1828–1895) kriya yoga
teacher

Sri Lahiri Baba, also called Yogiraj, was a modest but intensely pious and learned man. He was a disciple of the legendary BABAJI, an honored teacher of KRIYA YOGA, and a pioneer in women's education in India.

Born as Shyamacharan Lahiri to Gourmohan and Muktakeshi Lahiri on September 30, 1828, in the village of Ghurani in the Punjab, Lahiri Mahasaya was raised in a pious family of devout followers of Lord SHIVA. Gourmohan Lahiri was a recognized pundit and scholar of King Krishnanagar's court. In early childhood, Shyamacharan's mother would find him smeared in ashes and sitting in MEDITATION with his eyes closed. The most significant of these events took place when both mother and son were completely absorbed in the worship of Lord Shiva in the temple. Muktakeshi opened her eyes upon hearing "mother" from an unknown voice. Standing before her was a monk draped in a saffron cloth with locked and matted hair. The monk was the immortal yogi, Babaji. He told her that he had initiated her son for the purpose of liberating both saints and householders from worldly suffering using simple techniques of SELF-REALIZATION. He assured her that her son

would remain in the world and would be a highly respected being committed to the God-realization of others.

In 1832, a flood destroyed the family home and killed his mother. Shyamacharan moved with his father and sister first to Calcutta and then to BENARES (Varanasi), a city holy to Lord Shiva. As a boy, he was humble, quiet, calm, and detached. He attended an English school and studied SANSKRIT, Hindi, Urdu, Farsi, and English. At age 12 he entered Sanskrit University in Benares. In 1848 he completed a degree in English, with significant study of Indian philosophy and literature, as well as Western philosophy. He studied the VEDAS with the noted Maharashtrian Sanskrit scholar Pundit Nagabhatta. He later continued Sanskrit study under the tutelege of Pundit Devanarayan Ghosal Vidya Vachaspathi from Bengal. Gourmohan was proud of his son's achievement, but was also concerned that his quiet nature would lead him to asceticism, so he arranged for a marriage. The wedding took place in 1846; Shyamacharan was 18, and Kashimoni was 10, as was common practice of that time. During their 47-year marriage, she remained completely loyal and supportive of her husband's goal of self-realization. They lived a simple, impoverished life in the early years of their marriage. As Kashimoni grew older, she became an advocate of the education of women at a time when it was unpopular. Her husband taught her to read.

One day, Kashimoni had a profound vision and saw her husband to be none other than an incarnation of Lord Shiva himself. From this point onward, her commitment to God was intensified and her support for her husband's work increased. From 1851 to 1888, he worked as a clerk in public works and tutored children of kings and merchants. Some of these students would later take YOGA initiation from him. In 1888, he opened a Bengali school, of which he remained secretary throughout his life. He later established a school exclusively for women, an unprecedented action for the time.

On November 27, 1861, BABAJI called on him. Leaving his wife in Kashi (or Benares) he set out on a journey to Ranikhet, not knowing why. There he met Babaji, who claimed to have been waiting for him for quite some time. With just an extension of his hand onto Shyamacharan's head, an electromagnetic force passed through his body, and slowly he started to remember his past life as an ascetic. He now fully recognized Babaji and the place where they were. With their reunion, Shyamacharan's path was clearly defined, and thus began his life as Sri Lahiri Baba, also called Yogiraj. He went on to initiate many students, including his wife, in the lost practice of *kriya yoga*. This technique integrates the use of mantras and meditation to endow calmness and control on the body and mind. In his lifetime, Lahiri Baba did not author any books, but his teachings, when imparted, inspired many books by his disciples. He died on September 26, 1895.

Further reading: Paramahansa Prajnanananda, *Lahiri Mahasaya: Fountainhead of Kriya Yoga* (Orissa: Graphic Art Offset Press, 1999); Paramahansa Yogananda, *Autobiography of a Yogi* (Los Angeles: Self-Realization Fellowship, 1969).

Lakshmana   *See* RAMAYANA.

Lakshmi

Lakshmi is the wife of VISHNU and the GODDESS of wealth and happiness. She also is associated with beauty. Lakshmi sometimes goes by the name of Sri, though in very early times Sri seems to have had an independent identity and was only later conflated with her.

Laksmi is most often depicted seated on a lotus. She is golden or white in complexion. She has four arms; in two hands she holds lotuses and with an upraised hand and downward pointing hand she gives gestures that indicate well-being and prosperity. She is commonly depicted in her iconography being bathed by two celestial elephants holding a pot of water. When she stands beside VISHNU, her husband, she is generally shown with only two hands. Lakshmi is an extremely popular goddess.

Further reading: Upendra Nath Dhal, *Goddess Laksmi: Origin and Development* (New Delhi: Oriental, 1978); Niranjan Ghosh, *Concept and Iconography of the Goddess of Abundance and Fortune in Three Regions of India* (Burdwan: University of Burdwan, 1979); David Kinsley, *Hindu Goddesses* (Berkeley: University of California Press, 1986).

Lakshmanjoo (1907–1991) *teacher of Kashmiri Shaivism*

Rajanaka Lakshmana, known as Lakshmanjoo, was a popular and widely respected scholar and yoga master in the tradition of KASHMIRI SHAIVISM. He was the last living representative of the great lineage of teachers of Kashmir Shaivism, and the only remaining repository of its oral teachings.

Born in Srinagar, Kashmir, on May 9, 1907, Lakshmana was raised by his father, Sri Narayandas Raina, and his mother, Shrimati Aranyamali, both of whom were devotees and disciples of Swami Ram Joo. Sri Narayandas was a well-known builder of houseboats in Srinagar who had similar aspirations for his son. Yet, in early childhood, the boy exhibited actions of a spiritual nature and appeared to be on the path of becoming a yogi. At the age of three he made a clay Shiva for his worship. He spent long hours in MEDITATION, which caused him to act oddly. Out of concern for his well-being, his parents approached the family guru, Swami Ram Joo, who assumed care for the boy's spiritual education.

Lakshmana learned the discipline of Shaivism first under the guidance of Swami Ram, and then, when the latter died, under Swami Mahtab Kak. His father's illness forced him to look after the family business while still a teenager. He ended his formal education but continued to practice YOGA and study under Mahtab Kak. During this time he began to learn the Shaiva Sastras.

Lakshmana endured great struggles with his family as his spirituality developed. At the age of 13, he refused his parents' request for an arranged marriage. When he experienced SELF-REALIZATION for the first time at the age of 20, he became uninterested in his family's business and felt a strong urge to practice his SADHANA (spiritual search) in solitude. He left home and traveled to Sadha-malyun Ashram in Handawara, Kashmir. His parents searched frantically for him and eventually found him at the ashram. His father convinced him to return home only after promising to build an ashram for him. Four months later he moved into an ashram located on the slopes of a mountain opposite Srinagar. Lakshmanjoo continued his studies of the Shaivite Sastras for the next seven years under the guidance of the scholar Maheshuvar Nath Razdan. During this time he accepted the daughter of Sri Jai Lal Sopori, Sharika Devi, as a student and taught her the practice of Shaivite YOGA. After she attained self-realization under his guidance, the ashram attracted other devotees.

During the 1930s, Lakshmanjoo traveled throughout India, making the acquaintance of Mohandas Karamchand GANDHI in Sevagram, Sri AUROBINDO at Pondicherry, and RAMANA MAHARSHI at Tiruvannamalai.

In 1957, Lakshmanjoo commissioned a new ashram, Ishvara Ashrama, in the village of Ishaber, where his public teachings attracted a large number of devotees. Disciples began to call him Swami Ishvara Svarupa, a name given to him by Sharika Devi. Lakshmanjoo taught the Shaivite tantras (see TANTRISM) and other texts of the tradition to his disciples and to scholars from India and Europe. He gave Sunday talks on Shaivite yoga and received other spiritual teachers and scholars. As the last in an unbroken lineage of masters of an "oral tradition," he dedicated his life to the sacred teachings of Kashmiri Shaivism. He also established the Ishwara Ashram Trust and, in 1982, the Universal Shaivite Trust, which served as the foundation for the Universal Shaivite Fellowship.

Lakshmanjoo embodied the full yogic tradition, on both the practice side and the theoretical side. During his life he experienced all the transformative disciplines of the Shaivite tradition—he was a *jnani* (realized sage).

The knowledge of Kashmir Shaivism was traditionally passed along by oral communication or other unseen means, directly from master to disciple. Some material was written from the eighth century, but the texts were often intentionally obscure in an effort to prevent misunderstanding and misuse. The texts dealt with yogic experiences that are extremely individual and difficult to describe in words, and the practices involved are emotional. A living master, founded in the oral tradition, was always needed for guidance.

To forestall the loss of these oral traditions, Lakshmanjoo published works in Sanskrit, Hindi, and English. He was universally recognized for his scholarship as well as his perfection in Shaivite yoga. He received an honorary doctoral degree in 1965 from the Varanaseya Sanskrit University for his contribution to Sanskrit and to tantra. He is best known for reviving Kashmiri Shaivism as a vital philosophy. His influence on the scholarship of Shaivism extended into Europe and the United

States. He made his only trip to the United States in 1991 just months before his death on September 27, 1991.

Further reading: Vijnana Bhairava, *The Practice of Centering Awareness: Commentary by Swami Laksman Joo* (Varanasi: Indica Books, 2002); John Hughes, *Self-Realization in Kashmir Shaivism: The Oral Teachings of Swami Lakshmanjoo* (Albany: State University of New York Press, 1994); Swami Lakshman Jee, *Awakening to the Supreme Consciousness*. Edited by Jankinath Kaul (Delhi: Utpal, n.d.); ———, *Kashmir Shaivism: The Secret Supreme* (Albany, N.Y.: Universal Shaiva Trust, 1988); ———, *Self Realization in Kashmir Shaivism*. Edited by John Hughes (Albany: State University of New York Press, 1994); *Shiva Sutras: The Supreme Awakening, Revealed by Swami Lakshmanjoo*. Edited by John Hughes (Albany, N.Y.: Universal Shaiva Fellowship, 2002).

lalata chakra

The *lalata* (forehead) chakra is the seventh CHAKRA from the base of the spine in some systems of KUNDALINI YOGA. It is located at the crest of the forehead. A place of peace, calm, and contentment, the *lalata* chakra takes the YOGI to the verge of the highest consciousness, giving him or her every supranormal power. The associated deity is SHIVA himself or, in certain systems, Shiva and his consort in erotic embrace. The SHAKTI, or energy, of this chakra is the highest Shakti, or goddess herself. This chakra has eight bluish white petals.

Further reading: Harish Johari, *Chakras: Energy Centers of Transformation* (Rochester, Vt.: Destiny Books, 2000); John G. Woodroffe, *The Serpent Power,* 7th ed. (Madras: Ganesh, 1964).

Lalleshvari (14th century) *poet-saint*

Lalleshvari was a 14th-century poet-saint of the Kashmir region of India. Her songs are beloved among Kashmiris to this day. Her philosophical standpoint is in alignment with the tantric traditions of Kashmiri SHAIVISM.

Lalleshvari was born to the family of a Kashmiri BRAHMIN pandit in the village of Pandrenthan, four miles south of Srinagar. According to legend, she married the son she had borne in a previous life in the same village. In that life, when it was time for the 11-day purification ceremony after the son was born, Lalla (her given name) asked the priest, "What relation is this child to me?" The priest, amazed at the question, answered that the child was her son.

The mother answered that this was not the case. She said that she would soon die and be born as a female horse with certain obvious markings that the priest would know. If he were to find this foal, he would learn who her son really was. That very moment the woman died.

The priest hurried to the place where he was told the horse would be. He indeed found her, but when the foal told him she would soon be reborn as a puppy, the priest gave up the search. Lalla underwent six births in the animal world before she was finally reborn as a girl, who grew up to become the wife of the very son she had borne. When the same priest arrived to perform the wedding ceremony, Lalla confided in him the full story.

Lalla thus became the daughter-in-law of her former husband, who had remarried, and she went to live with the family. She was badly mistreated there, and after 12 years she left to become a disciple of the Shaivite SIDDHA Sri Kantha, the family priest she had known in her previous life. He lived in the village of Pampur and was a direct disciple of one of the founders of KASHMIRI SHAIVISM, Vasugupta.

Lalleshvari became a wandering *yogini*, going about naked, despite the ridicule and criticism she received. As the yogic scriptures state, she took praise and blame equally, not being swayed by either. She went about the Kashmir countryside and towns singing and dancing in mystical ecstasy and died, it is said, at an advanced age in Brijbi-hara, some miles southeast of Srinagar.

Her verses in the old Kashmiri language constitute a major contribution to the somewhat limited Kashmiri literature. They reveal a mystic perception that the notion of a god with character-istics and form, approaching a monistic absolute that comprehends infinity, both visible and invis-ible. She says:

> *In that place not even Shiva reigns supreme*
> *Nor the Shakti that belongs to him*
> *Only is the Unknown, like a dream,*
> *There pursuing a hidden sway*

Further reading: R. N. Kaul, *Kashmir's Mystic Poetess, Lalla Ded, Alias, Lalla Arifa* (New Delhi: S. Chand, 1999); Swami Muktananda, trans., *Lalleshwari: Spiri-tual Poems by a Great Siddha Yogini* (South Fallsburg, N.Y.: SYDA, 1981); Jaishree Kak Odin, *The Other Shore: Lalla's Life and Poetry* (New Delhi: Vitasta, 1999); B. N. Parimoo, trans., *The Ascent of Self: A Re-Interpretation of the Mystical Poetry of Lalla Ded* (Delhi: Motilal Banar-sidass, 1978); B. N. Parimoo, *Lalleshwari* (New Delhi: National Book Trust, India, 1987).

Lanka   *See* RAMAYANA.

Laws of Manu (c. 200)

The Laws of Manu is a seminal text in Indian social history. It gives greatest attention to the social obligations of BRAHMINS, whose supremacy in the social order is assumed, but it also outlines the obligations of rulers and other castes. It was the first of many systematizations of Hindu social law.

The book begins with the history of the world and the creation by the divine being of the social order, with the Brahmins at the top. It then outlines the elements of VEDIC education that are required in the BRAHMACHARYA or student stage of life. It gives an idealized description of the householder stage of life, dealing with mar-riage, children, ceremonies for ancestors, virtues such as generosity and merit, and a listing of the permitted occupations for a twice-born person, a person of the three top castes. Among other topics are the acceptance of food from various people, the types of foods that can or cannot be eaten, and things that will pollute a Brahmin by contact. It also discusses the forest dweller's (VANAPRASTHA's) duties and behavior that would be taken up when the householder reached that stage of life.

Two chapters deal extensively with the proper conduct of kings. There is a chapter on women that has become notorious for its call for their complete submission to men, and other sections on issues of inheritance and kingly justice. The book outlines the four-CASTE system and discusses the various mixed of castes. It has a chapter on restitution for various crimes; a lower-caste person is to be punished more severely than an upper-caste person. Finally it discusses issues of transmigration and KARMA.

Further reading: Wendy Doniger, with Brian K. Smith, *The Laws of Manu* (London: Penguin Books, 1991); Urmila Rustagi and Sudesh Narang, *Manu/Manu Smrti: An Appraisal* (Delhi: J. P., 1995).

Lekhraj, Dada   *See* BRAHMA KUMARIS.

lila

A common notion in Indian tradition is that there is no logical "reason" for things as they are in the universe; everything is merely the *lila* (play) of the divinity. This term is used only in association with a deity who can be seen as overseeing all of the universe. This would most often be VISHNU (or one of his incarnations), SHIVA, or the great GOD-DESS. Any such divinity will be said to have his or her divine *lila*.

Further reading: Harish Johari, *Leela: The Game of Self-knowledge* (Rochester, Vt.: Destiny Books, 1993).

lingam

The lingam or SHIVA LINGAM is a phallic-shaped icon that is a primary object of Shiva worship. The lingam always stands on a round base, which is representative of the YONI or vagina of the GODDESS.

The origin story for this cult object is well known. Shiva in his guise as a mad ascetic, naked, smeared with human ashes, and disheveled, appeared in the Pine Forest (deodar forest) where sages had retired with their wives to meditate. Mischievous and powerful, he began to brandish his erect penis before the women. Because of his divine power, the women were enthralled. However, the *rishis* were appalled and cursed the god so that he would lose his penis.

Instead of falling, Shiva's penis took off at lightning speed and fearsome energy and began rocketing around the universe causing endless destruction. The frightened *rishis* went to the gods to see how they could save the universe from destruction. The gods called upon the *devi* or goddess to offer her *yoni* as a safe place for the Shiva lingam to rest; thus it is that every Shiva lingam rests on a representation of the vagina of the goddess.

Main symbols of Lord Shiva: lingam and trident, in Gujarat *(Constance A. Jones)*

Further reading: Wendy Doniger O'Flaherty, *Siva the Erotic Ascetic* (New York: Oxford University Press, 1981); Stella Kramrisch, *The Presence of Siva* (Princeton, N.J.: Princeton University Press, 1981).

Lingayat sect   *See* VIRASHAIVAS.

Lokenath Divine Life Mission

Lokenath Divine Life Mission is an outgrowth of the work of Swami Shuddhananda (b. 1949), who has become a holy figure serving the poor of Calcutta (Kolkata), much as his late Roman Catholic counterpart Mother Teresa. His fellowship carries out its social and religious service in the areas where there are poverty and sickness. He has played a major role in developing schools and medical facilities, as well as economic activity, to provide nourishment, homes, and education for the underprivileged. The mission offers courses to transform stress into a positive power that produces success, peace, and harmony. The mission also sponsors programs to foster women's empowerment and sustainable rural development in India.

The fellowship is named for Baba Lokenath (1730–1890), who reportedly lived for 160 years as an embodiment of love, compassion, and humility. He taught his disciples that he would guide and help them forever, even after his death. The Lokenath Fellowship calls upon this promise and assumes that the enlightened sage watches over the social service organization devoted to his work in life.

As a young man, Shuddhananda emerged from school and university as a professor in business at Hyderabad University. Concerned about the religious and social service needs of underprivileged people he eventually left the academic arena and sought refuge in the Himalaya Mountains. He remained there several years searching his soul about how to help others.

As a very young man he had had visions of the 19th-century *rishi* and saint Baba Lokenath. The memories of the visions never left him. After his pilgrimage in the Himalayas he founded a social service and religious center where he could nurture those in need. The design of his mission and the scope of his services, from medicine to social support, are reminiscent of the work of Swami SHIVANANDA SARASWATI of Rishikish, the founder of the Divine Life Society.

During the 1990s Swami Shuddhananda traveled to the United States to share his spirituality and to talk about the way he has designed his social service mission. A small number of disciples have joined to learn from him and help with his charitable work in India. The Fellowship in the United States is located in Louisiana. The International Mission has headquarters in Calcutta.

Further reading: Anne Cushman and Jerry Jones, *From Here to Nirvana* (New York: Riverhead Books, 1998).

Long, Barry (1926–2003) *Australian teacher of realization*

Barry Long was a spiritual teacher from Australia whose realization of immortality in 1965 transformed his life and advanced him to realization of a higher consciousness.

Born in Sydney, Australia, in 1926, Long pursued a career in newspaper editing and politics. At the age of 31 he experienced a death of self and a dawning of a new sense of existence. The event sparked in him a lifelong quest for truth and self-knowledge. In the 1970s he traveled to London to secure publication of his experiences. There he continued writing and began meeting regularly with small groups of people interested in his teachings. In the 1980s he started holding meetings and meditation classes with larger audiences. His first widely circulated book, *The Origins of Man and the Universe,* published in 1984, increased his public recognition.

The Barry Long Foundation was established as an educational charity in England in 1985. Later that year, he founded the Barry Long Centre on the Gold Coast of Queensland. In England, North America, Australia, and New Zealand he taught seminars in his increasingly popular Course in Being. In 1993 Long began teaching a 16-day event called the Master Session, which took place annually in New South Wales. His teachings emphasize the living of truth and the realization that no duality exists between one's self and the greater power. Long's seminars introduce the stillness of being and the attainment of an inner place from which people can live their daily lives. The Barry Long Foundation headquartered in Australia does not have formal membership but continues to publish and distribute Long's written works through its publication branch, Barry Long Books.

Long died of prostate cancer on December 6, 2003.

Further reading: Barry Long, *Knowing Yourself: The True in the False* (London: Barry Long Foundation, 1996); ———, *Only Fear Dies* (London: Barry Long Foundation, 1994); ———, *The Origins of Man and the Universe* (London: Routledge & Kegan Paul, 1984); ———, *Wisdom and Where to Find It* (London: Barry Long Foundation, 1994).

Lozowick, Lee (1943–) *Western Baul teacher*

Lee Lozowick is an American teacher of the YOGA practices and syncretic Buddhist-Hindu philosophy of the BAUL SECT of Bengal. He is a prolific poet and writer, whose practice strongly emphasizes music—he and his followers have performed around the world.

Born on November 18, 1943, in Brooklyn, New York, to Russian Jewish parents, Lozowick describes his early life as "completely ordinary." His grandfather had been a *tzaddik*, or religious teacher, and his father, Louis, a successful artist. In 1970, while living in New Jersey, Lozowick became a teacher of Silva Mind Control and studied the human potential movement in depth. In 1975, after reading the works of ADI DA SAMRAJ (known at the time as Bubba Free John), which

he recognized as true, he became enlightened, or as he puts it, "woke up." He describes the process as completely impersonal and not the result of any training or discipline. In 1977, Lozowick went to India and met Yogi RAMSURATKUMAR, who was living at the ashram of RAMANA MAHARSHI in Tiruvannamalai, South India. Lozowick called the yogi his "father."

Lozowick relates that since 1975 he has been teaching in the Western Baul tradition. The Bauls of Bengal are a 500-year-old sect of ecstatic singers, love poets, and wandering minstrels who sprang from the folk tradition of rural Bengal. The Bauls blend tantric Buddhism and devotional Hinduism with music, dance, and yoga of sexual energy and breath, to form a path to God-realization through the body. Lozowick has adapted this tradition to serve spiritual seekers in the West.

Lozowick's teachings emphasize the practice of guru yoga, which he himself practiced for 25 years when his own guru was alive and continues to practice since his death. Lozowick functions as both guru and disciple. He has published over 1,000 poems to his master, Yogi Ramsuratkumar.

After awakening, Lozowick formed a small community called Hohm in New Jersey and began to teach spiritual devotees. In 1980, the community moved to Arizona, where both the Hohm Sahaj Mandir (temple) and Hohm Community are located. Lozowick also founded two ashrams, in France and India. Hohm Press has issued a number of publications on spiritual topics, natural health, Eastern religion, poetry, and parenting. Lozowick himself has written 18 books.

Lozowick is known for the poetry and music he has produced in the past 20 years. He is the lead singer in Sri, a blues band composed of members of his community that has produced nine albums and performs yearly tours to large audiences throughout Europe and the United States. His community also has a theater company, a gospel choir, a children's school, a publishing company, and several published authors. He is a passionate advocate for children and teaches practices for conscious parenting. For Lee Lozowick and his students, spiritual maturity is expressed in and through all aspects of life, and service to the divine is expressed through service of humanity.

Further reading: Georg Feuerstein, *Holy Madness: The Shock Tactics and Radical Teachings of Crazy-Wise Adepts, Holy Fools, and Rascal Gurus* (New York: Arkana, 1990); Lee Lozowick, *Alchemy of Transformation* (Prescott, Ariz.: Hohm Press, 1996); ———, *The Book of Unenlightenment/The Yoga of Enlightenment* (Prescott Valley, Ariz.: Hohm Press, 1980); ———, *In the Fire* (Tabor, N.J.: Hohm Press, 1978); ———, *Spiritual Slavery* (Tabor, N.J.: Hohm Press, 1975).

Lust, Benedict (1872–1945) *founder of naturopathy*

Benedict Lust was a pioneer in what has come to be called holistic medicine and a facilitator of the dissemination of YOGA in the United States. Lust was born in Michelbach, Baden, Germany. As a youth, he became ill and was cured by Fr. Sebastian Kneipp, a famous advocate of the water cure, a popular form of healing in the 19th century. He eventually traveled to the United States as Kneipp's official representative and in the late 1890s organized the water cure movement, especially among the many first generation German Americans.

Meanwhile, Lust studied osteopathy and various schools of healing that eschewed the use of drugs and surgery. By 1900, Lust was looking toward a new synthesis of nonintrusive healing arts, which he termed *naturopathy* (a name he actually purchased from a colleague).

In 1919, by which time Lust had launched his long-term battle to have the government recognize naturopathy, Lust met Sri YOGENDRA, a yogi who had traveled to New York from Bombay (Mumbai). Yogendra was a pioneer in reviving HATHA YOGA as a discipline for body and mind in India and had gone to the United States to conduct a set of scientific tests with the Life Extension Institute in New York. Lust quickly saw the value that hatha yoga might have in his repertoire of healing tools.

In 1924, Yogendra returned to Bombay. The restrictive, discriminatory immigration laws that went into effect at the time prevented him from making any return visits. Thus, Lust, through his naturopathy, was to become the major disseminating force for yoga in the next generation. Only after World War II did Asian teachers arrive in the United States once more to help popularize hatha yoga.

Lust died in 1945. Subsequently yoga has been deemphasized by naturopaths, and Lust's role in introducing yoga in America largely forgotten. The Benedict Lust Publication Company still offers books on naturopathy, health, and healing.

Further reading: Benedict Lust, *The Fountain of Youth* (New York: MacFadden, 1923); Paul Wendall, *Standardized Naturopathy* (Brooklyn, N.Y.: The Author, 1951).

M

Maa, Shree (1950–) *teacher of bhakti yoga*
After spending her childhood and early adult years meditating and worshipping virtually in solitude, Shree Maa emerged in the 1980s as a teacher and religious singer in India. In 1984 she founded the Devi Mandir temple in California and began spreading her teachings through worldwide tours and music recordings.

Shree Maa was born in Assam in northeastern India around 1950. Although no records exist for her name and date of birth, she reportedly was born in the year a great earthquake shook the region. She is from a family, that included businessmen as well as advanced yogis and is a descendant of the 18th-century Bengali poet-saint and KALI devotee Ramprasad Sen. She received her early education from her grandmother, whose attentiveness to worship in daily activities made a great impression upon her. She spent much of her childhood in meditation at the local temple and in the family shrine room.

In her early teens, Shree Maa spent many hours in solitude and worship, both at home and in the nearby caves of the Himalayas. She knew as a child that the 19th-century priest of Kali, Sri RAMAKRISHNA, would be her personal GURU. In high school and college she continued to live introspectively and to worship in seclusion, showing little interest in family and social gatherings. After completing college she left home and traveled to KAMAKHYA, the famous pilgrimage site in the foothills of the HIMALAYAS. She spent the next eight years wandering in the area living the life of an ascetic. Villagers always found her in deep meditation. She spoke very little and ate only basil leaves and sandal water. Devotees claimed that she reached *SAMADHI,* the highest state of consciousness, and gave her the name *Shree Maa,* Respected Holy Mother.

Breaking her solitude in the late 1970s, Shree Maa began worshipping in temples and singing publicly, exposure that drew an increasing audience of devotees. In 1980, at a temple in Bakreswar, West Bengal, Shree Maa met Swami Satyananda Saraswati, an American-born traveler who had been studying under a number of gurus in India since the 1960s. The two traveled together throughout India, performing religious rituals wherever they were invited.

In the early 1980s, Shree Maa received divine instruction from Sri Ramakrishna to move to America and teach the meaning of DHARMA, the path of righteousness. In 1984, with few possessions and almost no money she and Swami Satyananda

265

Saraswati arrived in California. Refusing to advertise or promote their presence, the two established a temple, Devi Mandir, in Martinez, California, and undertook the CHANDI YAJNA, a three-year fire ceremony. As word spread, people traveled from around the world to worship at the temple. In the early 1990s as a regular congregation formed, Devi Mandir moved to Napa Valley, California.

Since 1992, Shree Maa and Swami Satyananda have traveled much of the world offering programs and teachings of devotion and inspiration, while maintaining Devi Mandir. Shree Maa has recorded compositions inspired by Ramprasad and has produced several instructional videos demonstrating systems of worship. Following the tradition of Ramakrishna, she encourages worship and devotion in all places, insisting that all action can be a service to the divine.

Further reading: Linda Johnsen, *Daughters of the Goddess: The Women Saints of India* (St. Paul, Minn.: Yes International, 1994); Shree Maa and Swami Satyananda Saraswati, *Shree Maa: The Guru and the Goddess* (Napa, Calif.: Devi Mandir, 1996); Swami Satyananda Saraswati, *Shree Maa: The Life of a Saint* (Napa, Calif.: Devi Mandir, 1997).

Madhva (c. 1197 to 1276 C.E.) *Vedanta philosopher*

Madhva was a brilliant, prolific scholar of VEDANTA who developed his own DVAITA or dualist philosophy.

Madhva was born near Udipi in Karnataka in a village called Rajapitha, which may be the modern Kalyanapura. He was born into an orthodox Vaishnavite BRAHMIN family. He became the disciple of Acutyapreksha, a great teacher.

Madhva studied the writings of SHANKARA, the great non-dual (ADVAITA) philosopher, but concluded by rejecting his teachings. In fact, he eventually wrote tracts opposing 21 important philosophers in order to establish his own philosophy of *dvaita* or dualist VEDANTA. He made a

circuit of the south of India, going first to Trivandrum and staying in RAMESHVARAM, the famous Vaishnavite holy city in Tamil Nadu. As he spoke, he would argue against the various existing philosophical schools. He later traveled in North India, living in such places as HARIDVAR and Badarika. He is said to have converted many followers of Shankara in his travels. Eventually, he even converted his own GURU.

Madhva produced a massive corpus of work including commentaries on all the 13 orthodox Vedic Upanishads, the Vedanta Sutra, and the Bhagavad Gita. In these works he relentlessly argued for the idea that God and the human self or soul were completely distinct from each other, and that the world also was completely distinct from God. His profound dualism was a challenge to the non-dualist thinkers who preceded and followed him, who represent by far the largest school of Vedanta. He argued that only the grace of God, in the form of KRISHNA, could save a human being from the endless round of birth and rebirth, and only BHAKTI, or devotion to the divinity, could rescue humans from the abyss of successive rebirth.

Further reading: S. N. Dasgupta, *The History of Indian Philosophy* (Delhi: Motilal Banarsidas, 1975); Vasudeva Rao, *Living Traditions in Contemporary Contexts: The Madhva Matha of Udupi* (New Delhi: Orient Longman, 2002); B. N. K. Sharma, *Dvaita Philosophy as Expounded by Sri Madhvacarya* (Madras: University of Madras, 1996); Swami Tapsyananda, *Bhakti Schools of Vedanta* (Madras: Sri Ramakrishna Math, n.d.).

madya See PANCHA MAKARA.

Mahabalipuram (Mamallapuram)

Mahabalipuram was an ancient port city, known to Greek traders, which served as a provincial capital under the Pallava dynasty (sixth through eighth centuries). It is known for its extraordinary rock carvings.

Monolithic stone architecture in Mahabalipuram, Tamil Nadu *(Constance A. Jones)*

The city served as the port for the chief Pallava capital at KANCHIPURAM. It was situated at the mouth of the Palar River, 32 miles south of Madras (Chennai). The river long ago changed course.

A granite hill about 100 feet high and a half a mile in length, and a smaller granite outcropping farther south, provided the site and the raw material for the sculptures. Each work is carved out of solid stone, without the use of any brick or mortar, and without assembly of individual pieces. The technique was also used at the Kailasanatha temple at ELLORA TEMPLE contemporaneously.

The most dramatic carving, "Descent of the GANGES" (also known as ARJUNA'S Penance), covers an entire cliff 30 feet high and 60 feet wide. It shows the Ganges's descending from

heaven, flanked on both sides by NAGAS and NAGINIS. Deities, human beings, and animals all face the fissure in the rock where the Ganges descends in attitudes of adoration. A small shrine immediately to the left has a standing SHIVA image, before which bows Bhagiratha, who was responsible for the Ganges's descent. Above the temple Bhagiratha is shown doing penance, emaciated, holding his arms above his head, as was on the orthodox ascetic practice. There are monumental elephants to the right of him and a cat, delightfully imitating the ascetic posture of the sage. Mice are depicted at his feet and nearby are remarkably realistic carvings of deer and a monkey plucking fleas from its mate. The "ascetic" cat is faking asceticism to get mice, a not so subtle jab at renunciants who have not truly left behind desire.

The hills contain 10 carved-out *mandapas* (temple areas) with pillars. The largest is 25 feet wide and 15 to 20 feet high, with a depth of about 25 feet. The *mandapas* contain reliefs and statues of VARAHA and VAMANA (AVATARS of VISHNU), the Sun God SURYA, DURGA, and the special LAKSHMI, Gajalakshmi, a form showing her being bathed by celestial elephants.

Several *rathas* (chariot-shaped temples) can be found as well—the granite copying in every detail the shape and form of wooden buildings, although without finished interiors. They are dedicated variously to DRAUPADI, Arjuna, BHIMA, Dharmaraja, and Sahadeva. Some of these are of the oblong *chaitya* type, most often associated with Buddhist architecture.

Finally, there is an elaborate shore temple, with two towers, all carved from solid granite. It contains images of both SHIVA and Vishnu, quite unusual in Indian temples of any era.

Further reading: Michael Lockwood, *Mamallapuram: A Guide to the Monuments* (Madras: Tambaram Research Associates, 1993); M. Purushothama Rao, K. Lalitha, and M. C. Subramanyam, *Mahabalipuram* (Madras, Maps and Atlases Publications, 1970); C. Sivaramamurti, *Mahabalipuram* (New Delhi: Archaeological Survey of India, 1978).

Mahabharata

The Mahabharata (MBh), is one of the two great Indian epics (the other is the RAMAYANA). It tells the story of the descendents of BHARATA, the legendary leader of the early Indian tribes. It is the world's largest epic, containing at least 100,000 verses. It is often said in India that there is nothing that is not in the MBh and that which is not in the MBh is to be found nowhere. The story is said to have been dictated to the god GANESHA by the sage VYASA. Vyasa is the teller of the tale for our own era, but it is considered to have existed long before. From time to time Vyasa himself plays an important role in the epic.

The epic recounts a dynastic struggle that took place near Delhi in northern India. The eldest son in the dynasty of the Kurus is Pandu, whose wife, Kunti, has five sons (considered Pandu's sons, although each was fathered by a different god): YUDHISHTHIRA, ARJUNA, BHIMA, Nakula, and Sahadeva. Collectively they are known as the PANDAVAS. Because of a curse on Pandu that he will die if he has sexual intercourse with either of his wives (Kunti and Madri), Pandu is forced to give up his claim to the throne in favor of his blind brother, Dhritarashtra. Dhritarashtra has 100 sons, the oldest of whom is DURYODHANA. They are known collectively as the KAURAVAS.

Dhritarashtra becomes regent until Pandu's sons are of age, when one of them will rightfully assume the throne. Dhritarashtra is weak-willed and cannot resist his son Duryodhana's attempts to usurp power. The plotting of Duryodhana and his Kauravas against the Pandavas forms the central dynamic in this intriguing story. When their plot to murder the five Pandava brothers fails, they fleece them at dice and drive them into exile.

Finally, events culminate in open warfare between the two camps. The Pandavas are forced to fight against not only their evil cousins and uncles, but their venerable guru DRONA and their grand-uncle BHISHMA. In fact, part of the epic's greatness is that the story is not pure black and white, but instead shows shades of gray on both sides.

The god KRISHNA serves as the noncombatant charioteer of the brave Pandava, Arjuna. As the two pull up to look at the opposing armies before the war begins, Krishna recites the celebrated BHAGAVAD GITA, a profound poem that summarizes Hindu philosophy. On the battlefield of KURUKSHETRA a terrible carnage ensues, as the Pandavas eventually triumph and gain the kingdom.

This epic story is known to all Indians, many of whom are named for its heroes; place names in every part of India are taken from this story as well. There are versions in every one of the local Indian languages, as well as simplified folk dramas that act out its tales for those who cannot read.

Further reading: Peter Brook, director, *The Mahabharata* (videorecording), produced by Michael Propper (Chatsworth, Calif.: Image Entertainment, 2002); William Buck, *The Mahabharata* (Berkeley: University of California Press, 1973); J. A. B. Buitenen, *The Mahabharata,* 3 vols. (Chicago: University of Chicago Press, 1973–78); Alf Heiltebeitl, *The Cult of Draupadi,* 2 vols. (Chicago: University of Chicago Press, 1988–91).

Maha Kumbha Mela   *See* KUMBHA MELA.

Maharaj Ji, Guru   *See* RAWAT, PREM.

Mahashivaratri

The 14th day of the dark half of every lunar month (when the Moon is waning) is called Shivaratri (Shiva night). The Shivaratri of the month of Magha (February–March) is designated as Mahashivaratri (Great Shiva night) and is celebrated with a festival.

Several stories in the Skanda, Lingam, and Padma Puranas describe this festival, and the power associated with it. Once, it is said a hunter unknowingly fasted, watched over, and bathed a Shiva LINGAM all night, not knowing it was the Mahashivaratri time. For this simple deed he was rewarded by being taken directly to the abode of Shiva.

Mahashivaratri is the one major Hindu celebration that is not accompanied by revelry and gaiety. It is a solemn event that emphasizes restraint; devotees make vows such as forgiveness, truth telling, and noninjury to beings, which must be honored for the full 24 hours. Fasting and staying awake all night to worship Shiva are also important aspects of this observance. One spends the night reciting the MANTRA of SHIVA—*om namah shivaya*—and praying for forgiveness. If the rites are performed faithfully one is rewarded with worldly success and the heavenly realm of Shiva.

The festival and its vows probably originated around the fifth century C.E. In mythological terms the Mahashivaratri observance is often attributed to an episode that occurred on that day: when Shiva manifested himself as the fiery lingam (*jyotir* lingam), BRAHMA set off on his swan vehicle to find the lingam's top, and Vishnu set out in the form of a boar to root for its bottom. Neither of the two divinities was successful, thus proving that Shiva was supreme. In another story, Mahashivaratri was the day when Shiva, in order to save the world from destruction, drank the terrible poison that emerged when the MILK OCEAN was churned by the gods and demons to produce the nectar of immortality.

Further reading: Swami Harshananda, *Hindu Festivals and Sacred Days* (Bangalore: Ramakrishna Math, 1994); Nath Sharma, *Festivals of India* (New Delhi: Abhinav, 1978); Guy Welbon and Glenn Yocum, eds., *Religious Festivals in South India and Sri Lanka* (Delhi: Manohar, 1982).

mahat   *See* BUDDHI.

mahavakyas

The *mahavakyas* (*maha*, great; *vakya*, sayings) are usually a series of brief statements extracted from the UPANISHADS that are said to sum up their philosophy. Occasionally, they are from commentaries on the Upanishads or other sources that express Upanishadic philosophy. They are subjected to extensive exposition and exegesis in the different schools of VEDANTA.

Most commonly, only four *mahavakyas* are counted. These four statements are from the YAJUR, SAMA, RIG, and ATHARVA VEDAS in order. Some Vedic systems cite five, six, or even seven *mahavakyas*.

The first of the basic four is from BRIHADA-RANYAKA UPANISHAD I. 4. 10: "Aham brahmasmi" (I [aham] am [asmi] the ultimate reality [the brahman]). In other words, the individual self is identical to the ultimate reality of the brahman. From the CHANDOGYA UPANISHAD VI. 8. 7 is the second phrase, "Tat tvam asi" that [tat] (is what) you [tvam] are [asi]. That refers to the brahman, while you refers to the ATMAN, the individual soul or self within every human being. In Vedanta the atman as ultimate self and the brahman are seen to be one. This particular phrase is used in succession eight times in chapter 6 of the Chandogya Upanishad, and once each in sections 8 through 16, when Aruni, the father, is teaching his son the truth of the Atman, the Ultimate Self.

The third mahavakya is "ayam atma brahma" (This [ayam] self [atma] is brahma.) This means that the individual self is the Ultimate Reality, the All, the brahman. This phrase is found verbatim in MANDUKYA UPANISHAD I. 2 and is the logical conclusion of statements made by YAJNAVALKYA to two different questioners in Brihadaranyaka Upanishad, II.4. 1; II.4.2 and II. 5.1. The fourth phrase is taken from AITAREYA UPANISHAD, III.3.13: "prajnanam brahma." The Ultimate Reality is wisdom (or consciousness [prajnanam]).

Another mahavakya from the Upanishads that is sometimes cited is "sarvam khalu idam brahma" (All indeed is that [60]) (CHANDOGYA UPANISHAD III.14.1 and Maitri Upanishad IV.6 2). Other mahavakyas commonly cited are from the commentaries of specific Vedanta philosophers such as SHANKARA or from still other sources. The word can be used generically to refer to the "Great Sayings" of any particular person, for example, SAI BABA OF SHIRDI.

Further reading: Jan Gonda, *Notes on Brahman* (Utrecht: J. L. Beyers, 1950); M. P. Pandit, *Gleanings from the Upanishads* (Pondicherry: Dipti, 1969). R. Puligandla, *"That Thou Art": The Wisdom of the Upanishads* (Fremont, Calif.: Asian Humanities Press, 2002).

Mahavira (c. 599–527 B.C.E.) *Jain Arhat (omniscient being)*

Mahavira (great spiritual hero) is considered by Jains to be the last of the great disseminators of their faith in this half-era (*see* JAINISM). His life is celebrated in legends and festivals and is considered a model for all Jains to imitate.

He was born in 599 in Kundagrama, a large city near the modern city of Patna. His father, Siddhartha, belonged to the Jnatri clan, and his mother, Trishala, was the sister of the king of the area. The texts say they were followers of the earlier Jain TIRTHANKARA and teacher PARSHVANATH. They named their child Vardhamana, "he who brings prosperity." The SHVETAMBARA Jains believe that Mahavira was originally conceived by a Brahmin couple, Rishabhadatta and Devananda, and that the embryo was transferred into Trishala's womb magically. DIGAMBARA Jains do not accept this story.

Before Mahavira's birth Trishala had a series of auspicious dreams. Of the two major Jain sects, the SHVETAMBARAS say there were 14 dreams; the DIGAMBARAS say 16. In these dreams she saw (1) a white elephant, (2) a white bull, (3) a lion, (4) the Goddess Sri, (5) garlands of *mandara* flowers, (6) the full Moon, (7) the rising Sun, (8) a large and beautiful flag, (9) a vase of fine metal, (10) a lake full of lotuses, (11) an ocean of milk, (12) a celestial house in the sky, (13) a huge heap of gems, and (14) a blazing fire. Digambaras add (15) a lofty throne and (16) a pair of fish cavorting in a lake. Jains today recall and reenact these dreams when they celebrate the five auspicious moments of Mahavira's life.

It is said that Vardhamana remained very quiet inside the womb, exhibiting the Jain virtue of AHIMSA or noninjury. He only moved when by his powers he learned that his mother worried he was not alive. His birth was accompanied by many marvels as all beings celebrated the birth of the Tirthankara, the karmically special unique teacher, of this half-era.

Not much is known of his childhood. There is a story of his subduing a ferocious snake by his courage and calm. The Shvetambaras and Digambaras disagree about what occurred once Mahavira reached a marriageable age. The Shvetambaras say that he fulfilled his duties as a householder, married a princess called Yashoda, and fathered a daughter called Priyadarshana. They say that he did not become a mendicant until his parents died. The Digambaras believe that Mahavira never married. They stress the notion that he had an aversion to worldly matters from an early age.

When Mahavira was 30 years of age some gods went to him and urged him to renounce the world. A great ceremony took place when he embarked on his renunciation in a large park under an *ashoka* tree. According to the Digambaras he removed all his clothes and pulled out all his hair in five bunches (as is the norm for Jain monks and nuns even today), becoming a naked ascetic.

The Shvetambaras accept most of these details, but they believe he wore a small loincloth given to him by INDRA, king of the gods. They say that he wore this cloth for 13 months, when out of complete disregard for such things he let it fall from him and proceeded as a naked mendicant.

Mahavira wandered for 12 years, abstaining for long periods from water or food or both, ignoring all bodily pains or pleasures, not caring whether he was in the burning sunshine or the pouring rain. (Digambaras, however, believe he observed a vow of silence and solitude for these 12 years.) According to the Shvetambaras, he

Mahavira, 24th Tirthankara of Jainism, in Palitana, Gujarat *(Constance A. Jones)*

was approached during this period by the AJIVIKA ascetic Makkhali Gosala, who, upon seeing his magical yogic powers, became his disciple and companion. Unfortunately, they report, Gosala eventually broke away and declared himself a *jina* or spiritual victor, cursing Mahavira when the latter contradicted his claim.

After an amazingly difficult and extended period of austerity, in which Mahavira showed no concern for any bodily insult or trial, he ascended to *kevalajnana* enlightenment—an infinite supreme knowledge and intuition. He then became the 24th and final Tirthankara of the current half-era.

When he became enlightened and omniscient, the gods built him a vast assembly hall, where he sat quietly and uttered a divine sound that carried the essence of the Jain teaching. The Digambaras believe that the message was heard by all beings of every sort—heavenly beings, hell beings, humans, animals, and gods—all of whom gathered there in amazement; they also believe that Mahavira no longer ate, drank, slept, or aged, as a sign of his pure state. Shvetambaras believe that only the gods and a select few disciples heard his teaching. A Jain community began to form around him from that moment, though he made no effort to create it.

After his enlightenment, Mahavira lived for 30 years as an omniscient being, traveling from place to place. At the age of 72, after undergoing a series of ever more rigorous fasts, he took his death. He passed from this world, his soul heading toward the top of the universe, where it remains eternally in unlimited consciousness and bliss.

Historians believe that a Jain community of monks, nuns, and lay people emerged during Mahavira's lifetime. Nuns always outnumbered monks in the community by a significant margin.

Further reading: Paul Dundas, *The Jains* (London: Routledge, 1992); P. S. Jaini, *The Jaina Path of Purification* (Delhi: Motilal Banarsidass, 1990); L. C. Lalwani, *Kalpa Sutra* (Delhi: Motilal Banarsidass, 1979).

mahayuga

A Mahayuga or "great age," is a traditional Indian unit of TIME In Hindu tradition. It consists of four YUGAS in descending order, totaling 4,320,000 years.

Further reading: Cornelia Dimmitt and J. A. B. van Buitenen, *Classical Hindu Mythology: A Reader in the Sanskrit Puranas* (Philadelphia: Temple University Press, 1978); W. J. Wilkins, *Hindu Mythology, Vedic and Puranic*, 2d ed. (Calcutta: Rupa, 1973).

Mahendranath, Sri (Lawrence Amos Miles) (1911–1991) *tantric teacher*

Sri Mahendranath was a British-born student of a great variety of Eastern religious movements. He founded an ashram to teach his syncretic system of twilight YOGA. Lawrence Amos Miles was born on April 29, 1911, in London, England. As a child, he was interested in spiritual questions and the pagan way of life, and as a young man he had a series of unique experiences that forecast his devotion to the inner life.

In his early 20s Miles met Aleister Crowley (1875–1947), who suggested that he study the *I Ching* with Asian adepts. Miles went to India in 1953 and was initiated into SANNYAS (renunciation) by Sadguru Lokanath, a teacher in the Adinath branch of the Nath Sampradaya School (*see* NATH YOGIS). This tantric order (*see* TANTRISM) is unorthodox in its practices, which include wandering and nudity. During his 30 years as a renunciant in India, Miles studied with other GURUS and was initiated into two other schools, the Kaula and the Sahajiya, both of which are "left-handed" tantric sects, meaning that they use the impurities of life as a means of SELF-REALIZATION. He also went to Bhutan, where he was initiated into Tibetan Buddhism; to Malaysia, where he became a Taoist priest; and to Sri Lanka, where he became a Theravadin monk.

In 1975, he founded an ashram in Gujarat and began to teach a spiritual system called *twilight yoga,* which included elements of the *I Ching,* Tibetan Buddhism, Zen Buddhism, and SHAIVISM. In 1978 he established an East-West tantric order, the Arcane Magickal Order of the Knights of Shambhala/AMOOKOS. As a *sannyasi,* Mahendranath traveled to Sri Lanka, Southeast Asia, and Australia. He died at his ashram near the Vatrak River in the state of Gujarat on August 30, 1991.

Further reading: Lokanath Maharaj, "The Guru of Twilight Yoga," *Yoga Today* 6, no. 10 (February 1982): 10–12; Sri Gurudev Mahendranath, *The Amoral Way of Wizardry* (Oxford: Mandrake, n.d.); Muz Murray, *Seeking the Master: A Guide to the Ashrams of India* (Spearman Jersey, the Channel Isles: Spearman, 1980).

Mahesh Yogi, Maharishi (b. 1911 or 1917) *founder of Transcendental Meditation*

The Maharishi Mahesh Yogi played an important role in spreading the theory and practice of MEDITATION in the West. During the height of the Western "counterculture," he acquired a large degree of fame and notoriety.

Little is known about the Maharishi's early life. *Mahesh* is his family name, and *Maharishi* in Sanskrit means "great sage or saint." His date of birth has been variously given as either October 18, 1911, or January 12, 1917. Acquaintances in India claim that he is a native of Uttarkashi, a small town in the HIMALAYAS, and the son of a local income tax collector. According to his official biography, he received a degree in physics from Allahabad University in 1942 and then worked in a factory before studying SANSKRIT and Indian philosophy.

According to his biography, the Maharishi studied *ADVAITA* (non-dual) VEDANTA for 13 years under Swami Brahmananda Saraswati, Jagadguru and Shankaracharya of Jyotir Math, Himalayas (1870–1953). Upon the death of Brahmananda, he withdrew to a cave near Uttarkashi for two

years. On a visit to South India in 1955, he gave his first talks and became a popular lecturer on the wisdom of Hinduism.

In 1958 at a lecture in Madras (Chennai), the Maharishi spoke of his vision for the "spiritual regeneration of all mankind," which received a five-minute ovation. The next evening he announced the formation of the Spiritual Regeneration movement, dedicated to the accomplishment of that goal. Soon after, he began the first of more than 12 world tours. He first left India to settle in London, where he established the International Meditation Society. He taught primarily out of a small apartment in London's Knightsbridge section, as well as private homes and hotels.

He arrived in the United States in 1959 teaching a technique called TRANSCENDENTAL MEDITATION (T.M.), a practice that draws from Vedic science and employs a MANTRA, or chant, that is given to each student in an initiatory ritual. Each person's mantra is meant to saturate the mind and allow a peaceful state of mind, absent of thought. Initiates are encouraged to practice at least a half-hour in the morning and a half-hour in the evening. T.M. is well suited to life in the secular, technological West, as the practice does not require devotion or faith and claims a scientific rather than religious basis. In the 1960s the Beatles were his most celebrated followers.

In addition to the Spiritual Regeneration movement founded in 1958, the Maharishi formed the Students International Meditation Society and the International Meditation Society in the 1960s. In 1971, Maharishi International University was founded by the Maharishi in Iowa to train teachers of T.M.

The Maharishi returned to India in the late 1970s and moved to the Netherlands in 1990. His organization includes ashrams, clinics, schools, universities, and Vedic study centers. His teachings have stimulated a broad array of interest in Vedic literature. With over 5 million initiates, T.M. has expanded the reach of traditional yoga and Vedic philosophy.

Further reading: Martin Ebon, *Maharishi: The Guru: The Story of Maharishi Mahesh Yogi* (Bombay: Pearl, 1968); Jack Forem, *Transcendental Meditation* (New York: Dutton, 1974); Paul Mason, *The Maharishi: The Biography of the Man Who Gave Transcendental Meditation to the World* (Rockport, Mass.: Element, 1994); Helena Olsen and Roland Olsen, *Maharishi Mahesh Yogi: A Living Saint for the New Millennium* (Herndon, Va.: Lantern Books, 2001); Khushwant Singh, *Gurus, Godmen and Good People* (Bombay: Priya Adarkar, Orient Longman, 1975).

maithuna   *See PANCHA MAKARA.*

Malaysia

The earliest Hindu state to appear on the Malay Peninsula was Kamalanka, which emerged during the seventh century C.E. It appears to have developed out of the earlier kingdom of Lang-La-Tsiu, a dependency of the Cambodian kingdom of Funan. Eventually the Malay Peninsula became part of the Hindu kingdoms of Srivijaya (Sumatra) and Majapahit (Java). Hinduism as well as Buddhism were practiced throughout the peninsula, which became in 1957 the Federation of Malaya. Malaysia was formed in 1963 when the former British colonies of Singapore and Sabah and Sarawak (on Borneo) joined the federation.

Malaysia became a British colony during the 19th century; from the start, the colony accepted Hindu immigrants. Immigration from India continued until World War II, with peak numbers entering Malaysia during the Great Depression of the 1930s. The movement of laborers to Malaysia constituted one of the largest Indian out-migrations in history. Unlike in earlier periods (the era of Hindu expansion), emigrants were primarily from the lower castes, recruited to work in the sugar and rubber plantations, or in the fishing, forestry, and mining industries. Most migrants were from the state of Madras and

were culturally Tamil, although significant numbers were Telugu and Gujarati. SIKHS from the Punjab served in the military and police forces. The Tamil financier caste introduced worship of the deity Murugan, or KARTTIKEYA son of SHIVA, who became the principal deity recognized in Malaysia.

Today South Asians compose 8 percent of the population of the Malay Peninsula. Most Hindus do not practice orthodox Hinduism, but rather Tamil folk religion. Recently, Brahminical practices have become more popular, a process called Sanskritization. Hindu fundamentalism was growing among a minority, as in India, at the close of the 20th and beginning of the 21st cen-

Hindu temple in Kuala Lumpur, Malaysia *(Institute for the Study of American Religion, Santa Barbara, California)*

turies. Hindus have been very active in politics in Malaysia.

See also DIASPORA; INDONESIA.

Further reading: Crispin Bates ed., *Community, Empire, and Migration: South Asians in Diaspora* (New York: Palgrave, 2001); George Coedes, *The Indianized States of Southeast Asia.* Edited by Walter F. Vella (Canberra: Australian National University Press, 1968); K. S. Sandhu, *Indians in Malaya: Some Aspects of Their Immigration and Settlement (1786–1957)* (London: Cambridge University Press, 1969); K. S. Sandhu and A. Mani, eds., *Indian Communities in Southeast Asia* (Singapore: Times Academic Press and Institute of Southeast Asian Studies, 1993); Steven Vertovec, *The Hindu Diaspora: Comparative Patterns* (London: Routledge, 2000).

Mallinatha   *See* TIRTHANKARAS.

mamsa   *See* PANCHA MAKARA.

manas

Manas (mind) is the term for the mental capacity in the 24 categories that define reality in SAMKHYA and YOGA. It is seen to oversee the five capacities of action and the five capacities of perception directly. Above mind in the schema are the ego (*ahamkara*) and the intellect (*buddhi*). While *manas* is essential for the proper functioning of the human being, it is always understood to be subject to the whims of ego under the disguise of instinct or in terms of ego's role in creating the "grasping" self.

Further reading: S. N. Dasgupta, *History of Indian Philosophy,* Vol. 1 (Delhi: Motilal Banarsidass, 1975).

mandala   *See* YANTRA.

Mandukya Upanishad

The Mandukya is a short UPANISHAD (12 small stanzas) in the Atharva Veda, one of the most important for the ADVAITA (non-dual) VEDANTA of SHANKARA. Shankara's guru, GAUDAPADA, wrote a commentary on the Mandukya Upanishad that became important in that tradition.

In its first stanza the Upanishad establishes the supremacy of the syllable om, equating it to the ultimate BRAHMAN. Stanzas 3 through 7 outline the four STATES OF CONSCIOUSNESS. Stanzas 9 through 12 establish that the four parts of om (esoterically understood as *a, u, m,* and a fourth, which is beyond parts) are identical to the four states of consciousness, thus establishing om as the ATMAN or self.

Further reading: Patrick Olivelle, trans., *The Early Upanishads* (New York: Oxford University Press, 1998); S. Radhakrishnan, *The Principal Upanishads* (Atlantic Highlands, N.J.: Humanities Press, 1994); Thomas E. Wood, *The Mandukya Upanisad and the Agamasastra: An Investigation Into the Meaning of the Vedanta* (Honolulu: University of Hawaii Press, 1990).

mangala

Mangala is the name for the planet Mars in Indian tradition; in North Indian languages it is used as the name for Tuesday. Its widest meaning, however, is "auspicious." Along with its opposite, *amangala,* the term is constantly heard on a daily basis in Indian culture.

A number of factors can contribute to making something auspicious in India. It may be an astrological issue—the stars and conjunctions of planets can indicate that a particular day, month, or year will be *mangala* or *amangala.* Certain individuals are by definition *mangala,* such as GURUS, saints, and other holy men. Additionally, certain events can be described as auspicious, for instance, the arrival of an unexpected guest. Places, including rivers, mountains, and shrines, also can be seen as *mangala,* or auspicious, and yield benefits in both spiritual and worldly terms if they are visited.

A wide variety of places, times, locations, or objects can be described as *mangala*. In Jain tradition the *ashtamangala* or eight auspicious things are taken out for special occasions. They include a mirror and a pot full of water. In fact, the potential for auspicious or inauspicious occurrences is practically unlimited on a day-to-day basis in Indian tradition.

Further reading: John Carman and Frederique Apffel Marglin, eds., *Purity and Auspiciousness in Indian Society* (Leiden: E. J. Brill, 1985).

Manikkavacakar (c. ninth century) *Tamil poet-saint*

Manikkavacakar is often considered the Tamil people's most revered Shaivite poet-saint, even though he is not included in the traditional grouping of 63 saints. His works, Tirukkovaiyar and TIRUVACAKAM, form the eighth book of the Tamil Shaivite canonical work TIRUMURAI. There is hardly a Tamil Shaivite who does not know a line from these two poems, which express devotion to Lord SHIVA with great beauty and fervor.

Manikkavacakar was born in a Tamil Brahmin family in Tiruvatavur, a village on the Vaikai River, which also runs through the city of Madurai, and thus he has the proper name of Tirvatavur (He Who Belongs to the Sacred Village of Tiruvatavuras). But he is best known, Manikkavacakar (he whose utterances [*vacaka*] are like rubies [*manikkam*]). His father was an adviser to the Pandya king. The son followed in his father's footsteps and became chief minister to the Pandya monarch Arimarttanar.

The story goes that Manikkavacakar was sent by the monarch to a port city with a huge sum of money to buy horses. There Manikkavacakar, who was inclined to renounce the world, met his GURU, who was in fact a form of SHIVA himself. There he took teaching from the guru and asked to be taken

as a devotee. He surrendered to his guru all the treasure entrusted to him by the king. When the king found out, he imprisoned Manikkavacakar. Forced to stand in the hot sun so that he would agree to return the money, the saint prayed to Shiva, and a herd of beautiful horses was delivered to him to give to the king. Unfortunately, the horses were jackals who had been magically transformed and reverted to their former nature during the night.

The king again tormented Manikkavacakar in the hot sun. Eventually, when Shiva revealed himself to the king, Manikkavacakar was released. He was ordered by Shiva to go to three shrines to teach and to defeat the Buddhists in debate.

One of these shrines was the famous Shiva shrine of CHIDAMBARAM. It was there that most of the hymns that formed the Tiruvacakam were first sung (and probably written by his followers). It is said that the Buddhists there heard of the saint and sent someone to debate him. Manikkavacakar completely vanquished the Buddhists in debate, invoking SARASVATI to strike them dumb. The Buddhists then all became devotees of Shiva. Eventually, Shiva himself wrote all the poet's works, and the saint disappeared into the icon of Shiva in Chidambaram.

Further reading: G. U. Pope, *The Tiruvacakam* (Oxford: Clarendon Press, 1900); K. Ravi, *Saint Manikkavasagar's Verses of Wisdom: A Bio-Cosmic Worldview* (Madras: Anand Jothi, 2002); Glenn Yocum, *Hymns to the Dancing Siva: A Study of Manikkavacakar's Tiruvacakam* (Columbia, Mo.: South Asia Books, 1982).

manipura chakra

The *manipura* or "City of Jewels" CHAKRA is the third chakra from the base of the spine in the KUNDALINI YOGA system. It is situated on the spine at the level of the navel. This chakra is associated with the drive for power and accomplishment. Arrogance and vanity are the emotions that manifest from it. Its element is fire (*see PANCHA MAHAB-*

HUTAS). Its deity is RUDRA. Its SHAKTI, or presiding female divinity, is LAKINI, sometimes also called *Bhadrakali*. It has 10 blue petals.

Further reading: Harish Johari, *Chakras: Energy Centers of Transformation* (Rochester, Vt.: Destiny Books, 2000).

mantra

A mantra is a specially empowered spoken or chanted utterance, usually in SANSKRIT, although there are utterances called mantras in every Indian language. Mantras vary in size from one short syllable to a long chant, such as found in the "mantras" of the RIG VEDA. Etymologically *mantra* comes from the *man,* "think," and *tra,* "instrument," making a *mantra* literally an "instrument of thought," or more truly an "instrument of consciousness."

In the VEDAS the mantras were understood to be of superhuman origin, eternal and uncreated, and were received and recited by seers and reciters in order to call to divine powers. They were used for the removal of sins, diseases, and misfortune; the conquest of enemies; and innumerable other purposes.

In post-Vedic Hinduism the word *mantra* acquired a philosophical meaning. It was said to be derived from *man* (think) and *tra* (protect); a mantra then is that which conditions or protects consciousness and helps lead to liberation. All the old Vedic usages remained throughout Indian tradition, but the use of mantras to purify consciousness, identify with the divinity, and lead one toward liberation was always highly valued.

Mantras are used in India for building temples, for installing icons, and for worshiping them. Those who enter various orders are often given initiation mantras. Any Indian tradition has its *mula,* or basic mantra. Recitation of this mantra in *japa* or repetitive utterance is efficacious for all purposes. The Shaivite traditions use the mantra

om namah shivaya for this purpose. The Jains have what is called the mantra of five salutations, which is used for giving blessings and for asking for good fortune. Since Buddhism grew up on Indian soil, mantras are part of every sect of Buddhism, although their usage and interpretation may vary from those of the various Hindu sects.

The *bija mantra,* or seed mantra, is used most often in rituals. It is a one-syllable mantra, almost always ending with an *m* sound, which embodies the full power of a divinity. For instance, *gam* is the *bija mantra* for GANESHA and is always used in chanting to him.

All Hindu sects have slightly different philosophies of mantra, and all sects have long litanies of names of their divinities that can be recited for any purpose, including liberation. There is the famous VISHNU *sahasranama,* for instance, the Thousand Names of Vishnu, that VAISHNAVITES faithfully recited for all purposes.

In Hindu TANTRA it is common to understand the *mula* mantra, the basic mantra, as being the ultimate form of the divinity, more powerful and efficacious than either the *yantra* (the esoteric graphic form) or the image of the divinity itself. When one does a tantric mantra, one literally *becomes* the divinity, as the mantra is the divinity. Finally, according to tantra belief, by chanting the *mula* mantra or the litany of mantras to the divinity one can realize the *ajapa mantra,* or mantra that constantly recites itself. That is, the mantra begins to repeat itself in one's consciousness without further external utterance, thus totally transforming the adept. In the SHAKTA forms of tantra the Goddess mantras are called VIDYAS (wisdom), and the term *mantra* is reserved for utterances that relate to the male divinities only.

Behind the power and significance of mantra in India is the understanding that the universe itself is constituted of nothing but sound. The world is from *nada* BRAHMAN or ultimate sound. A mantra then is not a mere utterance, but must be understood to be intimately connected to the substance of the universe itself, and hence yields power when recited.

See also GAYATRI MANTRA.

Further reading: Harvey P. Alper, *Mantra* (Albany: State University of New York Press, 1989); Guy Beck, *Sonic Theology: Hinduism and Sacred Sound* (Columbia: University of South Carolina Press, 1993); Sharon Brown, *Om Namah Shivaya: A Mantra Experience* (Ganeshpuri: Shree Gurudev Ashram, 1977); Harold G. Coware and David J. Goa, *Mantra: Hearing the Divine in India and America* (New York: Columbia University Press, 2004); Jan Gonda, "The Indian Mantra," in *Selected Studies: History of Ancient Indian Religion* (Leiden: E. J. Brill, 1975), 4:248; Andre Padoux, *Vāc: The Concept of the Word in Selected Hindu Tantras.* Translated by Jacques Gontier (Albany: State University of New York Press, 1990); A. C. Bhaktivedanta Swami Prabhupada, *Chant and Be Happy—the Story of the Hare Krishna Mantra* (Los Angeles: Bhaktivedanta Book Trust, 1982); Ravi Shankar, *Chants of India* (sound recording) (New York: Angel Records, 1997); Swami Sivananda, *Japa Yoga: A Comprehensive Treatise on Mantra-Shastra* (Sivanandanagar: Divine Life Society, 1967).

Manu

Manu is the name of the first man in each of the designated ages or MANVANTARAS in Indian tradition, a progenitor somewhat akin to the Western biblical Adam. There have been an infinite number of ages in the past, as there will be in the future. Therefore the Manus are infinite in number.

According to TIME calculations in Hindu traditions, there are 14 MANVANTARAS in each eon or KALPA, which constitutes a day in the life of BRAHMA or 4,320,000,000 years. The first Manu of our *kalpa* was Svayambhuva Manu, who Indian tradition says composed the LAWS OF MANU, the famous text on social law. In all there have already been seven Manus in the current *kalpa,* each one leading off his designated age, includ-

ing the Manu who began the age we live in today, who is known as Vaivasvata. There will be seven more Manus in the remaining ages until our *kalpa* is ended.

Further reading: Cornelia Dimmitt and J. A. B. van Buitenen. *Classical Hindu Mythology: A Reader in the Sanskrit Puranas* (Philadelphia: Temple University Press, 1978); W. J. Wilkins, *Hindu Mythology, Vedic and Puranic,* 2d ed. (Calcutta: Rupa, 1973)

manvantara

A *manvantara* is one of the divisions of time in Hindu tradition, made up of 71 YUGAS. Fourteen *manvantaras* make up one KALPA, which constitutes one day in the life of the god Brahma or 4,320,000,000 years. Each *manvantara* has its associated MANU, or human progenitor. Each *manvantara* also has seven RISHIS (saints/seers), certain deities, and its own INDRA (king of the gods).

Further reading: Cornelia Dimmitt and J. A. B. van Buitenen, *Classical Hindu Mythology: A Reader in the Sanskrit Puranas* (Philadelphia: Temple University Press, 1978); W. J. Wilkins, *Hindu Mythology, Vedic and Puranic,* 2d ed. (Calcutta: Rupa, 1973).

Mariyamman

Mariyamman is the smallpox GODDESS of Tamil Nadu. She compares to SHITALA in other regions of India. Every village in Tamil Nadu has a temple to Mariyamman. It was understood that smallpox was both caused and cured by this goddess.

There were those who understood the disease to be in some way a blessing of the goddess upon them, with the white pustules seen as auspicious markings. However, the worship of Mariyamman was almost always intended to ward off the disease or to alleviate its effects. Because smallpox has been eliminated, Mariyamman is propitiated in the case of chickenpox and other diseases today.

Further reading: Pia Srinivasan Buonomo and S. A. Srinivasan, *The Goddess Mariyammann in Music and Sociology of Religion* (Reinbek: Dr. Inge Wezler Verlag für Orientalische Fachpublikationen, 1999); Paul Younger, *Playing Host to Deity: Festival Religion in the South Indian Tradition* (New York: Oxford University Press, 2002).

marriage   *See* ASHRAMAS.

Maruts

The Maruts were originally the storm and wind gods of the RIG VEDA. They accompanied INDRA, king of the gods, who holds a lightning bolt. In various references they are said to be 27, 49, or 180 in number. They throw thunderbolts, churn up wind, and cause the Earth to quake with their fury.

In the Puranas the Maruts are instead seen as the sons of Kashyapa and Diti. Having no child, Diti asked her RISHI husband for a boon. She wanted a child who could defeat Indra. Her husband said this could happen if she carried the son in her womb for 100 years while remaining completely pious and pure. At the 99th year, she is said to have faltered and Indra, anxiously observing, split the embryo into seven parts to become the seven Maruts. The name *Marut* was given to them by Indra when he told them not to cry (*rut*).

Further reading: Cornelia Dimmitt and J. A. B. van Buitenen, *Classical Hindu Mythology: A Reader in the Sanskrit Puranas* (Philadelphia: Temple University Press, 1978); E. Washburn Hopkins, *Epic Mythology* (Delhi: Motilal Banarsidass, 1986); W. J. Wilkins, *Hindu Mythology, Vedic and Puranic,* 2d ed. (Calcutta: Rupa, 1973).

Mata, Sri Daya (1914–) *prominent American Hindu leader*

Sri Daya Mata is the American-born third president of the SELF-REALIZATION FELLOWSHIP (SRF).

Faye Wright was born in Salt Lake City, Utah, and grew up in an environment of the Church of Latter-Day Saints (Mormons). As an elementary school student she first learned about India and quickly developed an emotional attachment that stayed with her as she grew up. Her reading of the BHAGAVAD GITA as a teenager set her on a quest for God that only began to be satisfied in 1931 when she attended a lecture given by Paramahansa YOGANANDA in her hometown.

Wright saw in Yogananda a person with a relationship to the divine that she wanted for herself; she resolved to follow him. Because of an illness that kept her out of school she was able to attend some of his classes, her face bandaged. During one class Yogananda approached her and announced that she would be healed within a week. His prophecy materialized. Two weeks later, with the permission of her parents, she entered Yogananda's ashram in Los Angeles.

Wright became one of Yogananda's closest associates in his Self-Realization Fellowship (SRF). She took vows of renunciation and was given a new name, Daya Mata. At the time of Yogananda's death, she was placed in charge of the movement's headquarters at Mount Washington, California, and James Lynn (Swami Rajasi Janakananda) was placed in charge of the SRF organization. Lynn died three years later. In 1955, Daya Mata succeeded Lynn as the third president of Self-Realization Fellowship, a position she has retained for decades.

She has been very active as president, overseeing a growing international organization, meeting frequent speaking engagements, and authoring several books. On March 5, 2005, she celebrated her 50th anniversary as the leader of SRF.

Further reading: Daya Mata, *Enter the Quiet Heart* (Los Angeles: Self-Realization Fellowship, 2005); ———,

Finding the Joy within You: Personal Counsel for God-Centered Living (Los Angeles: Self-Realization Fellowship, 2002); ———, *God Alone: The Life and Letters of a Saint* (Los Angeles: Self-Realization Fellowship, 1998); ———, *Only Love: Living the Spiritual Life in a Changing World* (Los Angeles: Self-Realization Fellowship, 1976).

Matagiri   *See* AUROBINDO, SRI.

math

Math is a word for monastery in the Hindi language. Many Hindu traditions established *maths* as austere residences where monks could live and study. Most famous are the four *maths* established by the great VEDANTA teacher SHANKARA (circa eighth century): BADRINATH in far northern India, DVARAKA (Dwarka) in Gujarat, Shringeri in Karnataka, and Puri in Orissa. Monks from the Dashanami order following Shankara's teachings now live at these locations. The abbot of each of these *maths* is referred to as the Shankaracharya (while Shankara himself is referred to as the Adishankaracharya, or first Shankaracharya).

Further reading: Austin B. Creel and Vasudha Narayanan, *Monastic Life in the Christian and Hindu Traditions: A Comparative Study* (New York: Edwin Mellen Press, 1990); Ram Niwas Pandy, *The Mathas of the Dasanami Sanyasis of Lalitpur, Kathmandu Valley* (Kathmandu: Royal Nepal Academy, 2002); Vasudeva Rao, *Living traditions in Contemporary Contexts: The Madhva Matha of Udupi* (New Delhi: Orient Longman, 2002).

matsya   *See* PANCHA MAKARA.

Matsya avatar

The Matsya (fish) AVATAR of VISHNU is said to have preserved the world from a cataclysmic flood in a previous cycle of time. According to the story,

the MANU (primordial man) of that era was a great king. He came upon a tiny fish as he was washing himself in the morning. The fish, speaking in a human voice, beseeched the king to save him. He promised to reward Manu by saving him in turn from an impending flood.

Manu agreed. He first put the fish in a bowl of water, but the fish grew very quickly and outgrew it. Then Manu put the fish in a pitcher, but it became too big for it overnight. Manu successively put it into a well, pond, and then the GANGES, but it outgrew them all. Finally, he put it in the ocean, where it became very huge. Once in the ocean the fish instructed Manu that after certain cataclysms a flood would wipe out all of the beings on Earth. The fish instructed Manu to build a huge boat, put the world's creatures in it, and tie a rope to it in preparation for that time. When the flood arrived, Manu attached the rope to the fish's horn and the fish took him to the northern mountain, where he attached the boat to a tree. Thus were all creatures rescued by the Matsya incarnation of VISHNU.

Further reading: Cornelia Dimmitt and J. A. B. van Buitenen, *Classical Hindu Mythology: A Reader in the Sanskrit Puranas* (Philadelphia: Temple University Press, 1978); E. Washburn Hopkins, *Epic Mythology* (Delhi: Motilal Banarsidass, 1986); W. J. Wilkins, *Hindu Mythology, Vedic and Puranic,* 2d ed. (Calcutta: Rupa, 1973).

Mauritius

The British acquired the island nation of Mauritius in the Indian Ocean from the French in 1814 as part of the Treaty of Paris. Sugar production on the island flourished under the British, who imported large numbers of African slaves to work on plantations. Prior to 1835, almost 70 percent of the population of Mauritius was of African descent. After the abolition of slavery, British officials began in 1835 to employ indentured servants from India to fill the labor shortage on the island. Since that time, the migration of Indians to the island has steadily increased. Indians of all faiths now constitute about 68 percent of the total population.

Most Hindus in Mauritius were from Bihar and Uttar Pradesh in northern India and Tamil Nadu and Andhra Pradesh in southern India. Many migrated to escape the drought and poverty that had ravaged regions of India during much of the mid-19th century. Others were enticed by the prospects of owning land. Large numbers of migrants from India continued to enter Mauritius until 1922, when contracts of indentured servitude were discontinued.

From their first days in Mauritius, Hindus were much more organized and had greater political leverage than their compatriots in other colonies with sizable Indian populations. Conditions for the indentured laborers were deplorable, but Hindus did not face severe persecution because of their religion. Throughout their residence in Mauritius, Hindus established temples, gained recognition of their religious festivals as public holidays, and maintained frequent contact with the Indian homeland. When MOHANDAS KARAMCHAND GANDHI visited Mauritius in the early 20th century he was impressed by the social justice and activism of the Hindu population on the island. Overall, Hinduism has enjoyed success and longevity there.

The earliest temples were constructed in the mid-1880s on the sugar estates by traders and indentured laborers. They were dedicated to Annam and KARTTIKEYAN, or Murugan. At present there are over 250 Hindu temples on Mauritius.

Temples serve as centers for many traditional Hindu festivals. MAHASHIVARATRI, SHIVA'S Great Night, is one of the largest. The annual celebration is designated a national holiday for those of North Indian descent. The festival involves a nine-day ceremony of fasting that concludes with a night-long worship service to Shiva. Other popular festivals in Mauritius include Thai Pusam, a celebration of the South Indian God Murugan. The festival is recognized officially as a Tamil holiday, but Hindus of all origins join the celebration of the deity. DIVALI, the festival of lights, is another popular festival proclaimed as a national holiday, in which both Hindus and non-Hindus celebrate. During the height of Divali observances, Hindu temples and Christian churches are lit with many earthen lamps to symbolize dispelling the darkness of ignorance. The festival of Divali represents religious solidarity across ethnic barriers.

Hindus in Mauritius have established strong traditions of both VAISHNAVISM and SHAIVISM. Additionally, reform movements such as ARYA SAMAJ have increased in popularity over recent years. In 2000, a celebration of the 125th anniversary of Arya Samaj drew over 15,000 people to more than 165 fire rituals.

Other organizations that have made their home in Mauritius over the decades include the INTERNATIONAL SOCIETY FOR KRISHNA CONSCIOUSNESS, the VEDANTA RAMAKRISHNA SOCIETIES MATH AND MISSION, the Chinmayananda Mission, and the Swami Lakshmanacharya Vishwa Santi Foundation. In 1983, Swami Krishnananda converted an infirmary established in 1888 in Calebassus into an ASHRAM and AYURVEDIC health care center that houses over 200 poor and needy residents.

Hindus in Mauritius still frequent pilgrimage centers in India, even as several sites have been established on the island for pilgrimages. One such destination is Spiritual Park, established in 1999 by Satguru Sivaya SUBRAMUNIYASWAMI, to house worship, music, education, and other activities. The park features three eight-foot statues of GANESHA, Dakshinamurti, and Lord Murugan (KARTTIKEYAN), hand-carved in MAHABALIPURAM, India.

Hinduism remains the dominant religion of Mauritius. A 2000 census estimated that there are over 500,000 Hindus on the island, making up to 44 percent of the total population.

See also DIASPORA.

Further reading: Somdath Bhuckory, *Profile of the Hindu Community* (Port Louis, Mauritius, n.p. 1972); Marina Carter, *Voices from Indenture: Experiences of Indian Migrants in the British Empire* (New York: Leicester University Press, 1996); Chand S. Seewoochurn, *Hindu festivals in Mauritius* (Quatre Bornes, Mauritius: Editions Capuchins, 1995).

maya

The term *maya* has several senses. In the VEDAS the term referred to the magic or power of the divinity. The term is still used in this sense in theistic branches of Hinduism to refer to the delusive and enthralling power of the personal divinity.

In SHANKARA'S *ADVAITA* VEDANTA the term developed a specialized meaning of "illusion," specifically, the illusory nature of the world of phenomena. It is an alternative term for *avidya* or ignorance—that is, ignorance of the unitary character of the ultimate reality. *Maya* in this context is the veil of illusion over the BRAHMAN or the highest reality. It neither exists nor nonexists, but is something that cannot be defined. *Maya,* the world as we sense it and know it, is thought to disappear as a fog does when the light of knowledge of the singular nature of the ultimate reality moves forward in consciousness.

In the SHAKTA traditions of GODDESS worship, the goddess as supreme divinity is sometimes called Maya or Mahamaya. In this case the word has no negative connotations, but simply refers to the goddess's supreme magic and power.

Further reading: Paul David Devandan, *The Concept of Maya* (London: Lutterworth Press, 1950); Margaret Dev and Neena Dev, *Maya: The Divine Power* (Piercy, Calif.: Chinmaya, 1999); L. Thomas O'Neil, *Maya in Sankara: Measuring the Immeasurable* (Delhi: Motilal Banarsidass, 1980); Tracy Pintchman, *The Rise of the Goddess in the Hindu Tradition* (Albany: State University of New York Press, 1994).

Ma Yoga Shakti International Mission (est. 1979)

The Ma Yoga Shakti International Mission, with ashrams and centers in India, the United Kingdom, and the United States, is dedicated to the spread of YOGA in the West. It offers instruction in a variety of yoga paths.

Ma Yoga Shakti (no birth name available) was born April 6, 1927, and raised in the holy city of BENARES (Varanasi), India. She spent her youth fascinated by high ideals and devoted herself to the quest of finding solutions to life's mysteries. She obtained an M.A. in political science and became principal of an all-women's college in Bihar, India. In 1956 she founded the Annie Besant Lodge of the THEOSOPHICAL SOCIETY in Chapra. In 1965, she took vows of SANNYAS, renouncing the worldly life, and became a *paramadesa* SANNYASI, or one who becomes a monastic without being initiated by another SANNYASI. She does not acknowledge any one GURU or Hindu lineage. She took the name Ma Yoga Shakti Saraswati. In 1969 she was given the name *Shakti Sant Shiromani* by several monastic orders of India at the KUMBHA MELA. She was given the title Maha Mandleshwar in 1974 by the Niranjani Akhara, one of India's largest orders of monks.

In 1979, following her intention to spread yoga to the West, she established the Ma Yoga Shakti International Mission, with ashrams in South Ozone Park, New York, and Palm Bay, Florida. Other ashrams are active in London and in five cities in India. Following the teaching of Ma Yoga Shakti, the mission emphasizes four forms of yoga—HATHA, raja, KARMA, and BHAKTI—and instructs students to pursue the yogic path that is most accessible to their inclinations and abilities. The mission publishes books by Ma Yoga Shakti in English and Hindi and offers a monthly periodical, *Yoga Shakti Mission Newsletter.* Each of the movement's ashrams offers retreats, devotional services, yoga and MEDITATION classes, and workshops.

Further reading: Guru Chetanshakti, *Guru Pushpanjali* (Calcutta: Yogashakti Mission Trust, 1977); Ma Yoga Shakti, *Prayers and Poems from Mother's Heart* (Melbourne, Fla.: Yogashakti Mission, 1976; ———, *Yoga Syzygy,* 2d ed. (Melbourne, Fla.: Yogashakti Mission, 1982); ———, *Yoog Vashishtha* (Gondia: Yogashakti Mission, 1970).

meat-eating

Meat-eating was apparently well established for all classes and castes in very ancient India. The VEDAS show BRAHMINS and others eating beef as well as an assortment of other meats. With the rise of the notion of AHIMSA (nonharm), first introduced by the Jains (*see* JAINISM) and Buddhists, meat-eating became less sanctioned.

In the *Manu Smriti* or *Manavadharma Shastra* (LAWS OF MANU) (c. 400 B.C.E.), a transitional stage can be seen; meat, including beef, that is killed as part of a Vedic ritual is allowed for Brahmins. However, non–ritually killed meat was not to be eaten by them. Eventually orthodox Brahmins adopted a Jain-like scrupulous VEGETARIANISM that became a cultural ideal of the faith.

However, many sectors of society in India still eat meat and fish. The most common meat eaten in India by Hindus is chicken, followed by lamb and goat. Water buffalo meat is also sometimes eaten. Only the lowest sectors of Hindu society eat pork or beef. Pork is raised by Dalit (untouchable) communities as a regular food source. Dalits also eat beef, taken as carrion.

Under British rule, tensions arose between Muslims and Hindus over the issue of beef. Muslims do not eat pork but do eat beef. Tensions have persisted into postindependence India. Particular offense can be taken if Muslims cook beef on a Hindu holiday, or in an area where Hindus can smell the process. Some cities, such as Delhi, have simply banned the slaughter of cows entirely. McDonalds, Wimpy's, and other international hamburger outlets have been open in India for a long time, but they never serve beef, usually substituting the meat of water buffalo.

Further reading: Sandria Freitag, *Collective Action and Community: Public Arenas and the Emergence of Communalism in North India* (Berkeley: University of California Press, 1989); D. N. Jha, *The Myth of the Holy Cow* (London: Verso, 2002); Brian K. Smith, "Eaters, Food and Social Hierarchy in Ancient India." *Journal of the Academy of Religion* 58, no. 2 (1990): 177–205; Francis Zimmerman, *The Jungle and the Aroma of Meats* (Berkeley: University of California Press, 1987).

meditation

The term *dhyana* (meditation) is used by Jains (*see* JAINISM), Buddhists, and Hindus, with somewhat different technical meanings.

The Jains may very well have been the first to practice meditation. Their tradition does not preserve a great deal of information about the early practice; there is no mention of PRANAYAMA or breath control, but *dharana* (focus), as known to the PATANJALI Yoga tradition, was apparently included.

Jain tradition has four types of *dhyana: artadhyana* (focus on things unpleasant or sorrowful), *raudradhyana* (focus on cruel and perverse things), *dharmyadhyana* (virtuous concentration), and *shukladhyana* (pure concentration). Most literature on the SIDDHA (perfected beings) and TIRTHANKARAS (most exalted personages) refers to the *shukladhyana* state, which involves intense concentration.

In the Hindu tradition, the term *dhyana* first appears in the Upanishads, in a handful of places, used as a rather generic term. By the time of the epics (c. seventh century B.C.E. to third century C.E.), *dhyana* was a well-established practice. Most later Hindu YOGA traditions derive from *raja yoga* or Patanjali Yoga, where *dhyana* is a refined meditative practice that is taken up after one has mastered *pranayama,* or breath control, and *dharana,* "mental focus." It is a deeper concentration of the mind, eventually leading to the SAMADHI state, which involves highly concentrated focus on the highest reality (or realities).

Wedding of Shiva and Minakshi, goddess of Madurai, Madurai Temple, Tamil Nadu *(Constance A. Jones)*

In other yogic traditions, those practicing *dhyana* focus on a MANTRA (recited word or phrase); a *YANTRA,* or sacred diagram; or an *ISHTA DEVATA,* or chosen divinity.

Further reading: Harold H. Bloomfield, Michael Peter Cain, Dennis T. Jaffe, and Robert B. Kory, *TM*: Discovering Inner Energy and Overcoming Stress* (New York: Delacorte Press, 1975); Georg Feurstein, *The Yoga-Sutra of Patanjali: A New Translation and Commentary* (Rochester, Vt.: Inner Traditions International, 1989); P. S. Jaini, *The Jaina Path of Purification* (Delhi: Motilal Banarsidass, 1990).

Meenakshi Temple, Madurai

The Meenakshi Sundareshvarar Temple at Madurai, dedicated to the goddess Meenakshi (MINAKSHI) and to SHIVA as the beautiful lord (Sundareshvarar), is one of the largest in India. The original temple was built by Kulasekara Pandyan, a king, sometime in the first millennium C.E., but it fell into ruins. The current structure was laid out by Viswanath Nayakar, a later monarch of Madurai, in the 16th century and was completed by Tirumalai Nayakar in the 17th century.

The original site was dedicated exclusively to the goddess Minakshi, whose presence in the area is very ancient. The current temple also contains, in addition to the inner sanctum with Minakshi's image, a LINGAM (phallus) for Shiva worship, as well as a striking, huge NATARAJA (Shiva as Lord of Dance) in one of its larger halls. Most notable are the 120-foot towers at each of the four entranceways. These are all elaborately decorated with myriad stucco-covered stone carvings of scenes from mythology, beautifully painted in bright colors.

Points of interest include the arched area of the eight SHAKTIS; the golden lotus pond near the Minakshi shrine, where people descend to bathe; the hall of the parrots, where parrots sing praises of the two divinities, Shiva and Minakshi; the 1,000-pillared hall; and the wall paintings that depict scenes from the Purana telling the story of the holy acts of Shiva. Each year during the CHITTIRAI FESTIVAL in April–May the wedding of Shiva and Minakshi is celebrated. Because VISHNU is said to be the brother of Minakshi and takes part in the wedding, the temple also houses depictions and sculptures representing Vishnu.

Further reading: Chris Fuller, *A Priesthood Renewed: Modernity and Traditionalism in a South Indian Temple* (Princeton, N.J.: Princeton University Press, 2003); ———, *Servants of the Goddess: The Priests of a South Indian Temple* (New York: Cambridge University Press); William P. Harman, *The Sacred Marriage of a Hindu Goddess* (Bloomington: Indiana University Press, 1989).

Meera, Mother (1960–) *embodiment of the Divine Mother*

Mother Meera is considered by her followers as an AVATAR of the Divine Mother. She is a silent teacher, primarily offering DARSHAN (eyegazing) to visitors to help them achieve health and happiness.

Born Kamala Reddy on December 26, 1960, Mother Meera was raised in the village of Chandrapalle in southern India. Her parents were not religious and raised her under no particular tradition. She was described as an unusual child, who often spoke of mysterious lights that visited her. She would later reveal that she received much of her love and spiritual guidance from visions. At the age of six she experienced her first SAMADHI, higher state of consciousness. Her uncle recognized the child's gift and invited her to stay with him in Pondicherry. In 1974 she visited

SRI AUROBINDO's ashram, attracting considerable attention there, and soon began giving DARSHAN, her own blessings to others. Her presence in Pondicherry attracted many and her popularity grew.

Devotees throughout the world consider Mother Meera an avatar of the Divine Mother, who has previously incarnated in other forms, such as KALI and the Virgin Mary. The appearance of the Mother is believed to offer people of the world healing, protection, and transformation in a time of crisis. Mother Meera has stated that the world is now in crisis and that her role is to give the transformative light of Paramatman, the Supreme Self, to everyone around the world. The light that she speaks of is the Supreme Being, which is an untapped energy permeating the world. Mother Meera believes that the ignition of supreme energy will give health, joy, and happiness to anyone who is open to it.

In 1982, Mother Meera married a German by the name of Herbert and relocated to Schaumburg, Germany. Thousands have met with her there and receive her *darshan*. Her teaching is not through words, but through silence. She greets all devotees who arrive for her blessing with an intense gaze. Looking into their eyes, she encounters every corner of their being in order to determine what help she can give.

Mother Meera meets with hundreds of visitors each year and offers regular *darshan*. She requires no devotion and is open to all individuals regardless of their religion. She continues to draw the interest of devotees from around the world.

Further reading: Martin Goodman, *In Search of the Divine Mother: The Mystery of Mother Meera* (London: Thorsons, 1998); Sonia L. Linebaugh, *At the Feet of Mother Meera: The Lessons of Silence* (United States: XLibris, 2003); Mother Meera, *Answers* (Ithaca, N.Y.: Meeramma, 1991); ———, *Bringing down the Light: Journey of a Soul after Death* (Ithaca, N.Y.: Meeramma, 1990); Adilakshmi Olati, *Mother Meera* (Thalheim, Germany: Mother Meera Publications, 1987).

Meher Baba (1894–1969) *God-Realized master said to be avatar of the age*

Meher Baba considered himself to be an AVATAR, a being who ushers in a new cosmic age.

Born Merwan Sheriar Irani to Persian parents on February 25, 1894, in Poona, India, Meher Baba (compassionate father) was exposed to a number of faiths early in life. His father, Sheriar Irani, was a devout Zoroastrian. Merwan went to a Christian high school in Poona and later attended Deccan College.

According to Meher Baba, five perfect masters exist in the world at all times. These masters can

Meher Baba (1894–1969), God-realized master from western India, said to be the avatar of the current age who bridged Hinduism and Sufism *(Courtesy Avatar Meher Baba Trust)*

summon an avatar when needed to assist the world. Although they appear to be five different individuals, they are actually Satgurus, who are in the unity of the one God. They "bring down" the avatar so that the world can escape MAYA, the cage of illusion, and experience reality. While in college, in 1913, Irani met the first perfect master, Hazrat Babajan, an Islamic woman saint who kissed him on the forehead and showed him indescribable bliss, which continued for about nine months. In 1914, Babajan gave him instant God-realization and made him aware of his spiritual calling and destiny.

Another perfect master, Upasni Maharaj, a Hindu who resided in Sakori, gave Merwan gnosis or divine knowledge over the course of seven years. Through these experiences he gained spiritual perfection. In 1921 his spiritual mission began when his first close disciples gathered around him. His disciples gave him the name Meher Baba.

After years of teaching disciples, Meher Baba founded a colony near Ahmednagar, called Meherabad. The colony included a school, hospital, dispensary, and shelter for the poor. From its inception, Meherabad did not recognize caste distinctions in training its students or serving the needy. Another important part of the work begun by Meher Baba is work with the *masts*, the advanced souls or "God-intoxicated" individuals who live perpetually in awareness of the highest realm of consciousness. He sought out *masts* and took care of their physical needs, which the *masts* themselves often ignored. He also washed the feet of and fed lepers and the destitute of India.

From July 10, 1925, Meher Baba observed silence, communicating with others and giving discourses only through dictation on an alphabet board. Much later, he abandoned the alphabet board and communicated through hand gestures unique to him.

He asserted that he was the Ancient One who had returned to redeem humankind from its bondage to ignorance and to show to all their true

Self, which is God. He was acknowledged by his followers to be the avatar of the age.

In 1959, when he was 65 years old, Meher Baba established the Avatar Meher Baba Trust to provide for disciples who were dependent on him and to care for his tomb and property. The trust oversees charitable activities in India and the United States and has created a development plan for Meherabad, the site of Meher Baba's tomb.

Meher Baba traveled to the United States six times between 1931 and 1958. His center in the West is located at Myrtle Beach, South Carolina. He left his body on July 31, 1969.

Further reading: Meher Baba, *The Everything and the Nothing* (Berkeley: Beguine Library, 1963); ———, *God Speaks* (New York: Dodd, Mead, 1973); ———, *The Path of Love* (Ahmed Nagar: Awakener Press, 1986); C. B. Purdom, *The God-Man: The Life, Journeys and Work of Meher Baba with an Interpretation of His Silence and Spiritual Teaching* (Crescent Beach, S.C.: Sheriar Press, 1964); Kevin Shepherd, *Meher Baba, an Iranian Liberal* (Cambridge: Anthropographia, 1986).

Meru, Mount

In ancient Indian cosmology Mount Meru is a golden mountain, supporting the heavens, located at the center of the known universe. Its location is at the center of the continent of Jambudvipa (the island of the rose-apple tree). The part of Jambud-vipa south of the mountain is called *Bharatavarsha,* which is identified with historical India. BRAHMA, SHIVA, and VISHNU are understood to reside on the summit of Mount Meru, accompanied by sages praising the gods, *apsarases* (celestial dancers), and GANDHARVAS (celestial musicians). The pole star is seen to shine directly over the summit of Meru.

The GANGES falls from heaven to the peak of Meru, where it is channeled to the four regions below. There are numerous mythological stories associated with this mountain. One says that Mount Meru and the god of the wind (VAYU) were

good friends. However, the mischievous sage Narada approached Vayu and instigated him to humble the mountain. Vayu blew with full force for one full year, but Meru did not yield. However, after a year Meru relaxed for a while, and taking advantage of this opportunity, Vayu increased in intensity. The top of the mountain was broken off and it fell into the sea. Thus was the island of Sri Lanka born.

Further reading: Cornelia Dimitt and J. A. van Buitenen, eds. and trans., *Classical Hindu Mythology: A Reader in the Sanskrit Puranas* (Philadelphia: Temple University Press, 1978); E. Washburn Hopkins, *Epic Mythology* (Delhi: Motilal Banarsidass, 1986).

Metamorphosis League for Monastic Studies (est. 1987)

The Metamorphosis League for Monastic Studies was founded by Kailasa Chandra Das (born Mark Goodwin) in 1987, in response to disputes within the INTERNATIONAL SOCIETY FOR KRISHNA CONSCIOUSNESS (ISKCON) between the leadership and some other disciples who had been trained and initiated by the founder, Swami A. C. Prabhupada BHAKTIVEDANTA. The stated goal of the league is to help define norms for a valid devotional Vaishnavite organization. These norms suggest that a GURU, teacher; YOGI, or spiritual guide must be a self-realized Vaishnavite, that is, a devotee of VISHNU who has traveled the spiritual path to enlightenment and God. This person also must have realized the supreme personality of the godhead, KRISHNA.

Those who seek help from the league are advised to leave any guru who attracts disciples by charisma only. The charismatic personality, the league believes, may not always follow spiritual rules and may succumb to the illusion of power and self-aggrandizement, which would mislead disciples on the path to SELF-REALIZATION. On the other hand, there is a danger that an institutional guru, with a following of disciples who have accepted him in a leadership role, might succumb to empty ritualism, devoid of spirituality. A genuine guru, according to this view, is modeled on the prototype of Bhaktivedanta Swami Pradhupada, who was said to derive his authority from God and to live his life in the purity of spirit.

The league upholds the paradigm of Pradhupada and advises that devotees be very careful about proclaiming allegiance to a guru who does not have a direct lineage to the godhead. The league follows the beliefs and principles of Prabhupada. Members must abide by all rules, including VEGETARIANISM, repetition of the Hare Krishna mantra, and abstinence from intoxicating substances. Members are also required to refrain from associating with members of ISKCON and consorting with "fake gurus" who are merely charismatic or who receive their status from a group that does not promote the truth as the league sees it. The league is headquartered in Beaverton, Oregon.

Milk Ocean

Between cosmic eras, Lord VISHNU is said to lie asleep on a couch made of the great snake Adishesha, who in turns floats upon a primordial ocean of milk. This ocean appears in another well-known Hindu myth: the churning of the MILK OCEAN by the gods and the ASURAS (the antigods).

The story goes that the irascible sage Durvasas once obtained a beautiful garland from a woman. Seeing Indra, king of the gods, go by on his white elephant Airavata, the sage offered the garland to him. INDRA placed the garland on the head of his elephant, who immediately took it with his trunk and tossed it on the ground.

Durvasas was outraged at this insult. He cursed Indra with the loss of his power to the *asuras,* who then triumphed over the gods. The gods went to Lord Vishnu to ask his help. Vishnu suggested that they go to the Milk Ocean along with the demons to churn out the powerful elixir of immortality (*amrita*). The demons agreed to this cooperative task, which could be accomplished if they all worked together.

At Vishnu's command, they gathered some herbs to throw into the ocean; took Mount Mandara, which props up Mount Meru, as a churning stick; and used Vishnu himself, incarnated as a tortoise, as the base for churning. They used the divine serpent Vasuki as the churning rope and began to churn.

In some versions of the story, the first thing to emerge from the churning ocean was a poison that could consume all the worlds. The gods begged SHIVA to control it, and he drank it up in one gulp. His wife, PARVATI, fearing for his life, grabbed his throat so the poison would not enter his stomach; the burn on his throat can be seen in his iconography as a dark blue marking. Fortunately, the next things to emerge from the Milk Ocean were more salubrious: Surabhi, the wish-fulfilling cow, came forth, followed by Sri, the goddess of prosperity and fortune (*see* LAKSHMI); Dhanavantari, the physician of the gods; the Kaustubha gem that always adorns Vishnu's chest; and other wondrous things and beings, until finally, the nectar of immortality was churned out.

Knowing that the demons would want to seize the nectar, Vishnu took the form of the enchantress MOHINI, and, while the demons were mesmerized with her beauty, she served the nectar to the gods alone. As only the gods were now immortal, when the demons attacked them they were easily routed; the world was once again in the hands of the gods.

Further reading: Guruseva Dasi, *Churning the Milk Ocean: A Young Reader's Edition of the Classic Story from the Puranas of Ancient India* (LaCrosse, Fla.: Bhavani Books, 2002); Cornelia Dimitt, and J. A. van Buitenen, eds. and trans., *Classical Hindu Mythology A Reader in the Sanskrit Puranas* (Philadelphia: Temple University Press, 1978); E. Washburn Hopkins, *Epic Mythology* (Delhi: Motilal Banarsidass, 1986); W. J. Wilkins, *Hindu Mythology: Vedic and Puranic,* 2d ed. (Calcutta: Rupa, 1973).

Mimamsa

Mimamsa (inquiry) is one of the six traditional orthodox schools of Indian philosophy. The Mimamsa SUTRAS of Jaimini (c. third century C.E.) is the first extant text of the tradition.

Mimamsa in its earliest form (Purva [early] Mimamsa) preserves a strict Vedic tradition; it sees the Vedas as eternal, divine texts that should guide all life and action. According to early Mimamsa one must do one's ritual duties and worldly duties precisely according to the Vedas. The Mimamsa texts, therefore, aim to clarify the precise meaning of each Vedic injunction, so that devotees can reach the heavenly realm after death. The Mimamsakas argue very strongly that even the UPANISHADS, valued by so many for their philosophy, should be read only to learn any requirements for action that they may contain.

Mimamsa cannot be said to be theistic or oriented toward gods in a true sense; the gods are at the beck and call of humans thanks to the power of the Vedic MANTRAS. Gods exist, but the Vedas supersede all. The soul or self is understood to exist in Mimamsa, as in all six orthodox Brahminical systems.

Early Mimamsa preserved the ancient Vedic understanding of the afterlife: after death, a person went to a heavenly realm somewhat like the earthly one, where one remained in a happy state, being fed by one's family. There is no overt mention of reincarnation in the Vedic mantras themselves, with the exception of the late ISHA UPANISHAD, which is appended to the mantras of the YAJUR VEDA. Salvation itself in Mimamsa put the soul in an inert state, liberated from the bonds of earthly existence through proper performance of Vedic duty. As Mimamsa developed and changed around the seventh century with the commentary of Shabaraswamin, it accepted the notion of karma and rebirth. In this respect it converged, as did YOGA, with the other VEDANTIC schools.

Two lines of teachers, drawing upon Prabhakara and Kumarila (eighth and ninth centuries), refined the doctrine further, using careful philosophical analysis of perception, causation, and the like, for the purposes of this school. This precise investigation was replicated in the commentary on the Upanishads that developed into VEDANTA. Because it was seen as an extension of the earlier Mimamsic investigative method, Vedanta is often called Uttara Mimamsa, or "later Mimamsa."

Further reading: Francis X. Clooney, *Thinking Ritually: Rediscovering the Purva Mimamsa of Jaimini* (Vienna: Institut für Indologie, 1990); S. N. Dasgupta, *A History of Indian Philosophy,* Vol. 1 (Delhi: Motilal Banarsidass, 1975).

Minakshi

Minakshi is the GODDESS of the city of Madurai. Her shrine is the site of one of India's most spectacular temples, the Meenakshi Sundareshvarar Temple. Her name (*mina,* fish; *aksha,* eye) is understood to mean "she whose eyes are the shape of lovely fishes," the translation of her original Tamil name, Ankayalkanni.

There is little question that Minakshi was the overseer of Madurai from very ancient times. However, as the Brahminical influence entered Tamil Nadu she was assimilated into the larger Brahminical culture as the wife of SHIVA.

The story goes that Minakshi's father and mother performed a special ritual to get a son. Instead of a son, a girl child emerged from the fire with three breasts. The parents were told to treat her as a prince would be treated and have her assume rulership. She was a powerful warrior and defeated all beings in all the directions. One day, however, she contended with SHIVA himself; upon seeing him, she fell in love. As this happened, she suddenly became bashful and timid (no doubt a patriarchal addition to the story!) and lost her third breast. She and Shiva were ceremoniously married, and he then became the king of Madurai and she the queen; the temple is now dedicated to both deities.

The kings of Madurai have retained their connection with Shiva, seeing themselves as ruling in his line. However, in the temple precincts Minakshi retains pride of place in the inner sanctum, which contains a small image of her.

Each year the CHITTIRAI FESTIVAL (in the lunar month of Chittirai) commemorates the marriage of Minakshi and Shiva. It is is marked by 10 days of pageantry and celebration; a huge temple chariot bearing the festival images of Minakshi and Shiva is paraded around. Because of her status in Madurai, a great many businesses there, from tire companies to restaurants, are named after the goddess.

Further reading: Chris Fuller, *A Priesthood Renewed: Modernity and Traditionalism in a South Indian Temple* (Princeton, N.J.: Princeton University Press, 2003); ———, *Servants of the Goddess: The Priests of a South Indian Temple* (New York: Cambridge University Press); William P. Harman, *The Sacred Marriage of a Hindu Goddess* (Bloomington: Indiana University Press, 1989).

Mirabai (c. 1450–1547) *mystic poet and devotee of Krishna*

Mirabai is one of the great mystic poets of India. A princess of the Rajput warrior clan in the Indian state of Rajasthan, she married a great prince of the famous town of Udaipur but was so devoted to Lord KRISHNA that she could not play the role of a proper wife. She eventually became the disciple of Raidas, a low-caste Hindu who was himself later worshipped as a saint.

Mirabai was persecuted by her husband and his family; it is said that they even gave her poison to drink, which failed to kill her. Finally Krishna appeared to her and told her to abandon family life and go to BRINDAVAN, his most sacred shrine. After spending some time there she settled at last in Gujarat in Dvaraka, where she died. Legend has it that she disappeared into the icon of Krishna in order to avoid a delegation from Rajasthan that was pleading for her to return.

Mirabai's works, written in the Hindi dialect Braj, show a passionate all-consuming devotion to Lord Krishna as the divine lover. As was the case with so many Vaishnavite (*see* VAISHNAVISM) saints, her songs often depict the agony of separation from God (Lord Krishna), who only rarely visits in mystical union. The mode of Mirabai very much resembles that of St. John of the Cross in his famous "Dark Night" (*Noche Oscura*). Mira's songs are known all over India but are sung particularly in Rajasthan.

Further reading: Robert Bly and Jane Hirshfield, *Mirabai: Ecstatic Poems* (Boston: Beacon Press, 2004); Rita Dalmiya, *Meerabai* (Calcutta: Writers Workshop, 1988); John Stratton Hawley, *Three Bhakti Voices: Mirabai, Surdas, and Kabir in Their Time and Ours* (New Delhi: Oxford University Press, 2005).

Mishra, Ramamurti (1923–1993) *(Swami Brahmananda Saraswati) teacher of raja yoga*

Ramamurti Mishra was an Indian-born yogi who founded the ANANDA ASHRAM in Monroe, New York. He wrote many books on YOGA and AYURVEDA and he commented upon many SANSKRIT texts.

Ramamurti Mishra was born in Benares (Varanasi), India, on March 6, 1923, into a religious Brahmin family. His mother was a spiritual teacher with many disciples and his father was a high court judge and practitioner of astrology. From an early age, Ramamurti was immersed in the study of Sanskrit, MEDITATION, and YOGA. At the age of six, he became ill and apparently died—for 36 hours, no vital signs of life, including respiration, were detected. As his father was about to light the fire for his cremation, the child sat upright and declared that he was alive. Ramamurti always considered this date, March 6, was his real birthday.

At a young age he left home to pursue the study of Sanskrit and medicine. He completed his first medical degrees in Ayurveda and Western medicine at Banares Hindu University. In 1955, he left India to study medicine in the United States and served as a resident in neurosurgery at Bellevue Hospital in New York City.

In 1964, he founded Ananda Ashram in Monroe, New York, where figures such as Timothy Leary and RAM DASS visited and taught. The ASHRAM continues to function as a year-round retreat for spiritual practice.

In 1966, Mishra resigned from his medical career to devote himself to spiritual discipline and the teaching of *raja yoga,* with a focus on the question, Who am I? Convinced that the cause of suffering is not in the body or the mind, but rather in ignorance of the true Self, he began to teach and explore the path to discovery of the "I AM" consciousness that he believed to be eternal and ever present.

In 1984 he was initiated into the vow of *sannyas* (renunciation) by Swami Gangeshvarananda and was given the name Brahmananda Saraswati. He was a prolific writer who published texts on yoga, meditation, *raja yoga,* Ayurveda, and commentaries on Sanskrit texts. He died on September 19, 1993.

Further reading: Ramamurti S. Mishra, *Fundamentals of Yoga* (Monroe, N.Y.: Baba Bhagavandas Publication Trust, 1996); ———, *Self Analysis and Self Knowledge* (Monroe, N.Y.: Baba Bhagavandas Publication Trust, 1997); ———, *The Textbook of Yoga Psychology* (Monroe, N.Y.: Baba Bhagavandas Publication Trust, 1997).

Mishra, Vachaspati (c. 840 C.E.) *Hindu scholar and commentator*

Vachaspati Mishra was a philosopher particularly celebrated for his *Bhamati,* a subcommentary on SHANKARA'S commentary on the VEDANTA SUTRA. He was a prolific scholar and writer whose name is attached to commentaries on NYAYA (logic), SAMKHYA, YOGA, and other subjects. Another of his well-known works was a subcommentary on the Veda Vyasa's authoritative commentary to the YOGA SUTRA of PATANJALI.

Further reading: S. N. Dasgupta, *History of Indian Philosophy,* 5 vols. (Delhi: Motilal Banarsidass, 1975).

Mitra

Mitra is a minor deity often mentioned in the Vedic hymns, especially in association with VARUNA. Many hymns and offerings are given to the pair Mitra-Varuna in the Vedic rituals. Some believe that Mitra was a form of Sun god who lost his ancient character. The Iranian *Avesta* has a prominent god named Mithra, who is clearly related historically to the Mitra of the VEDAS.

Further reading: Gonda, Jan. *The Vedic God Mitra* (Leiden: E. J. Brill, 1972).

Mohenjodaro (Mohenjo Daro) *See* INDUS VALLEY CIVILIZATION.

Mohini

The enchantress Mohini was a form that VISHNU took during the churning of the MILK OCEAN. The demons and gods had cooperated in churning the ocean to produce the nectar of immortality (AMRITA). Knowing that the demons would want to seize the nectar for themselves, Vishnu assumed the form of MOHINI, mesmerizing the demons with her beauty while she served the nectar to the gods alone. As only the gods were now immortal, when the demons attacked they were routed, and the world was once again in the hands of the gods.

Further reading: Guruseva Dasi, *Churning the Milk Ocean: A Young Reader's Edition of the Classic Story from the Puranas of Ancient India* (LaCrosse, Fla: Bhavani Books, 2002); Cornelia Dimitt, and J. A. van Buitenen, eds. and trans., *Classical Hindu Mythology A Reader in the Sanskrit Puranas* (Philadelphia: Temple University Press, 1978).

moksha

In a literal sense, *moksha* is the desire to be released from birth and rebirth, but the term has come to mean the release itself. It is used interchangeably with *mukti*. *Moksha* is the highest spiritual goal in the Hindu tradition (the term is used in JAINISM and SIKHISM as well). Traditional Hinduism recognizes four primary ENDS OF LIFE and *moksha* is the last in the list.

While every Hindu tradition sees *moksha* as the ideal, there are different understandings of its nature. Some traditions believe that one can be liberated while still alive—*JIVANMUKTA*. Some see liberation as a merging into a characterless BRAHMAN, while others see liberation as simply becoming one with God, or being liberated near God.

Further reading: M. C. Bharatiya, trans. and ed., *Moksa the Ultimate Goal of Indian Philosophy* (Ghaziabad: Indo-Vision, 1984); Balbir Singh, *Atman and Moksha: Self and Self-Realization* (Atlantic Highlands, N. J.: Humanities Press, 1981).

Mother, The (Mirra Richard) (1878–1973)
revered utopian yoga teacher

French-born Mirra Alfassa was a revered teacher of YOGA in a modern context and of utopian social thought. The title *Mother* was given to her by her associate, the great Indian sage Sri AUROBINDO. It indicated that she was considered a form of the GODDESS.

Mirra Alfassa was born to an Egyptian mother and Turkish father in Paris on February 21, 1878. Though she lived in a strictly atheistic household, young Mirra began to have spiritual and occult experiences as a young girl. She would often fall into a silent trance for minutes at a time. As she grew older she had experiences of distance sight and astral projection. As a young woman she took full advantage of the cultural excitement of Paris at the turn of the 20th century. Her first husband, with whom she had her only child, was an artist associated with the burgeoning modern art scene.

The Mother (1878–1973), spiritual partner of Sri Aurobindo and founder of Auroville Community, Tamil Nadu (*Courtesy Sri Aurobindo Archives, Pondicherry*)

At the age of 28 Mirra went to Algeria to study occultism under a little-known teacher, Max Theon, and his wife, Alma, but decided in the end that Theon was not a pure master. She felt that he was ego driven and self-centered. On a 1914 trip to India with her second husband, the diplomat Paul Richard, she met Sri Aurobindo, who had recently taken refuge in Pondicherry. She describes this visit dramatically in her diaries. She had dreamed of just such a person, with flowing robes and beard, when she was much younger and she felt that she had met a person of pure and powerful spirit. She relates how she was enveloped in his presence in the most profound silence of the mind. She did not, however, join Sri Aurobindo at that time, but went with her husband to Japan.

After leaving Japan and spending some time in Europe, Mirra Richard abandoned married life and joined Sri Aurobindo as his spiritual partner in 1916. At first there were questions about her status at his ASHRAM from people close to Sri Aurobindo, but he quelled them by declaring that his consciousness and the Mother's consciousness were one; it was he who gave her the important spiritual title, *Mother.* In his book *On the Mother* he explained her spiritual role in the new world.

The yoga that she and Sri Aurobindo practiced was worldly. Rather than the isolated transcendence of the renunciant in a cave, it was a transformative yoga aimed at changing all of reality in its wake. They wanted to bring to earth the divine superconsciousness, termed the *supramental,* by Aurobindo, which would, they thought, alter the nature of reality itself. The Integral Yoga, or complete yoga, of Sri Aurobindo and Mother was designed to orient its devotees yogically toward a life in the world that would progressively become divine.

In 1926 Sri Aurobindo went into seclusion in the ashram and left Mother in charge of day-to-day affairs. He declared that he had reached the Overmind in his yogic work and needed seclusion to work with the powerful forces in order to expand this into a supramental manifestation. Mother from then on managed all ashram affairs, designed the movement's educational programs, and provided inspiration to the burgeoning group of followers who began to attend more regularly.

Sri Aurobindo died in 1950 without completing his spiritual project. He declared that it was the Mother herself who would succeed in bringing about the supramental manifestation that would begin the transformation of all life, all matter, and all the cosmos toward perfect consciousness and bliss. In 1956 Mother announced that she had succeeded in bringing down the supramental and

proceeded from that day to prepare the world for the power of a new consciousness that she felt would now inevitably manifest.

Mother had already, in the early 1950s, envisioned a utopian ground where all nations could join to manifest the unity on Earth that she felt would accompany the new consciousness. This early vision of an international center for education gradually changed into the idea of a city to be built in South India under her auspices. In 1968 she broke ground for this city—AUROVILLE—which was to be a guide for the new earthly transformation. People from around the world flocked to the city to begin the new spiritual experiment.

Mother died in 1973 at the age of 95 and was buried in a tomb beside her beloved spiritual partner, Sri Aurobindo. She left a legacy of practice and commitment that few women spiritual teachers in the 20th century could match. Her writings were not vast as her mentor's were, but her words and wisdom were dutifully recorded by her student Satprem, who transformed them into a many-volume series, *The Mother's Agenda.*

Further reading: Kireet Joshi, *Sri Aurobindo and the Mother: Glimpses of Their Experiments, Experiences, and Realisations* (New Delhi: Motilal Banarsidass, Delhi, 1989); Satprem, *Mother's Agenda,* 12 vols. (Paris: Institut de recherches évolutives, 1991); George Van Vrekhem, *The Mother: The Story of Her Life* (New Delhi: HarperCollins Publishers India, 2000).

Mother India (1927)

Mother India was a controversial book, written in 1927 by Katherine Mayo, an American medical missionary and journalist, that condemned Hinduism as a cause of India's suffering.

The book was inspired by Mayo's encounters with Indian women and customs during her travels to the country in 1925 and 1926. It raised consciousness of important gender and caste issues that needed to be addressed; however, it also served as an indictment against Indian society and Hinduism in general.

Mayo claimed that Hindu customs were dangerous not only to India but to the entire world. She believed the customs weakened the human "stock" with poverty, disease, and physical and mental frailties. Historians have interpreted the book as a racist tract that emerged from the age of British and American imperialism. The book negatively influenced popular Western perceptions of India for decades and hindered support and sympathy for Indian independence around the world.

The main thesis of *Mother India* was an assertion that Hindu practices made Indians weak, incapable of self-rule, and unable to become economically self-sufficient. A primary indictment concerned the roles of women. Mayo charged that the Hindu religion enslaved women, forced them to be sexually subservient to men, and demanded that they follow social patterns that produced impoverishment and ignorance. Mayo cites factors such as child marriage, lack of education, the burdens of having many children, child widowhood, prostitution, and epidemics of venereal disease as significant problems for women in India.

Some American feminists during the 1970s revered Mayo as a pioneer who created awareness of the plight of Indian woman. Indian critics, by contrast, dispute *Mother India's* representation of all Indian women as weak, passive, and incapable of resistance. Mayo made no mention of the Indian women's movement or of efforts by the Indian National Congress to support women's rights. While depicting Indian women as helpless victims, the book lauds the British imperialists as a civilizing force, saving India from the customs of a decadent religion.

The book prompted outrage and criticism from Indian nationalists. Mohandas Karamchand GANDHI referred to it as a "gutter inspector's report," and it received further condemnation from Indian women's organizations. In Britain,

however, *Mother India* received enthusiastic reviews. Indignant Hindus in America rebutted the publication with many books and pamphlets; they tried to turn the tables by condemning American society as rampant with crime, political scandal, and marital infidelity.

The book did succeed in raising awareness of some issues and fostering British reforms in India, such as the Child Marriage Act of 1929. Ironically, *Mother India* also contributed to an alliance between Indian nationalists and women's movements, which organized to refute and neutralize Mayo's indictments. The alliance helped to pass the Sarada Act, a law enforcing a minimal age for marriage.

Mother India continues to influence Western perceptions of Hinduism and India. Its wholesale rejection of Hindu beliefs and practices and its depiction of a sexually deviant culture have influenced popular media to represent India as exotic, forbidden, and dangerous. Yet, *Mother India* remains inspirational to others who use its thesis to promote heightened awareness for reform in India.

Further reading: Elizabeth Bumiller, *May You Be the Mother of a Hundred Sons: A Journey among the Women of India* (New York: Random House, 1991); W. Estep, *An American Answers Mother India* (Excelsior Springs, Mo.: Super Mind Science, 1929); Katherine Mayo, *Mother India* (New York, Harcourt, Brace, 1927); ———, *The Isles of Fear; The Truth about the Philippines* (New York: Harcourt, Brace, 1925); Mrinalini Sinha, *Colonial Masculinity: The "Manly Englishman" and the "Effeminate Bengali" in the Late Nineteenth Century* (New York: Manchester University Press, 1995).

Mount Abu   *See* ABU, MOUNT.

Mount Kailasa   *See* KAILASA, MOUNT.

Mount Meru   *See* MERU, MOUNT.

mudra   *See* PANCHA MAKARA.

mudra

Mudra is a technical term used in both YOGA and Indian dance. In yoga the *mudras* are particular hand gestures or bodily attitudes that have spiritual or yogic meaning or purpose. In Indian dance the *mudras* are hand gestures accompanied by particular bodily stances. For example, in BHARATA NATYAM, the Indian national dance, *mudras* are used to communicate the moods of characters and their dramatic interactions.

Further reading: *Mudras in Symbols: Bharatnatya Manual Primer* (Madras: Centre for Promotion of the Traditional Arts, 1988); Swami Satyananda Saraswati, *Asana Pranayama Mudra Bandha* (Bihar: Bihar School of Yoga, 1999).

Muktananda, Swami (1908–1982)
Shaivite guru

Swami Muktananda was an influential teacher who formulated the Siddha Yoga philosophy and helped spread it around the world.

Muktananda (his birth name was Krishna) was born on May 16, 1908, into a prosperous farming family. His father was the headman of a village near Mangalore in Karnataka state. His mother, deeply pious, had prayed for the birth of a son, and from his earliest years she provided him with a strong religious foundation. While still in his teens he had several encounters with the wandering spiritual adept, Bhagawan NITYANANDA, who would later become his GURU. At the age of 15 Krishna decided to dedicate his life to attaining a direct experience of God and adopted one of the traditional Indian paths to that experience, that of a wandering SADHU, mendicant.

In the early 1920s, shortly after his travels began, Krishna went to Hubli in northern Karnataka, to the ASHRAM of Siddharudha Swami, a renowned VIRASHAIVA yogi. In Siddharudha's ashram, he studied VEDANTA, took vows of *sannyas* (renunciation), and received the name Muktananda (the bliss of freedom). In 1930, a year after Siddharudha's passing, Swami Muktananda began an extended period of wandering.

Muktananda once said that he walked across India three times. He traveled mostly on foot, carrying only a water bowl and staff as he moved from one teacher to the next. During this time he studied all of the major texts of the Hindu scriptural canon; he became adept at HATHA YOGA and AYURVEDIC medicine, and he met scores of holy beings. He became a renowned teacher in his own right, and still he kept searching.

In his spiritual autobiography, *Play of Consciousness*, Muktananda calls August 15, 1947,

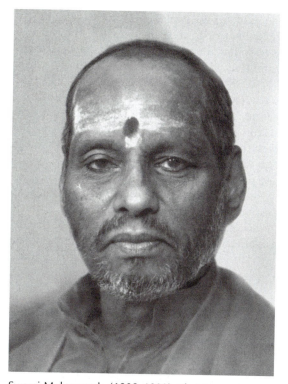

Swami Muktananda (1908–1982), Shaivite teacher, scholar, and founder of Siddha Yoga Dham (© SYDA Foundation)

"the most auspicious of all auspicious days", it was the day that Bhagawan Nityananda, by then living in Ganeshpuri, gave him *shaktipata* DIKSHA, spiritual initiation. This was followed by nine years of intense meditation under Nityananda's direction, until the guru declared that Muktananda was "one with BRAHMAN." In 1956 Bhagawan Nityananda installed Muktananda in a tiny ashram just down the road from his own. That spot, where Swami Muktananda's tomb and shrine now stand, remains the heart of what has become an international center for spiritual learning and the Siddha Yoga "mother" ashram, Gurudev Siddha Peeth.

Shortly before Nityananda's death in 1961, he made Swami Muktananda his spiritual successor. After his guru's passing, Muktananda began formalizing Nityananda's teachings, which he called the Siddha Yoga path. Siddha Yoga is the way of an enlightened, or SIDDHA, master; the practice is to follow the master's guidance and teachings with the aid of the master's enlivening grace. For all siddha yogis, the path begins as it did for Muktananda, with *shaktipata diksha*, spiritual initiation. The goal is permanent dwelling in a realization of the divinity that exists within and as everything. Muktananda's emblematic teaching, one that he repeated again and again throughout the two decades of his teaching mission, is "Meditate on your own Self. Worship your Self. Respect your Self. God lives within you as you." By the capitalized *s of Self,* he emphasized that he was referring not to one's individual ego but to an expanded identification of the Self with supreme consciousness.

Baba Muktananda, as he became known, traveled throughout India and completed three world tours, initiating and guiding students of Siddha Yoga meditation. He created the Siddha Yoga Shaktipat Intensive as the ideal environment for spiritual awakening. He founded ashrams around the world, established the SYDA Foundation to manage the Siddha Yoga mission, and created the canon of Siddha Yoga philosophy through his own writings and his synthesis of the teachings of VEDANTA, KASHMIRI SHAIVISM, and the writings of the BHAKTI poet-saints.

In 1982, Muktananda named his disciple Swami CHIDVILASANANDA to carry the Siddha Yoga lineage forward. The ceremony that announced and enacted this transmission was held publicly in Gurudev Siddha Peeth in May 1982. On October 2, 1982, on the full Moon night of Sharadpurnima, Baba Muktananda left his body (took *mahasamadhi*).

"Baba Muktananda's *shakti* [energy] is *sat* [being]," Guru Chidvilasananda has said. "It was experienced strongly in the past; it is powerfully with us now; and it will continue to be so in the future. His shakti awakens an ever-new life in all those it touches." Through his teachings, his ashrams, and the exemplary story of his own spiritual life related in *Play of Consciousness,* people continue to receive transmission of energy and spiritual awakening, which are the basis of his spiritual mission.

One of the first American disciples to receive *shaktipat* from Muktananda was Albert Rudolph (1928–73), who became Swami RUDRANANDA, a teacher of Shaivism in the United States. Later, Franklin Jones became a disciple of Muktananda and returned to the United States to become a spiritual teacher called Bubba Free John (now ADI DA SAMRAJ).

Further reading: Douglas Renfrew Brooks et al., *Meditation Revolution: A History and Theology of the Siddha Yoga Lineage* (South Fallsburg, N.Y.: Agama Press, 1997); *Swami Muktananda, from the Finite to the Infinite,* 2d ed. (South Fallsburg, N.Y.: SYDA Foundation, 1994); ———, *Play of Consciousness: A Spiritual Autobiography* (South Fallsburg, N.Y.: SYDA Foundation, 2000); [Pratibha Trivedi] Amma, *Swami Muktananda Paramahansa* (Ganeshpuri: Shree Gurudev Ashram, 1971).

mukti See MOKSHA.

muladhara chakra

In the *muladhara* (basic foundation) CHAKRA at the base of the spine rests the coiled KUNDALINI serpent, who awaits her awakening through YOGA to begin the journey upward to meet her transcendent counterpart SHIVA at the SAHASRARA juncture above the head. This chakra is associated with the most basic urge for survival and gross physicality. It is the site of the lower emotions, such as anger and greed. Its element is earth, the densest of the elements (*see* PANCHA BHUTAS). Its deity is BRAHMA and its ruler GANESHA. Its SHAKTI or energy power is dakini. It has 10 blue petals.

Further reading: Harish Johari, *Chakras: Energy Centers of Transformation* (Rochester, Vt.: Destiny Books, 2000).

muni

A *muni* is a saint, sage, ascetic, or hermit. This is a traditional term found in the epics and the Puranas, superseding the earlier VEDIC term *RISHI*. It is still used in modern Hinduism, although somewhat less than the terms *sadhu* and *swami*. The Jain tradition (*see* JAINISM) uses the term *muni* for a respected monk.

Further reading: Patrick Olivelle, trans., *Sannyasa Upanishads: Hindu Scriptures on Asceticism and Renunciation* (New York: Oxford University Press, 1992).

Murugan   *See* KARTTIKEYA.

myths of creation

The Hindu myths of creation are many and varied. The VEDAS, the most ancient scriptures, include several striking creation hymns. One hymn sees creation as emerging from a divine person, the PURUSHA, who is sacrificed in order for time to begin; creation results directly from his body and being. Another account, in the RIG VEDA, suggests that no one knows what existed before this world; only the one in the highest heaven knows, and perhaps not even he! Still another hymn speaks of a Golden Embryo that precedes all creation, out of which everything emerges.

The UPANISHADS, part of the Vedas, contain numerous cosmogonic (creation) stories. Several of them relate that the world was emitted from the supreme Self or ATMAN, which pervaded all reality. Others speak of reality's emerging from the one BRAHMAN, or ultimate all. Still others speak of the creation's beginning with PRAJAPATI, a male creator god or principle.

In the Puranas, written from about 400 C.E. to 1000 C.E., the god BRAHMA is usually said to be responsible for creation. He is depicted emerging from a lotus in the navel of VISHNU, who is sleeping on the primordial MILK OCEAN between eras. However, worshippers of either Vishnu or SHIVA often credited their chosen god with creating the entire universe.

Further reading: Cornelia Dimmitt and J. A. B. van Buitenen, *Classical Hindu Mythology: A Reader in the Sanskrit Puranas* (Philadelphia: Temple University Press, 1978); F. B. J. Kuiper, *Ancient Indian Cosmogony* (New Delhi: Vikas, 1983).

N

Nachiketas

In the BRAHMANAS, the explanatory portions of the ancient VEDAS, *nachiketas* was a special kind of fire. The word later became personalized as a character in the KATHA UPANISHAD. There, Nachiketas was a boy banished by his father's curse to the underworld. He arrived at the house of YAMA, the god of death, but was not greeted as a proper guest. When Yama returned, he offered Nachiketas three boons because he had neglected him.

Nachiketas asked to return to his father, to be restored to life, and to learn the secret of death—or rather deathlessness. Yama tried to dissuade Nachiketas from the third request, but the wise young man persisted. Yama then gave him a teaching on the nature of the BRAHMAN, the ultimate reality, and the nature of the Self, or universal soul.

Further reading: Eknath Easwaran, *Dialogue with Death: A Journey into Consciousness*, 2d ed. (Tomales, Calif.: Nilgiri Press, 1992); Mysore Sivaram, *Death and Nachiketas* (New Delhi: Vikas, 1981).

nadi

In certain YOGA systems, a *nadi* is a subtle bodily channel used to redirect PRANA (the life force found within the breath). The goals are to alter consciousness, strengthen the body, and help bring about the transformation needed for liberation from the cycle of births.

In HATHA YOGA, *prana* is forced through these channels to aid in raising the KUNDALINI at the base of the spine. The most commonly known *nadi* is the *sushumna nadi,* which travels up the spinal cord. The *ida* and *pingala nadis* are depicted as widely rippling waves that intersect at each CHAKRA (psychic center), exactly mirroring each other as they ascend around *sushumna.*

Further reading: Swami Sivananda Radha, *Hatha Yoga, the Hidden Language: Symbols, Secrets and Metaphor* (Boston: Shambala, 1989); Pancham Sinh, trans., *The Hatha Yoga Pradipika* (New Delhi: Munshiram Manoharlal, 1975).

Nagapanchami

The Nagapanchami snake-worshipping festival takes place on the fifth day of the lunar month of Shravana (July–August). The worship focuses on the cobra, to thank the snake for its auspicious presence and to palliate the serpent world so that it will not bite. The mythical and mysterious power of the serpent is recognized the world over; this festival is an ancient Indian tribute to its semidivine power, as a being that moves between this world and the powerful underworld.

On Nagapanchami, images of mythological serpents such as Vasuki are worshipped and given milk, considered a favored food of snakes (of course, Indian villagers often offer milk to live cobras on a daily basis). Figures of snakes may be drawn on walls with cow dung or on boards with red powder to be worshipped. Also, people go to abandoned termite hills and other places were snakes live to make offerings. Snake charmers may be invited to perform on this day, and in certain areas there are huge processions of men (and some women) who handle cobras in fulfillment of vows.

Further reading: Balaji Kundkur, *The Cult of the Serpent: An Interdisciplinary Survey of Its Manifestations and Origins* (Albany: State University of New York Press, 1983); Binod Chandra Sinha, *Serpent Worship in Ancient India* (New Delhi: Books Today, 1979).

nagas

The term *naga* appears in different contexts in Indian tradition. Its basic meaning is "serpent" or "snake," usually the cobra. NAGAPANCHAMI, for instance, is a snake festival celebrated on *panchami*, the fifth day of the lunar month of Shravana. The *nagakal* in South India are "snake stones," stone images of cobras placed under PIPAL (*ashvattha*) or neem trees. They are commonly worshipped by women who desire to have offspring.

The snake or *naga* plays a very important role in Indian folk religion. Villagers make shrines of abandoned termite hills, where snakes take up residence, give them offerings, and feed them milk. In southwestern India people have a *naga* shrine or grove in the corner of a garden. Most often the snakes are seen as protective, but they also connote immortality and fertility.

A divine, semidivine, or demonic *naga* is associated with all the foremost personages and divinities in the Buddhist, Jain, and Hindu traditions. The BUDDHA was said to have been guarded once by a semidivine serpent. The Jain TIRTHANKARA (saint) PARSHVANATH is depicted in his iconography protected by a huge multiheaded cobra being, or *naga*. SHIVA, too, has a *naga* or serpent around his neck as a necklace. VISHNU reclines on the divine serpent Ananta or ADISHESHA on the primordial MILK OCEAN. The huge serpent Vasuki was used as a churning rope when the gods and demons churned the Milk Ocean to get the nectar of immortality. KRISHNA, when he was young, vanquished the evil serpent Kaliya.

The term *naga* also denotes a category of semidivine creatures, the top half human and the bottom half snake, who guard precious gems and ores underground, similar to dragons in some Western mythology, but without their ferocity. Occasionally, these *nagas* can take fully human form; famous personages such as Nagarjuna are said to be their descendants.

Myths usually place the half-human *nagas* under the Earth, but they may also live under water or in mountain caves. They are beautiful and opulently attired. Their human heads are overarched by cobra hoods emerging out from the back of the neck. They have great wisdom and superhuman powers and indulge in pleasures that are the envy of the human world. These demigods play an important role in Buddhist, Jain, and Hindu traditions and are frequently encountered in the mythology of all three religions.

Further reading: James Fergusson, *Tree and Serpent Worship* (Delhi: Oriental Publishers, 1971); O. C. Handa, *Naga Cults and Traditions in the Western Himalaya* (New Delhi: Indus, 2004); E. Washburn Hopkins, *Epic Mythology* (Delhi: Motilal Banarsidass, 1986); Jean Philippe Vogel, *Indian Serpent Lore or the Nagas in Hindu Legend and Art* (Varanasi: Prithivi Prakashan, 1972).

Naga sect

The Naga is a sect of SADHUS or holy men devoted to SHIVA. Many of its followers go about naked, as the word *naga* implies. In doing this they follow the example of Lord Shiva, who was himself a naked mendicant. They often live in mountain caves completely naked, with the mountain snows outside. Following the example of Shiva, Naga sadhus smear their entire bodies with ashes from cremation grounds and wear dreadlocks. As does Shiva, they smoke great quantities of hashish, particularly when singing praises to that god.

The Nagas are also known as ascetic warriors. Though most Indian holy men are known as peaceful seekers of truth and higher consciousness, Nagas have been known to be extremely militant. In the past they have taken up arms against other sects of ascetics, Muslims, and the British.

Today Naga sadhus still carry weapons as they wander the countryside—sticks, spears, swords, and most especially the trident (which is a symbol of Shiva). At the KUMBHA MELA (festival) at ALLA-HABAD, these sadhus are usually the first to have the honor of entering the confluence of the waters of the YAMUNA and GANGES.

Further reading: Shashi Bhushan Dasgupta, *Obscure Religious Cults*, 2d rev. ed. (Calcutta: Firma K. L. Mukhopadhyay, 1962); Dolf Harsuiker, *Sadhus: Holy Men of India* (London: Thames & Hudson, 1993); John Campbell Oman, *The Mystics, Ascetics, and Saints of India: A Study of Sadhuism with an Account of the Yogis, Sanyasis, Bairagis, and Other Strange Hindu Sectarians* (New Delhi: Cosmos, 1984).

Nakula   *See* PANDAVAS.

namarupa

Namarupa (from *nama*, name, and *rupa*, form) is a term used in Hindu philosophy to refer to

Naked hermit of Naga sect at source of Ganges River, Gomulkh, near Gangotri, in the foothills of the Himalaya Mountains *(Constance A. Jones)*

the phenomenal world, the world of finiteness and limited nature, as opposed to the transcendent reality of the BRAHMAN or god. In Hindu thought, reality begins as an unmanifest infinity devoid of any manifestation or "thing." As things emerge that acquire a "name" and take a shape or "form," the manifest world or *namarupa* appears. Most Hindu traditions see liberation from birth and rebirth as a release or escape from the clutches of name and form, or *namarupa*. The term *namarupa* also appears in Buddhism with a quite different meaning, referring to the mind-body complex.

Further reading: Maryla Falk, *Nama-Rupa and Dharma-Rupa: Origin and Aspects of an Ancient Indian Conception* (Calcutta: University of Calcutta, 1943); Wilhelm Halbfass, ed., *Philology and Confrontation: Paul Hacker on Traditional and Modern Vedanta* (Albany: State University of New York Press, 1995).

namaste

Namaste is the common greeting and farewell in every part of India except Tamil Nadu. It is derived from the word *namas* (from the root *nam,* to bow) and *te* (to you). Thus it is understood as "obeisance," "homage," or "salutation." It is said to mean "I honor the god that is within you." If one wishes to be slightly more formal, one says *"Namaskar,"* with essentially the same meaning. The statement *"Namaste"* is accompanied, usually, by a gesture placing the palms of the hands together in front of one. (Even in Indian areas where the word *namaste* is not used, this gesture is found.)

Further reading: C. J. Fuller, *The Camphor Flame: Popular Hinduism and Society in India* (Princeton, N.J.: Princeton University Press, 1992); Richard Lannoy, *The Speaking Tree: A Study of Indian Culture and Society* (New York: Oxford University Press, 1974).

Nammalvar (c. 880–930 C.E.) *Tamil Vaishnavite poet-saint*

Nammalvar, "Our Own Alvar," was the 11th and greatest of the 12 ALVARS, the poet-saints, of Tamil VAISHNAVISM. He composed four works, of which the 1,100-verse Tiruvaymoli is most influential. Also celebrated are Tiruviruttam and Periyatiruvantati.

According to legend Nammalvar was born in a Vellala family (technically SHUDRA or servant class) to his father, Kariyar, and mother, Utaiyanankaiyar, in Kurugur (Tirunagari) in the Tirunelveli District of Tamil Nadu. The pair had prayed for a child at a temple at Tirukkurungudi and were told there that the child would be a part of VISHNU himself. Vishnu sent his minister Vishvaksena (theologically a part of Vishnu) to be incarnated as the child.

Maran (the later Nammalvar) was born only 43 days after KRISHNA himself passed from the world. As a baby, he is said never to have cried or drunk milk, but to have been possessed of a beatific, divine smile. After 11 days the parents took this divine child and placed him in the creche of a tamarind tree. The child, in a deep trance, opened neither mouth nor eyes for 16 years.

As Nammalvar was in this trance, the 10th of the Alvars, Mathurakavi, was traveling in the north of India. One night he saw a vision of blazing light in the south, which told him that a saint had been born there. He managed to find the young person seated in MEDITATION, looking impervious to the outside world. To see whether he could distract Nammalvar he dropped a stone on the ground and Nammalvar opened his eyes. Mathurakavi tested him with a difficult riddle; when he answered insightfully the older saint bowed down and accepted Nammalvar as his master. At this moment the transcendent vision overwhelmed Nammalvar and he began to pour forth his devotional songs in a continuous stream.

Further reading: John Carman and Vasudha Narayanan, *The Tamil Veda: Pillan's Interpretation of the Tiruvaymoli* (Chicago: University of Chicago Press, 1989); Alkondavilli Govindacharya, *The Holy Lives of the Azhvars or the Dravida Saints* (Bombay: Ananthacharya Indological Research Institute, 1982); A. K. Ramanujan, *Hymns for the Drowning* (Princeton, N.J.: Princeton University Press, 1981).

Nanak, Guru (1469–1539) *founder of the Sikh religion*

Guru Nanak was a charismatic religious and social reformer. He tried to bridge the gap between

Hindus and Muslims but instead founded a new religion, SIKHISM. Guru Nanak was born on April 15, 1469, in Talwandi-Rai-Bhoe in the district of Shekhupur, now in Pakistan. His father, Mehta Kalu, was a land surveyor and small farmer of the Khatri caste of the Bedi tribe.

In his early life Nanak showed great devotion to God and was often enveloped in spiritual meditation while watching over cattle. From age five he began to utter mysterious sayings; at seven, when taken to a teacher to learn to read, he would lapse into silence. Myths of miracles have been associated with his childhood. In response to such signs of withdrawal the local community suggested to his parents that he be married. His wife, Sulakhani, a Khatri of the Chona subcaste, eventually gave birth to two sons, Lakhmi Das and Siri Chand.

Nanak studied reading and writing in the local dialect, traditional scripture in SANSKRIT, and poetry in Persian. Throughout his life he had many mystical experiences; one story recounts how he went to the river to bathe and was visited by "messengers of God" who took him to a divine court and fed him nectar. For three days he remained missing, and upon his return he declared that there are no Hindus or Muslims, that all people are equal. His inner experiences gave him equanimity. He taught love, equality, justice, selfless service, and the worship of God. His teaching renounced religious hypocrisy.

Guru Nanak was considered to be a leader in the BHAKTI (path of devotion) movement but was also active in calling for reform of Indian social and religious customs that he saw as unjust. He was outspoken against caste oppression, discrimination, and injustice and committed to awakening the consciousness of people.

Guru Nanak criticized what he considered the empty rituals and sacrifices of Hinduism in his time. Working in the villages near his own he founded and developed the SIKH tradition, which integrated Buddhist, Hindu, and Islamic ideals of the virtuous life and enlightenment. According to Nanak, the process of realization involves the grace of both God and GURU. the spiritual master. The Sikh tradition maintains that the goal of all human beings is to achieve self-perfection in their lifetime and to help others do the same. Sikh philosophy states that self-transformation occurs through guru, guru's grace, guru's will, devotion, discernment, and detachment. He composed the Adi Granth, the sacred text later revered by Sikhs as the last guru. Today the Adi Granth is the only guru honored among traditional Sikhs. Guru Nanak died on September 7, 1539.

Guru Nanak (1469–1539), founder of the Sikh religion (*Erich Lessing/Art Resource, NY*)

Nandi, the divine bull and vehicle of Lord Shiva *(www.shutterstock.com/Arteki)*

Further reading: Anil Chandra Banerjee, *Guru Nanak and His Times* (Patalia: Punjabi University, 1971); Prithipal Singh Kapur, ed., *The Divine Master: Life and Teachings of Guru Nanak* (Jalandhar, India: ABS, 1988); W. H. McLeod, *Guru Nanak and the Sikh Religion* (London: Oxford University Press, 1968); Gurbachan Singh Talib, *Guru Nanak: His Personality and Vision* (Delhi: Gur Das Kapur & Sons, 1969).

Nandi

Nandi is the divine white bull who is the vehicle of SHIVA. He is the son of Kashyapa, a well-known RISHI (sage), and Surabhi (the wish-giving cow). In his form as Nandikeshvara, represented as a human with a bull's head, he is believed to be one of the great masters of music and dancing. He is a prominent iconic figure in many Shiva temples. Particularly notable is the massive 10-ton Nandi lying on his belly that greets all those who arrive at the BRIHADISHVARA TEMPLE in Tanjore.

Further reading: John Dowson, *A Classical Dictionary of Hindu Mythology and Religion, Geography, History, and Literature,* 12th ed. (Ludhiana: Lyall Book Depot, 1974); Margaret Stutley, *An Illustrated Dictionary of Hindu Iconography* (Boston: Routledge & Kegan Paul, 1985); W. J. Wilkins, *Hindu Mythology, Vedic and Puranic,* 2d ed. (Calcutta: Rupa, 1973).

Narada

The RISHI (sage) Narada appears in numerous contexts in Indian mythology. Though he is often taken to be the son of BRAHMA, there are varying accounts of his birth and exploits. In some contexts he is seen very positively: he is considered the inventor of the *vina* or Indian lute, and the one who revealed the DHARMASHASTRAS, or tracts on law. In other contexts he is seen as something of a troublemaker. It is Narada who informed Kamsa, the king who desired to kill KRISHNA, about Krishna's impending birth. Narada is also said to have cursed his own father, Brahma, to be worshipped by very few, to repay him for a curse that Brahma had placed on him.

Further reading: John Dowson, *A Classical Dictionary of Hindu Mythology and Religion, Geography, History, and Literature,* 12th ed. (Ludhiana: Lyall Book Depot, 1974); B. L. Raina, *Legends and Teachings of the Greatest Hindu Divine Sage Narada* (Mumbai: Bharatiya Vidya Bhavan, 1999); W. J. Wilkins, *Hindu Mythology, Vedic and Puranic,* 2d ed. (Calcutta: Rupa, 1973).

Narasimha avatar

Narasimha is the man-lion AVATAR of VISHNU. His story has many versions, all relating to the demon HIRANYAKASHIPU. The latter had undergone severe austerities to make himself superior to the gods and nearly invincible. BRAHMA had given him the boons that he could not be killed by man or beast, at night or during the day, outdoors or indoors. The gods beseeched Vishnu to intervene and put an end to the demon's depredations in the worlds.

Vishnu took up the man-lion form (neither man nor beast) and confronted Hiranyakashipu at the threshold of his palace (neither indoors nor outdoors) at twilight (neither day nor night). Thus he was able to kill Hiranyakashipu. The common iconographic depiction of Narasimha shows a sitting creature with a man's body and a lion's head, ripping into the supine demon lying on his knees.

Further reading: John Dowson, *A Classical Dictionary of Hindu Mythology and Religion, Geography, History, and Literature,* 12th ed. (Ludhiana: Lyall Book Depot, 1974); Margaret Stutley, *An Illustrated Dictionary of Hindu Iconography* (Boston: Routledge & Kegan Paul, 1985); W. J. Wilkins, *Hindu Mythology, Vedic and Puranic,* 2d ed. (Calcutta: Rupa, 1973).

Narayan, R. K. (1906–2001) *novelist of Hinduism*

R. K. Narayan was one of India's most celebrated modern novelists. Writing in English, he created works that are gentle evocations of small-town Indian life, the life of everyday Hindus.

Rasipuram Krishnaswami Ayyar Narayanaswami, better known by his pseudonym, R. K. Narayan, was born in the Prasawalkam section of Madras (Chennai) on October 10, 1906, and died May 13, 2001, at the age of 94. His father, R. V. Krishnaswami Iyer, moved the family to Mysore, where he became a schoolteacher and later headmaster of Maharajah's Collegiate High School. R. K. was not an outstanding student but managed to receive his bachelor of arts degree at the University of Mysore in 1923. Once he had graduated his natural path was to take a government job, but R. K. had already decided that he wanted to be a writer.

R. K.'s first published works appeared in magazines and in the newspaper *Hindu.* He eventually worked for that paper's Sunday edition. In 1934 he married for love, an unconventional move very much in line with his writing. His wife, Rajam, gave him one daughter, Hema, before she tragically passed away of typhoid in 1939, leaving him with a three-year-old daughter.

Most of R. K. Narayan's novels take place in the imaginary South Indian village of Malgudi, portrayed with brilliance and charm. He gives English readers who do not know his country a glimpse into the foibles and joys of the simple life and everyday piety of Hindu culture in India. He is also popular in India, where readers revel in seeing the India they know so brilliantly evoked in his deceptively simple prose.

There is always a breezy, easy quality to Narayan's work. It is not fraught with high philosophy or complex themes, but rather blessed with an accessibility that takes great skill to produce. His extraordinary productivity included many short stories and articles as well as his novels. On request, Narayan wrote popular versions of both the Ramayana and the Mahabharata.

In the late 1980s R. K. Narayan was elected to India's upper house of parliament, the Rajya Sabha. He was also honored with many literary awards, including India's Sahitya Akademi Award (for *The Guide*), the Royal Society of Literature's Christopher Benson Award, and Indian's second highest literary award, the Padma Vibhushan, in 2000. He also made the short list for the Nobel Prize in literature.

He died in 2001 after his own daughter's sad early demise, still working on another novel. Narayan was a great figure in world literature, whose own personal humility and desire to avoid pretense may have made him less widely known than he deserved.

Further reading: A. L. McLeod, ed., *R. K. Narayan: Critical Perspectives* (New Delhi: Sterling, 1994); R. K. Narayan, *An Astrologer's Day, and Other Stories* (Mysore: Indian Thought, 1968); ———, *The Bachelor of Arts* (Chicago: University of Chicago Press, 1980); ———, *Gods, Demons and Others* (New York: Viking Press, 1964); ———, *The Guide* (London: Bodley Head, 1970); ———, *The Mahabharata: A Shortened Modern Prose Version of the Indian Epic* (London: Heinemann, 1978); ———, *Malgudi Days* (London: Heinemann, 1982); ———, *My Days: A Memoir* (Hopewell, N.J.: Ecco Press, 1999); ———, *A Story-Teller's World* (New Delhi: Penguin Books, 1990).

Narayana   *See* VISHNU.

Narayanananda, Swami (1902–1968)
pioneer Hindu teacher in Scandinavia

Swami Narayanananda established VEDANTA centers throughout Europe and North America.

He was born in Coorg, a village in the state of Karnataka, in southern India. A bright boy, from an early age he showed a marked tendency to spiritual matters. He never married and at the age of 27 took the vows of the renounced life (*sannyas*) and began searching for a GURU. His pilgrimage around India eventually took him to the Belur Math of the VEDANTA/RAMAKRISHNA MATH AND MISSION, where he met Swami Shivananda, who became his teacher. Several years later, he was instructed by his guru to spend time alone in the Himalayas to strengthen his spiritual practice. In February 1933 he had a deep spiritual experience, which he described as merging into the formless aspect of God, that is, *nirvikalpa samadhi*.

He remained in seclusion until the partition of India in 1947. The violence of the period convinced him to dedicate his life to helping people; he left his retreat and began to accept disciples. In 1955, as a step toward building a more formal following, his devotees established a printing press and began to publish Narayananda's writings. It would be another 12 years, however, before the swami would consent to incorporating an organization, the Narayanananda Universal Yoga Trust. The first ASHRAM was opened in Denmark in 1967. The first ashram in the United States was opened in Chicago in the early 1970s.

Initially, the leaders of the rapidly expanding movement were all monks who had trained with Narayanananda in India, but in the course of the 1970s a number of Westerners took vows of *sannyas* and took on leadership roles. As in India, the monks live a life of celibacy and follow a spiritual discipline that includes twice-daily MEDITATION sessions with the community and the practice of HATHA YOGA.

Narayanananda died in 1988. His movement continues from its international headquarters in Gylling, Denmark, and the ashram in Chicago.

The various centers offer a range of instruction in hatha yoga and the teachings of Narayanananda.

Further reading: Swami Narayanananda, *The Ideal Life and Moksha (Freedom)* (Gylling, Denmark: N. U. Yoga Trust & Ashrama, 1979); ———, *The Mysteries of Man, Mind, and Mind-Functions: A Masterly Treatise on Psychology* (Rishikesh: Narayanananda Universal Yoga Trust, 1965); ———, *A Personal Guide to Samadhi* (Rishikesh: Narayanananda Universal Yoga Trust, 1966); ———, *The Primal Power in Man: Or, the Kundalini Shakti* (Rishikesh: Narayanananda Universal Yoga Trust, 1970); ———, *The Secrets of Prana, Pranayama and Yoga-Asanas* (Gylling, Denmark: N. U. Yoga Trust & Ashrama, 1979).

Nataraja

Nataraja, or Lord of the Dance (*nata*, dance; *raja*, king or lord), is one of the most popular iconic forms of SHIVA (the most common is the LINGAM). In his cosmic dance he creates, sustains, and eventually destroys the universe. When Shiva's dance is seen as symbolizing only the end of time, it is called the Tandava dance.

Nataraja is depicted in a pose from the BHARATA NATYAM dance, with his left leg raised and his right leg resting on a dwarflike being representing ignorance and delusion, sometimes called Apasmara (forgetfulness [of the truth of the divine]). He has four arms. In his upper right hand he holds the "shake-drum" (*damaru*) that can be sounded with one hand, a tethered ball striking either end of a small two-sided drum. His lower right hand is formed into the ABHAYA MUDRA, a gesture that removes fear. His upper left hand holds the flame that symbolizes the end of creation. His lower left hand points toward his upraised left foot. Around his head and in the circular frame to which he is attached is a halo of flames that show his divine energy.

Among Shiva's many celebrated dances: he danced in the sky with VISHNU; once he danced in the cremation ground to please KALI, his female counterpart; once he danced as a beggar for PARVATI's hand; once he danced a mad, erotic dance in the deodar forest for the wives of the RISHIS there; and he danced after the destruction of DAKSHA'S sacrifice. The great shrine at CHIDAMBARAMI in South India is perhaps the most famous one depicting Shiva's Nataraja form. There is also an awe-inspiring 20-foot-high Nataraja in black stone in the Meenakshi Temple at Madurai.

Further reading: Ananda K. Coomaraswamy, *The Dance of Siva: Essays on Indian Art and Culture.* Foreword by Romain Rolland (New York: Dover, 1985); Cornelia Dimmitt and J. A. van Buitenen, eds. and trans., *Classical Hindu Mythology: A Reader in the Sanskrit Puranas* (Philadelphia: Temple University Press, 1978); Stella Kramrisch, *The Presence of Siva* (Princeton, N.J.: Princeton University Press, 1981); Margaret Stutley, *The Illustrated Dictionary of Hindu Iconography* (Boston: Routledge & Kegan Paul, 1985).

Nathdwara

Literally, "the doorway to the Lord," Nathdwara is a sacred town near Udaipur in the Indian state of Rajasthan; it is the principal seat of the cult of Sri Sri NATHJI and of the VALLABHA sect. The town itself is sometimes called Sri Nathji.

Sri Sri Nathji is a form of KRISHNA. His image was taken to Nathdwara from Mathura in 1669 to prevent its destruction by the armies of the iconoclastic Mughal Muslim king Aurangzeb. The chief temple of Nathdwara enshrines the image of Krishna taken in 1669, which holds Govardhana Mountain, recalling the myth in which Krishna protected the cowherds of BRINDAVAN from storms caused by INDRA, king of the gods, by holding up this mountain as an umbrella.

Further reading: Amit Ambalal, *Krishna as Shrinathji: Rajasthani Paintings from Nathdvara* (Ahmedabad: Mapin, 1987); H. S. Verdia, *Religion and Social Structure in a Sacred Town, Nathdwara* (Delhi: Researchco, 1982).

Nath Yogis

The Nath Yogis emerged in the 12th and 13th centuries C.E. as a confederation of devotees of Shaivite (*see* SHAIVISM) and SIDDHA practices. The sect honors a legendary group of nine exemplars, called the nine *Naths*, or "lords," who give the sect its name. The nine exemplars are listed with a wide variety of names, but they usually include Matsyendranath and GORAKHNATH (with somewhat varying forms). These quasi-historical Naths are considered the original sources for the various Nath lineages. The forerunners of the Nath Yogis were probably the various radical Shaivite groups that arose in the early centuries of the Common Era.

The Nath Yogis were outsiders and very unconventional. They often adopted outrageous practices such as eating offal and public cursing, in order to emphasize their lack of fealty to any convention. They were extreme ascetics, practicing under the umbrella of TANTRISM, which sought above all to emphasize the dark and negative aspects of existence as the source of spiritual power and transformation. However, the Naths abstained from the sexual practices generally associated with tantrism, as they generally avoided women entirely.

Alchemy was an important element of Nath Yogi practice. Usually, this included not only changing base metals into gold via mercury, but also changing the body by the use of oxides of mercury to create an immortal body. This esoteric practice is combined with HATHA YOGA and the effort to raise the KUNDALINI at the base of the spine to effect complete spiritual transformation.

Further reading: Akshaya Kumar Banerjea, *Philosophy of Gorakhnath with Goraksha Vacana Samgraha* (Delhi: Motilal Benarsidass, 1988); George W. Briggs, *Gorakhnath and the Kanphata Yogis* (New Delhi: Motilal Banarsidass, 1982); David Gordon White, *The Alchemical Body* (Chicago: University of Chicago Press, 1996).

Natya Shastra

Natya Shastra, "the authoritative scripture [*shastra*] regarding drama [*natya*]," is often considered the "fifth VEDA." It was composed by the teacher Bharata around the second century C.E. Made up of over 5,000 verses, it delineates the art form of dance-drama of its time. The revived BHARATA NATYAM dance-drama form of modern India still follows the guidelines of this text.

The *Natya Shastra* claims that drama was created by the creator god BRAHMA himself. The text outlines every aspect of the drama, including the dress of the actors, the music, the stage, and the construction of the theater building. Indian drama has always relied greatly on dance; thus the steps, rhythms, and hand gestures or MUDRAS are carefully detailed. The text also suggests the most common themes that the drama can present, such as the battle between the gods and demons and the adventures of the individual gods. From a philosophical standpoint the two most important chapters are those that outline the principles of aesthetics in dramatic presentations. They present the distinctive theory of RASAS, the emotional "essences" that are communicated via the drama.

Further reading: *The Natya Sastra of Bharatamuni* (Delhi: Sri Satguru, 2003); Vasanta Vedam, *A Handbook of Natya Sastra* (Chennai: Vasanta Vedam, 2003).

Navaratri

The Navaratri (Navaratra) or Nine Nights festival is celebrated for nine days in the lunar month of Ashvin (September–October). It is a pan-Indian festival that takes different forms in different regions.

In most Hindi-speaking areas of North India Navaratri is celebrated as Rama Lila (the mysterious divine magic of Lord Rama), a commemoration of the RAMAYANA epic. Each day features readings from the medieval Hindi TULSIDAS Ramayana; in most places plays are presented depicting scenes from the Ramayana story, sometimes on a grand scale.

The largest of the Rama Lila plays is staged across the river from the holy city BENARES (Varanasi), where the kings have established an immense field as a stage for the Ramayana story. Actors go from station to station on different days as the story develops. On Vijayadashami, the day after Navaratri, effigies of Rama's enemies—the demon king RAVANA, his son Meghanada, and his brother KUMBHAKARNA—are burned to celebrate the victory of Rama over the demons or Rakshasas.

In Bihar, Bengal, and Assam Navaratri is celebrated as a DURGA festival. The festival begins by awakening Durga, who is asleep, and continues by manufacturing a temporary image of her that is enlivened for the purpose of the festival. PUJAS or worship services are performed for Durga on the last three days of the festival. On Vijayadashmi the image of Durga is taken in a great procession to be immersed and left in a tank, a river, or the ocean.

In South India SARASVATI, goddess of learning and the arts, is worshipped on the seventh day of the festival and Durga on the eighth day. On the ninth day there is a worship of instruments and implements of livelihood, which are taken out to be honored with mantras and small offerings.

Further reading: Diana L. Eck, *Banaras, City of Light* (New York: Columbia University Press, 1999); H. V. Shekar, *Festivals of India: Significance of the Celebrations* (Louisville, Ky.: Insight Books, 2000).

Nayanmars

A Nayanmar or Nayanar is a "leader" or "master." In the Tamil devotional tradition the Nayanmars were poet-saints who spread the message of devotion to SHIVA throughout Tamil Nadu. Tradition makes them 63 in number, but some of the names are probably legendary figures. The real Nayanars lived from roughly the sixth to the eighth century C.E. They sang the praise and love of Shiva at numerous holy places, shrines, and temples throughout the region, opposing the Jains, Buddhists, and VAISHNAVITES in their efforts to advance everyone to the grace of their Lord Shiva. They apparently participated in India's first known popular devotional movement, as all their verses are sung in Tamil, the spoken language of the local people, and not in SANSKRIT.

The last of the Nayanars, SUNDARAR, was granted a revelation by Lord Shiva himself at Tiruvarur, of the lives of the 62 saints who preceded him. His work is the first to give the entire list, to which his own name was later added. Nambi Andar Nambi (c. 1000 C.E.) is said to have compiled the songs of all of the Nayanars, adding to them the works of several other famous poet-saints, including MANIKKAVACAKAR, to form the basis of the TIRUMURAI, the basic Tamil Shaivite sacred canon. It consists of 12 books, 11 of them assembled by Nambi.

Included in Tirumurai is Nambi Andar Nambi's own account of the "holy labors" of the 63 saints, as well as his own story and verses. The 12th and final book is SEKKILAR's PERIYA PURANAM (c. 1200 C.E.); its more than 4,000 verses summarize and add to the earlier Nayanar compendiums and include the works of some other Shaivite saints.

The three best-known and most prolific of the Nayanars are APPAR, SAMBANTHAR, and Sundarar. Their hymns make up the TEVARAM, which serves as the primary liturgical scripture for Tamil Shaivites. These songs are strongly oriented toward particular sacred places, shrines, and temples that were visited by the three peripatetic saints as they pursued their PILGRIMAGE in order to sing Shiva. In Shaivite temples in Tamil Nadu today the Tevaram songs are sung in ritual worship, along with Sanskrit MANTRAS.

Most Nayanars were men, but a few were women. The most famous of the women saints is the first on the list of 63, Karaikal Ammaiyar. The saints were from every class and trade, from Brahmin (Sundarar and Sambanthar) to Dalit (untouchables) (Tirunalaipovanar, alias Nantanar).

Further reading: Vidya Dehejia, *Slaves of the Lord: The Path of the Tamil Saints* (New Delhi: Munshiram Manoharlal, 1988); Indira Viswanthan Peterson, *Poems to Siva: The Hymns of the Tamil Saints* (Princeton, N.J.: Princeton University Press, 1989); Kamil V. Zvelibil, *Tamil Literature* (Leiden: E. J. Brill, 1975).

Neem Karoli Baba (c. 1900–1973) *bhakti yoga teacher*

Neem Karoli Baba, popularly known as Maharaji, is one of the most influential GURUS from India to encounter the West. Although he never visited America or wrote any books, he graced the lives of many devotees during the 1960s and 1970s. Baba RAM DASS was particularly inspired by Maharaji and Ram Dass's works were among the first to introduce Eastern wisdom on a large scale to the West, particularly through portrayals of experiences with Neem Karoli.

Neem Karoli Baba (c. 1900–1973), teacher known for his dedication to devotion and service; guru of Baba Ram Dass *(Kashi Church, Sebastian, Florida)*

Neem Karoli was born Lakshmi Narayan Sharma to a BRAHMIN family in Akbarpur in Uttar Pradesh, India. In his childhood he was described as detached from desires of the material world. When he was 11 his family arranged a marriage with a girl from another Brahmin family. After the wedding, the groom left home and wandered the country as an ascetic for several years. His father, Sri Durga Prasad Sharma, eventually found him in the village of Neem Karoli (hence his name) and demanded that his son return home. The young man complied and spent the remainder of his life in dual roles as householder and saint.

Neem Karoli always considered the world as his larger family and stated that the key to attaining salvation is to love all, serve all, and feed all. Devotees who were close to him describe the GURU as one who radiated love. He based his teachings on a form of BHAKTI YOGA, emphasizing service and unconditional devotion to God. His techniques have been described as both subtle and literal, and his teachings varied from individual to individual. His advice was determined by the needs of the student, even though he always asserted that one's focus in life should be toward the welfare of others.

Neem Karoli established two ashrams, at Kainchi in Uttachal and at BRINDAVAN in Uttar Pradesh. Over 100 temples have also been founded in his name. American devotees, including Ram Dass, gathered together in 1977 to form a common place of worship in honor of Neem Karoli. The group proposed the construction of a statue representing HANUMAN, a deity most revered by Neem Karoli. The statue was commissioned in India and completed in 1978. It found its permanent home in Taos, New Mexico. Devotees formed the Neem Karoli Baba Ashram around the Hanuman figure and have since held annual celebrations in September, marking the *mahasamadhi* (death) of Neem Karoli Baba on September 11, 1973.

Further reading: Ram Dass, *Miracle of Love: Stories about Neem Karoli Baba* (New York: Dutton, 1979); Sudhir Mukerjee, *By His Grace: A Devotee's Story* (Santa Fe, N. Mex.: Hanuman Foundation, 1990).

Neminatha

Neminatha was the 22nd TIRTHANKARA (Jain saint) of our era, or, more precisely, half-era, as there are always 24 Tirthankaras in each half of a longer era. Unlike the 23rd Tirthankara in our time, PARSHVANATH, and the 24th, MAHAVIRA, both historical figures, Neminatha is not a historical figure.

Neminatha is said to have had his previous incarnation in the celestial abode. He was born to the king Shauripura and his wife, Shiva Devi. His birth was accompanied by many auspicious signs, including the appropriate auspicious markings on his body to indicate his special status. He never undertook the householder life. At the death of own parents he resolved to take up the path of a Jain renunciant, to the acclaim of the gods. He distributed his vast worldly wealth to the indigent.

As Neminatha ascended his royal palanquin for the last time to go to his place of renunciation, all beings hailed him and shouted their praises and encouragement. He arrived at a park named Revika and there removed all his garlands and ornaments and tonsured himself in the fashion of Jain monks by removing all his hair in five handfuls. At that time he took the vow of taking food only once every third day until he entered the order of the wandering monks.

For 54 days Neminatha lived completely ignoring his body in every way. On the 55th day on top of Mount Ajjinta, after reducing his food to once every fourth day, he attained to supreme knowledge and the status of a *kevalin,* having unobstructed wisdom. He attained, afterward, the status of a Tirthankara, a crosser of the ford, and omniscience, knowledge of all that occurred in the world at all times.

At this time he had a community of 18,000 monks, 40,000 nuns, 169,000 laymen, and 369,000 laywomen. With him were 400 monks who had achieved the highest wisdom short of being perfected and many other monks whose knowledge was developing. They say that Neminatha lived for 300 years as a bachelor, 54 days as a monk, and 700 years as an omniscient being. Thereupon, taking food once every month he fasted until he left his body and achieved NIRVANA. More than 84,000 years has elapsed since this event.

Further reading: Paul Dundas, *The Jains* (London: Routledge, 1992); P. S. Jaini, *The Jaina Path of Purification* (Delhi: Motilal Banarsidass, 1990); K. C. Lalwani, *Kalpa Sutra* (Delhi: Motilal Banarsidass, 1979).

new moon/ full moon ceremonies

New moon (*amavasya*) and full moon (*purnima*) observances and rituals have been held in India since VEDIC times at least. Many festivals and holy days occur on these days in contemporary India.

The following are some of the full moon celebrations: (1) Chaitra (or Chitra) Purnima is celebrated to recognize Chitragupta, assistant to the god of death YAMA. It is thought that if he is honored while people are alive he may be more lenient with them after death. (2) The full moon of the month of Ashvina (September–October) is a day for worshipping LAKSHMI for wealth. A vow is taken on that day to stay awake all night. (3) The full moon in the month of Shravana (July–August) is the time when certain BRAHMINS change their sacred threads. In the celebration of RAKSHABANDHAN sisters generally put a thread wristlet on brothers for good luck. (4) On the full moon in the month of Jyeshtha (May–June) occur the bathing of the images of the Jagannatha for the festival at Puri, and the observance of a fast day by married women in recognition of the devotion of SAVITRI, who retrieved her husband from the jaws of death. (5) In Chaitra (March–April) the birthday of HANUMAN, the monkey god, is observed on the full moon.

The following are some of the new moon observances: (1) In the month of Bhadrapada (August–September) the 15 days of the dark half of the Moon are for worshipping ancestors. (2) During the month of Magha (January–February) a day of silence is observed on the new Moon day; it is one of the important days of the Maha KUMBHA Mela (festival) at ALLAHABAD.

Further reading: Swami Harshananda, *Hindu Festivals and Sacred Days* (Bangalore: Ramakrishna Math, 1994); *Hindu Festivals* (Bombay: Central Chinmaya Mission Trust, 1989).

Nimbarka (c. 12th century) *Vedanta philosopher*

Nimbarka was a philosopher of the VEDANTA, who founded a sect of VAISHNAVISM centered in Mathura, North India, that focused on RADHA and KRISHNA.

Nimbarka was born in Andhra Pradesh; his name has been traced by some to the village Nimba or Nimbapura in the Bellary District. One myth explains his name more colorfully: once a wandering mendicant visited Nimbarka, who offered him food. Because the Sun had already set, the ascetic refused, saying that he had vowed not to eat after the Sun had set. Thereupon the philosopher took the last rays of the Sun (*arka*) and put them up in a neem tree (nimba tree) until food could be prepared and the ascetic could eat.

Formally, Nimbarka's Vedantic philosophy is called *dvaitavaita*, "both dualist and non-dualist," which makes it quite similar (but not identical) to the philosophy of RAMANUJA and his VISHISHTAD-VAITA, "non-dualism via differencing." *Dvaitadvaita*, as does non-dualism, understands that all is the divinity. All souls and all matter are the stuff of the divine. In this sense there is non-duality between the selves, between materiality and the ultimate. At the same time no individual soul (let alone matter) can ever be as supreme or sublime as the divine, so in that sense there is duality (a

difference) between the divinity and the world. Unlike SHANKARA'S VEDANTA, Nimbarka saw the world as real and not an illusion.

Less scholarship has been done on Nimbarka's philosophy than on several of the other major Vedanta philosophers. Eight major works in SAN-SKRIT are attributed to him but only three are available in published form: *Vedanta-parijata-saurabha,* his commentary on the Vedanta Sutra; a work called *Dasasloki,* which has only 10 verses; and *Krishna-stava-raja,* a devotional work. Several subcommentaries have been written on his work on the Vedanta Sutra.

Nimbarka's system took Krishna to be god, while the devotee took the role of Krishna's consort, Radha, in adoring him and serving him. Nimbarka is perhaps best known to modern India through the Vaishnavite sect named after him, the Nimbarki sect, which is also referred to as the Sanakadi or Hamsa sect of Vaishnavites, centered in Mathura.

Further reading: M. M. Agarwal, *The Philosophy of Nimbarka* (Varanasi: Chaukhamba Surbharati Prakashan, 1983); Unmesha Mishra, *Nimbarka School of Vedanta* (Allahabad: Tirabhukti, 1966); Swami Tapasyananda, *The Bhakti Schools of Vedanta* (Madras: Ramakrishna Mutt, 1990).

Nirankari movement (est. 1851)

The Nirankari movement developed within the larger Sikh community as an effort to revive a faltering SIKHISM. The founder, Baba Dyal (1783–1855), denounced new rites and rituals being introduced into Sikhism at the time, which he said were an indication that Sikhism was being absorbed into the more dominant Hinduism. The movement gained its name from his emphasis on Nirankar, or God the formless one.

In 1851, Baba Dyal formally organized his small following as the Nirankari Darbar. He was succeeded four years later by his son, Baba Darbara Singh. Among the emphases of the movement was abstinence from alcohol.

The movement remained small but received a boost in the 1930s from Boota Singh (1883–1944), who sought to revitalize it. He began to preach against all regulations based upon external habits and appearances, including all rules about what one wears, eats, or drinks (including the prohibition of alcohol).

Boota Singh received initiation from the SANT MAT lineage that looks back to Jaimal Singh (1838–1903). He not only passed the lineage to the present leader of the movement but also added the practice of *jnana,* the giving of knowledge by the GURU (or his representative) to each member of the movement. The giving of knowledge is a confidential aspect of the Nirankari faith, and members agree not to divulge its nature. Members also agree not to discriminate against people in respect to caste, sex, color, religion, or worldly status; not to criticize anyone because of his or her diet or dress; and to make no renunciation of the world.

Boota died in 1944, and he passed leadership of his small following within the larger Nirankari movement to Avtar Singh (1899–1969). The latter saw the partition of India and the movement of many Hindus from what is now Pakistan back into Indian territory. Operating from Delhi, he began to gather a following especially among the newly migrating Sikhs. In 1947 he formally organized the Nirankari Sant Mission, which held its first annual meeting (Samagam) the next year. The growth was such that Avtar Singh's following constituted the main body of Nirankaris.

In 1969, Avtar Singh was succeeded by Gurbachan Singh (1930–80), who would oversee significant growth of the movement outside India through the British Commonwealth and the United States. A major stimulant for growth was Gurbachan Singh's world tour the year before he became the head of the movement. Once in his leadership role, he formed a foreign section to stimulate further growth around the world. In 1971, he traveled to North America and organized the work in the United States and Canada. He also authored Avtar Bani, which serves as a holy book for the Nirankaris.

Gurbachan Singh asserted his belief that Nirankaris were Sikhs, in spite of their separate organization. Many Sikhs disputed these claims; against the tense background of Sikh demands for independence from India, intra-Sikh violence occasionally erupted. In 1980, Gurbachan Singh was assassinated. He was succeeded by Hardev Singh Ji Maharaj (b. 1954), who continues as head of the movement, now known as the Nirankari Sant Samagam of the Nirankari Universal Brotherhood Mission. Assisting Hardev Singh Ji Maharaj are seven men chosen by him and known as the Seven Stars.

Further reading: J. S. Chugh, *Fifty Years of Spiritual Bliss: Commemorative Souvenir of the Golden Jubilee Nirankari Sant Samagam,* November 6–10, 1997 (Delhi: Sant Nirankari Mandal, 1997); C. L. Gulotti, *A Mission for All* (Delhi: Sant Nirankari Mandal, 1997); Krishnan Lal, *The Mission and the Missionaries* (Delhi: Sant Nirankari Mandal, 1987); Nirankari Baba Hardev Singh, *Stream of Thoughts* (Delhi: Sant Nirankari Mandal, 1994).

Nirmala Devi, Mataji

See SAHAJA YOGA CENTER.

nirvana

Nirvana is the term used to refer to the state of liberation from the cycle of birth and rebirth, from worldly existence. The term probably originated within Buddhism. It literally means a "blowing out"—of the fires of worldly existence. In the early Buddhist context this implied the recognition that nothing is permanent and that there is no permanent self, but only a shifting combination of aspects that constitute themselves so as to make us believe in a permanent "self" or soul.

Early Buddhists tried not to describe this state elaborately as it is beyond human conception.

The Jain tradition also adopted the word to refer to the blissful, powerful, superconscious state of liberation from birth and rebirth. In the Brahminical tradition it came to mean union with the ultimate reality. This implies a realization of the infinite being, consciousness, and bliss of the godhead.

Further reading: George S. Arundale, *Nirvana: A Study in Synthetic Consciousness* (Adyar: Theosophical Publishing House, 1978); Muni Shivkumar, *The Doctrine of Liberation in Indian Religion: With Special Reference to Jainism* (New Delhi: Munshiram Manoharlal, 1984); Heinrich Zimmer, *Philosophies of India* (Princeton, N.J.: Princeton University Press, 1974).

Nisargadatta Maharaj (1897–1981)
advaita *teacher*

Maharaj Nisargadatta was a Bombay (Mumbai) merchant and householder, whose ADVAITA VEDANTA teachings and JNANA YOGA practices drew him a large following. His conversations, recorded by disciples and translated into English, ensured that his ideas would continue to spread after his death.

Born in Bombay in March 1897, Maruti (his birth name) was raised on a small family farm near Kandalgaon in Maharashtra. As a boy he became familiar with spiritual topics by listening to his parents discuss the spiritual life with a BRAHMIN friend, Vishnu Haribha Gore. When his father died in 1915, Maruti and his elder brother became responsible for supporting the family. They left home to seek employment in Bombay. Here, Maruti opened a shop selling *bidis*, handmade cigarettes. He became prosperous in the trade and established several more shops across Bombay. In 1924, Maruti married Sumatibai, and they later became the parents of a son and three daughters.

At age 34, Maruti began to seek answers to universal questions. His friend took him to Sri Siddharameshwar Maharaj, a teacher in Bombay in the Navnath Sampradaya, who gave Maruti a MANTRA and instructions on MEDITATION. Maruti quickly developed a practice, giving attention to nothing else than the sense of "I am." Soon, Maruti began to have visions and to experience trance states. Between 1933 and 1936, he experienced SELF-REALIZATION and reported that he lived in full awareness of the transcendent reality. He named himself Nisargadatta (One Given True Being).

After Sri Siddharameshwar's death in 1936, Nisargadatta left his family and business to live the renounced life of a SADHU, a wandering monk who owns nothing and begs for food, in the HIMALAYAS. His journey was short-lived, after a fellow disciple convinced him that his spiritual intentions would be more fruitful at home. Returning to Bombay he found his business in shambles. He reestablished one *bidi* shop, which sustained him and his family. Nisargadatta spent the remainder of his life tending his business and devoting himself to a strict discipline of daily observances and veneration of his GURU. He meditated and discussed his master's teachings with all who visited his *bidi* shop and did not visit saints or temples. As he began to speak to others, larger and larger groups of inquirers and students went to his shop to learn from his eloquence and wisdom.

Nisargadatta's teachings are based on *jnana* yoga and *advaita* Vedanta, a non-dualistic philosophy. His teachings emphasize the individual's direct experience with the eternal in the here and now. His typical recommendation to new students was to practice with discipline and follow the same instruction provided to him, which fostered SELF-REALIZATION. Nisargadatta encouraged seekers to draw attention to "I am." In doing so, he asserted that the practitioner's mind would soon gain self-realization in thought and feeling. Nisargadatta died in Bombay on September 8, 1981.

Ramesh S. Balsekar became one of Nisargadatta's closest disciples. Balsekar, a graduate of

London University and retired banker, met Sri Nisargadatta in 1970. He became entrusted with recording the conversations of Nisargadatta, the guru's primary method of teaching. Many of these were later published in the book *I Am That* (1972), which has become a classical treatise on how one person can realize the non-dual reality outside time and space. As more Westerners encountered Maharaj they furthered his teachings by translating his conversations into English, publishing them throughout North America and Europe.

After Nisargadatta Maharaj's death, Balsekar continued his guru's teachings and established the ADVAITA Fellowship in 1987. Since that time he has made annual visits to America and has become esteemed as a teacher of *advaita* Vedanta. The fellowship has its headquarters in Bombay (Mumbai), India, and in Redondo Beach, California.

Further reading: Ramesh S. Balsekar and Sudhakar S. Dikshit, *Explorations into the Eternal: Forays from the Teaching of Nisargadatta Maharaj* (Bombay: Chetana, 1987); Ramesh S. Balsekar and Sudhaker S. Dikshit, *Pointers from Nisargadatta Maharaj: Maharaj Points to the Eternal Truth That Is Before Time Ever Was* (Durham, N.C.: Acorn Press, 1990); Jean Dunn and Nisargadatta Maharaj, *Seeds of Consciousness: The Wisdom of Sri Nisargadatta Maharaj* (New York: Grove Press, 1982); Nisargadatta Maharaj, *I Am That*. Translated by Maurice Frydman (Bombay: Chetana, 1973).

Nityananda, Swami Bhagawan (c. 1900–1961) *Shaivite* siddha *yogi*

Swami Bhagawan Nityananda was an inspiring teacher of *siddha yoga* MEDITATION, who attracted thousands of followers and disciples.

The early years of Bhagawan Nityananda are shrouded in mystery of the sort that often characterizes the life of a saint from village India. From interviews with people who knew him in his early years, it appears that he was born near the turn of the 20th century in the town of Qualandi in Kerala state, South India, to parents who worked

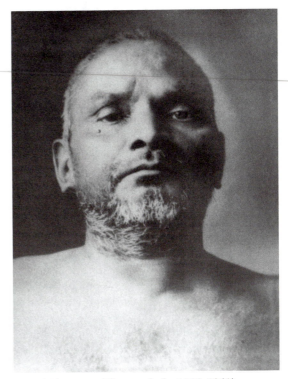

Swami Bhagawan Nityananda (c. 1900–1961), renowned devotee of Lord Shiva and *siddha* yogi *(Kashi Church, Sebastian, Florida)*

as servants in the house of a lawyer, Ishwara Iyer. His childhood name was Ram.

Even as a child Ram lived in an exalted state. Swami MUKTANANDA, Nityananda's successor, wrote of his GURU, "Beyond a shadow of a doubt he was a born SIDDHA [a person who is spiritually perfected]. Even though he was a self-born siddha still he had to have a *guru*. . . . It is the spiritual law—one has to have a guru." Nityananda considered his teacher to be Ishwara Iyer, who was not only his patron but also a devout BRAHMIN and a proficient YOGI. It was he who gave Nityananda his name. The story is that after spending a number of years in the HIMALAYAS, Nityananda returned to Qualandi to see Iyer, who was ill and praying for him to return. When Iyer saw the young yogi, he said, "Ah, my Nityananda has come!" From that point forward, he was known by that name, which means "eternal bliss."

Nityananda began manifesting miraculous powers while still in his teens, and he was a wandering SADHU (mendicant) before he was 20. There are accounts from Kerala and Karnataka states of the "sky-clad" (naked) yogi who traveled only on foot and ate only what was handed to him. In his presence, people had profound experiences of meditation and healing, both physical and spiritual. In the 1920s Nityananda built the Kanhangad Ashram around some jungle caves near the town of Kanhangad in Kerala, which is maintained to this day. By the 1930s, however, he left the region, again on foot. In 1936, Nityananda arrived in Ganeshpuri, the Maharashtrian village that was to be his home for the rest of his life. On the day he arrived, the caretaker of the local SHIVA temple built him a hut, and within a few years that *kutir* was enlarged to become Vaikuntha Ashram, the very spot where Bhagawan Nityananda's SAMA-DHI shrine stands today.

Bhagawan Nityananda is recognized in Ganeshpuri not only for his spiritual power but also for the material help he provided to the local people, who at that time were often living at a subsistence level. He distributed the offerings given to him, providing for the villagers food and clothing and establishing a local school and hospital and the Balbhojan (children's food) Center, which still functions in Ganeshpuri.

In the last two decades of his life, thousands of pilgrims traveled to Ganeshpuri for Nityananda's blessings and the experience of his DARSHAN. Swami Muktananda writes, "In his presence, everyone meditated spontaneously." Nityananda's hallmark teaching is "The heart is the hub of all sacred places. Go there and roam."

Shortly before Nityananda took *mahasamadhi* (died) on August 8, 1961, he passed on the guru's *gaddi*, the seat of power of his spiritual lineage, to Swami Muktananda, just as, years later, Swami Muktananda would pass it on to his disciple,

Gurumayi CHIDVILASANANDA, who has been carrying forward what is now known as the Siddha Yoga mission since 1982.

Further reading: Douglas Renfrew Brooks et al., *Meditation Revolution: A History and Theology of the Siddha Yoga Lineage* (South Fallsburg, N.Y.: Agama Press, 1997); Swami Muktananda, *Bhagawan Nityananda of Ganeshpuri* (South Fallsburg, N.Y.: SYDA Foundation, 1996); Shakti Smriti Interview Collection, Unpublished oral history manuscripts held by Shakti Punja, the SYDA Foundation archives, South Fallsburg, New York.

Nivedita, Sister (Margaret Noble) (1867–1911) *supporter of women's education in India*

Sister Nivedita, an Irish-born convert to VEDANTA, became a social activist and supporter of women's education in India.

Margaret Noble was born on October 28, 1867, to Samuel Noble and Mary Hamilton in Dunganon, Northern Ireland, in county Tyrone. Before Margaret was a year old, Samuel moved to Manchester, England, where he enrolled as a theological student of the Wesleyan church. The young baby was left with her maternal grandmother in Northern Ireland, where she enjoyed a happy childhood while her father studied and became ordained. At four years of age, she returned to live with her father, unhappy to leave her grandmother's home.

With her sister, she attended Halifax College, run by the Congregationalist Church. She learned personal sacrifice from the headmistress of Halifax, a member of the Plymouth Brethren. After her father was appointed minister of a church, she liked to listen to him preach and to imitate his expressions.

Margaret was a thoughtful girl who asked many questions. She had learned about the character of a nation from her paternal grandfather in his fight for home rule for Ireland. At age 18, in 1884, she received a post as teacher and became engaged in the movement to foster child-centered learning in schools. In 1885, she opened the Ruskin School in Wimbledon, for adults as well as children who wished to study modern educational methods. She was a cofounder of the Congress of Modern Pedagogy, centered on the child's experience of school. She also served as a welfare worker, while championing the underprivileged by writing pamphlets in London.

After Swami VIVEKANANDA's famous appearance at the WORLD PARLIAMENT OF RELIGIONS in Chicago in 1893, he stayed for three months in London; in 1885, Margaret met him and declared herself his disciple, calling him "Master." Through Vivekananda, she found a religion whose elements could be discussed scientifically and whose goal was expressed in terms of spiritual freedom rather than, as she thought, sin-defined slavery. While the swami was in England she followed his teaching assiduously, attending lectures four times a week. When Vivekananda left England in November 1895, Margaret began to study the swami's philosophical ideas in preparation for meeting him again, declaring herself a "monk."

In 1898 Margaret traveled to India to start her new life of service to education and women. In March of that year, she was initiated by Vivekananda and given the name Nivedita (she who had been dedicated). He asked her to live in an orthodox Hindu way. She opened a school for Indian girls in 1898 in a single room of her house in a poor section of Calcutta (Kolkata). While a plague raged in Calcutta, she nursed the sick and dying. She lectured on KALI, goddess of destruction and plagues, to audiences of thousands. She met and worked with Sri RAMAKRISHNA's widow, Sri SARADA DEVI (1853–1920), who was revered by the Ramakrishna monks as the embodiment of the Holy Mother.

In 1902 she left the Ramakrishna Order, after Vivekananda's death, because her political activities for Indian independence were declared incompatible with her status as a Hindu renunciant

(*brahmacharini*). The remainder of her life was spent in India working on behalf of Indian women. She died on October 13, 1911, in Calcutta.

Further reading: Atmaprana, *Sister Nivedita of Ramakrishna-Vivekananda* (Calcutta: Ramakrishna Math, 1999); Barbara Foxe, *Long Journey Home: A Biography of Margaret Noble* (London: Rider, 1975); Swami Ghambhirananda, *History of the Ramakrishna Math and Mission* (Calcutta: *advaita* Ashrama, 1957); Nivedita, *My Master As I Saw Him,* 10th ed. (Calcutta: Udbodhan Office, 1966); ———, *The Complete Works of Sister Nivedita* (Calcutta: Ramakrishna Sarada Mission, 1967); Lizelle Reymond, *The Dedicated: A Biography of Nivedita* (Madras: Samata, 1985).

niyama   *See* YOGA SUTRA.

nonviolence   *See* AHIMSA.

Nyaya-Vaisheshika

Nyaya and Vaisheshika represent two of the six "orthodox" systems of Indian philosophy. *Orthodox* here simply entails an acceptance of the VEDAS as an ultimate authority. In practice, even this requirement is observed only nominally in the case of one system, the SAMKHYA.

For many centuries these two schools have been integrated in a single philosophical system. However, certain of their distinctive and separate features are worth noting.

Vaisheshika, from the term *vishesha* (distinction), is usually thought of as the earlier of the two systems. There is strong evidence that this system began to take shape as early as 400 B.C.E., though the earliest extant texts are probably a little later. The 10 chapters of the Vaisheshika Sutra, by the sage Kanada, date around the second century C.E. They teach that salvation can be obtained only by "real knowledge" of things, as outlined in this SUTRA.

Vaisheshika admits of six philosophical categories, with a seventh controversial category added later. The six original categories are (1) substance, which consists of nine eternal realities that compose the foundation of the universe; substance is divided into (a) "atoms" of each of the five main elements or MAHABHUTAS and (b) time, ether, space, and soul; (2) attribute, of which there are 24; (3) karma, action or motion; (4) samanya, "generality," that which characterizes all the members of a given class; (5) vishesha or particularity, which distinguishes one member of a class from another; and (6) samavaya, "relation," or combination, that is, the relationship that exists between substance and its qualities. A seventh category, "non-existence" (abhava), was added later to deal with certain philosophical difficulties of the system.

Most important in the system of Vaisheshika is the understanding of the atomic nature of all the elements. This philosophy was originally realist and nontheistic in orientation. Only later was the notion of God imputed to it.

Nyaya was founded by Gautama (or Gotama) (c. 100 C.E.), who composed the Nyaya Sutra. Other famous philosophers of the Nyaya school are Vatsyayana and Gangesha. Nyaya can be loosely translated as "logic" or "argumentation," which is indeed the central thrust of the Nyaya tradition. Because it also had a strong realist bias, it was easily merged with the earlier Vaisheshika school.

Whereas the focus of Vaisheshika was the nature of things and how to categorize them, the focus of Nyaya is on the method of argument, syllogism, and the reliable means for knowing. The syllogisms that Nyaya constructed were similar, but not identical to those of Aristotle. Whatever the similarities, Nyaya developed a rigorous philosophical basis that makes it quite comparable to Western analytical philosophy.

The school of Navya Nyaya, or New Nyaya, that emerged in eastern India around the 14th century was particularly sophisticated philosophically. Nyaya developed proofs of the existence of God (which are not found in the Vaisheshika), which compare quite well to those developed in Christian theology. Though Nyaya-Vaisheshika has very few adherents today, it developed philosophical tools that all the other Hindu traditions used. They were particularly useful in refuting the heterodox Jains and Buddhists.

Further reading: Kisor Kumar Chakrabarti, *Classical Indian Philosophy: The Nyaya Dualist Tradition* (Albany: State University of New York Press, 1999); S. N. Dasgupta, *A History of Indian Philosophy*, Vol. 1 (Delhi: Motilal Banarsidass, 1975); Wilhelm Halbfass, *On Being and What There Is: Classical Vaisesika and the History of Indian Ontology* (Albany: State University of New York Press, 1992).

om

Om is the most important MANTRA in Hinduism. CHANDOGYA UPANISHAD discusses the significance of om. There it is given the highest value, equivalent to the RIG VEDA and SAMA VEDA combined; it is said to be speech and breath combined. Om is also said to be the Sama Vedic chant encapsulated.

In TAITTIRIYA UPANISHAD 1.8 om is variously said to be BRAHMAN or the entire world. The MANDUKYA UPANISHAD outlines the esoteric aspects of om. It is said to be all that is—past, present, and future—and to transcend time. Om is said to be the Self (ATMAN). Esoterically, it is said to encompass the four STATES OF CONSCIOUSNESS: the waking, dreaming, deep-sleep, and transcendent states. For this purpose, using SANSKRIT grammar, the letter *o* in the word om is understood to constitute an *a* and a *u*. *A* is the waking state, *u* the dreaming state, *m* the deep-sleep state; the fourth state has no external marker and is the non-dual reality.

Later texts understand om to encompass all visible and invisible worlds, and these are enumerated. It is seen to be the three gods: BRAHMA, VISHNU, and SHIVA; it is seen to be this world, the sky world, and the world of heaven; its letters are seen to be the manifest and unmanifest world; and so on. One of the most common MANTRAS

Om, the most revered syllable and mantra in Sanskrit, is believed to encompass all visible and invisible worlds. *(www.shutterstock.com/Junji Takemoto)*

using om is *om tat sat:* "om is that reality: all that exists."

For a YOGI, to focus on the mantra om is to focus on the ultimate reality. If the yogi pronounces om, it reaches the crown CHAKRA; if the yogi becomes absorbed meditationally in om, he becomes eternal. Om, too, is understood as the essence of the word *brahman* (*shabda brahman*) and is therefore, via its transcendent sound, the source of all manifest reality, where reality is known to be nothing but the congealing of sound. No mantra begins without *om* and most Vedic mantras end with *om* as well. Om is often referred to as *Omkara* (the *kara,* a meaningless marker), added to make it easier to distinguish visually in Sanskrit script. It is also called *pranava,* which literally means, "That which resounds."

Further reading: Cornelia Dimitt and J. A. van Buitenen, eds. and trans., *Classical Hindu Mythology: A Reader in the Sanskrit Puranas* (Philadelphia: Temple University Press, 1978); S. Ranganath, *Aum-Pranava in Indian Tradition* (Delhi: Eastern Book Linkers, 2001).

Omkara   *See* OM.

Omkarananda, Swami (1930–2000)
Vedanta teacher

Swami Omkarananda was a VEDANTA teacher who founded the first Hindu ASHRAM in Switzerland.

As a 16-year-old in South India the person later known as Swami Omkarananda suddenly left his home and traveled north to RISHIKISH in the foothills of the HIMALAYAS. There, the next year, he was initiated into the renounced life (*sannyas*) by Swami Sivananda Saraswati. He remained at Rishikish for study and in 1954 was awarded a degree by the Yoga Vedanta Forest University. In the following years he met and studied with several other prominent Indian teachers, but from 1962 to 1965 he entered a period of retreat.

In 1965, at the request of several Swiss intellectuals, he traveled to Switzerland to teach. He made a second visit in 1966; at that time he founded the Omkarananda International Ashram at Winterthur, Switzerland (near Zürich), the first permanent Hindu ashram in the country. The ashram grew and purchased a number of houses in Winterthur, identified by being painted blue.

By 1975, tension had developed in the town between the members of the ashram and their neighbors. As the tension increased, some members of the ashram bombed the home of a member of the government of the canton of Zürich.

The perpetrators were arrested, and the swami was also taken into custody and charged with complicity. He pleaded innocent but was convicted. After seven years in jail, he was released but banished from Switzerland. He settled in Austria, near the Swiss border, and resumed his teaching work. His followers initiated actions to have his conviction overturned and to restore his reputation, but he died in 2000 before that could be achieved.

In spite of the setback caused by the events of 1975, the ashram in Winterthur continues to operate, as does its sister branch in Rishikesh. Omkarananda wrote a number of books, many of which have been placed online at the Internet site posted by the ashram.

Further reading: *Omkarananda Ashram Himalayas.* Available online. URL: http://www.omkarananda-ashram. org/. Accessed August 16, 2005.

om tat sat   *See* OM.

Osho   *See* RAJNEESH, SRI.

P

pancha makara

In Hindu TANTRISM of the "left-handed" sort, the *pancha makara* or "Five *M*'s" (SANSKRIT words that begin with that letter), sometimes called the "five forbidden things (*pancha tattva*)," are the elements in a special esoteric ceremony. They are *mamsa* (meat, usually beef), *matsya* (fish), *madya* (wine), *mudra* (parched grain), and *maithuna* (sexual intercourse.) These five elements are meant to involve the participants (there may be one or more pairs in a tantric ritual circle) in forbidden actions that aid in realizing the divinity of mundane existence. By taking "forbidden" elements, they are confronted with the fact that even those things beyond the pale in human terms partake in the truth of the divinity, usually characterized as the goddess.

Beef is forbidden to all caste Hindus. It is highly polluting, and eating it is condemned by society. Fish is also not taken by most BRAHMINS and is believed to have aphrodisiac qualities. Parched grain also is known to stimulate sexual appetite and therefore is not considered desirable. Alcohol is probably the foremost of Brahminical prohibitions. In the *DHARMASHASTRA* of MANU drinking liquor is equated with killing a Brahmin. Sexuality outside marriage is looked upon as a negative thing. The female sexual partner in tantric sexuality is preferably of very low caste and not the male partner's wife.

Further reading: Agehananda Bharati, *The Tantric Tradition* (New York: Grove Press, 1975); N. N. Bhattacharyya, *History of the Tantric Religion: A Historical, Ritualistic and Philosophical Study* (Delhi: Manohar, 1982); Sanjukta Gupta, Dirk Jan Hoens, and Teun Goudriaan, *Hindu Tantrism* (Leiden: E. J. Brill, 1979).

Pancharatra

The Pancharatra (*pancha,* five; *ratra,* nights) sect was one of the early traditions that developed into VAISHNAVISM, the worship of VISHNU. It probably dates to the last centuries before the Common Era. The name may derive from the SHATAPATHA BRAHMANA XIII.6, where the god Narayana, the primordial and all-encompassing divinity, performs a special "five nights" sacrifice in order to transcend and encompass all beings. In later Vaishnavism Narayana became the name of the highest divinity; he was said to transcend BRAHMA, SHIVA, and even VISHNU.

In the Pancharatra system, creation emerges through *vyuhas* (arrangements) of the manifestations of the godhead. VASUDEVA, or KRISHNA, is the highest changeless god; Sankarshana is the Lord over all life; Pradyumna predominates over mind; and Aniruddha presides over ego. From Aniruddha derives BRAHMA, who then creates the physical universe. From Vasudeva on down, each of the phases or forms of the godhead derives from the previous form. The doctrine in certain ways is reminiscent of the Christian trinity, whereby the one god takes on different aspects.

The Pancharatra doctrines were elaborated in several important texts. The Bhaktisutras of Shandilya were central. The Pancharatra AGAMAS specified the temple cult, iconography, and ritual; they are no longer extant. Important extant Pancharatra texts are the Sasvatasamhita Ahirbudhnya Samhita and the Ishvara Samhita, which deal primarily with worship rituals.

Vedic sacrificial worship, the earliest known phase of Hinduism, did not involve permanent structures (temples) or icons. Those features emerged only after a long process of development, and both the Shaivite and Vaishnavite traditions had to develop texts to explain and justify these innovations in Vedic terms. The Pancharatras were the primary agents that performed this task for Vaishnavism.

Further reading: S. N. Dasgupta, *A History of Indian Philosophy,* vol. 3 (Delhi: Motilal Banarsidass, 1975); Sanjukta Gupta, trans., *Laksmi Tantra: A Pancaratra Text.* Orientalia Rheno-Trajectina, Vol. 15 (Leiden: E. J. Brill, 1972); S. Rangachar, *Philosophy of Pancaratras* (Mandya: Sridevi Prakashana, 1991).

Pandavas

The five Pandava brothers, among whom ARJUNA and YUDHISHTHIRA are best known, are central characters in the great Indian epic the MAHABHARATA. Their name is a patronymic derived from their father's name, *Pandu.* Through Pandu they descend from the ancient king Kuru and the more ancient progenitor BHARATA. Although they are considered Pandu's sons, they were not his natural sons, since a curse had been placed upon their father that he would die if he had sex with a woman. Their mother, Kunti (also known as Pritha, an aunt of KRISHNA), used boons she had previously received to bear children with several of the gods.

Kunti bore YUDHISHTHIRA, the eldest, by the god DHARMA; BHIMA by the wind god; and ARJUNA by INDRA. Kunti gave her remaining boons to Madri, Pandu's junior wife; the latter bore the youngest and least famous Pandavas, Nakula and Sahadeva, by the divine celestial twins, the ASHVINS. The five Pandavas shared a secret brother, Karna, who was born to Kunti by the Sun god, before her marriage to Pandu. Karna had been put into a reed basket and left to float away on a river.

After Pandu died while attempting intercourse with Madri, his brother Dhritarashtra, though blind, became regent. Pandu's sons were still considered the legitimate heirs, but Dhritarashtra's 100 sons, known as the KAURAVAS (descendants of Kuru—as were the Pandavas) and led by the eldest son, DURYODHANA, began plotting to destroy their cousins, the five Pandavas. Duryodhana, for instance, tried to poison Bhima but failed. The story of the epic revolves around the struggle for the kingdom between the Pandavas and their cousins. The conflict culminates in the great Bharata war, in which the Pandavas are triumphant, but with frightening losses.

Further reading: Peter Brook, director, *The Mahabharata* (videorecording), produced by Michael Propper (Chatsworth, Calif.: Image Entertainment, 2002); William Buck, *The Mahabharata* (Berkeley: University of California Press, 1975); J. A. B. van Buitenen, *The Mahabharata,* 3 vols. (Chicago: University of Chicago Press, 1973–78).

Panikkar, Raimundo   *See* CHRISTIAN-HINDU RELATIONS.

papa

In the KARMA system, *papa* is karmic demerit, often translated as "sin." All Hindu and Buddhist traditions used this term, which is the opposite of PUNYA or karmic merit. An accumulation of *papa* over a lifetime causes a rebirth into a status that accords with the sin. The various types of *papa*, or sins, are detailed in the texts on proper conduct or DHARMA. MANU'S DHARMASHASTRA, for example, has long lists of sins and transgressions. In the Indian context, however, there is no universal notion of sin. Instead, sin is determined by one's social place and rank.

A BRAHMIN committing a crime, for instance, will not be punished in any way as strictly as a SHUDRA (person of the servant class) would be for the same crime. On the other hand, a Brahmin who would use alcohol or eat beef would be seen to be committing a much greater sin than a Shudra who did.

Further reading: Wendy Doniger and Brian K. Smith, trans., *The Laws of Manu* (New York: Penguin Books, 1991); Wendy Doniger O'Flaherty, *Karma and Rebirth in Classical Indian Traditions* (Berkeley: University of California Press, 1980).

Paramananda, Swami (1884–1940) *pioneer teacher of Vedanta in the United States*

Swami Paramananda was a leading teacher of Vedanta in the United States. He founded the ANANDA ASHRAMA AND VEDANTA CENTRE, which carried on his teachings, including his respect for women as spiritual leaders.

Born on February 5, 1884, to an affluent East Bengali family in the village of Banaripara in what is now Bangladesh, Suresh Chandra Guhu Thakurta, the person who would later become Swami Paramananda, was cherished by his parents, Brahmamoyee and Ananda Mohan. His mother died when Suresh was only nine years old. When his father's second wife died, Suresh turned to an inner search. He began to read in his father's library and was introduced to the spirituality of Sri RAMAKRISHNA. He visited the RAMAKRISHNA MATH AND MISSION at Belur Math near Calcutta (Kolkata) and studied the life of the Bengali saint. In 1900, only four years after the death of Ramakrishna, Suresh ran away from home and joined the monastery. In 1902 he was initiated into the renounced life of *sannyas* by Swami VIVEKANANDA, student of Sri Ramakrishna and founder of the Ramakrishna Math and Mission.

Paramananda then spent four years in Madras (Chennai) with Swami Ramakrishnananda. While there he received a vision of a mission to the West. In 1906 he accompanied Swami ABHEDANANDA to New York and served as his assistant at the VEDANTA SOCIETY. He succeeded Abhedananda as director of the New York Vedanta Center and later founded Vedanta centers in Boston and Washington, D.C. While in New York, he became close to Sister Devamata (Laura Franklin Glenn) (1867–1942), who in the 1920s published his biography. He traveled widely and was a popular and sensitive spokesman for the message of VEDANTA.

As was his teacher Vivekananda, he was committed to including women in the spiritual life. His first disciple, Sister Devamata, was given considerable responsibility for giving talks and spiritual guidance when he was away. Her talks were published along with those of Paramananda. Some of the Boston students regarded her, rather than the SWAMI, as their spiritual teacher. Another of his students, Sister Daya (Georgina Jones Walton) (1882–1955), as did Sister Devamata, gave talks and spiritual guidance when Paramananda was not in town.

Beginning in 1915, Paramananda began to lecture and teach in Los Angeles, dividing his time between that city and Boston. In 1923 he opened the Ananda Ashrama at La Crescenta, California, and in 1929 opened a second ashram at Cohasset, Massachusetts.

Swami Paramananda died on June 21, 1940, at his Cohasset, Massachusetts, center. During his life, his three centers, in Boston, La Crescenta, and

Cohasset, were closely associated with the larger Vedanta Society in the United States, although organizationally independent. Since his death, the leadership of the ASHRAM has been held by women: Sister Devamata, Srimata Gayatri Devi, and Sister Sudha. The three centers, distrusting the attitude of some swamis toward women, refused to accept the new swamis sent by the Ramakrishna Math to lead their community. They applied to the Ramakrishna Math to be allowed to operate as a sisterhood, but no such permission was granted. In 1953 the Sarada Math, an order of women nuns, was founded in India, finally allowing women in the Ramakrishna-Vedanta tradition to take vows of renunciation. When the Paramananda community still refused to accept new male swamis as leaders, the parent order severed relations.

The Cohasset center and Ananda Ashrama continue to conduct daily shrine worship, give public services and classes, and publish Paramananda's books.

Further reading: Sister Devamata, *Swami Paramananda and His Work*, 2 vols. (La Crescenta, Calif.: Ananda Ashrama, 1926 and 1941); Sara Ann Levinsky, *A Bridge of Dreams: The Story of Paramananda, a Modern Mystic, and His Ideal of All-Conquering Love* (West Stockbridge, Mass.: Lindisfarne Press, 1984); Swami Paramananda, *Christ and Oriental Ideals* (Boston: Vedanta Centre, 1912); ———, *The Path of Devotion* (Boston: Vedanta Centre, 1907); ———, *Emerson and Vedanta* (Boston: Vedanta Centre, 1918).

paramatman *See* VEDANTA.

Parashurama avatar

Parashurama was an incarnation of VISHNU who fought the warrior class, who had tried to lord it over the Brahmins. It is said that Parasurama has wielded his fierce axe 22 times in different eras to destroy all the warriors on Earth—however, a few always managed to escape. Parashurama is also associated with the founding of the areas demarcated by the Indian state of Kerala.

The story goes that ARJUNA, hero of the MAHABHARATA, seized a cow from Jamadagni, the father of Parashurama. When the son returned to his father's hermitage, he became furious and went out after the great hero. In a dreadful and bloody battle he eventually beheaded Arjuna.

The sons of Arjuna, bent on revenge, went to the hermitage and killed Jamadagni. The furious Parasurama determined to extirpate the warrior race once and for all. This is when he first launched his 22 campaigns.

In another story, Parasurama's mother went to fetch water and became enamored of a king bathing there. So enthralled was she that she forgot to return to do her requisite sacrifices. When she finally returned, Jamadagni ordered his sons to kill their mother. When they refused, he ordered Parashurama to kill both his brothers and his mother. Knowing the power of his father, he did as ordered and received a boon in return. His wish, ironically, was that his brothers and mother be restored to life and that he forget all that had occurred. His father agreed. Other versions of this matricidal story are found in Indian folk tradition.

Further reading: Cornelia Dimmitt and J. A. B. van Buitenen, *Classical Hindu Mythology: A Reader in the Sanskrit Puranas* (Philadelphia: Temple University Press, 1978); John Dowson, *A Classical Dictionary of Hindu Mythology and Religion, Geography, History, and Literature,* 12th ed. (Ludhiana: Lyall Book Depot, 1974); Swami Bangovind Parampanthi, *Bhagawan Parshuram and Evolution of Culture in North-East India* (Delhi: Daya Publishing House, 1987).

Parshvanath (c. 900 B.C.E.) *Tirthankara in the Jain tradition*

Parshvanath was the 23rd TIRTHANKARA (saint) of our cosmic half-era, in the Jain tradition (*see* JAINISM). MAHAVIRA, the partly historical promulgator of Jain tradition, was the 24th and last for our

Parshvanath, 23rd Jain Tirthankara of this era, in Benares (Varanasi) *(Constance A. Jones)*

half-era. There are indications that Parsvanath, too, was a historical figure, who preached an early version of the Jain doctrine of strict worldly renunciation and very strict noninjury to creatures as the only means to liberation from birth and rebirth.

The Kalpa Sutra of BHADRABAHU (c. 500 C.E.) of the SHVETAMBARA Jains tells the story of the life of Parshvanath. It is said that he lived as a householder for 30 years, as a monk for 83 nights, and as an omniscient being for a little less than 70 years, for a total of 100 years.

In his previous life Parshvanath was a divinity in heaven (in the Jain tradition one cannot reach liberation as a divinity, but only as a human).

When that life ended he descended into the womb of Vama Devi, the wife of a king of the warrior caste, in the city of BENARES (Varanasi). It is said that on the night he was born the world was bright with the ascending and descending of gods and goddesses with sounds of beings inquiring what grand event was taking place.

Possessed of immense knowledge and faith, at the age of 30 Parshva took up the life of a renunciant, giving away his massive princely wealth to indigents. Outside the city in a park under an Ashoka tree he took off his finery and pulled out his hair in five handfuls (the custom when one becomes a Jain monk). He began vows of severe fasting and joined the community of homeless monks.

For 83 days, they say, he gave up the care of his body completely and bore every hardship as though it were not hardship. He adopted all the circumspect practices of the monk—careful movement, measured speech, guarded desires, restraint of his mind and physical activities—so as to leave the ego behind completely. During these 83 days he reached omniscience and proceeded to terminate the bonds of KARMA. Eight major followers joined him and he created a community of 350 monks, which grew and grew as his perfection affected more and more people. After 70 years as an omniscient being, he adopted the vow of taking food without water once a month on Mount Sammeta and became perfected (a SIDDHA) and liberated, his soul going to the top of the universe to dwell in effulgence forever.

Further reading: P. S. Jaini, *The Jaina Path of Purification* (Delhi: Motilal Banarsidass, 1990); Kastur Chand Lalwani, *Kalpa Sutra of Bhadrabahu Svami* (Delhi: Motilal Banarsidass, 1979).

Parthasarathi Rajagopalachari, Sri
(1927–) *teacher of* sahaja *yoga*

Sri Parthasarathi Rajagopalachari is the leader of the SRI RAM CHANDRA MISSION.

Born in 1927 near Madras (Chennai) in the village of Vayalur, the boy who was to become Sri Parthasarathi Rajagopalachari became devoted at age 18 to the teachings of the Bhagavad Gita, and experienced a spiritual awakening as he read the ancient book. He went on to graduate from Banaras Hindu University with a B.S. and followed a career as a chemical engineer and executive until his retirement in 1985.

In 1964 he discovered Sri Maharaj RAM CHANDRA and became a student of *sahaja* (spontaneous or innate) YOGA as the teaching had been handed down from Sri Ram's guru, Sri Ram Chandraji of Fategarh.

Parthasarathi Rajagopalachari, referred to as *Chariji,* travels widely teaching a message of spiritual awakening and enlightenment through *sahaja* yoga. He conducts public seminars throughout the world on a regular schedule.

Further reading: Parthasarathi Rajagopalachari, *The Principles of Sahaj Marg,* vol. 8 (Shahjahanpur: Shri Ram Chandra Mission, 1994); ———, *Revealing the Personality* (Shahjahanpur: Shri Ram Chandra Mission, 1993); ———, *Role of the Master in Human Evolution* (Munich: Shri Ram Chandra Mission, 1986).

Parvati/Uma

In Hindu mythology Parvati (she who belongs to the mountains) is the daughter of HIMAVAT and Mena, and the wife of the ascetic god SHIVA. She is considered the REINCARNATION of Shiva's first wife, SATI. She also goes by the name Uma. The first textual mention of Parvati/Uma is in the KENA UPANISHAD (c. 600 B.C.E.). Many scholars believe that Parvati was a mountain goddess of the indigenous, non-Aryan people of India who was absorbed into the Brahminical tradition.

Parvati is born, according to most stories, to lure Shiva away from asceticism so that he will produce a son. The gods are desperate for this to happen, since only a son of Shiva can kill the otherwise invincible demon Taraka. However, Shiva ignores all of Parvati's seductions. The gods send the god of love to make Shiva lustful, but Shiva opens his third eye and destroys him.

Parvati then sets out on a quest to gain Shiva's love by doing austerities of her own. She does the most difficult austerities, such as standing on one leg for many years, and gains great merit. The gods, noticing the tremendous power that Parvati is accruing, ask Shiva to grant her wish to marry him. Shiva, impressed by Parvati's devotion and steadfastness, agrees to marry her. The marriage is often described, depicted, and enacted in Indian literature and tradition. All the gods take part in the wedding party. The stories all include a humorous interlude when Shiva's mother-in-law, Mena, is outraged at his ascetic appearance—he is smeared with ashes from the cremation ground, and wears a garland made of a serpent and other disreputable items.

Shiva and Parvati go to live in Mount KAILASA. Some folklore shows Parvati as dissatisfied with living in a mountain cave instead of a proper house. Nevertheless, the lovemaking of Shiva and Parvati is so intense that it shakes the cosmos. One story recounts that Shiva's amorous enthrallment with Parvati turns all the animals, insects, and plants in the pleasure grove where they make love female. A hapless king who enters the grove also turns into a woman, although he wins a partial remission of this condition. (He is only required to be female half of any month.)

As fate would have it, just as Shiva is about to impregnate Parvati, the gods interrupt them and his semen flies off, leaping from one container to another till it finds a safe place only in the GANGES River, which thus becomes the mother of Shiva's son, KARTIKKEYA. GANESHA, a second son, is born in a similarly unconventional way: Parvati rubs her arms, covered with sweet powder, before her bath; takes the residue; and forms a child of it. Parvati then has the child guard her bath (sometimes bedchamber). Unknowingly, Shiva encounters the child and thinks it an intruder. He cuts its head off. When Parvati emerges she chastises Shiva and has him find another head immediately. In a rush he gets a newly severed elephant head, and thus the younger son Ganesha has the head of an elephant.

Parvati is often said to play dice with Shiva, and she always wins. She argues with him about his constant smoking of marijuana (a staple of Shaivite mendicants). Some stories connect Parvati with KALI, saying that she was originally dark in color but because of Shiva's teasing she changed to a light color. In other stories, Parvati is actually the left half of Shiva in his form as ARDHANARISH-VARA. As with other female divinities, Parvati is sometimes conflated with the great goddess or creator and protector of all the universe; she gains supremacy in some mythological contexts.

Further reading: Cornelia Dimmitt and J. A. B. van Buitenen, *Classical Hindu Mythology: A Reader in the Sanskrit Puranas* (Philadelphia: Temple University Press, 1978); John Stratton Hawley and Donnie Marie Wulff, eds., *The Divine Consort: Radha and the Goddesses of India* (Boston: Beacon Press, 1986); David R. Kinsley, *Hindu Goddesses* (Berkeley: University of California Press, 1988).

Pashupati   *See* SHIVA.

Patanjali (c. second century B.C.E.) *author of* Yoga Sutra

In Indian tradition two books are ascribed to Patanjali: the Mahabhashya (the primary commentary to the grammar of Panini) and the commentary on the YOGA SUTRA. Western scholarship, however, dates the first work to around 200 B.C.E., and the Yoga Sutra to around 200 C.E., making it impossible for the two Patanjalis to be the same.

Tradition has it that Patanjali was an incarnation of the divine serpent ADISHESHA, upon whom VISHNU reclines between ages on the MILK OCEAN. Patanjali's name, it is said, is from this serpent, which in very tiny form fell (*pat*) onto the palm

(*anjali*) of either Panini himself or his mother, Gonika, or fell from her womb (*anjali*) (the word *anjali* has many meanings). Patanjali is sometimes also referred to as Gonikaputra (son of Gonika).

Iconographically, Patanjali is depicted with the lower body of a snake and a canopy of five serpent heads over his head. He is shown offering *anjali* MUDRA with his palms joined. This clearly refers to the second element of his name.

Further reading: Georg Feuerstein, trans., *The Yoga-Sutra of Patanjali* (Rochester, Vt.: Inner Traditions, 1990); F. Kielhorn, *Katyayana and Patanjali: Their Relation to Each Other and to Panini* (Varanasi: Indological Book House, 1963); Baij Nath Puri, *India in the Time of Patanjali* (Bombay: Bharatiya Vidya Bhavan, 1957); Ian Whicher, *The Integrity of the Yoga Darsana: A Reconsideration of Classical Yoga* (Albany: State University of New York Press, 1998).

Periya Puranam

The Tamil Periya Puranam of SEKKILAR forms the 12th and final book of the TIRUMURAI, the Tamil Shaivite sacred canon. *Periya Puranam* means "Great *Purana*," or great ancient story. It comprises over 4,200 stanzas.

Composed in the 12th century, the book tells the stories of the 63 NAYANMARS or Shaivite saints. These stories were originally recorded by the eighth-century poet SUNDARAR in the *Tondartokai*, or "compendium of the lives of the saints." At royal order the list of saints was expanded in the 10th century by Nambi Andar Nambi. Sekkilar, a minister of the Chola empire, provides the most complete compendium in his Periya Puranam. It is said that he was inspired to create the work to wean the Chola king Anapaya Chola away from reading the highly erotic but heretical Jain text Jivaka Cintamani. Sekkilar is said to have recited this work at the Shaivite sacred shrine of CHID-AMBARAM.

The book has 13 chapters. The longest story is about Sambanthar (1256 quatrains), followed by the account of Appar (429 verses). The writing follows a simple lively style and was probably designed to be sung. It contains beautiful descriptions of each saint's village or town; the longer stories dwell on the spiritual development of the saints.

Further reading: G. Vanmikinathan, *Periya Puranam, a Tamil Classic on the Great Saiva Saints of South India* (Madras: Ramakrishna Math, 1985); Kamil V. Zvelibil, "Tamil Literature," in Jan Gonda, ed., *The History of Indian Literature,* Vol. 10, Fascicle 1 (Wiesbaden: Otto Harrassowitz, 1974).

pilgrimage

Visiting holy sites is one of the central activities in Hinduism. Many pilgrims visit shrines, rivers, sacred mountains, and sacred groves to obtain spiritual benefits; others go to achieve the worldly benefits that can also accrue from visiting a holy place. Women commonly vow to visit the shrine of a certain saint or god in order to have a child, especially a son. Some may visit a shrine and shave their heads there in order to win success at an exam or important business deal.

All sects in Hinduism do pilgrimage. SHAIVITES, SHAKTAS, and VAISHNAVITES alike have myriad important sites. Vaishnavites target the many places where RAMA or KRISHNA visited or lived, as well as the many temples where other forms of VISHNU are enshrined. Mathura, BRINDAVAN, and DVARAKA are particularly important for the devotees of Krishna, while AYODHYA is visited as the birthplace of Rama. Shaivites visit the many

Religious mendicants on pilgrimage in Sonnamarg, Kashmir *(Constance A. Jones)*

temples and shrines with SHIVA LINGAM, in addition to many other temples to Shiva that can be pilgrimage destinations. SHAKTAS or goddess worshippers have 53 shrines where parts of the goddess are said to have fallen when she was cut into pieces.

Among important pilgrimage cities are Gaya, BENARES (Varanasi), HARIDVAR, and Ujjain. Important rivers are GANGES, YAMUNA, Godavari, Narmada, and CAUVERY.

Perhaps the most significant pilgrimage site for Hindus is Benares. The primary aim of pilgrims in Benares is to bathe in the holy Ganges, which is said to confer heaven upon those who bathe in her. People nearing the end of their lives often go there, so that their ashes can be thrown into the river, and they can reach liberation from birth and rebirth.

Further reading: Anne Feldhaus, *Connected Places: Region, Pilgrimage and Geographical Imagination in India* (New York: Palgrave Macmillan, 2003); Baidyanath Saraswati, *Traditions of Tirthas in India: The Anthropology of Hindu Pilgrimage* (Varanasi: N. K. Bose Memorial Foundation, 1983); Man Mohan Sharma, *Yatra: Pilgrimages in the Western Himalayas* (Noida: Trishul, 1989).

pingala   *See* NADI.

pipal tree

The fig or pipal tree is foremost among the sacred trees of Indian tradition. This lush tree can grow to a huge size with a large canopy. It has large, rather thin leaves that make a rustling sound in a breeze, which tradition compares to the sound of the lute or *veena*. No one is allowed to cut down, remove branches, or tear off leaves from a pipal tree.

Some associate the pipal tree particularly with VISHNU, who is said to have been born under one. Often a pipal tree is officially "married" to a margosa tree when they are planted together.

A solemn ceremony mimicking an actual marriage ceremony is performed, often before an entire village. Sometimes the tree is also invested with the sacred thread, as a BRAHMIN is. The tree plays a role in certain brahminical rituals, and sometimes in marriage ceremonies. Branches of pipal wood were used in the VEDIC fire ritual. It was under a pipal tree that the BUDDHA reached his enlightenment. Many legends, myths, and stories in Indian literature refer to events and occurrences that take place under this, the most sacred of Indian trees.

Further reading: James Fergusson, *Tree and Serpent Worship* (Delhi: Oriental, 1971); P. Thomas, *Hindu Religion Customs and Manners*, 3d ed. (Bombay: D. B. Taraporevala Sons, 1956).

pitri   *See* ANCESTOR WORSHIP.

pollution/purity

Pollution and purity have been important social and religious concepts in Hinduism from ancient times. Pollution often entails substances related to birth, death, blood, bodily processes, and leftover food.

The concepts of purity and pollution are central to the notion of caste in India. People whose traditional occupations put them in contact with leather, dead animals, toilets and sewers, and sweeping (leftover substances) are usually considered outcastes or UNTOUCHABLES (Dalit). At the other social extreme are BRAHMINS, who never have contact with such substances and, ideally, deal only with learning, books, or temple rituals. They are considered pure. Middle castes, which sometimes have contact with polluting substances in their traditional work, have an intermediate purity status. For example, barbers, who have contact with bodily substances as they cut people's hair, are seen as lower caste, though not untouchable.

For Brahmins, purity is maintained by tradition and occupation and reinforced by vegetarianism. In Vedic times Brahmins were avid meat eaters and even ate beef. As the traditional specialists in ritual sacrifice, they were entitled to the leftover meat from each animal offering.

As new ideas of purity began to develop, Brahmins became the strictest vegetarians, even eschewing eggs in most regions of India. When they became the measure of purity, those who did eat meat were given lower status. Because of their purity, Brahmins may offer cooked food to anyone; thus, they are often hired as cooks in restaurants. Conversely, Brahmins can accept food from and eat together with only a very limited group of people, their own subcaste of Brahmins. Commensality—eating food together—is a sign of an equal level of purity. People who by tradition have different levels of purity traditionally would not eat in the same place or from the same source. Furthermore, any food that has been eaten by anyone else is highly polluting, unless that person is one's infant child or husband; beef is always considered the most impure and reviled of foods. In villages, different castes still draw water from different wells.

In social contexts feet are considered the most polluting body part and must never touch someone else. However, people do touch the feet of a mother, father, elder brother, GURU, or god out of honor, respect, or worship. Any association with blood or death is considered polluting.

Further reading: G. Morris Carstairs, *The Twice-Born* (Bloomington: Indiana University Press, 1967); Brian K. Smith, *Classifying the Universe: The Ancient Indian Varna System and the Origins of Caste* (New York: Oxford University Press, 1994).

Pongal

Pongal is an important festival in the Tamil region, celebrated in the Tamil month of Tai (January–February). Technically, the month starts when the Sun enters the sign of Capricorn. Pongal is a celebration of the harvest, which in Tamil Nadu occurs when the rainy season ends in December.

The word Pongal is from the Tamil root *pongu*, which means to boil. During the festival, a pot is filled with rice, ghee, milk, and sugar or jaggery (palm sugar) and is heated to boiling. The pot is supposed to boil over to show the abundance of the harvest. The day before Pongal old implements and clothing are discarded to be replaced by new ones. On this day cows and other cattle are directly worshipped and are allowed to run free. Bullfights are staged, and young men chase wild bulls, in a somewhat gentler version of the running of the bulls in Pamplona, Spain.

Further reading: M. Arunachalam, *Festivals of Tamil Nadu* (Tiruchitrambalam: Gandhi Vidyalayam, 1980); Anita Ganeri, *Hindu Festivals throughout the Year* (Mankato, Minn.: Smart Apple Media, 2003).

Pongala

Pongala, which means "prosperity," is a 10-day festival celebrated at the Attukal Amma Temple in Tiruvananthapuram (Trivandrum) in Kerala. It begins in the month of Kumbham (February–March). The main festival ritual, the boiling of rice in a pot, is connected to the Sunday ritual to the Sun in ancient Dravidian culture, and to the Tamil New Year celebration of Pongal, which has a similar name because the basic ritual is the same. The Pongala ritual has become the largest gathering of women for festival purposes in the world.

A high point of the festival is the recitation of the song of Kannaki, found in classical form in the ancient Tamil text *Cilappatikaram*. In this version, a boy is sacrificed and Kannaki tears off a breast to destroy the city of Madurai. On the ninth day, when the boy is sacrificed and Kannaki tears off her breast, the Pongala ritual fire is lit in the temple. All the women who are gathered simultaneously light their fires to cook rice. The overflow of the rice pot (or, in the case of BRAH-

MINS, the near overflow) indicates that the woman has received the grace of the goddess. No men are directly involved.

As part of the festival young boys ritually (and painlessly) pierce their skin with silver needles, to honor the goddess Attukal Amma. Unmarried girls under the age of 12 offer plates of rice, coconut, areca nut, and flowers to the goddess, to ensure that they remain healthy and protected.

Further reading: Dianne Jenett, "Red Rice for Bhagavati: Pongala Ritual at the Attukal Temple in Kerala," *ReVision* 20, no. 3 (1998): 37–43. Vikraman Kokkanathala, *The Glory of Attukal.* Translated by Kamala Bai (Thiruvananthapuram: Sunce Publishing Division, 1997); K. R. Vaidyanathan, *Temples and Legends of Kerala* (Bombay: Bharatiya Vidya Bhavan, 1994).

Poonja, Sri Harilal (Poonjaji, Papaji)
(1910–1997) *teacher of enlightenment*

Sri Harilal Poonja was a prominent spiritual teacher in Lucknow who had a number of influential students.

Born on October 13, 1910, in an area of the Punjab now a part of Pakistan, H. W. L. Poonja was part of a family of devotees. His mother was a devoted follower of the Lord KRISHNA, and his maternal uncle was Swami RAMA TIRTHA, a celebrated saint. At age eight, the boy had his first transcendental experience, became a devotee of Lord Krishna, and began a MANTRA practice day and night.

At age 20, he entered into an arranged marriage and later had two children. He served in the army for less than two years, leaving to pursue his spiritual quest. While living in his father's house with his wife and children, he received a vision of Bhagavan Sri RAMANA MAHARSHI, an enlightened master, who directed him to Ramana's ashram in Tiruvannamalai in southern India.

During the partition of India, Poonjaji moved his family from the Punjab to Lucknow, Uttar

Sri Harilal Poonja (Poonjaji), teacher of *advaita* Vedanta *(Courtesy of Eli Jaxon-Bear)*

Pradesh, where he worked as a salesman and mining manager. He later became a revered teacher in Lucknow, giving daily *satsangs* (teachings). His home and a nearby community building have been visited by hundreds of spiritual seekers and students. The main characteristic of his teaching was his capacity to awaken seekers to their true Self in his presence. The American teachers of enlightenment GANGAJI and Andrew COHEN are two of his best-known students.

In 1993, the Avadhuta Foundation was set up to further the teachings of Poonjaji and to archive and distribute audiotapes and videotapes of meetings with him. He died in Lucknow on September 6, 1997.

Further reading: David Godman, *Nothing Ever Happened: Biography of H. W. L. Poonja,* 3 vols. (Boulder, Colo.:

Avadhuta Foundation, 1993); H. W. L. Poonja, *Wake Up and Roar: Satsang with H. W. L. Poonja* (Kula, Hawaii: Pacific Center, 1992).

Prahlada

Prahlada, son of the demon HIRANYAKASHIPU, whom VISHNU slew in his "man-lion" incarnation (NARASIMHA), is known as one of the great devotees of Vishnu.

The story goes that Prahlada would admit, upon being questioned by his demonic father in his father's court, that he was a devotee of Vishnu, his father's sworn enemy. At one point, Hiranyakashipu became enraged and ordered his courtiers to kill his "traitorous" son. But God protected Prahlada, who was not harmed by the many weapons thrown at him. Further enraged, Hiranyakashipu commanded serpents to fall upon his disobedient son. The serpents too could not harm him.

Then Prahlada was made to endure the crushing feet of celestial elephants and again was unharmed. Hiranyakashipu then sent ferocious fire upon his son, to no effect, followed by equally inefficacious poison and a fiery magical female being. Summoned to the court to explain how he had survived these ordeals, Prahlada claimed no work of magic but only the blessing of Lord Vishnu. His father resumed his efforts, having the son thrown from the top of the palace and having an enchanter put a deadly spell on him; neither attempt succeeded. Prahlada was tossed to the bottom of the ocean and covered with rocks; he did not die. Somehow after all this the father and son were reconciled, though the son continued to testify that he had Vishnu "within his heart." When Vishnu eventually killed his father, Prahlada became the head of the demons.

Further reading: A. C. Bhaktivedanta Swami Prabhupada, *Transcendental Teachings of Prahlada Maharaja* (Los Angeles: Bhaktivedanta Book Trust, 1991); Cornelia Dimmitt and J. A. B. van Buitenen, *Classical Hindu Mythology: A Reader in the Sanskrit Puranas* (Philadelphia: Temple University Press, 1978); John Dowson, *A Classical Dictionary of Hindu Mythology and Religion, Geography, History, and Literature,* 12th ed. (Ludhiana: Lyall Book Depot, 1974).

Prajapati

Prajapati, "lord of all born beings," was a Vedic divinity of some importance. In the period of the BRAHMANAS his status rose even higher, as he was ritually identified with the cosmic PURUSHA, the source of all reality.

In the Rig Veda, the cosmic Purusha allowed himself to be dismembered to create all reality. This story was ritually reenacted each year in the *AGNICHAYANA*—the ritual building of the fire altar—but in the ritual Prajapati's name is substituted for Purusha's. Prajapati retained his aggrandized status in the UPANISHADS, but in later Hindu mythology he reverts to the status of "lord of all born beings." In some cases, BRAHMA, the creator god, takes on his role.

Further reading: Jan Gonda, *Prajapati's Relations with Brahman, Brihaspati and Brahma* (Amsterdam: North Holland, 1989); Frits Staal, C. V. Somayajipad, and M. Itti Nambudri, *Agni: The Vedic Ritual of the Fire Altar* (Delhi: Motilal Banarsidass, 1986).

prakriti

In the list of 24 categories of reality in SAMKHYA and YOGA, *prakriti* refers to nature or the phenomenal universe. It is seen as an eternal reality that always existed and always will exist. That is to say, phenomenal reality is *not* a created entity but is an eternal real that always was and always will be.

Prakriti is seen as an unconscious force that creates and dissolves universes; when a universe is dissolved, *prakriti* becomes an inert unmanifest reality, which will once again come forward to produce a new creation. The task of Samkhya and most yogas is to learn how to dissociate the intellect, the highest discriminatory faculty, as much as possible from the whirl of *prakriti,* phenomenal existence.

This task requires the devotee to develop an immunity of sorts to the pulls and pushes of manifest reality. Meditative practice and other yogic practices are designed to firm up the discriminative faculty against the pull of the fluctuations of reality. A yogi learns not to be influenced by either the good or the bad that comes her or his way, but to remain calm and steady in the face of all phenomena. When the highest discrimination (*viveka*) is awakened in the intellect, then the dormant consciousness or PURUSHA becomes fully aware that it is not of the stuff of *prakriti* or nature but is a conscious eternal entity of its own sort. Then occurs release from *prakriti* and the cycles of birth and rebirth, though one may remain in a bodily state afterward.

Further reading: Knut A. Jacobsen, *Prakrti in Samkhya-Yoga: Material Principle, Religious Experience, Ethical Implications* (New York: Peter Lang, 1999); Gerald Larson and Ram Shankar Bhattacharya, eds., *Encyclopedia of Indian Philosophies: Samkhya a Dualist Tradition in Indian Philosophy,* vol. 4 (Princeton, N.J.: Princeton University Press, 1987); Kapila Vatsyayan, ed., *Prakrti: The Integral Vision,* 5 vols. (New Delhi: Indira Gandhi National Centre for the Arts, 1995).

pralaya   See TIME IN HINDU TRADITION.

pramana

A *pramana* is a criterion for valid argument in Indian philosophy. From its earliest days Indian philosophy sought to delimit the grounds upon which valid argument could be made. Different philosophical schools varied widely as to which grounds they accepted, but they all had from one to six or more explicit *pramanas.*

Examples of *pramanas* are *pratyaksha,* or direct perception; ANUMANA, or inference; and SHRUTI, or

scripture. The CHARVAKAS, the Indian materialists, believed that only direct perception or *pratyaksha* was valid and there is no point in trying to draw any conclusions by analogy or any other way. The MIMAMSA school, on the other hand, saw *shruti* or the Vedic scripture to be the most important pramana. NYAYA-VAISHESHIKA, the most philosophical school, strongly relied on inference, or *anumana.*

Further reading: S. N. Dasgupta, *The History of Indian Philosophy* (Delhi: Motilal Banarsidass, 1971–75); R. I. Inagalalli, *Sabda Pramana, an Epistemological Analysis* (Delhi: Sri Satguru, 1988).

prana

Prana is the vital air or life's breath. According to older yogic theory there are five breaths or *pranas.* The breathing breath is called *prana;* the breath that goes downward out the anus is called *apana* (but sometimes *apana* is used to refer to the "out-breath" in contrast to the "in-breath" of *prana*); the digestive breath is called *samana;* the breath that is diffused throughout the whole body is called *vyana;* and the breath that goes up the throat and enters into the head is called *udana.* These five breaths, or *pranas,* resemble the humors of earlier Western medicine.

Further reading: Benimadhab Barua, *A History of Pre-Buddhistic Indian Philosophy* (Delhi: Motilal Banarsidass, 1970); Swami Naranjananda Saraswati, *Prana, Pranayama, Prana Vidya* (Munger: Bihar School of Yoga, 1994).

pranayama

Pranayama (lit. breath control) is one of the elements in the eightfold path of YOGA found in PATANJALI's YOGA SUTRA and other sources. Watching the breath is an element of virtually every yoga that emerged in India, whether Hindu, Buddhist, or Jain. The practice of PRANAYAMA is one of not only focusing on the breath but learning to control it in its three phases of inhalation (*puraka*), exhalation (*recaka*), and suspension of breath between the two (*kumbhaka*). Each must be controlled so that the three fill equal durations of time. One must gradually develop the ability to prolong all three.

Further reading: Swami Narayananda, *The Secrets of Prana, Pranayama and Yoga-Asanas*, 5th rev. ed. (Gylling, Denmark: Narayanananda Universal Yoga Trust & Ashrama, 1979); Swami Naranjananda Saraswati, *Prana, Pranayama, Prana Vidya* (Munger: Bihar School of Yoga, 1994).

Prana Yoga Ashram (est. 1975)

Prana Yoga Ashram is one of several centers founded by Swami Vignanananda (Who Has the Bliss of Wisdom), who represents the lineage of Swami SHIVANANDA of Rishikesh.

Swami Vignanananda (previously known as Swami Sivalingam), a devotee of Swami SHIVANANDA Saraswati, was born in Thinnanore, Trichy District, in Tamil Nadu on June 14, 1932. He studied with Shivananda at his Yoga Vedanta Forest Academy on the banks of the GANGES River in Rishikesh, beginning his spiritual journey there with four years of intense study of HATHA YOGA, from 1959 to 1963.

Upon leaving the academy, he began mission work outside India to disseminate the teaching and practice of Sivananda. In 1963, he left on a mission to Asia, establishing Sivananda Yoga Centers in Japan and Hong Kong. After teaching in Japan for 10 years, he entered the United States in 1973 and founded the Prana Yoga Foundation in 1974, the Prana Yoga Ashram in Berkeley in 1975, the Prana Yoga Center in 1976, and the Ayodhyanagar Retreat in 1977. During 1975 he traveled to Canada and established his work there. In all, he established nine centers in North America.

Vignanananda has passed on the synthesis of yoga teachings he learned at the academy. His teaching centers on HATHA YOGA with its postures (asanas) and the practice of PRANAYAMA (regulation of breathing patterns). Through a prescribed pattern of breathing and bodily postures, *prana* or spiritual energy is generated and dispersed throughout the nervous system. The effect is cleansing, healing, and energizing to the entire body.

The ashrams publish the periodical *Prana Yoga Life* through their headquarters in Berkeley, California.

Further reading: *Prana Yoga Centers, International.* Available online. URL: http://www.proliberty.com/pranayoga/. Accessed August 16, 2005; Swami Sivalingam, *Wings of Divine Wisdom* (Berkeley, Calif.: Prana Yoga Ashrams, 1977).

prasada

Prasada (to sit inclined toward someone) means "grace." It derives theologically from VAISHNAVISM but is used in other contexts as well. In theistic Hinduism the grace of God can free one from the bonds of KARMA, the cycle of birth and rebirth. Also, grace can give one blessings in life.

Grace can be conferred by visible means in a number of ways. Most commonly food or flowers will be offered to the divinity in a temple or shrine; once the deity has partaken of and blessed the offering, it is distributed to devotees and called *prasada*. Another very common way of receiving grace is from the *arati* lamp or PUJA lamp that is waved before the divinity. One can put one's hands over the flame and then touch one's head and/or face to receive the blessing of the divinity. Things given to a person by a guru or other religious personage also can confer grace. In fact, any object placed before an icon in order to be blessed may be given *prasada*, or grace.

Further reading: R. N. Dandekar, "God in Hindu Thought," *Annals of the Bhandarkar Oriental Research Institute* 48–49 (1968), 433–625; Klaus Klostermaier, *A Survey of Hinduism* (Albany: State University of New York Press, 1994); Richard Lannoy, *The Speaking Tree:*

A Study of Indian Culture and Society (London and New York: Oxford University Press, 1971).

pratyahara   See YOGA SUTRA.

pratyaksha   See PRAMANA.

Prayag   See ALLAHABAD.

Premananda, Swami   See SELF-REVELATION CHURCH OF ABSOLUTE MONISM.

prithivi

Prithivi is earth, one of the five ELEMENTS (*mahabhutas*) of reality. The word is also a name of the earth goddess in the Vedas. In the RIG VEDA and ATHARVA VEDA *prithivi,* or the "Earth," is called the *mother,* while the sky is considered *father.* Together they are frequently called parents, or even the parents of the gods; frequently the Sun is mentioned as their child. The Earth is seen as protecting, sustaining, and nourishing but is only rarely referred to without reference to the sky. In later Hindu mythology the earth goddess was called Bhumi Devi.

Further reading: Ralph R. T. Griffith, *The Rig Veda* (New York: Motilal Banarsidass, 1992); Marta Vannucci, *Ecological Readings in the Veda* (New Delhi: D. K. Print World, 1994).

PROUT (est. 1959)

PROUT is an acronym for *PROgressive Utilization Theory,* a socioeconomic philosophy developed by Prabhat Ranjan Sarkar (1923–90), better known to the world as Sri Sri ANANDAMURTI, the founder of the ANANDA MARGA YOGA SOCIETY. Sarkar saw PROUT as an alternative to both capitalism and communism, the major economic systems of the 20th century. Sarkar suggested that both capitalism and communism had failed to address the mental and spiritual needs of humankind. He called for a balance between more abstract concerns, such as economic growth, social development, and environmental sustainability, and individual and collective human interests.

Sarkar assumed that humanity is heading toward the experience of a higher consciousness as part of the essence of the race's evolution. Material and intellectual gains lose their significance unless accompanied by spiritual progress. He advocated a decentralized economy with decision making in the hands of local people. The democratization of economic power implied that there would be strict limits on the individual accumulation of wealth.

Alongside the decentralization of economic life, Sarkar saw the need for a world governance system, including a global bill of rights, constitution, and common penal code. Such a world government would institute many of the values he advocated, such as guaranteed necessities of life for all people, moral and principled leaders dedicated to the service of society, individual freedom, cultural diversity, and equal rights for women.

The PROUT system has gained some support from a few intellectuals, but has yet to find implementation on a large scale.

Further reading: Ravi Batra, *The Downfall of Capitalism and Communism: Can Capitalism Be Saved?* (Richardson, Tex.: Liberty Press, 1990); ———, *Great American Deception: What Politicians Won't Tell You about Our Economy and Your Future* (New York: John Wiley & Sons, 1996); Dada Maheshvarananda, *After Capitalism: PROUT's Vision for a New World* (Washington, D.C.: Proutist Universal Publications, 2003); Prabhat Ranjan Sarkar, *Universal Humanism: Selected Social Writings of P. R. Sarkar.* Edited by Timothy G. Anderson (Washington, D.C.: Proutist Universal Publications, 1983).

puja

Puja, or "worship," is perhaps the central ceremonial practice of Hinduism. A *puja* minimally entails an offering and some MANTRAS. It can take place at any site where worship can occur, either of a divinity, a GURU, or SWAMI, a being, a person (such as a wife, husband, brother, or sister), or spirit. It can take place in a home or a temple, or at a tree, river, or any other place understood to be sacred.

Incense, fruit, flowers, leaves, water, and sweets are the most common offerings in the *puja.* Also, common is the *arati* or waving of a lighted lamp. The most elaborate *puja,* the temple *puja* before the icon, includes the following elements accompanied by the appropriate mantras (usually in SANSKRIT): invitation to the deity, offering of a

Brahmin priest performing *puja* to Lord Vishnu, in Belur, Bengal *(Constance A. Jones)*

seat to the divinity; greeting of the divinity; washing of the feet of the divinity; rinsing of its mouth and hands; offering of water or a honey mixture; pouring of water upon it; putting of clothing upon it (if it has not been already clothed for the day); giving of perfume, flowers, incense, lamps, or food; prostration; and taking of leave.

In temples the iconic image of the divinity is always treated as a person of royalty would be treated. Therefore, a *puja* will be done in early morning accompanied by songs to awaken the deity. The deity is then bathed, dressed, and fed, and then more fully worshipped. *Pujas* go on throughout the day to the deity, as local traditions require.

In the Jain tradition temple *puja* is actively done only among the SHVETAMBARAS, but it can take on a different aspect. When the *puja* is done to the main image of the temple, a TIRTHANKARA or ARHAT (saint), no grace can be expected in exchange, as the Tirthankara is a released being only and not a god. Shvetambara Jains do other *pujas* to subsidiary gods and goddesses and spiritual personages other than the *arhats,* which can confer desired results.

Further reading: John Cort, *Jains in the World: Religious Values and Ideology in India* (New York: Oxford University Press, 2001); Klaus Klostermaier, *A Survey of Hinduism* (Albany: State University of New York Press, 1994); Donald S. Lopez, ed., *Religions of India in Practice* (Princeton, N.J.: Princeton University Press, 1995); Hillary Peter Rodrigues, *Ritual Worship of the Great Goddess: The Liturgy of the Durga Puja with Interpretations* (Albany: State University of New York Press, 2003).

punya

Punya is karmic merit. Its opposite is PAPA, sin or karmic demerit. This is a pervasive and important concept in Indian culture. *Punya* originally was accrued by sponsoring or performing sacrifices, by giving to BRAHMINS, or by giving of appropriate charity to others. As Hinduism developed, fasting and pilgrimages became additional means of

Lord Krishna's birthplace, where his *puranic* tale begins, in Mathura, Uttar Pradesh *(Constance A. Jones)*

acquiring *punya*, along with general good works. Generally *punya* was accrued in order to gain a better birth in the next life, although it could also help in the longer path to liberation. The term is used in a general sense in the Jain tradition, too, where the term *punya-karma* is used to mean "wholesome karma."

Further reading: Wendy Doniger and Brian K. Smith, trans., *The Laws of Manu* (New York: Penguin Books, 1991); Wendy Doniger O'Flaherty, *Karma and Rebirth in Classical Indian Traditions* (Berkeley: University of California Press, 1980).

puraka See YOGA SUTRA.

puranas

A *purana* is a story about the deeds and life of a divinity. These stories supply a rich backdrop to Hinduism, and, together with the epics, the RAMAYANA and MAHABHARATA, form the mythological infrastructure of the culture. Jains have their own *puranic* literature, but it dwells on the lives of the great teachers, the TIRTHANKARAS and other holy personages who have broken the bonds of karma, rather than on the gods.

There are 18 traditional *puranas* in Hinduism, all written in SANSKRIT. Though their names could be taken to indicate a sectarian focus (as, for example, the Shiva Purana), most often they contain both SHAIVITE and Vaishnavite stories. At times stories outline the supremacy of the GODDESS, such as those in the Markandeya Purana, but even these are juxtaposed with stories from the other two sects.

Included in the category of *purana* are very important local stories, usually in Sanskrit, but sometimes in local languages. In particular, the Tamil language of South India contains many stories like this. These *sthala puranas,* or *puranas* of "place," tell the origin stories of the vast number of local divinities who populate the Indian landscape. An example of this would be the Tiruvilayadal Puranam, written in Tamil in the 16th century, which tells the story of MINAKSHI from the Brahminical point of view, showing how she became subordinated to SHIVA, who became her husband.

Further reading: Vettam Mani, *Puranic Encyclopaedia: A Comprehensive Work with Special Reference to the Epic and Puranic Literature* (Delhi: Motilal Banarsidass, 2002); David Shulman, *Tamil Temple Myths: Sacrifice and Divine Marriage in the South Indian Saiva Tradition* (Princeton, N.J.: Princeton University Press, 1980).

Pururavas and Urvashi *See* APSARAS.

purusha

The term *purusha* has two meanings. In the ancient RIG VEDA, X. 90, the Purusha (usually spelled in English with a capital *P*) is the divine being who existed before time and was sacrificed to create both the transcendent and the material realms. The major Vedic ritual, the AGNICHAYANA, was seen as a reenactment of this primordial creation, and Purusha was seen as being sacrificed once again to mirror the myth. In that context the Purusha began to be called PRAJAPATI.

The second sense of the word *purusha* is found in the SAMKHYA and YOGA traditions, where *purusha* is the individual self. In the early understanding the *purushas* were infinite in number and all eternally distinct from one another. In the later understanding, affected by VEDANTIC thinking, the

purushas merged with the ultimate self, or ATMAN, when they achieved liberation. In current yoga, the term *purusha* is just another term for atman or "worldly self."

Further reading: S. N. Dasgupta, *History of Indian Philosophy,* 5 vols. (Delhi: Motilal Banarsidass, 1971–75; Klaus Klostermaier, *A Survey of Hinduism* (Albany: State University of New York Press, 1994); Heinrich Zimmer, *Philosophies of India* (Princeton, N.J.: Princeton University Press, 1974).

purusharthas *See* ENDS OF LIFE, FIVE.

Purvas (c. 700 B.C.E.)

The Purvas are 14 Prakrit (a language derived from SANSKRIT) language works that are understood to be the original texts of the Jain canon; they are no longer extant. BHADRABAHU (c. 300 B.C.E.) is said to be the last Jain teacher to know all 14 of these texts by heart. Brief descriptions of the Purvas appear in later literature. They must have included cosmology, speculations on the karmic substance that holds a soul in transmigration, polemics, astrology, astronomy, and disquisitions on esoteric powers and YOGAS. The Purvas were transmitted orally and preached by MAHAVIRA, the last TIRTHANKARA (saint) of our half-era.

Further reading: Padmanabh S. Jaini, *The Jain Path of Purification* (Delhi: Motilal Banarsidass, 1990).

Pushan

Pushan is a Vedic divinity associated with the Sun. He is the guardian of travelers and herd animals. He is frequently linked in the VEDAS to SOMA (who in addition to being a divine drink taken by BRAHMINS at the Vedic ritual is also the god of the Moon). Pushan is known to be an escort on the path to the next world. He is often listed as one of the 12 ADITYAS.

Further reading: Samuel Atkins, *Pusan in the Rig Veda* (Princeton, N.J.: Princeton University Press, 1941); Jan Gonda, *Pushan and Sarasvati* (Amsterdam: North-Holland, 1985).

Pushkara

Pushkara (Blue Lotus) is the site of the only large shrine to the god BRAHMA, the creator god. (A smaller shrine to Brahma exists at Itar on the border of Rajasthan and Gujarat). It is located at a blue lotus pond near Ajmer in Rajasthan in western India. The site was referred to in the MAHABHARATA as a place for the worship of Brahma; thus, it has probably been a pilgrimage site for nearly 2,000 years.

Some sources consider Pushkara a premier pilgrimage place, visiting which is equal to visiting all other pilgrimage sites. The current shrine appears to have been built in the 1970s. It is known today for its huge annual camel festival, held on the full Moon in the month of Karttika (October–November). Thousands of camels are taken to the site to be consecrated, displayed, and raced.

Further reading: Tarapada Bhattacharya, *The Cult of Brahma* (Varanasi: Chowkhamba Sanskrit Series Office, 1969); C. Cesary, *Indian Gods, Sages and Cities* (Delhi: Mittal, 1987); Diwan Bahadur Har Bilas and P. Seshadri, *Ajmer: Historical and Descriptive* (Ajmer: Fine Art Printing Press, 1941); Trilok Chandra Miupuria, *Erwan Shrine and Brahma Worship in Thailand: With Reference to India and Nepal* (Bangkok: Techpress Service, 1987).

R

Radha

Radha is a popular female figure in Hindu mythology and literature. She is usually presented as the primary consort of KRISHNA; their passionate love has served as a spiritual model and inspiration in Indian culture.

Radha appears in association with Krishna in textual fragments dated as early as the third century C.E., although she is not mentioned by name in the authoritative Vishnu Purana (c. fifth century C.E.) or in the equally important BHAGAVATA PURANA (10th century C.E.). By the 12th century, however, her role as Krishna's consort was assured, as in the magnificent GITAGOVINDA of Jayadeva.

The more Krishna became associated in the devotional literature with a divine "sweetness," the more his sweet, poignant love of the cowherd woman Radha and her reciprocal love became the guide for devotees to the god everywhere in India. As the *Gitagovinda* describes Radha's shifting moods of love, anticipation, pique, disappointment, and eventual union, the writer evokes a passion that seems to extend to the elements of nature, the trees, the wind, and the Moon. Radha is love incarnate.

Theologically, the *Gitagovinda* presents Radha as an energy, a SHAKTI (the Hladini Shakti), of Krishna himself. In the Bengali Vaishnavite tradition, which eventually extended its influence to BRINDAVAN and beyond, one has the sense that Krishna too cannot exist without the love of his counterpart. The devotee becomes, in effect, essential to God. Sometimes the tradition goes so far as to say (in devotional hyperbole) that it is better to worship the devotee than God himself.

Occasionally, in the Vaishnavite tradition, Radha is actually portrayed as Krishna's wife and partner. This attempt to sanitize their relationship distorts it: the power of their attraction is theologically understood to reside in her unavailability: she is married to someone else. Krishna and Radha are eternal paramours and not spouses. It should not go unsaid that Radha is not just a cowherd woman, but the goddess herself. Some elements of the great GODDESS (Mahadevi) can be found in her literary image.

Further reading: Edward C. Dimock, *The Place of the Hidden Moon: Erotic Mysticism in the Vaisnava Sajiya Cult of Bengal* (Chicago: University of Chicago Press, 1966); Lee Siegel, *Sacred and Profane Dimensions of Love in the Indian Traditions as Exemplified in the Gitagovinda of Jayadeva* (London: Oxford University Press, 1978); John Stratton Hawley, *The Divine Consort: Radha and the Goddesses of India* (Berkeley: Religious Studies Series and Delhi: Motilal Banarsidass, 1982); Donna Marie Wulff, "Radha, Consort and Conqueror of Krishna," in John Stratton Hawley and Donna Marie Wulff, eds., *Devi: The Goddesses of India* (Berkeley: University of California Press, 1996).

Radha, Swami Shivananda (1911–1995)
kundalini yoga teacher

The German-born Swami Shivananda Radha helped to spread KUNDALINI YOGA and other Indian teachings in Canada. She founded the Yasodhara Ashram Society in British Columbia, an important spiritual center.

Sylvia Hellman was born in Berlin, Germany. Before World War II, she established a successful career as a dancer and writer. She and her husband helped the persecuted escape Nazi Germany during the war. Her husband eventually lost his life in this cause. After the war Hellman remarried, but misfortune struck again when her second husband had a sudden stroke and died in 1949. Distraught over her losses, Hellman relocated to Montreal, Quebec, in 1951 with the intention of starting a new life. It was during this period of mourning that Hellman began questioning the meaning of life and pursuing a spiritual practice. In 1954, while at the SELF-REALIZATION FELLOWSHIP, founded by Paramahansa YOGANANDA, she experienced a vision of Swami SHIVANANDA SARASWATI. Feeling compelled by this vision, she traveled to RISHIKESH, India, in 1955 to meet and study with the swami. After only a few months, Swami Shivananda gave her MANTRA initiation and gave her the name Swami Shivananda Radha. From that moment forward, she devoted herself completely to studying Indian wisdom and introducing what she had learned to the West. While in Rishikesh, she encountered the eternal yogi BABAJI, the famous guru in Yogananda's line of KRIYA YOGA gurus, and received an intense experience of light and expanded consciousness.

After six months in Rishikesh, Swami Radha returned to Canada at the request of her guru. In 1956 she formed the Shivananda Ashram in Vancouver, British Columbia, which was later to become the Yasodhara Ashram in Kootenay Bay, British Columbia. The ashram has served as a major center in the West for the teaching of KUNDALINI practices and has remained independent of the various branches of Shivananda's Divine Life Society.

Swami Radha's teachings rely on practical techniques that make spirituality accessible to modern everyday life. Kundalini and other forms of yogic practice are used to direct individuals toward holistic development and independence. Radha taught what she learned from encounters with Babaji; her methods used visualized healing and divine energy. She often merged yogic teachings with Western psychology and symbolism, effecting an understanding between the Eastern and Western mind.

The Yasodhara Ashram Society publishes an internationally recognized yoga magazine called *Ascent,* which Swami Radha instituted in 1969. Timeless Books publishing company was established by Radha in 1978. Located today in Spokane, Washington, Timeless Books publishes works on kundalini, MEDITATION, mantras, and dream analysis.

In 1992, Swami Radha oversaw the completion of the Temple of Divine Light Dedicated to All Religions located in Kootenay Bay. She also founded the Association for the Development of Human Potential, dedicated to helping individuals achieve their spiritual path. Over 100 members have joined the Yasodhara Ashram Society with affiliated centers called Radha houses located throughout Europe and North America. The centers serve as a continuing resource for Swami Radha's teachings.

Further reading: Julie McKay, *Glimpses of a Mystical Affair: Spiritual Experiences of Swami Sivananda Radha* (Spokane, Wash.: Timeless Books, 1996); Swami Sivananda Radha, *Hatha Yoga: The Hidden Language: Symbols, Secrets and Metaphor* (Spokane, Wash.: Timeless Books, 1995); ———, *Kundalini Yoga for the West: A Foundation for Character Building, Courage, and Awareness* (Spokane, Wash.: Timeless Books, 1993); ———, *Mantras: Words of Power* (Spokane, Wash.: Timeless Books, 1994); ———, *Realities of the Dreaming Mind* (Spokane, Wash.: Timeless Books, 1994).

Radhakrishnan, Sarvepalli (1888–1975)
philosopher and political figure

Sarvepalli Radhakrishnan was one of the great philosophers and thinkers of modern India. He wrote prolifically and held distinguished academic positions in both the East and the West. As was the case for many of his compatriots, he participated in the movement for India's independence and held several distinguished positions in the new government of independent India, including the post of president of India.

Sarvepalli Radhakrishnan was born on September 5, 1888, at Tiruttani, near Madras (Chennai), in South India. His early years were spent there and in Tirupati, both famous as pilgrimage centers. As was the custom, he married young, at the age of 16; he and his wife, Sivakamuamma, had five daughters and one son. He graduated with a master's degree in arts from Madras Christian College in 1908. In partial fulfillment of his M.A. degree, Radhakrishnan wrote a thesis, *The Ethics of the Vedanta and Its Metaphysical Presuppositions*, which was a reply to the charge that the Vedanta system had no room for ethics. This thesis was immediately published as a book, when he was still only 20 years old.

In 1909, Radhakrishnan took a position in the Department of Philosophy at the Madras Presidency College. In 1918, he was appointed professor of philosophy in the University of Mysore. Three years later, he was appointed to the most important philosophy chair in India, King George V Chair of Mental and Moral Science in the University of Calcutta (Kolkata).

Radhakrishnan represented the University of Calcutta at the Congress of the Universities of the British Empire in June 1926 and the International Congress of Philosophy at Harvard University. In 1929, he took a post at Manchester College, Oxford, and from 1936 to 1939 served as Spalding Professor of Eastern Religions and Ethics at Oxford. In 1939, he was elected fellow of the British Academy. From 1939 to 1948, he was the vice chancellor of Banaras Hindu University.

S. Radhakrishnan later held distinguished positions in government. He was the leader of the Indian delegation to UNESCO during 1946–52 and served as ambassador to the Soviet Union in 1949–52. He was the vice president of India from 1952 to 1962 and the president of the General Conference of UNESCO from 1952 to 1954. He held the office of the chancellor at the University of Delhi from 1953 to 1962. From May 1962 to May 1967, he was the president of India. Sarvepalli Radhakrishnan passed away on April 17, 1975. In India, September 5 (his birthday) is celebrated as Teacher's Day in his honor.

Radhakrishnan devoted his life to making India's philosophical and religious riches known to the world. As had the great ACHARYAS of VEDANTA before him, he translated and commented on the UPANISHADS, VEDANTA SUTRA, and BHAGAVAD GITA; all of those works remain in print.

Radhakrishnan, by training, was the rare philosopher who could genuinely appreciate and compare Eastern and Western philosophy. In nearly every book he wrote he included detailed comparisons of various philosophical views, with the understanding that all spiritual paths have certain commonalities at their core. Part of his mission was to assess and evaluate both traditions on their own terms. He always remained, however, a true student of the Vedanta and saw the limits of approaches that do not at some point transcend the rational.

As did his compatriot MOHANDAS KARAMCHAND GANDHI, Radhakrishnan believed in an India that was spiritually aware and grounded in its ancient spirituality, but not bound by inherited social conventions destructive of freedom and justice. As others did, he criticized Indian traditions such as the caste system and customs that degraded women, and he fought to establish a pluralistic and democratic society that would fulfill the highest ideals of Indian tradition.

Further reading: Sudarshan Agarwal, ed., *Sarvepalli Radhakrishnan: A Commemorative Volume, 1888–1988* (New Delhi: Prentice Hall of India, 1988); Anjan Kumar Banerji, ed., *Sarvepalli Radhakrishnan: A Centenary Tribute* (Varanasi: Banaras Hindu University, 1991–92); S. S. Rama Rao Pappu, ed., *New Essays in the Philosophy of Sarvepalli Radhakrishnan* (Delhi: Sri Satguru, 1995); Glyn Richards, ed., *A Source-Book of Modern Hinduism* (London: Curzon Press, 1985); Paul Arthur Schilpp, ed., *The Philosophy of Sarvepalli Radhakrishnan* (LaSalle, Ill.: Open Court, 1991).

Radhasoami Movement (est. 1861)

The Radhasoami Movement began in Agra, India, in the 1860s with the teachings of Swami Shiv Dayal Singh. He himself reflected a variety of Hindu influences, including devotion to KABIR, SIKHISM, NATH YOGA, and the Vaishnavite tradition. Each of these emphasized the importance of sacred words and the guidance of a spiritual master in transforming the self.

Singh became known as Soamiji Maharaj, because he was believed to be the incarnation of the Supreme Being Radhasoami Dayal (or Merciful Radhasoami). In 1861, Shiv Dayal Singh began holding *satsangs* (gatherings) in Agra, preaching *Radhasoami* as the true name of God. Although Singh himself was greatly influenced by Guru NANAK, the founding teacher of Sikhism, the Radhasoami movement is not to be understood as an offshoot of Sikhism. It is often considered heretical by orthodox Sikhs because it does not adhere to the Adi Granth, the Sikh scripture, as the only guru. Orthodox Hindus treat the movement with suspicion because of its disregard of caste.

The Radhasoami tradition blends progressive leadership with esoteric beliefs and spiritual practices, a contradiction that gives this movement a unique personality. Radhasoamis practice a type of yogic meditation known as *surat-shabd* (spirit-sound), which they believe is based on scientific principles alone, not faith. The experience of *shabd*, or sound current, is an internally heard vibration from God that allows for spiritual evolution. The movement accepts a hierarchy of leadership with one major teacher in charge at all times; a Sant Sat Guru is considered to be a human being who has taken birth from the highest spiritual plane and has reached an exalted state by practice of *surat-sabd* yoga. A Sadguru is next in this structure, having received understanding from the Sant Sat Guru and practice of *surat-sabd* yoga. A Satsangi is a follower who learns the practice of *surat-sabd* yoga under the direction of a Sadguru.

Singh's students were mostly members of the urban merchant caste community, both householders and ascetics. After his death in 1878, there were many splits in the movement due to the lack of a clearly established method for selecting a successor. The succeeding masters gave birth to over 20 Radhasoami lineages, most of which have disappeared. Today the most famous branches include Radhasoami Agra, Radhasoami Dayal Bagh, and Radhasoami Beas.

Radhasoami Agra occupies the original site at Soami Bagh in Agra, where a memorial shrine for the founder, Soamiji Maharaj, has been in construction since 1904. Soamiji Maharaj's fourth successor, Babuji Maharaj, died in 1949, leaving the community to await the coming of the sixth Sant Sat Guru. A spacious residential colony and institution are administered by the movement's Central Administrative Council, which was originally established in 1902 by Maharaj Saheb (second successor).

The Dayal Bagh branch was founded by Kamta Prasad Sinha at Ghazipur in 1907. In 1913 Sinha's successor, Anand Swarup, moved the organization's headquarters to Agra, directly across from Soami Bagh. The two communities have remained separate, each maintaining a large residential colony, shops, post office, and bank. *Satsangs* (gatherings) are held every evening, drawing crowds in the hundreds.

The Beas branch was created in 1892 under Baba Jaimal Singh and is located in Punjab. Further splits in this group have produced the Ruhani Satsang founded by Kirpal SINGH, known as Kirpal Light Satsang; the movement became popular in the United States under the leadership of Kirpal's successor, Thakar Singh. The colony at Beas is a utopian city unto itself and draws thousands of attendees annually. *Satsangs* of this group gather near the Beas River and in Delhi and Bombay with thousands of people in attendance.

The movement at large claims over 1 million initiates in South Asia and tens of thousands more throughout the rest of the world.

See also SANT MAT MOVEMENT.

Further reading: Mark Juergensmeyer, *Radhasoami Reality: The Logic of a Modern Faith* (Princeton, N.J.: Princeton University Press, 1991); Om Prakash Kaushal, *The Radha Soami Movement: 1891–1997* (Jalandhar: ABS Publications, n.d.); David Christopher Lane, *The Radhasoami Tradition: A Critical History of Guru Successorship* (New York: Garland, 1992).

rajas   *See* GUNA.

rajasuya

The *rajasuya* was an important VEDIC ritual used for the installation of a king (*raja*). It proclaimed the sovereignty of the king and invoked the fealty of his subjects. A number of SOMA offerings were made that could take as long as two years to complete. The king would take symbolic steps in four directions to assure sovereignty everywhere. He would ride a chariot about and shoot at a mockup of a rival, to show his kingly prowess. The

rite ended with a throw of the dice; the winning throw would assure the king's good luck in the future. A losing throw would make him cautious in his rule.

Further reading: Jan Gonda, *Ancient Indian Kingship from a Religious Point of View* (Leiden: E. J. Brill, 1969); J. C. Heesterman, *The Ancient Royal Consecration: The Rajasuya Described According to the Yajus Texts and Annotated* (Gravenhage: Mouton, 1957).

raja yoga   *See* YOGA SUTRA.

Rajneesh, Bhagwan Sri (1931–1990) *guru who taught a syncretic path to enlightenment*

Sri Bhagwan Rajneesh was a controversial guru whose syncretic teachings and antinomian philosophy attracted a wide following in India and the United States. Legal problems eventually led to expulsion from the United States.

Born Rajneesh Chandra Mohan on December 11, 1931, in Kuchwara, a small village in central India, Rajneesh was the eldest of 12 children. His parents, Swami Devateerth Bharti and Ma Amrit Saraswati, practiced JAINISM, and Rajneesh remained a strict vegetarian throughout his life in consonance with Jain teachings. Interested since childhood in philosophical questions and the matter of death, he developed critical skills and studied philosophy at Jabalrur University. After receiving a master's degree in philosophy he taught for several years at Madhya State University.

In 1966, Rajneesh received enlightenment and began to travel throughout India instructing students and gaining a following. From 1969 to 1974 he taught at Mount ABU in Rajasthan. In 1974 he opened the Rajneesh Ashram in Poona. Here many Americans and other Western devotees attended his *satsangs* (gatherings) and lived in residence. Some have estimated that 50,000 sought enlightenment with him in Poona. In 1981, he fled Poona because of tax evasion charges and opened an ASHRAM on the 65,000-acre Big Muddy Ranch near Antelope, Oregon, in the United States, which he named Rajneeshpuram. Trouble dogged the ashram, including charges of poisoning, arms stockpiling, and antinomian sexual practices among top aides, although not by Rajneesh himself. The ashram was closed and Rajneesh sought sanctuary in North Carolina but was arrested there for visa violations. He was given a suspended sentence and a fine on condition that he leave the United States. He returned to Poona, where his health continued to fail. Here he abandoned the name of Rajneesh and adopted Osho, a name derived from the expression *oceanic experience* coined by William James. He died in Poona on January 19, 1990.

Rajneesh was well versed in the scriptures and teachings of many world religions. He created a syncretic spiritual path that combined elements of Hinduism, Jainism, Buddhism, Taoism, Christianity, Greek philosophy, humanistic psychology, and modern forms of therapy and meditation. Basically he taught the non-dualism of ADVAITA Hinduism, believing that all reality is one in essence. Consistently with *advaita,* he taught that souls experience REINCARNATION until they receive enlightenment and the realization of the God that is within each person.

He was known as the "sex guru" because he espoused open sex and freedom from inhibitions. He initiated his disciplines into "neo-*sannyas*" that did not require the total renunciation of traditional Hindu *sannyas.* Men were given the title *Swami* and women were called *Ma.* He favored dismantling the nuclear family and wanted it replaced with alternate forms of community and methods of child care. Prior to 1985, disciples wore red robes and a *mala* (necklace) of 108 beads with a picture of Rajneesh attached.

The movement at its peak claimed about 200,000 members and 600 centers around the world. It was targeted by anticult groups as an evil organization bent on mind control. Before his death, Osho appointed a group of 21 individuals to administer the meditation resort in Poona and the organization. They now operate 20 meditation centers worldwide and publish the *On Line Osho Times* newsletter. The current organization, Osho International, sponsors a number of Web sites and local communities.

Further reading: James S. Gordon, *The Golden Guru* (Lexington, Mass.: Stephen Green Press, 1987); Osho, *Autobiography of a Spiritually Incorrect Mystic* (New York: St. Martin's Press, 2000); ———, *Meditation: The First and Last Freedom* (New York: St. Martin's Press, 1997); Bhagwan Sri Rajneesh, *Words Like Fire* (San Francisco: Harper & Row, 1976).

Rakshabandhan (Rakhibandhan)

The Raksabandhan festival, which takes place on the full Moon of the lunar month of Shravana (July–August), is one of the most popular in India. On this day sisters tie an amulet of red or yellow threads on their brother's wrists to guard them for the year. If they are more learned, they may utter a well-known SANSKRIT MANTRA. The brothers then offer them presents. The observance is said to have originated after INDRA, king of the gods, was defeated in battle by the *asuras,* or antigods. It is said that he was able to regain his sovereignty when his wife, Shaci, put an amulet on his hand after performing some austerities.

Further reading: Stanley A. Freed and Ruth S. Freed, *Hindu Festivals in a North Indian Village,* (Seattle: University of Washington Press, 1998); C. J. Fuller, *The Camphor Flame: Popular Hinduism and Society in India* (Princeton, N.J.: Princeton University Press, 1992); Anita Ganeri, *Hindu Festivals throughout the Year* (Mankato, Minn.: Smart Apple Media, 2003).

Rama (Ram)

Rama is a god worshipped over all of India. He is considered to be an AVATAR or descended form of Lord VISHNU. Rama's full story is told in the RAMAYANA epic.

In that famous epic, the gods ask Vishnu to incarnate in the world as a man, in order to kill the demon Ravana, who was tormenting all the worlds. Ravana has a boon that he cannot be killed by any god or demon, but, in his arrogance, he never imagines he can be killed by a human. Thus the avatar of Rama is arranged.

Rama is born to Dasharatha, king of AYODHYA, and his wife, Kaushalya. In his youth Rama is sent to the sage Vishvamitra's hermitage to help defend it from beings who are trying to disrupt the sacred Vedic rites. There he slays the female being Tataka who was tormenting the sages. He receives certain celestial weapons and is obliged to kill the demons Marica and Subahu.

Rama later wins a contest to bend the bow of SHIVA; as his prize he wins the hand of SITA, daughter of the king of VIDEHA. In Ayodhya another wife of Dasharatha, Kaikeyi, plots to have her son, Bharata, put on the throne in place of Rama. As a result Rama is forced into exile for 14 years. His wife, Sita, and his brother, Lakshmana, follow him.

Rama, an incarnation of Vishnu, with his wife, Sita (right), and his brother, Lakshmana (left) (Institute for the Study of American Religion, Santa Barbara, California)

During his exile Rama's wife, Sita, is abducted by the demon king Ravana and taken to the island of Lanka. Making friends with a group of monkeys, including the faithful HANUMAN, Rama carries out his divine duty in defeating Ravana and winning back his wife. When he doubts her faithfulness, Sita passes a trial by fire. She is taken back, and the rule of Rama begins in all its perfection. Some versions of the Ramayana, such as the Kambaramayanam in Tamil, end at this point.

In other versions the story continues. New questions are raised concerning Sita's faithfulness, and Rama has his brother Lakshmana take her to the forest. He does not realize that she is pregnant with twins. Rama's sons Kusha and Lava are born in the forest ASHRAM of Valmiki. Eventually, they end up in a war with Rama's troops and defeat them.

At this point Rama realizes he has sons and wants Sita to return to live with him. She goes before him and in disgust at her two rejections asks the Earth to swallow her up. Rama continues his just rule and dies, as all avatars must, being human forms of the divinity. Rama is worshipped throughout India and celebrated in regional folklore and high culture alike. Sita is always included, and Hanuman and Lakshmana are rarely omitted in any iconographic or pictorial presentation.

Further reading: Ashok K. Banker, *Prince of Ayodhya* (New York: Time Warner Book Group, 2004); P. Bannerjee, *Rama in Indian Literature, Art and Thought*, 2 vols. (Delhi: Sundeep Prakashan, 1986); Stuart Blackburn, *Inside the Drama-House: Rama Stories and the Shadow Puppets in South India* (Berkeley: University of California Press, 1996); J. L. Brockington, *Righteous Rama: The Evolution of an Epic* (Delhi: Oxford University Press, 1985); Vidya Dehejia, ed., *Legend of Rama: Artistic Visions* (Bombay: Marg, 1994); Frank Whaling, *The Rise of the Religious Significance of Rama* (Delhi: Motilal Banarsidass, 1980).

Rama, Swami   *See* HIMALAYAN INTERNATIONAL INSTITUTE.

Ramacharaka, Yogi (1862–1932) *yoga popularizer*

The American-born Yogi Ramacharaka was a popular author in the New Thought movement in the United States. He later became the first major popularizer of Hindu thought in America.

Born in Baltimore, Maryland, to William and Emma Atkinson, William Walker Atkinson was an important and influential figure in the early days of the New Thought movement, which included a number of religious organizations devoted to the application of metaphysical principles to healing. He married Margaret Foster Black of Beverley, New Jersey, in 1889 and they had two children. He pursued a business career from 1882 onward, and in 1894 he was admitted as an attorney to the Pennsylvania Bar. The pressures of his profession caused a complete physical and mental breakdown and financial disaster. He sought healing, and in the late 1880s, he discovered New Thought, through which he attained health, mental vigor, and prosperity. By the early 1890s Chicago had become a major center for New Thought, mainly through the work of Emma Curtis Hopkins, and Atkinson decided to move there, where he became an active promoter of the movement as an editor and author.

In 1889 Atkinson's article "A Mental Science Catechism" appeared in Charles Fillmore's new periodical, *Modern Thought*. In 1900, he became editor of *Suggestion,* a New Thought periodical, and he continued to write for and edit another periodical, *New Thought*. He founded a Psychic Club and the Atkinson School of Mental Science and became a prominent metaphysical writer, publishing ten books on psychic, occult, and New Thought topics between 1901 and 1911. His Mental Science included lessons in personal magnetism, psychic influence, thought-force, concentration, will-power, and practical Mental Science.

While performing his *New Thought* editorial job, Atkinson became interested in Hinduism. He met a pupil of the late Yogi Ramacharaka, Baba BHARATI, who had become acquainted with Atkinson's writings. Atkinson and Bharati shared similar ideas. They collaborated, and with Bharati providing the material and Atkinson the writing talent, they wrote a series of books, which they attributed to Yogi Ramacharaka as a measure of their respect. Beginning in 1903, Atkinson eventually wrote 13 books under this pseudonym. All the titles were published by the Yogi Publication Society in Chicago; they reached a wider audience than Atkinson's New Thought works ever had. All of his books on yoga are still in print; their continued popularity is a credit to both Baba Bharati and Atkinson.

Under the name Yogi Ramacharaka, Atkinson became the first popularizer of Hindu thought and practice in the United States. He also continued his career as an attorney, being admitted to the Illinois Bar in 1903, and he continued to write well-received books on New Thought. In 1916 he began writing articles for Elizabeth Towne's magazine *The Nautilus,* and from 1916 to 1919 he edited the journal *Advanced Thought.* For a time he was honorary president of the International New Thought Alliance.

William Walker Atkinson died on November 22, 1932, in California.

Further reading: William Walker Atkinson [Yogi Ramacharaka], *Dynamic Thought* (Los Angeles: Segnogram, 1906); ———, *Hatha Yoga* (Chicago: Yogi Publication Society, 1931); ———, *The Mastery of Being* (Holyoke, Mass.: Elizabeth Towne, 1911); ———, *Raja Yoga* (Chicago: Yogi Publication Society, 1905).

Ramakrishna, Sri (1836–1886) *influential mystic and priest of goddess Kali*

Recognized as one of the greatest spiritual geniuses of modern Hinduism, Sri Ramakrishna was influential through his own example and through the work of his disciple Swami VIVEKANANDA.

Sri Ramakrishna (1836–1886), Bengali mystic and famous exponent of universal religion *(Courtesy Vedanta Society, San Francisco)*

Sri Ramakrishna was born on February 18, 1836, as Gadadhar Chattopadhyay to a poor Bengali BRAHMIN family. He had his first spiritual experience at the age of six or seven and entered into trancelike states throughout his childhood. He neglected his studies, preferring to spend his time in solitary MEDITATION, singing, and performing of Hindu stories. For much of his life he served as priest at the KALI Temple at Dakshineshwar near Calcutta, living a life of renunciation, but he stopped performing priestly functions when the "divine madness" took over his conscious awareness.

Sri Ramakrishna married SARADA DEVI, whom he viewed as the GODDESS incarnate; she looked upon her husband as her GURU, or spiritual teacher. He did not found a movement or establish an organization, although he was the inspiration of a generation of Indian Hindus. His influence spread throughout the world through the VEDANTA SOCIETIES/RAMAKRISHNA MATH AND MISSION, founded by Swami Vivekananda.

He remained devoted to the goddess Kali throughout his life, and he was also initiated into tantric practice (see TANTRISM). His teacher Tota Puri taught him ADVAITA VEDANTA and the practice of absorption in the formless, which he quickly achieved. His whole life was an uninterrupted contemplation and union with God. His life and teaching appeal to seekers in all religions, as he taught that the revelation of God can take place at all times and that God-realization is not the monopoly of any one religion or faith. He took up various disciplines associated with other religions, specifically Christianity and Islam, and taught that all paths lead to the same God-realization. His message of the harmony of religions was based on unity in diversity and a fellowship of religions based on their common goal of God-consciousness. Sri Ramakrishna died on August 16, 1886.

His famous disciple Swami Vivekananda founded the Ramakrishna Math and Mission at Belur Math, near Calcutta (Kolkata) to propagate the teachings of his guru. Sarada Devi, his widow, also began to assert the leadership role that Ramakrishna had specified for her, and she became known as the mother of the movement that Ramakrishna inspired. These missions offer spiritual, medical, and educational services to the people of India. Outside India, in 18 countries on five continents, the same organization is known as the Vedanta Society and is headed by swamis initiated and trained at Belur Math.

Further reading: Swami Ghanananda, *Sri Ramakrishna and His Unique Message* (London: Ramakrishna Vedanta Centre, 1937); Christopher Isherwood, *Ramakrishna and His Disciples* (Calcutta: *advaita* Ashrama, 1965); Sri Ramakrishna, *The Gospel of Sri Ramakrishna.* Translated by Swami Nikhilananda (New York: Vedanta Society, 1907); Romain Rolland, *The Life of Sri Ramakrishna* (Calcutta: *advaita* Ashrama, 1944).

Ramakrishna Math and Mission   *See* VEDANTA SOCIETIES/RAMAKRISHNA MATH AND MISSION.

Ramana Maharshi (1879–1950) advaita
Vedanta teacher and mystic

Ramana Maharshi was a GURU of international renown from southern India who taught the nondual philosophy of ADVAITA VEDANTA.

Ramana was born on December 30, 1879, as Venkataraman Ayyar at Tiruchuli near Madurai

Ramana Maharshi (1879–1950), widely recognized teacher, mystic, and foremost exemplar of *advaita* (nondual) consciousness *(Courtesy Sri Ramanashramam, Tiruvannamalai, Tamil Nadu)*

in the state of Tamil Nadu. He was the son of Shundaram Ayyar, a scribe and country lawyer. The family was religious, giving ritual offerings to the family deity and visiting temples. As a child, Ramana was largely uninterested in school; throughout his life he showed a marked inclination toward introspection and self-analysis.

In 1896, at age 17 he entered an altered state of consciousness that had a profound effect on him. He experienced what he understood to be his own death and return to life. Without any training by a teacher or any personal discipline, he attained a profound experience of the true Self and realized that the body dies but consciousness is not touched by death. He saw the real "I" as immortal consciousness, as a powerful living truth experienced directly. Thereafter, all attention was drawn to this "I" or Self and he remained conscious of his identity with the absolute at all times. All fear of death was permanently extinguished.

Ramana ran away from home to the holy mountain Arunachala near Tiruvannamalai. He spent 10 years in silent Self-absorption at the temple there, at the foot of the mountain, and in various caves on the mountain. Throughout these years he remained silent and maintained disciplines of spiritual purification and nonattachment. Against the pleas of his family, he refused to return home. His absorption in higher consciousness was so deep that he neglected care of his body and was at times famished and chewed by insects. Disciples began to gather around him to take care of his physical needs and to gain awareness of his non-dual state of consciousness. His disciples gave him sacred books, and he became conversant with the religious traditions of South India.

When Ramana broke his silence, he responded to questions about Self-consciousness. His teaching was given largely through conversations with guests who visited him on the mountain, where his ASHRAM began to develop. His advice to those who sought SELF-REALIZATION was to direct them to the question "Who am I?"—a self-inquiry that he insisted be used tirelessly as each student discovered deeper and deeper levels of awareness. The aim of this inquiry was for each person to find an awareness of non-duality, in which the oneness of the Self and cosmos could be perceived. He taught that a person who is not attached to the results of action can live in the world as an actor who plays a role in a drama but is immune to emotional disturbance, because the person realizes that action is only play acting on the stage of life.

Ramana remained at Arunachala for the duration of his life, welcoming visitors from East and West, while becoming a living example of non-dual consciousness. He died there of cancer on April 14, 1950, sitting in a lotus position.

The Ramanashramam exists today as a sanctuary that houses Ramana's grave, his cave residence, and accommodation for many visitors.

Further reading: Paul Brunton, *A Search in Secret India* (Bombay: B. I., 1934); David Godman, *Be As You Are: The Teachings of Sri Ramana Maharshi* (New York: Penguin, 1989); Arthur Osbourne, *Ramana Maharshi and the Path of Self-Knowledge* (New York: S. Weiser, 1970); Arthur Osbourne, ed., *The Collected Works of Ramana Maharshi* (New York: Samuel Weiser, 1970); *Talks with Sri Ramana Maharshi* (Turuvannamalai: Sri Ramanashramam, 1984).

Rama Navami

Rama Navami is a special day of worship of Lord RAMA. It takes place on the ninth day of the bright half of the lunar month Chaitra (April–May), considered the birthday of Lord RAMA; he was born at noon. All devotees of Rama must perform this worship, and others may do it optionally. It is accompanied by a vow of fasting beginning the previous night. If one performs the veneration properly, one is said to have one's sins destroyed and may even acquire MOKSHA or release from birth and rebirth.

Rama Navami is a popular observance. After a night of fasting, the following day the devotee performs worship before an image of Rama and makes a fire offering for Rama in a small specially created shrine; the celebration continues with a *japa*, or repetition of the MANTRA to Rama, the second night. Once the observance is complete the image is given to a learned BRAHMIN.

Only the most orthodox perform the full ritual these days. It is, however, observed en masse in places significant for Rama such as AYODHYA and Rameshvaram.

Further reading: C. J. Fuller, *The Camphor Flame: Popular Hinduism and Society in India* (Princeton, N.J.: Princeton University Press, 1992); Anita Ganeri, *Hindu Festivals Throughout the Year* (Mankato, Minn.: Smart Apple Media, 2003); Swami Harshananda, *Hindu Festivals and Sacred Days* (Bangalore: Ramakrishna Math, 1994).

Ramanuja (Ramanujacharya) (1077–1157 C.E.) (dated by his tradition from 1017 to 1137) *philosopher of Vedanta*

Ramanuja was the founder of the philosophical school known as Vishistadvaita or "special non-dualism."

Ramanuja was born in the city of KANCHIPURAM near present-day Chennai (Madras). His father was a Vedic BRAHMIN who was known as a brilliant student of the SANSKRIT scriptures. His first GURU, Yadava Prakasha, had a system that was not to the liking of this student genius. It soon became clear that he would develop his own system, which would challenge that of his teacher. Ramanuja's guru is said to have arranged to have him killed, while luring him on a PILGRIMAGE to the holy city of BENARES (Varanasi) on the GANGES. Ramanuja was miraculously saved and eventually his guru bowed to his feet and accepted Ramunuja himself as his teacher.

Ramanuja's system of VEDANTA combines the view of a unitary divinity found in the UPANISHADS with the theism of later Hinduism. For Ramanuja the divinity is endowed with innumerable auspicious attributes, as opposed to the view of SHAN-

KARA, who saw the ultimate reality or BRAHMAN as completely beyond characteristics or characterization. Where as Shankara's *brahman* was an inert, transcendental reality upon which the world was lain as a false conception, Ramanuja's *brahman* was the Lord VISNHU, who was the soul to the universe, which was seen as his body.

Along with many philosophic works in Sanskrit, Ramanuja wrote incisive Sanskrit commentaries on the BRAHMA SUTRAS and the BHAGAVAD GITA in his effort to refute the earlier and well-accepted school of Shankara. In his work, he validated the mystical vision of the Vaishnavite saints of Tamil Nadu, the ALVARS, whose Tamil songs were later collected as the main text for Tamil Vaishnavites, the *Nalayiradivyaprabandham*.

The movement in India that follows the teachings of Ramanuja and the Alvars is known as Sri Vaishnavism. It is a tradition of temple worship, in which both Tamil and Sanskrit scriptures are recited in the temples. The most important site for this tradition is the temple to Lord Ranganatha (Vishnu) at Shrirangam in Tamil Nadu. There is a secondary shrine in the smaller community of Sri Vaishnavites at Melkote in Karnataka.

Further reading: John Carman, *The Theology of Ramanuja: An Essay in Interreligious Understanding* (New Haven, Conn.: Yale University Press, 1974); Julius J. Lipner, *The Face of Truth: A Study of Mean and Metaphysics in the Vedantic Theology of Ramanuja* (Houndmills, England: Macmillan, 1986); Swami Tapasyananda, *Bhakti Schools of Vedanta* (Madras: Sri Ramakrishna Math, n.d.); P. B. Vidyarthi, *Divine Personality and Human Life in Ramanuja* (New Delhi: Oriental, 1978).

Rama Tirtha, Swami (1873–1906) *devotee of Krishna and Vedanta philosophy*

In his brief life, Swami Rama Tirtha managed to spread the teaching of Vedanta philosophy and spirituality in India and around the world.

Gossain Tirtha Rama was born at Murariwala, a village in the district of Gujranwala in the Punjab, to a family of Gosain BRAHMINS, distant descendants of the famous author of the RAMAYANA, Gosain TULSIDAS. When he was only a few days old his mother died and young Rama was reared by his father, his aunt, and his elder brother, Gossain Gurudas. Throughout his childhood he demonstrated unusual intelligence, a contemplative nature, and a love of solitude. He listened to recitations of scripture and discussed spiritual topics with religious teachers. At age 10, Rama was put under the care of his father's friend Bhakta Dhana Rama, a teacher who taught simplicity and purity to the young Rama.

A good student, Rama demonstrated a love of mathematics and achieved high marks at the undergraduate and master's levels. After completing college, he served as professor of mathematics at Forman Christian College in Lahore and, for a short time, reader at Lahore Oriental College. He began to read the BHAGAVAD GITA and became an ardent devotee (*bhakta*) of Lord KRISHNA. He could read Persian, English, Hindi, Urdu, and SANSKRIT literature. He studied VEDANTA with Sri Madhava Tirtha of the Dwaraka Math. His meeting with the famous Swami VIVEKANANDA in Lahore was decisive in turning Rama toward the vow of SANNYAS (renunciation) and wearing of the ochre robe.

In 1900, he went to Brahmapuri, on the banks of the GANGES near RISHIKESH in the foothills of the Himalayas, to become a forest dweller with his wife, his two children, and a few others. Because of ill health, his wife soon left the forest with one of the children. In the forest, he realized the all-inclusive bliss of SATCHITANANDA, or SELF-REALIZATION. Then he returned to the plains to teach Vedanta. He traveled to Japan, America, and Egypt and spent a year and a half in San Francisco, where he founded the Hermetic Brotherhood, dedicated to the study of Vedanta. In St. Louis, he spoke at the Religious League of the St. Louis Exhibition. Hailed as a torch of divine knowledge, he lectured in Christian churches all over the United States.

On his return to India, he continued to teach in the plains, but his health grew worse. He returned to the Himalayas and took residence at Vasishtha Ashram, where he died at age 33 on the banks of the Ganges River on October 17, 1906.

Considered a saint of modern India, Swami Rama taught the oneness and all-pervasive nature of God. He began as a devotee of BHAKTI YOGA, devoted to the image of Krishna, but he became more and more an ascetic and mystic who experienced the non-dual nature of reality consistent with Vedanta.

Under the guidance of a direct disciple of Swami Rama, Sri R. S. Narayana Swami, the Rama Tirtha Publication League was established in Lucknow; it has published most of Swami Rama's writings in several volumes.

Further reading: Rama Tirtha Publication League, *Swami Rama: Various Aspects of His Life by the Eminent Scholars of India* (Lucknow: Dayal Printing Works, 1939); Swami Rama Tirtha, *In Woods of God-Realization: The Complete Works of Rama Tirtha*, 19 vols. (Lucknow: Rama Tirtha Publication League, 1909–48).

Ramayana

The Ramayana, the story of the "adventures" (*ayana*) of RAMA, is one of the two great Hindu epics. It was composed originally in SANSKRIT in an epic of about 25,000 verses. The author, VALMIKI, is called the "first poet" of India and the Ramayana is considered the first long poem composed by humans (as opposed to the VEDAS, which are much older and are considered to be eternal and uncreated).

The SANSKRIT Ramayana dates to 600 to 400 B.C.E. Told in seven chapters, the story is in brief as follows: the gods ask VISHNU to take a human incarnation in order to fight the demon king RAVANA, who gained powers by extreme austerities and cannot be defeated by a god. Vishnu agrees to incarnate as RAMA. Rama is born to King Dasharatha and his wife, Kaushalya. Dasharatha has three other sons: Bharata, Lakshmana, and Shatrughna.

While Dasharatha is joyfully preparing to retire from the world and leave the kingdom to his virtuous oldest son Rama, a second wife of his, Kaikeyi, demands, as the fulfillment of a boon he had given her, that her own son, Bharata, be raised to the throne and that Rama be exiled in the forest for 14 years. Dasharatha, true to his word, must grant her wish, but he dies soon after of a broken heart. Rama, the most obedient of sons, accepts his father's request with equanimity and prepares to go to the forest. Lakshmana, his younger brother, will go with him. Sita, his wife, is asked to stay behind, as travel in the forest will involve great travail, but she argues strongly that she wants to be at her husband's side. Rama relents and allows her to go with him.

As they enter the forest, they are found by Bharata. Bharata insists he has no desire for the kingdom and asks that Rama give him his sandals to put on the throne during his absence, as a sign that it is Rama who is king. Wandering in the forest, Rama and Lakshmana meet Shurpanakha, sister of the demon king Ravana. She becomes smitten with Rama and changes her horrific form into that of a beautiful maiden.

Rama sees through Shurpanakha's guise, but to play a joke on his brother he tells her that while he himself is married, Lakshmana is not. When she approaches Lakshmana with passion, Lakshmana enters into the joke by sending her back to Rama, saying he is unworthy of her. Shurpanakha then returns to Rama and jealously tries to kill Sita. At this Lakshmana cuts off her nose and ears.

Eventually, Surpanakha persuades her brother Ravana to try to steal Sita away from Rama. Ravana has the demon Maricha take the form of a golden deer. When Rama chases after the deer, by means of ruses Ravana carries off Sita in his flying chariot and takes her to his island kingdom of Lanka.

In a frantic search for Sita, Rama and Lakshmana befriend the monkey Sugriva and his friends, including the virtuous and faithful HANUMAN. Hanuman is sent to Lanka to reconnoiter. He finds Sita but is caught by the demon Rakshasas. They put a cloth on his tail and set it afire, but he escapes and burns Lanka by jumping from building to building with his tail in flames.

Hanuman returns to Rama, and they make a plan to defeat Ravana and his demon hordes and get Sita back. They are successful and Sita returns, but Rama and others question her fidelity. She offers to undergo a trial by fire, passes the test, and joins Rama on the throne.

The last and final chapter, omitted in some vernacular versions, tells of the origin of the *rakshasas,* the demon hordes, and the history of Ravana. It also tells of Hanuman's childhood and other diverse tales. Sita's faithfulness, however, is once more questioned.

Sita is forced to flee to the forest while pregnant with Rama's two sons. She goes to live at the ashram of none other than Valmiki himself, the author of the RAMAYANA story. Some years later, while Rama is conducting an *ashva medha* (HORSE SACRIFICE), Valmiki arrives with his two disciples, Kusha and Lava, the sons of Rama. They recite the Ramayana story for Rama and he learns of their existence. He calls Sita back to court, where she admonishes him and asks the Earth to swallow her up rather than that she return to a husband who has wronged her.

The Ramayana story is an ocean from which a vast array of stories, myths, plays, and celebrations have emerged in Sanskrit and every vernacular. It is one of the central narratives of Indian culture; every region of the country has a variety of sites for pilgrimage and visitation that are connected to its characters—Rama, Lakshmana, Hanuman, and the others.

Celebrated versions of the Ramayana have been written in nearly every Indian language, including the Islamic-associated Urdu. Among such notable and beloved vernacular Ramayanas are the Krittivas Ramayana in Bengali, the Tulsidas Ramcaritmanas in Old Hindi, the Tamil Kambaramayanam, the Pampa Ramayana of Nagachandra in Kannada, Ranganatha's Ramayana in Telugu, and the Vilanka Ramayana in Oriya. Numerous Sanskrit versions of the story have also been composed, including the Adhyatma Ramayana and Yogavasishtha Ramayana.

Tales in Sanskrit about the Rama dynasty both before and after the events in the Ramayana have proliferated, such as *Raghuvamsha* and *Uttararamacharita*. The Jains as well tell stories of Rama, Ravana, and other characters from the Ramayana in Sanskrit and other languages. Every year in northern India the Ram Lila festival is celebrated, culminating in a grand burning of the effigies of Ravana, his son, and his brother.

The Ramayana story also traveled widely outside India. Thai and Indonesian versions are still popular.

Further reading: S. P. Bahadur, trans., *The Complete Works of Gosvami Tulsidas* (Varanasi: Prachya Prakashan, 1978–2005); J. L. Brockington, *Righteous Rama: The Evolution of an Epic* (Delhi: Oxford University Press, 1985); Harry M. Buck, *The Figure of Rama in Buddhist Cultures* (Bhubaneswar: Mayur, 1995); Robert Goldman, trans. and ed., *The Ramayana of Valmiki*, 6 vols. (Princeton, N.J.: Princeton University Press, 1984–2005); George L. Hart and Hank Heifetz, trans., *The Forest Book of Kampan* (Berkeley: University of California Press, 1988); Phillip Lutgendorf, *The Life of a Text: Performing the Ramcaritmanas of Tulsidas* (Berkeley: University of California Press, 1991); Shantilal Nagar, trans., *Jain Ramayana-Paumacariu* (Delhi: B. R., 2002); Sheldon I. Pollock, *Ramayana*, book 2, *Ayodhya* by Valmiki (New York: New York University Press, JJC Foundation, 2005); Paula Richman, ed., *Many Ramayanas: The Diversity of a Narrative Tradition in South Asia* (Berkeley: University of California Press, 1991); Paula Richman, ed., *Questioning Ramayanas: A South Asian Tradition* (Berkeley: University of California Press, 2001).

Ram Chandra, Sri Maharaj (1899–1983)
teacher of raja yoga

The boy who became Sri Ram Chandra later in life was born in Shahjahanpur, Uttar Pradesh state on April 30, 1899, into a BRAHMIN family. Following in the footsteps of his scholarly father he began his education with a particular interest in philosophy, literature, and geography. Reports indicated that he was not an outstanding scholar but could hold his own intellectually. He joined the judicial services, married, and raised children.

On July 3, 1922, he sought out Guru Sri Ram Chandra of Fategarh, who preserved and followed an ancient form of yoga called Pranahuti (divine transmission), which the younger Ram Chandra perceived to be superior to the newer methods. He himself had been practicing a form of PRANAYAMA or breathing technique for the previous seven years, but he abandoned this and adopted the spiritual practices of his new guru, who died in 1931.

Sri Ram Chandra felt that he had absorbed the teachings from his spiritual leader and was qualified to carry on his inspiration. He believed that he and his guru had spiritually merged. In 1932, he received a powerful transmission of spiritual energy from his guru. In 1944, he had a vision of white light that revealed Lord KRISHNA's true nature. He knew that his mission was to carry on the work of his master.

Sri Ram Chandra founded the Sri Ram Chandra Mission in 1945 in honor of his guru and in 1976 built an ashram in Shahjahanpur. Throughout these years he taught raja yoga and gave spiritual guidance to many.

Sri Ram Chandra Maharaj died on April 19, 1983, after many years of service to raja yoga. The lineage is preserved through his disciple Sri Parthasarathi Rajagopalachari of Madras (Chennai), who assumed the mantle at his bedside and is now the president of Sri Ram Chandra Mission. He is affectionately known as "Chariji."

Further reading: Sri Ram Chandra, *Complete Works of Ram Chandra,* Vol. 1 (Pacific Grove, Calif.: Sri Ram Chandra Mission, 1989); ———, *Down Memory Lane,* Vol. 1 (Shahjahanpur: Sri Ram Chandra Mission, 1993); ———, *Truth Eternal* (Shahjahanpur: Sri Ram Chandra Mission, 1986).

Ram Das   *See* SIKHISM.

Ramdas, Swami (1884–1963) *devotee of Ram and founder of Ananda Ashram*

The child Vittal Rao was born in 1884 at Hosdrug, in the South Indian state of Kerala, to a devout couple, Sri Balakrishna Rao and Srimata Lalita Bai. As a child, he exhibited an extraordinary luster in his eyes and considerable wit. Largely uninterested in formal schooling, he completed high school but did not pursue higher education. With his marriage in 1908 he became a householder, and he remained so until age 36. As a young husband and father, he vacillated between periods of employment as a spinning master in a cotton mill and periods of unemployment and idleness.

In 1920, in response to a number of trials and challenges in his worldly life, he began to inquire into the meaning of life and to chant the name of God, RAM. An intense spiritual transformation occurred: he realized the futility of worldly pursuits and the higher need for everlasting peace and happiness. He became convinced that God alone can give eternal peace and happiness. He decided on a life of self-surrender, as attachments to family, friends, and business dropped away. At that time, his father gave him the Ram MANTRA, *Om Sri Ram Jai Ram Jai Jai Ram,* to recite, and his detachment from worldly pursuits increased as the mantra took a place in his life. He then renounced the life of the world and became a wandering mendicant, a SADHU. He began his life of pilgrimage in December 1922, vowing to accept everything that happened as proceeding from the will of Ram alone. At Srirangam, he bathed in the CAUVERY RIVER and offered up his old white clothes to the river. He donned the ochre robes of a SANNYASI and took the name *Ramdas.* He never referred to himself in the first person again.

In 1922, he met the sage of Arunachala mountain, RAMANA MAHARSHI, and spent 20 days near Ramana in a cave there, chanting his mantra. He emerged from the cave and saw a strange light with a landscape completely changed: everything was Ram.

In 1931, after his years of traveling in faith, his devotees established Anandashram for him in Kanhangad, Kerala, where he lived with Mother KRISHNABAI, a realized saint of South India. Together they worked to improve the living conditions of the local people, founded a children's school, established a medical clinic, and formed a cooperative for weavers. They toured India together and conducted a world tour in 1954–55, with the purpose of sharing a message of universal love and service. Swami Ramdas died on August 2, 1963.

Ramdas wrote many books, all currently in print.

Further reading: Swami Ramdas, *God-Experience* (Bombay: For Anandashram by Bharatiya Vidya Bhavan, 1963); ———, *In Quest of God: The Saga of an Extraordinary Pilgrimage/Swami Ramdas* (San Diego, Calif.: Blue Dove Press, 1994); Swami Satchidananda, *The Gospel of Swami Ramdas* (Bombay: For Anandashram by Bharatiya Vidya Bhavan, 1979).

Ram Dass (1933–) *American psychologist and teacher of Hinduism*

Ram Dass was an important figure in the American counterculture of the 1970s. He drew wide public attention to yoga and Hindu spirituality and has continued his teachings since.

Richard Alpert was born in Boston, Massachusetts, on April 6, 1933, the son of a prominent corporate attorney who also served as president of the New York–New Haven Railroad and was a

Baba Ram Dass (b. 1933), popular American guru and founder of Hanuman Foundation *(Photo by Richard Alpert. Courtesy of Hanuman Foundation)*

founder of Brandeis University. Richard grew up on the New Hampshire estate of his father.

A student of psychology, Alpert received a B.A. degree in 1952 from Tufts University, an M.A. from Wesleyan University in 1954, and a Ph.D. in 1957 from Stanford University. From 1958 to 1963, Alpert taught and conducted research at the Department of Social Relations and the Graduate School of Education at Harvard University. In 1961, he first took psilocybin with his Harvard colleague Timothy Leary (1920–96) and became an integral part in the Harvard Psilocybin Project. With Leary and

Ralph Metzner, he wrote *The Psychedelic Experience,* a recapitulation of the *Tibetan Book of the Dead* intended to be a manual for establishing an appropriate setting for experiencing psychedelic drugs such as lysergic acid diethylamide (LSD), psilocybin, mescaline, and dimethyltryptamine (DMT). While at Harvard, Alpert began research into human consciousness and, with Timothy Leary, Aldous Huxley, Allen Ginsberg, and others, conducted research into LSD and other psychedelics. Because of the controversial nature of this research, Alpert and Leary were dismissed from their teaching positions at Harvard in 1963.

Alpert continued his collaboration with Leary on psychedelics. He became involved with attempts to realize a utopia as presented in *Island* by Aldous Huxley, and the *Glass Bead Game* by Hermann Hesse. He participated in utopian organizations, including the Zihuatanejo Project and the International Foundation for Internal Freedom. During the mid-1960s he lived for a while at the Millbrook estate in New York, a center for psychedelic religion, together with Leary and Swami Abhayananda (Bill Haines).

In 1967, he traveled to India, where he met Baba HARI DASS (b. 1923) and NEEM KAROLI BABA (d. 1973), both noted gurus who provided disciplined study on a spiritual path. They became role models for him and he replaced his attraction for drugs with a higher spiritual calling induced through MEDITATION and yoga. Neem Karoli Baba, also called Maharaji, gave Alpert his spiritual name *Ram Dass* (servant of God) and taught him *raja* yoga, a form of yoga that utilizes meditation as the primary means of moving from mundane reality to the invisible supersensible world of higher consciousness (SAMADHI). Ram Dass says that Neem Karoli allowed him for the first time to see his life in spiritual terms. Overall, he spent nearly two years with Neem Karoli before Neem Karoli's death in 1973. His *Miracle of Love* is a collection of stories about Neem Karoli, from the homely to the miraculous. Not a devotee of any one particular philosophy or method, Neem

Karoli tried to inculcate in others the path of love and service.

Upon returning to the United States, Ram Dass wrote his most famous book, *Be Here Now* (1971), which suggested that one can live only in the present moment. The past has vanished into history and the future is not yet here. In order to be fully present in one's life, Ram Dass advocated the simple proposition of residing in and being aware of the present moment and position in the world. Ram Dass believes that all people are on a spiritual path to enlightenment. Each has individual needs, including GURUS (teachers) of different kinds; some gurus may not be in the physical body, but meditation allows one access to the invisible world and communication with those gurus who no longer have a physical body. His book offered an alternative to psychedelics in his emphasis on gurus and spiritual pathways to guide one out of immersion in the drug culture. *Be Here Now* propelled Ram Dass into a role as a major teacher of the New Age counterculture and remains in print to the present time.

In the 1970s, Ram Dass took on a vigorous schedule of speaking, teaching, and traveling from his base in New Hampshire. Various organizations emerged around his many interests. For example, he and Bo Lozoff developed the Prison Ashram Library, which distributed literature to prison populations. It particularly taught lessons in meditation for inmates who wanted to live a life of service while incarcerated. This service has grown to include halfway houses and mental health programs.

In the mid-1970s, Ram Dass had become involved with several female gurus—Hilda Charlton (d. 1988) and Joya Santana (now known as Ma JAYA SATI BHAGAVATI of the Kashi Ashram). His interaction with them led to a spiritual crisis that he discussed in a famous *Yoga Journal* article, "Egg on My Beard." He assumed a low profile for a brief period but soon reemerged as a major writer and speaker. Before the decade was out, he had produced three important books: *The Only Dance*

There Is (1976), *Grist for the Mill* (1977), and *Journey of Awakening* (1978).

Ram Dass instituted the Hanuman Temple in Taos, New Mexico, to implement worship of HANUMAN, the god of service, and to honor his guru, Neem Karoli Baba.

In pursuit of the goals of KARMA YOGA, Ram Dass initiated several organizations devoted to service and community development. In 1974, he organized the HANUMAN FOUNDATION inspired by the devoted servant of the Hindu god RAM in the RAMAYANA, which is the organizing vehicle for Ram Dass's lectures and workshops and administers many social projects, including the Prison Ashram Project, designed to help inmates grow spiritually during incarceration, and the Living Dying Project, designed to foster conscious dying.

He is cofounder, with Larry Brilliant (b. 1946), and board member of the Seva Foundation, an international organization dedicated to relieving suffering in the world (*seva* means "service" in SANSKRIT). Seva sponsors diverse activities, including programs in India and Nepal to erase curable blindness, Guatemalan programs to restore the agricultural life of impoverished villagers, and programs in the United States to call attention to the issues of homelessness and environmental degradation.

On February 19, 1997, Ram Dass suffered a massive cerebral hemorrhagic stroke in his left brain. The stroke left him with extensive right side paralysis, expressive aphasia, and a number of recurring and threatening health problems. Since this event he has returned to a limited schedule of appearances and talks. He lives in San Anselmo, California, and Hawaii.

Mickey Lemle's documentary *Ram Dass: Fierce Grace* documents the biography of Ram Dass through friends' and family members' reminiscences and archival footage of his days of communal living. It shows the physical and psychological effects of the stroke and the spiritual lessons he has learned from his disability.

Further reading: Richard Alpert, Timothy Leary, and Ralph Metzner, *The Psychedelic Experience: A Manual Based upon the Tibetan Book of the Dead* (New York: University Books, 1964); Ram Dass, *Be Here Now* (Albuquerque, N. Mex.: Lama Foundation, 1971); ———, *Miracle of Love: Stories about Neem Karoli Baba* (New York: Dutton, 1979); ———, *The Only Dance There Is* (New York: J. Aronson, 1976); ———, *Still Here: Embracing Aging, Changing, and Dying* (New York: Riverhead, 2000); Ram Dass with Mirabai Bush, *Compassion in Action: Setting Out on the Path of Service* (New York: Bell Tower, 1992); Ram Dass with Paul Gorman, *How Can I Help: Stories and Reflections on Service* (New York: Alfred A. Knopf, 1985); Ram Dass with Steven Levine, *Grist for the Mill* (London: Wildwood House, 1977).

Rameshvaram

Rameshvaram is an island off the coast of Tamil Nadu whose name, "Rama the god," indicates its sacred status. It is told in the RAMAYANA that Lord RAMA, wishing to purify himself after killing his enemy, the demon king RAVANA, stopped at Rameshvaram. He sent HANUMAN, the monkey god, to BENARES (Varanasi) to get a SHIVA LINGAM for him to worship. While Hanuman was gone, Rama's wife, SITA made a lingam out of sand and began to worship it. When Hanuman returned, Rama ordered him to get rid of the sand lingam and install his own. Hanuman could not dislodge the lingam created by Sita. The second lingam then was set up beside the first so that both could be worshipped.

Rameshvaram is one of the most visited PILGRIMAGE sites in India and is accepted in Hinduism as one of the four major sites in India to visit (along with BADRINATH, Puri, and DWARAKA). The main temple on the island is dedicated to Shiva and is said to have been established by Rama himself. Historically, the present temple bears the architecture of the seventh through 13th centuries. There are a number of sacred places on the island associated with Rama, including the spot from which Rama allegedly shot his bow to destroy the bridge to Lanka after the war.

Further reading: Anne Feldhaus, *Connected Places: Region, Pilgrimage and Geographical Imagination in India* (New York: Palgrave Macmillan, 2003); N. Vanamamali Pillai, *Temples of the Setu and Rameswaram* (Delhi: Kunj, 1982); Baidyanath Saraswati, *Traditions of Tirthas in India: the Anthropology of Hindu Pilgrimage* (Varanasi: N. K. Bose Memorial Foundation, 1983).

Ram Lila   *See* NAVARATI.

Ramprasad   *See* SEN, RAMPRASAD.

Ramsuratkumar, Yogi (1918–2001)
enlightened yogi from South India

The revered South Indian beggar saint Yogi Ramsuratkumar attracted a large following through his ascetic piety and God-intoxication.

Ramsurat Kunwar was born on December 1, 1918, in a small village on the GANGES River five miles from BENARES (Varanasi) in Uttar Pradesh. The son of a devout rural BRAHMIN family, he was a natural mystic and brilliant student, who graduated from Ewing Christian College in ALLAHABAD with a B.A. in English literature in 1939. Pressured by his family to assume the responsibilities of family life, he was married in 1938. For some years he taught high school English in Bihar state, but he was consumed by a passionate longing for the divine that finally compelled him to make, in 1947, the first of many trips to South India to search for his GURU.

Yogi Ramsuratkumar said he had three "spiritual fathers" who initiated him into the spiritual path: Sri AUROBINDO, RAMANA MAHARSHI, and Swami (Papa) RAMDAS. After the deaths of the first two, Ramsurat returned to Swami Ramdas at Anandashram in 1952. At that time Ramdas initiated him

Yogi Ramsuratkumar (1918–2001), enlightened beggar yogi of South India *(Yogi Ramsuratkumar Ashram, Tiruvannamalai)*

into the MANTRA, *Om Sri Ram Jai Ram Jai Jai Ram;* after a week of repeating the mantra, Ramsurat was permanently cast into a state of God-intoxication. Referring to this permanent annihilation of his personal identity in the divine, he often said, "In 1952 Ramdas killed this beggar; this beggar is no more."

Swami Ramdas sent Ramsurat Kunwar away from Anandashram, telling him, "You cannot live in the ashram. . . . Remember, under a big tree, another big tree cannot grow. Go and beg." A divine madness similar to that of Sri CHAITANYA had taken over Ramsurat Kunwar, and at the cost of great personal anguish, he was compelled to enter the life of a wandering mendicant beggar. For seven years (1952–59) he traveled throughout India, finally arriving in 1959 at the foot of holy Mount Arunachala in Tiruvannamalai, where he lived for the remainder of his life.

Ramsurat would often visit Ramanashram, the ashram of Ramana Maharshi. One of Ramana Maharshi's senior disciples, T. K. Sundaresan Iyer, recognized the divine state of the unusual 40-year-old beggar and gave him the name *Yogi Ramsuratkumar.* For many years Yogi Ramsuratkumar was a "hidden saint," living on the streets of Tiruvannamalai and subsisting entirely on the

food and clothing that were given to him by local people who recognized his radiance and sanctity. The sublime countenance of the beggar yogi, his spontaneous outbursts—ecstatic song, chanting of the name of God, and blessing of all who were drawn to him—began to capture the hearts of seekers. By 1980 he had become widely recognized by countless numbers of people, including the American spiritual teacher Lee LOZOWICK, who became an ardent disciple.

In 1994 the Yogi Ramsuratkumar Ashram at Tiruvannamalai was built by his devotees. Dressed in the ragged shawls and stained *dhotis* of a beggar, with nothing but a country palm fan and coconut bowl, Yogi Ramsuratkumar gave DARSHAN twice a day in the temple of his ashram from 1994 through 2001. He did not teach by linear discourse, but through transmission of divine presence, instructing his disciples to repeat the name of God, using his name, Yogi Ramsuratkumar, as a mantra to invoke divine blessings. His vision of the unity of all life was often given in his words "My Father alone exists! There is nothing else, nobody else—past, present, future—here, there, everywhere, anywhere!

Today, *darshan*, chanting, Vedic rituals, and celebrations are regularly observed at the Yogi Ramsuratkumar Ashram. The *mahasamadhi* (tomb) of Yogi Ramsuratkumar is housed there. Farther south, a temple complex dedicated to Yogi Ramsuratkumar is situated near the ocean at Kanya Kumari in the small village of Kanimadam. Completed in 1993, this temple conducts daily BHAJANS, worship, and Vedic rituals.

Lee Lozowick has established ashrams in the United States, France, and India where the name of Yogi Ramsuratkumar is chanted.

Yogi Ramsuratkumar died on February 20, 2001.

Further reading: Vijayalakshmi, *Waves of Love* (Tiruvannamalai: Yogi Ramsuratkumar Ashram, 2002); M. Young, *As It Is: A Year on the Road with a Tantric Teacher* (Prescott, Ariz: Hohm Press, 2000); ———,

Yogi Ramsuratkumar: Under the Punnai Tree (Prescott, Ariz: Hohm Press, 2003).

rasa

Rasa (taste) is an important Indian aesthetic concept applied to literature, drama, and occasionally mythology. Literally, *rasa* is the taste, savor, or essence of something. In aesthetics *rasa* is the essential sentiment embedded in a work of art that evokes a corresponding emotion in the reader, listener, or viewer.

Works of art are often classified according to their predominant *rasa*. The literature variously lists eight to 11 of them. The most common listed are 10: *shringara* (love), *hasya* (mirth), *karuna* (pity), *raudra* (anger), *vira* (heroism), *bhayanaka* (fear), *bibhatsa* (disgust), and *adbhuta* (wonder); some add *shanta* (tranquillity) and *vatsalya* (parental fondness).

Further reading: Hari Ram Mishra, *The Theory of Rasa in Sanskrit Drama, with a Comparative Study of General Dramatic Literature* (Bhopal: Vindhyachal Prakashan, 1964); Tapasvi S. Nandi, *The Origin and Development of the Theory of Rasa and Dhvani in Sanskrit Poetics* (Ahmedabad: Gujarat University, 1973); V. Raghavan, *Abhinavagupta and His Works* (Varanasi: Chaukhambha Orientalia, 1980); ———, *The Number of Rasas*, 3d rev. ed. (Madras: Adyar Library and Research Centre, 1975).

rasa lila

The *rasa lila*, "round of passion" or "play of passion," is the circle dance performed by Lord KRISHNA with the cowherd women (*GOPIS*). Krishna stood at the center of the circle and multiplied himself so that he could dance individually with each of them. Devotees of Krishna understand this dance as a metaphor for the relationship between God and the individual soul. God is complete and isolated unto himself, while also residing intimately at the center of everyone's soul.

Further reading: Graham M. Schweig, trans., *Dance of Divine Love: The Rasa Lila of Krishna from the Bhagavata Purana, India's Classic Sacred Love Story* (Princeton, N.J.: Princeton University Press, 2005); B. V. Tripurari, *Aesthetic Vedanta: The Sacred Path of Passionate Love* (Eugene, Ore.: Mandala Publishing Group, 1998).

Rashtriya Swayam Sevak Sangh (RSS)
(est. 1925)

The Rashtriya Swayam Sevak Sangh (National Volunteer Corps) was for decades the most important organization advocating cultural and political HINDU NATIONALISM. It still wields influence and has been involved in a number of violent disputes with ethnic or religious minorities.

The RSS was first formed in 1925, but the movement has its origins in the ideology of Bal Gangadhar Tilak, who was convicted of murdering several British officials at the turn of the 20th century. Tilak had been influenced by the reformist goals of the reformer Rammohun ROY, but not by the liberal means that Roy championed.

The RSS was formed as a cultural and social organization, whose goal was to transform India from a secular state into a Hindu nation. Some call it "Hindu fundamentalist," but in actuality the ideology of *Hindutva*, or Hinduness, only relates to certain aspects of Hinduism. For example, while the RSS extols many of the achievements of the Indian past, its doctrines are not based on the four VEDAS, the most ancient Hindu sacred texts.

The RSS has argued that India fell under British rule because it lacked discipline and aggressiveness. It promotes a hypernationalistic, militaristic agenda seeking the expulsion of Muslims and the establishment of Hindu supremacy in India.

RSS rejects the pluralism found in traditional Hinduism. Instead, it has a goal of creating a single Hindu doctrine for India. It also wants to eliminate Islam and opposes Buddhism and JAINISM. It opposes preferences that the Indian government has extended to the lower CASTES; some of its support can be attributed to a reaction by higher-caste

Hindus to the government's equalization policy. In fact, its supporters generally are from the upper castes. While they criticize the distortions of the caste system (which they blame on Muslim influence), critics believe they really want to return to a time when caste was rigidly enforced.

RSS members conduct daily drills of martial arts wearing khaki uniforms, mimicking the Italian and German fascists they have long admired. Their disciplined members are often the first to arrive at the site of natural disasters, a practice that earns them support. The women's wing of the RSS is the Rashtriya Sevika Samiti; its structure is not unlike the male sections.

The political wing of the RSS is the BHARATIYA JANATA PARTY. It was founded in 1951 on a platform of an undivided India and aimed to unify all Hindus under a single doctrine, whereas in the past Hindus have tolerated a wide diversity of thought, and has rejected what it sees as European influences on modern Hindu thought and practice. At first it also rejected industrialization, but that orientation was eventually discarded.

During the 1940s M. S. Golwalker transformed the RSS into the most powerful of all the nationalist movements in India. Their influence expanded over time through missionary work. In February 1983 the RSS was implicated with nationalists and local police in Assam in a massacre of Muslim immigrants. The rioters also killed local Hindus who coexisted with the Moslems.

The RSS was also involved, along with the SHIV SENA movement and Bharatiya Janata Party, in the controversy that arose around the Babri Masjid Mosque in the Uttar Pradesh city of AYODHYA. This mosque was built in 1528 on a site that is believed to be the birthplace of RAMA, the AVATAR of VISHNU.

As early as the 1940s RSS members managed to erect an image of Rama in the mosque. Later the government sealed off the mosque to try to dampen the dispute. In the 1980s, the RSS started to protest the very existence of the Babri Mosque. Lal Krishnan Advani, a leader of the VISHVA HINDU PARISHAD (another nationalist group) led the protests; he was recently indicted for his role in the affair. The RSS protesters eventually attacked and destroyed the mosque in 1992. Nationwide communal riots resulted, in which 3,000 people were killed.

Further reading: Gwilym Beckerlegge and Anthony Copley, eds., *Saffron and Seva (Hinduism in Public and Private)* (New York: Oxford University Press, 2003); Chetan Bhatt, *Hindu Nationalism: Origins, Ideologies, and Modern Myth* (Oxford: Oxford University Press, 2001); Gerrie ter Haar and James J. Busuttil, eds., *The Freedom to Do God's Will: Religious Fundamentalism and Social Change* (London: Routledge, 2003); Blom Thomas Hanson, *The Saffron Way: Democracy and Nationalism in Modern India* (Princeton, N.J.: Princeton University Press, 1999); Santosh C. Saha, ed., *Religious Fundamentalism in the Contemporary World: Critical Social and Political Issues* (Lanham, Md.: Lexington Books, 2004); Santosh C. Saha and Thomas K. Carr, eds., *Religious Fundamentalism in Developing Countries* (Westport, Conn.: Greenwood Press, 2001); Peter van der Veer, *Religious Nationalism, Hindus and Muslims in India* (Berkeley: University of California Press, 1994).

Rati

In Indian mythology Rati, Desire, is the wife of the god of love KAMADEVA. Some stories say that she was created from the sweat of the RISHI DAKSHA, SHIVA's future father-in-law. Other stories make her the daughter of BRAHMA, who killed herself when Brahma, ashamed of his own lust, killed himself. Both were revived by Vishnu and she then was given to Kamadeva, the god of love, in marriage.

Rati's most celebrated achievement was to persuade Shiva to revive her husband, after he had burned him to ashes with his third eye. In the best known version of this story, Shiva restores Kamadeva to life but makes him invisible. In other versions, Rati tries to revive her husband by feats of asceticism but is stopped by the *rishi* NARADA, who forces her to serve as a demon's housemaid, under the name Mayavati. In still other versions, Rati, in the guise of Mayavati, raises Kamadeva to life and they are married once again.

Further reading: Cornelia Dimmitt and J. A. B. van Buitenen, *Classical Hindu Mythology: A Reader in the Sanskrit Puranas* (Philadelphia: Temple University Press, 1978); John Dowson, *A Classical Dictionary of Hindu Mythology and Religion, Geography, History, and Literature,* 12th ed. (Ludhiana: Lyall Book Depot, 1974).

Ravana   *See* RAMAYANA.

Rawat, Prem (Guru Maharaj Ji) (1957–)
head of Divine Light Mission and creator of Elan Vital
Prem Rawat, or Guru Maharaj Ji, is a teacher in the Sant Mat tradition who won a large following in the United States in the 1960s and early 1970s.

Prem Rawat was born on December 10, 1957, near Dehra Dun in Uttaranchal state, India, the youngest son of Sri Han Maharaj Ji, an established spiritual teacher. Prem received formal education at St. Joseph's Academy, but his spiritual direction was from his father. At age three, he began speaking to audiences about inner peace. When his father died in 1966 he became spiritual leader of the Divine Light Mission (DLM), a foundation Sri Han had established in the 1930s.

Under his leadership the mission continued to teach his father's main techniques, derived from the SANT MAT tradition. The tradition teaches that knowledge, as the energy and source of life, is obtained through four forms of MEDITATION, each of which focuses attention on inner life. Maharaj Ji presented the teaching as a cultivation of inner peace through maintaining silence, watching the process of breathing, and focusing the senses inward. Devotees who take initiation into DLM are said to "gain knowledge" and are called "premies."

Many members of the counterculture in the United States were impressed by Maharaj Ji's message of peace during his tours in the later 1960s, when he was still a teenager. In 1971, after his visits to Los Angeles and Boulder, Colorado, the United States DLM was established in Denver, Colorado. By 1972 the movement spread across the country. Ashrams were established in major cities and the publications *Divine Times* and *It is Divine* distributed.

In 1973 the DLM rented the Houston Astrodome for a gathering of peace coinciding with the birthday of Sri Han. The event failed to generate large attendance and became a financial loss. Programs and ASHRAMS were soon closed in order to pay off debt and many premies began to leave the movement. In 1974 Guru Maharaj Ji married a Western premie named Marolyn Johnson, a marriage that created conflict between Maharaj Ji and his mother. The fracture caused further troubles for the DLM when his mother returned to India and reestablished the DLM under her eldest son's name.

In the late 1970s the DLM reorganized and moved its headquarters to Miami, Florida. Maharaj Ji distanced himself from the religious association to make his teachings more universal. In the 1980s he encouraged followers to leave the monastic life and to regard him simply as a humanitarian leader. By 1983, he had ordered all Western ashrams to close.

In the mid-1980s, the DLM was renamed the Elan Vital and discarded all religious affiliation. Guru Maharaj Ji changed his name to Prem Rawat, believing that the divinity ascribed to him obstructed his message. Elan Vital became a much smaller organization. He increased his speaking engagements and produced video and sound recordings to spread his ideas.

Elan Vital, now headquartered in Agoura Hills, California, retains its status as a charitable organization, organizing events for Prem Rawat, raising funds, producing and distributing tapes of his messages, and archiving the history of his work.

Supported largely by volunteer staff and sales of his products, Elan Vital is active in the United States, Britain, and Australia.

At present, Rawat continues to give talks on knowledge throughout the world. According to the Elan Vital, his teachings have spread to more than 80 countries and its publications are available in 60 languages.

Prem Rawat lives with his wife in Malibu, California.

Further reading: Charles Cameron, *Who Is Guru Maharaj Ji?* (New York: Bantam Books, 1973); Sophia Collier, *Soul Rush: The Odyssey of a Young Woman of the '70s* (New York: Morrow, 1978); James V. Downton, *Sacred Journeys: The Conversion of Young Americans to Divine Light Mission* (New York: Columbia University Press, 1979); Guru Maharaj Ji, *The Living Master: Quotes from Guru Maharaj Ji* (Denver: Divine Light Mission, 1978).

rechaka   *See* PRANAYAMA.

reincarnation/rebirth

The Indian belief in the "cycle of lives" has ancient origin. Souls are believed to cycle through human or animal lives until they are liberated and merge with a higher reality. On rare occasions the tradition refers to reincarnation into a plant or stationary object.

The concept appears to have emerged in late Vedic times. Some argue that the idea was present in the Vedic tradition from the beginning, but little evidence can be found in any of the Vedic collections of MANTRAS, and only very occasional references are found in the BRAHMANAS, the explanatory portions of the Vedic collections. By the time of the UPANISHADS the notion of reincarnation seems to have become centrally important.

Some sects in ancient times appear to have believed that every soul must travel through a fixed number of births; one text puts the number at 8,400,000. The Ajivika sect believed that these births were all inevitable and could not be escaped; one could reach liberation only after they were all completed.

Many early sects adopted extreme ascetic practices, avoiding any taint of worldly passion, in order not to add to the accumulation of KARMA that had occurred from previous lives. Later Hinduism, as well as Buddhism and JAINISM, made the notion of reincarnation central to spiritual and religious practice, enshrining the notions of karma and SAMSARA (the round of birth and rebirth) in Indian culture and practice.

In these traditions, reincarnation results from one's actions in one's previous life, one's karma. In the process of time one might endure a huge number of highly undesirable births; *samsara,* or worldly existence, was thus a trap one tried to escape.

Such escape of rebirth has been the primary obsession of all practice in nearly all Indian traditions (except Islam) up to the present day. MOKSHA or NIRVANA, the liberation or release from this cycle, became the highest goal in all the major traditions. Release could occur in several ways. One path was severe, world-denying asceticism; even today there are such practitioners hidden away in mountain caves. Meditative yoga was seen as another way, which allowed one's mind or consciousness to remove itself from attachment to worldly life and thereby pave the way to liberation. Alternatively, a focus upon God could earn the grace of the divinity and God could help break the bonds of karma. Traditionally it has been said in Hinduism, too, that a true GURU can literally strip away one's karma, and thus devotion to gurus has become a strong feature of Hinduism.

Further reading: C. F. Keyes and E. Valentine Daniel, *Karma: An Anthropological Inquiry* (Berkeley: University of California Press, 1983); Wendy O'Flaherty, ed., *Karma and Rebirth in Classical Indian Traditions* (Berkeley: University of California Press, 1980).

Rig Veda

The Rig Veda is the earliest of the four VEDAS central to the Brahminical tradition. According to tradition it was compiled by VYASA. It is usually dated from 1500 to 1000 B.C.E., but since it is an anthology, some of its more than 1,000 hymns might well be older. The great majority of the hymns are from five to 20 lines in length; very few exceed 50 lines in length.

The Rig Veda contains hymns of praise to a pantheon of divinities. It also includes some cosmogonic hymns—hymns that tell of the creation of the universe—that are extremely important for the development of later Hinduism. By far the greatest number of the hymns of the Rig Veda are devoted to INDRA, king of the gods, a deity connected with the storms and rain who holds a thunderbolt, and AGNI, the god of fire. The rest of the hymns are devoted to an array of gods, most prominently MITRA, VARUNA, SAVITRI, SOMA, and the ASHVINS.

Less frequently mentioned in Rig Veda are the gods who became most important in the later Hindu pantheon, VISHNU and RUDRA (one of whose epithets was SHIVA, the benign). A number of goddesses are mentioned, most frequently USHAS, goddess of the dawn. ADITI (she without limit) is a goddess who is said to be the mother of the gods.

The Rig Veda, as are the other Vedas, is understood to be "composed by no man" (apaurasheya). It was considered to be an eternal text that is rediscovered during each new cosmic era. Commonly, the Rig Veda is divided into eight cycles, or mandalas, but in it is also traditionally learned in 10 books.

The RISHIS, poet-sages, are said to be responsible for "seeing" or hearing the verses in their divine form and recording them. Each Rig Vedic hymn has a rishi's name attached and some full books or partial books are said to have been received by a single rishi. Prominent among the rishis are Vishvamitra, Atri, Bharadvaja, Vasishtha, Kashyapa, Jamadagni, and Gautama.

Many of the other rishis are descendants of these major rishis.

Book III of the Rig Veda, for instance, is said to be received by Vishvamitra and his descendants. Nearly all the hymns of book VI are said to be from Bharadvaja. All the hymns of book VII are from Vasishtha. Most of book IV is said to have been received by the rishi Vamadeva, the son of the rishi Gotama. All of book II is said to have been received by the rishi Gritsmada. There were apparently some women who received Vedic hymns, including Apala of the Atri family; Ghosha, grand-daughter of Dirghatamas; Romasha; and Shashvati. The great majority of rishis were Brahmins and Kshatriyas, the two highest castes, but some verses were received by others.

Scholars believe books I and X were recorded later than the others. Book X contains several cosmogonic hymns such as the PURUSHA Sukta, the Hymn of the Divine Man (Rig Veda X. 90), which highlight the theme of cosmic unity. The hymns were very influential in later Indian thought. Most hymns of the Rig Veda, however, are not philosophical; rather, they are directed toward various divinities as part of a ritual cult, which is explicitly detailed in the BRAHMANAS. There are very few hymns of the Rig Veda that do not involve reference to some ritual.

The Rig Veda, as the other Vedas, was passed down from mouth to ear for millennia. It was forbidden to write them, as they were the exclusive preserve of those authorized and qualified to use them properly. Much as in a shamanistic tradition, the Vedas were shared only among initiates who learned from a Vedic GURU. The earliest written texts appeared around the 15th century C.E.

Further reading: S. N. Dasgupta, *History of Indian Philosophy,* vol. I (Delhi: Motilal Banarsidass, 1975); J. C. Heesterman, *The Broken World of Sacrifice: An Essay on Ancient Indian Ritual* (Chicago: University of California Press, 1993); ———, *The Inner Conflict of Tradition: Essays in Indian Ritual, Kingship and Society* (Chicago: University of Chicago Press, 1985); Ralph T. H. Griffith, trans., *Sacred Writings*. Edited by Jaroslav Pelikan, vol. 5, *The Rig Veda* (New York: Book-of-the-Month Club, 1992); Wendy O'Flaherty, *The Rig Veda: An Anthology* (Baltimore: Penguin, 1982); J. Frits Staal, *AGNI: The Altar of Fire*, 2 vols. (Berkeley, Calif.: Asian Humanities Press, 1983).

Rishabha

Rishabha was the first Jain TIRTHANKARA (saint) of our half-era (*see* JAINISM). He was followed by 23 others, the last of whom was MAHAVIRA.

Rishabha's life was marked by four auspicious events, which all took place when the Moon was in conjunction with the same star: he entered the womb after a previous life in a heavenly realm, he was born into the world, he left the life of a householder, and he attained infinite knowledge.

In the land of Kosala, he entered the womb of Marudevi, wife of Nabhi, a member of a warrior class family on the fourth day in the dark half of the month of Ashadha (June–July). His mother, as was customary for those who would bear a future ARHAT, an enlightened being, had had 14 auspicious dreams, such as seeing a white elephant and an ox. In the eighth day of the dark half of the month of Chaitra (March–April), he was born. Gods, goddesses, animal divinities, and others descended to greet this great birth and showered down jewels, gold, and silver.

Rishabha lived as a prince and as a monarch for thousands of years. Even as a monarch he was known for his many virtues and for his great teachings of the various arts. In his kingly life his children included the famed BHARATA and BAHUBALI.

In the month of Chaitra (March–April), he gave away all his wealth, mounted his kingly palanquin for the last time, and went to his place of renunciation to become a monk. He sat under a sacred tree; took off all his clothes, finery, and ornaments; and pulled out all his hair in five tufts, as was the custom for one who was to become a Jain monk.

For 1,000 years Rishabha ignored his body in every way, enduring every hardship without complaint or acknowledgment. He would walk very slowly, talk very quietly, and move about very lightly so as not to harm any being visible or invisible. He saw offal and gold as the same and would accept only that which had not been prepared specially for him.

Rishabha spent 1,000 years contemplating himself and doing penance in right conduct on the road to liberation. Finally, taking water only once every four days, he sat under a tree and reached the ultimate insight of full knowledge. Thereupon he became a spiritual victor, a *jina*, and became omniscient. At this time the gods and all other beings went to listen to him preach the Jain doctrine in an awesome and beautiful pavilion they built.

It is said that the Tirthankara Rishabha had 84 disciples who were very close to him and another 84 who assisted him. He had a total of 84,000 monks and 300,000 nuns. He remained seating in a lotus position, omniscient, for 100,000 years. Finally he met his death and his soul ascended to the top of the universe to exist there in eternal effulgence and bliss.

Further reading: Champat Rai Jain, *Rishabha Deva, the Founder of Jainism* (Allahabhad: Indian Press, 1929); P. S. Jaini, *The Jaina Path of Purification* (Delhi: Motilal Banarsidass, 1990); K. C. Lalwani, *Kalpa Sutra* (Delhi: Motilal Banarsidass, 1979).

rishi

A *rishi* in its most ancient Vedic sense was a seer and an inspired poet. The original *rishis* were those who saw or called forth the eternal verses of the VEDAS. The Vedas were not seen as written by anyone; the *rishis* were conduits for them. Most of the Vedic MANTRAS include the name of the *rishi* who recorded them. Seven of these ancient *rishis* are seen as the starting points for the orthodox BRAHMIN lineages: Kashyapa, Atri,

Vasishtha, Vishvamitra, Gautama, Jamadagni, and Bharadvaja.

In the later epics and Puranas, or mythical lore, *rishis* inhabited ASHRAMS or retreat places in the wilderness, where they performed their austerities. These *rishis* were sages, not necessarily connected with the transmission of the Vedas. Some of them were composers or compilers of the epics, such as the *rishi* VALMIKI who compiled the RAMAYANA, and the *rishi* VYASA who gave us the MAHABHARATA. The *rishis* encountered in this later literature often are known for the frightening curses they imposed upon those who had not treated them with due deference and respect.

Rishi today is an honorific term, for instance, in the case of MAHARISHI (great *rishi*) Mahesh Yogi, who founded the TRANSCENDENTAL MEDITATION movement. Few such people today are considered comparable to the great *rishis* of the past.

See also SAPTA RISHI.

Further reading: John Dowson, *A Classical Dictionary of Hindu Mythology and Religion, Geography, History, and Literature,* 12th ed. (Ludhiana: Lyall Book Depot, 1974); John E. Mitchiner, *Traditions of the Seven Rsis* (Delhi: Motilal Banarsidass, 1982); C. Sivaramamurti, *Rishis in Indian Art and Literature* (New Delhi: Kanak, 1981).

Rishikesh

Rishikesh (the RISHI's hair, or possibly a corruption of, *Hrishikesha,* an epithet of ARJUNA) is an important Indian PILGRIMAGE center. Many SWAMIS taught or lived there, including SWAMI SHIVANANDA and the MAHARISHI MAHESH YOGI, who founded the TRANSCENDENTAL MEDITATION movement.

Rishkesh lies in northern Uttar Pradesh in the foothills of the HIMALAYAS, on the GANGES. At the Triveni Ghat, the steps down to the Ganges, many offerings are made and ablutions done, for the Ganges is the purest of rivers, and at Rishikesh its water is very cold and fast. At sunset there is a custom there of setting little lamps adrift on the Ganges in worship to Ganga Devi, the river GOD-

DESS. Rishikesh is filled at all times with swamis, SADHUS, mendicants, and peregrinating pilgrims who seek this holy shrine for purification and devotion. Rishikesh is not far from HARIDVAR and is a waystation for pilgrims going farther up the Himalayas to BADRINATH.

Further reading: Augusthy Keemattam, *The Hermits of Rishikesh: A Sociological Study* (New Delhi: Intercultural, 1997); Reeta Khullar and Rupinder Khullar, *Gateway to the Gods: Haridwar, Rishikesh, Yamunotri, Gangotri-Kedarnath-Badrinath* (Dehradun: Uttaranchal Tourism and UBS Publisher's Distributors, 2004).

rita

Rita is a VEDIC concept that means "cosmic order." VARUNA was most specifically charged with its maintenance, but many other gods such as AGNI and INDRA were sometimes also said to maintain *rita.* It was understood that the Vedic rituals were necessary to maintain the cosmic order. In fact the greatest of the ancient Vedic rituals, the AGNICHAYANA, or fire ritual, was seen to re-create the entire cosmic order each year. The concept of *rita* is most important as a precursor to the notion of DHARMA, although the latter was extended into social law and social organization as well.

Further reading: Madhu Khanna, ed., *Rita, the Cosmic Order* (New Delhi: D. K. Printworld in association with the Indira Gandhi National Centre for the Arts, 2004); Jeanine Miller, *The Vision of the Cosmic Order in the Vedas* (London: Routledge & Kegan Paul, 1985).

Roerich, Nicholas and Helena   See AGNI YOGA SOCIETY.

Roy, Raja Rammohun   (1772–1833) *founder of Brahmo Samaj*

Rammohun Roy was a central figure in the Bengal Renaissance of the late 19th century and the founder of the reform movement BRAHMO SAMAJ.

He was born in Radhanagar, Bengal, on May 22, 1772, to a Bengali BRAHMIN, but religiously diverse family. His father worshipped VISHNU, while his mother was a devotee of the GODDESS. He was raised in Patna, a center of Muslim learning, and was influenced by Islamic teachings against images. Later, in Calcutta (Kolkata), he was exposed to Christianity. A scholar, he knew Bengali, SANSKRIT, and other Indian languages, as well as Arabic, Persian, Hebrew, Greek, and Latin. With his liberal education, he was inclined to reject the traditional orthodoxy of Hinduism

Raja Rammohun Roy (1772–1833), "Founder of Modern India" and creator of the Brahmo Samaj movement *(Victoria and Albert Museum/London/Art Resource, NY)*

and to accept the common aspects of different faiths, including Buddhism, JAINISM, Hinduism, and Christianity.

Although he read many of the world's scriptures in their original languages, he sought a way to free his own tradition, Hinduism, from superstition and prejudice. He claimed that the unifying doctrines he sought were contained in the UPANISHADS. With this renewed appreciation of the teachings of the Upanishads, he advocated that Indians learn their own tradition as well as science, philosophy, and modern perspectives. He adamantly rejected image worship, burning of widows (SATI), and the power that the Brahminic priesthood had over the populace. These practices he considered superstitious, prejudiced, and contrary to rationality. Once he became acquainted with Unitarianism through missionaries in India, he allied his movement with the principles of Unitarian philosophy.

Known for his work toward the abolition of *sati*, the immolation of widows on their husbands's funeral pyre; the disadvantages of polygamy; and challenges to the authority of the Hindu priesthood, Roy became a voice of tolerance and a continuing influence on traditional Indian practices. The first president of India, Jawaharlal Nehru, called Roy a "pioneer of modern India," and Swami VIVEKANANDA extolled Roy's love, which extended to Muslims as well as Hindus.

In 1831, he traveled to the United Kingdom and visited France. He died on September 27, 1833.

See also UNITED KINGDOM; UNITED STATES.

Further reading: Piyus Kanti Das, *Raja Rammohun Roy and Brahmoism* (Calcutta: Author, 1970); David Kopf, *The Brahmo Samaj and the Shaping of the Modern Indian Mind* (Princeton, N.J.: Princeton University Press, 1979); Spencer Lavan, *Unitarians and India: A Study in Encounter and Response* (Chicago: Exploration Press, 1991); J. Tuckerman, "Is Rammohun Roy a Christian?" *The Christian Examiner* 3, no. 5 (September–October 1826): 361–369.

Rudra

Rudra, "the howler," is the father of the MARUTS, the storm gods of the RIG VEDA, but is also known for causing disease and for healing. The epithet SHIVA, "the benign," is given to him in the Rig Veda (though he is most often fierce), and thus he is conflated in Indian tradition with Shiva himself. In scholarship the term *Rudra-Shiva* is commonly used in the description of Shiva. The explicit identification of Rudra and Shiva as Lord is first made in the SHVETASHVATARA UPANISHAD of perhaps the fourth century B.C.E.

Uncharacteristically honored alone and not in concert with other divinities, as so many Vedic divinities are, Rudra causes diseases of cattle and men with his bow and arrows and is propitiated and appeased rather than loved. In his fierceness he is associated with desolate and distant places.

Further reading: Cornelia Dimmitt and J. A. B. van Buitenen, *Classical Hindu Mythology: A Reader in the Sanskrit Puranas* (Philadelphia: Temple University Press, 1978); Stella Kramrisch and Praful C. Patel, *The Presence of Siva* (Princeton, N.J.: Princeton University Press, 1981).

Rudrananda, Swami (1928–1973) *American teacher of Shaivism and Siddha Yoga*

Swami Rudrananda, a Brooklyn-born disciple of the Shaivite GURU NITYANANDA, was a popular spiritual teacher in the United States.

Born Albert Rudolph in Brooklyn, New York, Swami Rudrananda grew up in the Depression era without a father. He relates that as a child he demonstrated psychic gifts and could go into trance and tell fortunes. At the age of six he saw two Tibetan lamas materialize and prophesy that the spiritual gifts they were implanting in him would be realized at age 31. As a young adult, he owned and operated an Oriental art shop in New York City.

In 1958 at age 30, Albert traveled to India to find a spiritual teacher. There he met his guru, Swami NITYANANDA, at Ganeshpuri, near Bombay (Mumbai). The meeting with Nityananda was to change the course of his life. Nityananda was a *mahasiddha*, always in a state of bliss and trance, who did not write or found any organization. His teachings were his direct transmission of spiritual force, and his utterances given in a profoundly immersed state were recorded by his pupils. Nityananda transmitted the creative life force or SHAKTI directly to disciples. Through this transmission or *shaktipat,* the power of kundalini was aroused in the disciple, who could experience an identity with the divine.

Albert had many extraordinary experiences with Nityananda, who even after his death appeared to Rudi and transmitted Shakti to him. However, it was Swami MUKTANANDA, one of the primary disciples of Nityananda, who initiated him into SANNYAS in 1966 and gave him the name *Rudrananda* (affectionately shortened to *Rudi*). Rudi was Muktananda's first Western disciple, and it was Rudi who took Muktananda to the United States. In 1971 Rudi broke with Muktananda, who wanted him to turn over his ASHRAMS and students.

Rudi's practice, as was that of Nityananda and Muktananda, was in essence *Shaivite,* although he did not focus on the philosophical aspects. Instead he was concerned to extract the content from the container. His entire teaching was centered on providing spiritual nourishment to his students, to insist that they develop a real practice so that they could create their own internal spiritual mechanism and connection to higher spiritual forces. Rudi was known for assuming his student's KARMA or spiritual tension, a negative energy that prohibits spiritual growth. This appropriation of others' karma he called *spiritual cannibalism* (the title of his autobiography). Rudi was said to have removed cancer from one disciple by taking on that person's karma.

In 1973 Rudi died in the crash of a small plane, en route to a lecture.

Rudi taught from his own center in New York City and opened his first ashram in the United States in Big Indian, New York. Eventually nine

Rudrananda Ashrams were established in seven states. He directly initiated several persons to become teachers in his practice, including Swami Khecaranatha, Swami CHETANANANDA, and Stuart Perrin.

Further reading: Rudi, *Spiritual Cannibalism* (Woodstock, N.Y.: The Overlook Press, 1978); J. Mann, ed., *Behind the Cosmic Curtain: The Further Writings of Swami Rudrananda* (Arlington, Mass.: Neolog, 1984); J. Mann, *Rudi: 14 Years with My Teacher* (Cambridge, Mass.: Rudra Press, 1987).

Ruhani Satsang *See* RADHASOAMI MOVEMENT.

Rukmini *See* KRISHNA.

S

sacred cow

The English idiom *sacred cow* was coined with reference to the veneration of cows that is common in India, but it reflects a degree of misunderstanding. Hindus do venerate and respect cows, but they do not regularly worship them; nor do they consider them in the category of icons or sacred objects. Bulls do have some sanctity, as a bull is the iconic vehicle of Lord SHIVA.

The weight of academic evidence shows that in VEDIC times (c. 1500–800 B.C.E.) bulls and barren cows were sacrificed by BRAHMINS, who then ate the animals. Other Indians also regularly ate beef. It was the Jains, and to some extent the Buddhists, who impressed Indian tradition with the notion of AHIMSA, the avoidance of harm to any being. Only gradually did society, led by the orthodox Brahmins, embrace VEGETARIANISM as the ideal diet and abandon the eating of meat almost completely.

The only Hindus who still regularly eat beef are the Dalit (UNTOUCHABLE) carrion gatherers. As *ahimsa* became the ideal the cow began to assume an iconic role and could not be killed. Since ancient times cow's milk has been a food staple; cow's milk and clarified butter are still used in ritual worship.

A sadhu and a sacred cow dressed for a festival in Mathura, Uttar Pradesh *(Gustasp Irani)*

The mythological wish-giving cow Surabhi is an indication of the magic inherent in the species. A late Atharva Vedic hymn (c. 300 B.C.E.) does treat the cow as holy, proclaiming it the universe itself—the Sun, the Moon, the rain. The imagery recalls the first verses of the BRIHADARANYAKA UPANISHAD, which gives sacred, cosmological meaning to the HORSE SACRIFICE as an object of MEDITATION.

No one knows exactly how the cow gained its special status in India, but it is believed that the development of *ahimsa* combined with the near-totemic status of the cow made the animal inviolable. Cows are often allowed to wander the streets to forage. Extreme consequences occur when a cow is struck by a vehicle (the driver might be physically attacked), so cows are scrupulously given the right of way on the somewhat anarchic Indian roadways. Even ownerless bulls are given similar deference.

India, because of its monsoon climate, possesses no pastureland to compare with that of North America, Europe, Argentina, or Australia. As a result, the raising of beef is not economical (although many ecologists claim that feeding grain directly to people is more efficient anywhere than converting it to beef). Therefore, the preservation of all cows for the dairy industry (and for their dung) has local economic logic. When cattle die they are considered carrion and may be taken away and eaten by Dalits (untouchables), who may be desperately poor, lack other food sources and process the skin for leather.

Further reading: M. K. Gandhi, *How to Serve the Cow* (Ahmedabad: Navjivan, 1954); Alan Heston, "An Approach to the Sacred Cow of India." *Current Anthropology*, 12 (1971): 191–210; D. N. Jha, *The Myth of the Holy Cow* (London: Verso, 2002); Brian K. Smith, "Eaters, Food and Social Hierarchy in Ancient India," *Journal of the Academy of Religion* 58, 2 (1990): 177–205.

sacred thread

The sacred thread is a cord worn by upper-caste Hindu males over the right shoulder, running across the chest and around the left side of the body. It consists of three strands before marriage and six or more thereafter. This thread can be worn by any of the three upper castes (*jatis*), BRAHMIN (priestly), KSHATRIYA (warrior), or VAISHYA (merchant). In practice, Brahmins (the priestly caste) commonly wear the thread, while Kshatriya (warriors) and Vaishya (merchants) wear it less often.

For Brahmins the investiture of the thread traditionally marks the beginning of the "student life" and is a very important ceremony. It is usually done at a young age (eight–12 years) and is considered a "second birth."

Further reading: Klaus K. Klostermaier, *A Survey of Hinduism* (Albany: State University of New York Press, 1989); Abbé J. A. Dubois, *Hindu Manners, Customs and Ceremonies.* Translated from the French and edited by Henry K. Beauchamp, 3d ed. (Oxford: Clarendon Press, 1959); V. Pandian, *Upanayana in Social Perspective* (Madras: Vijaya Vanamahdevi, 1980).

sadhaka

A *sadhaka* (from the SANSKRIT root *sadh*, complete, accomplish) is anyone who is accomplished in a special skill, or striving to be so. For example, one may be a "literary *sadhaka*." The term is often used to describe a spiritual seeker. In certain contexts the term is translated as "adept," but "spiritual aspirant" is also a good translation. The term is particularly used in TANTRA, where it refers to someone who is devoted to the path, but other traditions use it as well, for example, the tradition of SRI AUROBINDO and THE MOTHER.

Further reading: Agehananda Bharati, *The Tantric Tradition* (New York: Grove Press, 1975); Rachel Fell McDermott, *Mother of My Heart, Daughter of My Dreams: Kali and Uma in the Devotional Poetry of Bengal* (New York: Oxford University Press, 2001); Swami Narayananda, *A Word to Sadhaka: Spiritual Aspirant,* 3d rev. ed. (Gylling, Denmark: N. U. Yoga Trust & Ashrama, 1979).

sadhana

Sadhana (from the SANSKRIT root sadh, complete, accomplish) is used generically for any spiritual practice but is most frequently used to refer to Hindu TANTRIC practice.

Further reading: Pandit Madhav Pundalik, *Bases of Tantra Sadhana* (Pondicherry: Dipti, 1972); Sir John Woodroffe and Swami Pratyagatmananda, *Sadhana for Self-Realization: Mantras, Yantras and Tantras* (Madras: Ganesh, 1963).

sadhu

A sadhu (from Sanskrit *ƒisadhvi*, "good") is a renunciant, most commonly a mendicant who wanders in search of alms. Such people are regarded as good, pure, and religiously devoted. The terms sadhu and SANNYASI (more rarely their feminine forms *sadhvi* and *sannyasini*) are generally used interchangeably for wandering mendicants. The name SWAMI is also sometimes used.

Customs and characteristics vary greatly among sadhus and depend upon the sect to which they belong. They may be devoted to any divinity or to the BRAHMAN, the ultimate reality. Celibacy is universally required. Sadhus who worship Lord SHIVA may freely partake of hashish and marijuana to inspire their devotional chanting; for all others such drugs are strictly forbidden. Sadhus are very often devoted to a particular GURU (almost always a man) and follow his dictates strictly.

The sadhu or wandering mendicant is a very familiar feature of the Indian landscape and a distinctive aspect of Hinduism. While they are typically welcomed, there has always been some skepticism about their authenticity as well.

Further reading: Ramesh Bedi and Rajesh Bedi, *Sadhus: The Holy Men of India* (New Delhi: Brijbasi Printers, 1991); Agehananda Bharati, *The Ochre Robe: An Autobiography,* 2d ed. (Santa Barbara, Calif.: Ross-Erikson, 1980); Robert Lewis Gross, *The Sadhus of India: A Study of Hindu Asceticism* (Jaipur: Rawat, 1992); Dolf Hartsui-ker, *Sadhus: India's Mystic Holy Men* (London: Thames & Hudson, 1993).

Sahadeva   *See* PANDAVAS.

Sahaja Yoga Center (est. 1970s)

Sahaja Yoga was founded by Sri Mataji Nirmala Devi (b. March 21, 1923), an Indian girl born to a Christian family in Chindawara, India. Her parents, Prasad and Cornelia Salve, were direct descendants of a royal household in India. She is said to have been born with complete self-realization and to have known from childhood that she had a spiritual mission to help humankind. Early in her life, she displayed great wisdom, intelligence, and an understanding of the human nervous system and it energetic components.

Her parents were active in the Indian independence movement. Her father was a renowned scholar, a close associate of MOHANDAS KARAMCHAND GANDHI, who served on the Assembly of Free India; he helped to draft India's Constitution. As a child, Nirmala lived with her parents in Gandhi's ashram and served as a youth leader in the independence movement. Gandhi recognized her spiritual gifts and often engaged with her in conversation about the principle of Sahaja Yoga (the union with the divine innate in all people). Both agreed that fundamentalism and religious competition were obstacles to SELF-REALIZATION.

Nirmala studied medicine and psychology at the Christian Medical College in Lahore, Pakistan. In the late 1940s she married C. P. Srivastava, a member of the Indian Civil Service and later a diplomat. They had two daughters.

In May 1970, Nirmala had a transformative experience. She felt an opening in the crown CHAKRA at the top of her head. The KUNDALINI energy coiled at the base of the spine began to uncoil and to open the other energy centers along the spine. Empowered with this spiritual energy, she decided to assume the role of GURU and teach others how to experience this divine energy. She is believed to be a direct channel for divine power and energy, which flow directly through her. In her teaching she offers self-realization as a beginning process of spiritual or yogic practices. She is said to cause the rising of kundalini in her students when they are in her presence, triggering the awakening of the kundalini spiritual power in masses of individuals simultaneously. The goal of her personal appearances is to guide the individual practitioner to immediate and spontaneous enlightenment.

Since 1970, Nirmala has traveled the world to teach the techniques of Sahaja Yoga meditation. She does not charge fees for her lectures or for the experiences that students have in her presence.

The Sahaja Yoga Center has locations in the United States, Canada, India, and England and issues a periodical, *Nirmala Yoga*. Nirmala has created a number of nongovernmental organizations, including an international hospital in Bombay (Mumbai), an international cancer research center there, an international music school in Nagpur, and a charity house for the poor in Delhi.

Further reading: Shri Mataji Nirmala Devi, *Meta Modern Era* (Delhi: Nirmala Yoga, 1992); ———, *Sahaja Yoga* (Delhi: Nirmala Yoga, 1992); "The Russians' Love for Yoga: Nirmala Devi Shares Her Adventure," *Hinduism Today* 12, no. 10 (October 1990): 1, 7.

sahasrara chakra

The *sahasrara* (*sahasra*, thousand; *ara*, petaled) CHAKRA is not, properly speaking, a chakra (energy center along the spine). This "eighth chakra" in the KUNDALINI YOGA system represents the highest transcendent state that a practitioner can reach. It is depicted as a lotus with many petals floating 12 fingers above the head.

Sahasrara chakra is the meeting place of the divine feminine in the form of the kundalini with *paramashiva*, or highest SHIVA. Here the full inte-

gration of the transcendent and the earthly takes place, and the yogi can experience all of reality as divinity. The deity of this chakra is *paramashiva*. The SHAKTI is *mahashakti*, or the highest form of the GODDESS. The 1,000 petals are said to be of every color.

Further reading: Harish Johari, *Chakras: Energy Centers of Transformation* (Rochester, Vt.: Destiny Books, 2000); John G. Woodroffe, *The Serpent Power*, 7th ed. (Madras: Ganesh, 1964).

Sai Baba of Shirdi (c. 1856–1918) *revered ascetic*

Sai Baba was a highly charismatic ascetic and teacher of the early 20th century, whose influence carries to the present.

The early life of this Indian holy man is almost completely unknown. It is believed that he was born to a BRAHMIN family in a village in Hyderabad state, India, but the particulars of his family and lineage have not been discovered. He left home when he was eight to follow a Muslim teacher. When this teacher died, he associated with a Hindu guru named Venkusa. At age 16 he appeared in Shirdi, a village in Maharashtra state, where he kept to himself, remained silent except in response to questions, and begged for food.

After he had for some years appeared in public in Shirdi, people reported miracles and spontaneous ecstasy in his presence. He reportedly visited people in their dreams and healed the sick. In 1908 he began to be worshipped as a god.

Sai Baba's teaching emphasized devotion to a guru. He advocated VEGETARIANISM, taken from Hinduism, but also used Muslim MANTRAS and prayers. He advised all to remain in the faith in which they were born but to attend the festivals of other religions.

Sai Baba's grave in Shirdi is a shrine and place of pilgrimage. He is considered one of India's

Sai Baba of Shirdi (c. 1856–1918), the shrine of a holy man and miracle worker in Maharashtra *(Gustasp Irani)*

most famous holy men. His influence extends through several spiritual teachers who were influenced by him. MEHER BABA spent time with both Sai Baba and one of Sai Baba's followers, Sri Upasani Baba. SATYA SAI BABA considers himself the reincarnation of Sai Baba of Shirdi. Both Meher Baba and Satya Sai Baba have worldwide movements.

Further reading: Arthur Osborne, *The Incredible Sai Baba* (New Delhi: Orient Longmans, 1957); P. D. Sham Rao, *Five Contemporary Gurus in the Shirdi (Sai Baba) Tradition* (Madras: Christian Literature Society, 1972); Kevin R. D. Shepherd, *Gurus Rediscovered: Biographies of Sai Baba of Shirdi and Upasni Maharaj of Sakori* (Cambridge: Anthropographia, 1986).

Saiva Siddhanta

Saiva Siddhanta is a form of SHAIVISM practiced in Tamil-speaking regions, particularly Tamil Nadu and northern Sri Lanka. It is based on the 28 Shaivite AGAMAS, authoritative texts that interpret and extend Vedic knowledge, and on the teachings of the 63 NAYANMARS, the Tamil Shaivite saints. Other authorities include MANIKKAVACAKAR, who wrote the beloved TIRUVACAKAM (Sacred utterances) (c. 10th century), and Meykanda, with his Sivajnanabodham (Awareness of the knowledge of Siva) (c. 13th century).

Saiva Siddhanta focuses on the three categories of *pati, pashu,* and *pasha. Pati* is SHIVA, transcendent and pristine. Though he takes on a manifest aspect to enter the world, the world is always and eternally separate from Shiva. One can realize one's Shiva nature at the core of one's soul, but souls are eternally separate from one another and separate from Shiva. In this sense Saiva Siddhanta is a completely dualistic system. *Pashu* is the individual self that strives to realize its "Shiva nature." *Pasha* are the bonds of KARMA that hold one. Knowing one's Shiva nature confers liberation from birth and rebirth. Shiva can be realized only by worship, knowledge, and the aid of a GURU.

Saiva Siddhanta is characterized by its abject devotion and the sense of helplessness of the individual self in the face of a supreme that it can only understand, but with which it can never merge. Grace plays an important role in Saiva Siddhanta. There is an element of the system that speaks of Shiva/SHAKTI, or the divine masculine/divine feminine, which constitutes the totality of Shiva; this differs from the similar tantric idea, in which there is a complete identity between the level of the soul and the ultimate.

Further reading: S. N. Dasgupta, *History of Indian Philosophy*, vol. 5 (Delhi: Motilal Banarsidass, 1975); T. M. P. Mahadevan, *The Idea of God in Saiva-Siddhanta* (Madras: Annamalai University, 1955); S. N. Singaravelu, *Glimpses of Saiva Siddhanta* (Madras: Saiva Siddhanta Perumanram, 1992).

Saiva Siddhanta Church (est. 1957)

Founded in 1957 in San Francisco, California, by Satguru SUBRAMUNIYASWAMI (1927–2001), the Saiva Siddhanta Church promotes temple worship and propagates the teachings of SHAIVITE Hinduism through a temple/school complex.

The church serves Shaivism worldwide by initiating monks, publishing the writings of Subramuniyaswami and other Shaivite teachers, leading pilgrimages to holy sites of Shaivism, and promoting the study of Hinduism among Hindus and non-Hindus. Since 1957, centers have been established throughout the world. The Sri Subramuniya Ashram in Alaveddy, Sri Lanka, begun in 1949 by Subramuniyaswami, serves the needs of the Shaivite community near Jaffna.

In the first years of the church in San Francisco, monastics lived in apartments near the church on Sacramento Street and were self-supporting. Later, as the church grew, monks were able to live lives of cloistered study.

At their inception, the temple and school in San Francisco offered Hindu education through classes taught by Subramuniyaswami. The church transcribed and printed the lectures and sermons of their leader and disseminated these in a series of lessons, called the San Marga Master Course. As part of its mission to promote contemporary understanding of Shaivism's scriptures and teachings, the church also established the Himalayan Academy, its publishing house. Today the SANNYASIS (renunciants) of the church design, typeset, and illustrate the publications of the Himalayan Academy in Kapaa, Hawaii.

Temple worship is fundamental to Shaivite practice and has been central in the history of the church. Worshippers are encouraged to develop devotion (BHAKTI) to the congregation in each family's shrine room, and in daily life. In addition to the Ganesha Temple, dedicated in 1957 in San Francisco, California, Subramuniyaswami founded Kadavul Hindu Temple at Kauai Aadheenam on the island of Kauai on March 12, 1973. A number of images of deities from the Shaivite tradition are in the temples, and PUJA is celebrated several times each day. All major Shaivite festival days are observed through the year.

Publications include a partial translation in American English of Saint Tiruvalluvar's Tirukural, a book on Lord GANESHA, a progressive four-part series of premonastic and monastic vows concluding with the vow of SANNYAS (total renunciation), and a catechism and creed for Shaivite Hindus, which are Lessons One and Two of the San Marga Master Course.

In the early years of the church, families lived largely in and around the city of San Francisco, but, with increasing publications and dissemination of the teaching, the church has expanded to other areas, including Hawaii, Canada, and New York. As of 1980, two Dharmasalas, formally organized groups of church families, were in existence—one in Flushing, New York, and the other in San Francisco, California. Following the patterns of the American church structure, members of the Dharmasala work together to strengthen their lives through education, religious observance, shared culture, and economic cooperation. Their organization is overseen by a senior group of elders and a council on ministries.

A core group of church members formed in Alaveddy, Sri Lanka, the site of Subramuniyaswami's first ASHRAM. The ashram serves the Sri Lankan community through its children's school of religion, English classes, courses in Shaivite culture, and a full-fledged religious and cultural center for adults. At present, the church has members in many countries, including England, Mauritius, Canada, Sri Lanka, Thailand, India, South Africa, and Australia. The entire church membership now is made up of approximately 70 percent born Shaivites and 30 percent converts.

Further reading: *Hinduism Today* (1979–present); Satguru Sivaya Subramuniyaswami, *Dancing with Siva: Hinduism's Contemporary Catechism* (Concord, Calif.: Himalayan Academy, 1993); ———, *Loving Ganesa: Hinduism's Endearing Elephant-Faced God* (Kapaa, Hawaii: Himalayan Academy, 1996); ———, *Merging with Siva: Hinduism's Contemporary Metaphysics* (Kapaa, Hawaii: Himalayan Academy, 1999).

samadhi

Samadhi refers to the highest state of concentration and absorption in YOGA; the term in used in various yoga traditions. In some systems it is accompanied by a trance, whereby the yogi is completely detached from any external stimuli. *Samadhi* is a technical term in the yoga of PATANJALI, describing the next stage for the adept

after concentration skills (*dharana*) have been developed and deep involvement in MEDITATION (DHYANA) has been achieved.

There are two levels of *samadhi*: *samprajnata samadhi*, in which the yogi is still aware of a degree of worldly differentiation, and *asamprajnata samadhi*, in which there is a full realization of the self, or PURUSHA, and its consciousness, and there is no involvement in worldly differentiation. *Samprajnata samadhi* is said to retain the "seeds" of awareness of the external world of differentiation, while *aprajnata samadhi* is said to be "seedless": it no longer engenders thoughts tied to the external world. Neither of these states can be precisely described, because both take consciousness beyond language into indescribable realms.

Samprajnata samadhi is seen by Patanjali to have four steps. At the *savitarka* step the adept can look directly into the essence of real things, but only at the gross level. This step is still bound by conventional understandings, such as that time is divided into past, present, and future.

The second step is *nirvitarka*. At this point, conventional understandings, verbal and logical associations, cease. One transcends the cognitive or perceptive act itself, and one's consciousness meets directly with true reality. However, this meeting is still at a gross and not a subtle level.

At the third or *savichara* level consciousness is able to go beyond the surface of reality to its subtle level. One is still, however, bound by a certain residue of time and space (not as a felt experience, but as categories). Experience at this subtle level engenders the fourth step in this type of *samadhi*, the *nirvichara* level, in which consciousness descends into the very essence of the real world, no longer mediated by "concept."

Beyond the fourth stage of *samprajnata samadhi* is true *asampranjata samadhi*, in which concept is lost completely; there is a direct realization of the consciousness power of the self, with no limitation. This is sometimes also called *dharma-megha-samadhi*. Here one becomes completely aware that the self and its power of consciousness are not the body. All "knowledge" and all "consciousness" merge into an undifferentiated awareness that is absorbed in being itself. This does not mean that the person cannot and does not exist and act in the world as before. It merely implies that that person's awareness is no longer in any way affected or perturbed by that worldly reality. The yogi is then in the "isolated state" (*kaivalya*) and functions on a level beyond ordinary categories.

Further reading: Swami Hariharananda Aranya, *Yoga Philosophy of Patanjali: Containing His Yoga Aphorisms with Vyas's Commentary in Sanskrit and Translation with Annotations Including Many Suggestions for the Practice of Yoga*. Translated into English by P. N. Mukherji (Albany: State University of New York Press, 1983); Sri Chinmoy, *The Summits of God-life: Samadhi and Siddhi* (Jamaica, N.Y.: Agni Press, 1974); Ian Whicher, *Cognitive Samadhi in the Yoga Sutras* (Chennai: Adyar Library and Research Centre, 1997).

Sama Veda

Sama Veda, or "VEDA of the sung chants," is one of the three original Vedas that form the foundation of Hindu tradition (a fourth Veda was added sometime later). Most of its hymns are devoted to the god SOMA. This god was invoked in many Vedic rituals and was particularly honored by the preparation of a psychedelic substance that took the same name as the god: Soma. The honoring of the god and the preparation of the drug were the particular realm of the Sama Vedic priests.

Any public Vedic ritual required the recitation of passages from the Sama Veda. Many public rites also required the consumption of the Soma drug. The priests of the Sama Veda were known for their sonorous chanting, which is considered the origin of Indian music.

Further reading: Barend Faddegon, *Studies on the Samaveda* (Amsterdam: North-Holland, 1951); S. V. Ganapati, trans., *Sama Veda* (Delhi: Motilal Banarsidass, 1992); G. H. Tarlekar, *Saman Chants, in Theory and Present Practice* (Delhi: Sri Satguru, 1995).

Sambanthar *(Jnanasambanthar)*

(c. 570–670 C.E.) *Tamil Shaivite poet-saint*

Sambanthar (he connected to God through divine wisdom) is among the trio of most prominent Tamil SHAIVITE saints whose hymns appear in the central liturgical and literary text of the Tamil Shaivas, the TEVARAM.

Born to a BRAHMIN family in Cirkali, Tamil Nadu, near the famous Shaivite shrine of CHIDAMBARAM, Sambanthar was a child prodigy; it was said that he began composing hymns in praise of SHIVA when he was just a child. He is said to have mastered Vedic learning at age three and received by a miracle the ability to compose sacred poetry from Shiva himself.

While still quite young Sambanthar completed four great pilgrimages to shrines of the Tamil region, accompanied by other devotees. A minstrel who accompanied him on these journeys set his hymns to music—or, most likely, simply recorded the melodies that the young saint spontaneously sang; they are still sung by devotees today.

Sambanthar's hymns frequently condemn the Buddhists and Jains (*see* JAINISM). He is said to have converted the Pandyan king of Madurai from JAINISM to Shaivism. Many miracles are associated with his life. Legend says that when his parents, at last, arranged his marriage, Shiva appeared as a great blaze of light and invited the saint to merge with him. The wedding party and bride joined the saint in final union with God, before his marriage could be finalized.

Further reading: A. Kandiah, *Mystic Love in the Tevaram* (Colombo: A. Kaniah, 1987); Indira Viswanathan Peterson, *Poems to Siva: The Hymns of the Tamil Saints* (Princeton, N.J.: Princeton University Press, 1989); P. S. Somasundaram, *Tirujnanasambandhar: Philosophy and Religion* (Madras: Vani Patippakam, 1986).

Samkhya (Sankhya)

Samkhya is one of the six orthodox systems of Hinduism that were first developed in ancient times. It is traditionally believed to have originated with the sage KAPILA (c. 500 B.C.E.); its most authoritative text is the Samkhya Karika of Ishvarakrishna (c. 200 C.E.). Today the system has few adherents, and many of its ideas are preserved in YOGA traditions, including modern-day HATHA YOGA. (The word *samkhya* means "enumerate," a reference to the precise categories within the philosophy.)

Samkhya was dualist: the everyday world of matter and the world of the soul or self were considered to be two completely separate and distinct realms. Early Samkhya was nontheistic; it did not include any divine being or god.

In Samkhya PRAKRITI—nature or the manifest universe—was understood to be eternal. It had always existed and would always exist, though it might from time to time contract into an unmanifest form, awaiting the next manifestation. The selves or souls, which were also eternal but shared nothing in common with nature, were called PURUSHAS. There was an infinite number of them, and they were all separate and distinct from one another.

Each self or soul contained an inexplicable magnetism, which drew *prakriti* to collect or aggregate around it and give it life, a body, and birth. KARMA, the actions committed in the previous birth, would determine each new aggregation. In spiritual terms, this was seen as a constantly renewed trap for the self; the purpose of Samkhya was to show a way to escape the trap.

With the right state of mind, one could move one's point of view above the whirl of nature so that one's consciousness could focus on the soul itself and not be distracted by the pull of phenomena. The earthly realm of elements was considered to be characterized by inertia (*tamas*); the organs of action such as hands and feet were seen to constitute a realm of self-binding action (*rajas*); but the senses, mind, and intellect pointed toward the realm of purity (*SATTVA*). These three aspects of nature, the *GUNAS*, were experienced only in combination, with one or another mode predominating at any one moment.

MEDITATION could help one rise above the *gunas* or intertwined characteristics of nature. Intellect, or higher mind (*BUDDHI*), was the purest aspect of the human being and so was used as an instrument for the transcendence of matter. But even mind needed to be left behind for total release. Release occurred when the soul was freed from the body into its own self-reflective consciousness.

Yoga soon emerged as the practical way to realize the ideals of Samkhya. PATANJALI's YOGA SUTRA showed the practices that could be used and delineated the various stages of the process. By the first century C.E. the system was practically combined into one, and called Samkhya-Yoga.

Further reading: S. N. Dasgupta, *History of Indian Philosophy*, Vol. 1 (Delhi: Motilal Banarsidass, 1975); Gerald Larson and Ram Shankar Bhattacharya, *Samkhya: A Dualist Tradition in Indian Philosophy* (Princeton, N.J.: Princeton University Press, 1987); Heinrich Zimmer, *Philosophies of India* (Princeton, N.J.: Princeton University Press, 1974).

samsara

Samsara is the round or cycle of birth and rebirth that all beings are subject to in the Hindu worldview. By extension it is often used to designate the world, where birth and rebirth are the human destiny. The term is also used in JAINISM, Buddhism, and SIKHISM.

The negative evaluation of samsara, so prevalent in Hindu belief, began to color the ancient VEDIC tradition only in the era of UPANISHADS, some of which begin to show attitudes that would directly lead to the development of world-denying philosophies. The Vedic MANTRAS themselves are life-affirming and envision a peaceful, joyful heaven as the result of merit in one's life. There is no trace in them of REINCARNATION, of the hopeless mire of birth and rebirth. Reincarnation appears in the Upanishads, the small texts that were appended to the prose portions (BRAHMANAS) of the Vedas, along with the first evidence of the sense of entrapment in a web of endless births. The Buddhist and Jain traditions also focus on KARMA and the hopeless trap of the world.

Further reading: Rajeshwari Vijay Pandharipande, *The Eternal Self and the Cycle of Samsara: Introduction to Asian Mythology and Religion,* 3d ed. (Needham Heights, Mass.: Simon & Schuster Custom, 1996); Heinrich Zimmer, *Philosophies of India* (Princeton, N.J.: Princeton University Press, 1974).

samskara

Samskaras (from the Sanskrit *samskri*, refined, the source of the word SANSKRIT) are ritual ceremonies that mark and purify life cycle events. Every *samskara* requires a BRAHMIN priest to preside and includes prayers, oblations, offerings, and a fire ritual.

Rituals are performed to encourage impregnation and to obtain a male child. A special rite is performed at birth. The *annaprashana* is usually performed at the sixth month after birth to mark the feeding of the first solid food. The investiture of the SACRED THREAD, the *upanayana* ceremony, is performed for twice-born (high-caste) Hindu males when they are between ages eight and 12.

Perhaps the two most important *samskaras* for Hindus are the wedding ceremony and the *sraddha,* or death ceremony. The *sraddha* can be performed only by a male child. It ensures that a soul does not remain as a ghost but goes on either to liberation or to its next birth. A yearly ritual is performed to feed the deceased, in particular Brahmins, lest they fall from heaven. This ancient ritual of feeding the ancestor seems to conflict with the belief that nearly everyone is reincarnated, and that few proceed directly to heaven.

Further reading: R. B. Pandy, *Hindu Samskaras: Socio-Religious Study of the Hindu Sacraments* (Delhi: Motilal Banarsidass, 1969); Prem Sahai, *Hindu Marriage Samskara* (Ahmedabad: Wheeler, 1993).

samyagdarshana   *See* JAINISM.

samyagjnana   *See* JAINISM.

samyakcharitra   *See* JAINISM.

sanatana dharma

Sanatana dharma (eternal way) is a term created in 19th-century India as a more meaningful synonym for *Hinduism.* The word *Hindu,* after all, was not indigenous to the culture, but was coined by ancient Persians (based on their pronunciation of *Sindhu,* the Indus River). Indian spiritual traditions had typically described themselves as "the DHARMA." Dharma admits of many English translations; it refers to an essential set of rules and prescriptions that make up a given religious path. Those who coined the term *sanatana dharma* wanted to emphasize the Indian sense that their "way" was an eternal one that had had no beginning in time.

Because of the universality of certain Hindu notions, and the acceptance of a wide diversity of spiritual paths within the Hindu fold, the term *sanatana dharma* sometimes is taken to mean the ancient truth behind all religions (not just those of India), the truth that all seek in their own unique ways. In that sense, the *santana dharma* is not merely the religions practiced by the inhabitants of India who look upon the VEDAS as the supreme wisdom, but the "way" of all who seek the highest truth, whatever their religion.

Further reading: Balasubramania N. Aiyer, *Principles and Practice of Hindu Religion, Sanatana Dharma Sastra: A Comparative Study of the Ancient Tradition and the Perennial Philosophy* (Mumbai: Bharatiya Vidya Bhavan,

1999); Param Dayal Faqir, *Satya Sanatan Dharam: Or, True Religion of Humanity.* Translated by B. R. Kamal and Swami Yogeshwar Ananda Saraswati (Hoshiarpur: Manavta Mandir, 1978); Swami Rama Tirtha, *Sanatan Dharma* (Lucknow: Rama Tirtha Pratisthan, 1990).

sannyas   *See* SANNYASI.

sannyasi (f. sannyasini)

A *sannyasi* is a male renunciant who has "thrown everything down." (Rarely, there will be female

An ochre-robed wandering *sannyasi* in Benares (Varanasi) *(Constance A. Jones)*

sannyasinis.) Many sects in India have *sannyasis,* men who are seen as no longer a part of the everyday world (only a very few allow women renunciants). The rules or vows vary in the different traditions, but until modern times, *sannyasis* were expected to shun worldly occupations, living only through alms or in a monastic environment.

The vows for *sannyasis* all entail dietary restrictions that limit the number and size of meals, avoidance of women, prohibition on use of alcohol, and a focus on the divine at all times. *Sannyasi* is the fourth stage of life or ASHRAMA FOR BRAHMIN males, the point at which they ideally throw down all conventional life and take up a life of wandering as they focus on God or BRAHMAN.

Further reading: Patrick Olivelle, "Contributions to the Semantic History of Samnyasa," *Journal of the American Oriental Society* 101 (1981): 265–274; ———, *Renunciation in Hinduism: A Mediaeval Debate,* 2 vols. (Vienna: University of Vienna, 1986–87).

Sanskrit (Samskritam)

Sanskrit (*sam,* complete; *krita,* done, i.e., that which is done completely, the perfected, the refined) is the ancient liturgical or ritual language of India. In the Sanskrit language itself the language is called Samskritam.

Sanskrit is the oldest extant Indo-European language. It is linguistically related to such European languages as English, French, and German and such Asian languages as Persian. The earliest evidence for Sanskrit is in the ancient Indian texts, the VEDAS, the earliest of which, the RIG VEDA, dates from approximately 1500 B.C.E. The Vedas were received as divine revelation by seers called RISHIS, who recorded them. The Sanskrit of the Vedas is noticeably different from its classical form, as defined authoritatively by the grammarian Panini around 450 B.C.E.

After Panini, virtually no changes were accepted into the language. Today Sanskrit is still spoken by *pandits* (scholars) and those learned in Indian philosophy. There are several Sanskrit universities today in India, where all classes are conducted in that language. There are a few million Indians who can truly speak Sanskrit today in a population of over a billion or more; none of them speaks Sanskrit only.

There are many theories regarding the Sanskrit language; the different philosophical schools and sects in India have developed their own viewpoints. Most of them believe that the Vedas themselves are eternal and always existed; therefore, Sanskrit itself is similarly eternal, rather than an arbitrary language created by humans; it is the "language of the gods" (devavani).

When JAINISM and Buddhism began to develop scriptures and liturgies that departed from the Vedic ritual tradition, they made use of the Prakrits, the regional vernacular languages that had begun to develop out of Sanskrit. In that era (c. 800 to 0 B.C.E.), Sanskrit was still the spoken language of the educated classes and the language of Vedic high culture. By the turn of the millennium, however, even Buddhists and Jains began to write their works in Sanskrit, an indication that the cultural force of developing Hinduism had overwhelmed these heterodox traditions at least in that respect.

Sanskrit, thus, is the cultural link language of India. It has been used as the language of high culture for nearly 3,000 years. The body of extant writing in the language is vast. The Vedas, which are basically collections of MANTRAS, are accompanied by the BRAHMANAS, the ARANYAKAS, and the classical UPANISHADS. Hundreds of later texts called "Upanishads" exist independently of the Vedas.

The Sanskrit epics, the RAMAYANA and the MAHABHARATA, were written somewhat later. The Ramayana is itself about 40,000 verses in length and the Mahabharata over 100,000 verses. Included alongside the epics are the 18 Puranas that tell the tales of the divinities. There are also 18 minor Puranas and hundreds of Sthalapuranas or local works that tell the tales of local divinities.

Other prolific genres emerged over the long history of Sanskrit. There are hundreds of plays, longer poems, and other classical literary forms. There are works on aesthetics, erotics, medicine, philosophy and theology, and logic; there are devotional hymns, dictionaries, works on astronomy and astrology, works on mathematics, ritual, law, architecture, TANTRISM, history, music, sculpture, and painting. Additionally, there is much panegyric literature and many inscriptions. Every one of these Sanskrit genres has examples in the Jain tradition as well. All told, there are hundreds of thousands of texts and manuscripts, most of which have not been studied for centuries and are not edited, let alone translated.

Sanskrit is written in the DEVANAGARI script, which is made up of 48 to 51 letters, depending on the precise system. The script appears to have been devised during the Gupta era (fourth to sixth centuries C.E.).

Most Indian languages rely on Sanskrit-derived vocabulary. Even in a Dravidian language such as Telegu, more than 50 percent of the vocabulary is derived from Sanskrit.

At about the time of the arrival of the Muslims in India in the 13th century, Sanskrit learning began to decline. The vital and central role that Sanskrit had played in Indian culture for 3,000 years began to fade, and the vernacular languages began to develop as literary alternatives. (In South India, Tamil has long had a developed literature, still extant, dating to before the Common Era.)

Even then Sanskrit did not die out. Many texts continued to be written in the language through the 18th century; in fact, many works are still composed in Sanskrit. On Indian television and radio one can hear Sanskrit newscasts and bulletins. There also are a few Sanskrit newspapers.

Further reading: K. C. Aryan, *The Little Goddesses (Matrikas)* (New Delhi: Rekha, 1980); T. Burrow, *The Sanskrit Language* (London: Faber, 1973); Jan Gonda, ed., *A History of Sanskrit Literature*, 10 vols. (Wiesbaden: Otto Harrosowitz, 1975–82); John Grimes, *A*

Concise Dictionary of Indian Philosophy: Sanskrit Terms Defined in English (Albany: State University of New York Press, 1989); Arthur Berriedale Keith, *Classical Sanskrit Literature* (Calcutta: Y. M. C. A. Publishing House, 1947); ———, *A History of Sanskrit Literature* (London: Oxford University Press, 1920); Diana Morrison, *A Glossary of Sanskrit from the Spiritual Tradition of India* (Petaluma, Calif.: Nilgiri Press, 1977); Sheldon Pollock, ed., *Literary Cultures in History: Reconstructions from South Asia* (Berkeley: University of California Press, 2003); M. N. Srinivas, *The Cohesive Role of Sanskritization and Other Essays* (Delhi: Oxford University Press, 1989); Judith M. Tyberg, *The Language of the Gods: Sanskrit Keys to India's Wisdom* (Los Angeles: East-West Cultural Centre, 1970).

Sant Mat

The Sant Mat (View of the Saints) was a heterogeneous group of travelling poet-saints dating from the 14th to 17th centuries who had a profound impact on the religion of northern and central India. These poets included KABIR, Surdas, TUKARAM, and Ravidas. Their most important characteristics were a desire for social reform and a criticism of ritualism and caste. They stressed that the pursuit of spirituality was not limited to religion. The search for truth could be guided by any authentic experience of the One, however defined.

These teachers often ignored religious boundaries and mingled easily with Muslim Sufis. The Sant spirit was carried forward in the Sikh tradition by GURU NANAK, who had gone on pilgrimage and on the Hajj to show that the true God belonged to no particular religion. The Kabir tradition, in particular, has survived to the present, although it does not have the creative vigor and openness it once had; it seems to have become another sect of Hinduism.

Further reading: Daniel Gold, *The Lord as Guru: Hindi Saints in North Indian Tradition* (New York: Oxford University Press, 1987); David N. Lorenzen, ed., *Religious Movements in South Asia 600–1800* (New York: Oxford University Press, 2004); Karine Schomer and W. H. McCleod, eds., *The Sant Tradition of India* (Berkeley: Berkeley Religious Studies Series and Motilal Banarsidass, 1987).

Sant Mat movement (est. 1861)

The Sant Mat movement, also known as the RADHASOAMI MOVEMENT, emerged in the middle of the 19th century in the Punjab, as one of several movements that sought to revitalize the Sikh community after its government was defeated and replaced by the British. The new movement was introduced by Shiv Dayal Singh (1818–78), generally known as Soami Ji, and was distinctive because its leader was a living master, a person serving as an initiating GURU (a structure previously foreign to SIKHISM).

The new guru aimed to teach his followers *surat shabd* (sound current) yoga, as a technique to overcome *kal,* the negative forces that rule this world, and contact the divine. God had created the world by his word; therefore, through the repetition of MANTRAS (*japa yoga*), humans could establish contact with God. Soami Ji's teachings resonated with devotion to the name of God (*bhakti nam*), which had always been important in the Sikh tradition.

Shiv Dayal Singh introduced *surat shabd* yoga in 1861 at Agra, Uttar Pradesh, in northern India. He initiated some 4,000 people and then passed leadership to Rai Salig Ram (1829–98). At the same time, he also sent Jaimal Singh (1838–1903) to spread the movement in the Punjab.

The relocation of Jaimal Singh to Beas in the Punjab divided the movement; the Beas center became the larger of the two. Jaimal Singh's successor, Sawan Singh (1858–1948), built the Beas branch into the largest of what by then had become several segments of the original movement. He initiated over 125,000 people. However, his career was eclipsed by that of one of the 20th-century Beas leaders, Charan Singh (1916–90), who was said to have initiated over a million disciples.

Throughout the 20th century, the Sant Mat movement emerged into both an important minority movement in India and a global movement with centers throughout the West. At the same time, it splintered into a variety of separate groups, each of which professed to have the true lineage from Soami Ji. More often than not, when a lineage holder died, several claimants to successorship emerged and vied for the allegiance of his following. In some cases, those who did not receive the official sanction as the successor have been able to win large followings. Such was the case for Kirpal Singh (1896–1974), founder of the Ruhani Satsang.

The Indian-based Sant Mat groups all teach largely the same doctrine. In the West, some of the more prominent Sant Mat teachers have been Darshan Singh (1921–89), Rajinder Singh, and Thakur Singh (b. 1929). The American scholar David Christopher Lane has catalogued the dozens of Sant Mat gurus and the movements they led.

Some of the most interesting developments in the Sant Mat tradition have been created by non-Indian leaders who have assumed the role of living master and have built independent movements. For example, Master Ching Hai Wu Shang Shih, one of the very few women leaders in Sant Mat, learned the teachings from Thakur Singh. She has moved on to build a Chinese Sant Mat organization and changed the name of *surat shabd* yoga to the Quan Yin Method of Sound and Light Meditation, in order to present the teaching to a Buddhist Chinese-speaking audience; as her work has grown, it has expanded to include people from a variety of backgrounds and languages.

In the United States, a Westernized Sant Mat group called ECKANKAR (ECK) was started by Paul Twitchell (1909–70), a former student of Kirpal Singh. Twitchell ignored Kirpal Singh's lineage and proclaimed himself the 971st ECK Master, the recipient of a previously unknown tradition said to reach back into prehistory. Eckankar, Twitchell's organization, has spawned several groups. A somewhat similar group is the Movement for Spiritual Inner Awareness, formed by John-Roger Hinkins. "JR," as he is affectionately known, mixed elements of Christianity and Western esotericism with the Sant Mat teachings, resulting in a new eclectic perspective.

Indian religions have been carried into Africa in a similar manner by immigrants throughout the 20th century. A new branch of Sant Mat emerged in Uganda in 1957. It was founded by Dr. Jozzewaffe Kaggwa Kaguwa Kaggalanda Mugonza, more popularly known as simply Bambi Baaba. While he traveled to India and met with various Sant Mat teachers, he claims an entirely independent revelation of the teachings in a direct manner. In the 1970s, under the government of Idi Amin, he was charged with introducing a foreign religion in the country and forcing his members into a VEGETARIAN and alcohol-free diet.

Another interesting Sant Mat teacher in the West is Guru Maharaj Ji (PREM RAWAT) (b. 1957), who entered the United States in the early 1970s while still a teenager. His organization, originally called Divine Light Mission, now is identified as Elan Vital. He sees his teachings as independent of cultures, religion, beliefs, and lifestyles. Though adopting a secular overlay, he continues to present the Sant Mat teachings and to offer people initiation into the secret knowledge revealed only to initiates.

Further reading: Marvin Henry Harper, *Gurus, Swamis, and Avatars: Spiritual Masters and Their American Disciples* (Philadelphia: Westminster Press, 1972); Mark Juergensmeyer, *Radhasoami Reality* (Princeton, N.J.: Princeton University Press, 1991); David Christopher Lane, *The Radhasoami Tradition: A Critical History of Guru Successorship* (New York and London: Garland, 1992); Karine Schomer and W. H. McLeod, eds., *The Sants: Studies in a Devotional Tradition of India* (Delhi: Motilal Banarsidass, 1987).

saptamatrika

The *saptamatrika* (*sapta,* seven; *matrika,* mothers) are a grouping of seven goddesses found in the VEDAS, and possibly cited on seals of the ancient INDUS VALLEY CIVILIZATION. They are worshipped in both India and Nepal and have their own iconography. Their names only appear in the post-Vedic period. Six of the seven are considered wives of Hindu gods, as reflected in their names: Brahmani, Maheshvari, Kaumari, Vaishnavi, Varahi, and Indrani are married, respectively, to BRAHMA, SHIVA, Kumara (KARTTIKEYA), VISHNU, VARAHA, and INDRA. CHAMUNDA, the seventh, is most often seen as a form of DURGA.

Further reading: Shivaji K. Panikkar, *Saptamatrka Worship and Sculptures: An Iconological Interpretation of Conflicts and Resolutions in the Storied Brahmanical Icons* (New Delhi: D. K. Printworld, 1997).

sapta rishi (saptarshi)

The *sapta rishi* were a grouping of seven (*sapta*) RISHIS (seers), who are said to have received some of the most important books and verses of the VEDAS. They are considered to be the progenitors of the orthodox BRAHMIN lineages (GOTRAS). They are usually listed as Kashyapa, Atri, Bharadvaja, Vishvamitra, Gotama, Jamadagni, and Vasishtha. (There is another tradition that lists the chief *rishis* as Marici, Atri, Angiras, Pulastya, Kratu, Bhrisu, and Vasishtha; in that tradition, they are not necessarily the source for the Brahminical lineages.)

Those in the first list are frequently encountered in the epics and PURANAS, the Indian mythological literature. In the month of Bhadrapada (August–September) the seven *rishis* are honored on the fifth day of the bright half of the month, when the Moon is waxing. The ritual in their honor can be performed by anyone. Worship is offered to images of the seven, and celibacy and a vegetarian diet are observed for the celebration. The images of the *rishis* (often fashioned by hand) are offered to Brahmins alongside seven pots. This observance guarantees happiness, progeny, and freedom from sin and other difficulties.

The second list of *rishis* are usually worshipped in the seven days that begin on the first day of the bright half of the month of Chaitra (March–April), the New Year's month. Fruits, flowers, and cow's milk are offered to the *saptarshi.* A single meal is to be taken, only after sundown.

Further reading: Ravi Prakash Arya and Ram Narain Arya, *Vedic Concordance of Mantras as Per Devata and Rsi* (Rohtak: Indian Foundation for Vedic Science, 2003); John E. Mitchiner, *Traditions of the Seven Rishis* (Delhi: Motilal Banarsidass, 1982).

Sarada Devi, Sri (1853–1920) *incarnation of Holy Mother*

Sri Sarada Devi, wife of the Kali priest Sri RAMAKRISHNA, was a very popular teacher in her own right, considered to be an incarnation of Holy Mother. She became an important activist in helping the poor and in advancing educational opportunities for women.

Sarada Devi was born in the rural village of Jayrambati, west of Kamarpurkur in Bengal, on December 22, 1853. The eldest of seven children of Ram Chandra Mukhopadhyay and Shyamasundari Devi, Sarada was raised in a poor BRAHMIN household where she assisted her parents in household duties, worked in the fields, and cared for her younger siblings. She was described as a gentle, humble, hardworking, and diligent child. When time permitted, she attended school and learned to read and write.

At the age of five, Sarada married Sri RAMAKRISHNA, a Bengali priest of goddess KALI who was 17 years her senior. By that time, Sri Ramakrishna had experienced his first vision of the divine mother, the goddess KALI, and was living in an ecstatic state of communication with the divine. His mother, concerned with his strange behavior, sought to restore him to worldly life by finding

Sri Sarada Devi (1853–1920), wife of Sri Ramakrishna, incarnation of Holy Mother, and inspiration for Sarada Math/Monastery *(Courtesy Vedanta Society, San Francisco, California)*

him a suitable spouse. She found Sarada Devi in a neighboring village. After the marriage, Sarada Devi returned to her family and Sri Ramakrishna continued his spiritual practice and priestly duties at Dakshineswar Temple near Calcutta (Kolkata).

At the age of 18, hearing rumors that her husband was suffering from mental illness, she went to him at the temple. Finding him deeply engaged in spiritual disciplines, she became his first disciple and began her own spiritual journey under his direction and care. He instructed her in the spiritual life as well as the importance of household duties and their role in the meditative life. Ramakrishna considered her an embodied representative of the Divine Mother. From this time forward, Sarada Devi became known as the Holy Mother and spent the rest of her life sharing the wisdom and insight of Sri Ramakrishna's teachings to all who went to her.

Sri Ramakrishna died in 1886, leaving the 33-year old Sarada Devi as the lineage holder of the Ramakrishna Order. In addition to teaching and caring for her disciples, she guided the activities of the Ramakrishna Organizations, spending most of her time in service to rural communities in Bengal and the disciples of the Ramakrishna Order in Calcutta. Serving the poor and disadvantaged women of Bengal, she became committed to advancing the education of women to promote women's independence and social awareness.

From 1886 until her death, Sarada Devi touched the lives of hundreds of devotees through her simple and pure devotion to the spiritual life. As Holy Mother, she never turned away anyone in need. She valued equality and did not discriminate among disciples by caste, religion, gender, or nationality. Her unconditional compassion inspired a new spiritual movement. The core of her teaching, as of Ramakrishna's, was the recognition of the divine in everything. She died in Calcutta on July 21, 1920, 34 years after the death of her husband.

The Sri Sarada Math, the world's largest independent women's monastic order, was established in 1954 as the women's complement to the Vedanta Societies Ramakrishna Math and Mission, to perpetuate the teachings of Sri Ramakrishna, Sri Sarada Devi, and Swami Vivekananda. The *math* is located on the bank of the Ganges River near Dakshineswar Temple, where Sri Ramakrishna served as priest. Sri Sarada Math has nuns in residence in centers throughout the world.

See also Nivedita.

Further reading: Amalaprana, *Eternal Mother* (Calcutta: Kolkata Paperback, 2004); Atmaprana, *Sri Sarada Devi and Sri Sarada Math* (New Delhi: New Delhi Paperbacks, 2003); Swami Gambhirananda, *Holy Mother Shri Sarada Devi* (Mylapore: Ramakrishna Math, 1955); Swami Nirvedananda, *The Holy Mother* (Calcutta: Calcutta Paperbacks, 1983); Lizelle Reymond, *The Dedicated: A Biography of Nivedita* (Madras:

Samata, 1985); Swami Tapasyananda, *Sri Sarada Devi: The Holy Mother* (Mylapore: Sri Ramakrishna Math, 1958).

Sarasvati

The Sarasvati was one of the great rivers of RIG VEDIC times and was worshipped as a divine goddess in the VEDAS. A handful of verses in the Vedas also associate her with the stream of the dead, which is crossed by all who die.

The river Sarasvati dried up in ancient times. However, it is said still to be flowing invisibly, joining the GANGES and YAMUNA at Prayag (ALLAHABAD), one of the sites of the KUMBHA MELA festival.

In a stray verse or two of RIG VEDA, Sarasvati is seen as the goddess of knowledge—all the arts and sciences; this later becomes the primary identification of the name. She is iconographically represented as holding a *vina* or lute in her hands. She is the wife of BRAHMA. Her vehicle is the swan or peacock.

Further reading: Kanailal Bhattacharyya, *Sarasvati: A Study in Her Concept and Iconography* (Calcutta: Saraswat Library, 1983); N. N. Godbole, *Rig Vedic Sarasvati* (Jaipur: Government of Rajasthan, 1963); Jan Gonda, *Pushan and Sarasvati* (Amsterdam: North-Holland, 1985); David R. Kinsley, *Hindu Goddesses* (Berkeley: University of California Press, 1988).

sat   See SAT-CIT-ANANDA.

Satchidananda, Swami (1914–2002) *founder of Integral Yoga Institutes and Yogaville*

Swami Satchidanada was a great popularizer of yoga both within India and around the world. His interfaith emphasis and his organizational efforts, especially in the United States, continue to bear fruit.

Ramaswamy was born on December 22, 1914, to a devout family in Chettipalam, near Coimbatore in Tamil Nadu state. His father, Sri Kalyanasunderam, was the village's unofficial headman and his mother, Sri Velammai, entertained the visiting poets, musicians, philosophers, and astrologers who frequented the family home. As a youth, Ramaswamy met SADHUS and SANNYASIS (holy men and penitents) in his own home, as he pursued skills in agriculture, mechanics, electronics, and cinematography.

At age 28, he began a full-time spiritual quest that included meeting RAMANA Maharshi and Sri AUROBINDO. He became a disciple of Swami SIVANANDA of RISHIKESH and took SANNYAS initiation from him in 1949. He taught as a professor of HATHA and *raja* YOGA at Sivananda's Vedanta Forest Academy in Rishikesh and made extensive lecture tours throughout the world. He spread the teachings and the organization of Sivananda's Divine Life Society in many parts of Asia, particularly Sri Lanka, Malaysia, Singapore, Hong Kong, Japan, and the Philippines. In 1958 he completed a pilgrimage to Mount KAILASH in Tibet.

In 1966, Satchidananda made his first global tour, sponsored by an American devotee. The intended two-day visit to New York extended to five months as he was surrounded by hundreds of students, eager for his teachings and guidance. The Integral Yoga Institutes were founded under his direction, and today there are Integral Yoga Institutes and Centers throughout the world. In 1976, he became a U.S. citizen.

Satchidananda has been named patron and adviser to various organizations around the world, including the European Union of National Yoga Federations, the International Association of Yoga Teachers, Unity in Yoga, and the Temple of Understanding. He received many honors for his service, including: the Martin Buber Award for Outstanding Service to Humanity, the Juliet Hollister Interfaith Award, the B'nai Brith Anti-Defamation League's Humanitarian Award, the Albert Schweitzer Humanitarian Award, and the U Thant

Peace Award. He was also the recipient of several honorary doctorates and honorary titles.

Satchidananda's teaching centers around the principle "Truth Is One, Paths Are Many." He sponsored many interfaith symposia, retreats, and worship services around the world. In 1986, he created a center dedicated to the light of all faiths and to world peace, called the Light of Truth Universal Shrine (LOTUS), located at Satchidananda Ashram at Yogaville in Virginia. Yogaville serves as the international headquarters of the Integral Yoga Institutes and Centers.

He died on August 19, 2002, in his native Tamil Nadu, South India.

Further reading: Sita Wiener, *Swami Satchidananda: His Biography* (San Francisco: Straight Arrow, 1970).

sat-chit-ananda (sacchidananda)

Sat-chit-ananda is a philosophical term used in VEDANTA and other Hindu systems; it describes the ultimate reality or the ultimate character of a god or goddess.

In Vedanta, words can convey only a conventional description of the *brahman* or ultimate reality, which is beyond any characterizing or characteristics. Nevertheless, the combination of *sat* (Being as an ultimate category), *chit* (unlimited consciousness), and *ananda* (unlimited bliss) is often used to describe the ultimate. Those who achieve the highest level in YOGA, who realize oneness with the ultimate, are believed to be capable of knowing these categories beyond the words. Therefore, many realized SWAMIS use this appellation for themselves.

The use of these terms to identify the supreme BRAHMAN began in the UPANISHADS (c. 600 B.C.E.); it became a common practice as later Vedanta developed.

Further reading: Troy Wilson Organ, *The One: East and West* (Lanham: University Press of America, 1991); Swami Sachchidanand, *My Experiences*. Translated by P. J. Soni. (Ahmedabad: Gurjar Prakashan, 1989).

Sati

Sati is the first wife of SHIVA, later reincarnated as PARVATI or Uma. She is the daughter of the sage DAKSHA, himself the son of BRAHMA. Brahma was concerned that the human universe would not come about if Shiva did not take a wife, so he compelled Daksha to produce a daughter, Sati, who was a form of the Great Goddess. He arranged to have her marry Shiva. To seduce Shiva, who was devoted to asceticism and did not want to marry, Sati practiced austerities and won his attention. They were quickly married with Brahma serving as the marriage priest.

Daksha was not happy to have Shiva as his son-in-law. He held a great Vedic sacrifice and pointedly did not invite his daughter and son-in-law. When Sati complained to her father, he upbraided her. There are two versions of the succeeding events. In one, she immolated herself in a fire. The later Hindu practice of a widow's immolating herself on her husband's funeral pyre took on the name of *sati* (suttee).

In the second version, Daksha had been under a curse, that if he were to show disrespect to his daughter, she would die; when he upbraided her she simply fell to the ground dead. Shiva rushed to the site of the sacrifice, killed Daksha, and destroyed the entire ritual sacrifice ground. Both Daksha and the sacrifice were later restored in some versions—but not Sati. Shiva lifted Sati's body and mournfully began to carry it about India. Since a dead body is considered highly polluting, Lord VISHNU followed Shiva, gradually cutting off pieces of Sati as they went along. Everywhere a piece of her fell, a shrine was established to the Great Goddess. These are variously said to number 54, 108, or some other number.

sati (suttee) *widow self-immolation*

Sati, the practice of burning widows on their husbands' funeral pyres (as had happened with the goddess Sati), developed in post-Vedic India, as the rights of women, especially widows, greatly deteriorated. Widows were almost considered to be dead. They had to shave their heads and dress in white with no decoration. They were considered inauspicious and were often confined to the home.

Because of the practice of marriage outside one's clan in North India, spouses generally were from distant villages. As all marriages were patrilocal, a woman whose husband had died would find herself living with unrelated in-laws, who often did not look upon her kindly. If the woman had several children and particularly a son, she might draw comfort and status from them, but if she were newly married with no children, she looked forward to a life of ascetic denial and loneliness as remarriage was strictly forbidden. As a result, many women succumbed to the social pressure of self-immolation on the fires of their husbands; it is documented that many others were coerced to do so. As an added incentive, in certain regions, the woman who became a *sati* was deified.

In the 19th century the British colonial administrators outlawed *sati*. Independent India also outlawed the practice, and it largely fell into disuse after independence. However, the debate over the practice never completely ceased. With the modern Hindu revival some have argued that this traditional practice should be encouraged; this idea has spurred furious opposition from secularists and women's groups.

Further reading: John Stratton Hawley, ed., *Sati, the Blessing and the Curse: The Burning of Wives in India* (New York: Oxford University Press, 1994); John S. Hawley and Donna M. Wulff, eds., *Devi: Goddesses of India* (Berkeley: University of California Press, 1996); Stella Kramrisch, *The Presence of Siva* (Princeton, N.J.: Princeton University Press, 1981); Rajeswari Sunder Rajan, *Real and Imagined Women: Gender, Culture, and Postcolonialism* (London/New York: Routledge, 1993).

sattva   *See* GUNAS.

satyagraha   *See* GANDHI, MOHANDAS KARAMCHAND.

Satyananda Saraswati, Swami   *See* INTERNATIONAL YOGA FELLOWSHIP.

Satya Sai Baba (1926–   ) *popular spiritual teacher and miracle worker*

Satya Sai Baba was born Satyanarayana Raju in the village of Puttaparthi, Andra Pradesh, to a pious KSHATRIYA family on November 23, 1926. At the age of 14 he quit school and disclosed to his parents that he was in fact the incarnation of SAI BABA OF SHIRDI, the revered South Indian saint of the late 19th and early 20th centuries. He left his family and stayed in the house of a BRAHMIN neighbor during adolescence; there he began to receive devotees.

In 1950, the first ashram dedicated to the work of Satya Sai Baba was established near Puttaparthi. Later, other ashrams were established near Bangalore and Ootakamund.

Satya Sai Baba is well known for his miraculous healings and materializations, and some claim that he has even raised the dead. He is known for materializing in his right hand objects such as rings, lockets, amulets, and fruits out of season. Devotees report that his photos in their homes in different parts of the world are repeatedly covered with holy ash, *vibhuti*, even when he is not nearby.

Satya Sai Baba has built several schools, universities, and one modern hospital in India. He is responsible for a number of social work programs: colleges for both boys and girls, educational courses on spirituality, community building projects, welfare programs for the poor, and clean water projects for South Indian communities.

Claiming to be a full incarnation of KALKI, avatar of the KALI YUGA, Sai Baba says that his task is to behave in a human way so that humankind can feel kinship with him, yet to rise to superhuman heights to protect the virtuous and destroy evil. Quoting Lord KRISHNA's words in the BHAGAVAD GITA, Sai Baba says that whenever disharmony overwhelms the world, the Lord will incarnate in human form to establish peace and to reeducate the human community.

Sai Baba's influence is considerable; active devotees and centers organized around his work and message exist throughout the world. His personal conduct, however, has been the subject of numerous charges, including sexual misconduct and fraud. His international headquarters are in Puttaparthi, Andra Pradesh, India.

Further reading: Roy Eugene Davis, *The Teachings of Sri Satya Sai Baba* (Lakemont, Ga.: CSA Press, 1991); Satya Pal Ruhela, *In Search of Sai Divine: A Comprehensive Research Review of Writings and Researches on Sri Sathya Sai Baba Avatar* (Delhi: Print House, n.d.); T. B. Singh, *Satya Sai Baba: Godman of India Today* (Delhi: Hind Pocket Books 1976); Brian Steel, *The Satya Sai Baba Compendium: A Guide to the First Seventy Years* (New York: Weiser, 1997).

Satyavan   *See* SAVITRI.

Satya Yuga   *See* KRITA YUGA.

Savitri   *mythic princess*

The story of Savitri and Satyavan, told in the Mahabharata, is one of the most poignant in Indian literature. The beautiful maiden Savitri falls in love with a hermit's son, Satyavan, and marries him. Savitri learns from his father that unbeknown to Satyavan the boy has only one year to live. Savitri forebears from telling Satyavan, in order to preserve their precious days of happiness.

The pair live in great delight as the bride tries to forget the curse that threatens their love. As the final day approaches Savitri furiously engages in prayers and penances to stave off the inevitable. On the final day she follows her husband closely into the woods where he has gone to fetch wood. Her husband soon collapses as the frightening figure of YAMA, god of death, appears before them with a noose in his hand.

Yama removes Satyavan's soul and heads toward his domain, with Savitri in desperate pursuit. Yama asks her to turn back, but she insists that she will follow him even to the underworld. Seeing her great devotion, Yama grants her any boon but that of having her husband restored to life. She takes this boon but insists on following farther. She gains two more similar boons but will not relent. Finally, Yama offers her a boon without exception and she asks that her husband be restored to life. The boon is granted and Satyavan returns to life.

SRI AUROBINDO wrote an elegant and enchanting epic poem celebrating this story, in which he outlines his conception of Integral Yoga and the power of the MOTHER to effect the complete supramental transformation of the universe.

Further reading: Sri Aurobindo, *Savitri: A Legend and a Symbol* (Pondicherry: Sri Aurobindo Ashram, 1951); Aaron Shepard with Vera Rosenberry, *Savitri: A Tale of Ancient India* (Morton Grove, Ill.: A. Whitman, 1992).

Savitri   *Vedic divinity*

Savitri is one name for the Vedic god of the Sun. Several gods in the RIG VEDA seem to be associated with the Sun, probably indicating that the Sun had different names at different times of the day or seasons of the year, or for different purposes. *Savitri* was often used in conjunction with *SURYA*, and the two may have been interchangeable.

Savitri is used in the famous GAYATRI MANTRA, recited every morning by BRAHMINS and others. In the Rig Veda, Savitri is connected with several important rites. It is said that those who desire heaven should do the AGNICHAYANA, or "building of the fire altar," ritual for Savitri.

The name is derived from the SANSKRIT *su* (to incite or impel). Savitri thus brings to life or compels thoughts and action. This seems only natural for the Sun, who wakens the world and keeps it alive by its life-giving rays.

Further reading: Alfred Hillebrandt, *Vedic Mythology* (Delhi: Motilal Banarsidass, 1990); P. Pandit, *Aditi and Other Deities in the Veda* (Pondicherry: Dipti, 1970); W. J. Wilkins, *Hindu Mythology, Vedic and Puranic* (Calcutta: Rupa, 1973).

Sawan Kirpal Ruhani Mission   *See* SANT MAT MOVEMENT.

Scandinavia

The Scandinavian countries were preponderantly Christian until the middle of the 20th century; the Lutheran Church had been the established religion for centuries. While a spectrum of Christian sects appeared during the 19th century, the first break in the Christian consensus appears to have occurred early in the 20th century with the spread of THEOSOPHY to Scandinavia and the subsequent formation of several esoteric groups such as the Martinus Institute, founded in Denmark in the 1940s.

Hinduism was introduced into Scandinavia in 1967 as a result of the teachings of Swami NARAYANANANDA (1902–88), a YOGA teacher from Bengal. He had been discovered by some Danes who were traveling in India and they created the first ashram for his work in Gylling, Denmark. In 1969 they erected a house for Swami Narayanananda, who made his first trip to Europe in 1971. He regularly visited Europe throughout the rest of his life, and the Narayanananda Universal Yoga Ashrams spread to the other Scandinavian countries.

As a youth, a Dane later known as Swami Janakananda (b. 1939) began practicing YOGA and MEDITATION. Then in 1968 he met Swami Satyananda Saraswati (b. 1923), founder of the INTERNATIONAL YOGA FELLOWSHIP MOVEMENT, and went to India to study at the Bihar School of Yoga. He became a SWAMI, was given his spiritual name, and returned to his homeland two years later to found the Scandinavian Yoga and Meditation School in Copenhagen. Shortly thereafter he published *Yoga, Tantra and Meditation in Daily Life,* later translated into nine languages.

In 1977, Janakananda organized "Meditation Yoga 77," an international yoga congress held in Stockholm. He invited an international list of speakers, reflecting the many Indian teachers who would visit the Scandinavian school in succeeding years. He later opened a retreat center in southern Sweden. As did Narayanananda's movement, the school spread to the other Scandinavian countries. The first affiliated Norwegian school opened in 1983. In more recent years, other yoga centers, such as the Ashtanga Yoga Center of Helsinki, have opened in major Scandinavian urban centers.

Already in the 1970s, the expansive INTERNATIONAL SOCIETY FOR KRISHNA CONSCIOUSNESS targeted the Scandinavian countries. They opened their first center in Sweden and eventually spread to Denmark and Finland. Today they maintain a large temple in Grodinge, some 25 miles south of Stockholm.

In 1974, Sri CHINMOY (b. 1931) visited Iceland and subsequently formed the only Hindu community on the island. Chinmoy, noted for his physical feats, once lifted the prime minister of Iceland as part of a weightlifting demonstration.

In the 1980s, a small number of Indians began to find their way to Denmark and Sweden. By the beginning of the 21st century, there were some 1,500 Hindus in Sweden and around 3,500 in Denmark. Wherever concentrations of immigrants settled, temples and community organizations began to appear, among the first the Hindu Union in Jönköping, Sweden, founded in 1974. The larger community in Stockholm now sponsors two temples, both of which were opened early in the new century. The VISHVA HINDU PARISHAD has also formed as a coordinating organization for the various Hindu centers. The Hindu community is just completing its first generation in Scandinavia, and forecasting its future is difficult. It may also be noted that Indian migration to Scandinavia has also included some Sikhs; as of 2005 five *gurudwaras* were operating, two in Norway, two in Sweden, and one in Denmark.

Further reading: Swami Narayanananda, *The Ideal Life and Moksha (Freedom)* (Gylling, Denmark: N. U. Yoga Trust & Ashrama, 1979); Swami Janakananda Saraswati, *Experience Yoga Nidra: Guided Deep Relaxation* (Copenhagen: Bindu, 2003); ———, *Yoga, Tantra and Meditation in Daily Life* (Westminster, Md.: Ballantine Books, 1976); Margareta Skog, *Det religiosa Sverige* (Örebro, Sweden: Bokforlaget Libris, 2001).

Sekkilar (12th century)

Sekkilar, whose given name was probably Ramatevar, is the author of PERIYA PURANAM, the 12th and final book of the Tamil Shaivite scripture, the TIRUMURAI. He was a Vellala, a high middle-caste designation. He is also known as Arunmolitevar, Sevaikkavalar, and Sekkilarnayanar (Sekkilar the saint).

Sekkilar was born in the village of Kundratur in northeastern Tamil Nadu. He was chief minister of the Chola emperor Anapaya Chola. He is said to have recited the Periya Puranam to the retired Chola king at the Shaivite sacred shrine of CHIDAMBARAM.

Further reading: G. Vanmikinathan, *Periya Puranam, a Tamil Classic on the Great Saiva Saints of South India* (Madras: Ramakrishna Math, 1985); Kamil V. Zvelibil, "Tamil Literature," in Jan Gonda, ed., *The History of Indian Literature,* Vol. 10, Fascicle 1 (Wiesbaden: Otto Harrassowitz, 1974).

self-realization

Self-realization, or living in constant awareness of the real Self, ATMAN, is considered the goal of most Hindu study and practice. Hinduism recognizes that individual abilities and interests vary considerably among people, so it acknowledges that self-realization can be achieved through devotion, study, faith, work in the world, or meditation. In this way, Hinduism includes disciplines for mind, emotions, body, and action in the world—all as valid ways to realization of ultimate reality, the atman.

See also MOKSHA; SAMADHI.

Self-Realization Fellowship (est. 1935)

The Self-Realization Fellowship (SRF) is an international religious organization founded in 1935 by Paramahansa YOGANANDA (1893–1952) to introduce people of all races, cultures, and creeds to the ancient science and philosophy of YOGA and MEDITATION. Through its worldwide service, the society seeks to foster a spirit of greater harmony and goodwill among the diverse people and nations of the world, and a deeper understanding of the underlying unity of all religions.

SRF traces its beginning to 1861 and the work of the legendary mahavatar BABAJI, who is said by Yogananda to have revived the ancient science of KRIYA YOGA. According to Yogananda, Babaji chose him to take the teachings to the West. In 1917, Yogananda founded the Yogoda Satsanga Society (YSS) of India, headquartered in Dakshineswar (near Calcutta [Kolkata]). Today the YSS has more than 20 educational and medical facilities, including a college of liberal arts and business, a medical college, several schools for boys and girls, and both allopathic and homeopathic hospitals and clinics. In 1920 Yogananda traveled to the United States to attend the tercentenary anniversary of the International Congress of Religious Liberals convening in Boston. One of the last Indians to enter America before the change in immigration laws limited Asian immigration, he decided to stay in the United States. He formed a center of the Yogoda Satsang in Boston, Massachusetts, and traveled widely in the eastern United States.

In 1924, Yogananda made his first trip across the country and founded the headquarters for his work at Mt. Washington in Los Angeles, California. He lectured in the principal cities of the United States, wrote inspirational works, and worked on a home study course on *kriya yoga*. After the founding of SRF in 1935, other centers were opened in California at Encinitas, San Diego, Hollywood, Long Beach, and Pacific Palisades, with smaller groups in other cities in the United States.

Entrance to the Self-Realization Fellowship Headquarters in Encinitas, California *(Institute for the Study of American Religion, Santa Barbara, California)*

During Yogananda's years in the United States, he initiated thousands of men and women into the teachings and methods of yoga and meditation. Central to his teaching and that of SRF is a yogic way to bliss (ANANDA) or SELF-REALIZATION, or God realization. The way to bliss is through scientific methods of concentration, including an advanced technique called *kriya yoga* as taught and passed down by the yogi Babaji. This technique is a system of awakening and energizing the psychic centers or CHAKRAS located along the spinal column. Through deep regular meditation, spiritual cosmic energies are focused and direct perception of the divine is experienced. The blood is decarbonized and recharged with oxygen, the atoms of which are transmuted into "life current" to rejuvenate the brain and spinal centers. The practice makes it possible to withdraw one's energy and attention from the usual turbulence of thoughts, emotions, and sensory perceptions. In the stillness that is discovered, one is able to experience peace and attunement with God. The term "Self-realization" as used by Yogananda, signifies realization of one's true Self, or soul—the individualized expression of the one universal spirit that animates and informs all life.

SRF also emphasizes the essential unity of Eastern and Western religious teachings. Services in SRF organizations include interpretations of parallel scriptural passages from the BHAGAVAD GITA and Christian scripture, especially the New Testament.

Yogananda was succeeded by Swami Rajasi Janakananda (James J. Lynn), who died in 1955 and was succeeded by Sri DAYA MATA (b. 1914), the current head of the fellowship.

SRF is coordinated by members of its monastic order. These monks and nuns serve Yogananda's vision through worldwide spiritual and humanitarian work, including over 100 meditation centers, retreats, youth programs, publishing and translating programs, temple services, and coordination of the Worldwide Prayer Circle, a network of groups and individuals dedicated to praying for those in need.

Under the direction of Sri Daya Mata SRF publishes the writings, lectures, and informal talks of Paramahansa Yogananda and of his close disciples. SRF also distributes audio and video recordings of Yogananda's teachings. SRF has a temple or center in 49 states in America and 49 countries in the world. The Yogoda Satsang Society of India has 32 centers and operates a variety of charitable facilities.

Further reading: Sri Daya Mata, *Only Love* (Los Angeles: Self-Realization Fellowship, 1976); Paramahansa Yogananda, *Autobiography of a Yogi* (Los Angeles: Self-Realization Fellowship, 1971); ———, *Descriptive Outlines of Yogoda* (Los Angeles: Yogoda Satsang Society, 1928); ———, *Man's Eternal Quest* (Los Angeles: Self-Realization Fellowship, 1975); ———, *Self-Realization Highlights* (Los Angeles: Self-Realization Fellowship, 1980); ———, *Whispers from Eternity* (Los Angeles: Self-Realization Fellowship, 1986).

Self-Revelation Church of Absolute Monism (est. 1928)

The Self-Realization Church of Absolute Monism was founded by Swami Premananda (1903–95), who was called in 1925 by Paramahansa YOGANANDA to move to the United States. While independent of Yogananda's primary organization in the United States, the Self-Realization Fellowship, the Church of Absolute Monism has much the same teaching focus. Both stress ADVAITA (non-dualist) VEDANTA, the life and philosophy of Mohandas Karamchand GANDHI, the unity of all religions, the practice of *kriya yoga,* and cultural appreciation. The name *absolute monism* refers to the ancient philosophy of *advaita* Vedanta, which affirms that ultimate reality is non-dual.

The church has linkages to the Mahatma Gandhi Memorial Foundation and has an accent on education and culture. The current leader of the church and of the Gandhi memorial center is Sri Mata Kamalananda. She was ordained a minister in the Swami Order in 1973, and a full swami in 1978. The group publishes the *Mystic Cross* and the *Gandhi Message* periodicals.

Further reading: Swami Premananda, *Light on Kriya Yoga* (Washington, D.C.: Swami Premananda Foundation, 1969); ———, The *Path of the Eternal Law* (Washington, D.C.: Self-Realization Fellowship, 1942); ———, *Prayers of Realization* (Washington, D.C.: Self-Realization Fellowship, 1943).

Sen, Keshab Chunder (1838–1884) *social reformer and philosopher*

Keshab Chunder Sen was a philosopher and social reformer, whose career reflected the variety of responses to the modern world that emerged in Hindu society.

Sen was born on November 19, 1838, into a wealthy family in Calcutta (Kolkata) who were very involved in both Bengali and Western cultural movements. He was recruited at age 19 by Debendranath Tagore, father of the poet RABINDRANATH TAGORE, to the celebrated BRAHMO SAMAJ reform movement, which attempted to purify Hinduism from practices such as caste, child marriage, *purdah* (seclusion of women), ill treatment of widows, and particularly idol worship. He became secretary of the movement in 1859. Sen broke away in 1865 because of personal disagreements and formed the Brahmo Samaj of India. This organization also split after Sen married his daughter to a maharajah when she was only 14 years old, an action that was seen as a major betrayal of the movement's principles.

In 1878 Sen formed the Sadharan Brahmo Samaj. His views had changed under the influence of the teacher RAMAKRISHNA, who persuaded him to accept image worship and see the Hindu pantheon in a new light, as a way for the ordinary devotee to engage the divinity concretely.

His New Dispensation, which he announced in 1879, has often been taken as tantamount to his conversion to Christianity, but it is more complicated. He considered his movement to be on a par with the Jewish and Christian traditions and as a fulfillment of Christ's prophecy. He also believed that his movement would lead to the harmonization of all religions. Though he referred to himself as Jesudas, servant of Jesus, he emphasized Christ's Asiatic character and saw Christ in a VEDANTIC light as the one god, who is worshipped under different names by all those who worship God.

He died on January 8, 1884.

Further reading: *Keshub Chunder Sen in England: Diaries, Sermons, Addresses and Epistles* (Calcutta: Writers Workshop, 1980); Glyn Richards, ed., *A Source Book of Modern Hinduism* (London: Curzon Press, 1985); David C. Scott, ed., *Keshub Chunder Sen: A Selection* (Madras: Christian Literature, 1979).

Sen, Ramprasad (c. 1718–c. 1780) *Bengali poet-saint and Kali devotee*

Ramprasad Sen, who is often referred to by his first name alone, was a beloved Bengali poet-saint, whose songs are known to every Bengali.

As for many of the poet-saints of India the details of his life are intermixed with myth. Similarly, as with KABIR, his name and fame impelled other writers to compose many beautiful verses in homage to his works, particularly his collection of songs known as *Padabali*. His other major attributed works are *Bidyasundar, Kalikirttan,* and *Krishnakirttan*.

Ramprasad was probably born to a higher-caste Vaidya family of traditional physicians, possibly BRAHMINS. He was educated in SANSKRIT and in Persian in addition to Bengali. He is said to have lived in the village of Kumarhatt, also known as Halishore, on the banks of the GANGES not far from Calcutta (Kolkata). It seems certain that he was patronized by the contemporary king, Maharaja Krishnachandra Ray Bahadur.

Ramprasad started out as a clerk for a wealthy household in or near Calcutta. It is said that he was constantly distracted from his duties by thoughts of the GODDESS DURGA or KALI. Legend says that one of his employers, upon seeing his beautiful verses to the goddess in his account books, told him to cease being an accountant and offered him a salary simply to continue composing devotional verse.

Legend also says that when Ramprasad was a little over 60 years old, he announced that on the day when the goddess was going to be immersed in the Ganges (either Kali or Durga Puja day), he also would be immersed with the Divine Mother. It is said that he slowly descended into the river, singing some of his farewell songs. He died singing a song to the goddess Tara.

In one of the amazing stories associated with Ramprasad he accompanied the maharajah on a journey on the Ganges. As usual he was singing his devotional songs. The Muslim ruler of the area happened to overhear the song and was enchanted by it. The ruler requested Ramprasad to sing for him so Ramprasad sang a song in Muslim style. The Nawab, the Muslim ruler, was not pleased and asked him to sing a song to Kali. The Muslim was moved to tears and offered patronage and high rank to Ramprasad, who declined them.

Most importantly Ramprasad is a central figure in the revival of Shaktism (*see* SHAKTA) or goddess worship in late 18th-century Bengal. His works typically show him drunk or mad with the goddess, and he cannot live without her. His work shows strong TANTRIC influence.

Ramprasad's poems to the goddess see her as a daughter, as a fierce wife of SHIVA, as the Divine Mother, and as his own mother. His sentiment in regard to her is very close to that of another famous Bengali, RAMAKRISHNA.

Further reading: Lex Hixon, *Mother of the Universe: Visions of the Goddess and Tantric Hymns of Enlightenment* (Wheaton, Ill.: Quest Books, 1994); Malcolm McLean, *Devoted to the Goddess: The Life and Work of Ramprasad* (Albany: State University of New York Press, 1998); J. McDaniel, *Madness of the Saints:*

Ecstatic Religion in Bengal (Chicago: University of Chicago Press, 1989).

Shaiva Siddhanta   *See* Saiva Siddhanta.

Shaivism

Shaivism is the formal name for the group of traditions that worship Shiva as the supreme divinity. A person who worships Shiva will be called a Shaiva in India or a Shaivite in academic parlance. This loose sect, which encompasses by far the large majority of Hindus, probably began to form around the fifth or fourth century B.C.E. Worship of Lord Shiva is mentioned in both the Ramayana and Mahabharata epics.

The first Shiva lingam authenticated archaeologically dates from about the first century C.E., but it is likely that this type of worship was already many centuries old. Scholars often point to a very ancient Indus Valley seal showing a seated figure with a water-buffalo-horned headdress and, apparently, an erect penis, both evocative of Shiva. It is called the Pashupati figure, "Lord of the Animals," which is also a later designation of Shiva. However, there is no other evidence to indicate worship of a Shiva-like being in the Indus Valley civilization. Some even discern a "yogic" seating posture in the figure, although Indians do traditionally sit in that cross-legged pattern.

The Shiva lingam is actually a sexual symbol showing the coitus of the divine male with the female. The sexual organ of the goddess is found in the surrounding circular stone that almost always encases the lingam. It is probably because of this primordial association of Shiva with the goddess that from his first appearance in mythology he is seen with a wife, Sati, who tragically dies. She is afterward reincarnated as Parvati. At times Shiva is also associated with Durga and Kali. With Parvati the divine family develops with an older son, the elephant-headed Ganesha, and a younger son, Karttikeya.

The first formal Shaivite text may well be a Tamil text relating the worship of the younger son of Shiva, Murugan, another name of Karttikeya, dating from approximately the third century C.E. The first known Shaivite saint, a female ascetic, Karaikkalammaiyar, dates from around the fourth century. Not long after, stone temples were built to Shiva in South India, around the sixth century. As later all around India the central shrine was almost always a Shiva lingam.

In a challenge to the Jains in Tamil Nadu, a group of great Shaivite saints began to wander from shrine to shrine and temple to temple singing the praises of Lord Shiva. The three great saints associated with the Tamil Shaivite scripture Tevaram date to the sixth to eighth centuries. They helped make Shaivism the most influential tradition in the region. The pattern repeated itself farther north in later centuries, as poet-saint devotees spread the word of Lord Shiva and popularized devotional worship.

Shaivite *puranas* were first written in Sanskrit around the sixth century. They told extraordinary stories of the ascetic-erotic Lord Shiva, the chaotic Lord, who resisted household life and children and made trouble for the world and the gods. These *puranas* form the Sanskrit backbone for the Shaivite cult.

By the 12th century Shaivism (as had Vaishnavism) in the Tamil country had fully assimilated the Sanskritic tradition of the north into the local traditions. Thus Shaivism developed a clear sense of continuity with northern Vedic Brahminism. Both Sanskrit and Tamil were honored as holy languages. Shiva undoubtedly had a northern Indian provenance. All the shrines that the southern Shaivite saints frequented were originally associated with local divinities, whom the saints recognized as forms of Shiva.

Farther north, the Virashaiva tradition developed in the 12th century in Karnataka. The Virashaivas did not accept icons and eschewed Vedic worship entirely. They were devoted only to Shiva as a formless indefinable divinity. Each Virashaiva would simply wear a lingam around the neck to show devotion. Caste was outlawed and women were made equals to men in the tradition. Their path was devotional, and their desire was to realize the divine truth that was Shiva.

Shaivite icons and temple artifacts appear much later in the north than in the south, but Shaivism was flourishing earlier nonetheless. Smaller shrines with Shiva lingams were apparently the norm, places where mendicants gathered, often to smoke hashish and sing the praises of the Lord who was everywhere.

Between the eighth and 12th centuries the NATH YOGIS became prominent among the Shaivite wandering mendicants. Famed among these was the great GURU GORAKHNATH. These wild, ascetic mendicants were antisocial and often frightening in appearance, carrying begging bowls made of skulls and smearing themselves with human ashes to mimic the chaotic Lord himself. They practiced alchemy in an attempt to achieve immortality. When in the south an organized literature, liturgy, and temple culture had already emerged, North India Shaivism seemed to move along different lines. The Shaivite temple cult began to develop in North India around the ninth or 10th century, but truly dramatic temples were not built until some 600 years after they had appeared in the south.

In the 12th century the great ABHINAVAGUPTA wrote his texts outlining KASHMIRI SHAIVISM, a TANTRIC tradition that relied on personal transformation and ritual to realize the total oneness of Shiva, rather than on a temple culture. His texts were no doubt based on traditions that had been maturing for centuries.

Further reading: C. V. Narayan Ayyar, *Origin and Early History of Saivism in South India* (Madras: University of Madras, 1936); R. G. Bhandarkar, *Vaisnavism, Saivism, and Minor Religious Systems* (New York: Garland Publishing, 1980); R. Nagaswamy, *Siva Bhakti* (New Delhi: Navrang, 1989); Moti Lal Pandit, *Saivism, a Religio-Philosophical History* (New Delhi: Theological Research and Communication Institute, 1987); S. Shivapadasundaram, *The Saiva School of Hinduism* (London: George Allen & Unwin, 1934).

Shaivite (Shaiva)   *See* SHAIVISM.

Shakta

The term *Shakta* refers both to the practitioner/devotee and to the faith, a female-centered religious tradition that evolved out of prehistoric Mother Goddess worship found in civilizations across the globe. The word *Shakta* derives from the divine feminine power or SHAKTI and indicates a worshipper of the Goddess primarily. Evidence of this Earth-based and female-centered tradition on the Indian subcontinent dates back perhaps as early as the INDUS VALLEY CIVILIZATION (3500 B.C.E.–1500 B.C.E.), where numerous Harrapan seals portraying female figures associated with vegetative symbolism have been found.

The pre-Vedic Hindu tradition, with its Goddess-centered worldview, is often traced to the art and archaeological remains of the Harrapan and Mohenjo-daro civilizations. Although the point is contested, many scholars believe these findings definitively point to an early Earth-based, female/goddess-centered religious tradition.

Evidence for this tradition is clear as early as the fourth century, although Shakta itself is a relatively late post–eighth century term applied to those cults, scripture, or persons associated with the worship of the Goddess as Shakti. Before this time the term used for this type of Goddess worship was *kula* or *kaula*, a word also used to refer to clans of a female lineage, as well as to menstrual and female sexual fluids. It seems that this belief system whether called *Kaula* or Shakta, centered on the Goddess and her YONI, or sexual organ, as the primordial force of Earth and cosmos.

A Shakta views the female principle as the animating, dynamic force behind all existence while the male principle, especially in the later medieval tantric traditions, is considered to be the quiescent, receptive force. In the Shakta tantric worldview, the masculine principle is a complementary force to the all-pervading female power. "Shiva without Shakti is but a corpse, it is said."

Central to Shakta theology is recognition of the interrelationships among the agricultural, lunar, and female reproductive cycles. All of existence is conceived as the power, wisdom, knowledge, and action of a Great Goddess. Shaktas perform magical rites in order to ensure the continuation of both humans' and Earth's fertility. Stones, trees, water, and iconic and aniconic images all are worshipped as embodiments of Shakti or the power of Goddess. Ritual practices also focus on placating deities in order to prevent natural disasters and illness. To a Shakta, the mysteries of death as well as birth are considered the Goddess's domain, stemming from the belief that we all originate from and will eventually return to the great Mother Goddess.

From earliest times Shaktas have worshipped deities in multiple as well as singular form; they believe that the collectives are ultimately just different aspects or manifestations of the supreme Goddess herself. These deities have strong associations with the natural and human landscape: trees, mountains, hills, bodies of water, and the female body—in particular the sex organs and sexual fluids. *Yakshis* and YAKSHAS (tree and nature spirits), Grahanis, Matrikas, and Yoginis (goddesses and semigoddesses who are always depicted with animal totems/vehicles) embody both benevolent and malevolent qualities. These deities are connected to the threshold experiences of women's existence: childbirth, menstruation, sex, illness, and death.

Devotees share the belief in the great goddess, Mahadevi, who assumes many forms to defeat any forces that are threatening the natural equilibrium of the Earth and cosmos. Each of these forms carries benevolent as well as malevolent qualities and all have crucial roles in the birth,

fruition, preservation, and inevitable destruction of existence.

Within the Brahminic fold, Shaktas today worship goddesses such as PARVATI, Gauri, Ganga, LAKSHMI, SARASVATI, and Uma for their pacific natures. At the same time the wrathful, often destructive goddesses such as DURGA, KALI, CHAMUNDA, and the Matrikas and Yoginis are propitiated, revered, and especially held in awe.

Within the Shakta worldview all women are regarded as inherently divine. The ebb and flow of women's menstrual cycles in accordance with the 28-day lunar cycle are important to this tradition. The potency of *kula,* menstrual blood or other female fluids, plays a central role in rites and practices. The blood is revered for its vibrational potency and is offered to deities such as Kali, Durga, and the Matrikas as a means to pacify as well as worship.

Although in orthodox practices animal sacrifice has in some cases apparently replaced menstrual blood offerings, no female animals are offered to the deities. In many of the tantra texts relevant to this tradition, one finds descriptions of women that honor and revere their female nature; for example: "Women are divinity, women are vital breath. Women are goddess, women are life. Be ever among women in thought." This is the nature of a Shakta. Contrary to the later Brahminic traditions' immaterial conception of the universe as BRAHMAN, the Shakta views the divinity as both immanent and transcendent.

Further reading: Narendra Nath Bhattacharya, *History of the Shakta Religion* (New Delhi: Munshiram Manoharial, 1996); ———, *History of the Tantric Religion* (New Delhi: Manohar, 1999); Vidya Dehejia, *Yogini Cult and Temples: A Tantric Tradition* (New Delhi: National Museum, 1986); Jadunath Sinha, *Shakta Monism: The Cult of Shakti* (Calcutta: Sinha Publishing House, 1966); David Gordon White, *Kiss of the Yogini* (Chicago and London: University of Chicago Press, 2003); Sir John Woodroffe, *Sakti and Sakta: Essays and Addresses* (Madras: Ganesh, 1965).

Shakti

Shakti is the primordial creative, sustaining and destructive power of all existence. Although conceived as female in nature, Shakti is not an individual goddess, but rather a dynamic quality that all goddesses (and even all women, at least within the SHAKTA TANTRIC tradition) are said to possess. Unbridled, uncontainable, spontaneous, ecstatic, blissful, and fierce, Shakti flows from manifestation to dissolution. She is the power to give forth and to withdraw.

The concept of Shakti is an ancient one and has pre-VEDIC, prepatriarchal origins. She is often traced to archaeological discoveries from the INDUS VALLEY CIVILIZATION (3500–1700 B.C.E.) and to other prehistoric cultures throughout western and central Asia. In India the belief and worship of her all-pervading nature were pushed underground during the Vedic period. Shakti regains importance in classical and medieval Hinduism, in which in many cases this primordial power is personified as Devi, the GODDESS, and held in even higher regard than the male deities. Epic texts such as the Devi Bhagavata, Devi Purana, Kalika Purana, Markandeya Purana, and Mahabhagavata Purana accept and worship Shakti as the supreme nature of reality.

From earliest times the concept of Shakti appears in discussions of fertility as well as in reverence of the divine as mother of nature and cosmos. In the RIG VEDA the term *Shakti* is not mentioned; however, various goddess manifestations (Ratri, USHAS, ADITI, PRITHIVI, Vac-Sarasvati, goddesses) indicate the presence and influence that would later develop into the central figures of the Shakti cult (KALI, DURGA, Ambika, Uma) that are worshipped today.

The later Shakta Upanishads and tantras (*see* TANTRISM) contain philosophical references to Shakti that equate her with BRAHMAN. In these texts the dynamic, all-pervading nature of *brahman* and Shakti as the fabric underlying all existence cannot be separated into two. In the Shakta UPANISHADS as well as in the later Shakta tantras we

find references to Shakti's independent omnipotent nature where the complementary receptive qualities of the masculine force as Shiva are "but a corpse" without her activating power.

In the epic RAMAYANA, Shakti does not have the independent cult status that we find in the later epics; however, she is held in high regard. In the MAHABHARATA, Shakti once again regains the agency and importance that are evident in the prepatriarchal traditions. Here we learn of her invincible power as Durga and the Matrikas. She is also referred to as Kalika, Ambika, Bhadrakali, Parvati, Mahadevi, and by other names.

Shakti continues to gain importance in the *puranic* texts, the earliest of which, the Markandeya Purana, with its 13 chapters called the Durga Saptasai and Devi Mahatmya, elaborate the primordial all-pervading power of Devi. Here she is philosophically conceived as pure consciousness; the creator, preserver, and destroyer; the one and the many manifestations of supreme divinity. Shakti is both immanent and transcendent, illusive and manifest, moving and unmoving. She is knowledge, will, and action behind all existence. Here we find Goddess as the absolute reality, and yet she incarnates from time to time to help the gods to carry out her divine work. She also appears to help her devotees conquer the bonds of human suffering and the limitations of the physical realm in order to achieve liberation.

In the Markandeya Purana, the goddess is identified with PRAKRITI, the natural sustaining power of existence. She takes on various roles as mother, nurturer, warrior, lover to experience the LILA (play) of her divine consciousness. In the Devi Bhagavata Purana, Shakti is divided into three forms or qualities of existence: *sattva* (purity), *rajas* (passion), *tamas* (inertia).

As Mahasarasvati, Mahalakshmi, Mahakali, the Goddess takes the universe from creation to destruction and back to creation again. The Goddess's distinct iconographic forms are expressions of her multiple nature. She has both benevolent and pacific as well as wrathful and terrifying qualities. Her benevolent manifestations include Uma, Gauri, Parvati, Lakshmi, Sarasvati; her terrifying ones include Chamunda, Kali, Durga, the Mahavidyas, the Yoginis, and Matrikas.

In the Shakta tantras Shakti becomes Parashakti, the supreme reality who before manifesting through the physical world remains in a state of unmanifest repose. In this respect she is ineffable and indescribable. She is worshipped as Mahamaya or Mahadevi in addition to the numerous epithets that emphasize the myriad facets of her all-pervading nature.

The acknowledgment and worship of the nature of reality as female, as the mobilizing energizing primordial force called Shakti, speaks strongly to the inherently autonomous nature of women. This concept of divinity as female ultimately lies in the biological reality of the female body, in particular the power of the womb. Today statues, YANTRAS, and other iconic objects of Shakti worship are not mere representations of Goddess and her ultimate power, but rather embodiments of her Shakti.

Further reading: Narendra Nath Bhattacharya, *History of the Shakta Religion* (New Delhi: Munshiram Manoharial, 1996); Pushpendra Kumar, *Shakti Cult in Ancient India* (Varanasi: Bhartiya Publishing House, 1974); Ajit Mookerjee, *Kali: The Feminine Force* (New York: Destiny Books, 1988); Jadunath Sinha, *Shakta Monism: The Cult of Shakti* (Calcutta: Sinha Publishing House, 1966); Jagdish Narain Tiwari, *Goddess Cults in Ancient India (with special reference to the first seven centuries A.D.)* (Delhi: Sundeep Prakashan, 1985); *David Gordon White, Kiss of the Yogini* (Chicago and London: University of Chicago Press, 2003); Sir John Woodroffe, *Sakti and Sakta: Essays and Addresses* (Madras: Ganesh, 1965).

shaktipat

Shaktipat (*pat*, descent, of *Shakti*, spiritual energy) is an act found in TANTRISM and tantric-derived traditions such as that of Swami MUKTANANDA'S SID-DHA YOGA, in which the GURU confers the grace of spiritual transformation upon the adept through touching. This touch is intended to awaken and make the KUNDALINI force rise from the base of the spine. The touching is usually done by the hand, but sometimes with a feather or other object, upon the adept's head.

Further reading: Swami Muktananda, *Kundalini: The Secret of Life South* (Fallsburg, N.Y.: SYDA Foundation, 1983); ———, *Play of Consciousness: Chitshakti Vilas: A Spiritual Autobiography*, 3d ed. (South Fallsburg, N.Y.: SYDA Fdn., 2000); Swami Sivom Tirth, *A Guide to Shaktipat* (Thune: Devatma Shakti Society, 1985).

shakti pithas

Shakti pithas (seats or altars of the SHAKTI) are sites sacred to the divine mother that are embedded in the Indian landscape. Legends around these sites can be found in the *puranas* and tantras (*see* TANTRISM), however, the stories and number of actual *pithas* vary; most commonly *shakti pithas* are located in India, Nepal, Tibet, Pakistan, and Bangladesh.

The most popular story of how these *pithas* were created is found in the Puranas and tantras (Devibhagavata, VII, ch. 30; Kalika Purana, XVIII) and dates to the late medieval period. In this later development of a much earlier legend, the god DAKSHA is hosting a YAJNA (fire sacrifice) but does not invite his daughter, SATI, because she has married the ascetic god SHIVA, and Daksha does not approve of Shiva's antisocial qualities.

When Sati learns that all the other deities have been invited to this ceremony and only she and her husband have been excluded, she is outraged and confronts her father at his temple. Staying true to his socially defiant ways, Shiva shows no concern about this family insult and refuses to go with her.

Sati arrives alone and confronts her father. According to this version of the myth, Daksha grossly insults both his daughter and her wayward husband. To assuage her grief, Sati throws herself on the fire. She dies but her body does not burn up in the flames. Hearing of the loss of his wife, Shiva becomes mad with grief. Inconsolable, he wanders the Earth carrying his beloved on his shoulder.

In order to stop Shiva's dance of destruction and to relieve him of the burden of his grief, the gods BRAHMA and VISHNU decide someone must intervene. Vishnu, the great preserver, follows Shiva and cuts away at Sati's body. The fallen pieces of her body and limbs create over 50 *shakti pithas*, which today are worshipped as sites sacred to one of the many manifestations of DEVI such as Kameshvari, Tara, Ambika, and Gauri. A *bhairava* or fierce form of her beloved Shiva is often associated with each of these sites. These *pithas* have also been associated with the 51 letters of the Sanskrit alphabet.

The earliest mythological explanation of the *pithas* can be found in the RIG VEDA (X.61.5–7). Here we find the earliest association between the sacrifice and desecration of body parts that later is central to the Sati dismemberment myth.

Other legends tell of four important *pithas* that are associated with the four cardinal directions. These four sites (Kamarupa, Uddiyana, Jalandhara, Purnagiri) have been important pilgrimage centers to yoginis and yogis. Some legends speak of seven *pithas*; others speak of as many as 108 across the subcontinent.

Clearly these sites point to local cults of worship of the goddess in various manifestations. Today many of these places have become pilgrimage centers to the goddess as Shakti: Ambika, Parvat, Sati, Durga, Kaliet, and others. The various legends in the tantras and Puranas are later mythological explanations for what were originally sacred Goddess sites.

For millennia the Goddess has been embedded in the natural landscape. Lakes, ponds, or pools have been conceived as her *yoni*; double hills or mountains, her breasts. The *pitha* associated with the Goddess's breasts at Jalandhara-giri, and her *yoni* or sexual organ at KAMAKHYA remain two of the most frequented and revered sites for contemporary pilgrims. To ancient peoples the Earth itself was the divine mother, and the popularity of these sites reflects an attempt of later cultures to integrate these earlier traditions into their worship in order to attract more followers.

At the *pithas* the Goddess is usually worshipped in an iconic form. Often she is revered as a stone that has been painted red (red is the color of Shakti). Sometimes eyes and other anthropomorphic features are added. Originally these sites were worshipped under various names of the local tribal deities that later became syncretized into the Brahminic fold of goddesses. This is evident, in part, from the great variations in the lists of *shakti pithas* and the names connected with them.

Further reading: K. C. Aryan, *The Little Goddesses (Matrikas)* (New Delhi: Rekha Prakashan, 1980); D. C. Sircar, *The Sakta Pithas* (Delhi: Motilal Banarsidass Publishers, 1973).

Shakuntala   *See* KALIDASA.

shalagrama

The *shalagrama* is a small stone sacred object, usually three or four inches across with several holes, used by devotees of VISHNU in their home worship. It is made of black ammonite, from Mount Gandaki in Nepal. A story in the BHAGAVATA PURANA (c. 1200 C.E.) explains why this black stone is used for worship; another account is in the TULSIDAS Ramcharitmanas (c. 1600 C.E.).

In the worship, water is dripped on the stone and collected beneath. The water is later drunk by the worshipper. Sometimes the *shalagrama* is shown to dying persons to ensure that they go to Vishnu's heaven Vaikuntha, as it is seen to have sacred power.

Further reading: Abee J. Dubois, A. *Hindu Manners, Customs and Ceremonies.* Translated and edited by Henry K. Beauchamp, 3d ed. (Oxford: Clarendon Press, 1959); W. J. Wilkins, *Hindu Mythology, Vedic and Puranic,* 2d ed. (Calcutta: Rupa, 1973).

Shankar, Sri Sri Ravi   *See* ART OF LIVING FOUNDATION.

Shankara (seventh century C.E.) *founder of Vedanta philosophy*

Shankara was the great seventh-century philosophical genius who created the first widely known school of VEDANTA. He is also known as Shankaracharya.

Shankara was born in Kerala to a family of Nambudiri BRAHMINS, a strict Vedic group. Legend has it that when he was eight years old he wanted to become a renunciant, but his mother would not hear of it. Not long afterward, he was attacked by a crocodile. He cried out to his mother to allow him to renounce the world a moment before death so that he could reach liberation from birth and rebirth. His mother consented, and Shankara was miraculously released from the mouth of the crocodile.

He then proceeded to tour India and debate all those whom he encountered. Eventually he became known as the most brilliant philosopher of his time. Following the lineage of his GURU's guru Gaudpada, he argued that the BRAHMAN of the UPANISHADS was the only reality. He saw the world as a mere trifle, an illusion, or MAYA, unreal from the point of view of the ultimate.

Shankara wrote commentaries on the VEDANTA SUTRA, the Upanishads, and the BHAGAVAD GITA. In a thoroughgoing analysis he found that they all expressed the understanding that only the path of knowledge, the true knowing of the *brahman,* could lead to liberation. Devotion and works were only secondary pursuits. He initiated a tradition of renunciant yogis (the SHANKARACHARYA

ORDER) who sought the full realization of the *brahman* in a state of being, consciousness, and bliss (SAT-CHIT-ANANDA). Shankara's name is also connected strongly to SHAIVISM and to the worship of the GODDESS, through texts that were later attributed to him.

Shankara's system of Vedanta is known as the ADVAITA, or non-dual, VEDANTA, or more properly, Kevala (absolute) *advaita* Vedanta.

Further reading: S. N. Dasgupts, *History of Indian Philosophy,* 5 vols. (Delhi: Motilal Banarsidass, 1975); Swami Gambhirananda, trans., *Eight Upanisads with the Commentary of Sankaracarya,* 2d ed. (Calcutta: *advaita* Ashrama, 1965–66); Karl Potter, *Encyclopedia of Indian Philosophies.* Vol. 3, *Advaita Vedanta Up to Sankara and His Pupils* (Delhi: Motilal Banarsidass, 1981).

Shankaracharya Order (est. seventh century C.E.)

The Shankaracharya Order is an order of renunciants said to have been founded by the great seventh-century VEDANTA philosopher SHANKARA (also known as Shankaracharya). It is formally known as the Dashanami (10 Names) Order, because its renunciants or SANNYASIS all take one of 10 names: Aranya, Ashrama, Bharati, Giri, Parvata, Puru, Sarasvati, Sagara, Tirtha, and Vana. They also add the affix ANANDA (transcendent bliss). Examples would be Brahmananda (he who has realized the bliss of BRAHMAN) Sarasvati and Agehananda (he who has realized bliss in homelessness) Bharati.

Shankaracharya's aim was to establish a rigorously disciplined, intellectually capable group of mendicants who could challenge and defeat the Buddhists of his time and who would debate the theistic Hindus who clung to Vedic orthodoxy. He established four centers or MATHS in four parts of India for this purpose: the Vimala Pitha at Puri in Orissa, the Jyoti Matha in BADRINATH in the HIMALAYAS, the Kalika Pitha in DVARAKA in

Gujarat, and the Sharada Pitha in Shringeri in Karnataka.

It is still said that the Dashanamis of the Shankaracharya Order are the most respected group of religious mendicants in India. They are highly learned in SANSKRIT and VEDANTA philosophy and often are educated in English as well. The order is devoted to noninjury and nonviolence; however, they hired militant mendicants carrying tridents to defend them against attacks by militant Vaishnavite SADHUS or mendicants. Battles between these groups are famous for their carnage. There are currently six "regiments" of Dashanami NAGAS, special naked renunciants who defend the faith.

The heads of the four *maths* are all named *Shankaracharya*. They oversee extensive organizations with schools and social outreach centers. These schools rely on a network of locally trained Sanskrit *pandits*, experts who train students in the traditions of Hinduism, making these *maths* a valuable cultural resource.

Further reading: Austin B. Creel and Vasudha Narayanan, eds., *Monastic Life in the Christian and Hindu Traditions: A Comparative Study* (Lewiston, N.Y.: Edwin Mellen Press, 1990); Klaus K. Klostermaier, *A Survey of Hinduism* (Albany: State University of New York Press, 1990).

shanti

Shanti (peace or calm) is an oft-repeated word in Hindu texts. The reference is not to world peace, but to the spiritual peace that is understood to accrue to an individual with MEDITATION and even more so with higher realization. Many MANTRAS in SANSKRIT end with the chant *om shantih shantih shantih*, or "OM, peace, peace, peace."

Further reading: Puran Bair, *Living from the Heart: Heart Rhythm Meditation for Energy, Clarity, Peace, Joy, and Inner Power* (New York: Three Rivers Press, 1998); Clint Willis, ed., *Why Meditate?* (New York: Marlowe, 2001).

Shanti Mandir (est. 1987)

The Shanti Mandir (Temple of Peace) was established by Swami Nityananda (b. 1962), brother of Gurumayi Chidvilasananda, not to be confused with Swami Nityananda, the guru of Swami MUKTANANDA, in 1987, to promote the Shaivite teachings of Swami Muktananda, head of the popular Siddha Yoga Dham. Shanti Mandir now has centers in Atul, Gujarat, India; Kankhal, Uttarandchal, India; and Walden, New York.

Prior to his death in 1982 Muktananda had chosen a brother and sister team—Nityananda and Swami CHIDVILASANANDA, to coadminister the huge worldwide organization he had built. In 1986 Nityananda withdrew from Siddha Yoga Dham amid tension, controversy, disruption, and questions about his ability to administer the group. He renounced his vows of SANNYAS, entered private life, and set up a MEDITATION practice in California.

In July 1987, he established Shanti Mandir (Temple of Peace), over the objections of Siddha Yoga Dham devotees who questioned his authenticity and authority. After two years of building Shanti Mandir on December 26, 1989, Nityananda took a quick plunge in the GANGES near HARIDVAR and reaffirmed his vows of *sannyas* and commitment to Muktananda.

The Mandir in all three of its locations offers courses and meditation intensives and initiates students, using the chanting of MANTRAS as a primary practice. Nityananda also holds seminars, retreats, and workshops in the United States, Australia, and Europe.

Further reading: "Nityananda, One of Swami's Muktananda's Successors, Retakes Sannyasin Vows," *Hinduism Today* 12, no. 14 (April 1990): 28.

Shanti Yoga Institute and Yoga Retreat (est. 1974)

Shanti Yoga Institute was founded in the United States by Yogi Shanti DESAI, a younger brother of Amrit DESAI, who founded the center for KRI-PALU YOGA in Lenox, Massachusetts. Both Desai brothers were students of Swami Kripalu and accomplished in yogic disciplines as well as the application of yogic principles to everyday life.

Shanti traveled to the United States to pursue graduate work at Drexel University. He was awarded his M.S. in 1964 and subsequently worked as a chemist until 1972, when he realized that yoga was his life's path. He returned to India and accepted a SHAKTIPAT initiation from his guru. Shaktipat involves an energy transfer from the guru to the student that releases the KUNDALINI believed to lie latent at the base of the spine.

Shanti Desai founded his institute upon his return from India. In Ocean City, New Jersey, he opened the doors of the Yoga Retreat, in 1974 and Prasad, a holistic health food store and restaurant in 1981. Shanti has designed his yoga teaching especially to address American perspectives. His writings are published by the Shanti Yoga Institute.

Further reading: Yogi Shanti Desai, *The Complete Practice Manual of Yoga* (Ocean City, N.J.: Shanti Yoga Institute, 1976); ———, *Meditation Practice Manual* (Ocean City, N. J.: Shanti Yoga Institute, 1981).

Shashthi

Shashthi, "the sixth," is a GODDESS meant to represent the sixth day after the birth of a child, when it is understood that danger to both the child and the mother has ended. She is believed to protect children from evil and illness. Shashthi is best known in Bengal, where she is worshipped by married women who desire children. She is represented as a golden-complexioned woman with a child in her arms, riding on a cat.

There is a Bengali belief that women should never harm a cat because doing so will incur the anger of Shashthi. Festivals are held several times a year to honor this goddess. The husband of a family must worship her on the sixth day after a child's birth. A wife must make offerings to her after the child's third month. Women who do not have children go to her to ask for children; many other gods are also approached for this purpose.

Further reading: Donald S. Lopez Jr., ed., *Religions of India in Practice* (Princeton, N.J.: Princeton University Press, 1995); Akos Ostor, *The Play of the Gods: Locality, Ideology, Structure and Time in the Festivals of a Bengali Town* (Chicago: University of Chicago Press, 1980).

shastra

Shastra (from *shas,* to order or enjoin) is a term for any authoritative scripture in the Brahminical or Hindu tradition. For example, the ARTHASHAS-TRA is an authoritative scripture on *artha* (worldly action) as it relates to a king. The DHARMASHAS-TRA is authoritative scripture concerning DHARMA (right conduct).

Further reading: A. L. Basham, *The Wonder That Was India* (Calcutta: Rupa, 1997); Klaus K. Klostermaier, *A Survey of Hinduism* (Albany: State University of New York Press, 1989).

Shatapatha Brahmana

The Shatapatha Brahmana (c. 700 B.C.E.) is one of the most important texts for the interpretation of late Vedic ritual (*see* VEDAS). Its treatment of certain ritual ideas may have strongly influenced later Hindu philosophical developments. This BRAHMANA is attached to the White YAJUR VEDA.

The most important part of the Shatapatha Brahmana is its elaboration on the grandest of public Vedic rites, the AGNICHAYANA or "building of the fire altar." It explains this ritual as a reenactment of the sacrifice of the primordial man or PURUSHA, which created the universe. The ritual thus becomes a cosmic process transcending every mundane action. The various BRAHMINS performing the ritual identify themselves in turn with various aspects of the universe; one Brahmin is water, another the Sun, another the wind, and so on.

This was the first Brahmana in the Vedas to make explicit the central notion that the ritual itself could represent all of reality, both seen and unseen. Over the centuries, as the ritual actors identified more and more with the ritual itself, an esoteric or highly secret form of ritual emerged, carried out within the body of the Brahmin rather than on a public ground. The priest (a highly initiated Brahmin) began to identify himself not only with the ritual, but with all reality. Thus was created the background for the philosophy of the UPANISHADS, in which the identity of the individual self merged with the ultimate reality, the BRAHMAN.

Further reading: G. V. Devasthali, *Religion and Mythology of the Brahmanas: With Particular Reference to the Satapatha-Brahmana* (Poona: University of Poona, 1965); Naama Drury, *The Sacrificial Ritual in the Satapatha Brahmana* (Delhi: Motilal Banarsidass, 1981); Julius Eggeling, trans., *The Satapatha-Brahmana: According to the Text of the Madhyandina School*, 5 vols. (Delhi: Motilal Banarsidass, 1963).

sheaths, five

The five sheaths, also called the *pancha kosha*, are five coverings of the soul or self enumerated in the TAITTIRIYA UPANISHAD. The outermost sheath, which coincides with the human body, is the "food" sheath, the grossest aspect of being. Within that in the body at a subtler level is the "breath" or "life" sheath, which assures bodily sustenance, along with food. Within that in the body at another level is the "mind" sheath, which guides grosser instinctual functions and the surface aspects of nervous activity. Within this sheath is the sheath of "understanding," which overlooks higher and more refined mental functioning. Finally, there is the "bliss" sheath, which is the covering for the soul itself.

Some VEDANTA philosophies see these sheaths as simply "not-soul"; the spiritual process gradu-

ally rejects them in favor of the self or soul within the heart. Another, more holistic view, sees the spiritual effort as a process of full realization of these sheaths, and their integration with the realized self, the secret foundation of the sheath that consists of bliss.

Further reading: Swami Nikhilananda, trans., *Self-knowledge (Atmabodha): An English Translation of Sankaracharya's Atmabodha* (New York: Ramakrishna-Vivekananda Center, 1946); S. Radhakrishnan, *The Principal Upanisads* (Atlantic Highlands, N.J.: Humanities Press, 1992).

Shesha   *See* ADISHESHA.

Shitala

Shitala is the GODDESS of smallpox. Her name in Sanskrit means "cold" and refers to chill that accompanies the fever of smallpox. Though smallpox has been eradicated, Shitala is still worshipped in India to prevent or allay any serious disease.

Shitala is understood both to cause disease and to cure it. Sometimes her worshippers paint marks on their faces to mimic the pox. In a way that is not completely clear, the disease itself is seen as grace of the goddess—and her grace removes the disease as well.

Shitala is worshipped all over northern India. In South India the same goddess is called MARI-YAMMAN. Shitala's shrines are mainly found in the countryside. Her iconography is a golden-complexioned female sitting on a lotus or riding on an ass. She is dressed in red clothes. When Shitala is worshipped, presents are made to her to gain her favor. If a person is cured, a larger gift is given. Her flower offerings are sometimes put in the hair of children after worship, to protect them against disease. A seriously ill individual might be placed directly in front of the image of Shitala to aid in the cure.

Further reading: Ruth S. Freed and Stanley A. Freed, *The Two Mother Goddess Ceremonies of Delhi State in the Great and Little Traditions* (Albuquerque: University of New Mexico Press, 1962); Donald S. Lopez Jr., ed., *Religions of India in Practice* (Princeton, N.J.: Princeton University Press, 1995); Subrata Kumar Mukhopadhyay, *Cult of Goddess Sitala in Bengal: An Enquiry into Folk Culture* (Calcutta: Firma KLM, 1994).

Shiva

Shiva, "the beneficent one," is the divinity at the center of the largest Hindu religious sect. The tradition identifies Shiva with the Vedic god RUDRA, a fierce divinity who caused diseases of cattle and men and was propitiated out of fear. Rudra was known by the epithet *shiva* (as he was known to relent).

Shiva as a separate divinity first appears in the RAMAYANA (c. 600–300 B.C.E.) and MAHABHARATA (c. 700 B.C.E.–100 C.E.) epics; he is cited in the SHVETASHVATARA UPANISHAD (c. 300 B.C.E.) as the highest divinity. Clearly Shiva has ancient roots in North India. Some see his form in a seal from the INDUS VALLEY CIVILIZATION (c. 2600 B.C.E.) showing a seated figure with a buffalo-horned headdress and an erect penis.

It is clear that the worship of Shiva is quite ancient, many centuries more ancient than the first extant SHIVA LINGAM, which dates to the first century C.E. The LINGAM is an erect penis; it is the aniconic form that represents Shiva in the inner sanctum of virtually all temples dedicated to him. The lingam is nearly always shown surrounded by a circular stone rim that represents the YONI, or sexual organ, of the goddess, indicating his association with the divine feminine from a very early time.

In the stories of Shiva he is found first with his wife, SATI, who tragically dies, and then with Sati's reincarnated form PARVATI. His divine family includes the amusing elephant-headed god GANESHA, Shiva and Parvati's elder son, and KARTTIKEYA, the eternal youth with his peacock vehicle.

The major deity Shiva as Nataraja, Lord of the Dance *(HIP/Art Resource, NY)*

The basic Shiva myth depicts him in his youth as a fierce, ascetic naked wanderer with matted locks and smeared with ashes from human cremation grounds. He gads about willfully, not observing any social convention.

This all changes after the gods learn that only a son of Shiva can defeat the demon that is trying to usurp their power. They send Parvati to seduce him and then send the god of love to induce him to succumb. The uncooperative Shiva simply burns the god of love to ashes.

Eventually, however, Shiva does take to Parvati, and their lovemaking is famous in the literature. As they make love in a beautiful pleasure grove, his passion is so strong that everything in the grove becomes female—including an unfortunate king who happens into the grove. Shiva's son was actually born by accident when he spilled his semen into fire. The fire could not contain the energy and so gave the seed to the GANGES. She, with all her coolness, could not contain it either, so she abandoned it in a bank of reeds. There Karttikeya was born, so named because he was weaned and raised as a child by a group of female stars called the Krittikas. The demon was eventually defeated.

Shiva is famed as Lord of the Dance; as such his NATARAJA form is known to all India and found in grand representation in many temples. He is also the Lord of chaos, who destroys all the universe with his final dance. But of course he may dance that same universe into existence again, if he so chooses.

Further reading: Stella Kramrisch, *The Presence of Shiva* (Princeton, N.J.: Princeton University Press, 1981); Wendy Doniger O'Flaherty, *Siva: The Erotic Ascetic* (New York: Oxford University Press, 1973).

Shivananda Saraswati, Swami (1887–1963) *founder of Divine Life Society*

Swami Shivananda Saraswati was an Indian saint, YOGA teacher, and author of more than 200 books on spirituality. Through his disciples, he played a major role in spreading Hinduism and YOGA throughout the world.

Kuppuswami Iyer was born on September 8, 1887. His father was a pious Hindu government official who sent him to college and to medical school. His father died before he finished medical training and Kuppuswami was forced to leave school. Nevertheless, he maintained his interest in medicine and began a medical journal that specialized in preventive medicine and the Indian AYURVEDIC system of health. He administered a hospital in Malaya, where his meeting with a wandering holy man inspired his own spiritual search.

Returning to India he began a pilgrimage around the country. He settled in the holy city of RISHIKESH, where he was initiated into SANNYAS (renunciation) by Swami Viswananda Saraswati and given the name Swami Shivananda Saraswati. Living at Swargashram on the GANGES River, he devoted himself to MEDITATION, study, and giving of spiritual guidance to a growing group of disciples. He emphasized BHAKTI YOGA and KARMA YOGA and opened a dispensary to serve the residents of the ASHRAM.

In 1934 he established his own ashram, Ananda Kutir (Abode of Bliss), across the river in Rishikesh. It had a dispensary and meditation rooms for silent retreats. In 1936 he founded the Divine Life Trust with the goal of spiritualizing all of India. The Divine Life Society was begun as an auxiliary to the trust, and a monthly periodical was begun. Swami Shivananda also began the Forest Academy to train students in his teaching. He died on July 14, 1963.

Although Swami Shivananda's health prevented him from visiting the West, he became one of the most influential forces in the dissemination of Hinduism and yoga throughout the world through his students and disciples. His student Swami Shivananda RADHA (Sylvia Hillman) founded the YASODHARA ASHRAM SOCIETY in Vancouver. Another student, Swami Vishnudevananda, founded a chain of SHIVANANDA YOGA VEDANTA CENTERS in the United States and Canada. In 1959, Swami Chidananda, Shivananda's successor as head of the Divine Life Society, organized the society in the United States. Another student, Swami JYOTIRMAYANANDA, founded the Yoga Research Society in 1962, and SWAMI SATCHIDANANDA created the Integral Yoga Institute in 1966. His disciple and secretary of the Divine Life Society, Swami KRISHNANANDA, although he did not travel to the West, wrote extensively and welcomed seekers from the West to the ashram in Rishikesh.

Further reading: Wami Krishnananda, *Swami Shivananda and the Spiritual Renaissance* (Shivanandanagar: Divine Life Society, 1959); Shiva Shivananda, *Sadhana* (Shivanandanagar: Divine Life Society, 1958); ———, *Science of Yoga,* 18 vols. (Shivanandanagar: Divine Life Society, 1977); ———, *Yoga Asanas* (Shivanandanagar: Divine Life Society, 1969); Swami Venkateshananda,

Gurudev Shivananda (Shivanandanagar: Divine Life Society, 1961).

Shivananda Yoga Vedanta Centers
(est. 1958)
Shivananda Yoga Vedanta Centers were founded by Swami Vishnudevananda (1927–93), based on the teachings of his GURU Swami Shivananda SARASWATI (1887–1963) of RISHIKESH. Shivananda developed an integral system of YOGA, joining the four traditional paths (BHAKTI, KARMA, JNANA, and *raja*) with the addition of *japa* (repetition of a mantra). He established an ASHRAM and dispensary in Rishikesh, India, and later established the Divine Life Society there.

Swami Vishnudevananda became a disciple of Swami Shivananda in 1947 after reading Sivananda's books. Over the course of a decade Vishnudevananda was personally trained by Shivananda and became one of his most accomplished yoga students, adept at hatha yoga and *raja* yoga. In 1957 Shivananda instructed Vishnudevananda to spread his teachings in North America. Vishnudevananda established headquarters the following year in Montreal, Quebec, and continued to found centers across the United States. In 1962 the Shivananda Ashram Yoga Camp in Quebec was formed and in 1967 Vishnudevananda established the Sivananda Ashram Yoga Retreat in the Bahamas. He also founded the True World Order, a peace mission that began in 1969 to organize demonstrations for nonviolent struggle. The organization is known for conducting air drops of leaflets and flowers over conflict-filled areas in the world. The most notable mission occurred in Belfast in 1970.

Although Shivananda never traveled to North America, Vishnudevananda assured the spread of his message. Sivananda's system of yoga continues to be a central teaching at the Vedanta centers, with an emphasis on hatha yoga and *raja* yoga. There are currently about 80 ashrams and centers around the world, including 14 in the United States. Over 10,000 teachers have been trained. The Shivananda Yoga Vedanta Centers have earned the reputation of preserving the quality and tradition of yoga.

Shivananda Yoga Vedanta Centers have published several books including Vishnudevananda's *The Complete Illustrated Book of Yoga*, which has sold millions of copies. The center also produces a periodical, *Yoga Life*, that is available free through the organization's Web site, www.sivananda.org.

Further reading: Sivananda Yoga Vedanta Centers, *The Sivananda Companion to Yoga* (New York: Simon & Schuster, 2000); ———, *The Yoga Cookbook: Vegetarian Food for Body and Mind* (New York: Simon & Schuster, 1999); ———, *Yoga Mind and Body* (New York: D.K., 1996); Vishnudevananda, Swami, *The Complete Illustrated Book of Yoga* (New York: Harmony Books, 1988); ———, *Meditation and Mantras* (New York: OM Lotus, 1978); ———, *The Sivananda Companion to Yoga* (New York: Simon & Schuster, 2000).

Shivaratri   *See* MAHASHIVARATRI.

Shiv Sena (est. 1966)
Shiv Sena is a Maharastrian nationalist group founded in 1966 as a response to a wave of immigrants to the state and the city of Bombay (Mumbai) from Tamil Nadu, Gujarat, and Punjab. The movement tries to protect the interests of middle-class Maharashtrians in the conflict for resources and power. Shiv Sena is primarily a political and ethnic movement, not a religious movement. However, it uses some religious doctrines to support its political and ideological claims.

The founder of the movement is Balasaheb (Bal) Thackeray (he currently uses the name Don Balasaheb), who is also editor of the Marathi newsletter *Marmik*, which promotes the group's ideology. By 1968, Shiv Sena turned their struggle against communists and Muslims. Their tactics are largely political, but they have not eschewed armed conflict. More recently Shiv Sena has begun to recruit members of the lower castes, particularly Dalits.

In 1992 Shiv Sena boasted that it played a central role in the destruction of the Babri Masjid Mosque in AYODHYA. In fact, Shiv Sena activists arrived after the demolition, but they were heavily involved in the riots that followed in Mumbai.

More recently Shiv Sena has formed an alliance with the BHARATIYA JANATA PARTY (BJP). Since the BJP losses in the 2004 election the alliance appears to be collapsing. As Bal Thackeray ages, much of the leadership has fallen to his sons, a condition that has weakened the group as a political force.

Further reading: Sikata Banerjee, *Warriors in Politics: Hindu Nationalism, Violence and the Shiv Sena in India* (Boulder, Colo.: Westview Press, 2000); Julia M. Eckert, *The Charisma of Direct Action: Power Politics and the Shiv Sena* (Oxford: Oxford University Press, 2003); Dipankar Gupta, *Nativism in the Metropolis: The Shiv Sena in Bombay* (New Delhi: Manohar, 1982); Mary Fainsod Katzenstein, *Ethnicity and Equality: The Shiv Sena Party and Preferential Politics in Bombay* (Ithaca, N.Y.: Cornell University Press, 1979).

shraddha   See FUNERAL RITES.

shrauta sutra   See VEDAS.

Shrirangam

Shrirangam is an island in the CAUVERY River in Tamil Nadu, near Trichinopoly (Tiruchchirappalli), where Lord Ranganatha, a form of VISHNU, resides. The Vaishnavite saint RAMANUJA taught and oversaw the temple here, as did the saint Periyalvar, whose daughter ANDAL reached sainthood here. The site has a long tradition and is a popular PILGRIMAGE center.

Further reading: V. N. Hari Rao, *History of the Srirangam Temple* (Tirupati: Sri Venkateswara University, 1976); M. Somasundaram, *The Island Shrine of Sri Ranganatha* (Tiruchirappalli: St. Joseph's Industrial School Press, 1965).

shruti

Shruti (from *shru,* to hear) refers to sacred texts that are received through a kind of revelation, rather than written by humans. *Shruti* texts are the primary authority in Hinduism; they are complemented, but never superseded, by *smriti,* or human-made texts.

Shruti texts are understood to be heard from a transcendent source. The VEDIC MANTRA texts and their adjuncts, the BRAHMANAS, which include in them the ARANYAKAS and UPANISHADS, are accepted by all as being *shruti*. These texts are considered to have been "heard" or "seen" by the Vedic RISHIS (seers). Other texts are sometimes given the status of *shruti* by certain groups or regional traditions, such as the BHAGAVAD GITA, the Tamil TEVARAM, or the TANTRIC AGAMAS.

Further reading: Kalus K. Klostermaier, *A Survey of Hinduism* (Albany: State University of New York Press, 1989); M. Winternitz, *History of Indian Literature.* Translated by S. Ketkar (New York: Russell & Russell, 1971).

Shudra

The term *Shudra* originates in the ancient RIG VEDA; it refers to the servant class, as the lowest group in a four-part division (VARNA) of human society. It is used in present-day India for castes that are low in the social hierarchy, such as barbers, washermen, and others who perform personal services.

Each region of India has its own notions of what constitutes a Shudra. Below the Shudras in the informal caste hierarchy (the caste system was legally abolished after independence) are the

Dalits, untouchables, who are sometimes referred to as the "fifth" and "unclean" stratum of society. Many of them are employed as sweepers, refuse removers, and leather workers (*See* UNTOUCHABILITY).

Further reading: Maurice Carstairs, *The Twice Born* (Bloomington: Indiana University Press, 1967); R. S. Sharma, *Sudras in Ancient India,* 2d ed. (Delhi: Motilal Banarsidass, 1980).

Shurpanakha   *See* RAMAYANA.

Shvetambara

Shvetambara is one of the two branches of JAINISM. The name, which means "one who wears white garments," refers to the fact that its monks may wear clothing, as opposed to the DIGAMBARA monks, who are required to be nude. The Shvetambaras prevail among the Jains of northern and western India.

There is little doubt that MAHAVIRA, the great leader and promulgator of the Jain tradition, was a naked ascetic, as were his early followers, but the scriptures that are recognized by the Shvetambaras do not require nudity. The Shvetambaras accept the extant version of the early Jain scriptures, the ANGAS, and they follow, study, and preach its teachings. The Digambaras believe the authentic versions have been lost. The only text mutually accepted by both Shvetambaras and Digambaras is the TATTVARTHA SUTRA.

Shvetambaras also believe that women may attain liberation. Because women are not allowed to be naked ascetics, Digambaras believe that they cannot reach the level of detachment needed to become liberated; a woman must be reborn in a male body to reach liberation. Shvetambaras believe that Mallinatha, one of the 24 TIRTHANKARAS (saints) of our half-era (*avasarpini*), was a woman.

In general Digambaras (who predominate in southern India) and Shvetambaras are in nearly complete doctrinal agreement, but their communities developed separately and do not share festivals or sacred events. The Shvetambaras celebrate their major festival Paryushan around the recitation of the Kalpa Sutra. In the past, the two communities have fought bitterly over control of certain shrines, but in general they live in comity in places where they overlap.

Further reading: Paul Dundas, *The Jains* (London: Routledge, 1992); Uttam Kamal Jain, *Jaina Sects and Schools* (Delhi: Concept, 1975); P. S. Jaini, *The Jaina Path of Purification* (Delhi: Motilal Banarsidass, 1990).

Shvetashvatara Upanishad

The Shvetashvatara Upanishad is generally dated around the third century B.C.E., making it one of the later UPANISHADS. It is the only orthodox Upanishad that refers to a sectarian divinity, in this case RUDRA-SHIVA. It understands Shiva to be the same as the BRAHMAN, the ultimate reality, who had not previously been characterized in purely theistic terms. The text equates the terms PURUSHA, which is the person from whom the world evolved in the Vedas, ATMAN (soul or self), BRAHMAN, and God, so as to make clear the identity of all designations for the highest. The theistic quality of this text is developed in later Hindu theism and in theistic or God-oriented VEDANTA.

Further reading: Swami Lokeshwarananda, trans., *Svetasvatara Upanisad* (Calcutta: Ramakrishna Mission Institute of Culture, 1994); Swami Nikhilananda, *The Upanishads: Katha, Isá, Kena, Mundaka, Sv'etasv'atara, Prasña, Mandukya, Aitareya, Brihadaranyaka, Taittiriya, and Chhandogya,* 4 vols. (New York: Harper & Row, 1964); Patrick Olivelle, trans., *The Early Upanisads* (Oxford: Oxford University Press, 1988).

Siddha

Siddha ([The] Perfected) refers to a historic group of YOGIS who achieved all of the SIDDHIS, or occult powers, and attained liberation from the cycle of birth and rebirth in the body (JIVANMUKTA).

The tradition of the Siddhas preserves a list of 84 masters of the lineage. Several of the names are shared in a corresponding Tibetan Buddhist Siddha tradition. The most famous Siddha master was GORAKHNATH (Gorakshanatha); his name is included in both Tibetan and Indian lists. In India he is supposed to have been born between 900 and 1200 C.E.

The Siddhas practiced alchemy, ingesting poisonous oxides of mercury to achieve bodily immortality. They were known for their extreme asceticism, antisocial behavior, frightening appearance, and supernatural powers. They were often also associated with magical healing. The Siddhas were tantric and accepted membership from any caste. The modern tradition of SWAMI MUKTANANDA refers to itself as Siddha Yoga; it reveres a lineage of Siddha masters who have characteristics in common with Siddhas elsewhere, but of course also the 84 Siddhas of tradition.

The Tamil Shaivite tradition has a body of literature dating from as early as 600 C.E. tracing what is called a Sittar tradition (the word is from the same Sanskrit root), which resembles the larger Siddha cult. The first of these Sittars was considered to be TIRUMULAR, who wrote Tirumantiram, perhaps the first important tantric text, outlining KUNDALINI YOGA and describing other tantric practices.

Further reading: George Weston Briggs, *Gorakhnath and the Kanphata Yogis* (New Delhi: Motilal Banarsidass, 1982); John Campbell Oman, *The Mystics, Ascetics and Saints of India* (Delhi: Oriental, 1983); David Gordon White, *The Alchemical Body: Siddha Traditions in Medieval India* (Chicago: University of Chicago Press, 1996); Kamil V. Zvelebil, *The Poets of the Powers* (London: Rider, 1973); ———, *The Siddha Quest for Immortality* (Oxford: Mandrake, 1996).

Siddhaswarupananda, Jagad Guru
(1948–   ) *independent bhakti yogi*
The American-born yogi Jagad Guru Siddhaswarupananda was a teacher in the INTERNATIONAL SOCIETY FOR KRISHNA CONSCIOUSNESS (ISKCON) before forming his own offshoot organization.

Chris Butler was born in 1948 in New Orleans, Louisiana, but moved to Hawaii as an infant and grew up in the islands. His interest in religion in general and YOGA in particular emerged during his last years of high school. He studied with the YOGA teachers available to him and experienced SAMADHI sublime consciousness. As a young man, he founded the Haiku School of Nirvana Yoga (also known as the Haiku Meditation Center) on the island of Maui, where he taught ASHTANGA YOGA and KUNDALINI YOGA.

Around 1970 he met Srila BHAKTIVEDANTA SWAMI PRABHUPADA, the founder of ISKCON. Butler accepted Bhaktivedanta's teaching of devotional or BHAKTI yoga and his emphasis on a personal deity, as opposed to Butler's previous belief in an impersonal divinity. Butler closed his work in Hawaii and accepted an initiation from Bhaktivedanta to join his movement. He remained with ISKCON until after Prabhupada died in 1977.

In the year after Bhaktivedanta died, Butler concluded that his GURU had emerged as a non-appointed pure devotee who held his status by virtue of his own spiritual attainment, not via his relationship to the GAUDIYA MATH center. Shortly before his death Bhaktivedanta, following the example of his guru, Bhaktisiddhanta, appointed 12 men to manage the *math*. Similarly, Bhaktivedanta appointed 12 men to manage ISKCON. None of these appointees was a guru by virtue of this appointment; each could be a guru only as an unappointed, but accomplished, devotee.

Butler assumed that he was such an unappointed guru, and, in 1978, as Jagad Guru Siddhaswarupananda, he began to initiate disciples. He founded the Science of Identity Foundation as a vehicle to facilitate his teachings. He has led a rather low-key existence, traveling constantly and staying in various locations for relatively short periods as he is invited by his initiates. He has written several short books and produced a variety of video and audio materials for his followers.

The Science of Identity Foundation (originally the Hari Nama or Holy Name Society) is located in Honolulu, Hawaii. Siddhaswarupananda became a founding member of the WORLD VAISHNAVITE ASSOCIATION.

Further reading: Jagad Guru Siddhaswarupananda, *God: Supremely Lovable* (Honolulu: Science of Identity Foundation, 1989); ———, *The Holy Name Real Protection* (Honolulu: Science of Identity Foundation, n.d.); ———, *Reincarnation Explained* (Honolulu: Science of Identity Foundation, 1987).

Siddha Yoga Dham   *See* CHIDVILASANANDA, SWAMI.

siddhi

Siddhi (attainment) is a special power attained through YOGA or refined practice. Traditionally, there are eight *siddhis*: (1) the ability to grow extremely small, (2) the ability to become extremely light, (3) the ability to become extremely heavy, (4) the ability to touch any object however distant, (5) irresistible will, (6) supremacy over body and mind, (7) dominion over the elements, (8) ability to fulfill all desires. Numerous other powers are also listed in the tradition, such as the ability to fly, physical immortality, the ability to enter another's body, and knowledge of the past, present, and future.

PATANJALI'S system and certain other yoga systems such as that of the Theravada Buddhists downplay *siddhis* as distractions from the path of liberation; adepts are warned not to indulge themselves in these powers, lest they be sidelined in their spiritual progress. Certain systems such as the TANTRA, though, encourage the attainment of *siddhi* and allow its usage to a greater or lesser degree, depending upon the particular sect.

Further reading: Sri Chinmoy, *The Summits of God-life: Samadhi and Siddhi* (Jamaica, N.Y.: Agni Press, 1974);

H. C. Mathur, *Siddhi: The Science of Supernatural Powers* (New Delhi: Shree, 1998).

Sikhism

The Sikh religion emerged at the beginning of 16th century C.E. in the Punjab, a territory hotly contested by Hindus and Muslims at the time. It aimed to find the truths common to both faiths, placing less emphasis on laws and rituals and soon emerged as a third, well-organized, Indian religious community.

Though raised as a Hindu, Sikhism's founder, NANAK (1469–1539), began his adult life in the employ of a Muslim, as was his father. A thoughtful and inwardly oriented youth, he spent periods each morning and evening as a young man in MEDITATION. In his 30th year, his communion with the divine led to an intense experience of God in which he experienced God as the one creator. As a result of the encounter, he quit his job and gave away all his possessions. He began to proclaim his unique message that there is no Hindu and no Muslim. Sikhism would emerge as he began to articulate his message, drawing together what he saw as the best from both faiths. He shared the message in a set of hymns.

His message sought to discover what he saw to be the essence of the religious teachings around him. In the place of many religious acts, from praying on a prayer mat or living as a renunciant, he called upon people to cultivate the virtues these actions symbolized. For example, he suggested that the essence of asceticism was to remain pure amid impurities. He also called for a casteless society without distinctions based on the family into which one is born. He traveled from Sri Lanka to Tibet spreading his message, although Kashmir and the Punjab proved most receptive.

Before his death in 1539, Nanak selected a disciple whom he had named Angad (1504–52) as his successor. Angad would be followed by eight additional GURUS who were selected to lead the Sikh community: Guru Amar Das (1479–1574), Guru Ram Das (1534–81), Guru Arjan Dev (1563–1606), Guru Hargobind (1595–1644), Guru Har Rai (1630–61), Guru Harkrishan (1656–64), Guru Tegh Bahadur (1621–75), and Guru Gobind SINGH (1666–1708).

Each of the 10 gurus made his contribution to the development of the faith. For example, the fourth guru began construction on what would become the Golden Temple in AMRITSAR, the physical center of the Sikh community. The formation of the Sikh community, the Khalsa (the pure ones), was completed by the 10th guru, Gobind Singh. He saw to the baptism of new members into the Khalsa by sprinkling with sweetened water stirred with a sword. At the time, each male adopted the name *Singh* (lion) as his family name. As a visible sign of membership in the community, each male also began to wear the five K's: (1) *kesh,* long hair; (2) *kangh,* a comb; (3) *kach,* short pants (for quick movement); (4) *kara,* a steel bracelet; and (5) *kirpan,* a knife.

Through the years, the writing of the gurus were compiled in a book, the Adi Granth. The fifth guru, upon the completion of the Golden Temple, formally installed the volume in the temple, much as Hindus installed statues of deities in their temples. After the death of Gobind

Sikh Gurudwara (temple) in Hong Kong *(Institute for the Study of American Religion, Santa Barbara, California)*

Singh, his contributions were added to the Adi Granth, and then the book was declared to be the new guru for the community. Since that time, while there are teachers of Sikhism who convey the faith to each new generation, there is no human to whom the status of GURU (teacher) is formerly ascribed.

Wherever Nanak traveled, he established local groups called *manjis*. Over the years, these would mature as *gurudwaras,* seats of the guru or Adi Granth, the worship centers in which Sikh communities gather on a weekly basis.

While it had been Nanak's goal to create a synthesis that would dissolve the differences between Muslim and Hindu, both faiths continued and Nanak's work had the effect of creating a new religion. A minority community, Sikhs were frequently forced to defend themselves and emerged with a reputation as great warriors. At times aligned with the British, they served with distinction in battles throughout the 19th century, in both India and abroad.

Since the death of the last guru, temporal authority in the community passed to the Sri AKAL TAKHT Sahib, a name used to refer to both a building close to the Golden Temple and the Sikh leader who operates from the building. All the issues of import to Sikhs are debated there, and the decrees issued from it are considered binding on the entire community internationally. Another important structure in the community is the Shromani Gurdwara Parbandhak Committee (S.G.P.C.). It oversees the administration of the worship centers (*gurudwaras*) in India and carries on an extensive publication and education program. In the 1930s, the S.G.P.C. assembled the most noted Sikh scholars and theologians to produce a consensus statement on the standards of Sikh belief and conduct. The result was the Reht Maryada, a defining document of Sikhism, which offers guidelines for conduct both inside the *gurudwaras* and in the daily life of Sikhs.

The Sikh community declined in the 19th century, in part because of the attractiveness of some of the new movements of the Hindu renaissance, such as the BRAHMO SAMAJ, which shared many affirmations (such as the idea of one God) with the Sikhs. Many Hindus looked upon the Sikhs as just another sect of Hinduism, a position not accepted by most Sikhs. Several revitalization efforts appeared, including the NIRANKARI and SANT MAT movements, but with limited appeal. However, it was the Singh Sabha, the governing body that oversees Sikh communities, that seemed to have the greatest effect with its calling the entire community to a new understanding of itself and its heritage. It called for a new allegiance to the writings of the gurus and an end to encroachments by Christianity and Hinduism into the *gurudwaras.*

The reemergence of the Sikh community was viewed with alarm in some quarters. Some saw it as a challenge to government authority (i.e., British rule). The growing popularity of Sikhism set the stage for the development of Sikh nationalism, with its demands that the Punjab, territory in which the Sikhs predominated, be separated from Hindu India. In the decades since World War I, the tension between the Sikhs and the British, and later the Indian, government has waxed and waned. More extreme elements among the Sikhs responded to government attempts to suppress nationalist aspirations with violence, followed by retaliation by the Indian government.

The most significant event in the ongoing battles between the government and the Sikh community occurred in June 1984. Sant Jarnail Singh Bhindranwale, a militant Sikh leader, and his followers took refuge in the Golden Temple. Unable to persuade him to surrender, under orders from Prime Minister Indira Gandhi, the Indian army invaded the temple, with significant damage to the sacred property and loss of life. The event was a call to arms for the community. Among other consequences, Sikhs living outside India formed the World Sikh Organization. Then in October, Sikhs who served as Indira Gandhi's bodyguards turned on her and assassinated her. Though the assassins were later executed, they became heroes to Sikhs.

Sikhs had largely been confined to India until the 20th century. Their migration outward was in part motivated by the same factors that sent other groups to the West, but was also stimulated by the tensions created in the Punjab as the community revived. Many Sikhs targeted by the government for their activity as Sikh nationalists migrated to continue their efforts from a base outside India. Before immigration was curtailed, several thousand Sikhs immigrated to western Canada and the United States. Others took advantage of regulations that allowed free movement through the British Commonwealth to settle in the United Kingdom.

Migration by Sikhs into the United States increased considerably after anti-Asian immigration laws were rescinded in 1965. Today, several hundred thousand Sikhs reside in North America. American Sikhs hosted Sikh leaders in 1984 for the founding of the World Sikh Organization, which took place in New York City. As the American Sikh community grew, it organized the Sikh Foundation in the 1970s, which has more recently been succeeded by the Sikh Council of North America. The council seeks to coordinate and provide communication among the many *gurudwaras* across the continent.

As the Sikh community expanded in the 1970s, it was faced with a new and different phenomenon. A man popularly known as Yogi BHAJAN arrived in Los Angeles and claimed to be a Sikh teacher, but also a teacher of HATHA and KUNDALINI and TANTRIC yoga. He organized a movement of mostly young adult men and women, which he called the Sikh Dharma, though it was better known through its educational arm, the HEALTHY, HAPPY, HOLY ORGANIZATION (3HO). After a period of controversy, the Sikh Dharma was recognized as a valid expression of Sikhism, but because of its growth through conversion of individual members, rather than growth through heredity, it has remained a separate organization.

Further reading: W. Owen Cole, *Teach Yourself Sikhism* (Chicago: NTC Publishing Group, 1994); K. S. Duggal, *The Sikh People Yesterday and Today* (New Delhi: UBSPD, 1993); Max Arthur Macauliffe, *The Sikh Religion, Its Gurus, Sacred Writings and Authors,* vols. 1–6 (New Delhi: S. Chand, 1985); Nikky-Guninder Kaur Singh, *Sikhism* (New York: Facts On File, 1993); H. S. Singha and Satwant Kaur, *Sikhism: A Complete Introduction* (New Delhi: Hemkunt Press, 1994).

Singapore

Indian migrants began to arrive in what was British Malaya during the 19th century, primarily with the intent of finding employment on the sugarcane and rubber plantations that British entrepreneurs had established. The Crown Colony of Singapore served as an initial point of arrival for Indian migrants, most of whom quickly moved north. However, many chose to stay on the island. Most were from lower-caste families, and more than 60 percent from Tamil Nadu state. By 1900 some 16,000 had arrived.

By the beginning of the 20th century, four Hindu temples had been established in Singapore. The oldest of these, Sri Mariammam, was started in 1827; the present structure was erected in 1843 and dedicated to the goddess MARIYAMMAN, revered for her healing powers. In 1905, after complaints of mismanagement affecting a variety of religious institutions, administration of the temples was turned over to the Mohammedan and Hindu Charitable Endowments Board. That board continued to exist until 1969, when it was split into two boards, one for each religion. In 1915, a second structure, the Hindu Advisory Board, was established to advise the government on Hinduism. Both boards continue to the present. In the meantime the number of temples had grown to around 30 and the number of Hindus of Indian extraction had risen to about 225,000. The Indian community is now the third largest ethnic group in Singapore behind the Chinese and Malays.

Hindu activity in Singapore is dominated by the majority Tamil-speaking community. Local temples tend to be home to devotees of both SHAIVISM and VAISHNAVISM and the major deities each reveres. It is also not uncommon to see Buddhist and even Christian images in the temples. This syncretism is promoted in line with official government policies focused on building religious harmony in the very diverse religious community of Singapore. In 1978, the community established the Hindu Center to facilitate the transmission of Hinduism to the younger generation.

The annual life of the community in Singapore is punctuated by several festivals, all of which have become public events attended by many non-Hindus. Especially notable is the annual Thaipusam festival, a Shaivite festival celebrating the birthday of Lord Subramaniam, the younger son of Lord SHIVA, which occurs toward the end of January each year. Interestingly, this festival was outlawed in India for many years because of bloody hook swinging and body piercing and Singapore is one of the few places where it survives. The week-long festival culminates in an all-day procession in which young men carry a heavy structure honoring the deity from one temple to another through Singapore.

Since the 1930s, the Hindu community in Singapore has witnessed impulses for reform, including resistance to BRAHMIN domination of the temples, elevation of the status of women, and the social equity of different castes.

Further reading: Jean Pierre Mialaret, *Hinduism in Singapore: A Guide to the Hindu Temples of Singapore* (Singapore: Asia Pacific Press, 1969); Jagat K. Motwani et al., eds., *Global Indian Diaspora: Yesterday, Today and Tomorrow* (New York: Global Organisation of People of Indian Origin, 1993); K. S. Sandhu and A. Mani, eds., *Indian Communities in South East Asia* (Singapore: Times Academic Press, 1993); Vineeta Sinha, *A New God in the Diaspora? Muneeswaran Worship in Contemporary Singapore* (Honolulu: University of Hawaii Press, 2005).

Singh *See* SIKHISM.

Singh, Charan *See* SANT MAT MOVEMENT.

Singh, Guru Gobind (1666–1708) *10th Sikh guru*

Guru Gobind Singh was the 10th and final Sikh GURU in the lineage of Guru NANAK, the founder of SIKHISM. He established the beliefs and practices that the community follows to this day, including the devotion to scripture as the only GURU.

Gobind Rai was born on December 22, 1666, to Guru Tegh Bahadur, the ninth Sikh guru, and Mata Gujari in Patna in Bihar state. The young boy was taught the language of Bihari and Gurumukhi script as a child and was schooled in the life and deeds of the previous gurus. He was given a comprehensive education of India: the historical, social, religious, and political context. In keeping with the Sikh tradition he was also trained in music, prayers, and the use of weapons. He was raised in a family who held close relations with both Hindus and Muslims. He spent much of his childhood playing on the banks of the GANGES River and was said to be bold, with all the makings of a leader.

Guru Gobind's father met a violent death when the boy was less than 10 years old; Sikhs claim he was executed by Emperor Aurangzeb, Mughal ruler of India, as part of a campaign to convert India to Islam. Controversy surrounds the details, but the martyrdom of Guru Tegh Bahadur remains part of the Sikh belief system.

In 1675, the family made a long journey to Punjab, and in November of that year Gobind Rai was initiated as the 10th Sikh guru. Although still a child, he was said to be very self-aware. He continued to train in philosophy, politics, and weaponry. The popularity of the Sikh tradition continued to spread across India, drawing both Muslim and Hindu disciples.

Guru Gobind Singh had three wives. His first marriage was to Mata Jeeto of Lahore, who gave birth to three sons, Jujhar, Zoravar, and Fateh. He later married Mata Sundari of Lahore, who gave birth to another son, Ajit. She survived Singh and was revered as a great teacher by Sikhs after her husband's death. His last wife, Mata Sahib Devi of the Jehlam District, went to Guru Gobind after vowing to marry no one else. He did not wish to marry but agreed to a platonic relationship in which she could share her life with him.

Singh taught the oneness of humankind, love and worship of God, self-awakening, and social justice, all part of the Sikh heritage. His unique contribution, however, was to organize the Khalsa (pure ones) order in 1699, probably in response to his father's martyrdom decades before. The purpose of the Khalsa was to promote sacrifice for DHARMA, the right way of living. Members were enjoined to resist any form of slavery based on class, caste, or religion and to prioritize their commitment to social justice. Guru Gobind even advocated the use of arms when in resistance to oppression. He also instituted the five K's, observed by male Sikhs to the present day: (1) *kesh,* long hair; (2) *kangh,* a comb; (3) *kach,* short pants (for quick movement); (4) *kara,* a steel bracelet; and (5) *kirpan,* a knife.

Guru Gobind Singh declared that upon his death the line of individual gurus would end and the authority of the guru would rest solely in the scripture—the Adi Granth (called the *Guru Granth Sahib*)—and in the Khalsa, the fellowship of pure followers. Guru Gobind Singh died on October 7, 1708.

Further reading: Surinder Singh Johar, *Guru Gobind Singh* (New Delhi: Enkay, 1987).

Singh, Jaimal   *See* RADHASOAMI MOVEMENT; SANT MAT MOVEMENT

Singh, Kirpal Maharaj (1894–1974) *teacher of Sant Mat and Radhasoami*

Kirpal Maharaj Singh was a dynamic and influential reformer and international champion of interfaith cooperation. He helped disseminate the Sant Mat teachings in India and around the world.

Kirpal Singh was born on Februrary 6, 1894, in Sayyad Kasran in the Rawalpindi District of the Punjab in what is now Pakistan. He was educated at the Edwards Church Mission High School in Peshawar. In January 1912 he signed up for government service in the Military Accounts Department, an occupation that he pursued until retirement in 1947 as deputy assistant controller of military accounts. Throughout his early life he studied the basic scriptures of the Sikhs, Christians, Muslims, Buddhists, and Zoroastrians and began to believe that various religious philosophies communicate the same basic truth, which is the need for each person to attain both self-knowledge and God-knowledge.

In 1917 he first had contact with his teacher, Baba Sawan Singh of the Beas lineage of RADHASOAMI teachers. He was later married and became the father of two sons. In February 1924 he was formally initiated by Baba Sawan Singh and given the name *Naam,* "the word." It is said that his teacher Sawan Singh passed all his spiritual knowledge onto his disciple through one look in the eyes. In 1935 he began writing and composing his text, *Gurmat Sidhant.* On April 2, 1948, after the death of his teacher, he began his ministry in the Radhasoami lineage. At the end of that year he started his mission and began giving regular initiations.

In June of 1951 he founded the Sawan Ashram in Shakti Nagar, Delhi. Four years later he went on his first world tour. In 1956 in Delhi, he gave the inaugural address to the Ninth General Session of UNESCO. In 1957 he became the founding president of the World Fellowship of Religions; he later presided over four World Religious Conferences over a period of 14 years. In 1962 he was the first non-Christian to be honored with the

Order of St. John of Jerusalem, Knights of Malta. His interfaith efforts reached a climax when he convened the first World Conference on Unity of Man in Delhi in February 1974, which inspired the Unity of Man movement.

His extensive knowledge of major religious faiths along with his dedication to teaching led to Kirpal Singh's wide acceptance in the West. He popularized Sant Mat teachings in India and the West and became one of the most well known teachers of Radhasoami. He died on August 21, 1974.

See also SANT MAT MOVEMENT.

Further reading: David Christopher Lane, *The Radhasoami Tradition: A Critical History of the Guru Successorship* (New York: Garland, 1992); Bhadra Sena, ed., *Ocean of Grace Divine* (Bowling Green, Va.: Sawan Kirpal, 1976); Kirpal Singh, *The Crown of Life* (Delhi: Ruhani Satsang, 1967); ———, *Surat Shabd Yoga: The Yoga of the Celestial Sound* (Berkeley: Images Press, 1975).

Singh, Sawan   *See* SANT MAT MOVEMENT.

Singh, Shiv Dayal   *See* RADHASOAMI MOVEMENT; SANT MAT MOVEMENT.

Sita

In the RAMAYANA Sita is the wife of RAMA. *Sita* means "furrow," and it is said that she was not born to her father Janaka, but was ploughed up by him during a sacrificial rite to gain progeny. Sita was won by Rama in a contest by bending SHIVA's bow.

Sita is considered the model for wifely fidelity and purity in India (though modern Indian women have begun to rebel against this model). In the epic, she was kidnapped by the demon king Ravana and taken to Lanka. Because of a curse he was unable to violate her, and she refused his advances. Her husband fought successfully for her freedom. However, he doubted that she had remained faithful and cruelly rejected her, saying he had only fought against Ravana to clear his name.

To clear her name, Sita underwent a "trial by fire" (*agnipravesha*), which she survived unscathed. Several vernacular versions of the Ramayana indicate that the real Sita never actually went into the fire, sending a substitute instead; in fact, in these versions she was not even really kidnapped, but had only been in hiding. These versions seem to show a later discomfort with the original SANSKRIT story.

After her trial by fire, Sita was then accepted by Rama, until people once more began to challenge her faithfulness and Rama asked Lakshmana to take her away to the forest, in exile once more. He did not know that she was pregnant with his two sons, Kusha and Lava. She gave birth to her sons in the ASHRAM of the very VALMIKI who is cited as the author of the epic.

On one occasion Rama initiated a HORSE SACRIFICE; in that ritual, a horse is allowed to roam at will for a year, followed by the king's soldiers. Whatever land the horse covers becomes part of the ruler's kingdom. Kusha and Lava as it happens captured the king's horse and defeated the king's army when it arrived, thus defeating, in an act of poetic justice, their father. When Rama heard from VALMIKI that these were his own sons he asked that they be taken to court, where they sang the Ramayana story. He then called for Sita to return and declared her innocence in open court. Sita, however, refused to return and asked Mother Earth, from which she had been born, to take her back, whereupon she disappeared.

Further reading: Jacqueline Suthren Hirst and Lyn Thomas, eds., *Playing for Real: Hindu Role Models, Religion and Gender* (New Delhi: Oxford University Press, 2004); C. Rajagopalachari, *Ramayana* (Bombay: Bharatiya Vidya Bhavan, 1972); Paula Richman, ed., *Many Ramayanas: The Diversity of Narrative Tradition in South Asia* (Berkeley: University of California Press,

1991); Paula Richman, ed., *Questioning Ramayanas: A South Asian Tradition* (Berkeley: University of California Press, 2001).

Skanda *See* KARTTIKEYA.

smriti

Smriti (from *smri,* to remember) is a term in the Hindu tradition used to refer to revered textual sources that were composed by humans, as opposed to those that are eternal and appeared through revelation (SHRUTI).

These texts were composed by men but usually memorized rather than committed to writing. They were considered authoritative, but less so than the *shruti,* or "heard," texts such as the VEDAS, which had been received by RISHIS (seers) during divine trances.

Because of the diverse nature of Hindu tradition there have been disagreements between sects as to what texts can be considered *smriti.* Some hold, for instance, that the BHAGAVAD GITA is *shruti,* divinely received, whereas others hold that it is *smriti.*

Further reading: A. L. Basham, *The Wonder That Was India* (Calcutta: Rupa, 1997); Ram Kishore Gupta, *Political Thought in the Smrti Literature* (Allahabad: University of Allahabad, 1968); Klaus K. Klostermaier, *A Survey of Hinduism* (Albany: State University of New York Press, 1989); L. Sternback, *Hindu Legends of Justice: Pancatantra and Smrti* (Delhi: Global Vision Publishing House, 2002).

Society of Abidance in Truth

The Society of Abidance in Truth (SAT) was formed in 1974 by devotees of RAMANA Maharshi (1879–1950). The purpose of the nonprofit society is to disseminate the teachings of ADVAITA (non-dual) VEDANTA. SAT follows two ancient traditions with roots in India and China. These include the wisdom originally found in the VEDAS and codified in the 19th century as the SANATANA DHARMA, and Ch'an (Zen) Buddhism, as developed during China's T'ang dynasty. Following the knowledge imparted by Ramana Maharshi, the society emphasizes self-inquiry and self-knowledge to further the realization that no difference exists between one's nature and the absolute. The teachings proclaim that the true identity of self resides in God. The society does not observe any religious ritual, formal meditative technique, or code of conduct. Rather, SAT relies on developing skills of self-observation so that one can experience the unity of self and the highest divinity. SAT holds that in awakening to true formless nature one will find peace, happiness, and freedom.

Nome and Russell Smith, who have backgrounds in *advaita* Vedanta and Zen Buddhism, respectively, offer spiritual leadership, weekly teaching sessions, and *satsangs* (meetings) in Santa Cruz, California. SAT publishes translations of ancient SANSKRIT texts and books relating to Ramana Maharshi's life. Membership is primarily concentrated in Santa Cruz, but devotees are present throughout the world. SAT welcomes the general public to participate in its events.

Further reading: *The Journey Home* (Santa Cruz, Calif.: Avadhut, 1986); Ramana Maharshi, *Be As You Are: The Teachings of Sri Ramana Maharshi* (Boston: Arkana, 1975); ———, *The Spiritual Teaching of Ramana Maharshi* (Berkeley: Shambala, 1972); ———, *Teachings of Ramana Maharshi* (Madras: Affiliated East-West Press, 1990).

Soma

Soma was a divine, intoxicating drink favored by INDRA, king of the gods, according to the Vedas. It was made from a celestial plant taken to Earth by an eagle and was said to confer immortality on gods and humans. BRAHMIN priests in Vedic times oversaw its preparation, offered it to the gods, and drank it themselves at their rituals. The drink was used in such quantities that the YAJUR VEDA includes a chant to alleviate the effects of excessive Soma drinking.

Soma was most used by the priests of the SAMA VEDA. A majority of hymns in the Sama Veda itself praise the Soma, personified as a god. In fact, Soma is said to have inspired the composition of Vedic hymns. The drink is said to be sweet and milky. Various attempts have been made to identify the Soma plant. Today it is the name of a vine that does not appear to have intoxicating properties.

The Vedic god Soma acts as the husband of the dawns, supports the Earth and sky, and makes the Sun light up. In late Vedic times Soma was connected to the Moon. In modern Hindu mythology Soma is the Moon god and the lord of all plants. Scholars identify the beverage Soma with the Haoma, which was also offered to the gods in the Avesta, the scripture of the ancient Persians.

Further reading: Alfred Hillebrandt, *Vedic Mythology.* Translated from the German by Sreeramula Rajeswara Sarma. Vol. 1 (Delhi: Motilal Banarsidass, 1990); J. Stevenson, trans., *Translation of the Samhita of the Sama Veda* (Varanasi: Indological Book House, 1961); David Stophlet and Martin Schwartz, *Haoma and Harmaline: The Botanical Identity of the Indo-Iranian Sacred Hallucinogen "Soma" and Its Legacy in Religion, Language, and Middle-Eastern Folklore* (Berkeley: University of California Press, 1989).

Sri   *See* LAKSHMI.

Sri Chaitanya Saraswat Mandal (est. 1980) The Sri Chaitanya Saraswat Mandal is an offshoot of the INTERNATIONAL SOCIETY FOR KRISHNA CONSCIOUSNESS (ISKCON), popularly known in North America as the Hare Krishna movement. The Mandal was founded in 1980 by Bhakti Rakasa Sridhara Deva Goswami (1895–1988) to carry on the teachings of his god-brother Swami A. C. Prabhupada BHAKTIVEDANTA (1896–1977), founder of ISKCON.

Before he died Prabupada is said to have told his disciples that if dissention occurred in the movement, it should be resolved by Sridhara; they were "god-brothers," as both received their initiation from Bhaktisiddanthanta Sarawati Takir in the GAUDIYA MATH in India. This group had been the central Krishna Consciousness organization in Bengal.

Prabhupada's death was in fact followed by intense infighting and theological unrest. Disputes were frequent and solutions hard to obtain. When some members of the upper ranks turned to Sridhara, as they had been advised to do, the eventual solution was the founding of a new order. The Sri Chaitanya Saraswat Mandal was formed as the branch that would serve the mission in the United States while remaining affiliated with the Gaudiya Math.

Since its founding the mandal has flourished and has engaged in an expansive publishing program. Guardian of Devotion Press has published a variety of Sridhara's literature in the field of religion and spirituality. There are affiliated centers in Mexico, Brazil, England, Venezuela, South Africa, Italy, the Netherlands, Australia, Austria, and Hungary.

Further reading: Sridhara Deva Goswami (Bhakti Raksaka), *Bhakti Parpanna Jivanmarta: Lifenectar of the Surrended Souls: Nabadwip Dham* (West Bengal: Sri Chaitanya Saraswat Math, 1988); ———, *The Search for Sri Krsna, Reality the Beautiful* (San Jose, Calif.: Guardian of Devotion Press, 1983).

Sri Krishna Chaitanya   *See* CHAITANYA.

Sri Lalita   *See* SRI VIDYA.

Sri Lanka   *See* RAMAYANA.

Sri Ram Chandra Mission (est. 1945)

Sri Ram Chandra Mission in India was founded by His Holiness Sri Maharaj RAM CHANDRAJI of Shahjahanpur, in 1945. He was popularly known as "Babuji." The mission was in memory, honor, and testimony to his teacher, Samarth Guru Mahatma Sri Ram Chandriji Maharaj of Fatehgar, Uttar Pradesh, who is devotedly referred to as "Lalaji." Today, the work is being carried forward by Sri PARTHASARATHI RAJAGOPALACHARI (b. 1927).

The mission's objectives are to educate and teach the masses in the art and science of YOGA, tailored for the modern world, and to encourage feelings of unconditional love to everyone inclusive of all castes, creeds, and colors. In addition, the mission seeks to establish research centers whose focus is the study of YOGA, helping those who wish to carry forth the mission.

Practice and life in the mission include rising before dawn for daily PUJA (worship to divinity through offerings such as incense or rice) or spiritual MANTRAS (chants). The honor code of devotees includes being truthful and harmless to others and being free from resentful motives. Typically, members assume a peaceful lifestyle that gives harmony and serenity to their surroundings. The disciples try to live a plain and simple lifestyle devoted to spirituality. The mission has several hundred centers around the world. The president of each center is responsible for the transmission of divine wisdom. More than 1,000 people have been trained to assist these presidents with the authenticity of the *raja* path or the royal road to divine wisdom.

The international headquarters of the mission is in Madras (Chennai), India, and the United States headquarters is in Molena, Georgia. *Sahaj Sandesh* is a service that periodically broadcasts news via e-mail about SRCM activities worldwide.

Further reading: Ram Chandra Maharaj, Shri, *Heart to Heart,* vol. 3 (Shahjahanpur: Shri Ram Chandra Mission, 1993); ———, *Letters of the Master.* Vols. 1 and 2 (Shahjahanpur: Shri Ram Chandra Mission, 1992); ———, *Letters of the Master,* vol. 3 (Shahjahanpur: Shri Ram Chandra Mission, 1996).

Sri Rama Foundation (est. 1971)   *See* NARI DASS, BABA.

Sri Sri Nathji

Sri Sri Nathji (the Lord of Sri) is a form of KRISHNA worshipped at NATHDWARA near Udaipur in Rajasthan. Nathdwara is one of the main shrines of the cult of the Hindu saint VALLABHA. The image has different forms, one of which shows Sri Sri Nathji

Sri Sri Nathji, a special icon of Lord Krishna revered by the Vallabha sect of Krishna devotees *(calendar print)*

lifting up the Govardhana mountain, which is part of the Krishna mythology.

The image here is treated as Krishna himself and the worship follows a cycle of the events of Krishna's life. The image was taken from Mathura in 1669 to preserve it from destruction by the iconoclastic Muslim Mughal king Aurangzeb.

Further reading: Amit Ambalal, *Krishna as Shrinathji: Rajasthani Paintings from Nathdvara* (Ahmedabad: Mapin, 1987); Anne-Marie Gaston, *Krishna's Musicians: Musicians and Music Making in the Temples of Nathdvara, Rajasthan* (New Delhi: Manohar, 1997).

Sri Vidya

Sri Vidya is an all-India cult of the worship of the GODDESS Sri Lalita or Tripurasundari. It initiates in the right-handed tantric tradition (*see* TANTRISM), which emphasizes Sri Lalita as the Great GODDESS. Iconographically, she is seen as a beautiful 16-year old with a parrot on her shoulder; however, this is just her gross form. Her subtle form is the Sri YANTRA or Sri CHAKRA, which is a geometric design around a basic point, showing four entranceways at its outer portion that are representative of temple entranceways.

The highest form of Sri Lalita is the 16-syllable MANTRA that is chanted in worship of her. As is the tantric norm, she *is* the mantra and one who chants the mantra *becomes* the goddess. She in effect enters that person and becomes that person. The Sri Vidya PUJA (worship and offering) is done at homes and not publicly. The devotee first burns his or her self up symbolically, readying for the transformation into the goddess. "One must become the Goddess to worship the Goddess" is the operative phrase. Doing ritual worship to the diagram of the Sri Yantra, one places mantras on one's body to transform it into the body of the goddess. The reverse is done when the *puja* is coming to a close. At the end of the ritual proper the 1,000 names of goddess Sri Lalita are usually chanted.

South India has a particularly strong cult of Sri Lalita, where the initiates tend to be BRAHMINS. Thus, though there are tantric aspects to this ritual, there is no consumption of forbidden things such as beef or alcohol, as in the left-handed rites. Substitutes are used to make the rites palatable to Brahmin practitioners. The philosophical system involved is a tantric ADVAITA non-dual system, understanding that the manifest world is real and an aspect of the supreme Goddess.

Further reading: Douglas Renfrew Brooks, *Auspicious Wisdom* (Albany: State University of New York Press, 1992); ———, *The Secret of the Three Cities* (Chicago: University of Chicago Press, 1990).

Sri Yantra   *See* YANTRA, SRI.

states of consciousness

There are four states of consciousness outlined in the MANDUKYA UPANISHAD, one of the classical Vedic UPANISHADS often cited in VEDANTA and other Indian traditions. The four states are *jagarita* (*jagrat*), the waking state; *svapna*, the dreaming state; *sushupti*, the deep sleep state; and *turiya*, the transcendent state beyond conventional consciousness, in which one realizes the BRAHMAN or ultimate reality. Some early Upanishads conflate the last two states.

Further reading: Swami Krishnananda, *The Mandukya Upanishad: An Exposition* (Shivanandanagar: Divine Life Society, 1977); Swami Nikhilananda, trans., *Self-Knowledge (Atmabodha): An English Translation of Sankaracharya's Atmabodha* (New York: Ramakrishna-Vivekananda Center, 1946); S. Radhakrishnan, *The Principal Upanisads* (Atlantic Highlands, N.J.: Humanities Press, 1992).

Sthanakavasi

The Sthanakavasis are a minority sect within the Jain community founded by a Jain layperson from

His community, which still exists today, adopted the practice of meeting only in halls (*sthanaka*) and not in temples, hence the name *Sthanakavasi* (inhabiters of halls). Lonka Shaha's fanatical opposition to the worship of icons may have been influenced by the iconoclastic Islam of his era. As a distinguishing feature, Stanakavasi monks wear a mouth covering to prevent injury to invisible beings that might be breathed in and killed.

Further reading: John E. Cort, *Jains in the World: Religious Values and Ideology in India* (New York: Oxford University Press, 2001); Paul Dundas, *The Jains* (London: Routledge, 1992); A. K. Roy, *History of the Jainas* (Colombia, Mo.: South Asia Books, 1984).

stotra

Stotras (from *stu*, to praise) are shorter or longer chants in praise of various divinities, gurus, and personages. They have been a timeless feature in all native Indian traditions, including Hinduism, Buddhism, JAINISM, and SIKHISM. There are *stotras* of 1,000 verses, such as *Vishnu Sahasranama* (in praise of Vishnu) and *Lalita Sahasranama* (in praise of Sri Lalita), that consist of 1,000 verses; many others consist of 108 verses, but verses of almost any length can be found.

From very early times Hindus believed that chanting *stotras* could induce the gods to grant benefits in this world and, if done with sufficient devotion and frequency, lead to liberation from birth and death. By contrast, in JAINISM and early Buddhism *stotras* could not gain benefit from spiritual teachers such as MAHAVIRA or BUDDHA, because such yogis (unlike gods) did not confer grace; *stotras* were merely capable of calming the mind.

Further reading: Jan Gonda, *Medieval Religious Literature in Sanskrit*. Vol. 2, Fascicle 1, *History of Indian Literature* (Wiesbaden: Otto Harrassowitz, 1977); Nancy Ann Nayar, *Poetry as Theology: The Srivaisnava Stotra in the Age of Ramanuja* (Wiesbaden: Otto Harrassowitz, 1992); Nancy Ann Nayar, trans., *Praise-Poems to Visnu and Sri:*

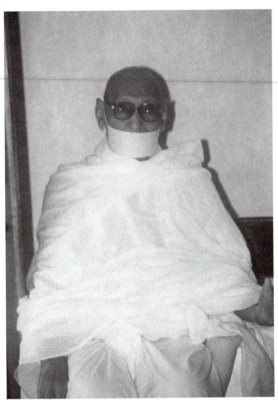

Sthanakavasi, a Jain monk with mouth covering to practice *ahimsa*, in Gujarat *(Constance A. Jones)*

Gujarat, Lonka Shaha, who in 1451 C.E. decided to form a new community based on a return to traditional values. He is said to have gained access to the basic texts of the Shvetambaras, which traditionally only the monks could read. In reading the texts he was stunned at the laxity shown by the monks of his day. He was convinced that the rituals performed by monks in the Jain temples had nothing to do with the Jain ideals; he felt that even the act of digging in the ground to establish temples and images involved such injury to Earth beings that it was in and of itself a violation of the Jain sacred principle of *ahimsa* or noninjury.

Shaha started a movement assisted by influential Jains to reexamine Jain life in view of the scriptures.

The Stotras of Ramanuja's Immediate Disciples (Bombay: Ananthacharya Indological Research Institute, 1994).

Subramaniya   *See* KARTTIKEYA.

Subramuniyaswami, Satguru (1927–2001)
American founder of the Saiva Siddhanta Church

The American-born Satguru Subramuniyaswami was an important teacher in the Saiva SIDDHANTA tradition. Through his organizational work, fundraising, and many books he helped spread Hindu teaching in America and around the world.

Born in Oakland, California, on January 5, 1927, and orphaned in 1938 at age 11, Robert Hansen spent his childhood and youth in the San Francisco Bay area and was, before he renounced the world, a lead dancer in the San Francisco Ballet Company. He was raised by a family friend who, as a student of Indian art, dance, and culture, had lived as a guest of the maharaja of Mysore, India. As a child, he wore Indian clothing and learned to appreciate many elements of Indian culture. As a teenager, he was exposed to Swami VIVEKANANDA's writings and the lectures of other SWAMIS. He relates that he studied MEDITATION and classical YOGA disciplines with several teachers.

At age 21 Hansen traveled to India and Sri Lanka, searching for a spiritual teacher. In Sri Lanka he studied with Shaivite elders and pundits (*see* SHAIVISM), one of whom, a member of the Chettiar caste, adopted him into his extended family and introduced him to temple worship. He meditated in the jungle caves at Jalani and attained SELF-REALIZATION by experiencing the absolute reality of SHIVA, which transcended all time, space, and form. This experience of Self-Realization became the cornerstone of his mystical teachings. Also in Sri Lanka, he met his GURU, Jnanaguru Yoganathan, also known as Shiva Yogaswami (1872–1964) who initiated him into the Shaivite tradition of *siddha yoga* and named him Subramuniya. Yogaswami was a direct descendent of the original gurus of this Sri Lankan lineage known as the Nandinatha Sampradaya, a tradition that has its roots in the 2,200-year-old sacred text Tirumantiram, by the saint TIRUMULAR. He followed his initiation with years of spiritual practice (SADHANA) and began to be referred to as *Satguru,* or "one who has attained God-realization and assumes responsibility for the spiritual life of his disciples." Upon the passing in 1964 of Shiva Yogaswami, Subramuniya (or *Gurudeva,* as he was affectionately known) became the spiritual successor of the lineage.

In 1950, he returned to the United States and continued his spiritual path, developing various psychic powers, including clairvoyance and clairaudience. In 1957, at age 30, he began his public ministry by founding the Subramuniya Yoga Order and the Christian Yoga Church, both in San Francisco, California. During the 1960s, the latter was disbanded; in 1970 the Subramuniya Yoga Order moved to Hawaii, where it was renamed the Wailua University of the Contemplative Arts. In 1973, the organization became the Saiva Siddhanta Yoga Order, and later the Saiva Siddhanta Church. Subramuniya called the Church the "first Hindu church, organized according to the American church system." In an attempt to sustain Shaivite orthodoxy, the church recognizes the celibate monk as the ideal spiritual practitioner and requires at least 12 years of adherence for a man to become a SANNYASI. Women may follow the celibate life of the BRAHMACHARINI, but they are not, strictly speaking, monastics in this church.

In addition to the church, Gurudeva created the Himalayan Academy, an educational publication house, and Hindu Heritage Endowment, a public service trust begun in 1995 to establish and maintain permanent sources of income for Hindu institutions worldwide. These organizations serve the growing Hindu DIASPORA. Local missions are on five continents. Subramuniya was instrumental in founding and building 37 Hindu temples around the world, including his own Iraivan Sivalingam temple on the island of Kauai, the first all-granite Agamic (built to Shaivite canoni-

cal specifications) temple ever built in the Western world. He founded Kauai's Hindu Monastery,
known officially as Kauai Aadheenam, the first
orthodox Shaivite monastery in the West.

Throughout his years of teaching, Subramuniyaswami traveled widely and met leaders of many
faiths and heads of state. He participated in the
World Parliament of Religions in Chicago in 1993.
In 1995, he named three of his longtime initiated
swamis as his consecutive successors, beginning
with the present *satguru*, Bodhinatha Veylanswami.

Subramuniya wrote over 30 books explaining
Hindu philosophy to adherents and others. His

Satguru Subramuniyaswami (1927–2001), founder of
Saiva Siddhanta Church and Hinduism Today *(Siva Siddhanta Church, Kapaa, Kauai, Hawaii)*

lessons on Shaivism are designed to preserve the
teachings among youth, and his illustrated Master
Course trilogy—three inspired 1,000-page texts—
summarize the religion, culture, and metaphysics
of Hinduism.

The academy's quarterly magazine, *Hinduism
Today*, originally begun as a newsletter in 1979,
seeks to promote Hindu solidarity in the face of
global pluralism and educate Hindus around the
world about their heritage. It covers the practices
and beliefs of all lineages and traditions within the
Hindu fold, and addresses the issues of the day in
light of orthodox Hindu teaching. The Web site
Hindu Resources Online, a public service inspired
by the message of Subramuniyaswami, is another
vehicle for dissemination of Shaivite teachings.

According to the teachings of Subramuniyaswami, Shaivism is ageless, the SANATANA DHARMA
or eternal faith. An enduring spirituality innate
in every man and woman, it is the source of all
religions on Earth.

Subramuniya died on November 12, 2001, at
age 74.

Further reading: Sivaya Subramuniya, *Dancing with
Siva*, 4th ed. (San Francisco: Himalayan Academy,
1993); ———, *Hindu Catechism* (San Francisco: Hima-
layan Academy, 1987); ———, *Merging with Siva:
Hinduism's Contemporary Metaphysics* (Kapaa, Hawaii:
Himalayan Academy, 1999); ———, *Raja Yoga* (San
Francisco: Himalayan Academy, 1973).

Sufism Reoriented   *See* DUCE, IVY O.

Sugriva   *See* RAMAYANA.

Sukul, Deva Ram (fl. 1920s–1940s) *teacher of raja yoga in the United States*

Deva Ram Sukul, founder of the Yoga Institute
of America, was one of a handful of independent
Hindu teachers active in the United States during

the years when the Asian Exclusion Act was in effect (1924–65).

Little is known of Deva Ram Sukul's early years, the work of his institute, or even his death. He emerges out of obscurity only as the author of a few books (*Yoga and Self-Culture* and *Yoga Navajivan*) and as a teacher of the American actress Mae West.

As director of the Yoga Institute, Sukul had become an acquaintance of the lawyer James A. Timony. At one point in the late 1920s, West became ill in reaction to the stress of several lawsuits against her. Timony introduced her to Sukul, who was able to heal her at their first meeting. Sukul subsequently joined her entourage and traveled with her through the next decade. West would later credit him with assisting her in developing a philosophy of life, although she was also interested in astrology and spiritualism.

In later years, Sukul lectured on raja yoga and taught the GAYATRI MANTRA. He also knew the pioneer San Francisco HATHA YOGA teacher Walt Baptiste (1917–2001) and he taught raja yoga in Baptiste's center in the 1940s.

Further reading: Deva Ram Sukul, *India and Tibet: Pilgrimage Lessons* (New York: Yoga Institute of America, 1941); ———, *Yoga and Self-Culture: Higher Laws of Spiritual Dynamics Including Outline of Philosophy of the Vedas, Upanishads, Bhagavad Gita, and the Six Systems of Hindu Philosophy* (New York: Yoga Institute of America, 1947); ———, *Yoga Navajivan (Path to New Life and Divine Realization): Introduction to Raja Yoga System of Self-Culture as Taught by Deva Ram Sukul* (New York: Yoga Institute of America, 1947); Jill Watts, *Mae West: An Icon in Black and White* (New York: Oxford University Press, 2001); Mae West, *Mae West on Sex, Health and ESP* (London: W. H. Allen, 1975).

Sundarar (c. end of seventh and beginning of eighth centuries C.E.) *Tamil Shaivite poet-saint*
Sundarar (also known as Nambi Arur and Suntharamurtti) is among the trio of the most prominent Tamil Shaivite saints (NAYANMARS) whose hymns appear in the central liturgical and literary text of the Tamil Shaivites, the TEVARAM.

Sundarar, "the Handsome One," was born a Shaivite BRAHMIN in Tirunavalur. SHIVA claimed Sundarar as his devotee, it is said, on Sundarar's wedding day, before his marriage could be completed. However, Sundarar later married a temple dancer, Paravai, whom he often mentions in his hymns, and a non-BRAHMIN, upper-caste woman, Cankili.

Sundarar lived in the Shaivite city of Tiruvarur, although as the other saints of the Tevaram did, he often traveled to other shrines to sing his devotion of Shiva. He also sang the praises of kings and local chieftains who were his benefactors. Sundarar, they say, went to heaven on a white elephant (perhaps the white elephant of Indra), accompanied by a Chera king. Sundarar is depicted in iconography with his two wives. His courtly life contrasted with the more austere life of his contemporaries APPAR and SAMBANTHAR, the others of the sacred trio of saints in Tamil Shaivism.

Further reading: Indira Viswanathan Peterson, *Poems to Siva: The Hymns of the Tamil Saints* (Princeton, N.J.: Princeton University Press, 1989); M. A. Dorai Rangaswamy, *The Religion and Philosophy of Tevaram, with Special Reference to Nampi Arurar (Sundarar)* (Madras: University of Madras, 1990).

Sun Temple *See* KONARAK.

Sunyata (Alfred Julius Emanuel Sorensen) (1890–1984) *Danish-born sadhu and teacher*
The youngest of three children on a small farm in northern Denmark, Emmanuel (indwelling God, the name he favored for himself) Sorensen worked during his childhood on his family's farm and attended school only to the eighth grade.

When he was 14, the family farm was sold and he entered four years of apprenticeship in horticulture. He had jobs in France and Italy and settled in England in 1911 and took up gardening on large estates. At one of those estates he met Rabindranath TAGORE, who was impressed with the quality of Emmanuel's silence. Tagore invited the young Dane to visit Shanti Niketan, Tagore's school in India, to "teach silence."

Sorensen arrived in India in 1930 at the age of 40 and began to teach. Immediately he was given the titles of BABA, *saint,* and GURU, but his gift to the people he met was not captured by these titles. In the four decades he spent in India, he traveled widely and offered his gift of "being" to those who went to him. In 1936 he met RAMANA MAHARSHI (1879–1950) at Arunachala and noted Ramana's quality of self-radiance, which nourished all around him. Ramana later called Sorensen a "rare-born mystic." On his third visit, Sorensen received a telepathic message from Ramana, "We are always aware SUNYATA." Sorenson wrote that he experienced the words as a "recognition, initiation, MANTRA, and name." Sorensen thereafter referred to himself and his hut as *sunyata* (a Buddhist term for void or emptiness). He acquired Indian citizenship in 1953.

Sunyata first lived in Haridvar, on a small island in the GANGES River, but eventually built himself a stone hut in the foothills of the HIMALAYAS near Almora. He accepted a small sum from the Birla Foundation in New Delhi, whose purpose is to assist saints and SADHUS (spiritual aspirants). He knew many teachers and saints of his day, including Lama Anagarika Govinda, Walter Evans-Wentz, Mohandas Karamchand GANDHI, Jawaharlal Nehru, Yashoda Ma, KRISHNA PREM, Sri ANIRVAN, J. KRISHNAMURTI, ANANDAMAYI MA, and NEEM KAROLI BABA. He remained uninterested in power, fame, or money, preferring nature, his own company, and silence. He did not heal, was not psychic, and did not perform miracles. He simply reminded all he met of the identity of each person

Sunyata (1890–1984), Danish sadhu and teacher
(Courtesy Sunyata Society)

and the divine in the words *Tat tvam asi*—thou are That.

Sunyata's dog Sri Wuji (Chinese for "a full emptiness") was his constant companion. The saint Anandamayi Ma accepted the dog along with Sunyata into her ashram with the words "Wuji is not a dog."

In 1973, a group of Americans from the Alan Watts Society invited Sunyata to California. At age 84, he arrived in California, where he gave DARSHAN (blessings) at Esalen and Palm Springs. In 1978 he moved to California permanently at age 88 and spent the last six years of his life there. At age 93, in 1984, he was struck by a car in Fairfax, California, and died soon afterward on August

13, 1984. The Sunyata Society of San Anselmo, California, publishes articles and books about his life and teaching.

Further reading: Betty Camhi and Elliott Isenberg, eds., *Sunyata: The Life and Sayings of a Rare-Born Mystic* (Berkeley, Calif.: North Atlantic Books, 1990); Sunyata Society, eds., *Sri Wuji,* vols. 1 and 2 (Berkeley: North Atlantic Books, 1990).

Surdas (Late 15th to late 16th century) *Hindi poet-saint*

Surdas was a poetic of mythic status in North India born in a village called Sihi, which was probably near BRINDAVAN, judging from the Braj dialect of his poems. Most of the biographical details of Surdas's life are in question.

Surdas is credited with writing *Sursagar* (The Ocean of Sur), a song of about 5,000 verses. As with many poet-saints in India, most of his poetry was written to be sung at public events; it is likely that these "songs" changed for each performance. His extant work is probably the careful textual recording of students and admirers. As is also the case in Indian tradition, his work may well include compositions of genius written by other authors that seemed worthy of inclusion among his. In the end this lack of clear biographical detail matters little in the perspective of the brilliant work represented under the name of Sur.

All the stories of his life agree that Surdas was blind, but there they part company. One story puts him at the court of the great Muslim king Akbar. In the other he was a follower of VALLABHA, the great devotee of KRISHNA, of Brindavan. It is said that Vallabha encouraged Sur to write about the child Krishna's divine play.

Sur's poetry is one of pure devotion. Millions of people in North India know his songs. His poetry is used for the temple liturgy of the Vallabhites. Classical vocalists always include his works in their repertoire, as do village singers. Many others read, recite, or sing his verses.

Further reading: Kenneth E. Bryant, *Poems to the Child-God: Structures and Strategies in the Poetry of Surdas* (Berkeley: University of California Press, 1978); John Stratton Hawley, *Three Bhakti Voices: Mirabai, Surdas, and Kabir in Their Time and Ours* (New Delhi: Oxford University Press, 2005); Usha Nilsson, trans. and ed., *Surdas: Poems* (New Delhi: Sahitya Akademi, 1982).

Surya

Surya is the most common of the names for the Sun in the VEDAS, which all seem to refer to different aspects of this divine body. (SAVITRI is the next most frequent Vedic Sun name.) The Sun is seen as crossing the sky each day on a chariot pulled by horses. In the Vedas Surya is sometimes said to be the son of ADITI and sometimes that of Dyaus (the heavens). Sometimes he is said to be the son or the husband of USHAS, the dawn. In the era of the PURANAS, Surya is seen as the son of Aditi and the sage Kashyapa. The Sun (under the name Savitri) is the object of worship each morning by twice-born (confirmed), upper-caste Hindu males who chant the GAYATRI MANTRA.

Further reading: Shakti M. Gupta, *Surya, the Sun God* (Bombay: Somaiya, 1977); Alfred Hillebrandt, *Vedic Mythology* (Delhi: Motilal Banarsidass, 1990); P. Pandit, *Aditi and Other Deities in the Veda* (Pondicherry: Dipti, 1970); W. J. Wilkins, *Hindu Mythology, Vedic and Puranic* (Calcutta: Rupa, 1973).

sushumna *See* KUNDALINI.

sushupti *See* STATES OF CONSCIOUSNESS.

sutra

A sutra (line, thread, or string) is a text (on any subject) composed of short, aphoristic verses, usually only of a few words. Most often the sutra form was used to facilitate easy memorization, as knowledge in India was most frequently communicated from memory. Because of the extreme conciseness of the lines of text, most verses are not comprehensible without reference to some sort of commentary. Buddhist and Jain traditions (*see* JAINISM) also frequently used this method in their texts (e.g., Acharanga Sutra of the Jains). Among the many such texts are the Dharma Sutra, YOGA SUTRA, and Vedanta Sutra.

Further reading: M. Winternitz, *History of Sanskrit Literature*, 3 vols. (Delhi: Motilal Banarsidass, 1963).

suttee   *See* SATI.

svadhishthana chakra

The *svadhishthana* CHAKRA is the second chakra (energy center) in KUNDALINI YOGA systems. It is situated on the spine in the genital region. It governs sexuality, excitement, and more refined physical sensation. It is associated with the element water. Its deity is VISHNU. Its SHAKTI is Rakini. All chakras are considered lotuses; *svadhisthana* has six red petals.

Further reading: Harish Johari, *Chakras: Energy Centers of Transformation* (Rochester, Vt.: Destiny Books, 2000).

svapna   *See* STATES OF CONSCIOUSNESS.

swami

A swami (one who has his own) is anyone who has proprietary rights, an owner, a lord, or a master. By extension, a person who is master of himself or herself, who has developed perfect yogic self-control, is a spiritual swami. Any religious or spiritual being of the highest order is called a swami. The word is usually added to proper names, for example, Swami MUKTANANDA or Swami SACCIDANANDA.

Further reading: Pagal Baba, *Temple of the Phallic Kin: The Mind of India, Yogis, Swamis, and Avataras* (New York: Simon & Schuster, 1973); Swami Agehananda Bharat, *The Ochre Robe* (Garden City, N.Y.: Doubleday, 1970); Marvin H. Harper, *Gurus, Swamis and Avataras: Spiritual Masters and Their American Disciples* (Philadelphia: Westminster Press, 1972).

Swami Kuvalayananda Yoga Foundation (est. 1972)

The Swami Kuvalayananda Foundation (SKY) of Philadelphia is devoted to the study and practice of HATHA YOGA. It was founded in 1972 as a nonreligious organization by Dr. Vijayendra Pratap, who received a Ph.D. in applied psychology from Bombay University. Dr. Pratap studied YOGA as a student of Swami Kuvalayananda (1883–1966), who founded the noted yoga center Kaivalyadhama in Bombay, where Pratap was assistant director before moving to America.

The SKY Foundation holds HATHA YOGA classes, from basic to the most advanced levels; trains teachers; and focuses on teachings from the ASHTANGA YOGA system of PATANJALI. One of the significant objectives of the foundation is to investigate the ancient as well as the more recent developments of yoga as they interface with contemporary times. Dr. Pratap's foundation has sponsored academic conferences to review what is known about science and yoga. At this point, he and his supporters consider the foundation an academic and research organization seeking ways that science and yogic practice can work together for the good of all humanity. The headquarters are in Philadelphia over the Garland of Letters bookstore, which is sponsored by the foundation.

Further reading: Vijayendra Pratap, *Beginning Yoga* (Rutland, Vt.: Chares E. Tuttle, 1997).

Swaminarayan movement

The Swaminarayan movement is a major worldwide Hindu movement. It is the contemporary expression of a religious revival started by Sri Sahajanand Swami (1781–1830), a monk generally known to his followers as Lord Swaminarayan.

Sahajanand was born at Chhapaiya, near AYODHYA in northern India. A precocious child, he showed an early inclination to the religious life. Upon his parents' deaths, when he was 11 years old, he adopted the life of a renunciant and pursued his spiritual quest. His seven-year PILGRIMAGE around India ended at Gujarat, where he spent a year with Muktanand Swami, who confirmed that Sahajanand was an incarnation of KRISHNA.

Swaminarayan (1781–1830), monk and founder of Swaminarayan movement, pointing to Lord Vishnu *(Courtesy Swaminarayan Headquarters, Bombay [Mumbai])*

Eventually Sahajanand assumed leadership of the devotees of Muktanand Swami.

Sahajanand began to reform the movement by recruiting a group of young SANNYASIS (renunciants) who were dedicated to his vision of uplifting humankind and involved themselves in various social service activities. He imposed five rules on the *sannyasis:* they were to avoid greed, worldly desires, attachments, and ego and live a life of celibacy. He also started holding large ceremonies called Vishnu Yajna with the goal of abolishing the popular sacrifice of animals. His actions attracted a large following throughout Gujarat. The non-*sannyasi* (householder) members were asked to avoid alcohol and intoxicating drugs, meat, food from improper sources, stealing, and debauchery.

Sahahanand authored the *Shikshapatri,* a work summarizing a code of conduct for his followers. As the movement expanded, followers began to affirm that Sahajanand was the incarnation of Lord Purushottama Narayana (i.e., Krishna).

Swaminarayan promoted a form of BHAKTI YOGA, the devotional path to God. He and the movement he founded believe God to be a person and focus their primary attention on Vishnu/ Krishna. Nevertheless, they fall within the larger scope of traditional Hinduism by affirming a philosophy of unity in diversity and acknowledging the common history and language of Hinduism.

Swaminarayan has been followed as head of the movement by a succession of leaders: Gunatitanand Swami (1785–1867), Bhagatji Maharaj (1829–97), Shastriji Maharaj (1865–1951), Yogiji Maharaj (1892–1971), and Pramukh Maharaj (b. 1921). In 1907 Shastriji Maharaj founded the Bochsanwasi Shri Akshar Purusottam Sanstha, which gave the movement its present corporate structure. He also exported the movement outside India, to East Africa. Later, in the 20th century, Pramukh Swami Maharaj carried the movement to the West, establishing the first center in England and subsequently overseeing the vast international spread of the movement through the post–World War II Indian DIASPORA.

At the beginning of the 1970s, Yogiji Maharaj sent four monks to America in response to a request from some immigrants from Gujarat. In 1972 the group who assembled in response to their visit established a center and purchased a temple on Long Island, New York. Pramukh Swami Maharaj in 1974 made the first of what were to be many journeys to the United States. He installed a group of deities for the community and has held similar ceremonies across North America in subsequent visits.

Today, international headquarters for the movement is in Ahmedabad, India. The group supports several institutions of higher learning such as the Pramuch Swami Medical College, the School of Architecture at S. P. University, and the Pramukh Swami Science College, all in Gujurat.

Internationally the movement has a following in Tanzania, Uganda, South Africa, Australia, Belgium, Germany, England, Canada, the United States, Singapore, and Thailand. Worldwide there are more than 3,000 centers.

Further reading: H. T. Dave, *Life and Philosophy of Shree Swaminarayan* (London: George Allen & Unwin, 1974); Sadhu Shantipriyadas, *Mandir Traditions and Belief* (Amdavad, India: Swaminarayan Aksaharpith, 1998); Sadhu Vivekjivandas and Sadhu Amrutvijaydas, *Basic Concepts of Swaminarayan Satsang* (Amdavad: Swaminarayan Aksaharpith, 2002); Raymond Brady Williams, *A New Face of Hinduism: The Swaminarayan Religion* (Cambridge: Cambridge University Press, 1984).

SYDA Foundation   *See* CHIDVILASANANDA, SWAMI.

T

Tagore, Rabindranath (1861–1941) *poet and writer*

Rabindranath Tagore, one of the great literary figures of the world and a fighter for social reform, was the first modern Indian writer to win a reputation around the world. He was the first Asian to win the Nobel Prize in literature.

Tagore was born May 7, 1861, in the Jorasanko District in Calcutta (Kolkata) in the state of Bengal, to the celebrated Hindu reformer Debendranath Tagore and Sarada Devi. His father's father had been a prominent, highly educated businessman and a supporter of the BRAHMO SAMAJ, the Hindu reform sect founded by RAMMOHUN ROY. His father had maintained this affiliation.

Rabindranath was the youngest of 14 children, all of whom were well educated, including the girls, in keeping with the newly emerging Bengali progressive tradition. Most of the children were educated in both Bengali and English and used their knowledge to publish magazines, write plays, and sponsor the arts; young Rabindranath had rich surroundings to allow his talent to grow.

In 1878, at the age of 17, Rabindranath went to England for a year to study in an elite public school in Brighton, and then at University College, London. He did not, however, complete his degree. In 1883, he married Mrinalini Devi, and the couple had two sons and three daughters. By this time he had begun to develop a literary reputation based on several Bengali works, including a long poem in the Maithili regional linguistic style originated by Vidyapati, the authorship of which he initially attempted to hide, and the poetry anthology, *Sandhya Sangit* (Twilight song), which he wrote in 1882. This work includes the famous poem *Nirjharer Svapnabhanga* (*The Cry of the Waterfall*).

In 1890, Tagore began to manage the family estates at Shelaidaha, a riverine region in what is now Bangladesh. There he lived modestly on a houseboat on a tributary of the Padma River. Works of poetry from this period include *Sonar Tari* (1894), *Chitra* (1896), and *Katha O Kahini* (1900). He also began to be known for his essays, plays, and short stories, often set in the local village and river life.

In 1901, Tagore moved to Shantiniketan, in west Bengal, where he started a pioneering educational experiment championing the outdoor classroom run in the ancient Indian way with one teacher and a very few students. Today this school is run by the government of India under the name Vishva Bharati. There he wrote *Naivedya* (1901)

Rabindranath Tagore (1861–1941), Bengali poet, educator, and Nobel Prize laureate *(Courtesy Library of Congress)*

and other works. Here, his wife died young and he lost a son and a daughter. His profound grief affected the tone of his work.

Tagore had developed a large following among Bengali readers; some English translations of his work had been made, but they were not of high quality. At the urging of some of his English admirers he started translating some of his own poems in free verse. In 1912, he went to England to read some of these. It was his fortune to be heard at these readings by the celebrated Irish poet William Butler Yeats. The English version of *Gitanjali (Song Offerings)* (1915) was later published by the India Society with an admiring preface by Yeats.

In November 1913 Tagore was awarded the Nobel Prize in literature, based on the attention that this translation had drawn.

His literary fame established at the age of 60, Tagore began to paint and exhibit his paintings in India and Europe. He painted in a wistful modernist style that was as impressive as his literary work. Deeply beloved in his home of Bengal, Tagore is the only person in the world to have composed two national anthems, India's and Bangladesh's. His love for his country, India, was well known and he joined others of his generation in doing what he could to contribute to the great struggle for independence. He carried on a correspondence, too, with Mohandas Karamchand GANDHI and they were mutual admirers.

As a result of his refined aesthetic sensibilities, his love of nature, and his extensive travels in Europe, America, the Middle East, and the Far East, Tagore developed a philosophy of universal brotherhood and cultural exchange. Above all he believed in the immanence of the divinity and the reflection of that divinity in human beings. As a result he is known and read as a philosopher as well as a literary figure. Perhaps because of his openness of spirit, Tagore's literature and philosophy have found an audience in realms far away from the quiet beauty of the Bengal of his time of which he so passionately wrote.

Further reading: Mohit Cakrabarti, *The Philosophy of Education of Rabindranath Tagore: A Critical Evaluation* (New Delhi: Atlantic and Distributors, 1988); Jose Chunkapura, *The God of Rabindranath Tagore: A Study of the Evolution of His Understanding of God* (Kolkata: Visva-Bharati, 2002); Vijay Dharwadkar and A. K. Ramanujan, eds., *Oxford Anthology of Modern Indian Poetry* (New York: Oxford University Press, 1994); Krishna Dutta and Mary Lago, eds., *Selected Short Stories of Rabindranath Tagore* (London: Macmillan, 1991); Kalyan Sen Gupta, *The Philosophy of Rabindranath Tagore* (Burlington, Vt.: Ashgate, 2005); Uma Das Gupta, *Rabindranath Tagore: A Biography* (New Delhi: Oxford University Press, 2004); Vishvanath Naravane, *An Introduction to Rabindranath Tagore* (Delhi: Macmillan Company of India, 1977); Rabindranath Tagore, *Collected Poems and Plays of Rabindranath Tagore* (New York: Macmillan, 1949); ———, *Gitanjali (Song Offerings)* (London: Macmillan, 1926); ———, *The Religions of Man* (London: Unwin Books, 1970).

Taittiriya Upanishad

The Taittiriya Upanishad is an UPANISHAD of the Black YAJUR VEDA. It is considered one of the oldest Upanishads. It consists of three sections.

The first section is devoted to teaching; it outlines elements of the sacred study of the VEDAS.

The second section is named for its description of the ANANDA (infinite bliss) of the BRAHMAN (ultimate reality). While in passing, defining the terms *self* and *ultimate reality,* it introduces the five SHEATHS that make up a human being. These are the sheath of food, the sheath of breath, the sheath of mind, the sheath of understanding, and the sheath of bliss.

In the final section, named after the teacher Bhrigu, these five levels of being are fully described: the sheath of food describes the external body and the sheath of bliss lies in the core of the heart, as the ultimate Self or *brahman.* The Upanishad concludes with a memorable chant, the vision of the sage who realizes *brahman:* "I am food; I am food; I am food. I am the food-eater; I am the food-eater; I am the food-eater. . . . Earlier than the gods; at the navel of immortality . . . [I see] the golden light!" The food is the manifest universe. The food-eater is the transcendent reality. The sage understands that in SELF-REALIZATION he encompasses all the manifest and unmanifest world.

Further reading: Swami Chinmayananda, *Discourses on Taittiriya Upanishad* (Madras: Chinmaya Publication Trust, 1962); Swami Gambhirananda, trans., *Eight Upanishads with the Commentary of Sankaracarya* (Calcutta: advaita Ashrama, 1972–73); Patrick Olivelle, trans., *The Early Upanishads* (New York: Oxford University Press, 1998); S. Radhakrishnan, *The Principal Upanishads* (Atlantic Highlands, N.J.: Humanities Press, 1994).

tamas See GUNAS.

tanmatra

The *tanmatras* (subtle elements) are categories in the SAMKHYA and YOGA list of 24 categories; they mediate between the five ELEMENTS (*panchabhuta*) and the five powers of knowing. The subtle elements are sound, touch, form, taste, and smell. Among the elements sound is connected to ether (*akasha*), contact is connected to air (*vayu*), form is connected to fire (*tejas* or *agni*), taste is connected to water (*ap* or *jalam*) and smell is connected to earth (*prithivi*).

Further reading: Lallanji Gopal, *Retrieving Samkhya History: An Ascent from Dawn to Meridian* (New Delhi: D. K. Printworld, 2000); Gerald Larson, *Classical Samkhya: An Interpretation of Its History and Meaning* (Delhi: Motilal Banarsidass, 1969); Jonn Mumford, *Magical Tattwas: A Complete System for Self-Development* (St. Paul, Minn.: Llewellyn Publications, 1997).

tantra   *See* TANTRISM.

tantric   *See* TANTRISM.

tantric ritual sex   *See* TANTRISM.

tantrism

Tantrism is a philosophical and religious stream that can be found in Buddhism, JAINISM, and Hinduism.

Tantrism derives from the term *tantra,* which in certain usages defines systems and texts that contrast themselves with the Vaidika or VEDIC tradition. While elements common to the tantric traditions can easily be enumerated and analyzed, the boundary between a system that is tantric and one that is not is not so easily defined.

Philosophically, most Hindu tantric systems focus on "desire" as a path of liberation. This involves a sophisticated reversal process that transforms what is commonly understood in Hinduism as a barrier to liberation, that is, desire, into an instrument for liberation. This method can be applied to numerous aspects of normative life and tradition that are purposely inverted or ignored in order to harness the "lower" aspects of existence and make them servants of liberation.

For instance, a tantric devotee might ritually eat beef, forbidden in normative Hinduism, in order to facilitate realization.

To be sure, many "tantric" elements infuse ordinary ritualistic, temple-oriented Hinduism. But the key to identifying tantrism are the distinctive rituals and practices that form a complex, usually taught to small groups of adepts by a special GURU. These rituals and practices are almost always practiced in secret, away from mainstream society. Thus tantrism as a fuller, secret complex contains an element, more or less obvious, that runs counter to the overt "sanctioned" philosophical streams.

Hindu tantrism seeks both supernatural powers (most often considered a distraction from the goal of liberation) *and* liberation, worldly enjoyment *and* release from the bonds of birth and rebirth. It does this by embracing what is usually eschewed. It takes the world, which is seen to be nothing but a barrier to liberation, as divine and by fully realizing its divinity learns to be its master, living in it in the full presence of the divine.

For the purposes of transformation, the transcendent is often seen as a passive masculine reality, and the feminine is seen as the same transcendent power in action. Using the polarity of masculine and feminine tantrics seek to realize both poles, finally embracing a totality that fuses, so to speak, that which is beyond with that which is here, or, more accurately, realizes that the two are already fused.

Once one understands the unity of the manifest and unmanifest, one also understands that the human is the microcosm of the macrocosm; the human *is* the universal. The tantric sexual ritual, *maithuna,* is based on these understandings. Sexual intercourse ritually replicates the truth of existence, that the masculine is the transcendent divinity and the feminine the immanent divinity, with two human bodies. But this ritual need not be practiced directly; many forms of tantrism practice *maithuna* metaphorically or simply understand it at a philosophical level.

Hindu tantrism can be understood as a marriage of practices and beliefs from the pre-ARYAN Goddess-oriented cults with the larger and more philosophically encompassing Aryan Vedic (but more directly UPANISHADIC) traditions. Tantrism as a distinct tradition has its beginnings with the settlement of the Aryans in fringe areas of India (e.g., Kashmir, Bengal, Tamil Nadu). As the two cultural complexes began to merge in the centuries before and after the start of the Common Era (with the Aryan Vedic always retaining its cultural supremacy), the forms of tantric practice began to become formalized.

Because of their derivation tantric practices are neither purely Vedic nor purely indigenous, but a fusion of the two. It is well known, for instance, that some contemporary non-Hindu tribal people of India still practice sexual rituals and even orgies in fields to promote agricultural (and human) fertility. This is a very ancient ritual, found all over the world in conjunction with early agriculture. It is based on the understanding that the female is the Earth and the male is the sky (and its rain). The two join in sexual embrace to create the fundaments of life. The use of sexual ritual in tantrism most surely derives from this precise process, but it is philosophically aggrandized or at least explicitly philosophized (as it may not have been before), as the union of God and Goddess.

Likewise it is well known that many subgroups in India, both Hindu castes and non-Hindu tribal people, worship the Goddess with alcohol, which is a most despised substance in Brahminical Hinduism. Vedic tradition does record the usage of very small quantities of alcohol in certain obscure rituals, but the drink is in general condemned. It is obvious again that the use of alcohol in certain tantric rituals, in which it is in fact ritually given to the female (the Goddess or SHAKTI) before sexual intercourse, is a remanent of the pre-Aryan traditions.

The ritual egalitarianism of tantrism, which does not observe caste divisions in ritual, also is probably a substratum tribal value taken up into the main complex, as mainstream Hinduism itself is highly oriented toward social stratification. Because the combination of pre-Aryan and Vedic needed philosophical interpretation, certain tantric practices such as the eating of beef can be derived only through philosophical reversal. Non-Hindu tribal people are not beef eaters, but they do eat and ritually use buffalo meat. Beef, of course, became the most forbidden substance for all Hindus. Therefore, the ritual eating of beef in tantric ritual is neither Aryan nor non-Aryan, but a philosophically constructed practice.

Perhaps ironically, tantrism as a system only became consolidated after BRAHMIN practitioners had written numerous texts in SANSKRIT to give it a certain orthodox sanction. Because Hinduism itself is a mixture of the same elements as tantrism, even some of its normative aspects can be said to have tantric roots.

Vedic tradition was not associated with place, probably because of the pastoral nature of society in the era of the Vedas. It was also quite clearly aniconic—not using visible, external forms of the divinities. Temple Hinduism, however, is place-based and uses ICONS. It is quite likely that the notions of a specific place that divinities inhabit is a non-Aryan notion. It is undoubtedly the case also that stone or wood images or symbols of divinities are also non-Aryan. It is thus no coincidence that the ritual texts that lay out the principles for temple design, the AGAMAS, are tantric in character and form part of the large tantric tradition.

The three most important tantric sects are the Vaishnavite tantrics, who have VISHNU as transcendent divinity; the Shaivite tantrics, who have Shiva as transcendent divinity; and the SHAKTA tantrics, who have the Goddess as the transcendent divinity. The last two are often difficult to distinguish as they use similar terminology and frameworks. The Ganapatyas (worshippers of GANESHA) constitute another, small tantric sect. Historically, there was a group of tantrics called

Sauras or Sun (SURYA) worshippers, but these do not appear to have an active sectarian presence in India.

There are numerous textual classifications and subclassifications of tantric groups and practice, but these seem to be more descriptive than practical. Any regional differences that once existed have by now disappeared.

The most important tantric system may be that of Kasmiri Shaivism, which has received the most study and has reached the West through teachers such as Swami MUKTANANDA. Generally, there is a tremendous amount of intentional obscuration and abstruseness in tantric texts to protect them from noninitiates. The Kashmiri Shaivite tradition, however, led by exemplars such as ABHINAVAGUPTA, seemed to make an effort to create philosophical systems that could vie with more orthodox or normative systems in the philosophical arena. Therefore, the Kashmiri Shaivite systems seem to be more clear and open than many others.

A second important subsystem is the SRI VIDYA Goddess-oriented tradition. This is, in fact, a modified and highly Brahminized tradition whose textual history has begun to attract significant scholarship.

Mention must also be made of SAIVA SIDDHANTA, a South Indian and Sri Lankan tantric system. Here, there is a significant body of literature not only in Sanskrit but also in Tamil. In fact, some of the texts originated around 600 C.E.

The various systems, while they share a common sexual paradigm to portray the relationship between the manifest and unmanifest worlds, are not philosophically uniform. Kashmiri Shaivism, for instance, is completely non-dual (ADVAITA), or monistic, whereas Shaivite Siddhanta is purely dualistic; one can realize oneself as a "small Shiva," but Paramashiva, or transcendent Shiva, is beyond the reach of the soul in transformational terms. That is, the highest Shiva is eternally distinct from the souls. The system of Bengali Vaishnavite Sahajiya, alternatively, retains the

Vaishnavite "quasi-non-dualistic" aspect, representing a third philosophical stream.

Tantric systems are divided into two tendencies that are referred to as left-handed and right-handed. The left-handed is most probably the original practice. It can be shockingly antinomian or antisocial. The AGHORIS are an example of this. These wanderers eat excrement and in other ways try to outrage people in public arenas in order to use the "reversed" energy to gain supernatural powers.

The extreme left-handed practices dating from very early in the history of tantrism have made the word *tantric* as despised in India as in the normative West. Formalized left-handed practice uses the PANCHA MAKARA, or five forbidden substances: meat, wine, sexual intercourse, parched grain, and fish. These are combined in a ritual context.

Right-handed practice could be considered a Brahminization of the left-handed stream. There, accepted entities or practices are substituted for the "forbidden" ones to align the practice more closely with social norms. This substitution might be a mental visualization of the practice rather than the practice itself; physical substitution, for instance, eating a particular vegetable instead of beef; or complete avoidance of any of the elements in favor of a purely philosophical approach.

Some important notions used in Hindu tantric practice include SADHANA, or adept practice; DIKSHA, the necessary initiation (distinct from the Vedic initiation); MANTRA, a distinctive usage of mantra practice; YANTRA, abstract designs used for ritual worship and MEDITATION; and MUDRAS, special hand gestures used in conjunction with meditation and ritual. KUNDALINI yoga is by definition a tantric practice and is a central part of many tantric systems. SHAKTIPAT (Shakti initiation) is also a practice done by some tantric gurus, who can transform an adept, or initiate him or her, by merely a touch that transfers the guru's Shakti, or grace, to the adept. Most tantric sects also develop a range of divinities or special powers that are worshipped only in the context of their particular cult.

There is some evidence of tantrism in Jain tradition, mostly limited to the use of tantric style mantras and certain hints of tantric sexuality. No full tantric practice is known to have emerged in JAINISM. This was primarily due to the severity of Jain asceticism, and the nature of reality according to Jainism, which left no room for pursuit of enlightenment through desire.

Further reading: Agehananda Bharati, *The Tantric Tradition* (New York: Grove Press, 1975); N. N. Bhattacharyya, *History of the Tantric Religion: A Historical, Ritualistic and Philosophical Study* (Delhi: Manohar, 1982); Douglas Renfrew Brooks, *Auspicious Wisdom: The Texts and Traditions of Sri Vidya Sakta Tantrism* (Albany: State University of New York Press, 1992); John Cort, "Worship of Bell-Ears the Great Hero, a Jain Tantric Deity," in David Gordon White, ed., *Tantra in Practice* (Princeton, N.J.: Princeton University Press, 2000); Shashibhusan Dasgupta, *Obscure Religious Cults* (Calcutta: Firma KLM, 1995); Edward C. Dimock, *The Place of the Hidden Moon: Erotic Mysticism in the Vaisnavasahajiya Cult of Bengal* (Chicago: University of Chicago Press, 1966); Michael Dyczkowski, *The Doctrine of Vibration: An Analysis of the Doctrines and Practices of Kashmir Shaivism* (Delhi: Motilal Banarsidass, 1975); Sanjukta Gupta, Dirk Jan Hoens, and Teun Goudriaan, *Hindu Tantrism* (Leiden: E. J. Brill, 1979); Mohanlal Bhagwandas Jhavery, *Comparative and Critical Study of Mantrasastra (with Special Treatment of the Jain Mantravada)* (Ahmedabad: Sarabhai Manilal Nawab, 1944); Paul Muller-Ortega, *The Triadic Heart of Siva* (Albany: State University of New York Press, 1969); Lilian Silburn, *Kundalini, the Energy of the Depths: A Comprehensive Study Based on the Scriptures of Nondualistic Kasmir Saivism.* Translated by Jacques Gontier (Albany: State University of New York Press, 1988); Sir John Woodruffe (Arthur Avalon), *Introduction to Tantra Shastra*, 2d ed. (Madras: Ganesh, 1952); ———, *Sakti and Sakta*, 6th ed. (Madras: Ganesh, 1965).

tapas (tapasya)

Tapas (heat) or *tapasya* is a concept of great importance in Hindu practices of austerity. The word refers to the sacred heat that is generated by bodily mortifications and ascetic denial. *Tapas* confers wondrous powers and abilities upon the YOGI and makes it easier for the adept to break the bonds of attachment to worldly life.

In a very literal example of *tapas,* ancient orthodox yogis used to sit surrounded by five fires under the noonday Sun in order to absorb the heat and gain spiritual power. Other ascetics doing *tapasya* would endure lengthy fasts or extreme bodily mortifications. There is some indication that the notion of *tapasya* developed within the Brahminical tradition as a result of association with the fires of the Vedic sacrifice.

Further reading: Walter O. Kaelber, *Tapta Marga: Asceticism and Initiation in Vedic India* (Albany: State University of New York Press, 1989); Klaus K. Klostermaier, *A Survey of Hinduism* (Albany: State University of New York Press, 1990); David M. Knipe, *In the Image of Fire: Vedic Experiences of Heat* (Delhi: Motilal Banarsidass, 1975).

tat tvam asi See VEDANTA.

Tattvartha Sutra (c. 200 C.E.)

The Tattvartha Sutra was composed by the great Jain Acarya (Saint) Umasvami (or Umasvati). It is the first text of JAINISM written in SANSKRIT (the earlier ones, which are no longer extant, were written in Prakrit, the vernacular tongue that developed from Sanskrit). The Tattvartha Sutra is the first extant text of the Jains, and it systematizes the canonical teachings into an integrated philosophical school. It is written in the concise aphoristic style typical of Indian texts designated as SUTRAS.

The Tattvartha Sutra plays a similar authoritative role in Jain tradition as the VEDANTA SUTRA of BADARAYANA or the YOGA SUTRA of PATANJALI in orthodox Hindu culture. In approximately 350 short verses, Umasvami surveys basic Jain doctrine. He discusses salvation; states of the soul; the human, celestial, and infernal realms; insentient reality; the nature of KARMA, karmic bondage, and the acquisition and removal of karma. The Tattvartha Sutra is the only Jain text that is accepted by both of the two main sects, the SHVETAMBARA and the DIGAMBARA.

Further reading: P. S. Jaini, *Jaina Path of Purification* (Delhi: Motilal Banarsidass, 1990); Nathmal Tatia, trans., *That Which Is: Tattvartha Sutra by Umasvami: With the Combined Commentaries of Umasvami, Pujyapada and Siddhasenagani* (San Francisco: HarperCollins, 1994).

Tegh Bahadur   *See* SIKHISM.

tejas (Agni)   *See* ELEMENTS, FIVE.

temple

The temple is the center of Hindu worship. It can vary in size from a small shrine with a simple thatched roof to vast complexes of stone and masonry.

During most times of the year the temple is devoted to individual or family worship or to greeting of the divinity. Since many houses in India have their own shrines set up for worship, the temple is reserved for special worship or for requests to the divinity, often by people who have made PILGRIMAGES. At festival times temples are given over to group worship, as devotees sing *BHAJANS* or *KIRTANS*, or to various rituals that commemorate special events in the life of the divinity, for example, the marriage of MINAKSHI at the Meenakshi Temple in Madurai.

The early worship of the VEDAS took the form of a ceremony around a fire or fires, without any permanent structures or icons. Location was unimportant. As Hinduism developed, it borrowed from other modes of worship, and both location and iconography became central features. Often geography determined temple location: high places that jut out from the countryside would usually have at least small temples at their summits, as would river junctions. In addition, places traditionally associated with events in the lives of a deity would often be marked with temples. The temple at RAMESHVARAM, for example, marks the place where RAMA had his monkey armies build a bridge to cross over and fight the demon king Ravana, according to the RAMAYANA.

Today, ICON worship is central to Indian temple worship. The stone itself is not worshipped. The icon is merely the place the divinity inhabits. A complex ritual must first be performed to install the divinity in the image. Thereafter, the image is treated as the divinity itself would be: it is bathed, dressed, sung to, fed, and feted each day. For SHAIVITES, most often the icon is the SHIVA LINGAM,

A typical Hindu temple tower. Shown here is the Krishna temple in Kanchipuram, Tamil Nadu.
(Constance A. Jones)

the erect phallus symbol of Shiva surrounded by the round *YONI* representing the goddess's sexual organ. For Vaishnavites the icon is a full representation of VISHNU in one of his forms; for SHAKTAS it is an image of the great GODDESS.

Often the inner sanctum of the temple, its most holy spot, holds a small, typically modest icon. The more elaborate statues and images are usually located in the larger temple precincts. Large temples often boast a huge array of images of gods and goddesses, usually depicting a particular event in their story. One might see, for instance, NARASIMHA, the man-lion AVATAR of Vishnu, ripping apart his demon foe HIRANYAKASHIPU, or see Shiva in his pose as the divine dancer, NATARAJA.

PUJA, the regular worship service including offerings and rites, is usually performed before the central icon at fixed times during the day. For a donation, devotees can dedicate certain features of a regular *puja*, such as the recitation of a particular MANTRA. They may also pay for *pujas* to be conducted by BRAHMIN priests at other times, simple or elaborate at their discretion, in support of certain prayers or pleas to the divinity. A woman might want to have a son, a man might want to gain success in business, or a student might seek success in exams. All worldly and salvational requests are taken to the divinity of the temple; popular temples are thronged with people year round.

The *puja* consists, at the minimum, of fruit, water, and flower offerings to the divinity, accompanied by the appropriate mantras. No *puja* is done without the ARATI, or waving of a lighted lamp before the divinity. At the end of the ritual people may step forward and waft the smoke from the lamp over their head or face to receive the blessing of the divinity. In certain temples one may receive a little of the food that had been offered to the divinity, called PRASADA, which will confer blessing when eaten.

Most temples in India, including all of the well-known temples, allow only Brahmins to perform the rituals. There are smaller and larger shrines all over the country, however, who have non-Brahmin and even SHUDRA (low-caste) priests. These are usually temples serving a smaller local community. By law, any member of any caste may enter any temple in India. Nevertheless, in practice Dalits (UNTOUCHABLES) are often barred. Certain temples admit only Hindus; Muslims and Christians will be excluded if they are identified. A famous case of temple exclusion took place when Indira Gandhi, prime minister of India, visited the JAGANNATH temple at Puri. She was excluded because she was married to a non-Hindu.

Many great Hindu temples deserve mention: the VISHVANATHA TEMPLE to Shiva in the holy city BENARES (Varanasi); the famous KALI temple at Kali Ghat in Calcutta (Kolkata); the JAGANNATH TEMPLE to KRISHNA in Puri; the temple for the goddess Kamakshi at KANCHIPURAM; the BRIHADISHVARA temple to Shiva in Tanjore; the MEENAKSHI TEMPLE to the goddess Minakshi and the Shrirangam temple to VISHNU, both in Tamil Nadu.

Most Jains also worship at temples. These can be quite elaborate, as at MT. ABU, or smaller buildings. The *puja* is similar to the Hindu *puja* in these Jain contexts, but since the TIRTHANKARAS, the exalted personages who are worshipped, are not gods, but human beings, there is no PRASADA or "blessed food" given, and technically no blessing can be given by the image or personage. Instead, worship is aimed largely at instilling values that will lead devotees toward the yogic perfection of the Tirthankara being worshipped.

Sikhs have only the Golden Temple at AMRITSAR, where the holy book of the Sikhs, Granth Sahib, is enshrined. Sikhs also have *gurudwaras*, or "entranceways to the guru," all over the world. These meeting places welcome anyone, but there is no iconic worship or *puja* there.

Recently many Hindu temples, Jain temples, and Sikh *gurudwaras* have been established in the West. They often have unusual features, as at the Shiva-Vishnu Temple in Livermore, California, where both Shiva and Vishnu are worshipped side by side. The Western temples are usually built in very traditional fashion, under the guidance of Brahmins and temple experts and artisans from India. However, each has its own unique style.

Further reading: Vasudeva S. Agrawala, *Evolution of the Hindu Temple and Other Essays* (Varanasi: Prithivi Prakashan, 1979); R. Champakalakshmi and Usha Kris, *The Hindu Temple* (New Delhi: Roli Books, 2001); Stella Kramrisch and Raymond Burnier, *The Hindu Temple* (Delhi: Motilal Banarsidass, 1976); George Mitchell, *The Hindu Temple: An Introduction to Its Meaning and Forms* (Chicago: University of Chicago Press, 1988); Malory Nye, *Place for Our Gods: The Construction of an Edinburgh Hindu Temple Community* (Richmond, England: Curzon Press, 1995); Paul Younger, *The Home of Dancing Shiva: The Traditions of the Hindu Temple in Citamparam* (New York: Oxford University Press, 1995).

Temple of Cosmic Religion

In 1966, while attending the KUMBHA MELA, a much-celebrated festival of ritual bathing at the confluence of the YAMUNA and GANGES rivers in ALLAHABAD, Lord Panduranga Vittala, an incarnation of KRISHNA, approached Satguru Sant KESHAVADAS (1934–97), an independent teacher of various paths of Indian philosophy, and told him, "Go to the West: spread the cosmic religion." Later, after returning home to Delhi, Keshavadas experienced a vision in which he understood the spiritual reason for such a journey. The key VEDANTA principle that there is only one truth, he realized, should be used to include, not exclude, others. Religion could be a force to gather together the sacred bonds that unite humanity.

The next year, 1967, Keshavadas toured Europe, the Middle East, and the United States. In 1968 he founded a small center in Washington, D.C., that would become the American headquarters of the Dasashram International Center, as it was known in India. In the mid-1970s he relocated the center to Southfield, Michigan, near Detroit, and changed its name to the Temple of Cosmic Religion.

Keshavadas had a primary goal of introducing the wisdom of Hinduism to the West. He wanted to usher in a cosmic religion founded on the principles that truth is one and that all paths lead to God. Keshavadas taught YOGA and MEDITATION as a way to know God and encouraged his followers to dance, sing, and chant. Central to Keshavadas's beliefs are the precepts of KARMA and REINCARNATION.

The world headquarters of the Temple of Cosmic Religion is now located in Bangalore, India; there are five other centers in India. The U.S. headquarters is currently in Oakland, California. Since the death of Keshavadas in 1997, the temple has been led by his widow, Guru Mata Keshavadas. The temple also has centers in Trinidad and England.

Further reading: Sant Keshavadasji, *The Doctrine of Reincarnation and Liberation* (Bangalore: Dasashrama Research, 1970); ———, *The Purpose of Life* (New York: Vantage Press, 1978); ———, *Satguru Speaks* (Washington, D.C.: Temple of Cosmic Religion, 1975); Mukundadas (Michael Allen Makosky), *Minstrel of Love* (Nevada City, Calif.: Hansa, 1980).

Temple of Kriya Yoga

The Temple of Kriya Yoga was established on the North Side in Chicago in the 1960s by the American Goswami Kriyananda (b. 1930), who had been teaching yoga since the 1940s. The headquarters of the temple is still located in Chicago. Goswami was born Melvin Higgins; he is not to be confused with his compatriot Swami KRIYANANDA of the ANANDA MOVEMENT.

Kriyananda studied YOGA and was initiated by his first GURU, Sri Shelliji, a disciple of Paramahansa YOGANANDA, founder of the SELF-REALIZATION FELLOWSHIP. Kriyananda, an excellent astrologer, also opened the College of Occult Sciences, which offered many courses in esoteric traditions.

During the 1970s Kriyananda established a retreat in South Haven, Michigan, and in 1977 founded the Kriyananda Healing Center as a holistic health facility. The center teaches nontraditional methods of healing, including biofeedback, MEDITATION, yoga, fasting, nutrition, and massage.

Kriyananda instructs students in Yogananda's KRIYA YOGA path of supreme bliss (*samadhi*); he teaches the oneness of God and a non-dual VENDANTIC cosmology. He has written several books about *kriya yoga,* astrology, and meditation.

The temple publishes a periodical, *The Flame of Kriya,* and maintains a Web site.

Further reading: Goswami Kriyananda, *The Bhagavad-Gita: The Song of God* (Chicago: Temple of Kriya Yoga, n.d.); ———, *Pathway to God-Consciousness* (Chicago: Temple of Kriya Yoga, 1970); ———, *Yoga, Text for Teachers and Advanced Students* (Chicago: Temple of Kriya Yoga, 1976).

Tevaram

The Tevaram is the collected hymns of the three most prominent NAYANMARS or Tamil SHAIVITE saints, APPAR, Jnanasambanthar (also known as SAMBANTHAR or Tirujnanasambanthar), and SUNDARAR (Suntharamurtti), whose lives spanned the sixth through eighth centuries C.E. These hymns, in the Tamil language, are considered by Tamil Shaivites to be equal in sanctity to the SANSKRIT VEDAS as scripture and MANTRA; in a sense, the Tevaram is a Veda. The text is memorized and sung by a hereditary community called Otuvars during daily temple rituals and ceremonials.

The hymns of the Tevaram celebrate SHIVA with passionate devotion, dwelling on the many tales of Shiva; his wives, SATI and PARVATI; and his two sons, GANESHA and KARTTIKEYA. They lovingly describe the deity's physical attributes and recount his visitations to famous devotees at the sites of many important Shaivite shrines in Tamil Nadu.

Further reading: Indira Viswanathan Peterson, *Poems to Siva: The Hymns of the Tamil Saints* (Princeton, N.J.:

Princeton University Press, 1989); R. Vijayalakshmy, *An Introduction to Religion and Philosophy—Tevaram and Tivviyappirapantam* (Chennai: International Institute of Tamil Studies, 2001); Kamil V. Zvelebil, *Tamil Literature* (Leiden: Brill, 1975).

Thailand

Contemporary Thailand is a predominantly Theravada Buddhist country, where Hinduism, animism, Islam, and Christianity are also practiced. The Hindu minority constitutes only about 1 percent of the population. Nevertheless, the historic influence of Hinduism is still apparent. The king of Thailand is always referred to as RAMA, the name of the title character of the Ramakien (the local version of the SANSKRIT RAMAYANA), and he is considered an AVATAR of VISHNU. Though the Thai monarchies date to the formation of the kingdom of Sukothai, the first king to take the title of Rama was Phraphutthayotfa Chulalok, who was named Rama I during the 18th century. The most famous Thai king was Rama V, also known as King Chulalongkorn, who defended Thailand's independence from European colonizers and introduced democracy. The West knows of him primarily as the child prince of King Mongkut (Rama IV) in the book *Anna and the King of Siam.* The current king, Adulyadej the Great, who rose to power in 1946, is called Rama IX.

The Ramakien is a central part of Thai culture. The epic is illustrated in the artwork of many temples and is often performed in dance and puppet plays. The best known image is a massive fresco painted on the wall of the Royal Temple (Temple of the Jade Buddha). Other Hindu imagery, such as YAKSHAS, who act as guardians of the doors, can be found within many Buddhist temples.

Monuments to the Hindu gods SHIVA and Vishnu are found in Thai Buddhist temples. The Royal Temple has a small group of BRAHMINS to conduct royal rituals, as Buddhist monks cannot preside over these rites. Thai Buddhism shares many beliefs with its parent religion Hinduism, most particularly the belief in liberation from the cycle of births, the cosmology of Hinduism, and the four major eras or YUGAS. Many of the laity fuse Hindu belief and ritual with Buddhist religion. Several Hindu temples exist in Thailand and most of the major deities are recognized. There are even temples and PUJAS (worship services) dedicated to the creator god BRAHMA alone, a rarity in India itself.

Further reading: Eliezer B. Ayal, ed., *The Study of Thailand: Analysis of Knowledge, Approaches, and Prospects in Anthropology, Art History, Economics, History, and Political Science* (Athens: Ohio Center for International Studies, South East Asia Program, 1978); John M. Cadet, *The Ramakien: The Thai Epic: Illustrated with the Bas-Reliefs of Wat Phra Jetubon* (Tokyo: Kodansha International, 1971); Georges Coedès, *The Indianized States of Southeast Asia.* Edited by Walter F. Vella translated by Susan Brown Cowing (Honolulu: East-West Center Press, 1968); Rajiv Malik, "Thailand Hinduism," *Hinduism Today* (July–August–September 2003); Stanley J. O'Conner, *Hindu Gods of Peninsular Siam* (Ascona, Switzerland: Artibus Asiae, 1972).

Theosophical Society (est. 1875)

The Theosophical Society was founded in 1875 in New York City by Helena Petrovna BLAVATSKY, Henry Steel Olcott, and William Q. Judge. The founders sought to promote the study of insights from various world religions, investigate spiritualist and other occult phenomena, and foster the brotherhood of all humankind. Olcott became the first president (1875–1907), although the writings and teachings of Blavatsky became synonymous with the teachings of the society. The society accepted her self-description as a disciple of highly evolved beings, *mahatmas*, who had instructed her in the ancient wisdom, the secret doctrine, the wisdom religion, or Theosophy. She claimed to have contacted an occult brotherhood of these *mahatmas* in her travels in the Far East,

particularly in Tibet. Their perennial philosophy became the basis of her writings.

Although Theosophy has no official dogma, it sees itself as a body of truths that are the basis of all valid religions. It is not a religion per se, but rather a restatement of the essence of religion itself. The three stated objectives of the society are (1) to form a nucleus of the Universal Brotherhood of Humanity without distinction of race, creed, sex, caste, or color; (2) to encourage the study of comparative religion, philosophy, and science; and (3) to investigate unexplained laws of nature and the powers latent in humans.

To Theosophists, the universe is a manifestation of one eternal, infinite reality, the divine, which underlies and pervades everything. Each person is a spark of the divine, a microcosm of the macrocosm, born in order to evolve from latent divinity to perfection. Through many incarnations, a soul entity or monad of the divine becomes perfect enough to be free from the cycle of birth and death.

Blavatsky expounded a cosmological scheme and description of the human body and soul, involving levels and hierarchies that express relationships among humanity, the angelic realms, and ultimately, the divine. Theosophical ideas are largely drawn from the cosmological and psychological teachings of Hinduism and Buddhism and are portrayed in an amalgam of Hindu and Buddhist terminology.

In 1879 Blavatsky and Olcott settled in India; in 1882 they established Theosophical Society headquarters at Adyar, near Madras (Chennai). In 1895, Judge, who headed the American section, severed its relations with the British and Indian branches. In 1896 Judge died and was succeeded by Katherine A. TINGLEY, who moved the American section's headquarters to Point Loma (San Diego), California. Further schisms of the Theosophical Society in America produced the Temple of the People (from the Syracuse, New York, branch) and the Theosophical Society of New York.

After Blavatsky's death in 1891, the Theosophical movement experienced a decade of internal dissent. Annie BESANT, an Englishwoman who joined the society after reading Blavatsky's work, succeeded her as head of the Esoteric Section, a small group who experimented with occult principles. When Olcott died in 1907 Besant became the new president of the society.

The first decades of the movement saw widespread interest in Theosophical principles in America, Europe, and India. The synthesis of East and West, religion and science, and esoteric and exoteric understanding made Theosophy compelling to cosmopolitan, liberal people, regardless of nationality, who had been disappointed by the dogmatism of both religion and science and sought to unite the diverse peoples of the world in a peaceful brotherhood.

Around the turn of the 20th century the movement had begun to decline, but under Besant's leadership many lodges in Europe, America, and India revived. In the Netherlands in 1926 Besant announced to the world gathering of Theosophists that the world teacher whom the society had anticipated since Blavatsky's time had been located. This teacher was the young Jiddu KRISHNAMURTI.

The occult formulations and esoteric teachings of the society have influenced many Western teachers and movements that do not use the name *Theosophy,* including Alice BAILEY and the Lucis Trust; Guy Ballard and the "I AM movement"; Elizabeth Clare Prophet and the Church Universal and Triumphant; and Rudolph Steiner and Anthroposophy. Theosophical publishing houses are responsible for making available to the general public many texts and writings of Hinduism.

Today the Theosophical movement includes the Judge-Tingley-dePurucker branch called the Theosophical Society, headquartered in Altadena, California. This organization sponsors the Theosophical Press, which publishes the periodical *Sunrise* and operates a large library. The Theosophical Society in America, part of the larger International Theosophical Society in India, is headquartered in Wheaton, Illinois. This organization sponsors the Theosophical Publishing House and Quest Books, publishes the *American Theosophist* and *Discovery,* and operates the Olcott Library at Wheaton. *The Theosophist,* founded in 1979, is still published at Adyar, India.

The United Lodge of Theosophy, founded in 1909 by Robert Crosbie, former member of the Point Loma community, is headquartered in Los Angeles and sponsors Theosophy Company, its publishing house. This organization publishes *Theosophy,* a monthly periodical. All of the Theosophical organizations cited here maintain Web sites.

Although current membership statistics are not available, adherents to the formal structure of Theosophy are becoming fewer. Yet its historic role in introducing Eastern thought and philosophy to the West remains secure.

Further reading: Bruce F. Campbell, *Ancient Wisdom Revisited* (Berkeley: University of California Press, 1980); Emmett A. Greenwalt, *California Utopia: Point Loma, 1897–1942* (San Diego: Point Loma, 1978); Howard Murphet, *When Daylight Comes: A Biography of Helena Petrovna Blavatsky* (Wheaton, Ill.: Theosophical Publishing House, 1975); Josephine Ransom, *A Short History of the Theosophical Society 1875–1937* (Adyar: Theosophical Publishing House, 1938); Charles J. Ryan, *H. P. Blavatsky and the Theosophical Movement* (Pasadena, Calif.: Theosophical University Press, 1975); *The Theosophical Movement, 1875–1950* (Los Angeles: Cunningham Press, 1951).

Therapanthi

The Therapanthis are a schismatic movement within the the STHANAKAVASI sect of Jains (*see* JAINISM). It emerged from the attempt by the 18th-century monk Bhikanji to deal with the perennial conflict faced by Jain monks: to eschew all worldliness or to work actively for the welfare and salvation of all beings.

Bhikanji's solution, radical for Jains, was that renunciation was more important than saving of an animal's life. He argued that if one were, for instance, to save the life of a dog, one would then be responsible for the violent KARMA of that animal in the rest of its life. Other Jains, shocked at this conclusion because of its apparent rejection of the Jain notion of AHIMSA or noninjury, predicted that Bhikanji would never have even 12 disciplines. Therefore, when the sect did in fact take hold, it became known as the Therapantha (the way of the 13).

Further reading: V. G. Nair, *Jainism and Therapanthism* (Bangalore: Adinatha Jaina Shvetambara Temple, 1970); Muni Nathmal, *Acarya Bhiksu: The Man and His Philosophy* (Churu: Adarsa Sahitya Sangha, 1968).

Thind, Bhagat Singh (1892–1967) *teacher of Sant Mat in the United States*

Bhagat Singh Thind, an Indian-American disciple of the reformist SANT MAT movement, became the subject of a court case in the 1920s that had far-reaching consequences for the American Indian community.

Thind, born in AMRITSAR, Punjab, and initiated by Sant Mat Satguru Sawan Singh (1858–1948), migrated to the UNITED STATES in 1913. He attended the University of California and earned his living, as did many Punjabis, working in the lumber mills in Oregon. During World War I he served in the U.S. Army. In 1920 he applied for and was granted citizenship.

Thind's move to become a naturalized citizen occurred in the wake of the passage of the Asian Exclusion Act of 1917, which included provisions that blocked further immigration from India. India's inclusion in the definition of "Asians" to be excluded had in part been prompted by the so-called "Hindoo riots" that occurred in Washington, Oregon, and northern California protesting the many jobs that were given to Punjabi men in the lumbering industry.

After the final approval of Thind's citizenship, a naturalization examiner challenged the court's decision. That challenge initiated a three-year court process that rested on a provision of an earlier 1790 law, which had opened citizenship to any "free white person" not otherwise encumbered. Thind argued that he was a "Caucasian" and hence a "white person." The case went to the United States Supreme Court, which in 1923, in an opinion written by Justice George Sutherland, ruled that not all Caucasians were white in the common understanding of that term and revoked Thind's citizenship. That ruling also led to the withdrawal of a number of other previous grants of citizenship to Indian Americans. The ruling in the Thind case stood as federal policy until changes were enacted in immigration law in 1965.

In the meantime, Thind remained in the United States and maintained his vocation as a Sant Mat teacher, though generally describing himself as a Sikh (see SIKHISM). He lectured widely across the United States, primarily to non-Indian audiences, and authored a number of books and booklets. He educated himself on American religion and argued for his faith, comparing it to transcendentalism and Christianity. In his mature years, cut off from the Sant Mat community, he developed his own unique, eclectic spiritual system.

He later married a French American, Vivian Davies, who worked for many years to introduce Indian culture into the United States. They had one son, David, who keeps his father's writings in print.

Further reading: David Christopher Lane, *The Radhasoami Tradition: A Critical History of Guru Successorship* (New York and London: Garland, 1992); Bhagat Singh Thind, *The Bible of Humanity for Supreme Wisdom* (New York: Author, n.d.); ———, *Divine Wisdom*, 2 vols. (New York: Author, n.d.); ———, *Radiant Road to Reality* (New York: Author, 1939); "*United States vs. Bhagat Singh Thind*, Decided February 19, 1923," *Supreme Court Reporter* 43, no. 10 (April 1, 1923).

time in Hindu tradition

Time in Hinduism is a cyclical concept. The universe arises and disappears in an infinite series of cycles.

In this time scheme, every "Great Age" (MAHA-YUGA) encompasses four successive Ages (YUGAS), beginning with an Age of Truth (KRITA, or Satya, YUGA) and progressively declining until an Age of Corruption (Kali Yuga, which has no relation to the goddess Kali, spelled differently in SANSKRIT). A long series of such oscillating Great Ages eventually plays out, until the universe dissolves and remains absent for a time equal to its previous presence. Then, it once again emerges into a new round of Great Ages. The Jain tradition shares this notion of cycles, defined somewhat differently. Buddhism has its own version of endless time, stretching in both directions, past and future.

Different traditions or *puranas* describe the story of time in varying ways. In one version, after the long night of BRAHMA, equal to 4,320,000,000 years, when the universe is in dissolution, the Supreme Being, VISHNU, stimulates the ever-present nature, or *PRAKRITI* (who exists in potential form while the universe is gone), to reemerge as the universe. The universe then begins a new Krita, or Satya, Yuga, now seen as a Golden Age, followed by a Treta (Silver) Age, a Dvapara (Bronze) Age, and finally a Kali (Iron) Age, the final Age of Corruption. We are currently in one such final age. Each Mahayuga, or Great Age, equals 12,000 god-years, each of which lasts 360 human years, for a total of 4,320,000,000 human years.

The Yugas decrease in duration: a Satya Yuga is 1,728,000 years, Treta is 1,296,000 years, Dvapara is 864,000 years, and Kali is 432,000 years. During this decline human stature, longevity, and morality also progressively decline.

One thousand Mahayugas, or cycles of four Yugas, make up a *kalpa* (eon), a day in the life of Lord BRAHMA, 4,320,000,000 years. Each *kalpa* is followed by a time of calamity and disaster, on the Earth and in all the worlds. All beings perish. Fire overtakes all of the worlds, followed by a massive flood. Finally all the elements return to the seed of primordial nature, or *prakriti*, and time itself ends, only to reemerge when the cosmic night has ended.

Within these cycles is another classification of time called the MANVANTARA, each of which is ruled by a MANU, or "first man," the progenitor of the human race in that period. Because the universe dissolves and reappears again and again, there are an infinite number of such figures. Each *kalpa* sees 14 Manus reign in succession. This means that a *manvantara* takes up approximately 71 Yugas. One *manvantara* thus lasts 367,020,000 years. Each *manvantara* has seven RISHIS (VEDIC seers), certain deities, an INDRA, and a Manu. The Manu of our era is known as Vaivasvata. He is the seventh Manu of our *kalpa*, or eon.

We are currently in the Kali Yuga, but there is no agreement among the sources as to precisely where we are in this 432,000-year cycle and when this age will end.

Further reading: Cornelia Dimmitt and J. A. B. van Buitenen, *Classical Hindu Mythology: A Reader in the Sanskrit Puranas* (Philadelphia: Temple University Press, 1978); F. B. J. Kuiper, "Cosmogony and Conception: A Query," *History of Religions* 10 (1970): 91–138; W. J. Wilkins, *Hindu Mythology, Vedic and Puranic*, 2d ed. (Calcutta: Rupa, 1973).

Tingley, Katherine (Augusta Westcott)
(1847–1929) *American Theosophical leader*

Katherine Augusta Westcott served as the head of the American Theosophical Society after it broke with Annie Wood BESANT (1847–1933).

Westcott was born in Newburyport, Massachusetts. Privately educated, she became interested in social work and founded the Society of Mercy, a relief organization on New York City's impoverished East Side.

Through her social work, she met William Q. Judge (1851–96), cofounder of the Theosophical Society. In 1891, another cofounder, Helena

Petrovna BLAVATSKY (1831–91) died. Previously, she and the third co-founder, Henry Steel Olcott (1832–1907), had moved to India, where each had absorbed elements of the Indian spiritual environment. Through the early 1890s, Judge challenged the role of Besant, a relatively new member of the society who emerged as head of its important Esoteric Section, in which Blavatsky had taught psychic development and occult practices.

Judge's challenge of Besant led the majority of the American section to break with the international society. Before he died in 1896 Judge designated Tingley, whom he had seen as a capable and dedicated leader, as his successor. Tingley stepped into her role immediately and traveled the globe on a World Crusade for Theosophy. When she returned to America, she set up headquarters at Point Loma at San Diego, California, where she founded the School for the Revival of the Lost Mysteries of Antiquity.

Tingley led the Theosophical Society in an interesting direction, mixing esoteric teachings with an experiment in communal living at Point Loma and developing a variety of outward-directed programs in the community. Among the more interesting programs was a relief work effort in Cuba that included taking a group of Cuban children to Point Loma.

Theosophy is basically a Western esoteric teaching, but it resonated with Hinduism at a variety of points. Most notably, it shared an understanding of the individual as essentially a substantial soul that reincarnated in different bodies through time. The youth division of the school at Point Loma was designated the Raja Yoga College, a designation Tingley took from the SANSKRIT sense of "royal union." She saw true education to consist in the harmonious development and balancing of all human faculties. As taught at the school, raja yoga was a system for developing psychic, intellectual, and spiritual powers and a union with one's higher self (the inner divine source of all).

The Tingley-led Theosophical Society opposed the emphasis placed on the role of Jiddu KRISHNAMURTI (1895–1986). Besant's designation of Krishnamurti as the vehicle of the World Savior in the 1920s attracted many new supporters to the international Theosophical Society, though most left when in 1929 Krishnamurti rejected his connection with Theosophy. Tingley's organization was crippled by Tingley's death in July 1929 in an automobile accident in Germany, and by the collapse of the stock market in October that year that plunged the world into an economic depression.

Tingley led every activity at Point Loma, and during her life the society flourished, though her inability to delegate authority and her neglect of the organization's other centers became evident after her death. The society remained vital through the 1930s but lost the land at Point Loma during World War II. In the later half of the 20th century, the International Theosophical Society recovered the support of the majority of American Theosophists.

Further reading: Bruce F. Campbell, *A History of the Theosophical Movement* (Berkeley: University of California Press, 1980); Emmet A. Greenwalt, *California Utopia: Point Loma, 1897–1942* (San Diego: Point Loma, 1978); Katherine Tingley, *Theosophy: The Path of the Mystic* (Pasadena, Calif.: Theosophical University Press, 1977); ———, *The Wine of Life* (Point Loma, Calif.: Woman's International Theosophical League, 1925); ———, *The Wisdom of the Heart: Katherine Tingley Speaks.* Compiled by Emmet Small (Point Loma, Calif.: Point Loma, 1978).

Tirthankara

The Tirthankaras (ford crossers), those who have crossed the ocean of birth and rebirth and have been released from the bonds of KARMA, are the central objects of devotion for Jains (*see* JAINISM). A Tirthankara is a karmically select being, not a god, but a perfected YOGI who has reached enlightenment. At rare intervals, such people appear in this world to teach and promulgate the tradition of the Jains. Technically, no one can become completely released from karma until death; Jains use the term Tirthankara in anticipation of the liberation from karma that these venerated beings have earned.

In each "half-era," 24 Tirthankaras manifest. Such events have transpired for an infinite number of eons and will do so in the future; thus, there have been an infinite number of Tirthankaras, in theory. Besides, Jain cosmology posits numerous other realms beyond our Earth where other Tirthankaras manifest, so it is understood that though we have no living Tirthankara here on Earth, there is always one alive somewhere in the universe.

In Jain temples the Tirthankara is often the central icon in the shrine, usually depicted at his or her moment of enlightenment and first teaching, surrounded above and around by all the gods, humans, and animals present to hear the teaching. The 24 Tirthankaras of the current half of a cosmic cycle: RISHABHA, Ajita, Sambhava, Abhinandana, Sumati, Padmaprabha, Suparshva, Chandraprabha, Suvidhi/Puspadanta, Shitala, Sreyamsa, Vasupujya, Vimala, Ananta, Dharma, Shanti, Kunthu, Ara, Malli, Munisuvrata, Nami, Nemi, PARSHVANATH/MAHAVIRA.

DIGAMBARA and SHVETAMBARA Jains agree on this list; however, the Shvetambara believe that Malli was a woman, while the Digambaras do not accept that women can achieve enlightenment or release from karma in a female birth. Most often the names of the Tirthankaras are followed by the term *Natha,* or "Lord," for example, Parshvanath. The final Tirthankara of our half of a cosmic cycle, MAHAVIRA, however, is generally not addressed this way. In iconography, the first Tirthankara and the last three are by far the most commonly seen.

Further reading: Jyotindra Jain and Eberhard Fischer, *Jaina Iconography,* 2 vols. (Leiden: E. J. Brill, 1978); P. S. Jaini, *The Jaina Path of Purification* (Delhi: Motilal Banarsidass, 1979); T. G. Kalghatgi, *Tirthankara Parsva-*

natha: A Study (Mysore: Dept. of Jainology and Prakrits, University of Mysore, 1977).

Tirumular (c. sixth century) *Tamil Shaivite saint*

Tirumular has a unique position in the Tamil literature. He is one of the 63 orthodox Shaivite (*see* SHAIVISM) saints of the Tamil pantheon, while also considered the first of the mysterious Sittars (SIDDHAS in Sanskrit), the antinomian, antiorthodox YOGIS of that tradition. Tirumular is so called because he entered his *mula* (body) by the grace of Tiru (the sacred one), the designation of SHIVA's bull NANDI. He says in one of his verses, "God created me, so that I might recreate Him in Tamil." Tirumular is known for his sixth-century poem Tirumanthiram, which forms the 10th book of the Tamil Shaivite canon, the TIRUMURAI.

Further reading: B. Natarajan, trans., *Tirumantiram, a Tamil Scriptural Classic by Tirumular* (Madras: Sri Ramakrishna Math, 1994); Kamil V. Zvelebil, *Tamil Literature* (Leiden: E. J. Brill, 1975).

Tirumurai

The Tirumurai is the Tamil Shaivite (*see* SHAIVISM) canon. This set of sacred texts, written in Tamil, holds a place in that tradition at least equal to the SANSKRIT texts about SHIVA. It is a collection of devotional hymns and stories of holy men and women, written over the course of 600 years by the 63 Tamil Shaivite poet-saints.

The entire 12-volume canon was assembled between 1080 and 1100 by Nambi Antar Nambi. Nambi began with the seven-volume TEVARAM, his collection of hymns by the three great saints SAMBANTHAR, APPAR, and SUNDARAR. Nambi then added MANIKKAVACAKAR's poems, the Tirukkovaiyar and TIRUVACAKAM, as the eighth book, and collected 28 hymns by nine other saints into the ninth book. He made the Tirumanthiram of TIRUMULAR the 10th book. The 11th book has two parts; the first contains 40 hymns by 12 other poets, and the second contains his own contribution, the Tirutontar Tiruvantathi. This work recounts the lives and achievements of the 63 saints, offers the story of his own life and work, and records some of his own hymns. Finally, Nambi made SEKKILAR'S PERIYA PURANAM, a larger summary of the lives and works of the Shaivite saints, the 12th book.

Thus, the Tirumurai is a vast heterogeneous collection. It spans the centuries from the first Shaivite saint, the woman Karakkal Ammaiyar (c. 500 C.E.), to Sekkilar in the 12th century. For a fuller list of the Shaivite saints see NAYANMARS.

Further reading: T. N. Ramachandran, trans., *Tirumurai the Sixth: St. Appar's Thaandaka Hymns* (Dharmapuram: Dharmapuram Aadheenam, 1995); V. C. Sasivalli, *Mysticism of Love in Saiva Tirumurais* (Madras: International Institute of Tamil Studies, 1995); Kamil V. Zvelebil, *Tamil Literature* (Leiden: E. J. Brill, 1975).

Tirupati

Tirupati (also known as Tirumala) is a site in southern Andhra Pradesh where a TEMPLE to VISHNU in the form of Venkateshvara stands on top of a sacred hill. It is one of the major PILGRIMAGE sites in India and may be India's richest temple. People go to see Venkateshvara for practical ends, with wishes for children, wealth, or success in education. It is very common for people to have their head shaved in the town of Tirupati, to fulfill a vow to the deity, who has been humbly beseeched.

As many as 30,000 pilgrims a day walk the long narrow winding roads to the top of Tirumala hill to the modest-sized temple there. There are rest houses along the walking route. A bus ride to the summit takes approximately one hour from the bottom. The summit is a dramatic 2,100 feet over the city of Tirupati. As are most Vaishnavite temples Tirupati is known for its delicious PRASADA, or "grace food," which is given to all who visit the Lord. The food is symbolically offered to God and divinely eaten by him before it is given

to the worshippers to take home. The temple is known both for allowing non-Hindus into its inner sanctum and for keeping the eyes of the image covered—its look is considered too potent for people to bear.

The temple is located amid the famous seven hills of the Sheshacalam mountain range, said to represent the seven hoods of the divine serpent ADISHESHA, the couch for the recumbent VISHNU as they float on the MILK OCEAN between eras. The oldest part of the temple dates to the ninth or 10th century. There is a credible tradition that the temple was originally a MURUGAN or SHIVA temple that was converted to Vishnu by the famous Vaishnava Acharya RAMANUJA in the 12th century. The temple was enlarged considerably under the VIJAYANAGARA kings, who took Venkateshvara as the patron deity of the royal family.

Further reading: Nandith Krishna, *Balaji, Venkateshwara, Lord of Tirumala-Tirupati—an Introduction* (Mumbai: Vakils Feffer & Simons, 2000); Velcheru Narayana Rao and David Shulman, *God on the Hill: Temple Poems from Tirupati* (New York: Oxford University Press, 2005).

Tiruvacakam

The Tiruvacakam is the celebrated collection of hymns by the Tamil Shaivite poet-saint MANIK-KAVACAKAR. Together with the shorter poem Tirukkovaiyar, it forms the eighth book of the Tamil Shaivite canon TIRUMURAI. Tiruvacakam contains 51 hymns comprising a total of 3,414 lines. The hymns range in length from eight to 400 lines and show a significant variety of metrical forms, with 14 subvarieties of meter. The hymns are usually rhymically recited or sung rather than read.

The work includes some unusual themes. Some have a woman in the role of devotee to the Lord, singing songs appropriate for playing games or doing village chores. One interesting poem is meant to be sung to awaken the divinity in the temple in the morning (a common part of Indian temple ritual). Because of its sacredness, Tiruva-cakam has no traditional commentaries attached to it.

Manikkavacakar's most important theme is the shadow of KARMA, which hovers over all as a specter. The poet calls to God to remove the bonds of karma and free him. He also speaks of impurity that takes him on the long road; when impurity has been removed, he becomes a slave to Lord SHIVA. (For both Shaivites and Vaishnavites, the truest devotee is often called a "slave to the feet" of the divinity.) Most importantly he asks for Shiva's grace to escape the hold of the senses, which lead one to impurity and destruction. Manikkavacakar is not, in the end, antisensual, but is wary, as many renunciants are, of the pull of the unrestrained senses.

Further reading: Ratna Navaratnam, *A New Approach to Tiruvacagam,* 2d ed. (Annamalainagar: Annamalai University, 1971); Radha Thiagarajan, *A Study of Mysticism in the Tiruvacakam* (Madurai: Madurai Kamaraj University, 1983); Glenn Yocum, *Hymns to the Dancing Siva: A Study of Manikkavacakar's Tiruvacakam* (Columbia, Mo.: South Asia Books, 1982).

Transcendental Meditation

Transcendental Mediation (T.M.) is a meditation practice taught first in the 1940s by Maharishi MAHESH YOGI, a disciple of Swami Brahmananda Saraswati (1869–1953), affectionately known as Guru Dev.

Maharishi has refused to discuss his early life and little has been discovered. It is known that he was born Mahesh Prasad Varma and that he graduated with a bachelor's degree from Allahabad University. Beginning in the 1940s, he spent 13 years in silent retreat with Guru Dev. After the death of Guru Dev in 1958, Maharishi started teaching publicly and began to gather disciples. He taught what he had learned from Guru Dev and added some of his own ideas to strengthen the work. His movement began to attract global attention when celebrities such as Mia Farrow, Jane Fonda, and the Beatles became involved.

In T.M., each student is given a private, individual MANTRA or sound for silent repetition. The overall strategy of Maharishi is revealed in his book *The Science of Being and Art of Living,* in which he spells out the groundwork for creating worlds of unmanifest being, with the goal of realizing God.

The theoretical base on which T.M. operates is termed the Science of Creative Intelligence (SCI); practitioners maintain that their objective is scientific and not religious; the basic technique for SELF-REALIZATION is derived from VEDIC science and technology. T.M. claims that its effectiveness has been scientifically proved in therapeutic settings involving criminals, drug abusers, and alcoholics.

The technique is described as a simple mental exercise that initiates deep relaxation and rest. It is generally practiced for 15 to 20 minutes in both the morning and evening. Although the technique was inspired by Vedic practices, instructors in T.M. and the Maharishi do not consider the practice to be specifically Hindu, as it does not require either belief in or devotion to a deity. The benefits of this practice (lowering of blood pressure, decreased effects of stress, and rehabilitation from dysfunctional habits) are said to have been verified by more than 500 scientific studies conducted at 214 independent universities and research institutes in over 27 countries. The research has been published in scientific journals in India, Europe, Canada, and the United States.

Transcendental Meditation has received acclaim for improving physiological functioning, developing mental potential, improving concentration, improving health, preventing disease, and bringing about positive effects on social behavior.

In 1977, T.M. announced its SIDDHA program to help initiates achieve paranormal abilities, including levitation of the body. A former teacher of the Siddha program eventually sued the council, claiming that these manifestations of unusual phenomena could not be achieved. He won a judgment of $138,000.

T.M. was largely introduced to the West through two organizations, the Spiritual Regeneration Movement and the Student International Meditation Society. In 1971, Maharishi purchased the defunct Parsons College in Fairfield, Iowa, and turned it into Maharishi International University, which in 1974 was renamed the Maharishi University of Management [of the Universe]). The school awards bachelor's, master's, and doctoral degrees in consciousness-based education. Currently, almost 800 students are enrolled in programs structured one course at a time in small classes over a period of four weeks. Degrees are granted in science, the humanities, and Vedic science.

In 1972, Maharishi revealed a World Plan to guide the nations of the world in using the insights derived from the practice of T.M. and the Science of Creative Intelligence. The World Plan includes a wide spectrum of activities for cultural renewal, health, freedom from war, and personal development. Over the last generation, a number of different organizations have been formed to implement the plan's ambitious goals.

According to the World Plan Council, T.M. is not a new religious group, but some observers disagree. In the United States controversy arose as T.M. teachers were receiving government funds to teach T.M. in places such as the public schools and the armed forces. In 1978, a federal district court in Newark, New Jersey, ruled that T.M. was indeed a religious practice and could not receive public funds; nor could government agencies promote its teachings and practice. After this ruling, the sharp upward trajectory of growth for the movement fell sharply, though it remains a substantial movement worldwide.

The New Jersey ruling pointed to the use of MANTRAS as a form of japa yoga; to T.M. initiations, which include traditional religious acts (most of which were never explained to Westerners); and to the acceptance of the movement in India as a form of SHAIVITE Hinduism.

Millions of people have taken T.M. courses. There are currently more than 7,000 authorized teachers working at 400 teaching centers. As the movement has grown, it has become to a large extent decentralized. In the United States, a Vedic City is being planned on land adjacent to the Maharishi University of Management. The many T.M.-related bodies are described in Web sites sponsored by the global movement.

During the 1980s the council introduced a line of AYURVEDIC medical products and opened a center adjacent to the university to promote them. The writer and physician Deepak Chopra emerged as a leading exponent of Maharishi's Ayurvedic (see AYURVEDA) program but has in recent years distanced himself from the organization.

Further reading: William Sims Bainbridge and Donald H. Jackson, "The Rise and Decline of Transcendental Meditation," in Rodney Stark and William Sims Bainbridge, eds., *The Future of Religion* (Berkeley: University of California Press, 1985); Harold H. Bloomfield, Michael Peter Cain, and Dennis Jafee, *T.M.: Discovering Inner Energy and Overcoming Stress* (New York: Delacorte Press, 1975); Martin Ebon, *Maharishi: The Guru (The Story of Maharishi Mahesh Yogi)* (Bombay: Pearl, 1968); Jack Forem, *Transcendental Meditation* (New York: Dutton, 1974); Maharishi Mahesh Yogi, *Life Supported by Natural Law* (Washington, D.C.: Age of Enlightenment Press, 1986); ———, *Transcendental Meditation* (New York: Signet, 1968); Paul Mason, *The Maharishi: The Biography of the Man Who Gave Transcendental Meditation to the West* (Shaftesbury, England: Element, 1994).

transmigration   *See* REINCARNATION.

Treta Yuga

All of the Yugas, or Ages in the Indian tradition, refer to throws in an ancient dice game. Treta Yuga is named after the 3, the second best throw. It always follows the KRITA, or SATYA, YUGA (the

Golden Age of Truth). It is 1,296,000 years in duration. The Sun God is its presiding divinity. Where in Krita Yuga pleasure was spontaneous, this ends in Treta Yuga. Where there were no permanent homes in the Krita Yuga, in the Treta Yuga trees become the homes for people. A beautiful honey (not made by bees) could be found in holes in the trees and was all the food people needed. People were all happy, well fed, and healthy.

However, passion and greed began to increase in this age. People remained truthful, but they focused on worldly success. As people cycled between greed and virtue, the trees would disappear and reappear. In their absence, people suffered from cold and heat and had to build shelters.

Toward the end of the Yuga, people grew more angry and more greedy, and men tried to possess each other's wives and wealth. In response, Lord BRAHMA emitted the warrior class, the KSHATRIYAS, to set limits in the world. Equality vanished as classes were formed.

Further reading: Cornelia Dimmitt and J. A. B. van Buitenen, *Classical Hindu Mythology: A Reader in the Sanskrit Puranas* (Philadelphia: Temple University Press, 1978); W. J. Wilkins, *Hindu Mythology, Vedic and Puranic*, 2d ed. (Calcutta: Rupa, 1973).

Image of the Hindu trinity: Brahma, Vishnu, and Shiva, Elephanta Caves, Bombay (Mumbai) *(Constance A. Jones)*

trimurti

Trimurti (*tri*, three; *murti*, forms) is a common term in Hindu texts, referring to the triad of divinities BRAHMA, VISHNU, and SHIVA. Brahma is the creator god, Vishnu is seen as the sustainer of the world, and Shiva is seen as its destroyer. In theistic Hinduism these three are often seen as aspects of one divinity, either Shiva or Vishnu.

Shiva and Vishnu are the two divinities around which the two great Hindu sects, SHAIVISM and VAISHNAVISM, constellate. Brahma is not a sectarian divinity, and there are only two temples dedicated solely to Brahma in all of India. Though it resembles the trinitarian conceptions of Christianity, the *trimurti* is a much looser concept and was not emphasized theologically or theorized upon in any way as the Trinity was in Christianity.

Further reading: Anant Ramchandra Kulkarni, *Buddha, the Trimurti, and Modern Hinduism* (Nagpur: Kulkarni, 1980); Kurian Mathothu, *The Development of the Concept of Trimurti in Hinduism* (Palai: Sebastian Vayalil, 1974); Margaret Stutley, *The Illustrated Dictionary of Hindu Iconography* (Boston: Routledge & Kegan Paul, 1985).

Trinidad

Hinduism first arrived on the Caribbean island of Trinidad on May 30, 1845, with a group of 197 indentured workers, who had endured a month-long voyage from Calcutta (Kolkata) aboard the *Fatal Kazack*. Trinidad had become a British colony in 1802, after a takeover from Spain. After Britain abolished slavery in 1833, African slaves left the sugar and cocoa plantations to pursue employment as free workers in urban areas. To fill the labor shortage on plantations, British officials developed a scheme to introduce indentured servants from India. Between 1845 and 1917 approximately 140,000 such workers arrived in Trinidad. Most were from Uttar Pradesh, Bihar, and Calcutta in northern India; others were from Madras (Chennai) in the south. About 60 percent of them were males. The majority left their homes in India to escape decades of famine, while others sought to escape increased British repression in India after the 1857 Sepoy Mutiny, the first of several revolutionary outbreaks of Indian nationalism.

Indentured servants were originally contracted to work five years, yet the majority remained in Trinidad and formed permanent settlements. They were enticed by the offer of free land and did not want to return to India, where conditions had not yet improved. Settlers soon converted the landscape, renaming streets and villages with familiar references to their Indian home.

Colonial officials initially sought Indian workers from the lower castes, claiming that BRAHMINS had "soft hands" for the hard work of the cane fields. British policy soon explicitly denied passage to the well educated in an effort to prevent Brahmins from stirring resistance among lower-caste workers. Nevertheless, approximately 10 percent of workers entering Trinidad were Brahmins, who secured passage by concealing their caste status and changing their name. Many arrived in response to the urgent plea for spiritual guidance. As more Hindus settled permanently on the island, Brahmins were able to practice their religious duties more openly. By 1870, public Hindu rituals were common in villages that had large populations of Indians.

Hindus in Trinidad followed the diverse forms of traditional worship and rituals common in their homeland. Over time, exposure to multicultural experiences and pressure by Brahmin leaders to make Hinduism a respected religion on the island combined to transform Hindu practices and make them distinct from Indian Hinduism. In the early 20th century the Brahmin caste consolidated and standardized doctrines and ritual practices in an official, organized orthodoxy now defined by the Sanatana Dharma Maha Sabha, the largest Hindu organization in Trinidad. This central organization prescribes congregationally centered practices, BHAKTI rituals (devotions), and the study of scriptures. The specification of a Hindu orthodoxy has placed Hinduism on a par with other religions, compatible with Christianity and Islam.

Changes in Hindu observance include the elimination of caste. Nevertheless, the Brahmin priest is recognized for ritual purposes. Brahmins were once considered to have lost their caste status once they traveled across the ocean, but the general population of Hindus today receive Brahmins with reverence as unique practitioners of essential and inherent duties. Today, many Brahmins in Trinidad are not full-time *pandits* (teachers) or priests but rather rely upon secular jobs for their income.

Hinduism has also made its impact on the larger culture of Trinidad. The popular Hindu festival DIVALI has become recognized as a national holiday in Trinidad with the growing influence of Hindu representation in government. Divali, also known as the festival of lights, is a much anticipated week-long event that honors LAKSHMI, the goddess of light, wealth, and prosperity. It is celebrated in the same way as Hindu communities observe Divali internationally: families and communities join together, homes are decorated with traditional clay lamps, and festive meals and sweets are prepared for the celebration. The climax of the holiday occurs with the lighting of the lamps, which are arranged in homes, on porches, along streets, and throughout villages. The thousands of lamps are lit to dispel darkness and ignorance.

In the 1920s, buildings known as *koutias* became a regular feature in the country's landscape. The structure, found throughout the Bhojpur region in India, traditionally served to house the temple caretaker. In Trinidad, *koutias* became additions to traditional temple structures and served as congregational halls. Many *koutias* were built in communities where there were no traditional temples, in order to attract visits from SWAMIS. The congregational halls became converted into central places of worship and began housing numerous Hindu deities. By the 1950s, the *koutia* temple became a unique feature of Trinidad's Hinduism. The structure of the *koutia* includes a long rectangular body with a flat or low-angled roof. When attached to a traditional temple it appears with a decorative dome at its front entrance. The temple typically holds up to 100 worshippers, who use the structure for congregational rituals, seminar talks with visiting swamis, and general worship services.

At present, approximately 300,000 Hindus reside in Trinidad and Tobago. They make up about 23 percent of the country's population and represent the second largest religion in the country after Christianity. Hinduism continues to thrive. Despite the incursion of secular influences, many young people remain interested in their faith and continue to support the preservation of Hindu traditions.

Further reading: K. O. Laurence, *A Question of Labour: Indentured Immigration into Trinidad and British Guiana, 1875–1917* (New York: St. Martin's Press, 1994); Ashram B. Maharaj, *The Pandits in Trinidad: A Study of a Hindu Institution* (Trinidad: Indian Review Press, 1991); Steven Vertovec, *The Hindu Diaspora: Comparative Patterns* (New York: Routledge, 2000); ———, *Hindu Trinidad: Religion, Ethnicity and Socio-Economic Change* (London: Macmillan Caribbean, 1992).

Tukaram (1608–1649) *Maharashtran poet-saint*
Tukaram was a Maharashtran poet-saint, who sang Marathi songs in praise of Vithoba or Vitthala, a local incarnation of KRISHNA.

He appears to have been low-caste in birth, probably SHUDRA. As with many of the poet-saints little is known of him for certain, and most of that is taken from autobiographical snippets found in his verses. The primary hagiographies, the *Bhaktililamrita* and the *Bhaktavijaya,* were both written by one Mahipati. They contain many miraculous events and much information that is probably not factual.

Poet-saints sometimes find the corpus of their works expand over the years as others mimic their style and wish to have verses of their own composition appear under the respected name of a saint. This phenomenon is evident in the case of Tukaram. Thus, there is no possibility of issuing a critical edition of Tukaram's words, though many editions and sets of verses have been attributed to him.

The hagiographical biography is as follows: Tukaram is born as an AVATAR of the Mahatrastran saint-poet Namdev at the behest of VISHNU himself, after his parents, Vaishnavite Bolhoba and Kanakai, sincerely entreat God for a saintly son. When Tukaram reaches manhood, his father gives him responsibility in his business. Because his first wife is feeble, Tukaram's father arranges a second for him. Tukaram proves inept at business, as he has otherworldly concerns; when he does have a successful venture he gives away all his profits to a needy BRAHMIN.

Tukaram falls into severe poverty and his elder wife starves to death. Then his eldest son dies. At this, Tukaram renounces the world and retires to a mountain to worship Vithoba. There Vithoba reveals himself to him. Tukaram's second wife continues to serve him as her husband but complains bitterly of his otherworldly nature.

Tukaram is known for his kindness and caring for all. He feeds the hungry by miracles, he aids a lame woman, he repairs a temple. Gradually, he attracts disciples and gains fame in his worship of Vithoba at Pandharpur. The famous Maratha king Shivaji visits Tukaram, who tells him to return to kingship and not renounce the world. Tukaram performs many miracles, including turning iron into gold. After many visitations, God himself escorts the glorious Tukaram to heaven.

Further reading: Justin Abbott, *Life of Tukaram* (Delhi: Motilal Banasidass, 1980); Ajit Lokhande, *Tukarama, His Person and His Religion: A Religio-Historical, Phenomenological and Typological Enquiry* (Frankfurt: Peter Lang, 1976); Eleanor Zelliot, "Four Radical Saints of Maharastra," in Milton Israel and N. K. Wagle, eds., *Religion and Society of Mahatrastra.* South Asian Papers, No. 1 (Toronto: Centre for South Asian Studies, University of Toronto, 1987); Eleanor Zelliot and Maxine Berntsen, *The Experience of Hinduism: Religion in Maharastra* (Albany: State University of New York Press, 1988).

tulsi (tulasi)

Tulsi (*Ocymum sanctum*) is a species of plant resembling European basil that is sacred to the Vaishnavites (worshippers of VISHNU) and is cultivated by them for use in PUJAS (worship services) and offerings. It is often put on a four-sided pedestal placed in a special location in one's house or near a place of worship. It is sometimes seen to be the wife of Vishnu, LAKSHMI herself.

One popular legend explains its origin: once Lakshmi and SARASVATI quarreled and cursed each other. Sarasvati's curse turned Lakshmi into a tulsi plant and forced her to live on Earth forever. Vishnu, however, intervened and modified the curse, saying that Lakshmi would remain on Earth as tulsi until the river Gandaki flowed from her body.

In another story tulsi is understood to be the plant incarnation of Vrindadevi, the primary and archetypal "forest goddess." She beautifies the flora and fauna of the ultimate spiritual forest, Vrindavana (BRINDAVAN). She appears in this world so that her leaves may be used in the worship of KRISHNA.

Tulsi is offered daily in Vaishnavite *pujas*, whether in the temple or at home. When an orthodox Vaishnavite BRAHMIN male dies, a tulsi plant is worshipped and a bit of root is placed in his mouth and leaves are placed on his face and eyes; he is sprinkled with a tulsi sprig that has been dipped in water. This ritual is said to guarantee heaven. Some say that even looking at this sacred plant confers release from sins.

Any illness or pollution from contact with polluting people or substances is said to be removed by worship of the plant. Tending the tulsi plant is said to assure liberation from birth and rebirth. Sprigs of tulsi are offered to Vishnu especially in the month of Karttika (October–November). Tulsi dipped in saffron will please Vishnu. A twig of tulsi given to someone can lift his or her troubles and anxieties.

Tulsi leaves are aromatic, and the plant is thought to help with coughs; it is taken as a folk medicine. Orthodox Vaishnavite Brahmins take it after meals to help digestion. It is also taken before and after rituals.

Further reading: Abbé J. A. Dubois, *Hindu Manners, Customs and Ceremonies.* Translated by Henry K. Beauchamp, 3d ed. (Oxford: Clarendon Press, 1959); Yash Rai, *Holy Basil, a Herb: A Unique Medicinal Plant.* Translated by K. K. Sata (Ahmedabad: Gala, 1992).

Tulsidas (1532–1623) *greatest Hindi poet*

It can be said without reservation that Tulsidas is the greatest poet to write in the Hindi language. Tulsidas was a BRAHMIN by birth and was believed to be a reincarnation of the author of the SANSKRIT RAMAYANA, VALMIKI.

Tulsidas was born in the village of Rajpur in Uttar Pradesh in 1532 C.E. He died in 1623 C.E. at the age of 91 at Asighat in BENARES (Varanasi). His father's name was Atmaram Shukla Dube and his mother's was Hulsi. Tulsidas's birth name was Tulsiram. The story of Tulsidas's life is not historically verifiable and many details clearly are intended to enhance the understanding that he was a saint. For example, he did not cry at birth and was born with 32 teeth. His early life was fraught with sorrow because his parents died when he was still young. Some say that his foster parents also passed away when he was young. We know he was married to a woman named Buddhimati or Ratnavali. It is said he had a son named Tarak.

Tulsidas was inordinately fond of his wife. One day she went to her father's house without telling her husband. When Tulsidas found out, he could not stay away from her and went to sleep with her in her father's house. Buddhimati, trying to resist his advances in embarrassment, said that if Tulsidas had half the love for Lord RAMA that he had for her lowly body, he would most certainly reach liberation from birth and rebirth. Shamed by this, Tulsidas resolved to leave the householder life and become an ascetic.

He spent the next 14 years visiting the various PILGRIMAGE sites of North India. Living in the wilderness, Tulsidas would spill the excess water after his ablutions on the root of a particular tree. This pleased the being within the tree, who offered Tulsidas a boon. Tulsidas asked for a direct vision of Lord Rama. The being told Tulsidas to go to a particular temple where HANUMAN, the monkey god, visited regularly in the form of a leper. He was told to approach Hanuman for his request. This he did, and he received DARSHAN of Lord Rama.

Tulsidas wrote 12 books, but, by far, the most important is the Ramcharitmanas (*The Holy Lake of the Acts of Ram*), a Ramayana written in old Hindi (*Avadhi*) couplets. The book was written under the direction of Hanuman himself. It is read all over North India, and particularly during the time of the Ramlila. It is sung aloud in large groups for devotional purposes. Vinaya Patrika is another excellent book said to be written by Tulsidas, who also authored Gitavali (1571), Kavitavali (1612), and Barvairamayana (1612)

Several stories demonstrate Tulsidas's special spiritual status. Once some thieves went to his ASHRAM to steal. They were frightened off by a dark-complexioned guard holding a bow and arrow in his hand. The next morning they asked Tulsidas about this unusual-looking guard. Tulsidas realized that it had been Lord Rama and was overcome with devotion. In thanks, he gave away all his wealth to the needy.

In another story it is said that Tulsidas, while visiting BENARES, was greeted by a murderer, asking alms in the name of Lord Rama. Tulsidas invited him to his house and gave him PRASADA, sacred food, from the worship of Rama. The BRAHMINS were angered; they thought it improper to give a criminal such a blessing and to sit and eat with him. The Brahmins challenged Tulsidas; they said they could approve giving alms to a murderer only if the temple icon of NANDI, Shiva's bull mount, would accept food from the hand of this murderer. Tulsidas took them up on this challenge, and the temple Nandi did indeed eat from the murderers hands.

In another tale saint Tulsidas restores a poor woman's husband to life. Finally, Tulsidas is said to have been jailed by the Mughal emperor; when he was freed by a band of monkeys, friends of Hanuman, the emperor himself, though a Muslim, recognized Tulsidas as a saint.

Further reading: A. G. Atkins, trans., *The Ramayana of Tulsidas* (New Delhi: Hindustan Times, 1954); S. P. Bahadur, *The Ramayana of Goswami Tulsidas* (Bombay: Jaico Publishing House, 1972); S. P. Bahadur, trans., *Complete Works of Gosvami Tulsidas* (Varanasi: Prachya Prakashan, 1978); S. R. Bakshi and Sangh Mitra, eds., *Saints of India* (New Delhi: Criterion, 2002); Ramdat Bharadwaj, *The Philosophy of Tulsidas* (New Delhi: Munshiram Manoharlal, 1979); *Sant Vani: Hindi Devotionals from Saint Poets* (Dum Dum: EMI: His Master's Voice, 1975); Devendra Singh, *Tulsidas* (Bombay: India Book House, 1971).

Turiya   *See* STATES OF CONSCIOUSNESS.

Turiyasangitananda, Swami (Alice Coltrane) (1937–) *jazz pianist and spiritual teacher*

Swami Turiyasangitananda combined her spiritual learning and musical talent to create a unique teaching in the YOGA tradition.

Born in Detroit, Michigan, on August 27, 1937, Alice MacLeod was a rare female jazz instrumentalist, playing piano, organ, and harp. She married the famous jazz musician John Coltrane in 1965. In 1968 she received a spiritual awakening and received initiation into SANNYAS (renunciation). She traveled to India with Swami SATCHIDANANDA, founder of the INTEGRAL YOGA INTERNATIONAL and studied his teachings. She began publishing books and recording devotional music, reflecting her spiritual life. In 1975 she was given the name Swami Turiyasangitananda and began to establish a small following in the United States. In 1983 she established the Vedantic Center on 48 acres of land in the Santa Monica Mountains near Agoura, California, and built an ASHRAM to serve its growing membership. The ashram was renamed Sai Anantam Ashram in Chumash Pradesh in 1994.

Sai Anantam incorporates both the teachings of Swami Satchidananda and Western spirituality. Music and singing have a central role at the ashram. Devotional compositions influenced by Turiyasangitananda's musical talents mix traditional BHAJANS with modern Western features. Studies at the center include readings from the VEDAS and the Hindu scriptures as well as Christian, Islamic, and Buddhist texts.

Sai Anantam is open to seekers of all faiths. Turiyasangitananda emphasizes basic Vedic principles including the advancement of human life, self-purification, selfless service, and unity with God. The center has primarily African American members. Approximately 30 residents live at Sai Anantam and others from the surrounding community attend regular worship services. Activities at the ashram include Sunday school for children, weekly worship, chanting of services, and prayer.

The ashram has a bookstore and a vegetarian restaurant. Radio and television programs are also produced by the center. Avatar Book Institute of Agoura Hills distributes Turiyasangitananda's writings and recordings.

Further reading: Alice Coltrane-Turiyasangitananda, *Endless Wisdom* (Los Angeles, Calif.: Avatar Book Institute, 1981); ———, *Monument Eternal* (Los Angeles, Calif.: Vedantic Book Press, 1977).

Twitchell, Paul   *See* ECKANKAR.

Tyberg, Judith M. (1902–1980) *Theosophist and U.S. Sri Aurobindo disciple*

Judith Tyberg was a convert to Hinduism who worked to introduce the faith to the West.

Judith was born on May 17, 1902, in California. Her parents were both Danish Theosophists; her mother reportedly chanted a Vedic hymn to the entering soul throughout her pregnancy carrying Judith. Her parents sent her to the THEOSOPHICAL SOCIETY's Point Loma Raja Yoga School and the Theosophical University. She earned an M.A. and Ph.D. in Religion and Philosophy with a concentration in Oriental thought and SANSKRIT studies. While working on her degrees, she began to teach at the Raja Yoga School. In 1932 she became its assistant principal, a position she left to become the dean of studies at the Theosophical University in 1935.

As a scholar, she began to work on the SANSKRIT terms that had been introduced into Theosophical teachings. Her first book, *Sanskrit Keys to the Wisdom-Religion,* appeared in 1940.

In 1947, Tyberg moved to India to pursue further studies at Benares Hindu University and to follow a spiritual quest that was leading her from Theosophy to Hinduism. Soon after her arrival, she was introduced to the writings of SRI AUROBINDO. Impressed, she traveled to Pondicherry and met the MOTHER, who related to Judith that both she and

Aurobindo had awaited her arrival. At the touch of the Mother's hand, Judith felt electric forces go through her being. Judith asked the Mother for a spiritual name and was given a piece of paper on which, in Aurobindo's handwriting, was written Jyotipriya (lover of light). While she would encounter a number of prominent Indian teachers over the next years, including ANANDAMAYI MA, Swami SHIVANANDA of RISHIKESH, Sri KRISHNA PREM, and RAMANA MAHARSHI, she had found her gurus in Aurobindo and the Mother.

Jyotipriya returned to the United States in 1950 and opened the East-West Cultural Center in Los Angeles in 1953, the first Aurobindo center in America. Eminent teachers from India, including Swami RAMDAS, Mother KRISHNABAI, Jagadguru Shankaracharya of Puri, Dilip Roy, Indra DEVI, Swami MUKTANANDA, Swami SATCHIDANANDA, and Swami VISHNUDEVANANDA, visited and lectured there. Besides offering regular meetings to share Aurobindo's teaching, the center became a welcoming place for Indian teachers to meet Westerners and to offer initial presentations of their ideas and practices.

She continued to work in Los Angeles until her death on October 3, 1980. The East-West Cultural Center evolved into the Sri Aurobindo Center of Los Angeles and continues to the present.

Further reading: Judith Tyberg, *First Lessons in Sanskrit Grammar and Reading* (Covina, Calif.: Theosophical University Press, 1944); ———, *The Language of the Gods: Sanskrit Keys to India's Wisdom* (Los Angeles, Calif.: East-West Cultural Centre, 1970); ———, *Sanskrit Keys to the Wisdom-Religion* (Point Loma, Calif.: Theosophical University Press, 1940).

U

udgatri   *See* VEDAS.

Uma   *See* PARVATI.

Umaswami (Umasvati)   *See* TATTVARTHA
SUTRA.

United Kingdom

The National Census of April 2001 reported
559,000 Hindus living in Britain, approximately
1 percent of the population, making Hinduism
Britain's third largest religion. In 1977, 70 percent of Hindu residents were Gujarati, 15 percent
Punjabi, and others originating from other Indian
locations, such as Uttar Pradesh, Tamil Nadu,
Maharashtra, as well as Sri Lanka.

The presence of Hinduism in Britain goes back
at least to the early 19th century, when Rammohun
ROY (1772–1833), founder of the BRAHMO SAMAJ,
visited England toward the end of his life and
died in Bristol in 1833. In 1870, Keshab Chunder
SEN, another representative of the Brahmo Samaj,
visited London and initiated the transmission of
Hindu thought and practice to the West. Only

later, in 1911, was a branch of this Hindu reformist organization established in London.

The substantial presence of Hindu communities in Britain can be traced to the late 1950s and
1960s, often the result of enforced alienation,
rather than employment. Hindus now have a
noticeable presence in numerous major British
cities. At the early stages of settlement, Hindu
communities rented premises for PUJA (worship
services). A decade later, during the late 1960s
and 1970s unused churches and some private
houses were converted into Hindu TEMPLES, and
a few temples were built dating from the 1990s.
There are some 150 *mandirs* (temples) in Britain:
the earliest is the Sri Geeta Bhawan in Birmingham (1967), and the largest is the Sri Swaminarayan Mandir in Neasden, completed in 1995.

Hinduism's main traditions are reflected in
Britain's religious landscape: Vaishnavite, Shaivite,
and SHAKTA, as well as some presence of the
NATH tradition. Within the Vaishnavite tradition,
the SWAMINARAYAN sect enjoys some prominence.
Although followers speak a variety of languages,
the use of SANSKRIT in worship is prevalent. All
major Hindu festivals are celebrated.

Hinduism has inevitably undergone adaptation in the DIASPORA. The most notable changes

have occurred in worship, as increasing emphasis is placed on congregational activity, scheduled to accommodate Western working hours. Rites of passage have undergone some change. Initially temples were not registered for the solemnization of marriage, thus necessitating a civil ceremony as well as a religious one. Hindu temples, however, are now formally recognized as places of worship, although the ceremony must incorporate elements necessitated by British law. FUNERAL rites have undergone some modification, to make them more compatible with crematorium arrangements. The CASTE system continues to prevail and remains relevant to POLLUTION, marriage, and eating prescriptions.

A number of umbrella organizations have been formed to champion the interests of British Hindus. These include the National Hindu Students Forum UK (founded 1993), the Hindu Council of the UK (founded 1994), and the National Council for Hindu Temples. The last of these was set up in the late 1980s, mainly by the INTERNATIONAL SOCIETY FOR KRISHNA CONSCIOUSNESS (ISKCON), to enlist the support of the wider Hindu community for ISKCON's activities.

Few indigenous Britons have converted to Hinduism in its traditional forms. However, a number of Hindu-related movements have emerged within the country and have proved attractive to Westerners. One early example was the RAMAKRISHNA

Swaminarayan Temple, completed 1995, in suburban London, England *(Institute for the Study of American Religion, Santa Barbara, California)*

VEDANTA CENTRE, founded by Swami Ghanananda in 1948. The MAHARISHI MAHESH YOGI lectured on TRANSCENDENTAL MEDITATION in London in 1960. In 1969 the Beatles hosted Swami A. C. Bhaktivedanta PRABHUPADA in London, and in 1973 George Harrison purchased Bhaktivedanta Manor for the International Society for Krishna Consciousness (ISKCON).

Other more recent Hindu groups include ANANDA MARGA YOGA SOCIETY (founded by P. R. Sarkar), BRAHMA KUMARIS WORLD SPIRITUAL ORGANIZATION (founded by Dada Lehraj), Prem RAWAT's movement (previously known as the Divine Light Mission and now called Elan Vital), Sahaja Yoga (led by Sri Mataji), the SELF-REALIZATION FELLOWSHIP (brought by YOGANANDA), Siddha Yoga Dham (founded by MUKTANANDA), and Sri CHINMOY centers. SATYA SAI BABA's movement remains controversial; SHIRDI SAI BABA (1838–1918), his allegedly previous incarnation, is followed in his own right by some of Britain's Asian community, who regard Satya Sai Baba as an imposter.

Western interest in Hindu spirituality has given rise to a number of Western GURUS who teach in the Indian tradition. The best known are Baba RAM DASS (born Richard Alpert, 1931), Avatar ADI DA SAMRAJ (born Franklin Jones, 1939), and Andrew COHEN (b. 1955).

See also UNITED STATES.

Further reading: R. Ballard, *Desh Pardesh: The South Asian Presence in Britain* (London: Hurst, 1994); G. Parsons, ed., *The Growth of Religious Diversity: Britain from 1945,* Vol. 1, *Traditions* (London: Routledge, 1993); T. Thomas, ed., *The British: Their Religious Beliefs and Practices 1800–1986* (London: Routledge, 1988); S. Vertovek, *The Hindu Diaspora: Comparative Patterns* (London: Routledge, 2000); P. Weller, *Religions in the U.K.: A Multi-Faith Directory* (Derby, England: University of Derby, 2003).

United States

The dissemination of Hindu thought and practice in the United States began before any Hindu teacher

Hindu temple in Malibu, California, a popular site for American Hindus *(Institute for the Study of American Religion, Santa Barbara, California)*

entered America. Ironically, the assimilation of immigrants from India has not been a primary vehicle for the introduction or popularization of Hindu teachings. The development of appreciation for Hindu traditions followed a standard American pattern—dependence on European scholarship and interpretation in the 17th, 18th, and 19th centuries and independent experimentation and selectivity in the 20th and 21st. During the 17th century, colonists and missionaries set up relationships with India that led to translation into English of some Hindu sacred texts. The BHAGAVAD GITA, translated in 1785, became important to Emerson, Thoreau, and other leaders of the transcendentalist movement early in the 19th century.

Before the transcendentalists, Americans showed little understanding of or sympathy for India and Hinduism. Cotton Mather, spokesman for militant Christianity, maintained a keen interest in the East, but only as a field in which Christian missionaries might preach, teach, and convert the "heathen." In 1721, Mather's *India Christiana* outlined the methods he felt were best suited to drawing Hindus into the flock of Christ.

Later in the 18th century, tangible evidence of contact with India reached American eyes. In 1784, the ship *United States* sailed to Pondicherry and returned to stock Boston, Salem, and Providence with cloth, teas, spices, and crafts. By 1799, William Bentley, minister of the Second Congregational Church of Salem, Massachusetts, set up the East India Marine Society and became the first notable collector in America of Oriental art and artifacts.

The first attempts to understand Hinduism and the East were those of American thinkers who were inheritors of the spirit of the Enlightenment, a time in which redefinition of religion was central. In Europe, Voltaire hailed Confucius as one of history's great men, and English deists found Oriental religions of equal merit with Christianity.

Old Vedanta temple in San Francisco, California, dedicated in 1905 *(Constance A. Jones)*

Attuned to this new thought, Benjamin Franklin maintained a friendship with Sir William Jones, the English Orientalist, who introduced the study of SANSKRIT to Western scholars. In the 1780s, while occupying a judgeship in Bengal, Sir William established the Asiatic Society and translated the *Laws of Manu* and Kalidasa's *Sakuntala*.

Joseph Priestley, scientist, scholar, and founder of English Unitarianism, traveled to America in 1794 and spent the last decade of his life there. His works of philosophy, science, and theology reveal a new understanding and respect for the Hindus, a people of "superior wisdom and civilization." Praising the culture, control, and traditions of the Hindus, Priestley stopped short of extolling their religion, which he dismissed as "absurd notions" and "complicated polytheism." As a reader of the translations of Sir William Jones, Priestley looked back toward European thinking and scholarship. As a resident in America, he exerted direct influence on John Adams, who heard the elderly Priestley lecture in Philadelphia in 1796. Adams, in turn, referred Thomas Jefferson to Priestley's writings.

At the turn of the century, Hannah Adams's *A View of Religion* (1801) encouraged greater acceptance of non-Christian faiths. In her study, Adams devotes considerable attention to Hinduism, describing the voluntary suffering to which the Indian submits in order to fulfill religious obligations and labeling Indian religion "the most tolerant of all." The open-mindedness of *A View of Religion* reflects a new liberality willing to dispute the supremacy of Christianity and to make religious questions and religious toleration a standard, at least among the informed.

Spreading this new liberality of interpretation was Unitarianism, with its emphasis on tolerance and the centrality of monotheism. In India, Hindus were responding to the impact of Christianity. Among the reformist movements in India was the BRAHMO SAMAJ, a movement based upon the assumed monotheism of the UPANISHADS and the abandonment of all image worship. The founder, Hindu Rammohun ROY, found spiritual affinity with Unitarianism and sought to apply Unitarian standards to Hinduism and to focus the attention of Unitarians on India. By 1820, Roy had published several Hindu texts in English and had developed his ideas on Hindu reform in articles and speeches, which were featured prominently in Unitarian periodicals published in the United States. Roy's writings and talks explaining Asia and Hinduism were the first expressions by a Hindu in Unitarian terms to which Americans had access. In the 1850s the Unitarian Charles Dall and the Brahmo Samaj's Keshub Chunder SEN developed a friendship that initiated a relationship between the two organizations that is still bearing fruit.

Later in the 19th century, leaders of the transcendentalist movement read newly translated Hindu scriptures and incorporated their ideas in an American philosophy. Emerson stressed eclectic theology; Thoreau, the immersion in nature; and Bronson Alcott, an interest in universal scriptures. Influenced by Emerson, Walt Whitman wrote poetry that expressed a remarkable similarity to Asian thought. In his writing he admits he had read "the ancient Hindoo poems," and he mentions BRAHMA and Hinduism in his "Song of Myself." While these figures created an intellectual climate receptive to the ideas of Hinduism, transcendentalism did not attempt to represent all of Hindu teachings, but rather selected elements consistent with their worldview.

Another American group, the Free Religious Association, made up largely of Quakers, Unitarians, and transcendentalists, turned to world religions to support their rejection of a faith based solely on the Bible. Their publications and meetings featured the works of the Oriental scholar Max Muller and championed the idea of a world Bible. Through this organization, active from 1865 through the late 1880s, the American consciousness was exposed to comparisons and contrasts of Christianity and Hinduism. In its 17 years of publication, *The Index,* journal of the Free Religious

Association, issued more than 500 separate works explaining and describing the East.

Beginning in 1875, the THEOSOPHICAL SOCIETY took to the United States an appreciation of Hinduism and Buddhism, interpreted through the lenses of its Western leaders, HELENA PETROVNA BLAVATSKY, Charles Leadbeater, and ANNIE WOOD BESANT, who traveled to India and took home firsthand impressions. Theosophists directly proclaimed an adherence to Asian thought but included elements of occultism and psychism as well. As a result of this synthesis, the contribution of Theosophy to the developing American consciousness was an amalgam of Hinduism, Buddhism, spiritualism, and rationalism. Helena Blavatsky's *Isis Unveiled* claimed direct revelation from Eastern adepts, called *Mahatmas,* and celebrated the traditional Hindu concepts of REINCARNATION and KARMA. In spite of its original association with spiritualism, Theosophy exerted a major influence in both India and the United States. By 1884, in addition to its success in the United States, over 100 branches of Theosophy flourished in India. Continuing until the present, various Theosophical publishing houses have been important disseminators in the United States of Hindu texts, commentaries, and histories. Much of what Americans grasp of Hinduism has been a result of the popularity of Theosophical publications.

Uniquely American religions, including New Thought and Christian Science, took up Hindu concepts. The New Thought churches, which include Religious Science, Divine Science, Unity School of Christianity, Mind Cure, and Applied Metaphysics, concentrated on VEDANTA philosophy and the concepts of REINCARNATION and KARMA. Indebted to the research of the Theosophists, exponents of New Thought gained for Hinduism a new kind of acceptance, however narrow, in the United States. No longer were the doctrines of the East damned as pagan nonsense; they were now incorporated into American religion. Christian Science, with its radical monism, its doctrine of eternal mind, its disavowal of the ultimate reality

of the world, and its unorthodox interpretation of Christ, demonstrated a mixture of Eastern and Western views of reality. The sources of the Christian Science founder Mary Baker Eddy's ideas remain in debate, but the result is clear: the incorporation in an organized American church of at least some of the ideas and values of Hinduism.

While religious movements and philosophical schools offered their interpretations of Hinduism, scholars were examining the East from their own perspective. The American Oriental Society, founded in 1842, provided a forum for scholarly exchange. It established a library and published the *Journal of the American Oriental Society,* which ran bibliographic essays reporting on Vedic research occurring in Germany, translations of religious texts that exposed ideas formerly unavailable to American readers, and essays on the philosophy of Hindu scriptures and on the various schools of Hinduism. These scholarly efforts lifted cultural, religious, and linguistic barriers. Leaders in the society were Edward Salisbury; William Dwight Whitney, who became America's greatest Oriental scholar; and Charles Rockwell Lanman, who, among other contributions, edited the *Harvard Oriental Series.*

Attempts to understand and explain surfaced in the general press as well. Although popular magazines did not carry reliable information about Asia, serious reviews served to foster escape from American isolation by looking analytically at Hindu ideas and scholarship. The *North American Review,* as did the *Edinburgh Review,* touched on many aspects of Indian culture and the Hindu religion. Book publishing reflected the new interest in the East. The popularity of Sir Edwin Arnold's *Light of Asia* (1879) and his free translation of the Bhagavad Gita (1885) drew the author to the United States for a lecture tour.

In 1883, the first Hindu GURU visited America. Protap Chunder Mozoomdar, a representative of the BRAHMO SAMAJ, delivered his first American address at the home of Ralph Waldo Emerson's widow in Concord, Massachusetts. He returned in 1893 to attend, along with many representatives of the religions of Asia, the WORLD PARLIAMENT OF RELIGIONS in Chicago. The congress was the first international gathering of representatives of the major Eastern and Western faiths. Speakers gave formal recognition to non-Christian faiths and made clear that Western thought had always drawn heavily on the East, and that Hinduism was a source of tolerance, introspection, self-discipline, and the opportunity for a full religious life, not mere idol worshipping or polytheism. This 17-day conference, which drew crowds far larger than any forecast, permitted non-Christians to speak about their own faiths and created an appreciation of the offerings of Eastern traditions. The experience affirmed that an interest in comparative religions was not simply the province of a few specialized or elite groups.

Swami VIVEKANANDA, another representative of Hinduism and a young disciple of the late Sri RAMAKRISHNA, was one of the parliament's most impressive speakers. He was hailed by the American press as the most persuasive speaker of the parliament. In several eloquent presentations, Vivekananda rejected formalism and delivered a universal gospel of unity in diversity by quoting from the sacred books of India. He chose to cite, "Whoever comes to Me, through whatsoever form, I reach him," and "All men are struggling through paths which in the end lead to Me." He spoke of the gods of all faiths, not only the God of a respective religion (Rolland, 1931).

His popularity established, Vivekananda followed the parliament session with a two-year tour of the United States. In 1895, he founded the first Hindu organization in the United States, the VEDANTA SOCIETY, and, upon his return to India, he organized the scattered disciplines of Sri Ramakrishna into the RAMAKRISHNA MATH AND MISSION. Two disciples, Swami ABHEDANANDA and Swami Turiyananda, traveled from Calcutta (Kolkata) to head the Vedanta centers in New York and San Francisco, respectively.

Establishment of the Vedanta centers coincided with the first small wave of immigrants from India to America, in the 1890s—a phenomenon that evoked riots and vitriolic reaction against a "Hindu invasion." But reason also existed and prompted a growing interest in Hinduism among non-Indians, the establishment of various societies, and the arrival of Indian teachers, partly to serve the immigrants. Among them, in 1902, was a young monk, Swami RAMA TIRTHA, who lectured for two years throughout the United States on the reasonableness of Hinduism—and the evils of the Indian CASTE system. In 1904, a Bengali Vaishnavite, Baba Premanand BHARATI, began a five-year tour, during which he formed the Krishna Samaj; in 1909, Swami PARAMANANDA, another member of the Ramakrishna Math in India, arrived, eventually to form another group of Vedantins.

From the time of the parliament onward, the United States saw the establishment of Hindu organizations and an expanding interest in the teachings of the religion. In large cities such as New York and Chicago, the press chronicled the exploits of visiting teachers from India. Emulating these emissaries, some Americans adopted the role of Hindu teacher and helped disseminate Hindu ideas through publications and formation of groups. In 1903, William Walker Atkinson, a New Thought teacher, assumed the title Yogi RAMACHARAKA and published widely on various YOGAS and Hindu philosophy. His many books remain in print a century later. Around 1909, PIERRE ARNOLD BERNARD, calling himself "Oom the Omnipotent," founded the Tantrick Order of America and demonstrated flamboyant stagecraft while dressed in Eastern garb. In spite of the demise of his movement after a few decades, his nephew, Theos Bernard (1908–47), wrote several texts on YOGA that remain reliable resources.

After two decades of growing interest in Hinduism from 1895 to 1915, the growth of Hindu groups waned during and after World War I. A string of American occultists created in the public mind the image of SWAMIS as fortune tellers and charlatans. After Sara Bull left the greater part of her half-million-dollar estate to the Vedanta Society, her daughter called for testimony of family servants, who reported frequent visits of swamis, a MEDITATION room, and séances. On the basis of their testimony, the court overturned Bull's will and awarded the money to her daughter. A series of articles in the press spewed forth, complaining that Americans, particularly women, were duped by Indian "holy men" and were forsaking the true Christian faith. A recurring theme was that Hinduism appealed to bored older women who had sizable fortunes to bequeath to their teachers. In 1914, Elizabeth Reed's *Hinduism in Europe and America* attacked alleged exploiters of naïve Westerners and blamed the tenets of Hinduism for their crimes.

Anti-Asian sentiment had direct political effect as well. Following immigration exclusion acts in 1882 and 1914 directed primarily against Chinese and Japanese immigrants, the Asian Exclusion Act of 1917 specifically denied immigration to Asians from India. By denying entry into the United States from most Asian countries, including India, the act effectively cut off immigration for several generations and halted what would have been, most probably, a significant growth of Hinduism. Several years later, the Supreme Court of the United States ruled that Indians were not eligible for citizenship and that the citizenship granted to previous Indian immigrants would be revoked. By 1921, a quota system allowed immigration from countries in proportion to each nationality's percentage in the United States. The quota for India was approximately 100 annually. This federal act of exclusion significantly curtailed the growth of Hindu movements. Of the organizations formed before 1917, only the Vedanta Society remained.

In 1927, Katherine Mayo's best-selling *MOTHER INDIA* damned all things Indian and heaped opprobrium on the worship of KALI. Mayo characterized Indians as inert, helpless, and weak: in all, slaves to superstition and oppressors of women and minorities. Perhaps no other writing damaged

Indo-American understanding so severely and so prejudiced an entire generation of Americans. From the early 1920s until 1960, anti-Indian feeling was strong, although Hinduism itself was not perceived as a political threat. This period includes two world wars, American isolationism after World War I, intense hatred of things Eastern because of Pearl Harbor, and the Korean conflict. That attacks on India and Indian traditions occurred is hardly surprising. What may be surprising are the viability and growth of interest in Hinduism throughout this period.

The Hindu community grew very slowly after the passage of the exclusion act. Teachers who immigrated prior to the exclusion act continued to lead and write. A Bengali playwright, Besudeb Bhattacharya, took the name Pundit Acharya and founded the Temple of Yoga, the Yoga Research Institute, and Prana Press in New York. Paramahansa YOGANANDA, charismatic teacher and author of the still-popular *Autobiography of a Yogi,* arrived in the United States in 1920 and organized the Yogoda-Satsang in 1926. Now known as SELF-REALIZATION FELLOWSHIP, Yogananda's organization has been extremely influential in disseminating Hindu thought through home correspondence courses and initiation into KRIYA YOGA disciplines.

Other teachers from India created organizations, taught Hindu ideas and practices, and fostered interfaith cooperation, including A. K. Mozumdar (The Messianic World Message), Swami Omkar (Shanti Ashrama), Sri DEVA RAM SUKUL (Dharma Mandal), Kedarnath Das Gupta (Fellowship of Faiths), Sant Ram Mandal (Universal Brotherhood Temple and School of Eastern Philosophy), Rishi Krishnananda (Para-Vidya Center), and Swami A. P. Mukerji (Transcendent Science Society).

Theosophy continued to contribute to the dissemination of Hindu ideas through its growing number of lodges and its reliable editions of Hindu and Buddhist texts. Theosophy also gained increasing popularity through its promotion of Jiddu KRISHNAMURTI as the vehicle for the coming world teacher, prophesied by spiritual adepts in the East. Krishnamurti, a poor BRAHMIN boy from South India, had been selected by the Theosophists to be groomed for acceptance of a higher consciousness that the world would need in the current era. He lectured throughout the 1920s as the anointed messiah but became disillusioned with the Theosophical enterprise and, in 1929, renounced the organization founded in his name. Upon leaving the Theosophical fold, he began his own career as an independent teacher, founding educational institutions in England, the United States, and India and lecturing until his death in 1986. Although Krishnamurti rejected any claim to represent Hinduism (or any organized religion), he nevertheless taught a form of self-analysis and self-observation that was congruent with Hindu and Buddhist disciplines. And, in his later years, after having shunned the study of sacred texts throughout his life, he became enamored of the VEDAS and the UPANISHADS. Americans who became familiar with Krishnamurti's teaching were drawn closer to Hindu thought and practice, although they did not identify themselves as "Hindu."

Later, in 1951, a Bengali philosopher, Haridas CHAUDHURI, founded the Cultural Integration Fellowship in San Francisco, which represented the first American influence of the famous philosopher and mystic Sri AUROBINDO. Chaudhuri was a charismatic proponent of Aurobindo's approach to integralism in philosophy and yoga, adding his own insights to his teacher's message through collaboration with other scholars of the East. In the 1960s Chaudhuri founded the California Institute of Asian Studies, an educational organization that exists today under the name California Institute of Integral Studies.

In the fall of 1965, the Asian Exclusion Act was repealed and immigration quotas for Asia became comparable to the quotas for Europe. The number of Indian immigrants rose dramatically. Between 1871 and 1965, only 16,013 Indians had been admitted to the United States. Between 1965 and 1975, over 96,000 were admitted, and the 1980 Census reported 387,223 Indians in the United States (Melton, 1985). By 1965, most large American cities had at least one Hindu center where lectures could be heard, texts purchased or read, and courses taught in Hindu philosophy. Although relatively small, these groups were significant in their stability and in their attempts to make Hindu literature available. Popular figures such as Edgar Cayce (1877–1945) made traditional Hindu concepts, such as reincarnation and karma, almost standard fare for spiritual seekers not bound to traditional denominations. But popularization has been accompanied by charges of violence, fraud, drug misuse, and emotional abuse leveled against some Indian and American promoters and leaders of Hindu and related New Age groups. Hinduism, in its various guises in the United States, has provided inspiration to spiritual seekers, an entry into countercultural pursuits, and groups who have experienced backlash from conservative quarters.

Most immigrants from India have not been teachers of Hinduism, but rather Hindu lay people seeking traditional venues and methods of practicing their religion. Unable to fund conventional structures, such as temples and shrines appropriate to their respective sects, they have joined other Hindus to create temples that serve several modes of Hindu worship—SHAIVITE, Vaishnavite, and SHAKTA—within one structure. Groups of Hindus have cooperated to recruit traditionally trained priests to the United States to preside over ritual activities at these temples.

Since the 1960s, elements of Hinduism have entered popular culture as components of various forms of spirituality, health practices, cosmetics, bumper stickers, and medical and psychological therapies. Somewhat independent of its source in Hinduism is the popular practice of HATHA YOGA, almost pervasive throughout the country in a variety of forms. Romain Rolland, French student of Vedanta, spoke in 1931 of the "strange moral and religious mentality of the modern United States" that was both cause and effect of the appropriation of Hindu thought in the 19th century. Simultaneous with stringent efforts to preserve traditional Hindu teachings intact and in toto is the more dominant American practice of eclecticism, which combines elements of any (or all) religions into idiosyncratic fusions designed to serve the individual.

See also DIASPORA; UNITED KINGDOM.

Further reading: Hannah Adams, *A View of Religion* (Boston: Manning & Loring, 1801); S. E. Ahlstrom, *A Religious History of the American People* (New Haven, Conn.: Yale University Press, 1972); Mrs. Gross Alexander, "American Women Going after Heathen Gods," *Methodist Quarterly Review* 62 no. 3 (July 1912): 495–512; Leona B. Bagai, *The East Indians and the Pakistanis in America* (Minneapolis: Lerner, 1967); J. H. Barrows, *The World's Parliament of Religions: An Illustrated and Popular Story of the World's First Parliament of Religions Held in Chicago in Connection with the Columbian Exposition of 1893,* 2 vols. (Chicago: Parliament, 1893); Theos Bernard, *Hatha Yoga: The Report of a Personal Experience* (New York: Columbia University Press, 1944); S. C. Bose, *The Life of Protap Chunder Mozoomdar.* Vol. 2 (Calcutta: Nababidhan Trust, 1927); Charles S. Braden, ed., *These Also Believe: A Study of Modern American Cults and Minority Religious Movements* (New York: Macmillan, 1951); Charles S. Braden, ed., *Varieties of American Religion* (Chicago: Willett, Clark, 1936); A. F. Buchanan, "The West and the Hindu Invasion," *Overland Monthly* 51, 4 (April 1908): 308–312; B. F. Campbell, *Ancient Wisdom Revived: A History of the Theosophical Movement* (Berkeley: University of California Press, 1980); Arthur Christy, *The Asian Legacy and American Life* (New York: Greenwood Press, 1968); ———, *The Orient in American Transcendentalism: A Study of Emerson, Thoreau, and Alcott* (New York: Columbia University Press, 1932); R. K. Das, *Hindustani Workers on the Pacific Coast* (Berlin: Walter de Gruyter, 1923); Robert S. Ellwood Jr., *Alternative Altars: Unconventional and Eastern Spirituality in America* (Chicago: University of Chicago Press, 1979); W. Estep, *An American Answers Mother India* (Excelsior Springs, Mo.: Super Mind Science Pubs., 1929); S. Gottschalk, *The Emergence of Christian Science in American Religious Life* (Berkeley: University of California Press, 1973); J. W. Hanson, ed., *The World's Congress of Religions* (Chicago: The Monarch Book, 1894); *Hinduism Comes to America: A Brief Account of the Purpose, Origin, and Spiritual Significance of the Vedanta Movement in America* (Chicago: Vedanta Society, 1933); Carl T. Jackson, *The Oriental Religions and American Thought: Nineteenth Century Explorations* (Westport, Conn.: Greenwood Press, 1981); Spencer Lavan, *Unitarians and India* (Boston: Skinner House, 1977); T. Jackson Lears, *No Place of Grace: Antimodernism and the Transformation of American Culture 1880–1920* (New York: Pantheon Books, 1981); Gurinder Singh Mann, Paul David Numrich, and Raymond Williams, *Buddhists, Hindus, and Sikhs in America* (Oxford: Oxford University Press, 2001); Katherine Mayo, *Mother India* (New York: Blue Ribbon Books, 1927); J. Gordon Melton, *A Bibliography of Hinduism in America Prior to 1940* (Evanston, Ill.: Institute for the Study of American Religion, 1985); P. C. Mozoomdar, *The Faith and Progress of the Brahmo Samaj* (Calcutta: Calcutta Central Press, 1882); F. Max Muller, *India: What Can It Teach Us?* (London: Longmans, Green, 1883, 1919); Jacob Needleman, *The New Religions* (Garden City, N.Y.: Doubleday, 1970); Joseph Priestly, *Disquisitions Relating to Matter and Spirit, 1777* (New York: Garland Pub., 1976); ———, *Letters to a Philosophical Unbeliever,* 2d ed. (Birmingham, England: J. Johnson, London, 1787); ———, *A Comparison of the Institutions of Moses with Those of the Hindoos and Other Ancient Nations* (Northumberland, Penn.: Printed for the author by A. Kennedy, 1799); H. G. Rawlinson, *Intercourse between India and the Western World* (Cambridge: University Press, 1916); H. G. Rawlinson, *Intercourse between India and the Western World* (Cambridge: University Press, 1916); J. P. R. Rayapati, *Early American Interest in Vedanta* (New York: Asia Publishing House, 1973); E. A. Reed, *Hinduism in Europe and America* (New York: G. P. Putnam's Sons, 1914); ———, *Hinduism Invades America* (New York: G. P. Putnam's Sons, 1914); Dale Riepe, *The Philosophy of India and Its Impact on American Thought* (Springfield, Ill.: Charles C Thomas, 1970); Romain Rolland, *The Life of Vivekananda and the Universal Gospel* (Almora: advaita Ashrama, 1931); Cybelle Shattuck, *Dharma in the Golden State: South Asian Traditions in California*

(Santa Barbara, Calif.: Fithian Press, 1996); Wendell Thomas, *Hinduism Invades America* (New York: Beacon Press, 1930); W. S. Urquhart, *Vedanta and Modern Thought* (New York: Oxford University Press, 1928); Paramahansa Yogananda, *Autobiography of a Yogi* (Bombay: Jaico Publishing House, 1946).

untouchability

The concept of untouchability has long played a role in the Hindu CASTE system of socioeconomic organization. Members of certain low-status castes were considered polluting and not allowed to touch any person of the upper castes, particularly BRAHMINS and members of the warrior and merchant castes. This practice was exaggerated even further in parts of South India, where certain people were considered unseeable and had to stay out of sight of the upper castes.

The history of untouchability no doubt tracks the rise of ARYAN cultural domination of India. There is evidence to suggest that certain tribal groups and peoples last integrated into the Aryan fold became classified as "out-castes" or the "fifth caste" (where the Aryans had a fourfold class system from great antiquity). The custom is supported by a very complex social conception of "POLLUTION" related to occupation. Purity is seen to reside in certain types of activity such as teaching and recitation of the VEDAS, and in habits such as VEGETARIANISM, while such essential social tasks as sweeping, the collecting of refuse, the removal of carrion animals, and the production of leather are considered severely polluting.

Caste, more properly *jati,* or birth, is in fact directly related in most cases to occupation, so untouchability is generally conferred by birth. (However, certain polluting situations within the family context, such as having someone recently die in the household, make any person, whatever the caste, polluting or "untouchable" for a limited time.)

It should be noted that almost all of the major freedom fighters in India who sought independence from Britain denounced the notion of caste and called for the abolition of untouchability. MOHANDAS KARAMCHAND GANDHI was most notable in this regard. He coined the term *harijan* (those born of God) to relieve the stigma from untouchables. The constitution of India was written by an untouchable (who also became a Buddhist), Dr. Babasaheb R. Ambedkar (1891–1956). In the setting up of India's central and state governments, untouchables were given designated quotas of positions, including parliamentary seats, to guarantee their advancement.

Today, India's untouchables have taken an increasingly militant political stance. They prefer to call themselves Dalit (the oppressed). Many of them have converted to Buddhism, following Dr. Ambedkar's conversion in late life. Buddhism was always opposed to caste notions and preached spiritual equality.

Further reading: B. R. Ambedkar, *What Congress and Gandhi Have Done to the Untouchables* (Bombay: Thacker, 1946); Mark Jurgensmeyer, *Religion as Social Vision: The Movement against Untouchability in 20th Century Punjab* (Berkeley: University of California Press, 1982); J. Michael Mahar, ed., *The Untouchables in Contemporary India* (Tucson: University of Arizona Press, 1972); Eleanor Zelliot, "Dalit—New Cultural Context of an Old Marathi Word," in Clarence Maloney, ed., *Language and Civilization Change in South Asia.* Vol. 11, *Contributions to Asian Studies* (Leiden: E. J. Brill, 1978), pp. 77–97.

upanayana   *See* SACRED THREAD.

Upanishads

There are thousands of texts referred to in Indian tradition as Upanishads. They all take this name to gain the authority of the original Upanishads, about 14 in number, which are considered part of the BRAHMANA or commentaries that are associated with the four VEDAS. (Each of the four is divided into a MANTRA portion, which consists of the chants themselves, and a BRAHMANA, or commentary. Both portions are considered SHRUTI, or revelation.)

Within the Brahmana portion of the Vedas are two classes of passages that later took the names ARANYAKA and Upanishad. The Aranyaka portions often closely resemble the Brahmana but often contain esoteric interpretations of the Vedic rituals. The further sections, sometimes within these Aranyaka sections, were termed Upanishads. While included in the Vedic literature, the Upanishads were composed somewhat later, roughly in the seventh to third centuries B.C.E., although they exist in the same ancient literary SANSKRIT.

Upanishad in its literal definition means "to sit down near." They represented secret teachings reserved for those who sat near their GURU in the forest. They contain a wide range of material. Some of it is indistinguishable from the rest of the Brahmana or Aranyaka, but other sections discuss the creation and nature of the universe. Most often, the discussions concern the BRAHMAN, or ultimate reality; the ATMAN, the ultimate self or soul; or their relationships with the individual self or soul.

In many places these Upanishads make clear that the individual self, seen from the highest consciousness, is nothing but the ultimate reality in all its glory. The exact relationship between the ultimate reality and the souls became the subject of centuries of discussion and mystic insights into the nature of things. The most commonly listed Upanishads are ISHA, KENA, KATHA, Prashna, Mundaka, MANDUKYA, TAITTARIYA, AITAREYA, CHANDOGYA, BRIHADARANYAKA, Pingala, and Jabala.

Further reading: S. M. Srinivas Chari, *The Philosophy of the Upanisads: A Study Based on the Evaluation of the Comments of Samkara, Ramanuja, and Madhva* (New Delhi: Munshiram Manoharlal, 2002); S. N. Dasgupta, *The History of Indian Philosophy.* Vol. 1 (Delhi: Motilal Banarsidas, 1975); S. Radhakrishnan, trans., *The Philosophy of the Upanisads* (London: G. Allen & Unwin, 1935); ———, *The Principal Upanishads* (Atlantic Highlands, N.J.: Humanities Press, 1994).

Urvashi and Pururavas   *See* APSARAS.

Ushas

Ushas is the Vedic goddess of the dawn. The night goddess, Ratri, is often called her sister. Some of the most beautiful hymns of the VEDAS are addressed to Ushas. Sometimes she is seen as the mother of the Sun god and sometimes his wife. She travels in a shining chariot drawn by red horses or cows.

She is seen as very beautiful, dressed in ornaments and fine raiments. She gives life and health to all beings. She is called the "life of all life" and the "breath of all breaths." She is a great power who revivifies Earth each day and makes all life that we know possible.

Further reading: Alfred Hillebrandt, *Vedic Mythology.* Translated by Sreeramula Rajeswara Sarma. Vol. 1 (Delhi: Motilal Banarsidass, 1990); W. J. Wilkins, *Hindu Mythology, Vedic and Puranic,* 2d ed. (Bombay: Rupa, 1973).

V

Vach (Vak)

Vach or Vak is Hindu goddess of speech, and the most prominent and important goddess in the VEDAS. In later times she becomes identified with SARASVATI, the goddess of learning, and loses her separate character, except in linguistic philosophy.

In Vedic tradition the words of SANSKRIT have a divine character. Words are not arbitrary or mere names, but are the essential truth of the object they represent. The sounds of the word *tree,* for instance, form the essence of a tree. All of reality can be seen as mere congealed speech.

Vedantic theory sees four levels of speech: (1) the transcendent level, where speech is the divine silence out of which emerges the manifest universe; (2) speech as it becomes incipient thought looking toward manifestation; (3) speech expressed as thought, but before external expression; and (4) speech as uttered words.

Further reading: Alfred Hillebrandt, *Vedic Mythology,* 2 vols. (Delhi: Motilal Banarsidass, 1990); Andre Padoux, *Vac: The Concept of the Word in Selected Hindu Tantras.* Translated by Jacques Gontier (Albany: State University of New York Press, 1990).

vaikuntha   See HEAVEN.

vairagya

Vairagya, freedom from any attachment, or renunciation, has been a central theme in Hinduism throughout the centuries. It was understood that attachment to worldly desires and ends can result only in continued rebirth, a continued circuit on the wheel of SAMSARA or worldly life.

The period from the eighth to the sixth centuries B.C.E., when JAINISM and Buddhism first emerged along with the UPANISHAD era within the VEDIC tradition, saw a great expansion in mendicancy and ascetic orders and a flowering of traditions of renunciation. The Vedas themselves, in their ancient MANTRA sections, upheld a very different, world-affirming point of view.

Ever since in India, it has been those who left the ordinary world behind and abandoned worldly concerns who have been credited with the greatest spiritual accomplishments. *Vairagya* in one form can mean simple avoidance of worldly externals, but in its most difficult form it might mean bodily mortification. In either case it is a central feature of Hindu religious life.

Further reading: Robert Lewis Gross, *The Sadhus of India: A Study of Hindu Asceticism* (Jaipur: Rawat, 1992); Patrick Olivelle, "Contributions to the Semantic

History of Samnyasa," *Journal of the American Oriental Society* 101 (1981): 265–274; ———, *Renunciation in Hinduism: A Mediaeval Debate,* 2 vols. (Vienna: University of Vienna, 1986–87).

Vaisheshika *See* Nyaya-Vaisheshika.

Vaishnavism

Vaishavism is the name for the group of traditions that adhere to the worship of Vishnu. An adherent of Vaishnavism is a Vaishnavite, "One who belongs to Vishnu."

Vishnu can be worshipped alone as Mahavishnu or "Supreme Vishnu," but Vaishnavites more commonly worship one of the two most prominent avatars or manifestations of the godhead, Rama or Krishna, along with their respective consorts, Sita or Radha. To be sure, every Vaishnavite reveres all 10 of Vishnu's avatars.

As all Hindu traditions do, Vaishnavism traces itself back to the Vedas and honors them as the ultimate authority. Vishnu, "The All-Pervading," is only a minor divinity in the Vedas, but the roots of a devotional cult that can be called Vaishnavite had been established by the later Vedic period in the sixth or fifth century B.C.E. The Mahabharata and Ramayana epics are both primarily Vaishnavite documents, highlighting the stories of Krishna and Rama, respectively.

The Bhagavad Gita within the Mahabharata is a sophisticated philosophical text that outlines the Vaishnavite path of devotion in the context of Vedic and Upanishadic visions of the divinity. The later temple-oriented Vaishnavism is based largely on the ancient Pancharatra tradition.

The followers of Vaishnavism are many fewer than those of Shaivism, numbering perhaps 200 million. If there is a distinctive character to Vaishnavism, aside from its doctrine of the avatar, it is in its commitment to the life of a householder. There are far fewer renunciants in the Vaishnavite sect than among the Shaivites. (Vishnu, after all, is the "preserver" of the world, whereas Shiva himself is a naked renunciant who is the world destroyer.)

Six sects of the Vaishnavites are prominent: the Shrivaishnavas founded in Shrirangam in Tamil Nadu, best known for their great 12th-century teacher Ramanuja; the Gaudiya Vaishnavites of Bengal, founded by the great 15th-century devotional mystic Chaitanya; the Vallabhas or Rudrasampradaya founded at Brindavan in the north by the great teacher Vallabha around the 15th century; the Madhva sect founded in the state of Karnataka at Udipi in the 13th century; the Nimbarka, or Nimbarki sect, based in Govardhana and founded by the 15th-century Vedantin philosopher Nimbarka; and the Sri sect founded by Ramananda, who was strongly influenced by the Ramanuja lineage, at Ayodhya.

Textually, Vaishnavites revere, in addition to the Vedas and Upanishads, the epics, the Bhagavad Gita, the Vishnu Purana, the Bhagavata Purana, and the hymns of the Alvars or other poet-saints of Vaishnavism. They focus, as does Shaivism, on temple worship, with, of course, their own distinctive ritual elements. Prasada in the form of "blessed food" is typically distributed at Vaishnavite temples and shrines and festivals after being offered to the divinity. This giving of blessed food is less common in Shaivite contexts.

Further reading: R. G. Bhandarkar, *Vaishnavism, Saivism and Minor Religious Systems* (Varanasi: Indological Book House, 1965); Manju Dube, *Conceptions of God in Vaishnava Philosophical Systems* (Varanasi: Sanjay Book Centre, 1984); Jan Gonda, *Aspects of Early Vishnuism* (Utrecht: A. Oosthoek, 1954); ———, *Vishnuism and Sivaism: A Comparison.* Jordan Lectures in Comparative Religion, no. 9 (London: Athlone Press, 1970); T. Rengarajan, *Dictionary of Vaishnavism* (Delhi: Eastern Book Linkers, 2004).

Vaishnavite (Vaishnava)   *See* VAISHNAVISM.

Vaishya

Vaishya is the term used in the ancient fourfold class (VARNA) system of India for the common people, including merchants and agriculturists. The earlier VEDIC term was *Vish*, from which the term *Vaishya* derived. They were "twice-born" as were the KSHATRIYAS (warriors) and BRAHMINS (priests), being invested with the sacred thread at eight to 12 years of age to symbolize a new birth into society. They were allowed to learn the VEDAS, though they probably studied them much less than the upper two classes. Vaishya merchants were known for their early support of JAINISM and Buddhism (c. 800 to 500 B.C.E.).

Further reading: Klaus K. Klostermaier, *A Survey of Hinduism* (Albany: State University of New York Press, 1994); Utsa Patnaik, *Peasant Class Differentiation: A Study in Method with Reference to Haryana* (Delhi: Oxford University Press, 1987); T. Ramaswamy, *Merchant Class: South India, 1336–1665* (Madurai: Mathi, 1997).

Vallabha (1473–1531) *Vedanta philosopher*

Vallabha was one of the great exponents of devotional VEDANTA. He was born in 1473 to a Telegu BRAHMIN, Lakshmana Bhatta, and his wife, Yellamma Garu, a member of an influential South Indian family. Her father had been a priest at the VIJAYANAGARA court.

Vallabha's father is said to have fled BENARES (Varanasi) while his wife was pregnant with Vallabha, because of a rumored Muslim invasion. While he hid in the forest near modern Raipur in Chattisgarh state, Vallabha emerged from his mother stillborn—but miraculously came to life. When the Muslim invasion did not take place, Vallabha's father returned.

As were many of the Vedantic ACHARYAS, or scholar-teachers, Vallabha was a precocious child who learned all the VEDAS and all the philosophical systems in four years of study. After his father died when he was just 11, Vallabha spent the next 20 years wandering India's sacred sites, remaining unmarried. At a mere 12 years old, he is said to have entered into a debate at the Vijayanagara court. He emerged victorious against the views of SHANKARA's Vedanta (absolute non-dualist) on the one hand and the views of MADHVA's supporters (dualist) on the other.

Vallabha stayed at the Vijanagara court for some three years, learning the BHAGAVATA PURANA and becoming familiar with the Madhva tradition (which he did not accept). By now he had followers of his own, as his debating victory had greatly enhanced his status.

At the age of 15 he set out on a long pilgrimage to a great many of India's sacred sites. One story relates that at Kaundiya Ashrama (*see* ASHRAM), Vallabha had a vision of the *rishi* (seer) Kaundinya, who preached to him the path of devotion, or BHAKTI; even the Vedas and the gods do not know VISHNU, Kaundinya said; only the one who concentrates his consciousness upon Vishnu and serves him every moment can merit that knowledge.

It is said that Vallabha spent time at the important centers of RAMANUJA's followers and Madhva's followers, learning all the nuances of the different philosophies. Heading north, Vallabha arrived in BRINDAVAN, the center of KRISHNA worship in India. Here he made Krishna his Lord and received the vision to establish a new sect, the Pushti Marga.

The last leg of this long pilgrimage took him to the HIMALAYAS. After returning to stay with his mother for one year, he headed to Maharashtra and Pandaripura, where he encountered the special form of Krishna, Vitthala. Here he received the divine command to marry, as he had up till now been a celibate, though not a SANNYASI (renunciant). When he arrived in Benares in about 1500, he encountered a man who offered him his daughter in marriage.

Vallabha's marriage produced two sons, one of whom was central in building his sect. While in the town of Gokula, near Mathura, Vallabha took the vow to establish his new sect. This new tradition was all his own, as he had never accepted anyone as his GURU. The initiatory MANTRA of his sect was *Sri Krishna Sharanam Mama,* "Shri Krishna is my refuge."

An auspicious miracle soon occurred near Gokula. An image of Krishna in his pose lifting the mountain Govardhana appeared out of a cave. It was said that Krishna would only accept food from the hand of Vallabha. On this spot Vallabha built a small temple, later supplanted by a large complex. The temple's image later had to be moved to Udaipur in Rajasthan, because of the Muslim invaders. There it is known as SRI SRI NATHJI.

Vallabha now embarked on a journey around the country that might be described as evangelical. He would debate the proponents of other systems, sharpen his own principles, and gain followers. His message resonated particularly in the area of Gujarat, thanks to the support of a famous devotional singer there.

There are many stories of Vallabha's meeting with his contemporary SRI CHAITANYA. Both made the BHAGAVATA PURANA the primary authority and both took Krishna as the fullest expression of divinity on Earth. The contrast was between Vallabha the intellectual, who prescribed worship of the child Krishna or the cowherd Krishna, and Chaitanya the ecstatic mystic, who preached "Love Devotion" based on the relationship between Krishna and his lover RADHA.

In all Vallabha wrote 17 books in SANSKRIT and five in medieval Hindi (Braj). All but one of his Sanskrit "books" were actually brief manuscripts. His longest book was in Sanskrit, *Essays on the Light of Knowledge,* a full exposition of his theology. Others of his books in Sanskrit are Vyasa Sutra Bhashya, Jaimini Sutra Bhasya, Bhagavata Tika Subodhini, Pushti Pravala Maryada, and Siddhanta Rahasya.

In the last year of his life Vallabha took vows of renunciation from the world. He wandered as a mendicant for only one year. The story has it that he plunged into the GANGES at HANUMAN Ghat in Benares and disappeared in 1531.

The philosophical system of Sri Vallabhacharya (to call him by his honorific) was technically called Shuddhadvaita (pure non-dualism). He did not believe that the world was illusory—all the universe was Krishna alone. The worldly, then, is a lower aspect of the divine, but still an expression of the being of the divinity. In Vallabha's system Krishna, as BRAHMAN, or the ultimate reality, was called *Purushottama,* the highest personage.

In practical terms, the Vedanta of Vallabhacharya was similar to that of both RAMANUJA and NIMBARKA. God is permanently transcendent; souls can reach union with God but remain distinct even in liberation.

Distinctive in Vallabha's system is the notion of inherent distinctions among souls. There are privileged souls who are destined for union with the divine, and other souls who are destined for eternal reincarnation without attainment of liberation (this Vallabha has in common with Madhva).

His Pushti Marga, or path of grace, is unique. *Pushti* literally means "nourishment," and later in the sect's history, this word began to be taken more literally, and the eating of vast amounts of PRASADA or sacred food became a sign of the sect. However, Vallabha seemed to intend "spiritual nourishment" or "grace." This effectively means that human efforts to reach the divine are secondary; primary are the will and grace of the divine.

Thus, in terms of the YOGAS of the BHAGAVAD GITA, the yoga of action (KARMA YOGA), the yoga of knowledge (JNANA YOGA), and even meditative yoga (raja yoga) are of almost no importance to Vallabha. Devotional yoga (BHAKTI YOGA) alone is enjoined to gain the grace (*PUSHTI*) of the divine.

This devotion is best developed through total service to the divinity and his servants.

Further reading: Richard Barz, *The Bhakti Sect of Vallabhacarya* (Faridabad: Thomson Press, 1976); G. H. Bhatt, *Sri Vallabhacarya and His Doctrines* (Delhi: Butala, 1980); Sharad Goswami, *Manual of the Devotional Path of Pusti.* Translated by M. R. Paleja (Gujarat: Sri Vallabhacarya Trust, 2002); James D. Redington, *The Grace of Lord Krishna: The Sixteen Verse Treatises (Sodasagranthah) of Vallabhacarya.* Sri Garib Das Oriental Series, no. 257 (Delhi: Satguru, 2000); Natvar Lal Gokal Das Shah, *A Life of Shri Vallabhacarya* (Baroda: Shri Vallabha, 1984); Jethlal G. Shah, *Shri Vallabhacarya: His Philosophy and Religion* (Nadiad: Pushitmargiya Pustakalaya, 1969); Brajnath R. Shastri, *Shrimad Vallabhacarya and His Doctrines.* Sri Vallabha Studies, no. 5 (Baroda: Shri Vallabha, 1984); G. V. Tagare, *Brahma-Vada Doctrine of Sri Vallabhacarya* (New Delhi: D. K. Printworld, 1998); Swami Tapasyananda, *The Bhakti Schools of Vedanta* (Madras: Ramakrishna Mutt, 1990).

Valmiki *author of the Ramayana*

Valmiki is the mythological author of India's great epic the RAMAYANA. His authorship, however, consisted simply in putting into a lasting composition a story that was related to him by the ancient RISHI (seer) NARADA.

Valmiki is said once to have seen a hunter shoot a male bird as it was making love to its mate. The female bird, seeing her mate bleeding and in distress, cried out piteously. In grief and sorrow, Valmiki uttered a poetic verse of two lines that upon reflection made a special meter. Because he received the line in sorrow (*shoka*), Valmiki termed the meter *shloka*. It is in this meter, suitable to be accompanied by the Indian lute (*vina*), that most of the Ramayana was composed.

Further reading: J. L. Brockington, *Righteous Rama: The Evolution of an Epic* (Delhi: Oxford University Press, 1985); Ilapavuluri Panduranga Rao, *Valmiki* (New Delhi: Sahitya Akademi, 1994).

Vamana Avatar

There are many versions of the stories about VISHNU's Vamana AVATAR (incarnation), as there are about his other manifestations.

In the best-known Vamana story, the avatar appeared in order to fight the *asura* (demon or antigod) Bali, who had succeeded by his religious austerities in gaining supreme power over the three worlds. Because of his own powers he was depriving the gods of the offerings that ordinarily went to them. They went to Vishnu to ask for assistance. He took on the form of a dwarf (*vamana* means "dwarf" in SANSKRIT) and approached the arrogant demon, BALI. The foolish demon king offered the dwarf the boon of having whatever territory he could cover in three paces. Thereupon the dwarf, who was Vishnu himself, took one step to possess the Earth, another to possess the sky, and another to possess heaven itself. (In some versions Vamana takes two paces to step over the whole universe and the last step onto Bali's head.) Thus did Vamana return the worlds to the gods.

Further reading: Nanditha Krishna, *The Book of Vishnu* (New Delhi: Viking, 2001); A. K. Ramanujan, *Hymns for the Drowning* (Princeton, N.J.: Princeton University Press, 1981); Pandrimalai Swamigal, *The Ten Incarnations: Dasvatara* (Bombay: Bharatiya Vidya Bhavan, 1982).

vanaprastha

In the orthodox Brahminical stages of life for men, *vanaprastha,* going into the forest, is the third stage or ASHRAMA. After he has completed his studentship and fulfilled his duty in life (when he has seen his children's children), the man enters the forest with or without his wife to devote himself to celibacy, austerity, study of the VEDAS, Vedic sacrifices, and spiritual discipline. This stage is also called the stage of SADHU. The man must wear animal skins, bark, or rags; leave his hair and nails uncut; and eat pure food. He may beg food, if necessary. The final stage is SANNYASI or mendicancy, when he emerges from the forest to wander alone, seeking alms. The *vanaprastha* and the *sannyasi* stage were clearly the most ideal course of conduct and were probably never followed completely by all BRAHMINS or other upper-CASTE men, for whom they were primarily intended.

Further reading: Patrick Olivelle, *The Asrama System: The History and Hermeneutics of a Religious Institution* (New York: Oxford University Press, 1993).

varada mudra

The *varada* (giving boons) *mudra* (*see* MUDRAS) is an important iconic gesture, with the fingers pointing downward and the palm facing straight outward from the body. The open palm indicates that the divinity or personage will bestow blessings upon the person who looks upon him or her with respect or devotion. Many iconic divinities, particularly those who have more than two hands, give this gesture with a left hand. This ancient mudra is found in the iconography of the Buddhists, Jains (*see* JAINISM), and Hindus. The BUDDHAS and the Jain TIRTHANKARAS are frequently seen using this hand gesture. This, as may any other mudra, may be used in any Indian dance when divinities are represented.

Further reading: Eva Rudy Jansen, *The Hindu Book of Imagery: The Gods and Their Symbols* (Havelte, Holland: Binkey Kok, 1995); Margaret Stutley, *An Illustrated Dictionary of Hindu Iconography* (Boston: Routledge & Kegan Paul, 1985).

Varaha Avatar

At the commencement of a new eon, when the Earth is covered by water in every direction, Vishnu takes the form of a huge boar (*varaha*).

The boar dives down to the bottom of the ocean and takes the Earth to the surface again so that life can reemerge.

Further reading: Nanditha Krishna, *The Book of Vishnu* (New Delhi: Viking, 2001); A. K. Ramanujan, *Hymns for the Drowning* (Princeton, N.J.: Princeton University Press, 1981); Pandrimalai Swamigal, *The Ten Incarnations: Dasvatara* (Bombay: Bharatiya Vidya Bhavan, 1982).

Varanasi   *See* BENARES.

varna

Varna (color) is the Vedic word for social class, in the class scheme found in Rig Veda X. 90. There the divine being is said to have offered himself in sacrifice to create reality. It is said that his mouth became the BRAHMIN, or priestly class; his arms became the Rajanya (KSHATRIYA), or warrior class; his thighs became the Vish (VAISHYA), or merchants, farmers; and his feet became the SHUDRAS, or the servant class.

The "mouth" of society is symbolically important in India because of the power of divine speech through the SANSKRIT language. The arms are obviously symbolic of the strong arms of the warrior. The thighs symbolize the ability to procreate and create prosperity for society. Feet have long been associated with impurity in Indian tradition, but it is a fact that no body can move without its feet.

There has been some debate about whether the use of the word *color* to denote class reflects an ancient racist system. At the present day Brahmins in any part of India tend to have slightly lighter skin than other classes, while the poorest elements of society often have much darker skin. When colors are traditionally assigned to the classes, white is for the Brahmin, red for the warrior, yellow for the merchants and farmers, and black for the servants.

This verse of the Vedas, which may in fact have been simply an ideal scheme for an integrated society, which could not function without any of its constituents, became the religious justification for the later concept of caste. *Caste* itself is a Portuguese word adopted into English; the more proper word for this type of social class is *jati,* or "birth." Nothing in this Vedic verse implies that *varna* is fixed at birth or that people can never alter their *varna*. It is well known, for instance, that the RISHI (seer) Vishvamitra, though born a warrior, became a Brahmin.

Further reading: Bharat Jhunjhunwala, *Varna Vyavastha: Governance through Caste System* (Jaipur: Rawat, 1999); Laurie L. Patton, ed., *Authority, Anxiety and Canon: Essays in Vedic Interpretation* (Albany: State University of New York Press, 1994); Brian K. Smith, *The Ancient Indian Varna System and the Origins of Caste* (Oxford: Oxford University Press, 1994).

Varuna

Varuna is a sky god of the VEDAS who has many, sometimes contradictory traits. He is the Indian counterpart of the Greek Ouranos. Varuna is paired with several deities in rituals and hymns, most commonly with MITRA. By himself, Varuna is seen as a guardian over the cosmic order. He is called the sovereign ruler of the universe, but this is said of other Vedic gods. Later he becomes the Indian god of the ocean.

Further reading: John Dowson, *A Classical Dictionary of Hindu Mythology and Religion, Geography, History, and Literature,* 12th ed. (Ludhiana: Lyall Book Depot, 1974); Alfred Hillebrandt, *Vedic Mythology,* 2 vols. (Delhi: Motilal Banarsidass, 1990); Heinrich Luders, *Varuna,* 2 vols. (Gottingen: Vanderhoeck & Ruprecht, 1951–59); W. J. Wilkins, *Hindu Mythology, Vedic and Puranic,* 2d ed. (Calcutta: Rupa, 1973).

Vasanta Panchami

Vasanta Panchami festival, literally "The 'Fifth Day of the Moon' in the Springtime," is celebrated on the fifth day of the bright half of the lunar month of Magha (January–February), the beginning of spring in India. It is dedicated to the worship of SARASVATI, the goddess of learning and fine arts. The worship is performed to a fashioned clay image, which is then put into a body of water such as a river or a tank. This festival is particularly popular in Bengal.

Some call this festival Sri Panchami and equate Sarasvati (who is usually the wife of Brahma) with LAKSHMI or Sri, the wife of VISHNU. Part of the day's observance is a preparation for the HOLI festival, which falls 40 days later. The devotee places a flammable image of the demoness Holika (after whom Holi is supposedly named) on a log, with an inflammable image of PRAHLADA (the great devotee of VISHNU) on her lap. During the 40 days people throw twigs and other flammable objects on the log, which is set on fire before the Holi festival commences.

Further reading: Swami Harshananda, *Hindu Festivals and Sacred Days* (Bangalore: Ramakrishna Math, 1994); H. V. Shekar, *Festivals of India: Significance of the Celebrations* (Louisville, Ky.: Insight Books, 2000).

Vasudeva

In Hindu mythology Vasudeva is the father of KRISHNA. He was particularly popular in the Jain tradition (*see* JAINISM), whose PURANAS abound with stories about his life. Krishna himself is known by the epithet *Vasudeva* (with a long *a* as the second letter, indicating that he is the son of Vasudeva).

Vasudeva was the chief minister of the evil king Kamsa of Mathura. Kamsa had learned that Vasudeva's wife, DEVAKI, was destined to bear a son who would eventually kill him. He kept the couple under constant guard and had their first six children killed. The seventh child, BALARAMA, was miraculously transferred to the womb of Vasudeva's other wife, Rohini. When the eighth child, KRISHNA, was born, a profound slumber fell upon the guards, and Vasudeva was able to sneak the child across the YAMUNA River and leave it with the cowherd Nanda and his wife, YASHODA, who thus becomes Krishna's (foster) mother.

The Jain *puranas* credit Vasudeva with 26 wives. The most complete story of the life of Vasudeva is found in the Jain text Vasudevahindi (c. third century C.E.), a work in the Prakrit language. The text was an adaptation of the earlier BRIHATKATHA story cycle, an ancient Indian story.

Further reading: Cornelia Dimitt and J. A. B. van Buitenen, eds. and trans., *Classical Hindu Mythology: A Reader in the Sanskrit Puranas* (Philadelphia: Temple University Press, 1978); Jagdishchandra Jain, *The Vasudevahindi: An Authentic Jain Version of the Brhatkatha.* L. D. Series 59 (Ahmedabad: L. D. Institute of Indology, 1977).

Vatsyayana (c. 400–500 C.E.)   *See KAMA SUTRA.*

Vayu

Vayu is the god of the wind in Indian mythology. He makes his first appearance in the VEDAS. He is associated with INDRA, king of the Vedic gods. He is seen as moving along in a chariot pulled by many horses. Most importantly he is regarded as the father of the monkey god HANUMAN. BHIMA, one of the five PANDAVA brothers in the MAHABHARATA, is said to be the son of Vayu. The term *vayu* is also used for one of the five elements in Hindu physics; in that context it is best translated as "air."

Further reading: Cornelia Dimitt and J. A. B. van Buitenen, eds. and trans., *Classical Hindu Mythology: A Reader in the Sanskrit Puranas* (Philadelphia: Temple University Press, 1978); Alfred Hillebrandt, *Vedic Mythology,* 2 vols. (Delhi: Motilal Banarsidass, 1990).

Veda(s)

Veda is derived from the word, *vid,* "to know." A Veda, then, would literally be a compendium of knowledge. In Indian tradition the four Vedas (sometimes collectively referred to as "the Veda") are the ancient scriptural texts that are considered the foundation for all of Hinduism. The four are the RIG, SAMA, YAJUR, and ATHARVA VEDAS.

The Rig Veda (c. 1500 B.C.E.), the most ancient extant Indian text, is the most important of the four. It consists of over 1,000 hymns, the great majority of them from five to 20 verses long. Very few exceed 50 verses. The hymns praise a pantheon of divinities. A few of them are cosmogonic—they tell of the creation of the universe; these were extremely important in the later development of Hinduism.

By far the greatest number of hymns in the Rig Veda are devoted to INDRA, king of the gods, a deity connected with storms and rain who holds a thunderbolt, and AGNI, the god of fire. The rest of the hymns are devoted to an array of gods, most prominently MITRA, VARUNA, SAVITRI, SOMA, and the ASHVINS. The most important gods in the later Hindu pantheon, VISHNU and SHIVA (in his Vedic guise as RUDRA), were far less frequently mentioned in the Rig Veda. A number of goddesses are mentioned, most frequently USHAS, GODDESS of the dawn. ADITI is said to be the mother of the gods.

Scholars have categorized the religion of the Rig Veda as henotheistic: that is, it was polytheistic, but it recognized each divinity in turn as supreme in certain ways. Later Hinduism maintained and enriched this henotheistic concept; in time Hindus have even been able to accept Christ and Allah as supreme "in turn."

A very powerful ritual tradition was central to the Rig Veda, with fire always a central feature. At public and private rituals (YAJNAS) worshippers spoke to and beseeched the divinities. Animal sacrifices were a regular feature of the larger public rites in the Vedic tradition.

Two of the other Vedas, the Yajur and Sama, were based on the Rig Veda. That is, it supplied most of their text, but the words were reorganized for the purposes of the rituals. Yajur Veda, the Veda of sacrificial formulas, has two branches, the

Black and the White Yajur Vedas; it contains the chants that accompanied most of the important ancient rites. The Sama Veda, the Veda of sung chants, is largely focused on the praise of the god Soma, the personification of a sacred drink imbibed during most rituals that probably had psychedelic properties. Priests of the three Vedas needed to be present for any larger, public ritual.

The Atharva Veda became part of the greater tradition somewhat later. It consists primarily of spells and charms used to ward off diseases or influence events. This text is considered the source document for Indian medicine (AYURVEDA). It also contains a number of cosmogonic hymns that show the development of the notion of divine unity in the tradition. A priest of the Atharva Veda was later included in all public rituals. From that time tradition spoke of four Vedas rather than three.

In the Vedic tradition, the Vedas are not considered to be human compositions. They were all "received" by RISHIS or seers whose names are frequently noted at the end of a hymn. Whatever their origin, none of the texts was written until the 15th century C.E. They were thus passed down from mouth to ear for at least 3,000 years. It is an oral tradition par excellence. The power of the word in the Vedic tradition is considered an oral and aural power, not a written one. The chanting itself has the power to provide material benefit and spiritual apotheosis. Great emphasis, therefore, was laid on correct pronunciation and on memorization. Any priest of the tradition was expected to have an entire Veda memorized, including all its components, as detailed in the following.

Each of the four Vedas is properly divided into two parts, the MANTRA, or verse portion, and the BRAHMANA, or explicatory portion. Both parts are considered revelation or SHRUTI. The Brahmanas comment on both the mantra text and the rituals associated with it, in very detailed, varied, and esoteric fashion. They repeatedly equate the rituals and those performing them with cosmic, terrestrial, and divine realities. Early Western scholars tended to discount these texts as priestly mumbo-jumbo, but later scholarship has recognized the central importance of the Brahmanas to the development of Indian thought and philosophy. It is not known when the various subdivisions of the Vedas were identified and named.

The name Brahmana derives from a central word in the tradition, BRAHMAN. Brahman is generically the name for "prayer," specifically the power or magic of the Vedic mantras. (It also was used to designate the "one who prays," hence the term BRAHMIN for priest). Brahman is from the root brih (to expand or grow) and refers to the expansion of the power of the prayer itself as the ritual proceeds. The brahman is said to be "stirred up" by the prayer. In later philosophy, brahman was the transcendent, all-encompassing reality.

The culmination of Brahmana philosophy is often said to be found in the SHATAPATHA BRAHMANA of the White Yajur Veda, which explicates the AGNICAYANA, the largest public ritual of the tradition. Shatapatha Brahmana makes clear that this public ritual is, in fact, a reenactment of the primordial ritual described in Rig Veda, X. 90, the most important cosmogonic hymn of the Vedas. That hymn describes the ritual immolation of a cosmic "man," who is parceled out to encompass all of the visible universe and everything beyond that is not visible. That is, the cosmic "man" is ritually sacrificed to create the universe. Through the annual agnichayana, the universe is essentially re-created every year. The Brahmana understands that, at its most perfect, the Vedic ritual ground is identical to all the universe, visible and invisible.

The Brahmanas contained two important subdivisions that were important in the development of later tradition. The first is called the ARANYAKA; this portion of the text apparently pertained to activity in the forest (aranya).

The Aranyakas contain evidence of an esoteric version of Vedic yajna, or ritual practice, that was done by adepts internally. They would essentially perform the ritual mentally, as though it were being done in their own body and being. This practice was not unprecedented, since the priests of the Atharva Veda, though present at all public rituals, perform their role mentally and do not chant. However, the esoteric Aranyaka rituals were performed only internally. From this we can see the development of the notion that the adept himself was *yajna* or ritual.

The UPANISHADS, a second subdivision within Brahmanas, were the last of the Vedic subdivisions, commonly found within the Aranyakas. Many of these texts, as did the Brahmanas in general, contained significant material reflecting on the nature of the Vedic sacrifice. In fact, the divisions among Brahmana proper, Aranyaka, and Upanishad are not always clear. The most important feature of the Upanishads was the emergence of a clear understanding of the identity between the individual self, or ATMAN, and the all-encompassing *brahman*, which now was understood as the totality of universal reality, both manifest and unmanifest.

The genesis of this Upanishadic view that the self was in unity with cosmic reality can be clearly traced. Firstly, Shatapatha Brahmana explained that the most perfect ritual was to be equated to the universe itself. More accurately it *was* the universe, visible and invisible. Second, the Aranyakas began to make clear that the initiated practitioner was to be equated to the ritual itself. So, if the ritual equals all reality, and the individual adept equals the ritual, one easily arrives at the idea that the individual equals all reality. The Upanishads, then, were the outgrowth not of philosophical speculation, but of self-conscious ritual practice. The later orthodox Upanishads (those physically associated with a Vedic collection) barely mention the rituals; they merely state the derived abstract concepts.

Another key breakthrough in the Upanishads was the explicit discussion of REINCARNATION and the theory of KARMA, the notion that actions in this birth would have consequence in a new birth. There is evidence that karma, or ethically conditioned rebirth, had its roots in earlier Vedic thought. But its full expression in VEDANTA (Hindu philosophy) had to wait for the Upanishads. There, the earlier notion of reaching unity with the ultimate reality was seen not merely as a spiritual apotheosis, but also as a way out of the trap of rebirth (and redeath).

Many texts have called themselves the "fifth Veda" to emphasize their importance in the tradition. The ARTHASHASTRA, the NATYASHASTRA, and the MAHABHARATA all have claimed that designation. Sometimes the TANTRA also refers to itself as the fifth Veda.

Tamil SHAIVITES or the Tamil Vaishnavites refer to their sacred texts, respectively, the TEVARAM and the Nalayira Divya Prabantham, as the Tamil Veda. Other local traditions in various languages do likewise.

The term Veda is also sometimes used generically in other fields of knowledge. Medicine, for example, is referred to as the "Veda of Life" (AYURVEDA), and the study of war is the "Veda of the Bow" (*Dhanurveda*).

Further reading: Faddegon Barend, *Studies in the Samaveda* (Amsterdam: North-Holland, 1951); S. N. Dasgupta, *History of Indian Philosophy.* Vol. 1 (Delhi: Motilal Banarsidass, 1975); Jan Gonda, *Vedic Literature (Samhitas and Brahmanas): A History of Indian Literature*, Vol. 1, no. 1 (Wiesbaden: Otto Harrassowitz, 1975); Thomas Hopkins, *The Hindu Religious Tradition* (Encino, Calif.: Dickenson, 1971); J. C. Heesterman, *The Broken World of Sacrifice: An Essay on Ancient Indian Ritual* (Chicago: University of Chicago Press, 1993); Brian K. Smith, *Reflections on Resemblance, Ritual and Religion* (New York: Oxford University Press, 1989); Frits Staal, *AGNI: The Altar of Fire,* 2 vols. (Berkeley, Calif.: Asian Humanities Press, 1983).

Vedangas

The Vedangas, or "branches of the VEDA," are six ancillary sciences of traditional Brahminical learning: *shiksha* (proper pronunciation), *kalpa* (mastery of the ritual details), *vyakarana* (SAN-SKRIT grammar), *nirukta* (etymology or derivation of Sanskrit words), *chandas* (prosody or verse metrics), and *jyotish* (astronomy/astrology). The adept had to know all these to be considered fully educated.

Further reading: Klaus K. Klostermaier, *A Survey of Hinduism* (Albany: State University of New York Press, 1994); Jagadguru Shankaracharya, *The Vedas and Vedangas* (Kumbakonam: Sri Kamakoti Research Centre, 1988).

Vedanta

Vedanta, literally the end or conclusion (*anta*) of the VEDA, is the most important philosophical school in Indian tradition. It is a wide and capacious field that includes those who adhere to a strict non-dualist (ADVAITA) perspective, those who believe in a non-dualism with certain reservations, and those who believe in the type of dualism (DVAITA) that states that God and the human soul will never be one.

The one basic requirement of Vedanta is that it rest upon the three basic texts: the UPANISHADS, the VEDANTA SUTRAS, and the BHAGAVAD GITA. Most commonly known in both India and the West is the Vedanta of SHANKARA, the seventh-century philosophical savant. This Vedanta understands that the world is illusory, MAYA, and only the transcendent ultimate reality, the BRAHMAN, is real. That *brahman* has no characteristics and does not act in any way. It is a pure plenum or totality that is sometimes characterized as infinite being (*sat*), infinite consciousness (*cit*), and infinite bliss (*ANANDA*). (*See* SAT-CHIT-ANANDA.)

A second type of Vedanta might best be described as BHAKTI Vedanta or devotional Vedanta. Here the oneness of the godhead is also understood, but the world is seen to be real and permeated by God in the form of VISHNU, usually, or his incarnations RAMA or KRISHNA. (Vedantas that emphasize SHIVA in this way are rare.) There is no

duality of soul, world, and God, but God is seen as supreme and all other realities as subsidiary. It is non-dualism with the reservation that the godhead has supreme power to act.

Finally, there is the rare minority sect of Vedanta championed by Sri MADHVA, who argues that the soul, the world, and God are all separated from each other eternally and will never be one. All is dependent upon the radically transcendent God.

In the Neo-Vedanta of the followers of RAMA-KRISHNA, reality is still one, but "God" may be characterized as "Allah" or "Christ" as well as in the usual Hindu ways. Because of the power of the word *Vedanta*, even systems like that of SRI AUROBINDO that resemble the TANTRA will be characterized as Vedanta. His followers have sometimes called his system Integral Vedanta.

All systems of Vedanta (except that of Aurobindo) agree that the highest goal is to break the bonds of KARMA and realize *mukti*, or liberation.

Further reading: Surendranath Dasgupta, *The History of Indian Philosophy*, 5 vols. (Delhi: Motilal Banarsidas, 1975); Swami Tapasyananda, *Bhakti Schools of Vedanta (Lives and Philosophies of Ramanuja, Nimbarka, Madhva, Vallabha and Chaitanya)* (Madras: Sri Ramakrishna Math, 1990).

Vedanta Centre/Ananda Ashrama   *See* PARAMANANDA.

Vedanta Societies/Ramakrishna Math and Mission

The Vedanta Societies are part of a missionary movement created by the monastic disciples of Sri RAMAKRISHNA Paramahansa (1836–86), the Indian saint of ADVAITA (non-dual) VEDANTA, who was considered an incarnation of God. Ramakrishna's message was that truth can be found in all of the world's religions. The basic tenet of Vedanta is that reality is non-dual and that one divine reality

Ramakrishna Temple, in Ramakrishna Math, Belur, Bengal *(Constance A. Jones)*

encompasses all. Swami VIVEKANANDA, a disciple of Sri Ramakrishna, first introduced Ramakrishna's ideas of Vedanta to the UNITED STATES when he addressed the WORLD PARLIAMENT OF RELIGIONS in Chicago in 1893. His message was so well received that he lectured throughout the country and founded the first Vedanta Society in the United States in New York City in 1896.

Other swamis or monastics in the order founded other Vedanta Societies in major cities. Swami ABHEDANANDA served the New York society and taught throughout the United States from 1897 to 1921. In San Francisco, Swami Trigunatita oversaw the construction of the first Hindu temple in the United States in 1906. Swami PARAMANANDA (1885–1940) lectured all over the United States and established centers in Los Angeles and Boston. In 1923 he established ANANDA ASHRAMA at La Crescenta, California. Swami Nikhilananda founded a center in Manhattan in 1933. Swami Prabhavananda (1914–76) established centers in Portland, Oregon, and Hol-

lywood, California. The Vedanta Society in Hollywood became the Vedanta Society of Southern California, with several monasteries, a convent, and the Vedanta Press. The writers Gerald Heard (1889–1971), Aldous Huxley (1894–1963), and Christopher ISHERWOOD (1904–86) were disciples of Prabhavananda.

The Vedanta Societies remain under the authority of the central monastery, the Ramakrishna Order, headquartered in Belur Math, India. The larger organization, the Ramakrishna Math and Mission, administers a network of Ramakrishna Missions in major cities and some rural areas of India. Missions sponsor hospitals in addition to religious services. SWAMIS are trained at the math and are sent to direct Vedanta centers outside India. At present, all swamis are male, although nuns are part of the organization and convents are provided for nuns through the Sarada Math, named for SARADA DEVI, the wife of Ramakrishna. Several swamis have left the Vedanta Society because of its traditional authority structure.

Further reading: Swami Gambhrananda, *History of the Ramakrishna Math and Mission* (Calcutta: Advaida Ashrama, 1957); Christopher Isherwood, *Ramakrishna, and His Disciples* (New York: Simon & Schuster, 1965); Carl T. Jackson, *Vedanta for the West: Ramakrishna Movement in the United States* (Bloomington: Indiana University Press, 1994); Romain Rolland, *The Life of Ramakrishna* (Mayavati: *advaita* Ashrama, 1931); ———, *The Life of Vivekananda and the Universal Gospel* (Mayavati: *advaita* Ashrama, 1931); ———, *Prophets of the New India.* Translated by E. F. Malcolm-Smith (New York: Albert & Charles Boni, 1930); Catherine Wessinger, "Hinduism Arrives in America: The Vedanta Movement and the Self-Realization Fellowship," in Timothy Miller, ed., *America's Alternative Religions,* 173–190 (Albany: State University of New York Press, 1995).

Vedanta Sutra (first century C.E.)
The Vedanta Sutra is said to have been composed by VYASA, but it is also known as Vedanta

Sutra and as such is attributed to Badarayana, an ancient sage. A SUTRA is a short aphoristic line of text; *Vedanta Sutra* can thus be translated as "lines relating to the VEDANTA." There are about 560 lines in this text.

The work was composed to resolve difficulties in the interpretation of the UPANISHADS and to refute the views of certain opposing schools. Chapter I systematically and with great specificity discusses the Upanishad passages dealing with BRAHMAN (the universal reality) and ATMAN (the soul or self). Chapter II is devoted to a refutation of the other interpretations, as presented by the schools of SAMKHYA, YOGA, NYAYA, VAISHESHIKA, MIMAMSA, CHARVAKA, Buddhism, and JAINISM. Chapter III discusses the PRAMANAS, the valid methods of obtaining knowledge (such as perception, inference, or scripture) in order to understand the *brahman* and atman. The fourth and final chapter discusses the results of *brahman* realization.

The Vedanta Sutra, Upanishads, and BHAGAVAD GITA form the traditional foundational texts for Vedantic philosophy. As a result, Vedanta Sutra has attracted numerous and varied commentaries. SHANKARA, RAMANUJA, and MADHVA all wrote extensive commentaries, which strongly disagree with one another, largely because the extremely concise style of the individual lines often admits to varied interpretations.

Further reading: V. M. Apte, trans., *Brahma-Sutra, Shankara-Bhashya: Badarayana's Brahma-Sutras with Shankaracharya's Commentary* (Bombay: Popular Book Depot, 1960); Swami Gambhirananda, trans., *Brahma-Sutra-Bhasya of Sri Sankaracarya* (Calcutta: *advaita Ashrama*, 1965); S. Radhakrishnan, trans., *The Brahma Sutra, the Philosophy of Spiritual Life* (New York: Greenwood Press, 1968); S. S. Raghavachar, *Sri Bhashya on the Philosophy of the Brahma-Sutra* (Bangalore: Sri Lakshmi Hayagreeva Seva Trust, 1986).

Vedantic Center   *See* TURYASANGITANANDA, SWAMI.

Vedic   *See* VEDA(S).

vegetarianism

Vegetarianism is highly valued in Indian culture. In general orthodox BRAHMINS will eat neither meat nor eggs. Castes who desire to gain respect and perhaps eventual advancement in the hierarchy will adopt vegetarianism as a way to "Sanskritize" or become more Brahminical. Hindus who are on any spiritual quest in India will remove meat and other things such as spices from their diet in order to ensure spiritual purity. Meat is considered to be *tamasic* (*see* GUNAS), or spiritually negative, and is believed to cause excessive desire for sexuality and a tendency toward violence.

Most scholars agree that vegetarianism was not originally part of the Vedic or Brahminical system, though this remains a controversial conclusion. The solid evidence of the Vedic texts themselves as well as authoritative DHARMA (right conduct) texts such as the *DHARMASHASTRA* of Manu, indicate quite clearly that meat, including beef, was eaten by all sectors of Indian society including Brahmins.

The Jains (*see* JAINISM) and Buddhists, however, were extremely critical of the Brahminical animal sacrifices and of the habit of eating meat. The Jains were most radical in this regard; Jain monks (and to a lesser degree the laity) practiced AHIMSA (noninjury) from as early as 900 B.C.E., as did the BUDDHA from around 600 B.C.E.

For the Jain monks, every motion of the body had to be calculated to minimize its effect on invisible microscopic beings that were believed to exist in air, water, fire, and earth. (This may have been the first human conception of microorganisms.) All the more did they refrain from slaughtering and eating large animals. Strict vegetarianism was required for monks, and the laity followed their example. One could never be a Jain in India, then or now, and eat meat or eggs. Buddhists were vegetarian in their monasteries but were allowed to eat meat received as alms. They were less absolute, but they too discouraged MEAT-EATING.

The Brahminical tradition began to move in the direction of *ahimsa* toward the end of the last millennium before the Common Era. Law codes such as the *Manu Smriti* or the *Dharmashastra* of Manu allow Brahmins to eat the meat of sacrificial animals, but other meat eating is discouraged. The influence of *ahimsa* is clear in the argument that ritually sacrificing an animal is not *himsa,* or "killing" per se.

As time went on, and Vedic ritual began to recede in importance in the culture, Brahmins took on strict vegetarianism as a sign of purity. They also followed the Jains and Buddhists in preventing any needless killing of any being. While Jainism and Buddhism remained localized or minority traditions, Brahmin conduct was always the model for the Hindu majority. Vegetarianism soon became the pan-Indian ideal.

Further reading: D. N. Jha, *The Myth of the Holy Cow* (London: Verso, 2002); Brian K. Smith, "Eaters, Food and Social Hierarchy in Ancient India," *Journal of the Academy of Religion* 58, no. 2 (1990): 177–205; Francis Zimmerman, *The Jungle and the Aroma of Meats* (Berkeley: University of California Press, 1987).

vehicles of the divinities

In the post-Vedic iconography of India, gods and goddesses are commonly seen in association with what is described in SANSKRIT as their *vahana* (vehicle). Often they are pictured astride an animal; at other times there is a depiction of the animal standing alone in the foreground or background. Vedic divinities did not have such mounts, but mounts were created for them in later times to make their images accord with those of the non-Vedic gods.

The vehicle of VISHNU is the man-eagle GARUDA; the vehicle of SHIVA is the bull NANDI; DURGA is often depicted astride a lion or tiger;

SARASVATI is seen in association with a swan or peacock; KARTTIKEYA, the younger son of Shiva and PARVATI, has a peacock vehicle; GANESHA, the elephant-headed divinity, is seen in association with the lowly rat. LAKSHMI is unique in having a lotus that she is always shown seated upon, which serves as her vehicle.

There are, however, many prominent divinities who do not have iconographic vehicles. These include RAMA and SITA, PARVATI and KRISHNA. Among the Jains the TIRTHANKARAS (perfected beings) were usually depicted in association with particular animals, perhaps in imitation of the Hindu notion. However, since the Jain tradition is so old, it is quite possible that the practice originated with them.

Further reading: Cornelia Dimitt and J. A. B. van Buitenen, eds. and trans., *Classical Hindu Mythology: A Reader in the Sanskrit Puranas* (Philadelphia: Temple University Press, 1978); Margaret Stutley, *An Illustrated Dictionary of Hindu Iconography* (Boston: Routledge & Kegan Paul, 1985).

Videha

Videha was an important region or country of ancient India, located in what is now northern Bihar state. With its capital Mithila it was mentioned in both the MAHABHARATA and the RAMAYANA. King Janaka of Videha was famous for his daughter SITA, who became Lord RAMA's wife, and for reaching a perfected state through action alone, as recounted in the BHAGAVAD GITA. The king is also mentioned in the UPANISHADS as a knower of BRAHMAN. Videha is also mentioned in the Buddhist Jataka stories and the *Majjhima Nikaya;* the Buddha traveled there. MAHAVIRA, the great Jain TIRTHANKARA (perfected being), was born in this country.

Further reading: Yogendra Mishra, *History of Videha: From the Earliest Times to the Foundation of the Gupta Empire, A.D. 319* (Patna: Janaki Prakashan, 1981).

vidya

Vidya (knowledge) from the SANSKRIT root "to know" is an important philosophical term in Hindu tradition. Initially it connoted the knowledge of the Vedic MANTRAS and ritual, and it bestowed great power. When the UPANISHADS concluded that Vedic rituals alone could not help break the cycle of birth and rebirth, Vedic knowledge began to be called the "lower knowledge" (*apara vidya*) while the Upanishadic knowledge was called the higher or liberating knowledge (*para vidya*). Buddhism also used the term to refer to knowledge of the path that breaks the cycle of birth and rebirth.

Further reading: Thomas Hopkins, *The Hindu Religious Tradition* (Encino, Calif.: Dickenson, 1971); Klaus K. Klostermaier, *A Survey of Hinduism* (Albany: State University of New York Press, 1994).

Vidyaranya (c. 1450 C.E.) *Vedantic philosopher*

Vidyaranya was a well-known philosopher in the tradition of SHANKARA. He is thought to be the brother of Sayana; Sayana is the commentator on the VEDAS. Vidyaranya composed several texts. The Sarvadarshanasangraha is a discussion of different philosophical views. The Panchapadika-vivarana is considered an excellent and thorough summary of the non-dualist philosophical perspective; Vivarnaprameyasangraha explores the same theme in a more scholarly fashion.

Vidyarana's Jivanmuktiviveka discusses those beings who have already been liberated from the cycle of birth and rebirth but remain in embodied existence. Finally, Panchadashi is a popular compendium in verse of Vedantic thought, known for its clarity and accessibility. Here he outlines his own understanding of the nature of the ultimate *brahman,* describing the *maya* or illusory world appearance as being in a sense a power of the BRAHMAN. *Brahman* is the underlying pure reality, while all names and forms are the false discoloration over the pure whiteness, as it were, of the ultimate reality.

Further reading: S. N. Dasgupta, *History of Indian Philosophy,* 5 vols. (Delhi: Motilal Banarsidass, 1975); T. M. P. Mahadevan, *The Philosophy of Advaita, with Special Reference to Bharatitirtha-Vidyaranya* (London: Luzac, 1938); Swami Tejomayananda, *Pancadasi of Svami Vidyaranya,* chaps. 5, 10, and 15 (Mumbai: Central Chinmaya Mission Trust, 1999).

Vijayadashami   *See* NAVARATRI.

Vijayanagara (1336–1630)

Vijayanagara, the "City of Victory," was a fortress city founded by an alliance of kings as a bulwark against the Muslims in the south of India. Its vast ruins can still be seen at the site of Hampi in Karnataka.

The city was the capital of a sprawling empire that controlled almost all of India south of the Krishna and the Tungabhadra Rivers at its height under King Krishnadevaraya. The empire took the name of the city, the Vijayanagara empire.

Vijayanagara played a key role in Hindu history, by successfully fending off many Muslim invasions and preserving and promoting Hindu culture for nearly 300 years, at a time when the rest of India was suffering complete Muslim domination. Two princes, Harihara and Bukka, created the kingdom in 1336. Harihara I (1336–57) planned and built the great new city of Vijayanagara, which became the capital of the empire in 1343. In 1346, the Hoysalas, the last remaining South Indian rivals to the Vijayanagara kingdom, were defeated.

The city covered 20 square miles and had seven concentric lines of fortifications. It had at its height a population of 500,000 people. It was an international city with wide trade ties, which helped finance beautifully carved and embellished buildings. The culture saw a flowering of South Indian civilization with support for all the sects of Hinduism, including Vaishnavite, Shaivite, and the GODDESS, and for the heterodox Jains as well (*see* JAINISM).

Further reading: K. A. Nilakanta Shastri, *A History of South India from Prehistoric Time to the Fall of Vijaja-nagar* (Madras: Oxford University Press, 1996); Burton Stein, *Vijayanagara* (Cambridge/New York: Cambridge University Press, 2005).

Vimalananda (1942–) *founder of Yoga House Ashram*

Vimalananda, founder of Yoga House Ashram and a former member and teacher of the ANANDA MARGA YOGA SOCIETY, currently teaches yoga throughout northern California.

Dadaji, as he in known to his friends and disciples, was born in 1942 to a BRAHMIN family in Badwel in South India. He had spiritual experiences as a young boy and at age six experienced a bright light filling his room and a voice urging him to commit himself to the inner path of enlightenment. Dadaji answered the call of the inner life; by the time he was 16 he was adept as a YOGA instructor.

In 1962 he developed a relationship with Sri ANANDAMURTI, founder and creator of the ANANDA MARGA YOGA SOCIETY. He delighted in the services the society provided for the sick, the poor, and the elderly. Very quickly he was promoted to yoga teacher. In 1966 Dadaji felt the need to spread the words and programs of the society to help humanity. He left India as an emissary of the society to found centers in Thailand, Singapore, Indonesia, Malaysia, Singapore, Hong Kong, and the Philippines. He was honored by the United Nations for his heroic work in the aftermath of the great earthquake that struck Manila in 1968.

In 1969 Dadaji went to the UNITED STATES and assisted in developing the Ananda Marga Society there. However, in the mid-1970s he left the society, created the Yoga House Ashram, and developed his own following. He settled in the San Francisco area and continued to teach that service to humanity was as important as yoga or MEDITATION. His life has been devoted to bridging the rivers that separate the East and West through traditional yoga techniques.

Further reading: Dadaji Vimalananda, *Yogamritam* (*The Nectar of Yoga*) (San Rafael, Calif.: Yoga House Ashram, 1977).

Vindhya Mountains

The Vindhya Mountains, 1,000 to 3,500 feet in elevation, are a range of hills forming a natural barrier between northern and southern India. They mark the northern edge of the central Indian or Deccan plateau. From Gujarat state on the west, they extend about 675 miles across Madhya Pradesh state to touch on the GANGES River valley near BENARES (Varanasi) in Uttar Pradesh. These mountains are mentioned in the Indian epics and are mythologically associated with numerous personages including AGASTYA, who is said to have caused them to bow down permanently in his travels to South India. DURGA is sometimes said to have her home in the Vindhyas in the form of the goddess VINDHYAVASINI.

Further reading: John Dowson, *A Classical Dictionary of Hindu Mythology* (New Delhi: Oriental Books Reprint, 1973); *History to Prehistory: Contribution of the Department to the Archaeology of the Ganga Valley and the Vindhyas* (Allahabad: Department of Ancient History, Culture, and Archaeology, University of Allahabad, 1980).

Vindhyavasini

Vindhyavasini (she who dwells in the VINDHYA MOUNTAINS) is an example of a local indigenous GODDESS who was incorporated in the larger tradition of the great Goddess in ingenious ways. Among the many Hindu local goddesses she is rare in maintaining the face of a bird and not a human, in keeping with non-Aryan tribal notions of divinity.

Vindhyavasini is depicted with the face of a bird and the body of a woman, having four arms.

In her hands are a conch, a club, a war discus, and the "fear not" gesture of the hand (ABHAYA MUDRA). Her vehicle is a lion. She is also depicted as KALI is with a garland of human skulls. To her right is the elephant GANESHA and to her left is a *yogini*, a demigoddess, seated on an elephant. Vindhyavasini is mentioned in the Devi Mahatmya, an important text that presents the various incarnations or forms of the great Goddess (Mahadevi). She is also mentioned in an early 19th-century local text called the *Vindhya Mahatmya*. In both she is understood to be the BRAHMAN, or ultimate reality, in its totality. She is also assimilated to Mahalakshmi, or LAKSHMI, conceived of as the ultimate divinity.

Vindhyavasini is primarily connected with the Vaishnavite tradition. The story goes that when KRISHNA was given to his foster mother Nanda to escape being killed by the evil king Kamsa, in exchange VASUDEVA, Krishna's father, received a divine child, Vindhyavasini. Kamsa, getting word that a birth might have occurred, went to Krishna's mother DEVAKI's house and tried to seize the new girl child. She escaped the king's grasp and prophesied, before returning to the Vindhyas, that Kamsa would be killed by Krishna.

A different account of Vindhyvasini's birth (resembling the tale that KALI emerged from PARVATI) tells of a goddess, Kaushiki, who was formed when Parvati shed her dark complexion to become golden or light in color (earning her the standing epithet *Gauri*, or white one). Kaushiki immediately went to the HIMALAYAS to take up her role as Vindhyavasini.

There is an active and elaborate PILGRIMAGE to Vindhyavasini around the village of Vindhyachal at the northern foothills of the Vindhyas, where they touch the GANGES between ALLAHABAD and BENARES (Varanasi). The temple of Vindhyavasini has elements that resemble those of Kali, and animal sacrifices are performed.

Further reading: John Stratton Hawley and Donna Marie Wulff, eds. *Devi: Goddesses of India* (Berkeley: University of California Press, 1996).

Virashaivas

The Virashaivas are a BHAKTI, or devotional, movement in the southern Indian state of Karnataka that was founded in the 12th century by their leader, BASAVANNA. The Virashaivas were socially radical, condemning all forms of caste, establishing equality of the sexes, and rejecting ritual of all kinds as empty posturing. Most important for them were the GURU, the saints as a group, a personal relationship with Lord SHIVA, and high regard for the wandering seeker who embraces poverty and defies convention. One Virashaivite saint, for example, AKKA MAHADEVI, was a woman who wandered about naked.

Virashaiva orthodoxy has eight elements: (1) the GURU who leads the self to Shiva; (2) the LINGAM, the sole symbol of Shiva, worn on a necklace by anyone; among the Virashaivas there is no indication that the lingam is considered a phallic symbol; (3) the *jangama*, the male or female wandering religious teacher who is considered God incarnate; the guru, lingam, and *jangama* all have sanctifying power; (4) the holy water that has touched the feet of the guru and been drunk as a sign of devotion; (5) PRASADA (grace), food blessed by the guru; devotees take this food from the feet of the guru together; commensality and community sharing occur regardless of CASTE, in defiance of ordinary social behavior in Indian tradition; (6) holy ash, which is worn as a sign of Shiva; (7) *rudraksa* beads, a necklace made of seeds from a special plant and worn as a sign of Shiva; they are sacred to all who worship Shiva; and (8) the five-syllable MANTRA, *Om Nama Shivaya*; this is an important mantra for all Shaivites.

The Virashaivas recognize a number of important saints born from the 10th to the 12th centuries. The poem-songs of these saints are sung and recited as part of devotion. These saints are Basavanna, Akka Mahadevi, Allama Prabhu, and Devara Dasimayya.

Further reading: Vinaya Chaitanya, *Songs for Siva: Vacanas of Akka Mahadevi* (Lanham, Md.: Alta Mira

Press, 2005); K. Ishwaran, *Speaking of Basava: Lingayat Religion and Culture in South Asia* (Boulder, Colo.: Westview, 1992); A. K. Ramanujan, trans., *Speaking of Siva* (New York: Penguin Books, 1973).

Vishishtadvaita

The term *Vishishtadvaita* is very commonly misinterpreted as "qualified" (or "modified") (*vishishta*) non-dualism (ADVAITA). A more accurate (though still imprecise) translation is "non-duality with differentiation." This reflects Vishishtadvaita's understanding of the three reals: Ishvara (God), *cit* (consciousness) and *acit* (unconsciousness). The conscious and unconscious existence are real aspects or attributes of God, non-dual or non-different from God from the point of view of God, but they are also eternally distinct (differentiated), in that they are attributes only.

God or BRAHMAN and the world are seen to have the relation of soul and body. The manifest universe is the body of God, but in his plentitude he is also an unchangeable infinity beyond the world, untouched in any way by the negatives or impurities of the world of manifestation.

Vishishhadvaita tradition begins with the 12 ALVARS, the mystic poet-singers of Tamil Nadu who date from the eighth to the 10th centuries. The songs of these Alvars inspired and shape the tradition of Vishishtadvaita. The philosophy expressed in these songs was first systematically explored by the teacher Nathamuni, probably in the ninth century C.E. Nathamuni is said to have received the verses of NAMMALVAR, which he put to music in Vedic style. These verses are still sung in the temples of Tamil Nadu, in addition to verses in SANSKRIT, and are part of the Vaishnavite VEDA in Tamil.

Nathamuni is credited with composing three Sanskrit texts that still inform the tradition. He had 11 disciples, the most important of whom were Pundarikaksha, Karukanatha, and Shrikrishna Lakshminatha. Pundarikaksha's student Rama Mishra became the guru of the famed Yamunacharya, who was also the grandson of Nathamuni. Yamunacharya was probably born in the early 10th century. He was a king who renounced everything to go to SRIRANGAM, one of the most important shrines for the Sri Vaishnavite tradition, which supports the philosophy of Vishishtadvaita.

Yamunacharya had many disciples, of whom 21 became prominent. RAMANUJA (born at the end of the 11th century), the greatest ACHARYA of the lineage, was born to the elder sister of one of Yamunacharya's disciples, Mahapurna. Yamunacharya composed six important Sanskrit works developing the philosophy of Vishishtadvaita. As with other great *acharyas* of the Vishishtadvaita tradition he was a great devotee, as well as a great scholar; one of the six works he composed was a praise poem to Lord KRISHNA.

Yamunacharya apparently lived to a ripe age but died before he could meet Ramanuja. Ramanuja's own guru understood that his student would one day outshine him and tried to have him killed, but Ramanuja was miraculously saved from this attempt. Eventually, Ramanuja took Mahapurna, his uncle, to be his guru and followed him to Srirangam. He arrived just after Yamunacharya died.

From seeing three of Yamuna's fingers twisted, after death, he learned that he should do three things: (1) convert the people to the Vaishnavite doctrine of surrender, (2) write a commentary to the VEDANTA SUTRA, and (3) write extensively on Sri Vaishnavism. All these things he did. Not long afterward, he renounced the householder life and went to Srirangam to head the order and devote himself to the divinity of that shrine. Ramanuja is famed for his Sri Bhashya, his commentary on the Vedanta Sutra, but he also wrote a commentary on the BHAGAVAD GITA and several other major Vedantic works.

All Ramanuja's works were written in Sanskrit. Two important philosophers followed Ramanuja, Parashara Bhattar, who wrote a Sanskrit commentary on the Sanskrit *Thousand Divine Names of Vishnu,* and Pillan or Kurukesha, who wrote a

Tamil commentary on the hymns of the Alvars, which became a philosophical backbone for later Vishishtadvaita thought. The most prolific later teacher among many later philosophers in this lineage was Venkatanatha of the 15th century, who wrote numerous works in Sanskrit and Tamil.

Most significant in the philosophy of Sri Vaishnavism is a vision of a personal divinity that is worshipped with great passion and devotion. At the same time that divinity, Vishnu, is understood to be the transcendent *brahman* of the UPANISHADS. The Alvar's faith was passionate and mystical. Ramanuja's commentaries were subtle philosophy that sought to legitimate their path in terms of Vedanta. The two paths together constitute what Sri Vaisnavas call the "Double Vedanta" (*Ubayavedanta*), which relies on both Sanskrit and Tamil textual bases.

Further reading: John Braisted Carmen, *The Theology of Ramanuja* (New Haven, Conn.: Yale University Press, 1974); S. N. Dasgupta, *A History of Indian Philosophy*, vol. 3 (Delhi: Motilal Banarsidass, 1975); A. K. Ramanujan, *Hymns for the Drowning* (Princeton, N.J.: Princeton University Press, 1981); Arvind Sharma, *Visistadvaita Vedanta: A Study* (New Delhi: Heritage, 1978).

Vishnu

Vishnu in his various forms is one of the most worshipped gods in the Indian pantheon. His tradition, known as VAISHNAVISM, constitutes the second largest sect within Hinduism.

Vishnu first appears in the VEDAS as a rather insignificant divinity, with only minor ritual importance. There are only 64 mentions of him in the RIG VEDA, most of them in passing, with only a handful of hymns addressed to him alone. He is celebrated in the Vedas mostly for his "three steps" that saved the world, in his incarnation as VAMANA AVATAR.

Vishnu first gains prominence in the later Vedic period, apparently after being identified with VASUDEVA, a non-Vedic god popular in western India in the last centuries before the Common Era, and with the god Narayana of the Vedic BRAHMANA literature. By the time of the MAHABHARATA and RAMAYANA epics his prominence was assured. He was identified both with the gods KRISHNA, hero of the Mahabharata, and RAMA, hero of the Ramayana.

Eventually, Vishnu's cult reached full development when he was recognized as Mahavishnu (great Vishnu), preserver of the universe, who entered into the world when needed in successive AVATARS or "descents." Before the world is created, Vishnu sleeps on the cosmic MILK OCEAN on the back of the divine serpent ADISHESHA. Out of his navel grows a lotus from which BRAHMA the creator god emerges to create the universe. Once

Lord Venkateshwara, popularly known as Balaji, is one of the manifestations of Lord Vishnu. (*Institute for the Study of American Religion, Santa Barbara, California*)

the world is created Vishnu reigns in his heavenly realm of Vaikuntha.

Iconographically, Vishnu is depicted as being of dark blue color with four arms. He is seated on a throne. In his four hands he holds a conch, a war discus, a mace, and a lotus. He wears the Kaustubha gem around his neck and has a tuft of hair on his chest called Shrivatsa. His vehicle is the man-eagle GARUDA. His spouse is LAKSHMI, or Sri. In the highest understanding he exists as all things and also transcends them.

Vishnu as the sustainer divinity takes human or animal incarnations when needed to maintain or defend the world. The BHAGAVAD GITA says that whenever there is a decrease in righteousness and an increase in unrighteousness in the world, Vishnu (there KRISHNA) sends himself forth. Only Vishnu among the gods is seen to take on incarnations as part of a divine duty. Other gods such as SHIVA and the Goddess will be found in various forms, but these will not be referred to in general as avatars or incarnations.

There are different lists of avatars or incarnations of Vishnu in different texts and traditions, variously containing 10, 12, or 22 god names. The most common list of avatars is MATSYA (fish), KURMA (tortoise), VARAHA (boar), Narasimha (man-lion), VAMANA (dwarf), PARASHURAMA (RAMA with the axe), Rama of the RAMAYANA, KRISHNA, BUDDHA, and KALKI (his future incarnation). Sometimes Krishna's brother BALARAMA is made the 11th avatar and sometimes both Krishna and Balarama are classified as one avatar.

Whenever Vishnu takes an avatar, he is subject to birth and death just as a human is. Krishna of the MAHABHARATA, for instance, dies by being shot in the heel.

Further reading: R. G. Bhandarkar, *Vaisnavism, Saivism, and Minor Religious Systems* (Poona: Bhandarkar Oriental Research Institute, 1982); K. Bharadvaja, *A Philosophical Study of the Concept of Visnu in the Puranas* (New Delhi: Pitambar, 1981); Kalpana S. Desai, *Iconography of Visnu (In Northern India, up to the Mediaeval*

Period) (New Delhi: Abhinav Publications, 1973); Cornelia Dimitt and J. A. B. van Buitenen, eds. and trans., *Classical Hindu Mythology: A Reader in the Sanskrit Puranas* (Philadelphia: Temple University Press, 1978); J. Gonda, *Aspects of Early Visnuism*, 2d ed. (Delhi: Motilal Banarsidass, 1969); ———, *Visnuism and Sivaism: A Comparison* (London: Athlone, 1970); Nanditha Krishna, *The Book of Vishnu* (New Delhi: Viking, 2001); Sushil Kumar Patel, *Hinduism in India: A Study of Visnu Worship* (Delhi: Amar Prakashan, 1992); A. K. Ramanujan, trans., *Hymns for the Drowning: Poems for Visnu by Nammalvar* (Princeton, N.J.: Princeton University Press, 1981); Margaret Stutley, *An Illustrated Dictionary of Hindu Iconography* (Boston: Routledge & Kegan Paul, 1985); Pandrimalai Swamigal, *The Ten Incarnations: Dasvatara* (Bombay: Bharatiya Vidya Bhavan, 1982).

Vishnudevananda, Swami (1927–1993)

See SHIVANANDA YOGA VEDANTA CENTERS.

vishuddha chakra

The *vishuddha* chakra is the fifth CHAKRA (energy center) from the base of the spine in the KUNDALINI YOGA system. It is located on the spine at the throat area. At this chakra worldly emotions are transcended and higher spiritual qualities begin to emerge, particularly higher spiritual insight (JNANA). Accordingly, its element is the refined element ether (*see* ELEMENTS, FIVE). Its deity is Panchavaktra Shiva or five-faced SHIVA. Its SHAKTI or energy is *shakini*, the embodiment of purity. It has 16 bluish gray petals.

Further reading: Harish Johari, *Chakras: Energy Centers of Transformation* (Rochester, Vt.: Destiny Books, 2000); John G. Woodroffe, *The Serpent Power,* 7th ed. (Madras: Ganesh, 1964).

Vishva Hindu Parishad

The Vishva Hindu Parishad (VHP or World Hindu Council) is one of the most visible of several

Hindu nationalist groups. It arose as the religious wing of the militant RASHTRIYA SVAYAM SEVAK SANGH (RSS).

The VHP was founded in 1964, in order to redefine *Hindutva,* or Hinduism, in a simplified but rigorous form that could compete with other world religions. It is an attempt to create a single, unified Hindu culture. Two leaders of the SHANKA-RACHARYA ORDER were present at its formation.

The VHP devised a uniform religious practice, which it publicized in the 1980s. All Hindus were expected to worship SURYA (the Sun) at dawn and dusk, wear the OM symbol around their neck, keep a copy of the BHAGAVAD GITA in their home, maintain a shrine to their personal deity, and attend temple services.

The VHP's writings give no importance to the four VEDAS, which have always been considered the most sacred Hindu scripture. Instead, they exalt the military ethos of the BHAGAVAD GITA and RAMAYANA. The focus of worship for the VHP has been on BHAKTI (devotional) practices, combined with sacrifices and PILGRIMAGES, with little attention to SELF-REALIZATION or renunciation. A unique practice introduced during the 1980s was the worship of bricks with the name of RAMA inscribed upon them. Bricks like these were used as weapons against Muslims in the murderous riots of 1992 and 2002 (*see* HINDU NATIONALISM). Though the VHP courts the lower castes, it exalts the KSHATRIYA or warrior caste.

In North America the VHP operates secretly. Its visual presence is best seen through the affiliated Hindu Student Congress.

Further reading: Gwilym Beckerlegge and Anthony Copley, eds., *Saffron and Seva (Hinduism in Public and Private)* (New York: Oxford University Press, 2003); Chetan Bhatt, *Hindu Nationalism: Origins, Ideologies, and Modern Myth* (Oxford: Oxford University Press, 2001); Gerrie ter Haar and James J. Busuttil, eds., *The Freedom to Do God's Will: Religious Fundamentalism and Social Change* (London: Routledge, 2003); Martin E. Mary and R. Scott Appleby, eds., *Religion, Ethnicity, and*

Self Identity: Nations in Turmoil (Hanover, N.H.: University Press of New England, 1997); Raheem Quraishi, *The Assam Bloodbath: Who Is Responsible?* (Indianapolis: Trust, 1984); Santosh C. Saha, ed., *Religious Fundamentalism in the Contemporary World: Critical Social and Political Issues* (Lanham, Md.: Lexington Books, 2004); Santosh C. Saha and Thomas K. Carr, eds., *Religious Fundamentalism in Developing Countries* (Westport, Conn.: Greenwood Press, 2001); Peter van der Veer, *Religious Nationalism, Hindus and Muslims in India* (Berkeley: University of California Press, 1994).

Vishvakarma

Vishvakarma, "the one who does all action," is the architect and artisan among the Vedic gods. He fashions buildings for them and makes their weapons and implements. On Earth he is said to have fashioned the entire world, including men and women. He shares in sacrifices made by people to the other gods. The Ribhus, who make chariots and other objects for the gods, are said to be his pupils.

Vishvakarma persists in the mythology of the PURANAS, where he maintains his role as divine architect and artisan. There he is the son of BRAHMA and is said to have three eyes, a club, a gold crown, and a gold necklace, though there is no proliferation of iconography of him.

Further reading: John Dowson, *A Classical Dictionary of Hindu Mythology,* 12th ed. (Ludhiana: Lyall Book Depot, 1974); Alfred Hillebrandt, *Vedic Mythology,* 2 vols. (Delhi: Motilal Banarsidass, 1990); W. J. Wilkins, *Hindu Mythology, Vedic and Puranic,* 2d ed. (Calcutta: Rupa, 1973).

Vishvanath Temple, Benares

The Vishvanath Temple to Lord SHIVA in BENARES (Varanasi) replaced a temple destroyed in the 17th century by the Mughal emperor Aurangzeb, who built a mosque on the same site. The temple was rebuilt beside that mosque in 1776 by Rani

Ahalyabai of Indore. Its magnificent 70-foot spire is totally covered with over a ton of gold plate, giving it its popular name of the Golden Temple. It enshrines a Shiva LINGAM that is considered one of the 12 *jyotirlingas*, or lingams of divine light, in India.

Further reading: Diana L. Eck, *Banaras, City of Light* (New York: Columbia University Press, 1999); Stella Kramrisch and Raymond Burnier, *The Hindu Temple* (Delhi: Motilal Banarsidass, 1976); K. K. Moorthy, *The Lord Shiva to Be Adored: A Mini-Compendium of 300 Saivite Shrines, Inclusive of the Dwadasa Jyotirlinga Kshetras, Pancabhutashtas, Pancharamas Plus Those Situated in Nepal Srilanka and Vietnam and Indonesia* (Tirupati, Andhra Pradesh: Message, 1995).

Vithoba (Vitthoba, Vitthala)

Vithoba is a form of VISHNU or KRISHNA; his main shrine is in Pandharpur, Maharashtra. This was the favored shrine of the Maharasthran saint TUKARAM, whose poetic songs are often addressed to this divinity. Vithoba is worshipped in Maharashtra and in Karnataka (where he is called Vitthala). The god is generally depicted standing on a brick (his name derives from the Marathi word for brick) with his arms resting on his hips. In one hand is a pouch with pebbles in it and in his other hand is a conch.

It is said that Krishna, accompanied by the RISHI (seer) NARADA, once went to visit a certain Pundalika to observe his devotion to his elderly parents. They arrived while he was taking care of his parents. Without stopping his work, he threw a brick at Krishna and asked him to wait.

Further reading: G. A. Deleury, *The Cult of Vithoba* (Poona: Deccan College, Postgraduate and Research Institute, 1960); Kusumawati Deshpande and M. V. Rajadhyaksha, *History of Marathi Literature* (New Delhi: Sahitya Akademi, 1988); Eleanor Zelliot and Maxine Bertsen, *The Experience of Hinduism: Religion in Maharastra* (Albany: State University of New York Press, 1988).

Swami Vivekananda (1863–1902), founder of the Vedanta Society in the United States and the Ramakrishna Math and Mission in India *(Courtesy Vedanta Society, San Francisco)*

Vivekananda, Swami (1863–1902)
founder of Vedanta Society and Ramakrishna Math and Mission

Swami Vivekananda was a great teacher of Hinduism for the modern world. His missionary work played a major role in the consolidation of ADVAITA VEDANTA in India and its spread to the West. He founded the VEDANTA SOCIETY in the United States and the RAMAKRISHNA MATH AND MISSION in India.

Narendranath Datta was born on January 12, 1863, in Calcutta (Kolkata), West Bengal, to aristocratic Bengali parents: Viswanath Dutta and Bhuvaneswari Devi. He meditated from a very early age and entertained spiritual questions from childhood. His inquiries about God led him as a youth to the BRAHMO SAMAJ, a reform movement founded by Rammohun ROY, but he was not satisfied with the spirituality of the movement.

In November 1881, while studying at Calcutta University, he visited Sri RAMAKRISHNA, the famous mystic and priest at the KALI temple of Dakshineswar near Calcutta. Narendra was fascinated by Ramakrisha's claim that he saw God clearly, and he wanted to know more. Although responsible for the care of his poverty-stricken family upon the death of his father, Narendra continued his work at the university and his study with Ramakrishna. He spent five years in training with Ramakrishna, during which he became committed to renouncing all of life in quest of God-realization. Ramakrishna died of throat cancer in August 1886. Then Narendra and a small group of Ramakrishna's disciples took vows to become monks and renounce the world. In 1887 he took the vow of SANNYAS and became Swami Vivekananda (bliss of discernment).

With some other young monks, Vivekananda wandered all over the subcontinent, begging for food and lodging. In his travels he learned firsthand of the imbalances in Indian society and the inhumanity of the CASTE system. He began to see the need for social service for millions of poor Indians, not traditionally an interest of spiritual seekers in India.

In 1893 Vivekananda attended the WORLD PARLIAMENT OF RELIGIONS in Chicago, with the intent of representing the message of Hinduism to the West. He was the most popular speaker at the parliament, giving classical, erudite dispositions on the nature and value of Hinduism, which excited many. From this success he began a tour of the United States, lecturing in the Midwest and New York City, where in 1895 he founded the Vedanta Society of New York, the first Hindu organization founded in the United States.

Upon his return to India in 1897, he found that his success in the West had increased his renown. He gathered his brother monks and founded the Ramakrishna Math and Mission, whose very name emphasized Ramakrishna's unification of the monastic life with social service. He found a site for the monastery at Belur and began relief work in nearby Calcutta. He worked with SARADA DEVI, Sri Ramakrishna's widow, to serve the poor. The Ramakrishna Math and Mission is today one of the largest monastic orders in Hinduism.

His teaching centered around *advaita* Vedanta and he constantly pointed to the identity of each person with the highest BRAHMAN. He believed that no one could be free until all are free. Even the desire for personal salvation should be relinquished in favor of tireless work for the salvation of others.

Vivekananda wanted to raise the inferior status of women in Hinduism by including them in spiritual life. He worked with many women in India, including Sarada Devi and Sister NIVEDITA, and with many Western disciples in promoting the education of and service to women. He insisted that the women of India must be able to meet the modern age with adequate education; it was the topic of one of his many books.

Vivekananda made a second visit to the West in 1899–1900, during which he founded other Vedanta Centers.

He was only 39 when he died on July 4, 1902, at Belur Math near Calcutta.

Further reading: Marie Louise Burke, *Swami Vivekananda in America: New Discoveries* (Calcutta: *advaita* Ashrama, 1958); Sailendra Nath Dhar, *A Comprehensive Biography of Swami Vivekananda,* 2 vols. (Madras: Vivekananda Prakashan Kendra, 1975); *Reminiscences of Swami Vivekananda by His Eastern and Western Admirers* (Calcutta: *advaita* Ashrama, 1961); Romain Rolland, *The Life of Vivekananda and the Universal Gospel* (Mayavati, Almora: *advaita* Ashrama, 1944); Swami Vivekananda, *The Complete Works of Swami Vivekananda,* 12 vols. (Calcutta: *advaita* Ashrama, 1965).

vows (vratas)

Vows or *vratas* are a central feature of Hinduism and JAINISM. They are undertaken for myriad reasons, but always with the desire of pleasing the divinity. Vows are often taken to do a particular thing in exchange for help from God. For instance, a mother might promise to donate a sum of money to a certain divinity's temple, if her gravely ill child should recover. A person might carry out a vow to shave his or her head and make a PILGRIMAGE to a god's temple in exchange for success on exams or to get a male child.

In times past very severe vows were sometimes taken. People were known to starve themselves to death in exchange for a divinity's promise to remove a curse on their family; others vowed that if a son were born they would offer him up to a renunciatory order upon his coming of age. Indian mythology records innumerable severe vows. Ravana the demon king, for instance, took a vow to stand on one toe for 10,000 years in order to win overlordship of the universe.

Most vows in modern times involve fasting, celibacy, pilgrimage, study of sacred books, feeding of BRAHMINS or mendicants, or limited vows of abstention. *Vratas* can be classified in different ways. One classification divides them into those that are bodily, those that pertain to speech, and those that pertain to the mind. Another type of classification is related to duration and timing of the vow, whether for a day, several years, until the fortnight is over, or until a certain star appears. A third classification is according to the divinity for whom the vow is performed. Last are vows that are specific to certain CASTES or communities.

To be valid, vows must almost always begin in a condition of ceremonial purity. Most vows begin early in the morning. Festivals, in general, often entail vows taken by various family members; typically they involve fasting, but they may also involve celibacy, service to the divinity, and pilgrimage.

There is a long list of special days appropriate to specific vows, usually entailing particular obligations of worship and observances. A devotee might vow to worship the Sun and fast on the day of Acalasaptami; to worship LAKSHMI at the base of a tree during Navaratri; to abstain from plowing on AMBUVACHI; to abstain from fish on Bakapancaka; or to bathe three times and make special offerings to the ancestors on Bhismapanchaka. Certain days of the month are auspicious for particular vows. The 11th of the month is observed as a fast day by many Hindus. The *Caturvargacintamani* of Hemadri (c. 13th century) lists nearly 700 such vows.

Further reading: Sudhir Ranjan Das, *A Study of Vrata-Rites*. Foreword by Nirmal Kumar Bose (Calcutta: S. C. Kar, 1953); Swami Harshananda, *Hindu Festivals and Holy Days* (Bangalore: Ramakrishna Math, 1994); Anne Mackenzie Pearson, *Because It Gives Me Peace: Ritual Fasts in the Religious Lives of Hindu Women* (Albany: State University of New York Press, 1996).

vratas   *See* VOWS.

Vrindavan   *See* BRINDAVAN.

Vyasa (or Vedavyasa)

Vyasa (arranger or compiler) is the sage or RISHI who compiled all the VEDAS. He did not "write"them—they are eternal MANTRAS that are received by different *rishis* in different eras, as the world is re-created. He is identified with the Vyasa who recited the ancient MAHABHARATA story to the god GANESHA, who wrote it down. In the Mahabharata Vyasa is also called Krishna Dvaipayana. The Vedavyasa who composed the most commonly consulted Sanskrit commentary on the YOGA SUTRA is also considered to be the same person.

Further reading: Bruce Sullivan, *Krsna Dvaipanaya Vyasa and the Mahabharata: A New Interpretation* (Leiden: E. J. Brill, 1990); ———, "The Religious Authority of the *Mahabharata*: Vyasa and Brahma in the Hindu Scriptural Tradition," *Journal of the American Academy of Religion* 62, no. 2 (1994): 377–401; ———, "The Unworshipped Avatar: Vyasa's Relationship to Vishnu and Brahma," *Journal of Vaisnava Studies* 4 (Summer 1996): 57–64.

women and Hinduism

Hinduism, because of its extreme diversity throughout the ages, has encompassed complex systems of thought and social hierarchies, which defy any simple generalizations. This overview of the status and role of women in Hindu India, and of the culture's attitudes toward them, reflects that variety. It should be born in mind that social correlates of gender, such as CASTE, class, stage of life, age, and family membership, are all variables that significantly affect the position of women in Hindu society, so that women in Hinduism demonstrate significant differences in their lives.

It is the case that in prehistory everywhere there were significantly more autonomy and sexual freedom for women (and men) than in later times. There are indications, certainly, that in pre-Vedic times in India (before 1500 B.C.E.), such freedom and autonomy existed among the pre-ARYAN tribal people who inhabited every corner of India. Tribal groups such as the Santals to this day do not restrict women's sexuality and action in any way as their more staid counterparts in the larger culture do. Ancient Tamil poetry, dated as early as 300 B.C.E., shows women freely choosing sexual partners before marriage and relying upon love marriages rather than family arrangements.

Also, groups such as the Nayars show that matriliny and matrilocality, which must be associated with more supportive lives for women, were probably fairly common in the Indian, pre-Aryan substratum that provides the cultural undergirding for much of later Hinduism.

A pattern develops, visible in the Brahminical texts, of women's having roles in the early Vedic culture (1500–800 B.C.E.) that began to be denied them even in the late Vedic period. Some RISHIS, for instance, were arguably women, and in the White YAJUR VEDA there are chants that can be performed only by a woman who knows Sanskrit. Though Hindu tradition even up to the present day understands that women were *never* allowed to recite the VEDAS or even witness a Vedic ritual, these examples indicate that this rule was not strictly observed in early Vedic tradition.

When hierarchies of society begin to be created in association with the creation of historical cities worldwide (in India beginning around 800 B.C.E.), such social developments generally result in the restriction of the rights of women. So was it in India, where women began to be subjugated more and more to family and husband and began to lose their role as independent actors. But as soon as the early urban period had come to fruition, perhaps as early as 400 C.E., women began to participate as direct actors in the devotional movements and play important roles there. A good example is Karaikkal Ammaiyar (400 C.E.), who became the first of the 63 Shaivite saints.

Movements like these pointed toward spiritual equality for women and, though the women saints form the exception to the rule of social constraints for women, they were prominent and numerous for many centuries leading up to the modern era. More than one movement, such as the VIRASHAI-VAS of Karnataka in the 11th century, called for spiritual equality for women and equal access to spiritual leadership. Sikhs, starting in the 15th century, held similar views, and the saint-poets of North India directly questioned the notion that gender should have any role in determining spiritual development or accomplishment.

When modernity comes forward in the 18th through 20th centuries and radically changes traditions such as child marriage, dowry, the ban on widow remarriage, and the custom of the childless wife's burning herself on the funeral pyre of her older husband, it must be understood that these traditions had not been unchallenged and contested in different regions and different movements within Hinduism's large umbrella. It is important to emphasize that modern India's legal rectification of these negative cultural sanctions upon women was complete, even though legal actions have not completely solved these problems. Histories of oppression are not solved overnight by the passing of just laws, but these bold legal measures are significant for a young postcolonial, independent nation.

MODERNIZATION

Modernization is dramatically affecting the social and religious lives of women in India. Since independence, India has sought to throw off the cloak of traditional prejudices related to caste, race, religion, and gender. While traditional practices that contribute to the low status of women in India, such as child marriage, *sati* (widow self-immola-

tion), dowry, and female infanticide, are illegal, these practices continue in some areas and among groups who have low socioeconomic status.

Traditional Indian cultural practices have usually been given religious justification, even when the scriptural bases for such practices were nonexistent, as was often the case with women's issues. In the extremely heterogeneous society that is India today, cultural practices cannot easily be distinguished from the religiously sanctioned prescriptions and proscriptions of Hinduism.

Hindu women in India occupy a broad range of statuses, varying from the most modernized, educated, and independent to some of the most traditional, least educated, and subordinate. Within India today, social class is more important in determining the status of women than is caste membership. Educated, urbanized women often marry outside caste, religion, and nationality. It is becoming more common for newly married couples to choose their own place of residence after marriage, so that they are not within the joint family system. As a result, many elderly women and men no longer receive care from younger generations but are being placed in nursing homes where neglect can be a problem.

FEMINISM

On the whole, Indian women, even proponents of women's rights and equality, resist the term *feminist,* which is often associated with aggressiveness, sexual permissiveness, immodesty, and a lack of womanly virtues; feminists are assumed to be against motherhood, family values, and men. For many the image of feminism is too directly discordant with the image of the "ideal woman" in Hindu society as defined in the Brahminic scriptures or *puranas*. Even filmmakers, writers, and artists whose work aims to castigate male privilege and sexist attitudes often reject the label *feminist*.

Modern reform movements to improve the status of women first arose in the 19th century, after the country had entered the mainstream of world civilization under British imperial rule. Both women and men worked together to improve the conditions of women's lives. Reform was strongest in Bengal and Maharashtra and tended to focus on ideals of family and society, rather than the independence and autonomy of women.

A new women's movement emerged in India in the 1970s, unaligned with any political parties and uninfluenced by foreign or government funding. Primarily composed of female volunteers, these women have sought to highlight the misogynist aspects inherent within Hinduism, advocate for women's rights over their own bodies and sexuality, and undermine tolerance for domestic violence. They have had to contend not only against nationalist elements, but also against Leftist resistance to discussing the oppression of women.

The opening up of the domestic economy to liberalization and globalization since the early 1990s has affected the outlook of the feminist movement in India. Various nongovernmental organizations funded by foreign aid have shown interest in some of the demands of the women's movement.

WOMEN AND THE SACRED

Hindu women have the feminine divine before them all the time, as the Hindu tradition preserves a worship of the GODDESS that probably dates from the Neolithic. Many divine tales recount the supremacy of the female aspect of the divine over the masculine. Through this access, women gain power in being and bearing; yet, in the social sphere, women have generally not been given freedom to reflect the powerful goddesses overtly. In Hindu society one can often hear a man say that his sister or wife is the "goddess" and, therefore, should be treated well and respected. Social conditions, however, support significant oppression of Indian women, especially those of lower social standing.

The goddesses who become role models for Indian women are not those that show autonomy and independence but those that embody subordinate roles. SITA, the obedient wife of Lord Rama, is the traditional role model for Hindu women. Women understand that the fierce goddesses (which Western women often view as inspiring) are goddesses that are not to be imitated. Uncontrolled by society and convention, powerful goddesses are not seen as role models. One of the greatest insults to an Indian woman is to be called a KALI.

As is the case in most of the world, women in India have throughout the centuries been the main cultural transmitters of myths and story and simple religious practices. While history records the lives of great male SWAMIS and teachers, little is recorded of the prayers, vows, and devotions of Hindu women who take on the tasks of assuring the welfare of their families by asking for divine intercession and aid. Yet, it is this integrative function performed by women that connects the everyday world to the cosmic order, even as it sacralizes the universe—an essential Hindu practice. While males, in the main, were free to develop philosophies and movements, women, forced into more limited roles, creatively reached out to the forces of the universe to preserve and protect their loved ones and provide for a harmonious and fruitful society. For every wandering ascetic who did his renunciation for higher spiritual gain, one could count, contemporaneously, thousands of individual women who practiced vows, fasts, and disciplines to ensure the welfare of those around them. This role of women as powerful religious and spiritual actors, although recognized in the culture, is largely unrecorded. The paucity of women saints in the history of Hindu tradition belies the agency that women have exerted in the temples, shrines, and households of India over the centuries. This agency has been central to the continuity of Hinduism over time.

Further reading: Frederique Apfel-Marglin, *Wives of the Godking* (Delhi: Oxford University Press, 1985); Mandakranta Bose, ed., *Faces of the Feminine in Ancient, Medieval, and Modern India* (Oxford: Oxford University Press, 2000); Thomas Coburn, *Encountering the God-*

dess: A Translation of the Devi Mahtamya and a Study of Its Interpretation (Albany: State University of New York Press, 1991); Vidya Dehejia, *Yogini Cult and Temples: A Tantric Tradition* (New Delhi: National Museum, 1986); Rita M. Gross, *Feminism and Religion* (Boston: Beacon Press, 1996); John Stratton Hawley and Donna Marie Wulff, eds., *The Divine Consort: Radha and the Goddesses of India* (Boston: Beacon Press, 1982); Alf Hiltebeitel and Kathleen M. Erndl, *Is the Goddess a Feminist? The Politics of South Asian Goddesses* (New York: New York University Press, 2000); Donna Jordan, "A Post Orientalist History of the Fierce Shakti of the Subaltern Domain." (Ph.D. diss., California Institute of Integral Studies, San Francisco, 1999); Julia Leslie, ed., *Roles and Rituals for Hindu Women* (Delhi: Motilal Banarsidass, 1991); Sara S. Mitter, *Dharma's Daughters* (New Brunswick, N.J.: Rutgers University Press, 1991); Vasudha Narayanan, "Brimming with Bhakti, Embodiments of Shakti: Devotees, Deities, Performers, Reformers, and Other Women of Power in the Hindu Tradition," in Arvind Sharma and Katherine K. Young, eds., *Feminism and World Religions* (Albany: State University of New York Press, 1999); Lucinda Joy Peach, *Women and World Religions* (Upper Saddle River, N.J.: Prentice Hall, 2002); David Smith, *Hinduism and Modernity* (Malden, Mass.: Blackwell, 2003); Katherine Young, "Hinduism," in Arvind Sharma, ed., *Women in World Religions* (Albany: State University of New York Press, 1987).

Woodroffe, Sir John (Arthur Avalon)
(1865–1936) *scholar of tantric texts*

Sir John Woodroffe was an Englishman, Indian civil servant, and scholar who pioneered the modern study of the tantric literary tradition.

Woodroffe was born December 15, 1865, the eldest son of James T. Woodroffe, advocate-general of Bengal and occasional member of the government of India, and his wife, Florence. John was educated at Woburn Park School and University College, Oxford, where he studied law. He was called to the Bar by the Inner Temple in 1889. He soon served as advocate of the Calcutta (Kolkata)

High Court and was made a fellow of Calcutta University and appointed Tagore Professor of Law. He served as judge on the High Court and in 1915 served as chief justice.

In addition to his practice and writing on jurisprudence, Woodruffe studied SANSKRIT and Hindu philosophy extensively, particularly TANTRIC literature. As a result of long and assiduous study of classical texts and contacts with tantric pundits of Bengal, he translated important tantric texts and added his own commentary and introductions. His publication *The Garland of Letters* is a clear and authoritative exposition of the *Mantra Shastra* and includes his explanation of the philosophy underlying tantric philosophy and practice.

Around 1910, Woodroffe was initiated by Shivachandra Vidyarnava. He did not take students, but rather remained a scholar, intent upon providing clear and authoritative translations and expositions that would be appreciated only decades after his death.

His publications have left an enduring legacy of original resources translated into English and valuable commentary on tantra. He collaborated with a fellow initiate, Atal Behari Ghose, in producing the first translations and interpretations of tantra in a Western language. Because Ghose remained anonymous in his publications, Woodroffe also published under a pseudonym, Arthur Avalon. Under the name Avalon, he published *Shakti and Shakta,* commentaries on the *Shakta Tantra Shastra,* and under the name Woodroffe, he published *The Garland of Letters,* a commentary on the *Mantra Shastra.* He lectured in England and India, including addresses to the Royal Asiatic Society and the Vivekananda Society. After retirement from legal work in India, he returned to England and served as reader in Indian law at the University of Oxford. He died there on January 18, 1936.

Further reading: Arthur Avalon, (Sir John Woodroffe), *Shakti and Shakta,* 2 vols. (Madras: Ganesh, 1959);

———, *The Tantra of the Great Liberation (Mahanirvana Tantra)* (London: Luzac, 1913); Shiva Chandra Vidyarnava Bhattacharya, *Principles of Tantra*, edited by Sir John Woodroffe, 5th ed. (Madras: Ganesh, 1978); Purnananda, *The Serpent Power*. Translated by Arthur Avalon, 4th ed. (Madras: Ganesh, 1950); Sir John George Woodroffe (Arthur Avalon), *Bharata Shakti: Collection of Addresses on Indian Culture*, 3d ed. (Madras: Ganesh, 1921); ———, *The Garland of Letters (Varnamala): Studies in the Mantra Shastra*, 3d ed. (Madras: Ganesh, 1955); ———, *Introduction to Tantra Shastra*, 2d ed. (Madras: Ganesh, 1952); ———, *The World as Power: Reality, Life, Mind, Matter, Causality and Continuity*, 3d ed. (Madras: Ganesh, 1966).

World Parliament of Religions
(Chicago, 1893)

The World Parliament of Religions was the first interfaith religious convention in the West to introduce major Eastern religions to a public audience. Held in conjunction with the Chicago World's Fair, the opening ceremonies were attended by 4,000 people in the newly opened Hall of Columbus. Originally the idea of Charles Carroll Bonney, a Chicago attorney with an interest in comparative religion, the parliament was organized by a Presbyterian minister, John Henry Barrows (1847–1902), as one of 20 congresses covering a number of topics, including women's progress, temperance, commerce, literature, music, and agriculture. Representatives of the Roman Catholic Church, Greek Orthodox Church, Confucianism, Buddhism, JAINISM, Hinduism, and Protestantism addressed the audiences over the course of two weeks, creating a climactic event for the closing of the 19th century. A number of Christian faiths refused to send representatives to a forum that would valorize "false faiths."

Unprecedented attention was given to Asian religions; their beliefs and practices were explained directly by adept practitioners from the Orient. Hinduism was represented by Swami VIVEKANANDA and Nara Sima Charyar; JAINISM by Virchand R.

Gandhi; the BRAHMO SAMAJ by Protap Chunder Mozoomdar and B. B. Nagarkar; and THEOSOPHY by G. N. Chakravarti. The largest Asian contingent was made up of representatives of Buddhism, from Sri Lanka and Japan. The goal was to have a personal spokesperson for every religion, an ambitious and impossible ideal to meet. In fact, major Asian religions were represented by practitioners of only one or two sects within each larger religious complex. In the case of Hinduism, Swami Vivekananda's remarks represented VEDANTA philosophy and practice but gave no understanding of popular forms of SHAIVISM or VAISHNAVISM.

Most presentations and papers focused on the areas of agreement between Western and Eastern religions. Several problems between East and West were addressed repeatedly, particularly the misrepresentations of Oriental religions in the West and the destructive ardor and arrogance of Christian missionaries in the East. The entire September 22 session was "Criticism and Discussion of Missionary Methods." Both negative and positive assessments of the parliament were made by missionaries, yet, whatever the final evaluation, missionary delegates revealed a new awareness of the appeal of Asian religion and the need for changes in missionary methods.

Protap Chunder Mozoomdar, representative of the Brahmo Samaj, while vociferously condemning the social abuses of India, explained the "world's religious debt to Asia." He cited a higher view of nature, recognition of the value of introspection, and the crucial roles of devotional activity and self-discipline in a full religious life. His prominence at the world parliament was the second time he had influenced American audiences with his words of tolerance. His visit in 1883–84 to the United States preceded the parliament by a decade and constituted the first visit of a Hindu teacher to the United States.

Swami Vivekananda, with fluency in the English language and a commanding stage presence, was a sensation with all of his addresses. He became a celebrity as he adroitly rejected, in memorable phrases and stories, Western notions of Hinduism as polytheistic and idolatrous. Vivekananda's clear exposition of tolerance toward other faiths as the essence of Hinduism was a revolutionary addition to the West's understanding.

The press noted the masterful oration and erudition of Oriental delegates and commented on the arrogance of Western churches that sent partially educated students of theology to instruct the wise and accomplished spiritual leaders of the East. One missionary to India for many years, the Reverend Thomas Slater of the London Missionary Society, observed, "The Hindus, by instinct and tradition, are the most religious people in the world."

A number of delegates from the East had been or were in 1893 members of the Theosophical Society. Peppered throughout the remarks from Asian representatives were ideas about synthetic religion, a clear influence from Theosophy. Theosophists termed the parliament a "distinctly Theosophical step."

Although most of the population of the UNITED STATES and the West in general were unaware of the proceedings of the parliament, the concluding remarks of the session lauded the event as perhaps the most important religious gathering ever assembled. The parliament encouraged a growing conviction that the features that believers held in common were essential characteristics of all religions, and that tolerance and charity among all religions were more important than differences in belief. Most certainly, the parliament created a new appreciation of Oriental religions.

Further reading: John Henry Barrows, ed., *The World's Parliament of Religions*, 2 vols. (Chicago: Parliament, 1893); Charles C. Bonney, "The Genesis of the World's Religious Congresses of 1893," *New Church Review* 1 (January 1894): 73–100; Walter R. Houghton, ed., *Neely's History of the Parliament of Religions and Religious Congresses of the World's Congress Auxiliary of the World's Columbian Exposition, Chicago, 1893,* 2 vols. (Chicago: Rand McNally, 1893); Carl T. Jackson, *The Oriental Religions and American Thought: Nineteenth-* *Century Explorations* (Westport, Conn.: Greenwood Press, 1981); Clay Lancaster, *The Incredible World's Parliament of Religions at the Chicago Columbian Exposition of 1893: A Comparative and Critical Study* (Fontwell, England: Centaur Press, 1987); Richard Hughes Seager, *The World's Parliament of Religions: The East/West Encounter, Chicago, 1893* (Bloomington: Indiana University Press, 1992).

World Plan Executive Council   *See* TRANSCENDENTAL MEDITATION.

World Vaishnavite Association (est. 1994)

The World Vaishnavite Association was formed in 1994, in large part to heal the splintering that had occurred around the International Society for Krishna Consciousness (ISKCON) in the years following the death of its founder, Srila A. C Bhaktivedanta Swami PRABHUPADA (1896–1977). ISKCON taught a form of devotional (BHAKTI) yoga in the tradition of CHAITANYA Mahaprabhu (1486–1533). ISKCON had been the leader and role model for this form of worship in the 20th century. It rapidly expanded during the 1960s, but in the years since Prabhupada's death in 1977, the organization has faced a variety of leadership problems and experienced a number of schisms in different parts of the world. Additionally, new organizations emerged in India from the GAUDIYA MATH, the spiritual home of Prabhupada prior to his founding of ISKCON.

The World Vaishnavite Association was formed to address issues and heal the divisions that had occurred within the movement. Despite unity of faith and practice, numerous differences concerning organization and the nature of leadership existed. Some groups thought that the leadership style followed by Sri Prabhupada should continue and that current SWAMIS should be venerated in the same exalted manner as Prabhupada. Others thought Prabhupada unique and eschewed any veneration of the current GURUS. More than two dozen factions emerged.

Efforts began in the 1980s to gather together the factions. Gradually the idea of forming an association emerged. At a meeting in 1994, the group convinced the 97-year-old Srila B. P. Puri Maharaj to take charge of the association. They also invited the leaders of splinter groups to participate. In February 1994, they published the initial copy of a periodical. The *World Vaisnava Association Newsletter* was distributed to every group from the Gaudiya Math lineage to keep them apprised of developments. In November 1994 a founding meeting was held with 120 participants. Twenty-eight ACHARYAS and SANNYASIS became founding members.

The WVA does not facilitate guru-student relationships; nor does it create ASHRAMS. Its role is to promote the teaching and spiritual enhancement of SANATANA DHARMA, the vital and legitimate teachings of Hinduism. Its theological approach is theist, a belief in a personal deity that deserves love and veneration. The WVA tries to help communities through troubling times in the regions where it has a presence and to promote missionary efforts outside India. The WVA attempts to mediate between affiliated groups. Any ISKCON-based group can join. The headquarters of the association is in the sacred city of BRINDAVAN, India, the mythological home of KRISHNA.

Further reading: *World Vaisnava Association.* Available online. URL: http://www.wva-vvrs.org/. Accessed August 16, 2005.

Y

yajna

Yajna is from the Sanskrit root *yaj*, "to honor a god with oblations." A *yajna* is a ritual involving oblations in the Vedic tradition. It may be simply an offering of clarified butter into a fire, or it may involve 17 priests in an elaborate 12-day ritual including the building of a large fire altar as in the Agnichayana. The ritual of the *yajna* always includes a fire, Sanskrit mantras, and some sort of offering. In the larger public rituals a sacrifice of some animal or animals has been common. The word *yajna* is frequently translated roughly as "sacrifice."

Further reading: Jan Gonda, *Vedic Literature (Samhitas and Brahmanas): A History of Indian Literature,* Vol. 1, no. 1 (Wiesbaden: Otto Harrassowitz, 1975); Thomas Hopkins, *The Hindu Religious Tradition* (Encino, Calif.: Dickenson, 1971); Frits Staal, *AGNI: The Altar of Fire,* 2 vols. (Berkeley, Calif.: Asian Humanities Press, 1983).

Yajnavalkya (c. 700 B.C.E.)

Yajnavalkya was the most prominent sage named in the Upanishads. He was a student of Aruni. His teachings are recorded in dialogues in the Brihadaranyaka Upanishad and the Chandogya Upanishad. In one teaching he is asked how many gods there are and he answers: "Three hundred and three and three thousand and three." Pressed to be clearer he says there are 33. He is questioned again and again and eventually arrives at the statement that there is only one "God," the Brahman, or all. In another dialogue one of his wives asks him whether wealth could make her immortal and he propounds a notion that everything that exists is underlain by one reality, which is what is to be held dear, not wealth.

Yajnavalkya was said to have been the source for the White Yajur Veda. The Yajnavalkya whose name is attached to an important text of Dharmashastra is unlikely to be the same individual.

Further reading: Swami Brahmananda, *The Philosophy of Sage Yajnavalkya: A Free Rendering of the Yajnavalkya Kanda of the Brihadaranyaka Upanishad as Expounded in the Atma Purana* (Shivanandanagar: Divine Life Society, 1981); Shoun Hino and K. P. Jog, eds. and trans., *Suresvara's Vartika on Yajnavalkya's Dialogue with Artabhaga and Others* (Delhi: Motilal Banarsidass, 1999); Swami Satchidanandendra Sarasvati, *The Vision of Atman: Yajnavalkya's Initiation of Maitreyi into the Intuition of Reality* (Holenarsipur: Adhyatma Prakasha Karyalaya, 1970).

Yajur Veda

The Yajur Veda is the VEDA of the sacrificial formula, the YAJUS. The priest of the Yajur Veda, the ADHVARYU, is responsible for the major sacrificial duties at the Vedic ritual, including pouring oblations and killing the sacrificial animals in the prescribed way. The formulas from the Yajur Veda must be uttered in proper fashion at the proper times.

The Yajur Veda consists to a large extent of passages from the RIG VEDA rearranged for sacrificial purposes. The Yajur Veda has two recensions: the White and the Black. The White Yajur Veda consists of hymns alone, numbering around 800. The Black Yajur Veda includes the exact same hymns, but it intersperses the explanatory. BRAH-MANA sections among the hymns. It is apparently this "muddied" or mixed aspect of the Veda that caused it to be named the Black Yajur Veda.

Further reading: J. Gonda, *Vedic Literature (Samhitas and Brahmanas): A History of Indian Literature*, Vol. 1, no. 1 (Wiesbaden: Otto Harrassowitz, 1975); R. T. Griffith, trans., *The Hymns of the Yajurveda* (Benares: Chowkhamba, 1957); Arthur Berriedale Keith, *The Religion and Philosophy of the Veda and Upanishads* (Westport, Conn.: Greenwood Press, 1971); ———, trans., *The Veda of the Black Yajus School, Entitled Taittiriya Sanhita* (Cambridge, Mass.: Harvard University Press, 1914).

yaksha (fem. yakshi)

In the VEDA a *yaksha* was a deity or divinity. Later the term designated certain semidivine beings. These *yakshas* could change form at will; they lived in caves, mountains, forests, trees, bodies of water, and even magic cities in the sky. They are roughly analogous to gnomes, fairies, or sprites in the European tradition. *Yakshas* or *yakshis* were often associated with sacred trees in villages. Indian temple iconography often depicts trees with beautiful *yakshis* sensuously entwined.

Such *yakshas* and *yakshis* turn up in the MAHAB-HARATA and the RAMAYANA, and in greater numbers in the PURANAS and in the works of such great SAN-SKRIT poets as KALIDASA and BHAVABHUTI. The earliest Indian sculptures, which tend to be Buddhist (c. 200 B.C.E.), are replete with *yaksas* and *yakshis;* they are well known in Buddhist literature as well.

Yakshas also appear in Jain sculpture and literature (*see* JAINISM). Some Jain temples show *yakshis* particularly in subsidiary shrines. Finally, in the Hindu *puranas, yakshas* are also frequently encountered. In physical form they tend to be very handsome or beautiful, and they are very prosperous as well. KUBERA, the god of wealth, is always depicted as attended by *yaksas.*

Further reading: Ananda K. Coomaraswamy, *Yakshas* (New Delhi: Munshiram Manoharlal, 2001); Ram Nath Misra, *Yaksha Cult and Iconography* (New Delhi: Munshiram Manoharlal, 1981).

Yama

Yama is the Indian god of death and the underworld. He is the son of Visvasvat, the Sun. In the VEDAS he is seen as the first mortal to die and thereby becomes king of the world of the dead. According to the Atharva Veda, he is accompanied by two four-eyed dogs in his realm. There he dwells with the ancestors, who receive offerings of food from men.

In the Vedic context, the realm of the dead is quite unlike the Christian hell; it is an afterworld of satisfaction and pleasures. One verse of the RIG VEDA mentions Yama's twin sister, Yami, who asks him to mate with her to create the human race. Yama refuses.

The ancient Iranian Avesta knows Yama by the name Yima. In later *puranic* descriptions Yama's realm is depicted less pleasantly; karmic retributions are even meted out (*see* KARMA). Yama in his role as guardian of the realm of the dead appears in many contexts in Indian tradition. In the KATHA UPANISHAD he offers the wisdom of BRAHMAN, ATMAN, and liberation to the young NACHIKETAS. In the MAHABHARATA he plays an important role in the story of SAVITRI and Satyavan.

Further reading: John Dowson, *A Classical Dictionary of Hindu Mythology and Religion, Geography, History, and Literature,* 12th ed. (Ludhiana: Lyall Book Depot, 1974); Alfred Hillebrandt, *Vedic Mythology* 2 vols. (Delhi: Motilal Banarsidass, 1990); Kusum P. Merh, *Yama, the Glorious Lord of the Other World* (New Delhi: D. K. Printworld, 1996); W. J. Wilkins, *Hindu Mythology, Vedic and Puranic,* 2d ed. (Calcutta: Rupa, 1973).

yama

The eightfold path (ASHTANGA) of Patanjali's yoga stresses observance of the "five *yamas*" or moral restraints: AHIMSA, avoiding causing pain or injury to any creature; *satya,* speaking the truth; *asteya,* not stealing; BRAHMACHARYA, sexual abstinence; and *aparigraha,* not being acquisitive. All of these restraints are developed to ever higher levels as YOGA progresses, so that "speaking the truth" becomes a struggle to avoid even the desire to lie.

Though some say that these constraints are not part of yoga per se, in fact a focus on these constraints is a common yogic practice. Furthermore, the other branches or elements of the eightfold path such as "concentration" (*dharana*) are seen as enhancing and perfecting the *yamas.*

Further reading: Swami Hariharananda Aranya, *Yoga Philosophy of Patanjali* (Albany: State University of New York Press, 1983); M. N. Dvivedi, trans., *The Yoga-Sutras of Patanjali: Sanskrit Text and English Translation Together, with an Introduction and an Appendix, and Notes on Each Sutra Based upon Several Authentic Commentaries* (Delhi: Sri Satguru, 1980); Ganganatha Jha, trans., *The Yoga-Darshana, Comprising the Sutras of Patanjali—with the Bhasya of Vyasa* (Madras: Theosophical Publishing House, 1934).

Yamuna (Jumna) River

The Yamuna River flows past Delhi and past the sacred sites of Mathura and BRINDAVAN and meets the GANGES at ALLAHABAD (Prayag). The deity Yamuna is seen as a GODDESS mounted on a tortoise, carrying a blue lotus, a fly whisk, and a water pot. (A beautiful sandstone statue of her is found at Aihole in Karnataka, dating from the seventh century.) Sometimes Yamuna is understood to be the sister of the god of death, YAMA. One of the greatest Indian festivals, the KUMBHA MELA, is celebrated at the conjunction of the Yamuna and the Ganges.

Further reading: David L. Haberman, *River of Love in an Age of Pollution: The Yamuna River of Northern India* (Berkeley: University of California Press, 2006); Sudhakar Pandey, *Ganga and Yamuna in Indian Art and Literature* (Chandigarh: Indra Prakashan, 1984).

yantra

A *yantra* is a meditative and ritual drawing or design used particularly in Indian TANTRIC YOGA. It is almost always drawn with colored powder on the floor or ground in a ritual process. It it usually a geometric pattern, with flowers or flower petals. Once it is completed, a MEDITATION is performed, focusing on the center of the *yantra,* which is most often the BINDU, a condensed point of consciousness out of which the universe is seen to evolve.

The *yantra* is usually seen as the subtle form of the divinity; when one creates a *yantra* one manifests an alternative form of the totality of the divinity for more focused ritual and worship. In ritual and meditation, one moves outward from the *bindu* to the other aspects and junctures of the design. Or, one may begin at the outer edge of the design and work inward toward the *bindu.* The *yantra* may in certain circumstances be worshipped in and of itself and in other circumstances will form a part of a much larger ritual. As with most tantric rituals, these are rarely performed in public.

Sometimes *yantras* are referred to as *mandalas.* The SRI YANTRA is sometimes called Sri Chakra. Buddhism and JAINISM also use *yantras,* though in Buddhism they will generally be referred to as *mandalas.*

Further reading: Madhu Khanna, *Yantra, the Tantric Symbol of Cosmic Unity* (Rochester, Vt.: Inner Traditions, 2003); P. H. Pott, *Yoga and Yantra: Their Interrelation and Their Significance for Indian Archaeology.* Translated from the Dutch by Rodney Needham (The Hague: M. Nijhoff, 1966); S. K. Ramachandra Rao, *Sri-Chakra: Its Yantra, Mantra, and Tantra* (Bangalore: Kalpatharu Research Academy, 1982).

Yantra, Sri

The Sri YANTRA, or Sri Chakra, is an important cult object for the SRI VIDYA tradition of TANTRISM. It is understood as being the subtle form of the goddess Sri Lalita.

The *yantra*'s geometric design combines five downward-pointing triangles representing the Goddess, or SHAKTI, with four upward-pointing triangles representing SHIVA. In the "nine circuits," all the parts of the design are worshiped in turn: the junctures of the triangles, the central BINDU, certain outlying features such as circles of lotus petals, and the outer border that looks like a set of four entrances to a temple. The process can either begin with the *bindu* and work out to the edge, or follow the opposite path.

A new Sri Chakra is always carefully drawn whenever a PUJA to Sri Yantra is performed. The *pujas* that are done in this tradition are always performed privately, except for *pujas* done to the few large Sri Yantras found in select temples. An example is the KANCHIPURAM temple to Kamakshi, who is sometimes identified with Sri Lalita. In this temple there is a very large Sri Yantra that is worshiped by a designated priest in a secret way. This ritual is never witnessed by anyone, except the priest.

Further reading: Madhu Khanna, *Yantra, the Tantric Symbol of Cosmic Unity* (Rochester, Vt.: Inner Traditions, 2003); S. K. Ramachandra Rao, *Sri-Chakra: Its Yantra, Mantra, and Tantra* (Bangalore: Kalpatharu Research Academy, 1982); S. Shankaranarayanan, *Sri Chakra* (Pondicherry: Dipti, 1970).

Sri Yantra, symbol of the Goddess and ritual design for meditation

Yashoda

Yashoda is the cowherd woman, wife of Nanda, who became the foster mother of KRISHNA. The evil king Kamsa had determined to kill the first male child of Krishna's mother, DEVAKI, wife of his minister VASUDEVA, to avoid a prophecy that he would die at the hand of a son of Devaki. By divine intervention, when Krishna was born, all of the king's guards who kept watch over the couple fell asleep and he was delivered to Yashoda, who raised him. Yashoda has a special place in Krishna worship; poems and songs to her and of her can be found in every part of India.

Further reading: Cornelia Dimmitt and J. A. B. van Buitenen, *Classical Hindu Mythology: A Reader in the Sanskrit Puranas* (Philadelphia: Temple University Press, 1978); John Dowson, *A Classical Dictionary of Hindu Mythology and Religion, Geography, History, and Literature,* 12th ed. (Ludhiana: Lyall Book Depot, 1974); John S. Hawley, *At Play with Krishna: Pilgrim-*

age Dramas from Brindavan (Princeton, N.J.: Princeton University Press, 1981).

Yasodhara Ashram Society   *See* RADHA, SWAMI SHIVANANDA.

Yayati   *See* DEVAYANI AND YAYATI.

yoga (yogi, yogini)

Yoga is an ancient Hindu practice and belief system that aims at releasing the adept from the bonds of the endless cycle of birth and rebirth. The word *yoga* is derived from the root *yuj*, "to yoke," probably because the early practice concentrated on restraining or "yoking in" the senses. Later the name was also seen as a metaphor for "linking" or "yoking to" God or the divine.

The earliest form of yoga may have been the Jain yoga (c. 900 B.C.E.), which involved severe sensual denial and restraint (*see* JAINISM). To free the soul from birth and rebirth Jains felt it was necessary to restrain the senses completely so as to be beyond both "love" and "hate," or more accurately, beyond any positive or negative emotion. The early Jain monks and TIRTHANKARAS (perfected beings) would train themselves to ignore the body completely and to train the mind to ignore even the strongest positive and negative stimuli. The details of these ancient Jain practices are lost to us. Jain yoga today is focused more on restraining oneself to prevent injury to any living being, which was always a concern in that tradition.

An element of worldly denial has always been part of all yoga, and even today yogis can be found who perform extreme feats of restraint. Yoga of this sort is ultimately about controlling all bodily functions, so that even the autonomic nervous system can be under the adept's control. When SWAMI RAMA first traveled to the United States in the 1970s, he demonstrated such control by stopping his heart completely for more than a minute while being attached to a heart monitor.

The BUDDHA's yoga (c. 600 B.C.E.) was created specifically to counter the earlier push toward complete bodily denial. He declared that mental control was the final object of yoga and did not need to be accomplished by hurting the body. Central to his yoga were watching of the breath and observing of the sensations of the body.

The UPANISHADS (c. 900–300 B.C.E.) do not discuss yoga per se, but they point toward a mental practice that aims to realize the unity of one's own self with the ultimate Self. This yoga is known as JNANA YOGA, sometimes called "the Yoga of Knowledge." Nothing is said about postures and only one Upanishad speaks of sitting in a quiet place to meditate. A form of MEDITATION, however, seems to have been central to this type of yoga. A number of passages in the Upanishads imply both bodily denial and attention to the breath.

The BHAGAVAD GITA (c. 200 B.C.E.) makes the first mention of a yoga that uses focus on God as the central practice (in the later YOGA SUTRA, a focus on God is an adjunct practice to the central disciplines). The yoga developed in the Bhagavad Gita was called "devotional yoga," or BHAKTI YOGA. One focused one's mind in the same yogic way as in other practices, but one used God as a focus point for all consciousness. Nowadays the chanting of the Gita itself or other texts will be part of the practice.

The Bhagavad Gita also contains the earliest reference to KARMA YOGA—in which the focus is on good conduct in the world. One acts in a disinterested way without regard to the fruits of one's actions. This makes everyday life a form of yoga. MOHANDAS KARAMCHAND GANDHI considered this the most important yoga; he wrote extensively about this practice.

The ASHTANGA (eight-limbed) YOGA of PATANJALI (c. second century C.E.) involved a sitting yoga, sometimes called raja yoga, which focused on breathing. As one observed the breath, one developed ways of concentrating the mind and eventually controlling the mind. ASANAS, or postures, are well developed in today's versions of

PATANJALI yoga, but his Yoga Sutra does not list any postures; these may have been later additions to the practice, or they may have developed separately and then merged with the Patanjalian school. There are strong resemblances between the practices found in the early Buddhist texts and those found in Patanjali.

HATHA YOGA is an amalgam of practices that may have emerged separately and were later combined. It includes the basic practices that can be found in Patanjali as well as postures. The term *hatha* originally meant "violent," and it is possible that this style of yoga originated in certain types of severe yoga that were softened for protection of the body.

In some systems hatha yoga includes KUNDALINI YOGA as part of its path. The focus of breath control becomes the "serpent" or "Goddess Energy" (kundalini) at the base of the spine, which must be awakened and forced upward to pierce the psychic centers or CHAKRAS that run parallel to the spine. The NADIS or subtle bodily channels are used to guide breath into the central spinal channel to help the raising of the kundalini through the centers. Finally, the rising kundalini meets the god SHIVA at a point above the head called SAHASRARA CHAKRA. This meeting provokes absolute enlightenment. Kundalini yoga practice itself can vary; the kundalini methods used in hatha yoga are somewhat different from those used in TANTRA yoga.

Tantra is the most esoteric of all of the yogas. All yogas, and in fact all paths toward spiritual advance in the Indian tradition, depend upon the guidance of a GURU. However, the tantra yoga practices are so complicated and often dangerous that a guru is of the utmost importance. The basic realization of tantra yoga is that the phenomenal world is nothing but the divine truth—the transcendent and the earthly divinity are one and the same. Whereas other yogas look toward a retreat from the sensual, tantra plunges into the dangers of the senses in order to reach the highest realization.

This is true in particular of the notorious practices of "left-handed" tantra. In the process of worship the devotee (most often a male) drinks alcohol, eats the forbidden beef, and has sexual intercourse with a low-caste partner or "goddess." The sexual union is seen as the union of the divinity in its transcendent form with the divinity in its mundane aspect. The practice aims to produce an understanding of the divinity in its totality. Alcohol too helps teach about the "bliss" of the infinite. Eating forbidden beef and other acts normally thought as "polluting" teach that even the dirt and refuse in the world are essentially divine. "Right-handed" tantra yoga does not resort to these forbidden practices. It includes much ritual and chanting of MANTRAS to guide the consciousness to its chosen goal.

Apart from these general categories of yoga, many specialized disciplines have emerged, including KRIYA YOGA and Integral Yoga (*see* Sri AUROBINDO).

Further reading: S. N. Dasgupta, *The History of Indian Philosophy* (Delhi: Motilal Banarsidass, 1975); Georg Feuerstein, *The Yoga Sutra of Patanjali* (Rochester, Vt.: Inner Traditions International, 1989); Trevor Leggett, *Realization of the Supreme Self: The Bhagavad Gita Yogas* (New York: Kegan Paul International, 1995); Robert Svoboda, *Aghora: At the Left Hand of God* (Albuquerque, N. Mex.: Brotherhood of Life, 1998); Ian Whicher and David Carpenter, eds., *Yogas: The Indian Tradition* (New York: Routledge Curzon, 2003); Sir John Woodroffe, *Sadhana for Self-Realization: Mantras, Yantras and Tantras* (Madras: Ganesh, 1963); Vivian Worthington, *A History of Yoga* (Boston: Routledge & Kegan Paul, 1982).

Yogananda, Paramahansa (1893–1952)
kriya yoga *teacher and founder of Self-Realization Fellowship*

The founder of the influential SELF-REALIZATION FELLOWSHIP (SRF), Paramahansa Yogananda was one of the most successful missionaries for yoga in the West.

Born Mukunda Lal Ghosh on January 5, 1893, into an affluent Bengali family in Gorakhpur,

Paramahansa Yogananda learned Hindu spirituality early in life. His father, a railway executive, was a disciple of LAHIRI MAHASAYA, one of those who revived KRIYA YOGA in the 20th century. Mukunda relates that, as a child, he was healed by a photograph of Lahiri. After high school, Mukunda joined a hermitage in BENARES (Varanasi), the Sri Bharat Charma Mahamandal, where he met Sri YUKESWAR Giri. Sri Yukeswar gave him the vows of SANNYAS (renunciation) in the Shankaracharya Order, Giri branch, in 1914 and he became Yogananda, meaning the "bliss that comes from yoga."

In 1916 he discovered the techniques of Yogoda, a system of life-energy control for physical and spiritual development, which, combined with traditional yoga, became the central concern of his teachings. Yogananda expressed a sustained interest in education. He attended Scottish Church College and later transferred to Serampore College to be near Yukteswar. In 1917, he founded a school for boys, Yogoda San-Sanga Brahmacharya Vidyalaya, at Dihik, Bengal, and in 1918 moved the school to Ranchi. His school included high school subjects as well as yoga and MEDITATION.

In 1920 Yogananda went to the United States to speak at the International Congress of Religious Liberals in Boston, where he remained to teach for three years. In 1924 he conducted a lecture tour of the United States that resulted in the establishment of several centers in his name. An American headquarters for these centers was set up at Mount Washington in Los Angeles. His personality was extremely effective in relaying his message and the ancient wisdom of India to a Western audience.

Yogananda taught *kriya yoga*, which he describes as a scientific technique for God-realization. The practice is conveyed in an initiation ceremony and involves meditation and visualization. His approach to *kriya yoga* is presented as a form of raja yoga but also includes concepts and exercises similar to those of KUNDALINI YOGA.

Yogananda originally called his work the Yogoda Satsang Society, but, in 1935, he incorpo-

Paramahansa Yogananda (1893–1952), master of *kriya yoga* and founder of Self-Realization Fellowship *(Courtesy Self-Realization Fellowship, Encinitas, California)*

rated his organization as the Self-Realization Fellowship. His lectures were collected into a home correspondence course for students to study in any location. Also in 1935, he visited India for the last time and was given the title *Paramahansa*, meaning "great swan," because his guru recognized that Yogananda had reached the state of *nirvikalpa samadhi* (irrevocable God-union).

Once back in the United States, Yogananda wrote his most famous book, *Autobiography of a Yogi*, perhaps the most widely read account of a Hindu teacher, published in 1946. His account is an absorbing story of a search for truth, interwoven with explanations of the subtle laws by which yogis perform miracles and attain self-mastery. He describes his years of training in India under Swami Sri Yukteswar Giri and his meetings with exceptional persons of the age, including Mohandas Karamchand GANDHI, Luther Burbank, Therese Neumann, and Rabindranath TAGORE. In 1942 he opened the Church of All Religions in Hollywood and later the Self-Realization Lake Shrine and Mahatma Gandhi World Peace Memorial in Pacific Palisades, California. Self-Realization Fellowship is currently headed by Sri Daya MATA at Mount Washington, California.

His death on March 7, 1952, was noted by his disciples as an extraordinary event because of the "absence of any visual signs of decay in the dead body of Paramahansa Yogananda . . . even twenty days after his death, according to a notarized testimony from Forest Lawn Mortuary in Glendale, California."

Further reading: Paramahansa Yogananda, *Autobiography of a Yogi* (Los Angeles: Self-Realization Fellowship, 1971); ———, *Whispers from Eternity* (Los Angeles: Self-Realization Fellowship, 1958); ———, *Yogoda* (Boston: Yogoda Satsang Society, 1924); *Paramahansa Yogananda, in Memoriam* (Los Angeles: Self-Realization Fellowship, 1958).

Yoga Sutra

The Yoga Sutra of PATANJALI outlining ASHTANGA YOGA is the earliest and most important text of the HATHA YOGA, or "posture yoga," tradition. It is dated around the second century C.E. The SUTRA designation refers to the text style: a collection of very concise lines that often need further explanation to be understood fully. The Yoga Sutra totals 195 sutras divided into four books: Book I is on concentration; Book II outlines the practice and means of reaching the highest goals; Book III details powers gained in the practice of yoga, including supranormal powers; Book IV describes various aspects of the nature of things but particularly the nature of the liberated state. Scholars believe the four chapters may have been written at different times, but all the hatha yoga traditions consider them to be a single authoritative text.

Book I begins with a definition: "Yoga is the practice of ceasing the false identification with the fluctuations of the mind." It then lists the types of mental fluctuations and discusses how to curb their influence on the self, soul, or PURUSHA. It deals with types of concentration (*dharana*), the obstacles that get in the way, and methods of overcoming them. Finally, it discusses God as a special self and presents the goal of a stable mind and attaining undisturbed calm.

Book II begins with methods for overcoming the mental "afflictions," things that cause distractions. It discusses the origin of KARMA, the causes of sorrow or pain, how to escape these through yoga, the eight branches of yoga (Ashtanga Yoga), abstentions (*yama*), observances (*niyama*), postures (*asana*), breath control (*pranayama*), and withdrawal of sense organs from their objects (*pratya hara*).

Book III begins by discussing the internal practices of yoga, including MEDITATION (*dhyana*) and various levels of concentration, including SAMADHI, the highest. It goes on to discuss seedless concentration (i.e., concentration without an object) and different categories of mental tranquility. Finally it discusses the attributes and powers one can achieve though these practices, including supernormal powers.

Book IV discusses philosophy, including arguments against other Indian philosophical systems. It ends with a discussion of the highest state of liberation and tranquility.

The Yoga Sutra is usually studied together with the ancient commentary of Vedavyasa (VYASA), which expands in detail upon each of the subjects covered in the brief sutras. Most yoga schools rely on this commentary explicitly or implicitly. There are many subcommentaries to the commentary of Vedavyasa, which are used by different schools in support of their particular practices.

Further reading: Swami Hariharananda Aranya, *Yoga Philosophy of Patanjali* (Albany: State University of New York Press, 1983); Ian Whicher, *Patañjali's*

Metaphysical Schematic: Purusa and Prakriti in the Yogasūtra, Adyar Library Pamphlet Series, no. 55 (Chennai: Adyar Library and Research Centre, 2001); Ian Whicher and David Carpenter, eds., *Yogas: The Indian Tradition* (New York: Routledge Curzon, 2003); James Haughton Woods, *The Yoga-System of Patanjali,* Harvard Oriental Series, Vol. 17 (Delhi: Motilal Banarsidass, 1972).

Yogendra, Sri (1897–1989) *pioneer teacher of hatha yoga*

Sri Yogendra was one of the important figures in the modern revival of HATHA YOGA, both in India and in the UNITED STATES. He founded the Yoga Institute and helped provide a scientific basis for the practice of yoga.

Yogendra was born on November 18, 1897, as Manibhai Harihai Desai in rural Gujarat, India. As a student at St. Xavier's College in Bombay (Mumbai), he met his GURU, Paramahansa Madhavadasaji. After several years, however, he ceased to be a disciple. Desai did not wish to lead a celibate life; instead, he wished to find out whether there could be a scientific underpinning for the practice of hatha yoga. In 1918 he founded the Yoga Institute of India.

In 1919, Desai, who had by this time assumed the name *Yogendra,* moved to the United States to work with several medical doctors who shared his interest in the yogic arts. Among the people he met was Benedict LUST (1872–1945), founder of the new medical system called naturopathy. Lust saw the value of hatha yoga for his work and studied it with Yogendra. Along with the early experiments on yoga, Yogendra completed his first books while in America: *Light on Hatha Yoga* and a volume on Rabindranath TAGORE.

In 1922 Yogendra returned to India. He planned a second visit to the United States in order to continue the research, but in 1924 Congress passed new immigration laws that prevented Asians from entering the country and Yogendra was not allowed to visit again. Lust was left to spread the practice of hatha yoga on his own.

Unable to continue his work in America, Yogendra threw himself into the task of building his Yoga Institute. He provided his own funding with royalties from his invention of a new type of boot polish. He found a helpmate in the form of Sita Devi, whom he married in 1927.

The 1930s became a time of significant expansion. A magazine, the *Journal of the Yoga Institute* (now *Yoga and Total Health*), was launched, and Yogendra wrote several books on the basics of hatha yoga, a practice that had largely disappeared over the centuries in India. Yogendra continued his efforts to present hatha yoga practice to the United States by working with an American student, Theos Bernard (1908–47), whose Ph.D. dissertation for Columbia University was eventually published as *Hatha Yoga: The Report of a Personal Experience* (1943). (*See* BERNARD, PIERRE ARNOLD.)

Aftr the disruptions of World War II, Yogendra purchased land in Mumbai as a permanent home for the institute. In the 1950s, the institute began to build a global reputation through the steady arrival of Westerners to study there. Yogendra continued to write, turning out a series of books. He was active well into his eighties, but in 1985 turned over directorship of the institute to his eldest son, Dr. Jayadeva Yogendra.

Further reading: Santan Rodrigues, *The Householder Yogi: Life of Sri Yogendra* (Bombay: Yoga Institute, 1982); Sri Yogendra, *Hatha Yoga Simplified* (Bombay: Yoga Institute, 1958); ———, *Yoga Asanas Simplified* (Bombay: Yoga Institute, 1939).

Yogoda Satsang Society *See* YOGANANDA, PARAMAHANSA.

yoni

The *yoni* (vagina or womb), seen as the embodiment of the great GODDESS, is worshipped in emblematic form in many Indian traditions. It can take the form of a pot or other vessel, a cleft rock, or a pond, lake, or pool. In certain esoteric rituals, a human vagina is worshipped directly. The association of female genitals with the divine female principle, and the correlation of women's reproductive and sexual cycles with the Earth's seasonal and vegetative cycles, have given the *yoni* cosmological significance.

Considered the gateway between life and death, as well as the generative force behind all existence, the *yoni* has had special importance particularly in the KAULA, SHAKTA, and TANTRA traditions. However, even ordinary Shaivite devotees worship the *yoni* together with the SHIVA LINGAM (phallus); the popular icon consists of a rounded stone shaft placed upright on a horizontal circular base that forms the *yoni*.

All of these practices are probably based on pre-Vedic, prepatriarchal civilizations. Many female figurines have been discovered in a pre-Harappan site in the Zhob Valley dating to the midfourth millennium B.C.E. Many of these figures had pronounced breasts and *yonis*, perhaps signifying their generative function. Cowry shells, a common representation of the vulva, were also found at these sites. Scholars believe women most likely used these objects in rituals, perhaps together with their own menstrual and sexual fluids, in order to ensure a fruitful harvest.

Numerous seals, ritual objects, and *yoni*/lingam structures from the later INDUS VALLEY CIVILIZATIONS of Mohenjo-daro and Harappa also point to an early understanding of the sanctity of female sexuality and its association with the Earth's fertility. Reverence of the female principle and the belief that it controls the perpetuation of the human and vegetative life cycles seems to lie at the base of these civilizations.

In the fourth century C.E., the cult of the goddess Lajja Gauri arose across the subcontinent. The most well-known images depict a woman with her legs bent and open and her vulva completely exposed. Often, her head has been replaced

with a pot filled with vegetation. In some depictions vegetation emerges from her *yoni*. These iconographical representations of the Goddess seem to have originated in the early Indus Valley, or even pre-Indus Valley civilizations. Lajja Gauri and another goddess of vegetation, Sakhambari, are worshipped today as the embodiment and generator of fertility, fortune, abundance, and life-force energy, qualities that are also associated with the *yoni*. The Goddess in general is conceived as the elemental source of all animal and plant life, as creative power personified.

Creative female sexual power is represented in various symbols even today. The lotus has become a quintessential symbol of the *yoni*. In SHAKTA and TANTRA texts, the *yoni*, as is the lotus, is a symbol of perfection, symmetry, and beauty. In Hindu cosmology waters are considered the perennial source and equated with the Goddess's womb. As the lotus rests on the water and remains unsaturated by water, not soiled by mud, to Shakta tantrics, so the *yoni* remains perpetually pure.

In Hindu architecture, the temple is conceived as a microcosmic representation of the macrocosmic whole. The inner sanctum of Hindu temples, regardless of religious sect, is called the *garbhagriha*, which means "womb-house." In Guwahati, Assam, at the site of the Kamarupa Temple, the Goddess in her form as the Great Yoni is worshipped. Here she is worshipped in aniconic form as a dark wet rock over which a natural spring flows. Each summer this water turns red and is worshipped as the Goddess's menstrual blood.

KAMAKHYA, in Assam, is a PILGRIMAGE site to Shaktas, Kaulas, and Tantrikas who worship a woman's menstrual blood as the sacred and potent elixir of life. In these traditions, women's menstrual cycles relate to processes of the universe. The body itself is considered the link between earth and cosmos, a microcosmic representation of the macrocosmic whole. In Kaula, Shakta, and tantric cosmogony women play a divine role due to the nature of their sex. In these ideologies liberation (MOKSHA) is possible to humans within this lifetime, but only through ritual sexual practices and the worship of the *yoni*, female sexual fluids, and menstrual blood.

In the first section of the Yoni Tantra, Shiva tells DEVI, the Goddess, that all gods and their power of creation, maintenance, and destruction originate in the *yoni*. In the Yoni Tantra the Mahavidyas, 10 tantric goddesses of spiritual liberation, are each associated with different parts of the *yoni*.

The tantric Sri Chakra cult also gives special importance to the *yoni*. The main iconic emblem of the Goddess, the SRI YANTRA, is composed of interlocking triangles. Five of these, symbolizing the *yoni*, point downward; the other four, symbolizing the LINGAM, point upward, in reference to the union of feminine and masculine qualities and representing the mysteries of creation and destruction.

Further reading: Arthur Avalon, *The Serpent Power: The Secrets of Tantric and Shaktic Yoga,* 7th ed. (New York: Dover, 1974); N. N. Bhattacharya, *History of the Tantric Religion* (New Delhi: Manohar, 1999); Carol Radcliffe Bolon, *Forms of the Goddess Lajja Gauri in Indian Art* (Delhi: Motilal Banarsidass, 1997); Madhu Khanna, *Yantra: The Tantric Symbol of Cosmic Unity* (London: Thames & Hudson, 1979); Michael Magee, *The Yoni Tantra*, Vol. 2 (Harrow, England: Worldwide Tantra Project, 1995); Ajit Mookerjee, *Kali: The Feminine Force* (New York: Destiny Books, 1988); David Gordon White, *Kiss of the Yogini* (Chicago and London: University of Chicago Press, 2003).

Yudhishthira

Yudhishthira, "he who is steadfast in war," is the oldest of the five PANDAVAS brothers of the MAHABHARATA story. He is the son of Kunti by the god Dharma. Yudhisthira has a prominent place in the story. He is addicted to gambling and, therefore, the source of sorrow for his brothers and their mutual wife DRAUPADI. Twice he loses in dice to the brothers' rivals the KAURAVAS; on the second occasion he loses everything, forcing the Pandavas and their wife into 13 years of exile. Generally, however, Yudhishthira is regarded as wise, righteous, and pure and is given the title "king of the right" (*dharmaraja*).

Further reading: Peter Brook, director, *The Mahabharata* (videorecording), produced by Michael Propper (Chatsworth, Calif.: Image Entertainment, 2002); William Buck, *The Mahabharata* (Berkeley: University of California Press, 1973); J. A. van Buitenen, *The Mahabharata,* 3 vols. (Chicago: University of Chicago Press, 1973–78); E. Washburn Hopkins, *Epic Mythology* (Delhi: Motilal Banarsidass, 1986).

Yuga

In Hindu cosmology a Yuga, or "Age," is the smallest unit of cosmological time. Four Yugas make up one MAHAYUGA, or Great Age: the Golden Age (KRITA, or Satya, YUGA), the Silver Age (TRETA YUGA), the Bronze Age (DVAPARA YUGA), and the Iron Age (KALI YUGA, no connection with the goddess Kali). The Yugas are named after an ancient dice game, in which a 1, or *kale*, was the worst throw and a 4, or *krita* (literally, the one that makes it!), is the best.

The Yugas decrease in duration: Satya Yuga lasts 1,728,000 years, Treta 1,296,000 years, Dvapara 864,000 years, and Kali 432,000 years. The figures are sometimes given in "god-years," each divine year equal to 360 human years. Then the Satya Yuga is 4,800 divine years; the Treta Yuga 3,600 divine years; the Dvapara Yuga 2,400 divine years; and the Kali Yuga 1,200 divine years. Each Mahayuga totals 12,000 divine years.

As the Yugas follow one another, every aspect of human life suffers a decline, including human height, longevity, and morality. We are currently in the Kali Yuga, the most corrupt of the ages. At its end, a new Satya Yuga will begin. Mahayugas follow one another cyclically; after a long series, the universe undergoes a dissolution, or *pralaya*. After this interlude, the progression of the Yugas resumes. The process goes on to infinity. Jain tradition has a similar progression of ages with different names.

Further reading: Cornelia Dimmitt and J. A. B. van Buitenen, *Classical Hindu Mythology: A Reader in the Sanskrit Puranas* (Philadelphia: Temple University Press, 1978); F. B. J. Kuiper, "Cosmogony and Conception: A Query," *History of Religions* 10 (1970): 91–138; W. J. Wilkins, *Hindu Mythology, Vedic and Puranic,* 2d ed. (Calcutta: Rupa, 1973).

Yukteswar, Sri (1855–1936) kriya yoga
teacher

Sri Yukteswar was an important link in the lineage that revived KRIYA YOGA, especially through his pupil Paramahansa YOGANANDA.

Priya Nath Karar was born in 1855 in Serampore, a suburb of Calcutta (Kolkata). He received his primary education at a modern English school and was later admitted into Calcutta University but left the university when he found his physics teacher to be incompetent. He continued to study informally by auditing classes in physics, chemistry, biology, physiology, and anatomy at the Calcutta Medical College. Especially talented in mathematics, he also studied astronomy and astrology. He would later become a famous spiritual teacher and astrologer. He married, but his wife died after giving birth to his daughter. As a widower, he cared for his daughter and widowed mother.

In 1883 he met LAHIRI MAHASAYA, who initiated him into the practice of *kriya yoga*. *Kriya* means "work," in this case a specific set of mental and physical practices for SELF-REALIZATION. He mastered the system and soon became a guru of *kriya yoga* himself.

Having been raised in Serampore, a center for Christian missionaries, Priya Nath was greatly influenced by the teachings of the Holy Bible and Jesus Christ. He wrote his own interpretation of the Bhagavad Gita and also drew comparisons between the teachings of KRISHNA and the teachings of Christ.

In 1894 Priya Nath went to ALLAHABAD for the KUMBHA MELA, a PILGRIMAGE festival that occurs four times every 12 years, attended by millions of people from all over the world. Here he first met BABAJI, his teacher's teacher, a semilegendary saint who appeared and reappeared at long intervals. Although not yet a SANNYASI (renunciant), he was honored as such by Babaji. In this encounter, Babaji encouraged Priya Nath to write about the similarities in the Hindu and Christian traditions, certain that the West could benefit from learning of these connections. Babaji assured him that they would meet again when the book was finished; indeed, when *Kaivalya Darshanam, the Holy Science,* was published, Babaji appeared under a tree near where Priya Nath took his daily bath in the GANGES River.

By the early 1900s Priya Nath was teaching to wider audiences; in 1902 he established Sat Sanga Sabha, a religious cultural institution that offered educational, social, and spiritual programs, including courses in *kriya yoga* and the Yogashastras. At this time, he received the vows of SANNYAS and was given the name Swami Sri Yukteshvar Giri (union with God) by Swami Krishna Dayal Giri. In 1913, he met his student Mukunda Lal, later known as YOGANANDA, and later bestowed on him the title of *Paramahansa* (great swan). Yukteswar took *mahasamadhi* (died) in 1936 while meditating in the lotus position. His body is buried in his ASHRAM; his tomb has become a sacred place for initiates of *kriya yoga*.

Further reading: Sailendra Bejoy Das Gupta, *Kriya Yoga and Swami Sriyukteshvar* (Calcutta: Uccharan, 1979); Swami Hariharananda Giri, *Kriyayoga: The Scientific Process of Soul-Culture and the Essence of All Religions* (Orissa: Karar Ashram, 1977); Paramahansa Yogananda, *Autobiography of a Yogi* (Los Angeles: Self-Realization Fellowship, 1971); Sri Yukteswar, *The Holy Science* (Los Angeles: Self-Realization Fellowship, 1968).

BIBLIOGRAPHY

Ali, Syed Mohammed. *Hinduism: A Select Bibliography.* Gurgaon: Indian Documentation Service, 1984.

Ashby, Phillip H. *Modern Trends in Hinduism.* New York: Columbia University Press, 1974.

Axel, Michaels, and Barbara Harshav. *Hinduism: Past and Present.* Princeton, N.J.: Princeton University Press, 2004.

Babb, Lawrence A. *Redemptive Encounters: Three Modern Styles in the Hindu Tradition.* Berkeley: University of California Press, 1986.

Bahadur, Om Lata. *The Book of Hindu Festivals and Ceremonies.* New Delhi: UBS, 1995.

Baird, Robert D., ed. *Religion in Modern India.* New Delhi: Manohar, 1995.

Basham, A. L. *The Origins and Development of Classical Hinduism.* Boston: Beacon Press, 1989.

———. *The Wonder That Was India.* New York: Taplinger, 1968.

Benjamin, Walker. *The Hindu World: An Encyclopedic Survey of Hinduism.* 2 vols. New York: Praeger, 1968.

Bhardwaj, S. M. *Hindu Places of Pilgrimage in India.* Berkeley: University of California Press, 1973.

Bhattacharyya, Narendra Nath. *Ancient Indian Rituals and Their Social Contents.* London: Curzon Press, 1975.

Bishop, D. H., ed. *Indian Thought: An Introduction.* New York: John Wiley, 1975.

Brockington, John L. *Hinduism and Christianity.* Houndmills, England: Macmillan, 1992.

———. The *Sacred Thread: Hinduism in Its Continuity and Diversity.* Edinburgh: Edinburgh University Press, 1981.

Camphausen, Rufus C. *The Encyclopedia of Sacred Sexuality: From Aphrodisiacs and Ecstasy to Yoni Worship and Zap-Lam Yoga.* Rochester, Vt.: Inner Traditions, 1999.

Carpenter, David, and Ian Whicher. *Yoga: The Indian Tradition.* New York: Routledge, 2003.

Chandola, Anoop. *The Way of True Worship: A Popular Story of Hinduism.* Lanham, Md.: University Press of America, 1990.

Chaudhuri, Nirad C. *Hinduism, a Religion to Live By.* New York: Oxford University Press, 1979.

Cole, W. Owen, and Piara Singh Sambhi. *A Popular Dictionary of Sikhism.* Calcutta: Rupa Paperback, 1990.

Copley, Anthony, ed. *Gurus and Their Followers: New Religious Reform Movements in Colonial India.* Oxford: Oxford University Press, 2000.

Dandekar, R. N. *Universe in Hindu Thought.* Bangalore: University of Bangalore, 1972.

Danielou, Alain. *Hindu Polytheism.* New York: Pantheon, 1964.

Dasgupta, Shashi Bhushan. *Obscure Religious Cults.* Calcutta: KLM, 1976.

Dasgupta, Surendranath. *A History of Indian Philosophy.* 5 vols. Cambridge: Cambridge University Press, 1922–55.

Davidson, Linda Kay, and David M. Gitlitz. *Pilgrimage from the Ganges to Graceland: An Encyclopedia.* Santa Barbara, Calif.: ABC-Clio, 2002.

Day, Harvey. *Yoga Illustrated Dictionary.* New York: Barnes & Noble, 1971.

Dell, David J. *Guide to Hindu Religion.* Boston: G. K. Hall, 1981.

de Michelis, Elizabeth. *A History of Modern Yoga.* London: Continuum, 2004.

Deussen, Paul. *The Philosophy of the Upanishads.* New York: Dover, 1966.

Deutsch, Eliot, and J. A. B. van Buitenen, eds. *A Source Book of Advaita Vedanta.* Honolulu: University of Hawaii Press, 1971.

Dhavamony, Mariasusai. *Hindu-Christian Dialogue: Theological Soundings and Perspectives.* New York: Rodopi, 2002.

Dimmitt, Cornelia, and J. A. B. van Buitenen, eds. and trans. *Classical Hindu Mythology: A Reader in the Sanskrit Puranas.* Philadelphia: Temple University Press, 1978.

Dimock, Edward C. *The Sound of Silent Guns and Other Essays.* Oxford: Oxford University Press, 1989.

Doniger, Wendy, ed. *Purana Perennis: Reciprocity and Transformation in Hindu and Jaina Texts.* Albany: State University of New York Press, 1993.

Dowson, John. *A Classical Dictionary of Hindu Mythology and Religion, Geography, History, and Literature.* London: Routledge & Kegan Paul, 1961.

Dubois, Abbe J. A. *Hindu Manners, Customs and Ceremonies.* 2d ed. Calcutta: Rupa, 1993.

Dundas, Paul. *The Jains.* New York: Routledge, 1992.

Eliot, Charles. *Hinduism and Buddhism: An Historical Sketch.* New York: Barnes & Noble, 1954.

Ellwood, Robert S. *Alternative Altars: Unconventional and Eastern Spirituality in America.* Chicago: University of Chicago Press, 1979.

Embree, Ainslee T., ed. *The Hindu Tradition.* New York: Random House, 1966.

Farquhar, J. N. *An Outline of the Religious Literature of India.* Delhi: Motilal Banarsidass, 1967.

Fenton, John Y. *Transplanting Religious Traditions: Asian Indians in America.* New York: Praeger, 1988.

Feuerstein, Georg. *Encyclopedic Dictionary of Yoga.* New York: Paragon House, 1991.

———. *The Shambala Encyclopedia of Yoga.* Boston: Shambhala, 1997.

Fischer-Schreiber, Ingrid, Franz-Karl Ehrhard, Kurt Friedrichs, and Michael S. Diener, eds. *The Encyclopedia of Eastern Philosophy and Religion: Buddhism, Hinduism, Taoism, Zen.* Boston: Shambhala, 1989.

Flood, Gavin D. *The Blackwell Companion to Hinduism.* Malden, Mass.: Blackwell, 2003.

———. *An Introduction to Hinduism.* Cambridge: Cambridge University Press, 1996.

Ghurye, G. S. *Indian Sadhus.* Bombay: Popular Prakashan, 1964.

Goodall, Dominic, ed. and trans. *Hindu Scriptures.* Berkeley: University of California Press, 1996.

Griswold, Henry DeWitt. *Insights into Modern Hinduism.* New York: Henry Holt, 1934.

Guénon, René. *Introduction to the Study of Hindu Doctrines.* New Delhi: Munshiram Manoharlal, 1993.

———. *Man and His Becoming According to the Vedanta.* New Delhi: Oriental Books, 1981.

Hartsuiker, Dolf. *Sadhus: Holy Men of India.* Singapore: Thames & Hudson, 1993.

Harvey, Andrew. *Teachings of the Hindu Mystics.* Boston: Shambala, 2001.

Hawley, John Stratton, and Donna Marie Wulff. *Devi: Goddesses of India.* Berkeley: University of California Press, 1997.

Hemenway, Priya. *Hindu Gods: The Spirit of the Divine.* San Francisco: Chronicle Books, 2003.

Holland, Barron, comp. *Popular Hinduism and Hindu Mythology (An Annotated Bibliography).* Westport, Conn.: Greenwood Press, 1979.

Hopkins, Thomas J. *The Hindu Religious Tradition.* Encino, Calif.: Dickenson, 1971.

Huyler, Stephen P. *Meeting God: Elements of Hindu Devotion.* New Haven, Conn.: Yale University Press, 1999.

Jackson, Carl T. *The Oriental Religions and American Thought: Nineteenth-Century Explorations.* Westport, Conn.: Greenwood Press, 1981.

Jackson, Robert, and Dermot Killingley. *Approaches to Hinduism.* London: John Murray, 1988.

Jain, Muni Uttam Kamal. *Jaina Sects and Schools.* Delhi: Concept, 1975.

Jarrell, Howard R. *International Yoga Bibliography 1950 to 1980.* Lanham, Md.: Scarecrow Press, 1981.

Johnson, Linda. *Daughters of the Goddess: The Women Saints of India.* St. Paul, Minn.: Yes International, 1994.

Kamath, M. V. *The United States and India, 1776–1976.* Washington, D.C.: Embassy of India, 1976.

Kapoor, S., ed. *Encyclopaedic Dictionary of Hinduism: Its Mythology, Religion, History, Literature and Pantheon.* New Delhi: Cosmo, 2004.

Keith, Arthur Berriedale. *The Religion and Philosophy of the Veda and Upanishads.* Cambridge, Mass.: Harvard University Press, 1925.

Kinsley, David. *Hindu Goddesses: Visions of the Divine Feminine in the Hindu Religious Tradition.* Berkeley: University of California Press, 1986.

———. *Hinduism: A Cultural Perspective.* Englewood Cliffs, N.J.: Prentice Hall, 1993.

———. *The Sword and the Flute: Kali and Krishna, Dark Visions of the Terrible and the Sublime in Hindu Mythology.* Berkeley: University of California Press, 1975.

Klostermaier, Klaus K. *Hindu Writings: A Short Introduction to the Major Sources.* Oxford: One World, 2000.

———. *Hinduism: A Short History.* Oxford: One World, 2000.

Knipe, David M. *Hinduism: Experiments in the Sacred.* San Francisco: Harper, 1991.

Knott, Kim. *Hinduism, A Very Short Introduction.* New York: Oxford University Press, 1998.

Krishnamurthy, Visvantha. *Essentials of Hinduism.* New Delhi: Narosa, 1989.

Lane, David Christopher. "Radhasoami Parampara in Definition and Classification." M.A. thesis, Graduate Theological Union, Berkeley, Calif., 1981.

———. *The Radhasoami Tradition: A Critical History of Guru Successorship.* New York: Garland, 1992.

Lele, Jayant, ed. *Tradition and Modernity in Bhakti Movements.* Leiden: E. J. Brill, 1981.

Liebert, Gosta. *Iconographic Dictionary of the Indian Religions: Hinduism, Buddhism, Jainism.* Leiden: E. J. Brill, 1976.

Macauliffe, Max Arthur. *The Sikh Religion.* 6 vols. New Delhi: S. Chand, 1978.

Madan, T. N., ed. *Religion in India.* New York: Oxford University Press, 1991.

Mann, Gurinder Singh, et al. *Buddhists, Hindus and Sikhs in America.* New York: Oxford University Press, 2001.

Marriot, McKim. *India through Hindu Categories.* New Delhi: Sage, 1990.

McKean, Lise. *Divine Enterprise: Gurus and the Hindu Nationalist Movement.* Chicago: University of Chicago Press, 1996.

McLeod, W. H. *Historical Dictionary of Sikhism.* Metuchen, N.J.: Scarecrow Press, 1995.

———. *The Sikhs.* Oxford: Clarendon Press, 1989.

———. *Who Is a Sikh?* Oxford: Clarendon Press, 1989.

Melton, J. Gordon. *The Encyclopedia of American Religions.* 7th ed. Detroit: Thomson/Gale, 2003.

———. *The Encyclopedic Handbook of Cults in America.* New York: Garland, 1992.

———. *Religious Leaders of America.* Detroit: Gale Research, 1991.

Melton, J. Gordon, and Martin Baumann, eds. *Religions of the World: A Comprehensive Encyclopedia of Beliefs and Practices.* 4 vols. Santa Barbara, Calif.: ABC-Clio, 2002.

Melton, J. Gordon, Aidan A. Kelly, and Jerome Clark. *New Age Encyclopedia.* Detroit: Gale Research, 1990.

Mishra, Vibhuti Bhushan. *Religious Beliefs and Practices of North India during the Early Medieval Period.* Leiden, Netherlands: E. J. Brill, 1973.

Mittal, Sushill, and G. R. Thursby. *The Hindu World.* New York: Routledge, 2004.

Mitter, Sara. *Dharma's Daughters: Contemporary Indian Women and Hindu Culture.* New Brunswick, N.J.: Rutgers University Press, 1991.

Mokashi, Digambar Balkrishna. *Palkhi: An Indian Pilgramage.* Albany: State University of New York Press, 1987.

Morgan, Kenneth W. *The Religion of the Hindus.* New York: Ronald Press, 1953.

Morinis, E. Alan. *Pilgrimage in the Hindu Tradition: A Case Study of West Bengal.* New York: Oxford University Press, 1984.

Nakamura, Hajime. *A History of Early Vedanta Philosophy.* Delhi: Motilal Banarsidass, 1983.

Narayanan, Vasudha. *Hinduism: Origins, Beliefs, Practices, Holy Texts, Sacred Places.* New York: Oxford University Press, 2004.

Nath, Rakhal Chandra. *The New Hindu Movement, 1886–1911.* Columbia, Mo.: South Asia Books, 1982.

O'Flaherty, Wendy Doniger. *Karma and Rebirth in Classical Indian Traditions.* Berkeley: University of California Press, 1980.

———. *The Origins of Evil in Hindu Mythology.* Berkeley: University of California Press, 1976.

Organ, Tory Wilson. *Hinduism: Its Historical Development.* Woodbury, N.Y.: Barron's Educational Series, 1974.

Pandey, Raj Bali. *Hindu Samskara: A Socio-Religious Study of Hindu Sacraments.* New Delhi: Motilal Banarsidass, 1969.

Pararignanar, Saiva Ilakkia. *The Development of Saivism in South India.* Kanchipuram: Dharmapuram Adhinam, 1964.

Pereira, Jose. *Hindu Theology.* Garden City, N.Y.: Doubleday, 1976.

Pintchman, Tracy. *The Rise of the Goddess in the Hindu Tradition.* Albany: State University of New York Press, 1994.

Radhakrishnan, Sarvepalli, and Charles A. Moore, eds. *A Sourcebook in Indian Philosophy.* Princeton, N.J.: Princeton University Press, 1957.

Raghavan, V. *The Great Integrators: The Saint-Singers of India.* Delhi: Publications Division, Ministry of Information and Broadcasting, 1966.

Rai, Ram Kumar, comp. *Encyclopedia of Indian Erotics.* Indological Reference Series 3. Varanasi: Prachya Prakashan, 1983.

Raju, P. T. *The Philosophical Tradition of India.* Pittsburgh: University of Pittsburgh Press, 1972.

Ramachandra Rao, S. K. *Encyclopedia of Indian Iconography, Hinduism, Buddhism and Jainism.* 3 vols. New Delhi: Sri Satguru, n.d.

Rawlinson, Andrew. *The Book of Enlightened Masters.* Chicago: Open Court, 1997.

Renou, Louis. *The Nature of Hinduism.* New York: Walker, 1962.

Rice, Edward. *Eastern Definitions: A Short Encyclopedia of Religions of the Orient with Terms from Hinduism, Sufism, Buddhism, Islam, Zen, Tao, the Sikhs, Zoroastrianism and Other Eastern Religions.* Garden City, N.Y.: Doubleday, 1978.

Richards, Glyn. *A Sourcebook of Modern Hinduism.* London: Curzon, 1985.

Rinehart, Robin. *Contemporary Hinduism: Ritual, Culture and Practice.* Santa Barbara, Calif.: ABC-CLIO, 2004.

Rosen, Steven. *The Six Goswamis of Vrindavan.* Brooklyn, N.Y.: Folk Books, 1991.

Roy, Ahim Kumar. *A History of the Jainas.* New Delhi: Gitanjali Press, 1984.

Rukmani, T. S., ed. *Hindu Diaspora: Global Perspectives.* Montreal: Concordia University, 1999.

Santucci, James A. *An Outline of Vedic Literature.* Missoula, Mont.: Scholars Press, 1976.

Saraswati, Swami Prakashanand. *The True History of the Religion of India: A Concise Encyclopedia of Authentic Hinduism.* Austin, Tex.: International Society of Divine Love, 2000.

Sharma, Arvind. *Classical Hindu Thought: An Introduction.* Oxford: Oxford University Press, 2000.

———. *Hinduism for Our Times.* Delhi: Oxford University Press, 1996.

Sholapurkar, G. R. *Religious Rites and Festivals of India.* Delhi: Bharatiya Vidya Prakashan, 1990.

Singer, Milton. *When a Great Tradition Modernizes: An Anthropological Approach to Indian Civilization.* Chicago: University of Chicago Press, 1972.

Singh, Harbans. *Encyclopedia of Sikhism.* n.p.: Punjabi University, 1995.

Smith, Bardwell L. *Hinduism: New Essays in the History of Religions.* Leiden: E. J. Brill, 1976.

Smith, David. *Hinduism and Modernity.* Malden, Mass.: Blackwell, 2003.

Srinivas, M. N. *Caste in Modern India and Other Essays.* Bombay: Asia Pub. House, 1962.

Stutley, Margaret, and James Stutley. *A Dictionary of Hinduism: Its Mythology, Folklore and Development 1500 B.C.–A.D. 1500.* London: Routledge & Kegan Paul, 1977.

Sugirtharajah, Sharada. *Imagining Hinduism: A Postcolonial Perspective.* New York: Routledge, 2003.

Sullivan, Bruce M. *The A to Z of Hinduism.* Lanham, Md.: Scarecrow Press, 2001.

———. *Historical Dictionary of Hinduism.* Lanham, Md.: Scarecrow Press, 1997.

Tatla, Darshan Singh. *Sikhs in America: An Annotated Bibliography.* New York: Greenwood Press, 1991.

Thapar, Romila. *Interpreting Early India.* New York: Oxford University Press, 1992.

Tripathi, B. D. *Sadhus of India.* Bombay: Popular Prakashan, 1978.

Uban, Sujan Singh. *The Gurus of India.* London: Fine Books, 1977.

Vertovec, Steven. *The Hindu Diaspora: Comparative Patterns.* London: Routledge, 2000.

Werner, Karel. *Popular Dictionary of Hinduism.* Chicago: NTC, 1997.

Wheeler, Robert Eric Mortimer. *Civilizations of the Indus Valley and Beyond.* New York: McGraw-Hill, 1966.

Whitehead, Henry. *The Village Gods of South India.* New York: Oxford University Press, 1916.

Williams, George M. *Handbook of Hindu Mythology.* Santa Barbara, Calif.: ABC-CLIO, 2003.

Williams, Raymond. *Religions of Immigrants from India and Pakistan: New Threads in the American Tapestry.* Cambridge: Cambridge University Press, 1988.

Wilson, H. H. *Religious Sects of the Hindus.* Calcutta: Susil Gupta, 1958.

Wuthnow, Robert. *After Heaven: Spirituality in America since the 1950's.* Berkeley: University of California Press, 1998.

Younger, Paul. *Playing Host to the Deity: Festival Religion in the South Indian Tradition.* New York: Oxford University Press, 2002.

Zaehner, R. C. *The Concise Encyclopedia of Living Faiths.* Boston: Beacon Press, 1959.

———. *Hinduism.* London: Oxford University Press, 1970.

Zimmer, Heinrich. *Artistic Form and Yoga in the Sacred Images of India.* Princeton, N.J.: Princeton University Press, 1984.

———. *Myths and Symbols in Indian Art and Civilization.* Washington, D.C.: Bollingen Series, Pantheon, 1946.

———. *Philosophies of India.* Princeton, N.J.: Princeton University Press, 1951.

INDEX